A Dictionary of Military History

and the Art of War

A Dictionary of Military History

and the Art of War

Edited by

André Corvisier

English Edition
Revised, expanded and edited by

John Childs

Translated from the French by

Chris Turner

Advisers to the English Edition

Simon Adams, Ian F. W. Beckett, J. B. Campbell,
Stephen J. Harris, Keith Neilson, Barrie Paskins, Alan
W. H. Pearsall, Glenn A. Steppler, Hew Strachan,
David Weston

Original French text copyright © Presses Universitaires de France, 1988

English translation and new material copyright © Basil Blackwell, 1994

Editorial organization for the English edition copyright © John Childs, 1994

The right of André Corvisier to be identified as editor of this work has been asserted in accordance with the Copyright, Designs and Patents Act 1988.

French edition first published 1988

English translation (with revisions and new material) first published 1994

Blackwell Publishers
108 Cowley Road
Oxford OX4 1JF
UK

238 Main Street
Cambridge, Massachusetts 02142
USA

British Library Cataloguing in Publication Data

A CIP catalogue record for this book is available from the British Library.

Library of Congress Cataloging-in-Publication Data

[Dictionnaire d'art et d'histoire militaires. English] A dictionary of military history and the art of war/ edited by André Corvisier; translated from the French by Chris Turner. —English ed./rev., exp. and edited by John Childs.
    p. cm.
Includes bibliographical references and index.
ISBN 0–631–16848–6
1. Military art and science—Encyclopedias.   2. Military history—Encyclopedias.
I. Corvisier, André.   II. Childs, John Charles Roger.
U24.D4913 1993
355′.003–dc20   92–46136
                                                                          CIP

ISBN 0–631–16848–6
Typeset in 10 on 11pt Times at The Spartan Press Ltd, Lymington, Hants
Printed and bound in Great Britain by Hartnolls Limited, Bodmin, Cornwall

This book is printed on acid-free paper

CONTENTS

CONTRIBUTORS TO THE FRENCH EDITION

Martine Acerra	CNRS, University of Paris-Sorbonne
Jean Allemand	colonel CR
Jean Bérenger	University of Strasbourg II
Gilbert Bodinier	Historical Service of the French Army
Jean-Pierre Bois	Lycée Joachim-du-Bellay (Angers)
József Borus	Institute of Historical Sciences, the Academy of Sciences, Budapest
François Buttner	general CR
Gérard Chaduc	Historical Service of the French Army
Jean Chagniot	University François-Rabelais, Tours
Jean-Paul Charnay	CNRS
Pierre Charrié	Council of the Sabretache
Philippe Contamine	University of Paris-Nanterre
André Corvisier	University of Paris-Sorbonne (emeritus)
Hervé Coutau-Bégarie	École Pratique des Hautes Études
Gilbert Dagron	Collège de France
Patrick Facon	Historical Service of the French Air Force
Michel Garrec	colonel and military magistrate
Jean-Marie Goenaga	colonel ER
Bernard Kroener	University of Bonn and Research Institute for Military History, Freiburg-im-Breisgau
Jean de Lassalle	colonel, Museum of the Army
Sophie de Lastours	
Joël Le Gall	University of Panthéon-Sorbonne (emeritus)
Joseph Le Gall	colonel ER
Raoul Lonis	University of Nancy II
Raimondo Luraghi	University of Genoa
Robert Mantran	University of Aix-Marseilles I
Philippe Masson	Historical Service of the French Navy
Jean Meyer	University of Paris-Sorbonne
Jean-Louis Miège	University of Aix-Marseilles I
Claude Nordmann	University of Lille III
Jean Nouzille	colonel ER
René Quatrefages	Centre for Military History and National Defence Studies at Montpellier
Daniel Reichel	Centre for Military History and Research, Morges
Cornelis M. Schulten	Historical Branch of the Dutch Army
Claude Sturgill	Florida State University
Arnaud Teyssier	Historical Service of the French Air Force

LIST OF CONTRIBUTORS TO THE FRENCH EDITION

Istvan Toth   Institute of Historical Sciences, the Academy of Sciences,
                       Budapest
Hervé de Weck   Lycée fédéral de Porrentruy

CONTRIBUTORS TO THE ENGLISH EDITION

Simon Adams	University of Strathclyde
Peter Barber	British Library
Thomas M. Barker	State University of New York
Ian F. W. Beckett	Royal Military Academy, Sandhurst
J. B. Campbell	Queen's University, Belfast
John Childs	University of Leeds
Andrew Cormack	London
John Gooch	University of Leeds
Jeffrey Grey	Australian Defence Force Academy, University of New South Wales
Peter Harrington	Brown University, Providence, Rhode Island
Stephen J. Harris	National Defence Headquarters, Ottawa
Brian Holden Reid	King's College, University of London, and Staff College, Camberley
Martin Kitchen	Simon Fraser University, British Columbia
Bruce Lenman	University of St Andrews
Keith Neilson	Royal Military College of Canada, Kingston
Barrie Paskins	King's College, University of London
Alan W. H. Pearsall	National Maritime Museum, Greenwich
Ian G. Robertson	National Army Museum
Gunther E. Rothenberg	Purdue University, Indiana
J. E. O. Screen	School of Slavonic and East European Studies, University of London
Glenn A. Steppler	London
Hew Strachan	University of Glasgow
Philip M. Taylor	University of Leeds
David Weston	London

Assistance was also received from Dr J. M. Winter, Pembroke College, Cambridge; Professor A. R. Millett, State University of Ohio; Professor Richard Hellie, University of Chicago; and Professor John B. Hattendorf of the Naval War College.

ACKNOWLEDGEMENTS

'Four brave men who do not know each other will not dare to attack a lion,' wrote Colonel Charles Ardant du Picq in *Battle Studies* (1880). 'Four less brave, but knowing and trusting each other well, will attack resolutely.' The editor wishes to thank all the contributors to the English edition for their co-operation, scholarship and respect for deadlines. Especial thanks go to Mrs Dorne Greensmith of the School of History in the University of Leeds for typing much of the manuscript, in some instances several times over, without uttering a word of complaint. Blackwell's reference editor, Alyn Shipton, and his assistant, Lorna Tunstall, have been helpful, practical and constructive.

However, after completing a book I always misquote Colonel John S. Mosby: 'writing loses a great deal of its romance after an author has published his first book.'

ILLUSTRATION ACKNOWLEDGEMENTS

Beken of Cowes: *navies*; Berwick Borough Museum: *barracks*; Bibliothèque Nationale: *Folard*; Board of Trustees of the Royal Armouries: *firearms*; Britannia Royal Naval College: *naval personnel*; British Library: *cartography*; *dockyards*; Camera Press: *Soviet military theorists*; *Zhukov*; Das Photo: *disarmament*; *fortification*; Don Pottinger: *museums*; Hulton-Deutsch Collection: *Mannerheim*; *Rocroi*; Imperial War Museum: *fortification, field*; *Lettow-Vorbeck*; Irish Tourist Board: *invalids*; KLM Luchtfotografie: *fortification*; Mansell Collection: *arsenals*; *iconography*; *Jomini*; *Jutland*; *Napier*; *Scharnhorst*; M.A.R.S.: *Ader*; *Estienne*; *honours and awards*; *tanks*; Mary Evans Picture Library: *iconography*; *Konev*; *Plevna*; *uniform*; 'MODUK': *terrorism*; National Maritime Museum: *naval warfare*; Peter Newark: *bases, naval*; Roger Scruton: *Symbolism*; Royal Collection of Her Majesty the Queen: *vexillology*; Thomas d'Hoste: *citadels*; Topham: *Maginot Line*; *Russo-Finnish War*; University of Leiden: *Stevin*; University and Society of Antiquaries, Newcastle upon Tyne: *frontiers*; U.S. Army Military History Institute: *Hamley*; Weimar Archive: *veterans*.

ABBREVIATIONS

AAT	Arme Automatique Transformable
ABM	anti-ballistic missile
ACOS	Assistant Chief of Staff
AHR	*American Historical Review*
AK	automatic Kalashnikov
ANZAC	Australian and New Zealand Army Corps
ANZUS	Australia – New Zealand – United States (1951 treaty for mutual security against armed attack in the Pacific)
ARM	anti-radiation missile
ARVN	Army of the Republic of Vietnam
AUTODIN	Automatic Data Information Network
AUTOSEVOCOM	Automatic Secure Voice Communication System
AUTOVON	Automatic (Telephone) Voice Network
AWACS	Airborne Warning and Control Systems
BAR	Browning automatic rifle
BCRA	Bureau Centrale de Renseignement et d'Action
BEF	British Expeditionary Force
BIHR	*Bulletin of the Institute of Historical Research*
BREN	Brno-Enfield (light machine gun)
CAL	carabine automatique légère
CAS	Chief of the Air Staff
CCF	Combined Cadet Force
CENTRO	Central Asian Treaty Organization
CIA	Central Intelligence Agency
CIGS	Chief of the Imperial General Staff
CFLN	Comité Français de Libération Nationale
CNO	Chief of Naval Operations
CNRS	Centre National de la recherche scientifique
COMINT	Communications Intelligence
CORF	Commission d'Organisation des Régions Fortifiées
CRS	Compagnies Républicaines de Sécurité
CS Gas	chlorinated gas used for riot control (chlorophenyl dicyanoethane)
CSCE	Conference on Security and Co-operation in Europe
DEFA	Direction des Études et Fabrications d'Armement
DES	Data Encryption System
DGDN	double-base propellant employing nitrodiglycol as the solvent for nitrocellulose
DGSE	Direction Générale de la Sécurité Éxtérieure
DNVP	Deutschnationale Volkspartei
EC	European Community
EDES	Greek Democratic National Union

EEC	European Economic Community
EHR	*English Historical Review*
ELAS	National Popular (Greek) Liberation Army
ELINT	Electronic Intelligence
EOKA	Ethniki Organosis Kipriakou Agonos (National Organization of Cypriot Struggle)
ERA	explosive reactive armour
ETA	Euzkadi Ta Azkatasuma, a Basque separatist movement
FAE	fuel-air explosives
FBI	Federal Bureau of Investigation
FLN	Front de Libération Nationale (Algeria)
FN	Fabrique Nationale d'Armes de Guerre (of Herstal, Belgium)
FNLA	Frente Nacional de Libertaçao Angola
FR	France
FRAC	Armed Revolutionary Forces of Columbia
FRELIMO	Frente de Libertaçao de Moçambique
FSA	fusil semi-automatique
GDR	German Democratic Republic
GHQ	general headquarters
GIGN	Groupement d'Intervention de la Gendarmerie Nationale
GNP	gross national product
GRU	intelligence directorate of the Soviet general staff
GUDOL	a German, triple-base, flashless propellant containing nitroguanidine
HE	high explosive
HEAT	high explosive anti-tank
HESH	high explosive squash head
HF	high frequency
HMX	tetramethylene tetranitramine (octogen)
IBM	International Business Machines
ICBM	inter-continental ballistic missile
INLA	Irish National Liberation Army
IPLO	Irish People's Liberation Organization
IRA	Irish Republican Army
IRBM	intermediate range ballistic missile
JHS	*Journal of Hellenic Studies*
JITDS	Joint Integrated Tactical Data System
JRA	Japanese Red Army
JRS	*Journal of Roman Studies*
JSAHR	*Journal of the Society for Army Historical Research*
KAR	King's African Rifles
KGB	Russian State Security Committee (the secret police of the USSR, 1953–91)
kiloton	a measurement of explosive force equal to that produced by 1,000 tons of TNT
KMT	Kuomintang (Chinese Nationalist Party)
MAC	Manufacture d'Armes de Châtellerault
MAD	Mutually Assured Destruction
MAS	Manufacture National d'Armes de St Etienne
MAT	Manufacture d'Armes de Tulle

megaton	a measurement of explosive force equal to that produced by 1,000,000 tons of TNT
MILSTAR	Military Strategic/Tactical and Relay System
MIRV	Multiple Independently Targeted Re-entry Vehicle
MPLA	Movimento Popular de Libertaçao de Angola
MTB	Motor Torpedo Boat
NAAFI	Navy, Army, and Air Force Institute
NATO	North Atlantic Treaty Organization
NC	nitrocellulose
NCO	non-commissioned officer
NG	nitroglycerine
NLF	National Liberation Front
NPT	(Nuclear) Non-Proliferation Treaty
NTDS	Naval Tactical Data System
NVA	North Vietnamese Army
NZEF	New Zealand Expeditionary Force
OAS	Organisation de l'Armée Secrète
OHL	Oberste Heeresleitung
OTC	Officer Training Corps
PAIGC	Partido Africano da Independência de Guiné e Cubo Verde
PETN	pentaerythritol tetranitrate
PIAT	Projectile Infantry Anti-Tank
PIRA	Provisional Irish Republican Army
PLA	People's Liberation Army
PLO	Palestine Liberation Organization
PSY OPS	Psychological (Warfare) Operations
RAF	Royal Air Force
RDF	radio direction finding/rapid deployment force
RDX	trimethylene trinitramine (cyclonite)
REME	Royal Electrical and Mechanical Engineers
RFC	Royal Flying Corps
RHA	rolled homogeneous steel armour
RN	Royal Navy
RNIA	Royal Netherlands Indies Army
ROAD	Reorganized Objective Army Division (US)
RUC	Royal Ulster Constabulary
RUSI	Royal United Services Institution
SA	Sturmabteilung
SALT	Strategic Arms Limitation Talks
SAM	surface-to-air missile
SAS	Special Air Service
SDECE	Service de Documentation Étrangère et de Contre-Espionage
SEATO	South-East Asian Treaty Organization
SIGINT	Signals Intelligence
SLBM	submarine-launched ballistic missile
SMLE	(Rifle), Short, Magazine, Lee-Enfield (0.303 in.)
SOE	Special Operations Executive
SSBN	nuclear-powered ballistic missile submarine
SSLP	Secretariat for (Swedish) Security Policy

SSM	surface-to-surface missile
START	Strategic Arms Reduction Talks
STOL	short-take-off-and-landing
TNT	trinitrotoluene
TOW	Tube-Launched, Optically Tracked, Wire Guided (anti-tank missile)
TWA	Trans-World Airlines
UDR	Ulster Defence Regiment
UN	United Nations
UNESCO	United Nations Educational, Scientific and Cultural Organization
UNITA	Uniao Nacional para Independência Total de Angola
UNO	United Nations Organization
USSR	Union of Soviet Socialist Republics
UP	Patriotic Front (of Columbia)
VC	Viet Cong
VHF	very high frequency
VTOL	vertical-take-off-and-landing

NOTES ON DATES

All dates given in the text are according to the Julian (Old Style) Calendar from 46 BC to 1582 and according to the Gregorian (New Style) Calendar after 1582.

French Revolutionary Calendar

In a number of entries, the French authors have utilized the French Revolutionary Calendar. Unfortunately, it is not possible to translate this into the Gregorian Calendar unless the day and month are stated in addition to the year. According to the Revolutionary Calendar, Year I commenced on 22 September 1792 and ran until 21 September 1793. The year of 365 days was divided into 12 months of 30 days; the additional five days were placed between 17–21 September and were regarded as public holidays. The week was abolished and the month was divided into three decades, each of ten days, the tenth day of which was a rest-day. The Revolutionary Calendar was abandoned in 1805 and on 1 January 1806 France returned to the Gregorian Calendar.

Year I	22 September 1792 to 21 September 1793
Year II	22 September 1793 to 21 September 1794
Year III	22 September 1794 to 21 September 1795
Year IV	22 September 1795 to 21 September 1796
Year V	22 September 1796 to 21 September 1797
Year VI	22 September 1797 to 21 September 1798
Year VII	22 September 1798 to 21 September 1799
Year VIII	22 September 1799 to 21 September 1800
Year IX	22 September 1800 to 21 September 1801
Year X	22 September 1801 to 21 September 1802
Year XI	22 September 1802 to 21 September 1803
Year XII	22 September 1803 to 21 September 1804
Year XIII	22 September 1804 to 21 September 1805

INTRODUCTION TO THE FRENCH EDITION

To publish a specialized dictionary bearing on an activity like warfare, which has occupied and is always likely to occupy an important place in the life of mankind, is a matter of some delicacy. Only a voluminous encyclopedia could aspire to achieve this objective. Even then, however richly detailed it might be, such a work would be necessarily uneven, incomplete and, given the current developments in technology, very soon outdated. There are, moreover, some highly respected military dictionaries in most major languages, though some of these are many years old, run to several volumes and, in some cases, derive from earlier works. We should, however, mention the *Encyclopaedia of Military History*, ed. R. E. and T. N. Dupuy (4th edn, New York, 1993).

The present work has a necessarily different purpose, which imposes more modest dimensions. When the Presses Universitaires de France asked me to produce a military dictionary of 800 pages covering all periods of history and all countries, my first reaction was to decline an invitation to take on what I regarded as an over-ambitious project. The enterprise also had no stated objective. None the less, after some hasty reflection, I agreed to assume the direction of this necessarily collective undertaking since I believed I had found a purpose that it could fulfil.

At the end of the twentieth century, military history is still feeling the effects of the disrepute into which it fell between 1925 and 1965. There were various reasons for this. In the first place, there was the disapproval generated by the bloodletting during the Great War (1914–18) followed by the experiences of the Second World War. Secondly, the *Annales* school condemned all event-based history, that which was centred on battles coming in for particular criticism. Finally, at least in France after 1940, the soldiers themselves condemned military history for sterilizing the imagination by lazy references to the glories of the past. For many, military history became a meaningless activity, a source of error and even of immorality. As a result, it was all but expelled from the discipline of history by those teaching in universities and relegated by military men to *ex cathedra* lectures. The only, or almost the only, people who remained faithful were the proponents of 'narrative history', who sought in it an escape, or military veterans still moved by memories of the ordeals that had marked their earlier years.

During the last twenty years a reaction has set in. Under the influence of sociologists, and indeed of conflict theorists, military men have rediscovered permanent underlying features beneath the evolutionary aspects of war. Scholars have become aware that, however distasteful it may be for certain sensibilities, military affairs have played a constant role in the development of technology, economies and mentalities (*mentalités*) and hence in the development of states and societies. It is symptomatic both that the teaching of military history has regained its place at the École de Guerre in the form of tutorials and that, in 1984, Fernand Braudel devoted the annual week-long conference of the Institut Datini de Prato to the theme of 'War and Economy', this constituting, in a sense, one of the last pronouncements of that great historian, the spiritual head of the *Annales* school.

Now it has to be admitted that the indispensable grounding the broad mass of the population must have for an understanding of military affairs no longer exists (as, indeed, is the case in religious matters also). A brief review of the content of the textbooks used in secondary and even primary schools in the period 1870–1914 shows that it is no exaggeration to speak of the existence of a genuine military culture. Yet today, there is a whole generation that has been denied even the most elementary framework of knowledge for understanding the nature of the great confrontations of the past by the education system. The phrase 'Marignano, 1515', which is smugly trotted out to stigmatize event-based history, has become a hollow formula which, if the cabaret singers are to be believed, some might be tempted to interpret either as a pre-1970 Paris telephone number or as the date of a treaty. Here and there a faintly discernible interest (though a fading one) in the heroes of historical romances or spy novels can be found on account of their engaging and adventurous character, though such figures are bathed in a mythic glow, and scant regard is paid to actual history.

This dictionary harbours no ambitions of reconciling the generations with military history. Its only objective is to lay some rudimentary information before those who have recognized this gap in their education. It will probably bring wry smiles from specialists in military instruction. None the less, it would be highly desirable if it could exert some influence on young officers.

To achieve this end, a non-encyclopedic dictionary was undoubtedly a tempting formula. Yet the right balance had to be struck between precise historical facts and general ideas. It would have been totally unacceptable to return to the type of military history that was written before the turn of the twentieth century. It was therefore necessary, except where the most technical articles were concerned, to let general ideas take the lead and give precedence to everything that could integrate military history into general history. In other words, it offered a means by which to reintroduce military history into the mainstream. It was also essential, while offering a broad sweep of information on the current state of the armed forces, not to neglect the roots of development in the past and in countries other than France. Lastly, and this was not the easiest task, it seemed appropriate to lower the barriers which too often exist between armies, navies and air forces.

These factors account for the choice of the title: *Dictionary of Military History and the Art of War*, with military institutions as an underlying theme. Quite clearly, it seemed to me, the main part of the work had to consist of a number of key elements selected to stimulate thinking on the whole field of military matters: this was why I chose to organize the material in 150 synthesizing articles dealing with broad subjects, often including related themes, rather than in a succession of analytical pieces. This approach will perhaps dismay some readers on account of the multiplicity of cross-references, whereas others will see in it the result of confused thinking. Yet this seemed the best method of highlighting the continuities, the reciprocal influences, the evolutionary developments and the discontinuities.

Among the synthesizing articles, entries concerning strategy, tactics, armament, discipline and the organization of the different parts of armies had to be high on the list of priorities, closely followed by entries dealing with factors which relate either directly or indirectly to the history of military personnel and armed conflict. Thus, articles on the laws of war, medical services and military law rub shoulders with entries on recruitment, logistics and arsenals. It is impossible to overstress that military history is not simply the history of leaders but also that of all men who have fought or have merely borne arms, and of all those who have suffered the effects of war. Although military men have often formed a more or less autonomous community, they have been completely isolated from society on very few occasions. Hence the need for frequent recourse to sociology and the study of mentalities (*mentalités*) to analyse such factors as the sense of military vocation, troop morale and conceptions of fatherland and nationality current in the societies from which the fighting men derived. The reader will, I think, agree that this is the only way to identify properly the specificity of the military calling and understand its expression in a particular language, culture and symbolism at a particular point in history. Also, it was necessary to examine the image of the military which has been portrayed in literature and art.

This dictionary of military history and the art of war offers neither narrative nor overall analysis of the great martial confrontations. It would not have made much sense to have devoted a few lines to the Punic Wars, the Crusades, the Thirty Years' War or the two world wars of the twentieth century. These subjects can be studied elsewhere. It seemed more useful to evoke the place which thirty or so peoples, from Antiquity to the modern period, have occupied in the development of military affairs, laying special emphasis on their contribution to the art of war. Remarkable continuities are revealed, the conquered party normally imitating the conqueror whenever and wherever possible. Thus, Frederick the Great belongs as much to the military history of France as to that of Germany, or vice versa in the case of Napoleon. Although distinct geographical areas can be identified – pre-Columbian America, China, the steppes of Asia, the European plains, and the colonial territories of the nineteenth century – the number of these regions has diminished over the centuries as a result of contacts between peoples. Currently, there are no longer great geographical differences in the practice of warfare, except those imposed by climate or population, and even where variations do exist they are by no means unknown elsewhere. The acceleration of history has particularly made itself felt in the field of military history. Even in the ancient Middle East, those discoveries which proved their worth – the horse, the chariot, the elephant – took less than a century to spread to other peoples. In the twentieth century, the time-lag has been reduced to a few months to the extent that the slightest failure to keep abreast of developments might be fatal. The only delays are those imposed by the potential for producing weapons or, perhaps, inertia. The military history of nations seems to be composed of high points during which they instruct their neighbours (Spain in the sixteenth century, France in the seventeenth century, Prussia in the eighteenth and nineteenth centuries, and the United States and China in the twentieth century) and long periods during which they receive and absorb lessons despite their attachment to national traditions. It is this interplay of influence and receptivity which is the central theme of the articles devoted to contributions to universal military history.

However, the book needed a backbone; in history this can only be provided through the establishment of chronology. The essential chronological reference points occur in the form of short entries relating to some 150 men and about 130 battles and sieges which have particularly marked the development of the art of war, though these are only covered to the extent to which they advanced the evolutionary process. Thus, the entry on Napoleon is brief as he was a genius at employing the innovations of others, whereas characters such as Folard, although less well known, have been granted more space as they exerted an immediate or later influence on military thinking. Other slightly unusual figures will also be found, such as Vitoria and Grotius, the spiritual fathers of international law, or Henri Dunant, the founder of the Red Cross. Moreover, the book does not present a roll of honour. The list of battles does not represent the annals of military glory; lesser encounters figure for the lessons they have provided whereas some battles of great political moment do not always receive a mention.

The chronological, geographic and thematic scope of the work meant that I could not undertake it alone. I have thus called upon some forty collaborators, notably eminent specialists in ancient history and the history of foreign countries and, for the entries of a technical character, on military officers, men of experience well-versed in the history and organization of a particular department of the armed forces. All have accepted the inevitable editorial directives, which often obliged the technical authors to make difficult sacrifices and the writers of the general entries to adopt a wide chronological and spatial field, which meant that they had to undertake a colossal amount of research.

In spite of everyone's efforts and in spite of the recourse to eight foreign collaborators, this dictionary remains somewhat gallocentric. I should, however, like to stress that, as members of the International Commission for Military History, two-thirds of the authors are accustomed to addressing a wide range of concerns and encounters between different points of view. No doubt, given that the material is very varied, some diversities of phraseology and even of conception will be noticeable between the different articles. I accept responsibility for this, as it seemed to me that I had to allow each contributor his own style rather than impose a somewhat artificial uniformity.

It remains for me to make an admission: the production of this work has caused me a great deal of worry. It also brought me much pleasure. First, the joy to which a collective work can give rise when a team is enthused by a single spirit. New friends were added to those of long standing, all of whom showed faith in the enterprise. To everyone concerned, whatever their contribution, I must express my deepest gratitude. I shall refrain from mentioning individual names except for that of Philippe Masson, who undertook the task of co-ordinating everything relating to naval affairs. I should also add that I felt a more personal pleasure in respect of the articles I wrote myself; not that I am satisfied with them. On each occasion it was a challenge to provide an account of a great wealth of material in just a few pages before broadening it out into an overall picture. That challenge, once accepted, has a stimulating effect on the mind, since it forces one to strip complexity to its essentials. I know that, while sometimes grumbling to their editor, the contributors to this dictionary, in spite of their original misgivings, also often shared this stimulation. I only hope that this same feeling communicates itself to the reader. In the literal sense of that word, this book is only an essay. Having thrown down the gauntlet, it is for others to take the work further by their reservations, criticisms and research.

ANDRÉ CORVISIER

INTRODUCTION TO THE ENGLISH EDITION

It did not take long to decide to accept the invitation to edit an English version of André Corvisier's *Dictionnaire d'Art et d'Histoire Militaires* (Presses Universitaires de France, Paris, 1988). Among the innumerable dictionaries, encyclopaedias and reference books devoted to military history, Professor Corvisier's work was new, original and approachably academic.

Rather than producing the traditional list of battles and potted biographies of famous generals, Professor Corvisier concentrated on important themes, topics and developments within military history. Engagements and soldiers only earned space if and where they had contributed to the advancement of the art of warfare. The recitation of the chronology of individual wars was also deliberately eschewed. Instead, Professor Corvisier devoted himself to studying the military history of the major countries of the world with a particular emphasis on the interplay between armed forces and societies. Additionally he investigated themes and sub-themes within military history, demonstrating its propinquity to the other branches of the historical discipline. It was this integrative and wide-ranging approach which struck a chord that was fresh and modern. A further attraction was the substantial nature of the major entries, many of article length, enabling the presentation of detailed arguments supported by sufficient illustration. Building on Professor Corvisier's original, which might be more accurately described as a set of thematically related essays rather than a dictionary, there seemed the opportunity to produce a reference book relevant to both the 'old' and the 'new' approaches to military history.

Professor Corvisier's scheme has been amended in two ways. First, accounts of some twentieth-century wars have been included. The Korean War and the Gulf War of 1991 have been included because they were new types of conflict: wars between forces of the United Nations and countries which had offended against its resolutions. Also, the original entry on the Battle of Suomussalmi has been replaced by an article on the Russo-Finnish War of 1939–40 as it was the entirety of the conflict which was historically important rather than just the one engagement. The colonial wars in Vietnam were searing experiences for France and the United States, too central to be omitted, while the Falklands War of 1982 contained many lessons about training, the advantages of professional armed forces and the limitations of modern armaments and logistics. Second, in an admirable attempt to achieve brevity and concision, a number of the smaller entries in the French book actually seemed to be too short to achieve their intended purpose. Consequently, many of the original pieces have been expanded to enhance the value of the *Dictionary* as a work of reference. Following the example of Professor Corvisier, the temptation to bring the thematic and national entries right up-to-date has been resisted as the work would have dated extremely quickly. Essentially, this is a book of military history.

Prima facie, military history appears to command a wide public interest in Great Britain but a closer look reveals that this is actually little more than a fascination with militaria and aspects of the First and Second World Wars. Although Professor Corvisier's reasons for writing the *Dictionnaire* specifically concerned the present condition of military history in France, the situation he describes is not dissimilar to that in Great Britain. Until the 1960s, military history was little taught in British universities and but slightly regarded by the academic profession. Its status has improved slightly since then, largely through the development of the 'new military history' in which battles and wars have been neglected in favour of studying armed forces in relation to society. To a considerable extent this was a conscious rationalization of military history in order to effect a compromise with the *Annales* school, a trend which reached a peak during the 1970s and early 1980s when it became quite normal to write books on armies and navies without actually mentioning the fact that their *raison d'être* was the perpetration of legalized violence. This imbalance is now being slowly corrected, especially as narrative history regains respectability. Professor Corvisier's volume presented an opportunity to present this emerging equilibrium by showing how the 'new military history' has enriched the old and vice versa.

Professor Corvisier's views on the state of history teaching in French schools could also easily be transplanted directly into Britain. It appears that children are no longer taught facts but vague historical 'techniques' without the contexts or the information to understand fully what they are trying to achieve. Such questionable classroom exercises as commenting on 'unseen' documents or writing an essay on 'How would you feel if you were Henry VIII's seventh wife?' commonly masquerade as history. 'Empathy' and 'imagination' are being encouraged at the expense of learning how to construct reasoned arguments from evidence. The military variety of history now plays a diminished and diminishing role even in that area where it might be expected to possess crucial importance: the education of British army, navy and air force officers. Professor Corvisier's didactic purpose is as relevant in Britain as in France. The English version of the *Dictionnaire* is thus intended to fulfil aims similar to those enunciated by Professor Corvisier with the essential addition that it is also a general and academic reference book illustrating both the current state of the subject and the fact that military history reaches back further than 1914.

Since work commenced on the production of an English version, further relevance has appeared. War has returned to Europe. After four and a half decades of peace beneath the nuclear umbrellas of NATO and the Warsaw Pact, the collapse of the rotten and corrupt regimes of Eastern Europe, culminating in the Second Russian Revolution of 1991, has ended European stability. At the time of writing, vicious civil wars are raging in Yugoslavia, a general Balkan war seems probable, states of the old Soviet Union are at war, and crude nationalism and racism are re-emerging across much of Central and Eastern Europe, while the co-operation and common purpose once promised by the European Community seem to have reached the limits of political and national acceptability and will almost certainly recede rather than expand. Once again, war in its numerous manifestations has become a central issue in European political and social development. There can be no more appropriate time for the publication of a book which attempts to investigate the trends, themes and common denominators which have shaped both the conduct of war and the political and social employment of war throughout history.

There were some problems in producing an English version of the French original arising from an inevitable national perspective. In order to prepare an edition for the Anglo-American market, the book had to be expanded and made to reflect more of the concerns and interests of the English-speaking reader. However, the latter point was not over-emphasized; no purpose would have been served by replacing a Gallocentric viewpoint with an Anglo-American equivalent. Indeed, by re-working parts of the original and by enlarging its scope and coverage, the French foundation of Professor Corvisier's book offered the chance to devise a more balanced, European approach. However, the English version could only be produced under certain material restraints. In the first place, the English publisher sanctioned additional material amounting to a maximum of 100,000 words. Second, building on Professor Corvisier's edition, instead of simply producing an English translation, entailed restrictions relating to the rights of intellectual property epitomized in the French *droit moral*. The interpretations and priorities of the original French contributors have thus remained fundamental to the book. This rigidity has been partially circumvented by the creation of over 100 new entries, the expansion of many existing articles and the total replacement of others. As a rule of thumb, where the French article demonstrated its principal points sufficiently, even if this was achieved mainly through the military history of France, then it has simply been translated and only necessary minor amendments and corrections effected. Where the original French entry was considered by the team of English-speaking consultants and contributors not to have fulfilled the requirements expected, then the entry has been either substantially modified or entirely reconstructed. Finally, the French edition lacked a general index. Although cross references were listed at the end of each entry, there was no means of cataloguing the multitude of potential cross references contained within the text. This lacuna has been filled. Overall, the task has not been easy nor the result ideal, but this version is intended as an enhancement of Professor Corvisier's pioneering book while remaining faithful to the original. As with most modern military history there remains a nagging sensation that the book is perhaps too Eurocentric. However, this can be readily justified: since 1500 the world has steadily adopted the military techniques, armaments and organizations of Europe to the extent that the armed forces of the world now display a remarkable homogeneity.

On reflection, the stress on one country, France, has actually proved advantageous. In the first place it presents a perspective not often available to the English-speaking reader. Secondly, France was in the van of numerous evolutions in military history: the Empire of Charlemagne; the development of feudalism; France and Spain were the arbiters of European martial history in the fifteenth and sixteenth centuries; she was in the forefront of the birth of the modern standing army during the seventeenth century; she was second only to Brandenburg-Prussia and Great Britain in the eighteenth century; and the world still owes much to the eclectic methods of Napoleon. The Franco-Prussian was the major European war of the nineteenth century and France was at the heart of the First World War. Only since 1919 has France partially fallen away as one of the premier military states of the Western world. A work of reference which uses one country as a yardstick, reinforced with examples and contradictions from elsewhere, is preferable to one whose entries are based on numerous scattered pieces of information relating to a large number of states. The former has structure whereas the latter can be rather diffuse.

The *Dictionary* clearly reveals the importance to the development of modern armies and techniques of war of two historical periods: the Ancient World of the Greeks and Romans and the changes which occurred in Western Europe during the sixteenth and seventeenth centuries. Indeed, these two periods are themselves closely related as many of the military reformers of the early modern period based their theories on Greek and Roman practice. The case for the prominence of Greece and Rome is firmly established while the phenomenon of early modern Europe is, it must be hoped, properly historical and not just the consequence of having both French and English general editors who happen to be interested in that period and whose historical thinking tends to converge. It is also apparent how many countries, races, states and nations have undergone similar military processes. Despite her non-martial traditions, the military development of England, or Great Britain after 1707, reveals far more similarities with continental European states than *sui generis* features. Likewise, tactics, strategy and weapons possess common principles and methods across the ages despite developments and changes in politics, economics, society and technology. Only with the coming of nuclear armaments did this continuity suffer a temporary interruption until more and more countries acquired the technical expertise to build their own atomic weapons regardless of attempts by international organizations to restrict their spread. Under this higher order of nuclear weapons, perhaps the first real manifestation of a natural law limiting the scale and scope of conflict, 'conventional war' reverted to development along established historical lines.

Where the original French entry has simply been translated and, if necessary, corrected, then only the French author's name has been appended. If new material has been added by an Anglo-American contributor, then joint names appear. Obviously, new entries carry just the name of the Anglo-American author. The reading lists after each entry are not bibliographies; they are works in which the reader can find additional information and delve more deeply into that subject. Wherever possible, books have been listed which are in English or in English translation. As far as was practical, other dictionaries and encyclopaedias have not been used in the preparation of this volume.[1] For one book of reference to take its information from another seems both undesirable and liable to compound error. The French edition contained a bibliography of general works on military history.[2] This has been omitted from the English version as the reading lists after each entry are far more extensive than those in Professor Corvisier's original, specific reading being more useful than the generalized, and the majority of the works cited were in French.

There remains one last justification for this book. During the nineteenth and twentieth centuries warfare has ceased to be a remote activity practised by professional armed forces. Mass conscription during the First and Second World Wars brought personal experience of the armed services, campaigns and battles to millions, while total war involves entire populations. Now, with the assistance of radio, television, and satellite broadcasting, populations of countries which are not at war can become vicarious observers. Wars, whether far away or close to home, can be brought into the living room of every house in every country, reported in real-time with live coverage from the front line. For non-participants, the experience of warfare is no longer restricted to the reconstructions of fiction; it is something which any individual equipped with a telecommunications receiver can choose to indulge vicariously at leisure. Montgomery and Patton in the Second World War were the original 'media generals' gaining publicity through the newsreels and consciously recognizing the need to deal with and assuage the press. The Vietnam War was the first televized conflict and has been followed by the British campaign in Northern Ireland, war in the Falklands (1982), the civil wars in the Lebanon, the Yugoslavian civil war which began in 1991, and the United Nations–Iraq conflict (the Gulf War, 1991). So dense was the media coverage of the opening stages of the last-named war that the armed forces seemed much pressed to maintain operational secrecy in the face of live television pictures of jets taking off and returning, air raids in progress, damage and casualties. To a regrettable extent, war has become a spectator sport, the ultimate blood sport, succeeding public hangings, bear baiting, cock fighting, boxing, wrestling, ice hockey, rugby, fox hunting, bull fighting and grid-iron football. This has always been the case, to a limited extent. Alexander Munro watched the Battle of Culloden (1746) and then rather wished he had been elsewhere; perched on rooftops the inhabitants of Boston enjoyed the Battle of Bunker Hill; Louis XIV regarded a good siege in Flanders as an enjoyable social occasion. But these were rarities, events which occurred to only a very few people. Now war exists for all to see. In 1991 during the United Nations–Iraq War, television sets suddenly appeared in business offices and school staff rooms, radio stations devoted entire channels to news from the Gulf, and the transmissions were viewed and listened to as though they were the Olympics,

Wimbledon or the World Cup Final. Cable news channels and the BBC even had reporters and camera crews stationed inside Iraq transmitting 'from the other side of the hill'. Whether exposure to this sort of material will help to create a wider anti-war movement and directly affect political reaction to war or whether the public will rapidly become inured to what they watch remains to be seen. Certainly, twenty years of media coverage of the 'troubles' in Northern Ireland has neither nauseated the British public nor achieved the aims of any of the sets of terrorists. The British public seem to have made the necessary adjustments. Probably, people will simply treat the coverage of war as a form of fiction, too unreal and too far away for profound concern. The current trend of television news broadcasts, and even some of the better newspapers, to resemble soap operas with their emphasis on the trivial and the 'human interest' aspects of stories might well have prepared the ground for the ultimate, negative public reaction. Will future battles have to stop for the occasional commercial break? More seriously, intensive media coverage of war will probably result in misrepresentation and distortion through partial editing, the emotive involvement of reporters and manipulative censorship. It will also focus public concern and interest solely on those wars which are covered by the media, forcing governments to adjust their foreign policies accordingly.

Like Professor Corvisier, the general editor of the English version has emerged with ambivalent reactions, ranging from deep concern to an occasional satisfaction. Obviously, if there had not been a basic agreement with Professor Corvisier's intellectual and historical approach it would have been absurd to have accepted this task. However, regardless of the substantial efforts of the numerous contributors, just as the French edition was moulded and shaped according to Professor Corvisier's thinking so the English version similarly reflects the general editor's overall views on the history of warfare.

JOHN CHILDS

1. See, *A Bibliography of Encyclopaedias and Dictionaries Dealing with Military, Naval and Maritime Affairs, 1577–1971*, ed. Hardin Craig (4th edn, Houston, Texas, 1971).
2. *Dictionnaire d'Art et d'Histoire Militaires*, ed. André Corvisier (Paris, 1988), pp. xi–xii.

A

Abraham, plains of *See* QUEBEC

Academies, military *See* TRAINING

Actium, Battle of (2 September 31 BC) A sandy promontory on the west coast of Greece at the entrance to the Ambracian Gulf, Actium was the site of the naval battle in which M. Antonius, supported by Queen Cleopatra of Egypt, was defeated by Octavian, the future Emperor Augustus. Accounts of the battle are confused and obscured by the propaganda of the victors. Antonius' fleet may have been trying to break out to a new position, but through either defeat or desertion much of it was captured by Octavian's admiral M. Agrippa, though Antonius and Cleopatra escaped to Egypt, where they subsequently committed suicide. Antonius' army at Actium surrendered soon afterwards, and Octavian's victory was complete, bringing the civil war to an end. Actium was more important for its political consequences than for military history; it ensured that Octavian would control the Roman world and that his view of Rome's political future and the role of her empire would prevail. *See also* ROME.

B. CAMPBELL

FURTHER READING
R. Syme, *The Roman Revolution* (Oxford, 1939), pp. 294–8.

Ader, Clément (1841–1925) This French engineer of roads and bridges, and inventor of genius, contrived to solve the problem of manned flight by adopting the methods of insects and birds. After fabricating a balloon during the Franco-Prussian War in 1870, he made a man-powered aeroplane in 1872 and a steam-powered, bat-like machine in 1886. In January 1890, he con-structed another steam-powered flying apparatus named *Eole*, which, in October 1892, succeeded in leaving the ground for a distance of 50 metres. With financial assistance from the French Ministry of War, a fourth machine was created in 1896, which proved capable of flight in 1897, but was severely damaged on its maiden attempt. This final disaster demoralized Ader and he abandoned experimentation.

Retiring to the town of his birth, Muret, he wrote a number of works, most notably *L'Aviation militaire* (1908), in which he expounded, with extraordinary prescience, the military applications of manned flight. Ader recognized the potential of this new weapon and laid down the organizational arrangements required for its realization. He described the range of weapons – bombs, machine-guns, cannon – with which it would be feasible to equip aircraft, in addition to various ancillary devices such as bomb sights. Finally, he envisaged the use, in due course, of aircraft flying from ships and anticipated the destruction of large cities, such as London, by air attack. Largely because of Ader's work, France was the first country to militarize the new science of flight. The name of his fourth flying machine, *Avion*, provided the French with their word for aircraft.

Orville and Wilbur Wright succeeded in flying a heavier-than-air machine at Kitty Hawk, North Carolina, on 17 December 1903. *See also* AIRCRAFT, BOMBER; AIRCRAFT, FIGHTER; AIRCRAFT, RECONNAISSANCE; AVIATION.

P. FACON
JOHN CHILDS
STEPHEN J. HARRIS

FURTHER READING
C. Christienne, P. Lissarague, A. Degardin, P. Facon, P. Biffotot and M. Hodeir, *Histoire de l'aviation militaire française* (Paris, 1980).

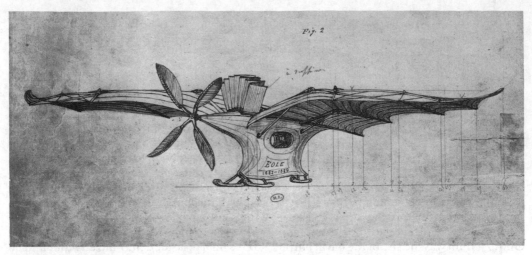

Ader's flying machine
(M.A.R.S.)

Administration, army Military administration originated with the establishment of permanent armies. In the citizen armies of the Ancient World or those made up of feudal contingents, its function was merely to verify the presence of the men who had been called up and to maintain them when their service was extended beyond the customary period. Mercenary armies handled their own administration, with problems of provisioning and supply being consigned by the army chiefs to financiers, such as Witte in the case of Wallenstein's army. In the royal armies of the modern era, the administration of companies was a task which fell to the captains and to their quartermasters, clerks, etc. With the development of the regiment, the general staff of these units included officers with essentially administrative functions, *majors* and *aide-majors* (France), majors and adjutants (England), and quartermasters in other armies. The function of the royal administration was, essentially, to manage the regiments and companies and maintain their strength.

The first coherent system of troop review appeared in France under Charles VII and developed rapidly in Spain from the beginning of the sixteenth century. In Charles V's armies, muster-masters carried out troop reviews several times a year, often without notice. On the strength of these muster-masters' declarations, the paymasters distributed the soldiers' pay to the commanders, as approved by the highest authorities, captains, generals or governors. The Spanish monarchy in the sixteenth century made great advances in military administration. The Master of the Accounts, *contador*, and the Treasurer, *pagador*, could not issue money without the authorization of the *Veedor*, muster-master-general. Similarly, the provision of rations was controlled by the *Proveedores* and the supply of arms by the Administrators of the Royal Arsenals. In Madrid, the *Contaduria mayor de Cuentas*, Revenue Court, exercised minute control over the whole of the Spanish army.

In France, administration of troops lay with the War Commissaries and the Paymasters and Controllers. The war effort for which Richelieu was responsible made the War Commissaries the principal agents of Royal government among the troops. To make this war effort more effective, the intendants were assigned the task of maintaining the armies in the field. All these administrators were members of the *noblesse de robe*, rather than of the old nobility, the *noblesse d'épée*. It was only after the Fronde, the revolts of the Paris *parlement* and elements of the nobility between 1648 and 1652, that the commissions of army intendants became distinct from those of provincial intendants. And indeed, the latter still retained control over the maintenance of troops stationed in their provinces and all jurisdiction over conflicts between troops and civilians. The administration of the royal militias created in 1688 also fell to them.

During the same period the Secretariat of State for War was set up. The concentration of military affairs in the hands of one of the secretaries of state began in about 1620, but the origin of the French Ministry of War can be dated to Scrvien in 1635. This ministry would thereafter continue to function, with only two interruptions, during the Regency, the Polysynod system, and during the Revolution, under the Committee of Public Safety. Under Louis XIV, thanks to Le Tellier and Louvois, a remarkable degree of structuring was achieved in military administration without any major innovations being made. That administration comprised:

1 The Secretariat of State for War, divided into a number of offices whose chief clerks shared out the 'business' according to their preferences and their skills. The Secretariat of State for War gradually came to incorporate the various army services, such as the artillery (controlled in theory by the Grand Master of the Artillery) and fortifications (formed into a single department in 1691). It was also responsible for general communications with frontier provinces including recently annexed provinces and, in time of war, with countries occupied by the French army.

2 The territorial military administration under the command of the provincial governors, who were responsible for order in the provinces where they represented the king's authority (with the assistance of the lieutenant-generals of the province and, in some cases, of military commanders). Individual town governors were subordinate to them. The king's lieutenants and the general staff of garrison towns were in fact subordinate to the War Secretariat. The provincial intendant worked closely with the governor while at the same time representing the will of the king. When an army was stationed in a prov-

ince, the governor had to defer to the commander-in-chief of that army.

3 Army intendants and War Commissaries were responsible for the administration of troops. After units ceased to be the property of their colonels and captains, *Conseils d'administration des corps de troupe* were set up (1776). These consisted of a colonel, adjutant-colonel, lieutenant-colonel, major and the senior captain, and survived in expanded form until 1934. However, routine administration remained the responsibility of adjutants, quartermasters and quartermaster-sergeants.

The French administrative system of the *ancien régime*, based on officers of the *noblesse de robe*, was copied in several countries, including Piedmont, where, in 1717, the Secretariat General of War, in conjunction with the local commissaries, became a genuine Secretariat. In Austria, on the other hand, it was the Spanish tradition of councils that was adopted. The *Generalkriegskommissariat* created in 1650, and supported by the *Generalproviantamt*, responsible for supplying the troops, did not really become separate from the *Hofkriegsrat* (the Aulic Council of War) until Haugwitz's reforms in 1752: problems of pay, discipline and the maintenance of troops fell to the *Generalkriegskommissariat*, and problems of command to the *Hofkriegsrat*. France succumbed for a short period to the temptation to adopt a council system (these were forms of collective ministries) when it introduced the Polysynod system.

In England, a genuine War Office was not created until 1855. Under Cromwell, military administration was the responsibility of the secretary to the general, and this official became the secretary at war after the Restoration in 1660. However, he was only a functionary charged with the movement and marching of troops, the political control and direction of the army resting with the secretaries of state. During the eighteenth century, the administration remained fragmented with the secretary at war responsible for the infantry and cavalry and the Board of Ordnance maintaining the artillery and fortifications. The Treasury supervised supply and issued money to the paymaster-general, the commissary-general mustered the army and the Board of General Officers, created in 1689, looked after strictly military matters. All of these officials were independent of each other but answerable to the secretaries of state, the commander-in-chief, when there was such a post, and the monarch. Only in 1798 did the secretary at war cease to be subordinate to the secretaries of state. The War Office Act 1870 firmly subordinated the commander-in-chief to the secretary of state and placed army administration in the hands of the commander-in-chief, the surveyor-general of the Ordnance and a financial secretary. The recommendations of the Esher Committee (1904) created an Army Council and a General Staff and re-organized the administration within the War Office. The Army Council decided matters of policy, while the War Office's responsibilities were divided between the chief of the general staff (operations, staff duties and training), the adjutant-general (maintenance and welfare of the troops), the quartermaster-general (supply and transport) and the master-general of the Ordnance (weapons manufacture, artillery and fortification). The War Office's functions were then delegated to admin-istrative military districts, which were dis-tinct from the districts of operational commands. In 1946, a Ministry of Defence was created to incorporate the Admiralty, the War Office and the Air Ministry. Be-tween 1964 and 1967, the Ministry of De-fence was reorganized. Instead of each service forming a separate section, the ministry was rearranged according to function – equipment, administration and, after 1971, procurement. The three services were reduced to merely administrative bodies within the overall ministry.

By contrast to England, where military administration remained under civilian control, in Prussia, the Directorate General of War; Finance and Domains, assisted in the provinces by Directors of Wars and Domains, showed how important military preoccupations were in governmental and administrative affairs. Russia followed suit.

In these two countries, the personnel of the military administration was made up of former soldiers, as was the staff of the civil administration.

However, in the second half of the eighteenth century, the role of soldiers in military administration expanded in all countries. In France, a soldier, the Maréchal de Belle-Isle, became secretary of state for war for the first time, in 1758. In 1788, a *Conseil de la Guerre* (War Council), composed of generals, was created to com-pensate for Louis XVI's lack of interest in his army and the limited skills of the secretary of state, Brienne.

Since the Middle Ages, military adminis-tration has often played a pioneering role in the history of administration, second only to that of the Navy. As a consequence, in France the Revolution did not need to make major changes to that organization. The Ministry of War, set up in 1791, confined itself to standardizing the adminis-tration of such services as the artillery and fortifications and passed responsibility for correspondence with the frontier provinces to the Ministry of the Interior. However, local military administration was simplified by a process which had begun in 1788. A military committee was set up in the As-semblies. In Year II, the Committee of Public Safety of the Convention reduced the role played by the Ministry of War and, on 1 April 1794, it was replaced by the *Commission de l'Organisation et du Mouve-ment des Armées*. The Committee of Public Safety had its own offices and its agents, the 'Commissioners to the Armies'. The Minis-try of War was re-established by the Con-stitution of Year III but in 1802, Bonaparte, alarmed by the extent of its power, divided it into two: it became the Ministry of War and the Ministry of the Administration of War (roughly a division between personnel and *matériel*). It was reunified in 1814.

Since then, in addition to the minister's own office the War Ministry has comprised a certain number of directorates, divided into offices reflecting the changing manner in which responsibilities have been appor-tioned. A certain number of consultative committees, councils and commissions, whose tasks have been to study technical problems generally concerning arms, material, etc., have also been attached to it. A similar pattern of organization is found in other countries.

Since the Second World War, the structures of war ministries have changed considerably, with a broadly similar process occurring in almost all countries. The names of the departments have changed: the French Ministry of War became the Ministry of National Defence, bringing together the War, Air and Naval Ministries, the Ministry of the Armies and the Ministry of Defence. Thus a general tendency to deal with defence problems on a wider scale has been seen. The effect of these issues on the life of the country concerned has led to the creation of information services for heads of state (in France since the Fifth Republic) or heads of government such as the General Secretariat for National Defence. Territorial administrations and the administration of units have also had to adapt to variations in staff size and to new developments in the art of war, notably, in paying more attention to military hardware and to psychological problems. *See also* ARM; CAVALRY; COMMAND; GENERAL STAFF; INFANTRY; INSPECTIONS; INTENDANTS; ORDNANCE.

A. CORVISIER

FURTHER READING
André Corvisier, *Armies and Societies in Europe, 1494–1789* (Bloomington, Ind., 1979); Owen Wheeler, *The War Office* (London, 1914); W. S. Hamer, *The British Army: civil – military relations, 1885–1905* (Oxford, 1970); R. F. Weigley, *History of the United States Army* (New York, 1967); Walther Hubatsch, *Frederick the Great* (London, 1975).

Administration, naval The term naval administration is used to cover the organization for directing, providing, manning and equipping the forces required for naval war, and their maintenance in an efficient condition.

In ancient and medieval times, when permanent naval forces were either small or non-existent, the necessary work could be carried out by a few individuals, usually drawn from the ruling group, and given the necessary authority to requisition and equip ships and vessels and to call up men to man them. There would usually be an official whose task was to look after the state's property in ships and arsenals.

Thus in Athens 'trierarchs', recruited from among the wealthiest strata of the population, were responsible for fitting out warships and recruiting their crews. In the Roman Republic, a different system was used, and their allies, the *socii navales*, provided most of the crews.

During the Middle Ages, Byzantium and Venice possessed genuine naval administrations, which to a large extent served as models for those of modern states, even if their emergence was at times belated. In Spain, for example, a 'ministry' was only created in the aftermath of the defeat of the 'Invincible Armada', and in France such a department did not appear until the seventeenth century.

In England a 'Keeper of the King's Ships' could be found as early as 1207, although in war the actual direction of the fleet lay with a great officer of state, the Lord High Admiral, who would take personal command or appoint a deputy.

With the progress of technology, and the increasing needs of states for permanent forces, such arrangements gave way to more extensive organizations. In England, this stage was reached in the reign of Henry VIII, whose European ambitions called for strong naval forces, and who was also a keen shipbuilder. In 1546 he set up the 'Navy Board', which, subject to the Lord High Admiral, was to administer naval affairs. Composed of four officials, each of whom held a post superintending one section of the business, this body inaugurated the English preference for a committee to run naval affairs; its instructions had to be signed by at least two of the four.

During the same reign, the king's yards began to expand both in size and in numbers, and the officers in charge of each also had a place on the Navy Board.

The system was found to be satisfactory during the reign of Elizabeth, notably through the influence of John Hawkins. Although subsequent results were less happy, this was largely on account of a lack

5

of interest in the Navy and shortage of money.

Revival took place when the Dutch Wars imposed much heavier burdens on the organization. Known under the Commonwealth as the Council of Admiralty, the system remained unchanged, but showed itself capable of providing and equipping the much larger fleets of the First Dutch War. While the Restoration in 1660 saw the old name restored, more precise instructions were laid down for the officials, and the influence of Samuel Pepys (1633–1703), the principal administrator of the Navy between 1660 and 1688, gave direction and clarity.

Serious deficiencies also emerged, however, and demonstrated the principle that administration had to extend its scope to meet real needs. Victualling so large a fleet had become a major undertaking, and when, even in peacetime, more ships were in commission, the contract method hitherto employed conspicuously failed. The care of sick and wounded seamen was likewise the subject of extempore arrangements, while, above all, the raising of seamen was a constant difficulty in every campaign.

The first two problems led to the creation of further boards on the same basis, the Victualling Board, which set about building up establishments to provide a constant and reliable supply of food, even if the methods of preservation available at the time were inadequate to ensure its lasting quality, and the Sick and Hurt Board, as well as the establishment of Greenwich Hospital as a refuge for disabled and aged mariners, and eventually naval hospitals. The third problem proved insoluble with the national administrative arrangements of the seventeenth and eighteenth centuries, hence the press had perforce to continue.

At the summit of the structure, 1688 brought an important change. Until that year, the Lord High Admiral continued to be an active post, long held by the Duke of York, later James II. His departure led to the office being placed 'in commission', so that yet another board appeared to provide the higher direction of the service – except for short periods under Queen Anne and George IV. The 'First Lord' became the political head of the Navy; several of the other Lords would be naval officers.

Until 1832 these four boards provided the administrative structure of the Royal Navy. While this somewhat complex structure has been much criticized, both at the time and since, for delays and corruption, it cannot be denied that, despite growing responsibilities and increased numbers of ships and men, the Navy was not unsuccessful. Moreover, the administration in the several dockyards operated the largest industrial establishments in the country and other specialized institutions – victualling yards, rope yards and hospitals. Indeed, political circles recognized that the Navy was a special case, which required special methods; the First Lord was often a naval officer, and the department was not so exposed to political jobbery as others. Consequently, the administration was reasonably efficient even if conservative and possibly open to internal feuds, and certainly superior to that of any other navy. It could do remarkable things, such as to send out at short notice the wherewithal to refit the Mediterranean fleet at Cadiz, build a new design of landing boat in three weeks, or victual large fleets as a matter of routine.

After 1815, a movement for 'economical government' found favour, and the Admiralty was consequently reformed in 1832. All the boards, except that of the Admiralty itself, were abolished, and the various functions were placed each under a chief official, responsible to one of the Lords of the Admiralty. While the change was not unsuccessful in abolishing much internal correspondence, it destroyed the 'strategic' function of the Board of Admiralty by overloading it with day-to-day work, at a time when the functions of the administration were vastly expanding with the coming of steam engines, iron and steel ships and continuous service for ratings, which both in themselves and in their consequences required more effort. The result was somewhat to discredit the Board system, and a demand arose for the Navy to be under a single secretary of state. To this end, changes in 1869 virtually abolished the Board, but the merits of its regular meetings were then realized, so that the former arrangement was restored. Nevertheless, the strategical aspect was still overwhelmed, and only after various indications of inadequacy had appeared were arrangements introduced in 1886 to prepare more thoroughly for war, while a full naval staff did not appear until the First World War. Following the problems of the 1880s, these arrangements proved satisfactory and the War Office was similarly reorganized after the Boer War, while the new Air Ministry of 1918 assumed a comparable structure. This lasted until 1946 when the three service departments were merged into a Ministry of Defence, although this new body retained elements of the board system.

For many years, the Navy of the United States was a much smaller administrative problem. During the past 220 years it has experimented with a variety of approaches:

The Continental Navy During the American War of Independence (1775–83), the Congress established in succession four different administrative bodies to deal with the Navy: the Naval Committee (October 1775–January 1776); the Marine Committee (January 1776–October 1779); and two regional committees under the authority of the Marine Committee – the Navy Board of the Middle Department, based at Philadelphia, and the Navy Board of the Eastern Department, based in Boston – to supervise manning, construction, repair and outfitting.

After experiencing little success in naval operations in 1777 and 1778, in October 1779 Congress decided to replace the Marine Committee with a Board of Admiralty, which directed the operations of the Navy until February 1781 when Congress superseded it with the office of Secretary of Marine in July 1781. Unable to find anyone willing to assume this position, the duties devolved on the Superintendent of Finance, who, in September 1781, received the additional title of Agent of Marine. When this individual retired from public office in November 1784, Congress saw no need to appoint a successor. As the remaining ships were sold off in 1784 and 1785, the newly established Board of Treasury dealt with the outstanding accounts and papers.

The US Navy When the constitution of the United States became effective in 1789, Congress assigned naval responsibilities to the Department of War, which carried them out until 1798. An ardent advocate of the Navy, President John Adams moved to establish a separate Navy Department, which was authorized by Congress on 30 April 1798. Under this arrangement, the Secretary of the Navy was responsible for executing all orders relating to the Navy received from the President. This began a long-standing tradition of decentralized authority and independent command for senior naval officers which lasted until the Second World War.

At the end of the War of 1812 there was a great deal of dissatisfaction with the administration of the Navy. There had been many administrative abuses resulting from the secretary's excessive number of duties, the need for closer supervision of naval agents, and the great latitude given to commanding officers. As a result, Congress established the Board of Navy Commissioners. Under the supervision of the Secretary of the Navy, this Board executed his ministerial duties. In September 1842, Congress reacted to a further public demand for naval reorganization and replaced the Board of Navy Commissioners with five naval bureaux subordinate to the Secretary of the Navy, functionally distributing the work of the Department between them. In 1862, Congress reorganized the Navy Department, dividing the responsibilities of some of the five existing bureaus and adding three others. The general principles behind this administrative structure, based on the functional division of effort, continued in effect until 1966.

In March 1915, Congress created the Office of the Chief of Naval Operations (CNO) for the senior officer of the Navy. When the United States entered the Second World War in December 1941, the CNO had authority under the Secretary of the Navy for the co-ordination of the functions of the naval establishment afloat and the determination of priorities for construction, repair and overhaul. The command of the fleet was vested in the three fleet commanders-in-chief, one of whom had the additional responsibility of being Commander-in-Chief, US Fleet. On 18 December 1941, President Franklin D. Roosevelt ordered that the principal headquarters of the Commander-in-Chief, US Fleet should be in Washington DC, and directed that he should keep the CNO advised of all logistic and other operating needs of the fleet. Two separate and distinct staffs operated side-by-side in Washington throughout the Second World War; however, from 26 March 1942 until 1945 Admiral Ernest J. King held both positions simultaneously. In August 1945, President Harry Truman combined the functions of the two positions in the person of the Chief of Naval Operations, making him 'the principal adviser to the President and to the Secretary of the Navy on the conduct of war' and commander of the operating forces, charged with the preparation, readiness and logistical support of both the fleet and the shore establishment.

Having reached its height during the Second World War, from 1946 the authority of the Chief of Naval Operations steadily declined. With the foundation of the Department of Defense in July 1947, the Secretary of the Navy came under the direction of the Secretary of Defense. At the same time, the CNO became a statutory member of the Joint Chiefs of Staff, the committee of service advisers to the President established in 1942 and modelled on Britain's Committee of Imperial Defence. The CNO's responsibility for independent command of the operating naval forces was weakened in 1947 by the creation of seven unified multi-service commands.

The Secretary of the Navy was removed entirely from the operational chain of command in 1958, which now ran from the President to the Secretary of Defense, through the Joint Chiefs to the unified commanders. The CNO's role became almost wholly administrative although he retained an element of command authority as a member of the Joint Chiefs. In 1966, the Secretary of Defense, Robert McNamara, replaced the bureau system as another step in his plan to create a stronger, more effective force while, at the same time, economizing. The Goldwater–Nichols Defense Act 1986 gave this further

impetus, increasing the power of the Chairman of the Joint Chiefs of Staff and requiring joint command.

In France there was no naval ministry before the time of Richelieu. Affairs were divided between the officials of the *Ponant* and the *Levant*, i.e. the Atlantic and the Mediterranean. Richelieu abolished the old offices of Constable and Admiral of France in 1627, appointing himself Superintendent of Commerce and Navigation. By thus systematically making use of the feudal and seigniorial structures, he cleared the ground for the fleet to become entirely controlled by the crown. Colbert, *de facto* Controller-General from 1661, unified the administration in the Secretariat of State for the Navy in 1669. This department was also responsible for trade and the colonies, tasks it continued to undertake until the coming of the Revolution, when a series of changes took place without great advantage. In other countries, there was no doubt of the primacy of the sea officers, but one of the drawbacks of the French system was the division of the officer corps into those 'of the sword', i.e. the sea officers, usually nobles, and those 'of the pen', or the civil administrators, both of equal standing, which produced constant friction, particularly as the institution by Colbert of *Intendants de la Marine* placed the 'pen' in charge of the ports. This power changed hands between the two during the eighteenth century, ending in favour of 'the sword', and under Napoleon, the intendants were replaced by Maritime Prefects drawn from the 'sword'. Centrally, the minister, with a very small staff, had to control shipbuilding, recruit and handle crews, and still plan operations.

Three factors should however be recalled. The French navy never had a general staff, and thus had a narrow dependence on the abilities of the secretary of state; second, the administrators could keep the machine functioning at the ports; and third, there was liable to be misappropriation of funds and materials. Furthermore, as with all navies, for the supply of materials, the administration had to be involved with the economic life of the country and of Europe. For its successful working, the administration had to function in close co-operation with the seamen and designers.

This arrangement in essentials, with expanded and often overlapping administrative departments, persisted through the nineteenth century. For many years, the minister was usually a naval officer, knowledgeable but without political standing. From 1887, civilian ministers were more common, but often had little naval knowledge, a lack which no part of the administration could supply despite the appearance of certain more or less consultative organizations, such as the *Conseil supérieur de la Marine*. Moreover, changes of minister were too frequent, with the corollary of many changes of policy, while operations became virtually the responsibility of the commander of the fleet, even in 1914–18, until a general staff was set up. Then, as in Great Britain, the staff formulated policy and directed the theatre commanders.

In Germany, another variation appeared, for not only was there a minister, often a service officer, of whom Tirpitz is best known, and an independent chief of the staff, but the Emperor took a close interest in naval affairs with a staff of his own. After 1918, however, the German administration depended on the Commander-in-Chief of the Navy, who had appropriate departments and staffs under him.

In fact, on the eve of the First World War, all the naval powers had adopted systems which derived from the French or British conceptions. In each, we see the existence of a minister, who is responsible for the defence of the interests of the navy in the political arena and a chief of the staff whose role is to ensure the development and maintenance of the fleet, in which he is assisted by the Staff (operations, intelligence, logistics) while central administrative departments supervised shipbuilding, supplies, personnel and health.

When put to the test, serious flaws appeared. In Germany, the conduct of naval operations caused much friction between the Emperor, the minister and the chief of staff, leading eventually to the resignation of Tirpitz. In France, the minister, recognizing his lack of competence, confined himself to a purely technical role, and the commander of the navy led the sea forces and directed operations. This was a singularly weighty task, which became practically impossible with the appearance of the submarine threat. Eventually a true general staff was created in Paris, with a special anti-submarine section. The British Admiralty found similar difficulties, and not only was an anti-submarine division set up in 1917, but the staff was greatly expanded.

Since then, all major navies have had general staffs acting as their operational headquarters, although with the theatre commanders having much authority within their areas. Since the end of the Second World War, independent naval ministries have been integrated into defence ministries combining the land, sea and air services. The three chiefs of staff find themselves under an overall chief of staff, who is responsible to the government for co-ordinating the development of the forces and their operational plans. *See also* BASES, NAVAL; COLBERT; DOCKYARDS; NAVAL PERSONNEL; NAVAL STORES; NAVAL WARFARE; NAVIES.

J. MEYER and P. MASSON
A. W. H. PEARSALL
JOHN B. HATTENDORF

FURTHER READING

Daniel Baugh, *British Naval Administration in the Age of Walpole* (Princeton, 1965); M. Oppenheim, *A History of the Administration of the Royal Navy, 1509–1660* (London, 1896); James Pritchard, *Louis XV's Navy, 1748–1762* (Kingston, Ont., 1987).

Adrianople, Battle of (9 August AD 378) To prevent the devastation of Thrace by the Goths, the Emperor Valens, without waiting for the rest of his Roman forces, marched against the Goths with an army which may have numbered about 60,000 men. The Goths, who probably did not have large cavalry forces, had been drawn up in a defensive position with their waggons in a circle. Battle was joined at Adrianople (Edirne, in European Turkey), and the Romans deployed cavalry on both wings with the legions in the centre. During the assault on the waggons, the Roman left wing became separated from the rest of the army and this was exploited by the cavalry of the Goths, who were able to isolate the Roman left wing while the rest of the battleline was rolled up from the flank by the infantry pouring out of its defensive position. The Roman legionaries were pushed into a confined area where they could not use their weapons effectively. Only a third of the Roman army escaped and many generals and officers were lost, including Valens himself, whose body was never recovered. *See also* ROME; WAGGON-LAAGER.

B. CAMPBELL

FURTHER READING
N. J. E. Austin, 'Ammianus' account of the Adrianople campaign: some strategic observations', *Acta Classica*, xv (1972), pp. 77–83; T. S. Burns, 'The Battle of Adrianople, a reconsideration', *Historia*, xxii (1973), pp. 336–45; J. F. Matthews, *The Roman Empire of Ammianus* (London, 1989), pp. 296–301.

Aeneas Tacticus A military theorist of the middle of the fourth century BC and the author of at least three military treatises, of which only that on the defence of the city-state against invasion and siege survives. Aeneas, who had seen service in the Peloponnese and Asia Minor, is probably to be identified with Aeneas of Stymphalus, a general of the Arcadian League in 367 BC. His work, based largely on personal experience and oral tradition, is a collection of the various formulas which are to be found in any treatise on the art of war from ancient times to the Middle Ages. Nevertheless, Aeneas belongs to the generation of pioneers who, at the end of the fifth and the beginning of the fourth century BC, began to publish fashionable reflections on military technique. Two aspects of his work are especially interesting. First, there is the wide range of advice which he offers besieged forces, including the mobilization of all available men, the practical organization of offensive and defensive positions, and various stratagems, even the use of masks against smoke and fire. In this way, he gives us an idea of what a siege was like in the period when the great technical advances of the second half of the fourth century BC had not yet revolutionized siege warfare. Second, Aeneas is a good observer of the mentality of men under siege. His emphasis on the fear of betrayal from within the city and the measures needed to counteract this, e.g. the use of passports, internment, censorship of letters, bans on meetings, surveillance of lodging houses and bonuses for people bringing in food and weaponry, gives a particularly revealing picture of fourth century BC social and political conditions in an environment of military conflict. *See also* ARRIAN; FRONTINUS; GREECE, ANCIENT; ONASANDER; ON MILITARY MATTERS; SIEGES; VEGETIUS RENATUS.

R. LONIS
B. CAMPBELL

FURTHER READING
T. S. Brown, 'Aeneas Tacticus, Herodotus and the Ionian revolt', *Historia*, xxx (1981), pp. 385–93; text and translation (Loeb Classical Library, Harvard 1923); D. Whitehead, *Aineias the Tactician, How to Survive under Siege* (Oxford, 1990).

Africa, pre-colonial *See* BLACK AFRICA

Agincourt (Pas-de-Calais), Battle of (25 October 1415) A battle fought between the army of the King of France, Charles VI (absent on grounds of insanity) and the English army commanded by Henry V in person. The latter, who had just captured Harfleur, won a crushing victory in spite of having many fewer men in the field. Indeed, although civil war had seriously depleted French financial and military resources, it was a fact that in October 1415 they clearly outnumbered the English, which led them first to bring Henry to battle and then to be drawn into launching an over-confident attack against English men-at-arms and archers drawn up in defensive formation (as at Crécy and at Poitiers in the previous century). The

French nobles and their retinues suffered terribly under a hail of arrows as they advanced over muddy ground. Agincourt brought Henry V immense popularity and in consequence he had little difficulty in raising money and troops for the expedition of 1417 which led, in 1419, to the conquest of Normandy. *See also* FRANCE; KNIGHTS AND CHIVALRY.

P. CONTAMINE

FURTHER READING
P. Contamine, *Azincourt* (Paris, 1964); John Keegan, *The Face of Battle* (London, 1976); *Henry V: the practice of kingship*, ed. G. L. Harriss (London, 1985).

Ain Djalout (the Spring of Goliath), Battle of (1260) Scene of a famous confrontation between two thirteenth-century great powers: the Mongols and the Mamluks of Egypt. After overcoming the Assassins and then shaking the whole Muslim world by capturing Baghdad, Mongol forces moved inexorably westwards to threaten Syria and Egypt. However, political problems and a shortage of fodder and pasturelands led the Mongol commander, Hulegu, to withdraw the greater part of his army. Thus the Mongols who remained in Syria under Kit-buqa's command found themselves outnumbered by the Mamluk army mustered by Sultan Qutuz. On 3 September 1260 they were defeated and Kit-buqa killed. Sometimes, though wrongly, seen as the single battle which halted the Mongol juggernaut, Ain Djalout was none the less of great psychological importance, proving that the supposedly invincible Mongols could, after all, be beaten. *See also* HULEGU; MIDDLE EAST; MONGOLS.

JOHN CHILDS

FURTHER READING
David Morgan, *The Mongols* (Oxford, 1986); Robert Irwin, *The Middle East in the Middle Ages* (London, 1986); J. M. Smith, 'Ayn Jalut: Mamluk success or Mongol failure?', *Harvard Journal of Asiatic Studies*, xliv (1984); Steven Runciman, *A History of the Crusades* (3 vols, London, 1951–5).

Airborne troops Using aircraft to carry men into battle was first suggested (in modern times) during the First World War by the American General William Mitchell who, in 1918, wanted to transport part of the US 1st Division by air to stage a parachute assault behind the German lines at Metz. Vetoed by General John Pershing, Mitchell's proposal was an imaginative (though at the time somewhat impracticable) solution to the tactical stalemate that so often existed along the Western Front. It sought to circumvent the enemy's main defensive line so that the troops could concentrate on attacking more important objectives to the rear.

The first practical military jump – which required a safe and reliable parachute – took place in Italy in 1927, and by the late 1930s the Italian army had three battalions of airborne troops. The United States and USSR also experimented with parachute and airborne operations, the Germans following in 1936, but it was in the Soviet Union that the greatest strides were taken. Under the command of Marshal Tukhachevsky, the Red Army formed its first airborne brigade in 1932, and in 1934 a force of 1,500 parachutists was dropped in an exercise opened to Western military attachés. (The year before, a combined force of 7,000 paratroops and airlifted infantry took part in a major exercise near Minsk.) By 1939, the Red Army had four airborne brigades.

Following Soviet developments closely, the Germans continued their experiments with parachute and glider units, and by the autumn of 1938 had formed an embryonic airborne division of nine battalions (seven air-portable, two parachute) in the *Luft-waffe*, and a year later the German army had also created an airborne division. France also had several units of air-portable infantry when the Second World War began, but the British army held back.

German parachute and airborne forces played a prominent role in the invasion of Norway and Denmark, where they were used to capture and hold vital bridges and airfields, and an even larger part in the invasion of France and the Low Countries. Major-General Kurt Student's glider troops captured the Belgian fortress of Eben-Emael, thus allowing armoured units to cross the Albert Canal, while in Holland parachute and air-landed units took bridges and airfields near Rotterdam. The Germans used their airborne forces equally well against the isthmus of Corinth during the Greek and Yugoslav campaigns of April 1941, but the heavy losses incurred during the airborne assault on Crete – which showed the limitations of such lightly equipped forces – so demoralized the German high command and Adolf Hitler that operations of this sort were never attempted again. Instead, the German paratroop divisions were used exclusively in land battles as regular infantry.

For their part, the Allies quickly built up their airborne capabilities, and the first large-scale operation took place in connection with the amphibious assault on Sicily in July 1943. However, the British and Americans' relative lack of experience led to heavy losses and produced some tragic errors, as when Allied anti-aircraft batteries shot down a number of their own planes. By comparison, the three divisions of airborne and parachute forces dropped behind the Normandy coast before the main landings on 6 June 1944 played an important role in the success of this undertaking, capturing and holding bridges and other key points to make an attempted German counter-attack more difficult, and to facilitate Allied progress forward. A number of other airborne operations were prepared during the Normandy campaign, the aim being to advance by leaps and bounds, but all were cancelled until September when, at Field Marshal Montgomery's instigation, a major effort was launched against Arnhem and the bridges leading to it – *Operation Market Garden*. Thirty-five thousand airborne troops, 2,000 vehicles and 568 pieces of artillery were landed or dropped by parachute, but these troops were not sufficiently well armed and equipped to hold off the strong German forces in the area. The operation, aimed at securing a bridgehead to allow the British 2nd Army to break out over the Rhine, was a failure. When an assault over the Rhine was made at Wesel, in March 1945, the Allies executed perhaps the best airborne operation (*Varsity*) of the

war to support the river-crossing. All landing and drop zones were within range of supporting artillery; troops were dropped directly on their objectives simultaneously in one large 'lift'; fighter support was continuous, with forward air controllers on the ground with the airborne units; resupply by air was immediate; and the link-up with ground forces was scheduled for the same day. In short, in contrast to *Market Garden*, little was left to chance, and the still relatively lightly equipped airborne army was not asked to stand and fight the enemy for too long.

Airborne forces were employed by both the Americans and Japanese in the Pacific theatre of war, but the Red Army, which had led the way in the 1930s, used their airborne units on a massive scale only once, on the Dnieper in September 1943, and did not achieve significant results. However, they, like everyone else, employed parachute troops for clandestine activities behind enemy lines.

Since the Second World War, the mobility of airborne forces has been exploited in almost all the struggles for colonial independence, often with success against enemies whose own forces were not concentrated and were extremely mobile. In some cases – particularly the French experience against the Viet Minh in the Indo-China war – too much was expected of the airborne arm, however, and supporting far-flung 'air heads' became costly operations and, as at Dien Bien Phu, highly symbolic traps. Although a political and strategic failure, the Anglo-French attack on Suez in 1956 was initially a major tactical success as paratroops took possession of the Canal and then awaited the arrival of amphibious units.

The Vietnam War and, to a lesser degree, the Algerian conflict introduced a new concept – air mobility, based on the use of helicopters to give traditional infantry and light artillery and armour the ability to conduct a war of movement and 'vertical envelopment'. During the 1970s, airborne forces proved their value in anti-terrorist and anti-subversive operations, the most spectacular examples being, perhaps, the Israeli raid on Entebbe airport in Uganda in

1976, where Israelis were being held hostage by hijackers, and the Belgian intervention of Kolwezi (Zaire) in 1978. *See also* AVIATION; INDIRECT WARFARE; PARACHUTE TROOPS; TRANSPORT, AIR.

P. FACON and A. TEYSSIER
STEPHEN J. HARRIS

FURTHER READING
M. Tugwell, *Airborne to Battle* (London, 1971); J. Weeks, *Assault from the Sky: a history of airborne warfare* (New York, 1978); C. Christienne, P. Lissarague, A. Degardin, P. Facon, P. Biffotot and M. Hodier, *Histoire de l'aviation militaire française* (Paris, 1980); P. Rocolle, *L'Arme aéroportée, clef de la victoire* (2 vols, Paris, 1948).

Aircraft, bomber The use of the aeroplane as a method of bombardment was envisaged in the earliest days of aviation. The contract between Clément Ader and the French Ministry of War, signed in 1891, actually provided for the production of a machine that could carry explosive or incendiary bombs. Ader, meanwhile, not only realized the destructive power of such a weapon of war, but also saw that the threat of air attack could be an effective deterrent. It was the Americans, however, who undertook the first experiments in aerial bombing, and the Italians who launched the first bombing raids in the course of their war with the Turks in Libya and Cyrenaica in 1911. In France, the government created a Michelin prize for performance in hitting a ground target from the air, but progress in the development of bombing machines was slow, chiefly for technical reasons: there were no aiming sights adapted for aerial use, and the light machines of the day, having weak airframes and small engines, could only carry very small bomb loads.

When the First World War broke out in August 1914 the Germans, British and French all raided enemy territory or attacked troops on the move, using reconstructed artillery shells and, in some cases, even steel darts. The first true bombing unit was set up by the French in 1914, to be followed by similar organizations in the British and German air forces, but the general staffs were then confronted by the most basic of questions: what should be bombed: objectives on or near the battlefield, or targets far to the rear, in enemy territory? France initially chose to carry out reprisal actions against German cities by day, but despite equipping its bombing machines with defensive armament, losses to anti-aircraft fire and fighters were so heavy that these daylight operations had to be abandoned in favour of night raids. This required the development of navigation beacons and the installation of searchlights around French aerodromes to allow crews to find their way back to base and land safely, but the technology of the day could not guide them to the target or facilitate accurate bombing. Eventually, the French gave up these large-scale strategic raids and concentrated instead on tactical bombing at or near the front line.

Although the intensity of their operations fluctuated, the British and Germans never abandoned the concept of strategic bombing. By the end of 1915, the Germans were regularly sending Zeppelin airships to bomb England, and when losses became too high, these were replaced by heavy, long-range bombers developed thanks to the extraordinary effort of the German aircraft industry. These attacked London and other cities through much of 1916 and all of 1917, and aroused considerable anger among the British population (in part because of the ineffectiveness of Britain's air defences). This dissatisfaction was of no small significance in the decision to create an Air Ministry which would control all service aviation and, subsequently, in the formation of an independent Royal Air Force (RAF) on 1 April 1918.

The main reason for the creation of the RAF was to improve the state of Britain's air defences, but its separate existence facilitated the formation of the Independent Force, which was to carry the strategic bombing offensive to the German war industry and civilian morale. Trenchard, first commander of the Independent Force, was not fully persuaded of the value of bombing, and preferred to see air power used to support the army, but following his orders faithfully he tried to convince his

French, Italian and American allies to join in a combined offensive. He failed, largely because the French would not alter their view. A British bombing offensive nevertheless took place, while the aerial attacks by the French, especially, helped halt the German offensive of March 1918 and supported Allied attacks later that year.

By the end of the war the design of bomber aircraft had advanced to the point that each machine was able to carry several hundred pounds of high-explosive bombs – a far cry from the artillery shells and steel darts thrown over the side in 1914. Still, the capabilities of bomber aircraft immediately after the war were nowhere near what was being assumed by the most extreme advocates of air power, who argued that strategic bombing was already capable of achieving decisive success. They had forgotten, it seems, that in over four years of war only a few dozen bombs had fallen on Britain, and that the damage caused by British attacks on Germany had not been severe. If, however, bombers carried gas bombs – something from which all concerned had shied away during the Great War – the potential for cataclysmic destruction and loss of life did exist.

The association between bombing and attacks on civilian populations allowed pacifist organizations to make bomber forces a focus of their attacks on military establishments – a prejudice that was reinforced in the 1920s by the theories of Douhet, Mitchell and Trenchard, all of whom argued that victory in the next war could only result from heavy air attacks on an enemy's vital industrial, agricultural and human resources. The defensive power of armies, they said, was such as to prohibit any land offensive from succeeding. Partly in response to these theories (and their impact on the public at large), a number of attempts were made to ban aerial bombing altogether, but the only real achievement came in an international agreement to ban the use of gas in air warfare. Otherwise, each country was free to do what it wished, according to its own needs.

Nearly disbanded at the time of the 1932 Geneva disarmament conference, the French bomber force was eventually sacrificed to budgetary considerations to such an extent that, in September 1939, the air force possessed no more than twenty or so modern bombing machines. In Germany, meanwhile, strategic bombing had been neglected (after 1937) in favour of the development and production of medium-range aircraft and dive-bombers intended for use with the army. Following the court martial of 'Billy' Mitchell in the United States, the influence of American advocates of strategic bombing weakened considerably, but left alone in a kind of splendid isolation they were able to develop their bombing doctrine and promote the design of heavy bombers like the B-17 and B-24, which would provide the backbone of the US bombing offensive in the Second World War.

It was in Britain that the exponents of bombing found their theories embraced most warmly. Even though the expansion of Bomber Command was slowed by the government's fear of the *Luftwaffe* after 1937, and emphasis given to building up the defensive forces of Fighter Command, plans for a large-scale bombing offensive against Germany were well developed by the outbreak of war, and developmental work on a whole series of heavy bombers – the Halifax, the Stirling and the Manchester, predecessor of the Lancaster – was well under way. Bomber Command was prevented from undertaking this offensive until after the German invasion of France, again because of the government's concern about what the *Luftwaffe* could achieve in raids on Britain, and when it was finally unleashed, its losses by day were so high that, like the French in the Great War, the RAF was forced to switch to night bombing. Having no navigation aids, however, crews had great difficulty in finding their targets, and if they did, their bombsights were not good enough to allow accurate bombing. Indeed, a study conducted in August 1941 found that, on average, only a quarter of the aircraft sent to the Ruhr actually came within 5 miles of their target.

Aware of these problems, in February 1942 the air staff, with Churchill's backing, embraced the idea of an 'area' bombing offensive in which the principal target was the German civilian population with any concomitant damage to industry being regarded as a fortunate by-product. By the end of the war, hundreds of thousands of sorties by Lancaster and Halifax heavy bombers had been launched against the principal cities of Germany, but destruction of near-cataclysmic proportions in single raids occurred only twice: at Hamburg in July 1943, and Dresden in February 1945, when intense firestorms devastated both cities and killed thousands. Otherwise, the British area bombing offensive failed to live up to expectations, despite the development of complex navigation and bombing aids and sophisticated electronic jamming equipment. German civilian morale did not crack, even during the Battle of Berlin during the winter of 1943–4, when Bomber Command concentrated on the enemy capital and Arthur Harris, its commander, boasted that the effort made by his command would cost Germany the war. In fact, it was Bomber Command that suffered nearly irredeemable losses, leading some to conclude that it was saved as an operational entity only because it was transferred, on 1 April 1944, to operations mainly in support of *Operation Overlord*, the Allied invasion of Normandy.

US doctrine was appreciably different. The Americans intended from the outset to conduct precision daylight attacks against German industry, and they never entirely wavered from this position despite the heavy losses they suffered before the appearance of the Mustang long-range escort fighter early in 1944. Once they enjoyed the air superiority won by the Mustang, the Americans were finally able to achieve useful results, causing tremendous damage and dislocation to the German aircraft industry, to Germany's fuel production and to its transportation and communications networks. On occasion, however, even the Americans could be tempted by area attacks, and they participated wholeheartedly in the destruction of Hamburg and Dresden. Their compunction against area attacks in Europe was hardly noticeable in the Pacific, where the B-29 force burnt out the major Japanese cities long before the atomic bombs were dropped on Hiroshima and Nagasaki in August 1945.

The advent of nuclear and thermonuclear bombs marked a new epoch in the history of air power and strategic bombing: the knock-out blow envisioned by Douhet, Mitchell and Trenchard was now possible. Bombers therefore became the principal weapon in the arsenals of the major powers, with the hope that the threat of massive retaliation would deter aggression. From the mid-1950s inter-continental ballistic missiles and advanced missile air defences threatened the future of the manned bomber, but it was soon realized that manned bombers could still play useful roles and offered better possibilities of recall than missiles. Bomber tactics were changed from high-altitude flight to low-level penetration, aided and abetted by electronic jamming equipment, and by the 1970s cruise missiles were designed to be launched by manned bombers at a safe distance from the enemy's main line of defence. Furthermore, bomber aircraft have been used in a number of non-nuclear conflicts, the best example being the American commitment of part of its B-52 fleet to the war in Vietnam, and development of very advanced types, like the American stealth bomber, continues. *See also* ADER; AIRCRAFT, FIGHTER; AIRCRAFT, RECONNAISSANCE; AVIATION; DOUHET; GERMANY, AIR BATTLE OF; MITCHELL; NUCLEAR WARFARE; TRENCHARD.

P. FACON and A. TEYSSIER
STEPHEN J. HARRIS

FURTHER READING
C. Christienne, P. Lissarague, A. Degardin, P. Facon, P. Biffotot and M. Hodier, *Histoire de l'aviation militaire française* (Paris, 1980); *Icare* (review); Robin Higham, *Air Power: a concise history* (New York, 1972); Basil Collier, *A History of Air Power* (New York, 1974); James L. Stokesbury, *A Short History of Airpower* (New York, 1986); *Aerospace Historian* (journal); Lee Kennett, *A History of Strategic Bombing* (New York, 1982); Malcolm Smith, *British Air Strategy between the Wars* (Oxford, 1984).

Aircraft, fighter The idea of aerial

combat is probably as old as man's dream about flight, but it required the advent of powered flight (with its inherent possibility of manoeuvre) to make air fighting a practical reality. By 1912 the French were considering the use of what they called 'destroyer' aircraft against the new German airships, rightly regarded as a threat, and were planning to fit these fighters with automatic weapons. Guns could always be mounted on the wings, of course, but the French realized from the beginning that it would be easier for pilots to aim and fire along their line of sight. As a result, engineers like Schneider and Saulnier were soon experimenting with systems that would allow machine-guns to fire through the area covered by the rotation of the propeller, but these proved to be of limited reliability and therefore dangerous – pilots could, in effect, shoot themselves down.

Accordingly, although aeroplanes met in combat a number of times during the first two months of the First World War, their crews were armed only with hand-held weapons – revolvers, shot-guns and rifles. Such engagements were usually inconclusive because of the near impossibility of taking effective aim from an unstable platform against a target moving through three dimensions. Attempts were therefore made by all sides to solve the problems involved in allowing fixed machine-guns to fire forward through the propeller's arc. The first workable solution was introduced by Roland Garros, who added armour to the propeller blades, but even this involved some risk, and wasted those bullets that hit the blades and were deflected away. The answer lay in synchronization, a system that would prevent the gun from firing while the propeller was in front of the barrel, and this was eventually produced by Fokker, a Dutch engineer working for the German aircraft industry.

Fokker's invention gave the Germans virtual air superiority over the Western Front in 1915. In part because of this technological advantage, the Germans were first to realize the benefits of employing their fighters in large groups, a tactic introduced at the start of their February 1916 offensive at Verdun. The French, who had meanwhile developed their own synchronizing gear, copied the German example, sent their best pilots to the Verdun sector and in time wrested mastery of the air away from the enemy.

The air battles at Verdun marked an important step in the development of aerial combat. Illustrating the value of co-ordinated combat, they marked the end of the era in which fighter pilots normally operated alone; instead, pilots would henceforth fly as part of an organized squadron and fight as a team. In time, the need to win air superiority over particular sectors of the front (to allow other friendly aircraft to support the army, for example) led to the creation of even larger formations such as wings, groups and, by 1918, air divisions, in which large numbers of squadrons were organic parts of a disciplined whole.

By the end of the war, very high quality fighter aircraft had emerged (Fokker DVII, Spad VII and XIII, Sopwith Camel) which could fly at speeds approaching 125 miles per hour and which carried multiple forward-firing guns. The air 'ace' had also emerged – legendary pilots like Guynemer, Fonck, Nungesser, Bishop, Navarre, Boelcke, Mannock, McCudden, and most famous of them all, Richthofen – whose exploits as knights of the air were communicated to an adoring public by mass circulation newspapers, and helped people forget the sombre realities of trench warfare.

Although the Great War had given the leading place to fighter aircraft and to these aces, developments in military aviation in the 1920s were dominated by the influence of those who, like Douhet, Trenchard and Mitchell, predicted that it was strategic bombing that would prove decisive in the next war. Furthermore, there were technological limits to what fighter aircraft could do in the defence of their country's airspace. By the mid-1930s, however, the growth of German air potential persuaded the French and British governments to give priority to fighter defence, a shift in policy that fitted well with the overall defensive strategy adopted by the Western democracies at that time. The Germans too built a large fighter force, but it was intended primarily to support the ground offensive.

By the eve of the Second World War, advances in aeronautical engineering, and particularly the replacement of the biplane by the monoplane, had produced a number of fighter aircraft with outstanding performance: the German Messerschmitt 109 and 110, the British Hawker Hurricane and Supermarine Spitfire, the French Dewoitine D520, and the Japanese Mitsubishi A 6M Zero.

The Second World War saw a considerable expansion of the roles given to fighter aircraft. In the successful blitzkrieg offensives against Poland, Norway and Western Europe, *Luftwaffe* fighters won air superiority and attacked opposing armies to good effect. During the Battle of Britain, the RAF succeeded in defeating Germany's air offensive by means of a well co-ordinated air defence system in which Fighter Command was supported by a comprehensive radar network and directed to enemy formations by a centralized command and control organization – a system which the Germans replicated when they came under heavy air attack after 1943. Furthermore, the development of airborne interception radars and other electronic devices allowed both the British and the Germans to create effective night-fighting capabilities. The strength of the German air defences compelled both the British and Americans to produce long-range escort fighters to support their bomber formations over enemy territory by day and, to a lesser extent, by night, and by 1944 these escorts – the Thunderbolt, Mustang and Mosquito – began to have an effect. By the time of the Normandy landings in June 1944, the Allies enjoyed virtual air superiority over north-west Europe. This superiority was put to good use by the fighters of the tactical air forces, who were free to operate in support of the Allied armies as they advanced from the English Channel to the Rhine and thence into Germany.

The major technological advance during the Second World War was the successful development of the jet engine, and by 1945 both the Germans and British were employing jet fighters on operations – the former using the Messerschmitt 262 both as an interceptor and as a fighter bomber, the latter employing their Gloster Meteors primarily against German V 1 flying bombs over England. The first air battle between jet fighters occurred during the Korean War in 1950.

By the end of the 1950s, more-powerful engines, advanced designs and new methods of construction allowed the production of jet fighters capable of flying at twice the speed of sound – about 1,300 miles per hour. At such speeds, old-style gun engagements seemed to be impossible, and most fighters were equipped with missiles which either were radar-guided or sought out the heat of an enemy aircraft's engines. The fighter's existence was threatened for a time by the predicted demise of the manned bomber and its replacement by the intercontinental ballistic missile, but the survival of the bomber, the outbreak of limited, regional, non-nuclear conflicts in which fighters could be put to good use, and the new strategy of flexible response all meant that fighters would survive as well. Today, fighter aircraft are fitted with advanced radars and automated fire control systems and can fly at well over twice the speed of sound, but the human element, particularly skill at manoeuvre, still has a part to play in air-to-air combat, as was proved over Vietnam, in the Arab–Israeli wars and during the Falklands conflict.

In some air forces, the roles allocated to fighter aircraft became so diversified that specialized types were developed – interceptor, air superiority and ground attack fighters, for example – but the cost of developing, producing and maintaining so many models can be prohibitive. Thus, with the help of new technologies, a number of multi-role fighter aircraft like the American F-18 and the European Tornado are in the inventories of contemporary air forces. *See also* AIRCRAFT, BOMBER; AIRCRAFT, RECONNAISSANCE; AVIATION; DOUHET; MITCHELL; TRENCHARD.

P. FACON and A. TEYSSIER
STEPHEN J. HARRIS

FURTHER READING
C. Christienne, P. Lissarague, A. Degardin, P. Facon, P. Biffotot and M. Hodeir, *Histoire de l'aviation militaire française* (Paris, 1980); *Icare*

(review); Robin Higham, *Air Power: a concise history* (New York, 1972); Basil Collier, *A History of Air Power* (New York, 1974); James L. Stokesbury, *A Short History of Airpower* (New York, 1986); *Aerospace Historian* (journal); N. Franks, *Aircraft versus Aircraft: the illustrated history of fighter pilot combat since 1914* (London, 1986); J. J. Halley, *The Role of the Fighter in Air Warfare* (London, 1979).

Aircraft, reconnaissance Reconnaissance, the search for and diffusion of information, is a specialized function often divided into strategic and tactical aspects. The methods and types of equipment used for reconnaissance have improved considerably from the earliest days, when visual observation was the only means available, and now include cameras and sensors (infra-red, radar, olfactory) capable of detecting the minutest details.

The idea of taking photographs from the air dates back at least as far as the first field experiments undertaken by the Frenchman Félix Tournachon in 1856, but the first military use of aerial photographic reconnaissance occurred during the American Civil War. Both sides utilized air reconnaissance during the Franco-Prussian war of 1870–1, and in time all armies had their own balloon sections. Further refinements in aerial photography were made by Major H. Elsdale, Royal Engineers, who took photographs of the fortress at Halifax, Nova Scotia, in 1883 using a clockwork-operated plate camera, and who subsequently commanded one of the first operational balloon sections in the British army during the 1890 expedition to Bechuanaland.

It was only natural, once powered flight was possible, that consideration should be given to mounting cameras on aircraft and to using aeroplanes in a reconnaissance role. During their 1911 manoeuvres, for example, the French employed army aircraft to detect and follow the movements of the 'enemy', but these experiments invoked the jealousy of the cavalry, who were traditionally responsible for military reconnaissance, and did not persuade the army high command to place too much confidence in the new technique. It was only after the Battle of the Marne, when both British and French aviators provided accurate information on German troop movements, that the value of aerial reconnaissance was clear to all.

Once the European battlefield became fixed, marked by trenchlines stretching from Switzerland to the English Channel, reconnaissance of the enemy's rear generally gave way to aerial observation of its front-line formations in order to direct artillery fire against gun positions and wire entanglements and to provide fire support for the infantry. The need for precise information, especially of enemy gun positions, led to improvements in the techniques of photographic interpretation, the provision of small-scale maps and better photographic kits.

The emphasis on immediate observation of the battlefield produced, over time, a mentality which ignored the importance of more long-range reconnaissance. As a result, the Allies failed to detect the build-up of forces for the great German offensive of March 1918; however, their expertise at short-range observation did provide them with sufficient warning of the July 1918 attacks.

The main question between the wars was not whether aerial reconnaissance and observation were useful, but whether they should be carried out by multi-seater aircraft or single-seaters; by fast fighters or slow but vulnerable reconnaissance machines. There was something to be said for each type, although using fighters for reconnaissance was not entirely practical until the perfection of oblique photography, where the remote-controlled camera was directed through a window in the side of the aircraft. This method gave rise to difficulties with focus and accuracy, problems which were not overcome until forward-facing cameras were employed in 1942. Although cameras first started to be installed on high-flying fighter aircraft in September 1939, the British still relied on slow, lumbering, low-flying Lysanders for observation and artillery detection. Long-range, high-altitude reconnaissance finally came into its own after Dunkirk, when the British had left the continent and desperately needed information on the results of their bombing offensive. Photo reconnaissance flights subsequently confirmed development of the German V-1 pilotless aircraft and V-2 rocket, identified new radars and found many of the locations to which crucial industries had been dispersed. On the other hand, although the Germans had made high-altitude reconnaissance flights over Britain from 1938 onwards, by 1944 the *Luftwaffe* was so weak, and the British air defences so strong, that they learned nothing of the Allied preparations for *Operation Overlord*.

Postwar developments in photographic techniques and sensing equipment have been spectacular, as has been the design of sophisticated, specialist, reconnaissance aircraft like the American U-2 and SR-71, and the Soviet MIG-25R. All could reach altitudes well above those possible for fighter aircraft, while the SR-71 and MIG-25R were faster than any conventional fighter. The postwar period has also seen the development of pilotless drones, which the Israelis have used to good effect in Lebanon and Syria.

Most recently, space has been the focus for strategic reconnaissance, and the major powers rely heavily on spy satellites to gather strategic, operational and tactical intelligence. The images received from satellites are so detailed that, in purely technical terms, no other form of reconnaissance is really required. However, satellites move along predictable orbits, and they cannot always provide constant or immediate images of particular objects. It seems likely, then, that reconnaissance aircraft will continue to be used for as long as there is a need for military defence and deterrence. Indeed, they may be used more frequently than ever before if the talks aimed at open skies, which commenced in 1990, prove fruitful. *See also* AVIATION, MILITARY; CAVALRY; INTELLIGENCE.

P. FACON and A. TEYSSIER
STEPHEN J. HARRIS

FURTHER READING
C. Christienne, P. Lissarague, A. Degardin, P. Facon, P. Biffotot and M. Hodeir, *Histoire de l'aviation militaire française* (Paris, 1980); *Icare* (review); Robin Higham, *Air Power: a concise history* (New York, 1972); Basil Collier, *A History of Air Power* (New York, 1974); James L. Stokesbury, *A Short History of Airpower* (New York, 1986); *Aerospace Historian* (journal).

Airmen, training of See AVIATION, MILITARY

Alamein, El, Battle of (1942) See EL ALAMEIN

Alba, Fernando Alvarez de Toledo, 3rd Duke of (1507–82) The most important Spanish commander after Gonsalvo de Córdoba, and the leading Habsburg general of the mid-sixteenth century, Alba can be considered the founder of the Spanish school of strategy, which was not successfully challenged until the Thirty Years' War. Having served in a number of Charles V's campaigns in the 1530s, the 1540s saw him become the most prominent Castilian nobleman on the Emperor's council. His military reputation was made by his conduct of the campaigns against the Schmalkaldic League, the alliance of German Lutheran towns and states, in 1546–7 and the victory of Mühlberg. Alba recognized the dangers of direct assaults against entrenched arquebusiers, and turned instead to a strategy of manoeuvre and the use of superior organization and resources to exhaust an enemy. He displayed the same skill on the defensive in Italy in 1555–7. As a councillor to Charles V and Philip II his advice on strategy and diplomacy was thoughtful and perceptive, but delivered with a truculence and arrogance that made him dangerous enemies. His most celebrated period of command followed his appointment in 1566 as captain-general in the Netherlands. His conduct of the campaigns against the Dutch rebels in 1568 and 1572 was extremely able. However, with an army he considered inadequate for its purposes, and without a navy, which he considered essential, he relied heavily on political and military repression to crush the revolt. Alba's notorious brutality did much to extend the hostility to 'Spanish' rule in the Netherlands, and popular resistance turned the Sieges of Zutphen, Naarden and Haarlem in 1572–3 into pyrrhic victories which led to his recall in December 1573. Despite the best efforts of his numerous enemies to remove him from Philip II's councils, he was employed again to command the invasion of Portugal in 1580–1, which he did with skill and success. As a commander Alba enjoyed international respect, and he clearly knew how to get the best out of a sixteenth-century army; his failure in the Netherlands should be seen as political rather than military. *See also* CÓRDOBA; MÜHLBERG; NETHERLANDS; PARMA; SPAIN.

SIMON ADAMS

FURTHER READING

William S. Maltby, *Alba: a biography of Fernando Alvarez de Toledo, 3rd Duke of Alba* (Berkeley, Calif., and London, 1983); S. Adams, 'Tactics or politics? The "military revolution" and the Hapsburg hegemony, 1525–1648', in *Tools of War: instruments, ideas and institutions of warfare, 1445–1871*, ed. John A. Lynn (Urbana and Chicago, Ill., 1990); *Epistolario del III Duque de Alba*, ed. Duke of Berwick and Alba (3 vols, Madrid, 1952).

Alesia, Siege of (52 BC) This Gallic town, where Vercingetorix took refuge after the failure of the cavalry attack he had launched against Caesar's army, was situated on Mount Auxois, which lies within the boundaries of present-day Alise-Sainte-Reine, near Dijon (Côte-d'Or). This is a plateau of about 240 acres, isolated between two valleys, whose very steep slopes are dominated by an insurmountable limestone cliff, and partly fortified by drystone walls. There are gushing springs on the plateau itself and at the foot of the cliff.

On reaching this stronghold, Caesar realized that it could be taken only by starving out the defenders and those who had taken shelter there by means of a total blockade which made good use of the possibilities offered by the terrain. When he had positioned his troops in fortified camps built on the plateaux partially surrounding Mount Auxois and on the plain to the west, Caesar had a continuous ring of siege works built, which the defenders were helpless to prevent. Meanwhile Vercingetorix dispatched his cavalry with the mission of raising a vast relieving army to attack the Romans in the rear. Caesar then brought his siege works nearer to the stronghold by reinforcing them still further, at least in the plain, with a trench 20 feet deep and, 400 feet behind this, two further trenches 15 feet wide and a 12 foot high rampart; all this was protected by auxiliary defences – a combination of pits with concealed man traps of sharpened stakes and iron hooks; he also built a similar line of fortifications facing outwards. The siege lasted for about six weeks, during which time it has been estimated that the Roman army built about 25 miles of campaign fortifications. The defenders had run out of provisions and the Romans themselves were beginning to go short when the relieving army arrived; but after three fierce and unsuccessful attacks on the Roman lines it was forced to disperse. Vercingetorix surrendered the following day.

The lay-out of the Roman siege works, first excavated in 1861–5 on the order of Napoleon III, has been substantially confirmed by recent investigations and aerial photography. *See also* CAESAR; FORTIFICATION, FIELD; ROME; SIEGES.

JOEL LE GALL
B. CAMPBELL

FURTHER READING

Napoleon III, *Histoire de Jules César* (Paris, 1865–6), ii; J. Harmand, *Une Campagne césarienne: Alésia* (Paris, 1967); J. Le Gall, *Alésia, archéologie et histoire* (2nd edn. Paris, 1980); J. Le Gall, E. de Saint-Denis, R. Weil and J. Marilier, *Alésia, textes littéraires antiques, textes médiévaux* (2nd edn. Paris, 1980); L. J. F. Keppie, *The Making of the Roman Army: from republic to empire* (London, 1984), pp. 89–94; Caesar's description – *De Bello Gallico (The Gallic War)*, vii, 66–90.

Alexander the Great (356–323 BC) The most notable feature of Alexander's brief career is the series of astonishingly rapid conquests by which he gained possession of an immense empire in the east and which is the basis for the prevailing view of Alexander as one of the greatest military leaders of all time. But his first achievements took place in Macedonia where, at the age of twenty, after the death of his father Philip, he imposed his authority on the Balkan peoples and then on Greece; here the speed of his interventions and the brutality of the destruction of Thebes silenced the stirrings of revolt among the Greek cities.

Alexander had from the outset a formidable instrument of conquest at his disposal in the army which his father had left him and whose renowned phalanx had already asserted its strength on the battlefields of Greece, notably at Chaeronea. But he introduced several important innovations. While he relied essentially on the phalanx in his first campaigns, adopting the oblique battle order perfected by Epaminondas, he used this unwieldy formation less and less in line battles (except at the River Hydaspes), preferring to set up mixed mobile groups, which were more effective in limited expeditions over difficult terrain. The light infantry, with its famous archers and Agrianian javelin throwers, became increasingly important as a consequence of this. But the arm he most favoured was the cavalry, which he employed not in the traditional role of protecting his infantry's flanks, but as an offensive unit, arrayed in triangular formation and proceeding by sudden charges intended to break up enemy formations. Similarly he discovered, after his confrontation with the Indian king, Porus, at the River Hydaspes, the advantages of using corps of elephants to neutralize enemy cavalry and break up the ranks of the opposing infantry.

But he was also skilled in battle preparation, according the greatest importance to two essential disciplines: logistics and intelligence. Following his father's example, he made considerable reductions in the slow wagon trains which followed Greek armies into the field, preferring to use swifter pack animals (mules, horses, camels), and making foot soldiers carry their own armour and equipment and some of their own supplies for the march. He made constant use of intelligence, both for reasons of strategy (information on enemy morale or on the resources of the country) and for tactical ends (systematically using his horsemen as scouts). Finally, Alexander gave the art of siege warfare a considerable boost: towers and various types of catapults became formidable war machines, serviced by engineers of renown, whose skills were particularly evident during the Siege of Tyre in 332 BC.

Alexander's military successes were also due in part to his qualities of personal leadership and physical courage on the battlefield, imperturbability, assured judgement, an instinctive ability to see his way out of difficult situations and to recognize where best in the line to commit his troops, and an imaginative, sometimes over-bold strategy. Nevertheless, this great conqueror's most outstanding quality was perhaps a capacity for adapting to circumstances and new techniques produced by a period of profound upheaval. *See also* CHAERONEA; EPAMINONDAS; GAUGAMELA; GRANICUS; GREECE, ANCIENT; HYDASPES; INFANTRY; ISSUS; LOGISTICS; SIEGES.

R. LONIS
B. CAMPBELL

FURTHER READING
From a wealth of literature, *see* P. Cloché, *Alexandre le Grand* (2nd edn, Paris, 1961); J. F. C. Fuller, *The Generalship of Alexander the Great* (New York, 1968); R. D. Milns, 'The army of Alexander the Great', *Entretiens Hardt*, xxii (1976), pp. 87–136; F. E. Adcock, *The Greek and Macedonian Art of War* (Berkeley, 1957); D. W. Engels, *Alexander the Great and the Logistics of the Macedonian Army* (Berkeley, 1978); M. M. Markle, 'Macedonian arms and tactics under Alexander the Great', in *Macedonia and Greece in Late Classical and Early Hellenistic Times* (Studies in the History of Art 10, Washington DC, 1982), pp. 87–111; A. B. Bosworth, *Conquest and Empire: the reign of Alexander the Great* (Cambridge, 1988).

Algiers, Siege of (1541) *See* TUNIS, SIEGE OF

Alliances Alliances are an essential complement to any defence policy and few powers will risk engaging in warfare if they are diplomatically isolated. As Monte-cucoli recalls in his monograph, *De foederibus Maximae*, the Romans achieved their progressive domination over Italy by first forming alliances with the neighbouring peoples, an essential preliminary in any offensive war. One of the finest examples of diplomatic preparation for a war of aggression was provided by H. de Lionne, who almost completely isolated the United Provinces in 1671, so that they found themselves at the beginning of the Dutch War in 1672 facing the military might of the French completely on their own. The bases of alliances are to be sought in the unstable equilibrium which characterizes international relations in the modern period. Christendom in general, and also regional sub-systems such as Italy or the Baltic, have been riven by competing interests. The formation of an alliance may be motivated by the egoism of princes or states, the conditions necessary for their survival or aggrandizement, or considerations of prestige. One could cite many examples from Renaissance Italy or post-1715 Europe.

Alliances may also have more solid foundations. When monarchies were still the keystone and the incarnation of the state, dynastic alliances played a very important role. The hegemonic power of the House of Austria, which lasted until the Peace of the Pyrenees, rested on a dynastic alliance. When Charles V abdicated in 1555, he divided his inheritance between his son, Philip, and his brother, the Archduke Ferdinand, but the House of Austria remained strongly united. The Spanish Empire could count on the support of the junior branch, which was less rich and powerful but equally ambitious. Marriages were consistently contracted between the representatives of the German and Spanish branches; and these marriage alliances dispensed the courts of Madrid and Vienna from the need to conclude formal alliance treaties. The reason Richelieu so greatly feared the Spanish dreams of hegemony was because the German branch acted as excellent seconders to the Spanish monarchy and served the imperialist designs of Olivarès, Philip IV's

formidable prime minister, while at the same time strengthening its own authority within the Empire. As a corollary to this point, it was also the case that numerous alliance treaties were sanctioned and reinforced by royal marriages. This was the thinking behind the 'Spanish marriages' arranged by Maria de' Medici: the Infanta, Anne of Austria, married Louis XIII and Elisabeth of Bourbon married the future Philip IV. However, simple matrimonial alliances were not enough to consolidate a policy of reconciliation between the two crowns, in so far as their interests did not coincide at the most fundamental level. As is well known, the marriage of the Dauphin (the future Louis XVI) to the Archduchess Marie-Antoinette came to an untimely end; conceived as a means of cementing the Franco-Austrian rapprochement of 1756, it only served to crystallize the French people's hatred of the royal family.

In times of great ideological conflict, alliances were often based on religious affinities. The Spanish monarchy declared that it was defending the interests of Catholicism against Protestantism, and of Christian Europe against Islam, but it was never able to convince the Republic of Venice or the King of France of the need to sacrifice their national interests. Moreover, such alliances, even when they were sincere, tended to turn minor powers into satellites of major ones and make the armies of these satellites into auxiliaries of the great powers.

One of the most effective binding forces for an alliance is the fear of a common enemy, of an invasion which threatens the existence of a nation or the way of life of its inhabitants. On several occasions, the Turkish threat led to the formation of alliances that were designed to halt the advance of the Ottoman armies through Central Europe or even to prevent them from landing in Italy. But in the sixteenth century such coalitions were short-lived: the naval victory at Lepanto was not exploited as neither Philip II nor Venice was willing to pursue their military collaboration once the danger had been removed. On the other hand, the efforts stimulated by the Siege of Vienna in 1683 produced a more durable anti-Ottoman alliance. The moving spirit behind this Holy League was Pope Innocent XI, whose efforts led to the recapture of the Hungarian plains from the Turks.

The practical application of alliances may take various forms, ranging from mere concerted diplomatic endeavours to joint military action, with various intermediate stages such as economic treaties and separate military operations which force the adversary to fight on a second front and divide his forces, thus making him more vulnerable. This was the theory behind the reverse alliance, used systematically by France against Austria. France had a series of allies in Northern and Eastern Europe which permitted it, when necessary, 'to keep the Emperor busy', whether this meant his having to deal with the Swedes, Poles, Hungarians, Transylvanians or Turks.

Distant allies may be limited to concerted diplomatic support. This was generally the role assigned by France to the Republic of Poland, and the one which Great Britain reserved for itself between 1660 and 1688. Charles II was unable to persuade his subjects to engage in military co-operation with France, but he at least prevented them from actively joining with her enemies.

The most common form of alliance was, for a long time, the economic treaty, by which an economically weak military power received funds from a richer ally, such as France under Louis XIV or Great Britain in the eighteenth century, which at that time subsidized Prussia and Austria in their military activities on the continent. This was technically easier than attempting combined operations, which were more difficult to put into effect, given the communication difficulties, the possibilities of one or other of the armies not being mobilized in time and the problems of reaching agreement on a plan of action and on common war objectives. A good example of this might be the Franco-Spanish plan to invade England in 1779 during the American War of Independence, which produced no concrete results. During the Thirty Years' War, French and Swedish armies operated separately in Germany, while in 1645, the Swedes and the Transylvanians attempted a combined operation against Vienna. It was only at the end of the war, from the 1645 campaign on, that the Weimarian forces of Marshal Turenne, the Hessians and the Swedish forces led by Wrangel took concerted action against the Austro-Bavarians and won decisive victories in 1648.

These examples, though largely dealing with events prior to the French Revolution, are still valid for the contemporary period. However, special mention should be made of international agreements intended to maintain the existing equilibrium and keep the peace, by intervention against an aggressor. The origins of this type of agreement may be seen in the Quadruple Alliance concluded against Spain and inspired by Alberoni, which became the Quintuple Alliance when Spain also joined (1715–25), and in the Holy Alliance concluded against Napoleon, which France would later also join (1815–30). The concept of such pacts was revived with the creation of the League of Nations and the United Nations Organization. It also has military effects since the signatories can mandate one or more of their number to stage a military intervention against a power posing a threat to peace and the established order (as in the Franco-Spanish wars of 1719 and 1823 and in the wars against North Korea in 1950 and Iraq in 1991), impose sanctions against them (as against Italy in 1935 for its acts of aggression against Ethiopia, and Iraq in 1990), or send an international peace-keeping force in order to keep the warring parties apart (i.e. the UN blue berets).

These international agreements have not prevented the formation of traditional alliances, which are offensive, or at least potentially offensive, despite being described in the majority of cases as defensive. In certain cases the term used is association rather than alliance, as, for example, when the United States refused to commit itself politically to the Allies in 1917, or when the Allies who had been fighting against Italy refused her the title of 'ally' in 1917. The division of Europe into Triple Alliance and Triple Entente in the years before 1914, and the Atlantic

Alliance (NATO) and the Warsaw Pact up to 1991, has taken the practice of forming alliances to enormous lengths. In fact, as early as 1918, the need was felt (at least on the Western Front) for a single command, which was entrusted to General Foch. Nowadays, this is felt to be insufficient and NATO and the Warsaw Pact, until the latter's dissolution in 1991, integrated parts of constituent forces into international armies, navies and air forces. *See also* ATTACHÉ; FOCH; LAWS OF WAR; NEUTRALITY.

J. BÉRENGER

FURTHER READING
Michael Donelan, *Elements of International Political Theory* (Oxford, 1990); George Liska, *Nations in Alliance* (Baltimore, 1968); *Coalition Warfare: an uneasy accord*, eds Keith Neilson and Roy A. Prete (Waterloo, Ont., 1983); Robert E. Osgood, *NATO, the Entangling Alliance* (Chicago, 1962).

BARRIE PASKINS

Andrea Doria (1466–1560) The leading admiral of the Christian principalities of the Mediterranean during the first half of the sixteenth century, Doria was one of the most successful examples of the late Renaissance military entrepreneur. A Genoese nobleman by birth, he entered papal service at an early age and until *c.*1510 served a number of Italian princes as a *condottiere*. In 1512, however, he supported the Genoese revolt against France and in the following years commanded the city's galleys. After Marignano, when Genoa returned to its alliance with France, Doria entered the service of Francis I. In 1527 he commanded the Genoese fleet which supported the French invasion of Naples. By the summer of 1528 it was blockading the Imperialist garrison of the city of Naples by sea while the French were investing it on land; then, in one of the more notorious episodes of the later Italian wars, a series of disputes with Francis led Doria to switch sides. As a result of his defection, Charles V was able to break the siege, and this defeat caused Francis ultimately to sue for peace in 1529. From 1528

until his death, Doria remained in the Habsburg service, his loyalty secured by a series of carefully negotiated and lucrative contracts which gave him the title of Captain General of the Sea and also protected Genoa's political and commericial interests. As Charles V's admiral, Doria played a prominent role in the Mediterranean naval campaigns of the 1530s and 1540s, commanding the Imperial fleets at Tunis in 1535 and Algiers in 1541. In 1538 he was once again at the centre of controversy, when, in command of a fleet assembled by Charles V, the Pope and Venice, he refused to attack Barbarossa's smaller fleet in its base at Prevesa on the coast of Greece. His motives were questioned at the time and are still debated. Doria's service to Charles V, like his defection from Francis I, was based on a finely balanced appraisal of his own interests and those of Genoa. He was one of a number of semi-independent commanders (Lazarus von Schwendi was another example) on whom the Habsburg military system depended. Like many earlier Italian *condottieri*, he was an excellent organizer and capable, on occasion, of bold and swift action, as demonstrated in his capture of Castel Nuovo in 1538. However, his caution was also legendary. His fleet was his livelihood and the basis of his influence; he was not prepared to risk its destruction in dangerous adventures. *See also* ITALY; MARIGNANO; MERCENARIES; NAVAL WARFARE; SCHWENDI; TUNIS.

SIMON ADAMS

FURTHER READING
J. F. Guilmartin, *Gunpowder and Galleys: changing technology and Mediterranean warfare at sea in the sixteenth century* (Cambridge, 1974), pp. 20–6, 42–5; R. J. Knecht, *Francis I* (Cambridge, 1982), pp. 215–18.

Angora, Battle of *See* ANKARA

Ankara, Battle of (20 July 1402) The Mongol leader, Tamerlain (Timur the Lame), had conquered Persia in 1386 and northern India and Delhi in 1398. He sacked Aleppo in 1399 before heading towards Jerusalem en route for Egypt until a swarm of locusts forced him to turn northwards to Baghdad and Damascus. From Damascus, Tamerlain sent a message to the Sultan of the Ottoman Turks, Bayazid I (1389–1403), who was besieging Constantinople, to return all the territories which the Ottomans had seized from the Byzantine Empire. Bayazid abandoned the siege and marched eastwards to meet Tamerlain's Mongolian–Turkish army. Bayazid's army consisted of Ottoman Turks, besides contingents of Serbs and Bulgars and levies from annexed lands. Tamerlain manoeuvred to cut off Bayazid from his water supply, thereby forcing him to engage in battle near Ankara on 20 July 1402. The janissaries (light infantry) in the Ottoman army held the more numerous Mongolian horsemen for most of the day until one third of the army deserted, probably by prior agreement. The Ottomans were then routed and Bayazid died a prisoner in Tamerlain's capital of Samarkand in the following year. The Mongols advanced into Asia Minor destroying Nicaea, Gemlik and Smyrna. However, Tamerlain then abandoned his westward expansion in favour of invading China. He died at Samarkand in 1405 in the midst of his preparations.

The Mongol victory at Ankara provided an opportunity for the states of Western Europe and Byzantium to drive the Ottoman Turks from Asia Minor. For ten years (1403–13), the Ottoman succession was disputed between Bayazid's three sons, Suleiman, Musa and Mehmet, until Mehmet re-established the sultanate as Mehmet I (1413–21). However, with England and France engaged in the Hundred Years' War, and Milan, Venice and Florence engaged in fifty years of warfare, there was little prospect of Western Christendom uniting to oppose the Ottomans. The sad fate of the 1396 Crusade was a further discouragement. As a result, the Ottoman conquest of the Byzantine Empire continued until little remained except Constantinople. *See also* BYZANTIUM; CONSTANTINOPLE; MONGOLS; NICOPOLIS; OTTOMAN TURKS; TAMERLAIN.

R. MANTRAN
JOHN CHILDS

FURTHER READING
René Grousset, *The Empire of the Steppes: a history of Central Asia* (New Brunswick, 1970); Colin Imber, *The Ottoman Empire, 1300–1481* (Istanbul, 1990).

Anson, George, 1st Baron (1697–1762) Anson's early career was uneventful: for several years he commanded a ship on the South Carolina station. In 1739, however, he was selected to command a squadron intended to harass the Spanish possessions in the Pacific. Although only one ship out of six completed the eventual circumnavigation, thanks to Anson's ability and determination the expedition succeeded and acquired a considerable amount of booty. Almost immediately on his return, Anson was appointed a Lord of the Admiralty and held this position for practically the remainder of his life. At times, he also commanded at sea, increasing his reputation with a victory over de la Jonquière in the first Battle of Finisterre (3 May 1747). He also established the blockading squadron off Brest as the basis for British naval policy in wars against France. In 1751, he was elevated to First Lord of the Admiralty and from this office he did much to increase the efficiency of both the navy and its dockyards, introducing the 74-gun ship. When war returned in 1756, he and General John, Lord Ligonier (1680–1770) acted as William Pitt's (1708–78) advisers in the strategic direction of operations. In contrast to earlier conflicts, Anson made sure that naval expeditions left England at the correct time of year in order to arrive at their destinations during suitable campaigning seasons. *See also* ADMINISTRATION, NAVAL; BASES, NAVAL; BLOCKADES; DOCKYARDS; HAWKE; NAVAL WARFARE; NAVIES.

A. W. H. PEARSALL

FURTHER READING
S. W. C. Pack, *Admiral Lord Anson* (London, 1960); Richard Walter, *A Voyage round the World by George Anson* (London, 1748); Glyndwr Williams, *Documents relating to Anson's Voyage round the World* (Navy Records Society, 1967); Julian S. Corbett, *England in the Seven Years' War* (London, 1907).

Antietam, Battle of (1862) At the beginning of September 1862, General Robert E. Lee, believing the Union armies to be exhausted and demoralized, led the Confederate army across the Potomac river. His objects in invading the North were to let his soldiers feed in the rich lands of Maryland and Pennsylvania and to win European recognition for the Southern states. However, the Union armies were reformed under George B. McClellan, a cautious general but an excellent organizer. On 13 September McClellan discovered that Lee had sent the major part of his army to deal with the Union garrison at Harper's Ferry, thus dividing his command. With 80,000 men to Lee's 50,000, McClellan had the opportunity to defeat the Southern force piecemeal. But McClellan's advance was slow. A defensive action at South Mountain on 14 September gave Lee time to concentrate in natural terrain behind the Antietam creek, a tributary of the Potomac. McClellan's plan was to roll up the Confederate left. However, his attacks on 17 September were poorly co-ordinated, and Lee had time to move his numerically inferior forces along the front and so meet the Union forces seriatim. By the middle of the day a gap had emerged in the Confederate centre, in front of Sharpsburg, but the Union forces were too exhausted – and McClellan too cautious – to exploit the opportunity. Late in the afternoon the last Confederate troops from Harper's Ferry arrived on the battlefield to drive into the Union left. McClellan's forces fell back. Tactically defeated, McClellan had none the less thwarted both Lee's strategic objectives. Moreover, total casualties on both sides were 23,000. Relatively speaking, such losses were far more serious for the straitened South. *See also* GETTYSBURG; LEE; UNITED STATES.

HEW STRACHAN

FURTHER READING
James M. McPherson *Battle Cry of Freedom: the civil war era* (Oxford, 1988); James F. Murfin, *The Gleam of Bayonets: the Battle of Antietam and Robert E. Lee's Maryland campaign, September 1862* (New York, 1965).

Anti-militarism *See* PACIFISM

Antwerp, Siege of (July 1584–17 August 1585) If it lacked the epic dimensions of those of Haarlem (1573), Leiden (1574) and Ostend (1601–4), the Siege of Antwerp was in technical terms the most impressive of the Dutch Revolt, and possibly of the entire sixteenth century. In 1584 Antwerp was one of the largest cities in Europe, with a walled circuit of five miles (rebuilt and embastioned by Charles V in 1543 and by Alba in 1567–9), and a garrison of 8,000–9,000 supported by a militia of 7,000–8,000. The Duke of Parma took the decision to invest it in June 1584, after regaining most of the towns of Flanders and Brabant by a combination of negotiation and military pressure during the previous three years. Since Parma already occupied much of the hinterland, the key to a siege would be the control of the Scheldt below the city, for on this its communications with the northern Provinces depended. To assure these communications, in 1583 William of Orange had advised the governor, his trusted lieutenant, Philippe de Marnix, Sieur de Ste Aldegonde, to open the dykes along the river and flood the pastures between Antwerp and the Scheldt estuary. In one of the most debated episodes of the siege, Ste Aldegonde (like Wentworth at Calais) postponed the decision at the request of the citizens, who were unwilling to see valuable land submerged. Since his field army then numbered only 10,000 men, Parma made no attempt to invest the city as a whole, but made the two main forts that defended the lower Scheldt his primary targets. Liefenshoek on the western bank fell on 10 July 1584, but Lillo on the eastern fought off the assault. Following this partial success Parma decided to build a fortified bridge across the Scheldt near Liefenshoek. The bridge was not completed until 25 February 1585 and until then Dutch ships continued to reach the city. In the meantime a second dimension to the siege had been created. During the attack on Lillo the defenders had finally opened the dykes and flooded the pastures of the eastern bank. Parma's bridge should have been outflanked, except that one dyke

25

(the Kouwenstein) still barred access to Antwerp, and this Parma moved quickly to fortify. During the spring of 1585 the bridge and the Kouwenstein were the scenes of four major attempts to break the siege. On 4 April the famous exploding ship, built in Antwerp by the Italian engineer Federico Giambelli, nearly destroyed the bridge, but the Dutch fleet in the estuary failed to react in time. On the night of 6 May the fleet surprised the Kouwenstein, but then the garrison of Antwerp failed to assist them. On 20 May the bridge was attacked a second time by fireships, but Parma was prepared, and the attempt failed. On 26 May a major combined assault by the fleet and the Antwerp garrison temporarily gained control of the Kouwenstein, but the ebb tide forced the fleet to retire, and Parma successfully counter-attacked. Although the city itself had not yet been threatened directly, this last failure led Ste Aldegonde to sue for terms. The Dutch had been counting on English intervention, and to this end they negotiated a treaty with Elizabeth I in July and August 1585; nevertheless Ste Aldegonde proceeded with the surrender, which was signed on 17 August. The siege was undoubtedly one of Parma's masterpieces, whatever he owed to the confusion in which Orange's assassination in June 1584 had left the Dutch government. Ste Aldegonde's decision to surrender was held to be premature, and he did not receive public employment again. *See also* ALBA; CALAIS; FORTIFICATION; NETHERLANDS; OSTEND; PARMA; SIEGES; SPAIN.

SIMON ADAMS

FURTHER READING
The most accessible narrative account is found in J. L. Motley, *The History of the United Provinces* (London, 1876 edn), i. The fullest is contained in L. van der Essen, *Alexandre Farnèse, duc de Parma* (Brussels, 1934), iii, iv.

Arab states *See* MIDDLE EAST

Arbela, Battle of *See* GAUGAMELA

Ardant du Picq, Charles (1821–70) Charles-Jean-Jacques-Joseph Ardant du Picq was a French colonel, military analyst and author, who was killed in an engagement near Metz during the early phases of the Franco-Prussian War. His *Études sur le combat* (*Battle Studies*) were published posthumously in 1880. Finding the military theory of his day too remote from the reality of battle, he relied on empirical evidence in the formulation of his concepts. The behaviour of men in action could only be understood by the collection of detailed information about actual conditions on the battlefield. To achieve this, in 1868 he circulated a detailed questionnaire among officers of all ranks in the French army.

Études sur le combat criticized the mediocrity of the French command during the Second Empire, which had resulted in the deterioration of combat discipline. Ardant du Picq affirmed the importance of morale in all forms of warfare; provided that he was well led, 'the soldier is capable of enduring a given amount of fear before he tries to escape from battle.' He analysed the nature of 'shock' as employed in military tactics and concluded that it did not really exist. Instead, he decided that an attack could only succeed through aimed fire and manoeuvre provided that the optimum conditions were first established. To achieve these he urged methodical tactics: artillery preparation; the infantry to attack in open formation preceded by skirmishers (half the battalion); and the avoidance of confusion between the distinct and separate acts of deploying the troops, usually in column, and advancing towards the enemy. A realistic appreciation of the exact battlefield conditions and a skilful use of terrain were deemed equally important.

On large battlefields dominated by breech-loading rifles and long-range artillery, Ardant du Picq saw little prospect of success for the new mass conscript armies. Amidst the smoke and noise, the regiments of conscripts would lose cohesion and the soldiers would 'go to ground'. The only manner in which warfare could be conducted under these new conditions was by professional, elite armies welded together by high morale and *esprit de corps*.

27

After the publication of the second edition of *Battle Studies* in 1903, Ardant du Picq's emphasis on the importance of morale was adopted out of context by the exponents of the notion that infantry displaying *élan* and the offensive spirit could overcome the hail of bullets sprayed out by entrenched infantry armed with magazine rifles and machine-guns. *See also* BLOCH; ESPRIT DE CORPS; GRANDMAISON; INFANTRY; MORALE.

A. CORVISIER
JOHN CHILDS

FURTHER READING
Charles Ardant du Picq, *Battle Studies* (New York, 1921, and Harrisburg, Pa., 1947); Azar Gat, *The Development of Military Thought: the nineteenth century* (Oxford, 1992), pp. 28–42.

Arm Contemporary usage groups soldiers serving in the infantry, cavalry and the artillery under the generic head of 'arm'. When, in the nineteenth century, the tactic of combining the three arms was referred to, it was this grouping which was meant, the navy occupying a separate place. In the nineteenth and twentieth centuries, technological progress was expressed in the development of new 'arms' or 'services', among which must be mentioned the engineers, signals, aviation, anti-aircraft defence, missile regiments, airborne and helicopter divisions, the marines and special units (responsible for raids, sabotage, etc.). The expansion of the battlefield, so that now it can cover entire countries, has led those French troops still considered as 'non-combatant' in the two world wars to be regarded as 'arms': the medical service, logistics and its many branches, including the women's auxiliary services and bodies such as civil defence.

The modern idea of 'arm' has developed from older concepts. It has retained certain characteristics of these older concepts and they make for a better understanding of its present nature. The categories of combatants that were used in the Ancient World and the Middle Ages were extremely varied, and troops were employed in a clearly differentiated fashion, depending on their particular skills and ethnic origins. A number of notable facts deserve examination in this context: the Assyrians had an intelligence arm, in the sense that its functions were given institutional status, while among the Israelites military chaplaincy assumed great importance. In the Greek world, where individual combatants played a central role, *hoplites* (heavily armed foot-soldiers) were deployed among the infantry of the line, which was reinforced on the flank by cavalry or chariots, and finally a light infantry composed of *peltasts* (foot-soldiers armed with a *pelte*, or light shield, and a short spear or javelin) was added. In conclusion, we must not forget the important part played by Greek engineers in fortifications and sieges.

For their part, the Romans set great store by experience acquired in battle. Their *triarii*, hardened veterans, made up the 'old guard' of their legions in the days before they were formed into the Praetorian Guard, which later wielded political power. Roman military organization relied on extensive assistance from allies and their special skills, e.g. the Balearic slingers. Finally the development of the *tercio* during the Renaissance marked the creation of the three distinct arms of the service (infantry, cavalry, artillery) with which battle was conducted throughout the modern era. In some countries, particularly in peacetime, these were placed under the leadership of separate inspectorates. In France Vauban's strong personality led to the creation of a body of engineers which became the separate arm of engineers or sappers. The end of the eighteenth century and the triumph of rationalism finally gave rise to that synthetic body, the division, conceived by Broglie and Guibert. This was the prototype of the 'inter-arm' structures which would be used by the high command after the French Revolution. The present-day 'arm' seems to be an institution which has inherited the professional traditions of the trade guilds (artillery, engineering, navy) and one in which efforts are made to retain the spirit of the military corps of earlier times. The continued use of the terms 'cavalry', 'hussars' and 'dragoons' among modern airborne, mobile and tank forces clearly demonstrates these points.

In the British army, the use of the term 'arm' is usually restricted to the actual fighting troops – infantry, cavalry and artillery. All other combatant or non-combatant organizations are generally referred to as 'branches' or 'corps': the Intelligence Corps, the Royal Corps of Transport, the Royal Army Medical Corps, etc. A similar pattern is followed in the US army. *See also* ADMINISTRATION, ARMY; ARTILLERY; CAVALRY; CHAPLAINS; ENGINEERS; INFANTRY; MARINES; MEDICAL SERVICES; ORDNANCE; SERVICES, ARMY; SIGNAL COMMUNICATION; TACTICAL ORGANIZATION; TRAINING.

D. REICHEL
JOHN CHILDS

FURTHER READING
C. C. King, *The British Army and Auxiliary Forces* (2 vols, London, 1892–7); J. F. C. Fuller, *Armament and History* (London, 1946).

Armada, voyage of the Spanish (July–September 1588)   Few naval battles have caused as many debates as the engagements in the English Channel in the summer of 1588. The nearest rival is Jutland, for like Jutland 'the Armada' was an encounter battle, where an English fleet that believed itself superior failed to inflict a decisive defeat on its opponent. However, unlike Jutland, the fragmentary sources leave the key episodes of the battle mysterious and many technical issues difficult, if not impossible, to resolve. The nineteenth-century belief that the battle saw the victory of a gun-armed fleet over one equipped only for boarding and that it thereby initiated modern naval warfare has inspired a running debate over the gunnery of both sides. More recently the Spanish planning for the operation has been re-examined, with the old argument that the expedition was totally misconceived challenged by one that it was a viable operation that failed only by accident. It has even been argued that the appearance of a Spanish battle fleet in the Channel represented a victory of sorts. The 'battle' itself was the consequence of an attempted invasion of England planned since 1585, in which a fleet was to sail from Spain to escort an expeditionary force from the Army of Flanders across the Straits of Dover, and to supply that force with reinforcements. Various delays meant that it was not until the end of July 1588 that the fleet of 122 ships arrived off Land's End. There it surprised an English fleet of sixty-six ships recently driven back from the Spanish coast and replenishing in Plymouth harbour. The English succeeded in escaping from Plymouth and secured the weather gage, but since the prevailing winds were westerlies, this meant that the two fleets were settled into a stern chase up the Channel towards the Armada's destination. The days that followed saw a number of gunnery engagements which caused some damage to the Armada, but also cost the English much ammunition: only two Spanish ships were lost, one by an accidental explosion, the other by a collision. Among the most debated aspects of the battle is the question of whether the Armada made a serious attempt to enter the Solent between 2 and 4 August, and consequently whether the English could claim 'success' in driving it off. On 6 August the Armada anchored in the roads of Calais in order to make contact with Flanders. Here, during the night of 7 August, the English, reinforced by a squadron stationed at Dover, attacked it with fireships. Although the fireships themselves did no damage, in escaping them the Armada was thrown into confusion, and a fresh English attack on 8 August achieved greater success: a galleass ran aground at Calais, two galleons ran aground off the Dutch coast, and a fourth ship foundered in the North Sea. The Armada was saved from disaster by the winds that drove it northward. Supply shortages forced the English to abandon their pursuit at the level of the Firth of Forth, and the Armada returned to Spain via the northerly route during the succeeding weeks. Thirty-four or thirty-five more ships were lost in this phase of the voyage, mainly from among the more weakly constructed or those damaged in the battle. During the Channel engagements the Spaniards maintained a tight and disciplined formation which served them well;

there appears to have been no tactical planning on the part of the English. For this reason it is difficult to consider the Armada a 'modern' naval battle similar to those of the later seventeenth century. What it did reveal, however, was that most of the fighting was done by a relatively small number (around twenty-five) major warships on both sides, and that the 'medieval' fleet of conscripted merchant vessels was now obsolete. *See also* COMBINED OPERATIONS; CORBETT; DRAKE; EXPEDITIONS; GREAT BRITAIN; JUTLAND; NAVAL WARFARE; NAVIES; PARMA; SPAIN.

SIMON ADAMS

FURTHER READING
The literature on the Armada is vast. The classic narrative is J. S. Corbett, *Drake and the Tudor Navy* (London, 1898), ii; with G. Mattingly, *The Defeat of the Spanish Armada* (London, 1959) providing a brilliant *tour d'horizon* of the wider context. The publications inspired by the quatercentenary in 1988 are surveyed in S. Adams, 'The *Gran Armada*: 1988 and after', *History*, lxxvi (1991), pp. 238–49. Of the English-language works the most important are C. Martin and G. Parker, *The Spanish Armada* (London, 1988); *Armada*, ed. M. J. Rodríguez-Salgado (London, 1988); *England, Spain and the Gran Armada, 1585–1604*, eds M. J. Rodríguez-Salgado and S. Adams (Edinburgh, 1991).

Armament, naval   *See* NAVIES

Armes blanches   *See* BLADE WEAPONS

Armistices   The terms 'truce', 'suspension of hostilities' and 'armistice' are often used interchangeably and refer to agreements between contending forces or, more generally, between warring powers, to bring about a temporary cessation of hostilities. These agreements often serve as a prelude to the re-establishment of peace. Hostilities may also be terminated by a surrender, which indicates acknowledgement of either local or general defeat and acceptance of the conditions laid down by the victor, and

implies an undertaking not to renew hostilities.

With the emergence of the worship of the dead came the introduction of temporary suspensions of hostilities in order that fallen warriors might be buried. It appears that these tacit or verbal agreements began to become increasingly rare in the seventeenth century. It should be noted that a 'Truce of God' was something rather different. It was inspired by the Church and was intended to proscribe hostilities during certain times of year or on certain days of the week.

If truces were to become permanent, they had to be followed by a peace treaty. The practice of making truces became very widespread in the seventeenth century, although the complexity of political relations in that period posed a number of difficulties.

Truces vary considerably in duration. They may mean a genuine cessation of hostilities lasting several weeks, as was the case in Italy during the war between France and Spain over the succession of Mantua and the possession of Casale (Montferrat). The two armies maintained their positions from the end of August until 15 October 1631, the set date for the renewal of hostilities. The consolidation of this truce represents Mazarin's first diplomatic success, when he was still only a young officer in the service of papal diplomacy. He succeeded in obtaining an agreement between the warring parties and separated the two armies at the last moment when they were already in battle order and preparing to renew the fighting.

Belligerents often baulk at signing long truces, since this may turn out to the enemy's advantage. One example of this was the negotiations at Münster and Osnabruck when the Allies refused to sign an armistice with the Imperial forces and continued fighting for three years (1645–8) while their diplomats were negotiating a peacy treaty. The Allies feared the truce would enable the Emperor to rebuild his forces and that he would take an even tougher stand in the negotiations. The truce Mazarin granted to the Elector of Bavaria in the spring of 1647 confirms this theory.

Turenne's successes during the campaign of 1646 had inflicted serious damage on the territory of Bavaria, the Emperor's 'sanctuary', and considerably diminished the resources of the Elector, who was the loyal ally of Emperor Ferdinand III. In spite of Turenne's warnings and the reticence of the Swedes, Mazarin agreed to a suspension of hostilities at Ulm in May 1647. He was soon obliged to face up to what had happened: Maximilian of Bavaria had only signed the armistice as an excuse to come to the Emperor's immediate aid in Bohemia and attack the Swedes. By autumn 1647, Mazarin found himself forced to proclaim the truce ended and hostilities resumed in the following spring, the ultimate outcome being the occupation of Bavaria by the Franco-Swedish army.

A truce may also in fact be a disguised peace treaty, and may thus be a kind of legal artifice, when one of the parties does not recognize the other in international law. The Ottoman Sultan was unable to sign a definitive or 'perpetual' peace treaty with the Infidels because, according to Islamic law, a state of war cannot exist in the *dar al-Islam*, the territories under the spiritual authority of the Caliph (the Commander of the Faithful). It dictates, on the contrary, that the Faithful should aim, by means of Holy War, to conquer the territories outside this domain. This, in effect, means that only truces, and not peace treaties, can be signed, though these may well be long-term and renewable, such as the truce signed with the Emperor in the seventeenth century after the Peace of Vienna in 1606. At that time, neither the Habsburgs nor the Sultan had the least interest in renewing hostilities in Hungary. During the same period, the government in Madrid was torn between two major concerns: how to achieve a cessation of hostilities between Spain and the United Provinces without recognizing the decisive secession of the Low Countries' northern provinces, which had broken away from their sovereign by the Union of Utrecht. This is what induced Spain to sign a twelve-year truce with the Estates General in 1609, which was not renewed in 1621, the 'war party' having triumphed both in

Madrid, with the coming to power of the Condé-Duque de Olivarès, and in the Hague, with the triumph of the Orange party and the Gomarists. By contrast, the Peace of Münster, signed in 1648, was of a more permanent nature.

Finally, it was only through the signing of a twenty-year truce between the Emperor and the Estates of the Empire on the one hand and the Kingdom of France on the other, at Ratisbon (Regensburg) in 1684, that Louis XIV was able to obtain recognition for the *Chambres de Réunion* and the annexation of Strasbourg. Leopold I had been uncompromising on the point of law and the Frankfurt Congress had been abandoned, with the *Deductio de juribus Imperii* of October 1682 reserving all the rights of the Imperial Princes whom the *Chambres de Réunion* had dispossessed. The Truce of Ratisbon resulted only in the provisional and *de facto* recognition of these annexations. Although this solution enabled both parties to save face, it was none the less a failure for French diplomacy and the problem was not solved conclusively until the Peace of Rijswijk (1697).

During the same period in the West, better definitions of what constituted a state of war and a state of peace were arrived at. Gradually, the distinction between an armistice binding belligerent states and a cessation of hostilities binding military leaders was made clear. An armistice implied a political agreement on a number of points and was often accompanied by preliminaries to a peace treaty. For example, the Peace of Vienna (2 May 1738) which brought an end to the War of the Polish Succession, was preceded, as early as 1735, by (secret) preliminaries between France and Austria (5 October) and an armistice between the Emperor, Spain and Sardinia (1 December), which brought hostilities to an end. After this date, this became common practice: e.g. at the Peace of Leoben (1797) and the Armistice of Villafranca (1859) between France and Austria. In some cases, an armistice might be accompanied by the capitulation of the defeated nation's capital city (e.g. Paris, in 1814, 1815 and 1871). In this last case, the armistice meant that France, as defeated

31

nation, was obliged to accept all the conditions laid down by the victors, as was Germany in 1918. The armistice of 8 May 1945 was a military surrender, the political government in Germany which the Allies had refused to accept having been replaced. Japan's capitulation on 2 September 1945 put the country entirely in the hands of the victorious Allies.

It should be noted that the armistice of 8 May 1945 was not followed by a formal peace treaty with Germany, which was divided into two separate states. At the present time, the tendency is for armistices to take the place of peace treaties or imply that peace has been achieved. However, the term 'armistice' is also used to refer to politico-military agreements, which are specific temporary arrangements (as in the civil war in Lebanon) and are regularly violated. The way in which the various terms are currently used is undergoing some transformation and it is thus difficult to provide a precise definition.

A. CORVISIER
J. BÉRENGER

The negotiation of truces is beset by an inescapable dilemma. If a brief form of words is agreed, by word-of-mouth or in writing, then the truce may break down through misunderstandings or accidents which could have been avoided by a fuller prior understanding. If opponents seek a very full form of agreement, then negotiations will inevitably be protracted, obstacles will be encountered which might better, in the interests of all parties, have been ignored, and subsequent breakdown of the painstakingly full agreement is likely to transmit messages of singular hostility between the opponents. There is no general solution to this dilemma, and certainly no substitute for negotiating skills, which are often very scarce when belligerents need them most. The civil wars which resulted in the breakup of Yugoslavia (1991–2) present a textbook case of many of the problems associated with ceasefires. One problem was that agreements of 200–300 words easily crumbled under the pressure of misunderstanding between passionate

enemies. Also, there was a tendency for the fighting to degenerate into scrapping between intensely localized sub-groups, so that the initiation of negotiations was made difficult by the problem of identifying bargaining partners who could be counted on to have the power to implement the measures they had agreed. As the misfortunes of those obliged to sign the 1918 Armistice on Germany's behalf remind us, there is very often a strong political imperative to avoid being identifiable as the signatory of a ceasefire.

BARRIE PASKINS

See also LAWS OF WAR; PRISONERS OF WAR; SURRENDER.

FURTHER READING
Sydney D. Bailey, *How Wars End: the United Nations and the termination of armed conflicts, 1946–1964* (2 vols, Oxford, 1982); Fred Charles Ikle, *Every War Must End* (New York, 1971).

Armour, personal Among the oldest pieces of defensive armour preserved, the helmet has pride of place. The Sumerian stela, 'the Vultures' (3rd millennium BC), shows us fighting men protected by a uniform item of headgear, equipped with a neck-guard. The 'Standard of Ur', a box with mosaic inlays depicting war scenes, provides evidence of the existence of a chin-strap. Assyrian helmets, worked in bronze leaf, and capable of being reinforced by padding, have also been found. From the earliest times, then, care has been taken to protect the warrior's head. But what of his body? We have much less information on this question, because leather (French *cuir*, which gives us the English term 'cuirass') keeps less well than metal. It does, however, seem that this material played an important role in the production of defensive armour during the first millennia of recorded history.

The Ancients tried to protect their soldiers from the hail of arrows with which battle generally commenced. The principal instrument was the shield, which took the most varied forms. The Greek *peltasts*, who were less exposed than the soldiers of the line, were equipped with a light wickerwork shield, covered with goatskin or sheepskin; a slit enhanced visibility and made it easier to parry arrows. The shield of a soldier of the line was either round or oblong. The Roman legionaries, when attacking ramparts, joined their shields edge to edge above their heads in the manoeuvre known as the *testudo*. Moreover, the Romans 'neutralized' their enemies' shields by making them the target of their *pilum* (heavy javelin), which could penetrate an inch of solid oak. Pulled down by a weapon stuck into it like a harpoon, the enemy's defensive shield was rendered useless. The Middle Ages turned the large shield or buckler into a symbol; it became the heraldic shield bearing the arms (armorial bearings) of the knight, though the *pavis* (assault shield) and the *rondache*, a small shield used in a manner reminiscent of the peltasts, were still employed. One original development was the welding of the knight's shield to his brassard (armour covering the arm). The modern and contemporary period has seen the reappearance of various kinds of shield: during the First World War, armoured shields were manufactured which imitated the shape of trees half-destroyed by shell-fire to serve as protection for snipers. Otherwise, the armour-plating of armoured combat vehicles has largely taken up the mantle of this defensive weapon, which is rarely used at all now in its primitive form, except by police forces engaged in public order operations.

Body armour occupies a central place in the development of defensive equipment. We should note here that of all forms of military equipment, it is one of the most expensive. The human body is, with all its complexity, extremely vulnerable. The degree of protection achieved depends on the price one is prepared – or able – to pay. One of the most costly forms of body armour was bronze armour, the Greek *thorax* or Roman *lorica*, cast 'to measure' on a mould of the torso of the soldier for whom it was being made (this development of a personalizing armaments technique may have had some influence upon the realism of ancient statuary). This piece of equipment was complemented by greaves (shin armour), which were also moulded to the body, and a helmet, providing almost total protection. This was the same helmet, we see worn by Pericles and Athena. The Roman legionary's armour, which was jointed and relatively light, was made up of iron plates riveted to leather straps. Seldom in history has so much attention been paid to providing the infantryman with such 'functional' protection. When a sense of civic duty disappeared from Rome, together with the military spirit, mercenaries, who were allotted the task of intervening where there was a threat, replaced the old Roman soldiers. These fighting men wore an almost total suit of armour made from scales of iron, chain mail, as indeed did their mounts. The form of their suit of armour would evolve to become that of the medieval knight.

The development of armour aimed to offer the most complete possible safety to the warrior. Insufficient documentation on losses makes it impossible to calculate a satisfactory coefficient of protection offered by the different forms of armour seen throughout history, but it does appear that the progress made in this field by the medieval armourers was, for economic reasons, achieved at the expense of a capacity to put sufficiently large armies into the field. Where the Roman legionary, who had perhaps 70 per cent protection, derived most of his security from his mobility and the impact of the great strength of his forces, the knight, who had perhaps 90 per cent protection, was unfailingly confronted with the problem of lack of numbers. Having said this, the development of his armour, like the development of blade weapons, reached a high point which would not subsequently be equalled. The coat of mail – which should not be confused with the leather jerkin worn under the armour – was made in different ways: 'rustred' if the rings, stitched onto cloth or leather, partly overlap; 'mascled' if the metal scales overlap like 'diamond tiling'. The classical model is known as 'barleycorn', in which the rings form genuine metal links. Though the coat of mail protected against blows struck crosswise, it could none the less be pierced by stabbing blows. In order to remedy this fatal defect, the armourers developed an armour made of metal plates. Their researches gave a great stimulus to metalworking and formed something of a prelude to the rise of modern industry. Another aspect of the development of armour is worthy of mention in this context: progress in the science of anatomy, closely bound up with a study of the faults in suits of armour, which was dearly bought in the course of hundreds of individual battles. The armour which was the fruit of these developments increasingly took the form of a miniature individual fortress. A chinpiece was added to the helmet, together with a gorget which covered the carotid artery. The pauldron was followed by brassard and gauntlet. The breastplate was connected to the humeral and back plate by straps, iron bards and hook-fastenings. The genitals were covered by a codpiece. The legs and feet were protected by cuisses, polyns, greaves and sabatons. A few centuries later, the engineers who were to develop the astronauts' space suits would study closely certain of the original solutions developed by the medieval armourers.

The use of defensive armour would never subsequently disappear altogether. In the eighteenth century, the horseman often still wore bullet-proof armour. In the nineteenth century, the use of campaign fortifications gradually came to replace the use of body armour, but in 1915 we again find the idea that the helmet is an indispensable item of the soldier's equipment. Later, the systematic study of injuries suffered in combat led most armies to equip their troops with helmets providing more-comprehensive protection. Lastly, there is the bullet-proof vest, for which new materials are used. The use of certain forms of highly resistant, superimposed meshes, which can fragment projectiles to absorb their impact, is one of the most recent developments. *See also* BLADE WEAPONS; CAVALRY; FIREARMS; INFANTRY; KNIGHTS AND CHIVALRY; TANKS; WEAPONS.

D. REICHEL

FURTHER READING

A. Snodgrass, *Arms and Armour of the Greeks* (London, 1982); P. Connolly, *Greece and Rome at War* (London, 1981); G. C. Stone, *A Glossary of the Construction, Decoration and Use of Arms and Armour* (New York, 1961); Claude Blair, *European Armour* (London, 1958).

Armour plate The notion of employing metal armour to protect military machinery and positions from small arms fire and gunfire emerged during the Crimean War (1854–6) in response to the development of the high explosive shell. The French constructed armoured floating batteries both in the Baltic and to attack the Russian fort at Kinburn at the mouth of the Dneiper in October 1855. In 1859, the French built the first 'ironclad' armoured warship, *La Gloire*, protected by a belt of wrought iron armour, 4.3–4.7 inches thick, backed by strong wooden planking. The British reciprocated with the much larger *Warrior* in 1861. Armoured warships were further developed during the American Civil War with the USS *Monitor* and the CSS *Virginia*, the former having a turret encased in 8 inches of iron armour. Also during the American conflict, iron armour was sometimes used to protect the embrasures of casemates in land fortifications. During the 1860s, the use of armour plate to protect casemates spread to the design of British coastal fortifications. Wrought iron was soon found to be insufficiently hard and it was combined with steel to form compound armour; the steel face provided the necessary hardness supported by the resilience of iron. The French firm Schneider et Cie invented an oil-tempering process to produce homogeneous steel armour (rolled plate with a uniform hardness throughout), which demonstrated good resistance to shell fire and better resilience than compound armour. During the late 1880s, the development of the armour-piercing shell required armour manufacturers to refine their product further. The American Hayward Augustus Harvey invented a face-hardening process by applying carbon to the face of steel at very high temperatures and for a considerable period of time. Harveyed armour thus had good face resistance and his use of a nickel–steel alloy rather than pure steel produced improved resilience, but it was prone to cracking. The German firm Krupp adopted a hot-gas tempering method and chromium was regularly added to nickel–steel.

During the First World War, rolled homogeneous steel armour (RHA) protected the majority of armoured warships, while thinner plate was applied to tanks and gun-shields. During the 1930s, molybdenum was combined with chromium –nickel–steel alloy and experiments were conducted into the lamination of a hard steel face-plate to RHA, but the bond tended to disintegrate when hit, besides being difficult and expensive to manufacture. Throughout the Second World War, alloy steel RHA continued to be the main protection for tanks, armoured vehicles and warships. By 1943, the armour on the majority of tanks was welded whereas previously the individual plates had been bolted onto steel frames. In addition, turrets were cast in one piece to eliminate weak points.

The effectiveness of RHA, which remained the basic protection for armoured vehicles into the 1970s, is increased by the angle at which the plate is laid relative to the vertical. At a slope of 60° to the vertical, the horizontal thickness of armour plate is doubled and the face presents a good angle to deflect approaching projectiles. For aircraft and light armoured vehicles (armoured cars, armoured personnel carriers), RHA is too heavy and aluminium armour is usually employed. Up to a thickness of 75 mm, aluminium resists penetration better than the equivalent weight of steel. However, because aluminium is less dense than steel, above a thickness of 75 mm an equivalent degree of protection from aluminium requires a far greater thickness than RHA. Aluminium armour is also pyrophoric when hit by a projectile (spontaneous combustion occurs on exposure to air). It has therefore never been suitable for large armoured fighting vehicles.

In order to combat modern armour-piercing shot (fin-stabilized, discarding-sabot, tungsten-steel projectiles) and shaped-charge warheads employing the 'Monroe Effect' (high explosive anti-tank – HEAT) (*see* EXPLOSIVES), armour has moved away from RHA to various forms of lamination. British Chobham armour consists of layers of titanium, nylon and ceramic material, which spread the kinetic energy of attacking projectiles over a wide area thus dissipating their force. Its layered structure also disrupts the formation of hypervelocity slugs formed by shaped charges. The glacis plate of the Russian T80 tank is a laminate of steel and glass fibre with a layer of lead-impregnated plastic to act as a spall liner (spalling is the breaking away of scabs of material from the inner surface of armour plate when hit by a projectile) and a radiation shield. Laminates of fibreglass, nylon or kevlar are now often used as armour against bullets and splinters on light armoured vehicles, aircraft and small warships. Titanium armour is also used in aircraft, mainly to protect the cockpit and fuel tanks (the Fairchild A-10).

To ward off the danger of the shaped charge, there have been two main developments. Spaced armour, thin plates positioned in advance of the main armour, induces the shaped charge to fire prematurely. German Mark IV tanks during the Second World War used wire mesh, later replaced by skirting plates, around their turrets to detonate shaped charges at a safe distance from the main armour. During the 1960s, Russian tanks were built with double-skinned armour; spalling from the inside of the first layer caused by HEAT rounds was unable to penetrate the second. Although of West German origin, explosive reactive armour (ERA) was first deployed by Israel on its Merkava tanks under the name Blazer. A steel box is bolted to the main armour. The front face of the box consists of two layers of steel separated by a sheet of explosive with a gap between this explosive sandwich and the tank's main armour. When hit by a shaped charge, the explosive detonates driving the first plate outwards and the rear plate inwards. Because the outer plate is moving under the force of the explosion, the jet from the shaped charge is obliged to penetrate a surface which is continually renewing itself. However, the jet moves much faster than the outer plate but the same principle applies to the inner plate which the jet next encounters. When the inner plate hits the main armour, it bounces outwards thus re-presenting its surface to the jet. The net effect is to so degrade the shaped charge that it cannot penetrate the main armour. ERA boxes are bolted onto the most vulnerable surfaces of the tank, particularly the turret. ERA proved effective in the Israeli attack on the Lebanon and it has been adopted by Russia on many of its main battle tanks. The combination of ERA and laminated armour has made most existing anti-tank weapons and missiles of questionable value. As a consequence, overfly top attack missiles are being developed which deliver shaped charges at the optimum angle to the most vulnerable part of an armoured vehicle (the top and forward slope of the turret). A second solution is the tandem warhead which contains two shaped charges, one to initiate the ERA and a second to penetrate the laminated armour. *See also* ARMOUR, PERSONAL; ARTILLERY; FORTIFICATION; NAVIES; TANKS.

JOHN CHILDS

FURTHER READING
G. Ferrari, 'The hows and whys of armour penetration', *Military Technology*, x (1985); P. R. Courtney-Green, *Ammunition for the Land Battle* (London, 1991); R. M. Ogorkiewicz, *Armoured Forces* (London, 1970).

Armoured vehicles *See* TANKS

Arrian (Flavius Arrianus) (second century AD)   A Greek from Bithynia who was a Roman senator and governor of the province of Cappadocia under Hadrian, when he defeated the invasion of the Alani *c.* AD 132. He described his military dispositions for this battle in a treatise – *Battle Formation against the Alani* – part of which survives. This is a unique source for the history of the Roman army and in it Arrian mentions an unusual defensive formation he adopted, apparently modelled on the Greek phalanx, to counter the enemy's heavy cavalry. The legionaries were drawn up in a densely packed mass eight ranks deep; the first four carried a long thrusting spear, while the rear ranks were armed with the usual throwing spear (*pilum*). Furthermore, archers, slingers and javelin men opened the battle with a concentrated barrage while the cavalry prevented any outflanking manoeuvres. Arrian also wrote a manual on the organization of the Greek phalanx, including an account of contemporary cavalry tactics and training. It is possible that Arrian and others who wrote on similar themes were offering practical instruction relevant to contemporary Roman military practice rather than providing mere antiquarian entertainment. Arrian is also remembered for his history of Alexander of Macedon. *See also* AENEAS TACTICUS; FRONTINUS; INFANTRY; ONASANDER ON MILITARY MATTERS; ROME; VEGETIUS.

B. CAMPBELL

FURTHER READING
A. B. Bosworth, 'Arrian and the Alani', *Harvard Studies in Classical Philology*, lxxxi (1977), pp. 217–55; P. A. Stadter, *Arrian of Nicomedia* (Chapel Hill, NC, 1980); J. B. Campbell, 'Teach yourself how to be a general', *JRS*, lxxvii (1987), pp. 13–29; Ann Hyland, *Training the Roman Cavalry: from Arrian's Ars Tactica* (Stroud, 1993).

Arsenals   Whereas all branches of the armed forces possess depots for the stockpiling of equipment, an arsenal is specifically a store or manufactory of weapons and ammunition. It probably derives from the Arabic *dar sinaʿa*, meaning a workshop. Archaeological excavations in Crete have revealed the existence inside the royal palace of rooms in which stood large earthenware vessels containing stocks of swords, arrow-heads, chariot wheels, etc. Naval dockyards – large industrial complexes covering everything connected with the fitting out of a fleet (Carthage, Venice) – are quite distinct from the arsenals of a land army. Ironically, the Venice Arsenal was actually a dockyard although it has given its name to army installations. Arsenals were designed originally for relatively small armies to serve as stores located at appropriate points throughout a country. Such stores gradually developed into manufacturing establishments. Frequently, the appellation has subsequently lost its original meaning but continues to be used

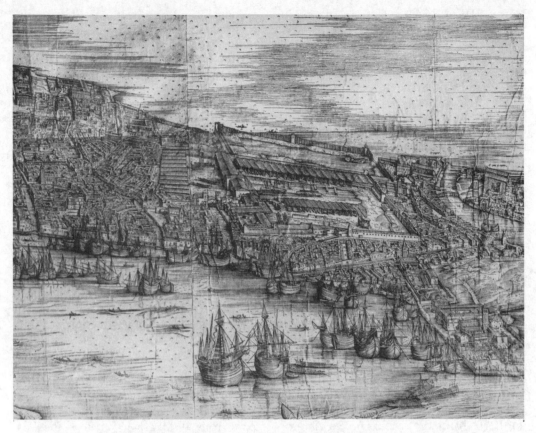

Possibly modelled on the Phoenician circular dockyard at Carthage, the Venice Arsenal was built in 1104 and continually expanded until the end of the seventeenth century. It employed over 4,000 workmen to construct, arm and maintain the Venetian fleet of war galleys. As a demonstration for the benefit of selected foreign dignitaries, the Arsenal could rig and equip one war galley in less than twenty minutes. The largest industrial enterprise of medieval Europe, the Arsenal was and remains a restricted and secure site.
(Mansell Collection/Archivi Alinari)

in a metaphorical sense in the names of roads or areas in cities (the Arsenal Football Club and district in north London).

The role of arsenals gradually became more varied. In the early modern period, they basically served as stores for artillery and engineering equipment. From the beginning of the sixteenth century, French arsenals; and the Ordnance Office in England, issued the cannon and equipment required by field armies. The English Ordnance Office was also responsible for all the professional gunners and cannon stationed in the garrisons and fixed fortifications. Arsenals then became responsible

for infantry weapons after the diversity of types and calibres had resulted in serious inefficiencies; the English Ordnance Office issued its first standard patterns in 1631. Finally, after the manufacture of gunpowder had become a matter of royal prerogative, it too was stored in arsenals.

Arsenals were next given the task of ensuring that sufficient equipment was stocked and that the appropriate quality was maintained. Since most military equipment in the sixteenth, seventeenth and eighteenth centuries was manufactured by private industry, it was essential to establish standards of design and quality. Artillery calibres were standardized by

Henry VIII in England, by Maximilian I in Germany and by Henry II in France. The points which inspectors verified were the quality of the metal, the calibre and the windage left for the easy passage of the cannon ball. Some products were, as a result, rejected and penalties were inflicted for non-compliance. In France, the function of inspection was extended in the eighteenth century to include the supervision of the state foundries and powder-mills. The English Ordnance Office also extended its role of inspection in the later eighteenth century as more work was put out to private contractors, especially Trotters of Soho.

Arsenals had to be located close to the points at which armies were likely to concentrate. In England, the Ordnance Office organized its various arsenals at Woolwich, the Minories, the Tower of London, Hull, Portsmouth and Plymouth, all ports from which the army might be shipped to the continent or the colonies. In addition, every county possessed an arsenal for the use of the militia. For the majority of European states, arsenals were situated in frontier fortresses. Henry II of France established arsenals at La Fère and Douai for the northern frontier; at Metz and Strasbourg for the eastern frontier, although these passed to Prussia in 1871; at Auxerre for the Jura region, later transferred to Besançon; and at Grenoble in the Alps to cover the border with Savoy, although this was moved to Lyons in 1871. In the eighteenth century, Brandenburg-Prussia had to position her arsenals throughout her territories to respond to threats from the south, east and west. The central arsenal in Berlin stocked general equipment, while musket and artillery ammunition was stored in the provincial capitals. The battalion artillery was parked in Berlin, Breslau, Magdeburg, Stettin and Königsberg and the heavy guns in the various fortresses. Bridging pontoons stood in Berlin, Magdeburg and Neisse, while the carts and field ovens were to be found in Berlin, Magdeburg, Stettin, Breslau, Glogau and Königsberg.

During the early nineteenth century, arsenals became centres of manufacturing and repair as states centralized their military activities and substantially reduced the amount of military production contracted to private industry. As a result, arsenals tended to move from the confines of fortresses into towns and cities, which were often unfortified, in order to take advantage of specialized labour and better communications. The adoption of conscription and the creation of divisional and corps districts dispersed the centralized stores held in arsenals into regional depots. A similar dispersal occurred in England after Cardwell's Army Reforms in 1870–1 had established permanent regimental depots.

Until the mid-nineteenth century, all British artillery was built at Woolwich Arsenal under the direct supervision of the Ordnance Office (the Department of Ordnance after 1855). With the adoption of the Armstrong Gun in 1858, a large majority of the work was transferred to Armstrong's Elswick Ordnance Works in Newcastle upon Tyne, but when production was stopped and the army reverted to rifled muzzle-loaders, the Woolwich Arsenal again resumed all production. However, the pressure for naval ordnance, coastal artillery and field guns during the Second Boer War led to increased demand, and Armstrong, Whitworth, Vickers, the Coventry Ordnance Works and Beardmore all began manufacturing on behalf of the Army Ordnance Department. Armstrong and Vickers designed guns to meet Woolwich specifications. After 1918, production was concentrated in the government's Royal Ordnance Factories although Vickers-Armstrong continued to make some guns. After 1945, nearly all guns were made in the Royal Ordnance Factory at Nottingham, while the installation at Leeds manufactured tanks. During the 1980s, the Royal Ordnance Factories were denationalized and sold to private industry, Vickers purchasing the factory at Leeds. The United States Ordnance Department manufactured the majority of its guns at Watervliet Arsenal in New York State (founded in 1812), while the development of carriages and the assembly of complete guns were concentrated at Rock Island Arsenal, Illinois. During the First World War, the US army purchased a considerable number of French and British cannon. US artillery is still largely produced at Watervliet. Japanese artillery was made at the Osaka Arsenal but the army re-equipped with American weapons after 1945.

However, not every army has centralized its development and production of weaponry within state arsenals. Between 1872 and 1875, Alfried Krupp re-armed the artillery of the German army and navy and Krupp produced the majority of the German army's heavy weapons during the Second World War. French arsenals produced most of the army's cannon until the mid-nineteenth century when the large companies of Schneider and St Chamond took over; they designed and produced nearly all French artillery until 1940. After 1945, the French army re-equipped with American guns. The Skoda Works at Pilsen provided artillery for the Austro-Hungarian army until 1918 when it found itself in the new Czechoslovakia. It still produces weaponry for the Czech army. *See also* ARTILLERY; BASES, NAVAL; DOCKYARDS; ENGINEERS; EXPLOSIVES; GRIBEAUVAL; ORDNANCE; PROPELLANTS.

J.-M. GOENAGA
JOHN CHILDS

FURTHER READING

A. Forbes, *A History of the Army Ordnance Services* (3 vols, London, 1929); Maurice Pearton, *The Knowledgeable State* (London, 1982); I. V. Hogg, *A History of Artillery* (London, 1974).

Arsenals, naval *See* BASES, NAVAL; DOCKYARDS; NAVAL STORES

Artillery In a modern army, 'artillery' is the collective noun for battlefield ordnance comprising anti-tank guns, anti-aircraft guns, field, medium and heavy guns, mountain guns and tactical missiles. 'Artillery' also refers to the branch of an army which operates these weapons. Historically, there are three broad categories of artillery: (1) where the projectile is propelled by torsional or tensional stress; (2) that which utilizes explosive propellants; and (3) where the method of propulsion is a rocket or a jet motor.

The first surviving record of the word 'artillery' occurred in 1248 but the existence of large catapults is mentioned in the Bible. The Persian army of Cyrus (559–529 BC) contained catapults, and these were later adopted by the Greeks. There were two basic types of machine. The ballista, which fired a missile on a low, flat trajectory, resembled a large crossbow; the cord was held on a hook and stretched by a windlass. Its ammunition consisted of barbed stakes, bundles of arrows or, less commonly, rounded stones. The catapult consisted of a wooden arm ending in a bowl-shaped receptacle, pivoted between two vertical uprights. It was strained backwards by a twisted skein of ropes which was tightened by a block and tackle. When released, the arm flew forward until its motion was arrested by a buffer placed between the two uprights. The stone projectiles might weigh as much as 1 cwt and could be hurled several hundred yards. Both catapults and ballistas could also discharge incendiary devices.

These machines were mainly employed in sieges but they did occasionally appear on a battlefield; the Spartans lost some of their artillery at the Battle of Mantinea (362 BC). Philip of Macedon had 150 catapults and both Alexander the Great and the Carthaginians made considerable use of artillery. At the Siege of Jerusalem (AD 70), Titus deployed 300 ballistas and 40 catapults. The Romans used artillery to attack strongholds, to defend their own camps, to cover troops who were engaged in river crossings, and in pitched battles. Artillery opened an engagement and could sometimes be moved from one position to another during the course of the action. Ballistas were mounted on a wheeled carriage while catapults, which were bulkier, could be dismantled and transported on waggons or pack animals. The ammunition, and certain parts of the machines themselves, were usually manufactured on site.

At the end of the Roman Empire, each century of 100 men possessed a ballista, and a catapult was assigned to every cohort. To

39

transport its 55 ballistas and 11 catapults, a legion required 400 horses. The cohort's artillery was commanded by a centurion and the artillery of the legion was the responsibility of a tribune. The equipment was constructed, maintained, provided with ammunition and operated by specialist personnel. A legion left gaps in its battle formation for ballistas while the catapults (which bore the nicknames 'scorpions' or 'wild asses') were positioned behind the frontline or on a commanding prominence. The nomenclature of the artillery pieces altered between the first and fourth centuries AD. The Roman army, which became progressively more static as it concentrated on frontier defence, equipped its camps with a considerable number and variety of machines but its opponents also adopted heavy weapons and some battles were dominated by artillery duels.

Similar machines were employed during the Middle Ages, mostly in attacks on towns and castles, more rarely in the defence of camps or in pitched battles. They were much used during the Crusades. The main source of supply was the Italian Republics; Venice provided the Fourth Crusade with 300 machines which discharged stone balls (perriers and mangonels). They were also deployed at the sieges of Nicaea and Jerusalem. Like the Byzantines, the Arabs also employed artillery, destroying Louis IX's machines in Egypt by setting them ablaze with 'Greek Fire'. Genghis Khan and Tamerlain also possessed artillery. The stone-launchers, called trebuchets, mangonels and perriers, had a see-saw action. A stout beam pivoted on an axis in such a way that the two parts were of unequal length; the shorter portion carried a counter-weight while the longer, which terminated in a sling, threw the projectile. *Ribaudequins*, which resembled ballistas, fired bolts.

The first firearms chiefly made use of the incendiary properties of gunpowder. Part of the charge exploded expelling the remainder as a jet of flame. 'Flamethrowers' of this type were employed both in China and in the West during the Middle Ages. The Byzantines shot 'Greek Fire' onto enemy ships through a tube, the first re-corded instance being at the Siege of Constantinople (AD 672–8). The first actual missiles launched by firearms were flaming arrows, later replaced by stones and metal balls. The early cannon (also called bombards on account of the noise which they made) were short, of small calibre, slightly tapered and mounted on a wooden plinth. The barrels were composed of strips of iron, welded together and reinforced with hoops. The charge was inserted via the muzzle, the powder tamped and the ball pushed on top and held fast by a plug. When, at a later date, the practice was introduced of firing incendiary (heated) cannon balls, a pad of earth was inserted between the projectile and the charge. The gunner ignited the powder with a red-hot iron bar through an aperture called the vent. Later a linstock (slow match) was substituted.

The first cannon appeared in Flanders around 1314, in England in 1321 and in France in 1326. The first manuscript reference dates from 1325. Principally, the early cannon were used for psychological effect; the three bombards employed by Edward III at Crécy (1346) were intended to terrify the Genoese and frighten the horses. When employed against castle and town walls, these early cannon proved relatively feeble as they fired stone ammunition with poor quality gunpowder. Iron cannon balls appeared around 1400. In 1343, the future John the Good of France had twenty-four cannon manufactured. Charles V ordered an artillery corps to be formed in 1367 and instructed cities to be equipped with cannon.

However, artillery did not play an important role in battle or siege until the fifteenth century. At the Siege of Orléans in 1429, the French cannon fired directly and the English indirectly (*see* GUNFIRE). The first employment of field artillery (cannon mounted on wheels or on trestles carried in waggons) was during the Hussite Wars (1419–34). Thanks to artillery produced by the Bureau brothers, Charles VII retook the cities and castles of Normandy from the English during the course of a single campaign. At Castillon (1453), artillery played a vital part on the battlefield. The cannon, which had been positioned within a fortified camp, inflicted damaging losses on the English army and Talbot, its commander, was mortally wounded. Charles the Bold of Burgundy was the first to form his guns into batteries.

Important technical advances were made in the mid-fifteenth century. Around 1460 in France, barrels were cast in bronze replacing the old welded and bound iron guns. By 1543, iron cannon were being cast in England. The strength of the cast guns allowed the employment of iron cannon balls propelled by the new 'corned' or 'granulated' powder. Casting around a core permitted the manufacture of longer barrels, which could shoot more accurately. Accuracy was further increased by the introduction of systematic procedures and instruments (gunner's quadrant) to assist in gun laying. Casting barrels allowed trunnions to be added by which the gun was mounted and pivoted on a carriage. Light, breech-loading cannon (petraras) were produced as well as giant muzzle-loaders with calibres of several tens of centimetres. At the Siege of Constantinople in 1453, Mehmet II deployed huge cannon and mortars. Mortars, short cannon of wide bore which shot at a high trajectory, propelled hollow balls filled with gunpowder ignited by a slow-burning taper which was lit before firing. Towards the end of the fifteenth century the mobile gun carriage was invented, formed by the addition of wheels to the cheeks of the original trestle mounting. This was then harnessed to a limber which was also furnished with two wheels on a single axle. The two portions were separated when the gun went into action. The newly developed trunnions rested in sockets in the cheeks of the mounting, an arrangement which allowed the barrel to be elevated and depressed.

Calibres were classified by the weight of the cannon ball and there was a degree of standardization among various armies to the extent that certain guns were given specific names. The robinet had a calibre of 1.5 in and fired a 1 lb shot; the falcon was 2.5 in, firing a 2.5 lb shot; the saker was 3.5 in, firing a 5 lb ball; a demi-culverin fired an 8 lb shot; the culverin was 5.5 in, firing a 16 lb shot; and a demi-cannon fired a 24 lb ball. The biggest gun in general use was the cannon, which had a calibre of 8 in and delivered a 60 lb ball. In France, the Bureau brothers standardized the royal artillery to seven types: 2, 4, 8, 16, 32, 48 and 64 lb. The length of a cannon was calculated at thirty times the diameter of the projectile.

At the close of the fifteenth century, artillery became more important and influential as the numbers of cannon grew. At Murten, Charles the Bold fielded 200 pieces of artillery. Charles VIII took 140 cannon and 126 light field pieces to Italy, serviced by 200 master gunners, 300 gunners, 600 carpenters, 6,200 pioneers, 1,000 master charcoal-burners, 200 ropemakers and 4,120 waggoners. Seven horses were required to tow a light field piece, while the heavy cannon needed more than twenty. The field cannon varied in weight between 1 and 4 tons. At Ravenna (1512), the light Spanish artillery was able to shift its position thus allowing the infantry and cavalry to retire in good order. At Marignano (1515), Francis I assembled 140 cannon, a ratio of 5 guns per 1,000 men. The Swiss infantry, whose basic tactic was to advance directly onto the artillery to effect its capture, were overwhelmed by the guns on this occasion and lost half their numbers. Learning from the lessons of the Battles of Marignano, La Bicocca (1522) and Pavia (1525), monarchs generally increased their strength in artillery. The army raised in 1544 by King Ferdinand of Hungary and Bohemia (1503–64) to fight the Turks included 60 siege cannon, 80 field guns, 200,000 cannon balls, and 500 tons of gunpowder, transported by 9,000 horses. During the second half of the sixteenth century, a ratio of at least 1 cannon per 1,000 men was considered essential. A typical army of 25,000 men would therefore require a theoretical total of 30 cannon together with 474 horses, 52,000 cannon balls, 60 powder waggons, 94 gunners and 1,500 pioneers.

Fresh technical advances appeared around the middle of the sixteenth century. Canister shot was improved and an explosive shell was perfected. Handbooks of ballistics were published showing the relationship between charge, range and weight of shot. Prince Maurice reduced the Dutch artillery to four calibres (6, 12, 24 and 48 lb) and had all cannon manufactured so that they could be mounted interchangeably on standardized carriages. This provoked little imitation until the Thirty Years' War. Spain continued to fight the Dutch with 50 models of cannon divided among 20 different calibres. King Gustav II Adolf (Gustavus Adolphus) of Sweden (1611–32) made considerable improvements in the manufacture and application of artillery. He divided his artillery into siege cannon (16 pounders and above), provided on a scale of 2 per 1,000 men; field guns (three 6 pounders and three 12 pounders per 1,000 men); and regimental artillery (4 light guns per 1,000 men). The Swedish army thus possessed 1 gun per 83 men, whereas their Imperial opponents in Germany had 1 gun per 2,000 men. He also reduced the length and weight of barrels giving the artillery greater mobility. To speed the rate of fire, the Swedes adopted wooden cartridges (the use of paper and cloth for artillery cartridges did not become general until the middle of the eighteenth century). The regimental artillery was very light (625 lb) and drawn by a single horse. Some were the famous 'leather guns', lightweight cast copper barrels tightly bound with leather and rope for reinforcement. Although they lacked the range and accuracy of cast-iron guns, on their light, two-wheeled carriages they could be moved rapidly around the battlefield. Gustav also concentrated his cannon into batteries, placed both in the centre and on flanks of his battle formation, and integrated the tactics of cavalry and artillery. After his death at Lützen (1632), many of his artillery reforms were allowed to lapse and were not extensively imitated by other armies.

Elevating or depressing the gun was initially a crude affair. Hand spikes and long levers were inserted between the gun and its carriage and the breech end raised or lowered until the correct point was registered on the gunner's quadrant. Blocks were then placed under the breech to hold the gun at the required angle. Greater control was later achieved by the gunner hammering a wooden wedge between the carriage and the breech. In 1571, an English gunner, John Skinner, invented the elevating screw, which was positioned between the breech and the carriage, allowing for precise control. Whereas elevation could be accurately defined, direction was crudely attained by the gunner squinting along the line of the barrel as cannon did not possess sights.

During the War of the Spanish Succession (1702–14), Marlborough began to reintroduce Swedish notions of a mobile artillery deployed in battle. At Malplaquet in 1709, he advanced a battery of 40 cannon into the core of the French lines where it wheeled and shattered the French cavalry reserve. The English and the Dutch developed howitzers of 8 in and 10 in calibres which fired hollow shells filled with gunpowder. The Prussian army introduced a 10 pounder howitzer in 1743 and an 18 pounder in 1744. By 1762, every Prussian infantry battalion was equipped with a 7 pounder 'battalion howitzer'. However, the gun carriages of the day prevented an elevation of more than 15–20°. While this permitted howitzers to fire over some obstacles, real high-trajectory fire had to be left to the mortars. The mortar had been invented by the Turks at the Siege of Constantinople in 1453. It was a short-barrelled weapon fired from a solid 'bed', usually a heavy block of wood. It had little or no adjustment for elevation and range depended on the weight of charge. Principally, it was employed at sieges, where its high elevation allowed the explosive shell to be lobbed over and into fortifications.

Artillery in a proliferation of types and calibres was widely employed by all the armies involved in the wars of Louis XIV. Between 1714 and 1730, Florent-Jean de Vallière (1667–1759), lieutenant-general of the King's Armies, undertook the massive task of standardization. His system, which was adopted in 1732, reduced the cannon to five types: 4-pounder (84 mm); 8-pounder (106 mm); 12-pounder (121 mm); 16-pounder (134 mm); and 24-pounder (151 mm). Two mortars were provided (225 and 325 mm) and a perrier of 405 mm. The

4-, 8- and 12-pounders ranked as field guns and the larger calibres as siege weapons. In 1731, von Linger reduced the Prussian artillery to four calibres – 3-, 6-, 12- and 24-pounders; Prince Joseph Wenzel Liechtenstein performed a similar service for the Austrian artillery; and Peter Shuvalov reformed some aspects of the Russian artillery. The French did not adopt howitzers until 1747. Although the 4-pounders could fire ten shots per minute, the rate of fire of the larger pieces rarely exceeded one or two shots per minute. The maximum range was between 3,000 and 5,000 yards, but the effective range for the field guns was around 800 yards. Siege cannon made little impact on earthwork fortifications at ranges over 200 yards. Bernard Forest de Bélidor demonstrated that range was not proportional to charge, allowing for a reduction in the weight of charge to one third of the weight of the shot. The introduction of chambered breeches also helped to reduce the weight of the barrels while increasing the muzzle velocity of the shot. Benjamin Robins, an English mathematician, invented a method of measuring muzzle velocity around 1740. In 1759, Frederick the Great formed a brigade of horse artillery. Light 6-pounders, complete with limbers containing shot, ammunition and spares, were towed by horses and all the gunners were mounted. Limbered horse artillery, which could offer mobile fire support at any point on the battlefield, was copied by the British and Austrians (1778) with their 'galloper guns'. Six-horse teams were adopted as standard and the gun weight was restricted to 30 cwt. However, the French did not adopt horse artillery until 1792.

J.-B. Vaquette de Gribeauval (1715–89), whose system was adopted in 1765, standardized French artillery types and rendered them lighter and more mobile by reducing the thickness and weight of the barrels. His 12-pounder weighed 900 lb and could be towed by a team of six horses, while Vallière's 12-pounder had weighed 1,600 lb and required nine horses. The guns were manufactured in accordance with the Maritz method whereby the barrels were cast as solid blocks which were then pierced and bored out instead of being cast around a core. This system was also applied to Gribeauval's new mortars. However, Gribeauval's system did not command wholehearted accord. His supporters, the 'Blues', triumphed over the defenders of Vallière, the 'Reds', only in 1774. The latter criticized Gribeauval's cannon as being too fragile, with an inadequate range. Four-pounder cannon of the Swedish type and 3-pounders of the Rostaing pattern were used sporadically as battalion guns in the French army during the War of the Austrian Succession.

Until the eighteenth century, the artillery train was operated by civilian contractors. In France, the artillery was militarized during the reign of Louis XIV. The artillery consisted of a group of officers without troops, together with the Royal Artillery Regiment and the Royal Bombardier Regiment. The two latter formations were combined in 1720 to form five battalions and the troopless officers of the Royal Group were put on the same footing as other artillery officers in 1722. A school was established for each battalion. In 1765, the battalions were expanded into seven regiments and, later, into artillery brigades. On the eve of the French Revolution, these regiments consisted of 20 companies of 71 men each, 6 companies of sappers of 82 men each, and 9 pioneer companies each of 71 men. The effectives of the French artillery amounted to 976 officers and 11,000 men, to which must be added the 127 officers and 2,000 men of the Royal Colonial Artillery. In Britain, the artillery was the concern of the Ordnance Office until 1716 when a permanent corps of artillery was founded. This was named the Royal Regiment of Artillery in 1727, and in 1741 the Royal Military Academy was opened at Woolwich to teach gunnery and military engineering. However, the growth in militarization was slow. As late as the 1740s Austrian gunners continued to regard themselves as a guild of skilled craftsmen and the British relied on civilian drivers and waggoners until the 1780s.

In action, the field artillery was divided into batteries, usually numbering between four and ten guns, and sited at intervals along the battle line. Two or three light 3- or 4-pounders were stationed with the foot battalions, often operated by the infantry themselves, firing canister or grape shot. Engagements usually commenced with a mutual cannonade, which might last for several hours, which was intended to dismount and damage the opposing artillery. Once the enemy artillery had been written down, the guns could support close quarter fighting with canister and grape shot. The remainder of the field artillery was sited in a favourable position to give covering fire to the whole army, to support a retreat or to protect a vulnerable point in the line. The heavier field guns rarely shifted their positions during an engagement. Frederick II, the Great, of Prussia (1740–86) provided an exception to this general use of artillery in a counter-battery role. At Leuthen (1757), massed Prussian field batteries decimated the Austrian infantry and the guns changed position on three occasions. Thereafter, Frederick ordered his guns to be brought forward 'continuously, as at Leuthen'. The artillery began each action by counter-battery missions but then oblique batteries concentrated their fire on the point(s) selected for infantry attack. Frederick almost realized a Napoleonic concentration of artillery fire.

In 1771, Du Puget proposed the adoption by the artillery of an organization which would make best use of its particular characteristics: he divided the cannon into four groups, of which one was in reserve. In 1778, Jean du Teil advocated the employment of massed artillery. Since it could be decisive in battle, he argued that it should be employed against infantry and cavalry rather than in counter-battery operations. Jacques Guibert (1743–90) also recommended the concentration of fire on a specific objective in order to gain decisive results. The French artillery gained a superior reputation in Europe, confirmed by d'Aboville's performance at Yorktown (1781) and Valmy (1792).

Napoleon made gun limbers a regular part of artillery equipment and militarized the French artillery train in 1800; until then the waggoners had been civilians. He also increased the ratio of guns to troops. There were 2 per 1,000 at Austerlitz in 1805; rising to 3 per 1,000 at Borodino in 1812 and to 3.5 during the campaign of 1813–14. At Waterloo in 1815, Napoleon had 3 guns per 1,000 men. Although Napoleon permitted a constant allocation of 10 guns and 2 howitzers to each infantry division and 3 guns and 1 howitzer to every cavalry division, he retained a large proportion of the artillery under his personal command in battle. He had in his own hands 80 guns at Austerlitz, 100 at Wagram (1809), 120 at Borodino, and 80 at Lützen (1813), Craonne (1814) and Waterloo. Napoleon's enemies likewise augmented their own artillery and out-gunned the French on several occasions. At Eylau (1807), the Russians possessed 400 guns while the French had only 200, but at this action and at Friedland (1807) Sénarmont moved his cannon as close as possible to the enemy to increase their effectiveness. The heaviest artillery bombardment occurred at Borodino where 400 guns fired more than 100,000 balls. More than 150,000 shot were fired at Dresden and Leipzig in 1813.

Between the end of the Napoleonic Wars in 1815 and the Crimean War in 1854, significant technical advances occurred in the art of gun-making: the production of explosive shells with time or percussion fuses; firing by means of a percussion cap; and rifled barrels firing pointed, cylindrical projectiles. These developments were prompted by the introduction of rifled muskets amongst the infantry. Foot soldiers were now able to shoot gun crews at ranges which made them virtually safe from retaliation. Unless the artillery could find a solution it would have to vacate the field of battle. After experiments in rifling by Baron Wahrendorff of Sweden and Chevalier Treuille de Beaulieu in France, William Armstrong of England brought about the artillery revolution in 1855. Instead of having its barrel cast in one solid piece and then bored out, the Armstrong Gun was built from a number of wrought, overlapping iron tubes or hoops sweated over each other. The Armstrong Gun was rifled (the shells were lead coated to grip in the rifling) and breech-loading. It was adopted by the British army in 1858. The French adopted Beaulieu's system. Each shell had six lugs which engaged with six grooves cut into the smooth-bore bronze barrel. In 1856, Alfried Krupp manufactured a 90 mm steel cannon and the Prussian army adopted Krupp steel, breech-loading cannon in 1864. Rifled cannon permitted the adoption of the cylindrical shell with a pointed nose. Fired from an identical calibre, a shell could be much heavier than a ball, the rifling giving it stability and longer range. However, the appearance of iron-clad warships in 1859 meant that heavy guns were required both for ships and coastal defence. The Armstrong Gun could not fire a heavy enough shell without damage to its fragile breech mechanism. In 1865, the British army went over to a system similar to the French with the Rifled Muzzle Loading gun in which a lugged shell engaged with grooves in the barrel.

In 1870, the French artillery was much inferior to the Prussian in both quality and quantity. The range of the German guns was 500 yards greater than that of the French and there were 4 per 1,000 infantrymen compared with the French ratio of 2.5 per 1,000. In addition, the German artillery benefited from a sound tactical doctrine which laid down the principle of concentration of fire while the French batteries were uncoordinated and lacked any concept of planned, concerted action. The German artillery caused 60 per cent of French losses but the French guns inflicted only 20 per cent of German casualties.

Improved propellants and slower-burning powders required longer barrels. In turn, this made muzzle-loading difficult and in 1878 the British army returned to breech-loading with Armstrong's 6 in and 8 in guns. Armstrong had solved the problem of manufacturing a reliable and secure breech by the interrupted screw. To seal the breech, the Armstrong cannon adapted the French de Bange system. Krupp, meanwhile, adopted brass cartridge cases rather than bagged charges as a means of sealing the breech against escaping gases, a method which was rapidly adopted by all armies. The remaining technical problem was recoil. Up to the end of the nineteenth century, cannon had recoiled on their wheeled carriages which then had to be pushed back into position by the gunners. Various experiments to control recoil or put it to work (disappearing carriages) with oil-filled cylinders finally found their solution in the hydraulic buffer fitted to the French 75 mm field gun in 1897. Field guns could now fire 20 rounds a minute; the crew sat with the gun and were protected from infantry fire by a shield. During the 1890s, small calibre, high-velocity magazine rifles were adopted by the infantry and the artillery had to conceal itself if it was to survive. This raised the question of how the artillery was to shoot if it could not see its target. Previously, all artillery fire had been 'direct fire' in which the target was in view of the gunners. Now, guns had to fire indirectly relying upon compass bearings derived from line of sight, maps and the observations of spotters. Around 1900, most armies possessed field guns of 75 or 77 mm firing shrapnel shells against troops in the open and howitzers of 100 mm which fired high-explosive shells on a steep trajectory to attack fortifications and dug-in positions.

In 1914, the German artillery was of higher quality than the French. It had greater range and possessed 3,500 heavy guns against the French 300. The First World War witnessed the return of the mortar as a weapon for trench fighting, artillery of all calibres and functions, anti-aircraft guns and, during the final days of the war, the 37 mm anti-tank gun. Long-range guns and guns mounted on railway trucks fired deep into rear areas. As the Great War was basically an artillery war, techniques developed rapidly. Aircraft and wireless were used to spot enemy batteries and correct fall of shot; sound ranging and flash spotting became sophisticated means of identifying enemy batteries and registering guns. 'Predicted fire' (*see* GUNFIRE) also became possible in 1917–18.

Before the war, artillery had been intended as a support to infantry attack. From 24 August 1914, Joffre altered this principle, which had shown itself to be erroneous, and ordered that artillery preparation was to precede infantry assaults. The huge consumption of shells rapidly led to a shortage of ammunition. The British Expeditionary Force went to war with 1,500 rounds for each field gun and 1,200 for every howitzer. Production of ammunition for the 18-pounder was only 10,000 rounds per month. During the French Champagne offensive in 1915, the French 75 mm guns fired 320,000 rounds per day plus 11,000 by the heavy artillery. By 1918, French factories were producing over 226,000 shells daily. Hasty wartime production procedures also resulted in poor quality guns and fuses; at the time of the Somme in 1916, 25 per cent of the British guns were out of action through mechanical faults. In August 1916, there were 25,000,000 unfilled and unfused shells in stock in Great Britain. Not until 1917 was the British artillery in a position to achieve battlefield dominance over the German guns. During the Champagne offensive, there was one French 75 mm gun per 32 yards of front and one heavy gun per 40 yards along a front of 22 miles. At Passchendaele in 1917, 2,686 British guns were opposed by 1,556 German cannon. The French Nivelle offensive in April 1917 consumed over 4,000,000 rounds of artillery ammunition.

Every attack was preceded by an artillery preparation lasting several hours and, after 1916, several days. Attacks were effectively made by the artillery and exploited by the infantry, who found it impossible to operate beyond the range of their own guns. Tonnages fired were enormous. At Verdun between 20 and 26 August 1916, 5 tons of shells were fired per yard of front and on 6 October there was one French gun for every 6 yards. Rolling barrages in front of the infantry were introduced in 1916 but the duration of barrages was reduced later in the war in an effort to achieve surprise. Between 1914 and 1918, the number of guns possessed by the French rose from 4,300 (4 guns per 1,000 infantry) to 13,400 in November 1918 (13 guns per 1,000 infantry). The artillery represented 38 per cent of the French fighting strength in 1918.

In the interwar period (1919–39),

artillery development was limited as all armies had an abundance of *matériel* remaining from the Great War. Although some experiments were made with self-propelled guns (the British 'Birch' gun of 1926), the major innovation of the period was the adoption of the anti-tank gun. By 1939, most armies were equipped with anti-tank guns of around 40 mm calibre, sufficient to deal with the light tanks in operation in the opening years of the war. As tanks became heavier and grew thicker armour, anti-tank guns responded. The British moved from a 57 mm weapon to 94 mm, the Americans from 37 mm to 90 mm, and the Germans from 50 mm, through 88 mm, to 128 mm. The latter weighed 10 tons and was no longer man-manoeuvreable. As a result, the recoilless gun was developed along with specialized anti-tank ammunition (shaped charge) which relied on chemical action rather than weight and muzzle velocity. Anti-aircraft guns also became heavier and of longer range to tackle the faster bombers and fighters (88 mm and 3.7 in). All armies developed self-propelled artillery, usually by mounting their standard artillery pieces into light tank or tracked chassis. The Germans developed the assault gun, which provided close fire support for the infantry. Anti-tank guns were also mounted on self-propelled chassis and dubbed 'tank destroyers'.

During the Second World War, as in the First, artillery became the principal weapon of all armies, providing both offensive and defensive firepower for undertrained conscript armies. Before Berlin in April 1945, the Russians had 25,000 guns and the US army possessed 23 guns per 1,000 men. In less than twelve months between 1944 and 1945, Patton's 3rd US army fired 12,000,000 rounds. In forcing the passage of the Rhine in March 1945, the British 2nd Army fired 434,232 rounds from 706 guns and twelve 30-barrelled rocket launchers. Artillery caused one half of the human losses in the war. In Korea (1950–3), the Americans made great use of artillery, preferring to expend shells rather than human lives. Anti-aircraft artillery improved markedly during the Second World War. In 1918, 17,000 rounds had been needed to shoot down an aircraft but better guns, mechanical computers (predicters) and the proximity fuse had reduced this to one in 300 by 1944.

After the Second World War, most armies lived off the fat of their Second World War stocks. The British Royal Artillery received no new equipment for ten years after 1945. However, the experience of the Second World War led to the search for greater accuracy and efficiency. The expenditure of ammunition by the British and the Americans in Europe in 1944–5 had been so huge and expensive that artillery had to become more cost-effective. To support the dropping of the 6th Airborne Division beyond the Rhine in March 1945, the British had fired 440 tons of artillery shells in an anti-flak programme and rained 500 tons of bombs on each enemy battery. Only one bomb had landed in a gun-pit. The solutions have been discovered in the guided missile and in the use of computers and electronics for target acquisition and verification.

Those countries belonging to NATO standardized their calibres at 105 mm and 155 mm but the Russians and the Warsaw Pact selected 122 mm and 152 mm. Self-propelled guns have been made proof against chemical and biological attack and nuclear fallout and towed pieces have been progressively lightened to make them air-portable by both helicopter and fixed-wing aircraft. Medium and heavy anti-aircraft guns disappeared after the war, replaced by guided missiles but light anti-aircraft guns (23–40 mm), guided by radar and computers, have since reappeared on the battlefield to deal with the menace of the helicopter. Towed and self-propelled anti-tank guns were phased out in favour of the recoilless rifle but this has now been largely replaced by the hand-held wire-guided missile. Electronics have rendered a considerable improvement in the accuracy of artillery shooting. Formerly, the method was to bracket the target and then, by observing the fall of shot, progressively to close with the target. It was slow, costly in shells, rendered the guns vulnerable to counter-battery fire, and could not operate against a moving target. Today, 'survey devices', laser range-finders and radars provide exact information and allow fire to be opened with a high certainty of hitting the objective. Surveillance satellites and drones are also used for artillery target acquisition. Since 1944, some tank and anti-tank guns have returned to the use of the smooth bore to fire discarding-sabot ammunition.

Rockets are first recorded as having been used on a battlefield in 1232 when the Chinese employed rocket-powered arrows against the Mongols. The rockets of Sir William Congreve were introduced into the British army in 1806 and used by Wellington. They ranged in size from 5 to 32 lb with different warheads for case, shell and carcass. They were inaccurate and often as dangerous to friendly troops as they were to enemies. 'I do not want to set fire to any town', remarked Wellington, 'and I do not know of any other use for the rockets.' In about 1930, the Russians experimented with battlefield rockets. They developed a solid-fuel powered 82 mm rocket carrying a 6.5 lb warhead, the Katyusha, or Stalin's Organ Pipes. It was first deployed against the Germans in July 1941 and was fired in salvoes from a bank of 36 launchers mounted on a truck. It was superseded by a 132 mm version. The Germans developed the *nebelwerfer* (smoke projector), a 150 mm rocket-mortar used to lay down smoke screens. Later, its warhead was changed to high explosive and the calibre increased to 210 mm, 280 mm and 310 mm. The *nebelwerfer* fired salvoes of five or six rockets with a range of between 7,500 and 8,600 yards. In 1940 and 1941, the British experimented with 3 in rockets as an anti-aircraft weapon. Later in the war, these rockets were mounted in launchers with 30 tubes (*Mattress*) and employed by the army and by the Royal Navy as a method of bombardment prior to amphibious landings. The United States developed a 4.5 in fin-stablized rocket fired in salvoes of 60. The German V-1 flying bomb and the V-2 rocket represented a new form of jet- and rocket-powered long-range artillery which was to lead to the development of the guided missile after 1945.

The 1986 pattern US division has a brigade of artillery, consisting of six battalions: a target establishment and ranging battalion; three battalions each armed with 24 155 mm guns; a mixed battalion of 16 303 mm guns and 9 multiple rocket launchers; and a ground-to-air battalion armed with 36 self-propelled, double-barrelled 40 mm cannon, 24 Chaparral missile carriers and 73 sections armed with the light, Stinger missile. Russian artillery is equipped with 120 mm mortars, 122 mm and 152 mm towed and self-propelled howitzers, 130 mm guns, and 40-barrelled multiple rocket launchers. The Russian ground-to-air artillery is armed with 23 mm cannon, 57 mm cannon, light missiles with a range of 3 miles and SA4 and SA6 missiles with ranges of 45 and 50 miles. Each division has a section armed with Frog 7 missiles, which can deliver either a nuclear or a chemical warhead. *See also* EXPLOSIVES; FIREARMS; FORTIFICATION; GRIBEAUVAL; GUNFIRE; KURSK; MARIGNANO; PARIS; PROPELLANTS; SIEGES; TEIL; VERDUN.

G. BODINIER
JOHN CHILDS

FURTHER READING
Shelford Bidwell, *Gunners at War* (London, 1972); Shelford Bidwell and Dominick Graham, *Fire-Power: British army weapons and theories of war, 1904–1945* (London, 1982); I. V. Hogg, *A History of Artillery* (London, 1974); O. F. G. Hogg, *English Artillery, 1326–1716* (London, 1963).

Assyrians Assyria roughly corresponds to present-day Kurdistan. Having resisted a great number of invaders, this mountainous country passed into the front rank of nations after the fall of the Hittite empire. The Assyrians acquired their independence in the ninth century BC and built a kingdom whose strength resided in the militias which were under the command of the local governments. Tiglath-Pileser III (745–727 BC) gave the monarchy increased authority, created a permanent army, and founded a genuine empire which his successors further extended, particularly Sargon II, and Ashurbanipal, who in the middle of the seventh century BC dominated the Near East and, for a short period, extended his power as far as Egypt.

The Sargonids' strategy consisted in building fortresses commanding a road network in the conquered lands and installing enlisted prisoners of war there. From these bases they launched expeditions among the neighbouring peoples which were aimed at raising tribute. Clearly these raids were directly sponsored by the state and they helped support the economy of the kingdom. Resistance was ferociously put down and gave rise to systematic retaliatory operations.

In the Assyrian monarchical system, the sovereign was champion of the gods, and it was a sin and a crime to resist him. Soldiers and civilians were part of a common form of social organization, which was based on the 'king's loyal men' (*ardenes*, plural of *ardu*) who owed him obedience in exchange for aid and protection, obligations which were established by an oath of allegiance (*adê*) sworn to him at a special ceremony. The *ardenes* provided the king with devoted civil servants, officers and soldiers. All his subjects had a duty to keep the king informed. Information was gathered and centralized by the 'king's guards', who were a sort of intelligence service. These 'eyes and ears of the king' used the services of *Dajjalis* (scouts) who were spread throughout subject lands, and the king maintained a great number of spies in foreign countries. Communications were maintained through express couriers (*Kalliu*) and by smoke signals.

The Assyrian army achieved a synthesis between the traditional Sumerian phalanx of heavy infantry and what they had learnt from the Hittites regarding cavalry, the use of iron and chariots. Their troops were organized in an extremely hierarchical command structure: commanders of squads of ten or fifty men, chiefs of thousands and, lastly, a *Turtanu* or commander-in-chief. The infantry was made up of archers and shield-bearers, heavy infantrymen armed with a pike, a thrusting sword and a large shield. The battle-line consisted of archer/shield-bearer pairs, the shield-bearer protecting the two men. The Assyrians developed chariots to a high level, and they became heavier, carrying a chariot-master, a charioteer, and one or two 'third chariot men'. Some also carried archer/shield-earer pairs. Moreover, chariots were used for transporting men and weapons, and in this way a kind of mounted infantry was formed.

The chariots could be made heavier because there was a parallel development in the cavalry. The first cavalry consisted merely of mounted infantrymen, one of whom held the bridle of the other's horse while he fired his arrow. Progress in riding techniques and the adoption of light armour, which meant that a soldier could dispense with a shield and leave his arms free, made each horseman independent. The cavalry showed its superiority by its speed and effectiveness in charges.

The Assyrians also developed a kind of engineering corps. Their pioneers built boat bridges carried on small craft, which were made of reeds plaited and covered with pitch, or on oxskins, while the men crossed the rivers using individual water skins which they inflated. The pioneers also played a major role in sieges, making traps and undermining walls of besieged towns. They used wheeled towers and rams manoeuvred by men protected by wheel-mounted wooden constructions.

The Assyrian empire was in part based on the terror it inspired in its enemies, which functioned as a deterrent. While the Annals they have left behind exalt the invincibility of their kings, their bas-reliefs smugly show the tortures they inflicted upon their enemies. By contrast, the correspondence which has been preserved gives a rather different, much more down-to-earth impression of a soldier's life. In any event, the Assyrians inspired a great deal of hatred and eventually succumbed to a coalition of neighbouring peoples – Babylonians, Scythians, Medes – and their capital, Nineveh, fell in 612 BC. *See also* EGYPT, ANCIENT; HITTITES; IRAN; ISRAEL, EARLY.

A. CORVISIER

FURTHER READING
F. Malbran-Labat, *L'Armée et l'organisation militaire de l'Assyrie d'après les lettres des Sargonides trouvées à Ninive* (Geneva/Paris, 1982); *Cambridge Ancient History*, ii, 2 (1975); *Cambridge Ancient History*, iii, 1 (1982).

Atlantic, Battle of the (1939–45) The outcome of the Second World War came to depend on the result of the struggle to control the waters of the North Atlantic, for if the Allies could not maintain supplies to Great Britain and convey troops and their equipment across that ocean, they could not attack a Europe under German control. Furthermore, the preservation of an adequate tonnage of merchant shipping was crucial to the Allied war effort everywhere; thus all their operations came to depend on the availability of merchant ships. Conversely, for the Germans, the destruction of shipping became one of their only hopes of defeating first Britain and then the United States.

The attack on shipping was anticipated by the British Admiralty not only from the experience gained in 1914–18, when many lessons had been learnt, even if only to be forgotten, but also from the emphasis placed by both Germany and Italy on building submarines, although it should be noted that treaty restrictions prevented Germany from building submarines until 1936. Probably as a consequence of these restrictions, Great Britain did not build any sizeable number of escort vessels until the last minute. It was, however, believed that the submarine menace would be reduced by the development of *asdic* (sonar), which would allow submarines to be located easily, and that improved depth charges would allow them to be sunk.

On the German side, construction of U-boats only recommenced in 1935–6, and many of the first built were small vessels. By 1939, the existing force was still inadequate, and indeed the *Kriegsmarine* was not ready for a war against Britain. It had, however, a sound basic design for the U-boat and a nucleus of many well-trained crews, while the commander of the U-boat arm, Dönitz, had developed new tactics.

At the outbreak of war, the British Admiralty applied much of its hard-won 1914–18 experience, instituting convoys immediately, and setting up the intelligence organization which was to be so fruitful.

It overlooked the value of air cover, which, if nothing else, could keep a U-boat submerged and therefore almost immobile, while effort was wasted in offensive patrols, which rarely saw a thing. The few U-boats had to travel great distances to their area of operations, but began taking a toll on convoys, which were often inadequately escorted, or from single ships after dispersal. Although the U-boats initially made some effort to conform to international law, its requirements for many reasons were impractical for submarines, and 'unrestricted' warfare was soon the rule.

The occupation of Norway and then France by Germany in mid-1940 changed the situation completely. The U-boats could now operate from French and Norwegian ports, thus greatly reducing the distance they had to travel to the scene of operations. The British eastern ports became largely unusable, while the southwestern approaches were too close to German bases; the majority of shipping had to use the North Channel to western ports. For a time too, forces had to be held in port in case of invasion, and escorts were therefore even scarcer. From September 1940 the crisis began.

The British position deteriorated sharply for other reasons too. Formerly, convoys required an escort for only the first or last part of their voyage; now it had to be given for much greater distances. Although some of the new escort vessels were in service, these greater needs resulted in many cases in the escort being a group of ships hurriedly assembled, not always well equipped and often inexperienced. Air cover was negligible, there being no long-range aircraft nor bases for them. To be effective depth charges had to explode close to the submarine; the *asdic* was found to have disadvantages, especially against surface vessels, and particularly when Dönitz introduced his new 'wolf pack' tactics of night attack on the surface by a group of U-boats, using their higher surface speed. Although there were still not enough U-boats, they had their first 'happy time', aided by the Kondor long-range aircraft operating from French bases.

The crisis was met resolutely, but the tide turned only slowly. In May 1940 Iceland was occupied, and its harbours became available to the Allies. The United States now realized that it too was threatened, and, beginning with the 'bases for destroyers' agreement of July 1940, ever more American assistance was given, culminating in the US navy taking over escort work in the western North Atlantic from May 1941. Meanwhile the strength of the Royal Canadian Navy was greatly increased, and new British ships steadily appeared. Special training methods were introduced, improved tactics were worked out and permanent escort groups were formed, but time was nevertheless needed for captains and crews to gain experience. Technical progress included the increase of depth charge capacity in escorts, fitting of radar and especially of high-frequency direction finding, which enabled escorts to locate the enemy. Air cover remained a problem owing to a shortage of suitable aircraft, for even though bases were set up in Iceland and western Ireland, a mid-Atlantic gap remained.

The intelligence war was closely balanced. As the German system of control needed numerous signals to direct their boats, the British, and later the Americans, were able to use them to establish an efficient submarine tracking system. The German service was able to decipher Allied signals traffic about convoys and this provided Dönitz with much detailed information, such as sailing times and occasionally routes. *Ultra* also made its contribution to Allied information. Both sides could therefore direct and regroup their forces at short notice.

Even so, despite all these factors, the vastness of the ocean no less than its often severe weather put limits on such changes, and acted as protection to the hard-pressed convoys, although indeed it must often have seemed more like a third combatant. Consequently, some convoys, even at the worst times, had uneventful voyages.

The eventual entry of the United States into the war rendered the ultimate outcome clear. Yet it was another 18 months before the struggle was decided, and, before that, owing to the slow American reaction to the extension of the war to the East Coast of North America, the U-boats, although working at the limit of their range, had another 'happy time' until the lessons of war were absorbed. Dönitz moved his attack first to the Caribbean, and then back to the North Atlantic, where the winter of 1942–3 was a grim struggle. By the end of 1942, however, new types of faster escorts appeared, with new equipment and new methods of firing depth charges ahead. More aircraft were working from Ireland, Iceland and Newfoundland, and at last some very long-range aircraft allowed the gap in mid-Atlantic to be covered after the summer of 1943. Support groups were formed to go to the aid of hard-pressed convoys, and escort aircraft carriers allowed aircraft to go with each convoy. While other methods had constantly been used to curb U-boats, such as bombing building yards or their bases, or attacking them while they were crossing the Bay of Biscay, none was truly effective, and the struggle was fought round the convoys. At last, in June 1943, Dönitz saw that his losses were exceeding results and withdrew his boats. Although U-boat warfare continued to occupy large resources on both sides, the Germans could only wait for the new Type XXIII with its fast submerged speed to restore their advantage, but none was ready until almost the end of the war. *See also* CONVOYS; DÖNITZ; GERMANY; NAVAL WARFARE; NAVIES; RAEDER.

A. W. H. PEARSALL

FURTHER READING

W. S. Chalmers, *Max Horton and the Western Approaches* (London, 1954); Karl Dönitz, *Memoirs: ten years and twenty days* (London, 1959); Donald Macintyre, *The Battle of the Atlantic* (London, 1961); S. E. Morison, *History of the United States Naval Operations in World War II. Vol. i, The Battle of the Atlantic, 1939–1943* (Boston, 1951); S. W. Roskill, *The War at Sea* (3 vols in 4, London, 1954–61); John Terraine, *Business in Great Waters* (London, 1989).

Attaché, military From ancient times through the Middle Ages, we find references to military officers accompanying or being sent to stay with ambassadors. In 1757, the King of France promoted Jean-Baptiste Vaquette de Gribeauval, an artillery officer, to the rank of lieutenant-colonel and sent him on a mission to Austria. The role played by the officers attached to the allied armies in the field during the French Revolutionary and Napoleonic Wars was important in developing the function of the attaché. In 1806, Napoleon appointed a captain of dragoons, Ange-François le Lièvre de la Grange, as second secretary in Vienna so that he could keep an eye on the strength of the Austrian regiments and their locations. In 1813, the Emperors of Austria and Russia and the King of Poland exchanged aides-de-camp. In 1816, France had diplomatic representatives in twenty-one European countries and the United States. The wars which raged in Europe and Asia between 1815 and 1914 led to the establishment of powerful and permanent national defence systems making it essential for states to acquire up-to-date intelligence and appreciations of their allies' and enemies' armed forces.

'The role of officers fulfilling the function of military attaché is to study the military system of the powers to which they are accredited' (1839). By the 1860s, the term military attaché was common; there were 30 in Europe by 1870 and 300 by 1914. He was given diplomatic immunity and was responsible locally to the ambassador, but was under the general orders of the commander-in-chief or the chief of the general staff.

In important embassies, the military attaché might be assisted by naval and air attachés as well as subordinate officers and non-commissioned officers. His task is to acquire information about the armed forces of the foreign country to which he is assigned through studying the press, attending reviews and demonstrations and personal contacts. His diplomatic status only allows him to acquire information through open channels. He also acts as technical adviser to the ambassador or head of mission and may serve as an agent for arms sales. The attaché is also responsible for military co-operation and co-ordination, hence the assignment of attachés to NATO. There is also an important public relations aspect to the post as the attaché is the observable representative of his country's armed forces. The opinion of attachés forms the basis for the reception of foreign VIPs in his own country and may influence the way in which military policy is conducted. He has long since cast off the old image of a spy and has become an essential communicator. Officers from field rank – majors and lieutenant-colonels – are usually selected for the post of attaché on a two- or three-year placement. *See also* ALLIANCES; INTELLIGENCE; SECRECY.

S. DE LASTOURS
JOHN CHILDS

FURTHER READING
Alfred Vagts, *The Military Attaché* (Princeton, 1967).

Attila, King of the Huns (AD 406–53) The Huns, a nomadic people from the great steppes of Central Asia, had pushed into Eastern Europe around the middle of the fourth century AD, displacing the peoples who occupied that region, many of whom attempted to take refuge within the Roman Empire. This was one of the causes of the 'Great Invasions' which broke over the empire at the end of the fourth and during the fifth century. A group of Huns finally settled in the middle reaches of the Danube and united under a series of kings, the best known of whom is Attila. He first invaded the territory of the Eastern Empire in 441–3, crossing the Danube and reaching the outskirts of Constantinople. Theodosius II was incapable of effective resistance and Attila imposed tribute and insisted on the return of escaped Roman prisoners unless ransomed. In 447 he led a second invasion, and a military victory enabled him to impose a higher tribute and insist that the emperor should evacuate the south bank of the Danube to a depth of five days' march. In 450 the new emperor, Marcian, put up more determined resistance and Attila began to turn his attention to the west. In the spring of 451, he crossed the Rhine, ravaged northeastern Gaul, and penetrated as far as Orléans, before he was forced to retreat towards Troyes by a powerful army organized by the Roman general Aetius, consisting of Romans and various allied contingents provided by barbarians who had already settled in Gaul – Burgundi, Franks, Alani – and especially by the Visigoths who occupied Aquitania. When they caught up with Attila in modern Champagne, a fierce battle was fought at a place known as 'Campi Catalaunici' or 'Mauriaci', the exact site of which is disputed. Although the battle was indecisive, casualties on both sides were enormous and Attila subsequently continued his retreat, which permitted the inhabitants of Gaul to celebrate it as a significant victory. In 452 Attila attacked Italy, captured Aquileia, whose inhabitants took refuge on an island (this is thought to be the origin of Venice), Pavia and Milan, but agreed to accord the western emperor a truce or a peace on condition that he provide tribute; this relatively fortunate outcome was attributed to the prestige of Pope Leo the Great who had been one of the negotiators. Attila's sudden death in 453 was followed by the immediate disintegration of his empire.

Attila was certainly an outstanding personality, a tough negotiator and an audacious commander, who was capable of acts of magnanimity towards his enemies. But he played more on the weakness of the two Roman empires of the east and west and terror spread by the ravages of his troops than on his military power; his Germanic subjects supplied more contingents to his army than the Huns themselves, who were too few in number. His expeditions tended to be raids aimed principally at destruction and plunder. *See also* ROME.

JOËL LE GALL
B. CAMPBELL

FURTHER READING
F. Altheim, *Attila und die Hunnen* (Baden-Baden, 1951); O. J. Maenchen-Helfen, *The World of the Huns: studies of their history and culture*, ed. M. Knight (Berkeley and Los Angeles, 1973).

Austerlitz, Battle of (2 December 1805) After the strategic victory which had enabled him to approach Vienna, Napoleon had established himself, with his 65,000 men, at the foot of the Pratzen plateau not far from Brno to await the armies of the Tsar and the Austrian emperor. He had extended his right flank, while his main forces were concentrated near the Brno road, his left resting on the Santon hill. The allied sovereigns, with some 90,000 men, occupied the Pratzen heights, where they established their centre. In the morning fog of 2 December 1805, they moved the major part of their forces down from the plateau, manoeuvring parallel to the enemy, with the intention of attacking and turning the French right flank. Napoleon then sent the corps of Marshal Nicolas de Soult (1769–1851) to occupy the Pratzen plateau where the allied defences had been depleted. From the breach thus opened up, a section of the French troops effected a pincer movement on the allied left flank. A Russian corps had to flee over frozen ponds which the French artillery bombarded with heavy fire, causing many to drown. On the allied right, the Russian general Peter Bagration (1765–1812) resisted vigorously but was surrounded by the corps of Marshal Jean Baptiste Bernadotte (1763–1844), which had also passed through the breach in the centre. By nightfall the allied armies were shattered. The French lost 9,000 men, the Austro-Russian forces 26,000, along with 185 guns and 45 flags.

Retrospectively, Napoleon presented Austerlitz as a victory for deception and bold manoeuvre – the deliberate weakness of the French right creating the opportunity to break the enemy centre and surround his flanks. In reality Napoleon's chances were made by headstrong allied offensive planning. His strengths were more traditional – his use of ground, and his tactical ability in the counter-attack. *See also* INFANTRY; JENA AND AUERSTÄDT; KUTUZOV; NAPOLEON.

A. CORVISIER
HEW STRACHAN

FURTHER READING
David Chandler, *The Campaigns of Napoleon* (London, 1967); Christopher Duffy, *Austerlitz 1805* (London, 1977); E. Lacombe, 'Recherche historique et recherche opérationnelle: notes d'un chercheur opérationnel sur la bataille d'Austerlitz', *Revue historique des armées*, no. 3 (1986), pp. 16–25.

Australia The military has occupied a marginal position in Australian society for most of the nation's history, but war and the fact of military service have been key determinants in the shaping of the national character and ethos. At the level of national policy, the search for security through alliance with 'great and powerful friends' has typified Australian defence and foreign relations since the late nineteenth century. Australians have often defined themselves in terms of their military past, although until very recently they have studiously avoided any consideration of the violent dispossession of the aboriginal people in this process.

The British army and the Royal Navy left an indelible stamp on the early Australian colonies, but this had little to do with the discharge of their most obvious military functions. The garrison of New South Wales was provided initially by several companies of the Royal Marines, who were succeeded in 1791 by the New South Wales Corps, a regiment recruited specifically for service in the colony. Following its involvement in the bloodless deposition of Governor William Bligh in January 1808 it was recalled to Britain and disbanded finally in 1818, and from 1809 the military force in the Australian colonies was provided by regiments of the British army, usually four in number at any one time. These provided guards for the convict labourers who made up the bulk of the settlement's early population, maintained internal law and order against the aboriginal population and escaped convicts, and provided a security guarantee against an external threat which, while frequently apprehended, never materialized. With the decline in transportation after 1840 the internal security function declined, and this together with the absence of a clearly identifiable external enemy led to a gradual rundown in the British garrison, although the last regiment was not withdrawn until 1870 in line with the recommendations of the Mills Committee of 1862.

The most important contribution of the British military was in 'nation-building'; most of the original transport and communications infrastructure of the colonies was created by officers of the Royal Engineers, who also supervised the early Mints, while the structure of executive government and administration was supplied by officers of the army and navy. The regiments and the ships of the Australia Station (created in 1859) played a dominant role in the social life of the colonies as well.

The achievement of self-governing status in the 1850s and 1860s, and especially the departure of the last garrison units, forced colonial governments back on their own resources for the provision of their own defence. The colonial military forces were never very effective militarily; they fulfilled an important social function for the middle classes but were subject equally to marked fluctuation in strength and the provision of equipment, especially during the major depression of the 1890s. On two occasions colonial forces played on a wider stage: in 1885 when New South Wales despatched a contingent of 770 men to the Sudan to avenge Gordon, and during the Boer War (1899–1902) when 16,175 men served in five colonial contingents and, following Federation in 1901, in three Commonwealth ones.

The period between the federation of the colonies in 1901 and the outbreak of war in 1914 was marked by considerable military activity, although initially the Commonwealth parliament was hostile to military spending. This changed with the Japanese victory against the Russians in 1905, coupled with dissatisfaction with existing arrangements for naval defence which entailed reliance on, but no control over, ships of the Royal Navy subsidized by the Commonwealth. Agitation for a greater say in the dispositions of naval defence led to the formation of an Australian naval squadron in 1914, while a system of universal military training was introduced in 1909 to provide a sizeable field force for the home defence of the Commonwealth. In both areas Australia adopted distinctly different solutions to its defence problems from either Britain or the other self-governing dominions.

The Boer War notwithstanding, participation in the Great War of 1914–18 was regarded widely as the nation's 'coming of age', and involvement in that war influenced Australian society for decades. Approximately half the eligible white males drawn from a total population of five million enlisted; 331,000 of these served overseas, of whom 60,000 were killed and a further 166,000 were wounded. It was a devastating introduction to modern industrial warfare, made worse by the deep divisions occasioned by the domestic disputes over conscription for overseas service.

The seizure of German colonial territories in the South Pacific in the war's opening months and the destruction of German commerce-raiders fully justified Australia's pre-war insistence on an Australian fleet, but the first major military commitment was to the defence of the Suez Canal and the opening of a front against Turkey in the Dardanelles. An unmitigated disaster at almost every level, Gallipoli is the foundation stone of the Australian military myth and provided the raw material of the self-regarding Anzac legend, which has dominated the Australian national image ever since. It was also a small epic of courage, endurance and sacrifice which demonstrated both that the Australians had the makings of very fine soldiers – something which various British observers had remarked on during the Boer War – and that they still had a long way to go. Of the 50,000 men who served on the peninsula over 26,000 became casualties, more than 8,000 of them killed, in just seven months.

The Australian Imperial Force was greatly enlarged and reorganized in January 1916; five infantry divisions departed for service on the Western Front while two mounted divisions remained in the eastern Mediterranean as part of the main strike force in the campaigns in Sinai and Palestine. In France the Australians fought on the Somme, losing 28,000 men in July–August 1916, and at Bullecourt,

Messines and Passchendaele, where they suffered another 58,000 casualties in the course of 1917. Formed into an Australian Corps at the end of that year, and from May 1918 commanded by an Australian militia officer, General Sir John Monash, the Australian divisions became one of the spearhead formations of the British 4th Army, heavily involved in the great advances of July–October 1918 which resulted in the final defeat of the German army, and during which they suffered a further 21,000 killed and wounded. The heavy losses in France led directly to agitation for the introduction of conscription in line with Britain and the other dominions. Dominated by the prime minster, William Morris Hughes, the domestic debate degenerated into a loyalty test into which various irrelevant considerations of religion and class were introduced by both sides, influenced by events in Ireland in 1916 and Russia in 1917. The electorate twice rejected the proposal, in October 1916 and December 1917, and by 1918 the home front was bitterly divided; recruitment in the last year failed significantly to keep pace with wastage, and many units in France operated at half strength or less.

The interwar years were marked by the same financial stringencies and political blindness experienced throughout the western democracies, in Australia's case influenced strongly by over-reliance on the Singapore strategy. The outbreak of war in 1939 saw Australia commit inadequately equipped forces to the Mediterranean once again, while the entry of the Japanese into the war in December 1941 revealed the bankruptcy of interwar strategy. Australian infantry divisions were involved heavily in the early defeats of the Italians in 1941 and in the see-sawing offensives against the Germans in North Africa, as well as comprising the main forces committed to the disasters in Greece and Crete. A division was lost at the fall of Singapore in February 1942, at which point the Australian government insisted on its right to withdraw its forces from Europe for the defence of its own territory. Under the command of General Douglas MacArthur in the American-created South-West Pacific Area, Australian formations defeated the Japanese in a succession of gruelling campaigns in Papua-New Guinea in 1942–3 until, eclipsed by the enormous build-up of US forces and denied a role in the reconquest of the Philippines, they were deflected into marginal campaigns away from the main axis of the Allies' northwards advance.

Australia fielded about 800,000 uniformed personnel during the war, and made as great an effort on the home front. As well as supplying its own needs it provisioned the US forces in the South-West Pacific theatre and continued to supply foodstuffs to Britain. War-related industries received a considerable boost, and large numbers of women entered non-traditional employment categories for the first time. So great was the strain on the domestic economy that the government began selective demobilization of the forces at the end of 1943 in order to meet the demands for labour. From February 1943 a limited form of conscription for overseas service applied; conscripted militiamen were required to serve only in Australia's immediate environs, and the successful passage of the legislation was the result of considerable persuasion within the Labor Party by the Labor prime minister, John Curtin. Dictated by the seriousness of Australia's strategic situation, it remains the only occasion on which the issue has not deeply polarized the wider community.

Postwar defence policy was characterized by three tendencies: forward defence and the concomitant involvement in a continuous series of conflicts throughout the 1950s and 1960s; the dominance of the regular services, especially the army, as the principal source of advice to government; and the centralization of defence administration. At the same time, Australian reliance on a major ally switched, gradually, from the United Kingdom to the United States. In the period immediately after the war Australia in fact re-emphasized the traditional links with Britain; through the 1950s Australian policy tried to balance British and American links and, although the major realignment of the armed forces along American lines began with equipment acquisition programmes announced in 1957, this policy continued until the final announcement of British withdrawal from southeast Asia in the late 1960s.

Involvement in the occupation of Japan (1946–51), the Korean War (1950–3), the Malayan Emergency (1950–60), Konfrontasi with Indonesia (1964–6) and the Vietnam War (1962–72) saw the services involved in operations more or less continuously for a quarter of a century. With the significant exception of Vietnam, these wars were fought entirely by regular service personnel; casualties were low and the operations generally successful, and involvement in these campaigns aroused little comment and almost no opposition at home. Although initially ignored by most, Vietnam became the most divisive war in half a century, especially after the first national servicemen were despatched in mid-1966. As in 1916–17 the issue for most was the use of conscripts overseas, although for the radical Left this soon led to a critique of the conduct of the war, the fact of Australian involvement, the US alliance, and the nature of society generally. The operations conducted by the 1st Australian Task Force were highly successful on the whole, and the casualty rates low: 501 killed, only 1 per cent of the total number involved, and around 3,000 wounded. These factors made little difference to the growing unease felt by middle Australia over government policy, nor to the mostly young demonstrators who took to the streets in 1970–1 in their tens of thousands. The Australian contribution was scaled down in 1969, and withdrawn in late 1971. Whether Vietnam was the key issue in unseating the government in the elections in December 1972 must be doubted, however.

Since 1975, and more particularly since 1983, Australia's defence posture has undergone some fundamental changes. While the alliance with the United States remains close, epitomized by the prompt despatch of a small naval task force to the Persian Gulf in late 1990, a series of reports has stressed the need for greater self-reliance in the task of defending Australian territory and interests. A large-scale equipment acquisition and replacement programme, commenced in the 1980s, will run through to the end of the century, and this has placed strain on the defence budget, but in other areas, especially the proclaimed intention to pass many functions back to the reserve forces, government policy seems intent on reversing many of the developments of the postwar era. *See also* DARDANELLES; ENGINEERS; GREAT BRITAIN; NEW ZEALAND; VIETNAM.

JEFFREY GREY

FURTHER READING
Jeffrey Grey, *A Military History of Australia* (Melbourne, 1990); *Australia: two centuries of war and peace*, eds Michael McKernan and Margaret Browne (Canberra, 1988); *Revue Internationale d'Histoire Militaire*, lxxii, edition Australienne, eds Peter Dennis and Jeffrey Grey (Canberra, 1990); Peter Pierce, Jeffrey Grey and Jeff Doyle, *Vietnam Days: Australia and the impact of Vietnam* (Ringwood, Victoria, 1991).

Austria The roots of the fully evolved Austrian army of later modern times may be traced back to the first half of the seventeenth century. Until the Thirty Years' War only the intermittently serving, relatively weak forces of the Holy Roman Emperor were recruited on the basis of feudal legal principles. Germany's nominal sovereign disposed of contingents raised by authority of the Reichstag. In his own hereditary domains he could employ militias (though they were not worth much) by arrangement with the provincial estates. Military enterprisers were already important in the sixteenth century and became crucially so after 1618. Men like Wallenstein provided the Viennese Court with most of the troops needed to defend strictly dynastic interests.

Numbers varied from year to year depending on the extent of the military danger and the funds available. At Ferdinand II's death in 1637 there were 88 cavalry and 66 infantry regiments of German, Walloon, Italian and Spanish provenance. A decree of 1649 confirmed the Austrian army's gradual birth over the preceding decades. Realizing that he required soldiers even in peacetime, Ferdinand III opted to maintain nine infantry regiments, nine of armoured cavalry (cuirassiers) and one of dragoons on a permanent basis – some 25,000 foot and 8,000 horse. In June 1650 Sweden recognized by treaty the existence of what was by now a standing or regular army.

Habsburg military institutions continued to develop in the later seventeenth and early eighteenth centuries in response to security threats from France and Turkey. The size of the host varied constantly, increasing at the start of wars and shrinking on the conclusion of a peace with an attendant reduction in the number of regiments. From 33,000 men in 1649 the Austrian army rose, by fits and starts, to 65,000 in 1672, 113,000 in 1705, 125,000 in 1716 and 271,000 in 1728. It was reduced to 80,000 men in 1740, but, by 1780, it had again grown to 200,000.

Though initially German in composition, the Austrian forces came to incorporate units recruited in East Central Europe as the Habsburgs annexed new territories. Hungary, however, maintained its own troops. This explains the organizational diversity of the different corps – something which Emperor Joseph would later remedy – and a multinational character that would characterize the army up to its very end. Its none the less real unity derived from a strong loyalty to the dynasty. The army, in its turn, being a sort of melting pot for the various nationalities, was to constitute a centripetal factor within the state until 1918.

From its inception the Habsburg army exercised a dual function determined by the need to fight both the Ottoman Empire in the East and the French, and later the Prussians, in the West. Hostilities with the Porte (the Ottoman court) gave it a singular character. In the first third of the eighteenth century Prince Eugene organized the 'military frontier', a vast region placed under a martial regime and protected by peasant-soldiers (*Grenzer*). The geography of the Danubian lands gave cause for maintaining a powerful and mobile cavalry. In 1649 there were more foot than *Reiter*. Subse-quently the cavalry became proportionately stronger than in exclusively Western European armies although the infantry expanded in its own right. Thus Austrian forces constitute a kind of relay station in the sphere of military art. Thereby troops of Eastern inspiration, such as the hussars, arrived in the West. One might also point out the importance the Habsburgs accorded to mountain troops, the fore-runners of the Tyrolean *Jäger*.

The structure of the Austrian army reflected both its Germanic background, namely in the character of the units (where much attention was given to soldiers' family problems, marriage and children), and the Spanish heritage (collegiate organization of the upper administrative levels of the army), with the *Generalkriegskommissariat* (set up in 1650) and the even older *Hofkriegsrat*. Haugwitz's reforms of 1752 laid down the duties of these two councils: the former handled problems of pay, discipline and logistics, and the latter had responsibility for command. Napoleon would take this division of tasks as a model. In the eighteenth century French influence made itself felt with the creation of the Theresian Military Academy at Wiener-Neustadt (1752), as, later, did the example of Prussia.

This was the framework of the army which confronted the French Revolutionary and Imperial troops. In 1791 the Austrian army had 59 regular infantry regiments together with another 17 for the *Grenzer* (77 per cent), while there were 32 cavalry regiments in all (23 per cent): 9 of armoured cavalry, 6 of dragoons, 9 of hussars, 7 of household cavalry and 1 of uhlans. At the time of Sadowa (1866) the ratio was reduced somewhat with 80 regiments of regular infantry (69 per cent) and 41 cavalry regiments (29 per cent).

After the Austro-Hungarian compromise of 1867 compulsory military service was introduced; two years later organizational reforms were undertaken. The Dual Monarchy's armed forces consisted of three elements: the Imperial and Royal (*k.u.k.*) army with its Austrian, Hungarian and (after 1878) Bosnian contingents, which was under the aegis of the imperial ministry of war, the Austrian *Landwehr* or reserve force, administered by the Austrian defence ministry, and the *Honvéd*, a reserve force made up of the *Landwehr* (the first ban) and the *Landsturm* (the second ban) under the direction of the Hungarian defence minister. In 1889 the Austro-Hungarian armed forces comprised 102 infantry regiments, 4 of *Tiroler Kaiserjäger*, 4 of Bosnian-Herzegovinan infantry (Bosnians) and 26 battalions of *Feldjäger*, 16 regiments of dragoons, 16 of hussars, 15 of uhlans, 14 artillery brigades and 6 fortress artillery regiments, 15 battalions of pioneers, 1 railway and telegraph regiment, 26 medical sections, and 3 regiments of the Service Corps. This meant there were 800,000 men on a war footing, buttressed by the Austrian *Landwehr* (26 infantry regiments and 6 of uhlans) and the *Honvéd* (28 infantry regiments and 10 of hussars). The number of regiments would vary but little up to 1914. During the First World War the Austro-Hungarian army still mirrored the heterogeneity of the Dual Monarchy owing to the diversity of the corps that made it up. It was a multinational army in which twelve languages were spoken, including two languages of command, German and Hungarian.

The St Germain peace treaty of 1919 reduced the now exclusively German-speaking Austrian army to 30,000 men recruited by twelve-year terms of service. The so-called *Bundesheer* was absorbed by the *Wehrmacht* after the *Anschluss* in 1938. The Austrian State Treaty of 1955 permitted a new army of 55,000 men. In 1985 it counted 38,000 men, 21,000 of whom were conscripts doing six months' military service. It is divided into two parts: a rapid deployment force (the *Bereitschaftstruppe* made up of a mechanized division and an air force division) and a regional militia (*Landwehr*) capable of putting into the field defence units and one reserve brigade per region within 48 hours. The *Bundesheer*, like Germany's *Bundeswehr*, seeks to maintain certain traditions of its pre-1918 forebear, but the links can hardly be considered organic in nature.

Navy The acquisition of lands in Italy prompted Charles VI to create a navy in 1719. Its first dockyard was located at Trieste. The Austrian navy attacked and destroyed maritime commerce in the Adriatic but was defeated in 1739. After the annexation of the Republic of Venice it was reconstituted (1797). In the nineteenth century it took part in the Battle of Heligoland (1864) against a Danish squadron. In 1866 Admiral Tegetthof, with his ironclads and old wooden ships, rammed and sank the modern steel-built vessels of the Italian Admiral Persano near the island of Lissa (Vis). After the loss of Venice the dockyard of Pola (Pula) replaced that of Venice. During the First World War the Austrian fleet and naval air arm were very active in the Adriatic. On 15 May 1917 Admiral Horthy's squadron of cruisers destroyed 14 Allied vessels in the Strait of Otranto. Austro-Hungarian submarines operated in the Mediterranean. On 31 October 1918, the Habsburg fleet was handed over to Serbia and provided a basis of sorts for the interwar Yugoslav navy though Italy later insisted upon the transfer of many of the ships to its control.

Danube flotilla In 1440 an arsenal was established at Vienna to build men-of-war for the Danube flotilla. During the siege of Vienna in 1529 this flotilla was wrecked by the Turks. A new one was built in 1532 to support the operations of the imperial army in Hungary. After the victory of the Kahlenberg in 1683 the Danube flotilla played its part in assisting the imperial army during the reconquest of Hungary. It was made up of galleys and the *Tschicken* (Viennese: *Tschinacke*) (narrow, oar-driven vessels also known as *Nassarenschiffe*). In 1692 this fleet possessed 12 vessels with a total of 860 sailors and 253 cannon. It was laid up in 1703. Reconstituted in 1715, by 1717 it counted 10 major warships with 200 cannon. Destroyed in 1719, it was resurrected in 1736 and fought some fierce riparian battles against Turkey in 1739. During most of the eighteenth century it transported supplies to the imperial army and conveyed the settlers who repopulated the desolated Banat. It also assisted in the surveillance of the Save and Danube frontiers. Though its strength varied over time, it was deployed in the Austro-Turkish war of 1788–91, against France in 1809, in 1848–9 against the Hungarians, and in 1866 against Prussia. During the First World War it participated in the campaigns against Serbia and Romania, while in 1918 it supported the Austro-German advance to the Ukraine and the Crimea. The Danube flotilla survived the Habsburgs. From 1919 onwards it was based at Linz and comprised some twenty river craft. It was incorporated into the German navy on 23 March 1938.

Aviation In July 1849, the balloonists of the Austrian army staged the first aerial bombardments in history by dropping their artefacts over Venice. The first military aeronautic unit was created in 1890, and a detachment of balloonists was installed at Fischamend in 1909. A military school for aircraft pilots organized the first training course for military pilots at Wiener-Neustadt in 1911. In July 1914, the Austrian army possessed 40 aircraft, 85 pilots and 11 aerodromes. Austrian aviation developed rapidly during the 1914–18 war and extended to the creation of a Fleet Air Arm at Pola in 1913, which operated over the Adriatic and along the Italian front.

See also ADMINISTRATION, ARMY; CAVALRY; CHARLES OF HABSBURG; CHARLES V, DUKE OF LORRAINE; EUGENE OF SAVOY; FRONTIERS; GERMANY; HUNGARY; LISSA; MONTECUCOLI; ST GOTTHARD ABBEY; VIENNA; WALLENSTEIN.

J. NOUZILLE
THOMAS M. BARKER

FURTHER READING
Thomas M. Barker, *Army, Aristocracy, Monarchy. Essays on war, society and government in Austria, 1618–1780* (New York, 1982); Thomas M. Barker, *Doppeladler und Halbmond: Entscheidungsjahr 1683* (Vienna, 1983); Christopher Duffy, *The Army of Maria Theresa* (London, 1977); Ernst Peter, *Die k. u. k. Luftschiffer- und Fliegertruppe Oesterreich-Ungarns, 1794–1919* (Stuttgart, 1981); Joseph Rechberger von Rechkron, *Geschichte der k.k. Kriegsmarine, 1848–1918* (Salzburg, 1967); Oskar Regele, *Der Oesterreichische Hofkriegsrat, 1556–1848* (Vienna, 1949); G. E. Rothenberg, *The Army of Francis Joseph* (West Lafayette, Ind., 1976); G. E. Rothenberg, *The Austrian Military Border in Croatia, 1522–1747* (Urbana, Ill., 1960).

Aviation, military The idea of using heavier-than-air machines in war existed long before the aeroplane was invented, and evidence of it can be found in such diverse sources as the drawings of Leonardo da Vinci and the poetry of Alfred, Lord Tennyson. Among the early pioneers in the field were Clément Ader, a Frenchman who conducted experiments with a steam-powered machine in the 1890s, having persuaded the French Ministry of War to provide financial support; the great German glider advocate, Otto Lilienthal; Hiram Maxim, in Great Britain; the American Samuel Langley; and Ferdinand Ferber, a French artillery officer. When the American Wright brothers finally achieved success at Kitty Hawk, North Carolina, on 17 December 1903, they too were aware of the military potential of the aeroplane, and in the next five years they travelled the world seeking to interest various armies in their designs. One of their 'competitors', the American Glenn Curtis, predicted in 1908 that 'the battle of the future will be fought in the air'.

It was the French, however, who first militarized air power, undoubtedly because of the catalytic effect of the ideas expressed by Clément Ader. His *Aviation in War*, published in 1908, was a seminal work by an inventor of genius, and it predicted a brilliant future for flying. He recognized the full potential of this new weapon, and specified the organizational arrangements that would allow its most effective use; he also described the range of weapons – bombs, machine-guns, cannon – with which it would be feasible to equip aircraft, as well as various ancillary devices, such as sights for bomb-aiming. Further, he envisaged the use, in due course, of ship-borne aeroplanes, and predicted the destruction of large cities, such as London, by attacks from the air.

The French army began training pilots (albeit in civilian schools) in 1910, and used aeroplanes, bought from several manufacturers, with some success during the manoeuvres held that year in Picardy. Also in 1910, General Roques was put in charge of military aviation, and the creation of this single command, and later a standing inspectorate, were the initial steps in a process that would lead to its independence from the artillery and engineers, the two branches of the army most closely involved in military flying. Three regional air commands were created in 1912, and in February 1913 a naval air service was organized.

Parallel developments occurred elsewhere. In Britain, the Royal Flying Corps was formed out of the Air Branch of the Royal Engineers in 1912, and the Royal Naval Air Service in 1914; Belgium had a military air service by 1913; and the Italians actually used aircraft against the Turks in Libya in 1911. In Germany, where the airships of Count Ferdinand von Zeppelin held sway, the French manoeuvres of 1910 and 1911 caused new interest in heavier-than-air technologies, but when the aeroplane was adopted the Inspector of Aviation Troops was subordinated to the Commander of Railways and Transport. In the United States, meanwhile, the army discontinued its aviation experiments in 1912; in Russia, still pre-industrial in many ways, development was scattered.

Thinking and experimentation nevertheless continued. In June 1910, the first trials involving the dropping of bombs on targets were conducted in the United States, while two years later, in France, the Michelin brothers instituted a competition for bombing accuracy. In addition, aeroplanes began to be fitted with machine-guns, and even with small calibre cannon.

In spite of these important advances, military aviation was still regarded, on the eve of the Great War, as a mere auxiliary of the army and navy, to be used by those services for reconnaissance and observation. The British, for example, decided to send six Royal Flying Corps squadrons to France to provide reconnaissance for each of the divisions of the British Expeditionary Force (BEF), while the French, despite having already divided their air force into three components – reconnaissance, artillery spotting and bombing – had no firm plans to carry out the third. Furthermore, at the outbreak of hostilities, the forces available on both sides numbered no more than a few hundred machines in total, together with a few dozen airships.

Yet even such marginal forces proved their worth in the Battle of Mons, when the reconnaissance planes of 4 and 5 Squadrons, Royal Flying Corps, persuaded Sir John French, commanding the British Expeditionary Force, that he should fight a defensive battle, an action which prevented the Germans from outflanking the BEF. Later, during the Battle of the Marne, the machines of the flying unit attached to the Paris defences as well as those of the Royal Flying Corps revealed that the German armies had turned eastward and were thus presenting an open flank to the Anglo-French counter-stroke which eventually halted their offensive. The German flying services, by comparison, were less effective in discovering the whereabouts of the Allies and in passing this information on to the army commanders.

With aircraft from both sides flying over the battle fronts, it was inevitable that combat would break out between them, but since pilots and observers only had rifles and pistols to use against the enemy, the initial air battles were extremely primitive. The first downing of a German aircraft by the Royal Flying Corps occurred on 26 August 1914 when three planes from 2 Squadron formatted around a German reconnaissance machine and simply forced it to land. The first victory by gunfire did not take place until 5 October, when a French crew (Frantz and Quenault) shot down a German observer near Reims.

Although the ground had been prepared for fighter combat, the creation of bomber formations came first. Indeed, before the end of 1914, both the British and French had bomber units which were given the task of attacking enemy territory. Though such missions took the form of retaliatory action at the outset, they rapidly turned into operations designed to strike at the enemy's economic potential and to undermine the morale of civilian populations. The losses suffered during daylight raids forced those in charge to change to night attacks, and to try to find solutions to the problems of navigating and bomb-aiming in the dark.

Bombing was not confined to these strategic objectives, however, and in time it came to play a direct and important part in the land battle, perhaps the most notable example coming during the fierce fighting on the Western Front in March 1918, when the Germans used air power to support their offensive while the Allies employed aeroplanes to plug gaps in their line. In this connection it should be noted that tremendous progress was made in the design of bomber aircraft. At the start of the war, in fact, there were no purpose-built bombers, but by the end of the war both sides had four-engined machines capable of carrying payloads of up to 1 ton over several hundred miles.

The evolution of fighter aircraft was just as spectacular. Created originally to sweep the sky clear of enemy observation aircraft and balloons, fighters were soon given the task of confronting enemy fighters in a battle for air superiority. Pistols and rifles were eventually replaced by machine-guns, mounted on the top wing or with the observer, but the most effective fighter tactics could not be employed until a way was found to synchronize the firing of the gun with the rotation of the propeller, to allow the pilot to fire forward, aiming along his own line-of-sight. Initial steps were taken by the French pilot Roland Garros, but the first workable system was designed by the Dutch manufacturer Anthony Fokker, who was working for the Germans. Once both sides had such a system, true air battles between aces began. The fixed forward-firing machine-gun also permitted more effective strafing of troops on the ground.

The demands of the Great War hastened the industrialization of aircraft manufacture. The French produced 52,000 airframes and 92,000 engines between August 1914 and November 1918, while the German figures were 41,000 and 48,000 respectively. Combined British and American production was even larger.

The pressing need for demobilization, the conversion of factory space back to the production of consumer goods, and general reductions in the size of all air forces following the war meant that, initially at least, they relied on old stocks, accumulated during the Great War. But the 1920s were also a period characterized by intensive studies of air power and several military thinkers (Douhet in Italy, Sykes and Trenchard in Great Britain, and Mitchell in the United States), stimulated by their experience in the recent war, worked out coherent sets of principles which, apart from differences in emphasis and detail, embodied the same fundamental ideas. Basing their views on the belief that it would, in future, be impossible for land forces to break through defensive systems, these writers argued that only the air arm was capable of winning a decisive victory, and that it might do this alone. In this scenario, they gave priority to strategic bombing, whose role would be to destroy an enemy's psychological and economic potential by terrorizing civilian populations and destroying its war industry. These doctrines exerted a profound influence in international military circles, and the potential of delivering chemical weapons by air became a preoccupation of both general staffs and the public at large throughout most of the 1920s.

The logical extension of these doctrines was that air forces should be autonomous. Although the processes which led to the independence of the various national air forces moved with varying speed in each instance, developments nevertheless took place according to the same general pattern: first, the creation of an air ministry or similar governmental authority and then the formation of an independent air arm. The British were first off the mark, having created the Air Ministry in 1917 and the Royal Air Force in April 1918, and were followed soon after the war by the Italians, for whom (particularly after Mussolini came to power) an autonomous air force symbolized the vigour and dynamism of their country (and the Fascist regime) to the whole world. The same kind of thinking lay behind Nazi Germany's creation of a powerful and independent *Luftwaffe* in 1935. France had to wait until 1933 for the establishment of an independent air force, five years after the creation of the French Air Ministry, and even then the existence of the *Armeé de l'Air* was not altogether welcomed by the army and navy. The United States army and navy were no better disposed toward the creation of a separate air force, and it was not until 1947 that the United States Air Force was able to translate the practical autonomy acquired during the Second World War into formal independence.

Still, the independence of air forces could be challenged. The separate existence of the Royal Air Force was threatened several times between the two wars, and it survived in the end in part because of the role it played in suppressing unrest in Britain's colonial possessions, particularly in India and Iraq – a role known technically as 'air control'. The French air arm was also used for the same purpose in the eastern Mediterranean and in Morocco's Rif War in the 1920s.

It was only after the technological revolution of the 1930s, however, that military air forces were able to extend their fields of activity to the point that they actually seemed capable of doing what the prophets of air power forecast. The biplane design gave way to the monoplane, fitted with retractable undercarriage; fighters were fitted with cannon, greatly increasing their firepower; and bomber aircraft grew larger, faster and, with the adoption of power-operated turrets, better able to defend themselves.

Air forces were given the opportunity to test their equipment and ideas in several of the localized conflicts – Spain, China, Ethiopia – which accompanied the general rise in international tension in the mid-1930s. Spain was by far the best proving ground. Dive-bombing had its first real operational trial; cities were subjected to bombing on a scale never before witnessed; and it was over Spain that the *Luftwaffe* developed its fighter tactics.

In the last few years before the Second World War the German and Italian re-armament programmes emphasized the development of the air force as an offensive weapon and more particularly, in Germany's case, as an army co-operation

air force. The spirit of the offensive also dominated British thinking in the early 1930s, although it took a different form: there the emphasis was on the deterrent power of Bomber Command or, if war broke out, its ability to do devastating damage to the enemy's war economy. From 1936, however, the growth of the *Luftwaffe* caused British politicians to believe that the United Kingdom (and specifically London) was vulnerable to air attack, and Fighter Command, designed for the air defence of Great Britain, began to grow at the expense of Bomber Command. In France, meanwhile, there had been talk in the early 1930s of abolishing the bomber force in order to satisfy pacifist opinion. Although the rise in tensions later in the decade meant that this did not happen, time was lost, and the bomber arm was not able to recover by 1939.

There were imbalances, then, between the Axis and Allied air forces when war broke out in 1939, and these were displayed in the battles of May and June 1940. Using the blitzkrieg technique involving close co-operation between armoured forces and aircraft, the Germans won a series of crushing victories over Poland (1939), Norway (April–June 1940), Western Europe (May–June 1940) and in the Balkans (April–May 1941), during which the *Luftwaffe*'s tactical superiority was strikingly evident. Its weakness as a strategic air force, however, became clear during the Battle of Britain (July–September 1940) when the Germans failed both to crush the RAF and to force Britain to sue for peace because of the damage inflicted upon London and other cities. The same deficiencies meant that while the *Luftwaffe* was able to control the skies over the battlefields on the Eastern Front for almost two years, it could not attack the large Russian industrial objectives located in the Urals.

As the war lengthened in duration, and extended over wider and wider areas, blitzkrieg tactics became obsolete, and the initiative in the air war passed to the Allies. At first the British, and then the Americans, were able to build huge fleets of aircraft and to conduct massive raids against Germany's cities, war industry and transportation and communication networks. Success did not come easily or quickly, and bomber losses were at times staggering, but by the spring of 1944 the German aircraft industry, rail and road networks and petroleum industries were under siege. In the long run, the campaign against the enemy's fuel resources paid the greatest dividends, while the mainly British area raids, aimed at civilian morale, failed to produce the psychological effects predicted by Douhet and Mitchell. Thus, strategic bombing revealed its limitations – until, in August 1945, the Americans made use of the atomic bomb against Japan.

Still, strategic bombing contributed in a significant way to the Allies' successful campaign to win air superiority over Western Europe. Once the Americans had long-range fighters to escort their bomber formations, they were able not only to fight their way to heavily defended targets, such as oil refineries and aircraft factories, but also to shoot down large numbers of German fighters in the process. Although the Germans were able to decentralize much of their aircraft production to avoid bombing, they could not replace the experienced crews lost in these air battles or develop new sources of fuel. Accordingly, by the time of the Normandy landings in June 1944, the Allies had undisputed mastery of the air and were able to prevent the *Luftwaffe* from interfering in the land battle. At the same time, the Allied tactical air forces were free to operate with little or no opposition.

The Allies developed their principles for the tactical use of aircraft during the desert war in North Africa and in Italy, and built up a strong force of medium bombers and rocket-equipped fighter bombers to attack lines of communication, armoured formations and other objectives on the ground. The tactical air forces were crucial in allowing the Allied armies to break out of Normandy and to advance to the Rhine. For their part, the Russians gave maximum emphasis to supporting their ground troops with a very highly developed tactical air arm whose spearhead was the Stormovik, a machine specifically designed for ground attack in level flight.

In the war at sea, aircraft were used against both surface ships and submarines. They protected Allied convoys in the Atlantic, flying not only off escort aircraft carriers, but also from coastal bases. Very long-range bombers, meanwhile, were capable of protecting shipping into mid-ocean, and their presence was a major factor in the Allies' eventual victory in the Battle of the Atlantic. In the Pacific, meanwhile, the aircraft carrier became the mainstay of navies, battleships proving vulnerable to air attack. The most powerful illustrations of this truth were the Japanese strike on Pearl Harbor on 7 December 1941, the destruction of the British warships *Repulse* and *Prince of Wales* by Japanese bombers flying from Indochina, the Battles of Midway Island and the Coral Sea, in which surface ships did not engage each other, and the sinking of Japan's super-battleship *Yamato* by 400 bombers of the US navy.

The development of transport aircraft also entered a new age during the Second World War, and these played a part in both the tactical and strategic spheres – in airborne operations, for example, but also when they were used as 'air bridges' as at Stalingrad and in the Burmese jungle.

The Second World War also saw important scientific and technological advances which produced guided missiles and bombs, jet engines in combat aircraft, electronic warfare and rockets. Aircraft production expanded to record levels: more than 675,000 machines were produced by the belligerents during the war, and by 1945 the US aircraft industry was capable of turning out 10,000 a month.

The development of the atomic bomb and its use against Japan by the United States in August 1945 opened a new era in the history of air power. A single aircraft and crew could now inflict damage equivalent to that produced by a 500-bomber raid dropping bombs of the conventional type. This revolutionary development represented the pinnacle of the strategic role of manned aircraft: they had become the war-winners depicted by Douhet, Mitchell and Trenchard twenty years before. Within ten years, however, the manned bomber had been superseded by the inter-continental ballistic missile, but bombers survived when it became clear that manned aircraft added an important degree of flexibility to a country's nuclear arsenal, and better command and control: bombers could always be recalled after take-off.

Interceptor (fighter) aircraft seemed also to be obsolete with the development of the missile, but they have survived, in part because bombers remain in service in the major air forces, but also because of their value in limited, non-nuclear, regional conflicts.

Still, the introduction of missiles has brought about major changes in air warfare. 'Traditional' air combat, in which two aircraft came into close contact, has in general been transformed into a battle conducted at long range (some tens of miles) featuring automatic target acquisition by complex radars. But 'dog-fighting' has not disappeared altogether. During the Yom Kippur War, Israeli pilots brought down a number of enemy machines solely by the use of their cannon.

Air defence systems combining quick-firing guns and several types of ground-to-air missiles – as seen over Hanoi and Haiphong during the Vietnam War, the Suez Canal during the Yom Kippur War and more recently in Lebanon – have become more complex and more effective, creating overlapping envelopes of defended air space each of which has to be overcome in order for an attacker to win air superiority. Flying very low to operate beneath the enemy's radar cover is one solution; jamming is another. In fact, it now seems clear, given what occurred in the Falklands War (1982) and in Afghanistan, that aircraft lacking electronic warfare equipment stand no chance of survival against a well-equipped enemy.

Now that space too can be militarized, air forces have arrived at a crucial turning point. Assuming that manoeuvre in space becomes feasible, and if there are no international agreements to limit the development of space weapons, air forces will have to determine their future roles in aerospace war. *See also* ADER; AIRBORNE TROOPS; AIRCRAFT, BOMBER; AIRCRAFT, FIGHTER; AIRCRAFT, RECONNAISSANCE; BASES, AIR FORCE; ATLANTIC, BATTLE OF THE; BRITAIN, BATTLE OF; DOUHET; GERMANY, AIR BATTLE OF; GUERNICA; MIDWAY ISLAND; MITCHELL; PARACHUTE TROOPS; TRANSPORT, AIR; TRENCHARD.

P. FACON
A. TEYSSIER
STEPHEN J. HARRIS

FURTHER READING
Charles Christienne, Pierre Lissarague, A. Degardin, P. Facon, P. Biffotot and M. Hodeir, *Histoire de l'aviation militaire française* (Paris, 1980); *Icare* (review); Robin Higham, *Air Power: a concise history* (New York, 1972); Basil Collier, *A History of Air Power* (New York, 1974); James L. Stokesbury, *A Short History of Airpower* (New York, 1986); *Aerospace Historian* (journal).

B

Bangladesh *See* PAKISTAN

Barfleur, Battle of *See* LA HOGUE AND BARFLEUR

Barracks Barracks, as such, hardly existed until relatively modern times. The word suggests buildings that were originally intended to be temporary. The German term 'kaserne' and the French 'caserne' are perhaps both derived from the Provençal 'cazerna', and all three probably emanate from the late Latin 'quaterna', which meant a square construction. In the field, the Roman legions used only camps (*castra*), in which there were rows of tents in summer and wooden huts in winter. Sections of the Praetorian Guard were housed together at the gates of Rome and a large number of strongholds and small forts were constructed along the line of the *limes* (the frontier of the Empire). The mile-castles and forts on Hadrian's Wall all contained stone barracks. In the later Imperial period, the *limitanei* (frontier army) requisitioned one third of civilian housing space as lodgings for the soldiers, who, by the law of AD 398, were officially known as 'guests'.

The construction of barracks as a regular policy seems to have been started by the French to accommodate the huge increase in the number of troops during the reign of Louis XIV. Financial constraints, however, compelled the government to rely on local expedients or to take over empty buildings, whenever the need arose. On several occasions royal pronouncements were made to the effect that all troops were to be quartered in barracks, but they were empty words. These edicts stressed that putting troops into barracks was the only way to maintain discipline and to alleviate the civilian population from having to share their houses with unwelcome strangers.

However, when lack of funds halted the building programme, the king approved the lodging of soldiers in towns. Rapid progress in the provision of barracks did not occur until after 1763 and was due to a new set of factors. In large towns, the police called, with increasing frequency, on the army's assistance in dealing with fires and mobs and in protecting markets. At Rouen, the Saint-Sever (1774) and Pré-au-Loup (1780) barracks were built to house a garrison capable of suppressing potential riots. Elsewhere, at Caen for example, the purpose was to avoid subjecting the public, especially its leading female members, to the offensive sight of soldiers. Steps were taken to seclude the troops as far as possible, iron bars being added to the windows of the new barracks in 1777. In addition, it became easier to accommodate a battalion or a squadron in a single building after Choiseul transferred the administration of companies from their captains to regimental boards.

During the English Civil War (1642–6) members of the Parliamentary army regularly used Anglican churches, especially cathedrals, as barracks for both themselves and their horses. After the Restoration in 1660, the standing army possessed some barracks in the Tower of London and the Savoy as well as in the various garrison towns dotted around the country. Portsmouth and Hull had purpose-built barracks but they were only sufficient to house less than half the garrison. The remainder were lodged on private and public householders. The Mutiny Act 1689, following on from the Disbandment Act 1679, made it illegal for soldiers to be billeted on a private house without the owner's consent. Throughout most of the eighteenth century, the British army was accommodated in groups of three or four men in public houses across the length and

The Ravensdowne Barracks at Berwick-upon-Tweed, designed in 1717, accommodated 600 men and 36 officers. They were the first purpose-built barracks in England. Eight men sleeping in four double beds shared each room. Initially there was neither hospital nor kitchen and the men prepared meals in their own chambers.
(Courtesy of Berwick Borough Museum)

breadth of the country. Barracks were built in the principal towns of Ireland after the end of the Jacobite Wars in 1691 and in Scotland after Culloden in 1746, but they were really blockhouses and police posts intended to suppress and control the countryside. Spurred by indiscipline, poor civil –military relations and the lack of opportunities for training, the British army was moved into municipal barracks between 1792 and 1858. In 1792, Parliament gave George III the right to erect permanent barracks. To begin with, their internal arrangements were appalling, with up to thirty men sleeping side-by-side on long benches which stretched from wall-to-wall. This changed after 1818 when the army took over the administration of barracks from the civilian authorities. The Duke of Wellington ordered them to be equipped with tiered iron bedsteads which gave each man his own bed but crammed as many men into a building as possible. Washrooms were situated at the end of each barracks. Cardwell's Army Reforms of 1870 fixed every regiment to a depot town complete with barracks.

The armies of Brandenburg-Prussia and Austria-Hungary were gradually transferred into barracks after 1763. Both Frederick the Great and Maria Theresa were exercised by the need to isolate their troops from the pernicious doctrines of the Enlightenment. Troops would only support absolute monarchy if they were sealed away from the ideas and emotions current within civilian society. Prussian barracks contained between twenty-five and thirty men, each bed being shared by two soldiers. In Austria, some purpose-built barracks appeared after 1748 but many men were housed in 'semi-barracks', usually dilapidated and abandoned houses. Living conditions were poor.

A fine example of an eighteenth-century British barracks survives in the Ravensdowne Barracks at Berwick-upon-Tweed. Designed in 1717, a battalion of 600 men was housed in two, three-storeyed main blocks on either side of a parade square. Thirty-six officers lodged in a pavilion on the third side of the parade and a two-storeyed office and storehouse block completed the quadrangle. The men slept eight to a room in four double-beds, each block being arranged around three staircases. There was initially no hospital and no kitchen, the men cooking in their own rooms. In Britain, France, Prussia and Austria, the cramped and insanitary barracks of the eighteenth century bred lice, fleas and epidemic disease among the soldiery. Until 1873, French soldiers still slept two to a bed and not until 1880 were the first barracks opened, at Bourges, according to the new 1873 pattern. The barracks were light, spacious and airy with each man having his own bed. Guard-rooms, sickbays, latrines, prison-block and cook-houses were all provided and sensibly situated. Unfortuately, the new barracks required a great deal of ground and this retarded their wide adoption. In Britain, barracks remained primitive and communal throughout the First and Second World Wars, the Korean War and the period of National Service. The coming of a freer and more affluent society in the 1960s led to a crisis in service recruitment. One of the ways of making army life more attractive was to provide each soldier with his own room, complete with sanitary facilities. The more recent trend has been to move away from the concept of barracks towards the provision of 'service housing' in which single men live in comfortable bed-sitting rooms and married NCOs and men occupy apartments or separate houses. The Knightsbridge Barracks of the Household Cavalry in London provide a fine modern example of service accom-modation.

Early modern European states were slow to accommodate their new standing armies in barracks because of the expense, even though the alternative of quartering the soldiers on the civilian population or employing cantonal systems of recruitment tended to integrate the military with civilian society rather than effect its isolation. Britain developed a barrack system during the first half of the nineteenth century in order to house its regular, professional army, largely due to the anti-military attitudes of the majority of the population. However, in much of Europe a barrack system was also found to be essential for the operation of mass conscription. In order to inculcate a military ethos and martial values into young conscripts within the short time available, isolation from civilian society was essential. Similar principles still pertain in those countries which have retained conscrip-tion, although the standard of barrack accommodation has improved immeasur-ably to bring it into line with the rising civilian standard of living. *See also* BILLETING; CAMPS; ETHOS; FORTIFICATION; FRONTIERS, MILITARY; MILITARY RESTRICTIONS ON USE OF LAND; PROPERTY OWNED BY THE MILITARY; RECRUITMENT; SOLDIERS AND SOCIETY.

J. CHAGNIOT
JOHN CHILDS

FURTHER READING
André Corvisier, *Armies and Societies in Europe, 1494–1789* (Bloomington, Ind., 1979); John Childs, *Armies and Warfare in Europe, 1648–1789* (Manchester, 1982); Reginald Hargreaves, 'Bivouacs, billets and barracks', *Army Quarterly*, lxxxv (1963), pp. 231–42; T. H. McGuffie, 'Life in the British army, 1793–1820' (MA thesis, University of London, 1940).

Bart, Jean (1650–1702) Jean Bart, the son of a Dunkirk fisherman, began his naval career in the Dutch fleet of de Ruyter and took part in the attack on the Medway in 1667. Returning to France in 1672, he commanded privateers, capturing fifty prizes between 1674 and 1678. In recogni-tion of these achievements, Louis XIV made him a lieutenant in the French navy, promotion to captain following in 1686. He was captured by the British in 1689 but managed to escape in a small boat. He commanded the *Alcyon* at Beachy Head (1690) before devoting himself to com-merce-raiding, in command of squadrons of fast royal frigates. In 1691 he captured ninety-six ships to the value of more than 1,500,000 livres and, in the next year, took an entire Dutch fishing fleet. 1694 saw his greatest triumph when he recaptured off the Texel a French grain convoy of over 100 vessels, a welcome exploit in that year of scarcity. He was rewarded by elevation to the nobility. On the Dogger Bank in 1696, Bart fought a fierce action against a Dutch convoy, destroying over eighty ships. He reached flag rank in 1697 and commanded the Flanders squadron. Bart was an associ-ate of Vauban, whose powerful fortress at Dunkirk he used to full effect as a base for the small frigate squadrons which both men advocated for the attack on Anglo-Dutch trade. They also urged, in vain, a landing at the estuary of the Thames. Bart's name is synonymous with the great success of

French commerce-raiding during the Nine Years' War (1688–97) and he is commemorated by a statue in Dunkirk. However, Bart's reputation has unfairly eclipsed that of his companion in adversity and glory, the Comte de Forbin (1656–1733). *See also* BEACHY HEAD; BLOCKADES; COMMERCE-RAIDING; CONVOYS; LA HOGUE AND BARFLEUR; NAVAL WARFARE; NAVIES; RUYTER; SEIGNELAY; SURCOUF; VAUBAN.

J. MEYER

FURTHER READING
E. H. Jenkins, *A History of the French Navy* (London, 1973); L. Lemaire, *Jean Bart* (Dunkirk, 1928); Geoffrey Symcox, *The Crisis of French Sea Power, 1688–97* (The Hague, 1974); Armel de Wismes, *Jean Bart et la guerre de la course* (Paris, 1965); J. S. Bromley, *Corsairs and Navies, 1660–1760* (London, 1987).

Bases, air force   The concept of an air base was only really developed during the inter-war years (1918–39) when military authorities came to appreciate the absolute need for their air forces to possess an appropriate infrastructure and when increasingly large machines proved too heavy for the simple grass strips of the First World War. From the late 1920s and early 1930s onwards, air bases became administrative and operational realities, the sites at which units were stationed and from which they would mount wartime missions. Installations grew large and complex, featuring permanent hangars and concrete runways.

During the Second World War, the number of operational air bases increased enormously, keeping pace with the geographical development of the conflict. Apart from a few common features, the character of these installations varied considerably from one region to another according to their function. Some consisted of no more than a rudimentary runway situated somewhere near the battle front which could be used by small aircraft (fighters, light bombers and reconnaissance machines) for tactical support missions. There were also large bases from which strategic bombers could operate, such as the British bases employed by the

Americans and the RAF for their raids on Germany, or those for logistical transport planes, such as the installations erected by the Americans in India and China to maintain supplies to the Chinese army. The long-range bombers which supported shipping during the Battle of the Atlantic required facilities for both land-based aircraft and seaplanes. The Americans established a number of bases in Africa and Latin America to refuel long-distance support aircraft and to provide air cover for Atlantic convoys.

The conquest, possession or creation of air bases was an essential element in the Pacific theatre of operations. From late 1942 onwards, the Americans, who now held the initiative, advanced systematically westwards using bases which they captured from the Japanese. By this 'leapfrogging' strategy they were able to bypass many enemy strongpoints, to intensify their bombing of Japanese industry and cities and to cut the enemy's lines of communication and supply. After the occupation of Iwo Jima in 1945, all Japan was exposed to uninterrupted attack from land-based US B-29s.

The importance of having access to a network of linked aerodromes was clear after the Second World War. It facilitated strategic bombing by bringing much of an enemy's territory within range and provided air cover for the army. Indeed, in the late 1940s and the 1950s, the United States, the Soviet Union, Britain and France all established networks in Europe and elsewhere. By the 1960s, however, following the development of guided missiles with improved navigation systems, it was evident that air bases would be particularly exposed targets in case of conflict, being vulnerable to both conventional and nuclear weapons. Both the United States and the Soviet Union developed 'counterforce' strategies which envisaged air bases as primary objects of attack in order to prevent retaliation.

A number of solutions have been considered to offset these risks. At the strategic level, more emphasis has been placed on submarine-launched missiles. At the operational or tactical level, short-take-off-and-landing (STOL) and vertical-take-off-and-landing (VTOL) aircraft, like the British Harrier, have been developed to reduce the air force's dependence on long runways and fixed installations and to permit dispersal.

Air bases have necessarily become involved in the economic and social life of the communities near which they are situated. These installations are often situated close to towns, and since air force personnel and their dependants are potential consumers, they provide income for local businesses and job opportunities for the local population. The threatened closure of a base usually provokes a hostile response on the part of the local community and, at times, bases of marginal importance and utility have been kept open because of these civilian considerations. On the other hand, the presence of a base can involve a certain amount of nuisance, particularly in the form of aircraft noise. There may also be a degree of risk; the city of Las Vegas, for example, is very near Nellis Air Force Base, which would be a prime target in the event of war between the United States and the USSR (Russia after 1991). *See also* AVIATION.

P. FACON and A. TEYSSIER
STEPHEN J. HARRIS

FURTHER READING
C. Christienne, P. Lissarague, A. Degardin, P. Facon, P. Biffotot and M. Hodeir, *Histoire de l'aviation française* (Paris, 1980); Philippe Masson, *Dictionnaire de la seconde guerre mondiale* (Paris, 1979); Robert Futrell, *Development of the AAF Base Facilities in the United States, 1939–1945* (Washington DC, 1951); Bruce B. Halpenny, *To Shatter the Sky: a bomber airfield at work* (Cambridge, 1984); Robin Higham, *Air Power: a concise history* (New York, 1972); Basil Collier, *A History of Air Power* (New York, 1974); James L. Stokesbury, *A Short History of Airpower* (New York, 1986).

Bases, naval Bases are one of the major elements of sea power. They have a dual role: to enable fleets to operate in their vicinity, and to permit the maintenance, refit and repair of warships. For reasons of their own security bases possess defensive armaments to deter enemy attacks. All nations with a navy will have one or more bases on their home territory; the overseas expansion of Western powers in the sixteenth to nineteenth centuries brought them many overseas bases, whose possession often became a matter of strife.

In all cases, a naval base must include a good harbour with sheltered anchorage, factors which usually account for their selection in the first place. Subsequent development depends upon circumstances. At the minimum, many would have stores for providing food and water, and perhaps masts and yards. Others would develop further with workshops, docks, and basins to become fully fledged dockyards, while a few might exist for one particular purpose, such as shipbuilding – e.g. Pembroke, Rochefort.

Bases first appear in Antiquity. In the dockyard of Piraeus, Athens possessed a full naval complex. During the Hellenistic period, Rhodes and Alexandria are examples of a similar type. Under the Roman Empire, the naval forces whose essential role was to police the Mediterranean were backed up by bases at Misenum, Ravenna and Alexandria.

In medieval times, Byzantium, Venice, Genoa and Tunis were major bases, before the appearance, from the thirteenth century, of permanent installations in the northern seas, such as Dover or the 'Clos des Galées' near Rouen.

From the sixteenth century, the great naval wars found the participating powers building up their bases at home, and more gradually abroad. In England, Deptford, Woolwich, Chatham and Portsmouth were supplemented by Plymouth in the late seventeenth century, while in France Toulon and Brest were the principal centres, Lorient being added later, with Amsterdam in the United Provinces, and El Ferrol, Cartagena and Cadiz in Spain. Bases abroad were at first largely points, usually good harbours, where ships on long voyages could recuperate. They often developed as the influence of the owning nation expanded. Such ports could change hands as the fortunes of war swayed back and forth, e.g. Minorca, which was the first

British overseas dockyard, many of the West Indian islands or the Cape of Good Hope. British success, with several bases, such as Mauritius and the Cape, captured during the long wars of 1793–1815, gave her after 1815 a fine series of bases throughout the world. French bases were fewer, as can be seen from Suffren's campaign in the Indian Ocean, when he had to operate from Île de France and from an improvised base at Trincomalee. Havana was an important Spanish overseas base, and indeed one of her principal shipbuilding centres.

The home dockyards of all nations were always, by the standards of their time, great industrial establishments, which could build ships, prepare masts and yards and make the necessary rope and numerous other articles as well as maintain large stores of materials of all kinds. Overseas bases were, however, rarely more than large store establishments, with perhaps a careening wharf and a sheerlegs (hoisting apparatus), as a sailing warship could, given the materials, refit herself. A good example of such a yard survives at Antigua.

During the nineteenth century, however, the requirements of an effective base greatly increased. With steam engines, and later iron and then steel hulls, much more was required, for the metal could not be worked aboard ship in the same way as timber. Moreover, metal ships in tropical waters fouled very quickly and dry docks were more necessary. Thus workshops, coal depots and dry docks had to be provided. At the same time, overseas expansion accelerated, and more powers acquired distant bases. So France acquired Saigon and Dakar, Russia Vladivostok and Germany Tsingtao, while Japan began her own series of home dockyards. Again the

The base of the Russian Baltic fleet had been founded at Kronstadt, an island off St Petersburg, by Peter the Great. Not only did Kronstadt protect the anchorage and dockyard, it also defended the city from naval attack. By the mid-nineteenth century, the main fortifications consisted of off-shore tiered, granite artillery casemates supplemented by open batteries on land.
(Peter Newark's Military Pictures)

British effort was exceptional, adding new bases such as Malta, Simon's Town, Aden, Trincomalee and Hong Kong. After 1907, *détente* with France and the development of German naval power led to a recasting of British home bases, Harwich, Rosyth, Invergordon and Scapa Flow being opened. In this period too, the United States, which had a number of navy yards on its own coasts, such as at Portsmouth (New Hampshire), Boston and New York, and later at San Francisco, San Diego and Bremerton on the west coast, developed a system far beyond its continental territory, with Guantánamo in Cuba, Pearl Harbor in Hawaii, and Guam and Subic Bay in the Philippines. The principal Russian dockyards were at Kronstadt and Sebastopol with Vladivostok coming later. Italy relied on La Spezia and Taranto, Germany on Kiel and Wilhelmshafen.

Between the two world wars, Britain began to develop Singapore, and Japan created a large base at Truk in the Caroline Islands. The US navy, faced with the vast distances and few harbours of the Pacific, developed the 'Fleet Train', a series of ships specially fitted to carry out all the functions of a base. The other naval powers were less well endowed. Neither in 1914 nor in 1939 was Germany, Italy or Russia in possession of overseas bases, which, apart from their own unfavourable geographic positions, automatically imposed serious limitations on the use of their naval forces. France had only a single overseas base, at Bizerta, and a small dockyard at Saigon.

In the Second World War, naval bases were vulnerable to air attack, and in this regard we need only recall the attacks on Taranto, Pearl Harbor or Truk. This threat gave rise to improved defences, as well as to the building of enormous concrete shelters such as those which protected German submarines at Brest, Lorient, La Pallice, Bergen or Trondheim. New bases were often urgently required to cater for new theatres of war. For this purpose, and also to replace heavily damaged dockyards, mobile bases, built by special construction parties ('Seabees'), or repair ships, with floating docks, were widely used, such as the development in the Pacific of forward bases at Espiritu Santo and Ulithi. Freetown in West Africa was another.

In the nuclear age, bases have lost none of their importance. The US navy has continued where the British Royal Navy left off, and now possesses a system of bases covering the globe. It has added Diego Garcia and Bahrein in the Indian Ocean, and Ascension Island, the Azores, Rota and Holy Loch. The Russian navy is less fortunate having mainly minor bases at its disposal with varied 'facilities'. Though bases remain indispensable, they are very vulnerable to nuclear attack. *See also* ADMINISTRATION, NAVAL; ARSENALS; DOCKYARDS; NAVAL STORES; NAVAL WARFARE; NAVIES; ORDNANCE.

P. MASSON
A. W. H. PEARSALL

FURTHER READING
See DOCKYARDS.

Bayeux Tapestry   *See* ICONOGRAPHY

Beachy Head (Bevéziers), Battle of (10 July 1690)

Having reached Brest from Toulon in 1689, in the following year the Comte de Tourville (1642–1701) was given command of the combined French fleet of seventy-five ships of the line. Working up the English Channel, he encountered the Anglo-Dutch fleet of fifty-nine ships of the line under Arthur Herbert, 1st Earl of Torrington (1647–1716). The latter initially acted cautiously so that his presence might deter the French from aggression but he was sent orders from Queen Mary and the Privy Council to fight. Accordingly, he moved to attack. While d'Estrées held off the English in the rear, Tourville slipped into the gap between the Dutch in the van and the main body of Torrington's fleet. The Allies lost fifteen ships and retired to the Thames, causing a panic in London. Tourville did not take full advantage of his success, ignoring the vulnerable communications of the English army in Ireland, and merely burned some ships and houses at Teignmouth in Devon (4 August 1690). The disappointment generated by Tourville's 'timidity of spirit' (Seignelay) caused Louis XIV and Louvois to rethink their strategic plans, which had been based on continental defence and naval offence. The Allied side made the mistake of trying to control their commander from a distance. Beachy Head also demonstrated the difficulty of achieving decisive military results with the blunt navies of the later seventeenth century. *See also* LA HOGUE AND BARFLEUR; NAVAL WARFARE; NAVIES; SEIGNELAY.

J. MEYER

FURTHER READING
Philip Aubrey, *The Defeat of James Stuart's Armada, 1692* (Leicester, 1979); J. Ehrman, *The Navy in the War of William III* (London, 1953); E. H. Jenkins, *A History of the French Navy* (London, 1973); Philippe Masson, *Histoire de la marine française* (Paris, 1981–3); Geoffrey Symcox, *The Crisis of French Sea Power, 1688–97* (The Hague, 1974).

Beaufre, André (1902–75) During his career this French general served in Indo-China, commanded a French corps during the Suez expedition in 1956 and occupied a number of posts within NATO. He played a key role in the development of strategic studies in France, establishing the *Institut français d'Études stratégiques* (French Institute for Strategic Studies) and publishing a number of key books.

H. COUTAU-BÉGARIE

Central to his contribution to the development of French strategic thought was the growing disillusionment in postwar France with the US nuclear guarantee to Western Europe. French strategic theorists such as Beaufre provided the theoretical justification for the French national deterrent. Beaufre was a proponent of the idea of 'multilateral deterrence'. He argued that while the nuclear forces of the Soviet Union and the United States provided a state of deterrence, there was no guarantee that the interests of their allies would coincide. He questioned whether the superpowers would take risks on what they might view as marginal issues. There was, therefore, a need for local, nationally controlled nuclear forces. However, he recognized that a multiplicity of nuclear forces could give rise to instability. He therefore further argued that national nuclear forces should be contained within an alliance structure. They would be in national hands but co-ordinated. He argued that this would increase the risks for an enemy since multiple decision centres would lead to uncertainty on the part of the enemy and therefore encourage caution. Thus, the deterrence value of each national force would be increased.

DAVID WESTON

See also DETERRENCE; FRANCE; NUCLEAR WARFARE; STRATEGY.

FURTHER READING
André Beaufre: *Deterrence and Strategy* (London, 1965); *An Introduction to Strategy* (London, 1965); *Strategy of Action* (London, 1967). For an examination of Beaufre's place in the development of strategic thinking, see Lawrence Freedman, *The Evolution of Nuclear Strategy* (London, 1981).

Belgium The provinces of the modern kingdom of Belgium once formed the 'cockpit of Europe', the central theatre of many international wars. For centuries, these territories formed part of larger political units – Lotharingia, the Burgundian states, France and the Spanish/Austrian Netherlands. The provinces were incorporated into France (1793–1815) and into the kingdom of the Netherlands (1815–31) before emerging as an independent state in 1831. The role of Belgium in military history has therefore been major but frequently passive. However, during the late Middle Ages and at the beginning of the sixteenth century, the Belgian provinces were more directly involved in the development of the art of war.

In 1302, the Battle of the Golden Spurs (or Courtrai) revealed the qualities of the Flemish foot soldiers, formed from militias attached to the guilds of weavers, when they inflicted a bloody defeat on the French cavalry. The victors contributed to the renaissance of infantry, which was also witnessed in the English successes in the

Hundred Years' War and in the military organization of the Swiss cantons. During the fifteenth century, the Netherlands, which formed a part of Charles the Bold's Burgundian state, profited from the advances which he made in military matters. During the Eighty Years' War (1567–1648) between the Dutch and the Spaniards, the southern Netherlands were both the base for the Spanish army and a testing ground for the *tercio* (*see* TACTICS), the Nassau Doctrine and the new techniques of siege warfare. The first permanent hospital of the modern period for wounded and disabled soldiers was founded by Philip II of Spain at Mechelen in 1585. In the reign of Louis XIV, some of Vauban's most sophisticated sieges were directed against the towns of the Spanish Netherlands and the neighbouring Bishopric of Liège – Mons, Ath, Ypres, Charleroi, Namur, Maastricht and Huy. The major towns and cities of the Spanish/ Austrian Netherlands were accordingly the recipients of the most up-to-date designs of fortifications. While under Austrian rule (1714–93), the southern Netherlands contributed regiments to the Austrian army, perhaps as many as 17,000 men during the Seven Years' War.

The independence of Belgium in 1831 was accompanied by neutrality; her military efforts were directed towards defence and fortification. In the '10 Day War' (August 1831), the new state of Belgium was invaded by a Dutch army of 40,000 under King William I of the Netherlands. Belgium was able to muster a motley array of only 30,000 men but the Dutch were forced to withdraw when a French army advanced into southern Belgium. In response, Belgium established a standing army of 60,000 men in 1832 in order to defend the key fortresses at Antwerp, Liège and Namur but the financial cost was extremely high and as the threat of invasion from the kingdom of the Netherlands receded so the army was gradually reduced. Belgium based her defence policy on deterring aggression by demanding a high price from the aggressor. If deterrence failed, she intended to safeguard her territory by employing a field army manoeuvring be-

hind modern fortifications and to maintain these operations until one of the powers which guaranteed Belgian neutrality intervened. Although her system of conscription (30–48 months' service) permitted substitution, Belgium possessed an army of 40,382 men and 3,406 officers in 1870. First-line reserves brought the total strength on mobilization to 168,439 men and 3,587 officers divided into four infantry and two cavalry divisions. In addition, there was an elite heavy cavalry *gendarmerie* of 3,079 men and the *Guarde Civique*, a militia of 35,000 men for the suppression of internal disturbances. The army was based on the camp at Antwerp, fortified by Henri Brialmont during the 1860s, in order to retain communications with the open sea. On mobilization, the army was detailed to defend Antwerp and the fortresses at Liège, Namur, Termonde and Diest. In 1914, Belgium mobilized 208,000 men but the field army amounted to only 118,000 men in six infantry divisions and one cavalry division. By 1918, the field army had grown to 170,000 in twelve infantry divisions and a single cavalry division. The Belgian army suffered 40,000 casualties during the First World War compared to 60,000 Belgian civilian casualties.

In the interwar period, Belgium reduced her period of conscription to between 10 and 13 months and additional fortifications were built, particularly Eben-Emael and the Antwerp–Liège line along the Albert Canal. In 1939, the army had a total mobilized strength of 900,000 divided between 20 infantry divisions and two of motorized cavalry. However, after taking 14,000 casualties, the Belgian army surrendered to the Germans on 27 May 1940. During the Second World War, 130,000 Belgians were involved in the Resistance, 17,000 of whom lost their lives. A Belgian Liberation Brigade of 3,000 men was formed in Britain and fought in Normandy in 1944. There was also a Belgian commando unit and a parachute squadron.

The Belgian army was re-created in 1945 around the nucleus of the Liberation Brigade and the parachute and commando units. By 1949, the army, which had been reorganized along American lines, numbered 95,000, 70,000 of whom were assigned to NATO. In 1950, 150,000 men in three divisions served with NATO forces, but this had been reduced to 96,000 by 1974. A reinforced battalion of 3,000 men fought in Korea (1951–4) and Belgian commandos and paratroopers were involved in the war in the Congo (1960–4). By 1968, American and Canadian military aid had ended and Belgium began to re-equip with French, British (Scimitar light tanks) and German (Leopard tanks) armaments. In 1991, 62,700 men (including 27,850 conscripts on 12 months' service) served in the Belgian army, 4,550 in the navy and 18,200 in the air force, which flies mainly American aircraft. Brussels is the headquarters of NATO and 22,500 Belgian soldiers serve with the NATO forces in Germany.

A small coastal defence navy was set up in 1831 but was disbanded in 1922. It was reconstituted in 1940 and is now based in Antwerp and Zeebrugge. It has 40 ships, 30 of which are minesweepers, including four 2,000 ton frigates. The Belgian Military Medical Service (4,500 personnel) provides support to all three services. *See also* AUSTRIA; CHARLES THE BOLD; FORTIFICATION; FRANCE; INFANTRY; NASSAU; NETHERLANDS; SPAIN.

A. CORVISIER
JOHN CHILDS

FURTHER READING
M. P. Gutmann, *War and Rural Life in the Early Modern Low Countries* (Princeton, 1980); Charles Terlinde, *Histoire militaire des Belges* (Brussels, 1931); E. Wanty, *Le Milieu militaire belge de 1831 à 1914* (Brussels, 1957); P. Roman, 'The Belgian land forces', *RUSI and Brassey's Defence Yearbook, 1977–78* (London, 1977), pp. 125–43.

Belgrade, Battle of (16 August 1717) Following their success against the Russians in 1711 and the Venetians in 1714, the Turks declared war on Austria in 1716 hoping to recapture those parts of Hungary which they had lost by the Treaty of Carlowitz in 1699. The Austrian commander-in-chief, Prince Eugene of Savoy, wanted to attack Belgrade but the Turks under the Grand Vizier Silahdar Ali Pasha reached the city first and then advanced to besiege Peterwardein. Eugene intercepted and defeated the Turks before Peterwardein on 5 August 1716.

Eugene besieged Belgrade in 1717. It was a strong fortress situated in a triangle of land between the Danube and the Sava, and garrisoned by 30,000 Turks. There was every danger that a Turkish field army under the new Grand Vizier, Halil Pasha, would advance to the relief of Belgrade. The Austrians protected their camp with lines of circumvallation and contravallation. The siege progressed slowly. During the first week of August, the Grand Vizier's army of 120,000 camped on a high plateau and bombarded the Austrian positions. After two weeks, the Austrians were on the point of collapse as sickness spread through their ranks. Leaving 10,000 to watch Belgrade, Eugene surprised the Turkish camp with his remaining 60,000 men early on the morning of 16 August. The Turkish army, the majority of which was composed of untrained levies, fled in panic towards Nish. Belgrade surrendered seven days later. The Treaty of Passarowitz was signed on 21 July 1718. The Turks surrendered the Banat of Temesvár, Belgrade and most of Serbia to Austria although they regained the Morea from the Venetians. *See also* AUSTRIA; EUGENE OF SAVOY; FORTIFICATION; OTTOMAN TURKS; SIEGES; ZENTA.

JOHN CHILDS

FURTHER READING
Derek Mckay, *Prince Eugene of Savoy* (London, 1977); Nicholas Henderson, *Prince Eugen of Savoy* (London, 1964).

Bélidor, Bernard Forest de (1694 or 1698–1761) Although orphaned almost from birth, this famous ballistics pioneer, artillerist and engineer, the son of a French officer, received an excellent education from one of his father's friends, an artillery officer. At fifteen he was employed by Cassini and La Hire in extending the Paris meridian northwards and, on their enthusiastic recommendation, the regent, the Duke of Orléans, appointed Bélidor professor of mathematics at the artillery school of La Fère. His courses and demonstrations soon attracted many distinguished foreigners, among them military men, often of high rank, but his research also attracted controversy. Through experimentation he showed that the quantity of powder used in artillery pieces could be significantly reduced without affecting the projectile's range, a discovery which led to the much lighter, more mobile guns of Gribeauval, and through them to an even more important role for artillery on the battlefield. It was a discovery of great significance but ran contrary to received wisdom and Bélidor, having given offence to the Prince des Dombes, the master general of artillery, was dismissed from his post. Subsequently he attached himself to the Maréchal de Belle-Isle and, after active service during the War of the Austrian Succession, was ultimately rewarded, being made maréchal de camp and ending his career as royal censor for mathematical works and inspector general of sappers and of the arsenal of Paris. His publications reflected his interest in mathematics, mechanics, ballistics and fortifications, and included: *Sommaire d'un cours d'architecture militaire, civile et hydraulique* (1720), *Cours de Mathématiques* (1725), *La Science de ingénieurs dans la conduite des travaux de fortification et d'architecture civile* (1729–49), *Le Bombardier français ou nouvelle méthode de jeter des bombes avec précision* (1731), *Traité des fortifications* (1735) and *Architecture hydraulique* (4 vols, 1737–54). *See also* ARTILLERY; GRIBEAUVAL; ROBINS.

G. A. STEPPLER

FURTHER READING
H. Duchêne-Marullaz, 'Forest de Bélidor, Bernard', *Dictionnaire de Biographie Française* (Paris, 1979), xiv, cols 441–2; Demusset-Pathay and Durozoir, 'Bélidor, Bernard Forest de', *Biographie Universelle, Ancienne et Moderne* (Paris, 1843), iii, 552; Léon Sagnet, 'Bélidor, Bernard Forest de', *La Grande Encyclopédie* (Paris, 1888), vi, 25.

Belisarius, Flavius (d. 565) Belisarius was born at Germana in Dacia and served as a *buccellarius* (a military retainer or body-guard officially employed by military officers) of Justinian when he was Master of the Soldiers. As emperor, Justinian appointed Belisarius in 529 as Master of the Soldiers *per Orientem* and in 530 he won a victory against the Persians at Dara. But after suffering a defeat in 531 Belisarius was recalled to Constantinople where he assisted Justinian in putting down serious public disturbances which had threatened to force the emperor to flee his capital. However, his reputation depended mainly on his reconquest of Africa from the Vandals (533–4), for which he was awarded the first triumph celebrated by someone outside the imperial family since 19 BC, and the wars in Italy against the Ostrogothic kingdom during which he won back Rome in 536, where he then withstood a year's siege; however disagreements with another of Justinian's generals, Narses, led to the capture and destruction of Milan by the Ostrogoths. Confirmed as supreme commander, Belisarius proceeded with the reconquest and Ravenna surrendered in 539. This great military success nevertheless had no great political consequences, and apparently was not accompanied by any important tactical innovations. Belisarius was subsequently recalled to Constantinople, and for a time served again as Master of the Soldiers *per Orientem*, but returned to Italy once more in 544 in the face of renewed Ostrogothic activity and in 547 managed to reoccupy the now abandoned city of Rome despite having inadequate forces. Recalled to Constantinople in 549, he organized the successful defence of the city against the Cotrigur Huns in 559. Belisarius, who kept a magnificent household including at one time 7,000 *buccellarii*, died in 565. His campaigns are known in detail because of the historical writings of his secretary, Procopius. *See also* BYZANTIUM; NARSES.

B. CAMPBELL

FURTHER READING
A. H. M. Jones, *The Later Roman Empire, 284–602* (2 vols, Oxford, 1964), pp. 271–8, 287–90, 293.

Bernhardi, Friedrich von (1849–1930) A German general and military theorist who held the influential position of head of the historical section of the German General Staff. Bernhardi is best remembered for a book, *Germany and the Next War* (1912), which was published three years after his retirement. The book is a revision of the polemical sections of a two-volume work, *On War Today*, published earlier in 1912. The latter was a comprehensive analysis of the relationship between force and numbers and of the technical aspects of warfare. It criticized the strategic concepts of the Chief of the General Staff, von Schlieffen, and the lack of emphasis he accorded to moral factors. Bernhardi believed that von Schlieffen had been instrumental in his removal from the historical section. Ironically, it was the Social Darwinist justification for preventive war and an aggressive foreign policy advanced in *Germany and the Next War*, which was translated into all major languages, that was held to express the militaristic state of mind of the German General Staff in the years leading up to 1914. Before the Great War, Bernhardi also wrote two theoretical works on cavalry. He returned to active service between 1914 and 1918 as a corps commander. After the Armistice, he continued his historical research, notably engaging in a prolonged dispute with Hans Delbrück about the merits of the generalship of Frederick the Great. *See also* GERMANY; DELBRÜCK; SCHLIEFFEN.

A. CORVISIER
IAN F. W. BECKETT

FURTHER READING
E. Carrias, *La Pensée militaire allemande* (Paris, 1947); F. Fischer, *War of Illusions* (London, 1975); G. Ritter, *The Sword and the Sceptre* (4 vols, London, 1972), ii; B. F. Schulte, *Die Deutsche Armee, 1900–1914* (Düsseldorf, 1977).

Bevéziers, Battle of   *See* BEACHY HEAD

Bicocca, La (Lombardy), Battle of (27 April 1522)   La Bicocca was a battle that should never have taken place. The fact that it did, however, made it the most dramatic example of the tactical realities of the Italian wars of the early sixteenth century: the Spanish reliance on field entrenchments, the wilfulness of the Swiss, and the French inability to exploit manoeuvre to advantage. The outbreak of the great struggle between Francis I and Charles V in 1521 saw the French commander in Milan (which had been conquered after Marignano), Odet de Foix, Marshal de Lautrec, facing a similar Spanish (now Habsburg)–Papal coalition to that which Nemours had fought at Ravenna in 1512. With only a small army and with local sentiment hostile to France, Lautrec had lost most of the duchy by the end of the year. However, in the spring of 1522, having received both reinforcements from France and a contingent of 16,000 Swiss, together with a promise of assistance from Venice, Lautrec took the offensive. The allied commander, Prospero Calonna, now held the city of Milan. Lautrec intended to eject him by manoeuvre, but his control over the campaign was inhibited by the Swiss, who, because they had not been paid since their arrival in Italy, threatened that if he did not make an immediate attack they would return home. Calonna had entrenched his army in the park of the house of La Bicocca 3 miles from Milan, a position that incorporated a sunken road running along one of the boundaries of the park. The assault was delivered on the morning of 27 April by two large columns, each containing some 4,000 Swiss pikemen, who refused to wait even for an artillery bombardment. The carnage in the sunken road was extensive and when the Swiss finally retired they left some 3,000 dead behind them. Lautrec had also sent a small cavalry force to sweep round the enemy. This force was successful in reaching Calonna's camp, but was not strong enough to make a difference and Lautrec declined to make a further frontal attack. On the 30th, their pay still not having arrived, the Swiss departed, and without them Lautrec considered his army too weak to continue the campaign. La Bicocca thus became another victory for Spanish tactics, but only thanks to the Swiss. It confirmed the lesson of Marignano and marked the final end of the legend of Swiss invincibility. It also supplied Machiavelli and other contemporary critics of the employment of mercenaries with vivid proof of the validity of their arguments. *See also* INFANTRY; MACHIAVELLI; MARIGNANO; RAVENNA; SWITZERLAND.

SIMON ADAMS

FURTHER READING
C. Oman, *A History of the Art of War in the Sixteenth Century* (London, 1937), pp. 172–85; R. J. Knecht, *Francis I* (Cambridge, 1982), pp. 113–15.

Billeting Billeting – the lodging of soldiers on civilians – did not become an important issue until the development of national standing armies in Western Europe during the seventeenth century. Simple and primitive governments which lacked the revenues and the organization to cater for their new armed forces could not provide either the accommodation or the supplies to house their troops centrally. All over the continent, soldiers were quartered in private houses, public houses, stables and empty buildings, leading to a loss of discipline and of unit cohesion. In order to reduce the burden on the population, the troops were quartered in small groups, often no more than three or four men, in towns and villages and moved to new billets at intervals which varied between 6 and 24 months. This prevented unhealthy liaisons between the military and the civil and ensured that the resources of a particular area were not permanently depleted. The life of the early modern soldier was itinerant. The artillery and the engineers were the first branches to enjoy more permanent stations, basing themselves close to their military academies or training establishments. Although royal guards accompanied their sovereigns on their travels, these formations tended to be located in the capital cities by the end of the seventeenth century. This was certainly the case in Paris and London by 1700. Line infantry tended to be housed in towns as 'garrisons' while the cavalry found quarters in villages and agricultural districts in order to feed their horses. In England, the foot were stationed in the main ports and 'garrison towns': Berwick-on-Tweed, Hull,

Chatham and Rochester, London, Portsmouth, the Isle of Wight, Plymouth, Chester and Carlisle. The cavalry were lodged in the Home counties, the Midlands and East Anglia. A similar pattern was followed in France with the infantry massed in the fortress towns of the eastern and north-eastern frontiers between Dunkirk and Briançon and the cavalry dispersed throughout the interior of the kingdom.

Billeting first became an issue in 1628 when the Petition of Right claimed that the quartering of troops on civilians, without their consent, was illegal. The Petition clearly implied that the government had been deliberately billeting soldiers on civilians in order to enforce the payment of unpopular taxation, a constant theme throughout the seventeenth and eighteenth centuries. 'Free quarter', whereby soldiers did not pay for their food and lodging but gave the householder a receipt which he could later reclaim from the Treasury, was the norm during the English Civil War. However, there was an enormous disparity between the technicalities of the regulations and the reality and, in effect, 'free quarter' was a precise description. In 1679, the Disbandment Act declared it illegal for soldiers to be billeted on civilians without their consent, and this was reinforced by the Mutiny Act 1689. These two statutes set the pattern for the eighteenth century. Troops could only be lodged in public houses and had to pay their bills in full before departure. After 1697, the Mutiny Act allowed innkeepers to pay infantrymen 4d a day and cavalrymen 6d for the privilege of not providing them with food. The soldiers still had to lodge in the public house but they were paid to provide their own provisions. Some barracks did exist, particularly in the main fortresses – Dover Castle, Portsmouth, Hull and Berwick – but they were insufficient to house more than a fraction of the numbers. Barracks were built in Ireland in the aftermath of the Jacobite Wars but they were intended as much as strong-points to control the country as accommodation for the troops. A similar development occurred in the Highlands of Scotland after Culloden in 1746. Spurred by the indiscipline, the lack of training facilities and the poor civil–military relations engendered by the billeting system, the British army was gradually moved into municipal barracks between 1792 and 1858, a process which could not have occurred without a richer and more proficient government. Cardwell's Army Reforms of 1870 fixed all regiments to a specific depot complete with barracks. Only with the mass conscription armies of 1914–18 and 1939–45 has billeting reappeared in Great Britain.

The armies of Brandenburg-Prussia and Austria-Hungary were mainly lodged with civilians until after the Seven Years' War when both states gradually transferred their soldiers into barracks. In both these countries, the cantonal method of recruiting greatly lessened the problem of accommodating soldiers. Sweden's *Indelningsverket* placed the soldier firmly within society and made his accommodation, employment and supply the responsibility of civilians. In France there were two methods of billeting. Along the main military routes leading from central France to her frontiers, and laterally along those borders, was a series of military staging posts each one march apart. These were the regular ports of call of soldiers travelling to, along and from the frontiers. Money was given to these towns and villages to provide lodging for the troops; needless to say, the money was rarely sufficient to meet the costs. Away from the military roads, communities which quartered soldiers were permitted to deduct the costs from the municipal taxes due to the government. This was a protracted affair and generally left the town or village out of pocket. Gradually, those communities liable to billeting paid a tax which was then distributed to the soldiers who paid for their quarters in cash. Some towns used this tax to build barracks or to purchase old property which could house soldiers and horses. By the end of the eighteenth century, most of the French army was accommodated in barracks, and regiments became fixed in their locations.

The increase of conscripts during the nineteenth century and the practice of locating barracks in towns were a possible factor in the depopulation of the French countryside. In 1906, 8 per cent of Breton labourers who had been conscripted from the countryside and accommodated in municipal barracks either remained in the town after their discharge or returned to it shortly afterwards. More than a third of the countrymen who had experienced the delights of Paris, Lyons and Marseilles as soldiers did not want to go home after discharge. The numbering of houses in streets arose from the needs of the billeting officer and the quartermaster; it was introduced in France in 1768 and Austria-Hungary in 1781.

Although many of the fortifications of the twentieth century have continued Vauban's practice of including barracks for the troops – Douaumont and the Verdun forts, the Maginot Line and the Siegfried Line – barracks have now mostly moved away from towns into specialized military camps, e.g. Aldershot in England or Mourmelon in France. This has been necessitated by the rising cost of urban land, the need for armies to exercise and train over huge stretches of terrain and the requirement for large premises for the instruction of conscripts.

The British army has moved to centres for infantry, artillery and armour on Salisbury Plain, in the Brecklands in Norfolk, in Northumberland, in Wales and in Essex. So vast has the military need for land become that it has crossed swords with the modern movements towards ecology and the protection of the environment. As a result, the British army now undertakes some of its training in Canada and California. *See also* BARRACKS; CAMPS; CITADELS; GARRISONS; PROPERTY OWNED BY THE MILITARY; SOLDIERS AND SOCIETY; STAGING POSTS.

JOHN CHILDS
J. CHAGNIOT

FURTHER READING
André Corvisier, *Armies and Societies in Europe, 1494–1789* (Bloomington, Ind., 1979); John Childs, *Armies and Warfare in Europe, 1648–1789* (Manchester, 1982); Reginald Hargreaves, 'Bivouacs, billets and barracks', *Army Quarterly*, lxxxv (1963), pp. 231–42.

Biological warfare *See* CHEMICAL AND BIOLOGICAL WARFARE

Black Africa (pre-colonial) The effects of military activity were felt throughout most aspects of daily life in pre-colonial Black Africa. The size of the geographical area, and the diversity of races and their socio-political structures, make it difficult for us to form an overall impression. In view of the size of this field and the complexity of the questions raised within it, the paucity of our sources and of the research under-taken soon becomes apparent.

Information comes primarily from travellers' tales, missionaries' accounts and the reports of soldiers engaged in colonial campaigns or struggles against local resist-ance movements. Such information is frag-mentary and comparisons are difficult to make on account of the diversity of the operations, the theatres of war and the number of different periods involved. These accounts are particularly un-satisfactory in that they frequently describe situations which had already been modified by the introduction of new weapons and the efforts of local chiefs to adapt, with varying degrees of success, to the conditions im-posed by the move from inter-tribal to anti-European struggles.

Three major types of military organiza-tion can be distinguished in the vast territ-ory of Africa. In traditional tribal societies, war does not seem to have been deified except by the inhabitants of Benin, who, in Ogun, honoured the gods of battle and of iron. Conflicts were determined in terms of a hierarchical order: confrontations within the tribe, internal combat between tribes of the same ethnic group (feuds) and external hostilities. Their object was less to make territorial conquests than to acquire cattle or slaves. There was often a close relationship between hunting and fighting. Both served as tests of manhood (e.g. the *Bétés* of the Ivory Coast) and were pre-pared for by common or similar initiation rites.

Cavalry was used in the Sudan and the Sahel where conditions were suitable for horses. Thus, in Central Africa, Fulah incursions were examples of genuine small armies in action. These were composed of a core of Fulah horsemen, together with mercenaries and slaves who had been captured young and trained in combat. These were the raids against which threatened tribes defended themselves by lines of lookouts, by retreating deep into the forests or by tributes paid in slaves. In the equatorial regions where sleeping sick-ness in animals was endemic, there were no war horses.

In ethnic societies, the nature of combat was different, centring here on territorial issues. This made for a different organiza-tion of troops: fully fledged armies, in some cases numbering up to 50,000 soldiers, were formed in some places. These military states appeared particularly in West and Central Africa (Luanda and Rwanda). The logical conclusion of this process was the appearance of the army nation, entirely organized around a military structure and composed of tribal regiments, recruited on a regional basis, and the king's regiments, organized according to age group.

As in the West, but under the influence of other factors (local rise in the birth rate), a powerful 'militarist, expansionist, predat-ory and parasitic' state was formed in Natal, in the south-eastern extremity of the sav-annah, at the beginning of the nineteenth century: the Zulu empire, formed by the amalgamation of several small independent communities. The strength of these troops derived from their fighting spirit, the charis-matic influence and personality of their leader, and also the possibility of both importing firearms and being able to service these new weapons by means of a nascent 'industry', which encouraged the develop-ment of village furnaces. A vast empire was thus formed by uniting a number of differ-ent groups under the banner of a bold warrior chieftain.

The same process was perhaps even more clearly evident in Black Islamic societies. In the Islamic world, particularly in West Africa, where the Empire of Samory Touré appeared, the traditional principles of Islamic armies, inspired by the belief in conquest as a sacred duty (*Jihad*), were applied. The work of Person provides a particularly good study of this form of organization in Islamic Africa. The troops of the Mahdi in eastern Sudan also pro-vided evidence of this synthesis of traditional tribal forces and Moslem military principles. The Mahdi's troops were split up into three large divisions, according to their ethnic origins: the black banner, the main force, formed of western Baggara nomads; the green banner, formed of Baggara tribesmen from Kordofan and the White Nile; and the red banner, recruited from among the Awlad-al-Balad. The distribution of the troops into five corps, and the use of a thrice repeated cavalry charge as an attacking strategy, derive essentially from the Islamic tradition.

The traditional offensive weapons used were the iron throwing knife (*Oubangui*) with wickerwork, plant fibre or ivory decoration, and wooden or iron clubs and bludgeons.

The cutting weapons ranged from the knife and dagger (Congo, Gabon, Chad) to the sabre (Dahomey, Ivory Coast) and included the assegai, a weapon with a single or multiple blade which, like arrows for bows, came in many different forms. The exceptional variety of forms and decoration for weapons was a result of the great range of functions for which they were used (battles, sacrifices, parades, hunting, magic). It is sometimes difficult to distinguish which of an object's functions – religious, military or aesthetic – represents its principal use. The defensive weapons used were shields, armour and coats of mail, often influenced by European techniques. Fortifications reflected both the nature of the civilization which constructed them and the materials available.

Military architecture was most often rather basic, consisting of ditches and ramparts made of earth and piled stones or stakes bound together. Sometimes defensive corps guarded the outskirts of a village (e.g. the Fang people).

Tata were fortified constructions. A detailed description of them has been given by Binger (in particular those of Niale and Sikasso) and Meillassoux has provided details of their structures. Wooden fortifications (*Diassa*) were more simple, and thorn and brushwood hedges (*Zaribas*) still more so.

Firearms were introduced at the end of the sixteenth century and imports increased steadily, especially from the eighteenth century onwards with missile weapons and in the nineteenth century with arms for barter, provided by the Belgians, the English and the French factory at Châtellerault which specialized in their manufacture. A single caravan going from Zanzibar to Masailand in 1847 carried more than 1,000 rifles. Sheikh Omar of Bornu possessed 2,000 rifles in 1866, half for his infantry, half for his cavalry. There are many examples of this kind. The introduction of firearms changed the nature of traditional armies, but the degree to which this occurred varied considerably from one region to another as a result of geographical conditions, particularly the greater or lesser proximity of European influence.

From an early date, the coastal regions in both East and West received abundant supplies of rifles and ammunition. These coastal states endeavoured to limit the spread of these arms, which gave them political independence and a position as intermediaries, to the interior. The control of this supply was one of the motives for the nineteenth-century Ashanti wars.

By the end of the nineteenth century, Africa was beginning to be swamped by arms supplies. From this time, several hundred thousand small firearms were brought in each year. In 1888, an English report estimated that there were more than 100,000 imports of this type on the east coast of Africa to the north of Mozambique alone.

The issue of arms smuggling fills boxes of correspondence in the archives. It was discussed at international conferences (Berlin 1885 and Brussels 1890) and its prohibition was mocked as often as it was respected.

The introduction of new weapons transformed traditional battle order. Infantries armed with rifles advanced on the enemy in closed ranks in a continuous line in order to increase the impact of their firepower and to be able more easily to recover their arms when losses were incurred. The uneven dissemination of these weapons influenced the distribution of power and created new regional balances. However, the relative modernity of African troops remained rather illusory where the economic and social base had remained archaic. *See also* COLONIAL TROOPS; COLONIAL WARS.

J.-L. MIÈGE

C. DUBOIS

FURTHER READING
Guerres de lignage et guerres d'état en Afrique, eds J. Bazin and E. Terray (Paris, 1980); M. R. Davie, *La Guerre dans les sociétés primitives* (Paris 1931); D. R. Headrich, *The Tools of Empire* (Oxford, 1981); *Journal of African History*, special edition, xii (1971); I. B. Kake, *Les Armées traditionelles de l'Afrique noire* (Libreville, 1980); A. S. Kanya-Forstner, *The Conquest of the Western Sudan* (Cambridge, 1969); J. Kugan, *The Ashanti Campaign* (London, 1967); R. Pankhurst, *An Introduction to the History of the Ethiopian Army* (Gembot, 1967); J. D. Omer Cooper, *The Zulu Aftermath* (London, 1970); *West African Resistance: military response to colonial occupation*, ed. M. Crowder (London, 1971); A. Isaacman, *The Tradition of Resistance in Mozambique: anti-colonial activity in the Zambezi Valley, 1850–1861* (Berkeley, 1976); *Protest and Power in Black Africa*, eds R. I. Rotbery and A. A. Mazrni (Oxford, 1970).

Black Prince *See* EDWARD, PRINCE OF WALES

Blade weapons The most ancient blade weapons date, in all probability, from the mesolithic era, when flint or obsidian daggers were fashioned. Some archaeologists have noted, in this connection, that flint mining (in England and Belgium) was perhaps one of the most ancient industries of Western Europe. During the period from 5000 to 3000 BC, the first experiments with bronze alloys seem to have been undertaken. From the third millennium to the Roman era bronze weapons predominated – except among the Hittites, who, towards the middle of the second millennium, discovered the more subtle possibilities of iron. The knowledge of this 'state-of-the-art technology' enabled them to maintain their supremacy over a large part of Asia Minor for several centuries. The Greeks, who knew of the existence of iron weapons, preferred bronze. The presence of daggers with iron blades and bronze handles in the Hallstatt tombs should also be mentioned here.

The Greek *xiphos* was a very short sword (about 20 in long); the *machaira* was even shorter. The longer *spathe* could be as long as 30 in. The *parazonion*, which became the Roman *parazonium* – the centurion's weapon – was a sort of elongated dagger (of about 15 in). One could add many other items to the list, revealing a great diversity of forms and influences. But if the form of these arms is known, the reasons which led to their being forged in a particular way are much less clear. This aspect of blade weapons deserves to be the subject of new research. One thing is certain: a knowledge of these weapons cannot be dissociated from a knowledge of combat by direct physical contact, of which hand-to-hand combat is the most striking expression.

The Romans made widespread use of iron, while essentially retaining the shape of Greek weapons. Their soldiers were equipped with the *gladius* or the *ligula* (shaped like an elongated tongue). The diversity of sword lengths seems to indicate that the Graeco-Roman world particularly took into account the height of their fighting men and that their weapons were, in a sense, 'made to measure'. It is well known that *hoplites* received extensive training in individual combat; the existence of weapons rooms where Roman legionaries were trained by former gladiators also seems to be generally accepted.

Arab and Asian blade weapons often have a characteristic curved form: daggers in the shape of billhooks, scimitars, yataghans, etc. It seems that striking with a horizontal blade (or chopping motion) was much more widespread among peoples using these weapons than it was in the Mediterranean world. On Trajan's Column a battle between Roman legionaries and Dacians is depicted in which the Dacians are slicing with their weapons while the Romans are stabbing with the points of their blades. Vegetius endorses the effectiveness of stabbing, where the wounds inflicted are deeper and reach the vital organs more easily than slicing blows, but he observes that stabbing requires greater coolness and training than the more primitive method. The technique for using the curved dagger, which has been retained right into the twentieth century – notably in Morocco – involves seeking to strike an upward blow which opens the opponent's abdomen. The scimitar, used by the Mamluks at the Battle of the Pyramids (1798), had a blade as sharp as a razor. Its saw-like shape enabled a horseman who struck his opponent's shoulder to cut through bone and penetrate right to his heart.

The Middle Ages took over the designs of the Ancient World, though these were modified and very elaborate improvements were made to hilts and handles, which became 'functional' parts of the weapon. Some forms, which reached perfection in their simplicity, like that of the Merovingian dagger, remained practically unchanged for more than eight centuries. Among the innovations of the late Middle Ages and the Renaissance, we should note: (1) a lengthening of the sword, which could now be as long as 3 ft 6 in and more. The increased weight gave greater effectiveness to sideways blows. It could also be used on horseback when the lance was broken. Swiss warriors and their German rivals, the *Landsknechte*, used two-handed swords which could be whirled around like the halberd; (2) the development of pliability in weapons, which allowed the art of fencing to develop to the full. The advances made by swordsmiths (especially at Toledo) enabled them to obtain an interior tension between the core of the blade and its outer casing, which gave it improved elasticity and resistance.

The short pike, which was both a hand weapon and a missile, appeared in very ancient times. It was part of the equipment of the light infantry and cavalry of the armies of the Ancient East, the Persians and the Greeks. The Romans also used the *pilum*, a heavy missile weapon able to penetrate light shields. The long pike was the weapon of heavy infantry. It was issued to the Macedonian phalanx. It was a shock weapon which a group of soldiers could use at charging pace and with which they could also form defensive 'hedgehogs', but this formation was not very manoeuvrable. Thanks to their strength and skill, the Swiss – soon followed by the German *Landsknechte* – brought the pike back into use. It was used by foot soldiers in close formation in the fifteenth century. When the musket became widespread, the pikeman was regarded as the protector of the musketeer while he reloaded his weapon. In the seventeenth century pikemen wore a breastplate, wedged their pikes against their right foot and held them in their left hand freeing their right hand to use a sword. During the Thirty Years' War, the ratio was two pikemen to every musketeer. The pike was regarded as the noble weapon of the infantry and the pikeman received higher pay than the musketeer or fusilier. The pursuit of increased firepower inevitably numbered the days of the pike, but it did not disappear until the bayonet enabled blade weapons to be incorporated into firearms. By contrast, among mounted troops, the lance, which had been lengthened and was no longer a missile weapon, continued to be issued to a part of the heavy cavalry. There were still lancers in the Polish army in 1939.

It was during the Renaissance that the blade weapon reached the highest point of its development, as is attested by the exceptional pieces that are preserved in the royal armouries. That development coincided with the tactical supremacy of impact or shock, which was regarded as the decisive element in combat. When the use of firearms came to be substituted – at least in part – for 'shock weapons', blade weapons were relegated to a secondary position (except in the cavalry, where the use of the sabre became widespread from the end of the seventeenth century onwards).

A new development revived the use of blades, however, when, at the end of the seventeenth century, a complement for firearms was discovered in the form of the socket bayonet (the original 'plug' bayonets were stuck into the gun-barrel by the hilt and thus made it impossible to fire). The invention of this simple weapon, which was particularly needed when poor weather rendered firearms unusable, made the infantry assault very effective. From the eighteenth century to our own day, the bayonet has thus been the main blade weapon. In one last development, in the Warsaw Pact forces, by means of an aperture made in the blade which fits into a pivot mounted on a special sheath, it has been turned into a device for cutting through barbed wire. In most of the wars of the contemporary period, we find battles in which there has been hand-to-hand knife fighting. During the Second World War, men sent on missions by the SOE (Special Operations Executive) were trained by Gurkhas (who always carry a knife) in the discipline of silent killing. Currently, such training is provided for the commando units in most armies. Here we see the blade weapon in its time-honoured function, as an instrument that provides an extension of man's own strength, whether it be called a cutlass, fauchard, dagger, kris or Malay dagger, *main gauche*, bayonet or trench knife. Paradoxically, we can see that this primitive arm takes its place alongside the most sophisticated weaponry with which modern armies are equipped. *See also* ARMOUR; CAVALRY; FIREARMS; INFANTRY; WEAPONS.

D. REICHEL

FURTHER READING
A. Snodgrass, *Arms and Armour of the Greeks* (London, 1982); G. C. Stone, *A Glossary of the Construction, Decoration and Use of Arms and Armour* (New York, 1961); F. Wilkinson, *Edged Weapons* (London, 1970).

Blenheim, Battle of (13 August 1704)   On 20 September 1703, Villars and the Elector Maximilian II Emmanuel of Bavaria (1679–1726) defeated the Imperialists under Count Styrum (d. 1704) at Höchstädt on the Danube. While the Comte de Tallard (1652–1728) observed the Imperial forces under the Margrave of Baden (1655–1707) in the Lines of Stollhofen (between the Rhine and the Black Forest, 10 miles north of Strasbourg), he also managed to capture Breisach and Landau, thus securing communications across the Rhine between France and her ally,

Bavaria. With the Holy Roman Emperor, Leopold I (1658–1705) distracted by the Rákóczi Revolt in Hungary and Prince Eugene of Savoy struggling to hold the Duc de Vendôme (1654–1712) in northern Italy, Villars urged the Elector of Bavaria to invade Austria and attack Vienna. Instead, he turned south into the Tyrol where his design to link up with Vendôme ended in ignominious failure.

Although France had lost one chance to knock Austria out of the War of the Spanish Succession in 1703, the situation appeared equally promising in 1704 although the decision of Victor Amadeus II of Savoy (1675–1730) to join the Grand Alliance brought an improvement in the Imperial position in northern Italy. To forestall a Franco-Bavarian invasion of Austria, which would have initiated the collapse of the Grand Alliance against France, the Duke of Marlborough decided to march the majority of the Anglo-Dutch army (40,000 men) from the Netherlands to Bavaria. Dutch fears that the French under Villeroi (1644–1730) would invade the Netherlands during his absence were allayed by the facts that Villeroi had orders from Louis XIV to follow Marlborough wherever he ventured and that Marlborough disguised the initial stages of his strategic march through Germany as a movement towards the Moselle. Marlborough departed from Bedburg, 20 miles to the north-west of Cologne, on 20 May. In the meantime, the Elector of Bavaria and Marsin (1656–1706), who had replaced Villars, were preparing to attack Austria along the line of the Danube with 50,000 men until news of Marlborough's southward movement necessarily placed French operations in abeyance.

Marlborough's march to Coblenz, over the Rhine to Mainz and on through Heidelberg to the Danube, was a considerable feat of logistics. He met Prince Eugene on 10 June at Mundelsheim where they agreed that Prince Eugene would observe Villeroi to prevent him from crossing the Rhine to intervene in Bavaria. On 2 July Marlborough seized the Danube bridging point of Donauwörth by storming the fortified heights of the Schellenberg. For a month, in conjunction with the Imperial forces under Baden, he proceeded to devastate the Bavarian countryside in an effort to bring the Elector and Marsin to battle. However, on 5 August, Tallard, who had led his corps through the Black Forest, joined the Elector and Marsin at Biberach south of Ulm. Realizing that Marlborough would be heavily outnumbered, Eugene left a covering screen to observe Villeroi and marched rapidly to join Marlborough and Baden at Schrobenhausen. Fortunately, Villeroi did not go on the offensive. The Franco-Bavarians decided to cross the Danube and attack Eugene's exposed Imperial army at Höchstädt, clearly not appreciating the close liaison between Marlborough and Eugene. Should this fail, they intended to march along the Danube to Donauwörth and threaten Marlborough's northward communications, a manoeuvre which would probably oblige him to evacuate Bavaria. Marlborough had reached Rain on 10 August when he received intelligence from Eugene that the Franco-Bavarians had crossed the Danube at Lauingen and were encamping around Höchstädt. Marlborough and Eugene resolved to attack.

The Battle of Blenheim (an Anglicization of Blindheim) was fought between two confederate armies: the Franco-Bavarian under Tallard, Marsin and the Elector (60,000 men), and the combination of Eugene's Imperial troops and Marlborough's English force, two-thirds of which was composed of German and Danish regiments (56,000 men). Baden had been dispatched on 9 August with 20,000 troops to besiege Ingolstadt. Advancing in nine columns, the Allied army spent the morning of 13 August deploying under cover of a cannonade. Tallard, who had not expected a battle, advanced from his camp to take up a position with the right resting on the fortified village of Blindheim (Blenheim) on the Danube and the left defended by woods and the village of Lutzingen. In the centre, at the junction of Tallard's command and that of the Elector and Marsin, was the village of Oberglau. Marlborough and Eugene had no master-

plan. Eugene marched his troops to the right to oppose Marsin and the Elector, while Marlborough stood opposite Tallard in the centre and left.

While Lord John Cutts (1661–1707) attacked the village of Blindheim forcing the French to commit more and more infantry to its defence, Marlborough led his centre and right across the Nebel stream despite French cannon fire. Marlborough's attempt to seize the village of Oberglau, the hinge of both the French and the Allied positions, failed and offered Tallard a fleeting chance to split Marlborough from Eugene and roll up the Allied lines. An Imperial cavalry charge restored the situation and sealed off Oberglau. Having poured infantry into Blindheim and Oberglau, Tallard's centre was now fatally weakened. To redeem the situation, he launched the mass of his cavalry against the Allied centre and left. However, Marlborough had arrayed his troops, virtually all across the Nebel by this time, in a unique formation – two lines of infantry sandwiched between two lines of cavalry. As the French horse charged down, the Allied cavalry retired between the intervals in the infantry line enabling the musketeers and battalion guns to halt the enemy horsemen. His last reserves committed, Tallard was unable to resist the Allied cavalry's counter-charge, which swept the French horse from the field before driving the remnants of his command towards the Danube. The 10,000 foot defending Blindheim held out for a while longer before capitulating. The Elector and Marsin, who had fought a furious duel with Eugene, withdrew their troops in better order towards Mörslingen. The Franco-Bavarians lost 38,000 men, many taken prisoner, while the Allied casualties amounted to 12,000; 43 per cent of the soldiers engaged in the battle had been killed, wounded or captured.

Until the final push by the Allied cavalry, the battle had been closely contested. Marlborough and Eugene, without a preconceived plan of battle, had relied upon the exploitation of Tallard's mistakes, of which there were several. In the first place, he had been taken by surprise and forced to deploy straight from camp into line of battle with the result that his troops had fought as two separate armies instead of in a combined whole. Another consequence of this hasty deployment was that the central pivotal position around Oberglau was occupied by cavalry rather than infantry. In addition, Tallard had deployed half a mile to the west of the Nebel instead of close to its bank. No doubt the intention had been to invite Marlborough to cross the stream before attacking him in the flank from Blindheim and Oberglau to press him back against the obstacle of the stream in his rear. Actually, Tallard's deployment permitted Marlborough to cross the stream, once he had secured his flanks at Blindheim and Oberglau, and form a bridgehead. Finally, Tallard allowed the bulk of his infantry to be sucked into the struggles for Blindheim and Oberglau; as a result, his defeated cavalry had no infantry support behind which to shelter and were, accordingly, swept from the field. The French advantage in artillery, not yet preponderant in battle, made no difference to the outcome.

Marlborough won because he was the more skilful and adaptable general. This was clearly demonstrated in Marlborough's unusual deployment of his horse and foot as well as in his crucial interventions around Blindheim and Oberglau. Marlborough commanded all his forces throughout the action; Tallard, partly because of his very short sight, was not consistently in personal control. The superior quality of the British and Allied cavalry was also vital. Marlborough and Eugene had demonstrated, as they were to do again at Oudenarde in 1708, that divided command and multinational armies could succeed provided that the leadership was united and co-operative. Blenheim was probably the most important land action of the War of the Spanish Succession although it had been Marlborough's strategic march towards Coblenz which had paralysed French plans for the invasion of Austria rather than the actual battle. It was the manoeuvre which had proved strategically decisive; the battle served as a confirmation. *See also* DENAIN; EUGENE OF SAVOY; MALPLAQUET; MARLBOROUGH; RAMILLIES; VILLARS.

JOHN CHILDS

FURTHER READING
C. T. Atkinson, *Marlborough and the Rise of the British Army* (London, 1921); Frank Taylor, *The Wars of Marlborough* (2 vols, Oxford, 1921); D. G. Chandler, *Marlborough as Military Commander* (London, 1973); Correlli Barnett, *Marlborough* (London, 1974).

Bloch, Jan (1836–1902) Sometimes referred to as Ivan or Jean, Jan Bloch was a Polish Jew whose entrepreneurial skills earned him the title of the 'King of Polish Railways'. A convinced pacifist, Bloch's financial expertise and familiarity with science and technology led him to conclude that states would be unable to sustain the economic consequences of mass modern warfare. Equally, the application of technology on the battlefield would have horrific results, creating an 'impassable zone of fire' and bringing attritional stalemate. Indeed, although some of Bloch's predictions were no more realistic than those of some other contemporary futurologists, his vivid description of that attritional stalemate did closely resemble what was to occur on the Western Front during the Great War, and is frequently quoted. Originally published in Polish in 1897, the six volumes of Bloch's military theories, collectively entitled *The War of the Future in its Technical, Economic and Political Aspects*, appeared in Russian in 1898 and in French and German editions in 1900. An English translation of the last volume was published in 1899 as *Is War Impossible?* Though Bloch had probably benefited from the co-operation of Russian soldiers such as General Puzyrevskii and Lieutenant Colonel Gulevich, his work had little impact on military theorists although it did apparently encourage Tsar Nicholas II to urge the convening of the Hague conference of 1899. *See also* DELBRÜCK; DISARMAMENT; INFANTRY; LAWS OF WAR; LOSSES OF LIFE.

IAN F. W. BECKETT

FURTHER READING
J. F. C. Fuller, *The Conduct of War, 1789–1961*

(London 1961); W. Pintner, 'Russian military thought', and M. Howard, 'The doctrine of the offensive', in *Makers of Modern Strategy*, ed. Peter Paret (Princeton, 1986), pp. 354–75, 510–26.

Blockades The term 'blocus fortin' appears in French during the sixteenth century to refer to the investment of a fortified place (*see* SIEGES). The use of the English word 'blockade' is first recorded by the *Oxford English Dictionary* in 1680. Under the *ancien régime*, there were two forms of blockade, the military and the civil, which soon grew indistinguishable.

The military blockading of France by Britain, aimed at the preservation of the natural separation of the French Mediterranean and Atlantic fleets to prevent their junction. This was achieved through a naval blockade of the great military ports, especially Brest. The restricted range of seventeenth-century warships limited the value of this tactic; only the Channel ports during the Nine Years' War (1688–97) and the War of the Spanish Succession (1702–14) were subjected to a blockade that was in any way effective. When, from the middle of the eighteenth century, relatively homogeneous fleets capable of staying at sea for many months appeared, the British blockade was intensified and extended to cover the entirety of the French and Spanish coasts, a task rendered easier by the possession of bases in Portugal and at Gibraltar and Minorca. Three factors, however, complicated the situation. First, military blockade presupposes empirical medical knowledge of how to combat the threat of scurvy, prevalent on long periods of sea service; second, it requires sophisticated logistical planning; and third, it needs sufficient finance. The first problem was solved by adopting, at the suggestion of Admiral Sir Edward Hawke, supply squadrons which conveyed fresh meat and vegetables to the blockading ships every two or three weeks. Later, lemon juice (the effectiveness of which had been known for many years but which loses its beneficent properties quickly unless it is mixed with navy rum, the alcohol in which preserves the vitamin C) was added, again by a process of trial and error, to the arsenal of anti-scorbutics (Nelson). In Napoleon's defeat by the British, lemon juice from Sicily played no small part. Blockade was greatly assisted by the fact that France possessed very few military ports with sufficient depth of water to accommodate capital ships – Brest, Toulon and, to a lesser extent, Rochefort.

The commercial blockade only assumed its true legal status, as understood in the nineteenth century, at a very late stage in history. In theory, international customary law upheld the freedom of the seas, but this was pure illusion. Corsairs and privateers hunted down the enemy's merchant ships, as did national fleets. The French responded to the *de facto* British blockade during the wars of the eighteenth century by relying on the merchant shipping of neutral countries (the Hanseatic towns of Hamburg and Lübeck, Portugal, Sweden, Denmark-Norway, and, when it was possible, Spain and the Dutch Republic). The Royal Navy showed increasing interest in monitoring this neutral shipping as it searched for 'war contraband' (weapons, ammunition, etc.). However, the definition of 'war contraband' rapidly expanded and came to include all supplies that an army and, more particularly, a navy, might require, such as timber from the Baltic, pitch, tar, hemp and iron. The French navy was soon paralysed. Since the bulk of these commodities originated from the Baltic littoral, trade wars resulted. Neutrals falsified their bills of lading enabling some 'naval munitions' to continue to reach French dockyards, but there was a growing need to rely on coastal convoys which 'flea hopped' under constant protection from the coast. These convoys did not always manage to get through, even under Napoleon (except in the summer months), leading to a mere trickle of supplies, delays, shortages and rising prices. All of these factors brought the French dockyards close to a standstill. The British blockade was combined with a skilful purchasing policy. In Russia and Scandinavia, the agents of the Royal Navy bought the best lots and dictated their price, leaving French buyers only the poorer quality lots at higher prices.

Though it operated indirectly, the blockade was a highly effective weapon and one of its main consequences was to increase the maintenance and ship construction costs of the French navy. Spain partially escaped blockade since one third of its ships of the line were built at Havana, using timber from the tropics. The interception of food convoys was not a component part of the blockade but frequently occurred as any enemy vessel was regarded as a legitimate target. There were some bitter battles around wheat convoys under Louis XIV and during the Revolutionary and Napoleonic Wars.

The financial effectiveness of the blockade was, however, very limited before 1780. It was not until that year, and only then after heated debates in Parliament, that London insurance companies were forbidden to sell policies on French merchant vessels. Until 1789, therefore, French commerce was able to tolerate its financial losses; after each war with Great Britain (1742–8; 1756–63; 1777–83) the number of French merchant ships rapidly returned to the pre-war level as though nothing had happened. This state of affairs changed, however, with the intensification of the naval war after 1792 and when the Directory prefigured the Napoleonic 'Continental System' (Berlin Decree of 1806 and Milan Decree of 1807). Although technically a form of blockade, this was a wide-ranging policy employed as a substitute for naval action, which properly belongs to the field of grand strategy and national politics.

The results of the enormous enterprise of the 'Continental System' were ambiguous. Admittedly, immediately after the Peace of Tilsit (1807), and even more effectively in 1810–11, Napoleon succeeded in ranging most of the continental states in a trade embargo against Britain – the French Empire itself; its subject states, such as the Netherlands, Denmark and Naples; the conquered states of Prussia and Austria; and countries with which France had recently become allied, like Russia and Sweden. Despite some stern ripostes, including a counter-prohibition of trade, the conquest of the Latin American and Far Eastern markets and the establishment of an extensive contraband operation from depots at Heligoland, Bornholm, Lissa and Malta, Great Britain felt the effects of the blockade. Exports collapsed, dropping from 61 million metric tons in 1810 to 43 million in 1811. The Baltic trade all but ceased. Many traders were bankrupted and riots broke out. However, this adverse situation proved to be serious rather than desperate; even when reduced to 43 million tons exports were still well above the 27 million at which they had stood in 1792. In particular, one crucial fact brought consolation to the British authorities: the continent was suffering even more from this economic warfare. Quite apart from the scarcity of coffee, chocolate and sugar, which had by this time become the familiar embellishments of social life, Europe was experiencing the effects of a critical shortage in certain raw materials – silk and cotton – which was linked to a lack of financial resources and to a loss of external markets. French goods, which gained the reputation of being expensive and shoddy, were boycotted in Central and Eastern Europe. The stagnation which affected the ports from Bremen and Hamburg to Venice was now compounded by stagnation in inland regions. The Rhineland, the Netherlands and Switzerland were no more exempt from this trend than France itself. In Russia, however, considerable stocks of raw materials were accumulated. Even more seriously, the 'Continental System' had pernicious political effects. By the hardship and vexation that it caused, it stirred up discontent among the populations of Europe. It contributed to the reawakening of national sentiment and played a vital role in the War of Liberation of 1813. It also contributed decisively to the break-up of the alliance between the French Empire, Sweden and Russia in 1811. Finally, this practically uninterrupted economic warfare running from 1793 to 1815 was a major factor in determining the economic orientation of France. At the end of the *ancien régime* the signs of an industrial revolution were appearing in the kingdom and maritime trade was encouraging the economies of the coastal regions.

For the first time in its history, France was looking towards the sea and its economy showed signs of emulating that of Great Britain. Following the Revolutionary and Napoleonic Wars, this orientation seems to have been reversed. The country was left with a smaller colonial empire, stagnating internal trade and a mediocre merchant fleet. Having been cut off from the sea for twenty years, the economic centre of gravity had shifted eastward and, until the middle of the twentieth century, the coastal regions of France would witness only limited economic progress. War and blockade had contributed, once again, to reinforcing France's atavistic attachment to the land.

Although tension on the high seas was reduced during the nineteenth century, the blockade remained an important weapon in certain conflicts. The American Civil War provides one of the best examples. The blockade of the coasts of the Southern States, which the Union navy mounted in April 1861, threw the whole Confederate strategy into disarray. In spite of the intense efforts of the 'blockade runners' the South was not able, as it had hoped, to trade its cotton for the arms and munitions which its troops needed, nor even to obtain essential manufactured products for the general population. Against a predominantly agricultural economy, the Northern blockade would ultimately prove to be one of the principal causes of the defeat of the Confederacy.

In 1870, the French navy attempted to mount a blockade of the ports of the North German Confederation from the North Sea to the Baltic. For want of appropriate ships, however, and because of the distance from her bases, bunkering difficulties and bad weather, the blockade, which was enforced on two separate occasions, and then only for a few weeks, had singularly little effect. It was merely an annoyance to German shipping and failed to prevent the re-routing of trade through Denmark and the Netherlands. By contrast, in 1885, Admiral Courbet was to be more successful. After the naval bombardments of Fuchou and Shihpu in 1884 during the Franco-Chinese war (1883–5), he mounted a blockade of the Yangtze, declaring rice to be war contraband. Threatened with a famine which would have affected the whole of northern China, the Peking government ultimately capitulated. On 6 April 1885, they agreed to cede their suzerainty over Annam and Tonkin to France.

During the First World War, the blockade was as extensively employed as during the Revolutionary and Napoleonic Wars, although the conditions in which it was applied were markedly different. To begin with, in 1912 the Royal Navy gave up its tried and tested technique of the 'close blockade'. Because of the danger posed by mines, submarines, torpedoes and even aircraft, the Navy was converted to the idea of a 'long-range blockade' which would be carried out from the bases at Scapa Flow, Rosyth and Harwich, though raids by the Grand Fleet between the 54th and 58th parallels were not excluded. These tactics, when combined with an economic blockade, were intended, in theory, to force the German High Seas Fleet, which was trapped in the North Sea, to give battle. This eventuality did not present itself – Jutland in 1916 was an indecisive action – but the Germans' refusal to engage in battle did not prevent the Allies from establishing an increasingly effective economic blockade against the Central Powers. From the autumn of 1914 onwards, Great Britain and France considerably enlarged the definition of war contraband. No longer was this limited to war *matériel* but covered raw materials, all manufactured goods and foodstuffs. In this they were pursuing a double objective: to paralyse German industry and induce a collapse of military and civilian morale through accumulating economic restrictions.

The North Sea shipping lanes were observed from the entrance to the English Channel and from a line of patrol established between Norway and Scotland. In the Mediterranean, the control points included the Strait of Otranto, Gibraltar and Port Said. Most of the world's shipping which ventured into European waters found itself subject to Allied inspection and the system became so extensive that it provoked strong protests from neutral states, particularly the United States. In response Germany used neighbouring countries – Denmark, Sweden and the Netherlands – as routes for her imports. The entry of the United States into the war in 1917 made the blockade total, enabling the Allies to impose harsh penalties on those neutral states which continued to supply the Central Powers. Germany's reaction was to resort to all-out submarine warfare.

At the end of the war, the blockade became the subject of heated controversy. Britain and America argued that it had been of prime importance in the defeat of Germany. France, traumatized by her massive losses, contested the point: the German army had not been short of weapons and the occupation of Romania and the Ukraine had enabled the Central Powers to mitigate the effects of the blockade. It was all a matter of degree and standpoint. Though the industry of the Reich had been able to meet the *matériel* needs of her armed forces, there is no doubt that the hardships suffered contributed to the deterioration in both civilian and military morale and accelerated the disintegration of Austria-Hungary. The blockade probably shortened the war by several months.

In the Second World War, however, the blockade tactic, which was applied from September 1939, was totally ineffective. Within the framework of a policy of autarky that had been several years in preparation, the Third Reich possessed considerable stocks of raw materials and a synthetics industry capable of producing petrol and rubber, quite apart from the economic agreements it had struck with Romania and the Soviet Union. From 1940 onwards, Germany was also able to exploit intensively the economic resources of virtually the whole of Europe. Despite the blockade, German industries lacked neither energy nor raw materials while the restrictions imposed on the civilian population remained tolerable and were not comparable with those endured between 1914 and 1918.

The failure of the blockade prompted the British and the Americans to intensify their strategic bombing campaign as a substitute means of dismantling the Reich's industry

and breaking the morale of the German people. Ironically, the Allied blockade contributed to the deteriorating condition of those countries which were subject to growing German economic levies. This phenomenon was felt in Vichy France between 1940 and 1942 and, most markedly, in Greece, where there was a terrible famine. Of all the belligerents, it was Japan that ultimately suffered most from blockade. From 1944 onwards, with the destruction of its merchant fleet by US submarines and aircraft, the Japanese archipelago was completely isolated and suffered progressive disruption in all sectors of its economy.

Since 1945, blockade operations have occurred within the context of limited conflicts. During the Cuban missile crisis in 1962, the US navy, as the forward force charged with the resolution of the incident, mounted a long-range blockade against Russian ships from its bases at Guantánamo and Florida. In 1972, during the North Vietnamese offensive, the US Naval Air Service undertook a direct blockade of the port of Haiphong using remote-controlled mines. During the Falklands War of 1982, the Royal Navy established a 200-mile 'exclusion zone' around the islands to isolate the Argentinian forces from supply and reinforcement. The blockade remains prominent among possible naval tactics in the event of limited or large-scale conflict. *See also* CASTEX; COMMERCE-RAIDING; CONVOYS; ECONOMIC WARFARE; NAVAL WARFARE; NAVIES; SIEGES; STRATEGY; WAR ECONOMY.

J. MEYER
P. MASSON

FURTHER READING
Julian S. Corbett and Henry Newbolt, *Naval Operations* (5 vols, London, 1920–31); F. Crouzet, *Le Blocus continental* (2 vols, Paris, 1957); L. Guichard, *Le Blocus naval, 1914–1918* (Paris, 1929); Richard Pares, *Colonial Blockade and Neutral Rights, 1739–1748* (Oxford, 1938, repr. Philadelphia, 1975).

Blücher, Gebhard Leberecht von, Prince of Wahlstatt (1742–1819) Blücher was one of the most popular German generals in the revolt against Napoleon in 1813–15. Born in Mecklenburg, the son of a Hessian captain, he served not only in the army of Frederick II of Prussia, but also in that of Sweden. Appointed commander-in-chief of the Silesian army in 1813, he fought at Lützen and at Bautzen, drove back the French under Jacques- [Étienne-Joseph-] Alexandre Macdonald at the Katzbach, won victories at Wartenberg and Möckern and, lastly, contributed to the defeat of Napoleon at Leipzig. Promoted field marshal on the spot, he was nicknamed Marshal *Vorwärts* ('Forwards'). It was partially thanks to the swift movement of his army, and its arrival on the field in the course of the battle, that Wellington was able to carry off victory at Waterloo. Himself a rather mediocre tactician, Blücher drew on the skills of his strategic advisers, Scharnhorst and Gneisenau, whose intellectual gifts were superior to his own. *See also* GERMANY; NAPOLEON; SCHARNHORST; WATERLOO; WELLINGTON.

B. KROENER

FURTHER READING
R. Parkinson, *The Hussar General: the life of Blücher, man of Waterloo* (London, 1975); Paul P. Vermeil de Tonchard, *Marshal Blücher as Portrayed in His Correspondence* (London, 1895); Wolfgang von Unger, *Blücher* (Berlin, 1907–8).

Bombardment, aerial *See* AIRCRAFT, BOMBER; AVIATION

Bombardment, land *See* ARTILLERY; FORTIFICATION; SIEGES

Bonnal, Henri (1844–1917) The son of an officer, Bonnal entered the military academy at St-Cyr in 1863 and fought in the Franco-Prussian War (1870–1) and at Annam in 1885. Between 1879 and 1884 he reorganized the École de Gymnastique at Joinville-le-Pont before being appointed Professor of Military History, Strategy and Tactics at the École Supérieure de Guerre in 1887. He left this position in 1896 and his military career came to an end in 1902 partly for political reasons. Through his pedagogy and his numerous publications, he did much to rekindle French public interest in military problems and he exerted a great influence on the young officers who studied under him. Bonnal devoted himself to an analysis of the strategic and tactical thought of Napoleon and Moltke. If he fully appreciated the salient characteristics of the German army, he undoubtedly underestimated its intellectual vigour. In his studies of Napoleon, Bonnal dismissed the notion that he conducted his operations according to a preconceived system and argued that the Emperor was more of an opportunist and a pragmatist. Consequently, he was accused of muddled and unreliable research. Bonnal introduced war gaming to the École Supérieure de Guerre in 1889 and was the inspiration behind the creation of the École de Guerre Navale. Although his ideas were strongly tainted with intellectualism and were almost immediately abandoned, Bonnal made the École Supérieure de Guerre the centre of the revival in French military thought. *See also* BERNHARDI; GERMANY; MOLTKE; NAPOLEON; TRAINING.

A. CORVISIER

FURTHER READING
E. Carrias, *La Pensée militaire française* (Paris, 1960); E. Muraise, *Introduction à l'histoire militaire* (Paris, 1964).

Borodino, Battle of (1812) In the summer of 1812 Napoleon invaded Russia with an army of 614,000 men. Foiled by slow progress and bad staff work in his bid to drive the Russian army up against the Pripet marshes and the River Bug, Napoleon had instead followed the Russians as they fell back eastwards. On 7 September, Kutuzov, who had assumed command of the Russian armies a week previously, fought a defensive action at Borodino, 70 miles west of Moscow. The fighting was bloody (both sides suffered in the region of 40,000 casualties out of 120,000 combatants) but indecisive. In the afternoon, the French, under the cover of a bombardment by 400 guns, broke into the Raevskii redoubt, the Russians' central position, but Napoleon refused to commit his reserves. Kutuzov was able to withdraw his army intact. Napoleon, now ill, was able to enter Moscow. However, his supply lines were over-extended and his foe still in the field. *See also* KUTUZOV; MOSCOW, RETREAT FROM; NAPOLEON; POLTAVA; RUSSIA/USSR.

HEW STRACHAN

FURTHER READING
David Chandler, *The Campaigns of Napoleon* (London, 1967); Christopher Duffy, *Borodino and the War of 1812* (London, 1972); E. V. Tarle, *Napoleon's Invasion of Russia, 1812* (Oxford, 1942).

Boulogne (Pas-de-Calais), Sieges of (1544 and 1549) The expansion of the Calais Pale by the conquest of Boulogne was an ambition that Henry VIII held throughout his reign. In 1543 he negotiated an alliance with Charles V for a combined Anglo-Imperial invasion of France and a march on Paris in 1544; with this ostensible purpose the largest English army of the century (28,000 English foot, 4,000 horse, and an expected 10,000 Burgundian and German mercenaries) assembled at Calais during June and July 1544. By the beginning of July the advanced guard had masked Boulogne and Montreuil. After Henry himself arrived on 14 July, he decided to invest Montreuil as a diversionary tactic, and concentrate on Boulogne, which had a garrison of only 2,000. The siege began in earnest on 19 July and the lower town was taken on the 21st. The upper town and the citadel held out until 13 September, having beaten off several assaults, and capitulated mainly as a result of the bombardment by the well-equipped English siege train. Henry was determined to retain the town, despite the fact that Charles V made peace with Francis I on 18 September, and left in it a garrison of 4,000 under John Dudley, Viscount Lisle. On 9 October the French mounted a surprise night attack – the *camisade* – which regained the lower town, but they were then driven out by an English counter-attack.

In 1545 and 1546 Henry spent some £122,000 refortifying Boulogne. The town was difficult to defend because it lay within the estuary of the River Lianne and the English had failed to capture the southern bank in 1544. To protect the harbour a large fortified mole had to be constructed in the middle of the river. Moreover, to maintain communications with Calais outlying fortifications were also necessary at Ambleteuse and Cap Gris Nez. These were all Italianate artillery fortifications similar to those later constructed in Scotland, but the outerworks were never developed beyond the level of earthworks.

Henry VIII's council was convinced that trying to hold Boulogne would be prohibitively expensive and a compromise was reached in the Treaty of Camp (June 1546) in which the English were to occupy Boulogne for eight years and further fortification was suspended. However, Henry II of France was no less determined to regain the town and, following the English difficulties in Scotland and the outbreak of major peasant uprisings, declared war in August 1549. The French quickly overran the outerworks and began bombarding the harbour, but were then bogged down by the onset of winter. This time the English council decided that the expense of reinforcement was too great and in March 1550 returned the town four years early in exchange for financial compensation. The English use of artillery fortifications at Boulogne and in Scotland was possibly the most extensive in Europe at the time. The Boulogne garrison was the first substantial English military force armed extensively with firearms. However, the benefits of military modernization did not compensate for the expense involved – a total of £750,000 between 1544 and 1550 – and Boulogne, like Calais, was ultimately untenable. *See also* CALAIS; DUDLEY, JOHN; FORTIFICATION; GREAT BRITAIN; SEYMOUR.

SIMON ADAMS

FURTHER READING
H. M. Colvin et al., *The History of the King's Works*, iii (London, 1975), pp. 383–93; C. Oman, *A History of the Art of War in the Sixteenth Century* (London, 1937), pp. 330–49; G. J. Millar, *Tudor Mercenaries and Auxiliaries*

1485–1547 (Charlottesville, Va., 1980), pp. 85ff.

Bourcet, Pierre Joseph de, Lieutenant-General (1700–80) A French engineer and artillery officer noted for his topographical skills and expertise in Alpine warfare, Bourcet has been credited with initiating the use of the all-arms division as a tactical formation and also with pioneering work in the creation of a true general staff. His full and eventful career began in the Alps in 1709 at his father's side and its long course was to expose him to the rigours of many campaigns and sieges in Italy, Germany and Corsica. He mapped the frontier of Dauphiné (1749–55) and held several commands in that region. In 1764 he opened a staff school at Grenoble but although this led to the beginnings of a permanent general staff, it was closed in 1776. Marshal de Broglie developed the notion of the division during the 1760s, but Bourcet had already made use of similar formations during the Alpine campaign of 1744 against Piedmont and, in his *Principes de la Guerre de Montagnes* (1764–71), he drew attention to the virtues of an army organized in a well-articulated divisional-like structure. Bourcet's *Principes* seems to have been a direct inspiration for Napoleon's Alpine campaign of 1794–6. *See also* GENERAL STAFF; TACTICAL ORGANIZATION.

G. A. STEPPLER

FURTHER READING
B. H. Liddell Hart, *The Ghost of Napoleon* (London, 1933); Spenser Wilkinson, *The Defence of Piedmont, 1742–1748* (Oxford, 1927); Spenser Wilkinson, *The Rise of General Bonaparte* (Oxford, 1930); R. S. Quimby, *The Background of Napoleonic Warfare* (New York, 1957).

Bouvines (near Lille), Battle of (27 July 1214) Fought between the army of the King of France, Philip Augustus, and a combined Anglo-German-Flemish army under the German Emperor, Otto IV, it marked the climax of King John's long military and diplomatic campaign to recover the Plantagenet territories (Normandy and Anjou), which Philip Augustus had seized in 1203–4. In February 1214 while Otto, with the help of the Counts of Flanders and Boulogne, kept the French troops occupied in the north-east, King John disembarked at La Rochelle. This forced Philip Augustus to divide his forces. He entrusted the defence of the west to his son Prince Louis. John's timidity led to his troops being routed at La Roche-aux-Moines (near Angers) on 2 July. A few weeks later Otto, whose army included an English contingent under the command of the Earl of Salisbury, forced the King of France's northern army to join battle at Bouvines, on a Sunday. For several hours the outcome remained undecided. At one stage Philip himself was in mortal danger. But in the end Otto fled, and Salisbury and the Counts of Flanders and Boulogne were captured. For King John the Battle of Bouvines marked the expensive and humiliating defeat of his whole strategy of reconquest. It led to rebellion and to Magna Carta. For Philip Augustus this crushing victory against a powerful coalition set the seal on a long and remarkably successful reign. The triumph was celebrated in the Latin epic verses of the *Philippidos*, composed by the king's chaplain, William the Breton. In William's view Bouvines was a victory for Right and for the God-fearing King of France, over the forces of Evil, willing to shed blood on a Sunday and led by an excommunicated sovereign. *See also* FRANCE.

P. CONTAMINE

FURTHER READING
G. Duby, *27 juillet 1214. Le Dimanche de Bouvines* (Paris, 1973); J. F. Verbruggen, *The Art of Warfare in Western Europe during the Middle Ages* (Amsterdam, 1977).

Bradley, Omar Nelson (1893–1981) Bradley graduated from the US Military Academy at West Point in 1915 in the same class as Eisenhower. In the interwar period, Bradley served in a number of posts, drawing the attention of George Marshall, under whom he served at the US Infantry School. In 1941, Marshall, then Chief of Staff, appointed Bradley commandant of the Infantry School. In February 1943, Bradley joined Eisenhower in the North

African campaign. In this campaign, Bradley initially served under Patton. In July 1943, Bradley led II Corps in the invasion of Sicily. Returning to England, Bradley was given command of the US First Army which invaded France on 6 June 1944 alongside the British Second Army (Operation *Overlord*). On 1 August 1944, Bradley assumed command of the US Twelfth Army Group, which included Patton's US Third Army in addition to the US First Army. During the invasion of Normandy, Bradley and the British commander, Montgomery, differed over strategy. Bradley preferred a wider advance, while Montgomery wanted to pursue a narrow thrust. At the Battle of the Bulge in December 1944–January 1945, Eisenhower offended Bradley by placing some of the latter's men under Montgomery's command. Bradley's forces were the first to cross the Rhine into Germany, and they linked up with the Soviet troops along the Elbe. In 1948, Bradley became Chief of Staff and the following year the first chairman of the Joint Chiefs of Staff, a position he held until his retirement in 1953. Bradley was a self-effacing, quiet man, but his rapid promotion throughout the war attested to his capabilities. After the war, he was instrumental in maintaining the strength of the US army in a period when nuclear weapons and air power threatened its existence. *See also* EISENHOWER; MARSHALL; MONTGOMERY; NORMANDY; PATTON; UNITED STATES.

KEITH NEILSON

FURTHER READING
Stephen Ambrose, *The Supreme Commander* (Garden City, NY, 1970); Charles Whiting, *Bradley* (New York, 1971); Russell F. Weigley, *Eisenhower's Lieutenants: the campaigns of France and Germany, 1944–1945* (Bloomington, Ind., 1981).

Braun, Werner von (1912–77) The work carried out by von Braun during the Second World War laid the foundations for the postwar development of missile technology and the US space programme.

Von Braun entered the Berlin rocket establishment at the age of nineteen. He demonstrated remarkable technical expert-

ise and in 1932 was appointed head of an experimental rocket station at Kummersdorf where he worked on the development of the A-4 rocket engine. He subsequently established the world's largest experimental rocket centre at Peenemünde. His experiments suffered a number of failures and Hitler was sceptical of the project, but with the continuing support of the military director of Peenemünde, General Dornberger, and a successful experimental firing of the rocket, in October 1942 Hitler authorized mass production of the A-4 (now known as the V-2). The V-2 was capable of carrying a 1 ton warhead 200 miles and was effectively the world's first intermediate range ballistic missile. It was first launched against London in September 1944, but was never available in sufficient numbers to affect the outcome of the war.

In May 1945 von Braun surrendered to US forces at Oberammergau, along with 450 other German scientists, including General Dornberger. They were taken to Paris and then on to the United States. He became a naturalized American citizen and, in 1950, was appointed director of the US army's Ballistic Missile Agency at the Redstone Arsenal, Huntsville, Alabama. Here he developed the Redstone SSBM (surface-to-surface ballistic missile) a modified version of which was used for the Mercury space rocket. Data gathered from the V-2 flights were also used by the USAF and by the US navy, where it culminated in the development of Polaris. He was a vociferous advocate of a US space programme even before the Sputnik launch by the Soviet Union and was involved in the development of the Jupiter V rocket which launched the first US satellite and was the moving spirit behind the Apollo space programme. *See also* NUCLEAR WARFARE.

A. CORVISIER
DAVID WESTON

FURTHER READING
Edward Schwiebert, *A History of the USAF Ballistic Missiles* (New York, 1965); John W. R. Taylor, *Rockets and Missiles* (London, 1970).

Breda, Siege of (23 April 1624–25 May 1625) The Siege of Breda is well known from a painting by Velásquez, 'The Surrender of Breda', and from the drawings of Jacques Callot. Breda, which was known as the family seat of the Nassau family, was regarded as an important symbol in the latter stages of the Eighty Years' War between the emergent Dutch Republic and Spain. It was besieged by Spinola and the Army of Flanders and, despite repeated efforts, Maurice of Nassau was unable to effect a relief. The Spaniards enclosed the city within two rings of field fortifications protected by 96 redoubts, 37 forts and 45 batteries. The besiegers did not fire on the bastions and works of the city itself, but allowed starvation to produce capitulation. Breda was recaptured by the Dutch in 1637. *See also* FORTIFICATION; NASSAU; NETHERLANDS; SIEGES.

A. CORVISIER

FURTHER READING
J. I. Israel, *The Dutch Republic and the Hispanic World, 1606–61* (Oxford, 1982); B. H. Nickle, *The Military Reforms of Prince Maurice of Orange* (Ann Arbor, MI, 1981).

Breitenfeld, Battle of (17 September 1631) Four and a half miles north of Leipzig, Tilly, with his 31,000 Imperial troops, attempted to halt Gustavus Adolphus, who had just joined 18,000 Saxons to his 23,000 Swedish soldiers. Tilly drew up his infantry in the centre in the old-style *tercios*, thirty ranks deep, and placed his cavalry on the wings. Gustavus Adolphus positioned his Swedish foot in the centre in linear formation only six ranks in depth, and put the untried Saxons on the left and the Swedish cavalry on the right. Pappenheim, at the head of the left wing of the Imperial horse, attempted to break through to Gustavus's reserve by outflanking the Swedish centre but was caught in a pincer movement between the Swedish reserve and the cavalry of the right wing. Tilly succeeded in driving the Saxons from the field but the Swedish infantry extended their formations to cover the gaps and the Swedish cavalry counter-attacked. Tilly's army was defeated by organized musketry and the heavy weight of artillery which the Swedes brought to bear. After holding Tilly's assaults, the Swedish infantry and cavalry advanced together and forced the Imperialists from the field. During the battle and the pursuit, two-thirds of Tilly's army was destroyed enabling Gustavus to advance into Leipzig and then into central and southern Germany. Breitenfeld testified to the efficacy and flexibility of Swedish tactical formations, the influence of decisive cavalry action and the growing importance of field artillery in battle.

There was a second battle at Breitenfeld on 2 November 1642 when the Swedes, under Lennart Torstensson, defeated an Imperial army commanded by the Archduke Leopold William. The Swedish victory was almost as complete as that of 1631, the Imperialists losing 5,000 killed and wounded and 5,000 prisoners. *See also* GUSTAVUS II ADOLPHUS; SWEDEN; TILLY.

A. CORVISIER
JOHN CHILDS

FURTHER READING
Michael Roberts, *Gustavus Adolphus: a history of Sweden, 1611–1632* (2 vols, London, 1953–8); Geoffrey Parker, *The Thirty Years' War* (London, 1984); Swedish Army General Staff, *Sveriges Krig, 1611–1632* (8 vols, Stockholm, 1936–9).

Britain, Battle of (1940) Between July and September 1940, after the defeat of France, the German air force (*Luftwaffe*) launched a massive offensive against the United Kingdom, aiming either to defeat Britain through air attack alone or to win air superiority over the south of England prior to a cross-Channel invasion. Air Chief Marshal Sir Hugh Dowding, Air Officer Commanding-in-Chief RAF Fighter Command, understood the German objective and decided that, while he could not let the *Luftwaffe* operate unopposed, he must nevertheless husband his resources carefully. The German force available (approximately 2,800 machines) outnumbered Fighter Command's first-line strength by about 4 to 1. Dowding's strategy was practicable because of the pioneering work done in Britain to integrate radar into the air defence system, a development which obviated the need for wasteful standing patrols, and which allowed smaller forces to be directed to precisely where they were needed most.

The first phase of the battle lasted from 10 July to 7 August 1940, and saw the *Luftwaffe* concentrate its effort against coastal shipping in the hope that this would draw Fighter Command into battle. When this failed, the Germans shifted focus in the second phase (8–23 August) and attacked airfields, command posts and radar installations, targets which Dowding had to defend. Beginning on 24 August the *Luftwaffe* confined its daylight operations mainly to attacks on airfields and aircraft industries in the south of England, particularly those near London, and succeeded in stretching Dowding's resources almost to the limit. However, on 7 September, in response to British raids on Berlin (which were themselves in retaliation for a German attack on London) the Germans focused their attack on the British capital.

This was a major blunder. Fighter Command had the respite it needed to repair airfields and damaged aircraft and Dowding, moreover, knew where the enemy was heading almost every day. The losses suffered during these daylight raids on London (involving as many as 600 bombers and fighter escorts) eventually forced the *Luftwaffe* high command to switch to night raids. This became the period of the Blitz, during which a number of cities, including London and Coventry, were heavily bombed and several hundred inhabitants killed. But damage and casualties of this sort were not sufficient to defeat Britain. The proposed invasion was postponed on 17 September, and cancelled on 12 October. Between 10 July and 31 October the Royal Air Force lost some 1,000 fighters, while the *Luftwaffe* had 1,733 aircraft destroyed. *See also* AIRCRAFT, FIGHTER; AVIATION.

P. FACON
STEPHEN J. HARRIS

FURTHER READING
Derek Wood and Derek Dempster, *The Narrow Margin: the Battle of Britain and the rise of air power, 1930–1940* (London, 1961); H. R. Allen, *Who Won the Battle of Britain?* (London, 1974); Richard Collier, *Eagle Day: the Battle of Britain, August 6–September 15, 1940* (London, 1966); John Terraine, *The Right of the Line: the Royal Air Force in the European war, 1939–45* (London, 1985); John Frayn Turner, *The Bader Wing* (Tunbridge Wells, 1981).

Britain, conquest of (AD 43) The invasion of Britain was ordered by the Emperor Claudius whose principal motive was probably the need to enhance his political prestige by a dramatic military campaign; moreover there was the precedent of Caesar's invasions of Britain in 55 and 54 BC, after which the Romans believed that the country was in their sphere of influence. A pretext was offered by the flight of the British king and Roman ally, Verica, seeking help from Claudius against the rising power of Togodumnus and Caratacus, kings of the Catuvellauni, which might threaten Roman interests. The expeditionary force assembled under the command of Aulus Plautius consisted of four legions: *IX Hispana* from Pannonia, *II Augusta* (under the command of the future emperor Vespasian), *XIV Gemina* and *XX Valeria Victrix* from the German provinces, and auxiliary troops. The main or only beachhead was established at Richborough and an unopposed landing was followed by a victorious advance to the River Medway where in a two-day battle the Romans fought their way across. First, auxiliary troops swam over in full battle gear and dispersed the British chariots, then an assault group led by Flavius Sabinus, Vespasian's elder brother, crossed at a different point to force the British back. The final phase occurred the following day with the crossing of the third Roman force, led by Hosidius Geta: this decided the battle. The British retreated to the River Thames where, near London, they suffered another defeat; subsequently Togodumnus was killed in a skirmish. At this point Claudius was summoned, probably as previously arranged, to take charge of the campaign. He arrived in August bringing elephants with him and stayed for sixteen days while he led the army to the capture of the British stronghold at Colchester where he received the surrender of many kings, though Caratacus was not taken until AD 51. Aulus Plautius, who clearly had instructions to create a province, continued the campaign with operations in the south-east, south-west and the midlands, before returning to Rome in AD 47 to celebrate an ovation. His successor, Ostorius Scapula, found most of this area firmly under Roman control and was able to attack centres of resistance in south Wales; there is no indication that the Romans intended to limit the expansion of the province at this stage by demarcating a frontier. Claudius celebrated a triumph, and in AD 51 a triumphal arch was dedicated to him in Rome by the senate and people 'because he received the surrender of eleven British kings who had been conquered without any setback, and was the first to bring under the control of the Roman people barbarian races beyond the Ocean'. *See also* GREAT BRITAIN; ROME.

B. CAMPBELL

FURTHER READING
S. Frere, *Britannia: a history of Roman Britain* (London, 1974), pp. 74–92; P. Salway, *Roman Britain* (Oxford, 1981), pp. 65–99; M. Todd, *Roman Britain, 55 BC–AD 400* (London, 1981), pp. 60–73; B. Jones and D. Mattingley, *An Atlas of Roman Britain* (Oxford, 1990).

Brooke, Alan Francis, 1st Viscount Alanbrooke (1883–1963) Brooke was born into a traditional Irish military family. He was raised in France and saw service in the British army in the First World War. During the interwar period, Brooke taught at both the Staff College at Camberley and the Imperial Defence College. In 1939, Brooke went to France as commander of the Second Corps of the British Expeditionary Force (BEF). Brooke was universally acknowledged as the commander whose efforts allowed the BEF to be successfully evacuated from Dunkirk in 1940. For his achievement he was appointed Commander-in-Chief of Home Forces. In 1941, he became Chief of the Imperial General Staff (CIGS). As CIGS, Brooke worked closely with Churchill, managing to temper the prime minister's imaginative strategic schemes with facts and sound judgement.

He also advised Churchill at major inter-Allied conferences, including Teheran. In November 1943, Brooke was disappointed at not being given the command of the invasion of Western Europe scheduled for 1944, but understood that it had to be given to Eisenhower for reasons of policy. While Brooke favoured close co-operation with the United States, he did not get along well with the US Chief of Staff, George Marshall. Brooke was known for his cool and rational approach to affairs. *See also* CHURCHILL; MARSHALL; MONTGOMERY.

KEITH NEILSON

FURTHER READING
David Fraser, *Alanbrooke* (London, 1982); Arthur Bryant, *The Turn of the Tide* (Garden City, NY, 1957).

Brusilov, Alexei Alexeievich (1853–1926) Entering the Russian army through the Corps of Pages in 1872, the well-connected Brusilov ably steered himself through endemic rivalry and factionalism to attain corps command in 1909, his military experience including campaign service in the Caucasus and the Russo-Turkish War as well as command of the Cavalry School. He was immediately appointed to the 8th Army in Galicia in August 1914 and also distinguished himself in the campaign in the Carpathians before being elevated to the command of the South Western Army Group comprising 7th, 8th, 9th and 11th Armies in April 1916. His subsequent offensive between the Pripet marshes and the Dniester, the beginning of which was brought forward to 4 June 1916 in order to relieve Austro-Hungarian pressure on the Italians, was characterized by the thoroughness of its preparation. It was also marked by the achievement of strategic surprise through being accompanied by little or no preliminary artillery bombardment and the combination of widely separated attacks by his four armies over a 280-mile front but with each thrust concentrated to achieve maximum penetration of the positions occupied by the Austro-Hungarians. Thus, despite the near parity of the forces involved, Brusilov had broken two of the four armies opposing him by 12 June, taking almost 193,000 prisoners and 216 guns. However, the dispersion of his armies robbed Brusilov of ready reserves with which to exploit his breakthrough fully, as did shortages in ammunition and transport and Brusilov's use of cavalry dismounted in an infantry role. By early July Brusilov's armies had suffered over 495,000 casualties and the offensive rapidly lost momentum. In demonstrating the virtues of limited rather than prolonged artillery preparation, Brusilov had further encouraged an emerging trend in the attempt to achieve a decisive breakthrough. In the process, he had also dealt a shattering blow to Austro-Hungarian morale and had encouraged Romania to join the Allies. Subsequently, Brusilov was one of those who urged the Tsar's abdication and he was appointed Commander-in-Chief by the provisional government in May 1917, only to be replaced by Kornilov in July. After being briefly imprisoned by the Bolsheviks, he threw in his lot with them, serving on a number of advisory committees, calling on other former Tsarist officers to return to the army during the Russo-Polish War and becoming Inspector of Cavalry, from which appointment he retired in 1924. *See also* LENIN; RUSSIA/USSR.

IAN F. W BECKETT

FURTHER READING
A. A. Brusilov, *A Soldier's Notebook, 1914–18* (London, 1930); N. Stone, *The Eastern Front, 1914–17* (London, 1975); A. K. Wildman, *The End of the Russian Imperial Army* (2 vols, Princeton, 1980–7).

Buccaneers *See* COMMERCE-RAIDING

Bugeaud, Thomas-Robert, Marquis de la Piconnerie, Marshal of France (1784–1849) Having joined the service in 1804 and been promoted to colonel in 1815 following distinguished service in Spain, Bugeaud was excluded from the army at the Restoration. Instead, he cultivated his estates, experimenting in agronomy. Recalled by the July Monarchy, Bugeaud was sent to Algeria in 1836. Appointed governor of Algeria in 1840, he moved from a restrained form of occupation to a campaign of conquest effected by flying columns in which the troops were more appropriately equipped than had previously been the case. He also made efforts at agricultural colonization in order to create an operational base (*ense et aratro*) and organized the Arab bureaux for the administration of the native population. At the Battle of the Isly (14 July 1844), Bugeaud ended Morocco's aid to Abdelkader (or Abd el Kader) and forced the latter to submit in 1847. Bugeaud practised a specific form of irregular warfare, often repeated in subsequent colonial conquests, which took particular account of the prevailing local conditions. *See also* COLONIAL TROOPS; COLONIAL WARFARE; GALLIÉNI; INDIRECT WARFARE; IRREGULAR WARFARE; LYAUTEY; MIDDLE EAST.

A. CORVISIER

FURTHER READING
Jean Gottmann, 'Bugeaud, Galliéni, Lyautey: the development of French colonial warfare', in *Makers of Modern Strategy*, ed. E. M. Earle (Princeton, 1943); Douglas Porch, 'Bugeaud, Galliéni, Lyautey: the development of French colonial warfare', in *Makers of Modern Strategy*, ed. Peter Paret (Princeton, 1986), pp. 376–407; A. T. Sullivan, *Thomas-Robert Bugeaud* (Hamden, Conn., 1983).

Bülow, Adam Heinrich Dietrich von (1757–1807) A minor Prussian aristocrat who, on the basis of a very short career of seven years as a military writer, established himself as one of the foremost military theorists and commentators of his day. A controversial figure, he has subsequently been hailed as the founder of modern military science, claimed as an early geopolitical scientist, and denounced as a crank. In 1790, after a disappointing eighteen years as a junior officer, Bülow left the Prussian army and began travelling, going as far afield as the United States, which became the subject of his first book in 1797. More than a dozen works were to follow, primarily on military subjects, but by 1806 his provocative manner and radical ideas had so aroused the Prussian government that he was arrested and declared insane. He died at Riga in the following year, allegedly from ill treatment at the hands of the Russians.

Although Bülow became a major advocate of the social and political changes created in France by the Revolution and of the 'new warfare' practised by the French armies, his first, and best-known, military work, *Geist des Neueren Kriegssystems* (1799), showed little awareness of these developments. Instead, he claimed to have discovered his own new system of warfare based on mathematical principles. Placing supreme importance on an army's line of supply (its line of operations), he suggested a completely geometrical science of strategy. Asserting that the outcome of any military operation could be predetermined precisely by the geometric relationship between its objective and its 'base', he went on to claim that his formula not only rendered battle unnecessary but, if projected onto the political plane, would mean the eradication of war itself. Bülow's new 'science of operations' was in fact an extreme statement of some of the theoretical notions of the military thinkers of the Enlightenment and, to that extent, was backward-looking but, more importantly, it was contradicted by the reality of warfare. His logic of supply was undermined by the apparently unorthodox, yet successful, campaigns of the French armies, while it missed entirely the central importance which Napoleon gave to battle. In time Bülow was to appreciate the military importance of many of the changes wrought by the French Revolution but he also persisted in trying to prove the validity of his original geometric conception of war. He offered a pioneering distinction between 'strategy' and 'tactics', but in this, as in much else, his thinking was flawed, as Clausewitz demonstrated. Though his grasp was unsteady, Bülow's ideas were not without influence, not least on Clausewitz himself, who credited him with the concept of a 'base of operations'. Bülow's extraordinary mixture of old and new ideas completed the shift of emphasis in European military thought from the organization and structure of armies to the actual conduct of operations. *See also* BOURCET; CLAUSEWITZ; FOLARD; GUIBERT; JOMINI; LLOYD; TEIL.

G. A. STEPPLER.

FURTHER READING
Azar Gat, *The Origins of Military Thought from the Enlightenment to Clausewitz* (Oxford, 1989); *Makers of Modern Strategy from Machiavelli to the Nuclear Age*, ed. Peter Paret (Princeton, 1986), pp. 91–119 *et passim*.

Byzantium

The Army
During the life of the Byzantine Empire (330–1453), the mode of recruitment, the structures, the weaponry and the tactics of its army underwent substantial changes.

Fourth–Seventh Centuries Initially, the Byzantine army was simply the Roman army of the Eastern Empire which, after 330, was regrouped around its new capital, Constantinople. After the reforms of Constantine (306–37), the army consisted of three main groups: the elite corps which replaced the old Praetorian Guard (*scholae palatinae*); a mobile field army (the *comitatenses*), which included certain 'crack' guard regiments (*palatini*); and the garrisons stationed on the frontiers (the *limitanei*). The latter rapidly evolved into a peasant militia settled on land which carried an hereditary obligation to military service. The *comitatenses* were commanded by the *magistri militum*, one for the cavalry and one for the infantry, who acted as inspectors-general of their arms and commanded them in the field. *Magistri equitum* and *peditum* were appointed to key frontier districts and, under them, certain frontier provinces or zones were entrusted to *duces* (*dux*).

Although the general obligation to military service remained in force, conscription was usually only enforced among sons of soldiers and the rural population. However, landowners could pay a monetary tax in lieu of the recruits which they were legally bound to provide from the *coloni* on their estates. Byzantine soldiers were thus mainly volunteers and, in this way, many foreigners (*barbari*) — Goths, Turko-Mongolians, Slavs from the Danubian frontier, Arabs from Syria-Palestine, Thracians, Isaurians and Armenians – entered the ranks. There were also the *foederati*, mercenary units under their own leaders raised from the tribes which were bound by treaty to supply soldiers to the Empire. At the time of Justinian I (527–65), leading generals became virtually *condottieri* recruiting their own personal guards and miniature armies (*buccellarii* and hypaspists). It was with a hybrid army of this type that Justinian's generals, Belisarius and Narses, attempted to reconquer Italy and North Africa, and his successors, Maurice (582–602) and Heraclius (610–41) faced invaders from the north (Avars, Slavs and Bulgars) and conquerors from the south (Persians and later, after the emergence of Islam, the Arabs).

The influence of these foreign peoples, particularly the nomads from the steppes, caused important technological and tactical changes in the Byzantine army. A treatise, the *Strategikon*, purportedly written by Emperor Maurice in *c*.600, describes some of these developments. From the Persians was borrowed a double-bow made from horn, drawn with a thumb-ring, and with great penetrative power up to a range of 200–350 metres. This was the distance, remarked Maurice, within which armies could be 'pinned to the ground'. Padded protective clothing was adopted for both men and horses, and the stirrup, an innovation which seems to have derived from China, was used in Byzantium long before it was taken up in the West and the Islamic countries of the East. In camp, the army lodged in round tents 'in the Avar style'. Also under the influence of the nomadic peoples, especially the Persians, the distinction between infantry and cavalry became blurred until a new model appeared: the all-round warrior (*cataphract*) armed with bow, sword and lance, both man and mount protected by armour of chain mail or metal plates.

Seventh–Tenth Centuries The poor condition of Byzantine finances and the Avar pressure on the Danubian frontier made it increasingly difficult to acquire Germanic mercenaries during the seventh century. The army was thrown back onto the human resources of the Empire and conscription became more frequent, especially among the newly conquered Armenian provinces. Maurice's *Strategikon* mentions military service for all male subjects up to the age of forty.

First the Persian and then the Arab conquest lopped off the Empire's eastern provinces (Egypt, Palestine, Syria and Cilicia), establishing the frontier between the Byzantine and the Islamic worlds in the Taurus and Armenian mountains for the next three centuries. At the same time, the Slavic invasions in the north isolated Thessalonica and even Constantinople. As Byzantium recovered some of her lost provinces in Thrace and Asia Minor, the territories were organized for their own defence. The old civil provinces were replaced by military districts (*themata* or *themes*). Three *themes* were created in Asia Minor each named after the army which it supported: the *Anatolikon*, the Army of the Orient; the *Opsikion*; and the *Armeniakon*, the Armenian army. *Strategoi* (military governors), *comes* in the case of the *Opsikion*, ruled over the *themes* and were, effectively, the successors to the *magistri militum*. The elite troops of the army (*epilekta*) – the *buccellarii*, the *optimates*, the *Thrakesioi* (Thracians) and the *foederati* – were permanently assigned to their own individual *themes*. The *themes* spread from Asia Minor into the European parts of the Empire and soon became civil and military administrative districts each supporting a specific army formation.

The *theme* (*c*.10–15,000 men) under the *strategos* was split into two or three *turmai* (divisions) of 5,000 men, each under a *turmarch*, who was both a military commander and an administrator. The *turma* was divided into five *banda* (1,000 men), each under a *drungario*, and each *bandon* was subdivided into five *pentarchies* (200 men) each commanded by a *komes*. Beneath each *komes* were five *pentekontarchoi* commanding *pentekontarchies* (40 men) and, finally, four *dekarchies* (10 men). Outside the *theme* organization were the *kleisurai*, commanded by *kleisuriarchs*. The *kleisurai* were the key frontier districts covering principal invasion routes; they were later raised to the rank of *themes*. The *akritai* (frontier defenders or margraves) were subordinated to the *kleisuriarchs*. Thus, outside Constantinople, the Empire became militarized in order to limit the damage caused by the Arabic and Slavic raiders. Along the frontier, a permanent state of war lasted for three centuries.

As a rule, the soldiers of the *themes* were peasants whose lands were encumbered with an obligation to perform military service but they could buy themselves out of the obligation or provide a substitute. Moreover, Armenian immigration into Cilicia and Mesopotamia, where there was a chronic shortage of population, ensured a supply of semi-professional frontier soldiers under the command of the great Byzantine or Armeno-Byzantine *akritai*. The *akritai* were characterized by their taste for independence and their code of honour as they carried on the petty warfare along the frontiers. The hero of the Byzantine national epic, Digenis, was an *akritas*, the son of a Greek mother and a converted Arab emir. His exploits reflect the frontier war of the tenth century, fighting with the infidel, robber bands and cattle-thieves (*apelatai*). The peasant soldiers in the *themes* and the *kleisurai* were mainly used for local defence; in large-scale campaigns, they merely made up numbers alongside the professional field army.

The nucleus of the professional army was stationed in and around Constantinople. There were four mounted *tagmata* (regiments of 1,500–4,000 men) – the *scholarii*, the *excubitores*, the *hikanatai* (each under the command of a *domesticus*) and the *arithmos* or *vigla* (the guard of the Imperial headquarters) commanded by a *drungario*. There was also an infantry regiment, the *numeri*, under a *domesticus*, plus a troop under the *comes* or *domesticus of the Walls* (the 'Long Walls' built by Anastasius I (491–518) 40 miles west of Constantinople). With the exception of the *Guard of the Walls*, all these troops went into battle with the Emperor under the centralized command of the domesticus of the scholarii, the highest ranking officer after the *strategos* of the *Anatolikon theme*. During the tenth century, the domesticus of the scholarii became commander-in-chief of the entire army. In the ninth century, the Byzantine field army probably numbered 120,000 men, a reduction from the 150,000 current during the first half of the sixth century. A document preserved from the tenth century describes in detail the complex infrastructure of the Imperial field army: the assembly camps; the requisitioning of men, mounts and beasts of burden; the delivery of various weapons by towns and regions; the ceremonial; the Emperor's travelling library which included treatises on tactics and books on interpreting omens; and the pay and financial structure.

Soldiers received relatively low wages. However, the peasant landholdings in the *themes* were a substantial compensation and provided the soldiers with their basic means of livelihood. For his first year of service, the soldier received one *solidus*, rising to a maximum of twelve *solidi* in his twelfth year. The soldiers of the *tagmata* and the subordinate officers in the *themes* received a maximum annual wage of eighteen *solidi*. Although the Imperial administration did its best to protect the peasant-soldier landholdings from rapacious landlords, there was a decline in the institution by the eleventh century, which led to a weakening of Byzantine defences. The disastrous defeat by the Seljuk Turks at Manzikert in 1071 and the Turkish occupation of most of Asia Minor by 1081 led to the collapse of the basic military system. The huge loss of territory forced the Byzantine army to rely upon mercenaries – Chazars, Patzinaks, Russians, Scandinavians, Georgians, Slavs, Arabs, Turks, Greeks and Latins. The *Varangian Guard* was mostly composed of Anglo-Saxons. By the early thirteenth century, the Byzantine army was an almost wholly mercenary organization.

The principal arm of the Byzantine army continued to be the cavalry (*caballaria themata*). The cataphracts attacked in mass formation, while the light horse (*trapezitae*), whose main weapon was the bow, carried out reconnaissance, harassed the enemy and specialized in rapid movement. Light infantry also employed the bow, although some units were armed with the javelin. Mail-clad heavy infantry carried spear, sword, shield and battle-axe. Every *bandon* possessed its own baggage train complete with numerous camp followers, mostly servants and slaves. The bridging train travelled with the heavy baggage and military engineering was well developed. There was also a medical service with doctors and ambulance waggons. Unfortunately, the emphasis on heavy cavalry increased the financial burden of the state.

The Byzantines regarded war as a practical and pragmatic art rather than a dogmatic science, moulding their methods to counter those of their various opponents. Emphasis was always placed on the defensive; the offensive was only stressed in siege operations. Frontier defence continued to rely on the old Roman system of the *limes* with additional fortified posts and small forts guarding the potential invasion routes. Towns in the interior were fortified and a system of signals announced the approach of an invader. If a raider broke through the frontier, infantry occupied the roads by which he might withdraw while he was constantly harried by light cavalry. In the meantime, the *strategos* collected his main forces to repel the attack and informed neighbouring *themes* of the danger. Each raid or invasion could be met by a measured riposte. Although regulations dictated the conduct of engagements, generals were expected to show initiative and originality; Cecaumenus urged generals on leave to study the Old Testament in order to discover martial stratagems. Casualties were to be kept as low as possible. The principles of this harassing warfare were laid down in various treatises (by Leo VI, Nicephorus II Phocas and Cecaumenus): making the optimum use of terrain, moving by night, choosing to attack the enemy when he was returning through the mountains laden with prisoners and booty, and relying on ambuscades, manoeuvre, sub-terfuge and mobility rather than full-scale battle. Morale among the troops was partially maintained by the religious contest present in so many of the campaigns.

In the fighting against the Arabs and, to a lesser extent, against the peoples of the Balkans and from north of the Black Sea (Bulgars, Hungarians, Pechenegs and Russians), an aristocracy of great military families was formed, solidly based on the frontier *themes*, which was critical of the bureaucracy in Constantinople and eventually assumed power. These great soldiers had their hour of glory when the divisions within Islam enabled Byzantium both to reconquer some of its lost territories – including Cilicia, Mesopotamia and Syria-Palestine as far as Jerusalem, which was threatened but not taken – and to react against a powerful, dangerous Bulgar state which had formed in the Balkans. There began a period, under the military emperors Nicephorus II Phocas (963–9), John I Tzimeskes (969–76) and Basil II (976–1025), in which a form of total war prevailed, with mass deportations, the destruction of towns and cities and the devastation of the countryside. The professional army was the major instrument of this 'Byzantine epic'; the high command, divided between a *domesticus of the west* and a *domesticus of the east* disposed between 30,000 and 40,000 men, at least 10,000 of whom were mounted, reinforced by elite corps (the 'Immortals', Russians and Scandinavians). This fever of reconquest enabled the military to gain the upper hand over the civilian authorities and new ideologies appeared concurrently; war was justified as the defence of Christianity and the protection of Christians living in Islamic countries and it was even suggested, unsuccessfully, that soldiers who died in battle against the infidel should be regarded as martyrs.

Eleventh–Fifteenth Centuries This unprecedented war effort and the resulting territorial annexations led to an illusion of peace. After 1025, the army of reconquest was gradually demobilized. Under the pressure of accelerated immigration of ethnic minorities (Armenians and Syrians) and the weakening of central government, the great military districts broke up into a multitude of little territories controlled, from their bases in small towns and villages, by local potentates each commanding a few hundred infantry. The Emperor now recruited his central forces almost entirely from mercenaries – Scandinavians, Russians, Normans, Franks, Pechenegs, Cumans and Turks – each group retaining its own weapons and military organizations. Hervé 'Frangopolous', Robert Crépin and Roussel de Bailleul were all famous Norman mercenary leaders who travelled from southern Italy to Constantinople, carved out fiefs for themselves and then raised their own taxes. It was a half-Western, half-Eastern army made up largely of foreign contingents which was defeated at Manzikert in 1071 by Alp Arslan's Turks. This disaster, which opened up Asia Minor to the invaders, simultaneously destroyed the base for Byzantine recruitment. One further step towards feudalization occurred when the *pronoia* (provision) was instituted. Land, to which was attached the obligation to provide soldiers, was granted to superior officers. The grant was only for a single lifetime and could not be inherited.

Despite the efforts of the Comneni emperors (1081–1185), after Manzikert there was neither the stable territorial base nor adequate fiscal resources to reconstitute a sound army organically rooted in the soil of the Empire. For its defence, Byzantium relied upon foreign support. The western Christians used the pretext of a call for mercenaries to launch the great process of the Crusades in the late eleventh century, which led to the occupation of Constantinople from 1204 to 1261. During the wars of that period, it was the model of the Frankish knight or the Turkish or Arab soldier that dominated the battlefields of Byzantium. Consequently, Byzantium did not experience the great technological and tactical changes of the fourteenth and fifteenth centuries: the revival of infantry and the introduction of gunpowder artillery. The most effective defenders of Constantinople in 1453, when Mehmet II launched his final attack, were a contingent of 700 Genoese commanded by Giustiniani.

The Navy

One might have expected that Byzantium, with its capital admirably situated on the Bosphorus and controlling the straits, would, throughout its history, have been a great maritime power. The paradoxical reality is, however, that Byzantium usually sacrificed opportunities for expansion by the deployment of its sea power on the altar of land defence and territorial consolidation. 'Its fleet is the glory of the Roman world,' wrote Cecaumenus, a landed aristocrat of the eleventh century, but the Empire relied militarily much more on its armies than on its fleet, just as its financial system depended more on taxes from land than revenue from trade. There are several distinct periods in the inconsistent Byzantine naval policy. For the Romans, the Mediterranean was *Mare Nostrum* and their fleet served as a floating police force rather than an instrument of aggression. The Vandal occupation of Carthage caused the Romans to take counter-measures in the western Mediterranean but by the time of Justinian (527–65) the sea had been restored to Roman control with only the occasional disturbance from Vandal pirates. Moreover, control of the Black Sea meant that Byzantium maintained trading links with the peoples of the north and the Asian interior. In the early seventh century, the Byzantine ships stationed along the coasts of the Aegean and Asia Minor constituted an unrivalled high seas fleet which experienced little difficulty in scattering the flotillas of Slavs and Avars which besieged Constantinople in 626. The Arabs, however, constructed their first war fleet in Syria in 645. Over the next two centuries it seized half the Byzantine coastline in addition to the large islands of Cyprus, Rhodes and, most importantly, Crete in 826–7. Arab attacks on Constantinople in 672–8 and 717–18 were repulsed with the help of 'Greek Fire' and the fleet. To combat this constant Arab menace, the Byzantines reorganized their fleet at the same time as the militarization of the Empire by extending the system of *themes* to cover naval recruitment.

During the eighth century two maritime *themes* were created – Cibyrrhaeots (south and south-west Asia Minor), and the Dodecanese or Aegean Sea. A third maritime *theme*, Samos (west Asia Minor), was added during the ninth century in response to a renewed Arab threat. Bases for the fleet were also provided in the European *themes*, especially Cephalonia. By the tenth century, there was an Imperial fleet of large ships for deep-sea operations based at Constantinople under the command of the *drungarios tou Ploimou*. The *strategoi* of the *themes* commanded smaller, lighter squadrons intended for coastal work. The organizational structure of the army was thus replicated in the fleet. The galleys of the main fleet were called *domon*, the largest having two banks of oars and a crew of up to 300 men, of whom 70 were marines and the remainder oarsmen and sailors. An average crew for a *domon* was in the region of 200 men. Lighter and more manoeuvrable ships were called *pamphyli* and the flagship of the admiral was always of this type. Reconnaissance and the carrying of dispatches were undertaken by fast, light ships with a single bank of oars. By the twelfth century, the oar-powered Byzantine ships were outclassed by the Italian merchantmen and warships as well as by the heavier, sail-powered Arab vessels. In action, the Byzantine ships relied on boarding and ramming but their principal weapon was 'Greek Fire', an invention of Callinicus, a Syrian Greek, and probably first used at the siege of Constantinople in 672–8. 'Greek Fire', probably a mixture based on saltpetre, sulphur and naphtha, which ignited on contact with water, was hurled from the bows of ships by catapults, thrown in small bombs and even projected through a tube by a variant of gunpowder. The manufacture of 'Greek Fire' was a Byzantine state secret until the Arabs discovered the formula during the ninth century. Byzantine naval tactics were not progressive and as late as the tenth century they still relied upon the principles of the old Roman fleet. Like the army, defence was the major concern.

The reorganization of the fleet did not lead to Byzantium regaining control of the sea; it failed to prevent the capture of Thessalonica in 904 and the deportation of its population. However, the reforms did permit the fleet to combat piracy successfully and to take part in the reconquests of the tenth century; Crete was retaken in 961, Cyprus in 965, and an attempt was made to recapture Sicily in 964. When the Seljuk Turks settled in Asia Minor after Manzikert in 1071 and the Normans installed themselves in southern Italy and Sicily, Byzantium attempted to protect its interests by calling for assistance from the Venetian fleet (after 1082) and, later, that of Genoa (1169). Byzantium was forced to concede huge commercial privileges to these powerful Italian cities, together with trading posts in the Empire. From that point onwards, the Byzantine fleet played only a supporting role in Mediterranean warfare despite attempts by Alexius I Comnenus (1081–1118) and Manuel I (1143–80) to rebuild the fleet and recapture the initiative in both the east and the west. *See also* ANKARA; BELISARIUS; CONSTANTINOPLE, FORTIFICATIONS OF; GREECE, ANCIENT; LEO VI; MANZIKERT; NARSES; NAVAL WARFARE; NAVIES; NICEPHORUS II PHOCAS; OTTOMAN TURKS; ROME; TACTICAL ORGANIZATION; WAGGON-LAAGER; YARMUK.

G. DAGRON
JOHN CHILDS

FURTHER READING

Louis Bréhier, *The Life and Death of Byzantium*, tr. Margaret Vaughan (Amsterdam, 1977); Sir Charles Oman, *A History of the Art of War in the Middle Ages* (2 vols, London, 1924); *Procopius*, tr. H. B. Dewing (7 vols, Cambridge, Mass., 1914–40, repr. 1961–2); M. Angold, *The Byzantine Empire, 1025–1204* (London, 1984); Hélène Ahrweiler, *Byzance et la mer* (Paris, 1966); G. Ostrogorsky, *History of the Byzantine State* (3rd edn, Oxford, 1968).

C

Caesar, Julius (100–44 BC) Gaius Julius Caesar was born into a famous patrician family. He possessed extraordinary gifts of intelligence, willpower and self-control, together with great talents as an orator and writer, an exceptional memory and immense physical endurance. In Rome there was no clear distinction beween civil and military functions and senators served the state as priests, administrators, judges and army commanders as required. So, Caesar was already Chief Priest when he was elected Praetor in 62, and in the following year he was sent to the province of Further Spain where he had to fight the peoples of northern Lusitania. His conduct as consul (one of the two chief magistrates of the state) in 59 clearly revealed his energy and determination to get his own way. During his consulship he had himself appointed proconsul (governor) of Illyricum (a small area of the former Yugoslavia) and Cisalpine Gaul (the plain of the River Po), to which the Senate added Transalpine Gaul (which stretched from Lake Geneva to the region of Toulouse and therefore bordered on independent Gaul). This command provided him with potentially great wealth and an army which he could inspire with personal loyalty and affection.

In the spring of 58 Caesar crossed the Rhône on the pretext that he was coming to the defence of Rome's allies, the Aedui, against the Helvetii and against the Germanic chieftain Ariovistus who was then occupying Upper Alsatia and threatening to extend his control beyond that area. Having conquered the Helvetii and Ariovistus, Caesar remained in Gaul, established winter quarters in the northeast of the region at the end of 58, and increasingly began to treat it as a conquered country, which provoked some fierce reactions, even though the peoples of Gaul had only gradually come to understand his

intentions. By 57 most of northern France was under his control, followed by the Atlantic coast in 56, so that he was able in 55–54 to turn his attention to Germany and Britain. Vercingetorix finally established an alliance of Gallic tribes against Rome, but Caesar's victory at Alesia in 52 was crucial in the establishment of permanent Roman control. After his enemies in Rome had attempted to relieve him of his proconsulship, and thus the command of his army, on 10 January 49 Caesar led some of his troops across the Rubicon, the river that marked the frontier of Cisalpine Gaul and Italy, and marched on Rome. This was the beginning of the civil war which he fought against his enemies, who favoured the traditional form of government dominated by the Senate, in Italy and Spain in 49, in Greece and Egypt in 48 and 47, and in Africa (modern Tunisia) in 47 and 46, and again in Spain in 45. He was victorious everywhere, and in 46 was appointed dictator for ten years and in 44 for life, but fell victim to conspirators' daggers on the Ides of March (15 March) in that year.

Caesar wrote seven books of commentaries, *On the Gallic War*; the eighth is the work of his friend Hirtius. Caesar also wrote *On the Civil War*, but the works *On the Alexandrine War*, *On the African War* and *On the Spanish War*, which complete the history of his military achievements, are not by him. Caesar's writings are concise, lucid and direct, and although they give us little information about either the composition of his army or the weapons used by enemy troops, they do give considerable attention to the spirit of his army – their devotion to their leader, their *esprit de corps*, their sense of comradeship and military honour. Naturally all these books sing Caesar's praises and emphasize his virtues as a military leader. His most outstanding quality was the speed with which he took decisions on the battlefield, especially where tactical movements were concerned; these were always effected with great dispatch in order to surprise the enemy. Caesar was also concerned to sustain the morale of his troops and their officers. Roman generals normally harangued their soldiers and Caesar never failed to address his men before they went into action, to tell them what was expected of them. He was even more careful to do so after a defeat, both to explain its causes to them and to restore their confidence. Moreover, he was attentive to their material interests; he doubled their pay in 49 and gave them large quantities of booty, particularly prisoners, whom they could later sell as slaves. He was also sensitive to their mood and would allow them to massacre enemies – men, women and children – whose resistance had especially irritated them. Notably, the commentaries demonstrate the care Caesar took in finding out in advance about the terrain, choosing the time and place for battle, organizing exactly the right formation, using the element of surprise, deceiving the enemy, and devising a good defence against unusual tactics. Above all, long and detailed descriptions of unusual operations and individual episodes, e.g. the naval battle against the Veneti, the two crossings of the straits of Dover, the building of a bridge on piles across the Rhine, the Sieges of Avaricum (Bourges), Uxellodunum (perhaps Le Puy d'Issolu), Alesia (Alise-Sainte-Reine), and Massilia (Marseilles), provide invaluable evidence for the level of sophistication of Roman military techniques, especially in bridge building and siege works. *See also* ALESIA; ROME.

JOËL LE GALL
B. CAMPBELL

FURTHER READING
Translations of Caesar's commentaries – *The Conquest of Gaul*, tr. S. A. Handford with an introduction by J. F. Gardner (Harmondsworth, 1982) and *The Civil War*, tr. J. F. Gardner (Harmondsworth, 1967); in general – R. Syme, *The Roman Revolution* (Oxford, 1939), pp. 47–96; M. Gelzer, *Caesar: Politician and Statesman* (Oxford, 1969); Z. Yavetz, *Julius Caesar and his Public Image* (London, 1983).

Calais (Pas-de-Calais), Siege of (1–7 January 1558) The town of Calais was the only part of France retained by the English after 1453 and, thanks to the French concession, it enjoyed an inflated reputation for impregnability. The key to its defence was the marshy valley of the River Hammes; to enable the marshes to be flooded in time, the smaller forts of the Pale (or defensive zone) had to delay a besieger. However, by 1558 all the fortifications were obsolescent, for modernization had been prevented by the expenditure in Scotland and at Boulogne in the previous decade. The garrison had been reduced to some 2,000 soldiers and 1,000 militia dispersed among the various forts. Yet neither the weaknesses of the fortress, nor the still debated failure of the Lord Deputy to take counter-measures until it was too late, detracts from the skill with which the Duke of Guise's attack was prepared or the audacity with which it was mounted. Guise invaded the Pale on 1 January 1558 with an army of 25,000 and advanced directly on the two minor forts that commanded the river and the harbour. Both fell on the 3rd, enabling him to surround the town and cut it off from England. After two days of bombardment the French waded across the upper harbour at low tide on the night of the 6th and assaulted the castle, which commanded the town. The castle was mined, but the mine failed to explode, and once a counter-attack was repulsed, the Lord Deputy surrendered early the next morning. The town of Guines, further up the Hammes and the strongest of the Pale forts, held out, but it was cut off from England and too small to stand a siege. After four days of bombardment and assault it surrendered on 22 January. The delay in the siege of Guines was caused by a major storm that broke on the 12th. Had Guise attacked later or Calais held out longer, the weather would probably have forced him to raise the Calais siege. It was a calculated risk that did much for his reputation. Nevertheless, the loss of Calais was also a dramatic illustration of the dangers of pre-artillery fortifications in the mid-sixteenth century; the forts of the Pale were too small to defend themselves and were little more than traps for their garrisons. As Boulogne had already shown, an English attempt to hold a continental outpost involved a level of expenditure on fortification that was greater than the outpost was worth. *See also* BOULOGNE; FORTIFICATION; GREAT BRITAIN; GUISE.

SIMON ADAMS

FURTHER READING
H. M. Colvin et al., *The History of the King's Works*, iv, pt 1 (London, 1975), pp. 337–74; D. M. Potter, 'The duc of Guise and the fall of Calais, 1557–1558', *English Historical Review*, xcviii (1983), pp. 481–512; C. S. L. Davies, 'England and the French war, 1557–9', in *The Mid-Tudor Polity c.1540–1560*, ed. J. Loach and R. Tittler (London, 1980), pp. 159–85.

Cambrai, Battle of (20 November–7 December 1917) Often regarded as the 'first modern battle', Cambrai was a large-scale British raid transformed into an attempt to break through the German Hindenburg Line on the Western Front. Launched without preliminary bombardment and using 378 tanks supported by infantry, artillery and aircraft in a ground attack role, the attack by General Byng's 3rd Army achieved a considerable degree of surprise. However, through the changes wrought in the original concept, there were insufficient reserves to exploit the initial success. Tanks were still too unreliable to be other than a 'break-in' as opposed to a 'breakthrough' weapon, and only 92 remained serviceable by 23 November. Consequently, while penetrating the positions of the German 2nd Army to a depth of 3 miles over a 6-mile frontage, the momentum of attack was lost in the struggle for Bourlon Wood. On 30 November the Germans counter-attacked, utilizing the fruits of their own careful study of the problems of breakthrough. Drawing on captured French manuals and honed in operations such as those at Tarnopol and Riga on the Eastern Front in July and September 1917 and at Caporetto on the Italian Front in October, the German infantry's new infiltration tactics accompanied by short and concentrated artillery bombardment had restored the front by 7 December. Both sides had suffered some 45,000 casualties but, in the process, had learned valuable lessons to be applied in the following year. *See also* CAPORETTO; FULLER; LIDDELL HART; TANKS.

IAN F. W. BECKETT

FURTHER READING
B. Cooper, *The Ironclads of Cambrai* (London, 1967); A. J. Smithers, *The New Excalibur* (London, 1986); J. Williams, *Byng of Vimy* (London, 1983); Bruce I. Gudmundsson, *Stormtroop Tactics: innovation in the German army, 1914–1918* (New York, 1989).

Camps The old term for the construction and design of camps was *castrametation*, derived from the Latin *castra* (a camp) and *metari* (to lay out). It was still used in this sense in nineteenth-century training manuals. Castrametation concerned the choice of camp-site and the principles of construction. This had a direct bearing on tactics, as the objective of a camp was to allow a force to manoeuvre against or obstruct an opponent while safeguarding itself. Polybius described the principles and rules of castrametation during the Roman Republic, while Vegetius added detail from the period of the Roman Empire. Subsequent authors and engineers have largely followed their advice.

Three main operational requirements governed the position of a camp. First, it had to be secure; the site could be additionally protected by outposts, guards, patrols and entrenchments. Second, it had to be so sited that the troops could easily and quickly be marshalled for battle. Third, it had to be positioned to guarantee maximum freedom of action for its defenders while restricting the options of the enemy. Logistical considerations had also to be answered. A camp had to be close to a line of communication, which meant, for a very long period of history, a waterway, to pasturage for horses and to sources of timber for fires and palisades to strengthen entrenchments. In instances where there was insufficient wood, the destruction of nearby villages was the classic solution. Reasons of health led commanders to avoid dirty or marshy localities. They also needed tents or huts for the men and a source of clean water. When troops were forced to bivouac or sleep on the ground without cover, procedures which usually occurred only on the eve of or during battle, the incidence of sickness rose appreciably.

The Roman Legion The legionary camp was important, not only because the principles on which it was based were applied for several centuries, but because towns were built to the same pattern. It thus had a marked influence on urban planning.

While on the march, a legion camped every night. The site was chosen by the officers although the final decision rested with the *augures*. Two streets, the *via praetoria* and the *via decumana* or *principalis*, divided the ground plan into four rectangular spaces. Entry and exit were by four gates at the end of these streets. The quarters of the consul (*praetorium*), the tribunes and field officers occupied the centre, close to the stores (*quaestorium*). The tents of each century of the legion were arranged in lines at right angles to the main streets, the centurion's tent at the end. The cavalry and auxiliary troops followed similar arrangements.

On taking the decision to encamp, a tribune surveyed the terrain with a *groma* and caused the streets and lines to be indicated by red flags and spears. Half the legionaries and the *velites* then formed up between the camp site and the direction of the enemy while the remainder of the legion dug a ditch around the perimeter and used the excavated earth to build a rampart which was then mounted by a palisade. Spiked man-traps might also be placed beyond the ditch. Such modest protection was adequate when a force camped overnight or for a few days but it was made more elaborate for longer occupancies. During his campaign against the Belgae, Caesar's camp had a ditch 18 feet wide and a wall 12 feet high. Vespasian's camps in the Jewish wars were equipped with watchtowers and ballistas.

Legionary camps were abandoned when the troops marched but the durability of the entrenchments meant that they could often be reoccupied and rebuilt. Camps became permanent fortresses when they were sited on the *limites*, the imperial frontier zones. They were then constructed from stone or brick but followed a similar layout to the camps. Legionaries were not supposed to marry, hence close to the permanent camps grew up villages of small huts (*canabae*) housing the female camp followers and a host of traders and sutlers. These formed the bases for the towns (*vici*) which developed around Roman fortresses.

Early Modern Period During the Middle Ages, armies usually camped on the march and during siege operations but their camps' layouts were dominated more by social rank than military necessities. The re-emergence of standing armies in the sixteenth and seventeenth centuries made the camp a regular feature of all campaigns. In winter, troops were quartered in villages and towns; the early initiative in a campaign went to the side which was first to concentrate its forces and take the field. On campaign, apart from instances when certain troops were ordered to garrison fortresses, soldiers lived in tented camps. An entrenchment was dug to the front and flanks if the enemy was close or if the camp was intended for a lengthy occupation.

The Roman system of packing troops closely together in their camps was no longer appropriate in the face of the danger from artillery bombardment. Armies camped in battle order, usually in two lines, with the horse on the flanks and the infantry in the centre. Artillery and baggage were placed to the rear. Technically, provided that open space existed to the front, the army could leave its tents and form a line of battle in the shortest possible time. The front and flanks were protected by patrols and the occupation of neighbouring villages and farms by light troops, cavalry and artillery. Troops foraged to the front and flanks; the rear areas were left intact to sustain a retreat. Despite all these precautions, armies were surprised in their camps – Turenne at Mergentheim in 1645,

Luxembourg at Steenkirk in 1692, and Frederick the Great at Hochkirch in 1758. During the seventeenth and eighteenth centuries, the emphasis on campaigns of manoeuvre rather than combat meant that armies spent long periods in entrenched camps, often within sight of the enemy's encampment (i.e. the Confederate Army at Koekelberg in 1697; Frederick the Great at Bunzelwitz in 1761 and during the War of the Bavarian Succession, 1778–9).

Modern Period As the range of artillery increased and armies consisting of several corps became common, the troops had to encamp at a greater distance from the enemy, usually in villages and farms rather than tents. They were protected by strong advance-guards and patrols. On the Western Front during the First World War, rest camps were maintained behind the lines and the continuous and relatively stable front obviated the need for security. Increasingly, during the twentieth century, the word 'camp' has been applied to a variety of military installations, whether permanent or temporary.

Camps have been widely employed for training. As long as battles were fought at close quarters, combat training could be carried out on parade grounds and in riding schools. The ditches of fortresses made excellent musketry ranges. Long-range rifles and artillery and, later, mechanization caused battle training to expand spatially, usually into the countryside after the harvest. This pattern is still followed by NATO forces in Germany. Armies have also acquired large, permanent training areas – Salisbury Plain, the Brecklands, Otterburn – to which permanent camps and depots have been attached (Tidworth, Larkhill, etc.). Also, permanent peacetime training camps were established away from training areas in order to receive and train recruits – Châlons in France, Aldershot in England and Eisenborn in Germany.

France was the first modern nation to develop the concept of the training camp, where elements of the army came together for a designated period to practise tactical drills and evolutions. The first was at Pont de l'Arche, near Rouen, between 1480 and 1482, where French infantry were trained by the Swiss in the new infantry tactics; this was the birth of what became known as the 'Picardy Bands'. The English army trained at a camp on Hounslow Heath (1685–8) and during the eighteenth century, camps for training formations in battlefield evolutions and co-operation became common in all European armies. The French army tested the efficacy of the *ordre profond* (column) and the *ordre mince* (line) at a camp at Vaussieux in Normandy in 1778. Following the eighteenth-century Prussian model, nineteenth-century armies expanded their training camps into full-scale manoeuvres. *See also* FORTIFICATION, FIELD; MANOEUVRE AND MANOEUVRES; MILITARY RESTRICTIONS ON USE OF LAND; PROPERTY OWNED BY THE MILITARY; ROME; TRAINING; VEGETIUS RENATUS.

J.-M. GOENAGA
JOHN CHILDS

FURTHER READING
D. J. Breeze and B. Dobson, *Hadrian's Wall* (3rd edn, Harmondsworth, 1987); K. Mallory and A. Ottar, *The Architecture of Aggression* (London, 1973); J. A. Houlding, *Fit for Service* (Oxford, 1981).

Cannae, Battle of (216 BC) A village in the valley of the Aufidus River (modern Ofanto) in Apulia, Cannae was the site of Hannibal's great victory against the Roman army under the command of the consuls L. Aemilius Paullus and C. Terentius Varro. Hannibal, though greatly outnumbered, stationed his best troops on both wings while the centre was drawn up in crescent formation curving towards the enemy. The Romans had a traditional formation with the legions in the centre and cavalry on the wings. The Carthaginian centre fell back under attack from the legionaries but was not broken. So, the Romans were led into a trap which was closed by the African infantry on the wings and completed by the Celtic and Spanish cavalry positioned on Hannibal's left wing which routed the cavalry opposite, charged across behind the Roman line to engage the remaining Roman cavalry, and then returned to attack the rear of the infantry. The Romans suffered huge losses, Aemilius Paullus being among the dead.

Recent archaeological discoveries have not resolved the question whether the battle took place on the left or right bank of the Aufidus. Hannibal's manoeuvre at Cannae remains a subject of study for strategists and was used as a model by von Schlieffen. *See also* CARTHAGE; HANNIBAL; ROME; SCHLIEFFEN.

J. LE GALL
B. CAMPBELL

FURTHER READING
F. Cornelius, *Cannae. Das militärische und das literarische Problem* (Leipzig, 1932); F. W. Walbank, *A Historical Commentary on Polybius* (Oxford, 1957), i, 435–49; L. J. F. Keppie, *The Making of the Roman Army: from republic to empire* (London, 1984), pp. 26–8.

Cantons *See* MILITARY DISTRICTS

Capitulation *See* SURRENDER

Caporetto, Battle of (24 October–25 November 1917) General von Below's German 14th Army was dispatched to the Italian front in August 1917 to restore the situation following the withdrawal of Austro-Hungarian forces in the face of an Italian offensive. German and Austro-Hungarian formations were then concentrated against the sector held by the Italian 2nd, 3rd and 4th Armies along the Isonzo, the brunt of a wide-ranging counter-offensive falling on General Capello's 2nd Army in the vicinity of Caporetto. Not only had the Central Powers achieved strategic surprise but, for the first time in the west, infiltration tactics by German infantry and the kind of short 'hurricane' bombardments perfected on the Eastern Front by Colonel Georg Bruchmüller, which liberally mixed gas and explosive shells in an attempt to paralyse an opponent's command structure, added to the disruption. An advance of 12 miles was achieved on the first day and, although the Italian 3rd and 4th Armies were able to withdraw to the Piave in reasonable order,

over 275,000 Italian troops surrendered. British and French reinforcements were rushed to Italy and the Italian commander-in-chief, Cadorna, was replaced by General Diaz before the front was stabilized on the Piave. The new German methods would shortly be utilized in their counter-attack at Cambrai on the Western Front in November–December 1917. *See also* BRUSILOV; CAMBRAI; ROMMEL.

IAN F. W. BECKETT

FURTHER READING
C. Falls, *Caporetto 1917* (London, 1966); M. Isenghi, *I vinti di Caporetto nella letterattura di guerra* (Padua, 1967); R. Seth, *Caporetto: the scapegoat battle* (London, 1965); M. Silvestri, *Isonzo 1917* (Turin, 1965).

Carnot, Lazare (1753–1823) This military engineer, mathematician and politician was an important figure during the French Revolution. A graduate of the School of Engineering at Mézières in 1777, he was already a captain when he began his political career. In August 1793, he was appointed to the Committee of Public Safety where he was placed in charge of war administration and given the overall direction of military operations. In this office he acquired a reputation as 'the organizer of victory'. Although he had written a eulogy of Vauban in 1783, he soon adopted the military ideas of the revolutionaries, for which he provided a coherent formulation, especially in his *Système général des opérations de la campagne de 1794*. Here he laid down the principles governing the nation in arms, mass warfare and the attempt to achieve decisive acts of annihilation through the concentration of forces and the destruction of the main enemy in battle. However, these principles were not universally applied to French strategy. While Carnot wanted to destroy English trade by leading an offensive against the northern ports, Robespierre and Saint-Just favoured trying to establish a new balance of power throughout Europe by pushing the frontiers of the Holy Roman Empire back beyond the Rhine. Carnot preferred the security of firm frontiers embracing patriotic civilian populations to the export of revolution to

France's sister republics and achievement of the 'natural' frontiers of the Rhine and Alps. In his instructions to the army commanders he advised them to use spies and captive balloons to observe the enemy; to attack against the flanks and the rear rather than frontally; to use overwhelming force (the tactic of 'six against one'); and to concentrate their resources and spare no effort once the troops were engaged. He published numerous works on strategy and tactics. Though he was not especially innovative, he exerted a decisive influence on the generals of the Revolution. *See also* DAVOUT; GUIBERT; NAPOLEON; VAUBAN.

J.-P. CHARNAY

FURTHER READING
Marcel Reinhard, *Le Grand Carnot* (2 vols, Paris, 1950–2); J.-P. Charnay, *Lazare Carnot: révolution et mathématiques* (2 vols, Paris, 1984).

Carthage Tradition has it that Carthage was founded in 814 BC by Dido (or Elissa), Princess of Tyre; it was therefore a Phoenician city and this name was corrupted by the Romans to give us 'Punic'. It is probable, however, that the foundation occurred about half a century later. Founded by a seafaring people on the Gulf of Tunis, at the meeting point of the western and the eastern Mediterranean, and with a good harbour, Carthage was ideally situated to exploit maritime trade. As early as the seventh century BC, it outstripped the ancient Phoenician settlements in the west and emerged as a major power *c.*550 BC; in conjunction with the Etruscans the Carthaginian fleet fought its first recorded naval battle at Alalia *c.*535, in which it defeated the westward movement of the Greek communities, Massilia and Phocaea. Carthage proceeded to establish control in southern Sardinia and parts of southern Spain. Moreover, it fought with the Greek settlers in the eastern part of Sicily to establish its claim over the island. This rivalry was at the root of a series of wars, particularly in the fifth and fourth centuries. In 480 BC a Carthaginian invading army was defeated at Himera by Greek forces under the tyrants Gelon and Theron; continuing warfare throughout the fifth century eventually confined Carthage to western Sicily. Later, in an attempt to preserve its position in the central Mediterranean, Carthage came into conflict with Rome in the three Punic Wars (264–241; 218–201; 149–146) which ended with the destruction of the city after courageous resistance by its entire population.

The fleets of Carthage were among the best in the Ancient World but we know very little about them. The ships were certainly very similar to contemporary Greek ships. They were 'long boats', powered by oars, the oarsmen were well trained, and the captains and pilots were men of exceptional skill. During the First Punic War, the Romans gained the upper hand by inventing hinged gangways with grappling irons, which landed on the Punic ships and brought them to a halt alongside their own, enabling the Romans to board them. These over-complicated devices were not, however, used in later wars. Because there was no compulsory military service for Carthaginians, the armies of Carthage were made up of mercenaries, of doubtful loyalty, who came either from Europe (Spain, Gaul, Italy or Greece) or from Africa (especially cavalry from Numidia). Their equipment and style of fighting were in keeping with their own national customs and they were commanded by their own countrymen. However, the higher-ranking officers and the generals were members of the Carthaginian aristocracy, who controlled the oligarchic constitution, though the generals were often fearful of being condemned to death and crucified after a defeat since their actions were examined by a body of 104 'judges'. In its wars Carthage used elephants, then still found in north Africa, but these nervous animals often seem to have been as much a danger to their own side as to the enemy. *See also* CANNAE; HANNIBAL; ROME.

JOËL LE GALL
B. CAMPBELL

FURTHER READING
S. Gsell, *Histoire ancienne de l'Afrique du Nord* (Paris, 1912–29); G. C. Picard, *Carthage* (London, 1964); B. H. Warmington, *Carthage* (London, 1960).

Cartography The need to have representation of space and terrain goes back to Antiquity. It is felt by travellers who wish to know not only distances but also directions and the configuration of the countries they have to cross and, even more exactly, the difficulties they will encounter as a result of relief and terrain, together with the obstacles they will run up against or the assistance they will derive from the rivers, lakes and streams, etc. This same concern is shared by merchants and soldiers and Vegetius declares that a general must have 'tables drawn up exactly which show not only the distances in numbers of steps, but also the quality of the paths, shorter routes, what lodging is to be found there and the mountains and rivers'. In this, he is referring to the representation of space and terrain, the two essential goals which geographical and topographical maps seek to achieve. This representation, which may be expressed in lists enumerating, for example, staging posts on a route, very soon took on a graphic form. In fact, schematic representations of the road network of the Empire appeared as early as the Antonine period, in such maps as that from which the famous *Tabula Peutingeriana* was copied.

The concern to represent space and terrain almost disappeared in the Middle Ages where, for several centuries, little was produced except symbolic schemes placing Jerusalem in the centre of the world. A revival does, however, occur in the thirteenth century. The monk Gilles Colonne advised Philip the Fair to have maps made and, in England, the monk Matthew Paris produced relatively accurate maps of Palestine and Britain and itineraries resembling those of the *Tabula Peutingeriana*. The same concern is found everywhere an organized state takes care to maintain permanent road routes. This was the case in China and in the pre-Columbian empires.

Modern cartography, nevertheless, owes its greatest debt to Western Europe. From about 1300, European mariners employed simple coastal charts (*portolani*) complete with books of sailing instructions which described the prominent coastal features. The earliest surviving terrestrial globe, that of Martin Behaim, dates from 1491. From that date, the search for systems of projection which provide the least degree of deformation became particularly lively. The first coherent system was the projection of Mercator (d. 1594) as developed by Edward Wright (d. 1615).

The next requirement was exact measurement, which occurred in three phases. The first of these, based on the work of Huyghens and the French Academy in the 1680s as perfected by Harrison in the 1720s, was the precise calculation of longitude on land and at sea. The second occurred in the eighteenth century with advances in triangulation (the measurement of the distance between Dunkirk and Perpignan, missions to Lapland and Peru to measure the flattening of the Earth at the poles, etc.) itself derived from the work of Gemma Frisino in the early sixteenth century. The third phase would come in the twentieth century with satellite photography.

With the Renaissance, great advances were made. The first modern maps of military and administrative utility were produced in northern Italy in the mid-fifteenth century. With the advent of mail services, lists of halting places, such as Robert Estienne's *Le Guide des chemins de France*, proliferated. They did, however, only go part of the way to meeting the new needs of the political authorities to possess a thorough knowledge of their states. As P. de Dainville has shown, it is with frontiers that modern cartographic work begins. The political and administrative objective here is patent. The object was to define the limits of areas of sovereignty. There was also a military objective, since it was disputed lands that were involved, which were destined to become theatres of military operations. It was these needs which led to the creation of a series of relatively large-scale 'plats' of the coasts of England and of the Pale of Calais after 1529 and particularly in the period 1539–52 when England's dominions were repeatedly under threat of invasion from France, Spain and the Netherlands. After this, however, the impulse towards military mapping slackened

'A True & Exact Map of the Seat of War in Brabant & Flanders with ye Enemies Lines in their Just Dimensions' (London, 1705). The zig-zagged line from Antwerp to the Meuse below Namur depicts the field fortifications built by the French to protect the area of the Spanish Netherlands from which they collected contributions (*see* FORTIFICATION, FIELD). These Lines were forced by Marlborough in 1705 (*see* MARLBOROUGH).
(The British Library)

in England, with the leadership in this area passing first to the Netherlands and, in the seventeenth century, to France. In 1607, taking advantage of the skills acquired by Italian engineers, Henry IV of France ordered that a map of the frontiers and coasts of his kingdom should be drawn up. In each frontier province, one or two of the king's surveyors operated, assisted by clerks. Triangulation was introduced into the preparation of these maps and great efforts were made, particularly in the Dauphiné. Under Louis XIII, *géographes de cabinet* derived small-scale maps for the whole of the kingdom from this work. In the first part of the reign of Louis XIV, the *Cartes générales de toutes les provinces de France* of Nicolas Tassin became available (1633). In 1651, the *Théâtre de France* appeared. This was the work of Nicolas Sanson (1600–67), first of a family of famous cartographers. Towards the end of the reign, the Sanson dynasty was succeeded by that of the Jaillots. Nicolas Sanson's maps were still inexact as regards the representa-

tion of angles and, consequently, of surface area. Work carried out under the aegis of the Académie des Sciences by Huyghens, Jean-Dominique Cassini and the Abbé Picard gave rise to the publication, in 1684, of the *Carte de France corrigée par ordre du roi sur les observations de MM. de l'Académie des sciences* (*Map of France corrected by order of the king on the basis of the observations of the gentlemen of the Academy of Sciences*) which, for the first time, gave an adequate idea of the surface area of France. When congratulating those who had produced it, Louis XIV could not, however, restrain himself from remarking, 'Your work has cost me one third of my kingdom', as it had previously been thought that France extended further toward the West. In parallel with this development, the sixteenth century saw a proliferation of 'Pourtraicts' (Portraits) of towns and cities and bird's eye views, notably in the six volumes of Braun and Hagenberg's *Civitates Orbis Terrarum* (1572–1617) and, in the seventeenth century, many town plans were produced, including those by Gomboust (Paris, 1652; Rouen, 1656, etc.).

Military cartography increasingly marked itself off by the production of plans of fortifications and the interest devoted to terrain. Hachures made their appearance in the seventeenth century, though as yet without any rigorous basis, as did symbols to indicate forests, marshes, etc. Another aspect of military cartography was that it was intended to be kept secret. Thus the various sovereigns created map offices. Louvois accorded especial importance to Louis XIV's collection when the *Dépôt de la Guerre* was being set up in 1688. For France, there are no less than about twenty collections of plans of fortresses, the oldest of which date from the reign of Henry IV. Among the most famous, we may cite the *Recueil des plans des places du roi*, known as *The Louvois Atlas* (1683–8), the *Atlas de chacune des places fortes* drawn up as required by the circular of 1774, the *Atlas des places fortes offert à Mgr le duc d'Angoulême* (1824). In this same connection, we should also make special mention of the creation of the exceptional *Dépôt des Plans-Reliefs* in 1668.

It was in 1696 that the French corps of surveyors was formed, with the title 'Corps of Engineers of the Camps and Armies of the King'. This corps, which was first attached to the Department of Fortifications and later, in 1761, to the *Dépôt de la Guerre*, saw its members come under the orders of the directors of the Engineer Corps in 1776 and become progressively militarized. In 1784, the surveyors were issued with a uniform. After first being abolished in 1791, then almost immediately re-established with a military hierarchy, it became, in 1809, the Imperial Corps of Surveyors with a complement of 90, including six student members. Similar developments occurred in Prussia, Austria and Britain in the course of the eighteenth century. In 1831, the French surveyors were attached to the General Staff corps. When this disappeared after the war of 1870–1, the Army Geographical Service was set up in 1885, partly under the aegis of the *Dépôt de la Guerre*. From this time

onward, some of the maps which did not contain any particular military information, such as current topographical maps, could be made accessible to the public and put on sale. This led, after the armistice of 1940, to the creation of the French National Geographical Institute, which was formally constituted in 1946. The army, which was the major party involved, especially as the use of maps has continually expanded, maintained a permanent liaison with the only map-making establishment in France through the 'Geographical Section' of the Army, which is attached to the Army General Staff. Today, most non-European states keep their larger-scale official mapping secret and even in European democracies there are several categories of official mapping that are confidential. The dividing line between topographical maps and military maps in France was set at the 1:5,000 mark and military maps are not generally available to the public.

The first general topographical maps were usually produced as military undertakings though in France the initial impetus was civilian. The first topographical map of France was the so-called Cassini map (the name of another family of topographers), the work of Cassini de Thury (1714–84) and his son Jacques-Dominique Cassini, which was made up of 184 sheets, had a scale of 1:86,400 and used hachures in what was still a subjective manner. The earlier (1720–3) Austrian survey of the Milanese and Ferrari's map of the Netherlands, and the surveys of the Austrian crown lands executed after 1780, were conducted by the military and primarily served military purposes.

The idea of General Staff maps following the metric system and indicating relief in a more exact way became widespread in the early nineteenth century. The first sheets of the Prussian General Staff map came out in 1841, those of the French map following in 1844. Both were on a scale of 1:80,000. The drawing up of this kind of map was the occasion for real investigative work on the part of surveyors not only into terrain but also into populations and their activities. These topographical maps were based upon guiding plans with contours, on the basis of which hachures were made following the direction of slopes, spaced out one quarter of their length and thicker at the top than at the bottom. These maps were drawn up on the zenithal light system, according to which light is supposed to shine upon the terrain in such a way that the lightest surfaces are those which are closest to the horizontal. The symbols on these maps were simplified and increased in variety. The French General Staff map was revised in 1889. Other countries also equipped themselves with General Staff (or National Survey) maps, generally on a scale of 1:80,000 or 1:100,000. Some of these used oblique light, light being supposed to come from the north-western corner of the sheet. One occasionally finds horizontal hachure systems (e.g. Sweden). Though technically obsolete today, these hachured maps are none the less extremely expressive.

In the twentieth century, the need for precision and exactitude has led us generally to prefer contour maps that are both on a larger scale (1:50,000 or even 1:20,000) and in colour though mountainous countries such as Switzerland employ a mixture of both. Today remote imagery from satellites and the use of computers in the processes of surveying and map making are revolutionizing cartography, as they are revolutionizing the representation of the Earth in general. *See also* CHAMLAY; COEHOORN; ENGINEERS; FORTIFICATION; ICONOGRAPHY; LOUVOIS; STEVIN; VAUBAN.

A. CORVISIER
PETER BARBER

FURTHER READING
Cartographical Innovations: An International Handbook of Mapping Terms to 1900, eds H. M. Wallis and A. H. Robinson (Tring, 1987); *The History of the King's Works*, eds H. M. Colvin et al (London, 1975 and 1982), iii & iv; D. Buisseret, 'Les Ingénieurs du roi au temps du Henri IV', *Bulletin de la section de Géographie* (Bibliothèque Nationale de Paris), lxxvii (1963), pp. 13–84; Y. Hodson, 'Prince William, royal map collector', *The Map Collector*, xliv (1988), pp. 2–12; *Lexikon zur Geschichte der Kartographie von den Anfangen bis zum ersten Weltkrieg*, eds I. Kretschmer, J. Dörflinger and F. Wawrrink (Vienna, 1986).

Casilinum, Battle of *See* NARSES

Castex, Raoul (1878–1968) Entering the French navy in 1896, Castex came to prominence by producing, between 1904 and 1913, several works of maritime history. While continuing a distinguished naval career, he wrote in 1920 his *Synthèse de la guerre sous-marine*, in which he argued that the German use of submarines during the First World War had been legitimate, provoking a lively controversy between the British and the French at the Washington Conference on naval disarmament in 1922. In *Questions d'État-major* (1923–4), he argued for a rigorous organization of command. He then devoted himself to his major work, *Théories stratégiques*, the five volumes of which appeared between 1929 and 1935. The *Théories*, which synthesized and superseded all that had previously been written on the subject, considered all aspects of war at sea and the overall effects of sea power, presenting some remarkable prognostications. In particular, Castex demonstrated that decisive battles are very rare in history and there is no geographical determinism to enable one to conclude, as Mahan had done, that sea power is inevitably superior to land forces. The work had an enormous impact, particularly in the Mediterranean countries and Latin America, but the spread of its influence was halted by the outbreak of the Second World War. Castex was promoted to admiral in 1937 and in 1939 became Admiral of the French Northern Fleet. His warnings regarding the weakness of French military planning were prophetic yet considered pessimistic and he was retired in November 1939. His intense intellectual activity continued unabated until the early 1960s and he died at Villeneuve-de-Rivière on 10 January 1968. *See also* BLOCKADES; COMBINED OPERATIONS; COMMERCE-RAIDING; CORBETT; MAHAN; NAVAL WARFARE; NAVIES; STRATEGY.

H. COUTAU-BÉGARIE

FURTHER READING
Hervé Coutau-Bégarie, *La Puissance maritime: Castex et la stratégie navale* (Paris, 1985); Hervé Coutau-Bégarie, *Castex, la stratégie inconnu* (Paris, 1986).

Castles The word 'castle' is found in the Romance languages (in the form, 'chastel', from the Latin *castellum*) as early as the *Song of Roland*. It normally designates a construction enjoying a certain material autonomy in relation to its environment, a building marked off from other current forms of habitation by virtue of both its size and its overall style, which is intended to serve as a permanent or temporary residence for an individual or a family. In this sense, the castle can be distinguished from the mansion or private residence, which is both socially and economically integrated with its locality, and from the palace, which is specifically associated with functions of a public or an official nature, and from the citadel or fort, which has essentially a military role. It is the specific characteristic of a castle to dominate a certain territory, whether that domination be symbolic or real, informal or legal. The castle is a place of authority and power – at least psychological power. There is no break in continuity between the French castle of the medieval period and the château of modern times. Each is situated in a comparable social context, in spite of the 'military' appearance of the former and the 'civil' appearance of the latter. The appearance of the castle is also closely bound up with the establishment of feudal relations and with the rise of the feudal lords and their lineage.

The *fort château* of the Middle Ages was the expression of a social regime in which the lay ruling class, which was largely hereditary, normally preferred to deploy its activities in the field of war; war lords enjoyed acknowledged prestige, and the notion of a purely civil power did not exist. It was, second, the expression of an economic regime in which the rich and powerful derived the greater part of their resources and revenues from lands which, by various legal titles, belonged to them or fell under their authority. They had every reason and incentive to reside on their lands among the peasants who worked to provide for their living. It was, third, the expression of a military system which was unsuited, for want of the appropriate means, either for the task of establishing real frontiers on the periphery of the various political entities or for the task of safeguarding truly protected and immune central zones. It was, lastly, the expression of a regime in which power tended predominantly to be divided, fragmented and confused even if each of the various centres of power so created tended to have its place within a more or less rigorously defined hierarchy.

We must also emphasize the variation in the types of castles. The whole range is represented, running from the simple one- or two-storey tower with a tile or slate roof, somewhat akin to the common or garden *pigeonnier*, to the monumental construction which, over the generations, has come, after a variety of improvements and extensions, to take on the aspect and dimensions of a small town. One castle might be considered a 'key to power in a locality' and only a 'siege mounted by a prince' might be able to overcome it, while another would provide only a symbolic obstacle to a band of adventurers roaming the countryside in search of plunder. Some castles would give their names to proud lineages, whereas others would remain forever anonymous. Some would see populous areas – townships or cities – arise and develop within their shade; others would remain isolated and desolate on a rocky outcrop or lost in the depths of a forest. Some would offer a gloomy lair to rusty rapiered Don Quixotes, while others, by the magnificence of their architecture and their fine stone backdrops, would provide a setting for the most refined courtly life.

Castles must have increased in number from the last decade of the tenth century onwards in the form of the mote and bailey castle (or *motte castrale*), which could be built quickly and cheaply. For any particular region, the written documentation alone attests to a regular increase in the number of castles between the year 1000 and the fourteenth and fifteenth centuries. We may take the Charentais region as an example: there were 12 castles at the beginning of the eleventh century, 72 at the beginning of the twelfth and 88 at the beginning of the thirteenth. For Alsace, we find records of 16 before 1100, 76 before 1200, 234 before

115

1300, 394 before 1400 and 445 before 1500. This gives us, for the fifteenth century, one castle for every 30 km^2 (11.6 miles^2). In an area on the edge of the Forez and the Bourbonnais extending over 1,500 km^2 (580 miles^2), including some 100 parishes within its bounds, we find 29 castles before 1200, then a further 58 castles or fortified residences built by the end of the fourteenth century. Around 1380, there are 87 castles or fortified residences, which is almost one per parish.

Obviously, the geography of castles reflects the military preoccupations of those who built them. Castles are concentrated around rivers that various parties wish to control. This was the case in the Moselle valley, which was disputed by the Counts of Bar and Vaudémont, the Duke of Lorraine and the Bishops of Verdun and Metz. They are also found on the border between two competing powers, the classic example being the border between the French and the Norman Vexin regions, where for more than a century the Kings of France and the Kings of England, who were also Dukes of Normandy, were at odds.

Castles dominated the Rhine gorge enabling petty nobles and princes to exact tolls from river traffic. In Britain, a network of castles had secured England for the Normans after 1066 and the castle was the method by which Wales was gradually conquered and controlled between the eleventh and the fourteenth centuries. The castle was also the basis of the military power within the Crusader states in the Holy Land.

The location of a castle is also a function of relief and terrain. There are castles built on a plain surrounded by a moat filled with water (the *Wasserburgen* of the Münsterland) and mountain castles. It is also a function of population density: in the thirteenth century, in English Gascony, areas almost completely bereft of castles coexisted alongside others that were abundantly covered by them. This contrast can only partially be explained by the fortification of certain areas, including certain frontier territories, for defensive purposes. It was chiefly the result of endogenous political developments, the de-velopment of the feudal system and popula-tion distribution: whereas in 1280 there were only 35 castles in the vast triangle of the Landes, in the same period the Agenais contained 130 fortified buildings in 7,000 km^2 (2,700 miles^2), one castle for every 50 km^2 (20.76 miles^2).

The development of the structure of castles can only be explained, as might be expected, in terms of the military role they were expected to play. The builders had to take into consideration the state of the art of war in the period. There was the period of the mote and bailey castle, which de-veloped between the Loire and the Rhine during the last third of the tenth century, with its wooden tower, ditch and palisades. Then, before the year 1000, even in the heart of France, quadrangular stone keeps replaced the wooden towers (e.g. at Langeais, Loches, Loudun and Niort). In parallel with this development, the outer walls were also strengthened and the range of defensive obstacles extended. The climax of this period came with Château-Gaillard, which was built at the end of the twelfth century and is sometimes consid-ered the masterpiece of 'Norman' castle-building.

Castle construction entered upon a new phase after 1200: castles became more compact and self-contained and were more regular in construction whether or not they contained a keep. The prototype was Philip Augustus's Louvre with its vast square flanked by towers, its broad moat and its inner courtyard, in the centre of which stood the imposing cylindrical keep, three vaulted storeys high, topped with a conical roof. The Louvre 'must for a long time have seemed the consummate model, given its size, the quality of its construction and the revolutionary, functional conception which it represented, verging as it did upon perfection for the period in its strict geometry, its overall economy and the minute attention paid to the flanking of all its parts' (André Châtelain).

For a long time, no further major innova-tions were seen, though we ought to men-tion the introduction of higher curtain walls and also the introduction of terracing on the tops of towers. Let us note in passing that, as a product of the desire to shelter the French monarchy from the turbulent life of the capital, the huge château at Vincennes was a fortified forerunner of Versailles. Not until the fifteenth century did artillery have an impact on castle-building: boulevards, barbicans, loopholes, glacis and embankments at the foot of the towers and low, squat artillery towers giving rise, around 1500, to bastioned fortification.

However, the increasing efficiency and complexity of methods both of attack and of defence, together with the expulsion of military threats beyond the political frontiers of the various states (which, for France, occurred after the Hundred Years' War), gave rise to a decisive split in the history of castles; from this point on, we find, on the one hand, imposing citadels built by and for the state, which were almost exclusively military in character (the 'Châteaux' of Dijon, Beaune, Bordeaux, Bayonne, Chalon-sur-Saône, Perpignan, Salses) and, on the other hand, in the interior of the kingdom, what were known as country châteaux, in which the defensive aspect was either non-existent or merely symbolic.

In England, the relatively peaceful internal condition of the country led to an early transition from the castle to the unfortified country house. Despite the limited hiatus of the Wars of the Roses, this change had been accomplished by the middle of the fifteenth century. During this period, many older, 'military' castles were converted to a more domestic purpose. *See also* CHÂTEAU-GAILLARD; CITADELS; FORTIFICATION.

P. CONTAMINE
JOHN CHILDS

FURTHER READING

P. Rocolle, *2,000 ans de fortification française* (2 vols, Paris, 1972); W. Anderson, *Castles of the Middle Ages* (London, 1970); D. J. C. King, *The Castle in England and Wales: an interpretative history* (London, 1988).

Cavalry Cavalry developed as a major force in warfare principally in relatively flat, open country: the steppes of central Asia and the plains of northern Europe. Mountainous regions have produced fewer roles for mounted soldiers. The use of horses added another dimension to warfare. The cavalry became the arm entrusted with long-distance reconnaissance, shock action, manoeuvre and even conquest. It was on horseback that dynamic, warring peoples (the Germanic tribes, the Huns and the Mongols) succeeded in subjugating nations which were often more advanced and civilized than themselves.

Around 2000 BC, the Chinese possessed a large number of horsemen. They were also found in India and Assyria, where there is evidence of both armoured and light cavalry. These horsemen typically wore a light helmet and, sometimes, a breastplate, carried a shield, and fought with bows, javelins, swords and lances. The Egyptians had no national cavalry, relying on foreign mercenaries, but they adopted the Hittite model of battle chariots transporting bowmen. There does not appear to have been a cavalry in Persia until the time of Cyrus (559–529 BC). The Persians created a formidable force of mounted archers, perhaps 15–18 per cent of the army, but they do not appear to have been well organized and fought without ranging themselves in any tactical formation. They were defeated by the Greeks at Marathon (490 BC) and Plataea (479 BC). With the exception of the Thessalians and certain other colonies, the Greeks made little use of cavalry as their country was unsuitable to the large-scale breeding or deployment of horses. Greek cavalry, which was aristocratic in nature, was not used as a shock weapon, except by the Thessalians who wore armour, but to reconnoitre, harry and pursue the enemy. The horsemen carried half pikes, javelins and bows. Alexander created an equestrian phalanx, armed with glaives (broad swords) and lances, which he used for breaching enemy lines. Ten per cent of his troops were mounted.

For a long time, cavalry played only a minor role in the Roman army. At the Battle of Cannae (216 BC), 10 per cent of the Roman force were mounted compared to 25 per cent of the Carthaginian army. It was positioned on the flanks of the Roman army, a deployment which was to remain customary until the eighteenth century. At Cannae, the Carthaginian cavalry routed their Roman counterparts, who had dismounted to fight, before swinging round and descending on the rear of the Roman infantry. Thereafter, Rome relied on foreign, auxiliary cavalries but it never fully succeeded in adapting its army either to incorporate or to oppose mounted forces, and it suffered heavily at the hands of the Parthian and the Barbarian mounted formations. Cavalry became dominant in the Byzantine army reducing the infantry to a subordinate role as a support for the mounted arm. The horsed units were organized on a ternary system.

Stirrups originated in Arabia around AD 650 and they became widely available in the West during the eighth century. Until this invention, cavalry had been restricted as a shock weapon and had depended on light weapons and the bow. Stirrups provided a stable platform from which a horseman could deliver a blow with a lance at the gallop. A horseman could also stand in his stirrups and utilize the additional height to strike downwards with a heavy sword. Together with the development of iron horseshoes in the ninth century, which enabled horses to travel on metalled roads and over hard and rocky terrain, stirrups revolutionized mounted warfare and heavy, armoured cavalry became the dominant military arm for the next seven centuries. These developments were enhanced by the fact that the conquerors of the Roman Empire – the Germanic tribes, the Huns and the Saracens – fought primarily on horseback. Cavalry also played an important role in the Frankish army, the Battle of Poitiers (732) being essentially a conflict between two cavalries. Only the rich could afford to maintain horses and so under the Carolingians it was the nobility who were compelled to perform military service as cavalry. Again, the growth of a feudal society encouraged this trend.

During the Middle Ages, feudal military organization was based almost entirely around the knight. The knight was attended and assisted by a number of fighting men, and together they were known as a 'lance'. Besides the cavalry, there emerged a serjeantry which, although less prestigious because it was recruited from outside the aristocracy, was also less costly and less heavily armed. Armour evolved from the coat of mail worn by the Carolingians to a complete armour weighing around 65 lb, the horses also being protected by metal plates. Knights charged in hedge formation carrying lances which increased in length from 8 ft in the eleventh century to almost 15 ft by the end of the Middle Ages. When his lance was broken or became unusable, the knight seized his sword and advanced cutting and thrusting using his shield to protect himself. Combat was thus between individuals and tactics were unsophisticated. The light cavalry was not highly regarded. Its function was to reconnoitre, to pursue the enemy and also, in conjunction with the infantry, to overpower routed enemy cavalry with the axe and the mace.

The methods employed by the Mongols were quite different. Their horsemen were grouped in units of 10, 100 and 1,000 men. They manoeuvred in extended order, relied on surprise, attacked from all sides simultaneously and pursued the enemy until he was annihilated. Battle commenced with continual harrying using the bow but in the final confrontation sabres were employed. The Mongols triumphed over almost all the forces they encountered: Chinese, Muslim and Christian.

The Hundred Years' War between England and France witnessed the final eclipse of the knight, partly because of his lack of discipline in combat, but principally because firearms pierced his armour. The initiative passed to the infantry armed with missile weapons. In 1494, 66 per cent of the army of Charles VIII of France consisted of pikemen, archers and hand gunners, the remainder being composed of heavy cavalry and their attendants. Thirty years later, heavy cavalry amounted to no more than 10 per cent of the army of Francis I and only 8 per cent of the Spanish army. However, despite its relative decline cavalry retained its importance in reconnaissance and as the only truly mobile force on the battlefield. During the sixteenth century, as the weight of infantry firepower increased, the charge of heavy cavalry became more and more costly until the horsemen were only able to operate against infantry whose formation and morale had already been broken. Both heavy and light cavalry began to manoeuvre in caracoles. Arranged in squadrons, a practice which appears to have been spread by German *Reiter*, the riders in the front lines discharged their pistols at the adversary before counter-marching to the rear to reload. Only when the enemy was sufficiently shaken by fire did they ride in with the sword. Perhaps the only European cavalry not to adopt the caracole was that of Poland, which continued to charge with lance and sabre.

Gustavus Adolphus of Sweden (1611–32) transformed cavalry organization and tactics by adopting the Polish model. He armed his cuirassiers with a sword and two pistols and assembled them in four ranks rather than the customary six. With the fourth acting as a reserve, the front three ranks trotted to within 150 yards of the enemy and then rode home with the sabre, reserving their pistols for the mêlée. Swedish dragoons were equipped with muskets, sabres and battleaxes and were trained to fight either on foot or as light cavalry. Previously, it had been the custom for infantry to fight infantry and for cavalry to fight cavalry, with the latter only coming to the former's assistance once it had defeated the opposing cavalry. Sometimes, Gustavus used his infantry, cavalry and artillery in combination instead of engaging them separately but he usually withheld his cavalry ready for intervention at the critical point in the battle. Variants of the Swedish approach were adopted in the British (Cromwell and Marlborough), French and Dutch armies and the caracole had disappeared by 1700, the Austrians being its last practitioners.

During the later seventeenth and eighteenth centuries, the dragoons lost their role as mounted infantry and became general purpose cavalry. Light cavalry retained its function of reconnaissance and patrolling while the cuirassiers charged in battle. The French and British cavalry charged in three ranks while the Austrian horse operated in two. The Prussian cavalry, which fought with particular distinction under Seydlitz at Rossbach (1757), became the best in Europe. Between 1741

and 1759, the cuirassiers evolved a two-rank formation in which the files stood knee-to-knee. They trotted to within 200 yards of the enemy before breaking into a gallop. Behind them waited the dragoons, poised to support the cuirassiers or attack the enemy's flanks, and in a third line stood the hussars to cover the dragoons and cuirassiers and participate in any pursuit. British cavalry developed a similar tradition, which dated back to the tactics of the New Model Army. The cuirassiers and dragoons deployed in three ranks, knee-to-knee, and charged at the trot, sabre in hand. The task of cavalry on the battlefield was to defeat the opposing mounted troops, attack disorganized infantry and pursue a beaten foe.

Cavalry regiments were created in France in 1635: 24 of cuirassiers, 1 of carabineers and 6 of dragoons. The *gendarmerie* continued in existence and the king's military household contained a number of mounted troops. In 1690, the French cavalry numbered 102 regiments but in 1790 there were only 58: 24 of cuirassiers, 18 of dragoons, 2 of carabineers, 12 of light cavalry and 2 of hussars. The English New Model Army of 1645 contained eleven regiments of cavalry of 600 men each plus a regiment of 1,000 dragoons. The Restoration Army of Charles II initially contained two regiments of cuirassiers, no dragoons being added to the establishment until 1683. Each regiment was usually divided into two or three squadrons each composed of between two and four troops. The squadron was the tactical unit while the troop (30–50 men) was the administrative formation. In Prussia, the problems posed by this duality were solved by abandoning the troop and forming each regiment into five squadrons for both tactical and administrative purposes. A similar rationalization was achieved in Austria, but in France and England the incoherent structure endured.

During the seventeenth and eighteenth centuries, the cavalry in an army was between one third and one quarter of the size of the infantry. Gradually, heavy armour was abandoned although a single French regiment of cuirassiers perpetuated the old style. The Polish cavalry also continued to sport coats of mail and carry scimitars, maces and battleaxes. Frederick the Great's Prussian cuirassiers wore iron breast plates, as did the Austrian troopers. Tricorn hats frequently disguised iron skull caps. Napoleon reintroduced body armour and helmets into the French heavy cavalry. The lance was reintroduced into France by Maurice de Saxe in 1743 and the Prussian *Bosniaken* sported this weapon. British light cavalry also adopted the lance and it was the weapon of the German uhlans. However, it was the single or double-edged straight or curved sabre, which had long been in use in Asia, which was the cavalryman's principal weapon.

Although cavalry was usually placed on the flanks of an army, the great captains adapted their formations to suit the terrain. Cromwell at Marston Moor and Naseby, Eugene of Savoy at Zenta, Marlborough at Blenheim and Seydlitz at Rossbach were able to manoeuvre their mounted troops and engage them in positions appropriate for achieving decisive results. Like the infantry, cavalry regiments were grouped into brigades to aid tactical control on the battlefield, and in 1797 the French formed four cavalry divisions.

Napoleon detailed a small section of the cavalry to provide him with reconnaissance information and cover. A light cavalry brigade was provided for each of his army corps and cavalry regiments were available to reinforce the infantry divisions when necessary. He created cavalry divisions to act as a general battlefield reserve. These divisions made mass surprise attacks, charging in lines 300 to 500 metres long, (1) to decide the outcome of the battle, as at Wagram (1809), (2) to outflank enemy forces, as at Essling (1809), or (3) to pursue the enemy in order to turn a defeat into a rout, as at Jena–Auerstädt (1806). Cavalry divisions, comprising 4–6 regiments with 120 horse artillery pieces, were also responsible for reconnaissance. During the nineteenth century there were no significant developments. In 1899, Switzerland introduced *mitrailleuses* drawn by pack horses into its cavalry, a practice adopted by France in 1907. During the First

World War, cavalry divisions were equipped with machine-guns and medium artillery, but, apart from this, they differed little from their fore-runners of the Napoleonic period, retaining the distinctions between cuirassiers, dragoons, light cavalry, hussars and lancers.

The increase in the firepower of the artillery and the infantry placed the battlefield role of cavalry in jeopardy. Already, during the Battle of Waterloo in 1815, the French cavalry had been unable to shake Wellington's unbroken infantry, while the charge of the British Light Brigade at Balaclava in 1854 demonstrated the impotence of horsemen in the face of modern weapons. During the American Civil War, both the Union and Confederate cavalries successfully adapted themselves to the new conditions by becoming mounted infantry. In other words, they reverted to the function of dragoons, fighting on foot but marching on horseback. The American cavalries were profitably employed in reconnaissance, patrolling and in executing raids deep into enemy territory, principally to destroy railroads. However, in the Franco-Prussian War (1870–1) the lessons from America had not been fully heeded by the French high command. French cavalry patrolled ineffectually, leaving their commanders largely ignorant of German movements, because their main task remained the delivery of the decisive charge in battle. Though valiant, the charges at Froeschwiller and Vionville showed that cavalry could not operate against infantry armed with breech-loading rifles. The charge of von Bredow's cavalry brigade at Vionville was probably the last successful cavalry charge in Western Europe; he lost 380 out of 800 men. Between 1800 and 1900, the average proportion of cavalry in European armies dropped from one sixth to one tenth. In 1914, France possessed 10 cavalry divisions and 84 infantry divisions.

Although this mode of mounted combat was now outdated, tradition continued the anachronism into the First World War. On 12 August 1914, the German mounted troops, in accordance with their regulations which stated that 'combat on horseback must be the cavalry's main method of combat', launched a lance and sabre attack on a division of Belgian cavalry who dismounted and inflicted heavy losses with their Mauser carbines. From the outset in 1914, the German army used its cavalry, particularly its uhlans, for reconnaissance. When the French army retreated to the Marne, the cavalry operated as mounted infantry to fight rearguard actions. On 8 September 1914, the 5th French cavalry division infiltrated the German lines and seized an airfield. In the trench warfare on the Western Front, cavalry were virtually useless although they were sometimes employed to close breaches in the line. In more open theatres there remained a role for cavalry. Having learned from the American Civil War and the second Boer War, British cavalry were trained to operate as mounted infantry. During the Megiddo campaign in 1918, Allenby used his cavalry to exploit a gap in the Turkish lines created by his infantry and artillery. Having ridden well into the enemy rear, the British cavalry dismounted and set up blocking positions with their rifles and machine-guns. Because of the huge distances involved, cavalry played an important role on the Eastern Front. A German cavalry corps led the pursuit after the Battle of the Masurian Lakes in 1914 and a Bavarian cavalry division attacked a Russian rearguard in Lithuania in 1915.

Effectively, apart from certain highly specialized functions, the Great War proved that the horse was obsolete in modern war but a number of general staffs were slow to grasp the consequences. Cavalry officers were usually hostile to motorization and mechanization; in France, tank units belonged to the infantry. In Britain a new tank corps was created but the cavalry regiments were converted to armoured formations only very slowly and reluctantly during the 1930s. Even then, many of the mechanized cavalry regiments retained their ancient traditions and attitudes. By 1939, the German *Wehrmacht* had only one cavalry division whereas the French army possessed three although they operated as mounted infantry. The countries of Eastern Europe still retained sizeable cavalries and the Soviet army increased its cavalry divisions from 16 to 41 during the Second World War because of inadequate motorization. The Russians found cavalry of great value for rapid movement during winter operations. Marshal Zhukov successfully combined infantry, tanks and cavalry. On the Russian front and in the Balkans, the Germans deployed cavalry to fight partisans and execute reconnaissance missions and raids deep into enemy territory. Even the *Waffen-SS* contained two cavalry divisions.

Cavalry corps disappeared steadily after 1945. They remained well suited to certain overseas theatres and the Indian army still had cavalry formations in 1947. Switzerland was the last European army to field effective cavalry units, but these were abolished in 1973. Cavalry now retains only a ceremonial function but even the British Life Guards and Blues and Royals operate as armoured regiments in wartime. However, if the horse has disappeared the cavalry ethos continues to exist in so far as armoured regiments have adopted both its traditions and its operational role, to reconnoitre and make shock attacks, by arming themseves with the one thing which cavalry lacked and which caused it to atrophy – firepower.

Mounted troops have a reputation for being an aristocratic branch of the army. The cavalry has always been well represented in royal military households and knights derived from higher social strata than foot soldiers. In the British army, cavalry commissions were taken by young men from the best families. In Prussia, between 1815 and 1860, 80 per cent of cavalry officers were members of the nobility. Up to the present day, there has always been a higher proportion of aristocrats in the cavalry than in other arms, and those who were not themselves noblemen adopted an exaggerated version of the latter's characteristics and, indeed, their faults.

The cavalry has a very deep sense of honour and tradition which has provoked many heroic and costly charges and has endured into the twentieth century as was shown by the manner in which the Saumur cadets fought in 1940 or the British mechanized cavalry operated in the Western Desert in 1941. The cavalry can be reproached for having shown excessive disdain for organization and the meticulous preparation of operations, cavalry officers preferring to trust to their own inventiveness and ability to improvise in the field. The study of tactical innovations and methods has been neglected at times and this has been imputed to a conservative attitude on the part of the officers towards both social and military issues. These officers have also been criticized for not having paid enough attention to the instruction of their troops and for having delegated this responsibility to subalterns. According to Lyautey, young French officers knew the horses in their unit better than they knew their men while in the British army it was a tradition that the welfare of the horses took precedence over that of the troopers. Cavalry officers have been accused of paying too much attention to equestrian technique, which developed into a sport – polo and hunting in the British army – or even an art (dressage), to the detriment of military aspects. In part, this was due to the close relationship between the rider and his mount. As far back as the *Iliad*, Arabic tales and medieval epics, the horse – man's most noble conquest – has been a true companion. Certain horses have been deified and some princes even had their horses buried with them. *See also* ARMOUR, PERSONAL; ARTILLERY; BLADE WEAPONS; BYZANTIUM; CANNAE; DRAGOONS; FIREARMS; GREECE, ANCIENT; HUSSARS; INFANTRY; KNIGHTS AND CHIVALRY; MONGOLS; ROME; TACTICAL ORGANIZATION; TANKS.

G. BODINIER
JOHN CHILDS

FURTHER READING
G. T. Denison, *A History of Cavalry from the Earliest Times* (London, 1877, 2nd edn 1913); G. C. H. V. Paget, Marquess of Anglesey, *A History of British Cavalry, 1816–1919* (4 vols, London, 1973–); J. M. Brereton, *The Horse in War* (Newton Abbot, 1976).

Cavalry, light *See* CAVALRY

Ceremonies, military A distinction can be made here between ceremonies internal to the army and those of a public character in which the army is associated with the population as a whole.

In all armies, the reviewing of troops, saluting the colours, handing over command and funerals are the occasion for ceremonies, though, in many cases, these are only very brief. By causing the troops to be isolated from the population, the practice of quartering soldiers in barracks has increased the number of parades, which in these circumstances take on an aspect of distraction for the men, particularly in professional armies. This is the case for those parades – very common in the countries of northern Europe – which mark the ending of the day, such as the Tattoo which takes place by torchlight in the barracks yard. The Tattoo (which is of Dutch origin, 'tap toe' being the onomatopoeic expression representing the corking of bottles which indicates that no more alcohol is to be drunk) spread to England with William of Orange and subsequently passed into those armies with Anglo-Saxon traditions. The German armies have a similar ceremony, the *Zapfenstreich*. In France, the *retraite aux flambeaux* (torchlight tattoo) has almost entirely lost its military character.

Armies have always been involved in public ceremonial and this has often first been laid down by tradition before being codified in regulations. For a long time, military ceremonies continued to be of a religious character. To declare war against a distant nation, the Romans had recourse to a symbolic rite: the *fetials* would throw a javelin on to the ground in front of the Temple of Bellona, which was outside the walls of the *Urbs*, and was taken to represent enemy territory. If the enemy was closer at hand, the javelin was thrown across the border with the offending nation. The *imperator*, accompanied by his soldiers, would ascend the Capitol to offer his victory to Jupiter; his triumphal procession was rather like the *pompa circensis*, the procession which preceded the circus games. In later ages, the armies of the Christian princes had their standards blessed in cathedrals before embarking on a campaign. The generals returned there afterwards bringing with them the colours they had captured from the enemy to hang from the walls. After victories or after signing peace treaties, public rejoicing was organized and *Te Deums* were sung. Success in war could only be expressed indirectly, through sacred music, whether it be in Latin in Catholic Europe (e.g. the *Te Deum* of Marc-Antoine Charpentier or the *Exaudiat te* of Charles-Hubert Gervais) or in English at the Chapel Royal, Westminster. There, in 1743, after the Battle of Dettingen, Handel celebrated with choirs and trumpets the definitive victory which the Lord of the heavenly hosts had won over death. There was no explicit reference to the prince's courage nor to the talents of his generals since, until round about the middle of the eighteenth century, warriors cast off their own glory at the altars of their churches.

Since the beginning of the modern period, however, soldiers have been called upon to participate collectively in religious ceremonies, which they are seen to enhance either by their music, by parading or merely by their presence. The priests of the Parisian parishes praised the services of some of the *Gardes françaises* in order to encourage them to take part in their processions. The Lutheran Maurice de Saxe led all the soldiers in his regiment to Mass, with drums beating – and that included his Muslim troops! The imperial decree of 13 July 1804 and the ordonnance of 4 March 1831 relating to infantry exercises and manoeuvres laid down the honours that soldiers under arms should render to the holy sacrament. These practices were little more than the specific applications of the general principle that soldiers in uniform were publicly to pay the respect which every citizen of whatever status owed to certain clearly defined categories of persons and symbols. In the early years of the Third Republic, an officer could indicate his commitment to the 'Ordre Moral' by leading a detachment of his soldiers in a procession; refusal to do so, or mere reticence, was considered a mark of Republicanism.

Military ranks were regulated in France by an ordonnance of 1661. When an important figure (e.g. the king, a prince of the blood or a marshal of France) entered a garrison, he reviewed the troops, as they paraded before him. Usually, the soldiers marched at eighty 70 cm paces per minute to the slow rhythm of the drums or bugles playing *Aux Champs*. Each unit paraded in turn, leaving wide gaps between the files. When there were several regiments, they presented themselves in the traditional battle order, which was also an order of precedence. The closing up of ranks and files, which was adopted in imitation of the Prussians, made necessary the introduction, around 1750, of marching in step, starting off 'by the left'. Until that point, military parades in France had lacked lustre on account of the poor quality of the musical accompaniment and the monotonous nature of the marching. The Parisians tired of seeing the same exercises each year when the king came to review his two regiments of guards at the Plaine des Sablons or his household cavalry at Marly or Versailles.

When he authorized Maurice de Saxe to drill his uhlans on 28 November 1748 at Passy in front of a very large audience, Louis XV encouraged French officers to vary the drilling of their own troops; this then became, as in Germany, a genuine spectacle, with troops performing to the beat of excellent musicians. In the end, reviews of this kind gave urban crowds the impression of being present at the preparations for battle, with artillery and infantry salvoes and squadrons of men manoeuvring. The militias and *gardes bourgeoises*, who had previously satisfied town-dwellers' taste for military ceremonies, now proved incapable of competing with the machine-like precision of soldiers trained in the drill exercises codified in 1749 by the Comte de Bombelles. The marching speed of military parades tended to increase at the beginning of the nineteenth century with the drum roll *La Générale*, which set a rhythm of 110 steps per minute. Though the Foreign Legion has maintained this still relatively slow marching pace, very quick speeds of between 140 and 160 steps per minute, which were already mentioned in the regulations of 1774, have become widespread, against a musical background provided by such very lively marches as *Sambre-et-Meuse* and *Sidi-Brahim*. The light infantry and their bugle majors have always been renowned for the skill with which they execute military marches.

Awakened each morning by reveille, soldiers have long manoeuvred to the sound of drums, trumpets, fifes or bagpipes, which set the rhythm for their interminable marches. But military bands also had the task of accompanying charges and assaults, marking the end of sieges and honouring the soldiers who had fallen in battle; they thus contributed to solemnizing the most dramatic episodes of warfare. A besieged garrison would 'sound a parley' when its leader felt further resistance was impossible. After the capitulation of a town or the surrender of a fortified position, the defeated troops were sometimes accorded full military honours by the victors to reward them for their valiant defence. They then left their positions with arms and baggage, drums beating and flags flying, 'muskets loaded and matches alight', as if ready to recommence combat. Soldiers who have fallen in a just war have often had official homages pronounced in their honour. Even after the defeats of Chaeronea (338 BC) and Crannon (322 BC), the Athenians charged orators with the task of publicly praising the vain sacrifice of their fellow citizens. The ceremonial of military burials, for which regulations were laid down in France as early as 1768, has gradually become laden with symbols. The coffins of great leaders have been carried on gun carriages or on armoured cars between rows of soldiers with their rifles held beneath the arm and pointing towards the ground. Since 1921, French veterans' organizations have daily rekindled the flame on the tomb of the unknown soldier, to the sound of the bugle call *Aux morts*.

Lastly, the army is also called upon to take part in annual commemorations as an instrument and expression of political power. As different political forces have come and gone, French troops have paraded on 15 August, the feast of Saint Louis and of Saint Napoleon, on 2 December, the anniversary of Austerlitz, of a coronation and a coup d'état, on 1 May, the feast of Saint Philip, and on 14 July, in memory of the storming of the Bastille. This last-mentioned has come to be generally accepted as the date for military parades in France. The great parade at which, among other things, the prototypes of new weapons are revealed to the world thus refers back, paradoxically, to an event of little military significance and an act of insurrection jointly carried out by civilians and soldiers who had disobeyed orders. The choice of 14 July is, none the less, easy to explain given the interpretation that has been put upon that date in Republican France and in France's colonial empire: this ceremony links together the ideas of progress and political liberty with the theme of political order. By contrast, neither 11 November nor 8 May could seriously be considered an appropriate date for great military demonstrations. They have come, in fact, to symbolize peace rather than victory over an enemy who has now become an ally and a partner. None of the warlike display and joyful celebrations of 14 July are to be seen on those dates, which are an occasion for more discreet ceremonies at which the survivors of two world wars come together to remember their brothers in arms lost on the fields of battle.

The non-military traditions of England have resulted in martial ceremonies with a different emphasis: music, entertainment and remembrance. Military bands are widely employed to enhance sporting events, festivals, etc. The army also provides entertainment by demonstrating its skills and techniques at the Aldershot Tattoo, the Royal Tournament, the Edinburgh Tattoo and countless local fêtes and carnivals. Finally, the armed forces parade in great strength on 11 November, Armistice Day, to remember the fallen in the wars of the twentieth century. The British armed forces are kept separate from parliament and the political establishment. However, the close connection between the army and the crown is reaffirmed annually at the ceremony of the Trooping of the Colours on the monarch's official birthday. *See also* ETHOS; GLORY; ICONO-GRAPHY; MORALE; MUSIC; SYMBOLISM; VEXIL-LOLOGY.

J. CHAGNIOT
JOHN CHILDS

FURTHER READING
B. G. Baker, 'Some historic military reviews', *Journal of the Royal United Services Institution*, lxxx (1935), pp. 246–54; H. G. Farmer, *History of the Royal Artillery Band, 1762–1953* (London, 1954); L. S. Winstock, *Songs and Music of the Redcoats, 1642–1902* (London, 1970).

Ceresole (Piedmont), Battle of (14 April 1544) In 1544 Charles V and Henry VIII planned a major three-pronged invasion of France. The French commander in Piedmont, François de Bourbon-Vendôme, Comte d'Enghien (1519–46), persuaded Francis I to allow him to challenge the Italian wing of the invasion to an early battle by besieging Carignano. The Imperialist army, 12–13,000 foot and some 800 horse, under Alfonso d'Avalos, Marquis del Vasto (1502–46), marched to relieve the siege and was confronted by a slightly smaller French force of 11,000 foot and 1,100 horse. Both armies included considerable numbers of arquebusiers, who turned the main engagement into a bloody mêlée. The battle was won, however, by an encircling French cavalry charge (prefiguring the manoeuvre employed at Rocroi) that routed the Imperialist infantry. The Imperialists lost 6,000 on the field and 3,200 prisoners, the French some 2,000 dead. Ceresole had little immediate strategic importance, for the greater part of Enghien's army was then transferred north to meet the main Imperialist invasion. Its tactical significance was greater, however, for while it confirmed the lessons of the 1520s about the effectiveness of firepower, it also showed that cavalry charges at the decisive point could still bring victory. *See also* BOULOGNE; CAVALRY; MONLUC; ROCROI.

SIMON ADAMS

FURTHER READING
E. Hardy de Perini, *Batailles françaises* (6 vols, Paris, 1894–1908). Numbers engaged from F. Lot, *Recherches sur les effectives des armées françaises des guerres d'Italie aux guerres de religion, 1494–1562* (Paris, 1962). *Blaise de Monluc: The Habsburg–Valois Wars and the French Wars of Religion*, ed. Ian Roy (London, 1971), pp. 104–14, provides the best-known eyewitness account.

Cerisoles, Battle of *See* CERESOLE

Chaeronea, Battle of (338 BC) Chaeronea was the site in Boeotia of the battle between Philip II, King of Macedonia, and the combined forces of the Greek city-states, principally of Athens and Thebes. This was still mainly an infantry battle since Philip possessed only 2,000 cavalry as against 32,000 infantry, a proportion of 1:16 (under Philip's son Alexander this fell to 1:6). Significantly, two different types of formation met here: the Greek *hoplite* phalanx, which for three centuries had been the spearhead of Greek armies on every battlefield, and the Macedonian phalanx, armed with longer spears and smaller shields. Philip's experience, the training of his troops and Alexander's daring leadership of the cavalry all contributed to a decisive victory in spite of the resistance of the Sacred Band of Thebes. On the left of the Greek line the Athenians were protected by high ground and the town of Chaeronea, the Thebans on the right by a river. Philip placed the phalanx on the right of his line and, taking command himself, had it execute a planned fighting withdrawal. The Athenians, thinking that they had won, advanced incautiously opening up a gap in the line which Philip's son Alexander exploited with the cavalry; then Philip ordered the phalanx to change its withdrawal into a counter-attack and the victory was complete. This marked the beginning of a period of supremacy in warfare of the Macedonian phalanx allied with effective cavalry and light armed troops, which ended only with the appearance of the Roman legion. The political consequences of Chaeronea were incalculable since it marked the end of the independence of the Greek city-states which for many years were to fall under the domination of the kings of Macedonia. *See also* ALEXANDER THE GREAT; CYNOSCEPHALAE; GREECE, ANCIENT.

R. LONIS
B. CAMPBELL

FURTHER READING
G. L. Cawkwell, *Philip of Macedon* (London, 1978); J. Buckler, *The Theban Hegemony 371–362 BC* (Cambridge, Mass., 1980); J. K. Anderson, *Military Theory and Practice in the Age of Xenophon* (Berkeley, Calif., 1970).

Chamlay, Jules-Louis Bolé, Marquis of

(*c*.1650–1719) Having inherited the ill-defined office of Maréchal-Général des Logis aux Camps et Armées du Roi from his father, Chamlay was employed as a chief of staff by Turenne and Condé. Later, he became a member of Louvois's staff before being appointed as the special adviser on the planning of military operations to Louis XIV in 1689. He was an advocate of the strategic 'reunions' of territories but argued against the destruction of the Palatinate. In 1691, he declined the opportunity to succeed Louvois, allowing Barbezieux to take up the post. Though he remained in the wings, he undertook the duties of chief of general staff to Louis XIV, assisting the king to 'govern by cabinet'. Chamlay had a fine eye and a wonderful memory, qualities which helped to make him a brilliant topographer. He organized the *Dépôt des Cartes et Plans* within the *Dépôt de la Guerre*. He was also a man of action and an advocate of the offensive. His campaign plans, memoirs and correspondence fill 21 volumes in the *Dépôt de la Guerre*. His role has been compared to that played by Shaposhnikov alongside Stalin during the Second World War. *See also* CARTOGRAPHY; LOUVOIS; SHAPOSHNIKOV.

A. CORVISIER

FURTHER READING
A. Corvisier, *Louvois* (Paris, 1983); C. Rousset, *Histoire de Louvois* (4 vols, Paris, 1886); A. A. G. M. de Boislisle, *Le Marquis de Chamlay* (Paris, 1877).

Chaplains, military The moral supervision of troops has always involved armies having preachers or, in the case of revolutionary armies, political commissars. The importance of their role in the Hebrew armies is attested in the Bible but this religious supervision was not permanently established until armies became permanent. In Muslim countries, where there are no clergy (except among the Shi'ites), this has not posed a problem, since preachers (imams) can be chosen from among the servicemen. This has not been the case in Christian countries where, from a very early date, priests were forbidden to carry arms. Since the soldiers needed spiritual succour, the clerics who served them in their travels acquired a special status. Mention is made of bishops and preachers assigned to armies in the field as early as 743 and again during Charlemagne's reign. With the disintegration of the Carolingian Empire, clerics frequently became involved in military action and, in spite of canon law, served partly as active soldiers, partly as chaplains. Naturally, royal and seigneurial chaplains followed their lords into war but it appears to have been the Crusades which brought improvements in the nature of military chaplaincy in Europe. Religious supervision was accorded considerable importance among Joan of Arc's troops. Nevertheless, one cannot really talk of the existence of military chaplaincy outside the religious military orders of the Holy Land, Spain and Prussia, where a permanent spiritual structure existed for the knights.

The sixteenth century saw the emergence of religious organization at corps level, notably in France and Spain. Two ordinances issued by Henry II of France (1555 and 1558) stipulated that provision should be made for a chaplain for every company (and, later, for every regiment). A similar structure was adopted by the Spanish army. It was strengthened in 1579 by Alexander Farnese who maintained a *capellan* in every company, under the command of the *capellan mayor* of each *tercio*. Nevertheless, there was widespread discontent during the sixteenth century over the scandalous character of many chaplains. But what kind of men were they expected to be to pursue their ministry among hardened soldiers? Their poor reputation was often the result of *ad hoc* recruitment, which many a bishop saw as an opportunity to rid himself of the most questionable clerics in his diocese.

The recruitment and status of chaplains posed numerous problems. Under the more or less active control of the sovereign, various solutions presented themselves:

- Chaplains seconded from among the local clergy where the troops were stationed, who remained subordinate to their diocesan bishop and were authorized by him to follow the troops, should the need arise.
- Chaplains attached to corps who were recruited by their commanding officers, with the authorization of their bishop if they belonged to the secular clergy, or the superior of their order if they were part of the regular clergy.
- An overall structure, the vicariate to the armies, which was set up following an agreement between the sovereign and Rome.

The case of a 'vicariate apostolic to the armies' is well illustrated in Spain. A papal brief from Pope Innocent X (26 September 1644) appointed the initial chaplains and vicars-general. The latter were assisted by chaplains to the troops who were appointed by the king and received the canonic advowson from Rome. This initially fragile institution was consolidated by Philip V in 1705 with the creation of a single vicariate-general for the whole of Spain attached to the king's principal chaplain, which covered everything but the patriarchate of the Indies. In 1736, this institution was extended to continue into peacetime. The vicar-general did not have the status of a bishop but exercised jurisdiction over the military and civilian army personnel by delegation from the Pope. Military chaplains, who were appointed by the vicar-general and maintained by the king, were awarded the rank of captain in 1804. A similar structure was introduced for the navy in 1787. The vicariate-general was temporarily abolished under the two republics (1873 and 1932), re-established in 1937 by the nationalists and disappeared in 1979 as a consequence of the abolition of the concordat of 1953.

Austria also had a vicariate-general in the nineteenth century, with a structure based on the division into military regions. In addition to this, there were in certain regions also pastors and rabbis attached to the troops and Bosnia-Herzegovina even had two imams.

From the very beginning, armies in Protestant countries appointed chaplains, notably to assist sovereigns or leaders such as Gustavus Adolphus, Cromwell and the princes of the house of Nassau. In Lutheran countries a hierarchy of chaplains was set up with the king's chaplain at its head. Although Frederick II was himself an atheist, he considered this service to be indispensable in his armies. The Prussian army had a *Feldprobst*, a field bishop who was at the same time the preacher for the first battalion of the regiment of the Guard, and a *Feldprädiger* in every corps, whose role was to lead the troops in prayer for a quarter of an hour every morning and evening. In 1742, chaplains acquired a uniform modelled on the tunic of French abbots. The Prussian regiment was virtually organized like a parish. As there were a relatively large number of married men in that army, which recruited its men by the *Kantonsystem* (40 per cent of soldiers of the Berlin garrison were married), the *Feldprädiger* acted as registrars and kept baptism, marriage and burial records for the corps. These clergymen were normally trained at the University of Halle. A similar structure existed for the Calvinists, Catholics and Greek Orthodox. A statute of 1832 introduced a hierarchy composed of the head chaplain, chaplains of army corps and divisional chaplains. The army corps of the Rhineland had properly functioning Catholic chaplaincies. Chaplaincies were established at an early date within the Swiss regiments on foreign service and their traditions were adopted by the Swiss army, whose chaplaincy was non-hierarchical and had no central organization.

Regimental chaplains were mentioned in England in 1621 and both Royalist and Parliamentarian regiments in the Civil War

127

seem to have possessed chaplains. However, on its foundation in 1645, the New Model Army did not assign chaplains to regiments but maintained a pool of chaplains on the army staff. The corps sent to Dunkirk and Mardyke in 1658 had no chaplains at all. After the Restoration in 1660, every regiment had a Church of England chaplain appointed to its staff as a commissioned officer and this has remained the pattern in the British army up to the present day. Chaplains were well paid – 6s 8d per day, only 4d less than a lieutenant-colonel of foot – and so there was no shortage of candidates. Many military chaplains during the seventeenth and eighteenth centuries were part-time, holding livings in civilian parishes. The first chaplain-general was appointed in 1796 and this was the effective beginning of the Royal Army Chaplains Department. The purchase of chaplains' commissions was abolished in the same year. The growth of religious toleration in the nineteenth century saw a broadening of the Royal Army Chaplains Department to encompass the denominations. The Presbyterians became a separate branch in 1827; the Roman Catholics in 1836; the Methodists in 1881; and the Jews in 1889. The first Jewish chaplain was appointed in 1892. There were 117 army chaplains in 1914 but 3,475 in 1918. Of these, 172 were killed in action. During the Second World War, 96 army chaplains lost their lives. The Protestant chaplains were grouped into four boards in 1920 – Church of England, Presbyterian, Wesleyan and the United Board (Baptist, Congregationalist, Primitive Methodist and United Methodist). In 1932, the four boards were reorganized into Church of England, Presbyterian, Methodist and United Board (Congregationalist and Baptist). Separate sections continued to exist for Roman Catholics and Jews. Chaplains from the Protestant boards were attached to regiments and battalions according to the religious profile of the personnel. In 1947, the Royal Army Chaplains Department moved to its home at Bagshot Park.

The case of France was complex and fluctuated a great deal. We must in particular distinguish between the army and navy.

It might have been expected that a centralized military chaplaincy, such as that found in Spain or the Protestant countries, would have developed under the aegis of the *Grand Aumônier de France* (first chaplain to the king) who, during the second half of the sixteenth century, was still seen as the bishop of the armies and the superior of the diocesan chaplains, chaplains and preachers ministering to the troops. Such a development did not, however, occur. The bishops were not in favour of an 'army diocese' and the king was not tempted to try the Spanish system, one which gave Rome the opportunity to intervene in the army's affairs. The *Grand Aumônier de France* became little more than an arbitrator in matters of ecclesiastical law. During the reign of Louis XVI there were a number of projects for creating a general chaplaincy of the armies, none of which came to fruition.

Corps commanders, governors of fortified towns and, for the military hospitals, the provincial intendants and war commissars themselves recruited chaplains by negotiation with either the local bishops or the religious orders. During the siege of La Rochelle, however, Richelieu made plans for the creation of a type of general reserve of chaplains, provided by various different orders, who could meet any demand that might arise. The navy, by contrast, set up a coherent religious structure by creating three seminaries, at Le Folgoat (1681), transferred to Brest in 1686, Toulon and Rochefort to train their chaplains.

Under Louvois, every regiment was again obliged to employ a chaplain. The latter belonged with the regiment's non-commissioned officers, together with the surgeon and the assistant provost marshal. In 1716, during the reorganization of the army on a peace footing, the cavalry regiments, each numbering 200 men, lost their chaplains, who would only be restored to them in war time. A similar measure had been taken in 1663. At the beginning of the eighteenth century, the regimental chaplain was paid 180 francs a year, i.e. a little more than the emolument paid to a curate. They received better treatment from the time of Choiseul onwards and under Louis XVI received 600 francs in peacetime, 650 during campaigns, i.e. slightly less than the 'living' of a parish priest. However, they were entitled in addition to board and lodging. Since this did not provide an income which was sufficient for their upkeep and the upkeep of their chapel, the colonels granted them allowances, which were deducted from the captains' pay. In the infantry, the recruitment of chaplains appears to have been, relatively speaking, properly conducted. However, the regulations were rather unevenly applied in the cavalry regiments.

In the eighteenth century, 60–70 per cent of military chaplains belonged to the regular clergy. The majority were Recollects, especially in the hospitals, but there were also Capuchin friars, Lazarists and Jesuits, the Jesuits being particularly numerous in the navy. In Canada, there were members of the Congregation of the Holy Ghost and the Sulpicians. The regulars were often wrongly considered to be the dregs of the diocesan clergy. On the whole, army chaplains do not appear to have merited the criticisms directed at them. They worked in a difficult environment in which the soldier brotherhoods who had assisted them in their spiritual work at the beginning of the century were dying out. In spite of something of a revival during the last years of the *ancien régime*, instigated by officers anxious to maintain good discipline, the military chaplains were unable to halt the early decline of Christianity in the army.

The Protestant chaplains in the foreign corps were better protected by the army regulations and military hierarchy.

During the Revolution, Condé's armies were not without their chaplains and the Vendeans had soldier-priests. Official chaplains disappeared from the Republican armies in Year II but priests enlisted as soldiers continued clandestinely to bring a degree of spiritual succour to those who required it. Military chaplains reappeared during the Consulate and Napoleon gave the *Grand Aumônier* authority over them. Their status remained ill-defined and they were limited in numbers because of the decline of Christianity and the shortage of priests.

Under the Restoration a general chaplaincy was organized, for the first time in France, under the command of the *Grand Aumônier des armées*, with one chaplain of the rank of captain for every regiment, although these men's relationship with the diocesan bishops was not defined (1814). A chaplaincy was created for the navy in 1823, a head chaplain was appointed but no coherent structure existed. In 1870 during the Franco-Prussian war, the chaplains were volunteers. A law passed in 1874 made provision for one chaplain for every 2,000 men, assisted by auxiliary chaplains. He was to be attached to a garrison and would come under the authority of the local diocesan bishop. The bishops were not in favour of the centralized organization the military chaplains wanted. The military laws of 1889 and 1905, contemporaneous with the anti-clerical struggles, allowed for the continued existence of the military chaplains but their maintenance allowances were reduced. Under the law of 1913 they were accorded the same status as stretcher-bearers.

However, the introduction of compulsory military service led to the introduction of 'curates with kit bags', with the result that the number of clerics in the French army was greater than it had been for a long time. During the First World War, 25,000 men of the cloth were mobilized, and 4,000 of them (i.e. 16 per cent) were killed. They carried out their ministry as and when they could. In practice, the colonels allotted one soldier who was a priest to each battalion to act as chaplain.

The chaplaincy of today has its origins in the army of occupation in Germany after 1918 over which Mgr Rémond, the chaplain at Mainz, was appointed bishop. A decree of 1935 made provision for a volunteer chaplain, with a captain's salary, to be attached to each battalion in war time and in 1937 the vicariate to the armies, which came under the Department of the Adjutant General, was set up. Protestant and Jewish chaplains were in a comparable position. Finally, an imam was drafted to every regiment of *spahis* and *tirailleurs* (Algerian and Senegalese native rifle regiments). In 1940, GHQ defined the role of the chaplaincy as follows: 'The chaplaincy comes into the same category as the NAAFI and soldiers' clubs. They are benevolent institutions, which are optional rather than essential, and whose services are only used by those who so desire.'

In 1952, the present vicariate was created. It comprises the three chaplaincies of the army, navy and air force and, for the first time in French history, constitutes a genuine diocese with personal rather than territorial jurisdiction. It has 250 full-time chaplains, three-quarters of whom are secular clergy, and a number of part-time chaplains. The other faiths have adopted a similar structure and each one has a head chaplain for the armies. Since the Second World War, military chaplains from different countries have maintained links with one another and have regularly organized international military pilgrimages to Lourdes (since 1957) for the Catholics and to 'the Desert' (the Mas-Soubeyran in the Cévennes) for the Protestants. *See also* MORALE; RECRUITMENT; SAINTS.

A. CORVISIER
JOHN CHILDS

FURTHER READING
John Smyth, *In this Sign Conquer* (London, 1968); A. Crawley, *Ministers to the Soldiers of Scotland* (Edinburgh, 1962); P. Middleton Brumwell, *The Army Chaplain* (London, 1943).

Charlemagne (742–814) Charlemagne was probably the most successful conqueror in European history. After his brother's death in 771, he became sole ruler of Francia (roughly modern France plus the Rhineland). He then conquered Italy, Bavaria, Saxony and, south of the Pyrenees, the Spanish march. What is more, he was still in full control of this vastly extended empire when he died. This double achievement was essentially a triumph of organization. After 771 he disposed of enormous resources in terms of manpower, waggons, weapons and food supplies. He exploited these advantages to the utmost, often being able to dispatch several armies to a single theatre of war and feed them there. In consequence, some of his victims (e.g. the Lombard kings of Italy

in 773–4 and the Bavarians in 787) were probably wise in deciding fairly quickly to surrender. By contrast, some of the Saxons, led by Widukind, put up a fierce resistance; unfortunately for them, they found in Charlemagne a tireless and ruthless enemy. He himself led at least nineteen campaigns against them and, after their lands had been devastated time and time again, they too submitted. Ironically, the engagement for which he was most celebrated – in the 'Chanson de Roland' – was one of his few setbacks: the ambush of his rearguard at Roncesvalles in 778. His coronation as the western emperor at Rome on Christmas Day 800 was little more than a ceremonial recognition of his astonishingly consistent military and political success. *See also* FRANCE.

JOHN CHILDS

FURTHER READING
Donald Bullough, *The Age of Charlemagne* (London, 1973); P. D. King, *Charlemagne* (London, 1986); *Einhard and Notker the Stammerer: two lives of Charlemagne*, ed. Lewis Thorpe (Harmondsworth, 1969).

Charles of Habsburg (1771–1847) The Archduke Charles took part in Austria's campaigns against France from 1792. In 1801, he was promoted to field marshal and from that date until 1809 he was the Austrian Minister of War. He reformed the Austrian army, ending all recruitment from outside the hereditary lands (*Erblände*) in 1802, organizing the army into corps and divisions and, in 1808, creating a *Landwehr* of 150,000 men whose role was to reinforce the regiments of the regular army. At the Battles of Eckmühl, Essling and Wagram in 1809, he put up a stout resistance against Napoleon I. In tactics, he favoured the use of infantry as a shock force rather than as a source of firepower. *See also* AUSTRIA; FRANCE; INFANTRY; NAPOLEON; TACTICAL ORGANIZATION.

J. NOUZILLE

FURTHER READING
Azar Gat, *The Origins of Military Thought from the Enlightenment to Clausewitz* (Oxford, 1989), pp. 95–105; Gunther E. Rothenberg,

Napoleon's Great Adversaries: the Archduke Charles and the Austrian army, 1792–1814 (Bloomington, Ind., 1982); Helmut Hertenberger, *Erzherzog Carl* (Graz, 1983).

Charles the Bold (1433–77) (Duke of Burgundy, 1467–77) Few men devoted themselves so assiduously to the organization of war as Charles, the last Valois Duke of Burgundy, creator of one of the earliest standing armies in Europe. The Milanese ambassador to the court of Burgundy observed, 'that all his pleasure, his every thought, is in men-at-arms: to make them look good and move in good order. He never dismounts until the whole camp is lodged and he has inspected all round.' We can trace this fascination with war in a series of ordinances which Charles issued between 1468 (the year after he succeeded his father as Duke of Burgundy) and 1476, for – as another contemporary put it – 'scarcely a day passes in which he does not spend an hour or two alone writing and drawing up his ordinances.' In 1471 he established, at least on paper, permanent companies of paid soldiers, some 10,000 combatants. Here he was adapting and developing the fifteenth-century French system of *ordonnance* companies. Subsequent ordinances laid down the number of troops, their type – men-at-arms, each with three horses, mounted archers, mounted crossbowmen, pikemen, foot archers and handgunners (culverineers) – and the hierarchy of command. Inevitably, Charles also insisted on an up-to-date artillery train. The 1473 ordinance was particularly concerned with discipline; its section on training and drill seems to have been the earliest of its type. Equally remarkable were the provisions banning swearing, playing with dice and individual appropriation of women camp followers; each company was to have no more than thirty women, in common. His last ordinance, drawn up in Lausanne in May 1476, sets out in detail the order of march and battle which was to be observed in the war against the Swiss. Yet just one month later he was taken by surprise and routed at the Battle of Murten (or Morat). A born organizer, Charles was nothing like the general he fondly imagined himself to

be. The Swiss defeated him at Grandson (March 1476) as well as at Murten. In 1477 at the Battle of Nancy he was killed and his army shattered. The creator of the Burgundian standing army was also its destroyer. Only his military ordinances survived him, to influence the organization and discipline of virtually every army in sixteenth-century Europe. *See also* BELGIUM; GRANDSON; MURTEN.

A. CORVISIER
JOHN CHILDS

FURTHER READING
Richard Vaughan, *Charles the Bold* (London, 1973).

Charles V, Duke of Lorraine (1643–90) Having entered the service of the Habsburgs, he fought with distinction at the head of a regiment of cuirassiers at the Battle of St Gotthard Abbey in 1664 in the war against the Turks. During the Franco-Dutch War (1672–8), he commanded Imperial troops in the Rhine theatre and was promoted to field marshal in 1676. During the Turkish invasion of Austria and the Siege of Vienna in 1683, Lorraine was given charge of the Habsburg field army. With the assistance of Polish reinforcements under King John III Sobieski, he defeated the Turks at the Kahlenberg forcing them to raise the siege. A disciple of Montecucoli he reconquered Hungary using the Danube as the axis for his manoeuvres. After a failed attempt in 1684, he recaptured Buda in 1686 and occupied Transylvania after beating the Turks at Mohács in 1687. In 1689, he was transferred to the Rhine theatre at the opening of the Nine Years' War (1688–97), taking Mainz from the French. *See also* AUSTRIA; HUNGARY; MONTECUCOLI; VIENNA, SIEGE OF.

J. NOUZILLE
JOHN CHILDS

FURTHER READING
Paul Wentzcke, *Feldherr des Kaisers. Leben und Taten Herzog Karls V. von Lothringen* (Leipzig, 1943); Hans Urbansky, *Karl von Lothringen* (Munich, 1983).

Charles XI, King of Sweden (1655–97) Though he became king in

131

1660, his personal rule did not begin until 1672. After fighting a difficult war against Prussia and Denmark (1674–9), he set about restoring the Swedish forces, which had been weakened by long wars and the defence of the Baltic Empire. Charles was faced with the task of creating a standing army from a country which was agrarian but short of population. Between 1682 and 1691, he modified the recruiting system of Gustavus Adolphus into the *Indelningsverket*. Sweden and Finland were divided into provinces, each of which had to recruit and re-recruit an infantry regiment of 1,200 men; farms within the provinces were formed into pairs, 'files', which were called upon to recruit and support one soldier. This man was normally given a cottage and a plot of land in the 'file' and worked as an agricultural labourer when not required for military service. This cantonal system became the model for many states during the eighteenth century, including Brandenburg-Prussia, Hesse-Cassel and Austria-Hungary. The *Indelningsverket*, in conjunction with other military reforms like a thorough topographical survey of Sweden and Finland and the construction of a network of military roads throughout the Swedish Baltic Empire, was the foundation which supported the wars of Charles XII. *See also* CHARLES XII; GUSTAVUS II ADOLPHUS; RECRUITMENT; SWEDEN.

C. NORDMANN
JOHN CHILDS

FURTHER READING
Claude Nordmann, *Grandeur et liberté de la Suède 1660–1792* (Paris, 1971); Michael Roberts, *Sweden's Age of Greatness, 1632–1718* (London, 1973); Alf Åberg, 'The Swedish army, from Lützen to Narva', in *Sweden's Age of Greatness, 1632–1718*, ed. Michael Roberts (London, 1973), pp. 265–87.

Charles XII, King of Sweden (1682–1718) Ascending the throne in 1697 at the age of fifteen, Charles XII was to grow to maturity while exercising the command of an army on active service, his exploits making him one of the eighteenth century's 'modern heroes'. In many ways an enigmatic figure, his naïvety as a warrior-king who had little grasp of politics or diplomacy has often been exaggerated, and his ability as a general underestimated. As a strategist he was not without ability, while as a tactician and motivator of troops, he has possessed few equals. Faced with a coalition of Denmark, Poland and Russia which aimed at the dismemberment of the Swedish Baltic Empire, Charles rapidly defeated Russia at Narva in 1700, invaded Denmark and occupied much of Poland. In 1708, he launched an invasion of Russia which resulted in the ruin of the Swedish army at Poltava in the Ukraine (1709). Charles escaped into Turkey and did not return to Sweden until 1714. By this time, Sweden's Baltic Empire had been largely erased and Charles spent the remainder of his reign attempting to defend Sweden from invasion. He was killed at the Siege of Frederiksten in 1718.

JOHN CHILDS

Although Charles's uniqueness has in the past been overstated, as much Swedish practice derived from Western European models, Sweden itself can lay claim to being a pioneer of national armies, recruited and maintained territorially (the *Indelningsverket*, literally 'allotment system'), financed and supplied under firm central direction. Charles owed much to his father's reforms and to Swedish tradition. The offensive *gå-på* (literally 'go-on') tactics of the *armes blanches*, with a very limited, but none the less strictly controlled, use of firepower, as employed by Charles's armies, were the result of his father's (Charles XI) tactical experiments, and in their general spirit could be traced to the much earlier army of his great-great-uncle, Gustavus Adolphus. The cavalry, following instructions first laid down by his father, attacked at the full gallop, 'knee to knee', formed in a sort of shallow wedge. The Swedish artillery had been in the forefront of innovation in the seventeenth century and, if rather neglected in the early years of Charles XII, the final years of his reign saw great emphasis again on its improvement, and important Swedish innovations were later copied in Denmark, Russia and Germany. Charles's use of infantry columns of attack, although claimed to be characteristic of his style of fighting, supposedly foreshadowing the future of European warfare, was not a constant feature, being but a particular answer to a specific situation. Charles was constantly at pains to improve his army's tactics and is most noteworthy for his exceptional tactical flexibility. Although the pike had disappeared in Western Europe, Charles's Swedish infantry retained it, in proportions as high as one-third of company strength.

Charles died at the height of his innovative powers. For his campaign of 1718 he had introduced a permanent brigade (*indelningar*) and divisional (*tilldelningar*) organization and had created a small permanent staff to assist him as commander-in-chief. His influence on the general evolution of European warfare, however, has tended to be ignored, though it did in fact insinuate itself into Western European military thought by way of certain contemporary writers, most notably Folard, whose own experience with the Swedish army left him with a lasting admiration of Charles, of the organization of his army, and of its offensive tactics. *See also* CHARLES XI; FOLARD; GUSTAVUS II ADOLPHUS; NARVA; PETER THE GREAT; POLTAVA; SWEDEN.

G. A. STEPPLER

FURTHER READING
Ragnild Hatton, *Charles XII of Sweden* (London, 1968); F. G. Bengtsson, *The Life of Charles XII* (London, 1960); Gustavus Adlerfeld, *The Military History of Charles XII, King of Sweden* (2 vols, London, 1740); Claude Nordmann, *Grandeur et liberté de la Suède, 1600–1792* (Paris, 1971); Alf Åberg, 'The Swedish army from Lützen to Narva', in *Sweden's Age of Greatness*, ed. Michael Roberts (London, 1973), pp. 265–87.

Château-Gaillard (Eure) This superb fortress, with its remarkable curvilinear inner curtain, perched on a rocky spur overlooking the Seine between Rouen and Paris, was built by Richard the Lionheart, King of England and Duke of Normandy, at breakneck speed and at great expense in the years 1196–8. The castle itself was just part of a complex of fortifications involving the town and island of Andeli (Les Andelys) which served as the armed base from which Richard reconquered the Norman territory that had been seized by King Philip of France while the returning crusader languished in an Austrian prison. When John succeeded Richard in 1199, Château-Gaillard assumed a defensive role. However, instead of treating it as one element in a co-ordinated strategy of defence, John left it to its own devices, making no effort to relieve it or harass the blockading French troops after August 1203. Even in isolation the castle did its job, holding up Philip's invasion of Normandy throughout the summer and winter of 1203–4. In December 1203 John left Normandy, never to return. Given a free hand the French king mounted a masterly demonstration of siegecraft and finally forced the courageous garrison to surrender on 6 March 1204. In the fifteenth century Château-Gaillard was to play an important part in the later stages of the Hundred Years' War. *See also* FORTIFICATION; RICHARD I; SIEGES.

P. CONTAMINE
JOHN CHILDS

FURTHER READING
Kate Norgate, *England under the Angevin Kings* (London, 1987); F. M. Powicke, *The Loss of Normandy* (Manchester, 1960); John Gillingham, *Richard the Lionheart* (New York, 1980).

Chemical and biological warfare Conventional warfare relies on the use of kinetic energy to produce disabling effects on equipment or to physically harm personnel. Chemical and biological warfare may rely on kinetic energy for a means of delivery, but it achieves its results by chemical or biological reactions induced in its target. Although frequently bracketed together, chemical warfare and biological warfare are to be distinguished in their *modus operandi*. At the simplest level biological warfare involves the use of living organisms, such as bacteria, but also includes viruses and toxins produced by living organisms; chemical warfare relies upon the toxicity of chemical agents.

Biological Warfare The use of biological warfare techniques has a long history, although for the most part its practitioners have lacked any real scientific understanding of their work. It is only in the post-Second World War period that scientific research and development has focused on this form of unconventional warfare.

During long sieges the practice of well-poisoning was a common means of attacking the defending population. A similar practice, although the spread of disease was not understood at the time, was to hurl the corpses of men and animals killed by infectious disease into besieged cities in attempts to cause epidemics. In 1763 the British attempted to start a smallpox epidemic among North American Indians by supplying them with blankets that had been used in a smallpox hospital.

The employment of biological means of warfare has remained on an *ad hoc* basis and there has been no use as yet of any deadly living organisms isolated for that purpose. The main difficulty with the use of the biological weapon lies in the fact that it has remained a strategic rather than a tactical weapon since it has an effect against an area rather than a specific target. It also appears to be a weapon upon which it is very difficult to impose limitations; there is no guarantee that its effects will not spread to one's own forces or population. None the less, this limitation does not appear to have prevented research, development and some limited use of toxins.

Toxins are poisons that have been derived from organic material; simple food poisoning can be caused by toxins produced by decaying animal tissue. Toxin-based substances were used by the United States during the Vietnam War for defoliation purposes. The aim was to destroy the natural vegetation cover being used by the North Vietnamese guerillas. Despite laying waste to large areas and destroying crops as well as natural vegetation it proved to be an expensive but ineffective strategy. The substance that was used, known as Agent Orange, contained large amounts of dioxin and has been linked with cancer, skin, liver and kidney disease and birth defects.

Since the late 1960s there have been many reports emanating from South-East Asia and Yemen and, more recently, from Afghanistan of a substance known as Yellow Rain. From the accounts this appears to be another toxin-based substance delivered by aircraft covering large areas with a yellow powder or vapour. The targets appear to have been civilian populations. The effect on its victims has been to induce vomiting and internal bleeding.

Research has been carried out since 1945 on the transmission of disease as a weapon of war. The most notable example of such research is the case of anthrax. This is a disease that is transmitted by a bacillus commonly found in sheep and cattle but is communicable to the human population (known as woolsorter's disease). It can be highly infectious and the bacillus spores may remain dormant for many years. Britain, the United States, the Soviet Union, Japan and Germany all experimented with anthrax, and its use was considered by the Allied Powers against Germany during the Second World War. British experimentation with anthrax was carried out on the Isle of Gruinard, off north-west Scotland. The island was infected with anthrax spores and it is only in recent years that it has been declared clear. It is believed that the Soviet Union experimented with anthrax and that an outbreak of the disease in Sverdlovsk in April 1979 was as a result of biological warfare research.

Chemical Warfare Chemical warfare has been used more extensively than its biological counterpart. The different types of chemical agent have led to a wide range of uses from internal policing duties to large-scale area attacks against enemy troops. The emergence of chemical warfare in the twentieth century is largely due to the development of the chemicals industry during the latter part of the nineteenth century. The delivery of the chemical weapon to its target may be carried out by several means, ranging from hand-held projectiles to delivery by missile, artillery shell or aircraft drop. The choice of delivery method is dependent on the nature of the target and the intention of the user.

Chemical weapons, normally gas weapons, have two fundamental purposes; to harass and to kill. Within the first category are the gases which are labelled as irritants, such as tear-gas (CS), those which cause vomiting, and those which cause severe skin blistering, such as mustard gas. In the second category come the choking, blood and nerve agents. The most deadly of nerve agents can kill with only a minute amount on the skin.

Chemical warfare was used extensively during the First World War. The French military took the first operational supplies of a gas weapon; hand-grenades containing a tear-gas. At the end of 1914 the German army used a shell-delivered irritant against the British forces located in the Neuve-Chapelle area, although this proved ineffective. The first effective use of gas occurred in April 1915 when chlorine, released from gas cylinders and relying on the prevailing winds to deliver the cloud, was launched against the French position at Ypres. Gaps were opened in the French line, largely due to panic rather than to gas casualties, but the German troops were unable to exploit them. In May 1915 the German army employed a blister agent, phosgene, on the Russian front. In July 1917 mustard gas began to be used leading to eye damage, skin burns and respiratory problems. The great majority of the gases used throughout the First World War were non-lethal but still left many veterans badly scarred and in chronic discomfort and ill-health. Out of an estimated 1,300,000 gas casualties, 91,000 were fatalities.

Research continued during the interwar period and by 1936 German scientists were working on nerve agents such as Tabun, an agent which causes muscular spasms and contractions resulting in death. By 1945 Germany had developed other, more powerful but less easily manufactured agents such as Sarin and Soman. Despite possessing these agents restraint was exercised and they were not employed. Fear of retaliation was probably a major influencing factor but logistics and technical limitations also played their part.

After 1945 the Soviet Union took over many of the German nerve agent facilities. Britain and the United States also carried out research and development as well as limited stockpiling of nerve agents. Chemical weapons were used by both sides in the Iran–Iraq War, although principally by Iraq, the first confirmation of such use coming in 1984. Reports have spoken of the use of Tabun, but blister agents such as mustard gas have also been used illustrating their usefulness against an enemy who relies upon the use of massed manpower and lacks adequate protection. Other allegations of the use of chemical weapons have come from Afghanistan, where the rebel forces claim their use by both Soviet and Afghan forces, and in Chad where they are said to have been used by the attacking Libyan forces. Their employment in the Iran–Iraq conflict remains the best documented.

Modern developments have largely been concerned with improvements in the system as a whole rather than in the production of new, ever more lethal, agents. The delivery systems have benefited from general improvements in missile and rocket technology and from better dispersal techniques. Research and development, and limited production, are underway on 'binary' weapons design in which the constituent chemicals are not lethally mixed until just prior to delivery to the target. Along with other military technologies there has been a diffusion of chemical weapon know-how to the less developed world. The majority of Middle Eastern states possess their own indigenous production facilities and considerable stockpiles. Many other countries are in a similar position.

The vast majority of the world's police forces and paramilitary organizations possess (and many use) CS gas as a means of dealing with civil disturbances. This is a modern variety of tear-gas which was developed by the British Chemical Defence Experimental Establishment (CDEE) in the late 1950s as a replacement for the slower-acting and less persistent CN gas developed prior to the First World War. CS gas has been used extensively for riot control purposes and was used in Vietnam by the United States military for bunker-clearing operations.

The offensive use of chemical–biological warfare and the development of gases and agents that are able to penetrate through the skin have led to the development of protective measures. In the First World War once the use of chemical agents ceased to be a surprise it virtually ceased to be effective. Gas masks were developed and this was followed by the development of complete protective clothing. During the First World War the Russian army, which lacked protective equipment, suffered 39 per cent (500,000) of all chemical casualties of the war. The effectiveness of modern agents means that extensive protective clothing and decontamination facilities are required, with a concomitant reduction in troop efficiency and morale.

The international community has attempted to respond to the threat of chemical–biological warfare. In 1899 and 1907 the fear of the development of sulphur-based gases led to the Hague Convention banning the use of projectiles emitting asphyxiating or harmful gases. Clearly, the Hague Convention did little to prevent the development of gas warfare during the First World War. In June 1925 the Geneva Gas Protocol prohibited 'asphyxiating, poisonous or other gases and all analogous liquids, materials and devices'. By 1939 it had been signed by thirty-two countries but not by Japan, the Soviet Union or the United States. More recently, reductions in stockpiles and agreements between the United States and the Soviet Union for on-site inspections at chemical–biological facilities illustrate the desire of all sides to minimize the risk of chemical–biological warfare. It is the fear of retaliation and a lack of complete control over the more deadly agents which motivate these agreements. Against an enemy who is unable to retaliate in kind or in conditions of civil disorder, chemical–biological warfare remains an option. *See also* NUCLEAR WARFARE; SIEGES; STRATEGY; WEAPONS.

DAVID WESTON

FURTHER READING
Stockholm International Peace Research Insti-

tute, *The Problem of Chemical and Biological Warfare* (4 vols, New York, 1971); R. Harris & J. Paxman, *A Higher Form of Killing* (London, 1983); G. Evans, *The Yellow Rainmakers* (London, 1983); F. J. Brown, *Chemical Warfare: a study in restraint* (Princeton, 1968); L. F. Haber, *The Poisonous Cloud: chemical warfare in the First World War* (Oxford, 1986).

China The military history of China is marked by contradictory tendencies. This land of ancient rural civilization has suffered attack on numerous occasions by the nomadic peoples from the steppes of central or northern Asia. A symbol of the permanence of this threat was the building of the 1,900-mile-long Great Wall, which was frequently restored and improved between the third century BC and the seventeenth century AD. Such continuity in defensive preoccupations and strategy is exceptional and is evidence, also, of long periods in which Chinese military technique stagnated. However, the Great Wall has not always afforded China effective protection. She has been forced on a number of occasions to bow beneath the yoke of the invaders, such as the Khitan Mongols in the tenth century AD, the Mongol hordes unified under Genghis Khan in the thirteenth century and the Manchus in the seventeenth century. Most often, China has ended up more or less assimilating her active, but not particularly numerous, conquerors. It should be noted that southern China has most often formed a 'breakwater' against these invasions.

From the beginnings of Chinese civilization, the soldier has enjoyed a special position within society, though that position has been variable. He was a well-integrated and prominent figure in the predominantly peasant society in the years when China was governed by a feudal system with the Emperor at its head (Chou dynasty, eleventh to sixth centuries BC). He became dominant when the country was occupied by warlike foreign peoples who superimposed their own hierarchical socio-political systems on the traditional administrative structures of the Chinese empire. In these instances, however, there were no living links between the conquering soldiers and the defeated Chinese people. The army remained an alien force within the country and Chinese military men were reduced to playing a strictly controlled auxiliary role of providing the technical expertise to the new masters of the country. The Manchus even disarmed the population to a considerable extent. During the periods when Chinese civilization has been at its height, the soldier has had a relatively marginal place. Buddhism and Confucianism, the influence of which spread from the fifth century BC, promoted doctrines of non-violence and encouraged a degree of distrust of the military among people of culture. Under the Sui, T'ang and Sung dynasties (between the sixth century BC and the thirteenth century AD), the Chinese mandarins kept the army under the control of the civil administration. At the imperial court, the general-in-chief was appointed by the minister of the armies, a civilian. In the provinces, the recruitment and supply of the army were in the hands of civilian administrators, not military governors. Sheltered by the Great Wall and protected by a well-disciplined army, China experienced a long period of calm, a *pax sinica*, disturbed only by occasional attempts by generals to win back the place they had lost when there were weaker emperors on the imperial throne. One legacy of this period among the cultured, middle-class Chinese was a marked hostility towards things military. The gregarious and disciplined character of the peasant masses has, however, meant that they have been willing to accept a high degree of incorporation into the military apparatus. Under the Sung dynasty, for example, territorial armies which are said to have numbered one million men were formed. The creation by the Communist regime of a Chinese People's Army therefore follows an historical continuity.

The long military history of the Chinese world includes many periods either of political disorder, and apathy on the part of the population, or, by contrast, of relative security and prosperity during which the Chinese military proved unable to adapt to the progress made by their neighbours in the art of warfare. The adoption of new weapons led only to a pale imitation of developments elsewhere rather than a thorough rethinking of military theory and organization. This was the case in the eighteenth and nineteenth centuries. The history of China has also seen more fertile periods from the military point of view and some of these have produced results of a quite surprising originality. Chief among such periods are the era of the Warring States and that of the contemporary People's Republic.

The second Chinese dynasty, the Shang (sixteenth to eleventh centuries BC), regarded the Emperor as the descendant of the god of war and declared the warrior superior to the peasant. The succeeding Chou dynasty (eleventh to sixth centuries BC) saw the establishment of a hierarchical feudal society which, in some respects, prefigured the chivalric society of medieval Europe in its rules of combat. The warrior, protected by a breastplate, fought in a chariot driven by his servant. The villages had to provide the accompanying infantry. The Chou later formed a cavalry to fight against the peoples of the steppes and this gradually led to the decline of chariot combat. This military system, which enabled a brilliant civilization to develop, gave rise to an excessive sense of superiority and security. By the time military thinkers stimulated by Sun Wu and Sun-Tzu (fourth century BC) began to formulate their theories, China was once again threatened by the peoples of the steppes.

During the Warring States period (fifth to third centuries BC), there were remarkable developments in military technique. Generals were forced to plan long campaigns and had to be able, when the occasion demanded, to engage in siege warfare. This explains the development of a peasant infantry and advances in siegecraft. The building of the Great Wall – a continuous fortification running from the Liao-Tung peninsula to the province of Kansu, in which defence and observation towers are set at approximately 1-mile intervals – was then begun, though, for the moment, its construction did not prevent the Chinese armies from operating beyond it. The mode of recruitment of the Chinese army was also modified. The Emperors of the Han dynasty (206 BC to AD 220) preferred to use fewer, more highly trained mercenaries and created colonies of soldiers on land lying beyond the Great Wall. They launched expeditions into Sinkiang (Chinese Turkestan), Korea and Vietnam.

From the tenth century onwards, Chinese military power declined. However, military technique, which had become the province of specialists, continued to develop. Gunpowder was in use in China several centuries before it was discovered in Europe and the Chinese also had catapults which hurled a type of explosive bomb or flaming arrow. Genghis Khan, who conquered China, possessed a corps of engineers who were mainly Chinese.

The period from the Mongol invasion (1211–1356) to the Chinese Revolution is full of military activity, including actions outside the country. The Chinese Empire still showed its military strength from time to time, though this was largely because its opponents were relatively backward neighbours. After the rule of the Ming, who liberated China from the Mongols (1368–1644), the Manchus (Ch'ing) held China by the force of their campaign army (Army of the Banner) with the aid of a militia (Army of the Green Banner), but China closed its frontiers to Westerners. The Chinese army only partially and superficially adopted Western innovations and was unable to resist the Westerners once they decided to set up trading posts in the country (1833–60).

The Chinese revolution of 1911 opened China to Western influence. The Chinese adopted the military techniques of Europe, and later of America, without really adjusting to the demands of the thinking and discipline involved and proved incapable of creating a truly national army because of the deadweight of corruption and tradition. The efforts of Feng Yü-hsiang, who had taken steps to ensure the moral education of his soldiers and their training, proved in the end to have been futile. The troops, who were poorly supplied, indulged in banditry and the generals behaved like 'warlords', pursuing their own personal goals. Chiang Kai-Shek drew on the authoritarian methods of the communists and fascists in his efforts to overcome Chinese individualism. However, the German – and, subsequently, American – instructors he employed met with some resistance from the troops and the weapons and ammunition provided to them by the European powers were poorly used, if not indeed wasted and even, in some cases, sold to other parties. This period of chaotic military activity none the less played a part in habituating Chinese peasants to the idea of bearing arms.

It was the achievement of the Marxist people's revolution to reconstitute a peasant army, similar to those which had existed at different times in China's past, to motivate it and instruct it in the use of technically innovative weapons through rigorous training. The Chinese People's Liberation Army (PLA) was founded in Nanchang in 1931 but was reformed by Mao Tse-Tung after the 6,000 mile 'Long March' to Yenan in 1934–5. This army, whose officers shared the lives and hardships of their men and in which time not spent in combat was constantly occupied in military exercises and political education (Lenin circles), was able, in conjunction with the Nationalist forces, to defeat Japan in 1945. Then, with the help of captured Japanese equipment, the PLA defeated Chiang Kai-Shek's Nationalist Army in a civil war between 1947 and 1949. The People's Republic of China was founded on 1 October 1949.

Mao Tse-Tung and the generation of generals which emerged during this period achieved an original synthesis in which traditional doctrines dating back to Sun-Tzu merged with revolutionary warfare learnt from social theory, a combination well suited to a rural and peasant population. However, the primitive tactics led to extravagant losses during the Korean War (1950–3) and the Chinese Communist Army was no longer able to apply the guerilla methods of trading space for time. Forced to adopt rigid linear defence, the army decided to abandon its role as a peasant infantry force trained and equipped for guerilla operations and change into a modern professional and conscript army with the help of Soviet weaponry and assistance. After the withdrawal of Soviet technicians and advisers in 1960, China adopted a policy of military self-sufficiency. In 1976, the Chinese armed forces contained 3,500,000 men, of whom 250,000 served in the navy and 170,000 in the air force, of whom 10,000 were pilots. By 1991, the armed forces had shrunk to 3,030,000 men, of whom 1,350,000 were conscripts on three years' service: 2,300,000 served in the army, 260,000 in the navy and 470,000 in the air force. In 1991, China had *c*.8,000 main battle tanks, *c*.5,000 combat aircraft, 94 submarines and 56 principal surface ships. In 1966, China, for the first time, successfully tested a land-based missile tipped with a nuclear warhead; her nuclear forces currently consist of 8 ICBMs, 60 IRBMs and 1 ballistic missile-carrying submarine (SSBN). *See also* INDIRECT WARFARE; JAPAN; KOREAN WAR; MAO TSE-TUNG; POPULAR WARFARE; SUN-TZU.

A. CORVISIER
JOHN CHILDS

FURTHER READING
R. L. Powell, *The Rise of Chinese Military Power* (Princeton, 1956); F. F. Liu, *A Military History of Modern China, 1924–1949* (Princeton, 1956); *Chinese Ways in Warfare*, eds F. A. Kierman and J. K. Fairbank (Cambridge, Mass., 1974); H. W. Nelsen, *The Chinese Military System* (2nd edn, Boulder, Col., 1981).

Chivalry *See* KNIGHTS AND CHIVALRY

Churchill, Winston Spencer (1874–1965) This British statesman was constantly involved in the military affairs of his country. A graduate of the Royal Military College, Sandhurst, Churchill saw action in both the Sudan and South Africa. Entering Parliament in 1900, Churchill held a number of military portfolios: First Lord of the Admiralty (1911–15), Minister of Munitions (1917–18) and Secretary of State for War and Air (1919–21). As First Lord, Churchill favoured the use of British seapower against the Central Powers and was largely responsible for the unsuccessful Dardanelles campaign. Excluded from

power from 1929 to 1939, Churchill became First Lord of the Admiralty in September 1939 and Prime Minister the following May. The Second World War was Churchill's finest hour. In a Britain left to fight the war alone, he embodied the spirit of national defence, mobilizing all the moral and material resources of his nation: 'I have nothing to offer but blood, toil, tears and sweat.' As he had in the First World War, Churchill employed Britain's seapower to good advantage, utilizing it to support peripheral campaigns in Africa and to blockade Germany. Churchill believed that a combination of economic pressure and air attacks would defeat Nazi Germany. But Churchill was also a fervent advocate of close Anglo-American co-operation. When the United States entered the war in 1941, he persuaded Franklin D. Roosevelt, the US President, that the Allies should first concentrate their efforts against Germany. Churchill initially was able to persuade the Americans to follow his strategy of peripheral campaigns; however, the Americans gradually prevailed and insisted on the opening of a second front in Europe. In addition to regular warfare, Churchill also believed in special operations and intelligence work, which he supported warmly. In 1945, Churchill was voted out of office. In March 1946, he visited the United States, where he popularized the term 'iron curtain' in a speech at Fulton, Missouri. *See also* BROOKE; GREAT BRITAIN.

ANDRÉ CORVISIER
KEITH NEILSON

FURTHER READING
Randolph S. Churchill, *Winston S. Churchill* (2 vols, London, 1966–7); Martin Gilbert, *Winston S. Churchill* (8 vols, London, 1971–88); Robert Rhodes James, *Churchill: a study in failure, 1900–1939* (London, 1970); J. H. Plumb, 'Churchill the historian', in *Churchill: four faces and the man*, ed. A. J. P. Taylor (London, 1969).

Ciphers *See* SECRECY

Citadels 'Citadel' comes from the Italian

cittadella, the diminutive of *citta* (city or township). The citadel was a permanent, fortified structure standing alongside or within a town to serve as the final line of defence. Although separate from the main town walls, it was not a detached fort but an integral part of the principal fortifications. In the nineteenth century, citadels ceased to be militarily significant as the defence of towns was transferred to fortified camps and rings of detached forts.

However, a certain number have been preserved as historical monuments (e.g. Lille, Wesel, Liège, Namur, Sedan).

Citadels played both a political and military role. Politically, they guaranteed the domination and control of a conquered town. Housing a garrison of the occupying power, the citadel was built on the extremity of the town so that reinforcements from without were easily available. The Antonia fortress in Jerusalem, the

A modern view of the citadel of Lille, built by Vauban as part of the refortification of the city between 1667 and 1674. The central space, containing barracks, the governor's house, a church, an arsenal and other buildings, has a diameter of 180 metres. The ground plan is a regular pentagon and is a fine example of a mature *trace italienne* in Vauban's early style which was heavily influenced by Pagan (*see* FORTIFICATION; VAUBAN).
(Thomas d'Hoste)

citadels constructed by the English in Scotland and Ireland, and those built by Louis XIV in the Low Countries and the Rhineland belonged to this type. The second political function of the citadel was the exertion of monarchical authority over the subject population. This was fairly widespread in Western Europe during the sixteenth and seventeenth centuries. Vauban, when considering the refortification of Paris, thought that two citadels might be necessary if the population grew fractious. In fact, two already existed, the Louvre and the Bastille, the latter retaining its symbolic role until 1789. Although the Roman Capitol and the acropolises of Athens and Corinth were primarily religious complexes, protecting the gods who, in turn, protected the city, the former also served as a centre of government authority during the struggles between the plebs and the patricians (494–287 BC). The palaces of the Abbasid princes in Mesopotamia (750–1258) controlled the wide diversity of peoples and religions within their cities, even though the various communities were enclosed in separate areas. The religious obligations of the leaders meant that the palaces had to be erected close to the Great Mosque to ensure open and free access for all believers. From accommodation within the palace, the prince's household guard maintained public order and quelled popular resistance. The fortified towers which are so often to be seen in medieval Italian towns (e.g. San Gimignano, Siena, or the Palazzo della Signoria in Florence) cannot be classified as citadels as they were not erected by an external, subjugating power but by the citizens themselves in response to internal, factional rivalries.

The military role of the citadel was more important. Fortified towns were intended to command points along possible invasion routes where a potential enemy had to pass through mountains or cross a river. If besieged, the fortress town capitulated when its walls were breached; the citadel then became the last post of the defenders, fulfilling a role similar to that of a keep in a castle. If it had been well sited, the besieged citadel might still possess the ability to control the threatened strategic avenues. On occasion, surrender cartels permitted the garrison of a town to withdraw into the citadel. This was the case at Namur in 1695 and Lille in 1708, both defended by Marshal de Boufflers. Sieges could thus become two-stage operations: the capture of the town followed by the siege of the citadel.

Naturally strong sites were sought in the immediate vicinity of towns, on an eminence if possible. Traces of past fortifications sometimes made that search easier. The castle at Brest, for example, was built over ruined Roman fortifications, the citadel of Port-Louis in the Morbihan adapted and extended a Spanish fortress, while Entrevaux in the Alps similarly modified a dilapidated castle. Should entirely new citadels be required, then it was essential to find a situation where the citadel dominated the town rather than vice versa; at Besançon, the citadel had to be protected by a neighbouring fortification. However, in some cases there was plenty of space and the new citadel was separated from the town by a zone *non aedificandi*, or *esplanade*. This open area was commanded by the citadel's cannon and also formed a parade ground for the garrison (e.g. Lille, Strasbourg, Wesel). Citadels also had a logistic function. In the absence of municipal barracks, the garrison was housed in the citadel together with stores, workshops, an arsenal, an infirmary, water tanks and the apartments of the governor. The citadel was thus a centre in which power and its instruments were concentrated.

Citadels were usually quadrangular or pentagonal in trace, rarely having more sides. They repeated, in great concentration, the range of fortifications found before their parent towns and because of the regularity of their designs were positions of great strength – besiegers directed their attacks against the town rather than the citadel.

Citadels developed as a function of both politics and technology. From the twelfth and thirteenth centuries, they became normal features on the landscape as urban fortifications and strong central government gradually won the political battle against provincial power represented by the castle. The political and military justification for citadels was forcefully contested by Machiavelli and yet princes felt the need for them. The English even built one in Quebec as late as 1818, despite the fact that hardly any had been constructed in Europe during the eighteenth century. By the nineteenth century, towns were defended at longer range by detached forts rendering citadels obsolete. The swansong came in 1832 with the defence of the citadel of Antwerp, Pasciotto's masterpiece, which was later demolished by Henri Brialmont. Sometimes, their initial function was subsequently reversed: having been created alongside a small town, the latter expanded to absorb the citadel. The town then provided the citadel with logistic support through its commerce and artisans, and the garrison and its barracks would remove from the citadel into the town. *See also* ARSENALS; ARTILLERY; CAMPS; CASTLES; ENGINEERS; FORTIFICATION; SIEGES.

J.-M. GOENAGA
JOHN CHILDS

FURTHER READING
P. Rocolle, *2,000 ans de fortification française* (2 vols, Paris, 1972); Christopher Duffy, *The Fortress in the Early Modern World, 1494–1660* (London, 1979); Christopher Duffy, *The Fortress in the Age of Vauban and Frederick the Great, 1660–1789* (London, 1985).

Civil contribution of armies Apart from the defence of the country and, should occasion arise, the maintenance of internal order, the army has, throughout much of history, been called on to carry out tasks of a purely civilian nature. Little mention need be made here of the support once given to civil authorities in the collection of taxes, with the sending of men acting as bailiffs to the premises of civilians who showed a reluctance to pay (a common practice under the *ancien régime*), or to the administration by the army of colonial territories that lacked any developed administrative structure or, again, to the superimposition of a military administration on the civil one in occupied countries. The principal civil tasks of the army were relief work after natural disasters, organizing *cordons sanitaires* and taking part in public works or sundry other forms of employment. It is useful, in addition, to distinguish the types of unit which were called on to perform these civil tasks. It was the citizen militias and the national guards that had the duty of participating in the majority of these activities which contributed to the defence and good order of the country. Regular army units were called on to intervene in the case of difficulties which were particularly serious or which extended beyond city boundaries.

Combating the Effects of Natural Disasters In towns, the officials in charge of districts or the officers of citizen militias took charge, at an early date, of dealing with outbreaks of fire, often with the help of monks (particularly the Capuchins), or with cases of flooding. The national guards took over these tasks in the nineteenth century. (In the United States, the National Guard still retains the leading role, especially in the Southern states, which are frequently ravaged by cyclones, torrential rainstorms, droughts, etc.) In France, there was a long-standing tradition in garrison towns of calling on the royal troops for help, particularly for dealing with fires. In the period immediately prior to the Revolution, the *Gardes Françaises* rendered effective service in this way. Since this unit had been disbanded, Napoleon, in 1812, established the Paris Firefighting Regiment (*le régiment des Sapeurs-Pompiers*). Units stationed in garrison towns often made fire pickets available to municipal authorities to help in combating serious outbreaks. Although intended only for providing help in cases of emergency, the soldiers might sometimes be required to undertake preventive measures. This was true of the Paris Firefighting Regiment, which had authority to compel property owners and lessees to take steps that would reduce the risk of fire.

Cordons Sanitaires Military units were also used for organizing *cordons sanitaires*, which were designed to seal off areas subject to epidemics. For a long period, the tendency was to follow the Hippocratic precept, according to which the only defence against the plague was to flee, as far and as fast as possible. Kings and others in authority set the example. But while this stance saved some privileged persons, it still had the effect of spreading the plague. Towards the end of the Middle Ages, there began to be a vague realization of this fact. The first known regulation forbidding inhabitants from leaving a city's bounds during an epidemic was laid down at Udine in 1382. Since this could not be enforced without coercion, the municipal authorities used their militias first to cordon off houses, followed by 'plague-ridden' neighbourhoods and, finally, the whole area of the town. Exceptions to these measures were permitted, however, based on geography or on professional and social position. Confined to particular localities and poorly coordinated, steps of this kind had only a very modest success in limiting the effects of epidemics. Nevertheless, in ports, the compulsory quarantining, with the help of troops and warships, of vessels suspected of harbouring disease proved not ineffective.

The establishment of more modern state administrations in the sixteenth century, which shortly afterwards were given the power to use royal troops, proved of great assistance. Notably in the French provinces (e.g. Savoy, 1575; Provence, 1580), *cordons sanitaires* – then termed 'lines' – began to be set up in the form of a succession of guard-posts occupied by troops. One of the best known *cordons sanitaires* was put into effect during the Plague of Marseilles (1720–2); this was, in fact, the return of a ravaging disease which had not been seen for nearly forty years and which accordingly inspired too little fear for care to be taken over maintaining a strict quarantine. It was negligence at the outset, rather than the rats and other creatures which carried the plague, that contributed to spreading the epidemic throughout the whole of Provence and that threatened the neighbouring regions. Military controls were set up under the authority of army generals, and later of the Marshal de Berwick, in Languedoc. In all, more than 1,000 km of 'lines' were established across Provence, the eastern part of lower Languedoc, the Cévennes and Vaucluse, as the disease advanced: 25,000 infantry, 1,500 militiamen and 1,500 cavalry were used – in some instances, for as long as two years. At the outbreak of the epidemic, Marseilles was surrounded by 89 guardposts manned by 31 officers, 332 soldiers and 281 peasants. The troops had orders to shoot on sight anyone who tried to cross the 'line', and the death penalty was imposed on those who were suspected of having done so without first receiving permission. Troops were partly responsible for conquering the plague in Western Europe during the seventeenth and eighteenth centuries.

In the nineteenth century, the use of *cordons sanitaires* aroused violent opposition. The surgeon Lassis criticized them for providing no barrier to rats and for subjecting populations to pointless misery. They came under adverse comment, in particular, for serving as a cover for politico-military operations. For example, in 1822, France used the pretext of yellow fever to install a *cordon sanitaire* in the Pyrenees as a prelude to military intervention in Spain. It was claimed that the Austrians used this expedient as an excuse for troop concentrations on the frontiers of the Ottoman Empire, when they were in fact designed for keeping watch on the Russians.

Advances in medical science and in the prevention of disease removed the need for *cordons sanitaires*. It can, nevertheless, be said that they played a useful part; probably the finest battle that armies have ever fought has been that against the plague.

Public Works Armies have also taken part in public works. Roman soldiers left a reputation for building and road-making but the practice of using troops in this way was lost in the Middle Ages to such an extent that soldiers were reluctant to work on fortifications at the beginning of the seventeenth century, leading to the requisitioning of peasant labour. It was only in Louis XIV's reign, with the maintenance of a large standing army consisting in part of conscripts, that troops in France once again were seen taking part in public works. Louis XIV, Louvois and Vauban had troops participate in moving the huge quantities of earth required in the construction of the fortifications on the French frontiers. Later, volunteers from among the soldiers were called to assist in work that had no military application. It was thought that this would help maintain discipline among men prone to idleness and dissolute behaviour during their period in winter quarters. The soldiers who worked received payment from their employer, part of which had to be shared with the fellow-members of their company, while their rations were sold back to the contractors and the resulting profit divided among the company. Cases occasionally occurred in which whole units, under the control of some of their officers, were assigned to a work site. It was in this way that, in the park at Versailles between 1678 and 1682, the ornamental lake named after the Swiss Guards was excavated by members of that unit. When Louvois, the secretary of state for war, succeeded Colbert as superintendent of buildings, crafts and manufactures, he placed at the disposal of this department a large number of soldiers, in particular for the construction of an aqueduct to bring the waters of the Eure to Versailles. From 1685 to 1688, a camp housing 9,000 to 10,000 men was maintained near Maintenon; 30,000 soldiers were said to have passed through it. In the minister's mind, this was also a way of keeping on an active footing troops who could be rapidly deployed on operations, should the need arise. In the same way, a camp for 15,000 men was established at Bouquenon for clearing the forest in the Saar region, while simultaneously serving as a means of putting pressure on the German emperor. Subsequently, troops worked, particularly during periods in winter quarters, on digging the canals of Briare, Languedoc, Orléans, the Lys, Saint-Omer and Burgundy, and on draining the marshland of the Charente.

During the period of the Revolution and the Empire, continuous hostilities meant that troops took little part in public works. The colonial epoch saw a revival of the practice. Marshal Bugeaud provided it with an additional mystique, under the device of *ense et aratro* (with sword and ploughshare); hand-in-hand with the pacification of Algeria went works of land reclamation and road construction. The unit which most distinguished itself in these activities was the Foreign Legion. For a different reason – troop training – the construction of several minor railway lines was entrusted to companies of the 5th Engineer Railway Regiment.

Naturally, France is not the only country to have used military labour for public works. After the setting up of the English standing army in 1660, troops were employed to fight fires, especially during the Great Fire of London in 1666, labour on fortifications and excavate the Serpentine in Hyde Park and the canal in St James's Park. Frederick the Great used his troops to man the Malapane ironworks in Silesia in 1754 and soldiers dug the canals and dykes that drained the marshes of the Oder valley. Prussian troops then built the new colonial villages in East Prussia, West Prussia and Pomerania. The *Indelningsverket* system in Sweden meant that all regular soldiers worked as farm labourers when not on active service. In 1786, 2,000 Spanish soldiers were digging the Canal de Aragon. The employment of troops on public works declined during the nineteenth century as governments raised the means necessary to employ their own civilian labour force or civilian contractors. The use of troops on public works was an expedient made necessary by the primitive organization and the restricted revenues of the governments in Europe before the Industrial Revolution.

Miscellaneous Work Efforts were made in France, on several occasions, to employ soldiers in the production of manufactures during their period of inactivity in winter quarters. Of their own accord, individual soldiers knitted stockings in order to earn money. Louvois organized workshops at the Hôtel des Invalides for the manufacture of stockings, caps and shoes. This initiative was abandoned after about thirty years owing to lack of space, since the number of disabled soldiers accommodated had greatly increased, and also as a result of pressure from the trades that were threatened by this competition. In garrison towns during the eighteenth century, volunteers from among the troops hired their services to both local authorities and private individuals. In Paris, members of the *Gardes françaises* took walk-on parts in theatrical productions, acted as guinea pigs for scientific experiments, worked as casual domestic staff in great palaces, or cleaned houses and shops. When in the field, soldiers helped in the crop and grape harvests. At the end of the eighteenth century, soldiers were forbidden to take on this type of employment on the grounds that it was prejudicial to good discipline and regimental prestige. Since the end of the nineteenth century, appropriately qualified soldiers have been required to teach gymnastics or to give French lessons in the colonies. Currently, a number of conscripts are posted to a service called *Coopération*, largely to teach French in foreign countries.

During the seventeenth and eighteenth centuries, British soldiers garrisoned in London and the major towns took part-time civilian work, often resuming their former trades. The foreign conscripts of the eighteenth-century Prussian army provided much of the labour for the industries and services of Berlin. Austrian infantry of the mid-eighteenth century were actively encouraged to pursue their civilian trades and occupations. By these devices, governments kept military wages as low as possible, thus controlling the fiscal burden of the military in peacetime. The growth of conscript armies in Europe during the second half of the nineteenth century meant that the majority of citizen-soldiers no longer had sufficient spare time to pursue profitable extracurricular activities, while the housing of armies in barracks reduced contact with the civilian population and thus the opportunity to find work. The professional armies of postwar Europe, particularly that of Great Britain, have witnessed huge rises in the remuneration of troops rendering it unnecessary for soldiers to supplement their income. The intensity of modern training has also removed the long hours of enforced idleness. *See also* ADMINISTRATION, ARMY; CIVIL POWER, SUPPORT OF; ENGINEERS; MEDICAL SERVICES; ROME; SOLDIERS AND SOCIETY.

A. CORVISIER
JOHN CHILDS

FURTHER READING
John Childs, *Armies and Warfare in Europe, 1648–1789* (Manchester, 1982); Ulrich Bräker, *The Life Story and Real Adventures of the Poor Man of Toggenburg*, ed. D. Bowman (Edinburgh, 1970); J.-N. Biraben, *Histoire de la peste* (2 vols, Paris, 1976); William Taylor, *The Military Roads of Scotland* (Newton Abbot, 1976).

Civil power, support of Political authorities with responsibility for what in earlier times was termed 'public safety', and latterly 'the maintenance of order', can use for the purpose, apart from the police, either the army proper or paramilitary formations. Under the *ancien régime* in France, troops were said to be *appelée en mainforte* in the event of violent demonstrations directed against property or persons regardless of whether the motives were political. Since the nineteenth century, the word *réquisition* (commandeering) has been applied to the same practice. It has become commonplace and, like the establishment of units specially trained to maintain internal order, it raises the whole question of the balance between state power and the rights of the citizen. In the majority of modern nations, it is in fact the executive which is the sole judge of when it is appropriate to summon military aid. In France, governments with radical tendencies asserted unequivocally in a series of instructions issued to military commanders between 1903 and 1907 that the state had an absolute prerogative in the matter. The order of 20 August 1907, which was occasioned by riots in the wine-producing region of Languedoc, requested the troops to move immediately on receipt of a message by telegraph, without waiting for written confirmation. Democratic governments thus possess powers – the declaration of martial law (1789), a 'state of siege' (1849) or a 'state of emergency' (1955) – which even absolute monarchs found circumscribed by the law and public opinion.

'Martial law' implies the suspension of civilian law. In England the Riot Act of 1715 made into felons all persons above the number of twelve who remained in the area of a riot one hour after the reading of the proclamation contained in the statute. Although the law was unclear, it was generally assumed that the magistrate could summon military assistance after the expiry of the sixty minutes. In exceptional circumstances, *habeas corpus* could be suspended through the operation of the suspending power, a prerogative shared by monarch and parliament after 1689. In the nineteenth century, Ireland was governed by special laws which were renewed annually. In France, the law of 21 October 1789 gave details of the formal procedures that were to accompany the introduction of 'martial law' – the firing of an alarm gun and the hoisting of a red flag. Its purpose was to prohibit any unlawful assemblies that posed a threat to public order and it allowed troops to fire without prior warning on those taking part. Its employment on 17 July 1791 (the shooting in the Champ de Mars) left an unhappy memory and the phrase 'martial law' was dropped from later laws and replaced by 'state of siege'. This had been the expression traditionally employed to explain measures taken in cases of danger arising from an internal threat but was here extended to cover instances of insurrection. The 'state of siege' could be declared only after a parliamentary vote had passed a law denoting the region to which its provisions were applicable. In French colonies, the governor could proclaim a 'state of siege' but had to inform the home government immediately of his action; a decision on its continuation rested with the Chamber of Deputies and the Senate. The governor of a fortress could declare a 'state of siege' when circumstances arose as defined in the law of 10 July 1891 – encirclement by an enemy, sedition or armed assembly within a distance of 6 miles. He was required to inform the Minister of War of his action forthwith. The 'state of siege' made it legal to carry out searches,

to confiscate arms and ammunition in the possession of individuals, to remove persons judged to be a danger to public order and to prohibit assemblies of more than three people. The majority of these provisions are covered by the modern 'state of emergency', although they have been adapted in accordance with changes in legislation and with the new organization of the forces used to maintain order.

There were limits to the employment of 'mainforte' since it could not be directed against certain institutions. For example, under the *ancien régime* troops were not allowed to enter the precincts of ecclesiastical establishments, although this rule was frequently infringed. In May 1750, the Swiss Guard 'cleared' the Quinze-Vingts hospice in Paris, where rioters had taken refuge, but an effort was made to observe the formalities by putting in charge of this force some *exempts de la robe courte* (NCOs of the *maréchaussée*) who were provided with a legal warrant. More important was the immunity possessed by large towns where the local *parlement*, under normal circumstances, exercised overall responsibility for the preservation of order. The *parlements* usually sought to protect the civil population against excesses of severity. Armed forces called out *en mainforte* showed less resolution in major urban centres than in the countryside, since they were liable to have to account for their actions before magistrates. Recourse to the use of troops was automatic only when the law suspended normal jurisdiction in favour of that exercised by the *prévôt*, *ratione loci* (outside towns) or *ratione materiae* (after 1739, for the corn riots). The army waited for six months before entering Lyons, which was in revolt in 1744. However, at the end of the *ancien régime*, Turgot and Malesherbes made efforts to free the political authorities from the control of the judiciary over *mainforte*; this tendency was to gather pace during the Revolution.

From 1768 in England (St George's Fields Riots) and from 1775 in France, the commandeering of troops to aid the civil power can be seen as an aspect of political history rather than civilian law. Governments turned in preference to the army, which carried greater authority and was better disciplined, rather than the citizen militias and the other watch organizations, which did not inspire much confidence. Yet there remained the question of whether the military were prepared, on every occasion, to carry out a task which was not technically theirs. In 1768, a London magistrate said, 'I have always considered that riots should be suppressed without the help of the army.' In fact, during the Gordon Riots in 1780, line regiments showed a marked reluctance to fire on the crowd. In Paris, the failure by the *Gardes françaises* to take any action in 1775 during the 'grain war' is explained by their officers' unwillingness; their fraternization with the populace was the result of a propaganda campaign against the principle of *réquisition*, as representing an attack upon civil liberties. In these circumstances, it was seen as a confession of impotence on the part of the political authorities if foreign regiments were called out to restore order.

With the formation of armies based on universal national service, it became dangerous to commandeer troops too frequently, since there was a possibility that they might desert and join the insurgents. Although the army suppressed workers' revolts, indeed with bloodshed, at Fourmies in 1891 and at Draveil in 1908, expelled religious communities and broke down barricades erected by Catholics in 1905, the 17th line regiment, which had been recruited in the Midi, mutinied and sided with the wine-growers of Languedoc on 21 June 1907.

More than one reason, therefore, provided the impetus for the creation of units designed specifically for the task of maintaining order. It was envisaged that such units would combine three qualities: (1) the efficiency of a mobile, disciplined and well-armed force; (2) a rigorously professional character to safeguard against possible defection; and (3), more importantly, the ability to act with a degree of moderation in order to prevent internal conflicts becoming more inflamed. This last consideration led to a preference for cavalry. In 1777, the Comte de Thélis spoke

with regret of the recent abolition of musketeers but made the perceptive remark that 'in the case of riot, half a dozen horsemen with sabres would create a greater impression and have more effect than fifty men armed with flintlocks and bayonets, which cannot be used without endangering the lives of innocent people.'

The division of tasks between the army and supplementary units that have a responsibility for ensuring internal order has varied at different periods. The *maréchaussée* suffered particularly from its lack of numbers as was often proclaimed in the *cahiers de doléances*; it was frequently overwhelmed when it was called out to assist the civil power. The *gendarmerie*, which replaced it in 1790, underwent numerous changes, which did not, however, prevent it from playing an increasingly important role, notably in the coup d'état of 1851. On the other hand, it experienced a long eclipse during the first fifty years of the Third Republic, while troops from the army were regularly commandeered. It was not until the passage of the law of 21 July 1921 that there was established – in the form of the Mobile Republican Guard (called the *gendarmerie mobile* since 1955) – a force capable of intervening in every type of critical circumstance. Besides, a new attitude towards the nature of a police force has worked in the direction of withdrawing the army from its association with the maintenance and restoration of public order. This has led, since 1948, to the attachment to the Ministry of the Interior of some army units (*compagnies républicaines de sécurité*) responsible for that specific task.

J. CHAGNIOT

The scope and limits of legitimate aid to the civil power in the modern United Kingdom are ill-defined in strictly legal terms but reasonably clear in practice. The armed forces are, by law, ethos and training, strictly subordinate to civilian control. They are not called on to judge when aid to the civil power is required. The initiative for such assistance lies with the chief constable of the local police force who finds himself unable to cope by means of

147

ordinary policing. He is empowered to request, and the military under government control are empowered to provide, such assistance as the situation may seem to the political authorities to require. Thus in August 1969, the Inspector-General of the Royal Ulster Constabulary asked the Northern Ireland government for army assistance in Londonderry where serious rioting was threatening to get out of hand. The request was passed on to the government in London, whence orders to deploy troops were sent. In the years since 1969, British troops in Northern Ireland have been subject to stringent requirements that they employ only minimum force. The somewhat freer hand with which public order difficulties were formerly handled within the British Empire has given way to a regime of tight restraint. Training for duties in Northern Ireland has been altered to accustom troops to long periods of boredom and provocative danger without expecting to be able to achieve anything which can be regarded as victory.

BARRIE PASKINS

See also ADMINISTRATION, ARMY; CIVIL CONTRIBUTION OF ARMIES; GENDARMERIE; MILITARY RESTRICTIONS ON USE OF LAND; MILITIAS; NORTHERN IRELAND; SIEGES; SOLDIERS AND SOCIETY.

FURTHER READING
Jean Chagniot, *Paris et l'armée au XVIIIe siècle* (Paris, 1985); J. Jauffret, 'Armée et pouvoir politique. La question des troupes spéciales chargées du maintien de l'ordre en France de 1871 à 1914', *Revue historique*, no. 547 (1983), pp. 97–145; Tony Hayter, *The Army and the Crowd in Mid-Georgian England* (London, 1978); Peter Rowe, *Defence: the legal implications* (London, 1987); John Sweetman, *Civil–Military Relations in Britain: twentieth-century civil–military relations in Britain* (London, 1986).

Civil war The term 'civil war' is used for the situation which arises when those who live under a single effective form of government – whether their condition is that of subjects or citizens – engage in armed conflict with each other. It is distinct from tribal and private war. The former occurs where there is no overall rule; the latter,

where such rule is tenuous. Internal conflicts can be regarded as civil wars only if the opposing parties are conscious of belonging to one nation or if, in the result, they achieve a more cohesive unity. The struggle between the Armagnac and Burgundian factions during the Hundred Years' War is considered a civil war, and the same is true of all the uprisings that have since occurred in France. When the thirteen British colonies in America rose, the event was seen differently by the parties concerned; to the loyalists it was a rebellion, to the insurgents a revolution, and hence, a civil war. It was also a war of independence. The Americans call the conflict which tore apart the United States from 1861 to 1865 a civil war, while in countries not unsympathetic to the Southerners it is termed the War of Secession and regarded as an unsuccessful attempt to secure their independence.

An appreciable proportion of the population of a nation-state revolts against its government only when the authority of the latter is undermined, for example, by a disputed succession to the throne, or through its tyrannical exercise of power, or when sufficiently strong motives that all point in the same direction fuse into one. Through the existence of the Salic law (which excluded females from dynastic succession), France avoided civil wars like the Wars of the Roses, which ravaged England from 1455 to 1487, or the Carlist Wars in Spain in the nineteenth century. She also escaped wars of succession after the defeat of England in the Hundred Years' War. Civil wars can arise from diverse causes, such as governmental oppression, or from religious, political or ideological motives, to which social factors also often add their strength.

Since the time of St Thomas Aquinas, a distinction has been drawn between the tyrant who has usurped power, in which case revolt against him and tyrannicide are legitimate, and the tyrant who has acceded legally but violates the natural rights and liberties of his subjects and despoils them of their possessions. In modern states, the cause of revolts has often been the burden of taxation (e.g. the popular uprisings in France during Louis XIII's time), objections to a particular tax (which was one of the reasons for the insurrection of the thirteen British colonies in America) or the curtailment of regional rights by a centralized administration (which was one of the motives behind the Fronde). Although, in the majority of cases, such reasons are operative concurrently, a distinction can be drawn between revolts of a popular character (the *Jacquerie* of the fourteenth century, or those of the *Croquants* and the *Nu-Pieds* against the extortionate tax-collectors and excisemen of Louis XIII and Richelieu) and the aristocratic type, like the Fronde, whose object was to prevent the monarchy from developing in the direction of administrative absolutism. In the latter case, however, the leaders were very ready to make use of the disaffected lower classes as their main striking force.

In the sixteenth and seventeenth centuries, it was religious motives that provided the driving force for civil motives of extreme violence, whether they reflected a determination to secure victory for the 'true' religion, or only a resistance to persecution by the state (e.g. Ireland, the Camisard rebellion), or whether there were other associated social reasons (the Peasant War in Germany in 1525) or socio-political ones (the eighty years of war in the Netherlands against the monarchy which had become too Spanish). The century of the Enlightenment provided, in the shape of the French Revolution, the starting point for ideological wars (though the Vendée still had a religious aspect); these have included the federalist revolts, the Carlist Wars and, later, the Spanish Civil War of 1936–9. Although they frequently took the appearance of civil wars, insurrections against an authority set up by a foreign power (Dombrowski's Poland, Spain resisting Napoleon, Juárez's Mexico fighting against Maximilian, Afghanistan, etc.) cannot be put in this category, since they were wars of national resistance.

Where religions and ideologies are not confined within particular territorial frontiers, civil conflicts can expand into international wars. Thus the Wars of Religion in France saw intervention by England on the side of the Protestants, and then by

Spain on that of the Catholics. Further, sovereigns have often sought to profit from the difficulties of their opponents by supporting internal revolts against the latter. Policies of this kind were pursued reciprocally by the French and Spanish kings from 1635 to 1659. Nevertheless, they showed great restraint when there was any risk of contagion from social or political movements that questioned the very principles of the established order. This view even prevailed finally in regard to the Wars of Religion. The idea that a country's religion should be that of its sovereign became, in some ways, a rule of international law, except when it could be claimed that a state was violating its own laws (e.g. the assistance given to the Camisards by the Allies). Louis XVI was the first sovereign to have openly assisted a revolution of an ideological nature. Since then, intervention by foreign powers in the civil wars of others has become a more widespread practice, whether with the aim of helping a government to restore order (e.g. the intervention of Prussia against the opponents of the Netherlands in 1787, or of France in Spain, when so commissioned by the Holy Alliance in 1823) or of assisting insurgents (e.g. help to the Russian White Armies, 1918–22). Since there were interventions by European powers on both sides in the Spanish Civil War (1936–9), it developed into an international war. They ceased to send in combatant troops once the sides were in balance, but this did not prevent them from continuing to provide war material. Between 1945 and 1991 the portioning of the world into two rival blocs was the cause of the continuance of civil war in numerous countries (Lebanon, San Salvador, Angola, etc.).

In any event, a civil war can occur only with the help of favourable conditions, and the military systems adopted by a country have a direct bearing. In times before the structure of centralized government adopted by modern states had been established, if the power of monarchs weakened for any reason, their military systems actually encouraged civil war. In fact, the army was made up of contingents which were raised by provincial and town governors, though in theory in the name of the king. When a governor or a town rose against the sovereign, they induced the forces they had to go along with them. During the Wars of Religion, the Huguenots and, later, the members of the League made use of the existing military arrangements to raise their armies and to stir up the civil populations. The county militias formed the basis for the armies of both Charles I and Parliament during the opening stages of the English Civil War (1642–6). From Louis XIV's time onwards, allegiance was sworn to the king only, in other words, to the state, and this placed difficulties in the way of such action, except in special cases (e.g. rebellion by alien inhabitants already enjoying a degree of autonomy; colonies in revolt). It needed the mistakes made by the Revolution for the result to be civil war. When the army is the instrument of state power and is maintained by the state alone, it is naturally bound to defend the latter when any revolt occurs.

If the state's power is weakened, there can be danger in the possession of such a responsibility by the army, because it thereby acquires a political role and may be tempted to act on its own behalf. When asked to restore order and carry out the coups d'état of the Directory, the French army put into power one of its own generals. The 18th Brumaire (9 November 1799) was the first military coup d'état of modern times, though in the nineteenth century they became a political way of life in South American countries, there called *pronunciamientos*. Unless they either succeed or are put down at once, they unleash civil war. Latin America has had bitter experience of this ever since its states achieved independence. In modern times, it is only when a nation has suffered a severe emotional shock that a civil war can come about. Hence, its origin is frequently a revolution, or an attempted revolution, following a military defeat (the Paris Commune, 1871; the Russian Civil War of 1918–22).

Civil war has always had the reputation of being more fearsome than one against foreigners. It is much harder to control than the latter and, inasmuch as the civil population cannot remain aloof, it abolishes the distinction between soldiers and civilians, produces a spate of accusations of hostility, or even of treachery, provokes massacres, and the fury of the belligerents is often wreaked on hostages and the innocent. In the strict military sense, civil warfare has rarely borrowed from the classical procedures of war as practised in its period, except in the case of sieges. An exception to this rule, however, was the establishment of an almost continuous front during the Spanish Civil War. On the other hand, it makes continual use of indirect warfare. Here, operations consist of capturing strategic positions by bold *coups de main* for which the way has often been prepared by clandestine action. In 1936, there was a plan for a secret 'fifth column' inside Madrid to combine its efforts with those of four columns converging on the city. Cities are among the most prized objectives, inasmuch as they offer support in manpower and supplies to either side, but the countryside remains a place of refuge both in regions with a large rural population (China or the Vendée) or where few people live (the Cévennes).

Civil wars in the military sphere, like revolution in the political, play havoc with rank and the normal paths of promotion to higher positions. They bring to the fore leaders who are often young, and sometimes highly talented, although lacking previous experience – Cromwell or Napoleon Bonaparte. Particularly if a civil war continues for a long time, its evil effects are extensive, most of all in regard to the destruction of property and the loss of human life (5,000,000 killed in the Taiping war, 1,000,000 in the Spanish). Since they are characterized by violent emotions, civil wars often incite men to acts of great cruelty, sometimes extending to genocide, and to individuals taking the law into their own hands; and they usually leave behind the seeds of discord, which often take long years to wither. *See also* GUERILLA WARFARE; INDIRECT WARFARE; LAWS OF WAR; NATIONALISM; POPULAR WARFARE.

A. CORVISIER

FURTHER READING
Perez Zagorin, *Rebels and Rulers, 1500–1660* (2

vols, Cambridge, 1982); J. H. M. Salmon, *Society in Crisis: France in the 16th century* (London, 1975); Hugh Thomas, *The Spanish Civil War* (London, 1961); J. F. N. Bradley, *Civil War in Russia, 1917–1920* (London, 1975); J. M. McPherson, *The Battle Cry of Freedom* (Oxford, 1988).

Civil–military relations *See* BARRACKS; CIVIL CONTRIBUTION OF ARMIES; CIVIL POWER, SUPPORT OF; SOLDIERS AND SOCIETY

Clausewitz, Karl von (1780–1831) Clausewitz, probably the most important of all military theorists, joined the Prussian army at the age of twelve, and in 1793 saw action for the first time. He fought at Jena in 1806, France's crushing victory over the old unreformed order in Prussia. In 1812, disgusted by his monarch's accommodation of the French, he threw in his lot with Russia. In 1815, restored to the Prussian army, he served in the Waterloo campaign. In 1818 he was appointed director of the War Academy in Berlin. This was the base which enabled him to devote the remainder of his life to his studies of military history and, above all, to his principal work, *On War*. In 1831 he served as chief of staff to Gneisenau in the Polish campaign, contracted cholera, and died.

On War was published in 1832, but the revisions which Clausewitz planned were not complete and the text therefore carried contradictions and obscurities which restricted its immediate influence. Clausewitz argued that war was not limited of itself. Killing was an absolute. But in practice war was limited in two ways. First, war served the objects of politics: war had its own grammar but not its own logic. Therefore political realities, the purpose in going to war in the first place and the need for an eventual settlement, determined the level of violence and the application of resources. Second, war's own nature thwarted the achievement of absolute war. Clausewitz called this 'friction'. Sickness, exhaustion, fear, lack of intelligence, human error, poor morale – all multiplied according to the size of the forces engaged –

stood between the commander and his goals.

Much of *On War* is concerned with the conduct of war in the time of Napoleon and does not aspire to the universal relevance of its leading ideas. But even here there were important insights. Clausewitz saw the destruction of the enemy's forces, and the concentration on seeking a major battle, as war's most likely objective. On the other hand, influenced by his experiences in 1812, he recognized that an attack could pass its 'culminating point of victory' and that defence was the stronger means.

Clausewitz's writing is rooted in the technology of his own age. He did not anticipate that absolute war might come as close to reality as it has done in the twentieth century. But it is the experience of two world wars and the invention of nuclear weapons that have given his writings fresh relevance. *See also* GERMANY; JOMINI; NAPOLEON.

HEW STRACHAN

FURTHER READING
Raymond Aron, *Clausewitz: philosopher of war* (London, 1983); Carl von Clausewitz, *On War*, tr. Michael Howard and Peter Paret (Princeton, 1976); Michael Howard, *Clausewitz* (Oxford, 1983); Peter Paret, *Clausewitz and the State* (Oxford, 1976).

Coastal defence The 'maritime frontier' poses problems different from those of land frontiers. The latter are modified as a result of conquests, annexations and the return of various pieces of territory; in line with such changes, new positions are fortified. The coastline remains largely unchanged throughout millennia; the problem of coastal defence is how to deal with the military dangers that come from the sea. The sea is a means of communication and supply. Deep-sea shipping in every age maintains connections with far-off places, bringing in commodities that are important for industry and for daily life; coastal vessels deal with short-distance links and with distribution; fishing provides direct food supplies.

The sea is a source of danger for populations living close to the coast and for the

151

states which it borders. From time immemorial, and up to the seventeenth century in Europe, pirates engaged in pillage and raids, sometimes taking temporary bases (the Vikings), or semi-permanent ones, like the Saracens at La Garde Freinet in the Var. Invasions arrive from the sea – William the Conqueror in 1066, or the Allies in Normandy in 1944. A heavily indented coastline has always caused difficulties for defence forces. Their movements on land are thereby restricted and, if made on foot, are slower than those of ships, whether under sail or rowed; the difference is even more pronounced if the enemy is using steam or motor vessels. A similar problem arises where rivers make large cuts across territories (Rhine, Danube), although the area involved is more limited and the fact that crossings must inevitably take place at certain points means that the tactics and defence works used in purely land battles provide the answers.

States with strong navies secured their own coastlines by the fact of their maritime superiority (Great Britain from 1688 to 1945) but those with weaker navies (i.e. France) had to deploy their fleets in coastal defence and protect their coastal provinces with military organizations. In the nineteenth century, France built up an elaborate system based on armoured coastguard vessels – a type of defence with limited mobility and which had to be suitably stationed – together with what was called, in 1886, the 'young school', naval smallfry in the shape of torpedo boats, complemented by a network of controllable mines. Ultimately, the coastal submarine was able to provide unobtrusive surveillance and effective defensive action. Tethered mines having proved their effectiveness, a natural development was the minefields of 1914–18 and 1939–45. Airships and, later, aircraft provided help to coastal naval forces, both for surveillance and in battle (e.g. British Coastal Command during the Second World War).

Surveillance – the detection of a potential attacker and the tracking of his movements – is the primary task in coastal protection. Traditionally, it was always done from look-out posts situated on high points, in order to command a large field of vision. It appears that Charlemagne established such a system as a partial counter to the Vikings, as did, before him, the Romans of the later Empire along the North Sea coast. But most frequently, it was the small peasant communities that had to arrange their own safety measures. Look-out towers provided shelter for the watchmen who had the task of alerting the peasants so that the latter could move into the hinterland with their animals, or go back into the village if it had some semblance of fortification. The invaders were usually seeking only to secure booty or slaves, at minimum cost to themselves. These towers, which were made of wood or stone, were not part of a real defensive system, but provided a wider field of vision and sheltered the watchmen in case they did not have time to join their fellow-villagers. Church bells fulfilled the same function. Various look-out towers in Ireland, however, being more strongly built and with access via an upper floor, could play an active defensive role. These towers also served as aiming points or leading marks for the pilotage of ships.

From the twelfth century, states or principalities assumed responsibility for this task of surveillance. The components of the system were no longer provided by a village, or group of villages, and the watchmen were located within sight of each other at a distance of about 5–6 miles; the movement of invaders was tracked, and defence forces could then be assembled. This system was still more valuable in wartime. The proper consequence would have been to use it as the basis for a defence organization, but cost generally prevented this, except in the case of sections of coast which were particularly threatened. Surveillance assumed a different character when the aim was to prevent the importation of contraband goods, or the disembarkation or escape of intelligence agents. It was then carried out by customs and excise authorities, mobile police or troops. In wartime, troops assumed the responsibility for surveillance, taking up position on high points or hiding in coves. In modern times, air forces have been able to combine surveillance with active participation in defence.

Defence of a particular area can be secured: (1) on the coastline, by fortifications; (2) in front of the coastline, by naval forces; and (3) inland, by mobile land forces.

Fortifications represent the oldest method. In Great Britain, the remains have been excavated of a Roman coastal fortress, which was probably built by the usurper Carausius (AD 287–93). In England, after 1539, Henry VIII built strong fortifications along the coasts facing France. Later French governments made numerous additions to the number of coastal batteries. The same was true of Spain, Portugal and Italy. Even before 1812, the defence of her ports, roadsteads and landfalls engrossed the attention of the young American Republic.

Methods varied in accordance with the weapons available. In the time of the sailing ship and round shot, batteries were placed low down where they could fire with a flat trajectory, to hit the rigging, and also to prevent light craft from stealing along the coastline. When long-range artillery was introduced, the batteries were placed on high points to increase range and engage ships with 'plunging fire'. But an earlier development, particularly in America, was the construction of giant batteries, sometimes housing 100 guns, firing in a high arc, which could tear to pieces the enemy ships in front of them. Until the end of the nineteenth century, coastal guns were protected against fire from ships' armaments by thick stone walls fitted with embrasures. The British Martello towers were descendants of the 'Saracen towers' of the Mediterranean, and probably so called after the tower on Corsica at Cape Mortella which resisted the British in 1794. The British copied the design and erected a chain of these small, round forts along the coasts of Sussex, Kent and East Anglia between 1803 and 1805, in the face of the French invasion threat. Later, they were introduced into Canada, but were rendered redundant by later artillery. The heavy, rifled muzzle-loading coastal guns of the mid-nineteenth century were housed in casements, but the American Civil War showed that casements made good targets for naval artillery. Guns were moved into the open where the invention of the disappearing carriage allowed the weapon to be fired over the parapet before sinking into a pit for loading. As the gun was exposed for only a few seconds, retaliatory fire was virtually impossible. Increased ranges of coastal and naval guns in the early twentieth century meant that a small target, such as a coastal gun emplacement, was unlikely to be hit. Guns were thus placed 'in barbette', a reinforced concrete emplacement with the shielded barrel always above the parapet. Air power led to the adoption of roofed emplacements, virtually casemates, and armoured turrets. Faster-moving ships brought the question of fire control to the fore. The British adopted radar to control coastal guns in 1940. In America, the effectiveness of the artillery led to a gradual reduction in the number of strong points: in 1810, there were 33, but 20 in 1850, 18 in 1900 and 11 in 1940 for covering the whole coastline of New England. Her unquestioned naval supremacy did not prevent Britain from fortifying her coastline; batteries were built in 1915 after the Battle of Dogger Bank, and the Channel coast was covered with blockhouses.

The defence of ports has always been a problem. The method used in Antiquity was to stretch chains between two strong towers; such were used too, in the post-medieval era, at Constantinople and Rhodes. Later, the system was to defend the entrance with batteries, such as Fort St Elmo at Malta, or the gun positions along the Brest channel. The landward side too required protection – something that was found to be lacking at Singapore in 1942. Thus, major French and British naval bases have been fortified towns, often with a citadel, as at Plymouth.

Provision needed to be made for intervention by government troops against an enemy who had disembarked small units with the aim of destruction or plunder or of preparing the way for a larger-scale enterprise. Coastal communities began to be organized on military lines in England in the time of Henry VIII, and in France under Francis I. This placed certain responsibilities on inhabitants of parishes whose church towers were situated within a particular distance from the sea; in France, this was set at less than 5 miles but, in fact, it was often more. Colbert, the Minister for the Navy, established coastguard militias in 1681. These consisted of independent companies, which were later recruited by lot from among able-bodied men of 18 to 45, armed and grouped into coastguard formations under a captain, and watch companies, comprising the rest of the male population up to 60 years old. In order to deal more effectively with a serious attack, field battalions or even, where the coast was flat, regiments of coastguard dragoons were established in the eighteenth century. In 1778, the coastguard militias were reduced to companies of coastguard gunners. Under the Empire, a return to a more mobile form of defence became essential.

In 1801, Bonaparte stipulated that there should be patrols of 200 horsemen, commanded by naval officers. In 1811, when emperor, he ordered the formation of mobile columns of 1,000 to 1,500 men (200 of them mounted) with two field pieces. Islands had to arrange their own defence; the garrison of Belle-Île, for example, numbered 4,000. From that time on, in mobilization plans, it was envisaged that divisions of the second reserve would carry out these tasks. Artillery pieces moving on narrow-gauge track (164 or 274 cm) had been planned for Brittany as a means of reinforcing the mobile defence. The trend of military thinking moved towards the scheme of having large formations in a central position, and thus able to move rapidly in force to meet an enemy who, after disembarking, had not yet established himself. This mode of action proved successful in 1915, at Suvla Bay in the Dardanelles. It was not so in 1942–5, because of the disproportion of the attacking forces and the enormity of their firepower, despite the bitterness of the fighting in Italy, Normandy and in the islands of the Pacific.

Attacks on coasts are often made with the support of forces already established in the interior of the country attacked, or with the expected backing of its inhabitants. Defence of maritime frontiers needs close liaison between navy and army, which is not achieved without difficulty. Because of his mobility, the seaborne assailant has a fundamental advantage, since he can choose the place of his attack. He can concentrate his forces, effect surprise, slip away, provided that he possesses mastery of the sea or, in more recent times, air superiority. In addition, in the course of artillery duels, coastal batteries present static targets, while ships offer only mobile ones and shells from a fleet always hit something ashore. Therefore, there have often appeared two divergent theories of defence – should an enemy be prevented from disembarking forces of any size by a defence stationed more or less on the coastline, but which immobilizes and disperses large numbers of troops? Or should one accept that the enemy should be allowed to disembark at his chosen points, in order to drive him back into the sea when the defenders have had time to concentrate against him? The former doctrine was the one generally chosen by France, except from 1778 to 1801, when defence efforts were confined to protecting some strategic positions with coastal batteries. The same difference of opinion arose in 1944 between Rommel, who was a proponent of coastline defence, and von Rundstedt, who believed in powerful counter-attacks.

In France and Britain, it is the navy which has more often been charged with the task of coastal defence. However, special French army commands were established for a short period at Camaret (Brest) in 1694 and at Saint-Cast in 1758. In the latter year, the army was given responsibility for dealing with the coastguard militia and retained it for some further twenty years. A law of 1793 gave the army responsibility for the defence of coastal fortresses but, in 1913, the running of naval ports was handed over to the navy. In 1917, the Minister for the Navy was put in charge of the defence of coasts against a seaborne enemy. From that time, the maritime prefect has had at his disposal whatever sea and land forces are currently allocated to him.

Colbert and Seignelay organized the coastal fortification service but, on the death of the latter (1690), Louvois coupled with it the land fortification service. The merging of these two services took place in 1691, the result being a department of fortifications. Building work was the responsibility of the 'king's engineers', that is, the engineer corps. At the end of the nineteenth century, in France, a division of labour was established, whereby the engineers dealt with construction work that was 2 metres above the highest water mark, and the department of maritime works took over everything below that point (i.e. where there was 'sea risk'). In 1913, the department of maritime works took over responsibility for the fortifications at ports, and in 1933 that for all coastal defences. In Britain and the United States, army engineers have retained these tasks. In 1940, Germany set up a special organization for this purpose, named after its first head, Fritz Todt. Coastal artillery was largely abandoned between 1946 and 1956; it was considered redundant in the face of missiles and nuclear weapons. However, some countries – Norway, Spain, Sweden, Yugoslavia and Turkey – have retained their coastal artillery. The recent Falklands War (1982), the Iran–Iraq War (1980–8), and the Gulf War (1991) have demonstrated the value of batteries of land-based coastal defence missiles against shipping. *See also* ADMINISTRATION, NAVAL; ARTILLERY; COMBINED OPERATIONS; ENGINEERS; FORTIFICATION; NAVAL WARFARE.

J.-M. GOENAGA
A. CORVISIER

FURTHER READING
Ian V. Hogg, *Coast Defences of England and Wales, 1856–1956* (London, 1974); Raymond E. Lewis, *Seacoast Fortifications of the United States* (Washington DC, 1970); Quentin Hughes, *Military Architecture* (London, 1974); K. Mallory and A. Ottar, *The Architecture of Aggression* (London, 1973).

Codes *See* SECRECY

Coehoorn, Baron Menno van (1641–1704) This great Dutch military engineer was born in Friesland. His father, an infantry captain, familiarized him with military matters at an early age. After studying mathematics and fortification at the academy in Franeker, he joined the Dutch army in 1657. He was wounded at the Siege of Maastricht in 1673. In the following year he invented a small, portable mortar which became known as the 'Coehoorn Mortar', or simply as the 'Coehoorn'. In 1685, he published *Nieuwe Vestingbouw op een Natte of Lage Horisont*, which was translated into English by Thomas Savery under the title, *The New Method of Fortification*. In this work, which soon became authoritative, Coehoorn advocated a clear alternative method of fortification to that which was used in the Netherlands between 1678 and 1688. The 'new system' required enlarged bastions and ravelins (fortification outworks); curved, oblique bastion flanks; the replacement of outworks – 'useless furniture' – with counter-guards; a continuous 'envelope' around the fortress behind the covered way, which was reinforced; and a lowering of the masonry revetments so that they could not be seen from outside the fortress. Coehoorn also preached an active defence at every stage of a siege. During the Nine Years' War, Coehoorn modified a number of fortresses, most notably Namur, which he defended unsuccessfully in 1692 but recaptured in 1695. He was created Engineer-General of Fortifications in the Dutch Republic in 1695. Between 1698 and 1702, he directed a team of sixty engineers, who rebuilt and modified a number of Dutch fortresses according to his 'new Method', most notably Bergen-op-Zoom. *See also* FORTIFICATION; NETHERLANDS; SIEGES; STEVIN; VAUBAN.

C. M. SCHULTEN
JOHN CHILDS

FURTHER READING
Vesting. Vier eeuwen Vestingbouw in Nederland, eds J. Sneep, H. A. Treu and M. Tydeman (The Hague, 1982); Christopher Duffy, *The Fortress in the Age of Vauban and Frederick the Great* (London, 1985); J. P. C. M. van Hoof, 'Fortifications in the

Netherlands', *Revue Internationale d'Histoire Militaire*, lviii (The Hague, 1984), pp. 97–126.

Colbert, Jean-Baptiste (1619–83) As the son of a great landed, merchant family of the Champagne region who had obtained for himself a solid place within the offices of the crown, nothing in Colbert's background seemed to predispose him to become interested in the navy. However, it was he, even more than Richelieu, whose good work was to some extent undone under Mazarin, who was the real founder of the French navy. His interest seems to have been prompted by Mazarin's capital investments in shipping interests and by Fouquet's thinking on the role of the merchant marine and the grievances of the French ports. He played a major part, after 1662, in the purchase of Dunkirk. In 1664, after a series of broad enquiries into the numerical state of the merchant fleet he submitted his views to the king in a series of reports. He set himself the task of making France as powerful on the sea as she was on land. Aided by a remarkable group of advisers, who were quite prepared to force his hand when they saw need to do so (Nicolas Argoud, Colbert du Terron, the Chevalier de Clerville, Vauban, Savary des Brûlons, etc.), he determined the site of the great naval dockyards: Brest, Toulon and Rochefort, and Marseilles for galleys. These developed impressively as the maritime front came to be seen as part of the 'belt of iron' around France. Colbert's choice of sites, which was to have considerable consequences, was not in all cases the best that could have been made (e.g. Rochefort). Calling upon English, Dutch, Genoan and Venetian experience, Colbert built up the greatest war fleet of the age, which was constructed with great rapidity by the French master-shipbuilders. Thus, from 1670, if one includes the vessels of the fifth rank (fewer than fifty cannon) Louis XIV possessed a fleet of 120 ships of the line. To give the force the reserves of material that would be essential in time of war, Colbert engaged upon an intensified 'rational' exploitation of France's forests, improving the forest roads and the rivers down which timber could be floated. He also created forges, foundries and arsenals. The scale of legislative activity was enormous and continued after his death. It reached its high point in the two great naval ordonnances of 1681 and 1689. At the end of the eighteenth century, one of the highest ranking civil servants in the naval department, Pidansat de Mairobert, gathered together all Colbert's papers relating to his naval activities into a single corpus, which is an extremely valuable, but under-exploited historical source.

To equip this fleet, Colbert carried out a census of French sailors and introduced the first 'compulsory military service' in the highly controversial form of the 'system of classes', the forerunner of the *inscription maritime* system of seaboard conscription for the navy. Though relatively well accepted in Brittany, this did give rise to a series of revolts.

Colbert's enormous naval effort produced varied results. The merchant navy developed more than has at times been suggested, progressing from some 130–150,000 tons in 1664 to more than 200,000 tons in 1688. After some initial difficulties, the navy triumphed in its Sicilian campaign of 1675–6, though it had to abandon the Channel and the Atlantic to do so. When peace was restored, Colbert made immense efforts to drive the Barbary pirates from the Mediterranean but his endeavours met with only limited success. Colbert proved no more able than his successors to remedy the principal weakness of French naval power – the shortage of sailors. Between 1660 and 1789, the figure remained stuck at around 50,000 men. Unrepentant advocate as he was of civilian power, Colbert prevented the formation of a naval general staff. He has also been criticized for favouring the 'officers of the pen' over the corps of 'officers of the sword', who were usually former army men and generally, it must be admitted, terribly ill-disciplined. Colbert's work was continued by his son, Seignelay, who himself died in 1690. *See also* ADMINISTRATION, NAVAL; BASES, NAVAL; FRANCE; NAVAL PERSONNEL; NAVIES; VAUBAN.

J. MEYER

FURTHER READING
Jean Meyer, *Colbert* (Paris, 1981); Etienne Taillemitte, 'Colbert et la marine', and André Corvisier, 'Colbert et la guerre', in *Un Nouveau Colbert: Actes des Colloques Colbert 1983* (Paris, 1985); C. W. Cole, *Colbert and a Century of French Mercantilism* (2 vols, London, 1939).

Colleoni, Bartolomeo (*c*.1400–75) The superb equestrian statue which Venice commissioned from Verrochio and which still stands near the Church of St John and St Paul, has led to Colleoni being regarded as the perfect type of *Quattrocento condottiere*. The son of a noble family from the Bergamo region, he learned his trade in the service of a *condottiere* of comparable repute, Braccio da Montone. For more than twenty years, between 1431 and 1454, he served Venice and Milan alternately. His finest battles were fought during this period, principally the victories over French expeditionary forces at Bosco Marengo in 1447 and Romagnano Sesia in 1449. After 1454, he remained in Venetian pay living in the castle of Malpaga, south of Bergamo, which he defended for his employers. Charles the Bold sought in vain to tempt him into a contract with Burgundy. After his death, his son-in-law continued to serve Venice with a famous troop of cavalry, the Colleoneschi. *See also* ITALY; MERCENARIES.

P. CONTAMINE

FURTHER READING
M. E. Mallett and J. R. Hale, *The Military Organisation of a Renaissance State: Venice, c.1400 to 1617* (Cambridge, 1984); Michael Mallett, *Mercenaries and their Masters* (London, 1974).

Colonial troops There already existed independent companies of infantry posted to French men-of-war and convict ships when, in 1635 and 1636, Richelieu formed four specialist regiments of foot for sea service. Several others were added subsequently but the units proved generally unsatisfactory and they were returned to land duties. Until 1763, the defence of French colonies was in the hands of the navy's independent companies, the forces maintained by the Compagnie des Indes and Karrer's Swiss regiment, which was raised in 1719. These troops were demobilized after the Seven Years' War (1756–63) and replaced by regiments from the French standing army which took tours of duty in the colonies. Particular units were, however, permanently retained in Goré and French Guiana. Since the soldiers from France rapidly succumbed to disease in tropical climates, in 1766 a legion was raised locally in Santo Domingo and another in Mauritius, these being organized into five regiments in 1772, while two further regiments were raised in Guadeloupe and Martinique. In 1791, these colonial regiments were placed under the War Ministry, but they were almost all recalled into France and colonial defence became the responsibility of battalions from the French army.

Between 1822 and 1827, two regiments of *infanterie de marine* existed but the defence of the colonies then passed back to the army until 1831. Two more regiments of *infanterie de marine* were recruited in that year, increasing to four by 1856. In 1870, the *infanterie de marine* numbered 20,000 men. The *infanterie de marine* was controlled by the War Ministry but administered by the navy. It was reorganized in 1890 to comprise eight regiments stationed in France, four in the colonies plus units recruited from the local colonial populations. The *infanterie de marine* took part both in the conquest and control of colonies and in the defence of France. At the end of the nineteenth century, there was a strong feeling of discontent among the officers of the *infanterie de marine* as they were treated as inferiors by the navy. In addition, large bodies of troops were no longer required on board naval vessels while the numbers of the *infanterie de marine* were insufficient to undertake the conquest and defence of empire. In 1900, the *infanterie de marine* was fully attached to the War Ministry and its name changed to *infanterie coloniale*. Of its 19 regiments, 12 were based in France but were ready for colonial service; in France, their costs were met by the War Ministry but these were assumed by the ministry of the colonies when serving overseas. The Foreign Legion and the Algerian and Tunisian regiments of riflemen were also available to assist the *infanterie coloniale*. Except in North Africa, the *infanterie coloniale* included locally raised troops. The first battalion of Senegalese riflemen was formed in 1857 and this had increased to 92 battalions by 1918. Three Annamite regiments were created as well as four Tonkinese and three Madagascan. Between 1914 and 1918, the colonies sent 215,000 men to France and Algeria; there were 60 native battalions at the front in 1914 and 210 in 1918.

After 1919, part of the *infanterie coloniale* was amalgamated into two divisions while the remainder was dispersed among regular army formations. In 1939, there were eight divisions of *infanterie coloniale*, 63,000 men of whom 45,000 were natives. Its formations played major roles in the 1st French Army in 1944 and also in the wars in Indochina and Algeria where they provided a number of parachute battalions.

In 1961, the *infanterie coloniale* regained its former title of *infanterie de marine*; currently, colonial troops form part of the 11th Parachute Division, the 9th Division and the 31st Brigade of the *infanterie de marine*. They are intended primarily for service in external theatres but they also provide detachments for international organizations (the United Nations' force in the Lebanon and the multinational peace-keeping unit in Beirut) as well as technical assistance to numerous African countries. Two-thirds of the 34,000 men are professional soldiers. In 1984, the *infanterie de marine* consisted of 21 regiments stationed in France (9 regiments of motorized infantry, 1 mechanized regiment, 4 parachute regiments, 1 mixed regiment, an armoured regiment and 5 artillery regiments). Six mixed regiments, 1 infantry regiment and 2 infantry battalions served overseas.

Most European countries which acquired colonies followed practices similar to those of France; a combination of locally raised troops reinforced by units from the home army. The Dutch garrison of Cape Colony in 1697 comprised 700 German mercenaries. During the eighteenth century, the soldiers who defended the Dutch Empire were frequently natives; free blacks were recruited in Surinam, with Amboinese and Javanese in the East Indies. In 1808, 7 per cent of the 18,000 men defending Java were European. The Royal Netherlands Indies Army was born in 1816, a professional long-service force supposedly recruited from Europeans, most of whom were mercenaries. However, the supply of Europeans rapidly evaporated and the RNIA recruited natives. By 1927, the RNIA was largely an armed, internal police force supported by militias in towns. Spain adopted garrisons of regular European troops to defend the principal ports of her South American Empire against naval attack, assisted by militias raised from among the European townsmen; Panama had a garrison of 200 soldiers in 1667 with a similar sized force in Portobello. Increasingly, the regular troops were recruited locally although they remained white. In 1603, Chile had an army of 2,000 men to defend its southern frontier. By the time of Charles III (1759–88), the regular army in New Spain numbered 6,000 with a militia of 20,000. The Portuguese relied on *ad hoc* military formations in India until 1671, when a regiment was sent from Portugal. However, desertion was so high that natives had to be recruited. The Portuguese in India and Ceylon were one of the few colonial nations to risk employing negro slaves as soldiers. In South America, the Portuguese installed a garrison of European troops in Bahia in 1625. By 1700, this had grown to two regiments of 800 men each, although William Dampier found the units so under strength that the entire garrison only amounted to 400 men. The regiments were mixtures of whites from Brazil and Portugal, coloureds and mulattos. Rio de Janeiro was also garrisoned. In an effort to raise more European recruits, the term of service for troops from Portugal was reduced in 1731 to 10 years for Brazil and 6 years for Angola.

Great Britain adopted similar arrangements. A small royal garrison took possession of Bombay in 1661 but the colony was sold to the East India Company along with the troops in 1668. During the eighteenth century, the army of the East India Company was based around the three 'presidencies' of Madras, Calcutta and Bombay. The soldiers were native sepoys commanded by British officers trained at the Company's own academy at Addiscombe in Surrey. The army of the East India Company was entirely separate from the British army, although some regiments of the latter were stationed in India. In the conquests of the nineteenth century – Ceylon (1815), Nepal (1816), Sind (1843), Punjab (1849) and Burma (1852) – the British and the Company regiments fought side-by-side. At the time of the Indian Mutiny in 1857–8, there were only 40,000 European troops in the British and Company armies but 200,000 sepoys. As a result of the Mutiny, the Company army was reduced to 120,000 sepoys and transferred to the control of the crown through the viceroy while its European troops were moved into the British army. Both the British and the new Indian armies were commanded exclusively by British officers. The Indian army grew to be a major source of British colonial and world power, being larger than the British army, and fighting outside India on many occasions. During the Second World War, the Indian army made a major contribution to the British campaigns in Malaya, India and Burma, in North and East Africa, and in Italy.

During the eighteenth and nineteenth centuries, much of the British army was stationed overseas to defend the major bases which controlled the sea routes to India, the West Indies, Africa, Canada and North America (until 1783). The colonies themselves were usually defended by small garrisons of regular troops assisted by locally raised units under British officers and militias. Until 1902, the colonies of British East Africa, Uganda, British Central Africa and Somaliland were defended by locally raised black battalions commanded by British officers. In that year, these battalions were regimented into the King's African Rifles (KAR), which defended the colonies and kept the peace. During the First World War, the KAR expanded to 30,000 men. The KAR served until independence was granted to the African colonies in the wake of the Second World War. Until the reforms of Edward Cardwell in 1870–1, there was no uniform system of reliefs for regular battalions on colonial duty. Thereafter, reliefs were made every four years. Since 1945, the disintegration of the British Empire has witnessed the transformation of the local colonial forces into the embryonic standing armies of the new, independent states. Many, particularly India, Pakistan and Bangladesh, have retained British military traditions, uniforms and methods. *See also* BUGEAUD; COLONIAL WARFARE; COMBINED OPERATIONS; EXPEDITIONS; GALLIÉNI; GREAT BRITAIN; INDIA; INFANTRY; LYAUTEY; MARINES; NETHERLANDS; SPAIN.

G. BODINIER
JOHN CHILDS

FURTHER READING
L. Beautza, *Histoire et épopée des troupes coloniales* (Paris, 1956); Philip Mason, *A Matter of Honour: an account of the Indian army, its officers and men* (London, 1974); Myron Echenberg, *Colonial Conscripts: the Tirailleurs Sénégalais in French West Africa* (London, 1991).

Colonial warfare (post-1945) Many of the wars that have occurred since 1945 can be divided into two broad categories: conflicts which arose as a result of colonial powers attempting to maintain authority in the face of rising nationalism, or civil strife between competing factions as the colonial power withdrew. In the majority of cases, the colonial powers intended to retreat as peacefully as possible, although, for some, the decision to withdraw was taken only after it had become evident that the colonies could not be held or when the political will to continue the conflict had evaporated. The issues were complicated by the Cold War and the supposed threat of communism.

In the period immediately after the end of the Second World War, conflicts arose as displaced colonial powers tried to reassert themselves. In some cases, this even occurred after indigenous governments had been established in the aftermath of the defeat of Japan. In the Dutch East Indies (Indonesia) the Dutch armed forces did not arrive until late in 1946 to replace the British, who had initially accepted the Japanese surrender. The Dutch successfully took control of the cities but they were subjected to protracted guerilla warfare elsewhere from Ahmed Sukarno's nationalists. Faced with the prospect of a long campaign, the Dutch accepted a UN ceasefire early in 1949 and gave sovereignty to Indonesia.

A similar set of circumstances transpired in French Indo-China, except that the French, unlike the Dutch in Indonesia, were more than willing to fight the forces of the Viet Minh. In the north, the guerillas operated virtually unfettered by French activity and, with the support of China, were able to build up a regular North Vietnamese army. By 1953 they were capable of taking the offensive and inflicted a severe defeat on the French at Dien Bien Phu in 1954.

The British were more successful in South East Asia than the French or the Dutch. In 1948, the Malayan Communist Party initiated an armed struggle against colonial rule to which the British responded by mounting large-scale battalion-level sweeps against the insurgents. These failed, leading to a change of strategy in 1950. The emphasis was switched to civil, military and police co-operation to win 'hearts and minds'. Tactics focused on the employment of small patrols relying on intelligence gathered by the police. The importance of separating the insurgents from their source of supply, almost exclusively the Chinese villages along the jungle fringes, was also recognized and a policy of resettlement followed. 'New villages' were established in protected areas and often there was a marked improvement in their standards of living. These settlements soon became popular, depriving the insurgents of their bases. The military also attempted methodically to clear individual districts which were then 'protected' and exempted from the emergency laws. Few 'white zones', as the cleared areas were known, reverted to 'black zones'. In addition to the military initiatives, there were also political developments which led to Malayan independence in 1957. However, the British remained to support the final anti-guerilla campaigns until the state of emergency was lifted in 1960. The successful Malayan operation became the model for the conduct of other British colonial wars, notably in Kenya (1952–5) and Cyprus (1955–9).

In Kenya, the British again applied the tactics of dividing the insurgents from the people, employing a balanced force structure, and co-ordinating civil and military with complementary socio-economic policies. As with the Malayan communists, the insurgents in Kenya, the Mau Mau, were closely identified with a particular support base. Where the Malayan communists relied on Chinese villages, the Mau Mau were almost exclusively drawn from the Kikuyu tribe. Kenya also featured an urban campaign in Nairobi, but extensive British cordon and search operations in 1954 rounded up numerous Mau Mau guerillas and yielded intelligence that led to many more being detained. By the end of 1955, the guerillas had been virtually defeated although the state of emergency was not formally ended until 1960.

The situation in Cyprus was somewhat different. Not only did the Greek Cypriots wish to be rid of British rule but they also wanted *enosis*, union with Greece. Unlike both Malaya and Kenya, therefore, there was a degree of external support and also widespread acceptance among the Greek community for the aims of Archbishop Makarios and the terrorist organization EOKA, led by Colonel Grivas. EOKA strategy was not to engage the British directly but to grind them down through riots, demonstrations, strikes and selective attacks against government installations as well as police and military targets. The aim was to raise the political and economic costs of remaining in Cyprus to prohibitive levels. It was essentially a small terrorist campaign – active EOKA members only numbered about 300 but they were supported by a large body of sympathizers supplying aid and intelligence. Nevertheless, despite the relatively small size of

EOKA, and British counter-insurgency successes, they did manage to bring Britain to the negotiating table. Although an independent Cypriot state was established, *enosis* was not achieved and Britain retained its military bases. However, the rise in sectarian tensions between the Greek and Turkish communities indicated that the negotiated compromise of February 1959 might not endure. Indeed, by 1963 serious fighting had erupted between the two communities, which almost brought Greece and Turkey to war and resulted in the partitioning of the island.

Having suffered at the hands of the Viet Minh, France was challenged by the rise of guerilla activity in Algeria. Defeat in Indo-China led to the development of a counter-insurgency doctrine, the *guerre révolutionnaire*. This emphasized such devices as resettlement and frontier barriers to deprive the insurgents of support, in addition to 'hearts and minds' campaigns modelled on the British policy in Malaya. It also stressed the need for domestic politicians to give unwavering support to the security forces at the cutting edge of the battle against insurgency. The military believed that the politicians had let them down badly in Indo-China but over-reliance on the need for this support was to prove more costly in Algeria.

Constitutionally, Algeria was regarded as a part of France. One million out of its population of nine million were white settlers, known as *colons* or *pieds noirs*. The Algerian insurgents (Front de Libération Nationale – FLN) began their campaign in 1954. The French army initially contained them but when the FLN re-equipped and regrouped they were able to exploit the growing divisions in Algerian society and attacked the *pieds noirs*. The FLN enjoyed the internal support of thousands of Muslims and initial external backing from the Egyptian leader, Abdel Nasser, and they were permitted to use neighbouring Tunisia as a sanctuary and a base. The commitment of the French army became heavier, involving 300,000 troops at the height of the war. The tactics of the army were harsh, including the use of torture to extract intelligence. These severe methods came to the fore during the Battle of Algiers in 1957 and began to cause political problems in France even though some military successes were achieved. The French army limited infiltration from Tunisia by the extensive Marice Line and the *quadrillage* system of a grid of garrisons linked by mobile patrols. By 1960, the French army appeared to be on the verge of victory but the FLN was recognized by fifteen states abroad and still had 20,000 troops in Tunisia. Popular opinion in France was becoming disenchanted with the war and the proponents of the *guerre révolutionnaire* no longer believed that the politicians would give them unqualified support. They demanded the return of General Charles de Gaulle but, contrary to the military's expectations, he began to negotiate a settlement. There was an attempted coup d'état in April 1961 but de Gaulle retained power and an agreement was reached in 1962 which gave Algeria complete independence.

During the 1960s, Britain was involved in colonial conflicts in Borneo and Aden. In the first, shifts in the politics of the external power helped to resolve the conflict in Britain's favour; in the second, changes in domestic politics and in the resolve to carry on the war were instrumental in British failure. In 1963, Britain wanted its three territories in Borneo – Brunei, Sarawak and North Borneo (Sabah) – to join a Federation of Malaysia. Indonesia objected as she had her own territorial designs in this area. Anti-Malay rebels were quickly suppressed by Britain but Indonesia continued to back the insurgents and launched a guerilla incursion into North Borneo. Britain's main problem was border surveillance but, again, a 'hearts and minds' policy with frontier tribesmen proved successful. When Indonesia intensified the conflict and employed regular troops, Britain went over to the offensive and cross-border operations made the Indonesian bases untenable. The war continued until 1966 when Sukarno was overthrown and his successor followed a more conciliatory policy. In any case, the concept of a Malay Federation came to nothing because of tension between Malaysia and Singapore.

Like the Malay Federation, Britain had also developed a Federation of South Arabia to which Aden was added in 1963. Here, the local opposition came from the Yemen which claimed the territories and appealed to Pan-Arabism to eject the British. Many Federation members were receptive to this call and, in the same year, the National Liberation Front (NLF) was established and based in Yemen. NLF activity in the Radfan area was contained but not eradicated by the British and the Federal Regular Army but the real trouble erupted in Aden where urban guerilla war broke out and was to last until 1967 when the British withdrew. The campaign began in an amateurish fashion but the NLF soon became skilled urban guerillas and were able to establish a number of safe areas in the town – notably in the Crater district – and take an increasing toll of the security forces. A change of government in Britain in 1964 brought about an alteration in policy and in 1966 the Labour government announced that it would withdraw British forces from South Arabia on independence. The Federation, reliant on a British military presence after independence, collapsed and Britain negotiated a transfer of power to the NLF and to the Marxist People's Democratic Republic of Yemen.

Portugal followed a different colonial strategy. While Britain, by and large, was fighting a rearguard action to cover its retreat from empire, Portugal, even in the 1970s, aimed to maintain its African empire of Guinea-Bissau, Mozambique and Angola. Nationalist movements developed in all three countries. In Guinea the *Partido Africano da Independência da Guiné e Cubo Verde* (PAIGC) commenced guerilla action in 1963; in Mozambique the *Frente de Libertação de Moçambique* (FRELIMO) opened its campaign in 1964 while in Angola there were three competing movements which began their operations at different dates during the early 1960s – *Frente Nacional de Libertação Angola* (FNLA), *Movimento Popular de Libertação de Angola* (MPLA) and *Uniao Nacional para Independência Total de Angola* (UNITA). Although only a poor country with a small army, Portugal believed that colonial possessions gave her the international status that she otherwise lacked. The army was inexperienced while the various guerilla movements enjoyed popular support and external backing. Nevertheless, Portugal was able to achieve some limited successes aided by the internal problems of her opponents. In Angola, the three factions competed against one another and in Mozambique tribal divisions hindered the growth of FRELIMO. Only in Guinea did the guerillas achieve early results. By 1970 there were 150,000 Portuguese soldiers in Africa, over 75 per cent of the total armed forces. Domestic problems brought about a coup in 1974 and colonial commitments which had taken 11,000 lives and accounted for over 40 per cent of the national budget were reduced. PAIGC was recognized as the government of Guinea in September 1974, FRELIMO became the legal authority in Mozambique in June 1975, while in Angola civil war broke out between FNLA–UNITA and the Marxist MPLA, a contest in which the latter was victorious.

These were the main colonial conflicts in the post-war period although many others occurred as a result of withdrawal from empire: the Indo-Pakistan wars, Suez, the disputes between Morocco and Mauretania in the western Sahara (formerly Spanish Sahara) and in the Congo. However, most of these wars were not colonial in the sense that they involved the defence of colonial territory or an attempt to retreat from a colonial obligation. Rather, they were wars whose origins were colonial.

The colonial wars were mainly fought with guerilla tactics forcing the occupying powers to develop counter-insurgency techniques. It was soon recognized that to defeat such opponents it was necessary to cut them off from their bases of support and win over the population, in addition to acquiring sources of intelligence which enabled the military to strike rapidly and accurately. The need to work closely with the civil authorities and the police and to develop a co-ordinated campaign was also recognized. None of this was of any consequence, however, if it was not backed by the political will to maintain a possibly lengthy and costly campaign. For the nationalist insurgents, the prime lessons were political: the necessity to maintain the momentum of operations in order to wear down the will of the enemy to carry on the conflict. In Algeria, Aden and in the Portuguese colonies, the avoidance of defeat was sufficient for the anti-colonial forces. *See also* BUGEAUD; COLONIAL TROOPS; DE GAULLE; DIEN BIEN PHU; GALLIÉNI; GUERILLA WARFARE; LYAUTEY; PAKISTAN; POPULAR WARFARE; VIETNAM.

DAVID WESTON

FURTHER READING
Guy Arnold, *Wars in the Third World since 1945* (London, 1991); Michael Carver, *War since 1945* (London, 1980); Frank Kitson, *Low-intensity Operations: subversion, insurgency and peace-keeping* (London, 1971); Richard Taber, *The War of the Flea: a study of guerilla warfare and practice* (London, 1970); Anthony Clayton, *Counter-insurgency in Kenya, 1952–60* (Nairobi, 1976); Richard Clutterbuck, *The Long, Long War: the emergency in Malaya, 1948–60* (London, 1967); Charles Foley and William Scobie, *The Struggle for Cyprus* (Stanford, Calif., 1975); Alistair Horne, *A Savage War of Peace: Algeria, 1954–62* (London, 1977); Harold James and Denis Shiel-Small, *The Undeclared War: confrontation with Indonesia* (London, 1971); Julian Paget, *Last Post: Aden, 1964–7* (London, 1969); Peter Paret, *French Revolutionary Warfare from Indochina to Algeria: the analysis of a political and military doctrine* (London, 1964).

Combined operations Combined (or amphibious) operations, which involve using the sea as a means for bringing armed forces into action against positions on land, must be counted among the major achievements of warfare. There is an extremely varied range of such operations – raids for the sake of pillage, commando actions and landings on a limited or a huge scale, with the latter involving full-scale armies as part of the opening-up of whole operational theatres. The success of these affairs implies command of the sea, and later of the air, whether gained by battle or close blockade.

Ancient history reveals some grand combined operations, of which excellent examples can be seen in the first, and especially, the second Persian War. In 480 BC, Xerxes' plan for the conquest of Greece relied on a seaborne supply train to move alongside his advancing army. Salamis defeated this attempt. During the Peloponnesian War, Athens made use of her command of the sea to harry her enemy's shores continually, while at the same time mounting large-scale operations like the Sicilian expedition. During the Punic Wars, the ultimate aim of Rome's naval effort was to conquer Sicily and defeat Carthage on African soil. After Regulus' failure, combined operations made it possible to secure this result in 202 and 146 BC. Following the Battle of Actium (31 BC), it was his ability to put troops ashore that permitted Octavius to ensure his stranglehold on the Near East and on Egypt in particular.

After the interval of the *pax Romana*, all naval warfare in the Mediterranean during the medieval period, and up to the turning back of the Ottoman tide in the seventeenth century, was connected with combined operations, which were sometimes on a very considerable scale, as seen in the course of Justinian's attempt to rebuild the Roman Empire, in the Arab conquests or in the various sieges of Constantinople. In the eleventh century, the counter-offensive in the central Mediterranean by the Italian cities was also carried out by combined operations. In 1087, a fleet consisting of ships from Genoa, Pisa and Amalfi succeeded in capturing Mahdia in Tunisia and holding it for a year. At the same time, the Normans' hold on Sicily led them to make raids on the Greek coast and a fruitless attack on Byzantium.

The Crusades led to the organization of a huge sea transport system which was adapted to support ambitious combined operations, like the one that succeeded in taking Constantinople in 1204, or the landings conducted by St Louis in Egypt and Tunisia. After the fall of Constantinople in 1453, the Ottomans in turn, for more than three centuries, carried out combined operations in the Adriatic and in the eastern Mediterranean leading to the occupation of many islands.

Starting with Julius Caesar's landing in England, the northern seas were an especially active theatre of combined operations. From the ninth to the eleventh century, the Vikings conducted pillaging raids, eventually ranging over all the coasts of Western Europe and even the Mediterranean, though some of their operations had the aim of establishing colonies. William the Conqueror's landing in England in 1066 represents the crowning example of this amphibious strategy.

The Franco-British struggle of the twelfth to fourteenth centuries was marked by amphibious operations whose success depended on command of the sea. The naval defeat at Dover in 1217 forced Philip Augustus to negotiate the evacuation of the dauphin's army, which had made a bold foray into England and had been cut off. On the other hand, the French disasters at Crécy and Poitiers, and the fall of Calais, originated in the command of the sea which the English had won at Sluys. Despite a serious effort to build up naval strength, neither Charles V nor Charles VI succeeded in breaking down this naval supremacy and in accomplishing the great landing in England that was planned.

From the sixteenth century, with the appearance of colonial empires, the establishment of standing fleets by nation-states and the development of major European conflicts, there was new scope for combined operations of an increasingly impressive variety. During the second half of the sixteenth century, English 'sea dogs' like Hawkins, Frobisher and Drake initiated the era of long-range expeditions against Spanish possessions, with the aim of plunder; it was these which provided the impetus for Anson's astounding circumnavigation of the world in 1740–4, undertaken in the midst of the War of the Austrian Succession. Meanwhile, the Dutch and, shortly after them, the French copied the British example. In 1697, Pointis, in conjunction with freebooters, carried out a profitable raid on Cartagena; fifteen years later, in 1711, Duguay-Trouin conducted a successful operation of a similar type against Rio de Janeiro. William III of Orange's invasion of England in 1688 was, perhaps, one of the most successful combined operations in recent European history.

There were combined operations of much larger size in connection with colonies. The British deployed a considerable effort during the Seven Years' War, in the course of the struggle for the possession of Canada. In 1758, an imposing striking force comprising 22 ships of the line, 15 frigates, dozens of transports and 12,000 men brought about the fall of Louisbourg, on Cape Breton Island, which commands the entrance to the St Lawrence. In 1759, an expedition of the same size went up the St Lawrence and put Wolfe's forces ashore; this led to the defeat of Montcalm and the fall of Quebec.

Throughout the long Franco-British conflict, which terminated only in 1815, the British mounted operations of this type against the Antilles and the French possessions in the Indian Ocean. These were very frequently successful, though there were also instances which went seriously amiss. During the Revolutionary Wars, the British troops could not remain in the Antilles owing to the disastrous death-toll resulting from yellow fever. A number of French combined operations, in particular those connected with the effort to retain Canada, also fell victim to diseases such as scurvy or typhus. Apart from its value in these long-distance operations, Britain's preponderant naval power, which had become easier to maintain from the end of the seventeenth century as a result of improved tactical cohesion, could be turned to the conducting of harassing sorties against enemy coasts, as part of a strategy of attack at any point on the opponent's periphery. This policy, which was dear to members of the 'blue water' school, was perfected by William Pitt the Elder. First employed at the time of Louis XIV's major wars, the method achieved its fullest expression during the Seven Years' War, in the shape of limited raids on the French coasts. The actions at the island of Aix, Saint-Servan, Cherbourg and St Malo were examples. Success in such operations fell, on occasion, below expectations, and some ended with those who had landed having to be taken off in a sorry state. Even so, the threat of the 'red jackets' still produced considerable apprehension and forced the Versailles cabinet to tie up sizeable forces which would otherwise have joined the armies in Germany and so have increased the pressure on Prussia. This strategy continued during the Napoleonic Wars. At the time when the French armies dominated Europe, and made their entry into all the major capitals, Britain in effect extended her frontier right up to the French coastline. In the North Sea, the Atlantic and the Mediterranean, the British occupied all the important islands, and established anchorages in both the Bay of Douarnenez and the Gulf of Fos. Marine commandos carried out raids on the coastline and cut communications. The perpetual threat of a real landing constantly hung over the coasts of the imperial territory. Napoleon found himself obliged to fortify all vulnerable positions and to tie down valuable forces. He considered that 'with 30,000 men, the British have immobilized 300,000'. Sometimes, Great Britain launched out into large-scale operations with the aim of creating real second fronts. During the War of the Spanish Succession, the British government sent troops into the Spanish peninsula when it already had an army operating in Flanders. In collaboration with Portuguese forces and nine Imperial regiments, the British used Barcelona as their base. The operation was costly when account is taken of the huge mortality suffered aboard the ships transporting the troops between Britian and the Iberian peninsula. During the single year of 1708, out of 29,395 soldiers only 8,660 actually reached the fighting zone.

A century later, the progress made in medicine explains, in large part, the success of the combined operations carried out by the British in this same Iberian theatre. From 1809 to 1814, the forces commanded by Moore, and later by Wellesley, the future Duke of Wellington, could – because they enjoyed continuous logistic support from the Royal Navy – give fresh heart to the guerillas, threaten the French with landings in their rear and contribute to the wearing down of the *Grande Armée*. The

victory at Vitoria on 21 June 1813 proved of the first importance. It brought about a renewal of the coalition of the major continental powers, which was a prelude to the French loss of Germany and the fall of Napoleon's empire. The success of the operation in Spain should not, however, lead to the passing over in silence of resounding failures, like the landing at Walcheren in 1809.

British naval supremacy did not give her a monopoly of the ability to mount combined operations. On several occasions, the French navy attempted, and sometimes achieved, success with operations of this character. For example, both under Louis XIV and during the Revolution, small units landed in Ireland, though admittedly such successes could not be exploited on account of the absence of any real support from the Irish themselves and the lack of a genuine command of the sea. It was, basically, this last factor that caused the failure of Napoleon's expedition to Egypt and the complete collapse of all the projects for a landing in England. The French–Jacobite scheme to invade England in 1692 had to be dropped after the defeat at Barfleur. Choiseul's plan in 1759 led to the disasters at Lagos and Quiberon Bay. The Franco-Spanish attempt in 1779 came to an abrupt end as the result of a terrible epidemic which put the combined fleets into disarray. As for the 1805 scheme, it met its end at Trafalgar. All these attempts gambled on achieving surprise and catching the British squadrons out of position – in other words, on not having to meet them in battle. However, whenever a crisis threatened, the British Admiralty regrouped the major part of its forces in the Channel and, at the same time, marshalled a powerful coastal flotilla of light ships whose task was to deal directly with the forces attempting to land.

Despite the absence of large-scale naval warfare, combined operations occurred throughout the nineteenth century. These were concerned with intervention in Latin America or with the acquisition of colonies. Those most worthy of mention took place in connection with European conflicts with China – the Opium War of 1840, the Franco-British expedition of 1860, and the campaigns of Courbet with their landings on Formosa and the Pescadores Islands. The most important was the conquest of Algiers, which brought into play the Mediterranean squadrons, a fleet of 347 transports and a landing force of 37,000 men. The Crimean War was dominated by combined operations: in the Baltic, by the occupation of Bomarsund; in the Black Sea, by the combined operation at Varna, which forced the Russian armies to evacuate the Danube provinces; and by the landing at Eupatoria, which made it possible to organize the siege of Sebastopol. Throughout the conflict, the constant threat of Allied landings obliged the Russian commander to dispose his forces along a huge coastline – all the more so since the Tsarist Empire still lacked rail transport. The Crimean War proved once again the advantages of moving troops by sea rather than by land.

The American Civil War was also characterized by numerous combined operations, particularly on rivers. On the other hand, in 1870, in view of the disastrous outcome of the operations in Alsace and Lorraine, the French navy had to cancel the plan for landing an army corps (which was marshalled and ready at Cherbourg) on the north German coast, in co-operation with Denmark. No large combined operations then occurred until the period of the conflicts in the Far East. In 1894, during the war with China, the action of the Japanese fleet in securing command of the sea at the battle of the Yalu River made possible the landings on the Liaotung Peninsula and the capture of Port Arthur. During the 1904–5 war with Russia, the blockade of Port Arthur and the battle of the Yellow Sea gave the Japanese navy a further chance to conduct large-scale combined operations, which led to the siege and capture of Port Arthur, as well as to the successful campaign in Manchuria.

In spite of these precedents, the 1914–18 war seemed to mark a decline in the sphere of combined operations. After much hesitation, the British cabinet could not bring itself to agree to a landing on the German Baltic coasts, as advocated by Sir John Fisher, the First Sea Lord, or to a more limited operation on the Belgian coast, with the aim of outflanking the German positions. The only important operation, for which the initiative came from Churchill, was ultimately the Dardanelles. The strategic concept was sound, with the prospect which it offered of causing the fall of the Turkish Empire and creating a direct link with Russia, but the tactical execution turned it into a serious failure, for a variety of reasons, among them being a lack of secrecy, inadequate support fire and problems of logistics. But the basic reason, confirmed by experience on the Western Front, lay in infantry's complete inability to cope with fortified positions bristling with machine-guns and covered in front by barbed wire. This failure had the further result of casting a heavy shadow over the evolution of combined operations, as can be noted in Castex's *Strategic Theories*.

Contrary to all prognostications, combined operations provided the keynote of the Second World War: the conquest of South-East Asia by the Japanese, the victorious American counter-offensive from Tarawa to Okinawa, the reopening of a Western European theatre, with the operations in North Africa, Sicily and Italy paving the way for the landings in Normandy and Provence. The Germans themselves scored some notable successes, as in the occupation of Norway or the recapture of the Aegean Islands in the autumn of 1943. This impressive array included only rare failures, like the Dieppe raid in 1942. These achievements, in which the Japanese were the pioneers with their operations on the coasts of China from 1937 to 1941, can be ascribed to sound strategic doctrine and the use of carefully designed equipment. Success in such operations naturally requires command of the sea and an air superiority ensured by advanced airfields or groups of aircraft carriers. It presupposes also heavy supporting bombardment from naval guns and from bomber aircraft. A further essential is a specialized fleet of landing craft which can both disembark the first wave infantry, tanks and various kinds of equipment, and supply the troops after they are ashore. In fact, all Allied amphibious landings from 1942 onwards took lessons from Japanese experience and from the Dieppe failure, and – contrary to the general practice of the past – were made on beaches that were only lightly defended so as to capture from the rear ports which had been turned into fortresses. When required, as in Normandy, logistic support could be ensured by the use of artificial harbours or a submerged pipeline.

To prevent enemy reserves from being rushed to bridgeheads, landings in Europe were also combined with deception plans, whose object was to deceive the enemy about the location of the landing beaches. Hence, in 1943, the Germans expected a landing in the Balkans. In June/July 1944, *Operation Fortitude* succeeded in making the enemy believe that the Normandy landings were merely a prelude to a larger operation north of the Seine. Large German reserves were immobilized for weeks by this ruse. Such methods had no useful application in the Pacific, where landings were made on islands cut off from any land mass.

A certain number of combined operations have taken place since the Second World War. The most considerable of these was that at Suez in 1956, which was comparable in scale with those of 1943–4. The Americans mounted much smaller operations in the Lebanon in 1957 and, on several occasions, in the Caribbean. The most recent, and the one which provided the greatest lessons for the military world, was the Falklands operation of 1982. In spite of the employment of new weapons systems, it proved the inviolability of certain principles – the necessity of naval and air superiority, of support fire, etc. In order to deal with possible crises, all navies today possess amphibious equipment which they strive to keep up-to-date with the aim of being able to put into action strike forces like the American RDF (Rapid Deployment Force) or the French FAR (Force d'Action Rapide). Combined operations remain one of the main concerns of strategy. *See also* ACTIUM; AVIATION; CASTEX; EXPEDITIONS; MAHAN; NAVAL PERSONNEL; NAVAL WARFARE; PLANNING.

P. MASSON

FURTHER READING
E. B. Potter and C. W. Nimitz, *Sea Power, a Naval History* (New York, 1960); J. S. Corbett, *England in the Mediterranean* (2 vols, London, 1917); John Carswell, *The Descent on England* (London, 1969); B. L. Villa, *Unauthorised Action* (Oxford, 1989); Max Hastings, *Overlord* (London, 1984).

Command The object of command is to involve troops as closely as possible in their leader's desire to fulfil his mission. Command is achieved through leadership. The conditions in which command is exercised are infinitely diverse and the means at a leader's disposal are many and varied, but military command basically rests on three foundations: (1) the moral and physical qualities of the leader through which he inspires confidence in his men; (2) the authority with which the leader is invested by his political and military superiors; and (3) the discipline and abilities of his subordinates.

Personal charisma is vital to motivate both his immediate staff and higher subordinate commanders and, though less directly, the majority of his troops. Intellectual ability is equally important. The leader is expected to be capable of facing difficulties of all kinds, including the sordid realities of war; firmness of character must be a pronounced characteristic, along with mental and physical endurance. Before leading other men and demanding of them tasks which they often have no wish to perform, a future leader must learn to obey. The basis of all knowledge is the recognition of error. It is by executing ill-considered orders, by enduring often unjust reproaches from leaders who are themselves learning their trade, that the future leader learns. Gradually, he discovers that although men do not seem naturally predisposed to discipline, none the less they feel a need to prove themselves. The leader who allows them to do so – intervening judiciously to set an example, keeping his head and showing clarity of judgement – may win their confidence. The converse is also true – men who demonstrate loyalty to their leader contribute considerably to strengthening his resolution.

The chief objective of every leader is to win battles. In addition to his physical and mental attributes, much of his success is achieved through the acquisition of knowledge. Extensive study of the enemy has pride of place and the leader must have a sufficiently nimble mind to learn his language, his way of thinking and hence, in some way, to 'get under his skin'. In acquiring an intimate knowledge of the enemy's probable plan of action, he comes to realize his strong and weak points. He will be well advised to supplement this research with a series of concrete case studies, drawn from ancient and recent history, to acquaint himself with the details of numerous battles. A modern general might well train by employing a computer application or a simulator to create the uncertainty, tension and crisis characteristic of war. War games, peacetime manoeuvres and exercises, staff and defence colleges, and observation of foreign armies and wars also provide valuable instruction in the art of command. These methods will permit him to distinguish indicators which the uninitiated might miss and acquire the sureness of touch of the true professional. A few basic principles have been deduced from history which apply to most aspects of combat: security, economy of force, the need to concentrate on one central effort and the necessity of holding reserves.

The final, indispensable requirement of all commanders in all ages is an adequate supply of reliable and up-to-date information, relating both to their own forces and to those of the enemy. Because of its numerous levels, information is filtered as it passes upward through the hierarchy of command. When it reaches the commander-in-chief, the information can be out-of-date and hopelessly generalized. As late as the French Revolution, when generals personally commanded their own armies, intelligence was usually sent directly to the senior officer who could also see for himself the condition of his men. However, with the advent of divisions, corps, armies and army groups, the commander-in-chief was no longer in direct contact with his troops and became reliant solely on information passed to him by his subordinates. Despite the assistance and delegation provided by general staffs, in order to ensure that their orders were being obeyed precisely and that accurate information was reaching them promptly, many commanders employed teams of personal liaison officers who acted as their eyes and ears. The two most notable exponents of this practice were Napoleon and Field Marshal Bernard Montgomery. Since 1945, the advent of computers and satellite communications has produced a wealth of information for the use of commanders, but these modern systems have not resulted in a corresponding improvement in the methods of command. Partly, this has been due to the fact that too much information is now available and the process of refining and editing the information renders it obsolete by the time it becomes available to battlefield commanders. This was nowhere more apparent than amongst the US forces in Vietnam. Partly also, the abundance of computerized information has allowed command to move further and further into the rear, away from the battlefield. Detailed tactical information is available to both politician and military commander simultaneously. During the Vietnam War, battlefield command actually rested in the basement of the White House rather than with General Westmoreland in Saigon. However, effective command did not shift back into Hitler's bunkers in Berlin and Rastenburg (where he moved imaginary armies amidst a sea of ignorance), nor into Haig's General Headquarters on the Western Front (where tactical decisions were taken on inaccurate and false information) because detailed command was so distant from the battlefield that information, intelligence and decisions were obsolete by the time they were translated into tactical orders. Noticeably, during the Gulf War (1991), General Norman Schwarzkopf was left to command the war from the headquarters in Riyadh without apparent interference from the White House or from the Pentagon. The result appears to have been a successful war based largely upon a discreet and highly professional employment of electronic information and intelligence.

'War and sickness have this in common: people refuse to think about them' (Milliez). Doctors and military leaders have to take care of these things on their behalf. The task of the latter is, paradoxically, more difficult to perform and less appreciated in peacetime than in wartime, because the imagination has to substitute for the realism of battle. When a war situation arises – often where and when it is least expected – human reason is suddenly confronted with the brutal eruption of phenomena which belong to the world of the irrational. The forces unleashed have a revelatory effect on the characters involved, bringing to the fore people who are intensely cool-headed. Sensing, at last, that they are in their element, these men are led, from necessity, to invention, and – through that original form of creation which consists in giving form to a battle – to victory.

Although the principles involved in exercising command have proved constant, the methods of their execution have subtly altered over the years. From Antiquity through to the Crimean War, army, corps and divisional commanders were present on the battlefield and could exhort their subordinates both before and, to a lesser degree, during the action. Commanders, such as Alexander the Great, who actually fought in the ranks exercised a minimal control over the action once it had begun and their skill rested in the acquisition of intelligence, manoeuvre, deception and the deployment of their troops before battle. Once commanders refrained from personal combat and confined their role to battlefield command (Scipio Africanus, Julius Caesar), they were able to hold a closer rein on the tactical development of the battle, particularly the commitment of the reserve. Generals remained able to tour a battlefield, showing themselves to their men, sharing their dangers and improving morale. The appearance of the Duke of Wellington at danger points during the Battle of Waterloo is a good example. The growth in the size of armies, beginning with the French Revolutionary and Napoleonic Wars, brought the development of the army commander as a co-ordinator, a man not often seen by the majority of his troops.

From his central headquarters, he directed his battle by electric telegraph and later radio and telephone and, for a period, he came to resemble a chief executive or managing director rather than a military commander. This development reached its nadir during the First World War with the 'château generalship' of Haig. Consequently, the role of leadership and motivation became the task of battalion, company and platoon commanders, with special responsibility being placed on NCOs. The Second World War saw a deliberate reversion from this remoteness of command and generals such as Guderian, Rommel and Patton became front-line commanders, leading their men into combat and encouraging by personal example. In many ways, this was most unsuitable to large-scale mechanized warfare, although the tradition has been imitated in the armoured forces of the Israeli army. The more successful commanders of the Second World War (Montgomery, Slim, Bradley) struck a balance between personal leadership and remote direction.

They were greatly assisted by the growth of war-reporting through newspapers, cinema newsreels, radio and television. Generals could reach and communicate with their men through the media and, as a result, became media personalities in their own right. The media allowed commanders to regain touch with their own troops. Montgomery and Patton were perhaps the first of the 'media generals' who courted the press to boost their own popularity both within the army and on the home front. This trend has accelerated. Television coverage of the Korean War reached the United States within twenty-four hours, but during the Vietnam War, live news broadcasts were beamed by satellite into American homes every evening. Generals were not just media personalities; their decisions and leadership were subjected to instant public scrutiny and criticism. Command was no longer a secret, almost mystic military activity; it had become public. The Gulf War of 1991 between the auxiliaries of the United Nations and Iraq has further exacerbated this tendency with the various commanders, including the chairman of the

US Joint Chiefs of Staff and the commander-in-chief in the Gulf region, giving daily news conferences. The ability to handle and keep the press happy has become a major attribute of a successful commander.

Naval command has always been different from that of the land forces. All officers, from admiral down to petty officer, operate from ships, and all share common dangers from both the elements and the enemy. Naval leadership has always been highly personal. The air forces have seen a combination of the methods of the navy and the army. During the Second World War, many US Air Force generals and marshals of the Royal Air Force flew with bombing raids over Germany to encourage their fliers but whether their efforts were worth the trouble is hard to estimate. The very nature of combat flying – one man or a small crew locked inside an aircraft – means that the effective unit of command is the aircraft captain or pilot. Because of the speed of air combat and the huge three-dimensional spaces involved, it is impossible for an airborne commander to control more than a handful of aircraft. Large-scale command can only be exercised by radio and radar from the ground. An exception to this was during the bombing raids on Germany by the Royal Air Force during the Second World War. A 'master bomber' circled over the target, usually in a fast, small plane (Beaufighter, Mosquito), and directed the dropping of flares by the pathfinders (target markers) by radio and then adjusted the aim of later markers and bombers. However, this method of airborne command was only possible because of the comparatively low speed of the heavy bombers and could only be applied when a single target was attacked. Generally, once an air operation has been planned and launched, each aircraft is on its own. Above squadron, wing or, possibly, group level, air force command has tended to be more managerial in style. Arthur Harris, the commander-in-chief of Bomber Command from 1942 to 1945, never flew with his men and never once visited a bomber station. He was a remote and little-known figure operating as a manager from his headquarters in High Wycombe.

Besides the direction and motivation of men, the First and, in particular, the Second World War have introduced another element into command: the management and distribution of resources. Not only does this cover logistics but it involves decision-making about strategic and theatre priorities. *See also* DISCIPLINE; ETHOS; GENERAL STAFF; HIERARCHY; LANGUAGE; MORALE; RESERVES; SIGNAL COMMUNICATION; STRATEGY; TACTICS.

D. REICHEL
JOHN CHILDS

FURTHER READING
John Keegan, *The Mask of Command* (Harmondsworth, 1988); Martin van Creveld, *Command in War* (London, 1985); N. Dixon, *On the Psychology of Military Incompetence* (London, 1976).

Commerce-raiding Privateering, filibustering and piracy are all closely related forms of maritime 'trade' carried on by force of arms. Legally, there are great differences between these activities but, in practice, they are remarkably similar. Privateers were given official sanction in wartime by a sovereign's 'letters of marque'. Privateering was directed against an enemy's trade and any booty secured had to be shared between the privateer and his associates or investors, the crew and the monarch, the exact proportions being decided by a prize court. The royal derivation of the French term for privateering, 'course' and the date of its adoption (sixteenth century) point to a Mediterranean origin. Privateering was sometimes overlaid with filibustering. This word, from the Dutch *vrybuiter* (freebooter), appearing in English as 'flibutor' (1587), and in French as 'filibustier' in about 1667, described the multinational swarm – Dutch, English, French and Spanish – who based themselves in the West Indies and, from about 1530 to 1700, executed indiscriminate raids in the southern seas, 'trade at the spear's point', smuggled into Spanish America and systematically attacked Spanish convoys. In the main, filibustering disappeared after the Peace of Utrecht in 1714. In developing their own privateering operations, the British and French drew heavily on the general methods, crews and sailing techniques of the filibusters. Piracy differed from privateering and filibustering by reason of its longer history and the fact that it was a ubiquitous form of maritime robbery, which paid no heed to nationality, conditions of war and peace or the rights of individuals. Piracy is not dealt with in this article as it was a private enterprise and not an activity necessarily connected with war.

The history of commerce-raiding in the early modern and modern periods can be divided into three main geographical and chronological subject-areas:

1 The Mediterranean, where Christian galleys, or, from the mid-eighteenth century, xebecs, opposed the forces of Islam. Privateering by the North African coastal states and Christian counter-measures by the Knights of Malta, Spain and the small Italian maritime states lasted until the mid-nineteenth century.
2 The Americas. Despite the legendary episodes and glorious feats, privateering had died out in this theatre by the start of the eighteenth century.
3 Legal privateering by private traders from great commercial/maritime nations, which played a military role within well-defined national strategies.

Privateering in the Mediterranean Muslim privateering was aimed at the usual material targets – timber, weapons, money – but also at 'human booty', which was required for rowing the galleys and for the 'domestic' needs of the North African city-states (Algiers, Tunis, Tripoli, Djerba and Salli). It reached its zenith around 1620 when the small-scale conflict which it represented replaced major actions by squadrons of galleys. Thereafter, commercial realities and bombardments by Christian ships caused North African privateering to decline to a scale compatible with normal commerce. Fleets and squadrons from European states dispatched to attack the 'Barbary corsairs' sometimes achieved psychological results but their costs were high and they usually forced the privateers to retaliate. The evidence of marine insurance rates does not indicate any great

benefit from these expeditions. During the seventeenth century, French naval officers were 'trained' by joining the Knights of Malta on their drives against the Barbary privateers. Piracy off the North African coast was finally ended by the attacks on Algiers and Tripoli and the capture of the former in 1830.

Privateering/filibustering in the West Indies This was pursued during the sixteenth and seventeenth centuries by the great commercial cities of the European Atlantic seaboard: Bayonne, La Rochelle, St Malo, Bristol, etc. Together with the buccaneers, privateers operating on the Atlantic trade routes were a serious threat to the commerce between Spain and America in the years 1550–1650. In the long term, however, despite Drake's exploits, the losses inflicted by the privateers were less than those caused by the elements. On the other hand, privateering was the reason why the Dutch, the British and the French became installed in the West Indies and was the root of their later colonial power. When they began to endanger the growth of these colonies, the privateers were withdrawn. Even so, during the transitional period (1650–1710), filibusters took part in large-scale expeditions like Henry Morgan's raid on Panama in 1671 and de Pointis's attack on Cartagena in 1697.

Legal Privateering by Large Countries Significant operations of this type were first started by Britain during the first Anglo-Dutch War (1652–4). The British navy seized over 2,000 Dutch merchant ships, including a number of the famous *fluyts* (cargo ships). These successes provided the impulse for the development of a whole strategy which was enunciated by Vauban in a book published during the Franco-Dutch War (1672–8). The concept was to avoid the high costs of maintaining a standing fleet by substituting a sustained privateering offensive against enemy merchant shipping, the *guerre de course*. Essentially, this was a weapon of the weak as well as a compromise for those countries whose geographical position demanded the expensive necessity of making military commitments on land as well as at sea. In the era prior to the French Revolution, France engaged in the *guerre de course* on two occasions. Under Louis XIV, the poor harvests between 1692 and 1694 so reduced royal revenue that the French navy had to abandon fleet operations and turn to privateering. It was carried on by small squadrons of converted merchantmen and purpose-built vessels but, chiefly, by warships financed by private shipowners. Limited companies were constituted and sold shares to the general public. Dunkirk was the principal privateering base (Jean Bart and the Comte de Forbin), although St Malo was also important (DuGuay-Trouin). During the wars against Louis XIV the privateers stifled the development of the British merchant fleet; from 1695 to 1715, French privateers captured 6,900 ships and secured the payment of ransom on a further 2,700. The decline commenced at the opening of the War of the Spanish Succession in 1702 when the British and the Dutch introduced a well-organized convoy system and used their navies to conduct anti-privateering sweeps. The lure of the 'South Seas trade' also offered an alternative source for French investment.

After the long period of peace with Britain and the Netherlands (1714–44), the War of the Austrian Succession (1742–8) witnessed a break in the tradition as the French were reluctant to employ their valuable fleet, now much smaller than under Louis XIV, in commerce-raiding. Instead, the growing French merchant fleet was itself exposed to attack by British (Channel Islands, Bristol, London, etc.) and Dutch (Amsterdam and Flushing) privateers. This pattern continued during the Seven Years' War and the American War of Independence.

Despite the exploits of Surcouf, the balance-sheet of French privateering after 1744 showed a heavy deficit. Through both losses in action and in manning the privateers themselves, the French navy lost the services of a large number of trained seamen. Even between 1688 and 1714, it had acted as no more than a substitute operation which had results that were momentarily important but never decisive. However, paradoxically, between 1690 and 1714, it contributed greatly to the formation of a powerful group of shipping magnates which provided a basis for the development of French maritime trade during the remainder of the eighteenth century.

The second major bout of French privateering occurred during the American War of Independence. Detailed analysis of the 2,200 prizes taken by French privateers during the conflict shows that more than 90 per cent were captured by ships from the Channel ports. When the ports on the Atlantic and Mediterranean seaboards were not blockaded, they preferred, indeed much preferred, to carry on normal commerce. On the other hand, the English Channel and the North Sea, being narrow and with heavy maritime traffic, afforded plentiful opportunities for privateers. From her point of view, commerce-raiding continued to offer France military advantages while avoiding the risks and potential losses of fleet operations. La Motte-Piquet's squadrons in the West Indies again demonstrated the effectiveness of warships in this type of work. The American navy also contributed 600 prizes. Heavy losses were sustained by the British merchant fleet, including 60,000 seamen, but commerce-raiding never threatened Britain's commercial prosperity. For both the British and the French during this war, the convoy proved highly effective.

A similar set of circumstances occurred during the period of the French Revolution. The French navy became disorganized and, having failed during Year II to effect corrections, it was once again obliged to adopt commerce-raiding as a substitute for full-scale naval operations. The Convention declared: 'The British government may, if it so pleases, preen itself on its navy: France will confine herself to attacking them in what they hold most dear and brings them most happiness – their wealth.' Until 1801, this commerce-raiding proceeded on a scale not seen since the Nine Years' War and the Seven Years' War. Following past practice, light squadrons were employed. Ganteaume operated in this way in the Levant, Allemand on the west coast of Africa, Leissègues and Jean

Dutertre in the West Indies, and François Lemème Sercey and Robert Surcouf in the Indian Ocean. The most successful of all these squadron commanders was probably Richery. In October 1795, he successfully attacked the Smyrna convoy off Cape St Vincent, prior to sailing to Newfoundland to deal damaging blows to the fishing industry. With such intensive commerce-raiding, private individuals soon became involved. Ship owners from Bordeaux and Nantes operated in the western Atlantic, while the Channel was the preferred hunting ground for the privateers from Brest, St Malo, Boulogne, Calais and, above all, Dunkirk, whence sailed Jean Blanckmann and Louis Leveille. The British response was traditional – recourse to the neutral flag, sailing in convoy when travelling to distant destinations, and patrolling the regular routes through the English Channel and the North Sea. *Prima facie*, the results seemed considerable especially as the prize cargoes partially compensated for the disruption of normal French trade. Between 1793 and 1801, the French captured 5,557 British merchant vessels. For short periods there was genuine disquiet in Britain but, in reality, these losses were desperate but not serious. Despite the war, British maritime trade continued to grow, reaching a total of 61 million tons p.a. and employing 13,000–14,000 ships annually. In addition, from 1797, French commerce-raiding lost vigour. At the time of the signature of the Peace of Amiens (1802), 593 French ships had been lost and about 41,500 seamen were prisoners in Britain. Although there had been some brilliant successes, commerce-raiding had no effect on the outcome of the war.

After a short pause, commerce-raiding began again with the outbreak of war in 1803. Once more, light forces were deployed in the now traditional theatres – the Channel, North Sea, West Indies and the Indian Ocean – while they also extended into the Mediterranean. The British reacted by patrolling the sea lanes, organizing convoys, abusing neutral flags and attacking the privateering bases – St Pierre-et-Miquelon, Haiti, Curaçao, Martinique, Guadeloupe, Réunion and Mauritius. Initially the results were promising: 387 prizes in 1804, 571 in 1809 and 619 in 1810. By 1812, the Royal Navy had been obliged to increase the number of its escort vessels to 145 frigates and 421 lighter ships. Again, the growth of British commerce was not unduly hindered. Between 1803 and 1813, the volume of that trade totalled 2,350,000,000 livres while the value of the prizes taken by the French did not exceed 13,000,000 livres. During the opening six months of 1809, French raiders captured only 48 British ships from a total of 3,762 sailings. In 1815, the British mercantile marine numbered 24,000 vessels (2,500,000 tons). From 1810, French commerce-raiding declined as her shipping resources became exhausted; in 1814, 27,400 French privateering seamen were prisoners of war in England. Commerce-raiding had insufficient power to operate at a strategic level.

The nineteenth century witnessed a period of relative peace on the high seas with only occasional bursts of commerce-raiding. The Paris Declaration of 16 April 1856 brought an important change to international maritime law. All commerce-raiding by private persons (i.e. privateers) was prohibited. Warships could only raid commerce if they obeyed specified procedures – the boarding of the merchant vessel, the identification of her nationality, the examination of her cargo and the guarantee of the safety of her passengers and crew. The United States refused to ratify the Declaration.

Consequently, from the start of the American Civil War, the Confederates authorized the arming of private commerce-raiders against Union shipping. Initially, brilliant successes were achieved, but the number of sinkings then rapidly diminished as the privateers were unable to regain their home ports through the blockade by the Union fleet. Twenty Confederate commerce-raiders tried to lift this blockade by undertaking long-range sweeps against Union merchant vessels. The most famous was the *Alabama* which, until she was sunk by the *Kearsarge*, captured 71 Union ships in a cruise of 22 months which took her from Newfoundland to the East Indies.

The results of the Confederate effort again conformed to the usual pattern. Union ship owners transferred one third of their tonnage to neutral flags and the Confederates' sinking of 100,000 tons of Union shipping had no effect on the outcome of the war. There was, however, one noteworthy consequence; the Union had to divert a considerable part of its naval forces to the battle against the commerce-raiders, which meant that the blockade of the southern ports was occasionally relaxed. In the Franco-Prussian War (1870–1), commerce-raiding played only a symbolic role. The German corvette *Augusta* operated for a short period off Brest and the estuary of the Gironde before being blockaded in Vigo. She captured three small merchant ships.

Commerce-raiding made no appearance in the wars in the Far East but it was to play a role of cardinal importance during the First World War, although in an unexpected manner. The customary pattern was exemplified by some German surface vessels, like the *Emden*, the *Karlsruhe* and the *Leipzig*, which all operated with limited results off the eastern coasts of the Americas at the outset of the war. The cruise of the *Emden* in the Indian Ocean during the autumn of 1914 was the only operation that was notably successful. Until being sunk by the *Sydney*, she sent to the bottom 70,000 tons of merchant shipping and, momentarily, halted all ship movements in the Bay of Bengal. After the removal of these cruisers by the start of 1915, the only German surface commerce-raiders were some camouflaged merchantmen which operated in the Atlantic and the Pacific.

Commerce-raiding had now passed to the submarine. However, the raiding of commerce by submarine was no longer a *pis aller* but a strategy for destroying the enemy, in flagrant contradiction of international law. Whether operating on the surface or submerged, a submarine usually cannot identify its victim, examine her cargo or ensure the safety of her passengers and crew. Throughout the First World War, this new type of warfare was executed by French submarines in the Adriatic, by the British in the Baltic and the Sea of Marmora and, particularly, by the U-boats of the German navy in the North Sea, the Channel, the Atlantic and the Mediterranean. Unrestricted submarine warfare was carried out by the Germans in two phases, in 1915 and from 1917 to the armistice. It produced impressive results – 11,200,000 tons of shipping were sunk at the cost of 180 U-boats out of the 343 put into service.

After patrolling the sea lanes had proved ineffective, from the summer of 1917 the Allied navies succeeded in stifling this threat by adopting the traditional method of sailing in convoy. However, the protection of the convoys relied heavily on the mobilization of large resources and the development of new techniques of submarine hunting (hydrophones, depth charges, etc.). The French navy alone equipped more than 1,000 vessels and 1,260 aircraft for the battle against submarines. For the first time in history, commerce-raiding, admittedly in a new form, seemed to have the power to win a decisive strategic victory by paralysing the Allies' lines of communication.

Events in the Second World War followed a similar course. Until 1941, the Germans employed large surface ships to attack Allied merchant shipping but the results were modest, despite successful forays by the *Scharnhorst* and the *Gneisenau*, amounting to less than 800,000 tons. Some sorties, like those of the *Admiral Graf Spee* and the *Bismarck*, ended in disaster. Apart from a few camouflaged merchant ships, the essential weapon for the war against merchant shipping was the submarine. It was used to great effect by the British in the Mediterranean and by the Americans in the Pacific but, most spectacularly, by the Germans in the Atlantic. Their U-boats assumed the methods of 1914–18 adding such tactical innovations as attack by 'wolf packs', i.e. in groups by night and on the surface. They sank more than 13,000,000 tons of Allied shipping but lost over 780 of the 1,400 submarines put into service. The U-boat threat was not finally removed until 1943 thanks to the deployment of considerable air and sea resources as well as new methods of detection (sonar and radar) and the deciphering of the submarines' radio messages. To some extent, the Battle of the Atlantic was an obstacle to Anglo-American strategic plans. *See also* ATLANTIC, BATTLE OF THE; BART; BLOCKADES; CONVOYS; DRAKE; ECONOMIC WARFARE; NAVAL PERSONNEL; NAVAL WARFARE; NAVIES; SURCOUF.

J. MEYER
P. MASSON

FURTHER READING
Geoffrey Symcox, *The Crisis of French Sea Power, 1688–97* (The Hague, 1974); J. S. Bromley, *Corsairs and Navies, 1660–1760* (London, 1987); Kenneth R. Andrews, *Elizabethan Privateering during the Spanish War, 1585–1603* (Cambridge, 1964); *Course et Piraterie*, ed. Michel Mollat (2 vols, Paris, 1975); David J. Starkey, *British Privateering Enterprise in the Eighteenth Century* (Exeter, 1990).

Communication *See* SIGNAL COMMUNICATION

Condé, Louis II de Bourbon, Prince of (1621–86) After studying under the Jesuits at Bourges, Condé learned the business of war at a Parisian Academy in 1637 where he also studied law, mathematics and history. He entered the French army in 1640 and, at the tender age of twenty-two, won a victory over the Spaniards at Rocroi in 1643. The bold manoeuvre which achieved this success laid the foundation for an exaggerated reputation. In 1648 he was victorious at the Battle of Lens. Condé left French service during the Fronde and served under the Spaniards until the Treaty of the Pyrenees in 1659. During this time, he was defeated while at the head of a Spanish army by Turenne at the Battle of the Dunes, near Dunkirk, in 1658. He took major commands in the War of Devolution (1667–8) and the Franco-Dutch War (1672–8) until laid low by gout in 1675. He was a fine example of the gifted and independent soldier prince of the later seventeenth century. *See also* FRANCE; ROCROI; TURENNE.

A. CORVISIER
JOHN CHILDS

FURTHER READING
H. Malo, *Le Grand Condé* (Paris, 1937); G. Mongrédien, *Le Grand Condé* (Paris, 1959).

Conscription *See* MOBILIZATION; NATIONALISM; NAVAL PERSONNEL; NUMERICAL STRENGTH; OBLIGATIONS AND DUTIES; RECRUITMENT

Constantinople, fortifications of The land and sea walls of Constantinople, which are still standing today, were completed in only a few years, having been begun in 412–13. Even though the city's garrison was kept extremely small, in order to deter the possibility of a military coup against the emperor, these exceptional constructions enabled the Imperial capital both to resist the constant pressures of invaders from the north (Goths, Huns, Bulgars and Russians) and to withstand full-scale sieges. In 626, a Persian army, supported by the Avars and Slavs, encamped at Chalcedon and tried in vain to take the city. On two occasions (672–8 and 717–18) the Arabs laid siege to Constantinople for long periods, but the walls, in conjunction with the defensive boom which closed off the Golden Horn to enemy flotillas, were proof against attack. In 1203 and 1204, the Franks and Venetians on the Fourth Crusade took advantage of internal strife to capture the city for the first time. It was not, however, until 1453 that Mehmet II's Turks, equipped with large, modern artillery, succeeded in conquering the city by breaching its walls. *See also* BYZANTIUM.

G. DAGRON

FURTHER READING
Louis Bréhier, *The Life and Death of Byzantium* tr. Margaret Vaughan (Amsterdam, 1977); D. E. Queller, *The Fourth Crusade: the conquest of Constantinople, 1201–4* (London, 1978); Steven Runciman, *The Fall of Constantinople* (London, 1955).

Contributions *See* LOGISTICS

Convoys Convoys, whether composed of a number of armed merchant ships or enjoying the protection of naval vessels, appear in Antiquity and the Middle Ages; Venetian merchant galleys sailed together to ensure protection from privateers and pirates. In the modern period this arrangement assumed a grander scale both in wartime and, on occasion, during times of peace. In the mid-sixteenth century, the Spaniard Menendez de Avilez established a two-year pattern of convoys – one year out, the next year back – between the New World and the Iberian peninsula to protect the treasure *flota* from the depredations of the French corsairs and the English 'sea dogs', such as Hawkins, Drake and Frobisher. This proved effective, and the first major setback did not occur until 1628 when a Dutch squadron destroyed a convoy at Matanzas.

During the Anglo-Dutch Wars of the seventeenth century (1652–4, 1665–7, 1672–4) the adversaries made systematic use of convoys to maintain their trade. The convoy system greatly increased in scope during the Nine Years' War (1688–97) and the War of the Spanish Succession (1702–14) when both the Dutch and the British had to face strong attacks from French corsairs. Regular convoys were organized to the Baltic, the Levant, North America and the West Indies. Again, the method was effective, in spite of some unpleasant surprises such as a destruction of the Smyrna convoy by Tourville's fleet in 1693 off Lagos on the coast of Portugal.

The same arrangement, although in more substantial form, was seen throughout the wars of the eighteenth century, including the Revolutionary and Napoleonic Wars, with convoys leaving British waters at varying intervals: every week for the North Sea, once a fortnight for the Baltic, and each month, or less often, for more distant destinations like North America, the West Indies, the Iberian peninsula or the Indian Ocean. The size of these convoys ranged between 100 and 1,000 sail. Overall, the convoy system proved its worth in sustaining commerce, although it demanded considerable efforts and resources from the Royal Navy. In addition, overseas military expeditions were always afforded strong naval escorts; these military convoys were, and are, treated as distinct and special types of operation.

Convoys continued into the nineteenth century and were employed by France in the Algiers and Far Eastern expeditions. Convoys were used extensively during the First World War. At first they were mainly of the 'military type' (e.g. the Dardanelles expedition in 1915) but, as the German submarine threat developed to dangerous levels following Ludendorff's declaration of unrestricted submarine warfare in 1917, the Allied navies turned to the use of convoys for merchant shipping from the summer of 1917 onwards after the failure of the 'patrolled routes' strategy. The measure was successful; German U-boats were forced to attack while submerged and risk violent counter-attacks from escort vessels.

Convoys were adopted by the British and Allied governments from the very beginning of the Second World War, despite the fact that the system had a number of minor disadvantages. The merchant navy's productivity fell by more than 30 per cent on account of the time lost in forming and dispersing convoys and because convoys operated at the speed of the slowest vessel. After the fall of France in 1940, all convoy arrangements were completely revised. Great Britain maintained convoys on the North Atlantic and the Freetown route, but the shortage of escort ships meant that adequate naval protection was only possible, at first, in the eastern part of the Atlantic. The participation of the US navy, despite the technical neutrality of the United States, and the increasing number of ships from the Royal Canadian Navy, allowed complete trans-Atlantic protection to be provided from the autumn of 1941. After Pearl Harbor, there was total protection for convoys in the North Atlantic.

Convoys proved to be the sole means of defending merchant ships against both surface raiders and submarines. Proof of this fact can be deduced from the heavy losses suffered by American ships sailing alone off the east coast of the United States between January and May 1942. Convoys were not, however, a total panacea and the 'wolf pack' tactics developed by Dönitz enabled the U-boats to achieve spectacular successes up to the spring of 1943. Air cover for convoys had been found efficacious in 1917–18 but until the summer of 1943, an 'air gap' existed in the central Atlantic. The filling of this gap by long-range aircraft (Liberators, Catalinas and Sunderlands), the introduction of new escort vessels and the deciphering of German signals traffic finally brought immunity to the majority of convoys.

The system was also employed on the so-called 'Arctic' convoys which carried material aid to the northern ports of the USSR. 'Rapid convoys', more 'military' in type than mercantile, were used in the Mediterranean to supply Malta. The Axis powers adopted convoys, with some success, in the Mediterranean and the North Sea. Japan, however, only resorted to convoys after 1944 when the menace from US submarines had become acute. On the other hand, the Japanese doctrine that submarines were only to attack warships meant that the Americans never had to employ convoys in their Pacific operations. Since 1945, the convoy system has only been applied on rare occasions – the military expeditions to Suez in 1956 and the Falkland Islands in 1982. It is, however, quite probable that it would be re-employed by Western navies in the event of a generalized conflict. *See also* ATLANTIC, BATTLE OF THE; BLOCKADES; COMBINED OPERATIONS; COMMERCE-RAIDING; DARDANELLES; DÖNITZ; EXPEDITIONS; NAVAL WARFARE; SURCOUF.

P. MASSON

FURTHER READING
J. S. Bromley, *Corsairs and Navies, 1660–1760* (London, 1987); Julian S. Corbett and Henry Newbolt, *Naval Operations* (5 vols, London, 1920–31); R. Patrick Crowhurst, *The Defence of British Trade, 1689–1815* (Folkestone, 1977); *Course et Piraterie*, ed. Michel Mollat (2 vols, Paris, 1975); Bryan Ranft, 'The protection of British seaborne trade and the development of systematic planning for war, 1860–1906', in *Technical Change and British Naval Policy, 1860–1939*, ed. Bryan Ranft (London, 1977); S. W. Roskill, *The War at Sea* (3 vols in 4, London, 1954–61); Owen Rutter, *Red Ensign: a history of convoy* (London, 1943); John Winton, *Convoy: defence of sea trade* (London, 1983).

Corbett, Sir Julian Stafford (1854–1922) Corbett first trained for the law but later turned to art. Having private means and literary ability he travelled and wrote, publishing between 1886 and 1895 four novels with a historical background, together with two short biographies of Drake and Monk. His appointment as a correspondent for the *Pall Mall Gazette* with the Dongola Expedition in 1896, in addition to other influences aroused deeper historical interests. He began serious research, and in 1898 appeared the foundation of his historical reputation, *Drake and the Tudor Navy*, followed in 1900 by *The Successors of Drake*.

His work was of such quality that he soon received recognition. The new Naval War College was about to open; Corbett was appointed its Lecturer in History, and soon afterwards showed his widening interests by publishing *England in the Mediterranean* (1904), a study in national policy related to sea power. From this time on he was at pains to show that sea power was a complicated matter which had to be striven for at various levels and which, by itself, was not a British security panacea. This theme was expanded in *England in the Seven Years' War* (1907), while in *The Campaign of Trafalgar* (1910) he demonstrated his ability to combine matters of detail with a broad vision of the strategical whole, yet still write attractively. In 1911 he embodied his theoretical views in *Some Principles of Maritime Strategy*. In addition to these notable books, Corbett also edited several important volumes for the Navy Records Society, as well as contributing numerous articles to periodicals both on historical and modern subjects. He gained much influence in both naval and political circles, broadly supporting the Fisher reforms. In 1914, he had recently prepared a British official history of the Russo-Japanese War (printed for official use in 1915) and he turned to preparing the history of the new war, becoming Director of the Historical Section of the Committee of Imperial Defence. The first volume of *Naval Operations*, the official naval history of the 1914–18 war, was published in 1920, and two more were prepared by him before his death.

Although Corbett followed in the wake of two eminent British naval historians, John Knox Laughton and Philip Colomb, he carried the study of naval history to new lengths. He wrote during the period of great British naval expansion and his works received much attention because, while realizing the central role of the decisive battle, he could see other important aspects of the use of sea power in the need to maintain seaborne trade and in the ability to threaten enemy coasts. For their combination of detail and broad vision his books remain essential reading. *See also* CASTEX; MAHAN.

A. W. H. PEARSALL

FURTHER READING
Donald M. Schurman, *Julian S. Corbett, 1854–1922: historian of British maritime policy from Drake to Jellicoe* (London, 1981).

Córdoba, Gonsalvo de (1443–1515) Celebrated in his own lifetime as 'the Great Captain', Gonsalvo de Córdoba was the first of the pre-eminent Spanish commanders of the sixteenth century. Córdoba rose to prominence in the last of the wars of the *Reconquista* (1482–92) and commanded the small army Ferdinand of Aragon sent to Calabria in April 1495 to aid the King of Naples against Charles VIII of France. During this campaign (1495–6) Córdoba suffered several defeats at the hands of the French, whose tactical combination of heavy cavalry, pikemen (German, Swiss or French) and a mobile artillery train had demonstrated its effectiveness in the defeat of the Italian alliance at Fornovo (6 July 1495). Spanish armies of the *Reconquista* had consisted largely of light horse; heavy cavalry was limited in number, and the infantry poorly armed. Córdoba's defeats, however, inspired him to undertake a major reform of the Spanish infantry. His most important innovation was the extensive adoption of the arquebus, combined with lesser proportions of pikemen and sword and buckler-armed infantry intended to attack the opposing pike-mass at close quarters. No less significant, however, was

the employment of field entrenchments as a defence against cavalry. The second war for Naples (1501–4) saw the new tactics employed with dramatic success. At Cerignola (26 April 1503) a French attempt to storm Córdoba's entrenchments with both men-at-arms and Swiss pikemen was shot to pieces by arquebus fire. This defeat left the French with only one stronghold in Naples, the fortress of Gaeta. To relieve it Louis XII sent a fresh army to the peninsula. After considerable manoeuvring, the French mounted a major attack across the Garigliano in the face of Spanish entrenchments on 6 November 1503. This assault was also defeated by firepower. The French failure led to six weeks of stalemate along the river, until, on 29 December, Córdoba made an unopposed crossing upstream, taking the enemy by surprise and defeating them in detail. The survivors retired to Gaeta, but that fortress too capitulated on 1 January 1504. The immediate effect of Córdoba's success in 1503 was to secure Spanish control of Naples, but its longer-term significance was the establishment of the combination of firearms and field entrenchments as the key to Spanish tactics for the remainder of the Italian wars. *See also* FORTIFICATION, FIELD; INFANTRY; SPAIN.

SIMON ADAMS

FURTHER READING
C. Oman, *A History of the Art of War in the Sixteenth Century* (London, 1937), pp. 51–62, 115–29.

Cossacks *See* POLAND; RUSSIA/USSR

Cromwell, Oliver (1599–1658) The outbreak of the English Civil War in 1642 revealed an aptitude for soldiering in this landed gentleman from Huntingdonshire. After fighting in the Earl of Essex's army at Edgehill in 1642, he became a colonel of horse in the army of the Parliamentary Eastern Association in 1643 and lieutenant-general of the cavalry in the New Model Army in 1645. He participated, under the command of Sir Thomas Fairfax, in the defeat of Charles I at Naseby in 1645, the battle which effectively decided the First Civil War (1642–6). Cromwell achieved victories over the Scots at Preston in 1648 and Dunbar in 1650, before beating Charles II at Worcester in 1651. Between 1653 and 1658, he was Lord Protector of England. Cromwell's martial success was founded on the maintenance of firm discipline, good administration and organization rather than special tactical ability or innovation. He was methodical in approach but could, and did, act rapidly and decisively (Preston, 1648). His religion provided strong political and military motivation. However, his martial career has been shrouded in myth to the extent that some of his tactical errors have been overlooked, particularly at Dunbar in 1650. Similarly, the success of the New Model Army during the First (1642–6) and Second (1648) Civil Wars was due as much to the overall command of Sir Thomas Fairfax as it was to Cromwell. In politics he was often vacillating and contradictory. Although it would be an exaggeration to describe Cromwell's Protectorate as a 'military dictatorship', the New Model Army was both his power-base and the arbiter of national politics. This interference by the army in English political life was deeply resented by the established ruling elite and exacerbated the already strong dislike of standing armies. On the credit side, Cromwell's rule helped to modernize the fiscal and administrative methods of the English state and stimulated colonial development. *See also* GREAT BRITAIN; MARSTON MOOR.

JOHN CHILDS

FURTHER READING
Barry Coward, *Oliver Cromwell* (London, 1992); *Oliver Cromwell and the English Revolution*, ed. J. S. Morrill (London, 1990); Ian Gentles, *The New Model Army* (Oxford, 1991).

Crusades *See* HOLY WAR

Cryptography *See* SECRECY

Culture, protection of *The Contemporary Nature of the Problem* This is a recent development. In former times, when the most urgent demand was for defence, temples or churches were destroyed to build town walls. Also, in the desire to be rid of the monuments of a particular fanatical cause or ideology, libraries were burnt and statues of saints or kings knocked down, though this only occurred in the exceptional circumstances of civil wars or religious strife. Generally, there was simply an attitude of indifference to the damage war might inflict upon the works of the past.

The French Revolution, with its costs in terms of works of art, marked the beginning of a change in attitude. Tentative efforts were made to protect the cultural heritage during the Franco-Prussian War of 1870–1 and these were further developed during the 1914–18 war, the Spanish Civil War of 1936–9 and the Second World War. After the 1939–45 conflict, UNESCO made strides to lay down a general set of rules.

Buildings and Monuments If they are not physically attacked, great stone buildings will stand up to the ravages of time for centuries. On some occasions they can even resist modern weapons, as in the case of Cologne Cathedral which was left jutting from a landscape of ruins in 1945. The wooden constructions of the Middle Ages are not as long-lived and many have suffered repeated fire damage. They are especially vulnerable to incendiary bombs (Lübeck, 1942). From 1914 onwards, the façades of buildings and statues were protected by walls of sandbags supported on a wooden or metal framework. These sandbag barriers were ventilated at the base and were not pressed against the walls of the buildings. Vaulting or archways were reinforced by scaffolding, which differed according to whether the arch was semicircular or ogival. The complete encasement (side walls and a terrace) of the towers of Serrano at Valencia was achieved in 1937. The building housed a number of the most precious works of the Spanish cultural heritage.

1939 saw marked advances in the passive protection of buildings, monuments and statues, as well as features of their interiors

179

with the protection of memorial stones and tombs (such as that of Karel Van Gelder at Arnhem). This type of protection proved effective.

After the war, much effort was taken to reconstruct famous groups of old buildings using photographs and postcards as historical sources. This occurred in the town of St Malo and the old parts of Warsaw. Where such work was required, it was prepared by photogrammetric surveys, a task allotted in France to the National Geographical Institute.

Special shelters were erected for the protective storage of archives and works of art. During the 1939–45 war, a number of such shelters were built, particularly in the coastal dunes of the Netherlands and, later, in the Dutch interior. They were usually made of reinforced concrete or were of lighter construction but erected in quarries. They were built in the style of fortifications and were designed to resist a direct hit by a 250 kg bomb, but they could be effective against a 20 kiloton atomic bomb exploding at a distance of 200 metres.

Contents of Buildings This very broad category includes statues when these are movable, pictures, stained glass, the masterpieces of the great furniture makers and archaeological treasures. These have to be transferred to shelters and the work of preparation for this is particularly delicate. The criteria for selection are quality, ease of transport and time allotted for the transfer. The shelter may be located on the same site, as in the case of the *Koninklijke Museum voor Schone Kunsten* (Royal Museum of Fine Arts) at Antwerp which was built in a vaulted cellar when the building was being fortified in the aftermath of 1870 and was subsequently strengthened with reinforced concrete. It may also be used as a way-station before the items are sent on to a safer haven. From 1890 onwards, in this same museum, trap doors were built along the walls so that large pictures could be removed more easily. Similar facilities have since been created in other museums. Preparation for removing such works to safe havens is barely compatible with the haste required in a mobiliza-

tion. Stained glass windows, for example, have to be logged section by section and tagged to show the shelter to which they are removed. In this way, the Louvre was able to have on display again a selection of one hundred outstanding paintings only a few months after the liberation of Paris.

Cases and packing materials of an appropriate size also have to be available as must the necessary padding; advances in chemistry mean that we now have at our disposal materials which make this possible, such as phenol-based plastic foam and protective covers of vinyl chloride, and an appropriate relative humidity can be maintained in the packing cases.

The works in question have to be stored in conditions appropriate for their preservation. This means the right temperature and humidity or, in other words, very carefully planned air-conditioning and ventilation. It has to be possible for the state of the items to be checked; to this end, paintings, for example, are stored on panels which slide laterally without jolting or jarring.

Written Documents These are subject to natural deterioration and are also vulnerable to attack by insects and bacteria. The precautions which have to be taken are similar to those adopted for paintings or tapestries so far as the atmospheric conditions of the shelter are concerned.

In order to preserve visual records of these for future generations, UNESCO recommended in 1950 that copies be made on microfilm and that these be placed in locations in Australia, Poland, the United States and the United Kingdom. These recommendations also apply to works of art in general. The way in which they are to be packed and the atmospheric conditions are specified.

General Measures During the First World War, the Allied general staffs became preoccupied in 1917 with protection from shells and from airborne bombs, which at the time were still relatively small. Shortly before the Second World War, the International Council of Museums took into account more powerful weapons, but these were still of the 'conventional' type; the countries concerned again took the appropriate measures. The end of the Second World War saw the coming of the nuclear age, with considerably more powerful bombs, capable also of causing massive fire damage. UNESCO held a conference at The Hague between 21 April and 14 May 1954 on the subject of the protection of cultural property in case of armed conflict. This produced a convention, regulations for its enforcement and a protocol, which were ratified by a majority vote.

The following were defined as cultural property, whatever their origin and whoever their owner might be:

- items of great importance for the cultural heritage of a country, whether movable or otherwise (monuments, archaeological sites, groups of buildings, manuscripts, books, collections or reproductions, etc.);
- buildings in which such works are conserved or displayed, as well as 'refuges';
- centres of historical interest containing a considerable number of items belonging to the categories listed above.

The signatories agreed that these items or the arrangements set in place for protecting them were not to be used for ends which might make them targets for destruction. Where one country occupied another's territory, the occupying power had to support the action of the authorities of the occupied country. Special instruction was to be given to the armed forces. Special protection was conferred upon 'refuges' and 'centres of historic interest' which had to be located at an appropriate distance from large industrial centres or important military objectives. It was also laid down that military personnel or equipment was not allowed to pass through a 'centre of historic interest'. The items recognized as being of cultural importance in this way had to be placed on an international register. The transportation of these items could receive special protection. The belligerents appointed a representative for the items on their own territory and another for items in (potentially) occupied territory; the protecting powers also appointed delegates. A Commissioner General for Cultural Prop-

erty was chosen from an international list of personalities to act in each of the belligerent countries (monitoring, inspection, reports, representations, etc.). The placing of items on the register could be contested. A distinguishing blue and white mark enabled both the specially protected items and the authorized personnel to be recognized. The convention completed the arrangements made under the previous Hague Conventions of 29 July 1899 and 18 October 1907, together with the Washington Pact of 15 April 1907. However, the shelling of Dubrovnik during the Yugoslav Civil War (1991–2) demonstrated the difficulty of enforcing these arrangements. *See also* DEPREDATIONS; FORTIFICATION; ICONOGRAPHY; LAWS OF WAR.

J.-M. GOENAGA

FURTHER READING
André Noblecourt, *Protection of Cultural Property in the Event of Armed Conflict* (UNESCO, Museums and Monuments no. 8, Paris, 1958).

Cunningham, Andrew Browne, 1st Viscount of Hyndhope (1883–1963) Entering the Royal Navy in 1897, Cunningham commanded the destroyer *Scorpion* for seven years (1911–18) with unrelaxed efficiency, serving at the Dardanelles (1915) and in the Mediterranean, where his later service was also centred. As rear-admiral of destroyers in the Mediterranean from 1934–6, he contributed to bringing the Mediterranean fleet to a high standard of proficiency, which he inherited on assuming the chief command in 1940. Although his fleet was numerically inferior to that of Italy, he maintained a general activity in order to assert dominance and seize the initiative, marked by the pioneer air attack on Taranto (11–12 November 1940) and the destruction of cruisers at Matapan (28 March 1941). The appearance of the German air force circumscribed Cunningham's freedom of action and his fleet lost heavily off Crete in 1941 and in assisting Malta (1941–2). Later, he became naval commander of the North African and Italian campaigns (1942–3), before succeeding Dudley Pound as First Sea Lord in October 1943. In that post he contributed to the overall direction of Anglo-American strategy through membership of the Chiefs of Staff Committee. In 1945, he had to organize the movement of the fleet to the Pacific and deal with the problems posed by the end of the war. *See also* DARDANELLES; NAVAL WARFARE; NAVIES; TARANTO.

A. W. H. PEARSALL

FURTHER READING
A. B. Cunningham, *Sailor's Odyssey* (London, 1951); S. W. Roskill, *The War at Sea* (London, 1954–61); Oliver Warner, *Cunningham of Hyndhope* (London, 1967).

Cynoscephalae, Battle of (197 BC) Cynoscephalae was the site in Thessaly at the foot of a range of hills where Rome and her Greek allies under the command of Titus Quinctius Flamininus defeated Philip V, King of Macedonia, during the Second Macedonian War (200–196 BC). Philip permitted the battle to take place on rough terrain, leading part of his phalanx into action on his right wing; the Macedonians had the upper hand here until Flamininus used elephants to spearhead an attack against the left wing where the remainder of the Macedonian phalanx was still taking up its position. The battle was for a long time undecided, and the crucial point was the decision on his own initiative of a Roman military tribune to lead twenty maniples (tactical units of 120 men) in a surprise attack on the rear of the Macedonian phalanx on the right wing. This was the first time since its appearance on the military scene in the fourth century that the Macedonian phalanx had been defeated in pitched battle by a different type of formation. The Greek historian Polybius presented this victory as proof of the superiority of the legion over the phalanx; on rough terrain or in rapidly changing circumstances, the legion, which was more flexible and manoeuvrable by virtue of its division into maniples, had the advantage of mobility over the heavy, compact mass of the phalanx. The Roman victory at Cynoscephalae, following closely upon the legion's triumph against the Carthaginians at Zama (202), was the first in a long series of successes which Roman armies won over the armies of the Hellenistic sovereigns in the second and first centuries BC. It also ended the threat of Macedonian domination and opened the way for the advance of Roman influence in Greece. *See also* CHAERONEA; GREECE, ANCIENT; ROME; ZAMA.

R. LONIS
B. CAMPBELL

FURTHER READING
Polybius, 18. 21–32; R. M. Errington, *The Dawn of Empire: Rome's rise to world power* (London, 1971), pp. 151–5.

D

Dardanelles (16 February 1915–8 January 1916) The Dardanelles campaign was a bold attempt to break the deadlock that existed on the Western Front by utilizing Allied seapower to open a new front against Ottoman Turkey, which had joined the Central Powers in October 1914. Born out of frustration with the mounting casualties in France and Flanders, the strategy of the so-called 'Easterners' within the British political establishment, such as Churchill, Hankey and Lloyd George, assumed that a British expedition directed against Turkey would not only knock the Turks out of the war and dismember the Ottoman Empire but also encourage so far neutral states such as Italy, Greece, Bulgaria and Romania to join a Balkan League against Austria-Hungary. At the very least, Germany would be compelled to divert troops to support her weaker allies and knocking away her 'props' might well speed the collapse of Germany itself. The defeat of Turkey would also free Russian troops from the Caucasus – the Russians actually appealed for an Allied operation to relieve the pressure on them there on 2 January 1915 – while the opening of the strategically vital Dardanelles would allow the Allies to ship munitions to Russia in return for Russian grain shipped west. Two additional assumptions supported the strategy: the notion that the fleet, having forced the straits, could actually seize the city of Constantinople, and the supposed irresolution of Germany's allies. Preliminary bombardment of Turkish coastal defences began on 16 February but the main naval assault on 18 March resulted in the loss of three Allied capital ships from gunfire or mines. A decision had already been taken to send troops in support of the naval operation but administrative confusion and unfamiliarity with amphibious warfare delayed the initial landings on the Gallipoli peninsula until 25 April by which time the Turkish defences had been reorganized by the German general, Liman von Sanders. General Sir Ian Hamilton's 75,000-strong Mediterranean Expeditionary Force suffered relatively few casualties coming ashore at three out of five beaches at Cape Helles and at what became known as Anzac Cove, but little urgency was shown in exploiting success and opportunities were thrown away. A new offensive was mounted on 6 August to break the deadlock that had ensued opposite the original beachheads but the new landing at Suvla Bay was again characterized by lacklustre leadership and its failure sealed the fate of the campaign. Further offensives in August achieved little and the decision to abandon the enterprise was taken on 7 December 1915. Ironically, the withdrawal from Anzac and Suvla by 20 December and from Cape Helles by 8 January 1916 was accomplished in masterful fashion. Overall, Allied casualties amounted to 252,000 and Turkish casualties probably to 350,000. The failure further isolated Russia, especially after Bulgaria joined the Central Powers, although the Dardanelles campaign may have played some part in bringing Italy into the war on the Allied side in May 1915. Combined operations were thoroughly discredited and, notwithstanding other 'sideshows', the main British effort was to be concentrated on the Western Front. *See also* COMBINED OPERATIONS; EXPEDITIONS; STRATEGY.

IAN F. W. BECKETT

FURTHER READING
G. H. Cassar, *The French and the Dardanelles* (London, 1971); R. J. Marder, *From the Dardanelles to Oran* (London, 1974); A. Moorehead, *Gallipoli* (London, 1956); K. Neilson, *Strategy and Supply* (London, 1984); R. Rhodes James, *Gallipoli* (London, 1965).

Davout, Louis-Nicolas (1770–1823) The military tradition of the Avout family dates back to the Crusades. There is a Burgundian dialect saying which runs: 'Quand naît un Davo, une épée sort du fourro' ('When a Davo is born, a sword leaves its scabbard'). Louis-Nicolas, a graduate of the École Royale Militaire, inherited the military ethos of the *ancien régime*, the essentials of which he managed to integrate into the new structure of the French revolutionary armies. He was at Neerwinden in 1793, came to the attention of Desaix at Kehl (1796) and distinguished himself in Bonaparte's service in Egypt in 1798. He became commander of the 3rd Corps and a marshal of France. His actions decided the outcome on the right wing at the Battle of Austerlitz (1805). Having defeated the King of Prussia while outnumbered 3-to-1 at Auerstädt in 1806, he passed into history as the Duke d'Auerstädt. His original genius was confirmed at Eckmühl in 1809. Defending Hamburg in 1813–14, he kept the Russian army pinned down for six months by desperate defensive action. As Minister for War during the 'Hundred Days', he preserved the unity of the French army organizing the retreat to the Loire. *See also* AUSTERLITZ; FRANCE; JENA AND AUERSTÄDT; NAPOLEON.

D. REICHEL

FURTHER READING
Daniel Reichel, *Davout et l'art de la guerre* (Neuchâtel, 1975).

Dayan, Moshe (1915–81) Born on a kibbutz on the shore of the Sea of Galilee, Dayan joined the *Haganah*, an illegal Jewish military group, at the age of fifteen. In 1937, he was drawn into Orde Wingate's 'special night squadrons', mixtures of British soldiers and *Haganah* members, which were employed as anti-guerilla forces and carried out raids against Arab bands. It was here that Dayan learned the arts of guerilla warfare. When Britain switched to a pro-Arab policy in 1939, the *Haganah* was accordingly turned against its old master. Dayan was captured and imprisoned but was later released to fight against the Vichy French in Syria as a soldier in the *Palmach*, a full-time Jewish defence force raised by the *Haganah*. He lost an eye during these operations.

After the Second World War he was placed in charge of intelligence gathering within the *Haganah*. He fought in the 1948–9 war where he formed a 'jeep battalion' (commandos) and then commanded at Jerusalem. Between 1953 and 1958, he was chief of staff of the Israeli army, during which time he formulated the strategy of 'massive reprisal', developing a corps of commandos entrusted with reprisal attacks. Flexibility, speed, surprise, long-range raids and night fighting all became standard tactics of the Israeli Defence Forces. During the invasion of the Sinai peninsula in 1956, he showed his qualities as a strategist. Based on the concept that the riposte should 'come five minutes before the enemy attack', his conceptions were bold and the execution fast. He was appointed Minister of Defence six weeks before the Six Day War in 1967 and the overwhelming success raised his reputation to new heights. Although he was less well prepared for the scale of the Yom Kippur attack in 1973, Dayan has remained the symbol of Israeli military potency in the Middle East. *See also* GULF WAR; IRAN; IRAQ; ISRAEL, SINCE 1948.

A. CORVISIER
DAVID WESTON

FURTHER READING
Moshe Dayan, *Diary of the Sinai Campaign* (London, 1966); Edward Luttwak and Dan Horowitz, *The Israeli Army* (London, 1975); Shabatai Teveth, *Moshe Dayan* (London, 1972).

Decision *See* COMMAND

Decorations *See* GLORY; HONOURS AND AWARDS; ICONOGRAPHY; KNIGHTS AND CHIVALRY

De Gaulle, Charles André Joseph Marie (1890–1969) Born at Lille, de Gaulle entered St Cyr in 1909 and graduated in 1912. He was commissioned into the infantry. In 1916, he was wounded and taken prisoner.

Following his return to France after the First World War, de Gaulle was appointed to the French military mission to Poland in 1919–20. Opposing the prevailing orthodoxies, de Gaulle rejected the defensive doctrine of the French General Staff, who, relying on the Maginot Line, believed in the ideas of the continuous front and an advance under cover of the greatest possible firepower. For de Gaulle, tanks and aircraft were the main, not the supplementary, force. In 1934, drawing inspiration from General Estienne's ideas on the combined use of tanks and aircraft, de Gaulle published *Vers l'armée de métier* (translated as *The Army of the Future*, London, 1940) in which he advocated the formation of an army of 100,000 professional soldiers grouped in mechanized divisions and capable of forcing a war of movement on the enemy. This book had more influence with certain politicians (including Paul Reynaud) than with military men. During the campaign of 1940, de Gaulle commanded 4th armoured brigade and scored some local tactical victories (Montcornet, Abbeville). He joined Reynaud's government on 5 June 1940 as Under-secretary of State for Defence, but was hostile to the idea of an armistice. On 18 June, he launched his famous appeal from London, calling on his countrymen to continue the struggle against Germany under his command. De Gaulle commanded the 'Free French' forces for the remainder of the war, often proving a difficult ally for Churchill and Roosevelt. In August 1944, de Gaulle led his forces into Paris. He served briefly as the President of France in 1945–6. In 1958, as a result of the Algerian crisis, de Gaulle again became President, a post he held for eleven years. During his latter tenure in office, France developed an independent nuclear striking force and withdrew from NATO in 1966 as a result of a quarrel with the United States. *See also* ESTIENNE; FRANCE; TANKS.

A. CORVISIER
KEITH NEILSON

FURTHER READING
P. Huard, *Le Colonel De Gaulle et ses blindés* (Paris, 1980); François Kersaudy, *Churchill and De Gaulle* (London, 1981).

Delbrück, Hans (1848–1929) Delbrück's principal work, *A History of the Art of War in the light of Political History*, was published in seven volumes between 1900 and 1936, although only the first four volumes covering the period up to the end of the Napoleonic Wars were actually Delbrück's own work. He sought to establish the relationship between the constitutions of states, strategy and tactics within the context of world history. Indeed, he argued forcefully that military history was merely a branch of world history. He concentrated on the material conditions of past battles, in so far as these could be determined from often suspect sources and, in passing, exposed a number of impossibilities in generally accepted accounts, not least in those relating to the Persian Wars. Expanding on Clausewitz, Delbrück postulated two basic forms of strategy: exhaustion and annihilation. However, it was as an apparent advocate of the totality of war that he had an influence on the German General Staff prior to the First World War, especially on von Schlieffen. Some of his theories were challenged by other German theorists, including von der Goltz and von Bernhardi. *See also* BERNHARDI; CLAUSEWITZ; GERMANY; SCHLIEFFEN.

A. CORVISIER
IAN F. W. BECKETT

FURTHER READING
A. Bucholz, *Hans Delbrück and the German Military Establishment* (Iowa, 1985); E. Carrias, *La Pensée militaire allemande* (Paris, 1947); G. A. Craig, 'Delbrück: the military historian', in *Makers of Modern Strategy*, ed. Peter Paret (Oxford, 1986), pp. 326–53.

Demetrius Poliorcetes (336–283 BC) Son of Antigonus 'the One-eyed', one of the most prestigious generals of Alexander of Macedon. During the quarrels over the succession which followed the death of the king in 323, he actively helped his father to enforce his authority over a part of the empire, winning a great naval battle against Ptolemy I at Salamis in Cyprus (306 BC). After the death of Antigonus at the Battle of Ipsus (301), where Demetrius' blunder in pursuing his cavalry charge too far had contributed to his father's defeat, his position was precarious. He was eventually accepted as King of Macedonia (294) only to be ousted in 288, though he retained his other possessions in Greece. He subsequently led a Macedonian expedition to Asia to recapture Antigonus' empire but this ended in failure as his army melted away, and he surrendered to Seleucus in 285, dying of drink two years later.

Demetrius has always been regarded as one of the greatest military leaders of his generation and one of the greatest experts in the art of siegecraft. This is the origin of his nickname Poliorcetes ('the Besieger'). In fact, he was not always successful in capturing towns (he suffered a significant failure at Rhodes in 305–304), but justly earned the admiration of his contemporaries for the wide range of devices employed and his skill in inventing new ones. Some of the most spectacular inventions in siegecraft occurred at this time and this may in part be attributed to his influence on military engineers: battering rams mounted on winches, giant catapults and huge mobile towers. The tower used at the Siege of Rhodes had nine storeys and was 140 feet tall, mounted on a platform 75 feet long, with eight wheels 15 feet in diameter; the whole, equipped with various types of ballistic device (missile engines for firing stones or heavy bolts) on each level, and protected over its entire height by iron plates, weighed some 150 tonnes and required 3,400 men to operate it. In reality, it was better suited to strike the imagination of contemporaries than to be militarily effective. *See also* GREECE, ANCIENT; SIEGES.

R. LONIS
B. CAMPBELL

FURTHER READING
Y. Garlan, *Recherches de poliorcétique grecque* (Paris, 1974); M. Cary, *A History of the Greek World, 323 to 146 BC* (London, reprint 1963), pp. 36–52.

Denain, Battle of (24 July 1712) After the secret negotiations conducted by the ministry of Robert Harley (1661–1724) and Henry St John (1678–1751) had achieved acceptable terms with Louis XIV, Queen Anne (1702–14) issued 'restraining orders' to the Duke of Ormonde (1665–1745), the commander of the British contingent in the Confederate Army in the Low Countries. Ormonde was forbidden to commit the British troops to either siege or battle. Villars, commanding the French army, knew of these 'restraining orders', while Prince Eugene of Savoy, who had assumed the chief command of the Confederate Army in succession to the Duke of Marlborough in 1712, also suspected their existence. Eugene successfully besieged Le Quesnoy during the first week of July 1712 and launched 2,000 light cavalry on a sweep around Paris from Rheims to Metz. Ormonde separated the 12,000 native British troops from Eugene's army on 17 July and marched them to the coast.

Free to act on his own, Eugene attempted to force a corridor into the heart of France by besieging Landrecies, the fall of which would have opened the road to Paris. Louis XIV authorized Villars to attack Eugene in order to interrupt his operations. Because he was trying to break into France on a narrow front, Eugene had to conduct the siege at the end of a sixty-mile supply line which stretched back to Tournai via Le Quesnoy, Denain on the Scheldt, Marchiennes, and St Amand. Eugene dug lines of circumvallation to defend his conduct of the Siege of Landrecies and field fortifications from Douai on the Scarpe to Neuville on the Scheldt to protect his extremely vulnerable supply line. Nevertheless, Villars's concentration of 70,000 around Le Câteau (Câteau-Cambrésis) threatened the flank of Eugene's corridor.

Villars built bridges across the Sambre as if he intended to attack the rear of Eugene's siege works at Landrecies; Eugene responded by gathering his field army between Le Quesnoy and Landrecies. On 22 July, Villars's army marched southwards towards the Sambre bridges but, during the night of 22–23 July, he reversed his steps northward, conducting a 12-mile forced march which took him back towards Neuville with the intention of attacking Denain, which protected the vital bridging point of the Scheldt. The idea for this manoeuvre had originated with a magistrate, Robert Le Febvre d'Orval, but it was closely modelled on Marlborough's forcing of the Lines of Brabant in 1705 and his crossing of Villars's 'Ne Plus Ultra' Lines in 1711. Denain was defended by twelve cannon and seventeen German and Dutch battalions (8,000 men) under the command of Arnold Joost van Keppel, Earl of Albemarle (1669–1718). Eugene heard of Villars's manoeuvre early on the morning of 24 July and rapidly began to march his field army towards Denain, fifteen miles away, but his intervention proved too late. The French burst through four Dutch battalions at Neuville and then assaulted Denain at 1.00 p.m. After initial resistance, Albemarle ordered a retreat towards the single pontoon bridge over the Scheldt. Only 3,000 of the Denain garrison escaped; 2,000 died, many drowning in the river, and 3,000 were taken prisoner. The French lost 500 dead and 1,000 wounded.

Although it was a relatively minor action and the sole French victory in the Low Countries during the War of the Spanish Succession, in the words of Napoleon, 'Denain saved France'. Eugene was compelled to abandon his attempt to force a corridor through the last line of Vauban's frontier defences; the fortresses along the Scarpe, as well as Marchiennes, Douai and Bouchain, were all regained by Villars before the end of the year, providing France with a platform for the peace settlement at Utrecht in 1714. *See also* BLENHEIM; EUGENE OF SAVOY; FORTIFICATION, FIELD; MALPLAQUET; MARLBOROUGH; RAMILLIES; VILLARS.

A. CORVISIER
JOHN CHILDS

FURTHER READING
Maurice Suatai, *La manoeuvre de Denain* (Lille, 1902); C. C. Sturgill, *Marshal Villars and the War of the Spanish Succession* (Lexington, Ken., 1965); Derek Mackay, *Prince Eugene of Savoy* (London, 1977), pp. 136–41.

Depredations 'A peste, fame, belloque libera nos, Domine.' That prayer, repeated at Mass for centuries, accurately identified in a single breath the three calamities which evoked the profoundest dread. Indeed, epidemics, famines and wars are closely linked, the first two often appearing as a consequence of the third. Even so, when assessing the material destruction caused by war, account must be taken of the ills of which it cannot properly be called the cause, but whose development it fosters.

Destruction Resulting Directly from War
The aim of warfare among primitive societies is often to gain possession of the property of those living nearby, and it takes the form of raiding. Very soon, however, a balance or a form of co-operation becomes established between the raiding peoples and their victims, by the terms of which the latter pay tribute money to the former in exchange for their protection against other raiders. Relationships of this type frequently come about between nomadic peoples and those with a settled habitat. Nevertheless, such agreements are at the mercy of any climatic change that deleteriously affects agricultural conditions. In certain regions, raids continued until the beginning of the twentieth century.

At a more developed stage, war takes the form of a trial of strength, undertaken for a variety of motives, after all possibilities of agreement have been rejected by one of the parties. Since the aim is to force the enemy to yield, war need not continue to the point of his physical destruction, but will seek to break his powers of resistance by cutting off his means of subsistence. It is true too that war is always a costly venture, for which the stronger party seeks to make the conquered pay. 'War provides the nourishment for war,' as was said in the seventeenth century. The property of the enemy is treated with respect only if there is a chance of profiting from such action. Otherwise, the aim is to deprive him of it. Hence the deliberate destruction of property and of the means of production, whether by soldiers on the ground or, at governmental level, by politicians.

The methods most commonly used have been fire (whose effect was multiplied by detonating devices from the sixteenth century onwards, and by petrol which began to be used around 1860), explosives, mines, artillery projectiles and, more recently, the disintegration of matter by nuclear weapons. Water and poisons (e.g. poisoning of wells, asphyxiating gas) have been used as accessories.

Examples of destruction resulting directly from war vary according to circumstances. They may be associated with the course of military operations, or with the mere presence of troops, and they can have a tactical, or even a strategic, purpose. The passage of troops through, or their stay in, an area can lead to destruction of property. Further, there is a danger that they can devastate a region which fails to provide sufficient food for men and horses. During much of the seventeenth century, this devastation was as likely to occur within an army's own country as in the lands of the enemy. Every effort was therefore made to put troops into winter quarters in occupied or neighbouring territories. Frequently, when they departed, such troops left the country scarred by destruction of many different kinds – houses converted into billets or used as stables, furniture burnt for firewood, etc. Troops passing through were even more to be feared, because the area of damage was more extensive, and it was harder for a check to be kept on the men. In addition, the condition of roads was worsened by the passage of convoys and particularly of the artillery; trees were cut down and walls and houses flattened. However, armies in the nineteenth and twentieth centuries have enjoyed improved discipline and this type of indiscriminate damage has become less widespread.

Military operations are destructive. A distinction must, however, be drawn in this regard between a war of movement and one of fixed positions. The former spreads damage over a wider area, generally along the routes of movement, with particular places – the battlefields – where the destruction is more severe (houses destroyed, fields scarred). Tactical destruction is carried out on lines of communication, such as felled trees barring roads to hinder the enemy or broken bridges, and its scale is rendered increasingly formidable with advances in means of demolition and in shell-fire. It must be realized, however, that the process of reconstruction becomes more effective

too. Wars of movement have generally left no permanent trace. Most battlefields remained unmarked, such as Malplaquet (1709), despite the barricades of felled trees that were used there. The destruction of crops was soon made good, unless the peasantry had fled. At least, that was the case up to the wars of the twentieth century.

Positional wars restrict destruction to circumscribed areas, but their intensity can be sufficient to modify the landscape. Captured or besieged towns suffered intensive destruction, particularly from the time when incendiary bombs were first used. Houses that were closely packed together, and often of wooden construction with thatched roofs, assisted the spread of fires, while the blowing up of powder magazines, if the blaze reached them, could devastate a whole quarter. The avoidance of such destruction was a particular reason why besieged towns surrendered. Capitulation took the city and its inhabitants out of the war but did not always bring operations to an end if there was a citadel in which the garrison could take refuge. The suburbs always suffered severely. They were levelled by the besieged themselves so as to prevent the besieging forces from taking up position there, and to clear the fields of fire in front of the walls. Where fortifications were built on the Vauban pattern, suburbs disappeared or were moved to a distance, but in every siege it proved necessary to destroy the casual buildings which had sprung up despite prohibitions. In general, damage in towns was quite quickly repaired.

The front line of 1914–18 in France and Belgium (called the 'red zone') left marks that were visible for a very long period. On the battlefields of the Somme, Passchendaele and Verdun whole villages disappeared, the old road system and the divisions between properties were obliterated and large sections were classified as danger areas because the soil still remained full of unexploded shells and mines. On the areas of high ground, the terrain stripped bare by the conflict slowly recovered its old natural afforestation, after a long transitional period when only brushwood was visible.

War has also long been marked by cases of tactical, or strategic, destruction carried out aside from any actual fighting; in the seventeenth and eighteenth centuries this practice was called 'devastation', and later 'scorched earth policy'. It may be ordered by military commanders during the course of operations. During an offensive, partisans or light troops go into action in the enemy's rear in order to spread panic by setting ambushes or, less frequently, to hinder by acts of destruction the movement of the main body of his forces. On the other hand, an army's evacuation of an occupied country is often accompanied by a 'scorched earth policy', which consists of creating a desert behind it as an obstacle to pursuit by the enemy. Consequently, it destroys more or less systematically, depending on the speed of its retreat, everything that it cannot carry away and everything which could help the enemy to subsist – hence setting fire to houses and the massacre of cattle with the inevitable corollary of flight by the inhabitants who then seek a temporary refuge in neighbouring towns or forests. Destruction can also be carried out on an army's home territory, if it has been invaded.

Destruction can take on a strategic character. A few examples will suffice. Although the French destruction of the Palatinate has achieved lasting notoriety, it was not an isolated case. In the sixteenth century, devastation had already been raised to the level of strategy. Paradoxically, the Palatinate was a victim of the fact that Louix XIV had set a limit to his territorial ambitions and had adopted a defensive strategy. It appears that the idea of turning into a desert the part of the Palatinate that lay immediately outside the system of French fortifications was originally due to Chamlay, then adopted by Louvois and approved by Louis XIV. In any event, it was not the first time that the French had taken this sort of action in the area having previously ravaged the Palatinate in 1674. On 31 January 1689, the order was given to burn Mannheim and Heidelberg, and then, on 21 May, Worms, Spier, Oppenheim and, finally, Bingen. In this second operation, the instructions were to burn private houses but to spare the cathedrals. The inhabitants were given six days in which to leave, taking with them their furniture and belongings, and those who expressed a wish to settle in French territory were promised carts to help them with the move and exemption from taxes for ten years; they were also guaranteed the freedom to practise the Protestant religion in Alsace. The operation took place on 31 May and 1 June. The scale of the damage is hard to estimate. Reconstruction took quite a time and part of the castle at Heidelberg was left unrepaired so that it might bear witness to French barbarity.

Another example of devastation resulted from the flooding of their own country by the Dutch who took this action in 1672 in order to halt the advance of Louis XIV's troops. It appears that Louis XIV, Louvois and the chief military commanders had certainly envisaged this possibility but had dismissed the idea, perhaps because of the dry weather, or because they doubted whether such tactics, which risked ruining the countryside for ten years, would really be employed. Another reason was that they had no clear knowledge of which sluices they needed to capture in order to frustrate this operation. On 22 or 23 June, the Muiden sluices were opened some hours after the Dutch negotiators had arrived to see Louis XIV. A large strip of land, running from the Zuider Zee to the Rhine delta and to Bois-le-Duc, and areas north of the Zuider Zee and in front of Groningen, remained under water for a long period. These instances of flooding carried out in Holland achieved their object but the damage caused was considerable – all the more so since this operation prompted the French systematically to exploit the country and to do a great deal of destruction in the parts of the Dutch territory which they subsequently had to evacuate. In the longer term, the flooding played an important part in the war's long-term effects on the Dutch economy.

Another example of systematic destruction can be found in the flooding of mines in northern France by the retreating German army in October 1918. This action was intended to strike a blow at the French economy but it did not altogether achieve its object since the mines were very rapidly put back into working order, with a defeated Germany being forced to provide assistance, and were equipped with much more modern and cost-effective machinery than before. Wars in Eastern Europe have often given rise to cases of systematic destruction, particularly through the use made by the Russians of a scorched earth policy, as for example in advance of Napoleon in 1812 and of the German army in 1941–2. The overall effect of such destruction could only be proportionate to the density of built-up areas. Frontal battles, like those at Stalingrad and Leningrad, caused much more serious damage, because of the amount of artillery engaged.

Aircraft have provided an unprecedented means for destroying an enemy's nerve centres, by strategic bombing of air and naval bases, railway junctions, ports and armament factories. Besides, the term 'strategic objectives' has been given a much broader definition. Attempts to produce a psychological effect by the bombardment of civilians is not a new idea. In 1684, Seignelay ordered the fleet to bombard the city of Genoa in order to induce the doge to submit to French demands, and Algiers also had experience of this method. Sieges, of course, provide an opportunity for bombardments designed to affect morale, as shown by such examples as those of Luxembourg (1684) and Paris (1870–1). This was the aim behind the shelling of Paris by long-range German artillery in 1918. In the Second World War, this kind of operation became increasingly common. The bombing of Hamburg, Dresden, etc. by the Anglo-American air forces assumed a terrifying level of intensity. It was with the same end in view that atomic bombs were used in 1945 on Hiroshima and Nagasaki.

The destruction carried out during civil wars by many different means has been due to efforts to produce an effect on morale coupled with the passions which such conflicts provoke. Hence, the regions in the west of France which took part in the insurrection of the Vendée not only suffered massacres of their populations, possibly amounting to several hundred thousands, but also a systematic destruction of houses, crops and cattle, leaving gaps which took a long time to refill. The aim of the fires which were started in Paris by the Commune in 1871, and which had no military purpose, was to destroy public buildings as a symbolic gesture. The employment of petrol for this purpose, which was then a novelty, had a striking effect on public opinion.

Destruction as an Indirect Result of War Examples where this has been provoked on a dramatic scale occurred particularly in the Thirty Years' War (1618–48) and the two world wars.

During the Thirty Years' War, the armies perpetrated widespread devastation both by repeated destruction along the same lines of march and by the pillage which was practised alike by friendly and enemy troops – this led to a regime of banditry, with brutal treatment being inflicted on inhabitants of the countryside in order to make them give up anything which they had managed to hide. Many houses were of wood, rammed earth and thatch, and hence easily set on fire. The most serious result was that some localities were left unoccupied as a consequence of the inhabitants' flight, the temporary depopulation being extended by epidemics which the troops transmitted, and by famine due to inability to gather in or sow crops. In the abandoned houses, roofs which had fallen into disrepair exposed the mud walls to erosion by rain and frost. In cases where some inhabitants had stayed in the vicinity, or returned reasonably soon, they stripped abandoned houses of any still sound materials and used them to repair their own. In some regions of Germany, as much as two-thirds of real estate was destroyed. Reconstruction, which took nearly fifty years, was achieved by a virtual recolonization of affected territory.

It is impossible to estimate the destruction caused by wars, even within a limited area such as Europe. Where recent wars are concerned, the figures used in the calculation of 'war damage', for which the defeated countries were required to pay, cannot provide an exact picture of the reality. Thus, in France, the damage caused by the war of 1914–18 was estimated at 300,000 houses destroyed and 7.5 million acres of cultivable land ruined, of which part could not be reclaimed, since artillery bombardment had frequently stripped away the soil and left naked rock. The flooding of the mines in the north and east had reduced the production of iron ore by 60 per cent and had practically stopped the output of coal altogether. Industrial output had fallen by nearly 35 per cent. For its part, Great Britain had lost part of its merchant navy. The outcome in Russia had been even more disastrous. In total, Europe's agricultural potential had been reduced by 30 per cent, and its industrial by 40 per cent (Milza). Thanks, however, to new techniques, reconstruction was relatively rapid and it was scarcely a decade before everything that could be salvaged was back in production. An estimate of damage in the Second World War, given as a percentage of national income figures for 1938, puts it at 20 per cent for Italy and Great Britain, 135 per cent for Germany and almost the same for France, 250 per cent for the USSR (where the damage was restricted to the areas west of the Volga) and 300 per cent for Poland and Yugoslavia (Roncayolo).

Concentration here on material devastation should not lead to a disregard of the moral damage caused by war. As already remarked, the Thirty Years' War encouraged a fresh surge of violence and barbarity. Although such an effect was limited in the First World War, except in the eastern theatre, the Second World War saw a recrudescence with the virtual abolition of any distinction between civil populations and military forces – an outcome of the use of partisan warfare – and the wiping out of whole communities. An earlier instance was the massacre of Armenians in the Turkish Empire in 1915 and a later one the operation directed against the Jews from 1939 to 1945, though the latter was more an outcome of ideology than a result of war. *See also* LOSSES OF LIFE; SIEGES; TACTICS.

A. CORVISIER

FURTHER READING
G. Parker, *The Thirty Years' War* (London, 1984); John Childs, *Armies and Warfare in Europe, 1648–1789* (Manchester, 1982); M. P. Gutmann, *War and Rural Life in the Early Modern Low Countries* (Princeton, 1980); C. R. Friedrichs, *Urban Society in an Age of War* (Princeton, 1979).

De Rebus Bellicis *See* ON MILITARY MATTERS

Desertion A soldier has deserted when, after officially enlisting, he subsequently leaves his unit without permission. Desertion was endemic in all professional armies in the seventeenth and eighteenth centuries. Its increase started after the opening of the Thirty Years' War in 1618 coinciding with the reduction in the number of mutinies and mass refusals by soldiers to obey orders, outbreaks which had characterized the Spanish armies in the Low Countries during the Eighty Years' War against the rebellious Netherlands, 1567–1648.

An officer who left the colours was rarely treated as a deserter, even if he entered the service of a foreign power. The deserter was nearly always a soldier or a non-commissioned officer who defaulted on his contract of enlistment made with his commanding officer in which he undertook to serve his sovereign and defend his country. No distinction was made between the *billardeur*, a man who 'cannoned' from one regiment to another in order to receive several enlistment bounties, and the man who vanished completely either back into civilian life or into a foreign army. The soldier who deserted with his arms, equipment and uniform compounded his offence as his company commander was put to the expense of providing a new recruit complete with accoutrements and, in the British army, the deserter would not have finished paying his commanding officer for his clothing. Company officers went to considerable lengths, including advertising in newspapers, to recover their lost sheep. Desertion was treated as a very serious offence in all armies. It was, however, principally a problem confined to the ill- paid infantry; the better-off cavalrymen, usually from higher social strata, did not show the same distressing tendency to run from their colours.

Desertion was not a peculiarly military phenomenon. It was endemic in civilian life as well as in the army and the navy; servants ran from their employers, apprentices escaped from their masters, sailors fled from their ships and soldiers left their colours. Society was under-legislated and the notion of contract and social responsibility was ill-developed. Also, many of these lower-class occupations were little better than penal servitude into which young people had been forced against their wills. After 1693, British recruits were supposed to have their 'voluntary' enlistment 'attested' by a justice of the peace but, in reality, the majority of soldiers were directed into the army by poverty, destitution, the need to escape the law, press gangs, trickery and 'crimpers', kidnappers who took civilians forcibly from the streets before selling them to recruiting agencies. Soldiers were also very badly paid in comparison with even the most menial labourers. It was small wonder that many soldiers took the first opportunity to desert. A poor harvest might cause a dearth of agricultural employment leading to many labourers entering the army. In reverse, an upturn in agricultural employment could also lead to a spate of desertions. Desertion was also easy. British soldiers were billeted in groups of three or four in public houses across the country, irregularly supervised by non-commissioned officers. Soldiers quartered in London often had part-time jobs and did not see their officers for weeks on end. On active service, opposing armies were often in close physical contact making desertion to the other side a simple business. Indeed, most armies encouraged such desertion as it depleted the enemy, augmented one's own forces and provided intelligence of enemy movements and intentions. Frederick the Great enlisted the entire Saxon army into his own after the surrender at Pirna in 1756. Most of it evaporated within the next twelve months.

Despite the death penalty, service in the French galleys, flogging, running the gauntlet and other ferocious punishments, armies could not stem the flood of desertions. During the 1743 campaign in the War of the Austrian Succession (1742–8), it was common for forty Frenchmen to desert every day. Towards the end of the Seven Years' War (1756–63), the French lost 10,000 men a year through desertion despite a deserter having to run the gauntlet ten times for the first offence plus an additional eight-year enlistment, if he was caught, and fifteen years behind the oars of a Marseilles galley for a second offence. In the peacetime decade of the 1780s, an average of 3,000 men deserted every year. The Prussian army lost enormous numbers from among its foreign soldiers. Infantry regiment no. 39 lost 1,650 between 1756–63, and the Guard Regiment of Potsdam, one of the foremost in the whole army, saw 3 officers, 93 non-commissioned officers, 32 musicians and 1,525 men desert, besides 130 suicides and 29 executions. Prussian camps were guarded day and night to prevent desertion and a special detachment of the provost marched behind the rearguard to discourage deserters. Desertion reached its peaks among defeated and retreating armies. Thousands left the Prussian army during its withdrawal from Bohemia in 1744 and after the Battles of Zorndorf in 1758 and Kunersdorf in 1759, the Prussian army melted away from a combination of casualties and desertion. As the remnants of the Franco-Bavarian army fell back from Blenheim in 1704, it disintegrated amidst the mountain passes of the Black Forest. Desertion was the bane of George Washington's army during the American War of Independence. Even after the founding of the Continental Line Army, it proved almost impossible to prevent soldiers trickling homewards.

The coming of conscription during and after the French Revolutionary and Napoleonic Wars largely brought the problem of massive desertion to an end. It has continued on a small scale, both in wartime and in peacetime, and a clear distinction is now drawn between the deserter who simply leaves the forces without permission and the defector who flies abroad. Universal conscription and short-service enlistment have also done much to reduce the need for desertion, along with improvements in pay and status. Where all young males have to undergo a two- or three-year term of conscription, the duty becomes unavoidable and the social stigma attached to obvious desertion unacceptable. The wider the military recruitment net has been cast, the smaller has been the problem of desertion. During the nineteenth and twentieth centuries, the problem for European armies has been the avoidance of the draft rather than desertion. However, where foreign nationals have been mobilized by another power, especially if they have been coerced, massive desertion has continued to be the order of the day. Poles absconded from the Russian army, Czechs escaped from the Austrian and the Saxons deserted Napoleon. Desertion in peacetime is now a peripheral issue for armed forces but it remains a difficulty for certain armies in wartime. *See also* DISCIPLINE; ESPRIT DE CORPS; LAW, MILITARY; MORALE; RECRUITMENT.

JOHN CHILDS

FURTHER READING
André Corvisier, *Armies and Societies in Europe, 1494–1789* (Bloomington, Ind., 1979); John Childs, *Armies and Warfare in Europe, 1648–1789* (Manchester, 1982); C. Duffy, *The Army of Frederick the Great* (London, 1974); William Moore, *The Thin Yellow Line* (London, 1974).

Deterrence This term has only appeared in military vocabulary in quite recent times but the practice of deterrence can in fact be traced back to very distant origins. For a long time the word 'intimidation' was used to designate the threat of action that was intended to cause any potential aggressor – or anyone resisting one's demands – to hesitate. The Bible alludes to many massacres and these were not infrequent in the Ancient world. Without resorting to such extremes 'showing one's strength so as not to have to use it' formed the basis of the *pax romana* as it did of operations to pacify colonies. In the modern period troop concentrations or mobilization orders have sometimes been sufficient to prevent wars or the spread of an existing conflict.

The armed forces of the great powers have always fulfilled a deterrent function but this has only been visible sporadically, for example at moments of 'gunboat diplomacy'. Mahan occasionally used the word 'deterrence' but he did not attach any great importance to it. The problem was one of discovering how to make the enemy yield without war, if possible. The strategic concept of deterrence only really appeared in 1945. In the nuclear age deterrence has become the permanent and declared alternative to war. It is based around the concept of 'mass retaliation'. Central to this idea is the assumption that the aggressive use of military action would result in a retaliatory strike that would mean that any gains would be more than offset by the resultant losses. The enemy would therefore be dissuaded from the use of force since his losses would far outweigh any possible gains. This strategic situation became known as 'the balance of terror'. In the United States it was formulated in the doctrine of Mutually Assured Destruction (MAD). The central assumption behind this is that even if the enemy struck first at the nuclear forces of the United States there would still be sufficient forces remaining to ensure massive retaliation.

French strategic theorists refined this and developed the idea of a *force de frappe*. They argued that it was not necessary to ensure mass retaliation but that only a minimum was needed to maintain deterrence; the capacity to 'tear off an arm or a leg' (de Gaulle). Thus deterrence could be ensured by the maintenance of a small force that could survive a first-strike such as a sea-based deterrent.

For deterrence to be successful it needs to be able to satisfy the demands of communication, capability and credibility. While the United States had the capability to ensure massive retaliation it was not clear that it had either the communication or the credibility. For deterrence to be successful there needs to be communication between the parties involved; it has to be clearly communicated what the lines of demarcation are and what the response will be if those lines are crossed. The threats that are made also need to be credible.

It was seen that massive retaliation was not a credible option in those cases where aggression by the Soviet Union might be piecemeal or not directly threaten the interests of the United States. The response to this was the development of the idea of 'flexible response'. The response to any aggression or threat of aggression would be in proportion to the act or the threat. The flexible response strategy was formally adopted by NATO in 1967. The West European members were not entirely happy with this since it emphasized war-fighting capability. While the West Europeans recognized the need to maintain the credibility of a strong response they also believed in the need to maintain the element of assured destruction.

Since 1945 the world has seen no direct conflicts between the superpowers. This has been seen as proof of the effectiveness of deterrence although this is not verifiable. This does not mean, however, that mutual deterrence has become stabilized. As Raymond Aron has noted stability at the higher level logically engenders increased instability at the lower level: deterrence is accompanied by multiple crises which are supposed not to bring vital interests into play and yet the notion of vital interests cannot be defined in a rigid manner (uncertainty contributing to the success of deterrence) and, on the other hand, the dynamic events may always set off a process of escalation which may end in an unintended nuclear war.

Since the beginning of the 1970s there has been much talk of a decline of deterrence. The increase in accuracy and the miniaturization of warheads have lent credibility to a first strike against armed forces and the use of battlefield nuclear weapons. Technological progress also appears to be making protection against nuclear attack a future possibility. In 1983 President Reagan established the Strategic Defense Initiative ('Star Wars') although this has since been reduced in scope. Some have concluded that the United States is sliding from a strategy of deterrence into a war-fighting strategy. In fact, the change has occurred at the level of means rather than ends. The prospect of fighting a

nuclear war still remains as irrational as before since no defensive network will ever be able to ensure complete protection. Beyond the technological changes that have occurred and the doctrinal controversies between anti-city and anti-armed forces strategies there is still no substitute for deterrence. *See also* BEAUFRE; DISARMAMENT; KAHN; NUCLEAR WARFARE; STRATEGY.

H. COUTAU-BÉGARIE
DAVID WESTON

FURTHER READING
Bernard Brodie, *Strategy in the Missile Age* (Princeton, 1970); Colin S. Gray, *Strategic Studies and Public Policy* (Kentucky, 1982); Lawrence Freedman, *The Evolution of Nuclear Strategy* (London, 1981); Philip Green, *Deadly Logic* (Ohio, 1966); Morton Halperin, *Limited War in the Nuclear Age* (New York, 1963); Klaus Knorr, *On the Uses of Military Power in the Nuclear Age* (Princeton, 1966).

Dien Bien Phu (20 November 1953–7 May 1954) The war between the Viet Minh forces, under the political and military leadership of Ho Chi Minh and Vo Nguyen Giap, and the French colonial forces in Vietnam widened in 1953 when Giap's People's Liberation Army invaded northern Laos. The French responded by establishing air-supplied garrisons to block the route to the Laotian capital Vientiâne. With the onset of the rainy season the Viet Minh forces pulled back. This was interpreted as a victory by the French. The military commander, General Henri-Eugène Navarre, believed that any future Viet Minh invasion of Laos could be blocked by the use of air-supplied centres. He further believed that these centres could be used to entice the Viet Minh to attack where they could be defeated in open battle.

General Navarre ordered *Operation Castor* and on 20 November 1953 six French parachute battalions landed near the village of Dien Bien Phu about 220 miles west of Hanoi in the highlands near the Laotian border and on the Viet Minh supply route into Laos. By March 1954 the garrison had grown to some 15,000 men (French soldiers, Foreign Legion and Thai battalions) and a series of strong points had been established around the airstrip.

In the meantime General Giap, the commander of the Viet Minh forces, had been concentrating about 55,000 men, many trained and equipped by the Chinese army, around Dien Bien Phu as well as 200 artillery pieces, including anti-aircraft guns and rocket launchers (against the 28 French artillery pieces). The guns had been dragged through the jungle and were camouflaged from aerial observation.

The offensive against the garrison began in earnest on 13 March. Supply by air was made impossible first by the Viet Minh capturing the airstrip on 18 March and then by the anti-aircraft artillery which made airborne supply and reinforcement too dangerous. Under the command of Brigadier General de Castries, the French troops resisted for more than a month. They succumbed to a final assault on 7 May having neither rations nor ammunition left. The French lost 5,000 dead and 10,000 prisoners, while the Viet Minh casualties are estimated at 25,000 men. Dien Bien Phu saved Laos from further invasion by the Viet Minh but its effect on French morale was significant. The Asian revolutionary armies had shown themselves equal to Western powers in technical efficiency and, by exploiting their particular human and physical environment, they forced upon their opponents a style of warfare to which the French had difficulty in adapting.

On 20–21 July 1954, the French and the Viet Minh signed the Geneva Accords which established the independence of Laos, Cambodia and a divided Vietnam. In the North, Ho Chi Minh created the Democratic Republic of Vietnam. *See also* GIAP; VIETNAM.

A. CORVISIER
DAVID WESTON

FURTHER READING
Bernard Fall, *Hell in a Very Small Place: the siege of Dien Bien Phu* (New York, 1966); John Pimlott, *Vietnam: the decisive battles* (London, 1990); E. Bergot, *Les 170 jours de Dien Bien Phu* (Paris, 1979).

Dieppe (1942) The Dieppe raid of 19 August 1942 was the first attempt by the Western allies to strike a major direct military blow against the German forces on the Continent. The raid was designed to test the German defences, to assure the Soviet Union of the Western allies' commitment to an invasion of Europe and to force the Germans to concentrate more effort on the defence of France. The landing force at Dieppe was just over 6,000 strong, of which 5,100 were Canadians and the remainder British Commandos and American Rangers. The troops were to be landed at a number of places along the coast, and were to be supported by air strikes. In addition, tanks were to go ashore to provide mobile support for the troops. While the force was on its way to Dieppe, it encountered a German coastal patrol. Secrecy was compromised, and the German forces defending Dieppe were alerted. When the troops went ashore, losses were heavy, particularly among the Canadians. Nearly three-quarters of the Canadians were either killed, wounded or captured. The raid at Dieppe was a great failure but provided many useful lessons for the subsequent Allied invasions of Europe. The Dieppe raid remains a controversial topic for Canadians, since many believe that the planning for and execution of the raid were flawed and that Canadian troops were unnecessarily sacrificed. *See also* COMBINED OPERATIONS; EXPEDITIONS; NORMANDY; OVERLORD.

KEITH NEILSON

FURTHER READING
Terence Robertson, *The Shame and the Glory: Dieppe* (Toronto, 1962); T. Murray Hunter, *Canada at Dieppe* (Ottawa, 1982).

Disabled *See* INVALIDS

Disarmament Disarmament is a term denoting a concerted action whose aim is to limit, abolish or ban all armed forces maintained by states, or the manufacture or use of certain weapons; and it has been believed by some to be the best means of

Following the Hague Agreement of 1899 on procedures for the peaceful settlement of international disputes, a donation of US$1.5 million from Andrew Carnegie in 1903 enabled the Palace of Peace to be built in The Hague. It was opened in 1913 to house the Permanent Court of International Arbitration. It is now the seat of the International Court of Justice, an institution of the United Nations.
(Das Photo)

guaranteeing peace. Ever since ancient times, philosophers, theologians and politicians have tried to prohibit warfare. In the Middle Ages, through the influence of the Church and Christian thinking in general, success was achieved in establishing the Peace, or Truce, of God, in order to combat the scourge of private wars. The Church condemned new types of weapon. In 1139, the Lateran Council forbade the use of the crossbow, which was considered to be a treacherous weapon and too deadly. The development of modern types of state, the establishment of standing armies, and the excesses committed in the course of conflicts led certain thinkers to investigate ways of abolishing wars and of inaugurating a condition of permanent peace. France and the Swiss cantons signed a treaty of permanent peace in 1516. There was the 'grand design' of Henry IV of France. In 1693, William Penn's *Essay towards the Present and Future Peace of Europe* advocated the reduction of armaments and a plan for European federation. The abbé de Saint-Pierre, in his *Project for Establishing a Permanent Peace in Europe* (1713), proposed a 'Holy Alliance' on the basis of the territorial status quo. In 1787, France and England reached an agreement limiting their naval armaments.

In 1898, Nicholas II of Russia invited the states of Europe to send delegates to a congress which would study how to maintain overall peace and reduce excessive armaments. At the ensuing First Hague Peace Conference in 1899, twenty-six powers were represented. The conference adopted a resolution on the peaceful settlement of international differences and forbade both the use of poison gas and the firing of projectiles from airborne balloons. Forty-four countries attended the Second Hague Conference in 1907. It agreed thirteen conventions, of which seven concerned warfare at sea. In 1912, Great Britain tried, unsuccessfully, to conclude an agreement with Germany on the reciprocal limitation of naval armaments. After the First World War, 'in order to make possible the limiting of armaments by all nations', the Treaty of Versailles (1919) reduced the numerical strength of the German army, restricted the number and type of weapons it could employ, abolished conscription in Germany and set up inter-allied commissions of inspection. Similar measures were applied to the other defeated nations. In conformity with article 8 of its covenant, the League of Nations proposed that all armaments should be reduced to the minimum level compatible with national security. On 2 February 1924, the assembly of the League of Nations adopted the Geneva protocol, which forbade war in any circumstances, laid down a method of determining which party was the aggressor and made the use of sanctions obligatory. This protocol was never ratified.

The United States endeavoured to resolve the problem of naval armaments. The Washington Naval Treaty of 6 February 1922 limited the naval arms race between the United States, Japan, France, Great Britain and Italy. Another Geneva protocol of 17 June 1925, on ethical disarmament, banned the use of poison gases and bacteriological methods. On 27 August 1928, by the Paris Pact, the United States, France and a large number of other countries, renounced the employment of force as an instrument of national policy. The London Naval Treaty of 24 June 1930 allowed the United States, Great Britain and Japan to control the number of their warships. The conference on the limitation and reduction of armaments, which took place in Geneva from 1932 to 1934, was a failure. An Anglo-German naval agreement, signed on 18 June 1935, fixed the permitted ratios between the two navies. The London Naval Treaty of 25 March 1936

restricted the maximum tonnage of warships and the maximum calibre of their guns. However, in 1933, Germany and Japan had left the League of Nations and, from that date onwards, were preparing themselves for war.

During the Second World War, the Atlantic Charter, signed on 14 August 1941, made provision for the disarming of certain countries which had proved a menace to international peace. The appearance of nuclear weapons, and their employment against Japan in 1945, encouraged the resumption of negotiations on disarmament in the postwar period. The United Nations Organization (UNO), unlike the League of Nations, did not seek a general disarmament but, under article 26 of its charter, asked countries to contribute towards peace 'by directing only a minimum of the world's human and economic resources to armaments'. The aim of the negotiations was to remove the threat of the use of the weapons of mass destruction. From 1946 to 1950, these discussions took place within the Atomic Energy Committee and the Conventional Weapons Committee. A single Disarmament Committee was established in 1952, on which were represented the members of the Security Council. The purpose of this committee was to promote a general and complete disarmament under strict and effective international supervision. The rivalries of the two superpowers and the absence of supervision prevented this ambitious project from coming to fruition.

By the treaty of 1 December 1959, the United States and the USSR succeeded in reaching agreement on demilitarizing Antarctica. In the Soviet–American declaration of 20 September 1961, it was stated that the two superpowers had adopted a common attitude and were studying methods of disarmament. After the Cuban Crisis (1962), the United States directed its attention towards arms inspection, limitation and control as ways of reducing the risk of nuclear war. The Moscow Treaty of 5 August 1963 prohibited nuclear tests within the Earth's atmosphere, in space and under water. The treaty on the military uses of space of 27

197

January 1967 had laid down that the moon and other celestial bodies would not be militarized, as well as barred the sending of nuclear weapons into orbit around the Earth. The Treaty of Tlatelolco, 14 February 1967, created a non-nuclear zone in Latin America. The Treaty on the Non-Proliferation of Nuclear Weapons was initialled on 1 July 1968. A treaty of 11 February 1971 forbade the placing of nuclear weapons on the sea bed. On 30 September 1971, the United States and the USSR signed an agreement which aimed to reduce the risk of a war being started by accident. The convention of 10 April 1972 prohibited the manufacture and stocking of biological weapons. The Moscow agreement of 26 May 1972, known as SALT 1 (Strategic Arms Limitation Talks), restricted the deployment of anti-missile defences and fixed quantitative ceilings for strategic missiles. On 3 July 1974, in Moscow, the United States and the USSR signed agreements on the limitation of anti-ballistic missiles (ABMs) and on the abolition of all underground tests on nuclear weapons above 150 kilotons. The Vladivostok agreement of 24 November 1974 fixed the number of offensive weapons of both parties at 2,400 nuclear delivery vehicles.

An extraordinary session of the UNO in 1978 was devoted to disarmament. On 18 June 1979, the United States and the USSR signed the SALT 2 Treaty in Vienna, which fixed the number of nuclear warheads at 2,250 but the US Congress refused to ratify the agreement. On 18 November 1981, President Ronald Reagan proposed the abandonment of the SALT negotiations to enable fresh Strategic Arms Reduction Talks (START) with the Soviet Union to commence, the aim of these being to reduce strategic armaments. The talks began in Geneva on 29 June 1982 but were suspended in December 1983. Though limited results have been achieved by the two superpowers in the sphere of nuclear weapons, the discussions on the reduction of conventional weapons have failed completely. The conference which opened in Vienna on 30 October 1973, to study ways and means of securing a mutual and bal-

anced force reduction (MBFR), made little progress. The Conference on Security and Co-operation in Europe (CSCE), whose final agreement was signed at Helsinki on 1 August 1975, and which was followed by those in Belgrade (1977–8) and in Madrid (1980–2), studied the military aspects of European security and proposed measures for achieving mutual trust and disarmament. A new Disarmament Committee, with forty members, has been in session in Geneva since January 1979.

J. NOUZILLE

By the time that the Soviet Union ceased to exist at the end of 1991, an imposing body of theory and practice relating to disarmament was in existence. Theoretically, disarmament was distinguished from arms control. Disarmament was taken to involve the reduction or complete elimination of weapons whereas arms control meant the implementation of agreed levels of armament – in principle, an arms control agreement could permit *increases* of weaponry in the interests of stability. Theory suggested that both types of agreement were easier to negotiate between two powers than among many. The status and future of the numerous agreements between the superpowers was therefore a matter of grave uncertainty as the Soviet Union dissolved into numerous successor states, some of them more suspicious of each other than of their former opponent and negotiating partner in Washington.

BARRIE PASKINS

See also DETERRENCE; LAWS OF WAR; NUCLEAR WARFARE; WEAPONS.

FURTHER READING
F. H. Hinsley, *Power and the Pursuit of Peace* (Cambridge, 1963); Nicholas A. Sims, *Approaches to Disarmament: an introductory analysis* (London, 1979); Hedley Bull, *The Control of the Arms Race: disarmament and arms control in the missile age* (London, 1961); *Hawks, Doves and Owls: an agenda for avoiding nuclear war*, eds Graham T. Allison, Albert Carnesale and Joseph S. Nye, Jr (New York, 1985); *The Arms Race in an Era of Negotiations*, ed. David Carlton and Carlo Schaerf (Basingstoke, 1990); Christopher Driver, *The Disarmers: a study in protest* (London, 1964).

Discipline According to Maurice de Saxe, discipline is the 'soul of the entire military enterprise. If it were not established with wisdom and maintained with unswerving firmness, you could not depend upon having soldiers: regiments and armies would be nothing more than a base armed rabble, more dangerous to the State than its enemies themselves.' The greater the severity, the greater the achievements, but severity must be tempered by kindness. Napoleon thought that discipline was the first quality of the soldier, valour being only the second. Lyautey added that 'a less trained troop that is under control is better than a better trained troop that is less well-controlled.' In the French army regulations, discipline is described as the source of an army's strength.

Discipline is often severe and sometimes poorly understood and bitterly resented by subordinates. The degree of severity is justified by the objective. The armies that win battles are disciplined whereas the indiscipline of leaders and soldiers is to blame for many a defeat. Discipline must not however be based solely on a system of penalties. The leader must also know how to explain his actions to his men to make them understand and encourage them to emulation, particularly by way of rewards. The best discipline is that which is accepted by subordinates who respect and have confidence in their leaders. It has to be conceived differently depending upon whether one is dealing with a mercenary army, which has few ties to its employer except pay, or an army of citizen-soldiers who are defending their country and are sustained by patriotic sentiments. However, even in armies of citizen-soldiers, discipline may be very rigorous. Despite its apparent ferocity, military discipline is usually a sharper version of the current criminal code of civilian justice in a given society.

Among the Greeks, acts of indiscipline were punished by fines, corporal punishment, death and such humiliations as being forbidden to marry or attend civil or religious ceremonies. Discipline was even stricter in the Roman army. The legionary swore an oath that he would 'follow the leaders under whom he was called to fight against any enemy, that he would not abandon the standard, and that he would commit no action that was against the law.' Minor offences were punished by beatings with a rod; a soldier who fell asleep on sentry duty was condemned to death by stoning. When a unit showed weakness in battle, it was decimated. There were also humiliating penalties: legionaries could have their weapons taken away and cavalrymen could be deprived of their horses. Good soldiers did, however, receive many rewards.

Discipline was often indifferent among the Gauls and in the army of the Merovingian kings, in which there were many rebellions. In his capitularies, Charlemagne decreed various measures for maintaining discipline. There was capital punishment for desertion where a war was being fought against an invader and a fine of 60 gold *sous* (*heriban*) when it occurred during an expedition on to foreign soil. Theft and pillage in friendly countries were punished. The man who showed cowardice in battle was declared to be without honour and his oath could not be received in a court of law. In the feudal armies, a subordinate (vassal) was bound to his chief by an oath and the lack of cohesion among the troops and discipline in battle was to blame for a great many defeats.

In the Mongol armies, there was iron discipline. In Timur Lenk's army, individual pillage was punished by death and minor offences by fines amounting to one tenth of the offending soldier's pay. Among the janissaries, desertion, cowardice and abandoning one's post were also punishable by death. For theft from a comrade or lack of diligence in drilling the soldier received 50 strokes of the rod; for brawling, he got 25, and for returning to barracks after curfew, 12. The flogging was taken lying face down and the guilty man had to kiss the hand of the presiding officer or bow to him.

Discipline was far from established in Western armies at the time of the Renaissance and it was a cause of defeat, said La Noue. He added that discipline should be established with rods since they gave weight to words, but he also argued that this was not enough, since it was necessary to appeal

199

to 'goodwill rather than constraint'. A great number of ordonnances were issued regarding the maintenance of discipline but their repetition proves they had little effect. Punishments were none the less severe: the blasphemer was condemned to sit astride a cannon and, if he repeated the offence, to have his tongue pierced. Abandoning one's post or refusing to manoeuvre an artillery piece meant banishment, and theft, rape, flight, intelligence with the enemy and mutiny were punished by death. Noble officers could be stripped of their noble titles and banished. The peasants suffered a great deal at the hands of the soldiery, in spite of the severest punishments. Hanging and breaking on the wheel were laid down for those soldiers who took horses from the plough or pillaged and ransomed the inhabitants. Those who cut down vines or fruit trees had to pay a fine or receive corporal punishment.

Wrongdoing by soldiery was again particularly rife during the Thirty Years' War, yet there were many ordonnances which sought to stamp it out. That of 5 January 1627 forbade soldiers to cut the wheat or interrupt the harvest and another of January 1629 ordered them not to 'pilfer' in the villages. Any soldier guilty of theft or violence was to be punished by the strappado and, for cases of theft of linen or furniture, by hanging. Officers were made responsible for theft carried out by their men: they could be fined for a first offence and cashiered if it was repeated. Richelieu had officers who were guilty of pillage, cowardice or weakness executed. Under Louvois's ministry, discipline made important strides forward. Between 1684 and 1716, desertion was no longer punished by death but by the galleys. Other offences were severely punished: a soldier who struck an officer was sentenced to the galleys for life and to the death penalty if the act was committed while on duty.

In the other European armies, efforts were also made to improve the discipline of the troops. In the Swedish army, which had a national system of recruitment, Gustavus Adolphus abolished the use of the whip and degrading forms of punishment, though discipline remained strict. Gambling, blasphemy and bad language were forbidden and violence against allies was harshly dealt with. In Wallenstein's army, which practised pillage in enemy territory and was followed by a swarm of prostitutes, discipline on duty was draconian: the least failing was punishable by death, and mutilations and torture were carried out frequently. Cromwell also published a severe disciplinary code: for minor offences corporal punishment was administered, while abandoning one's post, flight, the loss of one's weapons, the wasting of powder, drunkenness and blasphemy incurred the death penalty. In Peter the Great's army, discipline was equally rigorous – men found guilty received between 200 and 300 strokes of the knout and sometimes died of their floggings. Officers found guilty of breach of trust, indiscipline or cowardice were punished by fortress arrest, exile to Siberia or death.

In the eighteenth century, discipline in European armies made great advances, with most generals outlawing pillage. Discipline was particularly severe in the Prussian army. It was hardly less so in the French army, which took its lead from Frederick II's methods, but the death penalty for desertion was abolished on 12 December 1775 and replaced by a sentence of eight years in the galleys and then, later, by a lengthening of a soldier's period of service and a number of strokes of the rod. Theft, acts of violence against a comrade or a superior were punishable by death. In cases of collective crimes, this penalty was applied to one soldier in three after the drawing of lots. For less serious offences, prison sentences or corporal punishment were meted out. The bastinado (beating on the soles of the feet) was particularly favoured in German regiments, though straps had been abandoned in favour of rifle cleaning-rods. Saint Germain replaced the various forms of corporal punishment by beating with the flat of the sabre which was already in use in the cavalry and the Prussian army. This innovation was not well received by the soldiers and was even resented by some of the officers who thought it degrading and unsuited to the mentality of the French soldier. It was abolished on 12 July 1789 and the other forms of corporal punishment followed on 20 October 1790. These did however continue in the British army until 1881. Other forms of punishment included sentry duty outside the guardroom, confinement to quarters, to the barrack-room or to the guardroom where the soldier was put on bread and water, being relegated to last in the company, dishonourable discharge and reduction to the ranks for non-commissioned officers. Officers could be punished by arrest and imprisonment. Although the ordonnance of 25 March 1778 made clear that the intention of the king was to see established 'a gradual . . . mild and paternal subordination . . . based on fairness and firmness' and that 'the soldiers should find their superiors to be beneficent guides', discipline was sometimes excessive in certain regiments and at the root of many cases of desertion. In this period, however, the population no longer had to suffer the ravages of the old undisciplined soldiery and the attitude of Rochambeau's army in America, for example, won it general praise.

This exemplary standard of discipline was imperilled in the early years of the French Revolution, though chiefly for political reasons. There were many cases of insubordination and even mutinies. The new code promulgated on 19 October 1791 was more flexible in the penalties it prescribed, as were the regulations of 24 June 1792, which laid down that 'a gradual subordination, which, though losing nothing of its force, should be gentle and paternal' should be established. However, the government 'desire[d] that the infantry should always show passive obedience towards their superiors and that all orders should be carried out literally and without delay', though these orders had to be within the law. Serious offences were punishable by death, others by reprimand, by privation of liberty – or of drink in the case of drunkards. On marches, soldiers receiving punishment were made to hold their rifle-butts in the air. Discipline, which had been destroyed at the beginning of the Revolution, was subsequently re-established with firmness by the 'representatives on mis-sion'. There were no problems enforcing it during the Napoleonic Wars, when it was solid in battle but relatively relaxed in other circumstances. The good relations which generally existed between officers and soldiers assisted the operation of discipline.

The regulations of 3 May 1818 made few modifications to those of 24 June 1792. Officers became 'benevolent' rather than 'beneficent' guides, and there was now no mention of orders having to be within the law, but 'the authority which issues them is responsible for them and protest against them may be registered by the soldiers who have obeyed them'. Under the Second Empire, discipline became strict and finicky, which is typical of a standing army in peacetime. There were a great number of appeals against judgements. Discipline under the Third Republic was similarly rigorous and exaggeratedly meticulous. The slightest offence was penalized and many themes found in popular songs of the period have become legendary. This harsh discipline was, however, relatively well accepted by the conscripts, whose patriotism had been fired and who had been indoctrinated with a desire for revenge against Germany. A certain advance can be seen after the publication of Lyautey's article on the social role of the officer. This advocated that discipline should be based on the special aptitude of the French for sociability. The French army bore the reverses of 1914 well and few serious lapses of discipline were to be seen until the mutinies of 1917. These can be explained by the length and harshness of the battles and some misjudgements on the part of the officers. The lapses of discipline in the German army – and particularly in the Russian – were equally serious. The good discipline which prevailed in the French army in this war can be explained by the understanding which existed between soldiers, NCOs and officers.

The years after 1919 saw an increase in anti-militarism, but its containment proved possible. The enforcement of discipline continued to be excessively formalistic: the slightest offences were penalized and there was an unnecessarily high number of punishments. This situation came about because every officer, right down to the lowest-ranking NCO, could inflict punishments, the scale of these varying with the rank of the officer who also had the option of requesting a higher degree of punishment from officers of senior rank when the offence was serious. The years since 1945 have seen a decline in patriotic sentiments and traditional values. Anti-militarism and conscientious objection have made considerable headway. In some Scandinavian countries and in Germany, the resolve even to resist an invader cannot be relied upon. Among the old imperialist powers, the wars fought to maintain colonialism have produced problems of conscience for a substantial number of conscripts and some political parties have even openly defended the native nationalists in their revolt against the colonial power. The object of military discipline has therefore become, as Ardant du Picq put it, to make people fight even though in many cases they do so in spite of themselves. Moreover, discipline was shaken to its very foundations in some countries by the introduction of systems of representatives negotiating with or taking a stance against their officers, in the form of legal trade unions and soldiers' representatives or illegal soldiers' committees.

In the United States, the blow which General Patton struck against a soldier who claimed to be suffering from a nervous disorder gave rise to a thorough going review of traditional military discipline (Doolittle Commission). The disciplinary powers of the unit commanders were abolished and officers and NCOs could only command their troops by obtaining the freely given consent of the soldiers in their charge. During the Korean War, there were many lapses of discipline, except among the Marines who were a part of the regular army and had kept the old forms of discipline: one third of prisoners collaborated with the enemy and 13 per cent took part in propaganda actions against their own country. It became clear at that point that it was no longer sufficient to rely on the patriotism of the fighting men and the Code of the Soldier published in 1955 showed a marked stiffening of discipline. This did, however, receive a further buffeting during the Vietnam War. The American garrison at Pacer contested the validity of orders it received on the grounds that they were unconstitutional. The crew of the aircraft carrier *Coral Sea* petitioned Congress not to send the vessel back to Vietnam. This was, however, not an entirely new phenomenon. Even at the time of the French Revolution, the crews of ships sent to the West Indies forced their commanding officers to sail back to France, while the troops on board refused to obey their officers and to restore order among protesters whose cause they themselves espoused. Naval mutinies have indeed been relatively frequent throughout history, one fairly recent example being the revolt of the French sailors in the Black Sea squadron after the 1914–18 war.

As a reaction against the militaristic values of the Hitler regime, forms of discipline were profoundly transformed in West Germany. In 1964, a new internal regime (*Innere Führung*) was adopted within the *Bundeswehr*. The formalistic aspects of military life were abolished: insignia disappeared, the extent of military ceremonial and outward shows of respect was reduced and soldiers wore civilian dress when off duty. The object of these measures was to make the German soldier just another civil servant. The power to give orders was strictly regulated and that of initiating proceedings began only at the rank of company commander, though he also had to consult the soldiers' representative and any infringement of the code, however minor, was handed over to be dealt with by civilian tribunals. Moreover, conscripts had avenues open to them to protest against abuses of authority. The soldier could refuse to obey orders which infringed the law and the right to conscientious objection was recognized. Systematic recourse to civil tribunals did, however, lead to an increase in legal formalities and the result was an extremely slow judicial process. Moreover, the sentences inflicted were heavier than those which the military authorities would have pronounced. These latter have subsequently regained the power to impose punishment, but the German army is one of the least outwardly militaristic of forces and its disciplinary system is extremely flexible.

French disciplinary regulations have been entirely recast in order to take into account the development of society. This recasting had to balance the rise in the intellectual level of conscripts with a widespread scepticism about the need for military obligations. The new regulations, published in 1966, reduced the number of situations in which soldiers are required to salute, relaxed the arrangements for leaving barracks, laid down more flexible conditions regarding the wearing of civilian dress and limited the right to inflict punishment to the corps commander, the subordinate ranks being able only to request penalties. This document stated clearly the right not to obey orders where they are against the law or contrary to the customs of war. What struck observers most at the time, however, was the establishment of a scale of punishments, which was intended to prevent arbitrariness in the level of penalties and which covered all possible offences. It did, however, appear that this scale was in fact rather harsher than the one actually being applied at the time and, moreover, the idea was far from being a novel one, since similar tables existed towards the end of the *ancien régime*. Thus shirking a fatigue duty is now punishable by six spells of guard duty, whereas 200 years ago a soldier would receive six strokes with the flat of the sabre for the same offence. The new list contains the following punishments: reprimand, the guard-room, open and close arrest. These two forms of arrest have replaced the old guard-house and prison, but the distinction is largely a terminological one, the substance of the punishment remaining very similar. Several minor modifications have been made to these new regulations. The wearing of civilian dress when off-duty has become the norm. Conscientious objectors are now recognized within the regulations and military tribunals have been abolished. *See also* ETHOS; LAW, MILITARY; RECRUITMENT.

G. BODINIER

FURTHER READING
Scott Claver, *Under the Lash. A history of*

corporal punishment in the British armed forces (London, 1954); C. Duffy, *The Army of Frederick the Great* (London, 1974); E. M. Spiers, *The Army and Society, 1815–1914* (London, 1980); André Corvisier, *L'Armée française de la fin du XVIIᵉ siècle au ministère de Choiseul: le soldat* (Paris, 1964).

Disembarkation *See* COMBINED OPERATIONS

Divisions *See* TACTICAL ORGANIZATION

Dockyards Among all the naval dockyards of Antiquity, such as Rhodes, Alexandria, Syracuse, Carthage, Misenum or Ravenna, the best known is that of Zea in the Piraeus. In the middle of the fifth century BC, it had 200 slips capable of sheltering the Athenian triremes during the winter as well as adjacent stores for their tackle and oars.

During the Middle Ages, a series of dockyards provided logistical support for Byzantine, Muslim and Italian fleets. The most celebrated by contemporaries, and currently the best preserved, was the Venetian Arsenal. Begun in 1104 and subsequently enlarged on several occasions, by the fifteenth century it employed a labour force of more than 4,000. It was one of the largest industrial complexes of the age, encompassing the three essentials of a naval base – construction, repair and a depot for stores and weapons. Northern countries also began to acquire dockyards although none attained the size of the Arsenal at Venice. Philip Augustus (1180–1223) and Charles V (1364–80) started to build up the naval strength of France, and a beginning was made with the 'Clos des Galées' near Rouen. As early as the thirteenth century, England possessed 'housings for the king's galleys' at Rye and Winchelsea, but Woolwich and Portsmouth, the first real English dockyards, only came into being at the beginning of the sixteenth century. The remainder of the sixteenth century and the seventeenth saw the development of further establishments at Chatham, Sheerness and Plymouth. These ensured that the Royal Navy had bases on the North Sea coast, in the English Channel and at the gateway to the Atlantic. In Spain, El Ferrol

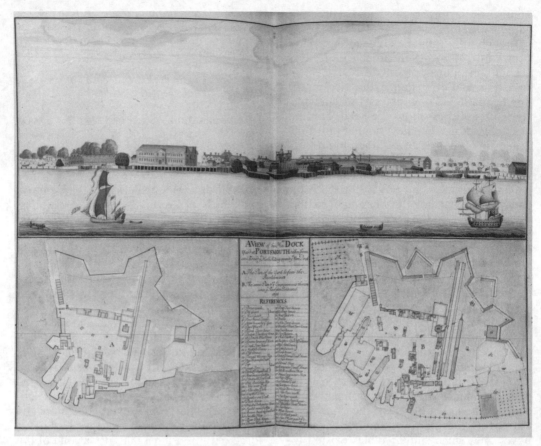

Portsmouth was the principal English naval dockyard after 1660. Its array of wet and dry docks, manufactories and storehouses made it the largest industrial complex in England until the nineteenth century.
(The British Library)

(North Atlantic), Cartagena (Mediterranean) and Cadiz (South Atlantic) supported the fleet.

From the middle of the seventeenth century, following unsuccessful attempts to set up bases at Le Havre and Brouage, the distribution of French dockyards assumed its final form. The principal establishments were at Brest (Atlantic and the English Channel), Rochefort (Atlantic) and Toulon (Mediterranean) for the deep water squadrons, and Marseilles for the galley fleet. The system was imperfect. Despite its admirable strategic position, shipping was frequently locked inside Brest because of the prevailing westerly winds while the neighbouring countryside could not provide sufficient foodstuffs and raw materials.

Although Rochefort benefited from a rich hinterland and a safe roadstead protected from the open sea by a chain of islands (Ré, Oléron and Aix), the dockyard was situated on an unhealthy site 15 miles from the sea. Vessels had to be hauled along the Charente, which was shallow and winding, with the fitting-out process still incomplete; the mounting of guns and the taking on board of provisions could only be accomplished in the roads. Except for a few periods of full activity, e.g. during the American War of Independence, Rochefort mainly served as a subsidiary partner to Brest. On the other hand, Toulon dockyard, which was built in 1682 in accordance with a logical plan, proved extremely satisfactory by reason of the 'ease of servicing' which it provided.

There was, however, one serious difficulty. The Mediterranean at Toulon has a minimal tide; it was not until 1778 that the first graving dock was installed. Besides these three major bases, the royal fleet could use the dockyard at Lorient after 1769 following the winding-up of the French East India Company. In general, the whole system gave a sensible distribution of services for the Mediterranean and the Atlantic but, unlike the Royal Navy, the French fleet lacked any substantial installation on the Channel coast. Louis XVI had a plan for closing this gap with an establishment at Cherbourg but the fortification work was not completed; a naval dockyard did not start operations at Cherbourg until 1853.

By 1750, the dockyard had become one of the largest industrial complexes in the era before the Industrial Revolution – dry docks, slipways, fitting-out berths, warehouses, workshops, rope-walks, mast-ponds, forges, offices, sawpits, cooperage, victualling stores and sheds. The rope-making shop was an early example of 'line' manufacture, starting with the raw hemp at one end and proceeding via the yarn stage to the finished rope. To seventeenth-century eyes, it was a building that illustrated an ideal co-ordination of form and function.

In the second half of the nineteenth century, dockyards began to undergo major changes arising from the revolution in naval warfare caused by the steam-powered warship armed with torpedoes and rifled guns firing explosive shells. Dockyards progressively abandoned construction in wood in favour of iron and steel. The most technically advanced became centres for the building of hulls and for the installation of the main and auxiliary engines, turrets and guns. The machinery was usually manufactured at inland sites and transported to the dockyards by rail. Both for building and for repairing damage suffered in battle, the dockyards were equipped with various forms of graving and dry dock capable of accommodating the largest vessels.

At the same time, because of the increase in the size and number of colonial territories possessed by European powers, the world map of dockyards underwent significant modifications. From 1860, the United States provided herself with installations at Portsmouth (New Hampshire), Boston, Brooklyn (New York), Philadelphia, Charleston, San Francisco, San Diego, Bremerton (Puget Sound) and, later, Pearl Harbor. Great Britain developed a world-wide network – Gibraltar, Malta, Aden, Singapore, Simonstown (the Cape), Trincomalee (Ceylon), Hong Kong, Sydney, Auckland, Halifax (Canada) and Esquimalt (Canada). Both in 1914 and 1939, the position of France was less favourable. Her navy had only one full-sized dockyard overseas at Bizerta and a secondary establishment at Saigon. On the eve of the Second World War, the base at Mers-el-Kebir had scarcely been started and nothing existed at Dakar.

At the beginning of the twentieth century, the principal Russian bases were at Kronstadt, Sebastopol and Vladivostok. The Italian navy relied mainly on La Spezia and Taranto. The Germans built facilities at Kiel and Wilhelmshafen. The appearance of a German fleet obliged the British to recast the geographical layout of their own system. Although the Channel dockyards were not abandoned, they were reduced in importance in favour of the North Sea bases – Harwich, Rosyth and Scapa Flow, the latter being raised to the status of a dockyard in 1940.

A fresh geographical distribution of dockyards can be an occasion for allocating specialized functions. Owing to the progressive abandonment of Rochefort in the first half of the twentieth century, France retained only four dockyards: Cherbourg concentrated on the construction of submarines, capital ships were built at Brest, Lorient built smaller vessels, while Toulon maintained the Mediterranean fleet. Despite all these changes, naval dockyards remain of fundamental importance whether for construction, maintenance or supply. *See also* ADMINISTRATION, NAVAL; ARSENALS; BASES, NAVAL; COLBERT; NAVAL STORES; NAVAL WARFARE; NAVIES; ORDNANCE.

M. ACERRA
P. MASSON

205

FURTHER READING
Daniel Baugh, *British Naval Administration in the Age of Walpole* (Princeton, 1965); Jonathan Coad, *Historic Architecture of the Royal Navy* (London, 1983); Jonathan Coad, *The Royal Dockyards, 1690–1850* (Aldershot, 1989); Roger A. Morriss, *The Royal Dockyards during the Revolutionary and Napoleonic Wars* (Leicester, 1983); 'Rochefort et la mer. Technique et politique maritimes aux XVIIᵉ et XVIIIᵉ siècles', *Publications de l'Université d'été Saintlonge-Québec* (Jonzac, 1985).

Dönitz, Karl (1891–1980) Dönitz joined the Imperial German Navy in 1910 and served in the *Breslau* in the Mediterranean and the Black Sea until 1916. He was then appointed to submarines and rose to command UB–68 but was captured during an attack on a convoy in 1918. He continued in the navy after the war serving in a variety of posts before assuming in 1935 the task of reconstituting the German submarine fleet. Although Raeder, the commander-in-chief of the *Kriegsmarine*, considered that large surface ships were still important, Dönitz was convinced that if they acted in groups, on the surface and under cover of darkness, submarines would be the most potent naval weapon in a war against Britain. The early stages of the Second World War proved him to be correct and these 'wolf pack' tactics enabled the U-boats to score great successes in the Atlantic. In January 1943, following the action in Barents Sea, Dönitz succeeded Raeder as commander-in-chief.

The promotion occurred when fortunes were changing in the Battle of the Atlantic as the Allies poured enormous resources into the contest. Dönitz continued the campaign with the aim of tying down considerable enemy air and sea forces while awaiting the introduction of high performance U-boats, though these did not come into service until the very end of the war. On 10 May 1945, Dönitz succeeded Hitler. The Grand-Admiral delayed the final surrender to enable hundreds of thousands of Germans to escape to the West. He thus remained at the head of the government in Flensburg until 23 May. At Nuremberg he was found guilty and sentenced to ten years' imprisonment, not for having conducted an unrestricted submarine campaign, but because he had prepared for a war of aggression. He was released in 1956. Without having fully subscribed to National Socialist doctrines, Dönitz had always shown great admiration for the Führer on account of his willpower and decisiveness. *See also* ATLANTIC, BATTLE OF THE; COMMERCE-RAIDING; CONVOYS; NAVAL WARFARE; NAVIES; RAEDER.

P. MASSON

FURTHER READING
K. Dönitz, *Zehn Jahre und Zwanzig Tage* (Bonn, 1958), English translation as *Memoirs: ten years and twenty days* (London, 1958); K. Dönitz, *Mein Wechselvolles Leben* (Göttingen, 1968).

Doria *See* ANDREA DORIA

Dorylaeum (Turkish: Eske Shehr), Battle of (1 July 1097) The armies of the First Crusade (1096–9) on their long march towards Jerusalem met the Turks in battle for the first time at Dorylaeum. The Crusaders' leading army was thrown into confusion by this first experience of an unfamiliar style of warfare, especially the elusiveness, mobility and archery of the Turkish cavalry. Only the arrival of a second Crusader army, taking the Turks by surprise, turned muddle into victory. But two points were significant about this battle. First, it opened up the road to Antioch and the Holy Land. Second, the leaders of the Crusade, above all the Norman, Bohemund – one of the finest generals of the age – learned from their mistakes at Dorylaeum. They worked out tactical counter-measures which, together with their possession of heavy armour, enabled them to face the Turks with more confidence. This was the military development which made the Crusades possible. *See also* HOLY WAR.

JOHN CHILDS

FURTHER READING
R. C. Smail, *Crusading Warfare, 1097–1193* (Cambridge, 1956); Steven Runciman, *A History of the Crusades* (3 vols, Cambridge, 1951–5).

Douhet, Giulio (1869–1930) Douhet graduated at the top of his class from the

Turin Military Academy, served in the artillery and subsequently commanded the first Italian aviation unit, the so-called Aeronautical Battalion, in the Great War. Highly critical of the Italian high command, which he charged with gross incompetence, Douhet was court-martialled and imprisoned, but subsequent investigations of the performance of the Italian army, particularly at Caporetto in 1917, confirmed what he had said, and he was appointed head of the Italian air service.

Douhet left the military in 1921, and wrote several works on air power, the most famous and influential of which was *Il dominio dell'aria* (1921), published in English as *The Command of the Air* in 1942. His main thesis was that the power of the defence in the land battle had grown to the point where armies could no longer win decisive victories; accordingly, it was up to the air force, flying over frontiers and bombing the enemy's vital resources, to win the next war. Tracing Douhet's direct influence is impossible, although it is known that the US Army Air Corps had a translation of *Il dominio dell'aria* in the mid-1920s. At the least, he was the first to set down – and set down powerfully – the ideas he shared with other air power advocates in the early 1920s. *See also* AVIATION; MITCHELL; TRENCHARD.

P. FACON
STEPHEN J. HARRIS

FURTHER READING
Giulio Douhet, *The Command of the Air* (London, 1942); Edward Warner, 'Douhet, Mitchell, Seversky: theorists of air warfare', in *Makers of Modern Strategy: military thought from Machiavelli to Hitler*, ed. E. M. Earle (Princeton, 1941); D. McIsaac, 'Voices from the Central Blue: the air power theorists', in *Makers of Modern Strategy: from Machiavelli to the nuclear age*, ed. P. Paret (Princeton, 1986).

Dragomirov, Mikhail Ivanovich (1830–1905) Dragomirov was the dominant figure in Russian tactical thought between the Crimean War and the First World War. He entered the Semionvski Guards in 1849, and graduated from the general staff academy in 1856. From 1863 to 1869 he was professor of tactics at the Nicholas Academy of the General Staff,

and in 1878 he returned to the Academy as its head. He left the Academy in 1889 to command the Kiev military district, whose chief of staff he had been in 1869–73. Dragomirov's tactical ideas were an amalgam of the Suvorov tradition and of his own observations while attached to the Sardinian army in the war of 1859. He argued that soldiers should be educated and encouraged rather than bullied and repressed. But he did so because he felt that morale was the key to battlefield performance. His service in the war against Turkey in 1877–8 did not lead him to a fuller recognition of the impact of new technology. In addition to his standard texts on tactics (1864 and 1879), he wrote histories of the wars of 1859 and 1866, and was the key figure in official works on training and field operations. *See also* PLEVNA; RUSSIA/USSR; SOLFERINO; SUVOROV.

HEW STRACHAN

FURTHER READING
Modern Encyclopaedia of Russian and Soviet History, ed. Joseph L. Wieczynski (Gulf Breeze, Fl., 1979), x.

Dragoons Dragoons were mounted infantrymen who moved on horseback but fought on foot. This type of soldier dates from ancient times. The *dimachai* (literally, 'two-knife men') in Alexander the Great's army fought on horseback or on foot. The Alamanni cavalry carried a lightly armed infantryman behind each rider who dismounted to fight. Heavy feudal cavalry often fought dismounted. In 1537, Strozzi had under his command mounted arquebusiers who operated as infantrymen. Other specialists, such as the *argoulets*, fulfilled similar functions – harassing the enemy, escorting convoys, occupying posts and covering the rear and head of columns. Despite this pedigree, the dragoon is supposed to have been invented by the Marshal de Cossé-Brissac in 1554. The name 'dragoon' appears at the beginning of the seventeenth century and is thought to have derived either from the dragon depicted on their standards or from their dragon-like 'fire-breathing' muskets.

The true creator of the corps of dragoons

was Gustavus Adolphus of Sweden whose methods were imitated by many European countries during the seventeenth century. The dragoon was armed with a musket, a sabre and a hatchet. He wore neither helmet nor armour and rode a small, inexpensive horse, or 'nag'; he was a cheap form of cavalry. In France, 15 companies of dragoons were combined in 1635 to form 6 regiments. They fought on horseback and on foot and the name 'dragoon' passed into official usage in 1668. By 1690, there were 43 dragoon regiments in the French army. A single regiment of 1,000 dragoons was included in the establishment of the New Model Army in 1645. The Russian army of Peter the Great possessed 24 dragoon regiments by 1710 and Frederick the Great had 12. However, by 1700 the dragoon had simply become a medium cavalryman; he no longer fought on foot but operated both on and off the battlefield as a general-purpose cavalrymen. The name 'dragoon' was retained in the majority of European armies but it no longer specified a particular function.

However, during the First World War, British cavalry reverted to a dragoon-style training: horses were used for mobility but the men fought dismounted with rifles and machine-guns. This proved particularly efficacious during Allenby's campaigns in Palestine in 1918. European armies converted their dragoon and cavalry formations into mechanized and armoured regiments in the interwar period. The Second World War saw a re-emergence of the concept of the dragoon. Armoured divisions transported their infantry contingents in armoured carriers and, by 1944, the British and Americans had motorized all their infantry divisions so that the foot soldiers once again 'rode' into battle but fought dismounted. This method of infantry fighting has been greatly extended since 1945, especially with the introduction of helicopters. The majority of modern infantry have the capacity to operate as air-transported or motorized dragoons. *See also* AIRBORNE TROOPS; CAVALRY; HUSSARS; INFANTRY.

G. BODINIER
JOHN CHILDS

FURTHER READING
G. C. H. V. Paget, Marquess of Anglesey, *A History of British Cavalry, 1816–1919* (5 vols, London, 1973–85); G. T. Denison, *A History of Cavalry from the Earliest Times* (London, 1877, 2nd edn 1913).

Drake, Sir Francis (1543–96) Drake began his career at sea in expeditions to West Africa for slaves and to the West Indies for booty; he was present at San Juan de Ulúa (1567) when Sir John Hawkins's (1532–95) expedition came to grief. His first command was a similar venture in 1572–3, destroying Nombre de Dios and intercepting a mule convoy on the Panamanian isthmus. Between 1577 and 1580, he made the first English circumnavigation of the globe (the second after Magellan's), sailing via Cape Horn, along the Pacific coast of South America pillaging and capturing valuable prizes, and then north to California and possibly beyond, before returning across the Pacific. The voyage met with the approval of Queen Elizabeth I, who had made a financial investment, and Drake was knighted in 1581. In 1585–6, another expedition to the West Indies enjoyed only a limited success but, in the following year, he led a daring attack on Cadiz which delayed the sailing of the Spanish Armada for twelve months. When that Armada did sail for England in 1588, Drake was second-in-command of the English fleet and played a prominent part in the fighting. Drake's counter-attack on Lisbon in 1589 failed because of a separation of the land and the sea forces and a series of disagreements. Drake's final great campaign to the West Indies (1595–6) was delayed and unsuccessful, the Spanish receiving prior warning. He died on the return voyage.

Although preceding the days of organized navies, and indeed for much of his life no more than a privateer, Drake set a standard for skill, determination and daring which has made his name a legend. *See also* COMMERCE-RAIDING; GREAT BRITAIN; NAVAL WARFARE; NAVIES.

J. MEYER
A. W. H. PEARSALL

FURTHER READING
K. R. Andrews, *Drake's Voyages* (London, 1967); Julian S. Corbett, *Drake and the Tudor Navy* (London, 1898).

Dudley, John, Duke of Northumberland (*c.*1504–53) The military career of the Duke of Northumberland has many similarities to that of his friend and later political rival, the Duke of Somerset. Like Somerset his first experience was gained in the invasions of France in the 1520s and his first major appointment that of Lord Warden of the Marches toward Scotland in 1542. In 1543 Dudley, by then Viscount Lisle, was appointed Lord Admiral, an office he held until 1547 and again in 1549. In those years he served actively on land and sea: he commanded the fleet in the 1544 attack on Edinburgh, took part in the Siege of Boulogne later in the year, and was the first commander of the English garrison there during the winter of 1544–5. In 1545 he commanded the fleet in the engagements with the French in the Solent and in the Channel. Under Edward VI he commanded the forward corps in the Pinkie campaign of 1547 and then in 1549 the army that brought the Norfolk rebellion to a quick end (the 'battle' of Dussindale, 27 August). 1549 also saw the beginning of the political manoeuvrings that led to his execution in 1553 following his attempt to place his daughter-in-law, Lady Jane Grey, on the throne. Northumberland enjoyed a high reputation among his contemporaries as a commander, so much so that the failure of his coup in 1553 caused considerable surprise. Yet unlike Somerset he has left no evidence of innovative strategic or tactical ideas. His one independent victory on land (Dussindale) displayed an effective use of heavy cavalry and arquebusiers against a larger (10,000+ to his 8,000) but much more poorly armed and organized army of rebels; he was never tested against a continental army. Northumberland is best described as 'a safe pair of hands', a commander of efficiency and energy with an eye for bolstering the morale of his men by the effective gesture. More significant, perhaps, was the role he shared with Somerset of patron to the younger officers of the campaigns of the 1540s, who later rose to prominence under Elizabeth and who formed a key element in the following of his son Robert Dudley, Earl of Leicester. *See also* BOULOGNE; DUDLEY, ROBERT; PINKIE; SEYMOUR; WILLIAMS.

SIMON ADAMS

FURTHER READING
B. L. Beer, *Northumberland* (Kent State, Ohio, 1973); W. K. Jordan, *Edward VI: the young king* (London, 1968), and *Edward VI: the threshold of power* (London, 1970); J. Cornwall, *Revolt of the Peasantry, 1549* (London, 1977), pp. 207–25, on Dussindale; S. Adams, 'The Dudley clientèle, 1553–1563', in *The Tudor Nobility*, ed. G. W. Bernard (Manchester, 1992), pp. 241–65.

Dudley, Robert, Earl of Leicester (1532–88) Owing to his notoriety as the leading courtier of Elizabeth I, Leicester has always occupied an ambiguous place in the military history of the reign. His appointments as Captain-General of the English army in the Netherlands between 1585 and 1587, and then of the army assembled to resist the Spanish Armada in 1588, have been criticized as examples of Elizabeth's favouritism and self-indulgence. Yet there is also a counter-school, which has granted him more significance as a military patron if not an active commander. Although Leicester may have accompanied his father Northumberland in the crushing of the Norfolk Rebellion of 1549, his one early experience of active service was as Master of the Ordnance to the English contingent in Philip II's army at the Siege of St Quentin in 1557. His career at the court of Elizabeth after 1558 inhibited further service, as at Le Havre in 1562 (where his brother commanded) or in Ireland in 1566 (where his brother-in-law commanded), prior to 1585. However, the military clientele he inherited from his father, together with a range of military interests and acquaintances (like Lazarus von Schwendi), made him the leading military patron of the reign. The patronage of officers like Roger Williams and his espousal of Protestant politics made him the natural advocate of military intervention in the Dutch Revolt. His

209

appointment as Captain-General in 1585 was the culmination of a decade of involvement in Dutch affairs. Although he deserves some credit for the creation of the Dutch field army, Leicester's conduct of operations against the Duke of Parma in 1586 met with mixed success. Inhibited by Elizabeth's insistence on a defensive campaign and the refusal of the Dutch to supply the finance they had promised, he was outmanoeuvred by Parma in the summer of 1586, enabling the Spaniards to seize several isolated Dutch towns. On the other hand, the exhaustion of Parma's supplies in the autumn gave Leicester the opportunity to strengthen the line of the Issel, although two key garrisons were lost later when two English officers defected. Leicester's return to the Netherlands in 1587 (which might not otherwise have occurred) was the result of Parma's investment of Sluys in May. By the time Leicester arrived in July the siege was well advanced and Parma too strongly dug in for a relief to be successful. Yet, whatever judgements are reached on his abilities as a commander, by infusing military patronage with religious allegiance and then linking it to service in the Netherlands, Leicester, more than anyone else, created the Anglo-Dutch connection, which provided the main form of English military education until 1640. *See also* ARMADA; DUDLEY, JOHN; NETHERLANDS; PARMA; ST QUENTIN; SCHWENDI; WILLIAMS.

SIMON ADAMS

FURTHER READING
For the early period, see S. Adams, 'The Dudley clientèle, 1553–1563', in *The Tudor Nobility*, ed. G. W. Bernard (Manchester, 1992), pp. 241–65. For the Netherlands, see F. G. Oosterhoff, *Leicester and the Netherlands, 1586–1587* (Utrecht, 1988).

Dunant, Henri (1828–1910) Henri Dunant was born in Geneva. Coming to Italy to meet Napoleon III in order to bring to his attention the state of affairs in Algeria, he involuntarily witnessed the plight of the wounded after the Battle of Solferino (24 June 1859). Deeply moved by their sufferings, which the contemporary medical services seemed unable to mitigate, he put all his energy into organizing assistance. In 1862, he published *Un Souvenir de Solférino* (reprinted Lausanne, 1969). The repercussions of this book helped to mobilize public opinion. Crowned heads of Europe, writers such as Charles Dickens, and personalities like Florence Nightingale, gave him their support. Partly through Dunant's lobbying, the first international conference met at Geneva in 1863. This resulted in the Geneva Convention and the foundation of the International Red Cross (1864). Despite having to leave Geneva in 1867 because of financial embarrassment, Dunant continued his philanthropic crusade, arguing for the abolition of slavery, disarmament, a method of arbitrating between states, humane treatment for prisoners of war and the establishment of a Jewish homeland. In 1901 he was awarded the first Nobel Peace Prize. Dunant died at Heiden in Switzerland. *See also* DISARMAMENT; LAWS OF WAR; MEDICAL SERVICES; SOLFERINO.

D. REICHEL
JOHN CHILDS

FURTHER READING
Ellen Hart, *Man Born to Live: the life and work of Henry Dunant, founder of the Red Cross* (London, 1953); H. N. Pandit, *The Red Cross and Henry Dunant* (London, 1969).

Dunkirk (1940) *See* FRANCE, BATTLE OF

E

Economic warfare   Ever since the dawn of history, men have realized that an enemy's strength could be undermined during a war by striking at his economic resources.

The earliest form of economic warfare was based on the elementary idea of starving out one's opponent (and his non-combatant population). A siege had, as its natural concomitant, a blockade, which represented a deliberate attempt to reduce to starvation in an enemy city those termed 'useless mouths' – women, old men and children – whose presence would be a source of weakness to the combatants. In this connection, the military history of the Ancient World and the Middle Ages is full of descriptions of sieges where the defenders ate cats, dogs and horses, not to mention instances of cannibalism. Reference need only be made to such examples as the sieges of Carthage 147–146 BC and Numantia 134–133 BC by the Romans where the system of starving the besieged wrote a new and separate chapter into the manual of military science.

In fact, this method was looked upon by the Romans rather as part of a military policy of 'deterrence' than as an end in itself. During the imperial period, the Roman political and military authorities wished to make it quite clearly understood that any revolt would lead not only to repression, but also to all the horrors of 'economic' war against the civil population. In other words, this method was not the result of any particular cruelty on the Romans' part, but represented a deliberate political and strategic choice, which did not aim at repression as such, but rather at avoiding it as far as possible, by 'deterring' subject peoples from following the path of rebellion.

The conclusion can be drawn that, both in Antiquity and the Middle Ages, economic warfare in the modern sense did not exist, the sole way possible of dealing an enemy a blow in this sphere being to starve his soldiers and his civil population. The devastation of farmland carried out by the Spartan armies in Attica during the Peloponnesian War, whose object was to induce famine inside the walls of Athens, was not an exception to that rule. The Romans, being masters of the sea, succeeded in cutting off Carthage completely from all outside sources, but Sparta was not in a position to do this to Athens. Without control of the sea, her strategy was doomed to failure.

The situation remained unchanged during the Renaissance and the opening part of the modern era, at least until the French Revolution; it must, however, be noted that the British naval blockade directed against France, like the continental counterpart decided on by Napoleon against the British Isles, was clearly quite different from modern economic warfare, since it was based on the principles of mercantilism, and therefore did not aim at dealing the enemy's commerce a mortal blow. The purpose was, indeed, very different, being to drive the enemy's commerce to the verge of ruin, in order to force him to negotiate. Certainly, Britain was pursuing complex objectives; she was really seeking to make the French understand that the continued existence of the Napoleonic empire would mean the end of French commercial profits, and that a far more worthwhile policy was to overthrow Napoleon and make a fresh start. However, given her practical outlook, would Britain have refused to sign a peace treaty if Napoleon had really wanted it and been willing to restore the conditions for a European balance of power?

Looked at in this context, economic warfare assuredly had an importance, but no one thought seriously of crushing an enemy completely by such means, the decisive blow being left to the armies and navies. After the Battle of Trafalgar, Britain contented herself for some time with enjoying undisputed monopoly of the commercial shipping routes. Then, the political leaders and the financial magnates of the City realized that the continental blockade was preventing the free sale of British goods in Europe. It was not, therefore, through fear that economic warfare would cause her military collapse, but to defend her trade that Britain decided to face her enemy in the field, and dispatched Wellington to Iberia, cleverly leaving the weightiest military tasks in Europe to the armies of the coalition of sovereigns. Economic warfare, then, played a part in the Napoleonic Wars, which cannot be too strongly stressed; but, as in the case of the Romans, it assisted but could not on its own win the war, whose outcome was decided, contrary to the views expressed by Mahan, on the fields of Leipzig and Waterloo.

The situation was utterly changed by the Industrial Revolution, which gave economic warfare unprecedented importance. It must be stated, however, that even in this period ideas of securing victory over an enemy by such means alone were shown to be illusory. The era that has taken its character from the Industrial Revolution has seen three major wars – the American Civil War and the two world wars. In the earliest of these wars, the North, which had complete control of the sea, immediately declared a blockade of the South. This required the gigantic effort of closing off 5,000 miles of coastline with four naval squadrons. The South responded by adopting a measure that was entirely new in economic warfare. The Paris Declaration of 1856 had outlawed privateers, i.e. armed commerce-raiders which captured enemy merchant ships (or ones carrying 'war contraband') and then took them to a friendly or neutral port where they were sold for the raiders' benefit. In this situation, the South had recourse to its naval cruisers proper which, instead of capturing ships together with their 'contraband', forced the sailors to take to the lifeboats, and then sank vessel and cargo. Thus the commerce destroyer

had taken the place of the privateer. This was unquestionably a revolution in the methods of naval warfare. The North was unsure how to react; it dispatched cruisers to hunt down the enemy ships and it finally succeeded in destroying them, but the damage done to the US merchant fleet was immense, since it was almost entirely swept from the sea. On the other hand, the Northern blockade did not yield positive results, because it could be broken, and thus the South's trade prospered. In 1864, after the blockade had been in continuous existence for three years, the South was receiving more merchandise of strategic value than when the war began. Naval men elsewhere took careful note of the American experience. In 1914, when the Entente governments declared a blockade of the Central Powers, the latter replied first with surface 'commerce destroyers', and then with submarines, a much more effective weapon.

From 1914 onwards, economic warfare underwent a transformation. In contradistinction to what happened in pre-industrial times, the industries producing the resources essential for the conduct of a war could now receive a death blow if seaborne trade was cut off. During the American Civil War, the South had received the great majority of its imported goods through neutral countries, e.g. the Bahamas (a British possession) and Mexico. Now, Britain formulated the doctrine of the 'continuous voyage', i.e. all goods considered to be 'war contraband' (the list included practically everything) that were sent to a neutral country 'closed' to the enemy were lawful prize. Since it was hazardous to keep Allied ships near to the German coast, recourse was made to blockade 'at a distance', though this could hardly be concealed and was confronted by the submarine threat. In 1917, Germany declared unrestricted submarine warfare: all ships entering a zone around Britain could be sunk without warning. After an unnecessary delay, Allied merchant shipping was grouped into convoys following the model which the Spaniards had adopted in the sixteenth century and the British and Dutch in the seventeenth. Thus, the kind of economic warfare that was only foreshadowed in 1861–5 was now fully exploited and demonstrated both its terrifying character and effectiveness. In 1917, Britain was at breaking-point, and American intervention helped rescue her from defeat. Nevertheless, the Allied blockade had not been without effect on the economy of Germany, and it had caused her to occupy the Ukraine as a source of grain and raw materials. This experience led Hitler, with his eyes on a future war, to develop within Germany an economy based on self-sufficiency, by putting the state machine on a war footing in advance of the event. His aim was to limit the effects of a blockade, in case of a prolonged war, and he also envisaged the occupation of countries which would, in consequence, play a part in the German war effort.

The Second World War was, in many respects, a repetition of the first, except that the blockade, like all-out submarine warfare, was initiated from the outset. The new factor was, however, aerial warfare. Both sides used aircraft in the war at sea, the Germans and Italians for attacking the merchant shipping of the Allies, and the latter for tracking down and sinking submarines. But much more spectacular was the air warfare conducted against cities, where the aim of destroying the economy was, however, combined with that of terrorizing the population. The British were partly motivated by the wish to take reprisals against the Germans who had unleashed this mode of operation with their raids on London and Coventry (1940–1). When, however, under pressure from the Americans, the air offensive was directed systematically against economic objectives (e.g. factories, petrol refineries),Germany began to feel the effects, and was pushed nearer and nearer to defeat.

Perhaps the main lesson of the two world wars was that economic objectives appeared increasingly to be of prime importance. They passed out of the sphere of mere logistics, and took their place in the operational, and even the strategic, plan. There was a dawning consciousness that it was more important to deal a mortal blow to an enemy's economic system than to annihilate his armies in accordance with the precepts of Clausewitz. The strongest army was reduced to impotence when its tanks, its aircraft and its ships were immobilized by the destruction of its supply depots or its sources of fuel. In short, economic warfare was no longer a means of exerting pressure on an enemy's soldiers through the threat of reducing their wives and children to starvation; populations were no longer the most important aspect of economic strategy. It was preferable to allocate military resources to massive attacks on real economic–strategic objectives, with a view to bringing an enemy's armies to defeat by depriving them of raw materials which had become indispensable to the war effort. Specialists have begun to realize the necessity for what has been termed a 'logistical strategy', whose aim is to concentrate systematically on the destruction of an enemy's economic 'sinews'. The basis of this 'logistical strategy' is the idea that, rather than 'encircle', 'isolate' or 'annihilate' an enemy's armies, it is far more important to cut off all his economic resources, and that the destruction of a large fuel store is much more important than that of a division or even of a whole army.

Nevertheless, what will a future war be like? Certainly, economic objectives will be at the forefront of military plans, since any general staff that chooses to ignore the necessity of thinking along these lines will be inevitably doomed to defeat. Secondly, the lesson of the two world wars will need to have been fully absorbed – that is to say, that terror bombing of populations is merely a waste – at once stupid and cruel – of military resources. Hence, it is easy to foresee that the nuclear weapon, in particular, will be used much more against economic and military objectives than against populations, with atomic terrorism being the least likely feature of a future war. As a consequence, the use of nuclear weapons against the systems on which the working of the economy depends (the destruction of a whole oil-producing or mining region, for example, being quite feasible) is a disagreeable probability. This was the view of Soviet strategists, who were ready to use nuclear weapons from the very start of a conflict since, unlike Westerners, they regarded them not as a deterrent, but as a weapon in the proper sense. It may well be thought that a power which uses these weapons for purposes of terror will be wasting its resources and will make its own defeat much more likely. Until the Russian Revolution of 1991, a terrifying intensification of submarine warfare was also probable, its aim being to destroy the resources which the NATO armies would receive from the United States; here too, Soviet strategists, such as Admiral Gorskov and Admiral Stalbo, had expressed themselves extremely clearly.

Hence, military staffs are confronted with the need to make a systematic study of a future logistical strategy. Such a strategy involves identifying the objectives of the main powers providing in advance the appropriate resources and, in particular, preparing minds for facing this kind of war. What is at stake is not solely, or even chiefly, victory, but the very survival of our civilization. *See also* AVIATION; BLOCKADES; COMMERCE-RAIDING; CONVOYS; FINANCES; MASADA; NAVAL WARFARE; SIEGES; STRATEGY; WAR ECONOMY; WEAPONS.

R. LURAGHI

FURTHER READING
R. Elberton Smith, *The Army and Economic Mobilization* (Washington, 1959); B. Fairchild and J. Grossman, *The Army and Industrial Manpower* (Washington, 1959); B. F. Cooling, *War, Business and American Society* (New York, 1977).

Economy   *See* WAR ECONOMY

Education   *See* TRAINING

Edward, Prince of Wales, known as the 'Black Prince' (1330–76)   This brilliant knight, whose tomb and armour can still be admired in Canterbury Cathedral, was also a great military leader, faithful to the judicious advice of his mentor, Sir John Chandos. He was the eldest son of Edward III, King of England, and although he fought alongside his father at Crécy (1346), his real career began in 1355 with his marauding expedition through Languedoc, from the Atlantic to the Mediterranean. In the following year, a new expedition, towards the Loire, culminated in the Battle of Poitiers where he defeated and captured the King of France, John the Good. In 1362, Edward III created him Prince of Aquitaine. For the next eight years, he maintained a substantial court, based at Bordeaux. In 1367, responding to an appeal from the King of Castile, Peter the Cruel, he won the Battle of Nájera over Peter's rival Henry of Trastámara and took Bertrand du Guesclin prisoner. He then contracted a serious illness which forced him to return to England in 1371. Henceforth, he played only a subordinate role in military affairs. However, he lived long enough to see the reconquest of the greater part of Aquitaine by the French armies of Charles V. *See also* FRANCE; GREAT BRITAIN; GUESCLIN.

P. CONTAMINE

FURTHER READING
Richard Barber, *Edward, Prince of Wales and Aquitaine* (London, 1978); Richard Barber, *The Life and Campaigns of the Black Prince* (Woodbridge, 1986); Herbert J. Hewitt, *The Black Prince's Expedition of 1355–1357* (Manchester, 1958).

Egypt, Ancient   The early history of Egypt provides little information on the art of war, so little indeed that it was for a long time thought that the country had originally been entirely peaceful and only drawn out of its inertia by invasions. However, the unification of the country by Menes in about 3100 BC could not have been achieved without warfare. Moreover, the Egyptians had to defend their rich river valley against the covetous desert nomads.

From the period known as the Old Kingdom (*c*.2686–*c*.2181 BC), military forces appeared under the command of a vizier, assisted by military commanders: 'Commanders of the Infantry' and 'Commanders of the Arsenals'. The pharaoh had about him a permanent guard in which there were foreign mercenaries, most notably Libyan archers and Nubian warriors. In time of war, recruits provided by the nomes (districts), towns and temples were called upon, and traces have been found of the existence of a commissariat administered by scribes.

After a period of turmoil, the pharaohs of the Middle Kingdom (c.2133–c. 1786 BC) created a permanent, structured army in which the national recruits formed a group apart, 'those who live in the army'. Funerary objects placed in a tomb at Meir and in the tomb of Mesehti at Asyut provide evidence of an infantry of the line armed with shields and short copper-tipped lances. There is also evidence for hatchets and maces, and archers using bows shooting arrows tipped with stone or bone. Citadels were built in the Suez isthmus and the upper Nile valley. These had walls of dried mud which could be as much as 30 feet wide at the base and reach a height of 80 feet. They were crenellated and had moats with scarps in front of them in a form of earthwork, which became standard throughout parts of east Africa. A standing army of several thousand men operated against the neighbouring peoples. With the accession of Pharaoh Sesostris III, the military virtues of the sovereign were extolled. However, this army was technically somewhat backward when compared with the armies of Asia and was outclassed by the Hyksos invaders, who used light cavalry and chariots, the hand axe, curved scimitars, and light armour.

After the Hyksos had been driven out, the pharaohs of the New Kingdom (c.1580–1090 BC) organized a kind of military feudal regime by distributing lands to those who had fought in the reconquest. These warriors, who swore fealty to the sovereign, had responsibility for recruiting the chariot crews and thus for constituting the main strike force. Through education, they could arrive at the highest offices of state. Soldiers were recruited either to the regulars or to the reserve within a framework of territorial districts each of which formed one corps, placed under the aegis of one of the major gods: the army of Amon, of Re, of Ptah and of Seth, each of which contained several thousand men. These corps were subdivided into something similar to battalions and platoons. This organization of the army can be seen in action at the Battle of Kadesh (c.1300 BC) under Ramesses II against the Hittites. The commander had around him a general staff of aides, quartermasters and scribes. The elite troops were often constituted by foreign mercenaries – the Shardana (perhaps prisoners and volunteers recruited from the Sea Peoples), Nubians, Canaanites and Amorites, all fighting with their own weapons and armour.

In their armament, the Egyptians borrowed a great deal from the armies of Asia. The use of metal became standard. The infantry was equipped with large shields which, when planted in the ground, formed a protective wall. The pharoah led the chariot force himself. The Egyptian chariot, which was lighter than its Asian equivalent, carried only two men, a driver and a 'fighting man' whose chief weapon was the double-curved bow. The use of the quiver also became more widespread.

When the hereditary principle was established, the warriors equipped by the king came to constitute a landed aristocracy. Their wealth, which came mainly from booty, compromised their vocation and corrupted their military virtues. When the Assyrians attacked Egypt, the Libyan mercenaries actually treated with the invaders (666 BC). At that point, the pharaohs called on Greek mercenaries, who enabled them to drive out the invaders, but did not defend them effectively against the Persian invasion of 525 BC. From this time onward, the military history of Egypt becomes part of the history of the Persian, Greek, Roman and Arabic worlds in turn. However, the victory won against the Syrians by the Ptolemaic sovereigns of Egypt at Raphia (217 BC), where native Egyptian forces fought in the phalanx, showed that the Egyptians could assimilate the military art of their conquerors. *See also* KADESH; RAPHIA.

A. CORVISIER

FURTHER READING
E. Drioton and J. Vandier, *L'Egypte* (Paris, 1952); *Cambridge Ancient History*, ii (1924); *Cambridge Ancient History*, i, 2 (1971); ii, 2

(1975); J. Baines and J. Málek, *Atlas of Ancient Egypt* (Oxford, 1980).

Eisenhower, Dwight David (1890–1969) Eisenhower was raised in Abilene, Kansas. He entered the US Military Academy at West Point in 1911 and graduated four years later. Eisenhower transferred to the tank corps but did not go to Europe during the First World War. During the 1920s, Eisenhower became friends with Patton and attended a number of army postgraduate schools. In the next decade, Eisenhower became MacArthur's aide, first at the Chief of Staff's office and then, after 1935, in the Philippines. In 1939, Eisenhower returned to the United States. By 1940, he had impressed sufficiently to be promoted to brigadier general. After Pearl Harbor, Eisenhower became head of the War Plans Division of the General Staff under the American Chief of Staff, George C. Marshall. Eisenhower was sent to London in April 1942 as Marshall's representative. In London, he formed an integrated Anglo-American General Staff that excluded the other allies. Eisenhower was made Allied Commander-in-Chief of the North African invasion, which began in November. In July 1943, he commanded the Allied invasion of Sicily. During this time and the subsequent invasion of Italy, Eisenhower worked closely with Patton and the British commander, Montgomery. In January 1944, Eisenhower returned to London where he was appointed the supreme commander of the Allied invasion of Europe (*Operation Overlord*). Once the landings had been accomplished, he used the enormous Anglo-American superiority in men and *matériel* to defeat the Germans, encircle the Ruhr, scatter the German forces and join up with the Soviet Army. For political reasons, Eisenhower agreed to de Gaulle's request that France should not have a military government imposed on it and that Allied troops should not march on either Berlin or Prague. After the war, Eisenhower became US Army Chief of Staff and retired in 1948. In 1950, President Harry S. Truman made Eisenhower the first commander of NATO. In 1952, he was elected President of the United States and served two terms in office. During his military career while shouldering the highest responsibilities, Eisenhower acted like a high-level businessman and diplomat, delegating authority and working closely with his staff. These traits, which he also followed as President, make him the model of the successful military leader in the age of industrial warfare. *See also* BRADLEY; BROOKE; CHURCHILL; MONTGOMERY; NORMANDY; OVERLORD; PATTON; UNITED STATES.

A. CORVISIER
KEITH NEILSON

FURTHER READING
Stephen Ambrose, *The Supreme Commander: the war years of Dwight D. Eisenhower* (Garden City NY, 1970); Kenneth Davis, *Eisenhower: American hero* (New York, 1969); Russell F. Weigley, *Eisenhower's Lieutenants: the campaigns in France and Germany, 1944–1945* (Bloomington, Ind., 1981).

El Alamein, Battle of (23 October–4 November 1942) The Battle of El Alamein was the turning point in the struggle for the control of North Africa during the Second World War. In 1940 Italian troops invaded Egypt from Libya. A British counter-attack threatened the Italians with defeat and in the spring of 1941 Hitler sent General Rommel and the *Afrika Korps* to secure the Axis position. In July 1942, Rommel's advance towards Egypt was checked at the first battle of El Alamein but Alexandria remained threatened. General Montgomery was given command of the British forces and, over the summer, rebuilt the British 8th Army. By the autumn, the British forces amounted to 150,000 men and 1,100 tanks, against which Rommel was able to range 96,000 (half of whom were German; the rest Italian) and 600 tanks. The two armies faced each other between the Mediterranean and the Qattara Depression, 40 miles inland. As the latter was impassable to wheeled vehicles, the battle front was limited. This allowed Montgomery, utilizing his superiority in *matériel*, to prepare a setpiece battle. On 23 October, 1,000 British field guns opened fire but Rommel had prepared careful defences in depth with imposing mine fields and the British attack was blunted. It was not until 4 November that the British broke through. Rommel, despite Hitler's orders to the contrary, ordered a retreat. Axis losses were heavy: 59,000 men either dead, wounded or taken prisoner (34,000 of them Germans), 500 tanks and 400 guns. The British lost 13,000 dead, wounded or missing, together with more than 400 tanks. The greatest battle of the desert war was a tactical, and above all a strategic, victory for the British. The Suez Canal was henceforth secure, and the clash had contributed to masking the scale of the preliminaries to the Allied landings in North Africa (8 November). The Battle of El Alamein thus marks the beginning of the Allied reconquest of North Africa. *See also* MONTGOMERY; ROMMEL; TANKS.

A. CORVISIER
KEITH NEILSON

FURTHER READING
Nigel Hamilton, *Montgomery. The making of a general 1887–1942* (London, 1981); James Lucas, *The War in the Desert: the Eighth Army at El Alamein* (London, 1982); Barrie Pitt, *The Crucible of War: year of Alamein 1942* (London, 1982).

Engels, Friedrich (1820–95) Engels, the German revolutionary, devoted considerable attention to military problems. His own experience in the 1848 revolution in Baden provided the stimulus for study which was not simply theoretical but was the necessary precondition for success in the future revolution. Schooled in the writings of Clausewitz and Jomini, Engels followed the events of the Crimean War, the Indian Mutiny, the American Civil War and the war of 1866. Most of his output was journalistic. Its focus was specific and technical, rather than political or theoretical. In particular the volunteer movement in Britain of 1859–60 provided the opportunity for analyses of tactics and weaponry. Not until 1878 in his *Anti-Dühring*, a specifically Marxist statement, did he forsake pragmatism. He argued that armies, by virtue of their equipment and organization, were themselves the product of a particular stage of economic evolution, and that wars were not decided by the genius of individuals. As he moved from revolutionary socialism in his later years, so Engels argued that universal conscription, the true nation in arms, was a principal agent for the democratization of states and the elimination of the militarism of the old order. *See also* CLAUSEWITZ; JOMINI; MARX.

HEW STRACHAN

FURTHER READING
Martin Berger, *Engels, Armies and Revolution* (Hamden, Conn., 1977); W. O. Henderson, *Engels as Military Critic* (Manchester, 1959); Sigmund Neumann, 'Engels and Marx: military concepts of the social revolutionaries', in *Makers of Modern Strategy*, ed. E. M. Earle (Princeton, 1943); *Marxism and the Science of War*, ed. Bernard Semmel (Oxford, 1981).

Engineers/engineering In a modern army, the engineers are responsible for (1) maintaining land communications, (2) designing and erecting fixed and field fortifications and field works, (3) constructing bridges, and (4) attacking and destroying enemy fortifications and structures. The military engineer is now a specialist in one of the above branches, having evolved from the multi-skilled expert of the past who was often a gunner as well as a builder of fortifications.

Origins Archaeology has revealed ancient fortifications which became more elaborate as the methods of attack and defence developed. The use and arrangement of blocks of stone, weighing tens or hundreds of tons, and the excavation of ditches in rock, required a considerable labour force and an obvious expertise. Absence of records prevents us from knowing who was in charge of the construction of such works but successive improvements suggest that there was some exchange of ideas among their designers. Carefully prepared plans were needed for the siege and assault of fortifications. Surveying a piece of ground and then raising its height in order to allow men and equipment to pass over ditches required experience in problems relating to the load-bearing characteristics of various types of terrain. Assault equipment – siege towers, battering rams, scaling ladders, 'tortoises' – must have been the work of skilled carpenters. It was not everyone who was conversant with the arts of mining. Furthermore, the construction of missile weapons, such as ballistas and catapults, required considerable expertise. Greek and Chinese authors provide some information about methods and stratagems but the only recorded names of leading figures in this field are Demetrius Poliorcetes at Rhodes in 305–304 BC and Archimedes at Syracuse in 213–212 BC. Nothing is known of the ways in which the experts who attacked and defended cities were recruited and rewarded. Even though all citizens might serve as soldiers and many might follow crafts, the designing of siege equipment was a speciality. The two greatest achievements of the military engineers of Antiquity were the Great Wall of China (c.210 BC) and Xerxes I's bridge across the Hellespont mounted on 676 pontoons (c.478 BC).

The Roman system of military engineering has been better recorded. The legionary was trained in building field works: laying out camps, moving earth, making roads and employing subject populations as a labour force. However, other abilities were needed to overcome physical obstacles and conduct sieges. Hence, legions contained a unit of specialists under the command of a prefect (*praefectus fabrum*). Its complement was about 150 men (a legion's total strength being 6,000) – miners, carpenters, smiths, etc. – who were able to build bridges, on both fixed and floating supports, mine under walls and construct missile and assault equipment. Their constructions are depicted on Trajan's Column and have been described by Caesar, Flavius Josephus and others. Factual evidence has been uncovered along the Rhine or at Dura-Europus in Syria, dating from the third century AD. It appears that such personnel did not count officially as soldiers but were organized into specialist groups. On the technical level, they gave instructions to the operators of the missile systems, the storekeepers, the fortress engineers and the bridging train. Tactical decisions rested with the field commander, though it may be that the prefects in charge of the specialist workers could override his authority.

Roman wars were not only fought against barbarians and associated with defence works as elaborate as the *limes*; their engineers showed their abilities in the sieges of the Punic Wars and, in particular, against the Parthians. The Roman model was copied by the Byzantines, whose army maintained, until the twelfth century, a wide variety of skilled specialists.

Engineers in the Middle Ages In old French, the word *engigneour* meant trickster or schemer and was sometimes applied to those who made use of stratagems in defence or attack. As in Antiquity, medieval military engineers were able to turn their hands to a wide range of activities – mining, building, demolition and, later, gunnery. In France, during the same period that cathedrals and country churches were rising, fortified castles were being built and towns were expanding to the limits of their confining Gallo-Roman walls. The new walls, incorporating technical improvements, were probably designed by fighting men and built by master-masons. There is no record of their names, of how they learned their crafts or of how they were selected.

The siege towers at Jerusalem in 1099 were constructed by Gaston de Béarn and a Genoese shipwright. William the Conqueror, when he intended to attack a town, included carpenters among his forces. There was a royal engineer in England by 1086, chiefly concerned with the design of castles, a custom continued by Henry I. Edward I appointed a chief engineer whose duties included road building and bridging, and a unit of sappers and carpenters appeared in England in 1282. Edward III took civilian smiths, miners from the Forest of Dean, pavilioners, carpenters, mortarers and ditchers on his expeditions into France; at the Siege of Calais in 1346, Edward had 314 engineers, gunners and artificers. By

1370, the engineers had established their headquarters in the Tower of London. The engineers employed forced or impressed civilian labour to build their castles and works. They were principally concerned with the fortresses on the Scottish border and the castles which coerced Wales and Ireland. Château-Gaillard was erected by Richard the Lionheart in two years. The methods available to the engineer had changed little since Antiquity but, by the end of the fifteenth century, the development of gunpowder and cannon had given rise to a new school of military engineering.

Architects during the Renaissance The engineers of the Italian Renaissance were mostly architects who also worked on fortifications. They were able to bring the new learning to their military tasks. These men were faced with the revolution in warfare brought about by the introduction of gunpowder: forged cannon firing metal balls demolished medieval walls of the overhanging type and explosive mines were more effective than the collapsible variety. Even before the turn of the fifteenth century, a good deal of research into the effectiveness of gunpowder weaponry had been carried out. Konrad Keyser initiated a pragmatic German school around 1400 which culminated with the work of Albrecht Dürer in 1527. Almost simultaneously, the Italians moved into the forefront of military engineering beginning with Francesco di Giorgio Martini, whose treatise dates from 1495, the Sangallo family during the years 1450–1550, Sanmicheli at Verona in 1527, and Leonardo da Vinci up to 1513. The remarkable construction executed by the Spaniard Ramirez at Salses in Roussillon 1497 should not be overlooked.

The new style of fortifications abandoned high walls. The ramparts were strengthened with well-tamped layers of earth and surfaces were sloped to deflect cannon shot. Listening and counter-mine galleries were built, but the principal innovation was the employment of the polygonal bastion as the core of the defence. Errard de Bar-le-Duc set out the new rules of fortification at the end of the sixteenth century. Italian expertise spread throughout Europe.

Leonardo da Vinci was appointed engineer to Louis XII of France in 1507, and the Knights of Malta sought Italian help at the sieges of Rhodes in 1522 and Malta in 1565. Fabrizio Siciliani seems to have worked at Boulogne in 1539 and to have taken part in fortifying Navarreux for Henri d'Albret. However, Henry VIII of England gave the task of fortifying his southern coast to a Bohemian, Conrad von Haschenburg, whose designs proved obsolete. The preeminence of the Italians continued into the early seventeenth century and even such countries as Russia and Hungary made use of their skills.

The increasing sophistication of fortress design and the advent of gunpowder weapons brought the beginnings of a more modern organization for military engineers. It was important to have cannon manufactured to precise specifications and engineers became responsible for the drawing up of standards and for testing. On the battlefield they were employed as gun-layers (master gunners). After 1420, Pierre Bessoneau, master-general of the artillery, brought order to the French artillery and he was succeeded by Gaspard Bureau in 1444. In Scotland, there was a law in 1456 relating to the manufacture of cannon. There was a chief of the train of artillery in England in the fourteenth and fifteenth centuries, raised to the rank of colonel by 1500. During the fifteenth century, the English Ordnance Office gradually evolved from the king's Privy Wardrobe. When Sir Thomas Seymour became Master of the Ordnance in 1544, his office was responsible for supervising the building of fortifications, barracks, artillery, the train and military manufacturing. The Master was elevated to Master-General in 1604. During the course of the seventeenth century, military engineers and gunners gradually separated into distinct specialities, a change which was reflected in the internal organization of the English Ordnance Office. Engineers were increasingly concerned with the construction of fortifications and the methods of their defence and attack. In addition they were entrusted with work on roads, bridges, canals and tunnels, some of which fell outside a military con-

219

text. They had no specialist troops attached and so called upon the services of conscripted peasants or the infantry.

Modern Military Engineers By the end of the sixteenth century, the bastioned style of fortification was well established. Having learned from the example of the Italian engineers, French engineers took a lead from Errard de Bar-le-Duc (1554–1610) whose *Fortification: its basic principles explained* dates from 1600. He was followed by De Ville (1596–1657), Pagan (1604–77) and, in particular, Vauban (1633–1707) who was the dominating European influence during the later seventeenth and eighteenth centuries. He had an extremely able rival in the Dutch artilleryman, Coehoorn (1641–1704).

These were practical men who built, improved, attacked and defended strongholds. They were in complete command of these operations and suffered heavy casualties. In France, they became properly established with their own hierarchy of ranks. The deaths of Colbert in 1683, Seignelay in 1690, and Louvois in 1691, led to the amalgamation of the two corps in 1691: the corps of Colbert and Seignelay had been responsible for ports and public works, whilst that of Louvois had been mainly concerned with military tasks. Nevertheless, the military engineers continued to undertake public works until 1750 when Trudaine created a corps devoted to roads and bridges. The sappers who dug the trenches and the miners were grouped into the regiment of the *Fusiliers du Roi*, which was formed in 1673, and became the *Royal Artillerie* in 1693. Two companies dealt with the repair of equipment and bridges. In 1700, the miners were concentrated in a depot at Verdun.

The corps of engineers in France was officially founded in 1755. The engineers were specialists, officers without troops, although there was a large number of subordinate officials to supervise works and public property. Any necessary labour was detailed from among the infantry by the local field commander. An important innovation was the foundation of the School at Mézières in 1749 which centralized the training of engineers. Engineers could now be directly recruited and instructed. The school, the second of its type in France having been preceded by the Bridges and Highways College in 1747, was followed by the School of Maritime Engineering in 1765 and of Mining in 1787. Mézières was distinguished by the high quality of its science instruction; Coulomb, Borda, Meunier de la Place and Malus were all graduates. Through the agency of Monge, one of its most eminent teachers, it was transferred to Metz in 1795 and its name changed to the École Polytechnique. Its direct descendant was the US School of Artillery and Military Engineering at West Point, founded in 1802.

Towards the close of the eighteenth century, there was a reaction against the orthodoxy of the bastioned system of fortification as taught at Mézières. The heretic was the Marquis de Montalembert, an artilleryman, who first published in 1776. His ideas were copied in Prussia and Austria (after 1815) as well as in the coastal fortifications of the young American Republic.

In 1716, the English artillery was separated from the engineers and formed into a regiment of four companies. In 1727, this became the Royal Regiment of Artillery. However, both the artillery and the engineers continued under the command of the Ordnance Office. The Royal Military Academy for the training of artillerymen and engineers was established at Woolwich in 1741, a model for the French school at Mézières. A company of artificers was formed at Gibraltar in 1772. This company, together with five others formed in 1787, were given the title of the Royal Engineers. Their motto is 'Ubique' – everywhere. The War Academy was founded in Vienna in 1717, the same year that the Austrians established an engineer college in Brussels. In 1732, a corps of engineers was created in the Austrian Netherlands which was later extended to the whole Austrian Empire. The proposal made in 1760 by Gribeauval for the formation of companies of sapper-miners was put into practice in 1762. In Spain, the corps of engineers was organized by Verboom, a Fleming. An engineering college, which had existed at

Barcelona since 1699, was moved to Alcala in 1760.

The Modern Era The cardinal development during the nineteenth century was the introduction of a system whereby engineering specialists worked with their own specialist troops. Engineers were no longer reliant on the infantry to provide labour. The engineers thus became the fourth arm of the army, taking precedence after the artillery.

The French engineers were reorganized into twelve battalions in 1793 and then into three regiments in 1818. In 1870, the engineers were given the title of sapper-miners and arranged into twenty battalions, one per army corps. Each battalion had a company of railway engineers. Signalling became a responsibility of the engineers and a battalion of telegraphists was formed in 1909. The French balloon service commenced between 1794 and 1796 and in 1886 there was one balloon company to each engineer regiment. Pontoneers were late in taking their place in the French engineer arm. Sappers were called upon to construct temporary bridges but they possessed neither the training nor the equipment with which to span wide gaps. Only the artillery trains carried the equipment and expertise for this task. Pontoons made of copper were produced in the seventeenth century and there were examples of these in the army of Gustavus Adolphus. Types made of wood appeared in 1801, of iron in 1901 and of aluminium in 1935. The earliest pontoneers belonged to the *Royal Artillerie*. A pontoon unit was created during the 1790s and this became the gunner-pontoneer regiment in 1840. A second regiment was formed in 1870. The pontoneers were transferred to the engineers in 1894 but pontoon bridging ceased to be a specialized aspect of engineering work. In the field of heavy railway bridges, reference should be made to the Marcille type, a precursor of the Bailey bridge, and also to the Bonnet-Schneider model. The need to ensure the correct functioning of the equipment in armoured fortifications led to the creation of the fortress sappers, of whom there were

16 companies in 1914. Later, the fortress sappers became the electro-mechanical engineers. Before 1939, there existed sapper cableway engineers in the French Alps.

A tendency to concentrate on a single activity began to manifest itself in engineering units. The workaday skills of the sapper-miners were inadequate to deal with specific technical requirements and this led to the creation of specialist railway, signalling, pontoon bridging and electro-mechanical units. The four regiments of 1875 reached a figure of eleven in 1914 plus five separate battalions. During the 1914–18 war, in which positions on the Western Front were occupied for long periods, various new categories of specialist engineers appeared – builders of hutments, lumber-jacks, electricians, road workers, water supply engineers and mechanics for motor vehicles. At the front, miners played a significant part, as also did the sappers who produced concrete bunkers, gas warfare units and the small-gauge railway sappers. During the war, the proportion of engineers in the French army rose from 3.6 per cent to 7.4 per cent. The French army followed a similar pattern during the Second World War except that, after 1944, it was equipped with American machinery and therefore adopted American engineering practices.

French engineers have been heavily involved in the building of fortifications: Lyons (1830–5), Paris (1840–7 and 1874–80), redesigning caused by the advent of the high explosive shell (1886–91), the armouring of emplacements (1910–13) and the building of the Maginot Line (1928–39). A large conscript army has also involved French engineers in the building of barracks and military depots.

'The engineers clear the way' has become a motto, especially among the combat engineers, referred to as field engineers in the British army. The combat engineer rose to importance during the First World War, his task being to handle explosives and cut barbed wire. In the German army, the pioneers became closely associated with the assault battalions. This role was extended in the Second World War and the combat engineer was called upon to clear and lay minefields, operate assault boats during opposed river crossings, assist in the demolition of enemy pill-boxes and concrete strong points and build bridges close to the front. In the German Panzer divisions, the combat engineers were really elite assault troops. Between 1939 and 1945, each division of the British army included three field companies of Royal Engineers. Particularly in offensive actions, field or combat engineers often found themselves in the vanguard of the attack and frequently suffered heavy casualties.

The Royal Engineers in Britain have followed a similar course of development to that of their French counterparts. There was a separate bridging train in Wellington's Peninsula army in 1813, a railway section was created in 1869 and a telegraph troop was formed in 1870. In 1812, the School for Military Field Work was established at Chatham, leaving the Academy at Woolwich solely to train artillery officers. In 1869, the institution was renamed the School of Military Engineering. A balloon section was added in 1890, the corps of electrical engineers was founded in 1907 and a wireless company was raised in 1909. In 1865, the course at Chatham included demolition, surveying and mapping, photography and chemistry, electricity, lithography, architecture and building, field fortifications and ballooning. The Royal Engineers also assisted in building public works, as in the construction of Pentonville 'Model' Prison in 1842. In India, Africa, Australia and New Zealand, British military engineers undertook surveys and mapping, built irrigation schemes, public buildings, roads, bridges, harbours and telegraph systems. By the Second World War, the Royal Engineers were divided into three sections: field and fortress, line of communications and transportation. Fortress companies existed only in overseas garrisons such as Malta and Gibraltar but the field companies were the engineering element in the fighting formations, the combat engineers. The line of communications units provided engineering services in the base areas and along lines of communication and the transportation units constructed and maintained roads, bridges, railways, waterways, docks and airfields.

For the *Overlord* landings in France in June 1944, the British provided a complete mechanized engineering division, the 79th Armoured Division, to assist the infantry and armour in leaving the beaches by clearing paths through minefields, demolishing fortifications, filling ditches and laying carpet roads and assault bridges. The Royal Engineers were responsible for the first complete mapping of the British Isles by triangulation, the Ordnance Survey. This began in Scotland in 1747, in England in 1783 and was finally completed in 1852. The responsibility of the engineers for signals ended in 1920 with the formation of the Royal Corps of Signals and the repair and maintenance of electrical and mechanical equipment, particularly motor vehicles, passed to the Royal Electrical and Mechanical Engineers (REME) in 1942. In 1967, the responsibilities of the Royal Engineers for transport passed to the new Royal Corps of Transport.

The United States have developed an original system, perhaps inspired by the engineers of the French Royal Corps which took part in the War of Independence. Prior to 1945, the US Army Corps of Engineers, whose motto is 'Essayons', was often given the task of carrying out public works on behalf of the government. During the nineteenth century, they surveyed, mapped, built roads, bridges and railways and generally played a vital role in opening the West. In the twentieth century, although they had to compete with state and federal agencies, the engineers worked on numerous projects, especially the Panama Canal and the Tennessee Valley Scheme. The engineers specialized in work on waterways, harbours and in flood control. The heavily indented American coastline makes it easy for potential enemies to approach major ports by sea, and so coastal fortification has been a principal function of the engineers. The first stage of the work began in 1816 under Simon Bernard, a French general who had emigrated at the Restoration. West Point was founded in 1802 to reduce the reliance on foreign engineers. It was used exclusively to train engineers until 1817 and was thus the first American college of technology. The engineers' important contribution to civil engineering, the contacts with businessmen and the practice of granting temporary ranks to personnel who were seconded to the military made it easy for the engineers to adapt to a large influx of men during a mobilization. During the Civil War, both sides formed railway and pontoon bridging units and developed field fortification sections. Robert E. Lee was an engineer. In the rear, camps, stores and hospitals had to be constructed for one million men in 1862, two million in 1917 and four million in 1941–2. The Second World War produced new responsibilities: beach engineering, in conjunction with the navy, and the construction of airfields, in collaboration with the air force. The war was waged with fully motorized engineer units. The huge amount of constructional work required by the Manhattan Project to build an atomic bomb was entrusted to an engineer general. Since 1945, the American engineers have become an exclusively military concern and are no longer involved in public works.

The majority of states with modern armies have followed a similar pattern of development to those in Britain and France. Engineers initially separated from the artillery and then branched into field and fortress sections. During the twentieth century, signals have become the responsibility of distinct corps. In most armies, the engineers are split into a fighting formation at the front and support services grouped in base areas. For a long period, the engineers were the source of scientific innovation in warfare but this role has almost entirely disappeared. Government departments and industries concerned with armaments and technology now undertake research and development and the engineer has been reduced to a practitioner. *See also* ARTILLERY; ASSYRIANS; COASTAL DEFENCE; COEHOORN; EXPLOSIVES; FORTIFICATION; FORTIFICATION, FIELD; MAGINOT LINE; MINING AND MINES; PROPELLANTS; SIEGES; SIGNAL COMMUNICATION; VAUBAN.

J.-M. GOENAGA
JOHN CHILDS

FURTHER READING
Whitworth Porter et al., *History of the Corps of Royal Engineers* (9 vols, London, 1889–

1958); B. Gille, *The Renaissance Engineers* (London, 1966); B. D. Coll, J. E. Keith and H. H. Rosenthal, *The Corps of Engineers: troops and equipment* (Washington, 1958).

Epaminondas (d. 362 BC) This political and military leader of Thebes, the principal community in Boeotia, contributed to the development of Theban power in 379–371 BC and was one of the commanders of the Theban army which opposed the invading Spartans at the Battle of Leuctra (371 BC). Here Epaminondas devised tactics which transformed the traditional phalanx method of warfare. First, he reinforced his left wing by massing the hoplites 50 ranks deep against the 12 ranks of the facing Spartans. Second, he deployed the remainder of his front diagonally (obliquely) so as to avoid immediate contact with the enemy at any other than the chosen point of impact (i.e. refusing his centre and right). This proved effective, enabling Epaminondas to scatter the Spartan right wing and win the battle, during which the Spartan king, Cleombrotus, was killed. The same tactics were employed against the Spartans at Mantinea in 362 BC but the death of Epaminondas during that engagement prevented the Thebans from exploiting their initial success. Epaminondas' tactics also influenced the innovations introduced by Philip II and Alexander of Macedon.

Epaminondas invaded the Peloponnese in 370–369 BC and assisted the Arcadians in achieving independence from Sparta. He then advanced along the valley of the River Eurotas itself, threatening Sparta directly and liberating the Messenians from Spartan control. He was also responsible for creating a Theban fleet, which he built from scratch, probably with technical assistance from the Carthaginians. This enabled him to strengthen the position of Thebes in the Aegean to the detriment of Athens. It was in great measure due to his efforts that Thebes was able to exert a preponderant influence in Greece between 371 and 362 BC. *See also* CHAERONEA; GREECE, ANCIENT; LEUCTRA; MANTINEA.

R. LONIS
B. CAMPBELL

FURTHER READING
J. Buckler, *The Theban Hegemony, 371–362 BC* (Cambridge, Mass., 1980); J. K. Anderson, *Military Theory and Practice in the Age of Xenophon* (Berkeley, 1970).

Errard de Bar-le-Duc, Jean (1554–1610)
See FORTIFICATION

Esprit de corps

Development and Constituents Every standing army displays an *esprit de corps*. It was invoked by the tribunes of the Roman legions to arouse their soldiers' ardour for battle. In the feudal era, its potency seemed to dwindle, or else merely to take the form of the sentiment that linked the inhabitants of any one lord's domain and approximated to a parochial loyalty. However, it reappeared in a corporate form with the advent of mercenary armies. In the royal armies of the pre-Revolutionary period, it combined the feeling of corporate solidarity and the faithful fulfilment of undertakings entered into with the captain, by written contract or – more often – orally, and through the medium of the captain, with the sovereign. Thus, the men remained attached to their companies. Besides, they lost their seniority if they transferred from one company to another. Nevertheless, in the course of the eighteenth century, enlistment in the army tended to become mainly a commitment to the sovereign and the state. This provided a broader and more persuasive justification, if not a profounder one, for *esprit de corps* which, it seems, reached its apogee in the second half of the eighteenth century, and remained on a high plateau for a century, with long-term military service instilling a professional attitude into soldiers. However, the French armies of volunteers and conscripts in Year II also felt an *esprit de corps*, and this did not disappear, even with the introduction of compulsory, short-term military service. One of its most enduring features is that it is made up more of bonds between men of different rank than of bonds between those of the same rank; in other words, vertical solidarity plays a larger part than the horizontal. That is why units of different sizes, when incorporated – the squad, the regiment, even an army or a whole theatre of operations – can form the bases for an *esprit de corps*.

Its various constituents are:

1 Primarily, loyalty to the unit and its officers, and regard for undertakings given.
2 A defensive stance, often a self-centred one, on the part of a unit's members against any outsiders, who may themselves be members of similar units. However, this attitude does not extend to militate against a feeling of belonging to a larger group which includes them all and which gives a certain unity to military society.
3 An *esprit de corps* implies sharing an ethos which attributes a special status to a particular military unit, and which claims an ability to prove it to others.
4 Pride in membership of a unit inspires a general will to excel and therefore to vie in excellence. Not only do men pride themselves in belonging to the best company in the best regiment but their *esprit de corps* can provide the will to turn this flattering opinion into reality, so as to uphold the unit's reputation.
5 Finally, the *esprit de corps* of a regiment outlasts, throughout its whole history, the men who compose it, as long as it keeps, to some extent, a homogeneous character. It is, therefore, obvious that the moulding and handing on of an *esprit de corps* depends very much on long service members of the regiment. This is why *esprit de corps* and military traditions are closely linked.

The Ways in which an Esprit de Corps Displays Itself A useful example is provided by the armies at the end of the pre-Revolutionary period, many of whose features remain relevant to the present day.

Concern to maintain the unit's reputation required recruits to prove and advertise that they possessed the necessary qualities. Hence arose the ordeals which the soldiers forced upon new arrivals. The aim was to test their spirit of comradeship and courage. Accordingly, there was no lack of rough jokes and provocations which ended in duels. It can be said that, in mercenary armies, when account is taken of the type of men recruited, an *esprit de corps* did a great deal towards knitting together their companies. Among the recruits, some were unable to assimilate themselves to the main body and rapidly deserted; others made up the solid core, which held the unit together amid the ordeals of war; others still remained in it for a greater or lesser period, somewhat on the fringes, and finished up either becoming genuinely incorporated or deserting. The drop in the number of deserters at the end of the pre-Revolutionary period, and in the armies of the nineteenth century, obviously produced a shift in the relative importance of the attitudes just outlined.

It is *esprit de corps* which initiates those instances of collective behaviour which impel men to extol the most glorious actions and to conceal others which are heinous. The memory of brilliant feats of arms is kept alive by the giving of soubriquets to a regiment or to members of it who have distinguished themselves, soubriquets which must not be confused with the stereotyped nicknames adopted by soldiers. Soubriquets can be employed also to stigmatize lapses and may drive the man to whom they are applied to leave the unit.

The desire to be the best led to a degree of rivalry and, sometimes, of competition between units, which on occasion hindered the execution of operations. Commanders, up to the middle of the eighteenth century, wasted time in getting regiments to take up their positions in set-piece battles, because precedences had to be respected. Louis XIV had to fix, in the case of regiments raised at the same time, the order of precedence which each should enjoy. A case is cited where two regiments upset the plans of the higher command by quarrelling over which of them should have the honour of occupying a particular position. However, in the majority of instances, *esprit de corps* had very positive effects and inspired many examples of self-sacrifice. In everyday life, on the other hand, incidents between units over matters of honour were not infrequent and then each came to the aid of his own.

The attitude taken by both the officers and men of a unit in the face of an offence committed by one of its members, sprang from a particular moral code and also from apprehensions over the consequences for the unit's reputation. Thus, to steal from a comrade seemed infinitely more serious than theft from the army or a civilian, because it could damage mutual trust. Cheating in games of chance was much less common among soldiers than in ordinary mixed social groups, because there was more danger of its ending in a man's death. When the offence might lead to prosecution by the civil authorities, and if the affair were not such as to damage the unit's reputation – for example, a duel – the officers exerted themselves to shield the guilty party, even to the extent of securing his admission into another regiment. When the case was otherwise, the man was dismissed under some pretext or other, before the law could lay hands on him, and abandoned to his fate.

Esprit de corps is the explanation for the maintenance of cohesion among the major part of French regiments during the Revolution. It prevented the spread of mutinies, restrained for a time officers who were thinking of emigrating, limited the activities of the political commissioners who were pressing for denunciations, and allowed suspects, noblemen, priests, etc., to take refuge in the army. In short, it contributed to the effectiveness of national defence.

The Institutional Expression of Esprit de Corps Maurice de Saxe was among the first to have written a considered piece on the need to build up *esprit de corps* but commanders had not waited until then to encourage it in practice. In the armies of the *condottieri*, the captains, as the 'owners' of their companies, were the chief beneficiaries. Since, in the seventeenth century, they clothed their men, every company had at least some distinguishing mark of dress. When the king prescribed a uniform for his army, the items of dress were all of the same pattern, but the colour of the facings and lappets, and the number of pocket buttons, varied from one unit to another. Later, the badges sewn on the sleeves or collars carried insignia denoting the arm of the service and the number of the regiment. In the nineteenth century, men apparently considered these marks to be inadequate. They adopted different cuts of beard and moustache according to their branch of the army and, in defiance of regulations, made efforts to vary their hair styles (e.g. straight, slanting, etc.). Later, the requirements of military secrecy would lead to the imposition of total uniformity (e.g. removal of all distinguishing marks), at least on operations.

Nevertheless, the military authorities certainly have not failed to give attention to *esprit de corps*. A proof of this is their care to maintain the lineal continuity of a regiment or to endow newly formed ones with predecessors. When viewed against the many changes that have occurred in the structure of armies, such a procedure has a degree of artificiality about it, yet it is evidently of no small value as a backing for the development of soldiers' morale. Thus, a unit's flag bears the name of its feats of arms and also displays the decorations which it has received. In this way, the flag acquires a personalized character. Another example can be quoted that belongs to the same line of thought – the monuments erected in honour of this or that unit at the actual sites of its exploits or at its home base. Mention can be made, too, of the proud soubriquets bestowed on some units and of the bold mottoes with which all have been eager to furnish themselves.

The high command has proved reasonably successful in controlling *esprit de corps* and in making use of it, through a policy, first started in the mid-eighteenth century, of cutting down the individual differences to which it leads, and of imposing clearly defined limits within which these are permissible. Even so, it has proved impossible to avoid completely the problems posed by the system of regional recruitment which, although making for cohesion, sometimes leads also to an imperfect standardization, owing to the greater latitude given to the way in which provincially raised units operate. Still, it is when it is focused entirely on the feeling of nationhood that we have the surest guarantee that *esprit de corps* will prove effective. *See also* DESERTION; DISCIPLINE; ETHOS; GLORY; HIERARCHY; HONOURS AND AWARDS; MORALE; MUSIC; NATIONALISM; SYMBOLISM; VEXILLOLOGY.

A. CORVISIER

FURTHER READING
John Keegan, *The Face of Battle* (London, 1976); John Baynes, *Morale: a study of men and courage* (London, 1967); Christopher Duffy, *The Military Experience in the Age of Reason* (London, 1987); Richard Holmes, *The Firing Line* (London, 1985).

Estienne, Jean-Baptiste (1860–1936) This artillery officer was regarded in France as the 'father of the tanks'. On 25 August 1914, Estienne, who was then a colonel, told his officers: 'Victory in this war will go to whichever of the two parties first succeeds in placing a 75 mm gun on a vehicle capable of moving over all types of terrain.' While pursuing the development of 'assault artillery' (*artillerie d'assaut*), he had the idea of equipping motor vehicles with armour plate and then with caterpillar tracks. Though the British army beat the French in putting these concepts into practice, Estienne, who had converted the French General Staff to the potential of this new weapon if it were employed in large

Although an artillery officer, Estienne experimented with aircraft for artillery observation from as early as 1910.
(M.A.R.S.)

enough numbers to create a breakthrough, was, through the development of the appropriate vehicles, one of the main architects of the effective role which tanks were to play in 1918. Appointed Inspector General of the Assault Artillery, he advocated the diversification of tank regiments into light tanks for close support, heavy tanks for effecting a breakthrough and medium tanks for pursuit, as well as the use of specialized armoured vehicles for liaison work. After the war, he continued to study the co-operation of tanks with other arms and came up with the idea of employing tank formations to force the enemy into a war of movement. *See also* FULLER; LIDDELL HART; TANKS.

A. CORVISIER

FURTHER READING
P. A. Bourget, *Le Général Estienne, penseur, ingénieur et soldat* (Paris, 1956).

Étapes   *See* BARRACKS; STAGING POSTS

Ethos, military   The ethos of war provides a soldier with a moral framework which enables him to resist the considerable pressures of combat. The development of this structure has been a complex and risky process because war is a phenomenon which verges upon the irrational; the moral structure has to function in the face of threats and suffering which often defy human reason.

To achieve this goal, early man resorted to magic, which he adapted by trial and error. By inducing a kind of trance in the warrior, the supernatural practices of magic enabled him to come into contact with natural forces over which he had little control. These primitive forms of preparation for battle were characterized by the initiation of the young male, often accompanied by physical ordeal and acute suffering, by rites which were designed to inculcate endurance and, lastly, by ceremonies in which solemnity, joy and exaltation all played a part. The tribal spirit was reinforced by these communal rituals, overcoming the selfish tendencies of the individual; human fear has always unleashed collective reflexes.

The Ancient World regarded war as a sacred art. The supreme commander, whether the pharoah, great king or emperor, was frequently deified. The mystique surrounding the leader occupied an important place in the ethos of the warrior. The epic was a literary genre which gave meaning to all aspects of life, whether it was daily routine, warfare or the death of a soldier. The *Iliad*, the *Odyssey* and the Book of Joshua contain a veritable typology of warfare in which the leitmotiv is the firm resolve of the leader. These epic narratives fed the imagination by showing that it was the gods themselves who fought beneath the outward appearance of the heroes. For their part, the latter often decorated their weapons with motifs borrowed from the supernatural world of mythology; thus the power to paralyse the enemy was attributed to Medusa, whose head was often depicted on shields. Preparation for battle was frequently accompanied by ceremonies. Music – singing psalms, certain rhymes or types of plainsong, such as the Phrygian mode – may have contributed to honing the warrior's ardour. Finally, military customs were codified into laws. Military thinking in the Asiatic world ran along similar lines. Great works like the *Bhagavad Gita* marked out a path which gave the warrior access to the highest moral values by gradually separating him from his enslavement to the material world.

The epic poets gave way to the philosophers. Socrates (469–399 BC), himself an old soldier, showed admirable detachment when condemned to drink hemlock. Plato (*c*.429–347 BC), in his *Republic*, demands four basic virtues in the guardians of the city: wisdom, bravery, temperance and justice. In *Cyropaedia*, Xenophon (*c*.427–*c*.354 BC) defines the basis of a military ethos in a remarkably modern manner – self-control and discipline with the leader setting a good example by his sang-froid and the soundness of his knowledge. In about 300 BC, at the Stoa Poikile, a public hall in Athens, Zeno (335–263 BC) founded the school of philosophy which came to be known as Stoicism. Only by devotion to understanding the highest intelligible law of the universe (*logos*) could a man succeed in emancipating himself from his instincts.

The thinking of the Hellenistic Stoics was passed on to the Roman world by Seneca (*c.*AD 1–65), Epictetus (AD 55–135) and the Emperor Marcus Aurelius (AD121–80), whose *Reflections* (also known as *Meditations*) reached a very elevated plane. The soldier was able to find in these writings, which contain a universal message, the certainty that his sacrifice was not made in vain and that the firmness of resolve of the man who does his duty to the bitter end enables him to achieve the greatest heights of spirituality. There were, however, other currents of philosophy. We know that in the first century AD the cult of Mithras, the god of light and truth, was widespread within the Roman army and contributed to motivating many legionaries. Superstition will always have its place among military men; any analysis of the military ethos, however brief, cannot disregard this fact.

When the reading of the Christian Gospels became relatively common in both the Eastern and Western Roman Empires, the soldier was able to discover, in certain passages, a justification for personal sacrifice of which the writings of the ancient philosophers had been harbingers: 'For whosoever will save his life shall lose it; but whosoever will lose his life for my sake, the same shall save it' (Luke, ix. 24).

The concept of a military ethos, resting on the Stoic and Christian tradition, has descended over two millennia without having undergone any profound modifications: the soldier is a man who accepts that he must face up to the most arduous difficulties. The warrior is prepared for his calling by being habituated to conquer obstacles and by being accustomed to discipline. As in the earliest times, the preparation is completed by ceremonies in which the irrational still plays a role – military honours, loyalty to the flag, the oath. Although the present age has had eager recourse to all the scientific resources, often imbued with materialism, which psychology and sociology have placed at its disposal, it has simply discovered that the military ethos had long ago already incorporated these, empirically, into its techniques of preparation for combat.

All the measures that are applied to integrate an individual into his group have this factor in common – they rarely leave a man on his own. Yet very often, in the realities of battle, and particularly when he is in a position of command, the soldier has to respond *alone* if he seriously accepts putting his life at risk. The response given will reveal the strength or weakness of his training, his cast of mind, his philosophy and his faith. Whether manifested as faith in his leader, faith in a god, self-sacrifice for a comrade or a cause, the military ethos is a force which permits a man to surpass himself and to identify himself with the community he is serving. But it is a force actuated by spirit: matter alone does not 'go over the top'. *See also* CEREMONIES; ESPRIT DE CORPS; GLORY; HONOURS AND AWARDS; ICONOGRAPHY; LOSSES OF LIFE; MORALE; SYMBOLISM; TRAINING; VEXILLOLOGY.

D. REICHEL

FURTHER READING
J. Glenn Gray, *The Warriors: reflections on men in battle* (New York, 1970); James A. Aho, *Religious Mythology and the Art of War: comparative religious symbolisms in military violence* (London, 1981); Nicholas Fotion and Gerard Elfstrom, *Military Ethics: guidelines for peace and war* (London, 1986); *Military Ethics: reflections on principles – the profession of arms, military leadership, ethical practices, war and morality, educating the citizen-soldier*, eds Malham Wakin, Kenneth Wenker and James Kempf (Washington, 1987).

Eugene of Savoy, Prince (1663–1736) Although born in Paris of Italian parentage, in 1683 Prince Eugene joined the Imperial service in preference to the French army. He fought against the Turks and France before rising to become Imperial commander-in-chief in Hungary in which capacity he won the decisive victory at Zenta in 1697. As President of the Imperial Council of War, he carried out the reorganization of the Austrian army in 1703 and distinguished himself as its field commander during the War of the Spanish Succession (1702–14). He fought in northern Italy in 1703, joined Marlborough during the campaign and victory at Blenheim in 1704 before returning to Italy in 1705–6. In 1706, he beat the Duke d'Orléans and Marsin (1656–1706) at Turin, although his expedition to take Toulon in the following year was a failure. He fought in Flanders with Marlborough in 1708 and 1709, beating the French at Oudenarde (1708) and Malplaquet (1709). Eugene was defeated by Villars at Denain in 1712. Going back to Hungary after the Peace of Utrecht in 1714, Eugene beat the Turks at Peterwardein in 1716 and Belgrade in 1717. During the ensuing peace (Treaty of Passarowitz, 1718), Eugene helped to establish the militarized frontier between the newly conquered lands and the remaining Turkish possessions in the Balkans. He also encouraged the colonization of these areas, particularly the Banat of Temesvár. He emerged from semi-retirement to command the Imperial forces on the Rhine, 1734–5, during the War of the Polish Succession (1733–5). Napoleon regarded him as one of the seven great captains in history. *See also* AUSTRIA; BELGRADE; BLENHEIM; DENAIN; FRONTIERS; MALPLA-QUET; MARLBOROUGH; ZENTA.

J. NOUZILLE
JOHN CHILDS

FURTHER READING
N. Henderson, *Prince Eugen of Savoy* (London, 1964); Derek McKay, *Prince Eugene of Savoy* (London, 1977); Max Braubach, *Prinz Eugen von Savoyen* (5 vols, Munich, 1963–5); *Feldzüge des Prinzen Eugen von Savoyen* (20 vols, K. K. Kriegsarchiv, Vienna, 1876–92).

Expeditions These are military operations undertaken against a distant objective and require special preparations for secrecy, training, security and supplies. There are small, individual expeditions, which have been known since the American Civil War as 'raids' (they were previously referred to as 'incursions'), and large-scale expeditions directed against distant targets for which an expeditionary force has to be organized.

Incursions or raids are bold thrusts into enemy territory, generally carried out against the enemy's rear by light troops – *Pandours*, cavalry, mounted infantry – to pillage, disorganize communications, destroy arsenals or spread terror. In the seventeenth century, the Hungarian hussars were capable of harassing the enemy up to distances of 250 miles from their bases (e.g. the raid on Vienna in 1703). In 1712, 2,000 Imperialists forayed for a fortnight behind the 'iron frontier', covering more than 125 miles. Fischer's light cavalry gave most effective assistance to the French army in Germany during the War of the Austrian Succession (1742–8).

The operations carried out along the coasts by the British navy during the wars of the eighteenth century and the Napoleonic Wars can also be seen as raids, as can the commando-style operations of the Second World War (e.g. Ouistreham, 1760, Bruneval and St Nazaire, 1941, Dieppe, 1942). Bombing operations directed against the enemy's rear have also been called 'raids'. Sea and air raids have steadily increased their operational range.

Long-distance operations are usually combined service operations, with the navy and, today, the air force transporting the expeditionary force and ensuring its protection. Julius Caesar and William the Conqueror's successful expeditions and the ill-fated example of the Spanish Armada in 1588 are good illustrations. Normally, these require a favourable military and political situation in the area chosen as the target. Thus French attempts to effect landings in the British Isles have most often been directed towards Ireland, where the people were supposedly ready to rise in revolt. The occupation of Corsica by the British in 1794–6 and the Quiberon expedition (1795) were based on the same kind of calculation. Sometimes the objective is to help a people to achieve independence (Rochambeau's expeditionary force to America) or to assist one of the parties in a civil war (Mexico, 1862). The pretext is often aid to one's own nationals in difficulty in a country outside Europe. This was the case with most colonial expeditions. In European history, the Crimean War provides the best example of the creation of a front against a country with which there is no shared frontier while Napoleon's Egyptian expedition (1798) and the Dardanelles expedition (1915) both sought to gain control of a position which was considered to be of prime strategic importance.

In all cases, an expeditionary force must be able to operate at a long range from its base. To this end, it is composed of troops from all arms, is supported by all the necessary services and the leader is given great freedom of action. For many centuries, such expeditions were rendered difficult on account of the dangers of sea transport and also by friction between the navy and the army. It is, therefore, also important to possess a base, such as the English held at Calais between 1347 and 1558, or to operate in a region where the local population will assist the operation.

The Second World War saw landings on such a scale that most cannot rank as mere military expeditions. Their speed and scale and the involvement of all armed services qualify them for the grander title of combined operations (the American landings in the Pacific, *Torch*, *Husky*, *Overlord*). *See also* AVIATION; CAVALRY; COMBINED OPERATIONS; HUSSARS; INFANTRY; OVERLORD.

A. CORVISIER

FURTHER READING
Archer Jones, *The Art of War in the Western World* (Oxford, 1989).

Explosives There are four groups of military explosives: (1) detonating, or high explosive, (2) deflagrating, or low explosive, which burns more slowly and develops lower pressure and is principally used as a propellant (*see* PROPELLANTS), (3) atomic explosives (*see* NUCLEAR WARFARE), and (4) fuel–air mixtures. Detonating, or high explosives (HE) are divided into two types: primary HE, which can be detonated by simple ignition (spark, flame or impact), and secondary HE, which requires a detonator and, sometimes, a booster. Military detonators usually consist of primary HE and are often fitted with percussion and timing devices. A booster consists of sensitive secondary HE which reinforces the shock waves from the primary HE in the detonator. Military HE needs to produce *brisance*, the ability to shatter steel, concrete and other hard substances. Until the middle of the nineteenth century, the sole military explosive was gunpowder (*see* PROPELLANTS).

During the mid-nineteenth century occurred two scientific developments which transformed the nature and capabilities of military explosives. In 1846, the Italian chemist Ascanio Sobrero (1812–88) discovered the explosive properties of liquid nitroglycerine (NG) while nitrocellulose (guncotton) was developed by T. J. Pelouze in 1838 and C. F. Schönbein in 1845. By treating ordinary cotton with nitric and sulphuric acids, nitrocellulose (NC) was formed. In its raw state it created an explosion too violent for use as a propellant but its purification by Sir Frederick Abel (1827–1902) in 1865 and the discovery by E. A. Brown in 1868 that dry compressed guncotton could be detonated by a fulminate detonator led to its adoption as a filling for shells. Russia employed guncotton as a shell filler after 1876 and the more stable moist guncotton was used after 1890. In 1867, the Swedish chemist and industrialist Alfred Nobel invented dynamite (basically stabilized NG) having invented a detonator filled with fulminate of mercury three years previously. By 1900, the majority of European armies were utilizing picric acid (trinitrophenol) as a high-explosive shell filling. It could be melted and cast into a shell but was sufficiently sensitive to be detonated by a percussion fuse. The British referred to picric acid as Lyddite (1888) after the siege artillery firing ranges at Lydd on Romney Marsh. Trinitrotoluene (TNT), first prepared by Wilbrand in 1863, is a derivative of NG and was employed as a military explosive by Germany in 1904. Although it could be safely melted by steam and cast into shells (its melting point was considerably lower than its flash point), TNT was expensive and somewhat unpredictable as a shell filler although it possessed the advantage of being capable of mixing with other ingredients. In 1914, the British imitated the Germans in adopting TNT as their shell filling but demand rapidly outstripped supply. As a compromise, they mixed TNT with ammonium nitrate to produce Amatol which became the standard British shell filling throughout the First and Second World Wars. The German V-1 flying bomb and V-2 rocket carried Amatol warheads.

In the interwar period, the British experimented with RDX (trimethylene trinitramine) or Cyclonite, which had been first discovered by the German, Henning, in 1899. RDX was manufactured at the Royal Ordnance Factory at Bridgewater from 1939. The Germans developed PETN (pentaerythritol tetranitrate). Although Amatol and TNT remained the main British shell fillings during the Second World War, increasing use was made of RDX and its superior derivative, HMX or Octogen (tetramethylene tetranitramine). Aluminium was often added to increase blast producing Torpex (TNT + RDX + aluminium). Since 1945, the most common high explosives in use in modern armies are TNT, RDX, HMX and PETN. They are also found in the following combinations: Composition B (60 per cent RDX + 40 per cent TNT + beeswax as a sensitizer); Pentolite (TNT + PETN); Cyclotol (granular RDX in molten TNT); Torpex, which induces the highest detonation pressure but not the highest *brisance*; and HBX (RDX + TNT + aluminium + wax), which produces the highest *brisance* and is much used in torpedoes, depth charges and naval mines. Plastic explosives are formed from RDX, HMX or PETN mixed with plasticizers and were first used militarily in 1942: Composition C is a plastic explosive composed of 90 per cent RDX + 10 per cent emulsifying oil. Explosive D (ammonium picric) is nearly as powerful as TNT and insensitive to both shock and moderately high temperatures; it is often used to fill armour-piercing shells and bombs where detonation must be delayed until the projectile has penetrated the surface of the target. Tetryl (trinitrophenyl methylnitramine) is more powerful than TNT and can act as a booster for small shells. When mixed with TNT it forms Tetrytol, which can be cast in blocks suitable for demolitions and engineering. Modern detonators employ either fulminate of mercury or lead azide. Red and white phosphorus are employed as fillings for incendiary shells, bombs, and grenades.

Between 1940 and 1945, the United States manufactured 30,000,000 tons of military HE and ammunition (700,000 tons in July 1945 alone). During 1945, the United States spent 5 billion dollars on HE and ammunition. Around 10,000,000 people died as a direct result of military action in the First World War compared with 31,000,000 during the Second World War. Each life cost $14,000 in the first conflict but $45,000 (at constant values) in the second.

As the armour plate of Second World War tanks and fighting vehicles grew thicker to resist tungsten core armour-piercing kinetic energy ammunition, a new approach was sought to the problem of defeating rolled homogeneous steel armour (RHA). In 1888, the American C. E. Munroe (1849–1938) was the first to investigate the hollow, or shaped, charge and his work was followed up by Neumann between 1920 and 1941. If a conical depression is made at the end of a column of explosive, the resulting shock wave is concentrated along the central axis of the charge (the Munroe–Neumann effect). Should the surface of the conical depression be lined with metal, usually copper, the shock waves degrade the liner into a jet followed by a slug and these are propelled forwards along the central axis of the explosion. The jet moves at exceptionally high speed – 8,000 metres per second – and can penetrate up to 50 cm of RHA. The following slug travels at a much lower speed (300 metres per second) and plays no effective role; it is often found lodged at the entrance to the hole created by the jet. Once it has penetrated the armour, the jet itself does enormous damage inside the vehicle, but it also causes the interior surface of the armour to 'spall' (i.e. scabs break off at high speed to cause a shrapnel effect within the fighting compartment). HMX or RDX–TNT are the usual explosives employed to create the hollow charge effect. The adoption of the hollow charge as an anti-armour weapon during the Second World War, because it uses chemical rather than kinetic energy, meant that the muzzle velocity of the gun was no longer important. Hence, anti-tank weapons could be hand-held (bazooka, *Panzerfaust*, PIAT), or the charge would be delivered by low-speed rocket projectiles, guided missiles, bombs and recoilless rifles. Hollow charge rounds are now known as HEAT (high explosive anti-tank).

Another development during the Second World War was HESH ammunition (high explosive squash-head). Originally designed to attack reinforced concrete bunkers and fortifications, it rapidly became adopted as an anti-armour weapon partly because of its effectiveness and partly because it did not rely on high muzzle velocity. When a HESH round strikes an armoured target, the explosive spreads over a substantial area of the surface before detonating to set up shock waves which travel through the armour. When the waves encounter the inner surface of the armour, they reflect back to meet waves coming in the opposite direction. This sets up very high pressures and tensions sufficient to cause the inner surface of the armour to spall as the waves discover the lines of weakness within the metal.

Fuel–air explosives (FAEs) create an aerosol cloud of fuel and air which is ignited to produce explosions with very high blast over-pressures. Unlike conventional high explosives, which concentrate their maximum blast at one point, FAEs spread their blast waves evenly over a wide area, up to a radius of 200 metres for a 1,000 lb bomb. Ammonium nitrate and fuel oil produced the first fuel–air mixtures which were used in First World War bombs and flamethrowers, but during the Second World War this was refined into Napalm, petrol thickened by aluminium salt, or petrol, oil, powdered magnesium and sodium nitrate. The American Daisy Cutter bomb (BLU-82) uses a mixture of ammonium nitrate, powdered aluminium and polystyrene soap to produce an explosion with blast over-pressure of 1,000 psi. FAEs can be up to ten times as destructive as an equivalent weight of TNT, generating high *brisance* sufficient to clear minefields, flatten concrete buildings and destroy armoured vehicles; they can be detonated underwater and in a vacuum, giving them potential uses in anti-submarine warfare and in space. They are, in some cases, as damaging as low-yield nuclear weapons. Their widespread use has been retarded by technical difficulties in evenly distributing the aerosol cloud when delivered at high speed. Once these have been solved, FAEs are likely to replace conventional HE in area attacks although not in precision operations. *See also* ARMOUR PLATE; ARTILLERY; CHEMICAL AND BIOLOGICAL WARFARE; FIREARMS; GUNFIRE; MINING AND MINES; NUCLEAR WARFARE; PROPELLANTS; WEAPONS.

JOHN CHILDS

FURTHER READING
T. Urbanski, *The Chemistry and Technology of Explosives* (3 vols, Oxford, 1964–7); M. A. Cook, *The Science of High Explosives* (New York, 1966); A. Bailey and S. G. Murray, *Explosives, Propellants and Pyrotechnics* (London, 1989); S. Fordham, *High Explosives and Propellants* (2nd edn, Oxford, 1980).

F

Falkland Islands, Battle of the (8 December 1914)   At the outbreak of war in August 1914, the German East Asiatic squadron, consisting of the armoured cruisers *Scharnhorst* and *Gneisenau* and the light cruisers *Nürnberg*, *Leipzig*, *Emden*, and *Dresden*, was commanded by Vice-Admiral von Spee. After detaching the *Emden* to attack commerce in the Bay of Bengal, he decided to attempt to return to Germany by way of the South Pacific and the Atlantic. Von Spee bombarded Papeete (Tahiti) on 22 September before making for Chile. Off Coronel on 1 November, he met and defeated a British squadron under Rear-Admiral Sir Christopher Cradock, sinking two cruisers, the *Good Hope* and the *Monmouth*.

Von Spee next decided to destroy the British wireless station and coaling stocks on the Falkland Islands. Approaching the islands on 8 December, he was surprised to find a British squadron of two battle-cruisers, the *Invincible* and the *Inflexible*, besides other cruisers, in the harbour at Port Stanley. These had been dispatched under Vice-Admiral Sturdee by the British Admiralty on receiving news of Coronel. Von Spee was presented with a unique opportunity as the British ships were coaling and at two hours' notice for steam. Missing this golden chance, von Spee did not attack but hurriedly withdrew. Sturdee was thus able to leave his anchorage and, benefiting from exceptionally good visibility and the greater speed of his ships, to overtake von Spee. Thanks to their superior firepower, the battle-cruisers sank the two armoured cruisers, the *Kent* sank the *Nürnberg* and the *Cornwall* and the *Glasgow* accounted for the *Leipzig*. The fast *Dresden* escaped but was eventually found and sunk at Mas-a-fuera on 14 March 1915 by the British cruisers. The Battle of the Falkland Islands, followed by the sinking of the *Emden* and

the *Königsberg* in the Indian Ocean, confirmed British dominance of the high seas. *See also* JUTLAND; NAVAL WARFARE; NAVIES.

P. MASSON

FURTHER READING
Geoffrey Bennett, *Coronel and the Falklands* (London, 1962); Richard Hough, *The Pursuit of Admiral von Spee* (London, 1969).

Falklands War (1982)   Argentina had been in dispute with Britain over the status of the Falkland Islands for more than a century and a half. Military action had been threatened on a number of occasions but in 1982, following vacillations by the British Foreign Office and contradictory political signals, Argentina believed that Britain would not have the political will to withstand a takeover of the islands and that such an action would, furthermore, bolster the diminishing reputation of the military junta then in power in Argentina. Consequently on 2 April 1982, General Galtieri, the head of the junta, accepted a plan proposed by the head of the navy, Admiral Anaya, and proceeded to resolve the issue by militarily occupying the Falklands. Britain had negligible forces on the islands and these were only able to mount token resistance. With the support of Parliament and, probably, the majority of the public, the British Cabinet immediately announced its intention to respond to this 'act of aggression' and to reoccupy the Falkland Islands. The decision marked the beginning of a campaign which was to last two and a half months and which can be divided into several phases.

The first of these was devoted to the task of mobilizing and concentrating a task force to operate at a distance of more than 8,000 nautical miles from the British Isles. This was facilitated by the support of a refuelling station at the American base of Wideawake

233

on Ascension Island which was made available to the British forces. This served as the forward base and it is here that the British Harrier aircraft were equipped with American SideWinder missiles, the latest air-to-air missile system, which were to prove crucial in the air war against the Argentinian air forces. By the end of April the task force was assembled off the Falklands under the command of Admiral Woodward. The fleet consisted of some fifty warships built around the aircraft carriers *Hermes* and *Invincible* and also included requisitioned merchant vessels that served as support vessels and troop ships such as the two liners *Queen Elizabeth II* and *Canberra*.

Following the best rules of naval strategy the Royal Navy gained absolute mastery of the seas when the nuclear assault submarine *Conqueror* torpedoed and sank the Argentinian cruiser *General Belgrano* on 2 May. Having no modern anti-submarine warfare equipment the Argentinian fleet, including the aircraft carrier *25 de Mayo*, remained in home ports unable to put to sea.

The first territory to be retaken by the British forces (26 April) was the island of South Georgia, a dependency of the Falklands. This operation had almost been a disaster as two Wessex helicopters were lost in the first attempt and a number of SAS soldiers had to be rescued. Nevertheless the second attempt succeeded and the small Argentinian force quickly surrendered. South Georgia had no military value and its recapture diverted scarce resources but it provided a 'victory' which was important in maintaining public confidence in the venture.

Preliminary operations against the Falkland Islands themselves began with commando raids and air attacks by Harriers operating from the aircraft carriers and by Victors from Ascension Island. The main landing took place on 20 May at San Carlos Bay. Ten thousand men from various units of the British army were involved. During this crucial phase the British fleet was subjected to determined attacks from the Argentinian fleet air arm and air force in the form of 200 Mirage II, Dagger, Skyhawk and Super-Étendard aircraft

operating at the extreme limit of their range. Both Exocet missiles and conventional munitions were employed in these attacks. The Argentinians suffered heavy losses (109 planes) but not without inflicting considerable damage on the British fleet. Two ships were hit and sunk by Exocet missiles, the destroyer *Sheffield* and the transport ship *Atlantic Conveyor*. The loss of the latter was particularly serious since it was carrying the helicopters intended for the forward lift of troops from San Carlos to Stanley, some 50 miles away. Another destroyer, *Coventry*, was also sunk, two frigates (*Antelope* and *Ardent*) were lost and two landing ships (*Sir Galahad* and *Sir Tristram*) were sent to the bottom. These attacks were not, however, able to prevent the landings and the subsequent advance of the troops across land. After capturing Goose Green the British troops advanced on Port Stanley at the end of May and, after the Argentine defensive line had been broken, the garrison surrendered on 13 June.

The whole affair, which ended in a complete British victory, taught many lessons. It emphasized the need for warships to reinforce their protective armour and their defences both against bombs and more especially against missiles. As regards logistics, it emphasized the superiority of sea over air transport. Though 5,800 men and 6,000 tonnes of equipment and supplies were carried by air to Ascension Island, the transport ships carried 9,000 men and 500,000 tonnes. The Falklands affair further showed the advantage of possessing a land intervention force working in tandem with air and naval forces including troop and supply ships and aircraft carriers. It also demonstrated the superiority of professional troops, well-trained for a specific type of action, over a conscript army. Finally, a number of the British ships which had been sunk had been lost through fires started by the initial explosion of bombs and missiles. The fires had spread rapidly along unprotected, commercially available, plastic-coated electrical cable which had been used in the vessels because of its low cost. The Falklands War showed that defence equipment must be manufactured to the highest possible specifications. *See also* COMBINED OPERATIONS; EXPEDITIONS; GREAT BRITAIN; NAVAL WARFARE.

P. MASSON
DAVID WESTON

FURTHER READING
Paul Eddy and Magnus Linklater, *War in the Falklands* (London, 1982); Max Hastings and Simon Jenkins, *Battle for the Falklands* (London, 1983); Martin Middlebrook, *The Fight for the Malvinas: the Argentinian forces in the Falklands War* (London, 1989); Julian Thompson, *No Picnic* (London, 1985); Sandy Woodward, *One Hundred Days: memoirs of the Falklands battle group commander* (London, 1992).

Families, military Ever since the disappearance of the Amazons and the death of Joan of Arc, the business of war, so long as it keeps within the rules, has generally been the preserve of young, adult males. For a considerable period, soldiers were advised not to marry, or even forbidden to do so. In keeping with the views of his time, Vauban said: 'men who are married are naturally less suitable for war than those who are not.' Though married men tended to desert less frequently, they were thought to be understandably cautious in the face of danger and often indulged in lucrative activities which had no connection with their military duties. Accommodation had to be provided for wives who accompanied their husbands, and financial provision had to be made for widows and orphans, all of which represented a heavy financial burden for the army and the state. In seventeenth and eighteenth century England, a soldier needed the permission of his captain to marry and recruiters were not permitted to enlist married men. Louis XIV was an exception. He encouraged foreign soldiers to marry in France, on condition – after 1685 – that they were Catholics, to tie them to their adopted country. Members of the British Brigade in the Dutch service in the seventeenth and eighteenth centuries also made numerous local marriages and this may have been officially favoured. Louis also encouraged the French guards, who always spent the winter in Paris, to take up part-time civilian employment and set up a home so as 'to escape from a life of debauchery'. Yet, in 1764, all married guardsmen were dismissed from this regiment so that it could be housed in barracks and its discipline tightened. In the case of officers, generally no action was taken except to discourage them from making unsuitable marriages, though the author of *Les Oisivetés* preferred them to devote their full attentions to their profession: 'I disapprove entirely of military men marrying.' The habitual propinquity of death, the continual movement of troops and the loose morals in garrison towns were not well calculated to develop in fighting men the qualities of husband and father.

Nevertheless, soldiers' wives and, more often, their women were tolerated within a society whose moral code did not conform with that of the civil community. In the sixteenth century, Spanish military writers considered that the presence of a few prostitutes in a *tercio*'s train was a lesser evil than a number of wives and children. Filippo Strozzi admitted that he had been quite wrong, in 1570, to throw into the Loire at Pont-de-Cé the 'girls' who infested his army. A large number of children, whether legitimate or not, were born in garrisons or nearby. It was possible to follow the line of march of French regiments, even as late as 1700, by studying the baptismal registers of the parishes where they had halted. The tone was set from the top. Vauban had three legitimate children and five known illegitimate children by five different mothers. Boys who had grown up in camps had a leaning towards the profession of arms; already soldiers *de facto*, they became so *de jure* as soon as they had attained the necessary bodily height. It grew to be the established custom in France to consider these army children as being in the service from birth. In 1766, Choiseul granted them half-pay from the age of six. From 1755, officers and war commissaries were trying to remove the prejudice against the married soldier. This reflected a current of opinion which was increasingly supported by writers on military matters, as demonstrated by the article on 'Pensioners' in the *Encyclopédie*. Their theme was that the royal army would profit by the hereditary transmission of soldierly qualities, a theory which at that time was still

235

uncontested. The general belief was that the sons of ordinary soldiers inherited their fathers' stout hearts and power of endurance, while the nobility were born with the privileges of valour and open-handedness.

The movement towards permanent and semi-permanent garrisons during the later seventeenth and eighteenth centuries fostered marriage. Frederick the Great favoured stable marriages for his foreign private soldiers 'so as to populate the country and to preserve the stock, which is admirable'. Out of 100,000 people who lived in Berlin in 1776, there were 17,056 NCOs and men, 5,526 army wives and 6,622 children. The wives lived with their husbands either in quarters or in barracks, in the latter case receiving a small wage for cleaning the rooms and making beds. Their husbands were granted a marriage allowance of 8 groschen a day. In wartime, wives who remained in garrison towns were given free bread and a small state pension and they could correspond with their husbands *gratis* provided their letters were stamped with the municipal seal. In every company of foot, between five and twelve wives accompanied the troops on campaign. Orphans were housed in the Potsdam Military Orphanage, which had 2,000 inmates in 1758. One in ten Austrian infantrymen was permitted to marry, the wives accompanying the troops on campaign. After 1774, Austrian military children were educated in regimental and military schools (*see* TRAINING).

Until 1851, British army wives had to live in barracks. In that year, the first official married quarters were established for the Foot Guards. Even so, soldiers paid only one shilling a day were not expected to be able to support a wife and family and the long periods (often 10 or 20 years) on colonial service militated against widespread marriage; only six women were allowed to go with each company overseas, increasing to twelve if the venue were New South Wales or India. The Royal Sappers and Miners had 20 per cent of their number married. Around the middle of the nineteenth century, the British army began to realize that marriage was good for discipline and contributed greatly to the well-being of the soldiers. Gradually, the number of men allowed to marry was increased and the number of women and wives permitted to travel overseas rose. The establishment of permanent regimental depots in 1870–1 further fostered military marriage.

In the twentieth century, professional regular armies are likely to contain a large proportion of married men as the army is a career occupying the soldier for the majority of his adult life. As a consequence, armed forces have to provide a complete range of social services: married quarters, nurseries, schools and welfare. On the other hand, conscript armies in peacetime have a low proportion of married men, as conscripts serve for only a short term and usually fulfil their military obligations before they reach marriageable age. In wartime, conscript armies begin by enlisting single men but casualties soon bring married men into the net, particularly in specialist services.

Montaigne wrote that 'the proper, sole and essential style for the nobility in France is the profession of arms.' Even after the foundation of standing armies in Europe in the sixteenth and seventeenth centuries, the nobility continued in the chivalric tradition and saw its *raison d'être* in war and armed service. As a result, the officer corps of the new armies were dominated by aristocrats, almost exclusively so in the cases of France and Prussia. A custom grew up in France which finally became the norm. As the Marquis de Quincy observed in 1726 in his *Maxims and Directions on the Military Art*, 'the usual procedure among men of rank or from a military background is to destine their eldest son to the profession of arms.' Families belonging to the *noblesse de robe* normally sent their younger sons into the army; some of these men founded military lines, like the families of Franquetot de Coigny and Potier de Gesvres. Such family associations with the army invested even commoners with a standing that justified conferment of nobility. The rare letters patent that were granted to officers or to life guards rewarded the merits of the whole family; this was the case with the gunner Mormès de Saint-Hilaire in 1651 and the sapper Delorme in 1745. The Comte d'Argenson regularized this practice in

1750 by his conferment of military nobility on officers who could show three generations of distinguished service. Frederick William I of Brandenburg-Prussia (1713–40) began the cult of the exclusively noble officer corps and, apart from influxes of bourgeois officers during wartime, it continued until 1918 and even into the army of the Third Reich. 'I always choose my officers from the nobility,' said Frederick the Great, 'for nobility nearly always has a sense of honour. It can be found among bourgeois of merit, but it is rarer, and in such cases it is better to keep them in one's service. If a noble loses his honour he is ostracized by his family; whereas a commoner who has committed some fraud can continue to run his father's business.' Many Prussian families – the Kleists, the Mansteins – served continuously in the German army from the eighteenth century to the twentieth. Between 1921 and 1934, 35 per cent of German officers were the sons of officers. However, it was easy to fake noble status – Yorck, Steuben and Clausewitz all originated from bogus aristocratic families – and forged aristocratic pedigrees were widely available for the bourgeoisie with money in their pockets.

Regimental officer corps were often family concerns. With patronage resting in the hands of the colonel, subalterns' commissions could be given to numerous relatives. This was particularly the case in foreign service formations – the British Brigade in the Netherlands or the Swiss, German and Irish units in the French army – where large military families might control whole regiments. Indeed, many colonels favoured applications from relatives when an ensign's or cornet's place fell vacant. Many a young officer married his captain's daughter, creating even wider blood connections. At a lower level, captains often preferred to recruit the sons of their sergeants and soldiers. There was also a tendency for NCOs and rankers to marry the widows of their deceased comrades. At all levels, family relationships were intertwined with networks of patronage reinforcing both *esprit de corps* and the cohesion of military society.

England, with her more limited martial traditions, boasted some military families, like the 'fighting Veres' of the sixteenth and seventeenth centuries. A number of families which suffered financially during the Civil Wars and Interregnum (1642–60) sent their sons into the armed forces after the Restoration. The three Churchill brothers – John, George and Charles – the Trelawneys and the Kirkes were prominent examples. From the seventeenth to the early twentieth century, the English (British) officer corps was the preserve of those who had the wealth to purchase commissions and to provide a private income. Class was not the sole arbiter. To some extent, this tended to militate against the gentry and the aristocracy in favour of the middle classes.

In France, family influence began to lose its potency during the second half of the eighteenth century. Choiseul, in 1763, removed the responsibility for recruitment from individual regiments and placed it with the civil authorities. Where a man was posted became a matter of chance and there was little likelihood that he would encounter relatives and neighbours. When armies began to enshrine the principle of service to the nation, the recruit was even more cut off from his roots; he joined a new family of which the colonel was father. As for the military vocation of the nobility, this was no longer considered a privilege of blood or of race, except in Prussia and some other German states. 'These distinctions are becoming alien to us,' wrote the author of *L'Esprit du militaire* in 1772. If courage was a continuing feature of some noble families, it was no longer thought of as being the result of a biological characteristic but rather as an individual psychological trait. In fact, any person of rank who had read Marmontel's *Belisarius* must have realized that he had a duty to devote himself to his country's service in order to discharge his debt for the advantages he had received at his birth. By 1830, only 21 per cent of British officers were aristocrats, 32 per cent came from the landed gentry and 47 per cent had middle-class origins. In the *Reichswehr*, 22 per cent of officers were noble in 1920, 21 per cent in 1926 and 24 per cent in 1932.

Conscription, the high degree of technical expertise now required and the overall decline of the values inherent in social class and aristocracy have turned modern officer corps into meritocracies open to talent adjudged by public application and examination. Certain small reservoirs of social exclusiveness remain in some guards regiments where a family tradition of service might be of some import but armed forces are now generally open societies. Nevertheless, there are still military families in the sense that it is the custom of that family to send its male offspring into one of the armed services. *See also* BARRACKS; BILLETING; GARRISONS; NAVAL PERSONNEL; PENSIONS; RECRUITMENT; TRAINING; VETERANS.

J. CHAGNIOT
JOHN CHILDS

FURTHER READING
André Corvisier, *Armies and Societies in Europe, 1494–1789* (Bloomington, Ind., 1979); Karl Demeter, *The German Officer-Corps in Society and State, 1650–1945* (London, 1965); V. Bamfield, *On the Strength: the story of the British army wife* (London, 1974); M. Trustram, *Women of the Regiment: marriage and the Victorian army* (New York, 1984).

Farnese *See* PARMA

Fatherland *See* NATIONALISM

Filibusters *See* COMMERCE-RAIDING

Finances, military 'Endless supplies of money', said Cicero, 'constitute the sinews of war.' The expenditure occasioned by the raising and maintenance of armed forces and the fighting of wars is one of the most important aspects of military history, but it is impossible to discover accurate data. What is generally called military expenditure only represents those direct expenses which have been met from regular funds and which therefore leave their trace in administrative records and are easy to identify. However, to establish true figures, we should have to add the many and varied forms of indirect expenditure sustained by the civil authorities and local administrative bodies, which are not always reimbursed by the military administration. However, this margin of uncertainty applies more in regard to army administration than to the administration of the navy. In spite of its necessary contacts with the merchant marine and other naval organizations, the naval administration has, over the years, formed a clearly circumscribed financial orbit. Another difficulty for the researcher is the secrecy that often surrounds military expenditure. From a government's point of view, to acknowledge that military expenditure is rising often means revealing its policy; hence the 'camouflaging' of some military expenditure in the interests of security. Lastly, the levels of military expenditure, even in the case of the most official expenditure, are more subject to variation than are those of any other activity of state. Obviously, a distinction has to be made between wartime and peacetime expenditure. These variations demand recourse to extraordinary and extremely varied means of raising finance. Problems of finance, like those of recruitment, cannot be dissociated from the economic and social preoccupations of a state and therefore from political problems.

We shall therefore examine means used to raise finance, military budgets and expenditure and, lastly, touch on the financial cost of fighting wars.

The Means of Raising Finance In the armies of tribal societies or within feudal societies where warriors or free men owed a service of arms at their own expense, the problems of finance remained very limited and a state of almost permanent war could be maintained. Matters were similar in many ancient cities. However, these principles did not absolve the sovereign, warlord, king or *demos* from the need to create a war treasure to meet the unforeseen costs of a potential conflict. This most often consisted of precious objects and was often placed for safe keeping in a temple, as was the case among the Hebrews and the Athenians. The idea of a war chest was to last into the era of well-financed states. On the death of Henry IV of France, that country possessed a treasury of 30 million livres which had been accumulated by Sully. Frederick William I of Brandenburg-Prussia left Frederick II a sum of 8 million taler for this purpose in 1740, and in 1895 the Germany of William II had a reserve of some 120 million taler as a war chest. Sovereigns who called upon the service of contingents of vassals or allies were usually obliged to pay them. Obviously this was also the case with mercenaries. The Bible relates that the King of Judah, Ametsia, took into his pay 100,000 (*sic*) valiant warriors for 100 silver talents. Such were the origins of state military expenditure.

The construction and maintenance of a fortress were largely provided for by statute labour or by making remuneration in kind to free workmen. It did, however, become necessary to pay certain specialist craftsmen in coin, as a monetary economy developed. Similarly, the suzerain who wished to retain his vassals for longer than the period laid down by custom (forty days or six weeks) had to maintain them. In order to meet these expenses, which were increasingly being paid in coin, he had recourse to feudal aids, a pecuniary contribution by a feudal vassal to his lord, which existed to provide for the lord when he was going to war. The king, as the highest lord among lords, used this same procedure for a long period. The evolution of the art of warfare and the development of a monetary economy made recourse to 'aids' increasingly frequent, to the point where it became necessary for the king to have such measures ratified by the representative assemblies or estates.

It was with the *Grande Ordonnance* of 1357, imposed by the Estates General in the aftermath of the disastrous defeat at Poitiers, that a national military tax was instituted in France. With the coming of a standing army, the tax continued to apply after the war. This was the *taille royale* (1439), which was initially regarded as a substitute for spilling blood and for that reason was not paid by those who gave, or were supposed to give, their blood in battle (the nobles) or by those who were forbidden to bear arms (the clergy). However, as the development of the state gave rise to an increase in the new non-military forms of expenditure funded from the *taille*, in 1539 Francis I created the *taillon*, a tax used exclusively to finance the maintenance of men at arms. In the sixteenth century, in France and Spain, a growing portion of the fiscal resources that arrived in the royal exchequer (which in France had become in 1523 the *trésor de l'Epargne*) was distributed to the army through special funds, though these did not prevent the financing of military activities from local taxes. However, the practice also became widespread of directly allocating certain financial duties or resources to a particular special fund. For example, the pensioners were maintained by the *droit d'oblat* paid by monasteries and a deduction from soldiers' pay. This diversity of revenues and expenditures makes it difficult to establish accurate total figures for military expenditure under the French *ancien régime*. The task is easier in Spain thanks to the archives of the omnipresent *Contaduria mayor de Cuentas*.

In the seventeenth century, the demands of the military made it necessary to call upon the most varied financial resources. Under Louis XIII and Richelieu, the fiscal burden was increased fourfold. Alongside the so-called 'ordinary resources' deriving from crown lands, 'extraordinary resources' (for this was the name still given to taxes in this period) were greatly increased. And it was also necessary to have recourse to short-term expedients: manipulation of the coinage, sale of offices (often created by dividing up existing offices), forms of forced loans, recourse to bankers, etc., which brought about the popular revolts of the time and the Fronde. Most of the monies raised in this way went to the army. After a brief period in which financial order was restored, the end of the reign of Louis XIV saw a return to the use of expedients, such as anticipations, which consisted of requiring the tax-farmers responsible for indirect taxes to pay the king the revenue for future years in advance.

The military policy of kings was to a large extent determined by their financial resources. The kings of France would have found it difficult to increase the overall fiscal burden, which was already very high, particularly since their intentions to make the privileged pay were thwarted. Such considerations forced Louis XV to negotiate the Treaty of Aix-la-Chapelle (1748).

Before – and more especially after – the American war (1783), to compensate for the expenses caused by the modernization of France's armaments, Louis XVI made swingeing reductions in the sums paid to military personnel. This kind of fiscal inhibition helped to maintain a lack of imagination which meant that only small resources could be deployed. This in turn contributed to keeping the financial administration of the army very complex, resulting in an endless process of 'muddling through'. It was not until Necker took the reins in 1788 that the idea was broached of substituting a single fund for the various different funds from which the army was financed: the ordinary war fund (for the old units), the extraordinary war fund (for all 'regular' troops), the ordinary artillery fund (arms and equipment), the extraordinary artillery fund (personnel) and the fortifications, invalids and Order of Saint-Louis funds, etc., which derived their income either directly or indirectly from the various fiscal resources. This reform was only really achieved by Petiet, Minister of War under the Directory, who established a proper military budget organized under separate heads in which, theoretically, no transfers between the different expenditure heads were permitted, except where a law had been passed to that effect by the legislative assemblies.

France is to some degree an untypical case. During the eighteenth century, the King of England, or rather the British Parliament, was able to impose much heavier taxes on the British people than was possible in France. Government revenues were made up as follows: 74 per cent from indirect taxes, 24 per cent from direct taxes and 2 per cent from income from crown lands. In France, the equivalent figures were 39 per cent, 49 per cent and 12 per cent. The more compliant nature of the British people in fiscal matters is explained by the fact that the burden was more equally shared among the various taxpayers and taxation levels were decided by Parliament. British public finance possessed considerable potential after the 'Financial Revolution', 1689–1750, which established an economy based on credit and banking.

With the creation in 1722 of the General Directory of War, Finance and Domains,

Frederick William I subordinated the economy of the kingdom of Prussia to the upkeep of his army. The main part of these resources came from excise duty, i.e. from indirect taxation. Specific taxes did still remain such as those earmarked for the remount depot. After 1751, the monies earmarked for the army were distributed by the *General-Kriegskasse* to the *Massow-kasse* for the maintenance of the army in peacetime. In time of war, these were distributed to the *Feld-Kriegskasse* (pay), the *Feld-Proviantamt* (magazines and transport), the *Feld-Bakerei* (bread supplies) and the *Lazarettkasse* (hospitals), all of which were directed by the *Feld-Kriegskommissariat*. The organization of the financial services of the Austrian and Russian armies was inspired by more or less the same principles.

In the nineteenth century, military finances were relatively uncomplicated and varied little in their organization between one state and another. They became more complicated again as warfare became more industrialized. It is sometimes difficult to distinguish military from civilian expenditure and some forms are 'mixed', such as spending on postal services, road building and railways. This also applies today in the case of scientific research at its various different levels.

Budgets and Military Expenditure The first military budgets dated from 1661 in England. The secretary-at-war or the paymaster-general, both royal officials, presented the king with a precisely itemized estimate of the next year's military expenditure on the army. A similar process was conducted for both the navy and the Ordnance Office. After 1689, these military estimates, or budgets, were proffered to the House of Commons who then voted the taxation to meet the commitments. On paper, these budgets looked neat and tidy but the production of an accurate budget was difficult. Spending varied according to the fluctuations of the military establishment: men on active service and in garrison were supplied on different financial bases; it was impossible to keep track of effectives in the field; and large items, such as fortifications, required varying levels of finance over a number of years. In France, Le Tellier invented the notion of an 'average man' which represented the average daily expenditure for the average strength of the armed forces over twelve months. This system was refined by d'Argenson in the eighteenth century. The figures provided by the archives of the French War Ministry are incomplete as some of the costs of garrisons and troops movements were paid from local resources or directly by the local population, matters on which only occasional evidence survives. However, these local sources of revenue only amounted to about 10 per cent of the money provided by the crown. In England, the costs of billeting troops were partially hidden by the providers of quarters often having to reclaim their outlays from the paymaster-general in London.

In the present day, military budgets are still quite often incomplete, since there is always extra-budgetary expenditure. Moreover, if some costs vary little over time – most notably maintenance costs – other expenses develop very rapidly. There are many cases where the production of weapons or research into new weapons has been rapidly cancelled either because the systems suddenly became outclassed or their development incurred unforeseen expenditure. In Britain until the 1980s, expenditure on the research, development and production of weapons systems was poorly controlled by government, leading to many projects running substantially over-budget. Military budgets are constantly being reviewed, sometimes even before they come into force. In effect,

military budgets have increasingly come to resemble expenditure programmes or medium-term financial plans. Nowadays, the division of the funds into separate heads is sometimes expressed in a flexible manner in order to make it easy to effect transfers, most notably between the design and production phases of the development of new arms and equipment. Lastly, some forms of weapons and equipment orginally produced for the national army may be sold to other armies, thus keeping down production costs and reducing overall military expenditure. The variations in expenditure are made all the greater by the fact that most armies are involved in some system of alliances and, in some cases, are members of military blocs (NATO). The distribution of costs between the various member nations changes with some frequency. This has extended to the development of multinational weapons systems with design and production costs spread among the members of the alliance (e.g. the European Fighter Aircraft project).

These various considerations mean that, essential as it may be, any comparison of the successive military budgets of a single country, as well as that of the military budgets of different countries at a particular point in time, must be interpreted with caution. With all these provisos, it is, however, interesting to consider the value of the military expenditure of certain states in a number of different periods. Below are some figures extracted from various authorities.

Table 1   *French military expenditure as a proportion of overall national expenditure*

	Total (in millions of livres)	Percentage	Debt servicing (%)	
1683	65.3	56.7	8.9	war
1692	140	79.8	8.8	
1699	74.3	16.5	76.5	
1726	65	35	33.5	
1751	107	42	28	
1775	124	30	38	
1788	159	25	41	
1949		19		Indo-China, Korea
1952		35		
1955		26		Suez, Algeria
1956		29		

Table 2 *The fiscal burden in France and England (in livres or francs germinal per inhabitant)*

	France	England
1715	p 7½	p 18½
1735	w 9⅓	p 18½
1745	w 10	w 21¾

p = years of peace; w = years of war

Table 3 *Overall tax burden (in livres tournois or francs germinal per inhabitant)*

	France	England		France	England
1715	p 7½	p 18½	1780	p 15½	p 32
1735	w 9⅓	p 18½	1790	p 17¾	p 41
1745	w 10	w 21¾	1800	w 22	w 66
1765	p 12¼	p 28⅓	1810	w 27	w 105
1775	p 13½	p 28			

p = years of peace; w = years of war

In 1765, in the Habsburg Empire and Prussia, the burden is 7 million livres at 1765 values. The percentage of military expenditure is greatest in Prussia, followed by the Habsburg Empire, France and England (navy included).

Let us now move on to the eve of the First World War to compare military spending in the various countries:

Table 4 *Military expenditure in 1910 (in gold francs)*

States	Military budget* (in millions)	Population (in millions)	Expenditure per inhabitant (in francs)
Germany	1,011	64.6	15.6
Austria-Hungary	559	52.6	10.6
Bulgaria	37	5.0	7.4
Spain	164	19.9	8.2
USA	844	92.0	9.1
France	872	39.5	22.1
Great Britain	681	48.0	14.2
Italy	364	34.4	10.6
Japan	219	50.5	4.3
Netherlands	60	5.9	10.2
Russia	1,370	150.0	9.1
Serbia	26	4.7	5.5
Sweden	75	5.5	13.6
Switzerland	40	3.7	10.8
Turkey	218	22.0	10.0
Belgium	57	7.4	7.7
Romania	61	5.2	11.7

* These are official figures given by the *Dictionnaire militaire rédigé par un comité d'officiers de toutes armes, supplément*, updated to 1 October 1911. It is clear that they should be treated with caution.

If we move forward to 1962–5, using the figures presented by General P. Hervieu in the *Encyclopaedia Universalis*, we may establish the following table, with all the requisite caution when dealing with figures for average capital expenditure:

Table 5   *Military expenditure levels in 1962–5 (in dollars)*

State	Military budget (in thousand millions)	Population (in millions)	Cost per inhabitant (in dollars)
United States	51.5	185	277
Great Britain	5	54	95
Federal Republic of Germany	4.5	57	78
France	3	47	63

The military budget of the USSR is thought to have risen from 12,400 million roubles in 1962 to 14,500 million in 1967, figures which do not take all expenditure into account. Western experts estimate that actual total spending in 1988 was between 18,200 and 32,000 million roubles. At the official rate of exchange, the official budget would be 20,000 million dollars, but treating the currencies in terms of pur-chasing power, it would be 42,000 million. The current military budget of China is officially 5,000 million dollars, but the highly decentralized administration of the People's Republic makes it possible for an unknown proportion of this expenditure to be borne by the regions.

Other estimates of the size of military budgets have been presented by Jean Meyer, *Le Poids de l'état*:

Table 6   *Percentage of official defence appropriation as a proportion of GNP*

Country	1965	1975	Trend
United States	7.57	6.0	− 1.57
Great Britain	5.87	5.0	− 0.87
France	5.17	3.5	− 1.67
West Germany	4.34	3.4	− 0.94
USSR	9.0	11–13	+ 2.0
GDR	3.3	5.7	+ 2.4
Czechoslovakia	5.5	3.5	− 2.0
Hungary	2.5	2.6	+ 0.1
Poland		3.6	
Romania		1.8	
Japan	0.95	0.9	− 0.05
Argentina	1.93	2.8	+ 0.87
Brazil	1.97	1.1	− 0.87
Egypt	9.20	37.0	+27.8
Israel		29.9	
India	3.7	10.9	+ 7.2

The Financial Cost of Wars   It is well known that many wars have exhausted a country's finances or left it with debts for many years, unless the country has freed itself from these debts by bankruptcy, as France did in 1721 or Germany in 1923. It should, none the less, be pointed out that the old adage that 'war should pay for war' has sometimes left the victor with a posi-tive financial balance. At the end of the Seven Years' War, Prussia, which had been ravaged by the fighting, had several million talers in its treasury after 20 per cent of its costs had been covered by its English allies, and Saxony had been forced to make huge contributions. Something similar applied to France in the Revolutionary Wars after 1794 and the Napoleonic Wars. The war against Prussia brought in 280 million gold francs as 'clear profit'. By contrast, the war in Spain was the first of the Napoleonic Wars to cost France money. However, in the first year of that war, hardly any more was spent than on the expedition of 1823 where the French army paid all its own costs. Overall, the Napoleonic Wars cost France 5,000 million francs, those of the Restoration period (Spain, Morea, Algiers) 286 million (the Algiers expedition yielding a profit as a result of the seizure of the treasury of the dey

of Algiers). The war in Italy, the Austro-Prussian War of 1866 and the Franco-Prussian War of 1870–1 each cost a total of approximately 1,500 million francs. By contrast, in the American Civil War, the costs were as high as 25,000–31,000 million francs depending on which of the various estimates one accepts. Reparations, war indemnities and 'ransoms' paid by the defeated party also have to be taken into account. Thus, for example, France had to pay 1,800 million francs to its conquerors after the fall of the Empire and 5,000 million francs after 1871. With the war of 1914–18, we move on to a completely new scale of expenditure. The figures cited in Dupuy and Dupuy's *Encyclopaedia of Military History* are as follows (these statistics are approximations):

Table 7 *Expenditure in the First and Second World Wars*

First World War (in millions of dollars):

France	49,877	Germany	58,072
British Empire	51,975	Austria-Hungary	23,706
Russia	25,600	Turkey	3,445
Italy	18,143	Bulgaria	1,015
United States	32,320		
Belgium	10,195		
Serbia	2,400		
Romania	2,601		
Greece	556		
Total	193,667	Total	86,238
Grand Total	279,905		

Second World War (in billions of dollars)

United States	350	Germany	300
United Kingdom	150	Italy	50
France	100	Japan	100
USSR	200		
China	?		
All other belligerents	350		
Grand total	1,600		

See also ADMINISTRATION, ARMY; ADMINISTRATION, NAVAL; PENSIONS; RECRUITMENT; WAR ECONOMY.

A. CORVISIER
JOHN CHILDS

FURTHER READING
John Brewer, *The Sinews of Power* (London, 1989); P. G. M. Dickson, *The Financial Revolution in England* (London, 1967); W. R. Lawson, *Modern Wars and War Taxes* (London, 1912); W. K. Hancock and M. M. Gowing, *British War Economy* (London, 1949); G. Hardach, *The First World War, 1914–1918* (Harmondsworth, 1987); A. S. Milward, *War, Economy and Society, 1939–45* (London, 1977).

Finland, pre-1809 *See* SWEDEN

Finland, since 1809 Between 1809 and

1917 Finland constituted an autonomous grand duchy within the Russian Empire: the Russian army and navy were responsible for its defence which assumed greater importance for the security of St Petersburg from the 1880s. After annexation by Russia the armed forces raised by Sweden in Finland (22,000 men) were dissolved and the Emperor declared that new Finnish troops would be raised only when Finland's resources permitted. Separate Finnish forces existed between 1812 and 1830 (six battalions) and between 1854/5 and 1867 (nine rifle battalions), local economic difficulties causing their disbandment. The Finnish military service law of 1878 (distinct from the Russian law of 1874 for constitutional reasons) took effect in 1881: nine rifle battalions and, from 1889, a dragoon regiment (totalling 5,800 men) were formed together with 32 reserve companies. The terms of service were shorter than in Russia, and Finland's defence burden was proportionately lower than Russia's. Russian determination to raise Finland's share prompted a new military service law in 1901 which was so opposed in Finland that the Finnish army was disbanded and personal military service replaced by national financial contributions. Even the prestigious Guards Finnish Rifle Battalion (raised 1812; became guards 1829), which had fought with distinction in Poland in 1831 and in the Russo-Turkish War of 1877–8, and survived in 1901, was disbanded in 1905. The Finnish Cadet Corps, dating from 1812, was abolished in 1903. It had enjoyed a privileged position in the Russian military educational system, training Finns as officers for all arms, the majority serving in the Russian army which, with the navy, afforded an attractive career for upper-class Finns for much of the period 1809–1917.

The presence of revolutionary Russian troops and local class tensions clouded Finland's declaration of independence on 6 December 1917. During 1917 Finnish socialists formed Red Guards and non-socialists White Guards to protect their interests. Civil War began with the socialist coup d'état in Helsinki on 27–28 January 1918; the White Guards, who had been declared government troops under the command of General Gustaf Mannerheim, disarmed Russian garrisons in Ostrobothnia on the same night. Industrial workers supported the Reds and farmers the Whites. Numerous weapons and limited help were provided for the Reds by the Russians (making the war for the Whites a War of Independence) but the Red Guards, which grew from 30,000 to 90,000 men, suffered from bad organization and leadership. The Whites improvised an effective army more successfully, helped by experienced Finnish officers from the Russian army (like Mannerheim), some Swedish volunteers, and by 1,800 anti-Russian Finns who had secretly left for Germany during the world war to receive military training in what became the 27th Royal Prussian *Jäger* Battalion. The return of most of these *Jägers* in February 1918 provided valuable leaders for newly conscripted units which fought alongside the White Guard volunteers and enlisted troops. The White army grew from 30,000 to 70,000 men, obtaining weapons from Germany, Sweden and from its enemies.

The Reds held populous southern Finland, a broken front running north of Pori, Tampere, Heinola and Viipuri. Strong Red offensives at Vilppula, Mäntyharju and in Karelia in February and March were defeated. The Whites attacked Tampere in mid-March; its fall on 6 April, after severe fighting, proved a decisive victory. At the same time German troops landed at Hanko and Loviisa in support of the Whites, the former force capturing Helsinki on 12 April. On 20 April Mannerheim began operations against Viipuri, which fell to his assault on 29 April. After some severe fighting, Red forces remaining in central and western Finland surrendered by 2 May. By 15 May the government was in complete control of Finland. Peace was concluded with the Soviet Union at Tartu in October 1920. Finnish volunteers, sometimes with official backing, had previously participated in 1918–20 in the anti-Russian and anti-Soviet campaigns of neighbouring Eastern Karelians, Ingrians and Estonians.

Despite political controversy, compulsory military service continued after the Civil War though not all men liable were trained. The officer corps became more homogeneous from the mid-1920s when those from the *Jäger* Battalion exerted political pressure to force out most of the older Russian- and Finnish-trained officers whom they regarded as remote from the needs and circumstances of the newly independent country. In 1932 the cadre system of mobilization was replaced by a territorial system for creating nine divisions. The peacetime army of three divisions and a cavalry brigade trained conscripts and provided covering troops in war. Finland contracted no effective defensive alliances although the Soviet Union was regarded as its potential enemy and fixed defences were built on the Karelian Isthmus in the 1920s and strengthened in the 1930s. There was a strong coastal artillery and a small navy and air force. However, the procurement of modern equipment, begun in 1931, proceeded slowly. The Civil Guard, which continued the traditions of the White Guards, supplemented the army with 100,000 volunteer reservists and 20,000 women auxiliaries.

The Russo-Finnish War of 1939–40 revealed the armed forces' deficiencies in equipment and trained men although they successfully frustrated Soviet plans of conquest. Some deficiencies were remedied in 1940–1 as Mannerheim, who continued as commander-in-chief, secured increased resources for defence. Strong new defensive positions were built, particularly between the Gulf of Finland and Lake Saimaa.

Dangerous isolation in the face of Soviet pressure was ended as Germany developed contacts with Finland beginning with an agreement in September 1940 for the transit of German troops through Finland to and from northern Norway. Finland hoped to regain its lost territory through participation in Germany's war against the Soviet Union and readily gave assistance over the start of German operations. German forces were permitted to deploy in Lapland where Finnish units were placed under German command. With great effort Finland mobilized 475,000 men (sixteen divisions) between mid-June and July 1941 and its formal neutrality – proclaimed when *Operation Barbarossa* began – ended after Soviet air raids on 25 June. The Finnish army redeployed for offensive operations. Between 10 July and 5 December 1941 Finnish forces advanced east in a series of successful but costly offensives, first north-east of Lake Ladoga, then on the Karelian Isthmus, and finally into Eastern Karelia. The army halted on tactically favourable positions on the Karelian, Olonets and Maaselkä isthmuses, having recovered the 1939 frontier and penetrated far (and controversially) into Soviet Eastern Karelia. Some troops were then demobilized and the front remained static while the strategic situation deteriorated in 1942–4. Mannerheim successfully resisted German pressure to attack Leningrad in 1941 and the Murmansk railway in late 1941 and 1942. Dependence on Germany for munitions and food did, however, hamper Finnish attempts to make peace with the Soviet Union.

In June 1944 the Red Army concentrated 450,000 men for offensive operations designed to remove Finland from the war. A powerful offensive began on the Karelian Isthmus on 9 June, with a 6-to-1 superiority in men and 20-to-1 in firepower. The Finns were rapidly driven back and Viipuri fell on 20 June. Finnish troops had to be withdrawn from the Olonets front to reinforce the Isthmus. A separate Soviet offensive, begun on 21 June, compelled the Finns to withdraw on the Olonets and Eastern Karelian fronts. However, a renewed Soviet offensive by ten divisions east of Viipuri between 20 June and 10 July was decisively defeated at Tali and Ihantala by four Finnish divisions and one brigade with strong artillery and air support (some German). Soviet assault forces, having failed to break through, were sent elsewhere and Finland, its army intact, avoided conquest or surrender. On 19 September 1944 it concluded an armistice with the Soviet Union, albeit on terms more severe than in 1940. The armistice required Finland to disarm German troops on its territory. Soviet pressure forced the Finns, at the same time as they were compelled to demobilize, to fight a bitter war, concluding in April 1945, to drive 220,000 German troops out of Lapland. Between 1941 and 1945 the

Finnish armed forces lost some 48,000 men killed (1,000 in the Lapland campaign).

Finland's armed forces were severely limited by the armistice and the ensuing Peace of Paris of 10 February 1947. The Civil Guard was disbanded. The armed forces, intended for internal security and frontier defence, were not to exceed 41,900 men and their equipment was restricted. However, Finland's obligation to defend its territory included in the Treaty of Friendship, Cooperation and Mutual Assistance with the Soviet Union of 6 April 1948 tacitly removed doubts about the permissibility of mobilizing reserves. Compulsory military service has continued and strong armed forces form an essential component in Finland's policy of neutrality. Since the 1970s all the armed forces have been equipped with a mixture of Soviet, Western and Finnish *matériel*. The peacetime army comprises eight brigades plus special and support troops; Finland could mobilize over 500,000 men. *See also* RUSSIA/USSR; RUSSO-FINNISH WAR; SWEDEN.

J. E. O. SCREEN

FURTHER READING
Thomas Ries, *Cold Will: the defence of Finland* (London, 1988); *Revue Internationale d'Histoire Militaire*, xxiii (1961); lxii (1985); J. O. Hannula, *Finland's War of Independence* (London, 1939); C. G. Mannerheim, *The Memoirs of Marshal Mannerheim* (London, 1954); *Guide to the Military Archives of Finland* (Helsinki, 1977), contains a brief historical outline of the organization of the Finnish armed forces and a bibliography.

Fire *See* GUNFIRE

Firearms The first small firearms appeared in the middle of the fourteenth century. Cylindrical in shape, they were attached to the ends of lances or staves and fired stones or small shot. In 1364, the town of Perugia ordered 500 of these rudimentary weapons, known as *scopette* ('scopetta' is Italian for 'broom'), and they were to be found across much of Western Europe by 1400. The 'hand gonne' was invented in the fifteenth century and was no more than a tube closed at one end. The lengthening of the tube to 5 feet and the addition of a curved handle and a butt created the arquebus which weighed about 34 lb and had to be supported on a forked rest for firing. It was ignited by a slow-match, the priming powder being placed in a receptacle known as the priming pan. Jan Ziska was the first to use firearms effectively, during the Hussite insurrection (1419–34). He also mounted light cannon on waggons to strengthen the 'wagenburg'.

Several improvements were soon made to the arquebus. First a 'serpentine' was added. This was an 'S'-shaped iron arm pivoting on an axis and thus bringing the slow-match into contact with the powder. This was then fitted with a spring and a trigger and the priming pan was covered to prevent the powder from falling out once the weapon had been primed, this mechanism being assembled on a lock-plate fixed to the right-hand side of the weapon. At the beginning of the sixteenth century the arquebus became considerably lighter: it weighed between 11 and 15 lb but, as its calibre was about 15 mm, its powers of penetration and range were limited. To remedy these deficiencies, the Spaniards adopted a 17 mm calibre musket in 1521, which could shoot a 1 oz bullet over a range of 330 yards. In France the musket only came into use belatedly, mainly on account of its weight, which was between 11 and 13 lb. But firearms were not adopted without resistance, since many, such as Bayard, considered them to be unfair weapons and according to Monluc they were the invention of the devil. At the end of the fifteenth century, an Italian *condottiere* had the eyes of soldiers put out and their hands cut off if they were captured in possession of an arquebus.

New discoveries made the weapon more manageable and improved its effectiveness. In the 'wheel-lock', ignition was achieved by the sparks produced by iron pyrites striking against a steel wheel. This mechanism was improved in various ways in the course of the sixteenth century. In the 'snaphaunce', a flint was placed in the jaws of the 'cock', which was freed by a catch when the trigger was pulled. Very soon, a shorter arquebus appeared, called the 'petronel' because the butt was pressed against the chest (Latin *pectus*), and this was used by cavalry. The invention of the wheel-lock allowed the use of this weapon to become common among mounted troops. In the middle of the sixteenth century mounted soldiers adopted an easy-to-load, wide-mouthed short weapon, the blunderbuss, and the wheel-lock pistol, which was later replaced by the flintlock pistol. The latter measured about 16 inches and was fired at arm's length. It was the favourite weapon of the German *Reiter*, who practised the tactic of the caracole in combat.

Infantry in Western Europe remained faithful to matchlock weapons until the end of the seventeenth century. The wheel-lock was more practical, since it was less affected by rain than the slow-match, which, moreover, allowed soldiers to be spotted at night, but its mechanism was delicate and fragile. The matchlock also had the advantage of being lighter and cheaper. In France, the arquebus disappeared after the Siege of La Rochelle (1627–8). The Swedish king, Gustavus Adolphus, had the musket made lighter, making it possible to use it without a rest. Around 1620, Marin Le Bourgeois improved the trigger mechanism by inventing a 'half-cock position' providing greater safety while the weapon was being loaded. The flintlock, which was incorporated into the wooden stock of the weapon, replaced the matchlock in most of the countries of northern Europe. The first flintlock muskets designed for mass use by the infantry appeared around 1635. They were lighter but of a lesser calibre than the matchlock and were, for many years, prohibited in the French army until matchlocks were finally proscribed in 1699 and disappeared in 1703. However, the Austrian army had adopted the flintlock as early as 1684 and the Swedes and the English followed suit between 1685 and 1697. In 1689, France replaced the plug bayonet with Vauban's improved socket version.

King Gustavus Adolphus of Sweden was the first to issue his troops with 'cartouches'. These paper containers carried all the various components: the priming powder, the charge and the bullet. The cartouche paper was torn between the teeth and used as wadding. The wooden rod used to drive down and tamp the charge was replaced in Austria by an iron rod in 1744 although this had been in use in the Prussian army since 1698. France adopted the cartouche much later than other armies – in 1702. Its adoption significantly increased the rate of fire from one shot in 10 minutes at the beginning of the sixteenth century to one shot a minute around 1700, and two to three shots a minute by the middle of the eighteenth century. However, in the Prussian army, where rapidity of fire rather than accuracy was demanded, the parade ground rate was as high as five to six shots a minute although this was halved in action. Although the elaborate sighting systems developed on arquebuses were still found, these subsequently disappeared or, at best, only the rudimentary 'bead' was preserved.

In 1717, a 17.5 mm calibre musket, which was intended to replace the diverse types of weapon with which the troops were issued, was made in France. It underwent several improvements and ultimately became the 1777 model, which was the first weapon to have been scientifically made and standardized. It fired a bullet of around 1 oz, weighed 10 lb 2 oz and measured 5 feet. It was used during the Revolutionary and Imperial Wars and was only slightly modified in 1801 and later in 1822. Both the light infantry and the dragoons were issued with a weapon 4 inches shorter. The British 'Brown Bess' musket was adopted during the War of the Spanish Succession although the first surviving model dates from 1717. The barrel was 46 inches long and of 0.75 calibre firing a bullet which weighed slightly over 1 oz. Light infantry employed a Brown Bess with 4 inches sawn from the barrel and the cavalry and dragoons had a carbine version. Only in 1794 was the Brown Bess gradually superseded by the Land Service Pattern and the India Pattern, themselves further modified in 1802.

Following Howard's discovery of fulminate of mercury in 1800, firearms developed percussion systems to replace the flintlock. Percussion sporting guns were in common use by 1820 but not until 1838 did the British army begin to replace its flintlocks with percussion locks, the Pattern 1838. Most European armies adopted the new device during the 1840s. Delvigne Pontcharra's rifled carbine of 1837, issued to the French infantry in Algeria after undergoing some modification, used this method of priming by percussion cap. Old weapons were modified to take the new system. The first rifled barrel was probably manufactured in Germany around 1520 and rifles were common as sporting guns throughout the seventeenth and eighteenth centuries. However, there was no need for accuracy in volley firing tactics and the tight-fitting spherical bullet was not conducive to fast reloading. Apart from small units equipped with the Baker and Brunswick rifles, the first British infantry firearm to be rifled was the Minié of 1851. This was rapidly superseded by the Enfield of 1853. The new rifles fired a spherical bullet with a hollow cup in its base; the force of the propellant charge expanded the skirt around the cup to engage with the rifling thereby imparting spin to the bullet.

This design enabled the bullet to be made to a smaller bore than the gun so that it could be loaded with the ease of a smoothbore musket. Rifles were also equipped with back and fore sights.

A concomitant but equally important innovation was breech-loading, which was faster than muzzle-loading and could be carried out while in the prone position. Many experimental weapons appeared during the period 1820–40 and in 1841 Prussia adopted the Dreyse rifle which was manufactured industrially from 1848. This weapon was of 15.43 mm calibre with a long, thin firing pin – hence the name 'needle gun' – which struck a priming pellet at the base of the powder charge. Prussia demonstrated unusual boldness in instantly adopting this new system whereas general staffs almost always showed hostility to innovations which were, apart from anything else, expensive; in this particular case there was a fear that it would only lead to soldiers wasting cartridges. Thus in 1857, the French army was equipped with a rifled

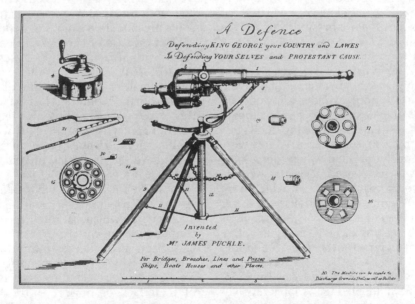

Puckle's Gun was one of the earliest attempts to design an automatic firearm. A patent was granted to James Puckle in 1718 for 'a portable gun or machine called a Defence that discharges so often and so many bullets and can be so quickly loaded as renders next to impossible to carry any ship by boarding'. The revolving chambers could be preloaded and speedily replaced. Although Puckle reserved round bullets for Christian enemies, square bullets being suitable for the Turks and other heathens, he made no provision for the necessary change of barrel. In any event, square bullets could not have been fired. (Board of Trustees of the Royal Armouries)

gun, but one which was still a muzzle-loader and Napoleon III did not succeed in adopting the 1864–6 breech-loading Remington rifle, which used metallic cartridges. It was only when there was a sudden worsening of the international situation that France adopted a breech-loading rifle, the Chassepot, in 1866. It was lighter, easier to load and had a better sealing system than the Dreyse rifle. It was 4 ft 3 in long, weighed 9 lb and had a calibre of 11 mm. Fired by means of a needle striking a percussion cap located at the base of the cartridge, its great defect was that it fouled rapidly. Various types of carbine were derived from this weapon. In 1870, there were a million Chassepot rifles in service. The British army was still equipped with the muzzle-loading 1851 Pattern Enfield rifle (issued from 1853). Rather than scrap its existing stock, it was decided to alter the Enfields to breech-loading by adopting the conversion designed by Jacob Snider. The Snider-Enfield was first issued in 1865. Old French army rifles were converted by the addition of the Schneider breech-loading mechanism, which was known as the *tabatière* or 'snuffbox'.

Ever since firearms had been invented, men had tried to increase their power by adding multiple barrels. But such weapons were heavy and cumbersome. The invention of the rotating cylinder allowed reliable repeating weapons to be developed. Although systems of this kind had been devised in the sixteenth century, they were only seriously pursued when percussion priming was introduced. The first weapon of this type was the 1835 Colt which went through several modifications. The Far West and the American Civil War made its reputation. It was an 11.17 mm gun with a six-shot cylinder; it measured 15½ in and weighed 4 lb 9 oz. In 1872 it was converted to receive metallic cartridges. In 1855, Great Britain adopted the Adams revolver of 1851. It fired more quickly than the Colt but was more fragile. The Confederate States of America acquired it together with the French Faucheux pistol of 1854. This latter, which was far superior to other weapons of the type, had the advantage of breech-loading. It employed Gévelot's pin cartridge and the navy adopted the 12 mm calibre 1858 model. The French army was issued with the Chamelot-Delvigne revolver in 1877, called the 'regulation revolver' (*revolver d'ordonnance*). It had a calibre of 11 mm and weighed 2 lb 3 oz.

The first repeating carbine was the 1860–2 Spencer, in which the magazine was located inside the butt. It was rapidly followed by other models of which the best known is the Winchester Model 1866 derived from the Henry carbine. This was a lever-action rifle and had a tubular magazine under the barrel. It was far superior to its contemporary the Chassepot, on account of its rate of fire, and with it one of Garibaldi's battalions was able to destroy a Prussian regiment in 1870, and in 1877 the Turks massacred charging Russian troops at Plevna. In 1871, Germany adopted the 11 mm calibre Mauser. This was a bolt-action rifle and it contained two innovations: a safety catch and a double-action trigger, but it had no ejection system. Following the introduction of the metallic cartridge, the French army was issued in 1874 with the Gras rifle, which had both an ejector and an extractor. It could fire nine shots a minute. In this period, all the world's major armies equipped themselves with arms of this type: Austria with the 1873–7 Werndl, the United States with the Springfield 'trap door' rifle of 1873–89, Japan with the Mourata. The best weapon of this type was undoubtedly the British Martini-Henry rifle of 1874. It was a 0.45 calibre rifle, and was extremely accurate but it did have the drawback of using a heavy cartridge.

In 1878, the French navy adopted the Austrian Kropatschek repeating rifle, the magazine of which, situated in the stock, contained seven cartridges. Although they had been used successfully during the American Civil War, repeating carbines were generally rejected by experts because of their lack of power. In 1884, Vieille discovered a smokeless colloidal powder with a consistent combustion, which he called 'B' Powder. This increased by a third the initial speed of a bullet for the least possible amount of charge, enabling calibres to come down to 8 mm and at the same time made for an improvement in accuracy.

The French 8 mm calibre Lebel rifle of 1886, modified in 1893, had a tubular magazine with eight cartridges in the stock. It measured 4 ft 3 in and weighed 9 lb. It was a weapon of great ballistic capacity but reloading was slow and it was impossible to use in close combat. It was progressively replaced by the Berthier rifle, which initially had a three-round clip (1907–15) and subsequently a five-round clip (1916).

Because of the time taken to reload magazines inside the butt or the stock, the system of a box magazine fixed at the breech, conceived by the American James P. Lee in 1879, gained in popularity. It was taken up by the Austrian Mannlicher (1886–8) and the German 1888 7.92 Mauser, which was improved in 1898, the American Springfield of 1903 (7.62 mm), the British Lee-Metford of 1889, and the SMLE (Short Magazine Lee-Enfield) of 1903.

If the repeating weapon appreciably increased the speed of fire, it still remained possible to increase this further by replacing manual reloading by the use of gases to reload weapons automatically. This system was employed in machine-guns and machine pistols. It was also used in those rifles which are called semi-automatic, firing individual rounds, to distinguish them from properly 'automatic' weapons which fired in bursts rather than rounds. Weapons of this type were tested at the end of the nineteenth century. The first model to be adopted was the rifle devised by the Mexican general, Mondragon, which Germany bought in 1914 for its airmen. In France, MAS produced the Model 1917 the breech of which was actuated by a gas cylinder contained in the stock. It had several defects and was replaced by a new model in 1918. It was the Russians who showed themselves the most innovative in this field with the adoption of the 6.5 mm Federov Avtomat in 1916, yet this weapon turned out to be fragile.

The first weapon which could properly be called a 'machine-gun' appeared in 1829 in Middletown, Ohio. Several prototypes were tested between 1840 and 1860. The first machine-gun to be used was the 1862 Gatling gun, worked by a hand crank. It was made of six barrels revolving around a central arbor. Its theoretical rate of fire was 300 shots a minute. Some of these guns were used in the Franco-Prussian War (1870–1). The Belgian Montigny machine-gun had 37 barrels firing simultaneously at a rate of 8 shots a minute. The French Reffye model of 1866 (13 mm) had 25 barrels and could be reloaded five or six times a minute. One hundred and seventy of these guns were in existence in 1870 but they were too heavy and, besides, were ill-used tactically. It was, indeed, on account of the poor use made of it during the Franco-Prussian War that this weapon fell out of favour.

The first machine-gun worthy of the name was the 1883 Maxim, adopted by the British, which was belt-fed and capable of firing 500–600 shots a minute. A short time afterwards the Mannlicher appeared in Austria in 1885, the Jouhandeau in 1889 in France, the Skoda in Austria in 1893 and the French Hotchkiss of 1897–1900, weighing 22 lb. This last-mentioned was used by the Japanese during the 1904–5 Russo-Japanese War, a conflict which revealed the lethal capacity of the weapon. The Saint-Etienne machine-gun of 1907 turned out to be rather mediocre and was replaced in 1914 by an 8 mm Hotchkiss. The German Maxim machine-gun of 1908 weighed 48½ lb and had a rate of fire of 300 shots a minute. In 1934 the Germans adopted the 7.92 mm MG (*Maschinengewehr*) 34. In the 1934–41 model the rate of fire was raised from 800 to 1,000 shots a minute and in that of 1942 to 1,100. France armed itself with the 13.2 mm MAC (*Manufacture d'armes de Châtellerault*), known as the Reibel, which used the side-feeding drum magazine of the 1930 Hotchkiss, and served as an anti-aircraft weapon. The American Browning machine-gun, a 12.7 mm calibre weapon, was in very widespread use in the Second World War, when it was employed either as an anti-aircraft weapon or against infantry. Because of their weight, machine-guns could not be moved at the same pace as the infantry, and thus, to complement them, lighter weapons with the same tactical properties were produced which could be carried by one soldier and fired while walking. The French Chauchat light machine-gun of 1903–7 was replaced in 1915 by the F–MCSRG of the same calibre as the Berthier rifle. In was 4 ft 6 in long and weighed 19 lb 8 oz. It was fed by a semi-circular magazine which held 20 rounds and its practical rate of fire was 120 shots a minute. The American Browning Automatic Rifle (BAR) of 1918 was also capable of single-shot fire. In the 1918 A2 model it had two firing speeds: 550 and 300 shots per minute. The British adopted a magazine- fed light machine-gun, the Lewis Gun, in 1915, and this was replaced by the BREN gun in 1937–9.

As the standard rifle cartridge with its truncated cone shape was ill-suited to clip-loaded weapons and especially to automatic weapons, France adopted a new 7.5 mm cartridge in 1924, following the example of German 7.92 mm ammunition. This cartridge was intended for the 1924 machine-gun which was modified in 1929. It was an automatic weapon functioning by gas intake at a point in the barrel. It had both single-shot and automatic fire, and was fed by magazines containing 25 rounds. The practical rate of fire of this weapon was 200 shots a minute and it weighed 19 lb 10 oz. Very strongly made and remarkably reliable in action, it was greatly superior to weapons of this type used in other armies.

There was renewed interest in weapons with a curved trajectory in the trenches during the Great War. So-called 'trench mortars' improvised by soldiers were subsequently replaced by mortars. Similarly, the grenades de fortune knocked up by soldiers for want of stocks of the 1888 and 1914 models of grenade, were replaced by mass-produced regulation missiles in 1915. The grenade is primarily a hand-thrown projectile and has been in use since the sixteenth century, when it consisted of a small metallic sphere and ignition of the charge was achieved by the burning of a slow match. It was used particularly during sieges. In 1843 a projectile fitted with a traction ignition system, which overcame the defects of the slow match, was adopted. Nowadays, a distinction is made between offensive grenades, which act through the effect of blast and have a range of only a few yards and are especially effective in confined spaces, and defensive grenades, which throw out shrapnel when their casings disintegrate. These latter are dangerous over a distance of several dozen yards and the thrower must therefore be sheltered. Grenades are fitted with an ignition cap which renders the projectile explosive about five seconds after the pin has been removed and it is thrown. Grenades also exist which explode on impact. Some are fitted with a shaft so that they may be thrown more easily. From the early days of firearms, plans have been devised for launching grenades from the muzzles of gun-barrels. In 1677 the troops of the Great Elector of Brandenburg used gun grenades at the Siege of Stettin. In 1739 British grenadiers were issued with a gun fitted with a grenade launcher. But this weapon was not seriously taken up because of the dangers involved in firing. It was in 1907 that a percussion rifle-grenade was perfected (Marten Hale), to be followed by a similar invention in Germany in 1913. France being backward in this field, her soldiers made use of ad hoc devices until the Feuillette grenade gun was manufactured in 1915. In 1916, the Viven-Bessières grenade was adopted which was fired by means of a grenade-launcher fitted at the end of the barrel. Subsequently guns were fitted with a launcher appropriate to the diameter of the grenade and with a sighting system. Recent gun grenades are feathered. There are also anti-riot (teargas and CS gas), smoke, incendiary (phosphorus base), and anti-tank grenades.

Between the wars, little perceptible progress was made in the field of light weapons except for the appearance of the sub-machine- (alias the 'tommy') gun. In 1936, the MAS 36 (MAS stood for Manufacture d'armes de Saint-Etienne) was brought into service. It was a bolt action rifle with a box magazine containing five rounds, weighed 8 lb 4 oz, with its cruciform bayonet and measured 3 ft 4 in. This weapon was sturdy, simple and very accurate. On the other hand, other French weapons were mediocre. The 1935-A and 1935-B automatic pistols lacked power as a result of their calibre (7.65 mm), as did the sub-machine-gun which appeared in the same year, fed by a 25-round magazine. The first submachine-gun was the Italian Vilar Perosa which was first produced in 1915. It had the prodigious rate of fire of 1,500 shots a minute. A little before the end of the First World War the Germans perfected the Bergmann MP 18 which used a 'snail' magazine of 32 cartridges. The American 11.43 mm Thompson M 1928 A1 sub-machine-gun was a weapon of great power but it suffered the drawback of being heavy. Its weight of 10 lb was made even greater by the weight of its cartridges, and all the more so since it was fed by a circular magazine containing 100 rounds, which was subsequently replaced by a vertical magazine allowing 20–30 shots. It was adopted by the US Marines after having proved itself among the gangsters of Chicago. Firing in bursts, the submachine-gun was well adapted to close combat. The best-known weapon of this type is the 1941 British sten gun, which fired single shots or automatically, with a 32-round magazine. It was widely used by the French Resistance. An Italian Beretta submachine-gun and a German *Maschinenpistole* were brought into service in 1938.

In 1935, the Germans equipped them-selves with the 7.92 mm Mauser 98k rifle. This was 3 ft 6 inches in length and weighed 8 lb 13 oz. This weapon was, however, wholly outclassed by the Soviet semi-automatic Tokarev SVT 38 with ten cartridges. After several setbacks, the Reich finally developed an excellent gun: the G43. During the Second World War the Americans used the automatically loaded Garand M1 gun which fires from an 8-round clip. This was adopted in 1936 and re-mained in service until 1957. The American M1 carbine of 1941 was fed by a 15-round clip. It weighed only 5 lb but its firepower left much to be desired.

During the Second World War the *Wehrmacht* was issued with a revolutionary weapon, the *Sturmgewehr* or assault rifle (MP 38/40). Automatically loaded, it com-bined the advantages of the rifle and the submachine-gun and could fire single shots or automatically at a speed of 800 shots a minute. After 1945, Germany, Spain, Portugal and Switzerland were issued with a weapon of 7.62 mm NATO calibre, de-rived from the Mauser 45M assault rifle. The Russian Kalashnikov automatic of 1947, known as the AK47, was inspired by the 43 and 44 Mauser models. Adopted by people's democracies and several other countries it is, with some 35 million in existence, the most widely distributed weapon in the world. The 5.56 mm NATO calibre Belgian CAL of 1969 has been bought by 30 countries. A machine-gun version of this weapon also exists. The 1951 American M16, which was used in the Vietnam War, was the first weapon to use a small calibre (5.56 mm). It is fed by a clip of 20 cartridges and uses ammunition weighing only 4 oz. The weapon weighs just 6 lb 10 oz. For several years there has been a general tendency to reduce the calibre and at the same time the weight of weapons. The Russian AKS 74 has a calibre of 5.45 mm, whilst the British Enfield L85A1 was designed in 4.85 mm calibre but was later changed to 5.56 mm.

After 1945, France lagged behind the major military powers in the field of small firearms. In 1949, she issued her forces with a semi-automatic rifle fed by a ten-round clip, which was modified in 1956 when an integral grenade launcher was added at the muzzle. It was 3 ft 4 in long and weighed 8 lb 9 oz. Loading was performed by the indirect action of gas on a moving mecha-nism which introduced a cartridge during its rearward movement and ejected the case during recoil. This weapon could be fitted with an infra-red sighting mechanism for night firing. Later, an image-intensifying sight was also developed.

In 1952, a 7.5 mm machine-gun (*fusil-mitrailleur*) known as the AAT-52 was brought into service. It weighed 22 lb, though a *mitrailleuse* version of this weapon exists which is heavier. The French army was also issued, in 1949, with a 9 mm sub-machine-gun called the MAT 49 (MAT stands for *Manufacture d'armes de Tulle*), fed by a 25-round clip. It is very strong and also has the advantage of a grip safety mechanism which reduces the risk of accidents, which are very frequent with this type of weapon. It was not until 1979 that the French army was issued with an assault

253

rifle which replaced the FSA rifle of 1949–56 and the 1949 submachine-gun which had long been outdated. The F1 MAS assault rifle, which is known as the *clarion* bugle, has a calibre of 5.56 mm, is 2 ft 6 in long, weighs 8 lb 2 oz and has a firing rate of 950 shots a minute. It is fitted with a bayonet and a grenade launcher. Like the AAT-52, it employs the direct action of gas on a non-locked breech, the recoil of which is slowed down by a system of inertia amplification.

For a long time ordinary weapons, using armour-piercing bullets, were employed for anti-tank combat but these were often unable to pierce armour-plating. The discovery of the hollow charge, which is also used in mines, has completely transformed anti-tank combat. Hollow charges are in fact able to pierce several inches of steel, and still more of concrete, and can therefore also be effectively used against pillboxes. Rockets carrying a hollow charge are self-propelled by a solid fuel. They are launched by means of a simple tube the sole function of which is to direct the missile towards the target. Ignition of the propellant is achieved by an electric mechanism. The British PIAT, the American bazooka and the German *Panzerfaust* were all man-portable anti-tank rocket-launchers using a hollow charge which were developed during the Second World War.

The French anti-tank rocket-launcher of 1950, which was developed from the American Bazooka, launched a rocket with a hollow charge 73 mm in diameter, which was capable of piercing 12 in of armour-plating over a maximum distance of 110 yards. A shield attached to the tube protected the firer from powder thrown out from the rocket but he had to take care not to have any obstacle behind his tube because of the powder thrown out as the rocket was launched. The American 2.31 inch M20 or 'superbazooka' was only a little better in its performance figures. The M72 A2, which was also American and had a range of 165 yards, was a single-shot weapon, which was jettisoned after use. The French 89 mm anti-tank rocket-launcher fires anti-tank, anti-personnel, smoke and incendiary rockets. It can penetrate 18 in of armour-plating at a range of 440 yards.

In addition to these portable short-range anti-tank weapons, more powerful missile weapons were also developed which were able to attack armoured vehicles from greater distances. One such was the American M47 or 'Dragoon', which has a range of 1,100 yards and has optical wire-guidance and infra-red sighting systems. The tube is jettisoned after use. The range of the German Cobra is 1.25 miles as is that of the French Milan, which is capable of penetrating 28 in of armour-plating.

The action of these missiles is completed by that of a range of yet more powerful long-range missiles fired from vehicles or helicopters. The first generation of these missiles was constituted in France by the ENTAC cable-guided missile, whose range was 1.8 miles, the SS10 and, later, the SS11, which all had similar guidance systems. They have today been replaced by the Hot missile, which weighs 13 lb, has a diameter of 5.3 in and a range of 2½ miles. Most of the great powers possess missiles of this type such as the British Swingfire, the Italian Sparviero, the Russian Sagger and Snapper and the American BGM Tow. *See also* ARTILLERY; BLADE WEAPONS; CAVALRY; EXPLOSIVES; GRENADIERS; INFANTRY; MINING AND MINES; PROPELLANTS; WEAPONS.

G. BODINIER

FURTHER READING
I. V. Hogg, *The Complete Machine Gun* (London, 1979); C. H. Roads, *The British Soldier's Firearm, 1850–1864* (London, 1964); H. L. Blackmore, *British Military Firearms, 1650–1850* (London, 1961); A. North and I. V. Hogg, *The Book of Guns and Gunsmiths* (London, 1978); H. Ricketts, *Firearms* (London, 1972).

Fisher, John Arbuthnot, 1st Baron of Kilverstone (1841–1920) Entering the Royal Navy in 1854, Fisher saw war service in China before progressing through the ranks of the peacetime navy, alternating sea with shore posts. He showed a marked technical aptitude. By the late 1860s, recognized as an authority on underwater weapons, he was selected to initiate torpedo training.

Subsequently, he became Captain of the Torpedo School and, eventually, Director of Naval Ordnance. In the 1890s he was successively Fourth Sea Lord, commander-in-chief in North America and then in the Mediterranean, and Second Sea Lord, in which position he reorganized officer training. After a spell as Commander-in-Chief Portsmouth, he became First Sea Lord from 1904 to 1910. He introduced, among a number of changes, the all-big-gun battleship (*Dreadnought*), redistributed the fleet and scrapped many aged vessels replacing them with up-to-date ships, including submarines. In so doing, he created much dissension within the navy. Retiring in 1910, he remained in touch with Winston Churchill, then First Lord of the Admiralty, and, early in the First World War, returned as First Sea Lord, inaugurating a large building programme. He resigned over the Dardanelles policy in 1915 and was subsequently chairman of the Board of Inventions. He had great technical understanding, drive and energy and maintained good relations with royalty, press and politicians but he made little contribution to the strategical and tactical aspects of the navy's work. *See also* CHURCHILL; DARDANELLES; JUTLAND; NAVAL WARFARE; NAVIES.

A. W. H. PEARSALL

FURTHER READING
Ruddock F. Mackay, *Fisher of Kilverstone* (Oxford, 1973); Arthur J. Marder, *Fear God and Dread Nought: the correspondence of Admiral of the Fleet Lord Fisher of Kilverstone* (London, 1952–9); Arthur J. Marder, *From Dreadnought to Scapa Flow: the Royal Navy in the Fisher era, 1904–19* (London, 1961–70).

Flags *See* ESPRIT DE CORPS; HONOURS AND AWARDS; VEXILLOLOGY

Flodden (Northumberland), Battle of (9 September 1513) Flodden was the first of three major military disasters suffered by minor powers in the sixteenth century (the others being Mohács (1526) and Al'Cazar-Kebir (1578)) that cost the lives of the king and the core of the nobility. Yet while the other two were comparatively straightforward encounters in which the defeated were simply overwhelmed by superior numbers, Flodden was more controversial. In August 1513, James IV of Scotland assembled a large army (estimated at 40,000, though no more than 30,000 actually took part in the battle) for an invasion of England to honour his alliance with Louis XII by retaliating against Henry VIII's invasion of France earlier in the year. It was the best equipped Scottish army of the period; there was an artillery train of seventeen large guns, while the infantry were armed with eighteen-foot pikes on the Swiss and German model. James's aims in the campaign have been much debated, for after besieging a few English border castles, he took up a defensive position on Flodden Hill at the beginning of September. Henry had given command against the Scots to Thomas Howard, Earl of Surrey, who by then had managed to assemble some 26,000 men. They were drawn largely from the shire levies of the northern counties and armed in the main with bows and bills. James's position at Flodden was too strong to be attacked directly, so Surrey advanced past him with the intention of cutting his communications with Scotland. James rejected the suggestion of attacking Surrey on the march but instead broke up his camp and retired to Branxton Hill several miles to the north. Here on the afternoon of 9 September the two armies encountered each other with the Scots facing north on the crest of the hill and the English at its foot. Despite recent heavy rain and the steep slope, James decided on a downhill advance in five large columns of pikemen. The combination of mud and the difficulty of arraying pikemen while descending a slope gave the English billmen the advantage. Although the Scottish left-hand column routed the Cheshire levies facing them, the centre columns were practically annihilated in a slaughter lasting little more than two hours. As many as 9,000 Scots were killed, including the king, two bishops, two abbots, nine earls and fourteen barons. Contemporaries compared the death of James IV to that of Charles the Bold at Nancy in 1477, but James was not defeated by superior numbers; his own tactical errors and his army's inexperience with a new weaponry were responsible. No less significant was the battle's effect on Henry VIII; such a dramatic success with traditional English weapons only encouraged his opposition to adopting the arquebuses and pikes of the continental armies. *See also* CHARLES THE BOLD; GREAT BRITAIN; INFANTRY; PINKIE.

SIMON ADAMS

FURTHER READING
W. Mackay Mackenzie, *The Secret of Flodden* (Edinburgh, 1931); N. Macdougall, *James IV* (Edinburgh, 1989).

Foch, Ferdinand (1851–1929) A future marshal of France and an honorary field marshal in both the British and the Polish armies, Foch left the École Polytechnique in 1873. In 1895, he became professor of military history and strategy and, in 1908, commandant of the École Militaire (then known as the École de Guerre). Commanding 20th Corps in 1914, Foch was elevated to the command of the 9th Army on 28 August and played an important role in the Battle of the Marne. Subsequently, in the 'race for the sea', he was given the task of co-ordinating the British, Belgian and French armies as commander of the Northern Army Group. After the Somme campaign, where he had advocated an 'artillery attack to be exploited by the infantry', but which, for want of adequate resources, had ended in semi-failure, he was sacrificed. However, after the crisis in the spring of 1917, he was appointed Chief of the General Staff before becoming Allied Supreme Commander on the Western Front on 26 March 1918. From this position he directed the Second Battle of the Marne, which marked the termination of the German spring offensives, and then conducted the allied counter-offensives leading to the Armistice. He was created a marshal of France in August 1918 but his contention that the Allies should retain military control of the Rhine brought him into conflict with both the Allies and his own political superiors.

As a military theorist he had published *The Principles of War* in 1903 and *The Conduct of War* in 1904. In these books he accorded a central role to the will to win and called for an offensive spirit but he insisted on historical methodology, arguing for the study and resolution of specific cases within 'military humanities'. Deriving much of his inspiration from Napoleon, Foch based his conception of the conduct of war on simple principles which could be adapted to all strategies: unity of action, which implied seeking out and destroying the main forces of the enemy; economy of force, which actually meant 'the art of having superior numbers, and applying that superiority at the chosen point of attack'; freedom of action, to avoid yielding to the enemy's will; and, finally, security, an area in which Foch emphasized the need to reduce uncertainty through sound intelligence. Although these views were generally in tune with those then current in the French army, Foch exerted great influence through his forceful articulation. *See also* FRANCE; JOFFRE; MARNE; STRATEGY; TACTICS.

A. CORVISIER

FURTHER READING
B. H. Liddell Hart, *Foch: man of Orléans* (London, 1931); J. Marshall-Cornwell, *Foch as Military Commander* (London, 1972).

Folard, Jean Charles, Chevalier de (1669–1752) Having been impressed at the age of fifteen by Caesar's *Com-mentaries*, Folard joined the French army and, in 1688, became an officer in a corps of partisans. He fought to the end of Louis XIV's wars, then passed into the service of Charles XII of Sweden, only returning to France on the occasion of the short Spanish war of 1718–20. He left the army as soon as peace returned without having progressed beyond the rank of *mestre de camp*, probably on account of his difficult character. He had already written a *Traité de la guerre des partisans*, which was still in manuscript when he began a career as a military theorist. He published the *Nouvelles découvertes sur l'art de la guerre* (1724) and the *Histoire de Polybe* (1727–30), which gave rise after his death to the *Abrégé des commentaires de M. de Folard* (1754).

Folard's treatises, although verbose, were erudite and vigorous. The fruits of experience and original thinking, they pro-

(Bibliothèque Nationale, Paris)

voked controversies to which he devoted the last years of his life. Maurice de Saxe, with whom he had discussed these questions, took him to task in particular for not having taken sufficient account of psychological factors or of the collaboration between the different arms, and for having referred too many things back to the Greeks and Romans. Folard based his analysis on the understanding of mistakes and was one of the first to produce case studies. He believed that the conduct of operations had to have the objective of annihilating the enemy army. To do this, rather than merely seizing the enemy's frontier posts, one had to seek a general engagement from the outset, for everything depended on how one began, on 'commencements'. If one was forced on to the defensive, it was best to practise 'active defence', covering one's lines of communication, using flying camps and creating destruction. An excellent intelligence service was considered indispensable. To win a victory, it was necessary to proceed with rapidity and resolve, engaging in hand-to-hand fighting, giving preference to shock action rather than firepower. The best means of obtaining a breakthrough was to attack in column, a veritable 'mobile rampart' of between one

and six battalions, whose exact number of ranks and files, together with its overall strength, would be determined by the nature of the terrain. Lastly, pursuit had to begin without delay. For this reason, the leader had to enjoy complete independence in the conduct of operations, and Folard repudiated the 'cabinet strategy' which was so much in favour under Louis XIV.

Folard's work covered almost all the fundamental principles of warfare. It had a great influence on Frederick II, who refuted Folard in a subtly nuanced work, *L'esprit du chevalier Folard* (1761), and on Mesnil-Durand, a partisan of deep battle columns as opposed to the shallow line. Through Guibert, Folard's work influenced the tactics of the French revolutionary armies and the thinking of Napoleon, who gave general currency to Folard's emphasis on attack and the complete destruction of the army. *See also* FREDERICK II; GUIBERT; SAXE; TACTICS.

A. CORVISIER

FURTHER READING
C. de Coynart, *Le Chevalier Folard, 1669–1752* (Paris, 1914); J. L. A. Colin, *L'Infanterie au XVIIIe siècle: la tactique* (Paris, 1907); L. Kennett, 'The Chevalier de Folard and the cult of antiquity', in *Soldier-Statesmen of the Age of the Enlightenment* (International Commission of Military History, Manhattan, Kansas, 1984); Emile Léonard, *L'Armée et ses problèmes au XVIIIe siècle* (Paris, 1958); Robert S. Quimby, *The Background of Napoleonic Warfare* (New York, 1957).

Fontenoy, Battle of (11 May 1745) The Battle of Fontenoy serves as an exemplar of Western European warfare in the mid-eighteenth century, though the oft-cited incident of a supposedly chivalrous exchange between Lord Charles Hay of the 1st Foot Guards and officers of the *Gardes françaises* when on the point of firing at each other has tended to obscure both the murderous reality of battle and the tactical ability of the best generals of the age.

At the end of April 1745, Marshal de Saxe, having cleverly masked his intentions, laid siege to Tournai in order to invoke an early encounter with the Duke of Cumberland's (1721–65) Allied army, then in the vicinity of Brussels. Over a period of ten days, Saxe selected the location for the coming battle, his final dispositions deploying about 52,000 men along a convex front on rising ground. His left was secured by the Forest of Barry (held by irregular light troops) and his extreme right by the village of Antoing on the banks of the Scheldt. The heavily defended village of Fontenoy lay in the centre. The French lines were further strengthened by earthen redoubts while the approaches to the centre and left were partly obstructed by marshy ground. Artillery was carefully sited in order to enfilade an attacker and the positioning of reserves was arranged with equal attention, notably on the left wing. Saxe's dispositions were a practical example of his belief that troops should be deployed with special regard to their strengths and weaknesses, while making every effort to place the enemy at a disadvantage. Having skilfully formed a numerically superior force on interior lines along a strong defensive front preceded by the type of terrain and obstacles which would tend naturally to fragment an attack, Saxe invited his enemies to dislodge him. He had set them a formidable task.

On 11 May, following a reconnaissance on the 10th, the Allied army of about 50,000 men attacked. After nine hours, they retreated in an orderly fashion having failed, largely through lack of co-ordination, to break Saxe's position. Advancing over difficult ground, in a remarkable display of discipline and courage, 15,000 British and Hanoverian troops under Cumberland's immediate command had initially pierced the French left between Fontenoy and the Forest of Barry until their attack lost direction and momentum while their unsecured flanks were subjected to a galling crossfire. Saxe succeeded in turning their penetration into a trap and by a combination of attacks by all arms finally forced the Allies to withdraw. Casualties were in excess of 7,000 on each side.

The excellence of the British and Hanoverian infantry in particular was unquestionable and even drew admiration from Saxe, but the generalship of the youthful Cumberland was a more contentious issue. If the very audacity of what might be fairly termed a reckless assault surprised the French and gave Cumberland a glimpse of victory, his success also proved his undoing as he seemed unequal to the task of exploiting his advantage. At the crisis, Saxe retained his composure and resolve and found in Cumberland's initial triumph the opportunity to effect his ruin. *See also* FRANCE; SAXE.

G. A. STEPPLER

FURTHER READING
Jacques Boudet, 'Fontenoy', in *Great Military Battles*, ed. Cyril Falls (New York, 1964), pp. 50–7; J. L. A. Colin, *Les Campagnes du Maréchal de Saxe* (3 vols, Paris, 1901–6), iii; F. H. Skrine, *Fontenoy and Britain's Share in the War of the Austrian Succession, 1741–48* (London, 1906); Jon Manchip White, *Marshal of France: the life and times of Maurice, Comte de Saxe, 1696–1750* (London, 1962).

Food supplies *See* RATIONS

Force, moral *See* ESPRIT DE CORPS; ETHOS; GLORY; HONOURS AND AWARDS; MORALE; TRAINING; VEXILLOLOGY

Foreign Legion *See* FOREIGNERS, SERVICE BY; MERCENARIES

Foreigners, service by Military service by foreigners is a matter of considerable importance because of the number of men who have engaged in it, and the variety of types of service. There has sometimes been a tendency to depreciate the practice, by looking upon it as a kind of mercenary service, but that is often unjustified. The impetus for foreign service is provided by an imbalance between a population's desire for the career of arms, or the numbers it could supply to an army, and a government's military requirements. Some states have, in fact, maintained an army which was larger than the human resources of their country allowed – whether through lack of numbers, military vocation or loyalty on the part of the population, or because of a wish not to endanger the economic life of the country – by having systematic recourse to the employment of foreigners. Maurice de Saxe's dictum in justification of the practice was: one foreign soldier is worth three men; he serves, he spares a man for the home economy and he reduces enemy numbers by one. On the other hand, certain countries have been looked upon as 'reservoirs of men', because of their population's natural military disposition. In Antiquity, this was true of some nations of 'barbarians' (i.e. those which lay outside the ambit of Graeco-Roman culture); and in more modern times, of countries where the density of population has been too great for the resources (e.g. Switzerland), or which, through lack of a large-scale army, were unable to retain those of their members who sought a military life (e.g. England and Ireland). Lastly, military service by foreigners can wear varied guises, ranging from normal service in a unit put at an ally's disposal to treason towards a native country, or again as devotion to a national or international cause.

The use of foreign units from other races has often been justified by their better knowledge of a particular terrain or by their skill in certain types of warfare. This was so in the case of units recruited in conquered countries or in colonies – hussars of the Imperial army in Hungary, Mamluks of the French army in Egypt, or again, zouaves and goums of the French armies in North Africa. There has been a regular tendency leading towards the use of such troops outside their native countries. Some units were directly recruited in foreign lands: the Scythian archers of Antiquity, the German *Landsknechte* and *Reiter*, the Albanian cavalry at the start of the sixteenth century. But we should not let these names confuse us: at a very early stage, they designated a particular type of fighting man and lost their ethnic aspect. The hussars can serve as an example. These were originally a light cavalry of Central Europe, highly skilled in horsemanship and adept at raids in depth. From Hungary, they passed into the Austrian army. The three regiments of hussars recruited by

Louis XIV in 1692 were made up of men of mixed origin but most of them came from Germany, the countries of the Ottoman Empire or ones abandoned by the Turks. They had already served in other armies but had a mutual bond through a community of language, way of life and general attitude, and were more attached to their unit than to the country in whose service they currently were. From 1750, however, recruitment dried up. In future, the hussars of the French army were to come almost entirely from the German-speaking provinces of Alsace and Lorraine and retained nothing of their origin but the uniform and some traditional practices.

The international character of the wars of religion increased the use of foreign units. This practice continued in almost all armies during the seventeenth and eighteenth centuries. Thus, the presence of regiments of Italians can be found in France and Spain, in particular; of Germans in France, Spain, England and Holland; of Walloons in France and Spain; of Irish and Scottish Jacobites in France and Spain; and of Swiss in practically all armies. With the exception of the last-named, who constituted a special case, foreign regiments were commissioned in accordance with the usual procedures and with the sovereign's more or less tacit agreement. In France, in the case of the German, Italian or Irish regiments, the language used in giving orders and the customs were those of the countries of origin; the pay was slightly higher than in French regiments but the discipline was harsher. The ordonnances which forbade these regiments to accept French recruits could not be observed in the case of the Irish Brigade once the Jacobite emigrations of the years 1691–1715 had ceased. Those units had to make do with the sons of Irishmen and with Frenchmen, and were kept in being solely for political reasons. German and Italian regiments preserved their racial character better, although in the former, German-speaking Frenchmen sometimes made up the major part. On the other hand, despite the ordonnances, foreigners still in the process of being assimilated were to be found in French regiments. Thus, the foreign units of an army did not give an accurate picture of the number of non-nationals who were actually serving in it.

The Swiss formed a category that was quite unique. Swiss regiments existed in all European armies, because they were highly prized, as is proved by the length of time of their employment by the following countries: Savoy-Piedmont (1480–1832), France (1496–1792 and 1815–30), Austria (1498–end of eighteenth century), Venice (1511–1719), Papal States (1506–1870), Spain (1515–1813), Genoa (1573–1779), England (1691–1856), Holland (1676–1828), Prussia (1696–1848), Saxony (1704–1814), Naples (1731–1859). In addition, there were Swiss companies in sovereigns' military households. Between the sixteenth and the eighteenth centuries, 35,000 Swiss were serving, at any one period, in peacetime, and this figure rose to 50,000 in time of war. That represented a ratio of men serving to the adult male population of 1 to 11, increasing, in wartime, to 1 to 7, a proportion surpassed only by Prussia and Sweden. In all, perhaps 400,000 Swiss undertook service in foreign countries, 40 per cent of them in France. The Swiss rarely enlisted as individuals. In some instances, regiments belonged to a canton which signed a convention with the contracting monarch, allowing him to use units recruited by the local Swiss authorities. In other cases, it was the colonel who carried out negotiations, and then recruited the unit within the scope of agreements reached with the cantons.

The Swiss regiments constituted an army within an army. They differed from all other foreign units by reason of having the highest pay, their own military law and special privileges (such as the captains' right to present their successors to the king). In addition, the agreements restricted their employment to particular theatres of operation. They could not serve overseas (with the exception of the Karrer regiment in France), and were not to be opposed to each other, if they came from the same canton. Indeed, they remained in contact with the latter, where recruiting offices were able to prevent abuses on the part of recruiting sergeants, and where they

could receive their pensions from the king who had employed them. The military calling thus often proved a way of relieving economic hardship. By serving under their own flag, but without reducing their loyalty to a foreign king, Swiss soldiers had the feeling of helping their own country. They did this, in fact, by the relief which their service rendered to the country's over-population and by the money which it earned. Nevertheless, the Swiss were sometimes hostage to the attractions of the country in which they were serving. So some were to be found in French regiments, to which they seem to have been drawn by the milder discipline.

Other powers put their troops at the disposal of a foreign sovereign. Instances of such action were those of Bernhard von Galen, Bishop of Münster, at the end of the seventeenth century, and of the Margrave of Hesse, at the end of the eighteenth, several of whose regiments fought in the English army against the American rebels. Service in a foreign army was not always voluntary. Thus, Frederick II forcibly incorporated in the Prussian army the Saxon forces which he had defeated in 1756 and recruited them with French prisoners taken in 1756 and 1757 to form 'deserter battalions' (*Freibataillonen Französischen Deserteuren*); desertion from these formations was astronomical.

The high point of service by foreigners seems to have been reached in the mid-eighteenth century. From the time of the Seven Years' War, the rise of nationalistic sentiments made it more difficult and, in addition, the regulations for foreign units were brought progressively into line with those for the troops of the host nations.

Some instances of service by foreigners arose from political alignments – the English or Scottish Jacobite units, and particularly, the Irish ones in the French and Spanish armies; the Polish regiments which remained loyal to Napoleon; and more recently, the Czech and Polish Legions of the First World War, or the Free French forces in the Second, before the French national army was re-established. There are cases where volunteers go off, at the prompting of their government, to serve within another army's organization – the German Condor Legion in the Spanish Civil War (1937), the Spanish Bluc Division and the Legion of French Volunteers in the German army (1943). The British army still contains Gurkha battalions recruited in Nepal.

The most original form of service by foreigners is represented by the Foreign Legion in France. It was first established in 1831 as a way of providing employment for numbers of political refugees, and then handed over to Spain in 1835. It was re-formed in France in 1836, and is recruited by voluntary enlistment. Recruits sign on as foreigners and there is no requirement to provide their exact identity. So long as a man's presence in thc Legion does not become known, he is protected by anonymity against any action from outside that is related to his past. Frenchmen and naturalized Frenchmen can serve with the permission of the Minister of War. In wartime, the legionary is excused, if he so wishes, from serving against his native country. The Legion has always been par-ticularly well qualified for overseas service. It has welcomed into its ranks men in search of adventure, or who are anxious to obliter-ate a dubious past, but especially those with a genuine military calling, as well as plenty of refugees from every revolution or victims of foreign conquests. The Legion, whose civil activities (on public works, rescues of various kinds, etc.) are as valuable as its military ones, has built up solid traditions (the annual 'celebratory day' for the Battle of Camerone, Boudin, the green tie and the white *képi*), and it makes every effort to maintain its standing as a crack unit. Its numbers have varied from 3,000 (in 1862 and 1872–80) to 35,000 (in 1940 and 1952).

Service by foreigners is, therefore, an extremely complex military phenomenon, and one which has also often assumed considerable dimensions. Under the later Roman Empire, it accounted for more than half the Roman army, up to 27 per cent of the French under Louis XIV, nearly 50 per cent of the Prussian under Frederick II, and over 50 per cent in the British army during the American War of Independence; it represented 8 per cent of the French

army in 1952, and one need hardly men-tion the foreign contingents which made up two-thirds of Napoleon's army in 1812. It thus has also a sizeable connection with the occurrence of movement by sec-tions of a population. *See also* ALLIANCES; HUSSARS; MERCENARIES; RECRUITMENT; ROME; SWITZERLAND.

A. CORVISIER

FURTHER READING
Fritz Redlich, *The German Military Enterpriser and his Work Force* (2 vols, Wiesbaden, 1964–5); J. C. O'Callaghan, *History of the Irish Brigades in the Service of France* (Glasgow, 1870, repr. Shannon, 1970); Rodney Atwood, *The Hessians* (Cambridge, 1980).

Formations *See* TACTICAL ORGANIZATION

Fortification The object of fortification is to strengthen the defensive military poten-tial of a natural or artificial site. Fortification can be either permanent or temporary. When permanent, part of its role is to protect populations and their possessions, but it may also serve to con-trol them and keep them in a state of dependency; in that case, it provides pro-tection for the forces of the ruling power. In the conduct of war, it provides cover for the formation of armies and a place to which they can fall back in case of need, armours offensive operations against counter-attacks and, lastly, its goal has long been to achieve a saving in the numbers of men deployed.

Fortification has been known since the earliest Antiquity. Although in archaeo-logical excavations it is not always easy to discern whether walls are those of sheepfolds or fortresses, as soon as arrow-heads, slingshots, multiple ditches and zig-zagging entrances are found, it is usually reasonable to assume that the site was a fortification. Fortifications enjoy a certain durability. While the huts of primi-tive peoples have disappeared, leaving only the traces of doorposts and fragments of pottery, the thick, heavy walls of a fortified construction survive the millennia more successfully. The site of habitation or refuge to be protected was chosen in order

Perhaps one of the best preserved examples of the *trace italienne*, the fortress of Naarden formed the northern hinge of the eastern edge of the 'Water Line', the combination of fortifications and inundations which defended the province of Holland. Originally fortified in the late sixteenth century according to the 'old Netherlands system', Naarden was largely refortified after 1672 according to the 'new Netherlands system'. The 'arrow head' bastions with deep curved flanks and the continuous envelope of counterguards sandwiched between wet ditches were typical of the style of Coehoorn, the chief exponent of the 'new Netherlands system'. A bastion according to the old system, its flanks joining the curtain at right angles, can be seen on the left of the picture. The majority of the roadways entering the town are modern.
(KLM Luchtfotografie)

to make its defence easier. It was often placed at the top of steep slopes and, if there was some degree of access, the weak point was barred off by a ditch or a wall, which is known as the 'barred spur'. When there was no natural prominence to use, an obstacle was created either by heaping up earth or rocks, to make motes, or by digging ditches. The castle and the mote – the latter a technical variant of the former – made their appearance as individual or family fortifications in periods of political disorganization, as in England after the

Norman Conquest. The same phenomenon occurred in towns which consisted of two distinct parts, the *ville comtale* or *ville épiscopale* on the one hand, and, on the other, the *bourg* (i.e. the 'borough' lying outside the walls) enjoying various freedoms. The late Middle Ages were characterized by the continual effort of kings or great feudal lords to win back for themselves alone the regalian prerogative to erect fortifications. This process began in England during the reign of Edward II.

Once kings had regained these rights,

fortification became an affair of state, the monarch deciding upon the building, maintenance or dismantling of fortified sites to conform with his policy. At times he even chose, going back to the model of the Roman *limes* or the Great Wall of China, to set up defensive lines or fortified marches barring the points at which rivers or mountains had to be crossed. Increasingly, as states took on fixed dimensions (though these could, of course, be changed through diplomacy or war), fortification became concentrated on the frontiers, with strongholds behind these lines to which troops could fall back. Lastly, with the coming of attacks from the air, the frontline combat mission began to be rivalled in importance by the need for active defence against the airborne enemy, and the passive protection of people and resources against bombing raids. As seapower had both offensive and defensive functions – to transport invasion forces and to counter invasion attempts – it required two types of fortification; its own bases required fortification whilst all points which might form the target of enemy seapower also needed protection.

The Ancients rarely wrote about fortification. However, some Byzantines, notably Emperor Leo VI and Philo of Byzantium, did record information relating to fortification and siege warfare. Demetrius Poliorcetes was renowned for his talents in this field but, in general, the skills were handed down by word of mouth and practical example from master masons or builders to their disciples. Certainly the Romans were prodigious in their use of both fieldworks and permanent defences. Their thick straight stretches of curtain strengthened by flanking towers was a basic design that survived until at least the Renaissance. Towns copied techniques from one another and great stretches of fortification like Hadrian's Wall, the Byzantine fortifications or those of the Crusaders could not have been built without directives and models passed from one generation to another.

In the late Middle Ages and during the Renaissance, written documents began to be kept. The earliest concerned the art of war and machines but there were also sketches of defensive works. A little later, we have the documents of the Italian architects who were also engineers. Those from the late Middle Ages – Villard de Honnecourt, Kyeser – did not build fortifications themselves but influenced others through the circulation of copies of their designs. The later medieval writers did have experience of early artillery. Following the appearance of French artillery in Italy, the Renaissance designers – Castriotto, Martini, Giuliano da Sangallo and Michelangelo – actually built fortifications. They developed and improved upon the bastioned, ramparted walls and exported their ideas throughout Europe, where their services were generally in demand. The Spaniards also built fortifications but wrote little on the subject. Machiavelli was the first of a long series of writers to enquire into the effectiveness of fortification and its rationale.

The seventeenth century saw the appearance of different schools which tended to codify the practice of a master and turn it into a catalogue of recipes instead of adapting themselves to the particular terrain. But at the preparatory level too, the Jesuit or Oratorian schools, which taught future engineers the necessary elements of mathematics, tended to present fortification as a science or, in other words, to deduce its ground-plans from theoretical data at a time when the resistance of materials, ballistics, the calculation of probability and descriptive geometry were still only at an early stage of development. The result in the schools was to be the myth of an ideal fortification, a standard frontage. Abler minds proved capable of avoiding the intellectual sclerosis of these schemes, realizing that fortification was, as a facet of strategy and tactics, the handmaiden of politics and the technological application of the sciences mentioned above. Sébastien Le Prestre de Vauban, Louis XIV's prolific engineer and soldier-statesman, was the supreme example of this, although his contemporary Menno van Coehoorn was scarcely less influential in the Netherlands.

The builder of fortifications has had to face *a range of constraints*: materials, weapons and nature, obliging him to justify his project to the political decision-makers in various ways.

Materials The materials chosen must be relatively easy to use, in good supply, durable and resistant to impact.

The first used was wood for building fences or palisades, for constructing traps or timber shielding. Wood possesses a certain elasticity, particularly in combination with earth (e.g. the Gauls at Avaricum). There are plentiful sources of supply since it is naturally renewed and it may be worked even with prehistoric stone axes. However, modern land clearance in certain places has sometimes made it difficult to build up reserves. Wood is perishable, even when not in use, nor is it sufficiently resistant to impact or flames. In the nineteenth century, the first armour-plating was made out of two sheets of iron separated by a layer of wood. During the early modern colonial wars, the first forts were built of wood, certain villages were surrounded by thorn hedges and the French conquerors of Algeria took with them a supply of wooden blockhouses. Wood reappeared in 1914–18 for the building of shelters in the trenches.

Earth is another natural material which, with some degree of stone content, is found everywhere. The first use of earth came in the digging of ditches which, by throwing earth up on to one's own side, also created an artificial escarpment. Legionary camps made use of it. The next development saw earth being combined with wooden beams in the ramparts built by the Gauls. Earth was also used to create those escarpments called motes; to avoid slopes slipping, layers of stone were intercalated between the layers of earth, as depicted in the Bayeux Tapestry. The material being divisible, the building of a mote, which might involve a hundred or so men labouring at the job for two months, was not a superhuman task. The material was also elastic, a factor which rendered it ideal to rampart – i.e. to buttress with a mass of earth – fragile stone walls against artillery. Although penetrable by projectiles, earth

slowed their progress; hence its use from 1856 to counter the great penetrative power of rifled artillery. From the American Civil War onwards, and particularly during the Russo-Japanese War of 1904–5 and the world war of 1914–18, it was used in trenches. Experience demonstrated that protection against heavy artillery could only be found at a depth of 20–30 metres, though this figure would rise to over 100 metres against the standard 20 kiloton atom bomb. Protection against atomic radiation can be afforded with earth at lesser cost than with concrete, though greater thicknesses are required.

Stone is also a natural material that has been used since the earliest years of ancient civilization. Since it does not deteriorate significantly, ancient stone fortifications can still be found in all parts of the world. Stone is highly resistant to compression, less so to violent impact. Thus the ballistic engines of Antiquity first destroyed the stone parapets and then the earthen ramparts. The damage soon became extensive when metal cannon balls appeared, giving rise to the use of supporting mounds of earth. Fragments of stone could wound the defenders; hence the rapid disappearance of fausse-brayes – retrenchments placed at the foot of walls. Stone which had originally been used to make enormous Cyclopean walls, made out of blocks with a normal weight of tons if not indeed hundreds of tons, came to be used in blocks of smaller height. To thwart the miner, stone dressed to a smooth and rounded surface was used, on which he could get no easy purchase and, to limit the effect of impact, the bossages were preserved. The high explosive shell of 1886 sounded the death knell of stone as a material.

Brick is an artificial material which is easy to produce and sun-dried bricks were used in dry countries from the earliest times. When kiln-fired, brick can resist the effects of weather. Its effectiveness against battering-rams depended on the thickness of the wall and the miner could breach it without great difficulty. Fired bricks were used in the Netherlands where there was a lack of stone. This was also to some extent the case at Bordeaux (Château-Trompette)

During the 1930s, Belgium improved her fixed defences between Antwerp and Maastricht along the line of the Albert Canal. Fort Eben-Emael covered the remaining gap between Maastricht and the complex of forts around Liège. It was immensely strong and earned the unenviable adjective of 'impregnable'. On 10 May 1940, ten gliders landed 78 German infantrymen on top of the fort, thus negating most of its close defences. An engineer platoon then crossed the Albert Canal in inflatable boats. A combination of satchel charges exploded around turret rims, flamethrowers directed through embrasures, and hollow charges placed on armoured cupolas, wrecked the fort. The garrison of 1,100 men was driven into the network of tunnels only to surrender a few days later.
(Das Photo)

and on the Île de Ré in the seventeenth century, for the same reason. When fired, its qualities are the same as those of stone.

With the use of concrete we come truly into the field of artificial materials. A monolithic material made of cement, sand and gravel, it affords good resistance against projectiles so long as these do not exceed a calibre of 150 mm. At a very early stage, however, it was replaced by reinforced concrete, which is also still referred to in French as *béton spécial armé* – or in English as 'armoured concrete' or 'ferroconcrete'; a fortification concrete with a very high cement content and very heavily reinforced. The reinforcements of mild steel are arranged in very dense layers near the outer (*extrados*) and inner (*intrados*) edges. This is done to counter the effect of the cracking off of the surface layers. Even if it does not pass through unreinforced concrete, the projectile produces serious fragmentation inside the concrete and causes the pieces that fragment to fall. This effect is also mitigated to some extent by interposing sheets of steel. In spite of the different proportions of steel used in different countries (the quantity is lower in Belgium than in France) reinforced concrete proved to be extremely effective – performing especially well at Verdun – and was reproduced in the same manner until 1939. For their Atlantic Wall,

265

the Germans used a simplified arrangement of steel in a cubic lattice-work.

Iron was used in Louis XI's reign for *moineaux*, a variety of *caponier*, in the ditches of Plessis-lez-Tours, then we hear nothing more of this material until 1830, when its use was advocated by Colonel Paixhans. The serious use of iron dates from the years 1875–80, when it was used first for look-out turrets and then for protective screens for artillery pieces when they were not firing. The navy had used iron first, in the building of *La Gloire*, a frigate armour-plated above the waterline in 1859. Iron was, however, too fragile and with the advances in iron and steel metallurgy (Bessemer 1856, Martin 1863, Thomas and Gilchrist 1881), the use of cast-iron then of steel was established definitively. With this, we see the coming of armour-plated fortification, first in casemates, then in revolving or disappearing turrets, and in conjunction with reinforced concrete for closing off embrasures.

Elastic materials which can absorb the effects of buckling have been employed in the past for certain purposes and these are still of some interest today in relation to the effects of shock waves. For example, just before the First World War the roof of Fort Douaumont at Verdun had been strengthened by a layer of sand between two concrete slabs.

Weapons Weapons raised the problems of where they were to be installed within the fortification and how their effects were to be resisted by the fortification, this latter problem being resolved historically through the selection and application of particular materials.

The war machines of Antiquity required a certain amount of 'clearance' behind them: hence the width of the tops of the walls. As they were able to fire with a curved trajectory, they could be concealed behind or below walls. The width of the parapet walks in some cases afforded the possibility of a defensive deployment of reserve troops up to the level of a genuine tactical manoeuvre, as on the Great Wall of China.

Missile weapons of the tensional type led to the creation of arrow-slits that were very narrow on the outside wall allowing downward vertical firing to reach the base of the wall. They could also accommodate different types of weapon, from a longbow to a crossbow.

The use of missile weapons that were employed vertically, for purely defensive purposes, led to the creation of machicolation and brattices.

Cannons occupy space and are heavy. It was not particularly safe to place them at the top of a medieval tower and they were usually fired through embrasures. However, the enemy gunner could attempt to hit the embrasure and this led to the introduction of moveable wooden screens. Cannons firing from casemates produced noxious fumes. They were therefore moved back to the top of the fortifications, where they fired *en barbette*. The French were for many years wary of casemates. The problem of gas or fumes remained and it has been solved in recent years by the use of mechanical ventilation.

By its curved trajectory, the mortar made it possible to strike against defences that were hidden from view. In response, raised casemates (designed by Baron Haxo) were constructed on the ramparts, then casemates from which the guns emerged before firing (Mougin) and, lastly, before the Second World War, the guns were protected by concreted casemates. Similar in style was the form of protection by screens known as 'traverses', which Vauban, who had himself invented ricochet fire, advocated to counter its effects.

The concentration of fire at the end of the nineteenth century turned forts into 'shell traps': hence the dispersion of the defensive artillery into outlying batteries.

The effect of blast is not a creation of the nuclear age. Sailors were the first to encounter it when firing their very heavy artillery pieces. Blast was channelled in the firing galleries, rendering its effects worse. These effects have been reduced by the use of deflectors and forms of spring or hydraulic recoil systems.

The shock effects caused by the impact of shelling have led to the use of elastic suspension systems and to living quarters being buried away deep beneath the surface.

Nature Even when modified, nature intervenes in the choice of a site.

The shape and relief of the land is easy to appreciate in mountainous regions where there is always a dominant position, though that position is pushed ever further back into the hills as the range of weapons increases. Briançon and the successive development of the outworks there provide a good illustration of this point. However, the question of relief is also posed in apparently flat country where the least undulation may provide cover for an attacker. One countermeasure was the forbidding by law of permanent construction, the exploitation of quarries or land clearance, up to a certain distance from the fortified place.

The site may be imposed by necessity when, for example, a bridge, a ford, a mountain pass or a narrow passage has to be held. To all intents and purposes, in spite of the efforts of Henry IV of France and his successors, it was only in the nineteenth century that the French road network became comprehensive. Before that, many roads could not carry long siege trains, enabling fortresses to be concentrated on the key routes. Moreover, political dealings played their part: Richelieu needed protected routes into Italy and Louis XIV needed routes into Germany before the Treaty of Ryswick. It was also necessary to bar the passages into Thiérache (the area around the River Serre, to the south-west of the Ardennes). Similarly, the forts of the 'Barrier' had to be held against France. All these points were given the name of *musoirs* ('pierheads') or *poternes* ('posterns').

It was also necessary for life to be carried on normally by the garrison. This does not seem difficult when we are looking at a town that became a fortified 'strong place', but if the garrison was as large or almost as large as the civilian population, well-stocked stores had to be maintained. It was also a good thing to have craftsmen among the population, and this was something sought after in the new towns like Neuf-Brisach or Montdauphin. Since water is of crucial importance, a variety of solutions have been adopted with, in each case, concern being shown for security: underground access to a spring (Megiddo), piping the water from the spring through an underground aqueduct (Hezekiah at Jerusalem) and cisterns. Although the concrete tops of the detached French forts were watertight, they were covered with a mass of earth which absorbed water; this was then purified for use by the garrison. Wells were drilled after 1935 in the larger works of the Maginot Line.

Modes of Fortification Modes of fortification are the ways in which an obstacle is created, although this obstacle only has value in so far as there are defenders to man it. The modes employed depend on the methods of siege warfare in use at any given time, but they may be divided simply into frontal or barring action, and lateral or flanking action.

Frontal action consists in attacking head on by scaling the wall, undermining it, knocking in the doors with a battering ram or opening breaches in the walls by the use of cannon which have been brought within range. To counter these methods, loopholes or arrow-slits are made in the walls. In low-built (or artillery) fortification, battlements are constructed for the marksmen while the cannon are sited on the curtain-walls or bastions or on cavaliers of raised earth ensuring them good command of the ground. Lateral action is already ensured, with vertical fire from the long arrow-slits and horizontal fire from the casemates or caponiers located in the ditches. With machines or guns becoming capable of long-range action on the battlefield, we shall see the 'barrier forts' of the 1870s, Seré de Rivières's system and the defensive blocks of the Maginot Line. This type of action was also practised by coastal batteries before the introduction of turrets, producing a plunging fire to the extent that the battery was higher up than the guns of the ships it was fighting. It was also obligatory for the dominant positions of mountain fortifications or the fortifications at the bottom of a gorge, called *chiuses*. In practice every attack ends with a frontal attack.

Lateral action is a privileged, effective mode of action and one that is economical as regards the means deployed, though it can only operate within a limited range from the actual site of fortification. The function of towers was not confined to reinforcing the curtain; they also enabled flanking or enfilading fire to be aimed at miners or ladder-bearers and made possible action against attackers who had scaled the walls. Apart from their heavy leaves and herses, the doors also had *assommoirs* in them, allowing for a type of vertical action, and, from the second millennium onwards, elaborate arrangements of obstacles such as murder-holes. The bastion had a similar role in the gunpowder era. In close defensive fighting, the low casemates known as 'caponiers' swept the bottom of the ditch with their flanking fire.

Fortification technique combines both frontal and lateral action. In entrenched camps, the forts protect one another, each firing in front of the other, and the late nineteenth-century concrete flanking 'casemate of Bourges' ensured great security for the guns charged with making this reverse fire. The fortification designed in 1923–7 (Maginot Line) was to take this principle to the extreme in the complete structuring of a battlefield, though frontal action was limited to some 10 km. For political reasons it was not possible for the guns to fire onto foreign territory.

The construction of fortifications has to be commensurate with the threat, taking into account the foreseeable increases in that threat. In a colonial setting without roads, it was senseless to envisage use even of the 24-pounder; but in Singapore, 1941, it would have been sensible to make provision for a land attack. In 1950 in Korea, it was illusory to count on the 100 kiloton bomb without adequate conventional defences on the ground.

History History reflects these criteria and contingencies with regard to aims, means and procedures.

The earliest fortifications belonged to relatively small tribes to shelter their herds and stores. The *enceintes* were vast and consisted of one or maybe two ditches, with walls of dry stone, which was, in some cases, hewn. The entrances sometimes had a zig-zag pattern. The living quarters were built on the periphery. Since great numbers of inhabitants have succeeded each other down the centuries, the actual living quarters tend to move around over time.

The formation of the city-states and the first empires gave a considerable boost to the building of fortifications, the mobilization of thousands of men making it possible to create megalithic constructions, not only for the defence of the capital, but also for the creation of fortresses and stores at enforced points of passage, thus closing them off. We see a first form of bastion appear among the Incas, and flanking by means of redans among the Canaanites who also organized their gateways for defensive purposes. Sun-dried or kiln-fired brick was a good material for the means of fortification employed in this period and size was a significant factor. The Ancients describe the walls of Babylon and the immense size of the city which was only conquered by Cyrus after the Euphrates had been diverted.

The Great Wall of China, built in the third century BC, was an open system of remarkable size, which only rested on natural obstacles at its extremities. It was not, however, the only fortification the Chinese built. They had fortified towns, some built in areas they had conquered, with a market, different areas for the different trades and occupations, and a redoubt for the governor and his forces. The characteristic element was the monumental building which surrounds the town gate with an inner courtyard behind. As a consequence of their particular form of organization, the Japanese mainly built castles. There was no communication between East and West on these matters; when the modern age arrived, Europeans constructed their own type of fortifications in the East, such as those built by Pigneau de Béhaigne at Hue or the British at Madras and Bombay.

The forts of the period of colonial conquest – the American West or Siberia – were made of wood, and when this material was absent, as for example in the Sudan, of rammed earth. There was moreover a huge mismatch between the defenders' weapons and those of the attackers. When the fighting was between populations of European origin, as in Canada and New England or the defence of Spanish America, the design was European. The plans for Louisbourg in Canada, which has now been restored, were drawn up by Vauban.

In their first phase, the Romans built no fortifications other than their legionary camps: the legionary camp became permanent and around it arose a town. The design of the camp was simply a ditch and a palisade, with sometimes loopholes to the front and, where possible, look-out or flanking towers. As conquest became a perpetual process, with the enemy standing at the gates of the Roman world and desiring only to come inside, a system had to be developed. The *limes* formula for frontier defence provided a solution. This 'open' arrangement was supported at its extremities by the sea (Antonine Wall, Hadrian's Wall) or by rivers (Agri Decumates) and played the role not so much of a barrier as of an alarm bell. In effect, apart from a ditch where the earth that had been dug out constituted an obstacle, its defence rested on small garrisons of auxiliaries and, most importantly of all, there was a strategic road along which patrols could pass and reinforcements could be brought. Thus any infiltrating forces could be detected, pursued and neutralized. Sixteen centuries later, the 'barrages' employed by the French army in Algeria would be of the same order, though they were built by other means. This arrangement could not offer resistance against mass invasions like those of the middle of the third century AD following which the towns of Gaul surrounded themselves with walls along boundaries which in many cases would remain fixed until the Middle Ages. The restored *limes* would continue to prove effective until the early years of the fifth century, though then they were held by Barbarian troops. In 270–5, Aurelian built the wall which bears his name in order to protect the 'Eternal City'. Six miles long with walls that are 13 ft thick and 380 towers, it resisted Alaric and his men for a year, before that leader starved Rome into submission in 410.

The Middle Ages were characterized by vertical military architecture. A wide view was needed to warn, assemble and shelter people and animals. A raised position afforded an advantage in that one could fire downwards on to attackers, hinder the manoeuvring of ladders, throw down rocks and boiling oil, etc. Stone constructions in this period were to reach a height of 100 feet. Before that, where only wood was available, the terrain would be raised by the building of a mote or mound of earth. The first castles were very simple, a doorless and windowless room on the ground floor for storing provisions, entrance being gained by the upper storey. There would be a room on the first floor where the lord of the castle lived and carried out his administrative functions, and a room on the second floor for his men at arms, though these were usually few in number. Complications of this basic pattern and relative comfort only came at a later date. Entrance was gained to the first floor by a flying bridge or a long ladder, an arrangement that is found in Ireland from the sixth century onwards. Such an arrangement was obviously not applicable to towns, for commercial reasons.

French towns initially used the Gallo-Roman walls and then improved and extended them as they expanded. The techniques employed were similar to those used in castles though they were introduced somewhat later and in more simplified forms for financial reasons. The great royal fortresses such as Richard I's Château-Gaillard or those of the religious orders from the Crusades onwards (Crak des Chevaliers in Syria), and the constructions built to control or defend towns, served as models.

Town walls were much less thick than those of castles. In some small towns, they were simply the outer walls of the outermost houses. The towers were also lower; this was the case in Italy though there the situation was dominated by internal family feuds. From the eleventh century onwards, the lower part of the walls had a batter built into it so that projectiles delivered from the top would rebound outwards. Lateral flanking fire could be provided from the tops of the towers. These were at first square or rectangular to allow a clearer field of fire, though they later became round making it less easy for the miner to dislodge blocks of stone from the base. One also finds spur-shaped towers which leave no dead angles and resist battering rams more effectively. The top, which is the active part, was equipped with putlog holes for beams on which hoardings were placed when necessary to protect the marksmen. The development of this was to lead to stone machicolations, i.e. corbelling with arches or crenellations separated by merlons with a hole at the base to allow downward fire. Over the years, these loopholes descended into the solid part of the wall, initially mid-way, then at the base level with the ditch (where there was one), the aperture becoming round for firearms. Loopholes were not made on the same vertical axis, in order not to weaken the wall.

Gateways required a great deal of attention. They faced a danger of direct impact first from battering rams and then later from cannon. This was countered by building an outwork called a barbican which forced the person entering to follow a path at right angles to the direction of the entrance. Against men who might have entered on foot, there was lateral flanking from the towers standing on either side of the gate, which were often quite close to one another, and vertical flanking from machicolations which in this case are called 'brattices'. Lastly, the door itself may be a double one, with *assommoirs*, passages through which projectiles could be thrown, being made beyond the herse. Typically, drawbridges (or bascule bridges) were also found, although mathematical studies were not yet devoted to the subject of their balancing, as was to be the case in the nineteenth century.

For areas near to the fortifications, a watch was kept from lookout turrets, known as 'bartizans', which continued to be built until the thirteenth century. For looking out over a greater distance, church towers or belfries were used, though these were not to be found everywhere and their function was more properly one of prestige. Unlike castles, towns did not have that additional storey known as a watchtower.

At this period, most towns in France were fortified, even quite small market towns. The kings or princes laid down that towns should be put in a state of readiness to defend themselves, with the costs being borne by the community, and they were granted permission to raise taxes for the purpose. As a consequence of the state of insecurity, underground refuges were used, and important farms and churches were fortified during the French Wars of Religion. Such density of strongholds was not widely found in Western Europe until the time of the Norman invasions and, even then, such fortifications were highly dispersed, whereas, from the time of Justinian, the defence of the Byzantine Empire was organized by the central government along a wide frontier zone.

During the Renaissance, the metal cannon ball marked the end of vertical architecture. Walls could be breached and the first tangible effect was the end of feudal castles and of local centres of power. Moreover, these latter no longer had the requisite financial capabilities, though Strasbourg, for example, still had its own artillery at the end of the sixteenth century. Henceforth, fortification meant the fortification of towns or of citadels within towns, with a slightly different slant to the problem when these were intended to control the population. There was one additional difference: the enemy was now the cannon.

The idea of merely reinforcing the walls was rapidly abandoned: it was soon realized that walls had to be built against a resilient mass of earth. The rampart produced by this development necessitated the demolition of nearby houses. At the same time, the walls were lowered, no longer leaving them directly open to an enemy strike. In order to reconstitute an obstacle that had to be scaled, the ditches, which were sometimes filled with water, were deepened. Two terms should be noted here: the scarp is the inner wall or slope of the ditch; the counterscarp is the outer wall or slope of the ditch. The latter is often reveted, i.e. faced with a wall of masonry. The lower towers no longer had command either over the floor of the ditch or the area beyond it. The solution to this problem was the development of the bastion (one already existed at Mont Saint-Michel in the thirteenth century). This is a projecting part of the wall, polygonal in shape. It has two 'faces' and two 'flanks', making possible flanking fire into the ditch or moat and for some distance forward, but not straight ahead. Firing ahead could only be done by the guns on the curtain between two bastions, the curtain thus being covered by lateral fire from the flanks of the bastions. There was much discussion of the ideal angles for the flanks and the curtain.

The sixteenth century was characterized by transitions in weapons systems and truly large-scale experiments. It opened in 1503 with the brilliantly sustained siege of the fortress of Salses (Pyrénées-Orientales) which had been designed in stone for artillery by Ramirez in 1497. During the Wars of Religion, the walls of the old castles or towns proved highly resistant. None the less, these designs had to be kept up to date.

The principle applied by the Italians was the lowering and ramparting of walls. The course of development ran as follows:

- Appearance of the bastion with *orillons* in 1501–3 built by Giuliano da Sangallo at Nettuno. These were rounded protections for retired flanks screening the guns that swept the scarp or the ditches. If the trace was a broken one, they were called shoulders.
- Semi-circular bastions to deflect cannon balls, practically without curtain walls, which were built for Henry VIII by von Haschenberg (a Bohemian) in the Cinque Port fortresses. The model was not copied elsewhere.
- Errard de Bar-le-Duc built a great many constructions and recorded many of his ideas. He insisted on flanking being built at right angles and set the length of the curtain wall as a function of the range of arquebus cross-fire. Lastly, in order to improve the defence of curtains or ditches, he advocated the building of ravelins. For frontal fire, he proposed cavaliers, mounds of earth above the curtains or bastions. His treatise on the subject was published in 1600 and he died in 1610. He it was who inspired d'Argencourt's constructions at Brouage (opposite the Île d'Oléron) and Montpellier.

Errard's conceptions were improved upon:

- By the Chevalier de Ville, who wanted more earth in the scarps and, particularly, calculated the placing of the defensive line on the basis of the range of a musket.
- By the Comte de Pagan, who also kept to musket range for the length of the defensive line, with the flanks running perpendicular to this and fire being concentrated on the ditches. In order to counter mining, he made provision for detached bastions and listening galleries of the sort that already existed at Salses, counter-guards, to cover the points of bastions, outworks with ditches and a covered way on the counterscarp. Lastly, even at this early stage, he also developed demilunes. In his *Treatise on Fortification*, which appeared in 1645, shortly after he had lost his sight, he also laid down the elements of classical bastioned fortification.
- The 'front' (as it was called at the end of the seventeenth century) was formed of two half-bastions (demibastions) with a curtain between them. This was the chief point for both the attacker and the defender; it was when it became evident that a breach could be made in the front that surrender would inevitably follow.
- The angle of the two faces of the bastion was more or less obtuse depending on

271

the number of bastions. It was acute in the case of the English 'star forts' which had four bastions; apart from certain exceptional cases, it was normally around 110–120 degrees.

- The angle formed by the flanks and the curtain, which was at first a right angle, tended to become more acute in order that the best conditions could be achieved in which to sweep the faces; an angle of 15 degrees enabled the defenders to dominate the foot of the curtain.
- The walls had a batter, a slant one quarter from the vertical, in order to make it easier to hold back the earthen bank. The height of this was around 26 feet which was the highest point that could be reached by manoeuvrable ladders. The slope of the bank was aligned with the slope of the external glacis, in order to ensure the continuity of fire of the fusiliers. Cannon could be placed on the top of the bank. It was not until the time of Vauban that pieces would be separated by traverses of earth, protecting them against ricochet fire seeking to dismount them.
- The ditches were wide – more than 22 yards. They were either left dry or filled with water, though later they could be filled with water only when necessary. Great importance would be attached to such 'water manoeuvres' in the later seventeenth century.
- Protected lines of communication called 'caponiers' sometimes connected the scarp to the counterscarp. A gallery was sometimes built into the base of the counterscarp to enable defenders to fire back into the ditch. One of the first examples was at Salses. This arrangement would again be employed after the end of bastioned fortification.
- The counterscarp was reveted with masonry on the side nearest the main body of the fortification, thus making the task of the miner more difficult. A covered way ran along the top making troop movements possible. Vauban would refer to this as the 'eyes and ears' of the fortification. Later parapets for riflemen would be built on the covered

way. Towards the outside, the terrain was formed into a glacis so as to increase the field of fire from the walls.

- As in medieval times, the gateways were defended by barbicans, which forced persons entering to follow a path with flanked angles.
- After Pagan, Errard's ravelins became lunettes, retrenchments in the bottom of the ditch parallel to the curtain. The demilunes were generally built of masonry and ramparted: triangular in shape, they were sited ahead of the curtains with ditches around them and fire could reach them from the faces of the bastions.
- The hornworks were outworks formed out of two half-bastions connected by a curtain; the couronne was a variant with two bastions. The elevation of these outworks meant that fire could reach them from the fortification proper.

From the beginning of the seventeenth century, fortresses or castles included some or all of these arrangements. During the Civil War, the English were to build them all in great number, often in *ad hoc* constructions, as in those built for the subjugation of Ireland. After this period, the only danger that counted was that which came from the sea and which the fleet was there to counter. By contrast, the rest of Europe was well provided with fortresses, whether reconstructed or improved, or captured from an enemy. During the Eighty Years' War with Spain the Dutch, adapting to the nature of their flat land, built a system on the same principles but did so to a very large extent by using the lines of streams and canals, earth, and, for want of stone, brick masonry.

The seventeenth century was dominated by the work of Vauban (1633–1707) and of Coehoorn in the Netherlands. Vauban had at his disposal the same theoretical armoury as his predecessors or his colleagues, who were in fact very talented. If his reputation now exceeds theirs, this can be attributed to his successes both in attack and defence and, particularly, to the fact that he refused to be confined within set ideas and proved able to adapt his plans to circumstances and terrain. What have been called his three systems reveal a mind that was constantly developing new ideas.

He says that he began by 'Paganizing' and in fact his first style was indeed that advocated by Pagan. When he came up against a standard fortress, the attacker would encounter successively:

- At the top of the glacis, fusiliers protected by the covered way or ready to counter-attack from the *places d'armes* built in that covered way. He would also be exposed to fire from the demilune and the curtain.
- Having crossed a first ditch under fire from the bastions and having occupied the demilune, he still had to cross a ditch to take the *tenaille*.
- Having done this, the attack on the curtain could only be made under fire from the flanks of the bastions and the fusiliers on the curtain.

Vauban's second system doubled the *enceinte* by a new defensive line constituted by the obtuse-angled *tenaille*, which was very much akin to detached bastions and not unlike the old counter-guards. Behind this there developed a continuous *enceinte* with straight curtains and the important innovation of bastion towers. These latter were massive masonry constructions, providing protection, within casemates, for artillery pieces which directed enfilade fire on to the ditch and the curtain. These cannon could no longer be dismounted by ricochet fire, which Vauban had just discovered, nor from a dominant position, as had been the case at Besançon or Belfort. This arrangement was suggestive of Montalembert's cannon towers and, more recently, the casemates of Bourges. Use of this system was not confined to rural sites, and he placed such confidence in the innovations that he thought the external *enceinte* was not of crucial importance. This system took form in his plans and constructions after 1687.

The third system differed from the preceding one in that the curtain was retired and double – and also bastioned – reveted redoubts were added in the demilunes, and

there were more limited revetments in the demilunes and counter-guards, though in fact live hedges were used to hold back the earth. The only complete example of this system was the fortification of Neuf-Brisach in 1698.

Vauban did not become obsessed with standard patterns of fortification with ditches and walls supported by banks of earth. In mountainous regions, he used the existing slopes and only employed a ditch in so far as it was necessary to bar the spur and, if direct fire was difficult, he did not hesitate to employ masonry towers. On the coast, the fortress could be the whole of a rock (la Conchée at Saint-Malo) or even a wood (Risban at Dunkirk). He also had the idea of entrenched camps, that is of works built away from the fortress proper which could provide protection for an army and act as a place where it could be reorganized and given a base. Camps of this kind were built at Lille, Dunkirk and Maubeuge; one was planned at Bayonne and was eventually constructed in 1814. We should not of course forget his plan of 1689 for the fortification of Paris.

It would be unfair to neglect his Dutch rival Coehoorn, who brilliantly reduced Namur (1695) which had been partially fortified by Vauban. Since, from the very outset, his fortifications were built on flat land with a high water-table, he made great use of broad wet ditches. In what is known as his first style, no communication was possible between the main building and the demilunes, except by footbridges. The curtains were reduced to redans prolonging the faces of the bastions whose flanks, in concave *orillons*, commanded the ditch. In his second style a sort of fausse-braye ran in front of the bastions, connected to the demilune, and a second continuous *enceinte*, or envelope, which was separate from both the demilunes and the main building. Having begun his career as a gunner, Coehoorn skilfully arranged the different tiers of fire one upon the other and he made provision for defensive action from the covered way by means of sunken redoubts enabling a grazing fire to be directed on the glacis. He died in 1704 aged 63 without having had a chance to elaborate a theory for areas of broken ground. The thinking of the eighteenth-century theorists was greatly influenced by his work.

The early years of the eighteenth century were overshadowed by the War of the Spanish Succession. All the fortresses designed or reconstructed by Vauban, which were later to be called the *Ceinture de Fer* ('Belt of Iron'), suffered serious damage up to Denain (1712), since these fortresses were not inviolable. The Peace of Utrecht opened up important breaches in the defensive lay-out by making France dismantle some of her fortifications, e.g. Dunkirk. In order to make up for these, from 1728 onwards, Cormontaigne undertook the fortification of Metz and Thionville and the fortifications at Briançon were built, chiefly under the direction of Bourcet. Finally, the loss of Arcadia led to the construction of the fortress of Louisbourg defending the mouth of the Saint Lawrence.

Vauban's style was present in all these works, though in a heavier form. Outworks became more numerous, with lunettes on the capitals of the bastions (the line drawn from the point of the bastion to the middle of the gorge) and the demi-lunes, etc. Without reaching the point of creating entrenched camps, detached works were installed on commanding patches of ground at Briançon (Salettes, Les Têtes) or to block a passage (harbour battery at Louisbourg). The whole arrangement was traditional but, at that point, advances in artillery began with the work of Vallière.

The second half of the century was, therefore, characterized by the development of new ideas; Maurice de Saxe advocated the separation of long-range action and close defence, the protection of the low *enceinte* with shields against long-range fire and lastly, and more originally, an earthern *enceinte* at some distance from the fortified place. Montalembert, who wished to do away with bastions, also attached a great deal of importance to long-range action and gave over the defence to stone casemates abundantly equipped with cannon, arranged so that some fired frontally and others delivered flanking fire. He seems to have been inspired by the Swede, Virgin. His detached scarps would be copied later by Carnot. Though his work was surrounded by controversy in France, he was copied by the Germans after 1815. The Austrians adopted massive 'Maximilian towers' for the fortifications at Linz, heavily equipped with artillery and, at Verona, a bastioned trace with detached scarps and glacis in reverse gradient on the counterscarp. The French at Lyons (1830) and Paris (1840) built extremely simplified bastioned defences without outworks. All these constructions included detached forts which played the role of entrenched camps.

The second half of the nineteenth century, with rifled cannon and later with high explosive, would see all these developments put in question. However, from the end of the eighteenth century, artillery of greater precision and shot of a better calibre had already enabled cannon-fire to demolish walls from a range of 1,000 or 1,300 feet, which made it unnecessary for siege batteries to be emplaced as close as the fortress's ditches.

The rifled cannon made it possible, if not to achieve plunging fire, then at least to fire over the relatively small undulations of uneven terrain. From that point, the scarp wall could be hit at its base over the covered way and the glacis; the result was a contracting of ditches, with no revetment on the counterscarp, and artillery being moved on to earthern cavaliers. Solid shot broke masonry or sank deep into earth. The explosive shell which was developed in the 1830s, blew away earth and, with its splinters or canister-shot, rendered riflemen or gun crews vulnerable. This caused the Germans and Austrians to move towards dispersal and the use of casemates.

As a result of the frontier changes that ensued, the period after the Franco-Prussian War was one of substantial efforts in the field of fortification both in Germany and in France; other countries also made similar efforts since in the middle of the 'long peace' no one could predict how long it would actually last. Strategic plans became marked out on the terrain in the form of the Metz-Thionville and Strasbourg-Mutzig complexes in Alsace-Lorraine and by the *rideaux* based on Seré de Rivières's lines of entrenched camps in France. Fortifications demarcated zones which were difficult to cross and between which the armies would operate.

Military engineers assimilated the most modern techniques: massive earthern mounds to counteract the penetrative power of shells, narrow courtyards and casemated barracks, defilading of the scarps calculated on the trajectory of missiles, a polygonal ground plan with caponiers to bar access to the ditches.

These substantial constructions, begun in 1874, would be rendered obsolete eleven years later by a new discovery – high explosive. This blew earthern and stone defences to pieces; though Mougin's cast-iron armour-plating was still serviceable, steel now took over. Iron- and steel-making made considerable progress at this point, partly as a result of military needs. In 1881, a 'special' chrome and tungsten steel made it possible to manufacture shells which, instead of disintegrating on striking hard cast iron, cracked the armour. From 1889 to 1891, chrome and then nickel steels and case-hardened steel made it possible to produce armour-plating against which shells fragmented. Artillerymen developed the longer cylindro-ogival shell with a more powerful charge. The speed of this shell at impact increased from 1,522 to 1,854 feet/second for the 155 mm gun at an angle of 56 degrees. The charge rose from 5.3 to 22.7 lb. The weight of the 220 mm shell increased from 176 to 260 lb with a charge of 80.7 instead of 8.8 lb. Similar advances were seen everywhere and each country organized competitions to improve on these levels. The whole business of fortification required rethinking.

The spacing out of possible targets was fixed on the basis of gaps three times the probable size of areas of explosion damage, 160 ft for the guns of the period. The result was a spreading out over a wider surface area, the forts of 1874 now being positive 'shell traps'. Weapons, whether cannon or machine-guns, were protected by reinforced concrete and armour-plating of special steel. Direct fire was provided by rotating turrets in the German army (Schumann) and in the French (Galopin) by rotating and 'disappearing' turrets which had an elaborate mechanical system of counterweights. The different parts of the fortification were connected by means of concreted galleries, the observatories were armour-plated and the riflemen's parapets were near to concrete shelters. Scarps and counterscarps were made of loose earth, with a defensive grating running along the ditch. A fort thus came to represent the organization of a battlefield, at least to a limited degree, and this was something that was entirely realized in the German *Feste* of 1907, which resembled battle zones rather than traditional closed forts, 100–200 hectares in area, sprinkled with fieldworks and gun batteries all interconnected by underground passages.

As there could be no question of abandoning existing constructions, the fortifications of 1874 were upgraded by levelling the enormous earthern cavaliers and, to compensate for their absence, concreting the casemates, adding turrets, casemates and casemates of Bourges around the principal fortified sites. The concrete designed to protect against the 220 mm shell was 9 feet thick and the armour-plating 8 in or 10 in thick. During the Ochakov experiments of 1913, they were to resist the 280 mm shells with total success.

The 1914–18 war put permanent fortifications rudely to the test. After a surprise attack on Liège, where the forts held out for eleven days, being successively overcome by fire from the German 420s and the Austrian 305s and the longer resistance put up by Maubeuge, doubts appeared, especially when Fort Manonviller, in Alsace, lasted for only 54 hours. However, the resistance of Maubeuge and Antwerp tied up forces that were consequently kept away from the Marne. In the East we should not forget the capture of the Austrian fortress of Przemysl after a six-month siege.

After the Marne, field fortification dominated the battlefield, as had been the case in 1904–5 during the Russo-Japanese

War. Trenches ran the length of the front and, to protect themselves against mortar-fire, the infantry made ever deeper dug-outs, while the Germans concreted some of their gun positions. The extremely long Battle of Verdun demonstrated the value of permanent fortifications against very heavy artillery – 420s in the German case, 400s on the French side. The experiences of these years would mould the post-war years.

In order to avoid the evils of an invasion of the kind that had occurred in 1914–18, the governments and high commands decided to build fortified lines: the Czechs built in the Sudetenland, the Belgians on the Albert Canal, and the French line ran principally along France's north-eastern frontier. The initial tactical conception, which was similar to that of Seré de Rivières, was to create fortified regions which were open in the rear with gaps left free for manoeuvre. The technical conception derived directly from the previous war.

It consisted in having an organized battlefield in each fortified region with a basic structure of large-scale fortifications for artillery, infantry casemates, anti-tank entanglements made of old railway lines, personnel bunkers, underground signalling centres, railways running from the depots and, in certain cases, inundations. Reinforced concrete was still used for protection, and this could be up to 11 ft 8 in thick to resist projectiles up to calibres of 520 mm (the Germans developed a 600 and an 800 which they would use at Sebastopol). Similarly the thickness of armour-plating increased to 12 in.

The larger sections had 'active blocks' at the front – turrets for 75s, 135s or machine-guns and casemates for 75s, 135s and 81s on the flanks. There was no heavy or long-range artillery, this being the preserve of the sector troops. The entrance blocks at the rear were some 650–850 yards from the forward blocks. The troop quarters, munitions and communications were buried in the ground at a depth of 100–130 feet.

The system was effective so long as the rules of the game were followed, as was the case in June 1940 in Alsace and Lorraine. It could not deal with the unexpected, as when the parachutists landed at Eben-Emael in Belgium or where a breakthrough at a weak spot meant that the enemy could manoeuvre around it, as at Sedan.

After the occupation of the Rhineland, the Germans built what became known as the Siegfried Line (*Westwall*). The idea behind this was totally different, being guided by a desire to build quickly. These were concrete blocks built to be occupied by troops in the field with their weapons. There was no protection for the gun embrasures, though there were anti-tank obstacles. In 1944 this system would prove less resistant than the old *Feste* of Metz when attacked by the Americans.

The Germans also built a line of coastal fortifications that was impressive at certain points. The Atlantic Wall was not remarkably effective but one has to bear in mind here the extent of the weapons ranged against it. The most outstanding feature was its submarine shelters which, with a slab of reinforced concrete 23 ft thick, topped with an anti-shellburst slab of 6 ft 7 in, remained practically undamaged after repeated bombing. We see here a commitment to passive defence, which can also be seen in the dispersal and protection of vital industrial complexes, the Churchill Forts and the anti-aircraft defence towers in Berlin. The Japanese did the same for their own sensitive installations in Tokyo. This course of development seems to reach its culmination not in the building of obstacles, but in the construction of protection for long-range weapons – rocket launch silos, or bunkers for communications systems and essential personnel. We see here the 'protected infrastructure' drawing on past experience and extrapolating from it to meet the needs of the new weaponry.

As a consequence of the continual struggle between cannon and armour, the men who dealt with fortification had to keep abreast of technological progress in gunnery. This was the case with the engineers of the Renaissance. It was also the case with those soldier-engineers who succeeded them, to the extent that for many years, together with the men of the artillery, and in close conjunction with them, they formed one of the two 'scientific arms'.

In regard to practical achievements, we should not forget such nineteenth-century engineers as the Belgian Henri Brialmont who installed the first armoured revolving turret (designed by the Englishman Colas) on the Scheldt in 1863; the Russian Todleben, known for his improvised defence of Sebastopol, who before 1870 installed the first armoured batteries at Kronstadt; and the Russian Velitchko, the creator of the fortifications of Port Arthur. After 1885, French, German and Austrian fortification was the collective work of officers grouped in Research and Development sections.

In the field of the applied sciences, the engineer-artillery combination contributed, together with the demands of ship-building, to progress in iron- and steel-making and in mechanical control systems. By its use of earth, bastioned fortification was instrumental in producing the science of soil mechanics, a tradition which, for French engineers, begins with Vauban, continues in the eighteenth century with Coulomb, and in the nineteenth century with Français and Poncelet.

Fortification originally arose as a necessity in response to a general state of insecurity. It subsequently became an affair of states and a reflection of political circumstances and relations. In each century, there have been cases where faith placed in fortifications has proved illusory. More often than not, this has been due to a misunderstanding of their potential and purpose. *See also* ARMOUR PLATE; ARTILLERY; CAMPS; CASTLES; CHÂTEAU-GAILLARD; CITADELS; COASTAL DEFENCE; COEHOORN; DEMETRIUS POLIORCETES; ENGINEERS; EXPLOSIVES; FORTIFICATION, FIELD; FRONTIERS; MAGINOT LINE; PARIS, SIEGE OF; PROPELLANTS; ROME; SIEGES; VAUBAN; WEAPONS.

J.-M. GOENAGA

FURTHER READING
P. Rocolle, *2,000 ans de fortification française* (2 vols, Paris, 1972); E. Viollet le Duc, *Annals of a Fortress*, tr. Benjamin Bucknall (London, 1875, repr. 1983); Christopher Duffy, *Siege Warfare: the Fortress in the Early Modern World, 1494–1660* (London, 1979); Christopher Duffy, *The Fortress in the Age of Vauban and Frederick the Great, 1660–1789* (London, 1985); Simon Pepper and Nicholas Adams, *Firearms and Fortifications: military architecture and siege warfare in 16th century Siena* (Chicago, 1986); Rolf Rudi and Peter Saal, *Fortress Europe* (Shrewsbury, 1988); W. Anderson, *Castles of the Middle Ages* (London, 1970); K. Mallory and A. Ottar, *The Architecture of Aggression* (London, 1973).

Fortification, field

Definition and Scope of Enquiry Field fortification is intended to achieve the same objectives as permanent fortification. It is either meant to create an obstacle or enhance an existing one, to protect defenders against enemy actions, and to allow the defenders to engage in offensive action. It is either created to meet the needs of a battle or for the occupation of a sensitive zone and, depending upon the way operations develop, it may sometimes remain in existence for several months and even for years. Since field fortification consists mainly in movements of earth, traces of it may remain in the ground for very long periods of time. It has been called field fortification, field defence or, since 1918, field works. Understood in this last sense, it has come to have a wider reference than before, being extended to cover operational infrastructure in so far as this involves peacetime preparations for demolitions.

Antiquity and the Middle Ages The classical type of field fortification in Antiquity is represented by the work of the Roman legionaries who, in the course of castrametation, i.e. laying out their camps, surrounded these with a ditch, with palisades above it and traps in front. During sieges, which sometimes lasted for months, the principle of having a retrenchment turned towards the fortified place and another turned towards the outside against possible relieving armies was respected in the form of lines of contravallation and circumvallation, troop camps being dispersed along the perimeter. By contrast with what was to happen in the seventeenth century, the troops did not camp in battle order; a parade ground created in the camp enabled tactical units to form up and they left the camp by gates that were, in some cases, protected by zig-zag passages.

After the fall of the Roman Empire, the long pre-eminence of cavalry began – heavy cavalry in the West, and in the East, light cavalry using bows. The Byzantines developed a form of protection for masses of infantry using breastworks and *chevaux de frise*. The important sieges of the Crusades were characterized by the use of con-travallation camps. The turning point in field defences for open battles came at Courtrai in 1302 with the ditch used to protect the Flemish infantry; this development was accentuated in 1356 at Poitiers with the use of hedges and abatis.

Modern Period The modern period saw the advent of the widespread use of firearms. As a consequence, the system of permanent fortification was transformed and the infantry came to play a greater role. The infantry also began to dig itself in, adopting techniques from the art of siege warfare.

'Defensive lines' became an important, though not always an effective, element of the new tactics. The object was to prevent an enemy from passing through a particular zone or region and to protect areas from contribution raids. In 1702–3, Villeroi built a continuous retrenchment which ran from the region of Antwerp to Namur (the 'Lines of Brabant'). With a parapet some 6 feet wide by 6 feet high, these continuous lines had no strong points, the troops being spread out evenly along them: the Duke of Marlborough had no trouble in breaking through. During the War of the Spanish Succession, there were also three sets of lines in Flanders and two in Alsace. They were made in areas that had little in the way of sound permanent fortifications and they made use of the lines of rivers or streams, and of villages, and also took advantage of forests for making abatis.

Similarly, 'entrenched camps' appeared as a place in which to form up or re-form an army. Protected by fire from fixed fortifications, a number of redoubts would be built, between which the troops would make their temporary entrenchments. These *camps retranchés* had little in common with the late nineteenth-century constructions of the same name which were permanent extensions to fortified places in response to long-range fire from the new artillery.

A 'battlefield', whether freely chosen or imposed, was subject to human organiza-tion, with abatis in wooded areas, ditches to break cavalry charges, and redoubts armed with cannon batteries. The sophistication of these works depended on the time avail-able; the Antoing redoubt at Fontenoy in 1745 was built in one night. The synthesis of all the various elements could be seen in a construction like the 'Torres Vedras Lines' in Portugal in 1810. Designed to accommo-date the armies of Wellington and, if need be, to protect their reembarkation, they barred the way to Masséna's army. The term 'lines' is incorrect here since what was involved was an arrangement of 59 re-doubts armed with cannon batteries, placed not as any systematic theory demanded, but as best suited the terrain. On a scale appropriate to the period, we can see here a forerunner of the *rideaux* of the later nineteenth century.

The material used was chiefly earth and armies were prepared to bring this from some distance if the ground was rocky, since splinters from stone are dangerous. A thickness of 6 feet gave protection from cannon balls, whilst 18 in was proof against bullets. The same thickness in gabions, made of intertwined branches and filled with brash, was equally effective. Timber was also employed to construct stockades, known as *palanks*, and *chevaux de frise*. Streams and rivers could be dammed or dykes broken to create flooded areas (inun-dations), a method which naturally proved most efficacious in the low-lying lands of Flanders and the Netherlands. However, at New Orleans in 1815 both the Americans and the British discovered their dams disin-tegrating and the water flowing back into the Mississippi. Sometimes the soldiers themselves laboured on these works but it was more usual, at least in well-populated regions, to requisition peasants.

Field fortifications tended to mirror the design of fixed defences since they were both the responsibility of the same military engineers. Apart from the Lines of Torres Vedras and a few 'indented traces' inspired by Montalembert, bastioned lines were the norm until the first half of the nineteenth century.

Contemporary Period This period begins with Todleben's creation of field defences at Sebastopol, which consisted of building a continuous extension to the permanent fortifications; his lines were dug into the terrain and his troops defended them yard by yard.

In the American Civil War each side made great use of retrenchments, trenches and abatis of all kinds, which were set in place as soon as the two armies came to a standstill. They built these defences instinctively, so to speak, without waiting for precise directives and their efforts were highly effective.

Each succeeding war saw a further development of field defences and revealed their effectiveness, whether it was to make up for the inadequacies of technically outdated forts as at Paris in 1870–1 or to complement forts as at Port Arthur in 1904–5 or to conduct a brilliant defence of a position as at Plevna in 1877, at Liao-Yang

The trench lines on the Western Front during the First World War (1914–18), which stretched from the coast of the English Channel to the Swiss border, were probably the most extensive lines of field fortifications ever constructed. However, they were rivalled by the extensive lines of field fortifications built in the Low Countries during the early modern period such as the Dutch Line of the Waal and the IJssel (1605) or the French 'Lines of Brabant' (1702–3) which stretched seventy miles from Namur to Antwerp.

(Imperial War Museum, London)

in Manchuria in 1904–5 and at Çatalca in the Balkans in 1912.

The 1914–18 war sank its network of trenches into the terrain; these were several hundred yards or, in some cases, several miles long. Over four years, from having been temporary, this fortification became in a sense permanent, with the positions and dug-outs being progressively reinforced. This painful experience was to influence later constructions (Maginot and Siegfried Lines, etc.). As the war progressed, the armies learned to exploit reverse slope positions and greater depth, with continuous trench lines gradually giving way to archipelagos of independent strong points and weapon pits, backed up by positions from which local counter-attacks could be launched. In periods of the fiercest fighting not even improvised field-works were considered safe, however, since they could still be registered by enemy observers. Instead, the troops often preferred to lurk in the unimproved shellholes that were scattered randomly across the battlefield.

The Second World War had, at the beginning, all the characteristics of a war of movement, though it lost these in Russia after 1942 despite large-scale offensives. The insecurity produced by the activities of partisan fighters and mobile spearheads brought about the creation of closed centres of resistance, providing protection for reserves and supplies especially in the winter of 1941–2. This 'hedgehog' technique which had proved only temporarily effective on the Somme in 1940 showed both its strengths and vulnerabilities at Tobruk and at Gazala–Bir Hakeim in Libya. By its bitter nature, the long urban Battle of Stalingrad was reminiscent of the Siege of Saragosia in 1808–9 and prefigured present or future battles in the conurbations.

The means of attack and protection developed throughout this period, as did the very objective of the protective action. At first the infantryman had to be protected against musket and rifle fire, cavalry charges and cannon; the gunner had to be able to fire without fear of being hit by rifle or cannon fire. Thicknesses of earth of

between 3 and 6 feet were adequate for the task. The breech-loading rifle and the explosive shell rendered this degree of cover inadequate. Attacks could no longer be made in dense battle columns; troops became more thinly spread on the battlefield. The bastioned retrenchment with its ditch, glacis and parapet gave way to the individual slit trench, made initially for the single rifleman lying flat, but deepened over time, before in turn giving way to the trench dug-out which entered the manuals shortly before 1870, and could be connected up in continuous lines. Battery positions were also dug in, in order to make them less protrusive. Research into camouflage and the concealment of positions began.

The redoubts built at Liao-Yang in 1904 in a flattened pentagon, surrounded by moats and double rows of barbed wire entanglements with *trous de loup* (shallow pits), artillery cavaliers and bomb-proof infantry casemates, were derived from forts of the 1880 type. Capturing them proved extremely onerous.

Wire (Knoxville, 1863, during the American Civil War) made attack difficult, but pathways had to be created through the entanglements to make possible counter-attacks. During the Boer War the wire was barbed, and the 'Bangalore torpedo' – a tube stuffed with explosive – was devised to destroy it. In 1914–18, wire was cut with wire-cutters or blown to pieces by the hail of shells. Mine and shell craters were often used in the fighting as the beginnings of trenches or positions.

Even before 1914, anti-personnel land mines had replaced the time-worn fougasses, which were simply pits filled with a charge of powder projecting fragments of iron or stone as required. There would be spectacular developments in the design of these new mines during the 1939–45 war and later wars, in conjunction with the construction of booby traps.

In 1916, the tank made its appearance. Anti-tank mines, which were shells with a pressure detonator on the fuse, date from 1917 and developed very quickly after 1934 towards heavy types which were designed to destroy the engine and not just the tracks. Today we are in the era of the 'smart' standoff mine with terminal homing. Tank attacks were also prevented by digging ditches, building entanglements of railway rails (France) and concrete blocks of various sizes (Germany) forcing the tank, as it surmounted these obstacles, to expose its vulnerable underbelly.

Just like barbed wire entanglements, these networks of mines and obstacles close off zones which the attacker must identify or neutralize in order to establish pathways for his approach. To this end, apart from detection by the classic 'mine detector', the 1939–45 war would see the creation of armoured vehicles, which had indeed been conceived as early as 1918, pushing heavy rollers or flailing the ground with chains. During the 1944 landings, the British 79th Armoured Division was equipped with machines of this kind. Tanks or tank destroyers came to be concealed in earthworks which were made with the aid of heavy earth-moving tractors and bulldozers, or improvised from the rubble of houses. The presence of heavy artillery on the battlefield also led to an increase in the number of dug-outs. Made at first from earth and logs, they came to be dug deeper and deeper and when they were constructed from reinforced concrete they resembled permanent fortifications.

The study of 'field works' as an intellectual discipline begins with the 1939–45 war. It was then realized that attention could not be confined solely to the battlefield proper but must also be given to the access to the battlefield, to communications, supply of material ('mobile fortification depots' were formed in France after 1936), and to prepared demolitions.

Already by the second half of the Great War, military doctrine prescribed that there should be a system of outposts in the front line, then a line of resistance some 5,000 metres behind it, which may come into play in a retarding action, and a further 5,000 metres behind this, the main line of resistance, with the reserves further in the rear. Experience showed, however, that this theoretical plan, which was still officially in force in 1943, was not adequate in conditions of fully motorized units, the rapid detection of artillery – which now had to be mobile – and modern signals systems. The emphasis then came to be put on centres of resistance, barrages and mobility. None the less, the basic principles were still valid: ensuring lines of sight, protecting one's flanks and maintaining security.

General Conceived and overseen by specialist engineers and the officers of the engineer corps, field defence or fortification was initially seen as a variety of permanent fortification, and in the writings devoted to it, it was regarded as being akin to the works aimed at preventing sorties by forces under siege. When, after 1820, it was taught in courses on the art of war in the French academies and, after 1840, codified in Laisné's *Aide-mémoire*, the thinking was inspired by bastioned fortification, except for the use of abatis and the castellation of villages. A number of authors, most notably the Belgian Captain Girard in 1874, sought to turn it into an independent field of study. After 1918, the French specialist literature and the manuals call for continuous lines whereas the Germans had adopted tactics of dispersion and the use of individual slit trenches. The war of movement of 1939–41 does not seem to have influenced the American manual of 1943. Postwar thinking laid emphasis on mobility, dispersion and 'commando' actions, while heavy fortification became a field exclusively reserved for specialists, aimed at protecting command posts whose role in the actual fighting was indirect. *See also* CAMPS; CASTLES; CITADELS; ENGINEERS; FORTIFICATION; MINING AND MINES; ROME; SIEGES; TODLEBEN; TORRES VEDRAS.

J.-M. GOENAGA

FURTHER READING
P. Contamine, *War in the Middle Ages* (Oxford, 1984); Tony Ashworth, *Trench Warfare, 1914–1918, the Live and Let Live System* (London, 1980); Edward Hagerman, *The American Civil War and the Origins of Modern Warfare* (Bloomington, Ind., 1988); K. Mallory and A. Ottar, *The Architecture of Aggression* (London, 1973).

France Though the military history of France only begins, properly speaking, in the twelfth century, military activity occupies a considerable place in the past of the various countries and provinces from which it was composed. As is generally the case elsewhere, the main facts which have come down to us relate to wars: the short-lived capture of Rome by Gauls (390 BC) and the Roman conquest of the Mediterranean seaboard of Gaul (122 BC). Gaul was divided among some sixty or so peoples of Celtic civilization who were based in fortified towns (*oppida*). The warrior held an important place in society. Only in exceptional circumstances did these somewhat turbulent peoples show themselves capable of uniting behind a common chief (the 'vergobret'), against an invader. This merely conjunctural form of organization did not prove sufficient to resist the will of Caesar and the solidity of his legions. After a success at Gergovia, Vercingetorix was besieged and defeated at Alesia (52 BC). It had taken 20,000 men only eight years to put down a vast country and some twelve million inhabitants (58–51 BC).

Gaul was then subjected not so much to occupation as to military control. It was covered with a network of camps and towns overlaying the network of *oppida*, with roads spread across the countryside by the Roman legions. The Roman military presence was much greater along the banks of the Rhine, the frontier with the 'Barbarian' world, where military colonies were established. The *pax romana*, which lasted for three centuries, was interrupted around AD 250 by an invasion of Germanic peoples who forced the towns to defend themselves with walls and then, in a second phase, by these peoples using more or less brutal means to settle in the country under the command of their war lords. A stop was put to these invasions in 451 when the Gallo-Romans and the Germans united to fight off Attila's Huns. By gaining a series of victories, Clovis, the King of the Franks, managed to bring the other Germanic peoples which had settled in Gaul under his rule. His descendants, the Merovingians, tore Gaul apart with incessant wars, during which the warrior established a position of primacy within society. The warriors, who came from the class of 'free men', became,

with the great landowners, the dominant element in society. An end was put to the prevailing anarchy by another dynasty, the Carolingians, who had distinguished themselves by repelling an Arab invasion at Poitiers (732) and seized the crown. Supported by a group formed out of the fusion of the great landowners and the warriors who owed him both personal military service and contingents of free men according to a system based on the agricultural exploitation (*manses*) of their lands, Charlemagne governed through counts, who were chosen from among the most powerful of these landowners and appointed by him. He extended his authority over the greater part of Western Christendom.

Wars which pitted Charlemagne's descendants against one another destroyed the Carolingian Empire and opened it up to pillaging raids by peoples who came from the sea – Saracens and, more especially, Normans. The task of defending the coasts against these raids was assumed by the counts, who had become the major landowners, the masters of the troops under their command, and who built fortified strongholds and made themselves virtually independent. The Norman threat diminished after a number of these invaders settled in the Lower Seine region, which served them as a base for their conquests outside *Francia occidentalis*, one of the kingdoms into which Charlemagne's empire had been divided in 843. Through heredity, the counts and other war lords consolidated their power and erected the feudal pyramid. Theirs was a society that was essentially military, based on the subordination of one man to another. The wars between the feudal barons which bathed the tenth and eleventh centuries in blood, saw increasingly heavily equipped cavalry and stone-built castles assuming a preponderant role. The Crusades in Spain and the Holy Land removed some of those feudal barons, impoverished others and enabled the Church to regulate the conduct of private wars (truces of God) while a new dynasty, the Capetians, very gradually reconstituted royal authority.

In the divine right monarchy established by the Carolingians, the king's position was that of supreme military leader of the kingdom and this was symbolized in the oriflamme of St Denis. With the restoration of royal power, this function once again became a reality. It allowed the king, when the kingdom was attacked by an external enemy to call up the *ban* and the *arrière-ban* of his vassals and the militias which had been created by the towns to which he had granted charters. This was the case, most notably, in 1214. The victory of Bouvines over the Emperor thus appears as the first national victory. The Hundred Years' War, which saw France opposed to England from 1337 to 1453, put the solidity of that 'feudal monarchy' to the test. The defeats at Crécy (1346), Poitiers (1356) and Agincourt (1415) proved that the feudal knights practising *la guerre guerriable* as a sport were ineffective compared to the mercenaries and the troops belonging to the king. The French were initially outclassed by the English at sea, and later on land on account of the indiscipline of the knights, the weakness of their militias and their paid infantry and, lastly, the effectiveness of the English bow, which was a less formidable weapon than the crossbow but capable of more rapid fire. The French thus reacted slowly on account of their internal divisions. Initially, du Guesclin refused to join battle and allowed the enemy to wear himself out in raids throughout the kingdom. Then, at the height of the crisis, the extraordinary part played by Joan of Arc, by revealing the existence of national sentiment, put an end to the succession of defeats (relief of Orleans, 1429). Lastly, Charles VII and his counsellors superimposed on the traditional military structures of the kingdom a first national army based on paid service. The cavalry was organized in ordinance companies. As regards infantry, efforts were made to avoid the need to call on mercenaries, who were often foreign and who ravaged the countryside during truces (the *grandes compagnies*), by raising companies of *francs archers* drawn from the population, an experiment which was to prove a failure. Lastly, the Bureau brothers created the first French artillery which showed its superiority on the battlefield.

Once delivered from the English peril, the kings launched themselves into the adventure of the Italian Wars which gave rise to a long duel between France and the House of Habsburg. These wars saw a profound transformation in military technique. That change, which was inspired by the Italians, was to mean that the Spanish armies would be dominant for more than a century, as advances were made in the use of firearms. Marignano (1515) was the first victory won by artillery and the French defeat at Pavia (1525) showed that the use of firearms meant new tactics had to be employed on the battlefield. At the same time, siege warfare expanded in scope and gained in importance. However, the persistence of the old traditional military structures of the kingdom allowed factions to lead provinces in rebellion and raise troops when the power of the monarchy faltered, thus making possible the Wars of Religion. Once this new crisis had been surmounted, the monarchy had under its command troops that were reliable, but limited in number: 20,000 men in the guard regiments, *Maison du Roi*, and the *vieux*, old-established provincial regiments. France had not, however, been able to create for itself a military administration comparable to that of Spain.

In 1635, France entered into a difficult war with Spain which forced the chief minister, Richelieu, to increase the absolutism of the crown. To increase the army to more than 150,000 men, it had been necessary to have recourse to officers – colonels and captains – who owned their own regiments or companies and to whom the king paid the sums necessary for raising and maintaining their troops. To keep the number of cases of fraud in check, the supervision and administration of these troops was entrusted to civilians whose authority was backed up by the Secretariat of State for War. The victory at Rocroi (1643) brought confirmation of the power of the new French army, which was led by commanders of great ability (Condé, Turenne). In spite of a fiercely fought civil war – the 'Fronde' – an exhausted France snatched final victory ('Peace of the Pyrenees,' 1659) and ensured itself a predominant position in Europe.

Thanks to Le Tellier and Louvois, Louis XIV was then able to maintain an army whose wartime numbers were to border upon 400,000 men. This meant that there was one soldier for every twelve adult males and one in every three nobles was in the army, usually serving as an officer. In 1688, the *milice royale* (royal militia) was created, soon to be recruited by drawing of lots. The army was to be developed into a very highly organized force: more exact supervision of numbers of men and of pay and supplies; wearing of uniform which enabled stricter discipline to be enforced; foundation of Les Invalides for old soldiers; advances in weapons (hand-guns and bayonets) achieved by the first steps being taken to structure their industrial production. In parallel with these developments, Colbert provided France with the first large fleet it had ever possessed (more than 100,000 tons) with a Secretariat of State for the Navy and he established a system of recruitment classes, imposing service in the king's vessels upon seamen, and instituted pensions. Given the possibility of achieving expansion both on land and at sea, Louis XIV accepted limitations on his territorial ambitions in order to keep a free hand at sea. While Vauban, who had raised the art of siege warfare to a new level of perfection, was creating the 'iron belt', a complex of fortifications established on secure frontiers intended to preserve the kingdom from invasion, the French navy was, for a time, able to stand up to the Dutch and English fleets. France's resistance during the difficult War of the Spanish Succession proved the strength of her national spirit and the efficiency of her military system.

After the death of Louis XIV, while the armies of Europe set about imitating the French model, the French army went through a period of relative stagnation which showed up in its defeat at Rossbach (1757) by the armies of Frederick II. This defeat prompted a military renaissance in France. Her Ministers of War, who included Choiseul, provided the country with a remarkably organized army (*École militaire*, end of the system of officers

owning their own regiments and companies, creation of divisions, advances in military training, Gribeauval's artillery, the 1777 model gun). However, the nobility's monopoly of commissions, an increasing tendency to quarter troops in barracks and stricter discipline provoked discontent among the lower-ranking officers and the men, who went over to the Revolution when it broke out. In the same period, the French navy, which had been restored by Sartine in particular, showed itself capable of facing up to the English navy during the American War of Independence.

From 1792 to 1815, France was subjected to the ordeal of uninterrupted warfare. After some initial setbacks partly attributable to a great number of its officers joining the emigration, the army – which had been brought closer to the people by the peril facing the nation, and which was swelled first by the call for volunteers, then by 'mass levies', and was commanded by excellent NCOs promoted rapidly to the highest ranks – was able to repel the invasion of Year II. In 1798, the Jourdan Law instituted conscription. By contrast, the navy collapsed. The professionalization of the army, which had been begun in the last years of the *ancien régime* and been reinforced by constant campaigning, and the place the army had assumed within the nation, contributed to the development of a military regime under the Empire. Greatly expanded in Napoleon's hands but maintaining its earlier structures, the French army defeated some of the nations of Europe (Austerlitz, 1805; Jena, 1806, etc.), but wore itself out in over-ambitious ventures (Peninsular War, invasion of Russia). Defeated at Leipzig by the army of twenty nations (1813), it succumbed to exhaustion in 1814 and by the time of the Battle of Waterloo in 1815, it was unable to stem the tide of events.

France quickly rebuilt its army and its navy. The Gouvion–St-Cyr law (1818) laid down the procedure for conscription, which was to be by drawing of lots. The limited wars of the Second Empire ended with the collapse of Sedan and the fall of Paris after a lengthy siege (1870–1). The defeat, which was due to a certain failure to match up to the demands of modern warfare and the absence of reserves, affected the nation deeply. While fighting colonial wars, France eagerly prepared its 'revenge' by a series of army bills which gradually established compulsory military service for all (for a period which rose to three years in 1913), developed military instruction and the training of officers and soldiers and gave the country a system of fortifications (Seré de Rivières) without abandoning the 'spirit of the offensive'. The heart of the entire nation beat with that of its army, which was capable of uniting citizens beyond their political passions, including those generated by the Dreyfus Affair. Anti-militarism, which had migrated from the Right to the Left, did not prevent the emergence of a *Union sacrée* in 1914. The 'Great War' saw the sacrifice of French lives reach extraordinary heights. The victory on the Marne in 1914 and the resistance at Verdun in 1916, together with the daily holding operation on the Western Front, cost France nearly one and a third of a million lives and produced at least as many invalids. In the longer term, the war had disastrous demographic and moral effects on France which were momentarily masked by the victory she had won at the head of the Allied armies commanded by Foch.

The French Empire reached its greatest extent at that point. Though the navy prepared itself appropriately to assume its mission, the army took little part in the renewal of military thinking which was taking place throughout the world and successive governments, feeling that peace could best be ensured by disarmament, only granted it the resources to carry out modernization at a late stage. Outstripped in only a few years by the German army, the French land forces fell apart almost at the first battle in 1940. The resistance against the occupying forces, which General de Gaulle rallied first from London and later from Algiers and in which the Empire gradually joined, actively laid the ground for liberation and played a part in its realization, while the units of Free French formed overseas undertook an important role in the Allied war effort.

From 1944, the army was rebuilt around a delicate balance of soldiers from the pre-war army, men from the African army, and ex-Resistance fighters. For its organization and equipment, the army modelled itself on the forces of the United States. Hardly had reconstitution occurred than it had to face wars of decolonization in which 'classical warfare' (defeat at Dien Bien Phu in 1954) was undermined by psychological and subversive action to an extent not previously witnessed. The nation was deeply divided by these wars and the army itself did not escape the crisis, part of it not accepting the abandonment of Algeria. Faced with the division of its former allies between two armed alliances, France initially joined NATO. She then developed her own nuclear weapons and left NATO, without however deserting the Western camp. Today, France takes part in the maintenance and re-establishment of order in those countries which call upon her assistance. *See also* ADMINISTRATION, ARMY; ADMINISTRATION, NAVAL; ARTILLERY; AVIATION; CARTOGRAPHY; CASTLES; CAVALRY; COLONIAL TROOPS; COLONIAL WARFARE; DRAGOONS; ENGINEERS; FINANCES; FORTIFICATION; FORTIFICATION, FIELD; GENDARMERIE; HUSSARS; INFANTRY; INVALIDS; KNIGHTS AND CHIVALRY; MAGINOT LINE; MEDICAL SERVICES; MERCENARIES; MILITIAS; NAVAL PERSONNEL; NAVAL WARFARE; NAVIES; NUMERICAL STRENGTH; PENSIONS; RECRUITMENT; RESISTANCE; SECRECY; SIGNAL COMMUNICATION.

ARDANT DU PICQ; BART; BEAUFRE; BUGEAUD; CARNOT; CASTEX; CHAMLAY; CHARLEMAGNE; CHARLES THE BOLD; COLBERT; DAVOUT; DE GAULLE; ESTIENNE; FOCH; FOLARD; GALLIÉNI; GRANDMAISON; GRASSE DE TILLY; GRIBEAUVAL; GUESCLIN; GUIBERT; JOFFRE; LOUVOIS; LUXEMBOURG; LYAUTEY; MONLUC; NAPOLEON; PÉTAIN; RICHELIEU; SAXE; SUFFREN; SURCOUF; TURENNE; VAUBAN; VILLARS; WILLIAM I .

AGINCOURT; ALESIA; AUSTERLITZ; BOUVINES; CERESOLE; CHÂTEAU-GAILLARD; DIEN BIEN PHU; FONTENOY; FRANCE, BATTLE OF; JEMAPPES; JENA AND AUERSTÄDT; LEIPZIG; LUXEMBOURG, SIEGE OF; MARIGNANO; MARNE; METZ; MOSCOW, RETREAT FROM; NORMANDY; ORLEANS; PARIS, SIEGE OF; PAVIA; POITIERS; QUIBERON BAY, BATTLE OF; QUIBERON BAY, LANDING OF ÉMIGRÉS AT;

RAVENNA; RIVOLI; ROCROI; ROSSBACH; SEDAN; SOLFERINO; TRAFALGAR; VALMY; VERDUN; WAGRAM; WATERLOO; YORKTOWN CAMPAIGN; YPRES.

A. CORVISIER

FURTHER READING
D. G. Chandler, *The Campaigns of Napoleon* (New York, 1966); Lee Kennett, *The French Armies in the Seven Years' War* (Durham, NC, 1967); Douglas Porch, *The March to the Marne* (Cambridge, 1981); Maxime Weygand, *Histoire de l'armée française* (Paris, 1961); P. M. de la Gorce, *The French Army* (New York, 1963).

France, Battle of (10 May–25 June 1940) The German offensive against France was launched at dawn on 10 May 1940. Initially, the Germans had planned to attack France through Holland and Belgium, in a fashion similar to the Schlieffen Plan of the First World War. However, General von Rundstedt and his chief of staff, General von Manstein, persuaded Hitler that the main concentration of the German attack should be through the Ardennes Forest, at the centre of the French defences. In this way, the initial German thrust against the Low Countries would serve to lure the French and Allied reserves northwards and the main German attack would encircle the entire defensive force. When the battle began, the German plan worked to perfection. The French and Allied troops, expecting an attack through Belgium, moved quickly into Belgium, taking up a defensive position between Antwerp and Namur. This placed them in an awkward position when the main German attack broke through the poorly defended Ardennes, an area which the French General Staff had considered impassable. On 13 May, the Meuse was crossed at Sedan, Monthermé and Haux by units of Kleist's army thanks to the superiority of the *Luftwaffe* (with its close-support tactics and dive-bomb attacks) and the skill of the German infantry. In spite of a number of counter-attacks (for example, by de Gaulle on 17 May and by the British four days later), nothing could stop Guderian's armoured divisions and he reached the Channel coast on 20 May, cutting the

Allied armies in two. The Dutch army had been forced to surrender on the 14th. The Belgians, and the French who had come to their aid, could not hold out on the Dyle, so Weygand, having replaced Gamelin as Commander-in-Chief of the Allied armies, on 19 May, tried to form a new front on the Somme and the Aisne. The capitulation of the Belgian army on 27 May put paid to the last remote chance of mounting a defence in the north of France. Hitler's decision on 24 May to stop the advance of German armoured units towards Dunkirk allowed the British to evacuate their forces from that port. From 28 May to 4 June, the British Admiralty, using requisitioned vessels, removed 338,000 men, of whom 112,000 were French and Belgian, from the beaches under the cover of the Royal Air Force. The second phase of the Battle of France, which began on 5 June, saw the Allies unable to hold the 'Weygand line', resulting in the complete breakthrough of the German armies into French territory. Paris fell on 14 June, and when an armistice was sought three days later, only the Maginot Line and the front established by the armies in the east of France still held. The campaign had cost the Allies 130,000 men, including 96,000 Frenchmen, while the Germans had lost 45,000.

The extraordinary strategic and tactical victory of the Germans was not due to any marked superiority in either numbers or in the quality of their equipment. Instead, it was the product of the Germans' planning and tactics (the combined use of aircraft, parachutists, armoured divisions and infantry), their attacking spirit and the unpreparedness of the French for a war of movement fought with modern weapons, the errors of the French command, the lack of co-ordination between the Allied forces and a want of confidence in certain units that were severely tested by the blitzkrieg. As Henri Michel has written: 'The disproportion lay not in the numbers of troops, but in the way in which they were used.' *See also* AVIATION; DE GAULLE; FRANCE; GERMANY; GUDERIAN; MANSTEIN; RUNDSTEDT; SCHLIEFFEN; TANKS.

A. CORVISIER
KEITH NEILSON

FURTHER READING
Henri Michel, *La Défaite de la France, Septembre 1939–40* (Paris, 1980); Brian Bond, *France and Belgium, 1939–1940* (London, 1975); Eleanor M. Gates, *End of the Affair: the collapse of the Anglo-French alliance, 1939–40* (Berkeley and Los Angeles, 1981).

Frederick II, 'the Great', King of Prussia

(1712–86)   As a young prince, this son of Frederick William I suffered a great deal from the irritable temperament of his father. This conflict greatly affected his character, giving rise to a general cynicism and a contempt for mankind.

He acceded to the Prussian throne on 31 May 1740 and in the same year took advantage of the death of the Emperor Charles VI to invade Silesia. Victorious in the three Wars of the Austrian Succession, he was allowed by the Treaty of Hubertusburg (1763) to keep Silesia and, through the First Partition of Poland in 1772, was finally able to join royal Prussia to the central provinces of Brandenburg. During the War of the Bavarian Succession (1778–9) he prevented Austria from annexing the territory of the Elector of Bavaria.

The king's military successes were the product of two essential factors, the first of which was his constant presence in the theatre of war. This enabled him at all times to take advantage of the operational situation; he was able to react more quickly than his opponents. The second was his most expert use of the military organization which his father had developed, and which he modified but little. So far as tactical developments were concerned, Frederick reintroduced the oblique order which, by reinforcing one wing, while weakening the other, allowed him to outflank an opponent. His brilliant tactical victory at Leuthen on 5 December 1757 was attributable to the revival of this tactical method. *See also* GERMANY; FREDERICK WILLIAM I; INFANTRY; LEUTHEN; ROSSBACH; TACTICS.

B. KROENER

FURTHER READING
Christopher Duffy, *Frederick the Great: a military life* (London, 1985); W. Elze, *Friedrich der Grosse* (Berlin, 1936); Pierre Gaxotte, *Frederick the Great* (London, 1941); R. Koser, *König Friedrich der Grosse* (4 vols, Berlin, 1914); Gehard Ritter, *Frederick the Great: an historical profile* (London, 1968).

Frederick William I, King of Prussia

(1688–1740)   Frederick-William's fascination with military affairs throughout his reign (1713–40) earned him the nickname of the 'Sergeant-King'. Conscious of the poverty of his kingdom, but also of the political role it could play, he saw the expansion of his army as an essential instrument of Prussian power. He put the national recruitment service into better order by the *Kantonsreglement* of 1733 and, with the founding of the General Directory of War, Finance and Domains in 1722, he completed the process of creating the efficient centralized administration which had been planned by his grandfather, Frederick William 'the Great Elector' (1640–88). Partly through the enlistment of substantial numbers of non-Prussians, the size of the army was more than doubled, to 83,000 men, becoming the fourth largest in Europe despite a native population of only 2.5 million. Frederick-William remained loyal to the emperors of the Holy Roman Empire and his reign was peaceful. The weakening of Sweden after the defeat of Charles XII at Poltava allowed him to acquire Western Pomerania (1720). *See also* GERMANY; FREDERICK II; RECRUITMENT; SWEDEN.

B. KROENER
G. A. STEPPLER

FURTHER READING
Robert Ergang, *The Potsdam Fuhrer: Frederich William I, father of Prussian militarism* (New York, 1941); Gordon A. Craig, *The Politics of the Prussian Army, 1640–1945* (New York and Oxford, 1955); Thomas Carlyle, *History of Friedrich II of Prussia, called Frederick the Great* (6 vols, London, 1858–65); Martin Kitchen, *A Military History of Germany from the Eighteenth Century to the Present Day* (London, 1975).

Frontiers, military

This term refers primarily to the unique military institution maintained by the Austrian Habsburg rulers along their boundary with the Ottoman Empire to protect their lands against the threat of Turkish incursions. The concept, however, is a very ancient one, dating back to a number of frontier defence experiments especially in the later Roman Empire. Such systems appeared when a state lacking adequate human and material resources had to protect a long frontier against raids by active and determined nomadic tribes. Usually these defence arrangements not only included fortified lines, but also the militarization of the population in the hinterland. In addition, frontier zones sometimes were shielded by dependent buffer-states.

Internally stable states, for example the Roman Empire in the time of Augustus, generally stationed their armies on their frontiers, often in permanent camps located at strategic points close to a fortified line such as the Great Wall of China or the Roman *limites*. The actual Roman defence line, the *limes*, consisted of a continuous rampart, *vallum*, reinforced with defensive works – forts and guard posts, *burgi* and *castella*, backed with fortified camps, *castra*, quarters for mobile reserves – operating on a road network. The most important *limes* covered the area between the Rhine and the Danube but the system, adapted to the specific terrain and whenever possible utilizing river lines, the Rhine, Danube, Tyne and Euphrates, was also used in northern Britain, Mauretania, South Tunisia and Syria. Employing growing numbers of auxiliaries recruited from 'barbarian' tribes, the *limites* assisted in Romanizing the frontier areas.

After the invasions of the third century AD revealed the defects of the Roman military establishment there were changes. The *limites* were garrisoned by local soldier-peasants, *limitanei*, living dispersed throughout the area. They guarded sections where the ramparts were not continuous, but disposed in depth provided a covering screen. The best troops formed

Housesteads Fort, one of the sixteen on Hadrian's Wall (AD 122–c.138), is 36.5 'wall miles' from South Shields and covers an area of 5 acres. It housed a garrison of around 1,000 men. Hadrian's Wall was part of a process, which had begun under the Emperor Domitian (AD 81–96), of artificially defining and defending the frontiers of the Roman Empire.
(University and Society of Antiquaries, Newcastle-upon-Tyne)

field armies, ready to move against major threats. During the great invasions, the defence of the Empire came to be entrusted to 'barbarian' tribes forming buffer-states. Charlemagne, too, organized military districts, 'marches', along the frontiers of his empire.

The Habsburgs' frontier defence system, however, was unique and merits a slightly extended description. A buffer zone between Christianity and Islam, peopled by hardy peasant-soldiers, it was progressively expanded between 1535 and the 1780s, ultimately stretching in a narrow belt from the Adriatic to the Carpathians. In 1522, King Louis II of Hungary had requested his brother-in-law, Ferdinand I of Austria, to assist in the defence of northern Croatia from the Adriatic to the Drave (Drava). After the disastrous Battle of Mohács in 1526, Ferdinand became King of Croatia and Hungary. To defend Croatia he first relied on mercenaries, augmented from 1522 by refugees, *uskoks*, from Serbia and Bosnia. In 1535, 1538, 1544 and 1564 he granted special privileges to these refugees. In return for hereditary military service, they were endowed with small grants of land and relieved from the usual manorial obligations. By 1573, available forces in the Croatian border zone totalled 5,913. Between 1578 and 1743 maintenance of this establishment became the responsibility of Inner Austria – Styria, Carinthia and Carniola. In 1579, Archduke Charles began construction of a central fortress, Karlstadt (Karlovać).

New refugees were granted similar charters in 1579 and 1598. Better to administer the growing number of frontier fighters, the organizational statute of 5 October 1630 divided the area into two generalcies, Karlstadt and Warasdin (Varazdin). The duties of the border fighters, *Grenzer* or *Graniçari*, were to patrol the frontier, repel or report incursions, harass Turkish penetrations, continually gather intelligence about the Ottomans, and protect the settlements. Each year, from spring to autumn, the border zones saw constant small wars, with raids conducted either by the Turks or by the *Grenzer*.

The border zones of Hungary extended for over 600 miles from the Drave to Transylvania. Following the Peace of Vasvár in 1664 they were guarded by a line of stockades and fortresses, the latter permanently garrisoned by imperial troops. Behind this fortified line lay a zone under military authority, its peasant-soldiers removed from the jurisdiction of the Hungarian diet and the large landowners (magnates). In 1682 the Hungarian border zones mustered 12,000 men, including 6,000 Hungarian irregulars.

The victory at the Kahlenberg on 12 September 1683 marked the beginning of the Turkish retreat from Central Europe and encouraged Austria to formulate a new policy in the south-east. Its main objectives were to gain a natural frontier in southern Hungary; to place Serb military settlers, subject to direct control by the Vienna Court War Council, in the new frontier regions; to develop devastated areas reconquered from the Turks by bringing in settlers of Serb or German origin; and finally to use these men to curb the ever turbulent Hungarian nobility. As a result of three Austro-Turkish wars, the Austrian frontiers advanced deep into the south-east – into the Lika and Krbve districts of Croatia in 1696, to the line of the Save, the Tisza (Theiss) and the Maros (Mureş) by 1699; and beyond the Save and Danube to include parts of Serbia and Wallachia up to the Olt in 1718. In 1739 Austria's boundaries consolidated along the Save and Danube until the occupation of Bosnia-Herzegovina in 1878.

The internal organization of the new frontier zones followed already established patterns including the particular socio-economic South Slav customs. Here the most important element was the *zadruga*, an extended family group living and working on its common land. The Austrian administration gave land to the family groups and not to individuals and in return each *zadruga* furnished a fixed number of fighters, the nuclei for larger units. *Grenzer* played an important, if auxiliary, role during the war of 1683–99 and Austrian commanders, including Eugene of Savoy, recommended expansion of the military frontier system.

In 1691, Emperor Leopold I granted charters to Serb refugees in southern Hungary and settled them in the Vojvodina, while in 1702 new colonies were formed in Slavonia and along the Tisza and Maros. In 1704 the Lika and Krbve formally became the Banal border, mustering 6,485 *Grenzer*. Elsewhere the count was lower. The Slavonian frontier militia, including the garrison of 90 fortified posts, *tschardacks*, located at 1- or 2-mile intervals along the Save, fielded only 3,199 fighters. The Tisza and Maros colonies mustered 1,900 militia, while the colonies in north Serbia had 2,300 defenders. Slavonian and Warasdin *Grenzer* participated in operations against the Rákóczi revolt, the *Kuruc War*, in 1703–11. Reorganization in Slavonia in 1718 raised strength to 13,750.

The Treaty of Belgrade in 1739 restored northern Serbia to Ottoman rule and fixed the frontiers of the Habsburg monarchy along the lines of the Save, Danube and the summit of the Transylvanian Alps. But in the meantime, the decline of Ottoman power and the recovery of Hungary created a crisis on the military borders. There was tension about the religious and economic privileges of the *Grenzer* coupled with complaints about abuses by the Austrian commanders. Insubordination and mutinies erupted in the Karlstadt generalcy in 1702, 1714, 1728 and 1735, while incidents in the Warasdin generalcy in 1695, 1719, 1728 and 1732 culminated in a major revolt in 1735. This brought a much-needed basic reorganization, carried out by Duke Joseph of Saxe-Hildburghausen between 1737 and 1749. While retaining the *zadruga* system, the Duke, beginning in the Warasdin, formed the *Grenzer* into regimental units on a fixed establishment, two foot regiments Warasdiners, four Karlstadters, three Slavonians and two in the Banal region, that is the Lika and Krbve districts nominally subject to the Croatian *Ban*. In addition, he created some light horse units, *Grenz-Husaren*, but these never reached full strength and soon were disbanded. The regiments were administrative organizations; battalions served in the field.

Impressed by the services of the *Grenzer* during the War of the Austrian Succession (1740–8) and in dire need of troops, Queen Maria Theresa decreed in 1747 that in future their units 'shall in all matters be treated as regulars' and serve not only on the frontier but wherever the monarchy needed them. However, bowing to insistent Hungarian demands, in 1751 the queen abolished the Tisza and Maros military districts. Transformation of the *Grenzer* into regulars, codified in the Military Border Code of 1754, was interrupted by a final major mutiny, the Warasdin revolt the following year. Order was re-established by concessions and threats in 1755.

The crisis was settled just in time. War with Prussia began the next year and altogether 88,000 *Grenzer*, albeit in rotation, served in the Seven Years' War, slightly more than a quarter of the field army, gaining a reputation as effective light troops. Recognizing their value, Maria Theresa ordered further reorganization and expansion of the Military Frontier. In 1763 the Karlstadt and Warasdin generalcies were combined, and in 1764 two *Szekler* and two Wallachian infantry regiments, together with a regiment of *Szekler* hussars, were formed in Transylvania. In the Banat of Temesvá one German and one Illyrian-Wallachian infrantry regiment, were organized between 1762 and 1765. In 1763, the *Tschaikisten* battalion, rivermen to patrol the Danube, Save, and Tisza with small gunboats, was formally established at the confluence of the Save and Danube. Although the formation of the Transylvanian regiments was not completed until the 1780s, the Military Frontier now extended over 1,000 miles from the Adriatic to the Bukovina. All mounted units, except for the *Szekler* hussars, were disbanded in 1786 and the forces of the Military Frontier comprised 17 infantry regiments with a peace establishment of 54,644, and double that number if required.

Grenzer participated in the War of the Bavarian Succession (1778–9) and in the last Austro-Turkish war (1788–91), as well as in the campaigns against the French Revolution and Napoleon. In 1807, the Border code was modified by a new basic statute defining *Grenzer* rights and duties. Even so, the Military Frontier could not escape the tide of nationalism and the changing socio-economic conditions penetrating the region. While during the 1848 Revolution most of the *Grenzer* units remained loyal to the Habsburgs, fighting in Italy, Hungary and in the reduction of revolutionary Vienna, the *Szekler* hussars joined the Hungarian revolt. No longer considered totally reliable and as soldier-peasants never quite reaching the combat proficiency of line troops, the end of the institution was near. In 1850 the Transylvanian regiments were disbanded while, following the Compromise of 1867 which created the Dual Monarchy, the existence of the Vienna-controlled military regions could not be reconciled with Hungary's regained independent status. Beginning with the Warasdin regiments in 1871, the institution was dismantled and finally abolished in 1881. During its existence, the Military Frontier had not only been a defence against the Turks; it had helped to restrain Hungarian aspirations, while also acting as a reservoir of cheap, trained manpower for all of the Habsburg wars.

Military frontiers, albeit in modified form, were tried by several colonial powers. Most recently Morocco has organized a similar system to defend the annexed Rio d'Oro region against the Polisario guerilla attacks. *See also* AUSTRIA; EUGENE OF SAVOY; FORTIFICATION; HUNGARY; MILITARY DISTRICTS; OTTOMAN TURKS; ROME.

GUNTHER E. ROTHENBERG
J. NOUZILLE

FURTHER READING
William H. McNeill, *Europe's Steppe Frontier, 1500–1800* (Chicago, 1964); Gunther E. Rothenberg, *The Austrian Military Border in Croatia, 1522–1747* (Urbana, Ill., 1960); Gunther E. Rothenberg, *The Military Border in Croatia, 1740–1881* (Chicago, 1966); Carol Göllner. *Die Siebenbürgische Militärgrenze* (Munich, 1974); Jakob Amstadt, *Die k. k. Militärgrenze* (2 vols, Würzburg, 1969).

Frontinus, Sextus Julius (*c*.AD 30–104) A Roman senator of the imperial period who had a distinguished career in many aspects of government; he was governor of Britain probably from AD 74–7 when he conducted a military campaign against the Silures in Wales, governor of Asia in 86, and in 97 was appointed senior official in charge of the aqueducts and water supply of Rome; in 100 he was consul for the third time, with the Emperor Trajan. Frontinus wrote a number of didactic works on practical subjects – land surveying, the management of the aqueducts, and Greek and Roman military science. The last work has not survived but there is extant Frontinus' *Strategemata*, a collection of exploits and stratagems mainly of earlier commanders, though there are some contemporary or nearly contemporary examples. The *Strategemata* includes methods for concealing your intentions and discovering those of the enemy, looking after the psychological welfare of the army, arranging to fight under favourable conditions, winning sieges and developing the art of generalship. Frontinus wrote for practising commanders: 'For in this way army commanders will be equipped with examples of good planning and foresight, and this will develop their own ability to think out and carry into effect similar operations. An added benefit will be that the commander will not be worried about the outcome of his own stratagem when he compares it with innovations already tested in practice.' Frontinus' *Strategemata* is one of a number of books written about tactics and generalship, especially in the first and second centuries AD of the Roman Empire, which may suggest that since the Romans lacked a systematic method of preparing men for military commands, textbooks of this kind were held to be of some importance in their training. *See also* ARRIAN; ONASANDER ON MILITARY MATTERS; ROME; VEGETIUS RENATUS.

B. CAMPBELL

FURTHER READING
Text – Loeb edition (1925); A. R. Birley, *The Fasti of Roman Britain* (London 1981), pp. 69–72; J. B. Campbell, 'Teach yourself how to be a general', *Journal of Roman Studies*, lxxvii (1987), pp. 13–29.

Frunze *See* SOVIET MILITARY THEORISTS

Fuller, John Frederick Charles (1878–1966) Fuller was one of the earliest exponents of mechanized warfare. Along with his close friend, Liddell Hart, Fuller was responsible for the development of the theories for the use of tanks that led to the blitzkrieg tactics used in the Second World War. Fuller was born in Chichester and was educated at Sandhurst. He entered the British army in 1898. During the First World War, Fuller became chief of staff of the British Tank Corps. He organized the British attack on Cambrai of 20 November 1917, the first successful use of tanks. The following year, Fuller drew up the campaign outline for 1919 (Plan 1919), which envisaged the employment of massive tank armies supported by bombers. The end of the First World War meant that this plan was never implemented. After the war, Fuller became chief instructor at the Staff College at Camberley. Throughout the interwar period, Fuller continued to advocate mechanized warfare, to the detriment of his own career. His publications concerning this subject include *The Foundations of the Science of War* (1926), *On Future Warfare* (1928) and *Machine Warfare: An Enquiry into the Influence of Mechanics on the Arts of War* (1942), and his influence was strong in both Germany and the Soviet Union. In 1933, he retired from the army owing to the continuing opposition to his ideas and became a war and military correspondent. Fuller's reputation suffered because of his joining the British Union of Fascists and espousing a virulent anti-Semitism. None the less, his writings on mechanized warfare and his studies in military history – including *A Military History of the Western World* (3 vols, New York, 1967) and *Decisive Battles of the Western World and their Influence upon History* (3 vols, London, 1954–56) – have ensured Fuller's reputation as a military intellectual. *See also* CAMBRAI; ESTIENNE; LIDDELL HART; TANKS.

A. CORVISIER
KEITH NEILSON

FURTHER READING
Brian Holden Reid, *J. F. C. Fuller: military thinker* (London, 1987); A. J. Trythall, *'Boney' Fuller: the intellectual general* (London, 1977).

G

Galliéni, Joseph Simon (1849–1916)
Galliéni was France's leading exponent of
colonial pacification. After St-Cyr he
joined the marines and served with distinction in the Franco-Prussian War. Like
other soldiers, he found consolation for
France's defeat in 1871 in the colonies.
He served in Réunion, in West Africa and
the Sudan, and in 1892–6 in Tonkin. This
last command formed the basis of his
ideas. Galliéni realized that against an opponent who would withdraw rather than
fight the answer was to occupy. In conjunction with the military posts, he aimed
to stimulate local economies and introduce efficient and just administration.
Thus the soldier's first task of conquest
gave way to that of settlement. Lyautey
served under Galliéni when the latter was
governor of Madagascar from 1896 to
1905 and learnt from him the precepts on
which he constructed his theories of
colonial pacification. In 1911 Galliéni was
considered for the post of chief of the
general staff but refused it on the grounds
of age in favour of another Madagascar
subordinate, Joffre. Recalled to service in
1914, Galliéni became military governor
of Paris and was responsible for the thrust
into the German right wing which formed
the most dramatic moment in the Battle
of the Marne (1914). The rivalry which
developed between Joffre and Galliéni as
to who was responsible for the victory
deepened when in October 1915 Galliéni
became Minister of War but found his
control of strategy limited by the powers
conferred on Joffre as commander-in-
chief. Disillusioned and sick, he resigned
in March 1916 and died a few weeks later.
See also BUGEAUD; COLONIAL TROOPS;
COLONIAL WARFARE; FRANCE; JOFFRE;
LYAUTEY; MARNE.

HEW STRACHAN

FURTHER READING
Jean Gottmann, 'Bugeaud, Galliéni, Lyautey:
the development of French colonial warfare', in
Makers of Modern Strategy, ed. E. M. Earle
(Princeton, 1943); Marc Michel, *Galliéni* (Paris,
1989); J. Kim Munholland, 'Collaboration
strategy and the French pacification of Tonkin,
1885–1897', *Historical Journal*, xxiv (1981), pp.
629–50.

Gambiez, Ferdinand (b.1903) Gambiez
graduated from St-Cyr in 1925 and fought
in the Battle of France in 1940. After
appointment to the general staff of the
army of Vichy France, in 1942 he escaped
into Spain. He was interned for a short
period before he succeeded in reaching
North Africa where he organized a battalion of commandos. A landing on Corsica
(13 September 1943) was followed by commando raids on the Italian coast as a
prelude to the recapture of Elba. He participated in the operations of the French
commando brigade on the Rhine and the
Danube (Belfort, Masevaux and Colmar).
A practitioner of indirect and guerila warfare, his commandos were trained to co-
operate with armour. After the Second
World War, he taught the essence of
surprise and assault at the *école militaire* at
Saint-Maixent. First in Indo-China, and
then in Tunisia and Algeria, he countered
subversion and guerila tactics by trying to
win 'the hearts and minds' of the local
population. Profiting from his experiences,
he expounded the theory of indirect warfare in his book, co-authored with Colonel
M. Suire: *The Sword of Damocles: indirect
warfare* (1967). *See also* COLONIAL WAR-
FARE; INDIRECT WARFARE.

A. CORVISIER

FURTHER READING
F. Gambiez and M. Suire, *L'Épée de Damoclès,
la guerre en style indirect* (Paris, 1967).

Garrisons The word derives from the French 'garnir' (to stock) and originally it designated the supplies and war equipment placed in a town so that it could serve, if need arose, as a military stronghold. Later, the term was applied to the troops stationed in such a town and to any place which accommodated soldiers. The fortified towns where sovereigns resided maintained garrisons both for defence against enemies from outside and to protect the king from his own subjects. Garrisons were regularly installed in towns which were situated along frontiers, which stood in strategic locations or whose loyalty it was desired to ensure. In the Middle Ages, to receive a garrison was a mark of vassal status and a loss of urban independence. As royal authority grew stronger, the sending of garrison troops was often regarded as a means of applying pressure on localities which seemed reluctant to pay taxes and on heretics whose conversion the state wished to hasten. In France in the Napoleonic era, troops were quartered on the families of political opponents and deserters. In cases where the kings were sure of the loyalty of the inhabitants, they entrusted the responsibility for garrisoning the town to the municipal authorities. In France, the cost of maintaining garrisons fell, for the most part, on the citizens.

When standing armies were established in the sixteenth century, the problem arose of finding quarters for the soldiers. At the beginning of the sixteenth century, when armies were comparatively small, they were based close to the residence of the sovereign and some detachments accompanied him on his travels. In France, the Wars of Religion caused the conflicting parties to force towns to accept the presence of their troops. The Huguenots had their right to garrison 'secure strongholds' recognized in the Edict of St Germain (1570) until it was cancelled by the Edict of Ales in 1629. During the Fronde, the rebels installed garrisons in the fortified places they had captured and the king did the same. At the start of the seventeenth century, after Henry IV had restored public order, provision was made to garrison the fortified towns of the realm with a total of 4,000 men divided into independent (i.e. non-regimented) companies. These companies were frequently composed of retired or discharged soldiers as much to rid towns of those who had sunk to begging as to ensure a military presence. In France, the number of troops in garrison reached its highest point between 1678 and 1702. Indeed, after the Peace of Nijmegen in 1678, the 'aggressive defence' advocated by Louis XIV and Louvois made it necessary to garrison a large number of strongholds. Garrison battalions were formed which constituted one third of the total number of infantry. In wartime these battalions acted as a reserve to the field army. After 1691, the most vigorous of the men who had been given a place in Les Invalides were dispatched to royal fortresses which were not endangered and formed into independent invalid companies. After 1714, garrison battalions were disbanded and only reappeared occasionally, as, for example, in 1776.

In the reigns of Henry VII and Henry VIII, there were over 100 garrison posts in England, the largest at Dover, Berwick, Carlisle and Calais. During the 1530s, the network of garrisons was extended by the major fortifications along the south coast to guard England from invasion. Henry VIII had over 3,000 troops in his numerous garrisons, enough to form the cadre for a standing army. During the Civil Wars and Interregnum (1642–60), numerous English towns received garrisons. At the Restoration in 1660, the number of royal garrisons was restored to the level of 1637 and an era of more extensive garrisoning was introduced. For the first time, England possessed a peacetime standing army which had to be housed in garrisons. The monarch in Whitehall was protected by the Foot Guards and the Life Guards who were quartered in the City of Westminster, the Tower of London, the Savoy and in the 'out parishes'; royal troops were forbidden to enter the City of London. Away from the capital, garrison companies were retained in the principal naval dockyards and harbours – Hull, Plymouth, Portsmouth, Chatham, Chester, Tynemouth, Sheerness and Gravesend; along the Scottish border in Berwick and Carlisle; and in certain strategic locations – York, the Isle of Wight, the Channel Islands and the Scilly Isles. The marching regiments of the standing army also quartered in these garrisons whenever possible. During the reign of James II, when the army was considerably expanded, the shortage of barracks in the garrison towns meant that a large proportion of the army had to billet in towns and villages which had not accommodated soldiers since the Civil War. As far as possible, the troops were quartered in public houses but the overflow had to be billeted on private householders, often without their consent although this was illegal. James II also employed his engorged standing army to garrison towns which were slow in surrendering their charters or were otherwise unenthusiastic about his policy of Catholicization. The Glorious Revolution of 1688 ended this development and during the eighteenth century, although wartime brought pressure on available quarters, the British standing army remained in its strategic garrisons and there was no further attempt to employ garrisons for political purposes.

French garrison companies were quartered in royal castles or in houses which towns let for that purpose. When, in exceptional circumstances, troops were present in larger numbers, quartering on members of the civil population became necessary. This was often the case in winter when, before Louis XIV's time, in France itself and even beyond its borders in operational areas, it was customary to move the inhabitants out of one or several quarters in a town in order to house the troops (hence the term, 'winter quarters').

At an early date, governments turned their attention to controlling the activities and conduct of garrisons in order to avoid clashes between the military and civilians. In France, the first set of rules dates from 1662 followed by a series of detailed regulations, such as the ordonnances of 1727 and 1768. English regulations concerning billeting began with the Petition of Right in 1628 and continued throughout the Restoration and the various incarnations of the Mutiny Act during the 1690s. Permanent garrisons were commanded by the governor.

It became the practice, very early on, not to leave troops in one peacetime garrison for any length of time in order to avoid a weakening of military discipline through over-fraternization between soldiers and civilians. In England, although independent garrison companies stayed *in situ*, companies and troops from the marching regiments were moved into new garrisons twice a year. In France, regiments stayed in garrison for periods between one and three years. Changes of garrison grew less frequent during the nineteenth century. In France, the introduction of compulsory military service brought with it a more regionally-based system of recruitment creating great loyalty and attachment between a town and its regiment. The reforms of Edward Cardwell in England in 1870 also introduced a locally-based recruiting system and established regiments in permanent depot towns. By this stage, the majority of soldiers were housed in barracks and were no longer a burden to the civilian population. Since that time, garrison towns have simply been those which have incorporated a military depot complete with barracks. Aldershot, Colchester and York are good modern examples.

For a long time, the presence of troops was disliked by civilians yet they brought considerable economic advantages. Soldiers were consumers who brought government money into a regular market for accommodation, food, drink, clothing and leisure. So great were the economic advantages to be gained from the presence of troops that certain French towns petitioned for garrisons during the nineteenth century. Army garrisons helped to rehabilitate provinces which were incorporated into France through the expansion of her frontiers. Soldiers helped to renew economic activity, military ceremonies brought a new sense of identity and recruiting eased unemployment. This was very much the case in Alsace and Lorraine after their return to France in 1919. *See also* BARRACKS; BILLETING; CITADELS;

FORTIFICATION; RECRUITMENT; SOLDIERS AND SOCIETY; STAGING POSTS.

A. CORVISIER
JOHN CHILDS

FURTHER READING
A. Corvisier, *Armies and Societies in Europe, 1494–1789* (Bloomington, Ind., 1979); John Childs, *Armies and Warfare in Europe, 1648–1789* (Manchester, 1982).

Gaugamela, Battle of (331 BC) After having defeated Darius III of Persia in two setpiece battles and secured possession of his territories in Phoenicia and Egypt, Alexander met him in a final battle, which took place in the plain of Gaugamela, near the town of Arbela in eastern Mesopotamia. The king had collected a force of considerable size and taken up a defensive position, planning to make use of his formidable scythed chariots. But Alexander, adopting oblique tactics similar to those employed by Epaminondas, held back his left wing and advanced to the right in echelon. When the king decided to commit his chariots they proved largely ineffective since the Macedonian phalanx opened its ranks to let them pass through and the light troops brought down the horses and killed the charioteers. After hard fighting, during which the Macedonian left wing under Parmenio was placed under great pressure, Alexander used a daring manoeuvre to attack the centre of the Persian position where the king was stationed. In danger of being surrounded, the king fled, and as soon as this news reached the rest of his troops, they hastened to withdraw. Victory was due to Alexander's use of tactics by which he attacked the enemy left wing in echelon and dealt with the threat of the scythed chariots, to his rapid change of troop dispositions for attacking the Persian centre, to his personal leadership and fighting spirit, and also to Parmenio who kept the left wing intact against superior outflanking forces. Gaugamela confirmed the effectiveness of cavalry formations in large-scale battles of this kind, and their role as an integral operational arm within armies. *See also*

ALEXANDER THE GREAT; EPAMINONDAS; GRANICUS; GREECE, ANCIENT; HYDASPES; ISSUS.

R. LONIS
B. CAMPBELL

FURTHER READING
E. W. Marsden, *The Campaign of Gaugamela* (Liverpool, 1964); A. B. Bosworth, *Conquest and Empire: the reign of Alexander the Great* (Cambridge, 1988), pp. 74–85.

Gendarmerie This term has been used for units of very different kinds. From the time of Charles VII of France, it denoted regular, paid cavalry troops, but later, heavy cavalry only. After the Revolution, it was synonymous with the force which had been called, under the *ancien régime*, the *maréchaussée*, and whose task was the maintenance of public order. It is in this last sense that the *gendarmerie* is discussed below.

The system originated in France. Its beginning can be identified in the placing of men-at-arms (*gens d'armes*) at the disposal of the *maréchaussée et connétablie de France*. The appearance of a body exercising military style criminal jurisdiction (i.e. one which combined the work of the police and the judicial authorities) can be detected in 1356 under the control of the *maréchaux de France* and of the *connétable*. It was under Francis I that small units of *archers* (officers) of the *maréchaussée* were formed. They were dispersed in small cities and towns of the realm but they formed part, organizationally, of companies under the *prévôt des maréchaux de la province*. Numerous ordonnances (of 1555, 1570, 1573, 1618 and 1661) laid down the duties of the *maréchaussée*, which was responsible for safety on the public highways and in the lowlands. The courts set up by the *prévôts des maréchaux* passed rapid judgement on *cas prévôtaux* (which included brawls, murders, armed robberies, etc.) and crimes detected in the act, but the *maréchaussée* should not be confused with the army police force consisting of the regimental *prévôt* and the watch, nor with the *connétablie*. In fact, the judicial functions of the *maréchaux de France* diminished as their military role grew in importance, while the post of *connétable* was not filled after 1631. Although the *maréchaux de France* continued, in theory, to have the right to act in a judicial role, only the most senior among them retained any non-military responsibilities. He alone actually presided as a judge, and he also assumed, with the *lieutenants* of the *maréchaux de France*, responsibility for the court that dealt with points of honour, which Louis XIV had set up to settle differences between gentlemen, and thus to remove the occasion for duels.

Although, under Louis XIV, it had become organized on more uniform and systematic lines, the *maréchaussée*, which then numbered nearly 4,000 men, proved rather ineffective. Despite the wishes of the States General, the *archers* of the *maréchaussée* were not soldiers and, most frequently, never had been. Their posts changed hands for money and were bought by citizens who frequently passed them on to their sons and even paid substitutes actually to carry out the duties.

Everything was to change when the edict of 1720 'militarized' the *maréchaussée*. Sale and purchase of positions were abolished. The companies commanded by *prévôts*, with the help of lieutenants and non-commissioned officers, were split into sections of five to six mounted men. Gradually, but increasingly, the latter were recruited from among old soldiers (20 per cent from 1720 to 1730, and 80 per cent from 1730 to 1760). In 1760, an ordonnance brought more into line the administrative arrangements covering the *maréchaussée* and the *prévôté des troupes*. The cavalrymen of the *maréchaussée* were admitted to Les Invalides and its officers could be awarded the Cross of St Louis.

Many of the cavalrymen of the *maréchaussée* served in their native areas; nevertheless, because they came from the army, its make-up – in the sense of the proportion recruited from the various regions of France – was reflected in the composition of their own force. On the eve of the Revolution, the men who came from the east of France made up an appreciable fraction of the cavalrymen of the *maré-chaussée* in the interior of the country. This mixture led the Ministry of War and its intendants (regional administrators) to encourage the association of local men, who had a knowledge of the area's dialect and customs, with men whose origin had been elsewhere, and who were thus less susceptible to local influence. Although the total strength had hardly increased (it numbered only 4,500 men for the whole realm in 1784), the *maréchaussée* was then sufficiently effective and well liked for the population of towns often to ask for a section to be stationed there.

The decree of 22 December 1790 established companies and sections in a corps which took the name of *Gendarmerie Nationale*. (The term *gendarmerie* was used as being more prestigious than *maréchaussée*, although the force was not made up of *gens d'armes*.) The law of 17 April 1799 (28 Germinal Year VII) laid down for the *gendarmerie*, in more specific terms, the responsibilities which had been those of the *maréchaussée*. The *gendarmerie*, described as 'the body whose purpose is to ensure, within the borders of the Republic, the maintenance of order and the execution of the laws', retained a special responsibility for the safety of the countryside and the main roads. It was provided with an inspectorate general in 1800. Its numbers had gradually increased – they reached nearly 8,000 men in 1801. In 1805, it had 144 foot companies and 68 mounted squadrons and it provided the army with sections for dealing with crimes and misdemeanours. The vast majority of its members threw in their lot with the Revolution, to which they were a valuable source of support; then, at the fall of the First Empire, the *gendarmerie* was reduced in size and 'purged', but the ordonnance of 1820 put it back on its previous footing. An ordonnance of September 1830 divided the force into a *gendarmerie* for the *départements* of France, another for ports and arsenals and a third for the colonies, the responsibility for the last two being put, in 1832, with the Minister for the Navy. Under the Third Republic, a force of native *gendarmes* (*Moghzanis*) was created in Algeria. In addition, from 1820 to 1860, a battalion of

297

Corsican light infantry acted as an auxiliary force of the *gendarmerie* on the island.

From an organizational point of view, the *gendarmerie* forms part of the army and counts as one of its branches. It is divided into legions, companies and sections. The system under which *départements* had their own legions has been dropped. At the headquarters of army divisions, the post of *commandant* of the *gendarmerie* of a region has been created. Posts as *gendarmes* are given to soldiers on the active list or who have completed the required length of service in the regular army. Officers are recruited by examination. Recently, a certain number of students from the *École Interarmes* (Joint Service College) of St-Cyr-Coëtquidan have chosen every year to serve in the *gendarmerie*. The staff headquarters of the *gendarmerie* is at Melun, as are also its administrative services, its records and its museum.

The *gendarmerie* has continued to grow in strength – it currently numbers 100,000 men – and to form new offshoots. In 1921, there was formed the Mobile Republican Guard, an operational force in which all *gendarmes* have to serve at least one tour of duty. The *gendarmerie mobile* is nicknamed the 'red *gendarmerie*', the *gendarmerie* of the *départements* the 'white', from the colour of their rank stripes. Later creations have been the motorized *gendarmerie* units attached to the road police, and the *Groupement d'Intervention de la Gendarmerie Nationale* (GIGN), for tasks that need careful handling and which require men who have had special training, particularly in regard to the battle against terrorism. In wartime, a portion of the *gendarmerie* is incorporated in the army *gendarmerie*.

Foreign countries have copied this institution, often even to the extent of adopting its name, e.g. *Landgendarmerie* and *Feldgendarmerie* (i.e. civil and military police) in Germany, the Mounted Police in Canada, the *Guardia Civil* in Spain and the *Carabinieri* in Italy. The *Guardia Civil* of Spain and the *Carabinieri* of Italy have used the French organizational pattern.

See also CIVIL POWER, SUPPORT OF; DISCIPLINE; LAW, MILITARY.

A. CORVISIER

FURTHER READING
L. Larrieu, *Histoire de la gendarmerie depuis les origines de la maréchaussée jusqu'à nos jours* (2 vols, Paris, 1927–33); S. F. Crozier, *The History of the Corps of Royal Military Police* (Aldershot, 1951).

General staff A staff is composed of officers who assist a commander to carry out his intentions. Its main tasks are to provide him with information, to plan operations, to assemble the required resources, and to draft and communicate instructions. This work is co-ordinated by a chief of staff, who assigns missions to his subordinates, monitors their performance and reports their completion to the commander. All units contain staffs whose form of organization is in principle the same as that employed in formations of the highest level, even though simplified to a greater or lesser degree.

The description which we possess of the forces of Pharaoh Thutmose (or Thotmes) I indicates that a staff existed, which was apparently concerned with intelligence gathering. Officers with special responsibility for supplies made their appearance, however, only at the end of the Ancient Egyptian era. The Assyrian army attained a high degree of excellence, but the way in which its staffs operated is unknown. Their methods were probably copied by the Persians, and it seems inconceivable that the latter's huge military operations could have taken place without detailed preparatory work by a staff. The Spartan kings made use of a rudimentary staff composed of one or two polemarchs, or aides-de-camp. Command in the Athenian army was exercised by a group, the ten 'generals' (*strategoi*), assisted by their taxiarchs, who were not specialists. It was with Philip of Macedon that the first proper staff made its appearance; this contained specialists in fortifications, ballistic weapons, siege operations and supplies. Alexander's staff was composed of *somatophylakes*, whose role is imperfectly understood, some of whom seem to have been specialists. The Roman legion had six tribunes, grouped in pairs, who took turns in commanding the force. The four tribunes whose turn it was not to command carried out the responsibilities of staff officers. There were also aides-de-camp (*contubernales*), and personnel whose task it was to gather intelligence (*speculatores*).

Though the art of war reached a high level of development at Byzantium, it was rudimentary in the West during the Middle Ages. The military organization of the English kings seems the one which was least haphazard; there, the presence can be noted of a staff in which the constable carried out the duties of a chief of staff. He was assisted by a marshal, a mustering officer, whose task was to keep a check on numbers, a chief supplies officer, a quartermaster for dealing with encampments, a baggage-master and an officer in charge of scouting parties.

In the sixteenth century, *landsknecht* units had a regimental staff. The sergeant-major was responsible for administration and training and transmitted the colonel's orders. The quartermaster dealt with the troops' billets and food supplies. These functions became the established responsibilities for a quartermaster in the English and Prussian armies, where he also dealt with intelligence and troop movements. Gustavus Adolphus perfected this system of organization, after it had already been improved by Maurice of Nassau. The staff of a Swedish regiment comprised a colonel, a lieutenant-colonel, a major whose task it was to transmit orders and to distribute supplies, a chief quartermaster, responsible for encampments, two legal officers, also four provosts and an assistant provost, four surgeons, two chaplains and secretaries. The staff of the army was organized on the same lines, but with the addition of a chief of staff, a commander of scouting parties, the commanders of the specialist arms and a highly developed supply section.

At the end of the sixteenth century, the French army was commanded by the constable, who could call on marshals, commanders of the various arms and specialists such as the master-general of the baggage train, the provost marshal and the judicial marshal, the master-general of scouting parties, the sergeant-major general and the *maréchal de camp*. These last two officers had particular responsibility for operations. The post of constable disappeared under Louis XIII; the army was then commanded by a marshal, assisted by a lieutenant-general and by the *maréchal de camp général*. The last named acted as chief of staff and conveyed orders to the majors in brigades. Richelieu added an administrative officer to deal with pay and provisions. In Louis XIV's time, the army was commanded by a prince of the royal family or by a marshal, with the help of a *maréchal de camp général*, who carried out the duties of a chief of staff, the *maréchal de bataille*, who was responsible for positioning troops in readiness for combat, and the *maréchal général des logis*, who prepared camps and arranged troop movements and supplies. Other officers who were found on the staff were a marshal- general of infantry and a marshal-general of cavalry, assisted by deputy majors and commissioners, whose duties were provisioning and the disbursement of pay. The staff of a regiment consisted of a sergeant-major (later termed 'major'), who was responsible for detailed administration and was assisted by a deputy major. A second deputy major was added in 1689, and the staff also included a chaplain and a surgeon.

In 1657, the Brandenburg staff consisted of a *maître de l'ordonnance* (commander-in-chief), who later had the title of 'general field marshal', a senior commissioner (chief of staff), a baggage-master general, responsible for the movement, encampment and positioning of troops for combat, two adjutant-generals, a prosecutor-general who was head of the military legal system, two quartermaster-generals dealing with engineer operations, a quartermaster for provisions, another for camps, an army paymaster, a chaplain, a dispenser, a surgeon, a chief baggage-master, a chief provost and eleven secretaries.

By the later seventeenth century, the central British staff was very like that of continental armies, particularly the Swedish and Dutch. It consisted of a paymaster-general, secretary at war, commissary-general of the musters, adjutant-general, quartermaster-general, judge advocate, physician-general, surgeon-general and apothecary-general. Deputies or representatives of these central staff officers accompanied British armies and expeditions overseas. Each regiment possessed a major, an adjutant, a quarter-master, a chaplain and a surgeon. On Marlborough's staff, there was as yet no definite sign of a responsibility for operations; that was exercised by the commander-in-chief himself with his personal assistants. The quartermaster-general dealt with the choice and layout of camp sites. Subsequently, British staff organization changed little until the end of the century.

In the eighteenth century, no large, structured troop formation yet existed. Brigades, like divisions (which did not make their appearance until 1759), were put together for limited periods only, and the generals who commanded them had nothing which could really be considered a staff. On the other hand, staffs did exist at regimental level. In 1788, the French regimental staff consisted of a colonel, a lieutenant-colonel, a major, a deputy major, a quartermaster-treasurer and two colour-bearers. The so-called *petit état-major* (i.e. the part comprising non-commissioned officers and soldiers), contained two sergeants, a surgeon-major, a chaplain, a drum-major, eight musicians, a master-tailor, a master-cobbler and a master-armourer. Staffs at army level were of a temporary nature and the officers employed in them received no special training. In 1748, the staff of the French army in Italy consisted of a *maréchal des logis* and eighteen deputies, a sergeant-major general of infantry and twelve deputies, and a *maréchal des logis* and six deputies from the cavalry. The staff at the camp in Rochambeau's expedition to America contained three brigadiers, one of whom acted as second-in-command, a sergeant-major general and two deputies, and four deputy *maréchaux des logis*, while each of the generals had several aides-de-camp. In the middle of the century, Bourcet evolved

modern methods of staff work. In 1766, he was put in charge of a unit of twenty-one officers whose task it was to carry out a topographical survey of the country. This unit's work ceased in 1771 for financial reasons, and it was abolished in 1776. In 1783, Marshal de Ségur established a staff unit for the army but this was abolished at the start of the French Revolution. The officers of this unit were distributed among the commanders of armies and divisions as adjutant-generals and, in Year VIII, took the name of deputy commanders. One of them, Berthier, when he became Bonaparte's chief of staff, proposed in 1796 that the work of the staff, under his supervision, should be split up between four adjutant-generals. The first had particular responsibility for legal matters, the movement of troops and for muster-rolls; the second, for weapons, supplies and the specialist arms; the third, for intelligence and operations; and the fourth, for camps. They were put at the head of proper departments and were assisted by deputies. The commanders of specialist arms and the aides-de-camp were also attached to the staff. In 1800, Paul Thibault, an adjutant-general, published a manual for staff officers, which was translated into Spanish, Russian, English and German and, for a long period, was regarded as authoritative. Napoleon's general headquarters consisted of a staff and his military household. The latter comprised aides-de-camp, often of senior rank, who were entrusted with important and delicate missions; a general duties group of junior officers used for reconnaissance work; and an office divided into three sections dealing with intelligence, topography and secretarial duties. The staff, supervised by Berthier, who also had a private staff of his own, was made up of deputy commanders responsible for services and non-tactical movements of troops, the commanders of specialist arms and aides-de-camp. There was also an administrative and logistic headquarters, distinct from the GHQ; this was sited in a rear area and was operated by Napoleon or Berthier. The latter had no direct access to intelligence, and Napoleon himself dealt with operational matters. Staff officers at that time received their training in the field; in 1818, Gouvion-St-Cyr established a recognized staff officer corps. In 1826, it was made a requirement for its members to do some service in an army unit; this stipulation was removed in 1833, and the quality of the staff officer corps declined. Among the defects in Napoleon III's army was the inadequate performance of its staffs.

On the other hand, the German staff had attained a high level of efficiency. The Prussian staff had been reshaped in 1802 and 1806 under the influence of Massenbach's ideas, and greatly transformed by Scharnhorst after the Battle of Jena (1806). The commanding general was understudied by a chief of staff, who was his partner and not his subordinate, as in other countries. In 1821, the staff was removed from the control of the Minister of War and put directly under the king. After 1870, the staff's powers were considerable and it frequently succeeded in imposing its will on the emperor and the government; hence, the Allies enforced its abolition in 1919. Hitler's government re-established it under the name of *Oberkommando*. In 1867, the supreme general staff was divided into the *Haupt-Etat*, which was the main section responsible for preparations for war, and the *Neben-Etat*, the secondary part, whose members filled the technical posts. The staffs of army corps had been organized, in 1826, into four sections, comprising the staff proper, a second section dealing with administrative matters, and legal and commissariat sections. Divisions had no chiefs of staff.

For their staff, the British drew inspiration from the corresponding organizations in France and Prussia, but succeeded in producing an original type. Wellington's consisted of his personal staff and two support units which comprised the adjutant-general's department, with particular responsibility for general correspondence and for discipline, and the quartermaster-general's, which dealt with the movement of troops, with camps and with equipment. Attached to the staff were the administrative services, the commanders of individual arms, who had their own staffs, the reconnaissance unit and the civilian sections, responsible for food supplies and pay. As on Napoleon's staff, there was no sharp division between the logistic and operational functions. The staff of a British division consisted of two officers from the adjutant-general's department, a deputy quartermaster-general, an assistant deputy quartermaster-general, two aides-de-camp, one or two engineer officers, a surgeon, a chaplain, a deputy commissary-general and his deputies, a deputy provost, a baggage-master and a stock-keeper. After Wellington's time, staff efficiency deteriorated. It was not until 1857 that a staff college was established, and it was not a success. At the end of the century, England lagged far behind Germany and France. It was the publication of Spenser Wilkinson's book *The Brain of an Army* and the Esher Report (1904) which gave rise to the reorganization of the War Office and the creation of a General Staff in 1908. This model was extended to the colonies as the Imperial General Staff in 1909. However, the Imperial General Staff was very different from its French and German cousins. Rather than the General Staff and its chief assuming the role of the virtual commander-in-chief through the primacy of the operations branch, the Imperial General Staff (operations and intelligence) was merely an equal partner on an Army Council along with the Quartermaster-General's Department (logistics), the Adjutant-General's Department (personnel), the Master-General of the Ordnance (weapons and equipment) and the civilian finance member, presided over by a politician, the Secretary of State for War. Few modifications were subsequently made to this system except that the creation of a Chiefs of Staff Committee during the Second World War elevated the CIGS to the effective head of the army, a position which he retains to the present day.

In Russia, Peter the Great appointed a quartermaster-general in 1701. The army regulations issued in 1716, which were based on Prussian and Swedish models, made him responsible, in particular, for the engineers, operations and intelligence;

but it was not until 1770 that – as urged by Frederick Wilhelm Baur, a Hessian major-general who had taken service in Russia – a proper staff, on the lines of the Prussian, was established. Intelligence, like topography, was highly developed, but staff work, in general, was inadequate. In 1813, Muraviev took action to train staff officers, but it was only in 1832 that a staff college was opened, in accordance with a plan put forward by Jomini in 1826. At the end of the year 1815, as also proposed by him, the staff was reorganized by the formation of a general staff, headed by an officer who had under him a quartermaster-general, who was, in fact, the chief of staff, with responsibility for movements, camps and operations, and a director of administrative affairs. This body was more akin to a ministry than a staff and, in 1836, was converted into a Ministry of War, containing a central unit controlled by the quartermaster-general, who had under him three sections: the first dealt with the movement and encampment of troops; the second had the name of 'Historical Section', and was concerned with intelligence; and the third handled financial accounts. The staffs of major formations were also reorganized at this period.

At the beginning of the twentieth century, the staff of the Russian army was divided into five departments. The quartermaster-general was responsible, in particular, for organization, equipment, supplies, camps, operations and training. The second quartermaster-general dealt chiefly with intelligence and mobilization; the third with general service and administrative matters; the fourth with communications; and the fifth with topography. In addition, four standing committees co-ordinated the work of the staff. No clear distinction seems to have been drawn between the logistic and the operational function; in any case, supply had always been a weak point in the Russian army. In large formations, the chief of staff had the position of deputy commander, as in the German system. The quartermaster-general was the real chief of staff, because the main staff work was carried out under his supervision. His office was divided into four sections – operations, reports (correspondence), which was given, in 1914, the)name of general service matters, reconnaissance (intelligence) and surveying. A fifth section – censorship – was added in 1914. At army level, the head of communications, on whom the logistic arrangements largely depended, came directly under the chief of staff. Below army level, the functions of the chief of staff and the quartermaster-general were merged into one.

The Red Army adopted the Tsarist army's system but attached political commissars to the military commanders. Between 1922 and 1935, Russian military doctrine was modelled on the German. According to regulations issued in 1936, the staff of an army contained sections dealing with operations, intelligence, organization and signals. The commanders of individual arms and services, particularly those concerned with logistics, were attached to it. In 1946, there was created the supreme commander's staff (*Stavka*), which provided the government with advice and drew up overall plans. Under its orders, the general staff worked out detailed plans but progressively the latter absorbed the former and became the general staff of the Soviet armed forces. It comprises seven departments – operations (headed by the deputy chief of staff), intelligence, mobilization, signals, fortified zones, surveying and history. There is also an armed forces' inspectorate. The commanders of the land, air and naval forces, and the head of operations in rear areas, as well as the specialist arms and administrative services, come directly under the minister of Defence. The land forces have no staff as such. The commander-in-chief fills this role through his staff, which has sections covering operations, intelligence, signals, organization and training. It also has charge of the specialist arms, but the artillery and armoured forces come directly under the minister of Defence.

Washington's staff was based on the British model. It consisted of an adjutant-general, a quartermaster-general, a commissary-general for stores and supplies, a paymaster-general, a muster-master general and an engineer commander; then, there were added a baggage-master and a supplies commissary for thc artillery and, later still, a medical and a military legal service. At the end of the year 1777, the post of inspector-general was created and its first holder was the Prussian, Steuben. He introduced into the United States the methods of Frederick the Great and improved the workings of the American staff. In accordance with the law of 1796, the staff was composed of a major-general, an inspector carrying out the functions of an adjutant-general, a quartermaster-general and a paymaster-general. Subsequently, the staff officers of the major formations were attached to it. This staff was, to a large extent, independent of the army command.

When the American Civil War broke out, there had been no advance of any appreciable nature in the organization of staffs since the War of Independence. McClellan, commander of the Army of the Potomac, provided it with a chief of staff, and his example was followed by the majority of the other generals in the Union army, but a similar post was not created in subordinate formations. General Grant's staff consisted of a chief of staff, two military secretaries, seven aides-de-camp, two assistant adjutant-generals, an inspector-general, a chief quartermaster, an assistant quartermaster, a supplies officer, an engineer commander, a provost-marshal and a deputy provost-marshal. After this war, no progress was made in American staff organization and the war with Spain exposed its weaknesses. The arrival of Elihu Root as Secretary of State for War in 1899 meant that considerable improvements could be carried out. In the following year, he founded the War College Board, the forerunner of a general staff, which was headed by William Ludlow, a follower of Wilkinson, and in 1901, he reorganized the training of senior army officers. Through his course on operational orders, Captain Swift introduced uniformity of method and clarity of thought and he also brought in the system of using real examples as exercises. In 1903, Root succeeded in abolishing the post of general-in-chief and replaced it with that of a chief of staff. A War College for staff training was also established. The chief of staff was given control of troops and of the departments of the staff which had hitherto been largely independent although within the realm of the secretary of state. These constituted the administrative staff, and comprised the departments of the adjutant-general, the inspector-general, the judge advocate and the quartermaster, as well as the services dealing with supplies, medical affairs, finance, equipment and manufacture of weapons, engineers, signals and artillery. The chief of staff's own staff assumed the title of 'general staff'. It had three departments: the first dealt with the regular army; the second, with intelligence; and the third, with training, military colleges, campaign plans and coastal fortification. In 1908, the general staff was divided into four sections: mobile forces; training; coastal artillery; militia.

The forces which were sent to Europe under General Pershing had staffs on the French model. All staffs were made up of five sections, each under a deputy chief of staff; these were administration and logistics, intelligence, operations, supplies and training. The staff also contained officers from the various arms and services. In 1921, the staff was reorganized, with four sections. The first dealt with personnel, the second with intelligence, the third with operations, and the fourth with supplies. In addition, a separate division was given the task of preparing war plans. In 1942, this was replaced by an operational division. Further changes were made in 1946. The staff then comprised six departments: personnel and administration; intelligence; organization and training; services, supplies, manufacture, purchases and sales; research and development; plans and operations. Each departmental head had the title of director, in place of assistant chief of staff (ACOS). In 1948, departments 4 and 5 were amalgamated into one of logistics. Further posts created were those of a vice-chief of staff for the army, an assistant chief for plans and operations and another for administration and logistics. The administrative services were placed directly under the control of the director of personnel and administration, the technical branches coming under the director of logistics. In 1949 there were further changes, with the creation of a chairman of the combined chiefs of staff, a deputy secretary, three assistant secretaries, a defence comptroller and a political committee for the armed forces. In 1956, the duties of the staff were split up between five assistant chiefs of staff, dealing with personnel, operations, logistics, audit, and research and development. In addition, five heads of services were placed directly under the chief of staff.

The post of chief of staff was established in France in 1871 and its holder acted, at the same time, as principal private secretary to the Minister of War. He had a section for dealing with general correspondence, and another called the 'War Depot', which was responsible for making preparations for operations. In 1874, four sections were set up: the first handled organization and mobilization, the second military statistics, i.e. intelligence, the third operations and the fourth transport. The general correspondence section became number 5 and, in 1878, was attached to the minister's private secretariat, and the 'War Depot', with responsibility for equipment and technical services, no.6. This system was abolished in 1878, when six directorates were brought into being – infantry, cavalry, artillery and military equipment, engineers, administrative services (later, commissariat), gunpowder and saltpetre. Two fresh directorates were added in 1882: medical services and audit; with further ones for legal matters and for the military law service (1899), for colonial troops (1900) and for aviation (1913). In 1890, the minister's general staff became the staff of the army. The army staff college disappeared in 1890, and was replaced by the Senior War College, whose creation owes much to General Lewel. The staff college was re-established in 1946, was closed down in 1972, but reappeared in 1980. It trains officers of lower rank than the Senior War College, and the students also tend to be from more technical arms. It was only in 1911 that the post of commander-in-chief of the armed forces was created, the holder being, in fact, the army's chief of staff. At the start of hostilities, he had a general headquarters consisting of two assistant chiefs of staff and three sections – organization and personnel, intelligence and operations. In November 1914, the directorate in charge of rear areas was made responsible for transport and communications and placed under a third assistant chief of staff. The minister could make use of the army's staff. In 1915, a fifth section was formed to handle information and propaganda.

In 1919, the staff of the army went back to its pre-war organization. During the 1919–39 period, new directorates were created: police, armament manufacture and passive defence. Each arm and each administrative service had also an inspectorate. There were three separate ministers – of War, the Air Force and the Navy – and the forces which came under each were independent entities. Their staffs were not directed by any overall staff organization and General Gamelin was given, at a late stage, merely the task of co-ordinating the organization of national defence. The Fourth Republic created a minister of National Defence with authority over the three secretaries of state for War, the Air Force and the Navy, and over the three armed forces' staffs, whose activities were co-ordinated by a combined general staff. The posts of the three secretaries of state were abolished under the Fifth Republic. In 1962, an armed forces' staff was created. The staff organization of the land army had been little changed. Overall, its work was supervised by a vice-chief of staff, with two assistant chiefs of staff whose responsibilities related to those of the four sections. The inspector-general of the army came directly under the minister of National Defence. The army chief of staff controlled the following directorates: personnel, engineers, signals, equipment, training, national service, higher level military instruction and military colleges. The audit department, the arms supply commission and the inspectorate-general came directly under the Minister of National Defence, the heads of the medical and of the fuel supply services under the armed forces' chief of staff. Today, the staff of the land army is supervised, under its chief of staff, by a vice-chief of staff who has three assistant chiefs of staff – covering studies, planning and finance, logistics, and operations – and also can make use of the head of the department dealing with methods and techniques of military action.

In France and the United States, the different departments are placed on the same level; in other countries, 'operations' has the leading position. The Americans draw a distinction between the 'General Staff' (which assists the high command) and the 'Special Staff', made up of technical advisers to the latter and who are normally the heads of individual arms and services. The United States and Britain, unlike Germany and Russia, have never accepted the idea of a supreme general staff on which the land forces carry most weight. In the USA, the chiefs of staff form, on a footing of equality, a combined chiefs of staff committee, whose chairman is drawn from outside their number, and which works through a staff drawn from the three different armed forces. *See also* ADMINISTRATION, ARMY; ADMINISTRATION, NAVAL; BOURCET; COMMAND; HIERARCHY; INSPECTIONS; INTELLIGENCE; INTENDANTS; LOGISTICS; RATIONS; SIGNAL COMMUNICATION; WILKINSON.

G. BODINIER

FURTHER READING
S. P. G. Ward, *Wellington's Headquarters: a study of the administrative problems in the Peninsula, 1809–1814* (London, 1957); Brian Bond, *The Victorian Army and the Staff College, 1854–1914* (London, 1972); W. Görlitz, *The German General Staff* (London, 1952); J. Hittle, *The Military Staff* (Harrisburg, Penn., 1961); Martin van Creveld, *Command in War* (Cambridge, Mass., 1985).

Genghis Khan (?1167–1227) Temuchin became Great Khan of the Mongols in 1206 under the title Genghis (meaning 'Oceanic', therefore, perhaps, 'Universal') Khan, after conquering, or unifying by force, the tribes of Mongolia. If he was to stay in power, he had to keep his followers well rewarded. The momentum of war, and the prospect of loot, had to be maintained. So he turned his newly created army against external enemies, initially neighbouring tribes and then, in 1206–17, China. The northern capital, near modern Peking, fell in 1215. In 1218, leaving the completion of the conquest of China to subordinates, he turned west. The crumbling empire of Qara-Khitai (south of Lake Balkhash) was overwhelmed. Finally, in a series of campaigns between 1218 and 1221, he conquered the Khwarizmian empire from Samarkand to the Caspian Sea. His death in 1227 did not mean the end of Mongol expansion; this was to continue for another half-century. None the less the Mongol empire was unquestionably Genghis Khan's creation. By 1227 it already stretched more than 3,000 miles from east to west.

As rulers over steppe nomads Genghis and his successors had available to them a cavalry force which could be rapidly mobilized, which was intensively trained by the daily lifestyle of herding and hunting, and which consisted, in theory at least, of the entire adult male population. Genghis Khan's organizational achievement was to exploit this potential in a disciplined and flexible manner with, at the core of his army, an imperial guard (*keshig*) some 10,000 strong. In military terms his career was characterized by the systematic use of the 'Hiroshima principle' – massacring the population of one city in order to persuade others to surrender without a fight. *See also* HULEGU; MONGOLS; TAMERLAIN.

JOHN CHILDS

FURTHER READING
H. D. Martin, *The Rise of Chingis Khan and his Conquest of North China* (Baltimore, 1950); David Morgan, *The Mongols* (Oxford, 1986); J. J. Saunders, *The History of the Mongol Conquests* (London, 1971).

Gentili, Alberico (1552–1608) In 1598, Gentili, an Italian jurist converted to Protestantism, who had taken refuge in England, published *De jure belli* which inspired Grotius. He originated the tendency within natural law traditions towards a positivistic, secular, nationalistic outlook receptive to the insights of sociology. His statement that war constitutes an 'armed, public and just struggle' is often quoted. Gentili argued that since princes and peoples have neither judge nor superior between them, the judgement of arms is therefore necessary. Though war always appears just to those who fight, it is none the less the case that preventive war against a certain peril is justified. It is also legitimate to come to the assistance of a third party. The final objective must nevertheless be to conclude a peace which both parties can accept. However, before resorting to war, Gentili recommended recourse to arbitration and sound reason. *See also* GROTIUS; LAWS OF WAR; SPINOZA; VATTEL; VITORIA.

A. CORVISIER

FURTHER READING
G. Livet, *Guerre et paix de Machiavel à Hobbes* (Paris, 1972); *The Languages of Political Theory in Early Modern Europe*, ed. Anthony Pagden (Cambridge, 1987); Richard Tuck, *Natural Rights Theories: their origin and development* (Cambridge, 1981).

Gergovie *See* ALESIA; FORTIFICATION; MASADA; SIEGES

Germany The military history of Germany is extremely complex. Initially little different from that of the other states formed from the Carolingian Empire, it was subsequently transformed by the decline of the Holy Roman Empire, which turned Germany into the battle-ravaged setting of the Thirty Years' War and, from the sixteenth century onwards, a country full of mercenaries (*Landsknechte* and *Reiter*). Thus the institution of modern state military forces came relatively late to the country. The role of Prussia more than that of Austria, which had turned its attention to the East, sets its stamp on the military development of Germany. Under Frederick II, and from 1866 to 1914, Prussia provided Germany with a model of military art and became the birthplace of an original form of military society, the destiny of which would eventually have disastrous results for Germany.

The military institutions of the Holy Roman Empire, bequeathed to it by the Carolingian army and based on the *Landfolge* (the duty to defend one's territory), passed into the service of the feudal lords when this territory was broken up. The vassal's duty to provide the Emperor with armed contingents (*Gerichtfolge*) was constantly invoked by Imperial ordinances. Appeal to this duty was made whenever there was an attack by a common enemy, whether he was Turkish or French.

In this way, when danger arose, an Imperial army was mustered, organized around the ten *Kreise* of the Empire established by the Emperor Maximilian (1500 and 1512), which would continue in force until 1805. All 'immediate' members of the Empire (that is, all direct vassals of the Emperor, ecclesiastical and lay principalities, and free towns) had to provide a contingent of soldiers proportionate to their size. In 1521, the Diet of Worms agreed on a *Simplum* (or first round of mobilization) totalling 4,000 cavalrymen and 20,000 foot soldiers. When the total number was not achieved or when more men were needed, further troops would be called up, the *Duplum*, *Triplum*, etc. The soldiers' pay was raised by the imposition of taxes known as *Roman months*. The number of 'Roman months' in a year was proportionate to the number of men and their length of armed service. Following an Imperial decree of 1681, the *Kreise* were obliged to provide 32,000 cavalrymen and 76,000 foot soldiers for the *Triplum*. However, during this period, the German princes were more concerned about their own armies than about the contingents they had to supply to the Empire and were unwilling to deprive their own forces of troops to provide for the latter. During the Nine Years' War (1688–97), an attempt to reorganize the Imperial army was made in the five western *Kreise* by the Margrave Ludwig-Wilhelm of Baden. Nothing remained of this after 1697. The last Imperial army was levied against France in 1793–5.

In fact, from the beginning of the Thirty Years' War, the Imperial army played a relatively insignificant role. The Emperor and the princes preferred to rely on 'military enterprisers' who were taken into their service together with the mercenary armies they owned. The German armies shared a number of common characteristics. Hence, in contrast to the armies in the Latin countries, soldiers were not strictly forbidden to marry, a fact which contributed to the relatively rapid development of social institutions for soldiers' families and orphans and also to the vigour of the military caste, particularly in Prussia.

Permanent armies did not become institutionalized in the Holy Roman Empire until after the 1654 Diet when the Emperor, Ferdinand III, officially granted the right to muster large bodies of armed men (*Armierte Reichsstände*) in peacetime to the princes, in particular to the lay Electors of, for example, Bavaria, Brandenburg, Saxony and, later, Hanover. The existence of an army enabled these states, which had low population densities, little economic power and, in most cases, had been ravaged and devastated by the Thirty Years' War, actively to exercise their sovereignty and become involved in the power struggles of the great European powers.

While Bavaria depended on an army backed up by regional militiamen (*Landfahnen*) of dubious worth and increasingly financed by subsidies, Prussia under Frederick William I, the 'Sergeant-King', established a revolutionary form of recruitment. The *Kantonsystem*, set up in 1733, gave the regimental leaders the right to enlist, in addition to foreign mercenaries, a certain number of the king's subjects, who had been volunteered, more or less willingly, by one of the cantons within the Prussian Kingdom. The boys were enrolled at the age of ten. Once past adolescence, those who were healthy and of suitable height and strength, were conscripted to serve from a year and a half to two years in order to provide them with adequate military training, and then for two or three months annually over a period of thirty to forty years. A rural system peculiar to the provinces east of the Elbe, where the landed aristocracy (*Junker*) and their vassals served respectively as officers and recruits, facilitated the establishment of a form of social militarization. Almost all of the responsibilities of army officers and the civilian administration were reserved for the nobility, which the king saw as the cornerstone of his state. In addition, the Royal dynasty gave the nobles the means to live off their land. Agricultural products, in particular wheat, were bought in advance at a price fixed by the king's council (*Kammerpreistaxe*) and stored either for the army's rations or to keep control of the price of cereals in times of scarcity. Society worked for the army, which represented the state. The middle class and the peoples of the western provinces were in general exempted from military service. Their task was to manufacture a large part of the equipment or contribute to the financing of the army. Prussian militarism depended on a stable equilibrium between all these social groups as regards the costs and profits of war and the army. In 1740, Frederick William I bequeathed to his son, Frederick II, an army of 83,000 men, which was disproportionately large for a population of 2,200,000.

At the same time, the beginning of the political and military dualism between the courts of Berlin and Vienna was accompanied by a decline in the military power of the other states in the Empire, which no longer played a decisive role in European politics. The hazardous policies of its sovereigns, Max-Emmanuel and his son Karl Albrecht, resulted in Bavaria increasingly ceding its predominance in the south of Germany to the Habsburgs while the forces of the Elector of Saxony and the King of Poland were crushed by Prussia in the Seven Years' War. Hanover, in its role as the 'sword of England' on the Continent, especially during the reign of Frederick II, fell in with the policies of its powerful Eastern neighbour. After the Seven Years' War, the King of Prussia, reflecting on his campaigns, wrote: 'Is it not clear that all these armies, through their precise co-operation and simultaneous action, would have beaten our regiments one after the other, and that, by continually advancing to the centre they would have finally reduced

307

our troops to defending the capital? . . . How many favourable moments they let pass, how many fine opportunities they wasted! In short, to what incredible errors we owe our security.'

In the mid-eighteenth century, all armies were closely linked to their support services, which were still limited and insufficient for the number of men and operational objectives involved. Frederick had some innovative ideas on this matter but these limitations prevented him from implementing them fully. 'Frederick II', wrote Émile Wanty, 'models the action to be taken on the balance of forces. His strategic views reflect the sum of his experiences and cover extremely varied forms of war.' According to Frederick II, 'superiority over one's enemy is achieved more through partisan methods than by regular warfare: by fighting his detachments and rearguard; by surprising his quarters if he has not made them secure; by depriving him of his provisions and stocks; by intercepting his communications; by a decisive battle if he is weak and badly positioned; by pretending to detach troops to force him to spread his forces and then attacking with all one's forces united.' This represents a combination of attrition, indirect and destructive strategies, which means that all the varied commentators on Frederick have been partially correct. However, this approach was never taken to its logical conclusion or exploited to the full. The genius of the great king, his position as king-constable which enabled him to react more quickly than his adversaries, who were always hampered by static bureaucracies, and his unexpected victories resulted in his army acquiring great technical skill and high morale.

It was not until after Prussia's total defeat by Napoleon I's armies at Jena–Auerstädt in 1806 that the reforms, which had until then always been limited, could be carried out in earnest. Scharnhorst, Gneisenau, Boyen and the famous Clausewitz promoted the concept of a nation in arms united loyally around a dynasty. With his guiding concepts, many of which remain valid in spite of the changes in the art of warfare, Clausewitz was the most important of the military theorists, thinkers and philosophers. His aim was not to set out a new method of warfare but, as he himself stressed, 'to bring together all the already established principles of military art and then reduce each one of them to its elementary simplicity. The "principles", which are always relevant are not confined solely to tactics but also concern the political, social, economic and moral development of a state.'

The decisively important but frequently misquoted phrase 'War is merely the continuation of politics by other means' is well known. War, then, must not be allowed to interrupt political relations. 'Do political situations between peoples and between their governments stop when diplomatic notes are no longer exchanged? Is war not just another expression of their thoughts, another form of speech or writing? Its grammar, indeed, may be its own, but not its logic.' Just as he promoted the idea of the subordination of war to politics, his works demonstrate that he was never the theorist of 'total war' as he was portrayed by General Ludendorff and others in Germany. In this connection, we should again return to his original text: 'War, which is subordinate to politics, necessarily takes on the character of the latter. The stronger and more powerful the latter, the more energetic it is. There is no limit to this and hence it is possible to arrive at absolute war.'

Clausewitz's contemporaries were not yet ready to understand him. Prussia's situation called for an organizer rather than a philosopher. Revolution from above was in some respects only a reform of Frederick William's finally modernized system. The programme of reform consisted in compulsory military service for all and the abolition of exemptions for the middle class and privileges for the nobility where army commissions were concerned. The popular struggle against Napoleon's armies was initially favourable to the reformers but the outcome of the Congress of Vienna, the Holy Alliance and the subsequent return to the pre-revolutionary system marked the definitive defeat of the reform ideas. The plan of having a permanent army (*Linie*) backed up by units from a middle-class militia (*Landwehr*) was eventually abandoned after a long struggle, but compulsory service for all subjects continued to operate. The other states in the German Confederation (e.g. the kingdoms of Saxony, Württemberg, Bavaria, Hanover and the Grand-Duchy of Baden) followed the French practice of drawing lots and substitution for the middle classes. From the 1850s onwards, developing industrialization made substitution increasingly difficult, and compulsory military service was introduced throughout Germany. While in Prussia the nobility dominated the army officer corps, in other contingents of the German Confederation there were officers of middle-class origin, who had more chance of social advancement by embarking on a military career. The split between the Royal army and middle-class society again came to the fore in Prussia, culminating in the uprisings of 1848–9.

When William I, and later Bismarck, worked towards the unification of Germany under Prussian domination and finally achieved it with the help of the Royal army during the wars of 1866 and 1870–1, the fulfilment of the liberal middle-class dream produced a rapprochement between the military rulers and the civilian majority. But this did not take the form of a coalition of equal partners, as it had in 1813. Soldiers now swore allegiance to the monarch, not to the constitution. Until the end of the monarchy, the army remained an instrument of Royal or Imperial power. The exaggerated degree of prestige accorded to the rank of officer reflected the militarization of German society, which varied in intensity between the states of the Empire in 1871. The majority of Germans believed Prussia owed its domination of the Empire to its invincible army. Compulsory military service and the training of conscripts had produced more widespread consent among the lower social strata. In the last decades of the nineteenth century, the exercising, weaponry and command structures of contingents were 'Prussianized', albeit with some modifications, in the other armies of the Empire; those of Bavaria, Saxony and Württemberg.

After the signing of the Franco-Russian Alliance (1894), Germany felt itself threatened on two diametrically opposed fronts. The only chance of avoiding being crushed between the two powers seemed to be to gain a rapid victory over the most dangerous of the two possible adversaries. The Chief of the General Staff, General von Schlieffen, opted for an offensive in the West. In 1905, the so-called 'Schlieffen Plan' was finalized. 'It is imperative', General von Schlieffen wrote, 'to try, by launching attacks on their left flank, to push the French back to the East, towards their Moselle fortifications, towards the Jura and Switzerland.' By anticipating the violation of Belgian neutrality, the Schlieffen Plan contradicted the principle enunciated by Clausewitz that political considerations should always take precedence over purely military factors. Moreover, Schlieffen's grandiose ideas took little account of the actual state of the German army and the possibilities open to it. In August 1914, neither the number of divisions available for the attacking force on the right wing of the German front nor the railway system (which could alone guarantee mobility and supplies) was adequate.

The German navy has a shorter history. Although the Great Elector cherished plans for naval expansion, his successors, the Kings of Prussia, neglected the navy. It was only under William II that the German Empire developed a desire to acquire an ocean-going fleet, inspired by Tirpitz, the real architect of the German navy. After the laws of 1898–1900, Germany's industrial strength enabled Tirpitz to put to sea the world's second greatest fleet, which resulted in an arms race with Great Britain. He then began the development of a submarine fleet.

On the eve of the First World War, social militarization had attained a peak, and not just in Prussia. The middle classes had come under the army's domination, uncritically accepting its norms. This was the psychological state of German society during the 1914–18 war. The blow dealt both to the army and to the ruling parties of the state by the Armistice and the Treaty of Versailles can well be imagined. Since the

Allies demanded that Germany should set up a professional army limited to 100,000 men rather than a conscript army, the recently formed Weimar Republic was unable to establish an armed force which identified with the parliamentary system. Instead the army remained isolated, traditional and anti-democratic. When Hitler took power, nearly all the officers and soldiers of the *Reichswehr* complied with the new regime. No doubt they hoped it would revise the Treaty of Versailles, one of the conditions of which was that the army should develop a closer relationship with society. Consent between the military and political elites persisted until the eve of the operations planned against Czechoslovakia. In 1938, the opposition which formed within the army high command confined itself to a critical analysis of the prospects for a German military attack, without ever questioning the political reasoning behind it. A second crisis of confidence between Hitler and his generals arose in the autumn of 1939 when the dictator gave the sudden order to attack France. The experience of the 1914–18 war meant that many of the officers had little faith in their equipment or the physical condition of their men.

The offensive plans prepared by the army's general staff were also felt by some officers to be questionable. General von Manstein, chief of staff of von Runstedt's army group, formulated a revolutionary solution based on an attack through the Ardennes, a region previously considered difficult for armoured and motorized divisions.

At the same time, Germany was rebuilding a formidable navy, essentially on the initiative of Admiral Raeder. The victory over France, after a campaign which lasted no more than a few weeks, surprised the majority of the German military leaders and gave rise to a sense of pride which already contained the seeds of their future defeat. Germany believed itself invincible, at least on the European continent. The war against the USSR in 1941, then conceived as its most ambitious blitzkrieg, marked the limits of the Reich's expansion policy. However the defeat before Moscow in 1941 marked the end of the blitzkrieg and led to the resignation of the commander-in-chief of the army.

Hitler personally took over the latter's functions, a fact which signified the start of more intense efforts to align the army with Nazi ideology. This process was further accelerated by the subsequent defeats at Stalingrad and Tunis. At the same time, resistance was mounting, principally in the offices of the army high command where the young staff officers were under no illusions as to the military's desperate situation. The extensive participation of these officers and others in the plot of 20 July 1944 produced a bloody reaction from the regime. About a hundred of the staff officers were subsequently executed after shabby trials. In 1944, the combat units were terrorized both by the regime and the prospect of unconditional surrender. The prospect of unconditional surrender and fearing the treatment they would receive as captives in the hands of their adversaries, especially in the East, continued to fight tenaciously.

If moral forces have played a significant role in Germany's recent military history, so too have the technical aspects of warfare, to which Frederick II, the generals of the Moltke school and the Third Reich ascribed such importance. The military's bold thinking in relation to the use of modern weapons was, for example, more significant than weapons superiority in the conflicts with France in 1870–1 and 1940. The German underestimation of tank warfare in 1916 is an exception. By contrast, the German general staff ascribed an important role to machine-guns and heavy artillery in 1914, and armoured divisions, dive-bombing and the use of flying bombs and rockets (V-2s) in the Second World War.

Ten years after the end of the war, in 1955, when the last prisoners of war were returning from the camps in Siberia, the German losses during the Second World War were calculated as being in the region of 4 million men. At the end of that year, after fierce parliamentary debates, the Federal Republic of Germany again decided to form an army, one that would be closely linked to its allies' armed forces and be assigned to NATO contingents. In 1989, the *Bundeswehr* (the armed forces of Western Germany) consisted of 495,000 officers and men, of which 340,000 were in the army, 110,700 in the air force, 38,300 in the navy and 6,000 in the reserve. Conscripts on 15 months' service constituted half the total, the remainder consisting of professional soldiers on engagements of between 21 months and 15 years. In the GDR, a 'people's army' (NVA) was formed which continued many of the traditions of the old Prussian army. The NVA was integrated into the Warsaw Pact. In 1990, the NVA was amalgamated with the *Bundeswehr* to form a unified German army under NATO command. *See also* ADMINISTRATION, ARMY; AIRBORNE TROOPS; ARMOUR; AVIATION; BERNHARDI; BLOCKADES; CHEMICAL AND BIOLOGICAL WARFARE; CLAUSEWITZ; COMBINED OPERATIONS; DELBRÜCK; DISCIPLINE; DÖNITZ; ECONOMIC WARFARE; ESPRIT DE CORPS; ETHOS; FREDERICK II; GENERAL STAFF; GERMANY, AIR BATTLE OF; GLORY; GUDERIAN; HIERARCHY; HINDENBURG; HITLER; INFANTRY; INTELLIGENCE; JENNA AND AUERSTÄDT; LEUTHEN; LOGISTICS; LOSSES OF LIFE; LUDENDORFF; MANSTEIN; MERCENARIES; MILITIAS; MOBILIATION; MOLTKE; MORALE; MUSIC; NATIONALISM; NAVAL WARFARE; NAVIES; PARIS, SIEGE OF; RAEDER; ROMMEL; ROSSBACH; RUNDSTEDT; SCHARNHORST; SCHLIEFFEN; SEDAN; SIGNAL COMMUNICATION; STALINGRAD; TANNENBERG (1410); TANNENBERG (1914); TIRPITZ; VERDUN.

B. KROENER

FURTHER READING
G. A. Craig, *The Politics of the Prussian Army* (Oxford, 1955); Karl Demeter, *The German Officer Corps in Society and State, 1650–1945* (London, 1965); Martin Kitchen, *A Military History of Germany from the Eighteenth Century to the Present Day* (London, 1975); F. C. Carsten, *The Reichswehr and Politics, 1918–1933* (Oxford, 1966); R. J. O'Neill, *The German Army and the Nazi Party* (London, 1966).

Germany, air battle of (1942–5) Plans for a strategic bombing offensive against Germany, to be mounted in daylight against the enemy's war economy, existed within the British Air Ministry from 1937, but these were by and large shelved when war broke out in September 1939. A shortage of resources and the unwillingness of the British government to initiate unrestricted bombing curtailed Bomber Command's activities, while the heavy losses suffered on the few day raids that took place determined that future operations would be confined mainly to night-time despite the difficulties crews would have finding their objectives. As a result, for the first 30 months of the war Bomber Command ineffectively nibbled at a variety of target systems. Indeed, by the winter of 1941–2 the high priority given to the development of a large bombing force was being challenged.

The future of Bomber Command and a massive British bombing offensive was saved when Air Chief Marshal Sir Arthur Harris was appointed Air Officer Commanding. His deft understanding of the need for an extraordinary, exemplary operation led to the first 1,000 bomber raid on Cologne in May 1942 and, with this success and Churchill's support, he was subsequently able to build up Bomber Command for its assault on the cities of Germany to destroy enemy morale.

But the decisive turning point in the air battle of Germany came when the Americans committed themselves to a daytime offensive from English, North African and, later, Italian bases. The Casablanca directive agreed by the Allied leaders in January 1943, and its subsequent modification (*Pointblank*) in June, established the basic principles for a coordinated, combined bombing offensive: the Americans would attack precise industrial targets by day, the British urban areas by night.

Until spring 1944 the Germans were able to mount an effective defence against both the British and Americans. Using airborne radars and ground control, and despite increasingly sophisticated electronic and other countermeasures, the *Luftwaffe* inflicted an overall loss rate of 3.6 per cent on Bomber Command from March 1943 to March 1944, but on some nights casualties exceeded 12 per cent. The Americans suffered even heavier losses by day until the appearance of the P51-D long-range fighter, which was able to escort bomber formations to Berlin and back and was the equal of all German fighters except the jet. With the Mustang, and following a concerted effort against German aircraft factories in February 1944, the Americans won air superiority over Europe by day. Bomber Command benefited from the losses the Americans inflicted on the *Luftwaffe*, but on occasion was hit hard by German night fighters as late as 1945.

The British offensive against civilian morale was in no way decisive despite the terrible damage done to cities like Hamburg (July 1943), Berlin (November 1943–March 1944) and Dresden (February 1945). Once the Americans had air superiority, their attacks on oil, synthetic fuels and lines of communication were extremely successful. Both the British and American offensives forced the Germans to devote significant attention and resources to air defence. In the process, Bomber Command lost 22,000 aircraft, and the Americans 18,000; together, they lost 160,000 lives. The 2,700,000 tonnes of bombs dropped on Germany caused some 300,000 civilian deaths and wounded a further 800,000. *See also* AIRCRAFT, BOMBER; AVIATION; EISENHOWER.

P. FACON
STEPHEN J. HARRIS

FURTHER READING
Anthony Verrier, *The Bomber Offensive* (London, 1968); John Terraine, *The Right of the Line: the Royal Air Force in the European war, 1939–1945* (London, 1985); Williamson Murray, *Luftwaffe* (Baltimore, MD, 1983); Max Hastings, *Bomber Command* (London, 1979); Norman Longmate, *The Bombers: the RAF offensive against Germany, 1939–1945* (London, 1983).

Gettysburg, Battle of (1–3 July 1863) In June 1863, to relieve the increasing pressure on the Confederate states, Robert E. Lee led his 76,000 men in an invasion of Pennsylvania. Union cavalry soon discovered Lee's movements and thereafter successfully screened their own army while depriving Lee of information. On 28 June Lee ordered his forces to concentrate in the region of Gettysburg in anticipation of a major action. In the event the battle began on 1 July without his intending it. A Confederate corps was engaged by Union cavalry at Gettysburg and both sides concentrated accordingly. George Meade, appointed by Lincoln to command the army of the Potomac only three days previously, took up a strong defensive position south of Gettysburg during the night of 1–2 July. He held the high ground and, with his main forces arrayed in a horseshoe formation, could use interior lines to strengthen threatened points. Lee resisted the advice that he turn Meade's southern flank and cut the Union army's communications with Washington. He opted instead for an attack against the Union's left wing while launching a feint against the right. Meade's left held and, though reinforced from his right, the Confederates did not exploit the opportunity thus created in that quarter. None the less, Lee still believed victory to be possible, and on 3 July ordered Pickett's division to head an attack against the centre of Meade's position. Despite artillery preparation, the Confederates suffered heavy casualties, Pickett's own division losing two-thirds of its strength. Meade did not counter-attack and Lee was able to break off the action unimpeded. But the effects were grievous for the Southern states. Lee's reputation was buckled; his total losses of 27,900 represented one third of his strength and the chances of international recognition for the Confederacy were finally gone. The battle proved to be the turning point in the American Civil War. *See also* LEE; UNITED STATES.

HEW STRACHAN

FURTHER READING
Edwin Coddington, *The Gettysburg Campaign: a study in command* (New York, 1968); James M. McPherson, *Battle Cry of Freedom* (Oxford, 1988); Glenn Tucker, *Lee and Longstreet at Gettysburg* (Indianapolis, 1968).

Giap, Vo Nguyen (b. 1912) Giap was both

a politician and a military leader. He fought against the Japanese, the French, the South Vietnamese and the Americans in turn and helped to make his country the foremost military power in South-East Asia. He was one of the leading theorists of revolutionary warfare. Believing that war is a continuation by arms of the political, social, cultural and economic struggle against the colonial powers, he advocated a strategy which used time and space to wear down the enemy.

With the armed propaganda groups which he organized in the remote villages of the Viet Bac in north-eastern Vietnam he was able to launch the August 1945 insurrection against the Japanese. This enabled the Viet Minh communists under Ho Chi Minh briefly to assume power in Vietnam. However, by 1946 the French had returned to Indo-China and after a period of uneasy peace conflict broke out between the Viet Minh and the French. The Viet Minh military forces led by Giap were unable to hold Hanoi and the port of Haiphong and they withdrew to their safe bases in the countryside. Urban guerilla fighting was kept up in order to tie down enemy forces but Giap concentrated his efforts on the countryside where he was able to hit isolated French outposts and garrisons.

This strategy proved successful and by 1950 Giap's People's Liberation Army of Vietnam had grown to 250,000 of which 60,000 were regular soldiers organized into five full divisions. In the northern area of the country they had virtual control with strong pockets in rural areas elsewhere. His military training camps taught the PLA cadres, or officers, political as well as military work. The army, with material support from China, consisted of guerilla-fighting militiamen, provincial troops who carried out liaison duties and regular units (known as the Chu Luc).

As a result of the 1950 Border Offensive which had secured Giap's bases in the north, established supply routes into China, and made the area virtually untenable for the French Giap felt able to go over to the third phase of revolutionary war in accordance with the pattern advocated by Mao Tse-Tung. Phase One involved the creation of safe bases in remote villages. In Phase Two guerilla warfare was launched in pinprick attacks against government forces and to protect the safe bases. Phase Three involved the transition from a guerilla army to regular units in order to take on the enemy in open battle. In this third phase Giap envisaged attacking ever larger concentrations of enemy forces until the war could be taken into the cities. However, Giap underestimated the abilities of the French military leadership and their willingness to fight. Once more he had to revert to the guerilla warfare phase.

There followed another period of reorganization but by October 1952 he was able to launch another offensive against the French. The culmination of this phase in the war was at the battle for Dien Bien Phu which finally fell to Giap's army on 7 May 1954 after a siege of 170 days.

After the peace settlement, Giap became Minister of Defence of the Democratic Republic of Vietnam. During the 1960s, the leadership turned its attention to South Vietnam and from 1965 onwards the North Vietnamese Army was the mainstay of the National Liberation Front which fought to rid the country of its pro-Western government and its American allies. The methods employed followed those used against the French. Giap remained the North's leading strategist even though he left an ever greater role to the generals he had trained, such as Van Tien Dung who captured Saigon in 1975 and subsequently succeeded Giap as his country's minister of defence. Giap entered virtual retirement although he was accredited with a responsibility for 'long-term defence planning'. *See also* DIEN BIEN PHU; GUERILLA WARFARE; MAO TSE-TUNG; POPULAR WARFARE; VIETNAM.

A. CORVISIER
DAVID WESTON

FURTHER READING
Vo Nguyen Giap, *People's War, People's Army* (New York, 1961); G. Boudrel, *Giap* (Paris, 1977); M. Maclear, *Vietnam: the ten thousand day war* (London, 1981); G. Lockhart, *Nation in Arms: the origin of the People's Army of Vietnam* (London, 1989); W. J. Duiker, *The Communist Road to Power* (Boulder, Col., 1981).

Glory Victorious leaders and valiant warriors legitimately aspire to glory. It is not, however, for them to sing their own praises, for fame does not favour the braggart. Whatever his exploits, the *miles gloriosus*, the self-styled swashbuckler or braggadocio, has at best only worn the mask of the hero. A great general sometimes brings the public homage bestowed on him into even greater relief by evading praise, Nicolas Catinat for example. Military glory has almost always been a cause for ritual celebration, the archetype of such rites being the 'triumph' of the Roman *imperator*. In his chariot drawn by white horses, the triumphant general, his face painted with rouge, dressed in a purple tunic adorned with gold embroidery and in the *toga picta* and gilded shoes, bearing a sceptre of ivory topped with an eagle, and wearing on his head a crown of laurels, was identified with Jupiter Feretrius; he would ascend the Capitol to offer the god the *spolia opima*. During the period of the Empire, all victories were attributed to the emperor, who, legally, was commander of all the armies. Trophies, statues and triumphal arches commemorated his good fortune; on medals he became the companion of the unconquered Sun and the equal of Hercules.

From the fifteenth century onwards, the *condottieri*, the great captains and the princes gave scholars and artists the task of enhancing their glory by drawing on the resources of Antiquity and mythology. In the *Galerie* which bears his name at Fontainebleau, Francis I appears in the guise of Aeneas and Achilles; in 1540, to honour Charles V on his visit to Paris, the city commissioned Giovanni di Bartolo to sculpt a statue of Hercules planting two columns in the ground bearing the device 'Plus oultre', which expressed the boundless power of the imperial guest. The Italian medallists and sculptors of the Renaissance were still intent upon grasping the physical and moral personalities of their models. By contrast, monarchist propaganda in France and Spain standardized the themes of encomiastic literature and of decorative programmes. As in the Roman imperial tradition, the sovereign alone won victories, whether we are speaking of Philip IV in the 'Battle Hall' of the Buen Retiro, now the Spanish army museum, the *Museo del Ejército*, or Louis XIV at Versailles in the *Salon de guerre*, which was completed and opened to the public in 1686. All the actors of war were personified in allegory. The capture of a fortified town or a crossing of the Rhine in 1672 thus lent themselves better to representation than did victories in open country: women crowned with crenellated towers and bearded rivers surrendered to splendid kings led by Minerva. After an eclipse in the eighteenth century, in a cosmopolitan Europe in which the arts of peace provided the princes with greater renown than they would have won from conquests, the symbols of war rediscovered their expressive force with the Napoleonic Empire: eagles reappeared above flags and Canova sculpted Napoleon as a naked hero holding a statue of Victory.

The renown of monarchs is more or less a consequence of their military successes. Posterity, under Voltaire's influence, judges harshly the victor of Narva later defeated at Poltava. Napoleon is an exception to this rule: in France, Austerlitz and Wagram are still celebrated with little concern being shown for Waterloo. The final catastrophe, with which the Romantic generation with its dreams of power identified, merely added further to the glory of the 'little corporal'. The reputation of generals attaches more to their purely military qualities: their bravery, clear-sightedness and sometimes their moderation. One failure is not therefore sufficient to discredit them. The fact that Condé went over to the enemy and was crushingly defeated at the Dunes in 1658 has barely detracted from the prestige that surrounded him in his younger days, when, as the Duc d'Enghien, he was victorious at Rocroi and became the hero of the *précieux* novels of Mme de La Fayette. In other ages, the defeats suffered by a Chanzy or a Rommel have not diminished their merit. Some valiant leaders such as la Palice at Pavia have even shared with the kings of Sparta the privilege of being immortalized even more by their sacrifices than by their victories. How many officer cadets must have meditated upon the sublime example of Leonidas massacred at Thermopylae with his 300 Spartan hoplites:

'Tell them in Lacedaemon, passer-by:
That here, obedient to their laws, we lie.'

Happier was the young hero who fell at the height of his triumph, like Gaston de Foix at Ravenna, who was solemnly buried in Milan cathedral and for whom his captains and soldiers grieved, saddened to see cut down this 'fine green blade of grass or pleasant flower in the merry month of May, before it knew the fierce heat of the Summer'. The Italian Wars marked the high point of a military ethic maintained by stories of battle and chivalric romances. The nobles were driven by the desire to establish their 'reputation' and to contribute to that of their lineage. Monluc wished to 'make his name known', Bayard hoped 'in no way to do dishonour' to his parents, Robert de la Marck sought to 'imitate the bold knights of old'. And even in the eighteenth century, we find this preoccupation with family honour being expressed once again: Mercoyrol de Beaulieu, a young officer in the Picardy regiment, is proud to hear the soldiers say of him in 1743, 'Young Beaulieu will be as good an officer as his uncle.' And this reader of Brantôme admires his colonel, who prefers the strains of warfare to the pleasures of the court, 'so that posterity may accord him the title of great captain'. But the ideal which emerged from the Renaissance set greater store by honour than by glory. The fighting man gained distinction by his feats of valour, but also by his acts of liberality, which were the mark of the high-born. This can be seen in the magnificent eulogies addressed to the Marquis of Pescara and the Duke of Sessa in Brantôme's *Memoirs*; their memory will not die, for they have given without counting the cost to render a disinterested homage to their fallen rivals, Bayard and Lautrec.

In the age of French classicism, the Church delivered some stern blows against the glory of the soldier. In his funeral oration on the death of Condé, Bossuet set at nought the merits of Alexander and all the great pagan generals. Deaf to the compliments of the living in the hell into which their pride has plunged them, they are left with merely a 'shadow of glory' and their derelict statues. The great Condé himself would have shared the same fate, were it not for the grace of a late conversion. The wisdom and moderation of Turenne are illuminated by a faith which leads Fléchier to compare him to Judas Maccabaeus. Though a military courage, very Roman in style, still figures in the mausoleum of the Duke of Montmorency at Moulins, it became the custom for sculptors to depict generals at the moment of their death – such as Turenne, Harcourt or Maurice de Saxe – as being more preoccupied with the judgment of God than with that of men. It is true that they were also honoured in colleges, learned academies and even in the theatre: Maurice de Saxe was crowned with laurels at the Paris Opera on 18 March 1746.

From the middle of the eighteenth century, the great leaders did, however, see their exclusive privilege to accede to glory contested by others. The epic narrative came to be democratized to some degree and the heroes of lower rank, who were numerous in the lists of the martyrs of battle, claimed the honour of being cited in the telling of its story: for had they not also been called to spill their blood in the service of the fatherland? The Chevalier d'Assas and Sergeant Dubois, who fell at Klosterkamp in 1760 and, later, Joseph Bara, killed by the Vendeans in 1793, are symbols of the sacrifice of soldiers who died doing their duty. At least they still have a name and a face. With the development of national armies in our own day, we have become accustomed to celebrating and commemorating the collective and anonymous self-sacrifice of citizen-soldiers. Modern total war, complete with conscription and the extension of the battlefield to the home front, has fostered the glorification of the ordinary members of society and of the armed forces whose self-sacrifice has helped the nation and its way of life to survive. Horst Wessel, the hero of the Nazi Party, was a street thug from Hamburg and Heroes of the Soviet Union were invariably common soldiers or agricultural or industrial labourers. Glory tended towards the anti-hero. After wars, every town and village and every public body erects a monument to its war dead. We have even been reduced to piling up corpses in bone-pits on the sites of battlefields, without always being able to remove all the human remains from the mud. The unidentified victims are those most seen as deserving of pity and most venerated: at each anniversary, the survivors go to the tomb of an unknown warrior to make their personal act of remembrance, or to a necropolis like that of Marasesti in Romania. The point of such actions is not now to keep alive an undying military glory, but to extol the spirit of sacrifice. This development is not, however, irreversible, for the wars of the twentieth century have again given rise to a glorification of individual valour. Inseparable from the anonymous sacrifice of the ordinary 'tommy', the exploits of a Guynemer and the unrelenting vigour of a Foch or a Pétain attest to the continued existence of military glory in its most traditional form.

Great Britain has proved more resistant to the cult of martial glory. The Duke of Marlborough (1650–1722) was much reviled, despite his victories, for his cult of self-glorification. The Duke of Wellington understated his own achievements and is one of the few examples of an Englishman rising to political prominence through military achievement. Another is Oliver Cromwell. Because of her geography, England has favoured the naval hero – Drake, Byng, Hawke, Nelson and Beatty – although only Nelson was honoured with an enduring physical monument. *See also* CEREMONIES; ETHOS; ICONOGRAPHY; MORALE; MUSEUMS; VEXILLOLOGY.

J. CHAGNIOT

FURTHER READING
Thomas Carlyle, *On Heroes, Hero-Worship and the Heroic in History* (London, 1841); J. W. M. Hichberger, *Images of the Army: the military in British art, 1815–1914* (Manchester, 1988); M. Hansen, *The Royal Facts of Life* (London, 1980); E. Dinter, *Hero or Coward. Pressures facing the soldier in battle* (London, 1985).

Grandmaison, Louis Loyzeau de (1867–1915) This brilliant officer, whose name was surrounded by controversy after 1914, is remembered primarily for two lectures which he delivered at the École de Guerre in 1911. As a consequence, he was held partly responsible for the massive French losses in 1914 on the grounds that he had advocated the offensive in excessive terms – 'imprudence in an offensive is the best of securities'. In reality, Grandmaison's theories should be seen in the context both of the crisis in French military thought at the beginning of the twentieth century and of the contemporary political climate. His intention was to repudiate 'passive defensive strategy' and to avoid submitting to the enemy's will by seeking to impose one's own will. Assuming that the German armies would pass through Belgium, Grandmaison believed that a breakthrough would occur at Sedan. He also believed that the French would have insufficient troops to outflank and counter-attack the Germans from the west or the north-west. It would therefore be necessary to plan a counter-attack in the centre towards Sedan (the so-called 'Austerlitz manoeuvre') making essential the control of the key points from which the counter-offensive could be mounted. Since 1906 Grandmaison had argued that advancing under fire was not feasible without artillery support and he placed considerable emphasis on inter-arms co-operation. In some respects, Grandmaison's lectures prepared the way for the appointment of Joffre as commander-in-chief (1911) and in 1913 Grandmaison was the architect of the field service regulations relating to larger formations. While these embodied Grandmaison's 'offensive spirit', the complementary regulations for smaller formations were not ready by the outbreak of war in 1914. This led to ill-considered attacks and cost many lives. Grandmaison was killed at Soissons. *See also* ARTILLERY; FRANCE; JOFFRE; INFANTRY.

A. CORVISIER

FURTHER READING
Eugène Carrias, *La Pensée militaire française* (Paris, 1960); Douglas Porch, *The March to the Marne* (Cambridge, 1981); Michael Howard,

'Men against fire: the doctrine of the offensive in 1914', in *Makers of Modern Strategy*, ed. Peter Paret (Oxford, 1986), pp. 510–26.

Grandson, Battle of (2 March 1476)   Relations between Duke Charles of Burgundy and some of the Swiss towns, notably Basel and Bern, had been tense for some years when, in 1475, he decided to attack Bern, the city which was impeding the passage of Italian recruits to the Burgundian army. On 12 February 1476 he crossed the frontier with an army of some 11,000 combatants and an impressive train of artillery. He captured the castle of Grandson on 28 February and hanged the garrison. Then, as he advanced towards Neuchâtel, he was attacked by Swiss pikemen. Charles was able to redeploy his troops but as more Swiss contingents arrived on the scene he found himself outnumbered. His cavalry could not break into the Swiss 'hedgehog', and when he ordered a tactical withdrawal, his troops panicked. 'God gave us luck so they fled,' wrote the Zurich chronicler. The duke's camp was over-run, his baggage train and artillery captured. However, Charles the Bold's confidence was undented and three months later he invaded again. *See also* CHARLES THE BOLD; INFANTRY; MURTEN; SWITZERLAND.

JOHN CHILDS

FURTHER READING
Richard Vaughan, *Charles the Bold* (London, 1973); *Grandson, 1476*, ed. D. Reichel (Lausanne, 1976).

Granicus, Battle of the River (334 BC)   This was the first of the great battles fought by Alexander of Macedon against the Persian king Darius. After launching his invasion of Persia by crossing the Hellespont, Alexander encountered the Persian army on the east bank of the River Granicus, which was an important natural defensive feature because of its steep banks. The exact disposition of the Persian forces is obscure, but Alexander's problem was how to effect a crossing of the river without exposing his infantry phalanx to devastating attack. He organized a mixed force on the right wing, including cavalry, javelin men and archers, which was directed to make an oblique crossing of the river ahead of the rest of the army with the objective of forcing its way onto the bank in a series of waves rather than in column formation, while holding off the Persian cavalry. Then Alexander himself crossed with the rest of the Macedonian cavalry and directed his attack at the Persian centre; meanwhile Parmenio, who was in charge of the left wing, was to establish a foothold on the other side of the river with the help of the Thessalian cavalry. After a hard battle on the right wing, Alexander's dashing leadership of the cavalry helped to secure the Macedonian position across the river. Then, as the rest of the Macedonian army crossed, the Persian centre gave way and fled; the battle ended with the virtual destruction of the Greek mercenary infantry fighting on the Persian side, which was offered no quarter and suffered significant casualties. This victory opened the way for Alexander's occupation of Asia Minor. *See also* ALEXANDER THE GREAT; GAUGAMELA; HYDASPES; ISSUS.

B. CAMPBELL

FURTHER READING
E. Badian, 'The battle of the Granicus: a new look', *Ancient Macedonia*, ii (1977), pp. 271–93; N. G. L. Hammond, 'The battle of the Granicus river', *JHS*, c (1980), pp. 73–88; A. B. Bosworth, *Conquest and Empire: the reign of Alexander the Great* (Cambridge, 1988), pp. 39–44.

Grant, Ulysses Simpson (1822–85)   Grant passed out low from West Point in 1843, evinced little interest in military theory and quitted the army after service in the Mexican war. He returned as a colonel in the Illinois Volunteers on the outbreak of the American Civil War. His reputation as a commander was made in the Vicksburg campaign of 1862–3. Unlike his contemporaries, he was prepared to forfeit his line of communications and live off the land. He was free of European orthodoxies about the importance of manoeuvre and battle, recognizing that individual engagements were but part of a flexible sequence serving long-range strategic goals. Although possessed of little charisma, in March 1864, after his victory at Chattanooga, he was appointed Commanding General of the Union Armies. His strategy was to employ the superior resources of the North in continuous fighting on as broad a front as possible in order, literally, to destroy Lee's army. His methods involved heavy losses; they included the acknowledgement that war would also be waged against the enemy's means of production. His style of fighting was therefore both a foreshadowing of twentieth-century war and a model for specifically American approaches to the conduct of war. But it aimed to achieve its results in short order. A protracted campaign could only have served the South's claim to recognition. While Sherman approached Atlanta and Georgia from the west, Grant engaged Lee round Petersburg and Richmond. In April 1865 Lee surrendered to Grant at Appomattox. In 1868 Grant was elected President of the United States, an office he held until 1876. *See also* LEE; SHERMAN; UNITED STATES.

HEW STRACHAN

FURTHER READING
Bruce Catton, *Grant Moves South* (Boston, 1960); Bruce Catton, *Grant Takes Command* (Boston, 1969); J. F. C. Fuller, *The Generalship of U. S. Grant* (London, 1929); John Keegan, *The Mask of Command* (London, 1987); Russell Weigley, *The American Way of War* (New York, 1973).

Grasse-Tilly, François-Joseph, Comte de (1722–88) After taking service with the Knights of Malta, de Grasse joined the French navy and gained much experience, being captured in the action of 15 May 1747. Appointed to flag rank in 1778, he participated in most of the engagements in the West Indies between 1779 and 1781. In the latter year he earned considerable credit for bringing his fleet into Chesapeake Bay from where he was able to thwart the English fleet under Thomas Graves (1713–87) on 5 September 1781. This prevented any relief for Cornwallis in Yorktown and ensured the independence of the United States. Despite the skilful opposition of Samuel Hood (1724–1816), in 1782 de Grasse captured St Kitts,

Montserrat and Nevis. He accepted battle with Rodney's fleet in April 1782 off Dominica (Battle of the Saints) in order to save two ships which had been damaged in a collision. Rodney broke the French line and was able to capture five French ships in the ensuing confusion, including de Grasse's flagship, the *Ville de Paris*. The Saints revealed de Grasse's limitations. By his rigid attachment to the tactics of the 'line', de Grasse had decided the outcome of the war. Through his excessive caution he had missed a number of opportunities before fighting a major action which, given his numerical inferiority, he ought to have avoided. *See also* FRANCE; NAVAL WARFARE; NAVIES; RODNEY; YORKTOWN CAMPAIGN.

J. MEYER

FURTHER READING
Jonathan R. Dull, *The French Navy and American Independence* (Princeton, 1975); W. M. James, *The Royal Navy in Adversity* (London, 1933); David Spinney, *Rodney* (London, 1969).

Gravelines, Battle of (13 July 1558) Gravelines was the last major engagement of the Habsburg–Valois Wars. Although much smaller in scale than St Quentin it confirmed several of the key tactical lessons of that battle. The success of the Duke of Guise in capturing Calais and then Thionville in the first half of 1558 led to a deadlock between the main French and Habsburg armies in Picardy during the summer. At the end of June the Marshal des Thermes, commander of the garrison of Calais, decided to exploit the stalemate by mounting a raid on the Flemish ports. With a force of between 7,000 and 9,000 French and German foot and 1,500 horse he advanced past the Habsburg garrison of Gravelines early in July to attack Dunkirk. Dunkirk surrendered after a brief bombardment, to be followed by Bergues several days later. On 10 July, his army now laden with plunder, Thermes decided to retire. The French withdrawal was conducted along the Flemish coast and by the 13th they had arrived at the River Aa near Gravelines. In the meantime, reports of the raid had led to the assembly of a rather miscellaneous force of between 10,000 and

16,000 foot from the garrisons of Flanders and the militias of the major towns together with some 2,000 horse, a mixture of the Flemish *gendarmerie* and German pistoleers, commanded by Lamoral, Count of Egmont and governor of Flanders, who had played a major role in the victory at St Quentin. By the 12th Egmont's cavalry had reached the coast to the west of the Aa. On the following day they intercepted the French as they were crossing the river. Egmont's initial charges were beaten off, but Thermes was forced to deploy those of his troops who had already crossed. Egmont then mounted a concerted charge of all his horse, the *gendarmerie* in the lead. This overwhelmed the cavalry on the French inland flank leaving their infantry surrounded. More curious was the simultaneous collapse of the German foot who occupied the coastal section of the French line. Although all the accounts do not agree, the cause may have been the chance appearance of a squadron of English warships which proceeded to enfilade the French line with their artillery, a repetition of their performance at Pinkie in 1547. Almost the entire French army surrendered; only a few of the cavalry succeeded in escaping to Calais. Gravelines has its unique features (although the Battle of Nieuport in 1600 was another example of an engagement fought on the Flemish coast) and (like Montmorency at St Quentin) much may be blamed on Thermes's recklessness. Nevertheless, as at St Quentin, it showed that cavalry could still win decisive victories, particularly in a surprise encounter and if the charge were launched in sufficient depth. *See also* CALAIS; GUISE; NIEUPORT; PINKIE; ST QUENTIN.

SIMON ADAMS

FURTHER READING
C. Oman, *A History of the Art of War in the Sixteenth Century* (London, 1937), pp. 274–80; F. Lot, *Recherches sur les effectifs des armées françaises des guerres d'Italie aux Guerres de Religion, 1494–1562* (Paris, 1962). For the strategic context, see M. J. Rodríguez-Salgado, *The Changing Face of Empire: Charles V, Philip II and Habsburg authority, 1551–1559* (Cambridge, 1988), pp. 170–83. The English naval intervention is discussed in T. Glasgow, 'The navy in Philip and Mary's war, 1557–1558', *Mariner's Mirror*, liii (1967), pp. 321–42.

Great Britain As an archipelago on the edge of Western Europe, Great Britain possesses an individual military history. Celtic influences from Scotland, Wales and Ireland have been strong but she has also absorbed European ideas and concepts through conquest by the Romans, Anglo-Saxons, Vikings and Normans and from her own invasion of France during the Hundred Years' War and involvement in continental warfare after 1689. England herself became centralized under Athelstan (924–39); Wales ceased to be a military danger after 1283 and was incorporated in 1536; Scotland was brought into a joint sovereignty in 1603 and united with England in 1707; and Ireland became part of the United Kingdom in 1801. Internal peace was not the corollary of this relatively early centralization. Scotland fought England in the Bishops' Wars (1639–40), was involved in the Civil Wars (1642–51) and was the seat for the Jacobite Rebellions of 1689, 1715 and 1745. Ireland has never been completely pacified and a low-intensity counterinsurgency war still continues in Ulster. However, compared to some of her European neighbours, Great Britain has generally enjoyed domestic peace and political stability. This has enabled her to engage in continental diplomacy and warfare at times of her own choosing. The exception was in 1688, when the invasion by William of Orange drew England into the Nine Years' War. After the Norman Conquest in 1066, England became part of an Anglo-Norman Empire until 1205. This was advantageous as it protected England from invasion at a time when the English navy was insufficiently developed to guarantee command of the seas. The naval victory at Sluys in 1340 and the dominance of the fleet made possible the establishment of a new English empire in France during the Hundred Years' War. After her retreat from France in 1453, English defence policy concentrated on the establishment of naval supremacy in the English Channel and the southern North Sea.

After the defeat of the Spanish Armada in 1588, England was successful in ruling the seas. The Netherlands were kept at bay (1652–4, 1665–7, 1672–4) as well as France (1692, 1696, 1744, 1805) and Germany in 1940. During the latter stages of the American War of Independence, the Royal Navy resisted the combined strengths of the French, Spanish and Dutch fleets. After the ruin of the French fleet at Trafalgar in 1805, England retained control of the seas until she joined NATO in 1949. The invasion by William of Orange in 1688 forms a notable exception, but the success of this expedition was due to political rather than military factors. The 'king's seas' constituted England's real frontiers and in *Mare Clausum* (1635) John Selden claimed that England had legal rights to those waters and repudiated the notion of freedom of the seas expounded by Grotius in *Mare Liberum* (1609). England also acted as though her effective frontiers rested on the shores of the Continent, hence her determination to possess the islands close to those coasts. The Channel Islands passed to England in 1106 and were retained despite French attempts at recapture between 1460 and 1463. England showed an interest in Heligoland between 1807 and 1896 and in acquiring Walcheren and territory within the delta of the Rhine and the Maas (1572–1604, 1672 and 1809). Every chance was taken to establish a hold over ports on the European coastline: Calais (1347–1558), Le Havre (1562–3), Rouen (1590–2) and Dunkirk (1658–62). The vulnerability of London and south-east England to invasion was clearly demonstrated in 1667, when the Dutch attacked the English fleet in the Medway. Working from Selden's ideas, the Stuart monarchs insisted that foreign warships lower their colours or topsails at the sight of an English man-of-war in 'English' waters in recognition of the legitimacy of their claims and the primacy of the Royal Navy. From the time of Elizabeth I until 1945, a major objective of English foreign policy was to ensure that the Channel ports did not fall into the hands of a hostile power.

The military history of Great Britain divides into four phases determined by considerations of security: (1) the period of the 'open seas', (2) the period of overseas conquest and control of the seas, (3) the modern period when the major threat has been posed by air power, and (4) post-1945 when English financial weakness forced her into military and economic alliance with Europe through NATO and the European Economic Community. The latter has resulted in a rail tunnel under the English Channel, a clear admission that the 'narrow seas' no longer represent a division of Britain from Europe.

The Navy Naval activity was often as much defensive as offensive. It was stimulated by the size of the seafaring population, which was proportionately greater than in France, by close contact with the North Sea and the Atlantic, which were among the most difficult seas in the world and hence places where excellent sailors were nurtured, and, lastly, by the overseas policies of the crown. British naval superiority was patiently acquired thanks to an aptitude for adopting innovations in seafaring technique, particularly those introduced by the Portuguese in the fifteenth century, and to the continuity in naval policy pursued by succeeding monarchs. Because of her geographical situation, Britain was able to concentrate her national resources on the navy. However, British maritime power only arose gradually. Drake and the Elizabethan privateers possibly represented its first phase, though their importance should not be over-estimated. James I (1603–25) must take credit for forming the first small, specialist war fleet, whilst it was Cromwell (1653–8) who first used that instrument to break Dutch maritime supremacy. The solid entrenchment of naval superiority really occurred after the Restoration in the reigns of Charles II (1660–85) and William III (1689–1702). The work of Samuel Pepys at the Admiralty provided the Royal Navy with a pool of professional officers while the series of Navigation Acts, beginning in 1651, encouraged English shipping, shipbuilding and seafaring. Above all, the revolution in public finance which occurred between 1689 and 1750 produced the money to support a large and modern navy.

In ship design and other technical matters, the Royal Navy was inferior to the French, the Spanish and the Dutch navies during the eighteenth century, but in terms of administration, professionalism, seamanship and finance the British were far superior. Some technical improvements were made – the introduction of lemon juice to counteract scurvy on long voyages, the invention of the chronometer to determine longitude, and copper sheathing to combat teredos, or ship worms, in tropical waters. The Navy fought in line astern, tactics which had first appeared during the Anglo-Dutch Wars and were to continue, in essence, up to Jutland in 1916.

As a seafaring nation, England paid much less attention than countries on the Continent to ensuring the regular recruitment of crews. However, from Anglo-Saxon times, coastal populations had been obliged to provide and equip a ship with sixty oarsmen for every 300 hydes or farms. The kings possessed a few ships of their own and hired or commandeered merchantmen in emergencies but during the reign of Edward the Confessor (1042–66) the Cinque Ports were founded – Sandwich, Dover, Hythe, Romney and Hastings. In return for some municipal privileges, they undertook to raise a fleet for the king, without payment, for a certain number of days a year. A charter of 1278 provided for 57 ships for 15 days. However, the silting up of some of the Cinque Ports and their oppressive monopoly caused later monarchs to revert to chartering merchantmen through contractors; William Cannynge of Bristol fitted out a complete expedition for Edward IV. In the more modern period, England had nothing comparable to the French system of 'maritime classes' and relied upon volunteers and the press gang. The press mostly operated among merchant seamen and other seafarers and, despite attempts at reform, it was not abolished until the establishment of voluntary long-term service in 1853. The Royal Naval Reserve was created in 1859 (1861 for officers) and the Royal Naval Volunteer Reserve followed in 1903.

The Industrial Revolution and the needs of empire gave Britain almost total naval superiority in the nineteenth century. For a short while, under the Second Empire, France attempted to catch up and, after that, the Russians and the Japanese developed navies, but the only serious rival to the Royal Navy was the German High Seas Fleet after 1890. In 1889, Britain declared herself committed to the 'Two Power Standard', by which her navy was to remain superior to the combined strength of the two next most powerful navies. British naval mastery was a vital factor in the Allied victory in the First World War but after 1918 her superiority was steadily overhauled by the United States. At the Washington Conference in 1921–2, Britain was permitted parity with the United States in surface capital ships; the united strength of the capital vessels in the American and Japanese navies outnumbered the British in a ratio of 8:5. *Operation Overlord* (1944), which set out from British ports, represented the last demonstration of Britain's naval superiority over continental Europe. Subsequent expeditions to Suez (1956) and the Falklands (1982) have shown the decline in naval strength. The financial catastrophes of two world wars, the membership of NATO in 1949 and the EEC in 1973, and the loss of the British Empire have sharply reduced the political need for a strong navy.

Britain's geographical position and her consequent naval power have created a slight preference for the adoption of a peripheral strategy in European and world wars. Although Britain has been fully prepared to commit large land armies into Europe to support her continental allies (Nine Years' War (1689–97); War of the Spanish Succession (1702–14); Seven Years' War (1756–63); French Revolutionary and Napoleonic Wars (1793–1815); First and Second World Wars (1914–18, 1939–45)), her naval power has permitted her to execute simultaneous strategies which were more varied, mobile and flexible. From an early stage, the British acquired great expertise in combined operations, especially during the numerous landings on the French coast in the eighteenth century. The landing of an Anglo-Russian army in Holland in 1798 was particularly successful, as was the recapture of Egypt in 1801. The Peninsular War (1808–14) relied on the strategic use of sea power. In 1915, Winston Churchill instigated the Dardanelles expedition to circumvent the deadlock on the Western Front. The 'Mediterranean Strategy' during the Second World War was predicated on the employment of sea power. Moreover, Britain developed an expertise in evacuating its over-adventurous expeditionary forces at minimum cost (Île de Ré, 1627; Corsica, 1796; Dardanelles, 1915; Dunkirk, 1940).

The Army The place occupied in British history by the navy has, to some extent, overshadowed the role of the army. British geography and her naval development have placed particular tasks on the British armed forces: defence of the realm by traditional militias, the formation of intervention forces to aid allies in Europe, and the protection of the colonies. Unlike France or Austria, Britain usually only had to fight on a single front and has generally avoided facing a coalition of enemies, except during the American War of Independence. She has therefore been able to apply the principles of unity of action and economy of force, even when employing peripheral and indirect strategies. However, Britain has usually had to fight on both land and sea, 'double forward commitment', which has proved financially expensive.

As long as the seas were open to all, the English army remained similar in nature to those in Europe. There were few differences between the troops of the Anglo-Saxon chiefs and those of the barbarian leaders in Gaul and Germany. They were recruited from among the *Gesithcundmen*, some being maintained by the chief and others enjoying allotments of land from their master. On the eve of the Norman Conquest in 1066, the Saxon army consisted of the king's own house-carls, professional bodyguards, in addition to the house-carls of his earls (*c*.2,000 men), together with the fyrd. Service with the fyrd was one of the three duties incumbent upon freemen, the others being the maintenance of bridges and fortifications, and each hundred was expected to produce five volunteers. Technically, *c*.50,000 were eligible for service but kings usually summoned a limited fyrd of *c*.20,000 men from among the better equipped peasants. Every thane was obliged by his holding of land to serve for up to two months in any one year. Local peasants also turned out if their homes seemed to be threatened.

The fyrd produced a good infantry but it was weak in cavalry and produced little permanent fortification. The Normans, with their numerous cavalry and experience in fortification, were able quickly to establish a military domination of England. William the Conqueror had mote and bailey castles built on strategic sites across the kingdom. He also distributed 180 enfeoffed tenures to his supporters, in exchange for the *servicium debitum* which provided the king with an army of between 5,000 and 6,000 horsemen, servants and vassals. In fact, the feudal army rarely existed in this form. Money fiefs had begun to replace landed fiefs from the time of the Conquest and by the time of Edward I, the feudal host had been virtually forgotten and the crown relied on paying wages and granting annuities to knights who agreed to fight when summoned. Improvements in this system led to indentures, formal contracts which laid down conditions of pay, length of service, numbers to be levied, etc. This new state-feudal military system was superimposed on the fyrd, which continued in effective operation, giving England a well-established principle of general military obligations. In 1181, Henry II proclaimed the 'Assize of Arms' which imposed a duty on every freeman with a revenue or personal estate worth 16 marks sterling (a knight's fee) to keep the weapons of a knight. Freemen with less wealth had to provide themselves with arms appropriate to their means. All those eligible were at the disposal of the king for forty days in any one year. This edict was periodically repeated, most notably in the Statute of Winchester in 1285. Substantial landholders might own several hundred knight's fees and were expected to send deputies. In theory, this meant that the king always had available a force of heavy cavalry to resist invasion or rebellion.

Obligations were extended to commoners in 1230, and in 1242 those who owned 40 solidates of land had to provide an archer. Those between the ages of 16 and 60 were liable for service, and approximately 100,000 were eligible for the militia in 1554. Commissioners of array supervised the militia in every shire, selecting the fittest and best men before sending them to the rendezvous. The entire militia was never called out as this would have deprived whole counties of their agricultural labour. There was also a geographical division; when the enemy was France, the southern militias were summoned and when the opponent was Scotland the militias north of the Trent were put into the field. A statute of Edward III's reign stated that the militia did not have to serve outside its county boundaries except to meet an invasion. Henry VIII raised his armies by hiring mercenaries, through contracts (indentures) and by raising sections of the militia (the old *fyrd*).

A statute of 1558 reorganized the Tudor militia to counter the threats posed by France and Spain. The military obligation of all male subjects between the ages of 16 and 60 beneath the rank of baron was reaffirmed. Freeholders were divided into ten classes – e.g. a man with an income between £5 and £10 per annum had to supply the full equipment of an infantryman; one with over £1,000 a year had to provide 16 horses, 80 coats of mail, 50 helmets and 20 arquebuses. The militia did not necessarily entail personal service, but rather represented a fiscal liability. The lord-lieutenant commanded the county militia and the officers were drawn from the gentry. They were assisted by the commissioners of the musters, the high constables of the hundreds and the constables and churchwardens of the rural parishes, all of whom kept lists of militiamen and were responsible for their armament. There were around one million names on the lists in 1570 but only about 100,000 were actually trained by the muster-masters. When the Revolt of the Northern Earls in 1569 revealed the failings of the militia, specially selected 'trained bands' were drawn from the general militia. The men in these units were better drilled and disciplined, and

received pay. Despite its organization, the militia always promised more than it delivered. After its Tudor hey-day, the militia went into decline. The Civil Wars and Cromwell's military rule made military service unpopular and, after 1660, there was a peacetime standing army which assumed many of the functions of the militia. However, periods of danger witnessed a resurrection of the militia. In 1757, on the initiative of George Townshend, the 'New Militia' was formed, with its soldiers chosen by ballot, and this became a permanent service in 1769. The regiments of fusiliers, known as 'Fencibles', who could be used for operations outside the county, were drawn from the New Militia. In time of war, the 'Supplementary Militia' was called up. This system was at its height between 1775 and 1802. The tradition still existed in 1940 when the Local Defence Volunteers, or 'Home Guard', was formed to face the threat of a German invasion.

During the Civil Wars (1642–48), England experienced a high level of military activity with regiments of conscripts, volunteers and mercenaries being raised by both sides. At the height of the wars in 1644, there were perhaps as many as 160,000 armed men in England. The Protectorate of Oliver Cromwell (1653–8) ushered in a short period when the army enjoyed a high political profile. The New Model Army was Cromwell's power base and Charles II (1660–85) maintained a peacetime standing army. His brother, James II (1685–8), augmented the standing army to over 20,000 men and used it as a coercive political police force in his quest for a stronger central government and toleration for Catholicism. The Glorious Revolution of 1688 halted these trends and, since then, the British army has largely remained outside politics. The result of the experiences in the seventeenth century was a fervent anti-militarism and a deep unpopularity for the army. As a consequence, the professional army in England remained small, rarely more than 20,000 men except in wartime, although more could be housed in Ireland and in the colonies. In 1783, there were 51,000 regular troops – 18,500 in England and Scotland, 12,500 in Ireland, 7,000 in

India and 13,000 in the remaining colonies. During the nineteenth century, the number of troops in the colonies increased as Britain added to her empire. There were 50,000 overseas in 1858, excluding the 60,000 men of the Indian Army.

Unlike many of her European neighbours, England did not adopt either partial or total conscription in the nineteenth century. Instead, she relied solely upon volunteers, although the press and other dubious methods had to be employed to fill the ranks during the wars of the eighteenth century. A reserve was established in 1867 but a major modernization of the army was not attempted until 1870 when secretary for war Edward Cardwell attempted to fit the British army to defend India and the colonies and to play a role in Europe. He introduced short-service enlistment for 12 years, 6 with the colours and 6 with the reserve. Cardwell also tried to solve the problem of recruitment by linking local militia regiments with line regiments, centred on a depot town. In this way, it was hoped that the militia would feed volunteers into the regular formations. Sixty-six districts were created, each commanded by a brigade, coinciding with county boundaries wherever possible. Further to improve martial spirit and enlistment, the pay of the private infantryman was increased to one shilling a day in addition to free meat and bread. The purchase of commissions was abolished. Cardwell's reforms, although important, were bedevilled by the regimental system of the British army which had developed and taken root during the later seventeenth century.

After the failure of the Boer War (1899–1902) and in the face of the growing menace of France and Germany in the colonies and in Europe, the British army was substantially modernized before the First World War. Working on the results of the Esher Committee (1904), a general staff was established and the War Office reorganized but the majority of the reforms had to wait until Richard Haldane became War Secretary in 1906. Haldane organized an expeditionary force of two corps to intervene in Europe and amalgamated the militia and volunteers into the Territorial Army, initially for home service only. The British Expeditionary Force (BEF) was expanded to over one million men by the end of 1914. Conscription was introduced in 1916. Between 1914 and 1918, the British army lost 744,702 men killed.

During the interwar years, the army was reduced to cadre size in order to save money and concentrated on its pre-war work of imperial defence. Despite this, considerable progress was made in both mechanization and motorization (the Experimental Mechanized Force of 1927 and manoeuvres in deep and rapid penetration between 1931 and 1934). However, as the task of the army was basically to protect colonies, there was not the imperative behind the drive towards mechanization that existed in the German and Soviet armies. There was also the problem of the Royal Air Force. This had become an independent third force in 1918 and because of the perceived threats from the bomber in the interwar years, the RAF received a high proportion of defence funds. The RAF became a bombing and counter-bombing force rather than an adjunct to the army to provide tactical air support. Conscription was reintroduced in 1938. On the outbreak of war in 1939, the British could field 5 divisions in the BEF to support France and Belgium, 7 divisions in the Middle East, 1 division and 1 brigade in India, 2 brigades in Malaya and a few colonial garrisons. The 14 divisions of the Territorial Army stood behind the regulars. The government decided to create an army of 55 divisions by September 1941 (32 British and 23 Imperial), a total which was later revised to 36.

Conscription was continued until 1960, a reflection of the tensions of the Cold War, the demands of the British army of occupation in Germany and the numerous small conflicts caused by the steady erosion of the British Empire. India was granted independence in 1947, the garrison of Palestine was withdrawn in 1948, Egypt was totally evacuated in 1954, and Cyprus in 1959 although military bases were retained. After the failure of the Suez expedition,

Britain abandoned her role as a conventionally equipped world power and retreated under the nuclear umbrella effectively as a client of the United States. Further sweeping changes were made by the Labour government in 1967; with the exception of minor forces in Hong Kong and Belize Cyprus and Gibraltar, Britain abandoned her world strategic role and concentrated on the British Army of the Rhine, her commitments to NATO and on the defence of the British Isles. The 'revolution' in Eastern Europe in 1989 and 1990, combined with the need to reduce defence expenditure, has brought about another major reduction in the size of the army and of the armed forces in general. As the EC steadily expands to encompass Eastern as well as Western Europe, a British defence role in Europe is not foreseen. The Argentinian invasion of the Falkland Islands in 1982 and the British contribution to the UN forces fighting for the expulsion of Iraq from Kuwait in 1991 demonstrate that Britain requires small, highly trained and professional armed forces equipped for rapid mobility and response. The defence of the United Kingdom has largely become a matter for the RAF although the Royal Navy continues to have an important role in keeping shipping lanes free from the menace of submarines and in transporting and supplying the army overseas. *See also* ADMINISTRATION, ARMY; ADMINISTRATION, NAVAL; AIRCRAFT, BOMBER; AIRCRAFT, FIGHTER; AIRCRAFT, RECONNAISSANCE; AVIATION; BASES, AIR FORCE; BASES, NAVAL; BLOCKADES; COASTAL DEFENCE; COLONIAL TROOPS; COLONIAL WARFARE; COMBINED OPERATIONS; COMMERCE-RAIDING; CONVOYS; DOCKYARDS; EXPEDITIONS; INTELLIGENCE; LOGISTICS; NAVAL PERSONNEL; NAVAL WARFARE; TANKS.

BROOKE; CHURCHILL; CROMWELL; DRAKE; EDWARD, PRINCE OF WALES; FULLER; HAIG; HAWKE; LIDDELL HART; MARLBOROUGH; MONTGOMERY; NELSON; RICHARD I; ROBINS; RODNEY; SHRAPNEL; TRENCHARD; WELLINGTON.

AGINCOURT; BLENHEIM; BRITAIN, BATTLE OF; BRITAIN, CONQUEST OF; DARDANELLES; EL ALAMEIN; FALKLAND ISLANDS; FALKLANDS WAR; FONTENOY; HASTINGS; JUTLAND; MARSTON MOOR; NORMANDY; PLASSEY; QUIBERON BAY, BATTLE OF; TORRES VEDRAS; TRAFALGAR; WATERLOO; YORKTOWN CAMPAIGN; YPRES.

A. CORVISIER
JOHN CHILDS

FURTHER READING
A Guide to the Sources of British Military History, ed. Robin Higham (London, 1972); *British Military History: a supplement to Robin Higham's Guide to the Sources*, ed. Gerald Jordan (New York, 1988); Sir John Fortescue, *History of the British Army* (13 vols, London, 1910–35); Correlli Barnett, *Britain and her Army, 1509–1970* (London, 1970); P. M. Kennedy, *The Rise and Fall of British Naval Mastery* (2nd edn, London, 1983); John Terraine, *The Right of the Line* (London, 1985). A new, multi-volume study, *The Manchester History of the British Army*, is now in preparation and will be published by the Manchester University Press from 1991.

Greece, Ancient Commentators are generally right to insist on the frequency of wars in Ancient Greece. It is not that the Greeks were more warlike than other peoples, but the division of the Greek world into innumerable cities, which constituted so many states jealously seeking to maintain their own independence, offered many opportunities for conflict. Then, when larger political units appeared – the Hellenistic kingdoms which were left after the dismemberment of Alexander the Great's empire – intense rivalries set them against one another or else they sought to impose their hegemony on isolated city-states or recalcitrant federations. In short, war was indeed the familiar horizon of the Greek throughout the greater part of his history.

The most striking factor in the history of Greek military art and technique and one of its most characteristic features is the priority accorded for the greater part of that history to heavy infantry over other formations.

From the seventh century BC onwards, most of the Greek city-states adopted what is normally known as the hoplite reform. Earlier, the confrontations we know from the Homeric epics consisted of two masses of combatants who, though less disorganized than is often thought, still lacked standardized weaponry, a coherent structure and rigorous discipline in the field. From this point on, the infantry were uniformly equipped with armour made up of a breastplate, a helmet, a shield, and greaves, and a long lance (7–8 feet) and short sword as offensive weapons. Tactics consisted of setting two masses of men, each armed and equipped with this bronze panoply, against each other by making them advance in step, to the sound of the pipe, in a compact formation between 8 and 10 ranks deep; victory belonged to the commander who, in a continuous thrust, forced the enemy to retreat to a point where, with his ranks broken up, he turned tail and abandoned the field; a 'trophy' – a kind of cruciform structure on which were hung the weapons of the defeated – was then erected at the spot where the outcome of the battle had been decided.

Over three centuries, these tactics underwent very few modifications, though the most noteworthy of these was the introduction of the successful oblique battleline formation by the Theban Epaminondas. From the mid-fourth century BC onwards, the appearance of the Macedonian phalanx which was to be victorious on various battlefields against hoplites, though without forcing these to disappear, is part of this same tradition of keeping faith with heavy infantry; it had the same compact mass, though with even more depth (16 ranks on average and as many as 32 at times), a longer lance (the *sarissa* which was some 13–23 feet long) and a round shield, which was fixed on the outside of the forearm, leaving both hands free to wield the heavy lance. This was a formidable formation, but one that could only manoeuvre well on relatively flat ground. It was this formation that enabled Macedon to triumph over the Greek city-states at Chaeronea and made that kingdom one of the great powers of the time. On some occasions, Alexander the Great preferred to use more mobile and efficient units, but his successors did not much follow his example and the phalanx played a pre-eminent role in most of the Hellenistic armies.

In the military history of Greece, it is interesting to note that the states which enjoyed military supremacy for various lengths of time were precisely those which best mastered the use of heavy infantry: Sparta from the sixth to the fourth centuries BC, Thebes from 371 to 362, Macedon from the middle of the fourth century onwards.

It is clear that in these conditions other formations, such as light infantry and cavalry, were neglected for a long time or considered as being of lesser importance. Light infantry (archers, slingers and javelin men) had only a minor place in Greek armies, particularly after the adoption of the hoplite reform. However, conflicts with non-Greek peoples skilled in the use of light arms, the development of the practice of ambushes and raids all led to a recrudescence of interest in light formations, which assumed increased importance from the mid-fifth century BC onwards. Their role did, however, remain secondary and was confined to certain specific operations. Then, at the beginning of the fourth century an Athenian, Iphicrates, introduced the peltasts, a type of formation that was more mobile than heavy infantry but better armed than light infantry. The Hellenistic period saw light infantrymen employed on a larger scale, with more systematic recourse to peoples who specialized in the use of particular missile weapons, e.g. Cretans, Thracians, Cypriots, Iberians.

Cavalry did not play an important role in battle in the earliest period. Admittedly, the horse made its appearance on the battlefield at a very early stage but it did so harnessed to the chariot, as is shown by the documents of the Mycenaean period in the last third of the second millennium BC. The chariot also appears in the Homeric epics (eighth century), though we may wonder whether at that period it was not merely a means of transport used to bring warriors to the battlefield rather than an operational machine. In the following century, horses were still used mainly by mounted hoplites who dismounted to fight. For example, the cavalrymen who constituted the warrior aristocracy in Euboea, the king's escorts in Sparta, or the 'Sacred Band' of Thebes, were in fact merely infantrymen on horseback. Only a few regions with a tradition of horsemanship, like Macedon or Thessaly, can have conducted mounted warfare at a very early stage. Other cities, such as Athens, Sparta or Thebes, came only very gradually to recognize the importance of cavalry, according it, in the fifth and fourth centuries BC, a greater place in the military machine. Its essential purpose, however, continued to be the harassment of an enemy army on the move, its pursuit after a rout or, more simply, the carrying out of reconnaissance.

It was not until the time of the kings of Macedon, first Philip and then, more especially, his son Alexander, that the cavalry became a highly regarded arm: it then came to play a decisive part in battle, as was the case most notably at Gaugamela. Alexander's successors did not however follow his example, preferring once again to give pride of place to the infantry or showing greater readiness to call upon elephants. The use of elephants, which was copied from the Indian armies, was one of the most remarkable innovations of the Hellenistic period. This was indeed the main lesson Alexander drew from the Battle of the Hydaspes, which he fought against the Indian prince Porus in 326 BC. After Alexander, every Hellenistic army worthy of the name would have elephants in its ranks.

In the naval sphere, Greek military history is characterized by the long predominance of the trireme, a ship with three superimposed banks of oars, the topmost being supported by an outrigger construction, and each oar being operated by a single oarsman. The trireme, which according to some sources was invented by the Corinthians, and according to others, by the Phoenicians, was adopted throughout the whole Mediterranean area in the seventh century BC. Its average crew of 170 oarsmen gave it great speed and remarkable mobility, thus making it capable of the most difficult manoeuvres: outflanking on the wings (*periplous*), passage between the enemy lines (*diekplous*), circle formation with the rams facing outward (*kyklos*), ramming or boarding. It could carry some fifteen marine infantrymen, whose role was decisive in the event of a boarding attack or in combined naval and land operations. The trireme was the favourite vessel in all

Greek war fleets until the beginning of the Hellenistic period.

First Alexander and then his successors did, however, adopt larger and larger vessels, with 4, 5 or 6 and even 20 or 30 'banks' of oarsmen, at least if we translate the names of these ships literally. In fact, some of these ships probably had rows of oars with several oarsmen and even, in some cases, a double hull. The most impressive ships (40 rows of oarsmen) were in fact merely ceremonial vessels which were probably unsuitable for use in warfare.

By virtue of the skill of their oarsmen and the quality of their shipyards, certain states gained mastery of the seas for a time in the eastern Mediterranean. This was the case with Athens in the fifth and fourth centuries, and with Rhodes and Ptolemaic Egypt in the Hellenistic period. The problem of providing crews was resolved in various different ways. At Athens, for example, crews were made up from those citizens or resident foreigners (metics) who did not have sufficient resources to equip themselves as hoplites. For want of men, other states had to either call upon mercenaries or enrol slaves. Recourse to this latter category of men was, however, still infrequent in the classical age. The Hellenistic states largely used mercenaries (something made possible by their more extensive financial resources), received contingents of men provided by those peoples among their vassals who had a maritime tradition (Phoenicians, Cypriots), or enrolled their non-Greek subjects (e.g. Egyptians in the navy of the Ptolemies).

The use of different formations was closely linked to a certain conception of space. In the age when the city-state was the predominant form of socio-political organization, the city and its territory were indissociable. It was important that the city protect the whole area of the territory, however tiny it might be, since without it the citizens could not survive; but it was just as important that the urban zone, which contained both the sanctuaries of the gods and the dwellings of men, should be protected from damage, if possible with the aid of solid ramparts. This double demand explains the uncertainties and hesitations in the strategy actually adopted.

When faced with an enemy attack, the inhabitants of a town had a choice: they could move out of the town in order to defend the territory; they could fall back within its walls, sacrificing the countryside; or they could seek to achieve a difficult combination of the two strategies. For their part, the attackers could confine themselves to pillaging the territory, in the hope of bringing the enemy out of the town and then confronting him in a pitched battle; they could undertake a long siege in the hope that the enemy would be forced to capitulate; or, lastly, mount an assault on the ramparts.

So long as siegecraft – the art of capturing towns – was still at the rudimentary stage, the territory was the major object of struggle and hoplite infantry was the main instrument used to defend or attack it. Hoplites alone were capable of winning a rapid victory over the enemy by crushing all his forces in open country, after having forced him to leave the town. However, when, at the beginning of the fourth century, the development of increasingly well-constructed siege engines made it possible to capture towns by direct assault, in spite of the concomitant advances in the art of fortification, it became necessary to adapt to this new situation. Light troops, peltasts and specialists in the use of siege-engines then came to occupy a more important place in the military apparatus, though despite this heavy infantry was not abandoned. Defending or taking a town became the essential preoccupation of a great number of generals, who won their reputations on the basis of their successes in this field. Treatises on siegecraft were published, such as that of Aeneas Tacticus, which met with considerable success.

This phenomenon was accentuated in the Hellenistic period, which was an age of larger political units, in which towns were not so much small entities sitting astride their territories as places of safety which, once occupied, made possible the control of entire regions. This was to be the golden age of siege warfare. The so-called ram tortoises (high, wheeled towers several storeys high), and increasingly sophisticated engines for firing arrows or throwing rocks (using compressed air or springs), brought fame on those engineers who invented them, such as Philon of Byzantium, or generals who knew how to use them, such as Demetrius I Poliorcetes ('the Besieger').

The development of the tactical use of the different formations can only be properly understood, on the other hand, if we take into account underlying social organization. Military affairs are intimately dependent upon the social reality and political structures with which they are bound up. Hence in a framework such as that constituted by the city-state, one of the obligations of the citizen was to take up arms for the defence of the community. Now, apart from the case of Sparta where the state provided the citizen with the land whose resources permitted him to fulfil his obligations, the citizen generally had to arm and equip himself at his own expense. The richest could purchase and maintain a horse and so served in the cavalry. The poorest contented themselves with serving as light infantrymen or as oarsmen in the navy. As for the hoplites, they were recruited mainly from the category of medium and small landowners who made up a substantial part of the population of the Greek cities. It was thanks to them that most of the city-states could be assured of finding the men they needed to establish the heavy infantry phalanx. Moreover, the shift in responsibility for the defence of the state from a few aristocrats to a substantial number of citizen farmers may have contributed to the developing political unrest and revolutions in the seventh century, in so far as those who had grievances of various kinds now had a chance to rectify them.

However, by the fourth century the financial burden imposed by the need for equipment, the growing disaffection of the citizen hoplites over campaigns that were too frequent and too long, and a certain weakening of civic spirit increasingly caused a certain number of city-states to call upon non-citizens and particularly upon mercenaries. The use of mercenaries, which had been known and practised in

Greece from the archaic period, developed considerably from the second half of the fifth century onwards. These mercenaries were most often used in the formations (light infantry and peltasts) or the tasks (siege engine service) which were then gaining in importance, not only because these corresponded to the development of tactical conceptions, but also because citizens were unwilling to fulfil their duties in less traditional formations. It was, moreover, partly to combat its citizens' evasion of their duty that, at the end of the fourth century, Athens reorganized the preparation of its young people for their civic and military obligations in what is commonly referred to as the *ephebia*.

It follows that in the Greek city-states, in the archaic and classical periods, the hierarchy of military formations was very often a reflection of the hierarchy of social categories from which they were recruited. The preferred use of certain of these formations was in many cases due to the importance of the social groups who made up their ranks. However, that use was very much dependent upon the availability of members of these groups. If they were unwilling to take up their duties, the tactical use of these formations could be modified to some extent or even threatened entirely.

On the other hand, states which possessed sufficient reserves of men, such as Macedon in the second half of the fourth century or the Hellenistic kingdoms of the East, or who could call upon substantial resources (mines, taxes, tribute), were not subject to the same chance factors. They could also make more widespread use of mercenaries – hence the prodigious development of the role of the mercenary in the Hellenistic period. This was a development which cannot simply be explained by the dislocation of the social structures of old Greece nor by the proximity of a market of men constituted by the barbarian or semi-hellenized regions; high rates of pay were also needed, such as could only be provided by rich states. Moreover, because of the cleruchy system (allotment of land in return for military and fiscal obligations), certain states such as Ptolemaic Egypt had at their disposal reserves of soldiers (first Greeks, then later native Egyptians) who were always willing to serve.

As can clearly be seen, the history of military art and technique is barely conceivable without reference to the evolution of social structures and the attitudes of citizen soldiers. Though there were few great innovations in the archaic and classical periods, those periods saw the perpetuation of methods of warfare and techniques which were well adapted to war between city-states. The Hellenistic period, by contrast, was accompanied, in this field as in many others, by a certain number of shifts and bold technical innovations, and gradually saw the emergence of a new type of warrior who was more of a professional. *See also* AENEAS TACTICUS; ALEXANDER THE GREAT; CHAERONEA; CYNOSCEPHALAE; DEMETRIUS POLIORCETES; EPAMINONDAS; GAUGAMELA; GRANICUS; HERON; HYDASPES; IPHICRATES; ISSUS; LEUCTRA; MANTINEA; MARATHON; NAVAL PERSONNEL; NAVAL WARFARE; NAVIES; PHILON OF BYZANTIUM; PLATAEA; POLYBIUS; RAPHIA; ROME; SALAMIS; SPARTA; THERMOPYLAE; XENOPHON.

R. LONIS

FURTHER READING

R. Lonis, *Guerre et religion en Grèce à l'époque classique* (Paris, 1979); R. Lonis, 'La guerre en Grèce, quinze années de recherches, 1968–1983', *Revue des études grecques*, xcviii (1985), pp. 321–79. Land warfare – W. W. Tarn, *Hellenistic Military and Naval Developments* (Cambridge, 1930); H. W. Parke, *Greek Mercenary Soldiers from the Earliest Times to the Battle of Ipsus* (Oxford, 1933); G. T. Griffin, *The Mercenaries of the Hellenistic World* (Cambridge, 1935); F. E. Adcock, *The Greek and Macedonian Art of War* (Berkeley, 1957); A. Snodgrass, *Early Greek Armour and Weapons; From the End of the Bronze Age to 600 BC* (Edinburgh, 1964); J. G. P. Best, *Thracian Peltasts and their Influence on Greek Warfare* (Groningen, 1969); E. W. Marsden, *Greek and Roman Artillery* (2 vols, Oxford, 1969–71); J. K. Anderson, *Military Theory and Practice in the Age of Xenophon* (Berkeley, 1970); H. H. Scullard, *The Elephant in the Greek and Roman World* (London, 1974); W. K. Pritchett, *The Greek State at War* (4 vols, Berkeley, 1974–85); Y. Garlan, *War in the Ancient World: a social history* (London, 1975); J. B. Salmon, 'Political hoplites?', *Journal of Hellenic Studies*, xcvii

(1977), pp. 84–101; A. W. Lawrence, *Greek Aims in Fortification* (Oxford, 1979); J. Lazenby, *The Spartan Army* (Warminster, 1985). Naval warfare – J. S. Morrison and R. T. Williams, *Greek Oared Ships* (Cambridge, 1968); L. Casson, *Ships and Seamanship in the Ancient World* (Princeton, 1971); J. S. Morrison and J. F. Coates, *The Athenian Trireme: the history and reconstruction of an ancient Greek warship* (Cambridge, 1986).

Grenades Supposedly named after 'pomegranates'. *See also* GRENADIERS.

Grenadiers This term originally referred to soldiers who specialized in the use of grenades, but it soon came to be applied to certain elite units. Grenades were employed from the end of the Middle Ages in the form of hollow iron shells stuffed with gunpowder, very similar to bombs or 'bombines', which were either thrown by hand or projected from slings or muskets after the fuse had been ignited. The soldiers given the dangerous task of casting them were volunteers who fought as 'enfants perdus' at the head of assault columns. The grenade had little function in open battle and was a weapon mostly reserved for siege and trench warfare.

The institutionalized development of grenadiers began in France. Grenades were first employed there at the Siege of Arles in 1536, but it was not until 1667 that four men from each infantry company were specially trained in the throwing of grenades and named grenadiers. After 1671, infantry regiments added one company of grenadiers to each battalion. The grenadiers were allotted especially hazardous and difficult tasks and formed a *corps d'élite* within the infantry battalion. They were equipped to meet varied tactical situations with a flintlock musket, bayonet, sword, hatchet and a grenade pouch, 'grenadière', containing between 12 and 15 grenades. Only strong, tall and agile men were selected for the grenadier companies. After the War of the Spanish Succession in 1714, grenades dropped out of use as an infantry weapon and became the preserve of the artillery and the engineers. Grenadier companies continued to adorn infantry battalions as crack troops but their equipment was reduced to that of the ordinary fusilier companies. However, they were distinguished by their fierce moustaches and their headgear. From their inception, the act of throwing a grenade overarm rendered the broad-brimmed hat unsuitable and grenadiers had adopted pointed caps. This developed into the grenadier's mitre decorated with a copper plate at the front. At the end of the eighteenth century it was sometimes covered with fur to produce the busby which was adopted by the French and British Guards.

Grenadier companies were introduced into British regiments in 1678 and most European armies had imitated the French example by 1690. In 1676, Louis XIV created a company of mounted grenadiers for the 'garde du roi' and this was copied in England in 1679 with the introduction of horse grenadier troops for each troop of the Life Guard. Every Prussian battalion had two grenadier companies but, on campaign, the grenadier companies were removed from their parent regiments and formed into special grenadier battalions charged with leading infantry assaults and other dangerous tasks. Austria-Hungary followed a similar pattern but established permanent grenadier battalions in 1769. France created a grenadier regiment, the Grenadiers of France, in 1748. Maurice de Saxe was highly critical of the practice of creaming off the best infantrymen into special companies and battalions as it weakened the overall strength of the army and aroused resentment. Gradually, after the Napoleonic Wars, the grenadier companies and battalions dropped out of use; they were finally abolished in France in 1868. The appelation 'grenadier' has survived into the present day to describe certain elite and guards formations, such as the British Grenadier Guards (1st Foot Guards).

During the First World War, the return to the techniques of siege warfare brought about a resuscitation of the grenade as an infantry weapon. Projected by hand or by rifle, the fragmentation grenade was perhaps the major infantry weapon in trench fighting by 1917 and the British General Staff bemoaned that the soldiers much preferred 'bombing' to musketry. Since 1918, the fragmentation grenade has remained a regular item of infantry equipment. Although the high-explosive fragmentation grenade remains the principal form, other variants of grenade have appeared since 1939. White and red phosphorus grenades are used to make smoke screens or for signalling, most tanks being equipped with short launching tubes. By employing hollow charges, anti-tank grenades can penetrate thin armour plate. Stun grenades do not fragment but seek to disorient an enemy by producing a loud noise, a blinding flash and slight blast. They are much used in anti-terrorist operations. Finally, the grenade is the ideal means of delivery for tear gases and CS gas during riot control operations. The majority of grenades can be delivered by hand projection, from an adapter fitted to the muzzle of a rifle, from special handguns, or by light cannon. In the three last cases, the grenade has to be fin-stabilized. *See also* CHEMICAL AND BIOLOGICAL WARFARE; EXPLOSIVES; FIREARMS; INFANTRY; MINING AND MINES; PROPELLANTS.

A. CORVISIER
JOHN CHILDS

FURTHER READING
F. H. Tyrell, 'Grenadiers: their history, dress and equipment', *United Services Magazine*, n.s. lii (1915), pp. 61–71; H. L. Blackmore, *British Military Firearms, 1650–1850* (London, 1961); P. R. Courtney-Green, *Ammunition for the Land Battle* (London, 1991), pp. 58–71.

Gribeauval, J.-B. Vaquette de (1715–89) Gribeauval was the son of a professional family, lawyers, administrators and soldiers, which had been recently ennobled; a typical example of social mobility by service to the state. He entered the artillery school of La Fère at the age of seventeen in 1732, the year of the adoption of the Vallière artillery system, and was taught by the famous Bélidor. He fought in the War of the Austrian Succession, served on a fact-finding mission to Prussia, and transferred to the Austrian service during the Seven Years' War. He distinguished himself in the defence of Schweidnitz during Frederick the Great's siege in 1762.

On returning to France he gained the confidence of the Duke of Choiseul, Minister of State for War and the Navy, and was appointed First Inspector General of the Artillery, Commandant in Chief of the Corps of Miners and, later, Lieutenant-General. In association with the technical expert Maritz, Commissioner of the King's Foundry at Strasbourg, and the clerk Dubois, he undertook an extensive redesign of the artillery *matériel*. However, his reforms, introduced in 1765, received a mixed reception, being attacked by the supporters of the Vallière system, the so-called Red Officers, and defended by his own partisans, designated the Blues. (The two sides took their titles from the colours with which the gun carriages of each system were painted.)

The dismissal of Choiseul in 1770 led to the suspension of these reforms, a period referred to as 'the downfall of the artillery'. However, Gribeauval regained his positions in 1776 and was raised to the vice-presidency of the Council of War in 1787.

Gribeauval's system increased the efficiency of artillery pieces by means of numerous improvements, among which may be mentioned the adjustable sight, the use of screwed-in vent pieces, which permitted easy replacement when the vent became enlarged with use, and the introduction of 'fixed' ammunition comprising charge, wad and projectile in one package, which greatly increased rates of fire. The safety of cannon was also significantly improved by Gribeauval's invention of an instrument which permitted not only the location but, more importantly, the accurate measurement of casting faults in the bore of the piece. This quality control system reduced the likelihood of defective barrels being accepted for use.

Greater mobility was achieved by means of the *prolonge*, a sort of tow rope, whereby the carriage could be dragged behind the limber at a distance of about 25 feet, using its iron-clad trail as a skid. The gun could thus halt periodically to fire and resume its movement immediately after discharge. The most significant aids to mobility however were the reduction in the weight of barrels and the construction of much stronger carriages. Though the latter were heavier than formerly, and included iron axles, the overall weight of the pieces was less than before and they were better balanced.

The standardization of the various components of the pieces was encapsulated in the Regulation of 1785 which codified all artillery vehicles. The rules included a single axle length for all carriages, the interchangeability of wheels between gun carriages and ammunition waggons, and standard screw threads for all nuts and bolts having the same function. These advances made mass production possible.

The Gribeauval system served throughout the wars of the Revolution and Empire and was only replaced by the Vallée system in 1825. *See also* ARTILLERY; BÉLIDOR; VALLIÈRE.

A. CORVISIER
A. CORMACK

FURTHER READING
H. O. De Scheel, *Treatise on Artillery* (repr. Museum Restoration Service, Bloomfield, Canada, 1984); P. d'Arcy, *Observations et expérience sur l'artillerie* (Alethopolis, c.1772); *Carnet de la Sabretache*, special numbers on artillery (1977, 1978); E. Picard and L. Jouan, *L'Artillerie française au XVIIIᵉ siècle* (Paris & Nancy, 1906); P. Nardin, *Gribeauval, Lieutenant Général des Armées du Roi, 1715–1789* (Paris, 1982); H. Rosen, 'The system Gribeauval: a study of technological development and institutional change in eighteenth century France' (Doctoral thesis, University of Chicago, 1981).

Grotius, or de Groot, Hugo (1583–1645) This eminent humanist, who became a renowned jurist, Latin poet, theologian and historian, was born in Delft. From his earliest youth, he showed himself to be a precocious and gifted thinker, arguing the case for free access to the ocean for all nations in *Mare Liberum* (1609) against the Englishman John Selden (1584–1654), whose theories were later expressed in *Mare Clausum* (1635). Being an ally of Johan van Oldenbarneveldt

(1547–1619), the Raadspensionaris of Holland who came into conflict with Maurice of Nassau, Grotius was condemned to life imprisonment in 1619 but escaped and took refuge in France. Here he published his *De Jure Belli ac Pacis* in 1625 complete with a dedication to Louis XIII. He was then appointed Swedish ambassador to Paris (1634–45). He died in Rostock. His works (e.g. *Obsidio Grollae* of 1629) and his correspondence are a mine of information about the contemporary practice of war. Reacting to the barbarism and amorality of contemporary warfare and international politics, Grotius sought to establish control, discipline and restraint both in the conduct of war and in the relations between states within a framework of natural law. He argued that the human rights which were discernible in natural law did not cease to exist because states were at war. On the contrary, war ought never to be conducted unless the belligerents agreed to abide by the conventions which were dictated by natural law. These rules and guidelines were apparent to reason – decent treatment of prisoners, humanity towards civilians, respect for property, honesty in the formulation of contracts and treaties, rights for neutrals, and resort to armed conflict only for good reasons. Grotius did much to bridge the gulf between the philosophical concept of natural law and the practical reality of an international law. His ideas reached a wide audience. *See also* GENTILI; LAWS OF WAR; NASSAU; NETHERLANDS; SPINOZA; VATTEL; VITORIA.

C. M. SCHULTEN
JOHN CHILDS

FURTHER READING
G. Livet, *Guerre et paix de Machiavel à Hobbes* (Paris, 1972); E. Dumbalud, *The Life and Legal Writings of Hugo Grotius* (Oklahoma, 1969); Richard Tuck, *Natural Rights Theories: their origin and development* (Cambridge, 1981).

Guadalcanal (July 1942–February 1943) One of the decisive battles in the war in the Pacific, the battle for Guadal-canal was a bitterly fought contest for the control of the Solomon Islands. The conflict began in July 1942, when the Japanese landed troops on Guadalcanal as part of their plan to isolate Australia by completing the conquest of the island group. The Japanese landing at Guadalcanal on 5 July clashed directly with the Americans' intention to take Guadalcanal as a stepping-stone to an attack on the Japanese base of Rabaul on the island of New Britain. Thus, on 7 August, an American naval task force landed some 11,000 Marines on Guadalcanal (a number soon increased to 16,000), beginning a seven-month struggle, both on land and at sea for control of the island and the surrounding waters.

In all, there were seven naval battles in the Guadalcanal campaign. These engagements were Savo Island (9 August), the Eastern Solomons (24 August), Cape Esperance (11 October), the Santa Cruz Islands (26 October), Guadalcanal (13–15 November), Tassafaronga (30 November) and Rennell's Island (30 January 1943). These engagements were accompanied by a host of other obscure actions conducted by submarines and torpedo boats and by nocturnal supply operations carried out by small craft from Rabaul – the so-called *Tokyo Express*. The naval losses were about even, with each side losing 24 ships, although the Japanese losses in tonnage were higher, 136,000 tonnes to the Americans' 126,000. More serious for the Japanese was the loss of some 600 aircraft in the aerial battles that accompanied the naval clashes.

The war on land was taxing, being fought in heavy jungle. The Japanese had been able to increase their forces on Guadalcanal by means of reinforcement from Rabaul; by October they outnumbered the 23,000 Americans. The Japanese attempts to dislodge the Americans from the latter's newly established air base, Henderson field, resulted in heavy casualties to the attacking forces. The naval battle at Guadalcanal on 13–15 November tipped the tables in the favour of the Marines: only 4,000 of the 12,000 Japanese troop reinforcements and 5 tons of the 10,000 tons of supplies that had accompanied the Japanese naval forces were able to land as a result of the American naval victory. The Japanese troops on the island were thus isolated, and the 13,000 survivors were evacuated early in February 1943. In all, the Japanese lost about 25,000 troops (9,000 alone to disease and hunger) in the Guadalcanal campaign; American losses were just over 1,000 dead and nearly 3,000 wounded. The Japanese defeat was not attributable to inferior resources, but to disastrous tactics on land, the failure of their medical services and the decision not to commit the major part of their naval forces to the battle. With the battle for Guadalcanal, the strategic initiative passed over to the Americans and their counter-offensive against Japan began to gather pace. *See also* COMBINED OPERATIONS; NAVAL WARFARE.

P. MASSON
KEITH NEILSON

FURTHER READING
S. B. Griffith, *The Battle for Guadalcanal* (New York, 1980); Graeme Kent, *Guadalcanal – Island Ordeal* (London, 1972); John Miller, Jr, *Guadalcanal – The First Offensive* (Washington, 1949).

Guards Units of very diverse character have been termed 'guards'. Those so-called may be found in the service of institutions that often have no relationship to each other, and their responsibilities may differ, even if they occasionally overlap. The main examples of such troops are the personal guard of sovereigns; an army's crack troops; some police forces; and some army reserves.

Sovereigns' Personal Guards and Military Households Rulers have always wanted to have about them a body of troops, small in number but of absolute loyalty, and these also sometimes constitute the flower of their army. An early example is provided by the 10,000 'Immortals' of the 'Great King' of the Persian Empire. Later, Roman emperors maintained a praetorian guard of several thousand men, whose purpose was to protect them and the government, and also to keep watch over the capital of the Empire. In periods when they were particularly subject to danger, kings surrounded themselves with some outstandingly loyal and devoted men as their close personal bodyguard, like the vassals of the Merovingian kings, the Saxon house-carls, or again, under Henry III of France, the 'Forty-Five', a third of whom were always on duty. Such guards have frequently remained in being for limited periods only. On the other hand, the guard of sergeants-at-arms which surrounded Philip Augustus in the Holy Land to protect him from the *Hashishin* (Assassins) was to develop into a company 150–200 strong, and was still in evidence round the Valois kings in the fifteenth century. At this period, however, their place seems to have been taken by two companies of 100 men of good birth, later called 'gentlemen of the halberd', who had ceased, in Louis XIV's time, to be more than a ceremonial show unit. Kings often preferred to be protected by foreigners, who would be less influenced by the intrigues of court circles; examples of such were Charles VII's Scottish guard and the Swiss Guards from Louis XI's time onwards. The expression *gardes du corps* made its appearance in France in the sixteenth century; an equivalent can be seen in England with its Life Guards, and in German-speaking countries with their *Leibkorps*.

The military household became a regular institution in France. From the time of Louis XI, the king had permanently at his disposal a certain number of units, of which the majority remained in being until the Revolution. Originally part of the royal household, these units turned in 1667 into the military household, and came to some degree under the Secretary for War in matters of discipline and administration. From then on, there was a distinction between the internal guard of the royal residence and the external one.

The internal guard comprised the following units:

1 The four bodyguard companies, of which the first, the Scottish company, dating from Charles VII, contained the 24 *Gardes de la Manche*, who provided the king's close protection, with a quarter of their number being permanently on duty. Each company's strength varied, over different periods, from 200 to 360, the equivalent of a contemporary cavalry regiment. Quartered near Paris, the bodyguards took duty at Versailles in rotation. Louis XIV, who in 1664 did away with the purchase of positions in this force, also turned it into a crack unit which took part in numerous battles, as well as into a school for producing officers. By the end of the reign, the bodyguard companies, which were generally composed of men of good birth, were drawn from the best cavalry units.

2 The two companies of cavalry (heavy and light) of the guard.

3 The two companies of musketeers which were formed in 1622 and 1660, and called respectively, after 1665, the 'grey' and the 'black' musketeers, from the colour of their horses. Saint-Germain chose an inopportune moment when, in 1776, he abolished these two companies, whose barracks were in Paris, and who were responsible in the eighteenth century for the policing of the capital.

4 The horsed grenadier company of the guard, formed in 1676, with a strength of 50.

5 The *Cent-Suisses*, the only foot unit in the royal household, and dating back to 1496.

The external guard was made up of a regiment of the *Gardes françaises* (French Guards), whose strength was raised by Louis XIV to 6 battalions (4,000 men), stationed in Paris, and the regiment of the Swiss Guards (4 battalions, 2,000 men), of whom 1 battalion served in Paris. In the middle of the eighteenth century, the former ceased to be a crack unit and turned into a force that played an essential part in the policing of the capital.

The military household of the French kings provided the pattern both for the personal guards of other contemporary sovereigns and for their crack troops, which were frequently quartered in or near the capital and which provided units to accompany them on their travels.

Henry VII of England established the Yeomen of the Guard 'for the safeguard and preservation of his own body', and in 1539 Henry VIII created the Corps of Gentleman Pensioners as an additional bodyguard. After the Restoration in 1660, Charles II slavishly imitated the French military household. He raised a Life Guard of three troops of between 150 and 200 men in each, even adding the refinement of three troops of Horse Grenadier Guards in 1679. He also established two regiments of foot guards, the first, later the Grenadier Guards, and the second, the Coldstream Guards. The mounted Life Guards not only protected the person of the sovereign but also acted as a training school for future officers.

In the Prussian army, certain crack units were attached to the Berlin garrison (which numbered 40,000 men), and provided the units that made up the king's personal guard (*Leibgardebataillon, Leibregiment zu Pferde, Leibkarabinieren, Leibjusaren, Grenadiergardebataillon*), but they had in the army a precedence corresponding to their date of formation only. Similarly, Peter the Great created in Russia the cuirassiers of the Guard, and Paul I later established the Mounted Guards, all men of good birth, while the Preobrazhenski and Semionovski regiments, which had their barracks in St Petersburg, acted also as a training school for young officers. Often units were given the appellation 'guards' merely as an honorary title, like the Walloon Guards, for example, who were a French-speaking regiment in the service of Spain.

With the French Revolution, the numbers in personal guards diminished, and it was the external guards that became the section of the army containing the crack units. In France, the royal military household was abolished in 1790; it was replaced by the king's Constitutional Guard (1,800 men), whose place was later taken by the Convention Guard (500), the Directory Guard (two companies, one horsed and one infantry, of 120 men each), and finally by the Consular Guard (2,090). At the Restoration, the companies of the bodyguard were re-established as the sovereign's personal guard. Napoleon III had his personal guard, which was called the *Cent-Gardes*. After the fall of the Second Empire, the Republican Guard became responsible for protecting the president of the Republic, and for providing formal military display at official state ceremonies. In the nineteenth century, royal guards shrank to a few hundred men, usually horsed, or to detachments provided by units stationed in the capital, such as the 20 battalions of the bodyguard (*gardes nobles*) of the Emperor of Austria.

It is noteworthy that the members of military households or sovereigns' personal guards enjoyed certain privileges, including a general rise in rank. Thus, in France the soldiers of bodyguards under the *ancien régime* were ranked as junior NCOs, its senior NCOs as lieutenants, etc., while members of the Republican Guards counted as senior NCOs. This meant that they received a higher rate of pay than they would have done in an ordinary unit. Officers in the English Life Guards copied this system: captains ranked as colonels, lieutenants as lieutenant-colonels, cornets and guidons as majors, and corporals as lieutenants. Officers of the foot guards enjoyed higher pay.

Guards – The Elite of Armies   Bonaparte revived the idea of the external palace guard or the quartering of regiments in the capital, and he increased the Consular Guard to 7,000 men. When it became the Imperial Guard, this force continued to grow by taking from other units their most tried and tested men. A greater than average height was also required for entry into the Guard. Its members enjoyed the privilege of a system of elevated ranking. The Imperial Guard reached a strength of 52,000 in 1811, and became a kind of army within the army, with its own infantry, cavalry, artillery and specialist units. Its numbers finally exceeded 80,000, representing one fifth of the whole army. It had no special role, but was used in battle like other units. Napoleon attached to it the 'honorary guards'. Formed in 1813, they numbered 10,000 and were made up of young volunteers who served at their own expense.

Others followed the example of the Imperial Guard. Alongside the bodyguards, the Restoration instituted a Royal Guard with a strength of 25,000 – a full-scale army corps – but this disappeared in 1830. Napoleon III re-formed the Imperial Guard in 1854, with a strength of 25,000–30,000. Germany had an Imperial Guard, consisting of an army corps (two infantry divisions and one cavalry). The same was true of Russia whose Imperial Guard numbered as many as 60,000. The SS (*Schutzstaffel*), which was in origin a political body, came in the end to resemble – in the shape of the Waffen-SS during the Second World War – the Imperial Guard.

Guards – Local Militia and Police Units
Towns have often drawn from their militias certain privileged units to which various titles have been given, but which can conveniently be grouped under the appellation of 'citizen guards'. In Paris, they came under the king. The most important of them was the Paris Guard, part of which was mounted, and which in the second half of the eighteenth century numbered nearly 1,000 men. The Revolution revived the old city militias in the shape of the national guards, whose members fitted themselves out at their own expense, and gave them a standard form of organization (law of 14 October 1791). The national guards became dormant at the time of the Consulate. After being kept in check by the Restoration government, the national guard reached the summit of its importance with the July Monarchy. It was opened to all in 1848, but proved unequal to its task in the July insurrection; in the suppression of this, some part was played by a short-lived Mobile Guard. Disbanded, and then reconstituted under the Second Empire on a new basis, the national guard had little to do. It was abolished on 25 August 1871. In the United States, all individual states maintain militias called the National Guard which form a reserve for the Federal Army in time of war and maintain law and order as well as frontier and coastal defence.

Guards as an Army Reserve Medieval monarchs had called on contingents from the urban militias (e.g. at the Battle of Bouvines) but, subsequently, militias or citizen guards were scarcely ever used except for the army's non-combatant tasks. Nevertheless, the national guards did make an appearance as a reserve at the time of Varennes. The Constituent Assembly voted that a part of the national guards should be placed on the active list, and this was followed by a call for national volunteers to join the army. On 30 July 1813, Napoleon called 90,000 national guards to the colours; they were divided into 'cohorts' of four companies (two of grenadiers, two of light cavalry) containing 50 men each, for the defence of the country. Finally, the Niel law established in 1868 the *Garde Nationale Mobile* as an auxiliary to the army for the defence of fortresses and for the maintenance of order internally. This mobile Guard was at the planning stage only in 1870 and disappeared under the terms of the military law of 1872.

Guards – As Units for the Maintenance of Order There have been offshoots from the Republican Guard, whose own responsibilities had gone beyond merely ensuring the safety of the head of state. These are the *Gardes républicaines mobiles* (formed in 1921), and – a later creation – the *Compagnies républicaines de sécurité* (CRS) intended for deployment in cases of internal unrest. They come under the Ministry of the Interior but carry out police duties in normal times.

The appellation 'Guards' has also been assumed by the paramilitary wings of political movements and revolutions. 'Red Guards' were at the forefront of the Chinese Cultural Revolution in 1966, and a political National Guard helped the Ba'ath Party to power in Iraq in 1963. *See also* GENDARMERIE; MILITIAS.

A. CORVISIER
JOHN CHILDS

FURTHER READING
Michael Rafter, *The Guards: or the household troops of England* (London, 1852); H. L. A. Fletcher, *A History of the Foot Guards to 1856* (London, 1927); H. Lachouque and A. S. K. Brown, *The Anatomy of Glory: Napoleon and his Guard* (Providence, RI, 1962).

Guderian, Heinz (1888–1954) From a military family, Guderian served as a staff officer in the First World War. Under the influence of such people as Liddell Hart, Guderian became an early advocate of mechanized warfare. Guderian's ideas brought him to Hitler's attention, and he rose rapidly in rank as a result. In 1938, Guderian became Chief of Mobile Troops. In the Polish campaign, Guderian's blitzkrieg (lightning war) tactics were vindicated by the rapid German victory. Guderian was prominent in the French campaign of 1940, commanding the Panzer corps that broke through the Ardennes and sealed the fate of France. He was promoted to colonel general as a result of this action. In the invasion of the Soviet Union, Guderian was given command of the Second Armoured Group, which was part of the Army Group Centre. Guderian was very successful in the early phases of the war. In August 1941, he argued unsuccessfully against the diversion of his Panzers to Kiev in the south, advocating instead the continuance of the drive towards Moscow. In late September, Guderian's force was returned to Army Group Centre for the final drive on Moscow. During the Battle for Moscow, on 20 December, Guderian was removed from his command for attempting to withdraw his forces from an exposed position resulting from the Soviet counter-offensive. He was made Inspector General of Armoured Troops in March 1943 after the German defeat at Stalingrad. In the aftermath of the July 1944 plot to assassinate Hitler, Guderian replaced Kurt Zeitzler as Chief of Staff, a position he held until March 1945. Guderian remains the most famous architect of blitzkrieg. *See also* FRANCE, BATTLE OF; FULLER; GERMANY; LIDDELL HART; MANSTEIN; TANKS.

B. KROENER
KEITH NEILSON

FURTHER READING
Heinz Guderian, *Panzer Leader* (London, 1952); Kenneth Macksey, *Guderian, Creator of the Blitzkrieg* (London, 1975).

Guerilla warfare This term, which appeared during the Peninsular War (1808–14), is applied to a form of warfare carried on by volunteers fighting for a national, religious or social cause who enjoy the support of the population, form and disperse rapidly, and engage primarily in *coups de main*. Guerilla warfare is the weapon of peoples who have no army with which to fight against occupying forces. It is a mode of fighting that is usually employed against an invader. Guerilla warfare played an important role at various times in Asia against the Mongols. It also constitutes one of the principles of the Arabic art of war (*rezzou*). It was also used by the Romans, however, in the fight against Hannibal (Fabius Cunctator) and in their turn the Roman legions encountered it in Spain, Gaul and Africa.

The history of guerilla warfare is marked by the interplay of two opposing principles.

1   The institutionalization of war by the chivalric code, the coming of mercenaries and the establishment of international law in the eighteenth century involved a condemnation of armed actions carried out by men who did not have military status. When caught red-handed in this way, civilians were summarily executed. This was the rule applied to *francs-tireurs* particularly during the Franco-Prussian War of 1870–1. However, armies did not repudiate all subversive action aimed at disorganizing the enemy's dispositions (elements of indirect strategy). Thus the eighteenth century saw a proliferation of regular troops practising skirmishing warfare (*petite guerre*) and equipped and trained for the purpose (hussars, light infantry, mixed legions of cavalry and infantry) operating as 'foraging parties' (*partis*), from which the French name, 'partisans', that was given to these regular soldiers in the seventeenth century, is derived.

2   Nevertheless, national (and sometimes religious) feelings give rise to resistance actions in countries that have been invaded or come under foreign domination. We may cite the exploits of 'Le Grand Ferré', the 'compagnons des Vaux de Vire' in France, during the Hundred Years' War, the 'Gueux des Bois' in the Netherlands (1566–8), the troubles in Ireland in 1641, the actions of the *Schnapans* in Swabia, the

Barbets in Piedmont against Louis XIV's armies, the actions of Andreas Hofer in the Tyrol or the Spaniards who gave this form of warfare its name in their struggle against the army of Napoleon. Guerilla warfare, as the weapon of the weak against the strong, was also used in uprisings of various types, such as the revolt of Stenka Razin in Russia (1667–70), the Camisards and the Chouans. It was the same in the wars of independence such as the struggle of the English colonies of America when the United States were founded, or that of Haiti, of Spanish America, and the movements of the nationalities in Europe: the Philiki Etaireia in Greece, the Haiduks of Transylvania, the Bulgarian 'Committees' against the Ottoman Empire and the Polish insurrectionists under Traugutt of 1863.

The generally very cautious attitude of the authorities towards guerilla warfare was always dictated by circumstances. In Islamic countries, guerilla warfare could be legitimized as a form of holy war. Until the seventeenth century in Europe, sovereigns of invaded countries would on occasion order their subjects to 'rush upon' the invaders. They might themselves use and direct this popular resistance, as did Charles V of France and du Guesclin. In Spain, Ferdinand VII's ministers sought to establish a legislative framework for guerilla warfare. Governments feared that, as a result, the *guerilleros* might threaten their authority, along with the established order. By contrast, even when war became institutionalized, they were tempted to encourage guerilla warfare in and against the countries they were fighting, by giving assistance to movements of national, religious, political and, more rarely, social revolt in order that they might tie down enemy forces and possibly serve as a support for their own armies. However, whereas the equivalent on the high seas, commerce-raiding, continued to be considered legitimate (letters of marque), guerilla warfare in fact seemed condemned to disappear as a result of the development of the laws of war, its lesser effectiveness as the art of warfare developed (*francs-tireurs* in 1870–1) and then, implicitly, the signing of the Hague Conventions.

However, guerilla warfare was rehabilitated, and came indeed to be even more highly regarded, during the Second World War. The terms 'resistance fighters' in Western Europe and 'partisans' in Italy and Eastern Europe (this latter the name taken by irregular fighters) became almost synonymous and the two were often associated. Even among invaded peoples, some professional soldiers repudiated this form of warfare. Others did, however, adapt to it, though not without some difficulty. The techniques remained the same as they had been in earlier periods, when allowance is made, of course, for the development of the military art. They included such things as intelligence-gathering, sabotage, destruction of property, attacks on isolated enemies, formation of groups of various sizes (underground fighters), where the geographical and human conditions allowed. This was the case in areas of difficult terrain, remote regions, forests, areas of low population density and places where movement was difficult. The effectiveness of these actions could be measured as much in terms of the immobilization of large numbers of enemy forces as in terms of the numbers of losses inflicted. Thus, since the Second World War, guerilla warfare has become a very widespread form of warfare (open warfare having become more difficult), particularly in the wars caused by anti-colonial movements.

In earliest times, guerilla warfare already had not only its practitioners, but also its theorists. In China in the fourth century BC, Sun-Tzu asserts that the 'peasants might serve you better than your own troops', and Wu-Zi studied the techniques of counter-insurgency warfare. The Arab world also had theorists of guerilla warfare. In 1811, in defeated Prussia, Gneisenau devised plans for a militia, the *Landsturm*, that would appear and disappear depending on the circumstances: 'If the enemy should show himself, the militia would appear as ordinary members of the population'. These conceptions ran counter to international law and were discarded. The Prussian *Landsturm* was in fact organized merely as a normal 'army reserve'.

The idea was, however, taken up by Engels, and later by Lenin, and was applied by Trotsky and Frunze against the White Russian armies. Guerilla warfare passed into the service of revolution. Stalin called for such action against the German invader in 1941. With Mao Tse-Tung, guerilla warfare was no longer a mere supporting tactic, but itself became the strategy. Partisans were to form the basic units of the army. From their rural bases, the partisans, who would move about among the people 'like fish in water', were to surround the towns. It would, however, fall to others to perfect the tactics of 'urban guerilla' fighting. Lin Piao saw guerilla warfare as the war of the Third World against America and Europe. Guerilla warfare was thus to become the true form of revolutionary warfare. *See also* GIAP; INDIRECT WARFARE; LENIN; MAO TSE-TUNG; POPULAR WARFARE; SUN-TZU; VIETNAM.

A. CORVISIER

FURTHER READING
Otto Heilbrunn, *Partisan Warfare* (London, 1962); *Civilian Resistance as a National Defence*, ed. Adam Roberts (Harmondsworth, 1969); Walter Laqueur, *Guerilla* (London, 1977); G. Fairbairn, *Revolutionary Guerilla Warfare* (Harmondsworth, 1974); R. B. Asprey, *War in the Shadows* (London, 1975); M. Cooper, *The Phantom War* (London, 1979); C. B. Ingrao, 'Guerilla warfare in early modern Europe', in *War and Society in East Central Europe*, eds B. K. Király and G. E. Rothenberg, i (New York, 1979), pp. 47–66.

Guernica (26 April 1937) The Spanish Civil War (1936–9) was to serve as a testing ground for a number of the European combatants in the Second World War, but it was the German high command and *Wehrmacht* that drew the most and best lessons from the conflict. On 26 April 1937, during operations in the Basque country in support of the campaign waged by the Nationalist armies to destroy resistance in the north, units of the German Condor Legion under the command of Wolfram von Richthofen bombed, dive-bombed and strafed the town of Guernica, a gathering point for refugees loyal to the Republic and site of the Renteria bridge, over which Republican forces were staging their withdrawal. Whether Richthofen's target was the bridge or the town in general is still debated, but facing no opposition, his crews were able to obliterate much of the latter. Two hundred were killed and 500 injured out of the population of 7,000 – a 10 per cent casualty rate caused by no more than three dozen aircraft in just a few minutes.

Subject of a painting by Picasso, the bombing of Guernica and the seemingly wanton destruction stirred world opinion. Demonstrating the immense power of modern air forces, the raid on Guernica also confirmed that, in the next war, civilians were likely to be bombed as targets of military value. When the bombing was over, the Renteria bridge still stood, and was used by Nationalist troops when they entered the town. *See also* AVIATION; SPAIN.

STEPHEN J. HARRIS
A. CORVISIER

FURTHER READING
P. Broué and E. Temine, *La Révolution et la guerre civile d'Espagne* (Paris, 1961); Hugh Thomas, *The Spanish Civil War* (London, 1961); Gordon Thomas and Max Morgan Witts, *Guernica: The crucible of World War II* (New York, 1975); Peter Monteath, 'Guernica reconsidered: fifty years of evidence', *War & Society*, v (1987), pp. 79–104.

Guesclin, Bertrand du (1314 or 1320–80) Du Guesclin, whose family belonged to the lesser nobility of Brittany, first came to prominence in the mid-1360s during the Hundred Years' War between England and France. He subsequently achieved fame as the leader of companies which he had taken to Spain to fight on their own account. Made Constable of France in 1370, he obeyed the orders of King Charles V and adopted a cautious strategy. Refusing to engage in pitched battles in which the French cavalry had been repeatedly defeated, he fought a war of skirmishes, ambushing English detachments and intercepting their supply convoys with the assistance of the local people. In this manner, several English marauding expeditions (*chevauchées*) across France were reduced to relative ineffectiveness. Simultaneously, Charles V was having castles and towns fortified in which people could take refuge and in which troops could shelter between actions. This strategy, though costly to the population and to the countryside as the English inflicted great damage as they passed, turned the tide of the war. By 1380, the English were on the retreat. *See also* INDIRECT WARFARE; POPULAR WARFARE.

A. CORVISIER

FURTHER READING
Siméon Luce, *Histoire de Bertrand du Guesclin et son époque. La jeunesse de Bertrand du Guesclin, 1320–1364* (Paris, 1976); J. Cuvelier, *Chronique de Bertrand du Guesclin* (2 vols, Paris, 1939).

Guibert, Jacques Antoine Hippolyte, Comte de (1743–90)   The son of General Charles de Guibert, who drew up regulations on field service and service in fortified places, the Comte de Guibert followed his father into the army at the age of thirteen and fought in the Seven Years' War. He rose to become a *maréchal de camp* in 1788 and a member and secretary of the Conseil de Guerre in the same year. A soldier-*philosophe* (he was a member of the Académie Française and a minor literary writer), he published his *Essai Général de Tactique* in 1772 and added to it a *Défense du Système de Guerre Moderne* in 1779. His work stands out as original mainly by the boldness of his conceptions. Starting from the idea that the national character of the French soldier disposed him more to the attack than to the passive resistance of fire, Guibert thought it advisable that the army should develop greater mobility and that the commander should be allowed freedom to choose his tactics at any point in a battle. Guibert took from Folard the idea of a generalized offensive and from Marshal de Broglie the idea of splitting the army into divisions operating in liaison with one another, hence the idea of a 'grand tactics' based on the interchangeable convertibility of line-of-march into line-of-battle: the idea of the 'march-manoeuvre', combining mobility and concentration. Speed became an essential element in the offensive, and fortifications were merely seen as incidental. This meant too that the supporting services of an army would have to be trimmed. Being aware of the growth in importance of firepower, he advocated the *ordre mince*. However, in the quarrel between the partisans of the *ordre mince* (line) and those of the *ordre profond* (column), i.e. of firepower against shock action, after the unconvincing Vaussieux camp manoeuvres of 1778, he produced a synthesis of previous experience and of the then fashionable ideas. He prepared the regulations of 1788, in which it was stated that battle would be joined initially by fire, concentrating the action of skirmishers on particular points of the enemy's positions, and would then be followed by charges in column to deliver the *coup de grâce*. Guibert was to exercise a real influence on young intellectual officers such as Bonaparte, and on the conduct of warfare during the Revolution. *See also* BOURCET; BÜLOW; CLAUSEWITZ; FOLARD; LLOYD; TACTICAL ORGANIZATION; TACTICS; TEIL.

J.-P. CHARNAY

FURTHER READING
Azar Gat, *The Origins of Military Thought from the Enlightenment to Clausewitz* (Oxford, 1989); B. H. Liddell Hart, *The Ghost of Napoleon* (London, 1933); R. R. Palmer, 'Frederick the Great, Guibert, Bülow: from dynastic to national war', in *Makers of Modern Strategy*, ed. Peter Paret (Oxford, 1986), pp. 91–119; Robert S. Quimby, *The Background of Napoleonic Warfare* (New York, 1957); Spenser Wilkinson, *The Rise of General Bonaparte* (Oxford, 1930).

Guise, François de Lorraine, 2nd Duke of (1519–63)   Like other talented princely or noble commanders of the sixteenth century, the Duke of Parma or the Duke of Somerset for example, the Duke of Guise was advanced quickly by rank to a position where his abilities could be deployed to effect. His father, Claude, a cadet of the ducal house of Lorraine, was a favourite of Francis I, who created him Duke of Guise in 1528. The 2nd duke saw his first service in the campaigns of the 1540s, but it was his skilful and successful conduct of the defence of Metz in 1552–3 that made his reputation. By then the dynastic and political ambitions of Guise and his numerous siblings had brought them to the centre of the factional politics of Henry II's court. Guise's own marriage to Anne d'Este (1549) gave him a personal interest in the continuation of the Italian wars, a policy opposed by his rival, the Constable Montmorency. Having encouraged Henry II to intervene in Italy in 1556, Guise himself commanded the expeditionary force. His campaign in Italy in 1557 met with little success, however, thanks to the skilful defensive tactics of his opponent, the Duke of Alba. In compensation, Montmorency's disastrous defeat at St Quentin led to the recall of Guise and his army. In 1558 he conducted his master-stroke, the rapid siege of Calais, which was followed in 1558 by those of Thionville (May–June) and Arlon (July). The Peace of Câteau-Cambrésis saw Guise at the height of his reputation. This and his large military clientèle strengthened his family's existing political influence as Guise assumed the leadership of the Catholic party in the factional struggles that led to the French Wars of Religion. After the Guise were expelled from the court in early 1561 the duke formed a political and military alliance with his old rival Montmorency. Guise's attack on a Protestant congregation at Vassy (March 1562) precipitated the First War of Religion, and he also achieved the first major Catholic success, the Siege of Rouen (October 1562). At the main encounter at Dreux (19 December 1562), Guise deliberately yielded the command of the Catholic army to Montmorency. However the Constable's capture early in the battle returned it to him and he was responsible for the marginal Catholic victory that followed. His command of the Catholic army was now unchallenged, but on 18 February 1563 he was assassinated while besieging the Protestant capital, Orléans. In the eyes of followers and admirers like Monluc, Guise was a model commander whose only flaw was the time he wasted through his insistence on writing his letters and orders in his own hand. No less famous was his studied affability and magnanimity – his own labour with pick and shovel was one of the legends of the Siege of Metz – though there was also a streak of cold-blooded ruthlessness in his character. At his best, Guise combined boldness with careful planning and his abilities were respected even by his enemies; but it was precisely these that made him such a dangerous and controversial figure in politics. *See also* ALBA; CALAIS; METZ (1552–3); MONLUC; PARMA; ST QUENTIN; SEYMOUR.

SIMON ADAMS

FURTHER READING
The destruction of Guise's papers in 1871 has prevented a modern biography. For his conduct of the Siege of Metz, see G. Zeller, *La Réunion de Metz à la France, 1552–1648* (Paris, 1926), i; for that of Calais, see D. M. Potter, 'The duc de Guise and the fall of Calais, 1557–1558', *English Historical Review*, xcviii (1983), pp. 481–512. See also N. M. Sutherland, 'The assassination of François duc de Guise, February 1563', in *Princes, Politics and Religion, 1547–1589* (London, 1984), pp. 139–56. For an admiring contemporary portrait, see *Blaise de Monluc: the Habsburg–Valois Wars and the French Wars of Religion*, ed. Ian Roy (London, 1971).

Gulf War (1991)   On 2 August 1990 Iraq invaded Kuwait following several months of dispute between the Iraqi leader, Saddam Hussein, and the Gulf States over oil production and pricing, and in particular disagreement with Kuwait over the Rumilla oilfield, which straddled the Iraq–Kuwait border, and other territorial issues.

The action was quickly condemned in the United Nations. The United States despatched troops and naval forces to the area followed by forces from other countries such as Britain. Two factors prompted this rapid response; an eagerness to demonstrate to Iraq that such aggression would not succeed and also a desire to protect Saudi Arabia (and Middle Eastern oil supplies) from any further military incursions by Iraq. It soon became clear that Iraq would not withdraw from Kuwait unconditionally, and Hussein's line hardened as he declared Kuwait an Iraqi province and began to hold Westerners as 'hostages' at key military–industrial sites.

By the end of October *Operation Desert Shield* had put in place 200,000 US and Coalition forces in Saudi Arabia. This soon increased to 500,000 as it became clear that the economic sanctions imposed by the UN would not, by themselves, dislodge the Iraqi forces and that the use of force was increasingly likely. At the end of November a UN Resolution authorized the Allies to use 'all necessary means' to oust the Iraqis if they remained in Kuwait beyond 15 January 1991. The Coalition forces consisted primarily of US troops (320,000) but also numbered significant contributions from Arab states, including Syria, and from Britain, which provided an armoured division and RAF Jaguars and Tornadoes, and France. A total of thirty countries militarily or financially assisted the Coalition forces.

On 16 January *Operation Desert Storm* began. This was a massive air assault launched against the military–industrial infrastructure of Iraq. The strategic aim was to destroy the command, control and communication network and the nuclear, chemical and biological facilities. The Coalition forces also hoped to achieve air superiority by destroying the Iraqi air defence system and airfields. The US and the Coalition forces fought a high-tech war. Electronic warfare aircraft with jamming equipment preceded air attacks to neutralize the Iraqi SAM systems, Airborne Warning and Control System (AWACS) aircraft operated over Saudi Arabia and were able to provide information on Iraqi air force positions, and the use of anti-radiation missiles (ARMs) against radar sites, 'droplet' mines, laser-guided munitions and cruise missiles, all contributed to air supremacy – not just superiority – being achieved by the end of January. The Iraqi air force was not wiped out (only 55 aircraft were destroyed in those first two weeks compared to 27 Coalition losses) but over 100 planes sought sanctuary in Iran and the remainder stayed out of the air rather than face the risks of confronting the Coalition air forces.

The Iraqi response was to launch its Scud surface-to-surface missiles (SSMs) against targets in Israel and Saudi Arabia. The aim was to widen the conflict by bringing in Israel which, if it had been successful, would have placed the Arab members of the Coalition in a difficult dilemma. Israel resisted the temptation to strike back against Iraq and the introduction of the Patriot SAM system and the promise of postwar aid from the United States helped to lessen the threat. It had been feared that the Scuds could have been equipped with chemical warheads but this proved not to be the case although the threat of chemical warfare remained ever-present.

The air bombardment continued into February with Iraqi positions in Kuwait being hit by both B-52 bombers and tactical aircraft. The 'softening up' continued until 24 February when the ground attack was launched. Massive firepower from the Coalition forces had effectively silenced Iraqi artillery, destroyed communications to the front-line and hit their armoured formations. The ground attack, *Operation Desert Sabre*, devised by the commander of the Coalition forces, the US General Norman Schwarzkopf, was a bold plan to encircle the whole Iraqi Army based in southern Iraq and Kuwait. Although some Iraqi forces were still able to put up a fight, many others simply collapsed. By 28 February Kuwait City was cleared. Almost 200,000 Iraqi soldiers were captured and estimates of Iraqi dead have ranged from 40,000 to over 100,000. Coalition casualties were fewer than 170 killed.

The Gulf War was the first real test of much of the advanced technology of the US forces. Designed primarily for combat along the Central European Front against the Soviet Union it performed spectacularly well. Other factors were equally important: the vastly superior training and preparation of the Coalition forces over an Iraqi conscript army using basically pre-1970 equipment; the value to the logistical exercise of the pre-positioned equipment in Saudi Arabia as well as in Europe which helped to reduce the burden of shipping an army of half a million men and their associated equipment. There was also an element of luck in the timing of the conflict. Without the decline of Soviet power in

Eastern Europe troops and equipment could not have been released for the Gulf. The end of the enmity between the Soviet Union and the United States also paved the way for the important resolutions passed at the United Nations. The building of the coalition by the United States was an undoubted success. Not so successful was the postwar phase. Despite the Iraqi defeat and the liberation of Kuwait, Saddam Hussein remained in absolute power in Baghdad. Although his overthrow was not the aim of the war, it was clearly the dominant sub-theme. Restrictions were placed on his domestic and foreign policies and inspections were carried out at military establishments suspected of harbouring nuclear facilities. Important questions were also raised concerning the arms sales policies of the Western powers which had largely been responsible for creating the Iraqi military machine. The defeat did not prevent Saddam Hussein from tightening his grip on his country and executing aggressive policies towards those groups which opposed him, specifically the Kurds and the Shi'ites. The war was a clear-cut military victory but a satisfactory peace and political settlement have yet to be attained. *See also* IRAN; IRAQ; ISRAEL, SINCE 1948; MIDDLE EAST.

DAVID WESTON

FURTHER READING
L. Freedman and E. Karsh, *The Gulf Conflict, 1990–1991* (London, 1993); Norman Friedman, *Desert Victory: the war for Kuwait* (Annapolis, Maryland, 1991); Dilip Hiro, *Desert Shield to Desert Storm: the Second Gulf War* (London, 1992); Bruce Watson et al., *Military Lessons of the Gulf War* (London, 1991).

Gunfire Gunfire emanates from artillery; it is distinct from musketry, small arms fire and rocketry. Gunfire is an accessory to and a support for the main action by infantry, cavalry and armoured fighting vehicles. Until the advent of rifled, long-range guns towards the end of the nineteenth century, particularly the French 75 mm quick-firing gun of 1897, the majority of artillery fire was *direct* (over open sights), i.e. the target was within the gunners' view. However,

although the hydrostatic or hydraulic buffer and recuperator enabled a field gun to recoil on its carriage without losing its settings, smokeless powder and high velocity musketry made the forward battlefield a dangerous place for artillery. The lessons from the Boer War (1899–1902) and the Russo-Japanese War (1904–5) made it plain that artillery had to withdraw from the front line, if it was to continue to support the infantry, and deliver *indirect fire* from covered and concealed positions. The gunners could no longer see their targets because of intervening ridges, woods or buildings but they could lay their guns on the correct map bearing with the *goniometric sight* (*panoramic* or *dial sight*), fire being adjusted onto the target by an *observer* in contact with the *battery* (usually 4, 6 or 8 guns) via telephone or radio. Indirect was slower than direct fire but the guns were not in immediate danger and were hidden from instant counter-battery attack. Indirect fire also had the advantage of concentrating the fire of many guns onto a single target without having to pack the cannon into a visible 'gun-line'; any number of indirect batteries could bring oblique fire to bear.

There was nothing new in this principle. For 400 years, mortars had been firing indirectly during sieges and since the mid-eighteenth century, Austrian and Prussian howitzers had been firing over the heads of their own infantry. However, during the Great War, indirect fire became the norm for field and heavy artillery with direct fire reserved for emergencies, tank guns, anti-tank guns and infantry-support guns. At sea, gunfire was mostly direct, i.e. aimed at a target in view, although the advent of radar-assisted gun laying during the Second World War brought an element of indirect fire into naval gunnery. Anti-aircraft artillery likewise fires directly.

Guns, which usually possess a length to bore ratio (calibres) of above 40:1, provide accurate, long-range (often over 32,000 yards), high velocity fire on a flat trajectory, always less than 45° (grazing fire). Anti-tank and anti-aircraft guns also belong to this type. Howitzers, normally less than 30 calibres, lob lower velocity projectiles in parabolic trajectories in excess of 45° (plunging fire) over ranges up to 20,000 yards. Because of the lower muzzle velocity of the howitzer, the shells have thinner walls as they do not have to endure the higher barrel pressures present in high-velocity guns. Howitzer shells thus contain larger explosive charges and are particularly useful against area targets – troop concentrations, route junctions, etc. The high trajectory, which can be altered by utilizing different amounts of propellant, makes howitzers especially efficacious against targets occupying positions on reverse slopes. Gun-howitzers (30–40 calibres) are compromise weapons which combine the muzzle-velocity and accuracy of the gun with the parabolic trajectory and larger shells of the howitzer. They are currently replacing both guns and howitzers in modern armed forces. Mortars are the simplest and cheapest artillery pieces, firing their fin-stabilized bombs at very low muzzle velocities on high, parabolic trajectories over ranges between 100 and 4,000 yards. The bombs, which travel at very slow speeds, are thin-skinned, containing heavy explosive charges. Modern mortars vary in calibre (diameter of bore) from 50 to 120 mm.

Gunfire cannot be totally accurate; artillery is an area weapon rather than one designed for pin-point accuracy. Every shell fired from the same gun varies fractionally in its dimensions while the characteristics of the barrel are constantly changing due to wear. The temperature of the propellant can also affect the behaviour of a projectile. Also, shells travel relatively slowly and their trajectory is affected by air temperature, barometric pressure and wind. Starting during the Somme in 1916, meteor messages were periodically given to the artillery indicating air temperature, pressure and wind direction. During major battles in the Second World War, the British artillery received meteor messages every six hours. From firing tables accumulated during previous test firings, compensation for the prevailing atmospheric conditions could be calculated.

The prime requirements for gunnery are accurate, reliable survey leading to excellent maps; indirect fire in its many forms relies basically upon large-scale maps (1:10,000 or 1:20,000) of the target area. On fast-moving battlefields in foreign countries, accurate maps are not always available but, given the opportunity, the artillery prepares its own maps from its own survey. Between 1914 amd 1917, the British surveyed 12,000 square miles of their sector of the Western Front, primarily for gunnery and target identification. Computerized mapping from satellite photography has greatly assisted the modern gunner in his search for reliable maps.

During the planning of a battle, either defensive or offensive, a fire-plan is worked out for the artillery in which each battery is given a series of targets which it is to engage for specific lengths of time. Every target is identified by map co-ordinates and each gun is then registered; a forward observer watches the fall of shot on the target and adjusts the fire by means of radio or telephone contact with the battery. Once registered, the batteries await the onset of the action. Although registration assures a relatively high degree of accuracy from indirect fire, it often cannot be used after the opening stages of a battle and is unsuitable for engaging targets of opportunity. For these fire missions, forward observers, or indeed the tanks and the infantry themselves, call upon mission batteries to fire on map co-ordinates and then adjust the fall of shot. Targets which lie some distance behind the front often cannot be observed, even though during the First and Second World Wars artillery observers frequently operated from light aircraft to improve the range of observed fire. For targets beyond observation, predicted fire is employed, sometimes called shooting by the map. The map co-ordinates, range and bearing of the target, plus the meteor message and the characteristics of the gun and ammunition were all fed into firing tables (1914–18), mechanical computers called predictors (1939–45) and electronic computers (present day) to obtain the lay of the gun. Through computers, laser range-finders and radars, modern predicted fire is extremely accurate and, because of its greater psychological impact, it is often preferred to observed fire.

A gunnery mission consists of the effect to be achieved, the target and the tactical conditions of its execution. The effects desired are either destruction of the target (at least 50 per cent of the enemy personnel and hardware put out of action), neutralization (preventing the enemy from fulfilling his mission for a given length of time) or harassment (posing the enemy constant problems). The different effects are achieved through density of fire. Fire may be opened on the initiative of the gunners themselves, at the request of the troops being supported or according to a schedule. Fire may be successional (laid down as the advance is made), box fire (concentrating upon a specific area of terrain), or a barrage (shells falling in a line, first employed at Neuve Chapelle in 1915). A barrage can be standing, the shells falling along a fixed line, or rolling or creeping, where the barrage lifts in pre-arranged jumps to keep just ahead of advancing troops. Much gunfire is counter-battery fire with the objective of destroying or neutralizing the enemy artillery. Enemy battery positions can be ascertained by flash-spotting, sound-ranging, aerial reconnaissance and, increasingly, satellite observation and photography. Registration also reveals the position of a battery to counter-battery fire.

Preparatory fire is made before the launching of an attack whilst supporting fire reinforces the action of a unit or formation. Accompanying fire consists of close support fire, which gives immediate support to forward troops, and protective fire which is aimed at enemy counter-attack concentrations. Counter-preparatory fire is directed at the offensive weapons of the enemy when he is preparing an attack, while a standing barrage is intended to halt an enemy attack by intense fire. Final protective fire is a barrage laid down close to defensive positions as a final line of defence. *See also* ARTILLERY; FIREARMS; FORTIFICATION; NAVAL WARFARE; NAVIES; SIEGES; WEAPONS.

JOHN CHILDS

FURTHER READING

S. Bidwell and D. Graham, *Fire-Power: British army weapons and theories of war, 1904–1945* (London, 1982); I. V. Hogg, *The Guns, 1914–18* (London, 1971); I. V. Hogg, *A History of Artillery* (London, 1974).

Gunpowder *See* EXPLOSIVES; PROPELLANTS

Gustavus II Adolphus, King of Sweden (1594–1632) Ascending the throne at the age of seventeen at a time when Sweden was under threat from Denmark, Gustavus had to consent to the charter of 1612 which limited the royal prerogative and gave greater power to the *Rad* (Council) and the aristocracy which dominated the *Riksdag* (representative assembly). Having been well instructed by J. Skytte, who taught him the theories of Justus Lipsius, his military education familiarized him with the Dutch and Spanish methods of war, as well as the writings of Vegetius and Frontinus. However, circumstances and his own Protestantism inclined him to follow and adapt the military methods of Maurice of Nassau.

His gifts as a strategist and tactician enabled him to put an end to Sweden's conflicts with Denmark, Russia and Poland. He improved upon the military reforms of Maurice of Nassau by reducing the infantry ranks from ten to six for musketeers and to five for pikemen and by adding light field guns to boost the firepower of the infantry. The pike was made shorter and lighter and cartridges were introduced for both the infantry and the artillery. Recognizing the weakness of the contemporary arquebus and musket, Gustavus increased the proportion of pikemen to musketeers within the foot battalion in order to augment the shock action of infantry in the attack. Similarly, Swedish cavalry ceased to employ the caracole but changed to the Polish model of shock action employing the sabre. Gustavus's armies were characterized by intensive training, stern discipline and high morale. Part of the army was raised by national recruitment (*indelta*) but much was composed of mercenaries. Its superior firepower, numbers and tactical flexibility made the Swedish army highly successful after its entry into the Thirty Years' War (1618–48) in Germany in 1629. Gustavus's victory at Breitenfeld in 1631 was a contest between the old and new schools of warfare. However, the Battle of Lützen in 1632, where Gustavus fell, demonstrated that the Imperial armies had rapidly assimilated the Swedish techniques. Gustavus laid the foundations of the Swedish Baltic Empire, raising his country temporarily to the status of a major European power. *See also* ARTILLERY; BREITENFELD; CAVALRY; INFANTRY; LÜTZEN; NASSAU; RECRUITMENT; SWEDEN; TILLY; WALLENSTEIN.

C. NORDMANN
JOHN CHILDS

FURTHER READING
Michael Roberts, *Gustavus Adolphus* (2 vols, London, 1953–8); Michael Roberts, *The Swedish Imperial Experience, 1560–1718* (Cambridge, 1979); Swedish Army General Staff, *Sveriges Krig, 1611–1632* (8 vols, Stockholm, 1936–9).

H

Hague Conferences *See* DISARMAMENT

Haig, Douglas (1861–1928) Haig remains one of the most controversial figures in British military historiography, for ever linked with the attritional battles of the Somme and Third Ypres, popularly known as Passchendaele. Entering Sandhurst from Oxford, where illness had prevented him from fulfilling the residential qualification required for a degree, Haig was commissioned into the 7th Hussars in 1885. Dour and inarticulate, he was more professional than most Victorian army officers but much of the professionalism and progressivism was expended in the cause of a branch of the service rendered anachronistic by the development of firepower and technology. His own particular narrowness of vision was epitomized by his *Cavalry Studies* published in 1907. Haig's concept of the immutability of warfare and the true function of a commander, which he absorbed as a Staff College student in 1896–7, was to have a stultifying effect on the military system over which he was eventually to preside. Chief of staff to the cavalry division in South Africa, Haig was then Inspector of Cavalry in India in 1903, Director of Military Training and then Director of Staff Duties at the War Office from 1906 to 1909 and Chief of the General Staff in India from 1909 until returning to command the First Corps at Aldershot in 1912. After the initial campaigns on the Western Front, First Corps became First Army in December 1914 and Haig then succeeded Sir John French as Commander-in-Chief in France and Flanders in December 1915, his elevation owing not a little to his intrigues against his former superior. Haig's headquarters became rapidly isolated both physically and mentally from his army. Obsessed with fears for his health and for the judgment of posterity, dabbling in spiritualism and surrounded by the sycophantic mediocrities whose company he preferred, Haig engendered an atmosphere of fear through his demand for an absolute loyalty abrogating genuine discussion. Army commanders, in turn, were compelled to operate in a curious command vacuum created by Haig's alternating detachment from and interference in the planning process. For all the *post facto* justification of the Somme or Passchendaele as necessary attrition of German manpower, Haig remained wedded to an elusive decisive breakthrough that was not technically attainable before late 1917. Even then, victory was not without great cost since the average daily casualty rate in the last 'hundred days to victory' exceeded that of both the Somme and Passchendaele offensives. Promoted field marshal in 1917, Haig received an earldom in September 1918 and finished his service as Commander-in-Chief of Home Forces in 1920, devoting his remaining years to the establishment of the British Legion for ex-servicemen. *See also* COMMAND; FOCH; INFANTRY; TACTICS; YPRES.

IAN F. W. BECKETT

FURTHER READING
Gerard de Groot, *Douglas Haig, 1861–1928* (London, 1988); Keith Simpson, 'The reputation of Douglas Haig', in *The First World War and British Military History*, ed. Brian Bond (Oxford, 1991), pp. 141–68; Tim Travers, *The Killing Ground* (London, 1987); David Woodward, *Lloyd George and the Generals* (Newark, Del., 1983).

Hamley, Sir Edward (1824–93) E. B. Hamley was probably the best-known military writer of Victorian Britain. A gunner, his own active career was limited. He served in the Crimean War and published defensive accounts of the army's conduct in *Blackwood's Magazine*. His subsequent books on the war, especially *The War in the Crimea* (1891), remain valuable accounts. In 1857, he was appointed the first professor of military history at the newly created Staff College. His didactic use of military history was best exemplified in *The Operations of War* (1866), a text-book which taught principles by means of historical case studies. His approach and outlook owed much to Jomini. Hamley's work emphasized the continuity in the rules of strategy; it was not sensitive to changing tactical conditions, and its precepts rested on the idea of small armies fighting limited wars. But it did provide a basis for the education of British officers, and the last edition did not appear until 1923. Hamley himself went on to be a successful commandant of the Staff College from 1870 to 1877 and a divisional commander in Egypt in 1882. Here he clashed with Garnet Wolseley, his commanding officer, and the subsequent controversy effectively finished his career. *See also* JOMINI; SEBASTOPOL; TRAINING.

HEW STRACHAN

FURTHER READING
Jay Luvaas, *The Education of an Army* (London, 1965); A. I. Shand, *Life of General Sir Edward Bruce Hamley* (Edinburgh, 1895).

(U.S. Army Military History Institute)

Hannibal (247–183/2 BC)   Hannibal was a member of the illustrious Carthaginian family, the Barcidae. His father, Hamilcar Barca, had been the greatest Carthaginian general of the First Punic War and had crushed the revolt of the mercenaries brought back to Africa from Sicily when Carthage had been forced to cease hostilities. Hamilcar sailed to Spain in 237 BC in order to develop Carthage's economic and military interests there. Before leaving he had made his eldest son Hannibal who accompanied him swear never to be friends with Rome, but it is not clear if at this stage he was aiming at a full-scale confrontation with the Romans. On Hamilcar's death in 229 his son-in-law Hasdrubal succeeded to the command in Spain, but after his murder in 221 as a result of a private dispute, Hannibal took over the leadership of the Carthaginian forces; he was twenty-five years of age.

Hannibal continued the war in Spain and in 219, after an eight months' siege, captured Saguntum, a town on the east coast of Spain which was a Roman ally. This led to war, and since the Roman fleets were more powerful than the Carthaginian, Hannibal decided to wage war against Rome on land and to weaken Rome by setting against it the peoples of Cisalpine Gaul (i.e. the plain of the Po) which Rome at that time was attempting to subjugate, together with the peoples of the peninsula who did not always readily accept Roman domination. His bold strategy was to march from Spain to the Rhône and then force the passage of the Alps. He used diplomacy and force where necessary, avoided the Roman army which had landed near the mouth of the Rhône, and succeeded in crossing the Alps, despite many privations for his army, which numbered only 26,000 when he arrived in the plain of the river Po. Here he won a first victory beside Lake Trebia in December 218, through an out-flanking manoeuvre by his cavalry and elephants and an unexpected attack by concealed troops under the command of his brother, Mago. In the following spring he crossed the Apennines and, on 21 June 217, he destroyed the army of the consul Flaminius beside Lake Trasimenus. Hannibal's clever deployment of his troops trapped the

Roman army on unfavourable ground between the lake and the surrounding hills, and about 15,000 legionaries were killed. From there he advanced into southern Italy where his operations were obstructed by the skilful tactics of Quintus Fabius Maximus Cunctator ('the Delayer'), appointed to the emergency office of dictator, who harassed him while consistently refusing battle. But in the following year Hannibal gained his most famous victory, at Cannae on 2 August 216 BC. This won over to his side a large part of southern Italy, notably Capua, though other cities did remain faithful to Rome and those which disassociated themselves from it turned out to be disappointing allies for the Carthaginians. Central and northern Italy remained loyal to Rome and Hannibal was unable to force the Romans to surrender or fight another pitched battle. His brother, Hasdrubal the younger, left Spain to come to his assistance, but was defeated and killed at the River Metaurus in 207. In 204 the consul P. Scipio landed near Utica in Africa and soon gained important successes. Hannibal, who had remained in Italy for sixteen years without suffering a major reverse, was recalled. He returned to Africa in the autumn of 203 with his best troops and organized an army by adding some African elements. But he was defeated by Scipio at the Battle of Zama in 202 and, having escaped to Carthage, advised that peace be concluded. Subsequently he became one of the chief magistrates of Carthage, and then introduced constitutional and economic reforms. But political rivalry and Roman suspicion led to his flight from Carthage, first to King Antiochus of Syria, and then to Prusias of Bithynia; he committed suicide in 183 or 182 to avoid extradition to Rome.

The Ancients passed contradictory judgments on Hannibal's character, though stories of his cruelty and treachery are doubtless at least in part the product of Roman propaganda. But everyone acknowledges his military genius, which was certainly nourished by his study of the campaigns of Alexander, of the great generals of the Hellenistic period, and of his father. As a commander Hannibal developed an imaginative and courageous concept of strategy; tactically he displayed great attention to the detailed preparation for battle and fully exploited the co-operation of infantry and cavalry, especially in outflanking manoeuvres, and the use of ambuscades. Moreover, he was first and foremost a leader of men; his army of mercenaries was made up of a nucleus of veterans to which he added contingents recruited as opportunity presented itself. He sacrificed these first, in order to spare the veterans, whom he kept back so that they could play a vital role. He acted decisively, moving quickly and avoiding sieges, because they took up too much time and also perhaps because he did not have the resources to conduct them successfully. The Numidian cavalry was often his main weapon because of its rapidity and hardiness. He also set great store by military intelligence, diplomacy and the acts of treason to which both could give rise among his enemies. *See also* CANNAE; CARTHAGE; ROME; SCIPIO AFRICANUS; ZAMA.

JOËL LE GALL
B. CAMPBELL

FURTHER READING
G. C. Picard, *Hannibal* (Paris, 1967); R. M. Errington, *The Dawn of Empire: Rome's rise to world power* (London, 1971), pp. 49–128; J. F. Lazenby, *Hannibal's War: a military history of the Second Punic War* (Warminster, 1978); B. Caven, *The Punic Wars* (London, 1980).

Hastings, Battle of (14 October 1066)   The Battle of Hastings was fought between William, Duke of Normandy, and Harold, King of England. It was one of the very few battles of the time whose course can be followed fairly closely on account of the detailed nature of the source material. Against Harold's men, all of whom were ranged along the top of a hill on foot, William sent his three corps combining archers, infantrymen and cavalry. The early hours of the action were very difficult for the attackers. William was almost killed more than once and his army began to fall back in some disorder. This tempted some of the English to leave the hill in pursuit where they were rapidly cut down. William, moreover, managed to regain control of his forces and mounted fresh attacks, some probably stemming from feigned retreats. At the end of the day, Harold was killed by an arrow and on the point at which he fell would stand the high altar of Battle Abbey, founded by William as an act of thanksgiving. On the evening of 14 October, the Duke of Normandy was master of the field. He was clear to advance on London and begin the conquest of England. *See also* ICONOGRAPHY; WILLIAM I.

P. CONTAMINE

FURTHER READING
R. A. Brown, 'The Battle of Hastings', in *Proceedings of the Battle Conference on Anglo-Norman Studies*, ed. R. A. Brown, iii (1980); C. H. Lemmon, 'The campaign of 1066', in *The Norman Conquest, its Setting and Impact*, ed. D. Whitelock (London, 1966); John Gillingham, 'William the Bastard at war', in *Studies in Medieval History Presented to R. Allen Brown*, ed. C. Harper-Bill (Woodbridge, 1989).

Hattin (Israel), Battle of (4 July 1187) The Battle of Hattin was a victory for Saladin, the Sultan of Egypt and Syria. At the head of an army of 12,000 well-equipped and well-trained men he overcame a disparate army under the command of the King of Jerusalem, Guy de Lusignan, while the latter was seeking to relieve the nearby castle of Tiberias. After a bitter engagement, Guy de Lusignan was taken prisoner and the Crusaders lost possession of the relics of the true cross. The harassing tactics of the Saracen troops had been successful over the massed charges of the Frankish cavalry. In the same year, Jerusalem fell to Saladin. However, the Franks retained a few of their coastal bases and the leaders of Christendom resolved to respond to the loss of Jerusalem by a new crusade, the third, in which the Holy Roman Emperor, Frederick Barbarossa, the King of England, Richard the Lionheart, and the King of France, Philip Augustus, were to take part. *See also* HOLY WAR; NUR-AD-DIN; RICHARD I; SALADIN.

P. CONTAMINE

FURTHER READING
R. C. Smail, *Crusading Warfare, 1097–1193* (Cambridge, 1956); Joshua Prawer, *Crusader*

Institutions (Oxford, 1980); R. C. Smail, 'The predicaments of Guy of Lusignan, 1183–1187', in *Outremer*, ed. B. Z. Kedar (Jerusalem, 1982).

Hawke, Edward, 1st Baron (1705–81) After entering the Royal Navy in 1720, Edward Hawke first attracted attention when, as captain of the *Berwick*, he captured the Spanish ship *Poder*, the only success in the unfortunate battle off Toulon (11 February 1744). Reaching flag rank in 1747, he commanded a squadron which successfully intercepted a French convoy under l'Étenduère bound for the West Indies, capturing six of the escort (14 October 1747). During the Seven Years' War (1756–63), Hawke was dispatched to restore the situation in the Mediterranean after John Byng's (1704–57) failure at Minorca in 1756. In the following year, he commanded the Channel Fleet, concluding with the Rochefort expedition in the autumn, where he was exasperated by the indecision of the generals. In 1758, he gave up his command after taking offence at the appointment of Richard Howe (1726–99) to command the landing squadrons at St Malo and Cherbourg. However, in 1759 he was reappointed to command the Channel squadron and doggedly maintained the first strict blockade of Brest. When the French fleet did escape, Hawke pursued it into Quiberon Bay where it was dispersed and destroyed. He continued to command the Channel Fleet until 1762. From 1766 to 1770, Hawke was First Lord of the Admiralty. A fine seaman, he was relentless and aggressive in the presence of the enemy. *See also* ANSON; BLOCKADES; NAVAL WARFARE; QUIBERON BAY, BATTLE OF.

A. W. H. PEARSALL

FURTHER READING
R. F. Mackay, *Admiral Hawke* (Oxford, 1965); Julian S. Corbett, *England in the Seven Years' War* (London, 1907).

Headquarters *See* GENERAL STAFF

Henry IV, King of France (1533–1610) Although he was the one European monarch of the later sixteenth century to command actively in the field, the military abilities and influence of Henry IV are not easy to assess. His early experience was gained in the semi-guerilla warfare of the later French Wars of Religion (1575–89). During these campaigns the Huguenot cavalry abandoned the lance for the sword and pistol, while their infantry (though this was a general trend) suffered from a substantial decline in the number of pikemen, thus increasing the proportion of shot. The simplification of their equipment made the Huguenot armies highly mobile, and the tactical advantages of their armament were demonstrated in Henry's first major victory, Courtras (20 October 1587). Here the charge of the thin line of lancers of the Royalist–Catholic army of the Duke of Joyeuse was first disrupted by the fire of the Huguenot arquebusiers, and then smashed by the counter-charge of the deeply arrayed Huguenot horse. Courtras confirmed Henry's belief in the decisive effect of the cavalry charge, but its aftermath revealed the king's casual approach to strategy and logistics. Henry's success in the campaigns of the 1590s was a mixed one. His most impressive victory was obtained at Arques near Dieppe (21 September 1589), where skilfully placed entrenchments in a defile enabled him to fight off the superior numbers of the Duke of Mayenne. His third major victory, Ivry (14 March 1590), also against Mayenne, was like Courtras essentially the destruction of a long, thin line of lancers by fire and counter-charge. In more complex manoeuvres Henry's touch was less sure. His attempts to besiege Paris in 1589 and 1590 had to be abandoned, and he was completely outmanoeuvred by the Duke of Parma during the siege of Rouen in 1591 and 1592. It was Henry's political decision to convert to Catholicism that brought the civil wars to an end, not military success. The war against Spain (1595–8), in which the king commanded only occasionally, was conducted badly, although Henry's financial weakness, which made it impossible for him to field sufficiently large armies, was also responsible. His 'war' against the Duke of Savoy in 1600, on the other hand, was impressive.

Although Savoy was not a serious opponent, and Henry's aims were limited to the regaining of territory Savoy had occupied during the French civil wars, he conducted a lightning campaign which forced a quick settlement on Savoy before Spain, always nervous about northern Italy, could intervene. His assassination on his departure for a campaign against Spain in 1610 makes it impossible to assess the effects of the reorganization of the army since 1600. Henry was at his best as a battlefield commander, where he possessed the winning combination of personal bravery, panache and (like the Duke of Guise) affability, and this particular type of military reputation greatly assisted him in reconciling Catholic France to his kingship. Yet the moral effects of his leadership were vitiated by his failure to exploit his victories strategically and the careless manner in which his armies were supplied and maintained. Parma's jibe that Henry was a mere captain of light horse may have been sarcastic, but even his lieutenant the Duke of Sully was one of his critics. When faced by an opponent of Parma's calibre, Henry lacked the requisite seriousness of approach or the skill in infantry tactics for success. *See also* CAVALRY; FRANCE; GUISE; INFANTRY; PARMA.

SIMON ADAMS

FURTHER READING
The most accessible recent assessment of Henry IV as both commander and king is D. Buisseret, *Henry IV* (Paris, 1984). His battles are analysed in C. Oman, *A History of the Art of War in the Sixteenth Century* (London, 1937) and a vivid account of Courtras can be found in G. Mattingly, *The Defeat of the Spanish Armada* (London, 1959).

Heritage, national *See* CULTURE, PROTECTION OF; MUSEUMS

Heron Heron of Alexandria flourished probably in the second half of the first century AD. He was a mathematician and inventor whose writings include treatises on measurement, geometrical definitions, the construction of machines powered by compressed air or steam, the design and use

351

of sighting instruments for the calculation of distance, and military catapults. In the *Cheiroballistra*, he produced a highly technical discussion on the specification and construction of a war catapult, which can have been comprehensible only to experts. However, in the *Belopoeica*, Heron set out to write about the basic principles of artillery construction in a way that everyone could understand, and describes the construction of a non-torsion engine which fired arrows, and then the development and design of torsion catapults down to *c.*270 BC, relying heavily on an earlier work of the Alexandrian engineer Ctesibius. The *Belopoeica* will have retained a practical value for anyone interested in the construction of catapults, and could be supplemented by additional information in the work of the Roman writer Vitruvius. *See also* ARTILLERY; PHILON OF BYZANTIUM.

B. CAMPBELL

FURTHER READING
E. W. Marsden, *Greek and Roman Artillery* (2 vols, Oxford, 1969–71).

Hierarchy Though today the military hierarchy may seem straightforward, with precise designations of rank which are almost exactly equivalent between one army and another, this has not always been the case. In fact, military hierarchy has often combined various notions of office, function, rank, post, title and designation.

Office The early modern concept of 'office' was not necessarily military. It related to both civil and military posts, of which the holder, who was appointed by the king, was himself the owner. From the end of the sixteenth century, in a number of countries, of which France was one, certain military offices, including those of colonel, *mestre de camp* and, in some cases, captain, became hereditary and purchasable, though ability and, of course, the approval of the appointing authority were still taken into account. This development was paralleled in civil offices. The value of military offices varied according to the law of supply and demand but it also fluctuated with the prestige of the corps in which it gave command. Thus it was not unusual to see a captaincy in a company of the King's Household, or indeed in an old permanent regiment, being worth more than a colonelcy in a temporary regiment. In 1776, a law was passed in France by which the sale of military offices was to disappear by stages (with the loss of a quarter of the original value each time an office was passed on) and the practice was completely suppressed at the Revolution. In Britain, the purchase of commissions was not abolished until 1871.

Function The term 'function' refers to a transient situation among the officer corps. Where its leader has been killed or when it is on some special mission, a regiment is sometimes commanded by a lieutenant-colonel or a company by a lieutenant and sometimes colonels perform the function of generals on a temporary basis. In the British army, battalions are always commanded by a lieutenant-colonel, only full regiments being commanded by colonels. The latter is frequently an honorary position. The British also make much use of the system of brevets whereby officers are given temporary rank above their actual or substantive rank. Brevets only function in peacetime; in war, much use is made of acting or temporary rank whereby an officer can be promoted several steps above his substantive rank. In the Second World War it was not unusual to find lieutenant-colonels holding the temporary rank of lieutenant-general.

Post The post an officer actually holds often depends on more general circumstances. At the end of hostilities, reductions in the size of the armed forces have often involved the disbanding of a large number of units. In some cases, the title of 'reformado' was given to officers who could no longer be employed but who would be given a new command as soon as one fell vacant. These officers often became supernumerary officers of the units which were retained and could, where necessary, take the place of the commissioned incumbent.

Rank It is rank which has become the simplest of the various notions listed above.

A commission confers on an officer the ownership of his rank and indicates his position in the military hierarchy and his right to a particular command. A rank is generally linked to a particular task: for example, a company is commanded by a captain. However, the development of general staffs and services has led to the creation of commissioned and non-commissioned officers without troops who, in some cases, have specific titles. In the British army, for example, the Brigadier General Staff is the chief of staff of a corps or an army, while the Major-General Royal Artillery commands the artillery of an army. In the British army, a soldier is called a private in the infantry, a trooper in cavalry regiments, a gunner in the artillery, a sapper in the engineers, a signalman in the Royal Signals and a guardsman in the foot guards. Lance-corporals and corporals (bombardiers in the artillery), sergeants and warrant officers first and second class constitute the non-commissioned officers. Commissioned officers of subaltern rank include second and first lieutenants and captains; those of field rank are majors, lieutenant-colonels and colonels; while general officers include brigadiers, major-generals, lieutenant-generals, generals and field marshals. The army of the United States has adopted the same commissioned ranks as the British army except that the field-marshal is termed general of the army. In the Royal Navy, the non-commissioned ranks run from ordinary seaman, to able seaman, leading seaman, petty officer and chief petty officer. The commissioned ranks are midshipman (cadet), sub-lieutenant, lieutenant, lieutenant-commander, commander, captain, commodore, rear-admiral, vice-admiral, admiral and admiral of the fleet. In the Royal Air Force, the non-commissioned ranks are aircraftman 2nd and 1st class, leading aircraftman, corporal, sergeant, flight sergeant and warrant officer. The commissioned ranks are pilot officer, flying officer, flight lieutenant, squadron leader, wing commander, group captain, air commodore, air vice-marshal, air marshal, air chief marshal and marshal of the Royal Air Force.

History The Athenian army was commanded by ten *strategoi*, each playing the role of commander-in-chief in turn. They were assisted by two hipparchs at the head of the two cavalry wings and by taxiarchs, whose task it was to organize marches, camps and supplies. The *lochoi*, or bands, were led by *lochagoi* and the cavalry units by phylarchs. The army of the Roman Republic was commanded by the two consuls in turn. The commanders of the legions were its six tribunes, who exercised command in pairs for periods of two months. They had the centurions as subalterns and the decurions each commanded groups of ten men. The senior centurion took the title of *primus pilus* and he was often the real commander of the legion since the tribunes were often inexperienced. The distinguishing marks of rank were expressed in the shape of ornamentation of the crest of the helmet. In Imperial Rome, ranks became further diversified. The armies were commanded by proconsuls, legions by legates and praetors, with the assistance of prefects who had responsibility for troop movements and encampment. Constantine created a *magister peditum*, or leader of the infantry, and a *magister equitum*, or commander of the cavalry. The prefects then took on various administrative functions and, towards the end of the Empire, their role eventually became to some extent that of a military governor. By the time the Empire fell, the old ranks had disappeared and the military leaders bore such titles as duke, count and patrician (*patricius*).

In medieval times in the West, the political leaders and the holders of the major offices at court were also military leaders. In other countries, where the armies were better organized, the military hierarchy was differentiated from the civil and social hierarchy. The officers in the Mongol army were originally elected but their posts became permanent and even hereditary. Above the *yuzbachi* (*centenar*), who continued to be elected, all appointments were in the hands of the khan. In Tamerlain's army, a unit of ten men was led by an *ombachi*, one of a hundred by a *yuzbachi* and one of a thousand by a *ginbachi*.

Under the early Capetian kings, the

French army was commanded by the seneschal; under Philip Augustus command passed to the constable, who had initially been the chief officer of the stables. The troops were raised by agents of the king called legates, who gradually took over command under the name of *bannerets*. The *maréchal de France* appeared as a military commander at the end of the twelfth century. Saint Louis created a second, Charles VII a third, Francis I a fourth and Charles IX a fifth. From the reign of Henry III onward, no limit was put on their numbers. Beneath the constable and the *Maréchal* there were officers performing temporary functions, including the *maréchal de camp général* who had the responsibility of ensuring orders were carried out, and a *commissaire général* who passed the orders to the cavalry *commandants* and to the *maréchaux des logis* (quartermasters) of the infantry. The companies were commanded by captains. Since there was no intermediate rank between general and captain, it was the most senior captain who had command of a 'troop', which grouped together several companies.

The captain who was the commander of an 'ordinance' (i.e. cavalry) company was assisted by a lieutenant, an ensign, a guidon and a *maréchal des logis*. The captain commanding a band of *francs-archers* had a lieutenant and an ensign under him, together with centenars, *cinquanteniers* and *dizeniers* to command the sub-divisions. Francis I created the legions in 1534. Each legion contained six bands. One of the six captains of the legion served as its colonel, while another assisted him as *mestre de camp* and a third as *sergent-major*. The captain commanding a band had under him two lieutenants, two ensigns, ten centenars, forty *caps d'escadre*, four quartermaster sergeants, six *sergents de bataille*, a provost marshal (*prévôt*), aided by four sergeants. The captains were appointed by the king and then chose their officers and men themselves.

The bands of Picardy and Piedmont had at their head a captain assisted by a lieutenant and an ensign. In 1508, twelve *lance-pessades* (anspessades) were added, which were posts reserved for young noblemen, and subsequently sergeants (who were officers) drawn from among the soldiers, and from the corporals, who were originally the agents of the provost marshal. With the creation of sergeants and corporals, the *centenars*, *cinquanteniers* and *caps d'escadre* gradually disappeared. At that time, the *fourrier* (quartermaster sergeant) also appeared, whose duties included the keeping of accounts. In the early sixteenth century in Spain, the companies were commanded by coroneles under the command of a coronel-general. The *tercio*, created in 1534, was commanded by a *maestro de campo*, assisted by a *sergeant-major* whose duties covered administration and training and a quartermaster-general responsible for billeting and encampment.

The term *colonel*, which is Spanish in origin, replaced the term *capitaine général* in the French army and was adopted in England in the sixteenth century. In French armies, this officer commanded a battalion, which was made up of a variable number of bands; he was assisted by a *mestre de camp*, a *sergeant-major* and a provost marshal. Like the *mestre de camp*, he also commanded his own band. The function was originally merely a temporary one, but on 22 May 1542, Francis I appointed a colonel general of the bands of Piedmont (east of the mountains) and, in 1544, a colonel general of the bands of Picardy (west of the mountains) and, in 1547, colonels general of the Italian and Corsican bands and of the *landsknechte*. The two offices relating to the French infantry were merged in 1571 and a colonel general of Swiss and Grisons troops was created. Subsequently, colonels general were created for the cavalry, the dragoons and the hussars. From the seventeenth century onwards, these offices became mainly honorary, as did that of Grand Master of the Artillery, which succeeded that of Grand Master of the Crossbowmen.

Generally speaking, each French army contained three *maréchaux de camp*, a title first identified in 1522, one in the vanguard and two in the main body. It was their task to handle matters of supply and billeting and to manage troop movements and the disposition of units on the battlefield. The constable commanded the vanguard while the king had command of the main body. Charles IX created a post of marshal general of the cavalry which was similar in nature to that of marshal general of the infantry. The *maréchal général des logis*, who came under the authority of a marshal, had responsibility for organizing marches and quartering. The *maréchal de bataille* was his adjutant in time of battle. Subsequently the marshals had under them *lieutenants généraux*, the first of whom was appointed in 1621.

The term *mestre de camp* appeared in 1547. This officer commanded the bands when the colonel general was absent. The company of the colonel general of the infantry was commanded by a lieutenant who was subsequently given the name of lieutenant-colonel and became the second in rank in the regiment. In the seventeenth century, the regiments were commanded by *mestres de camp* or by colonels (they bore this latter title when there was no colonel general).

When armies began to reach a considerable size, Louis XIV and Louvois gradually laid down a number of principles which were adopted abroad. The commissioned officers, who received their commissions from the king, were distinguished from the *officiers à la baguette* who were appointed by the regimental commander and were thus the officers of lesser rank. These appellations survive in the British Army where such officers are known as 'non-commissioned officers' or NCOs. There was no rank of 'battalion commander' or 'squadron commander', these units being commanded by the lieutenant-colonel or the senior captain. The regimental staff comprised a *sergent-major* of the rank of captain, who was later called *major*, an *aide-major* (adjutant) of the rank of lieutenant, a second *aide-major* (created in 1689), a *maréchal des logis* (quartermaster) of the rank of ensign, and an assistant provost marshal. In an infantry company, one found a captain, a lieutenant, an ensign, two sergeants, two or three corporals and four or six anspessades. With periodic decreases in the size of companies, the rank of ensign was on several occasions

abolished. A career structure was created which made it possible to bypass the purchasable offices of captain and colonel and therefore, to a certain extent, to circumvent the wealth barrier. This structure ran from lieutenant, through captain of grenadiers, *aide-major* and *major* (administrative functions) to lieutenant-colonel. The title of infantry, cavalry or dragoon brigadier which was conferred from 1668 onwards on certain colonels or lieutenant-colonels gave officers of great merit the opportunity of becoming a 'general officer'. The *ordre du tableau* of 1675 introduced promotion by seniority into the rules for promotion, though it did not exclude promotion by selection. In practice, the command of a group of similar units fell to the most senior officer of the highest rank. Lastly, rank or, where this was not possible, the status to which a rank would usually entitle the holder was conferred on the members of the most prestigious corps through a system of recognition of 'equivalent ranks'. Thus the king's lifeguards had equivalent status with non-commissioned officers in other units, the *exempts* (NCOs) with captains and the lieutenants with *mestres de camp*. The captains were chosen from among the marshals of France. These principles were also in force in the *Gardes françaises*. Later on, they were applied to the Imperial Guard.

There were few changes in the eighteenth century. The lowest officer rank, that of ensign in the infantry or cornet in the cavalry, disappeared in 1762 and was replaced by that of second lieutenant. Their functions were taken over by the 'colour bearer' (infantry), 'standard bearer' (cavalry) and the 'guidon' (dragoons) from among the NCOs. At the same time there appeared the quartermaster-treasurer who had charge of the regimental funds. The *aides-majors* and *sous-aides-majors* disappeared in 1776 and an increasing diversity of NCOs emerged. The *fourrier* (quartermaster), introduced in 1758, was responsible for the quartering of troops and the sergeant-major (or, in the cavalry, the *maréchal des logis-chef*), created in 1776, had responsibility for order, discipline, training and armament. The *adjudant*, who

355

appeared in the same year, was a member of the battalion staff. Having as his main task the training of the rank and file, he became the 'eyes' of the colonel. In 1776, a rank of second colonel was created, which was replaced in 1788 by that of a second major. These were ranks reserved for the sons of the upper nobility, men who were destined later to command regiments. In the same period, *colonels attachés* were also created. There were also supernumerary officers and, in the cavalry, *capitaines réformés* who were not on the active service list. They could of course subsequently be recalled to active service, as could the 'substitute' captains and second lieutenants. The officers of the army general staff were known by special names. There was, for example, a *major général des logis* of the army, *majors généraux* of the infantry, the cavalry and the dragoons, assisted by aides (officers on the active list or supernumeraries) who had 'equivalent' ranks, as was the case among the King's Household troops where the ranks of NCOs often corresponded in fact to field officer ranks and officer ranks to those of generals. The artillery officers who bore special names – *officier pointeur*, ordinary commissary and extraordinary commissary – were gradually brought into line with other officers, as were the royal engineers, but not the war commissaries, who were also known as provincial commissaries and commissaries-in-charge. Since all ranks had to wear uniform, the minister, d'Argenson, planned to differentiate commissioned officers from NCOs by the form of their gorgets and, in 1758, Marshal de Belle-Isle introduced different types of epaulettes for the different ranks. Choiseul made the wearing of these obligatory.

Under the revolutionary governments, the name of *chef de bataillon* reappeared, but this time as a replacement for the title 'lieutenant-colonel', while the colonel became a *chef de brigade*, the maréchal de camp *général de brigade* and the lieutenant general *général de division*. The ranks *maréchal de camp* and lieutenant general were revived on 16 May 1814 and finally abolished on 28 February 1848. The Revolution also created *adjudants-majors* who

were employed on the regimental staff and held the rank of lieutenant, and *adjudants-généraux* on the staffs of the larger units holding the rank of lieutenant-colonel or colonel. These latter subsequently came to be called *adjudants-commandants*. In 1790, the name of *bas-officier* was replaced by that of *sous-officier*.

Very few changes have been introduced during the nineteenth and twentieth centuries. The *chef de bataillon* has become distinct from the lieutenant-colonel and has replaced the rank of *major*. The rank of army corps general has been created, together with that of *aspirant*, a rank bestowed on a young officer, of *adjudant-chef* (created in 1912), *sergent-chef*, *caporal-chef* and *major*, the highest NCO rank, which was created in 1975. The rank of *sergent-major* which was held by soldiers employed in book-keeping duties was abolished.

The British army rank structure developed at the Restoration in 1660 and has scarcely changed since. Initially, the 2nd lieutenant in an infantry company was termed the ensign, and in the cavalry he was known as the cornet, but these nomenclatures gradually died out in the eighteenth century. The rank of field marshal was introduced in 1736. The development of the structure of military ranks in the major states has shown fewer and fewer local particularities since the seventeenth century. Around 1900, the ranks in almost all armies were similar to those in the French. In Britain rank and function may diverge considerably: within a single battalion, two or three companies may be commanded by majors and the others by captains. Similarly, general officers do not have functions specific to each rank, but undertake a variety of tasks at an appropriate level of responsiblility. In In terms of hierarchy, the US army took its lead from the British. In Russia, ranks were for many years predominantly titles and there was no clear correlation between rank and post. In Spain, it was possible for many years for officers to hold one or two honorary ranks which were higher than their substantive rank. The Belgian army has retained the Austrian army titles for its general officers (general major, lieutenant general). In the Swiss army, the title 'general' is reserved for the commander-in-chief of the army on a war footing. The highest rank in peacetime is that of colonel. Depending on their particular posts, the colonels are called *colonel brigadiers*, *colonels divisionnaires* or *colonels commandants de corps d'armée*. *See also* ADMINISTRATION, ARMY; ADMINISTRATION, NAVAL; FAMILIES; PROMOTION; RECRUITMENT; TACTICAL ORGANIZATION; TRAINING.

A. CORVISIER

FURTHER READING
W. B. R. Hill, 'Brevet rank', *JSAHR*, xlviii (1970), pp. 85–104; T. H. McGuffie, 'The significance of military rank in the British army between 1790 and 1820', *BIHR*, xxx (1957), 207–24; I. F. Burton and A. N. Newman, 'Sir John Cope: promotion in the 18th century army', *EHR*, lxxviii (1963), pp. 655–68.

Hindenburg, Paul von Beneckendorff und von (1847–1934) Having fought in Prussia's wars against Austria (1866) and France (1870–1), Hindenburg subsequently served on the General Staff and was commanding IV Army Corps at the time of his retirement in 1911. He was recalled to the active list on 22 August 1914 to command the 8th Army in East Prussia where he replaced General von Prittwitz, who had been dismissed for withdrawing before a Russian offensive. In fact, von Prittwitz had already determined to counter-attack before his removal and Hindenburg and his chief of staff, Major-General Erich Ludendorff, inherited the offensive plans which had been drawn up by Colonel Max Hoffmann. The subsequent encircling operations resulted in the defeat of the Russian Second Army at Tannenberg in August and of the Russian First Army around the Masurian Lakes in September 1914. On 28 August 1916, Hindenburg succeeded Erich von Falkenhayn, with whose strategy he disagreed, as Chief of the German General Staff. Ludendorff accompanied him in the position of First Quartermaster General and, to a large extent, manipulated his superior. Faced

with a weakened government, Hindenburg and Ludendorff created what has been described as a 'silent dictatorship' enjoying a critical influence over both foreign and domestic policy, not least in the formulation of war aims. Opponents such as the Chancellor, Bethmann-Hollweg, were eased from office. Despite the massive failure of Hindenburg and Ludendorff to preserve Germany, Hindenburg was regarded as a living symbol of the tenacity and valour of the German army. While Ludendorff's resignation was accepted in October 1918, Hindenburg remained in office until July 1919. Elected President of the Weimar Republic in April 1925 and re-elected in 1932, Hindenburg remained a monarchist at heart. As President, he appointed Hitler to the Chancellorship in January 1933. *See also* GERMANY; LUDENDORFF; TANNENBERG (1914).

B. KROENER
IAN F. W. BECKETT

FURTHER READING
Eugène Carrias, *La Pensée militaire allemande* (Paris, 1948); Martin Kitchen, *The Silent Dictatorship* (London, 1976); Martin Kitchen, 'Hindenburg', in *Soldiers as Statesmen*, ed. Peter Dennis and Adrian Preston (London, 1976), pp. 55–78; John Wheeler-Bennett, *The Wooden Titan* (2nd edn, London, 1967).

Hitler, Adolf (1889–1945) Hitler was born in Braunau on the Austro-German border. He was educated at Linz and twice competed unsuccessfully for a place at the Academy of Fine Arts in Vienna. Having a modest inheritance, Hitler lived in Vienna from 1908 to 1913, imbibing the anti-Semitism and German nationalism prevalent at the time. In 1913, Hitler moved to Munich to avoid military service in the Austro-Hungarian forces. But, in 1914, he enlisted in the German army, was twice decorated for bravery, finally reaching the rank of corporal. Hitler was gassed in 1918 and temporarily blinded. When the war ended, he remained in the army and was assigned to keep watch on the many revolutionary parties flourishing in Munich. In the autumn of 1919, Hitler joined what would shortly become the National Socialist German Workers' Party (Nazis). His oratorical skills soon won him a prominent position in the Party. In 1923, Hitler led the Nazis' paramilitary force, the *Sturmabteilung* (SA), in a failed *putsch*, an action which resulted in his being sent to gaol. During his time in prison, Hitler wrote *Mein Kampf*, a book outlining his views on politics and the future of Germany. The Nazi Party was unsuccessful until the Great Depression. By September 1930, the Nazis were the second largest party in Germany and Hitler was appointed Chancellor in January 1933. He moved ruthlessly to consolidate power and, by 1934, Germany had become a one-party state. Hitler had the officer corps of the German army swear an oath of personal allegiance to him. From 1934 to 1938, Hitler strengthened the German armed forces, beginning a massive plan of rearmament and gradually repudiating the clauses of the Treaty of Versailles that limited Germany's armed might. In 1936, German troops reoccupied the Rhineland and in 1938 an *Anschluss* with Austria occurred. Later that year, Nazi Germany annexed part of Czechoslovakia under the terms of the Munich settlement. In August 1939, Hitler's representatives negotiated the Nazi-Soviet Non-aggression Pact with Stalin's Russia, clearing the way for the invasion of Poland and the outbreak of the Second World War. Hitler was an advocate of mechanized warfare and close land–air co-operation. This style of warfare, known as blitzkrieg (lightning war), proved highly effective. The rapid victory in Poland was followed by similar successes against Norway (April 1940) and France (May–June 1940). When the German air force was unable to subdue the British, Hitler turned the German army against the Soviet Union. The invasion was launched on 22 June 1941. By December, the Germans had invested Leningrad, taken Kiev and were at the gates of Moscow. A strong Soviet counter-attack at Moscow ended the German hope of victory in one short campaign, but Hitler took personal command of the German army and his decision that German troops should stand fast prevented any major Soviet success. In 1942, Hitler

made Rostov, Stalingrad and the oil fields of the Caucasus the German target. Despite initial successes, the German Sixth Army was surrounded at Stalingrad. Hitler ordered it to stand fast but the Sixth Army was forced to surrender in February 1943, a major setback. In a final attempt to win the war in the east, Hitler authorized an assault on the Soviet salient at Kursk. The stalemate there in July 1943 was the turning point. The Germans never recovered from their losses and 1944 and 1945 were years of retreat. Hitler's health declined during these years and he became progressively detached from reality. Hitler committed suicide in April 1945. *See also* GERMANY; GUDERIAN; KURSK SALIENT; MANSTEIN; MOSCOW, BATTLE OF; RUNDSTEDT; STALINGRAD.

KEITH NEILSON

FURTHER READING
Alan Bullock, *Hitler: a study in tyranny* (Harmondsworth, 1967); Joachim Fest, *Hitler: a biography* (New York, 1970); David Irving, *Hitler's War* (London, 1977).

Hittites Though less well known than the Assyrians and the Persians, the Hittites nevertheless played a considerable role in the development of the art of war in the Ancient World. These Indo-Europeans who arrived in the Near East by stages and settled in Asia Minor around 2000 BC, under King Mursilis I (*c*.1620–1590 BC) destroyed the powerful kingdom of Babylon founded by Hammurabi and created a state in Anatolia which reached its peak under Suppiluliumas I (*c*.1380), who dominated Mesopotamia and Syria. It was the Hittites who under Muwatallis halted the expansion of Ramesses II at the Battle of Kadesh (*c*.1300). The most important section of the Hittite people, its aristocracy, remained a separate class, many of them owning large estates granted as fiefs by the king. The assembly of the *Pankus*, which consisted of fighting men, servants and grandees, could act as a court of law and also ensured that the contracts binding vassals to their sovereign were respected; the vassals promised fidelity, the payment of a tribute and military aid, but only in return for protection and good government.

The Hittites were technologically far more advanced than their enemies in that they made well-controlled use of horses and also employed iron. Their iron-smiths had succeeded in quenching steel using techniques which were kept secret. Both by their quality and lightness, their blade weapons outclassed those made of bronze, just as their carefully selected and well-trained horses outclassed asses and onagers by their speed and hardiness. The archives at Boghazköy contain a treatise of the fourteenth century BC by Kikkuli of the land of Mitanni, on the care and training of horses. Similarly, they built light chariots of a wholly new design with two, six-spoke wheels instead of four solid wheels as used by their enemies. Each chariot contained three men – the driver, the archer and the shield-bearer – to form a unit which excelled in terms of speed, surprise and shock effect. The main weapons were the lance and the bow, with a rectangular shield, sometimes designed like the head of a double axe.

The chariotry was the preserve of the nobility. It was reinforced by infantry made up of mercenaries, vassals and allies. At Kadesh, the Hittites are said to have had 3,500 chariots and 8,000 infantrymen in the field. A relief from the 'King's gate' at Boghazköy suggests that some infantrymen wore a short belted kilt and helmet with plume and ear protectors, and carried a small axe and curved sword. The Hittites did not employ cavalry, though there were some lightly armed mounted troops (*Sutu*) used for rapid surprise attacks. Based in fortresses and entrenched camps (the Hittites were skilled in the art of military fortifications, as the massive remains of the defensive walls at Boghazköy show), the Hittite warriors were mobilized in summer either for general manoeuvres or for war. They were subject to strict discipline. Troops were brought together at concentration points which were well ordered in terms of transport and supplies. There were pioneers to prepare the way for the army and to serve in sieges. The use of new techniques and their level of organization, explain the Hittites' strategy, which was based on mobility. The peoples who surrendered to them were spared and took an oath of allegiance, while those who did not were pillaged, after which the booty was carefully divided. The indisputable superiority of the Hittites came to an end when the neighbouring peoples adopted their technical innovations. *See also* ASSYRIANS; EGYPT, ANCIENT; KADESH.

A. CORVISIER
B. CAMPBELL

FURTHER READING
J.-F. Rolland, 'Aristocrates et mercenaires du Moyen-Orient', in *Histoire universelle des armées*, ed. J. Boudet (4 vols, Paris, 1965–66), i; O. R. Gurney, *The Hittites* (Harmondsworth, repr. 1966).

Holy War The military clash between religions has often proved a potent inspiration for warriors. Islam and Christianity have both fought each other in holy wars although the degree and nature of their motivation has differed.

Harb al Muqadasa, Holy War, is often confused with *Jihad fi Sabil Allah*, effort directed along the path of God, which elevates the Muslim to a state transcending politics and earthly concerns. The *Jihad* is the driving force and justification for the battle of Islam against unbelief. Islam divided the world into those regions where Islam prevailed, called *dar al-Islam* (the world of Islam), and those yet to be converted, *dar al-Harb* (the world of war). Enduring peace between the two was impossible and the result was incessant warfare along the Christian and Muslim frontiers. Mohammed preached that the *Jihad* was one of the five obligations of the true believer. The very act of taking part in the *Jihad* ensures that the faithful Muslim will enter paradise if he falls in battle. Those among the vanquished who are converted to Islam become the equals of the victors and share the rights and duties of the *Jihad*. When conquest has been accomplished, those who do not convert may retain their own faiths and enjoy a certain measure of protection so long as they pay tribute, but they have none of the rights accorded to the faithful. However, a distinction is made between pagans and monotheists. Arabs, to whom Allah first directed his message, are dealt with harshly if they refuse to accept Islam, whereas monotheistic Jews and Christians are treated somewhat better as their religions lean towards Islam. Nevertheless, any form of resistance or revolt places the infidels beyond the law and, in the eyes of the believers, justifies massacre which can also be carried out as a preventive measure (the Christians in the Balkans, the Armenians in 1916).

The power to proclaim holy war belonged to the descendants of the Prophet, the Caliphs, and was one of the principal factors in Arab and Muslim territorial expansion. Being also temporal sovereigns, they could declare holy war when their states were in political conflict with infidel powers (the Sultan of Turkey in 1914). The Turkish Caliphs' call to holy war was directed, in theory, to the whole of Islam but, in practice, it only applied to the Muslims of the Ottoman Empire. Occasionally, it awakened a sense of solidarity amongst other Muslim peoples. Some African prophets (*Mahdis*) have proclaimed holy wars (Mohammed Ali in 1881–5 against the British in Sudan). Besides full-scale *Jihad*, other wars against infidels have assumed a certain sacred character. In the early fourteenth century, Barbary piracy made its appearance and was conducted as a veiled holy war against unbelievers.

Christianity has also fought to convert or exterminate non-believers. The clearest examples were the wars fought by Charlemagne against the Saxons, conflicts which were later carried on by the Knights of the Teutonic Order against Prussia and the Baltic lands. After achieving conversion, these wars degenerated into conquest. The Crusades to the Holy Land were different in character. Their deeper origins are found in the ecclesiastical prescriptions of the ninth century which sanctified battle against the infidel to order to protect Christians who were suffering oppression, but when the Byzantine Emperor Nicephorus II Phocas sought to have soldiers killed in battle against Muslims

regarded as martyrs he met with resistance from the Church (tenth century). However, Pope John VIII granted absolution to warriors who might die defending Christians against Saracens. More precisely, in 1063, Pope Alexander II applied this absolution to those who were fighting the Moors in Spain. After the Battle of Manzikert (1071), the threatened Byzantine Empire called on the Pope for assistance but the plan failed. Whether or not he had been called upon by Emperor Alexius I Comnenus, in 1095 Pope Urban II preached the First Crusade, the starting point of five centuries of effort initially intended to keep open the possibility of making pilgrimages to Jerusalem and, later, to contain the thrust of the Turks towards Europe.

The vows of the Crusader were different from those of the pilgrim, which did not permit him to take up arms. Saint Bernard compared the Crusader's vow to taking holy orders. The Crusader received certain privileges whilst his family and possessions were placed under the protection of the Church. The expeditions against the Muslims in Spain were placed on the same footing as the Crusades to recover Jerusalem and the Iberian Crusaders were awarded the same privileges (1147). Lesser indulgences, equivalent to those earned by a pilgrimage to Rome, were granted to men who fought to defend the young Christian communities in the Baltic countries. The Crusades spawned religious and military orders: the Templars, the Hospitallers and the Knights of St Mary's Hospital at Jerusalem. The latter were transplanted to the Baltic, where they merged with the Knights of the Sword and the survivors of the orders of Santiago, Alcántara and Calatrava from Spain to form the Teutonic Knights. The Hospitallers, who took refuge in Malta, continued the fight against Islam by combatting the Barbary pirates at sea. Crusades were also preached against the Albigensian heretics (1209–31) and even against the temporal enemies of the Papal States. The Crusader spirit revived momentarily with the Turkish threat against Constantinople (1453) and Vienna

(1683). *See also* DORYLAEUM; ETHOS; LAWS OF WAR; MANZIKERT; MIDDLE EAST; OTTOMAN TURKS; SPAIN.

A. CORVISIER

FURTHER READING
E. Christiansen, *The Northern Crusades: the Baltic and the Catholic frontier, 1100–1525* (London, 1980); Steven Runciman, *A History of the Crusades* (3 vols, Cambridge, 1951–5); Eric Carlton, *War and Ideology* (London, 1990).

Honours and awards In the era of the Roman Republic, successful soldiers could look forward to a share of the booty as well as decorations for bravery. Julius Caesar celebrated his victory at Thapsus (46 BC) by presenting 20,000 sesterces to each of his veterans, twice that amount to his centurions and quadruple to the tribunes of the legions. During the Empire the opportunities for gaining booty through warfare diminished and emperors kept their soldiers happy by making peacetime handouts (donatives), often equal to five years' pay. Donatives were usually made when a new emperor came to the throne, and after the death of Nero (AD 68), when four emperors succeeded one another in rapid succession, the donative was an important political tool. The Praetorian Guard was offered ten years' pay to support Galba's claim to the throne (AD 68); Galba's non-payment of the promised donative was a principal cause of his assassination by the Praetorians in the following year. Under the Republic, military decorations were won on merit regardless of rank (javelins of honour, decorative bosses for shields, silver and gold cups). The Empire was more hierarchical and certain decorations were reserved for officers of particular rank (gold and silver medals, crowns of gold and oak leaves, torques and armbands). In addition to pecuniary rewards and medals, after maximum service of 25 years soldiers retired and received either a grant of land, usually in a frontier military colony, or a gratuity.

The award of medals encouraged a desire to emulate the feats of others; retirement gratuities promoted the successful integration of the retired legionary into civil life

and the continuance of a hereditary military calling; donatives purchased, for several months, the loyalty of an army in the eventuality of a new war between Romans. In general, however, the different types of military honours and awards have to some extent merged with one another. Awards of honours have often in history brought with them a rise in the social hierarchy or carried at least a pension; there have been cases too where regimes that fear for their future have decorated their supporters, and have not merely divided amongst them the material spoils of power.

Hence, the majority of the orders of chivalry established in the monarchical European states of the Middle Ages and early modern period were destined gradually to degenerate. They were conceived at the outset as a fellowship of a limited number of warriors, all fired by the same spirit of sacrifice to an ideal; but, in the end, they were used as a way of honouring leading servants of the state, whether their posts had been of a military character or otherwise. Ranks made their appearance in the orders and then blossomed out into a whole hierarchy of dignities and offices; inevitably, promotions tended to be based on length of service. In France, the *Ordre de l'Étoile* was too short-lived to fall away from the ideals of religion and chivalry which had inspired its founder, John the Good. But the *Ordre de Saint-Michel*, founded in 1469 by Louis XI, and even the *Ordre du Saint-Esprit*, established by Henry III in 1578, served little purpose other than to build up a trustworthy circle around the king, and one which imposed a heavy burden on the state finances. The same was true of the Dukes of Burgundy's *Order of the Golden Fleece*.

In Britain the orders of chivalry have endured to the present day, due to the continuity in British social and political life and the fact that the military orders had lost many of their strictly martial connotations by the sixteenth century (Order of the Garter, 1344; Order of the Bath, 1399; Order of the Thistle, 1687; Order of St Patrick, 1788). Throughout the nineteenth and into the twentieth century, Britain has continued to create orders of chivalry to reward long and distinguished service in both military and civilian life (Order of St Michael and St George, 1818; Order of the Star of India, 1861; Order of the Indian Empire, 1877; Royal Victoria Order, 1896; Order of Merit, 1902). With the exception of the latter, these orders are sub-divided into three or five classes.

When the military calling began to take on a professional form, there was felt a need to give those who served an award which was peculiar to them and which would encourage them to continue with their careers. The royal and military *Order de Saint-Louis*, founded by the edict of April 1692, at first took into account merely length of service; in the end, there was even a regulation laying down the seniority in rank required for the award of the cross. The rituals of this order differed from those of its predecessors, in that the Church played no part in them. The king alone presided and it was to him that the oath was sworn. The members of the order could not owe allegiance to any other authority; hence, Knights of Malta were not admitted. Another new departure was that possession of noble birth was not a condition of membership. Louis XIV and his successors brought together, as joint celebrants of their glory, the sons of the old military nobility and officers who were commoners, without any other consideration than merit. The members had to profess the Catholic faith. In order to be able to reward Protestant foreigners, Louis XV created the *Ordre du Mérite militaire*, which came under the same regulations and administration. The *Ordre de Saint-Louis* served as a model for the foundation of such others as the Order of the Sword in Sweden (1748), of St George in Russia (1769) and of Merit in Prussia (which was restricted to military members in 1810).

An idea that began to gain support at this time was the desirability of providing some compensation for the risks inherent in military life in the shape of welfare benefits, some of which would be transferable to widows and children. The giving of retirement pensions to officers gradually became a standard practice. Other ranks, too, found the state prepared to recognize its indebtedness. For example, the authorities in charge of Les Invalides were instructed in 1764 to pension its old soldiers, who received full pay after 24 years of service and half-pay after 16. On the other hand, when an officer died, his sons – if they had already taken up a military career – were often accorded the privilege of drawing a part of the allowances previously paid to him.

In a society of sharply defined social strata like France under the *ancien régime*, the most gratifying award, and at the same time the most profitable one, remained the grant of a hereditary title of nobility. However, although there was a profusion of those who had been ennobled on account of their civilian posts, military officers who had been admitted to that rank by a personal decision on the king's part were quite rare. To issue a few documents conferring titles of nobility, which generally gave a list of the whole family's services, was viewed as merely a matter of correcting an anomaly; it seemed quite improper that a *maréchal de camp* should be a commoner. Perhaps the traditional requirement for all officers to be noble – to which its supporters from time to time called attention, but which was always being infringed – delayed the establishment of a military nobility. It was not until the edict of November 1750 that all general officers and all other officers whose fathers and grandfathers had, owing to length of service, received exemption for life from taxation were ennobled, provided that they themselves had received the Cross of St Louis. About 200 families acquired military nobility before the Revolution, though a privileged position which had been attained purely by a legal fiat was insufficient to procure them immediate acceptance into the society of the established nobility. In a state such as Prussia, where those who possessed nobility by birth had retained all their traditional prerogatives, there was pressure to ensure that ennobled officers who came from the middle class were kept in subordinate posts and possessed only a very limited social influence.

Throughout the whole of the period preceding the French Revolution, the views of official departments and of military men were out of step with each other; the former increasingly viewed merit and length of service as identical, while the latter stressed instead outstanding feats of arms as being deserving of reward. Vauban carefully listed in his *Oisivetés* the noteworthy actions which, in his opinion, should be taken into account for promoting officers or for awarding other ranks a period of leave in advance of the time due. It became commonplace, at the end of the *ancien régime*, for demands along these lines to be put forward; there were visions of simple grenadiers being made officers by their colonel after an assault on a fortress. But the organizational and social structure of the army in monarchical times was not of a type to work in favour of such spectacular rises in rank.

Matters were quite otherwise in the army of the Revolution and the Empire. Citizens who took up arms in defence of the country and of liberty were not assumed to have any interest in making a military career; to arouse a spirit of emulation among such soldiers, commissioners attached to armies presented in Year II some 'swords of honour' to battalions which had particu-larly distinguished themselves. Later, Bonaparte made a systematic use of this method in the shape of personal awards during his campaigns in Italy and Egypt, and subsequently the Consulate accorded official recognition to such honours, which had been given, since 1792, solely to those who had performed feats of arms. Between 1800 and 1804, a modest-sized company of 2,104 heroes had come into being. At first, they were merely granted double pay but, later, they were put into the lowest grade of imperial honours, most of the holders of which were in the army. In 1814, in fact, 87 per cent of the members of the *Légion d'honneur* were in the armed forces, as were 59 per cent of those ennobled under the Empire. As the heir of the Jacobins, Bonaparte at first gave ordinary soldiers the same type of awards as Scipio Aemilianus; when he became the new Caesar, Napoleon presented imperial eagles to his regiments on the morrow of his coronation but he also gave his generals, on whom land, pensions and titles had already been showered, a leading position in the aristocracy which he intended to establish.

An array of British medals from the Second World War. Among the most notable are (*top row from the left*) the Victoria Cross, the Distinguished Service Order, the Military Cross, the Distinguished Flying Cross, the Air Force Cross; (*middle row, left*) Military Medal. (M.A.R.S.)

Since the beginning of the nineteenth century, French decorations have reflected the enduring continuity of meritorious conduct on the part of individuals and also the insecure nature of political institutions. The effigies change – the obverse shows Napoleon, Henry IV or the Republic, the reverse, the eagle, the lilies or the flags. On the other hand, the mottoes remain unchanged. 'Honour and native land' continue to appear on the insignia of the *Légion d'honneur*; so do 'Courage and discipline' on the *Médaille militaire*, which dates from 1852 and which is awarded to senior NCOs and other ranks, as well as to officers in general, for length of service or for distinguished conduct in the field.

With the development of conscription and of a national army, there appeared a number of service or campaign medals which all ex-soldiers are entitled to wear. Medals of this type are too commonplace to give those who possess them any standing; but men in political positions sometimes make use of them to give fresh life to a military glory of which they claim to be the inheritors. Napoleon III, for example, in 1857 created a St Helena medal for the surviving members of the old Imperial army.

Decorations awarded for courageous acts during a war come into a quite different category, examples being the Prussian Iron Cross, created in 1813, the British Victoria Cross (1856) and the French *Croix de guerre*. In France, since the period of the First Empire, outstanding actions have been the subject of individual, or collective, citations – devoted, in the latter case, to a regiment, a brigade, a division, a corps or an army. These take the form of a text giving the reasons for the award and the wearing of a *Croix de guerre* or a *Croix de la valeur militaire*; the palm, for citations in army orders, and the lanyard, worn in certain units that have received honours on several occasions, add to the lustre given by the exceptional tributes. These are frequently given posthumously. This proves that, despite political changes which sometimes cause a reduction in the standing of military decorations and titles, the modern era remains faithful to the age of chivalry's ideal of disinterested self-sacrifice.

British decorations for gallantry have followed a similar pattern with different awards applicable to particular ranks and services. Only the Victoria Cross (1856) and the Military Division of the George Cross (1940) can be won by all ranks. The Distinguished Service Order (DSO) can be awarded to commissioned officers of all three services; the Distinguished Service Cross (DSC) to naval and marine officers below the relative rank of lieutenant-commander and to warrant officers; the Military Cross (MC) to army officers below the rank of captain and to warrant officers; the Distinguished Flying Cross (DFC) to officers and warrant officers of the Royal Air Force. For other ranks, the Royal Air Force awards the Air Force Cross (AFC) and the Distinguished Flying Medal (DFM); the Distinguished Conduct Medal (DCM) and the Military Medal (MM) are given by the army; whilst the navy and the marines grant the Conspicuous Gallantry Medal (CGM) and the Distinguished Service Medal (DSM). The George Medal (GM) is awarded to civilians for valour. There are also medals for long service and good conduct which were instituted by the army in 1830, the navy in 1831 and the Royal Air Force in 1919. *See also* ESPRIT DE CORPS; ETHOS; GLORY; KNIGHTS AND CHIVALRY; MORALE; PENSIONS; PROMOTION; VETERANS; VEXILLOLOGY.

J. CHAGNIOT
JOHN CHILDS

FURTHER READING
L. L. Gordon, *British Battles and Medals* (4th edn, London, 1971); P. E. Abbott and J. M. A. Tamplin, *British Gallantry Awards* (London, 1971); J. H. Mayo, *Medals and Decorations of the British Army and Navy* (2 vols, London, 1897); A. R. Litherland and B. T. Simpkin, *Standard Catalogue of British and Associated Orders, Decorations and Medals* (London, 1990).

Hulegu (1217–65) Hulegu Khan, the grandson of Genghis Khan and the supreme commander of the Mongol forces in western Asia, is famed for having destroyed Alamut and other fortresses of the Ismailite sect – the Assassins – in

Mazandaran (1256) and, more particularly, for having taken Baghdad in 1258, where he put an end to the Abbasid caliphate and destroyed the city. He also captured Aleppo and Damascus. Muslims were the victims of his conquests; Christians were spared. In 1259 Hulegu's brother, the Great Khan Mongke, died in China so Hulegu returned to the East leaving only a remnant of his army in Syria. *See also* AIN DJALOUT; GENGHIS KHAN; MONGOLS; TAMERLAIN.

R. MANTRAN

FURTHER READING
The Cambridge History of Iran, ed. J. A. Boyle (Cambridge, 1968), vol. v; B. Lewis, *The Assassins: a radical sect in Islam* (London, 1967); J. J. Saunders, *The History of the Mongol Conquests* (London, 1971); David Morgan, *The Mongols* (Oxford, 1986).

Hungary The forebears of the present-day Hungarians occupied the Hungarian Plain under the leadership of Prince Arpad at the end of the ninth century AD. In the following century, Hungarian warriors conducted pillaging campaigns into Italy, German and French territories and against the Byzantine Empire. The Battle of Augsburg of 955, at which Emperor Otto I defeated the Hungarians, put an end to their westward incursions.

With the first Hungarian king, Stephen I (or Istvan or Vajk) (997–1038), a member of the Arpad dynasty, the Christian state of Hungary was formed. From that point onward, it was to be Hungary's fate to fight a great number of wars against her neighbours: in the east against the succeeding waves of invaders from Asia and, in the west, against the Holy Roman Empire, which aimed to reduce Hungary to a subject state. A brief enumeration of these wars is essential if we are to understand the military role of Hungary in Europe. In the eleventh century, the army of the young Hungarian kingdom successfully resisted successive invasions by the German Emperors.

In the twelfth century, Hungarian warriors fought wars against the Russian principalities and defended themselves against the Byzantine threat. In 1096, 1147 and 1188, the Crusaders crossed Hungary on their way to the Holy Land. In 1217, the Hungarian king Andrew (Endre or Andras) II was himself the leader of a short crusade. The Mongols arrived in Hungary in 1241 and, at the Battle of Mohi, they annihilated the army of Bela IV. They invaded the country and laid it waste, but departed again a few months later. As had been the case after the Hungarian incursions into Western Europe three centuries before, a wave of castle-building in Hungary followed this Mongol invasion.

The line of Arpad died out in 1301 and, after a civil war, the Angevin monarch, Charles I (Karoly Robert or Carobert of Anjou) strengthened the central government. His son, Louis the Great (Lajos Nagy), fought several wars in an attempt to conquer the Kingdom of Naples. At the end of the century, a new enemy appeared in the south of the Hungarian kingdom: the Turks. In 1396, a Christian coalition was formed against them. To King Sigismund's warriors, numbering between twelve and fourteen thousand, were added some one thousand French knights. At Nicopolis, however, Sultan Bayezid I scattered the Christian army.

In the middle of the fifteenth century, John (or János) Hunyadi, a talented military leader who had gained his military experience as a *condottiere* in Italy and in the wars against the Hussites, led the Hungarian army against the Turks. After the successes of the 'long campaign' of 1443, in the following year he was defeated at the Battle of Varna, at which King Vladislas I of the Jagiellion dynasty met his death. Hunyadi defeated the sultan in 1456, three years after the fall of Constantinople, beneath the walls of Belgrade castle, but he died of the plague three weeks later. His son, King Matthias I Corvinus (or Matyas Corvin) (1458–90), formed a permanent army of mercenaries, the famous 'Black Army', and occupied a part of Bohemia and Vienna.

In 1526, at the Battle of Mohács, the Hungarian army was destroyed by the Turks. King Louis II died, along with 7 bishops, 28 barons and most of his army

(4,000 cavalry and 10,000 infantry). In the decades that followed, the Turks occupied central Hungary and the royal capital of Buda, which had fallen into their hands in 1541 without a siege. After the failed siege of Vienna in 1529, Süleyman launched a new campaign three years later against the Austrian capital, but he avoided engaging Charles V's army in battle. After this, he chose not to attack Austria, but fought several major campaigns in Hungary, until his death beneath the walls of Szigetvar castle in 1566. Along the border between Christian and Turkish Hungary two chains of castles sprung up during the sixteenth century and skirmishing continued between their garrisons even in periods of relative peace, causing the country to be devastated. After the 'long war' (1593–1606), the status quo was re-established: with a balance achieved between the various forces, the Turks settled in to a lasting military occupation. The rulers of Transylvania launched wars against the Habsburgs with the support of the Hungarian nobles (István Bocskai, Gábor Bethlen, György Rákóczi).

Yet again, the Turkish empire attempted to conquer Vienna. After the Battle of the Kahlenberg (1683) and the Turkish defeat, a European coalition formed to liberate Hungary. Buda was recaptured in 1686 and, after a long war in which the chief battles were those of Szalánkemén in 1691 and Zenta in 1697, the Turks withdrew from Hungary and the country became a subject state of the Habsburg emperors of Austria.

In the favourable military situation created by the War of the Spanish Succession, a war of independence broke out against the Habsburgs (1703–11) and Ferenc II Rákóczi was elected prince of Transylvania and Hungary. At the beginning of the war, there were some 60,000 or 70,000 soldiers in his army, which was made up of regular and irregular troops. Light cavalry were the dominant force within that army; its weak link was the artillery.

For seven centuries Hungary had been a land of confrontation between the armies of Christian Europe and those of invaders from Asia. It thus played an important role in the exchanges of military techniques and tactical ideas between east and west, a role it continued to exercise in the following period.

I. G. TÓTH

After the failure of Rákóczi's attempt to liberate the country in 1711, there was for a long period no independent Hungarian state, nor an Hungarian army. Within the framework of the Habsburg army, the Hungarian regiments of hussars and haiduks were organized and their forces, comprising 12 regiments of hussars and 16 infantry regiments at the end of the Napoleonic Wars, amounted to a quarter of the Imperial army. These regiments were recruited on what was historically Hungarian territory and their uniforms and, in part, their armament were different from those of other regiments. In the beginning, the language of command was Hungarian and several elements of Hungarian military terminology have been borrowed by other European languages (e.g. hussar, shako). The Hungarian regiments were under the control of the Army Council in Vienna. They took part in the wars of the Habsburg Empire and lost at least 150,000 soldiers in the wars against the French Revolution and Napoleon.

In the spring of 1848, revolution broke out in Hungary. A Hungarian government was formed. Within a few months, a Hungarian army was created out of battalions from imperial regiments and soldiers recruited in Hungary. This basically new army reached 156 battalions and 18 regiments of hussars by the summer of 1849, making a total of 200,000 soldiers and a substantial artillery. This army fought most effectively against the Imperial army, and the Habsburgs were only able to defeat it by drawing on support from the army of the Russian tsar.

After 1849, the unity of the Habsburg army was re-established and several new Hungarian regiments were organized, military service having become compulsory in 1852. After the Austro-Hungarian compromise of 1867, a Royal Hungarian Army was organized as an independent part of the

Imperial army. This contained infantry and cavalry and, after 1912, artillery.

In 1914, 47 regiments of infantry, 8 battalions of light infantry, 16 regiments of hussars of the Imperial army, 32 infantry regiments and 10 regiments of hussars of the Royal army were recruited within the territory of Hungary.

In autumn 1918, at the end of the First World War, a revolution broke out in Hungary and on 21 March 1919, the Soviet Republic was proclaimed. This Soviet Republic organized its own army, which fought against the Czechs and the Romanians who invaded the country, but it eventually succumbed to the superior military force of the Entente powers. By the Trianon Treaty, Hungary lost two-thirds of its territory, its army was limited to 35,000 soldiers and it was allowed neither armoured divisions nor an air force. The army, which was made up of professional soldiers, again began to develop after 1938. Because of financial problems and its lack of industrial potential, Hungary was not able to create a truly modern army. It fought in the war against the Soviet Union from 1941 onwards (having three armies in the field in 1944) and was re-equipped on the Soviet model after the Second World War. *See also* AUSTRIA; EUGENE OF SAVOY; FRONTIERS; GERMANY; HUSSARS; MONGOLS; NICOPOLIS; OTTOMAN TURKS; ST GOTTHARD ABBEY; VIENNA; ZENTA.

J. BORUS

FURTHER READING
Christopher Duffy, *The Army of Maria Theresa* (London, 1977); G. E. Rothenberg, *The Army of Francis Joseph* (West Lafayette, Ind., 1976); *War and Society in East Central Europe*, eds B. K. Király and G. E. Rothenberg, i (New York, 1979), pp. 67–111; *War and Society in East Central Europe*, eds B. K. Király, P. Pastor and I. Sanders, vi (New York, 1982).

Hussars In fifteenth-century Poland, hussars, in the form of heavy cavalry and infantry, were raised to fight the Turk but this was a false beginning for the history of hussars in European armies. At the same time, hussars appeared as auxiliary light cavalry in Hungary during the reign of Matthias I Corvinus (1458–90).

Etymologists are divided over the derivation of the word 'hussar'. For a long time it was thought that its origin was to be found in the prefix 'husz', which, in Magyar, means 'twenty'. Thus, a hussar might be a soldier raised by taking each twentieth man, one man paid twenty kreutzers or an officer commanding twenty men. Today, many scholars believe that the word is from the Latin 'cursus', meaning 'raid', and that it passed into the Hungarian language by way of the Croatians. From this root also springs 'kuruts', a description of the Hungarian rebels who were adept at long-distance raiding.

When recruited in the fifteenth century, hussars were irregular horsemen paid for the duration of a single campaign. Gradually they came to be formed into regular regiments on account of their cheapness and bravery. Following the death of Ferenc I Rákóczi in 1676 and the failure of the Hungarians to acquire independence from Austria (1676–81), many Hungarian refugees joined other European armies including those of Austria, the German and Italian states, Spain, Portugal, Prussia, the United Provinces, Denmark, Sweden, Russia, Great Britain, Poland and France.

In 1692, Baron de Cronenberg, acting on the authority of Louis XIV, raised a unit of German and Hungarian hussars. This was the beginning of a series of hussar regiments in the eighteenth-century French army. However, although the initial regiments were formed from exiled Hungarians, they were increasingly recruited from among deserters from enemy armies and, after 1750, from Rhinelanders and men from the eastern provinces of France. By 1786, there were only 45 Hungarians out of a total of 6,320 hussars. Despite a uniform which recalled their Hungarian origins, the 14 hussar regiments in the army in 1812 were definitely French. Consequently, their numbers have fluctuated to meet the needs of various campaigns: 6 in 1815; 8 in 1870; 17 in 1915; 4 in 1922; 9 in 1958; and 4 in 1984.

Hussars first appeared in the Prussian army in 1721. The initial 30 men were Hungarian deserters and renegades but the 5 regiments of 1741 and the 10 regiments of 1773 were composed of Prussians attracted by the lure of plunder. Austria possessed 8 hussar regiments in 1740 and hussars entered the Russian army between 1725 and 1740. Between 1807 and 1862, it became fashionable for certain light dragoon regiments of the British army to be re-designated 'hussars'. Across Europe, the hussars retained their national 'Hungarian' costume of the 'dolman' shell jacket, fur-lined pelisse, busby and tight trousers and boots. To this day, the ceremonial dress of the British Royal Horse Artillery is based on the hussar uniform.

Hussars were designed for the 'little war' of ambushes, patrols and reconnaissance. During the twentieth century they have been transformed into light armoured troops thus retaining their roles of reconnaissance, security and raiding. *See also* CAVALRY; HUNGARY; INDIRECT WARFARE.

G. CHADUC
JOHN CHILDS

FURTHER READING
Hervé de Weck, *La Cavalerie à travers les âges* (Lausanne, 1980); G. T. Denison, *A History of Cavalry, from the Earliest Times, with Lessons for the Future* (London, 1877, 2nd edn 1913); Marquess of Anglesey, *A History of British Cavalry, 1816–1919* (5 vols, London, 1973–85).

Hussites *See* WAGGON-LAAGER

Hydaspes, Battle of the River (326 BC)   This battle between Alexander of Macedon and the Indian prince Porus took place on the banks of the Hydaspes, a tributary of the Indus, where Porus attempted to halt the Macedonian invasion of his kingdom. To Alexander it seemed that the main danger came from the enemy's elephants of which Porus had a substantial force, capable of causing considerable damage in the ranks of the Macedonian phalanx and putting the horses out of action, since they were frightened by the elephants' smell and their trumpeting. In order to force the crossing of the river, Alexander, having established a base camp under the command of Craterus with large numbers of infantry and cavalry, staged daily and nightly attacks along the bank to divert attention from the crossing point he had chosen opposite an island midstream. During a thunderstorm his main force crossed un-opposed and deployed on the opposite bank. Porus concentrated his forces against Alexander and arranged his battle line with cavalry and chariots on the flanks and infantry interspersed with elephants in the centre. Alexander led his cavalry across in front of his battle line in an attack on the Indian left wing. Then the infantry moved forward, opening its ranks to allow the elephants to pass through while Alexander's light cavalry concentrated their arrows and javelins on the mahouts, and the members of the phalanx also worked to unseat them with their long pikes. The elephants were forced back and caused confusion in the Indian line which was now under attack from the phalanx as Alexander's cavalry completed the rout of the left wing. The Indian line broke and fled and the remainder of the Macedonian force under Craterus crossed the Hydaspes and pursued the fugitives. Porus himself was wounded in the battle. Alexander's military expertise is seen in the crossing of the river and in the tactics employed to deal with the elephants. He drew lessons from the battle in respect of how a large elephant corps, if better handled, could be successfully deployed against cavalry. He incorporated a certain number of elephants into his army and, following his example, the Hellenistic rulers subsequently made regular use of them. *See also* ALEXANDER THE GREAT; GAUGAMELA; GRANICUS; GREECE, ANCIENT; ISSUS.

R. LONIS
B. CAMPBELL

FURTHER READING
J. R. Hamilton, 'The cavalry battle at the Hydaspes', *JHS*, lxxvi (1956), pp. 26–31; A. B. Bosworth, *Conquest and Empire: the reign of Alexander the Great* (Cambridge, 1988), pp. 126–30.

I

Iconography, military This vast and varied field possesses its own parameters often far removed from those which surround purely military concerns. However, iconographical creations are frequently of service to military research because of their documentary character. Moreover, works of art which deal with military subjects reflect the interests, sensibilities and opinions of individuals, and, in many cases, of a society, in relation to military matters whether through iconographic, sculptural, decorative or technical expression.

Distinctions must be drawn between works commissioned by official bodies, both those inspired by the needs of propaganda and those of a militant or educative nature, and more freely inspired works which are devoted to scenes from military life and are usually anecdotal or picturesque in character. A final category is more technical: relief models, photographs, panoramas and film.

Official Works of Art Glorifying Battle
From a very early period, rulers built monuments which were intended to preserve and commemorate the great military deeds of their reign. The Romans have left some fine examples in their columns and arches, such as the Column of the Emperor Trajan (AD 98–117), which is the major

Section 36 of the Bayeux Tapestry (*c.*1067–77) depicts the provisioning of the fleet of around 300 ships which conveyed William of Normandy's mercenary army to England on 27–28 September 1066. The majority of the hastily constructed vessels were 45–55 feet long, carrying either 60 men or 30 men and 10 horses. Each ship required about 20 large trees to provide its basic planking, keel and ribs. (Mansell Collection)

369

documentary source on the army of his day. The Bayeux Tapestry, which has sometimes been compared with a strip cartoon, also qualifies as an official work of art. It is the best representation we possess of the nature of the armies and navies of the eleventh century. The depiction of military achievements waned during the Middle Ages until the Renaissance, with its concern for personal glory, witnessed a revival. Classical symbolism reappeared in the guise of trophies and weapons at the expense of exact and anecdotal representation. This tendency peaked during the seventeenth century in the decoration of royal palaces such as the Retiro in Madrid (1630–40) and the Galerie des Glaces at Versailles. It was also manifest in Louis XIV's triumphal arches (at the Porte St-Denis and the Porte St-Martin) and, later, in the structures of Napoleon (the Arcs de Triomphe at the Carrousel and at the Place de l'Étoile). The same trend can be seen in the statues of kings and military leaders, whether depicted on foot or on horseback, or in the sombre decoration of the Hôtel des Invalides and the Royal Hospital at Chelsea. Military symbolism also expressed itself in the eighteenth century in the form of scrolls at the head of discharge certificates and in the ornamental borders or headings on note-paper. One constant feature of these symbolic representations was the expunging of any reference to death, which was merely suggested in the shape of a few fallen enemy soldiers.

In a parallel development, the use of engraving for the representation of battles and sieges enabled the artist to render technical aspects by showing precise details of relief, troop positions and movements and, in the foreground, close-ups of weaponry. Symbols were only to be found in the margins. The desire for exact depiction was introduced into battle paintings by, most notably, the Fleming Pieter Snayers (b.1593), whilst the Baroque element was excised from battle paintings by Adam van der Meulen (1632–90) in his frescos at Les Invalides. Battle painters became genuine experts: they followed the armies, took notes, and consulted accounts of battles. Their works were offered as aids to tactical thinking and officer training. The eighteenth century saw similar, although less majestic, works (e.g. the paintings of Pierre-François Cozette (1714–1801). After the French Revolution, a less conventional way of fighting sounded the death knell of this wide-angled style of depicting battles and gave way to more limited combat scenes, as in the works of Elizabeth Thompson, Lady Butler (1844–1933). However, the older approaches were never completely abandoned and the practice of depicting whole battlefields was resumed through panoramas and dioramas of Waterloo, by Sir William Allan (1782–1850), Borodino, Rezonville, etc., and, more recently, by animated versions (Arromanches, Quebec, etc.). In France, Édouard Detaille (1848–1912), a student of Jean-Louis-Ernest Meissonier (1813–91), was greatly renowned among battle painters.

Military and Educational Works These employ all forms of artistic expression. Sometimes they may have been commissioned by an official body to illustrate a passage of arms or an act of heroism or, in other cases, the artist may have produced the work for sale in the open market. In the second half of the eighteenth century, this type of picture reached a popular audience through the technique of engraving. In France, the period following the Franco-Prussian War (1870–1) saw a proliferation of pictures evoking the heroism of the defeated (*gloria victis*) or the lost provinces to be reconquered by rising generations. These works were frequently characterized by a degree of symbolism. During the nineteenth century, great efforts were made to familiarize the French people with military life, right down to the production of printed military handkerchiefs. Works of this kind often took the form of popular engravings as, for example, with the *images d'Épinal* which, to a very great extent, were devoted to the army and military subjects. Lastly, from the eighteenth century onwards, recruiting posters constituted an important aspect of military iconography. These were originally commissioned by colonels to recruit their own regiments but were later adopted by government.

Monuments to the dead occupy a special place in military iconography. Up to the seventeenth century, the mausoleums of famous warriors can only be distinguished from those of other personalities by the dead man's military dress or accoutrements. Turenne's tomb in Les Invalides set the pattern for the new type of military mausoleum in which it was not only the glory of the hero that was represented in the symbols and other features, but also that of the king and the nation he had served. During the French Revolution, the Parisian sections posted up the lists of their fallen volunteers, accompanied by symbolic images. The period after the Battle of Leipzig (1813), and particularly after Waterloo (1815), gave rise to military tombs of officers and monuments to the glory of the dead of a specific unit, complete with names engraved, erected on the very site of their sacrifice, as on the battlefields of the American Civil War (1861–5). The Franco-Prussian War witnessed a remarkable development in the evolution of battlefield war memorials dedicated to the dead of a particular unit and of monuments to the dead of a *département* erected in its chief town. The 1914–18 war brought a new dimension to war memorial building. Apart from the creation of necropolises on the scale of the massacres they were built to commemorate (the Tannenberg Memorial), it led to the building of some 30,000 village war memorials in France in less than fifteen years, together with the erection of plinths in the headquarters of service associations, public and private offices, educational establishments, etc. These works, which were rarely realistic and more often theatrical, and in many cases hastily erected and stereotypical, sometimes attained great artistic value or at least an eloquent sobriety (the Cenotaph in Whitehall, 1920). The Second World War did not lead to a further burgeoning of war memorials: usually, the names of the dead of 1939–45 were simply added to those of 1914–18, as have been the names of those who have fallen in more recent wars.

Scenes from Military Life These are often

'Soldiers attracted to war by promise of reward', by Jacques Callot (1592–1635). Born in Nancy, Callot was moved to compose his *Malheurs de la Guerre* (1633) after witnessing the behaviour of the troops of Louis XIII of France during their invasion of his native Lorraine. Romeyn de Hooghe composed a similar set of anti-war engravings, *The cruelties committed by the French* (1673), following the invasion of the Dutch Republic in 1672. These etchings were essentially propaganda but mirrored the intellectual climate, created by the excesses of the Thirty Years' War (1618–48), which sought to limit the effects of war on civilians.
(Mary Evans Picture Library)

anecdotal in character and are extremely varied, running from the depiction of scenes of individual combat and heroic death, through the miseries of war, to the evocation of the daily life of soldiers in peacetime.

It was really with Jacques Callot (1592–1635) that this genre reached maturity. His series of etchings 'Les malheurs de la Guerre' ('The miseries of war') is of considerable interest as an historical document. In the eighteenth century, first Jean-Antoine Watteau (1684–1721) then Charles Parrocel (1648–1704) depicted the most varied scenes from military life. The reappearance of the representation of death does not take place in this type of work until the beginning of the nineteenth century, when it was induced by the advent of Romanticism, the vogue for history painting, and the experience of the charnel- houses of the Revolutionary and Napoleonic Wars. However, anecdote, the picturesque, close interest in uniforms, and the search for the ideal and the typical invaded the field of military iconography through the work of Nicolas-Toussaint Charlet (1792–1845) and Auguste Raffet (1804–60). Subsequently, the works of eye-witnesses who were painters, such as Charles Fouqueray (1872–1956), or of amateurs, assumed a more prominent place, particularly during the First World War; they produced works which are a valuable evocation of the daily life of the serviceman away from the field of battle.

Iconology of a Technical Character Old maps and plans only belong to military iconology through the symbolic decoration of their borders. In contrast, relief models and photographs must be included even though, for the most part, they are not products of strictly artistic endeavour.

The admirable collection of relief models of the fortresses of the Kingdom of France housed in the Hôtel des Invalides, the preservation of which is currently under threat as a result of a curious decision to move it, was first instituted in 1688 by the good offices of Louvois and new acquisitions were made right up to the nineteenth century. Its scrupulous precision makes it a unique collection, presenting a comprehensive picture of the art of fortification at a given historical moment and, moreover, reconstituting the urban and architectural context and giving a clear view of how the fortress fitted into its immediate environment.

Photography has added new dimensions to military iconography with the depiction of scenes of military life, both by official reporters and amateurs, and also through photographs gathered for the purposes of information, particularly aerial and, more recently, satellite photography of military targets and the effects of bombing. Official photography again includes the components of approved iconography: information (where this is not covered by secrecy laws), and propaganda. Amateur photography has sometimes been subjected to censorship.

Cine-photography is also used and television news bulletins have even made it possible for a large viewing public to see combat scenes from the point of view of those involved in the unfolding battle. Film is employed extensively for propaganda. Thus, late in 1914, a film was made of the 'Marne taxis' when they were no longer actually being used, in order to preserve the memory of their heroic action. Lastly, war films, whether official or otherwise, sometimes produce interesting depictions of battle, even if, having an eye to cinematic effect, the film-makers do not always heed the opinions of their technical advisers. All armies possess photographic and cinematographic branches.

A. CORVISIER

FURTHER READING
Arsène Alexandre, *Histoire de la peinture militaire en France* (Paris, 1889); Jean Humbert, *Édouard Detaille, l'héroïsme d'un siècle* (Paris, 1979); Germain Bapst, *Essai sur l'histoire des panoramas et dioramas* (Paris, 1981); André Corvisier, *Arts et sociétés en Europe au XVIIIe siècle* (Paris, 1978); André Corvisier, 'La more du soldat depuis la fin du Moyen Age', *Revue historique*, ccliv (1975), pp. 3–30; C. Pincemaille, 'La guerre de Hollande dans le programme iconographique de la Grand Galerie de Versailles', *Histoire, Economie, Société* (1985), pp. 313–34; *Histoire universelle des armées*, ed. Jacques Boudet (4 vols, Paris, 1965–6), contains some very fine reproductions.

The artistic representation of soldiers in peace and war can be traced back to classical antiquity when it was common to depict the military victories on the tombs of great generals or on other monuments such as Trajan's Column in Rome. A thousand years later, the Bayeux Tapestry (c.1067–77) recorded the whole military campaign of William of Normandy over the Saxons of England. Other military events were represented in the illustrated chronicles of the medieval period although many scenes of battles such as Crécy, Poitiers or Navarette were produced over a century later. These hieratic drawings, as Oman calls them, of 'a battle' or 'a siege' demonstrated little knowledge of the event or the topography. Their only aim was representational. The Renaissance saw the appearance of paintings celebrating military feats and personal glory as a result of the increase in commissions from the nobility, one example being Paolo Uccello's 'The Rout of San Romano, 1432'. Here the artist completely ignored the defeated army in favour of celebrating the victor, Niccolo da Tolentino, who is prominently depicted as the central horseman. All other figures were secondary to the general. In 1505, Michelangelo produced a full-size cartoon of an intended large fresco of the Battle of Cascina showing violent combat between figures wearing contemporary costume and others dressed in classical armour. Military themes, particularly instruments of death, appeared in the work of Leonardo da Vinci who also painted a monumental piece depicting 'The Battle of Anghiari 1440'. Albrecht Dürer captured the intricacies of armour and weaponry. 'Glorifying pictures', such as Uccello's, became common in the Italian High Renaissance and into the sixteenth century with Rubens' two battle pieces – 'Charles V at the Battle of Tunis 1535' and 'Henry IV at the Battle of Ivry 1590'.

The seventeenth century was a milestone in military iconography with an immense outpouring of paintings and prints emanating from Central Europe. The Thirty Years' War was a catalyst for countless pictures by French, German and Dutch artists depicting combat. The majority of these were studio paintings which had little regard to the actual military operations. Such 'generic' battle scenes were painted by Jacques Courtois (Il Bourgognone), Philips Wouvermans, Salvator Rosa and Jan Hughtenburgh. Many of Courtois's paintings included a central rearing horse bearing the victorious commander of the day. The wars of the period inspired anti-war pictures also representing the cruelties inflicted on mankind. Jacques Callot, for one, captured in a series of graphic engravings the miseries of war, while P. Bruegel the Younger produced a series of pictures entitled 'The Disasters of War'. Callot had earlier produced large engravings of the sieges of Breda and La Rochelle in which the sieges were represented in schematic form with the towns represented from aerial perspectives. These picture plans began to appear in the sixteenth century and represented an analytical style of battle painting, as Cederhof calls it, in which the artist tried to create a pictorial analysis of the strategical and tactical conduct of battles and sieges. In addition to battle paintings and engravings, countless engravings appeared in the sixteenth and seventeenth centuries depicting mercenaries, particularly the *landsknechte* of Germany and Switzerland. Two other forms of military iconography which became prominent in the seventeenth century were the martial portrait inspired by the works of Van Dyck, and the numerous military treatises outlining the latest ideas in the science of warfare. Engravings of siege operations and tactics were frequently found in such texts.

The glorifying military picture was taken a step further in the paintings of A. F. van der Meulen and Charles Le Brun in the late seventeenth-century. While earlier artists had been commissioned by patrons to depict campaigns, it was Louis XIV who set the standard by immortalizing himself in paintings by these artists. The majority of these pictures placed the monarch in a conspicuous position usually on horseback directing a battle or siege, but two canvases by Le Brun ('The Siege of Douai' and 'The Siege of Tournai' both in 1667) broke with this tradition by placing the king on foot in a trench behind breastworks. Military tapestries glorifying generals, monarchs or other personages were an outgrowth of late seventeenth-century military art and were particularly popularized during and after the War of the Spanish Succession; examples include the various tapestry sets commissioned by the Duke of Marlborough and several of his generals commemorating their victories. Military genre scenes by such artists as Georg Philipp Rugendas, who also painted combat pieces, Charles Parrocel and Jean-Antoine Watteau, depicting soldiers pursuing more peaceful activities or figure studies, became common in the early part of the century particularly as subjects for prints.

Heroic battle pieces were to continue throughout the eighteenth century reaching their pinnacle in Benjamin West's 'Death of Wolfe' painted in 1771. This and other 'death tableaux' represented the interest of High Art with military subjects and many leading artists like John Singleton Copley and John Trumbull produced battle pieces depicting the death of the hero. The death of Nelson in 1805 caused similar pictures to be reproduced.

Napoleonic France witnessed a vast array of military iconography devoted to hero-worship in all its forms from the triumphal arches at the Arc de Triomphe, the Place de l'Étoile, and the elaborate tombs and memorials to Napoleon's officers, to the portraits and battle pieces commissioned by the Emperor to adorn the walls of Versailles. Artists such as Pierre-Jean David, François Gérard, Baron Gros and Horace Vernet made their reputations recording the victories of Napoleon or his likeness. Some of these paintings captured particular incidents while others recorded events in panoramic style. Such panoramic battle paintings were also popular in Britain through the paintings by Sir William Allan of Waterloo, and panoramas depicting other great military events were common fare throughout the nineteenth century. The wars against France also inspired thousands of anti-war caricatures by many of the leading satirical artists of the day including James Gillray and Thomas Rowlandson.

Later French painters such as Auguste Raffet, Nicolas Toussaint Charlet and Hippolyte Bellange perpetuated the myth of Napoleon in the first half of the nineteenth century in countless lithographic images of battles, soldiers resting, or veterans recounting their exploits; while Jean-Louis Géricault and particularly Eugène Delacroix produced military scenes inspired by the Romantic movement in France, an example being the latter's 'Massacre of Chios' (1824). Anti-war sentiments were represented in Goya's painting of the atrocities committed in Spain during the Peninsula War. Elsewhere in Europe, the affordability of lithography made prints more accessible and military subjects, particularly prints of elegant uniforms, lent themselves to graphic depiction.

The mid-nineteenth century saw the appearance on the battlefield and in the barrack yard of the photographer. Roger Fenton and James Robertson captured the events in the Crimea while Matthew Brady and Alexander Gardner recorded the impressions of the American Civil War. Added to this, the popularity of the illustrated press and the 'special artists' including William Simpson, Melton Prior and Frederick Remington, who were sent out by the newspapers to record wars, made military events familiar to society. None the less, as the camera was still in its infancy, it was left up to the artist to capture many of the important conflicts. The late nineteenth century saw new schools of military art springing up all over Europe and America. Military subjects were popular with the realists who sought to capture every detail of weaponry and uniform. In France, Alphonse De Neuville and Édouard Detaille, who had both participated in the Franco-Prussian War, and Jean Meissonier, captured moments in contemporary as well as historical battle paintings. Likewise, in Britain, Lady Butler, Richard Caton Woodville and Ernest Crofts began to focus more on the incident in battle as opposed to recording the whole action. These paintings were more democratic in that they often focused on the ranks rather than the generals, an outgrowth of the Crimean War. This brought about a more general realization of the sufferings of the common soldier in war. Elsewhere, Emil Hünten, Georg Bleibtreu and Carl Röchling, in Germany, Gilbert Gaul, William Trego and Julian Scott in America, and Vassili Verestchagin in Russia, were all producing military scenes although the latter's works were clearly anti-war in sentiment.

The Great War forever changed the depiction of the soldier. While early pictures of the fighting bordered on the heroic with more than a hint of propaganda thrown in, the allied governments in 1917–18 commissioned artists to go to the front and record what they saw, not what they imagined. The results, from the brushes of Christopher Nevinson, John Nash, William Rothenstein and others, captured the grim realities of war as never before. With the peace came thousands of war memorials and cenotaphs, many the work of the finest sculptors and architects of the day; Sir Edwin Lutyens designed the cenotaph in Whitehall which was erected in 1920. While monuments to the fallen had appeared as far back as prehistory, and had become particularly common in the second half of the nineteenth century, it was the world wars of the twentieth century and the subsequent conflicts that saw the overwhelming impact of monumental art devoted to memorializing the fallen. With the horrors of the Western Front still fresh in the memory, many early twentieth-century artists conveyed anti-war sentiments, none more so than Pablo Picasso who portrayed the violence of the aerial bombardment of Guernica during the Spanish Civil War. However, with the advent of the movie camera and later television, the realities of war could be brought home to millions of people and the images manipulated to influence public perception. Nevertheless, in modern campaigns, artists can still be found sketching the minutiae of military life; an official war artist accompanied the British expedition to the Falkland Islands in 1982. *See also* CULTURE, PROTECTION OF; GLORY; GUERNICA; PSYCHOLOGICAL WARFARE OPERATIONS; SYMBOLISM.

PETER HARRINGTON

FURTHER READING

Olle Cederhof, 'The battle painting as a historical source', *Revue internationale d'histoire militaire*, vii (1967), pp. 119–44; J. R. Hale, *Artists and Warfare in the Renaissance* (Yale, CT, 1990); Meirion and Susie Harries, *The War Artists: British official war art of the twentieth century* (London, 1983); J. W. M. Hichberger, *Images of the Army: the military in British art, 1815–1914* (Manchester, 1988); Sir Charles Oman, 'Early military pictures', *The Archaeological Journal*, xcv (1939), pp. 337–54.

India The history of India is made up of almost incessant internal or defensive wars, except during the period of the stable British Raj (1858–1947). The case of the great Mauryan Emperor Asoka (269–232 BC) is only a partial exception based, like the peace of the British Raj after the Sikh Wars and the Great Mutiny of 1857–8, on the absence of any serious challenge after the conquest of Kalinga (modern Orissa). In ancient India, war was a normal state activity: there was no exchange of permanent ambassadors between the different sovereigns and no supra-national authority, such as the Church, to preach peace. Peace by mutual agreement is indeed only one of six means of governing listed in the *Arthasastra*, the others all involving recourse to war or duplicity. This treatise, which dates from the fourth century BC, puts forward the idea that it must be the policy of each king to subjugate his neighbours. The 'theory of circles' sees the state as an entity surrounded by enemy states; these latter in turn have further enemies around them who, by that very token, are the friends of the first states. This goes on from circle to circle, so that the aim of policy becomes the achievement of a series of mutual alliances. Other writings place glory above power. The Laws of Manu (second–third centuries) advocate battle as a giant tournament with chivalric rules. Although there were casuists who made out a case for the violation of these rules, it seems that from the fall of the Maurya empire onwards (second century BC), warfare was conducted in a more humane way in India than elsewhere. There does not seem to have been systematic pillage although the notion of honour did not appear until quite a late stage.

In the earlier Vedic period (1500–600 BC), it had been incumbent upon all free men to fulfil military obligations but by the end of that era a fourfold division of society was regarded as divinely ordained. Below the highest order, the brahmans, was the kshatriya or warrior varna. This was an order capable of incorporating invaders (such as the ancestors of the Rajputs) and other martial groups, to the extent that such groups agreed to conform to certain rules of Hinduism's holy law. The order or varna of warriors had its own specific usages. However, it did not hold a monopoly of arms and it became transformed into complexes of regional castes or jatis whose members were no longer even bound to pursue a military career.

The first known organized army is that of Candragupta Maurya (321–300 BC), founder of the Maurya empire. This army, which was described by the Seleucid ambassador, Megasthenes, at the beginning of the third century BC, seems to have been very large, containing hundreds of thousands of men. The hereditary troops, who for the most part belonged to the order of warriors, formed its backbone. Alongside these, the army contained mercenaries, militias recruited by the guilds (*shreni*) to perform specific tasks such as the protection of caravans, troops provided by subject or allied states, deserters from enemy armies and the so-called 'wild' troops, who were a type of guerilla fighter used for operations in the jungle or the mountains. Instead of paying taxes in money, some villages provided soldiers.

The army comprised four arms: an infantry, which was the main force, from which was extracted a sort of Praetorian Guard, whose men were bound to the ruler by an oath taken during a banquet; a cavalry, which was ineffective against the mounted archers of the Parthians or the Greeks; chariotry, which was the main fighting arm in the Vedic period but which degenerated into a means of transportation and became obsolete about the dawn of the Christian era. An elephant corps played both the role of modern tanks in breaking through lines of resistance and that of bridge trains in fording rivers. The elephants were clad in coats of leather and their armour was studded with metal spikes. Besides the mahout, they also carried two or three men armed with bows and long lances and they were protected by infantry. Enemies very soon discovered a counter-thrust, since elephants panic at the sight of fire and this often threw an army into confusion.

The army was composed of mixed units (*patti*) made up of one elephant, one chariot, three cavalrymen and five infantrymen. These units were grouped either three by three or ten by ten into a corps. In their weaponry the Indians were very much like other people. However, they did use long bamboo bows which had to be wedged with one foot when firing, two-handed swords and a long lance used by soldiers mounted on elephants (*tomara*). Defensive equipment included a rattan shield covered with leather or metal and a light armour, also of leather or metal. The army moved slowly, travelling 10 miles a day at the quickest. Battle was joined by following, as closely as possible, a ritual procedure the date and time of which was fixed by astrologers. The heavy infantry was placed at the centre and the other corps on the wings. Sieges were an important part of ancient Indian warfare. Though pre-Muslim fortresses in India have been modified to destroy any impression of their original state, archaeology has revealed remains of rough stone defensive walls, as well as pre-Gupta brick city walls in Orissa, and even of timber defences of Mauryan date at Patna. Timber defences were deprecated because of the fire hazard, but cheap and convenient. Lastly, ancient India seems to have had no navy, there being merely a few ships armed to fight pirates.

These military structures were profoundly modified by the experience of a succession of invaders who both borrowed from purely Indian traditions, notably the use of armoured fighting elephants, and gave new equipment and tactics, notably a new emphasis on the use of cavalry. Here native Indian rulers were at a considerable disadvantage, because horses did not thrive in most of Hindustan, and rulers with access to bloodstock imports from Central Asia and Persia held the upper hand. These tended to be the invading powers or their immediate heirs settled across the vital trade routes which crossed the Punjab. As a result, the western part of the Indo-Gangetic Plain was conquered by the Rajput people (sixth century AD), then by Muslims, the Ghaznavid Turks (late tenth century), and the Mongols (early fourteenth century), with Tamerlain taking Delhi in 1398. None of these warrior peoples built an empire centred on India. Most treated it simply as a target for massive raids. Some who settled were absorbed by Hindu society, like the Rajputs.

The impact of Islam began in the early eighth century when the Umayyad governor of Iraq launched a punitive column of 1,000 Syrian horse and 1,000 Iraqi camels against the piratical rajas of Sind, but only became disruptive with the Ghaznavid invasions from the high plateau of Afghanistan after 997. Islamic armies enjoyed vastly superior mobility to the unwieldy Hindu hosts, whose numbers are absurdly inflated by chroniclers whose figures make more sense as total potential military manpower. Nevertheless, they were still big enough, predominantly infantry, and accompanied by a vast non-combatant 'tail' several times their own size. Successive Muslim ascendancies culminated in the rule of the tribally-based Afghan Lodi sultans of Delhi in the early sixteenth century.

In 1526, thanks to the use of Turkic horse archers and artillery, the Timurid, Babur, captured Delhi with 25,000 men against a defensive force of 100,000 Indians. The centre of his battle array was formed by groups of waggons lashed together, between which his Turkish gunners operated. The cavalry was positioned on the wings. His grandson Akbar (1542–1605) refounded the Mughal Empire which dominated Hindustan and began to expand into the Deccan. The army had as its core a heavy cavalry force under the Emperor. This was always some 85 per cent Muslim, with 70 per cent of these coming from outside India. The state was a semi-fossilized army, though Akbar did seek to create a synthetic unifying imperial religion and culture. The culture proved enduring: the religious syncretism was bankrupt by the reign of the last great emperor, Aurangzeb, a rigorously orthodox Sunni Muslim.

The Empire of the Great Mughal over-extended itself deep into the Deccan under Aurangzeb (1659–1707). The Mughal armies, though reinforced by huge local levies, were none too effective against the Hindu reaction of the Marathas, who employed guerilla and 'scorched earth' tactics. Involvement in the Deccan made it difficult for the Mughals to suppress the rise of the Sikhs, galvanized by their monotheistic faith which was an offshoot of Hinduism. Meanwhile, fire-arms became even more widely available, entering the country through the Portuguese (after 1511), Dutch (1598), British (1600) and French (1668) factories. European trading companies, led by the French, discovered the cheapness and effectiveness of Indian mercenaries trained and disciplined in the European fashion – the sepoys. After Clive's victory over the Nawab of Bengal at Plassey (1757) and the Treaty of Paris which reduced French possessions to her five factories, the British East India Company set about patiently organizing three enormous sepoy armies. The Indian Army, which remained based on the Bombay, Madras and Calcutta forces, was restructured after the Indian Mutiny (1857–8). It only became a unitary force in the twentieth century, but it was an important source of British power, being bigger than the UK army. It took into its ranks a considerable number of Sikhs and Gurkhas, crack ethnic troops who, when they were needed, also fought in theatres outside India. Since independence (1947), the successor states, India, Pakistan, Sri Lanka and Bangladesh, have inherited the traditions of the old Indian Army. In Pakistan and Bangladesh the army, in typical Islamic fashion, has dominated politics. In India civilian leadership has built up an enormous army, much the biggest in the Third World and many times bigger than external security requires.

See also COLONIAL TROOPS; IRAN; MONGOLS; PAKISTAN; PLASSEY.

A. CORVISIER
B. P. LENMAN

FURTHER READING
H. H. Dodwell, *The Cambridge History of India* (6 vols, Cambridge, 1922–53); A. L. Bashan, *The Wonder that was India* (London, 1954); Philip Mason, *A Matter of Honour: An account of the Indian Army, its officers and men* (London, 1974); J. P. Lawford, *Britain's army in India: from its origins to the conquest of Bengal* (London, 1978).

Indirect warfare The brief analysis of the subject given here is based on a survey produced by Eric Muraise. Conventional warfare can take two forms. In the direct type, the aim is to meet the enemy face to face and then to bring about his collapse in a decisive battle; the indirect tries to wear down the opponent, or rather, to break his morale and disorganize, or destroy, his supplies and equipment, with the battle supervening merely to complete his ruin. These two methods have been employed in every part of the world. Nevertheless, the direct form of warfare has, in general, been instinctively preferred by Western nations. Hans Delbrück has asserted, in his *History of the Art of War in the Light of Political History*, that to do so is an attribute of Europeans, as being naturally of fixed habitation and attached to the defence of their soil, a trait which limits their freedom of action. Indirect warfare would seem likely to be more natural to nomads used to wandering through vast and featureless open spaces – a fact that Plano Carpino, as René Grousset has told us, understood very thoroughly during his stay with the Mongols. Indirect warfare requires the employment of light infantry, light cavalry or light armoured vehicles. It uses the tactics of the feigned retreat which can rapidly turn into a fresh advance, or of raiding parties which retire as soon as their immediate aim has been achieved, and of the kind of harassing action characterized by repeated ambushes.

Indirect warfare consists of continually surprising the enemy by moves which appear unconventional, such as feigning to give battle whilst, in reality, a withdrawal is taking place. If a battle has to be fought, the right course is to pretend to give way in front of the enemy and thus to draw him forward by the force of his own momentum into an unfavourable position, so that he can be destroyed. The extreme case occurred at Cannae where Hannibal allowed his centre to be worsted. E. Muraise has compared direct warfare to boxing, indirect to judo.

Among military thinkers, indirect warfare has had its supporters and its critics. Clausewitz believed that it was impossible to drain an enemy's strength in this way. In his view, indirect warfare could be no more than complementary to the direct type and could only be employed against an invader. The supporters of the theory of indirect warfare are not found only in the East, as there is a current tendency to believe, but also in the West. Mao Tse-Tung is often quoted but it is worth recalling that, 2,500 years ago, Sun Wu and Sun-Tzu founded strategy on patience and guile, the aim being to wear down the enemy by hunger, sleeplessness and nervous prostration, while avoiding a full-scale battle. 'The whole art of war is based on deception. If we are ready to make an attack, we should have the air of being incapable of it; if we are using our forces, we should seem inactive; if we are near the enemy, we should make him believe that we are far away, and if we are far away, that we are near by . . . when the enemy advances, we retire; when he tries to slip away, we harass him; when he retreats, we pursue him; when he is tired, we attack him . . . if you have ten times more troops than the enemy, surround him; if five times more, attack him; otherwise, avoid battle.' Mao Tse-Tung expressed the same idea: 'Our strategy is one against ten; our tactics are ten against one.' A quotation from Maurice de Saxe discloses a similar line of thought, even if stated in more measured terms: 'All possible means of securing victory should be used to the full, before any engagement takes place; able generals seek not so much to fight battles – where both parties run equal risks – as to bring down the enemy by other means.' Nearer our own time, General Gambiez has appeared as an exponent of the 'indirect style' of warfare.

Naturally, indirect warfare had practitioners long before Mao Tse-Tung and we need only quote a few examples here. Du Guesclin retired within the walls of castles and towns, leaving the enemy nothing but a vacuum. The four English sweeps across France had the same fate as the five 'extermination campaigns' waged by Chiang Kai-Shek against Mao. The Byzantines had already used the same type of strategy. The armies of the period before the divisional formation was adopted made a practice of attacking an enemy's bases and communications and it was as a result of his skilful stroke at Huy (1746) that Maurice de Saxe placed the Imperial armies in difficulty and secured Namur. Much warfare of the late seventeenth century relied on deception and the wearing down of the enemy's economic resources. Wellington and the Spaniards, as also the Russians, used the methods of indirect warfare against Napoleon. The Boers did the same against the British. Sherman's march through Georgia was a classic indirect manoeuvre.

Nevertheless, if indirect warfare is to be waged in a *systematic* fashion, safe refuges are a necessity. These may be provided by geography – in the shape of mountains, marshlands or extensive space. Invaders have proved incapable of taking a grip on the whole of Russia or China. Refuges may equally well be groups (not lines) of fortified positions which support each other mutually. The 'iron frontier' established by Vauban in the north of France held for four years, and in the end was not crossed. The final 'refuge' is the population itself; that allows a war to be carried on as a people's (or revolutionary) struggle.

At the end of the eighteenth century, the development of more complex and effective equipment, which necessitated fuller training for its handling, then conscription which made possible the use of larger forces, and lastly the introduction of the divisional formation, seemed to spell the end of indirect warfare, often called the 'little war', a form of warfare that seemed to breed indiscipline. The nineteenth century saw the heyday of direct warfare, though there were occasions where a people who had been invaded showed themselves ready to turn to guerilla activity. Today, aircraft and armoured fighting vehicles have allowed a return to indirect warfare, in the shape of action against an enemy's rear, and particularly in the destruction of his supply bases.

There is no lack of methods which have been used to ward off the threat posed by indirect warfare. Four are quoted by E. Muraise. These are (1) close formations like those used by Xenophon when, during the 'Anabasis', he brought his heavily-armed infantry and baggage train back to safety over a distance of 1,250 miles, keeping the Persians at bay with repeated charges by his small force of cavalry, and with the missiles from his slingers; Bonaparte's squares against the Mamluks at the Battle of the Pyramids; and the 'boar's head' formation adopted by Bugeaud at the Battle of the Isly (1844); (2) the use of ground which renders movement difficult and which makes feasible the establishment of posts for observation and for making checks (Roman *limes*, frontier barriers in Algeria); (3) the employment as auxiliary troops of those who themselves practice indirect methods of warfare, such as some North Africans (Numidian cavalry in the Roman army), or the Croats in the Austrian); (4) the conversion of regular troops to indirect warfare, a method practised with success by the Byzantines, or the light troops (the mixed legions of the eighteenth century) used against the Pandours and guerillas, or assault commandos.

Indirect warfare can pass beyond the sphere of the conventional type, since it can receive the help of civilian combatants. It then becomes akin to a people's, or revolutionary, war. *See also* CAVALRY; GAMBIEZ; GUERILLA WARFARE; GUESCLIN; INFANTRY; MAO TSE-TUNG; MONGOLS; POPULAR WARFARE; PSYCHOLOGICAL WARFARE OPERATIONS; SAXE; STRATEGY; SUN-TZU.

A. CORVISIER
JOHN CHILDS

FURTHER READING
E. Muraise, *Introduction à l'histoire militaire*

(Paris, 1964); Archer Jones, *The Art of War in the Western World* (Oxford, 1989); B. H. Liddell Hart, *Strategy: the Indirect Approach* (New York, 1961); Otto Heilbrunn, *Warfare in the Enemy's Rear* (London, 1963).

Infantry This arm is composed of soldiers called infantrymen who fight on foot and are equipped with weapons that can be easily carried. Infanty is divided into two types – heavy and light – so-called on account of the weight of their weapons, armour and equipment. Light infantry are more mobile. The word 'infantry' derives from the Italian *fante*, a young retainer who followed his lord to war, and from it came *fanteria* and *fantaccino*. During the sixteenth century, these passed into the French language as *fanterie* and, finally, *infanterie*. Napoleon described the infantry as 'the lord of the battlefield' and it usually forms the majority of an army except among certain Asiatic peoples and during the Middle Ages when it was relegated to the position of an auxiliary to cavalry.

As early as the Old Egyptian Kingdom, the two types can be distinguished. There was a line of heavy infantry who carried shields of hide, short spears with copper points, and, at a later date, axes, boomerangs and a variety of other weapons. The light infantry were basically archers who sometimes caried daggers and axes. The foot soldier wore a headdress of leather strengthened with metal plates, a leather body protector or a coat of bronze scale armour. Food and water were carried over the shoulder.

The Assyrian army was organized in regional and national units. The heavy infantryman wore a breastplate and a conical helmet and was armed with a long spear or pike, a thrusting sword and a large metal shield. The light infantry were bowmen equipped with a wicker shield and helmet. In the line of battle, pikemen and archers stood in pairs so that the former's shield protected both men. The Persian infantryman had a breastplate and a small shield and was armed with a cutting sword or an axe. The corps of the 10,000 'Immortals' was divided into hundreds, tens and fives. The bow was the main weapon of the Persians and most Oriental nations but it was not highly favoured by the Greeks or the Romans. By placing his left foot against the bottom point of the bow, which he fixed in the ground, the Persian archer was able to shoot accurately and with considerable force. In Oriental armies, the infantry was formed up for battle in a closely packed mass with little internal articulation. The archers were positioned at the front behind a line of shields which had been placed in the ground, the front rank firing directly and the rear ranks indirectly. Having discharged their arrows and javelins, the missile men withdrew and the heavy infantry attacked, if the situation was considered favourable.

Aristotle states that in archaic Greece the marshalling of infantry in regular formations was unknown. Minoan (3000–1000 BC) and Mycenaean (1580–1120 BC) soldiers carried a shield of ox hide, which was secured round the neck by a strap, a helmet and a long sword. In the middle of the seventh century BC there appeared the device of a loop attached to the back of the shield through which a soldier could pass his arm while his hand held a weapon. The shield thus became smaller. During the classical epoch, the heavy infantryman, or hoplite, wore a helmet ornamented with a crest, a leather or linen jerkin covered with metal scales, and greaves. He was armed with a seven-foot spear, tipped with iron at each end, and held in both hands. His iron, or usually bronze, sword was 2 feet long, straight and with two cutting edges. In the case of the Athenians, the shield was round. The accoutrements weighed 75 lb; for this reason, the infantryman was accompanied by a servant who helped to carry his equipment together with sufficient food for three days. The wealthiest citizens served in the cavalry while the poorest were found in the light infantry, or peltasts (from the fifth century BC), slingers or archers who carried a wicker shield. There were also the *psiloi*, skirmishers who harassed the enemy and were skilled in fighting over rough terrain.

Greek infantry fighting was decided by the weight of manpower and weaponry. The heavy infantry formed up in a phalanx, whose numerical strength varied though in its most common form it comprised 4,096 men arrayed in 8–10. The massive nature of the phalanx was accentuated in its Macedonian version (359 BC) in which up to 16 ranks were employed. The spears grew in length to between 13 and 23 feet and, when lowered, formed a wall through which cavalry could not penetrate. The standard tactical unit was the *taxis* (1,500 men) which was subdivided into companies (*lochoi*) and sections (*dekades*). Greek military strength derived also from the quality of its fighting men, especially the Spartans who, as professional warriors, underwent an intensive training which eliminated those unable to meet the required standards. Both the Greek and Macedonian phalanxes were capable of manoeuvre on the battlefield. To secure action by the phalanx in unison with that of the cavalry was to be one of Alexander the Great's achievements.

After remaining a formidable and undefeated system for about 200 years, the Macedonian phalanx was finally outclassed by the Roman legion. Like the Greeks, the Romans possessed a mobile light infantry, the *velites*, who were armed with a thrusting sword and a javelin and were protected by a round shield and a leather helmet. The heavy infantry legion was divided into *hastati*, the youngest legionaries, who fought in the first line, the *principes*, older men placed in the second line, and the *triarii*, the oldest and most experienced soldiers forming the third line. The legionary was well equipped. He wore a metal helmet, a leather cuirass reinforced with metal plates and carried an oval shield. His weapons were the javelin, *pilum*, which was thrown during the opening phase of a battle, and a thrusting sword. This was later superseded by the Spanish type, which was short and broad and could be used for both cut and thrust in close-quarter fighting. The strength of the legionary, as of the hoplite, was the result of his protective accoutrements but the Roman equipment was lighter than the Greek allowing the legionary to move more quickly. Greek and Roman fighting efficiency was similar, both systems being based on rigorous training. The legion's superiority over the phalanx arose from its greater capacity for man-

oeuvre due to its division into *maniples* (12 files of 10 men) which paraded with gaps between them allowing the legion to operate over difficult ground.

The phalanx occupied a front of 560 yards with a depth of 38 yards; the legion of the fourth century BC had a front of 975 yards and a depth between 110 and 130 yards. By the first century BC, these distances had extended to 2,160 by 220 yards. The *velites* fought in front of and in the spaces between the *maniples* but they were abolished in the time of Gaius Marius (*c*.157–*c*.85 BC) as was the distinction between the *hastati*, *principes* and *triarii*. The numerical strength of the legion was raised from 4,000 to 6,000 men but its cavalry element was reduced to 300 and used mainly for reconnaissance. Over the course of centuries the legion underwent a number of major changes. Under the Empire, the cuirass and the helmet were partially abandoned as the legion turned to the extensive use of the bow and missile weapons to combat the Barbarian cavalry. The sword was lengthened and the javelin shortened while the bow, which the legionary had once despised, became a standard weapon. At the end of the Empire during the reign of Constantine the Great (306–37) the legion disappeared to be replaced by lighter units with cavalry playing an increasingly important role – forming a third of the total numbers under Diocletian (284–305) – in order to counter the mounted forces of the Germans, Parthians and Huns.

The heavy infantry of the Eastern or Byzantine Empire were armed with lances, thrusting swords, bows and crossbows, and the light troops with bows, slings, thrusting swords and javelins. After the defeat at Adrianople (378), the Byzantine army turned to the employment of mass cavalry, infantry being relegated to sustaining the horse in retreat as well as holding strong points and guarding camps. Although the majority of the Barbarian armies were mounted, the armies of the Franks and Merovingians were almost entirely composed of infantry and fought without any tactical system or ability to manoeuvre. As a consequence, the infantry of the Western Roman Empire retained its dominance for a little longer than its Eastern counterpart. However, the defeat of the Frankish infantry by the Roman cavalry at Casilinum (554) marked the end of reliance upon infantry. For many centuries, cavalry was the principal arm in European armies. Only in England, until the Norman Conquest in 1066, did infantry remain effective.

During the period when aristocratic heavy cavalry ruled the battlefield, the bulk of the infantry was provided by commoners although the crossbowmen were usually mercenaries. Despite the fact that the feudal levies could produce large bodies of infantry, their lack of uniform armament and training rendered them ineffective in the face of heavily armoured horsemen and they were relegated to protecting camps and assisting at sieges. Occasionally they were employed as light troops to open an engagement. The cavalry had nothing but contempt for the infantry and it was not unknown for the cavalry to ride down their own infantry in their eagerness to charge. However, infantry did achieve some successes. Before the Battle of Courtrai (1302), Robert d'Artois declared that 'a hundred mounted men-at-arms are worth a thousand foot soldiers', but his charging cavalry were held by the Flemish infantry and then pushed back into a river. The Duke of Athens was beaten by infantry in 1311.

During the fourteenth century, infantry underwent a renaissance through the emergence of mercenary companies in Italy and France, the use of the Welsh longbow in England and the tactics of the Swiss phalanx. The longbow was first employed *en masse* at Falkirk in 1298; after the Scottish infantry had been riddled by a hail of arrows at a range of 200 yards, they were charged and dispersed by the English heavy cavalry. During the Hundred Years' War, the English archers operated defensively from behind sharpened stakes set in the ground and inflicted severe defeats on the French heavy cavalry at Crécy (1346), Poitiers (1356) and Agincourt (1415). Just as the English were demonstrating that heavy cavalry could be defeated by light infantry firing missile weapons, the Swiss looked back to the infantry tactics of

ancient Greece and Rome. In 1386, 1,300 men from the Swiss mountains routed, in open country, a force of 3,000 cavalry from Lorraine; in 1444, 2,000 Swiss fought an heroic action against 14,000 men from the Dauphin's army; and in 1476, they defeated the Burgundian Charles the Bold at Grandson and Murten. The achievements of the Swiss infantry resulted less from the combination of weapons employed – pike, halberd, axe, bow, crossbow and arquebus – than from their tactical formations which looked back to both the Greek phalanx and the spaced maniples of the Roman legion. The Swiss infantry were also thoroughly trained. During the fifteenth century, the Swiss adopted an extended pike (nearly 20 feet in length) and were early users of firearms. Each battalion formed a compact square, composed of 7 or 9 ranks of pikemen in the centre, with the crossbowmen or arquebusiers on the flanks. The pikemen formed a 'hedgehog' when facing cavalry into which the crossbowmen and hand gunners retired after they had skirmished with the enemy during the opening stages of the action in order to cover the advance of the phalanxes. Against cavalry, the end of the pike was planted on the ground resting against the soldier's foot; against infantry, it was held in both hands. In the attack, the pikemen pressed forward and then opened their ranks to allow the halberdiers, bearers of two-handed swords, 'morning stars', and 'Lucerne hammers' to wreak havoc among the opposing infantry and cavalry. Swiss phalanxes were capable of rapid and co-ordinated movement both on and off the battlefield, partly because they eschewed heavy armour.

Working from the basis established by Charles VII in 1448, between 1479 and 1483, in the aftermath of the Hundred Years' War, Louis XI of France organized an embryonic standing army trained according to Swiss methods. Each of these 'Picardy Bands', supplemented by the 'Piedmont Bands' in 1504, contained 800 pikemen and 200 crossbowmen although the latter weapon was steadily superseded by the arquebus. By the reign of Francis I (1515–47), the arquebusiers composed between 10 per cent and 50 per cent of the strength of these 'legions'. However, the Spaniards were the principal heirs to the methods of the Swiss. The Spanish infantry had been reorganized by Gonsalvo de Córdoba at the beginning of the sixteenth century. Half the troops were armed with the long Swiss pike, a third with a round shield and thrusting sword, and the remaining sixth with the arquebus. Gradually, the swordsmen were replaced by additional arquebusiers. In 1505, Córdoba grouped the companies into twenty *colunelas* (later *coronelias*), commanded by *coroneles*, under the overall charge of a colonel-general. This system of organization gave way, in 1534, to the *tercio*, which was based on the Roman legion. A *maestro de campo* commanded 3,000 men, divided into three *coronelias* (1,000 men), each of four companies (250 men). In 1636, the Spanish company was standardized at 200 men (11 officers, 30 musketeers, 60 arquebusiers and 99 pikemen).

In 1560, Duke François of Guise reorganized the French infantry into three regiments along the lines of the *tercio*, each containing about twelve *enseignes*. The Huguenots raised nine regiments, each of 2,000 men, in the following year. From 1567, these French formations became the progenitors of the regiments which were to form the French army of the seventeenth century. The German infantry in the Spanish service were formed into regiments of 3,000 men, divided into ten companies of 300 (50 per cent musketeers and 50 per cent pikemen). Similar organizations were adopted by the Italian, Burgundian, English and Walloon infantries.

As European armies grew larger during the second half of the sixteenth and into the seventeenth century, infantry became the predominant arm basically because it was far cheaper to equip and train a foot soldier than a cavalryman. The latter fell into relative decline. Infantry firearms and artillery had blunted his shock action to such an extent that cavalry had given up the lance and degenerated into little more than mounted pistoleers. During the middle stages (1590–1600) of the Eighty Years' War against Spain, the Dutch leader, Maurice of Nassau, returned to the Roman model of well-articulated infantry. Just as the legion had been made smaller during the later Empire, so Maurice broke up the regiments and *tercios* into battalions of *c.*500 men which fought in ten ranks, the pikes in the centre and the arquebusiers on the flanks. The arquebusiers could maintain a continuous fire as each rank successively discharged its weapons and then counter-marched to the rear to reload. The pikemen protected the arquebusiers from attack by cavalry and assisted in an infantry charge. With a high proportion of officers and non-commissioned officers, the Dutch battalions were well articulated and balanced. However, the new shallow battalions were vulnerable in their flanks and rear; this could only be circumvented by armies adopting a basically linear or chequer-board battle formation with each battalion protecting its neighbours' flanks. The flanks of the army were anchored on natural obstacles, easy enough to find in the Netherlands, or were protected by cavalry. Also, the new, smaller battalions had to be grouped into brigades for ease of command in battle. Overall, the Dutch formations required a high level of drill, discipline and training, factors which strongly influenced the move towards permanent, standing forces. However, despite its limitations, the battalion of between 500 and 700 men has remained the basic infantry formation up to the present day.

Gustavus Adolphus of Sweden refined the Dutch system. Matchlock muskets replaced the arquebus and the battalions fought in six ranks thus increasing the frontage and the density of fire. Gustavus also introduced 'volley firing' by advancing the three rear ranks of musketeers into the intervals between the front three ranks. The Swedish battalions were supported by two or three light, 3-pounder cannon – 'infantry guns'.

The new battalions had to concentrate on volley firing. The inaccurate matchlock and flintlock muskets were only effective if a number were simultaneously discharged. As efficiency and the rate of fire increased during the seventeenth and eighteenth centuries, the number of ranks of musketeers was gradually reduced to create a longer battalion frontage. Unfortunately, as the ranks diminished in number and the frontage grew, it became almost impossible for a battalion to defend its flanks and rear. The solution was for each battalion to butt onto its neighbours, forming a continuous, though thin, line of battle. The flintlock musket had virtually replaced the matchlock by 1700, on account of its higher rate of fire and greater reliability. However, the principal change was the abolition of the pike and the adoption of the bayonet. The early plug bayonet appeared in France in 1647 to be replaced by the socket bayonet in 1689. It was adopted by Brandenburg-Prussia in the same year and by Denmark in 1690. By the end of the War of the Spanish Succession in 1714, European infantry fought in linear battalions, three or four ranks deep, each man armed with a flintlock musket tipped with a socket bayonet. He could combat cavalry and engage all opponents with volley firing. Heavy and light infantry had been temporarily combined.

Maurice of Nassau had provided 'skirmishers' for his new battalions and these made a reappearance during the eighteenth century as light infantry. Although not differently equipped to the line infantry, the light troops had a distinct function. They took part in reconnaissances and raids, were trained to use aimed instead of volley fire and, after 1750, were often armed with the rifle rather than the musket. On the battlefield they acted as skirmishers to mask the deployment of the battalion lines and operated from cover on the flanks. At Lauffeld in 1747, swarms of French light infantry used aimed musket fire to shield the deployment of the main columns. As Broglie advanced to Minden in 1759, his march was preceded by a cloud of light troops, infantry and cavalry, who seized river crossings, made feint attacks and gained intelligence. There were 5,000 light infantry in the French army in 1748 and 25 per cent of the Austrian army were thus qualified by 1763. Light troops also proved of great value in colonial warfare.

By the Seven Years' War (1756–63), infantry battalions fought in three ranks, the Prussians achieving a rate of fire of three enormously inaccurate shots a minute. The Prussians also fired on the move.

The weight of musketry was now sufficient to allow gaps between the battalions in the battle line, any infiltrators being met by heavy flanking fire. Frederick the Great proceeded to abandon the straight line of battle and adopt an echeloned, 'oblique', formation which enabled him to concentrate his main effort against the decisive point while preventing his opponent from committing reinforcements from other sectors of the line. Towards the end of the eighteenth century, the French experimented with infantry in column, between six and twelve ranks deep. This suited the less than perfectly trained volunteers and conscripts of the French Revolutionary Wars but it also complemented the revolutionary spirit. Napoleon's infantry fought in line in three ranks with the front protected by skirmishers (*voltigeurs*) while reserves waited in column ready for the assault. As the quality of his infantry declined, Napoleon relied increasingly on the column. After 1808, the British infantry operated in two ranks, emphasis being placed on accuracy and rate of musketry.

In the middle of the nineteenth century appeared the rifled, breech-loading firearm. Prussia adopted the Dreyse 'needle gun' in 1848, the British adapted the Enfield-Snider in 1867 and the French introduced the Chassepot in 1866. An infantryman could now lie down to reload and fire six aimed shots a minute at ranges of up to 800 metres. At Sadowa in 1866, the Dreyse rifle was partly responsible for the Prussian victory over the Austrians. Equipped with the Chassepot, a company of 200 men had the firepower of a whole battalion at the time of the French Revolutionary and Napoleonic Wars. Battalions could now spread out, seek cover and abandon volley firing. All infantrymen were translated into light infantrymen. A Prussian regulation of 1847 split up the massed columns of the battalion into lighter, company-strength elements. The interval between soldiers was set at between one and five paces. Formations had to adapt to the ground, which resulted in their men becoming spread over larger areas so that battalion and company commanders could no longer exercise direct control. Increasing importance was attached to platoons and sections with the non-commissioned officers assuming tactical responsibilities; in 1914, the 'fire cell' of a British battalion was a section of ten men commanded by a corporal. Unable to give orders by word of mouth, battalion and company commanders had to designate objectives to their subordinates and then concentrate on deploying reserves to close a gap or exploit a breakthrough. Battalion and company commanders were unable to resume a tighter control over their formations until the widespread introduction of light, portable radios during the Second World War. However, the speed of these changes should not be exaggerated; the new weaponry brought much uncertainty and indecision about the most appropriate tactics to adopt. The French fought in dispersed formations in Algeria, but used massed battalions in Italy and the Crimea. Useful lessons were, however, drawn from Sadowa. Instead of marching towards the enemy in column of companies, a formation in two echelons was adopted which allowed an alternation between firing and moving rapidly from one piece of cover to another – 'fire and movement'. Although the Franco-Prussian War demonstrated that infantry attacks in close ranks (column of platoons or column of companies) were doomed in the face of massed rifle fire, there was a reversion to close order in both France and Germany during the 1880s and 1890s. It was not until the slaughter of the German, French, Russian and British infantry in 1914 and 1915 that old tactical notions finally withered.

The invention of smokeless powder in 1884, the magazine rifle during the 1860s and the Maxim machine-gun in 1883 produced a further revolution in infantry fighting. The range and weight of fire was so great that many theorists, particularly Jan Bloch, believed that it would be impossible for infantry to cross the 'beaten zone'. After 1875, the Germans temporarily abandoned close formations; the skirmishing and the main lines would advance in open order, using and firing from cover, the main line being used to thicken the skirmish line until it lapped around the flanks of the enemy position and forced him to withdraw. The achievement of fire superiority was also seen as vital to a successful attack. However, as Ardant du Picq observed, the infantry now fought in extended formations, each man on his own in a fog of fear, smoke and confusion. He was no longer buoyed up by the propinquity of his comrades and officers. In the new battle, he might 'go to ground', a tendency exacerbated by the fact that the new infantry were mostly short-service conscripts rather than professional regular soldiers. These fears, that the officer might lose control over his men, resulted in the German Regulations of 1888 which encouraged the infantry to attack in column of platoons on a front of 25 metres. The French and, despite their experiences in the Boer War, the British advocated that the only way across the 'beaten zone' was to charge with the bayonet in massed formations thereby achieving a moral ascendancy over the defender. The Russo-Japanese War encouraged this optimism. Japanese infantry crossed the 'beaten zone', although at considerable cost, with the help of artillery barrages and covering rifle and machine-gun fire up to the instant of the attack. Also, the adoption of eighteenth-century siege techniques presented another method of crossing the 'beaten zone'; the infantry dug trenches, advanced by saps and only exposed themselves to an open assault when they were extremely close to the enemy positions. Casualties, however, were very high.

In the open, infantry was unable to advance without the support of artillery; in defence, infantry could only shelter from artillery by digging in. The First World War was an artillery contest. On the Western Front and in Gallipoli, infantry adopted the siege methods which had reappeared during the American Civil War and the Russo-Japanese War – trenches, dug-outs, saps, mines, hand-grenades and mortars. In the trenches, the defensive power of the machine-gun became overwhelming. The failure of the offensives in 1914 and 1915 proved that even in an age of Social Darwinism, the bayonet alone could not break through modern defences. After 1915, all offensives had to be preceded and supported by continuous, heavy artillery fire. At the Somme in 1916, Haig believed that the Germans would be shattered by the preliminary barrage allowing his infantry to advance in line and occupy deserted trenches. Of 120,000 men who advanced on 1 July, 60,000 became casualties within the first few hours. Gradually, during 1916, 1917 and 1918, the combatants tried to discover a means to overcome the tactical stasis and advance beyond the range of their own artillery support. Automatic weapons and light machine-guns were introduced along with rifle grenades and flame-throwers. The British and French deployed portable artillery in the form of tanks while the Germans developed 'fire and movement' through infiltration tactics. All sides abandoned continuous lines, both in defence and in attack, concentrating on area defence and on small squads and sections in the assault. By 1917, the huge casualties had reduced the quality of the infantry on all sides, a tendency made worse by the hasty training given to conscripts. However, by 1918 the British army had developed a weapons system – accurate artillery, machine-guns, light machine-guns, light mortars, rifle grenades, tanks and aircraft – which enabled the infantry to advance successfully against heavily defended field fortifications.

Infantry during the Second World War possessed much the same weapons as during the 1914–18 conflict and relied just as heavily on artillery support both in attack and in defence. However, infantry had to face new weapons, principally the tank and the aircraft. Anti-tank guns and anti-aircraft guns became standard infantry weapons during the Second World War and in the British and French armies, special 'infantry tanks' were assigned to the foot soldiers to assist in both attack and defence. Infantry also became more mobile. German and British armoured divisions contained a sizeable body of infantry which was carried in lorries or in armoured carriers (mechanized infantry). The British and American armies also motorized their infantry divisions so that by 1944 infantry had achieved a considerable tactical and strategic mobility (motorized infantry). Infantry were hence converted into dragoons – mounted soldiers who used transport for mobility but fought on foot. However, in 1944 and 1945, as the weight of firepower on the battlefield increased, certain sections of the German motorized infantry (*panzergrenadiers*) were designated armoured infantry (*gepanzerte*) and were carried right onto their objectives in their armoured half-track carriers. They even used their weapons directly from the vehicle, firing over the sides. In defence, infantry fought from dug-in positions, supported by machine-guns, light machine-guns, mortars and artillery. In the attack, rifle squads grouped around a light machine-gun employed infiltration tactics but continued to rely heavily on supporting artillery barrages. The British rifle section remained at ten men. In both attack and in defence, British infantry adopted a triangular formation. In a company of 119 men and five officers, two platoons fought in the line with the third in reserve; the three battalions in an infantry brigade adopted a similar formation of 'two up and one in reserve'.

Modern offensive infantry tactics have remained similar to those practised during the Second World War; 'fire and movement' and infiltration. In defence, weight of firepower from concealed positions and the counter-attack still constitute the basis of all infantry tactics. Since 1945, of the major powers, only China has retained large forces of marching infantry equipped with towed artillery. The main world armies still possess some motorized infantry plus some light infantry in the form of specialized Commando or Ranger units but the vast majority of modern infantry is mechanized. It carries out a diversity of roles. On a nuclear battlefield, or a conventional battlefield dominated by electronically controlled weaponry of high yield, the infantryman has continued to function as a modern dragoon operating from armoured and hermetically sealed carriers, his task being to occupy ground captured by automatic and missile weapons. The Second World War German concept of armoured infantry has reappeared, especially in the Russian army, with foot soldiers firing their small arms from their armoured personnel

carriers and being transported directly onto their objectives. On the nuclear or chemical battlefield, it has become essential for the infantry to operate from their carriers. The vehicles themselves have ceased to be simply carriers and now possess heavier armour and often small turrets armed with heavy machine-guns or light cannon; the carrier has now become an all-purpose combat vehicle (the US M113 or the Russian BTR 52 and 60). Some theorists even doubt whether infantry can actually survive on the modern, electronic battlefield. Battalions have to operate in widely dispersed formations so that in the event of the explosion of a tactical nuclear weapon no more than a single company will be destroyed. However, with modern mechanization and signals, this wide dispersion does not present an obstacle to rapid concentration and deployment. Infantry is now part of an all-arms, all-mounted army equipped with tracked vehicles capable of operating in most terrain. The helicopter and the helicopter gunship have provided infantry with an air-portable capability and close fire support. The tactical potential of this mobility was demonstrated in Vietnam and is widely employed by rapid reaction forces. Infantry has played the leading role in combatting guerilla campaigns in the Third World where traditional forms of fighting have been combined with modern techniques. Increasingly, infantry is deployed on low-intensity operations to counter terrorist campaigns and various forms of urban warfare. The British deployment in Northern Ireland is the most obvious example. It is in these types of conflict, as well as in close and mountainous terrain, that infantry will continue to play the primary role. In large-scale conventional or nuclear war, infantry will be confined to mopping-up operations after the ground has been taken by tanks, artillery and missiles.
See also AIRBORNE TROOPS; ARMOUR, PERSONAL; ARTILLERY; BLADE WEAPONS; BLOCH; CAVALRY; DRAGOONS; FIREARMS; GREECE, ANCIENT; GRENADIERS; GUSTAVUS II ADOLPHUS; HIERARCHY; NASSAU; ROME; SALDERN; SPAIN; SPARTA; SWITZERLAND; TACTICAL ORGANIZATION; TACTICS; WEAPONS.

G. BODINIER
JOHN CHILDS

FURTHER READING
Archer Jones, *The Art of War in the Western World* (Oxford, 1989); E. M. Lloyd, *A Review of the History of Infantry* (London, 1908).

Inspections A governmental policy of carrying out inspections of military personnel, equipment and supplies at regular intervals or unexpectedly has three basic aims. It combats wastage of public funds by ensuring that money is paid only for services actually rendered; it checks the operational efficiency of armed forces; and it ascertains that the army does not possess more men than can be paid. The earliest form of inspection was the muster. Essentially, a troop or company was mustered before an official who verified that the officers and men present on parade corresponded with the names and numbers on the muster roll which had been presented to him by the commander. If all was well, the roll was signed and sent to the paymaster who issued pay to that company or troop according to the ranks and numbers listed on the roll. Company and troop commanders devised a number of frauds to inflate their commands on the day of the muster: hiring additional men, having one man answer to two names, retaining dead men on the rolls, etc. As the period between musters was often three to six months, captains could make a handsome sum of money by pocketing the pay of deceased or non-existent soldiers. Mustering was a constant war between captains trying to cheat the system and the central military administration. In the sixteenth century, the Spanish authorities made the *tercios* undergo *revistas* (inspections) or *muestras* (musters). The *veedor* (inspector) made a particular point of parading the men whose names were borne on the nominal rolls. Following these inspections, reports, in several copies, were drafted in a standard form of presentation. There were even marginal notes recording the amount of pay earmarked for men who were absent or on leave, as well as the names of colleagues authorized to draw pay on their behalf.

Until the time of Louvois, the French system of mustering was highly inefficient and ineffective. Captains of companies were given a fixed sum of money for a given period and they were then at liberty to pay their officers and men at whatever rates they chose. Neither does there seem to have been a reliable check upon numbers. Under Louvois's rod of iron, inspections were carried out by a *commissaire des guerres* enabling accurate assessments of expenditure to be calculated. The minister severely penalized officers and *commissaires* who were found guilty of conniving at the inclusion of bogus soldiers on the muster rolls. The change for the better was almost complete by 1725; the *commissaires des guerres* now regularly prepared three copies of each inspection report. One was sent to the secretary of state for war, another to the *intendant de province* and the third to the treasurer responsible for making the payment. The exactitude with which the *commissaires* carried out their task seemed guaranteed by the requirement that they should put up a surety, set at a standard level of 70,000 livres in 1785, and which the state could sequester if they failed in the performance of their duties. They exercised the right to dismiss recruits whom they thought were unfit for military service but they could grant a bonus payment to any captains who paraded their companies at full strength. The British system of mustering was closely modelled on the French methods of Louvois. After 1747, British companies were mustered twice a year but captains were required to make monthly returns of strength 'upon honour'.

There was a virtual synonymity between musters and inspections in the seventeenth century but, during the eighteenth century, the two began to separate. French *commissaires des guerres* initiated inspections of the civilian contractors who furnished bread to the soldiers, checked horse fodder and inspected the hospitals. In England and Ireland, William III introduced specific tours of inspection by trusted officers, a full inspection of the Irish army being carried out in 1696. A regular pattern of regimental inspections was commenced in 1716 and this developed into an annual inspection for all British regiments in England, Scotland and Ireland in 1720. For all armies, ceremonial reviews also served as inspections as did annual manoeuvres in the eighteenth, nineteenth and twentieth centuries. Frederick the Great established a royal commission of inspectors in 1763, initially five for the cavalry and six for the infantry. This had increased to seven and ten by 1786. The inspectors were not members of the army staff but were personally responsible to the king. Each inspector toured his province and supervised anything up to 21 battalions of infantry or 75 squadrons of cavalry. The inspectors assisted the king at the spring reviews and autumn manoeuvres. By 1850, the British army possessed inspectors of the cavalry, fortifications and military schools. The army of the United States appointed inspectors during the War of Independence and the war with Britain in 1812 and an inspector-general's office was added to the general staff in 1821. The inspector-general now reports directly to the chief of staff. If an army inspector is to be effective, then he must be directly subordinate to the effective head of the army and not have to answer to intermediate staff levels or headquarters. The inspectorate forms an essential part of the personal 'eyes and ears' of the commander through which he can bypass the official hierarchy and receive up-to-date and accurate information on the state of the forces at his disposal. *See also* ADMINISTRATION, ARMY; CEREMONIES; COMMAND; DISCIPLINE; FINANCES; INTENDANTS; NUMERICAL STRENGTH; RECRUITMENT.

J. CHAGNIOT
JOHN CHILDS

FURTHER READING
A. Corvisier, *Armies and Societies in Europe, 1494–1789* (Bloomington, Ind., 1979); John Childs, *Armies and Warfare in Europe, 1648–1789* (Manchester, 1982).

Intelligence In its earliest manifestion, intelligence took the form of keeping a watch on the activities of a current, or possible future, adversary – particularly by means of spying. Hence, there are references in remote antiquity. Joshua made use of information provided by a prostitute to capture the city of Jericho. The Assyrians maintained an espionage service, and the Great King of the Persian Empire raised intelligence, both inside and outside his territories, to a very high level of sophistication. The same was true of ancient China. Intelligence also played an important part in the conflicts between Christians and Moslems, thanks to the co-operation of co-religionists on both sides. The spread of written communication and the development of administrative systems, from the fifteenth century onwards, particularly in the Italian states, produced new forms of intelligence. Sovereigns and military commanders had their intelligence agents, but for sovereigns military intelligence constituted one part only of the quest for information. Louvois, who combined the functions of secretary of state for war and of postmaster-general, raised the conduct of Louis XIV's state business to a high pitch of efficiency by the systematic use of intelligence. Under Louis XIV, there was a close relationship between intelligence and subversive activity directed against an enemy. The eighteenth century witnessed the growth of postal censorship, which monitored the correspondence of persons on whom a watch was being kept. While monarchs provided themselves with genuine intelligence services, military commanders still employed only an occasional agent. An exception was the Duke of Luxembourg, who used agents and spies regularly during his campaigns in the Low Countries (1690–4). In the nineteenth century, however, military intelligence services attached to general staffs were established – the British Intelligence Service, the German *Abwehr* and the French *Deuxième bureau*, which was set up in 1874 as one of the four departments of the general staff with representatives on the staffs of units. Even so, intelligence in the military sphere seemed to monarchs or to governments impossible to separate from a system which would cover the complete range of state affairs and, in the twentieth century, more and more services designed specifically for those purposes came into being.

Intelligence and information are synonymous. Intelligence services, therefore, are bodies which, in order to provide information for those whom they serve, operate in a manner that is peculiar to them, secret and often termed 'special'. The results of such activities, where they do not consist of 'open information', are called 'intelligence'.

General Aspects The intelligence to be sought will relate to the current and future situations, to the intentions of the 'other side', and can be concerned with various military or civil spheres. It has to be transmitted first to the authority whose responsibility it is to make a decision based on the information. Subsequently, it is passed on for utilization to sections which build up an overall intelligence picture and sometimes, after this analysis, to special services responsible for action such as putting a stop to leakages or producing disinformation, as well as to any others able to take such follow-up measures as it may require. The use to which intelligence is put is always determined by a decision of an official civil department or a military headquarters. One or other of these decides on the orientation of any disinformation or 'deception' which the counter-espionage service will execute. The counter-espionage service is responsible for curtailing the activities of enemy agencies that are seeking to acquire information. It is consequently best placed to use double agents. It lures enemy agents by first arranging for them to obtain pieces of accurate, but unimportant information ('chicken feed') and then information which is to a greater, or lesser, degree false and which is sufficient to cause the other side to modify its plans and actions in the desired sense. Obviously, a counter-espionage service operating in this offensive role will be in a position to note the effect of this disinformation. On the other hand, counter-espionage in its defensive aspect can, by putting the counter-espionage police to work (i.e. in the suppression of espionage activities), neutralize the operations of enemy services, but must at the same time avoid 'eliminating' the enemy's sources and continue to make its disinformation plausible.

Since the work of these services is not restricted to seeking and assembling intelligence, expressions such as 'secret services' or 'special services' seem preferable to that of 'intelligence services', particularly on account of their methods, procedures and modes of action, which are clandestine – indeed, on the borderline of legality. Nevertheless, the core of this work is to seek, assemble, protect, transmit and, at least in part, exploit intelligence.

Various Branches of the Special Services It is logical for the search for, and assembly of, intelligence to be carried out in accordance with its relevance and its nature, and by the appropriate means. Where relevance is concerned, a distinction must be drawn between 'macro-intelligence' (which will be the outcome of a comprehensive study) and 'micro-intelligence', which has value only when linked with many other pieces of information. As for its nature, intelligence can be concerned with politics, the armed forces, the police, economics (in both its technological and industrial aspects), science and even banking and cultural life. Dealing with each of these categories is an organization which fits together pieces of micro-intelligence and tries to blend them into macro-intelligence. These different organizations constitute the intelligence services and are themselves subdivided into agencies and into intelligence groups. Each of these groups has as its target a certain number of objectives laid down by governmental authorities or the high command. It sometimes happens, however, that these groups begin devoting themselves to objectives that lie closer to their own particular interests. The means by which intelligence can be sought and acquired can be divided into the following categories:

1 The traditional means, which rely essentially on human beings. At the head of organizations are officers known as 'controls', whose trustworthiness is absolute; it is on them that an intelligence service rests. Below them come the agents, of whom Sun-Tzu (fourth century BC) provided a classification that is still partly valid, but needs to be adapted to the present day, based on the sex of agents, their profession, their racial background, their political outlook and their circumstances. Agents require to be handled with finesse and firmness, particularly with regard to the hold which the service has over them (via, for example, their self-interest or weaknesses, and sometimes also their ideals). On a higher level are the 'honorary correspondents', who are generally unpaid and are most commonly nationals; the work which they do in the course of their normal professions puts them in a position to collect certain information, which they generally do for patriotic or ideological reasons.

2 Alongside these are found an increasing range of technical sources of intelligence. The oldest is the monitoring of the mail, used in earlier times and widely applied during the First World War in particular. More recent are telephone-tapping and radio monitoring (this latter being backed by direction finding techniques), together with microphonic eavesdropping, electronic detectors and the interception of radio waves, termed SIGINT (signal intelligence). SIGINT is subdivided into COMINT (communications intelligence, which deals with verbal communications) and ELINT (electronic intelligence, which is the service dealing specifically with electronic warfare, and which handles material that is non-verbal and purely technical in nature, but which allows important positions to be fixed). There is also observation from the air by U2 type aircraft, from space by satellites (including those designed for the detection of ballistic missile launches, and even for their destruction) and on the ground or underwater by robots. In line with technical advances, these methods are undergoing constant refinement, some of them being based on cryptanalysis (e.g. the British source of intelligence on the Germans called 'ULTRA', which was pooled among the Allies during the Second World War, or the American 'MAGIC' on the Japanese).

Protection of intelligence and of its sources, which belong to the category of 'top secret', is carried out by the security services. They are the concrete expression of preventive counter-espionage and need to show a high degree of positive activity, basing their work on documentary sources of the widest-ranging and most accurate kind possible, particularly in relation to individuals (computer files), and making use of the most sophisticated information techniques and of especially powerful computers. All personnel recruited for intelligence work have to be scrutinized by the counter-espionage service. The security services maintain surveillance of targets which could be of interest to the services of foreign powers, particularly in wartime, but also in peacetime, and monitor their own side's radio traffic and the enciphering of messages by departments that deal with these functions, in order to prevent any slip that might give real or potential opponents information about the code.

The transmission of intelligence, of whatever kind, is a delicate operation – whether carried out by means of personal rendezvous, telephone, couriers of written messages, 'dead letter boxes', or radio – because the special services of the other side possess comparable methods and techniques.

Use can be made of intelligence in many fields, depending on its nature, and it will thus be a task for various organizations, not all of them necessarily belonging to the special services, which are responsible for one particular aspect of this use, following a decision, in cases where such is required, from the governmental authorities or the high command. These intelligence-using organizations are:

- the Intelligence Service itself in seeking information supplementary to some preliminary information which is defective or incomplete;
- the Counter-Espionage Service, in connection with the repressive side of its work, for making arrests and neutralizing an enemy spy network or, in its offensive role, for disinformation and, if required, deception plans;
- the *Action Service*, which in France dates from the Second World War, when Colonel Passy's *Bureau central de Renseignement et d'Action* (BCRA) was

given the role of exploiting in certain fields, by 'discreet' methods, intelligence in regard to targets (both material and human) which could not be dealt with by the classic and official means (i.e. the army or the police). Subsequently, such operations were put in the hands of the *Service de Documentation étrangère et de Contre-Espionnage* (SDECE), and later, of the *Direction générale de la Sécurité extérieure* (DGSE). Such missions comprise a large part of the operations which the Americans set out in 1948 in the National Security Council's directive NSC 1012 – a document, moreover, of which the USSR secured knowledge; these were sabotage, destruction, 'springing' of individuals, assistance to subversive resistance movements, attacks, including those on people, and kidnaps – such tasks and the operations required to accomplish them being the responsibility of specialist personnel using appropriate and often sophisticated equipment.

All countries will be found to possess, in general, the following branches, their greater or lesser integration with each other depending on the political nature of the state concerned: (1) intelligence service (search for, and assembly of, information by the standard methods); (2) counter-espionage service – preventive (whether or not in the form of a security service), defensive (whether or not combined with a police force responsible for suppressing dangerous elements), and offensive (combined with, or attached to, services dealing with psychological warfare and deception plans); (3) services for action against human and material targets; (4) technical services containing a research section, often combined with the radio and code-breaking wing of the intelligence service, a transmissions section, a section for counter-espionage (particularly in the form of radio direction finding) and an equipment section.

Some Examples of Special Services. In Russia/USSR, up to the revolution of 1991, there were two main organizations, the

391

KGB and the GRU. The KGB (State Security Committee) was a full ministry, with a staff of 500,000 (300,000 of them being frontier guards); it had a chairman and was attached to the Council of Ministers but, in reality, came under the Central Committee of the Party (the Politburo). It consisted of five general directorates (suppression of internal activities hostile to the state, intelligence, internal surveillance, frontier guards and schools), and a dozen ordinary directorates or services (among them, counter-espionage, disinformation or deception, action, etc.). The GRU (a department of the general staff) dealt with military espionage (tactical, strategic and technical) and with paramilitary operations. It came under the control of one of the ordinary directorates of the KGB that maintained surveillance over the military forces of the country. During the Second World War, it achieved remarkable results. Both organizations also carried out economic and technical espionage. The KGB was often a stepping stone to high official positions (Yuri Andropov being an example).

The special services of the United States employ nearly 200,000 agents divided between the Central Intelligence Agency (CIA), responsible for external intelligence and counter-espionage; the Federal Bureau of Investigation (FBI), concerned with internal counter-espionage; military intelligence and counter-espionage, which comprises, apart from its general services, some armed operational elements; internal intelligence and presidential protection; specialized external intelligence (narcotics and nuclear energy).

In France, at present, there are the *Direction générale de la Sécurité extérieure* (DGSE), which replaced the SDECE in 1982, and which deals with external intelligence and counter-espionage, as well as with code-breaking and external action; the *Direction de la Surveillance du Territoire* (DST), responsible for internal counter-espionage; a group of directorates under the prime minister, the minister of defence (e.g. the DGSE) or the minister of the interior (*Direction des Renseignements généraux* or DRG), *Direction de la Gendarmerie nationale*, *Direction de la Protection, de la Sécurité et de la Défense* (PSD), which has replaced the old *Sécurité militaire, Groupement interministériel de Contrôle* (GIC), etc.

The Cold War brought about a considerable expansion of these services. *See also* ATTACHÉS; COMMAND; INDIRECT WARFARE; PSYCHOLOGICAL WARFARE OPERATIONS; SECRECY; SIGNAL COMMUNICATION; SUN-TZU.

J. ALLEMAND

FURTHER READING
G. Mattingly, *Renaissance Diplomacy* (Boston, 1955); Christopher Andrew, *Secret Service: the making of the British intelligence community* (London, 1985); John Ranelagh, *The Agency: the rise and decline of the CIA* (New York, 1987); Nigel West, *GCHQ: the secret wireless war, 1900–86* (London, 1986); *Knowing One's Enemy: intelligence assessment before the two world wars*, ed. E. R. May (Princeton, 1984); *The Missing Dimension: governments and intelligence communities in the twentieth century*, eds. Christopher Andrew and David Dilks (London, 1984).

Intendants Military administration assumes an institutionalized form characterized by the economic, social and political structures of different states at different periods in their histories. Long before Vegetius and Richelieu, Xenophon had already emphasized the vital task of regular supply to the troops. In Antiquity, soldiers maintained themselves by pillage, and the invaders of continental Europe during the Dark Ages – the Arabs and the Norsemen – acted in the same fashion. Only with the advent of nation-states during the fifteenth, sixteenth and seventeeth centuries could the more centralized and better-funded governments begin to assume some responsibility for the maintenance of their armed forces. Modern military administration was the product of the development of the national standing army.

Modern logistics really commenced with the Genoese and the Venetians at the time of the Second and Third Crusades when it was necessary to assemble considerable stocks of weapons, horses and foodstuffs to sustain the Christian armies in the Holy

Land. France adopted a new system during the Hundred Years' War. After the disaster of the Battle of Poitiers, the Estates-General forced on the king the 'Grande Ordonnance' of 1357 which laid down the principle that every Frenchman had an obligation to assist in the defence of his country, financed the mobilization and maintenance of the king's army and appointed commissaries to regulate the pay of the soldiers. The commissaries carried out musters to see whether the stated number of men were actually present with their units. Those responsible for the maintenance of modern armies originated as administrators of pay rather than of provisions. Soon, these gentlemen graduated to become the king's war commissaries. Their duties included checking the numerical strength of units, the ability of men and horses to undertake a campaign and ensuring that the relevant ordonnances were observed. As they had to be numerate and literate, the commissaries were generally members of the bourgeoisie; military administation was originally a matter for civilians.

Spain drew lessons from both the Italian and the French experiences becoming the first country to set up a coherent system of military administration complete with a departmentalized bureaucracy. The inspectors of the musters (*veedores*) were the linchpin of the organization. The paymaster (*contador*) and the treasurer (*pagador*) could do nothing without their written approval. The *veedores* were accompanied by halberdiers to emphasize their authority. The kings of Spain also took a partial control over the supply of food. Although the captains of units largely dealt with private traders, the government supervised the issue of foodstuffs through inspectors (*proveedores de viveres*) and in 1594 this was extended to the provision of clothing. Central stores of weapons and foodstuffs were stocked by the *proveedores* making arrangements with either private merchants or official supply officers. After 1590, horses were supplied on credit, their cost being deducted from pay. This latter use of a hire-purchase system became the norm for the provision of uniform and weaponry in many European armies. The whole organization was controlled from Madrid by the *Contaduria mayor de Cuentas* (the Revenue Court).

The French kings tried to imitate the Spanish system. Just as in Spain, military administration was a civilian function. Besides the royal commissaries, whose title was changed to war commissaries in 1567, there were also war auditors responsible for handling financial matters. During periods of warfare, commissaries for foodstuffs were appointed.

Louis XIII and Richelieu had to maintain 150,000 soldiers during the Thirty Years' War. With the aim of increasing the effectiveness and efficiency of the government's military administration, intendants were sent to the armies and to the various provinces of France. They were recruited from among the officials of the Royal Council. Intendants of the army were appointed to an army for a single campaign while the intendants for legal, organizational and financial affairs were appointed to a province for varying lengths of time. The latter had the additional responsibility of supervising the maintenance of troops stationed in, or passing through, their 'généralité'. In 1648, the Fronde forced the regent, Anne of Austria, to recall the provincial intendants but the intendants of the army remained at their posts and assumed the administration of the frontier provinces and did much to rescue France from the disruption caused by the insurrection.

Under Louis XIV and Louvois, the system of intendancy developed along different lines. Nevertheless, the provincial intendants retained their responsibility for the maintenance and discipline of the soldiers in their areas until 1788, a task which became more burdensome as military administration increased in scope. On these gentlemen fell the duty of raising and supporting the royal militia, a force created in 1688. The army intendants, who were fewer in number, were only commissioned in time of war. They had to monitor army supplies and act as intermediaries between the captains of units and the official treasurers, taking over some of the functions of the defunct war auditors. A distinction was drawn between the campaigning season (May to September) and winter quarters (October to May). During the months in winter quarters, the soldiers received full pay but had to buy their own food; when on campaign, food was provided by the king against a stoppage in pay. At the end of the seventeenth century, the system was altered; the whole body of troops was fed throughout the year from deductions in pay, the captains using the money to purchase supplies. The wars of Louis XIV resulted in a considerable increase in the burden of providing for armed forces owing to the development of weaponry, the adoption of compulsory uniform, the beginnings of a policy of providing regular barracks, the establishment of military stores and the tightening of discipline.

The war commissaries continued to execute the detailed work of military administration under the supervision of the intendants. In 1664, the position of war commissary, which had been based on a royal commission, was made a state post and opened to purchase. The ordonnance of 1692 fixed the number of commissaries at 180 and listed their powers. As a consequence, their status rose and, at the end of the eighteenth century, the cost of purchasing such a position amounted to 100,000 livres (c.£4,800), more than an infantry colonelcy. As these civilian administrators had the task of exposing any abuses at which the colonels and captains had connived, the relations between the two parties were often strained. However, under Louis XIV a new generation of senior officers emerged who began to look upon the war commissaries as indispensable collaborators. Slowly, the war commissaries gained military status. They attended courts martial and in 1735 they were allowed to speak and vote. In 1727 they received the same scale of allowances as infantry captains in staging areas. In 1746 they were given a uniform and from 1772 they were placed upon the same establishment as infantry captains. Complete integration into the army had to wait until after the French Revolution.

A hierarchy was created among the grades of commissary. In 1595, provincial commissaries, whose place of duty was fixed, appeared alongside the commissaries who dealt with the marching regiments. Commissaries-in-charge were created in 1635 taking station under the intendants in order to supervise the ordinary commissaries. As the position of the commissaries rose, so that of the army intendant declined. Few army intendants were commissioned during the eighteenth century and the office lost its importance as the king took away the supporting regiments and companies. They disappeared altogether in 1788. When Saint-Germain was Minister of War, he appointed two *intendants généraux* to inspect the administration of the army. The ordonnance of June 1788 transferred to the commissary-in-chief part of the responsibilities which had previously fallen to the provincial and army intendants.

The Revolution retained the position of war commissary but, at the same time, abolished the system whereby it could be bought and sold. Many of the holders under the *ancien régime* remained at their posts. The law of 14 October 1791 transformed the war commissaries into military magistrates. The commissaries-in-chief became high court judges and presided over courts martial; the commissary-auditors exercised governmental authority while monitoring army administration; and the ordinary commissaries undertook the detailed work. Civilian administration had returned but not for long. The law of 11 September 1793 established the principle that military men should be recruited into the commissariat. The law of 17 January 1795 (28 Nivôse III) laid down the responsibilities of the war commissaries which, by and large, remained unchanged until 1882. They were members of courts martial where they ranked immediately below the presiding judge; they audited the disbursal of pay; supervised the administration of units; provisioned armies and fortresses; distributed foodstuffs, forage, fuel and clothing; organized hospitals; arranged transport for foodstuffs and the artillery; levied taxes and contributions on occupied countries; and managed staging posts and areas. Their structure of rank was fixed at: senior commissary-in-chief, who ranked immediately beneath general officers; commissaries-in-chief; and war commissaries.

The next stage was to establish a means of checking the activities of the commissaries. Bonaparte took the step of separating the executive payment for military supplies from its auditing. The *arrêté* of 30 January 1800 created two corps of officials. The duties of the 60 *inspecteurs aux revues*, who were independent of military commanders, were to inspect, verify and audit. The war commissaries, numbering several hundred, remained subordinate to the military commanders and carried out the work of provisioning and administration. With men like Petiet and Daru supplying the impetus, this system, which retained the name 'intendance' from long-established usage, succeeded, despite the chaotic conditions, in supplying the necessary provisions from the resources of occupied countries for large and mobile armies.

The ordonnance of 29 July 1817 re-established a single corps of officials, called 'military intendants', subdivided into the grades of intendant, deputy-intendant and assistant intendant. These were equivalent to the military ranks of *maréchal de camp* (brigadier-general), colonel and lieutenant-colonel. The titles remained in force until 1928 when they were replaced by those of *intendants généraux* and *intendants*. Originally, recruitment was intended to be among civilians but from 1822 intendants were drawn from army personnel.

In 1829, a standing consultative committee for war administration was established consisting of five chief intendants, the forerunners of the *intendants généraux inspecteurs* who were created in 1856. After the Franco-Prussian War, the law of 16 March 1882 redefined the administration of the army. It laid down the principle that the administrative services were subordinate to the military command and that financial auditing was independent of the commissariat. To this end, a corps of auditor-generals was founded.

The sphere of responsibility of intendance remained considerable, even though it had shed direct involvement in regimental and medical affairs. The tasks of intendance have increased in the twentieth century to such an extent that intendance can be confused with the general administration of the army and its supporting services. However, administrative and technical services can be distinguished from intendance. Intendance covers:

1 The financial administration of the army In particular, the accounting of income and expenditure and auditing.

2 The supply of foodstuffs In 1557, in imitation of the Spanish system, there were established in France commissaries for victuals who were responsible for maintaining stores along routes of march. There were also commissaries for forage. The commissaries bought their supplies from private merchants and from the state. Richelieu, by the ordonnance of 1629, tried to ensure that the state fed its soldiers, but his initiative was premature and was abandoned during the Fronde. Under Louis XIV and Louvois, there was a return to a more flexible system which made use of both private contractors and state-controlled enterprises together with the stockpiling of main magazines and mobile stores. The minister turned most frequently to firms like Lacour, which provided bread to the French armies of the north and east during the War of the Spanish Succession. The Pâris brothers were also important. Taking Prussia as his model, Saint-Germain tried in 1775 to establish a system of independent firms working on contract but, in 1778, responsibility for the provision of foodstuffs was handed over to army units under the overall supervision of a foodstuffs directorate.

During the Revolution, use was made of every system: state-controlled enterprises, purchasing committees, agencies, private firms and requisition. In Year VIII, Bonaparte had recourse to a new type of enterprise in which the state had a financial interest and the director-general of foodstuffs served as the manager. It worked rather poorly and various attempts were made to improve its performance. Some notable advances were made under the July Monarchy with the foundation of a corps of administrative officers who took their instructions from the military intendants. In 1844, the purchasing of foodstuffs, which was executed by intendants through tendering, was separated from the reception, storage and distributions of foodstuffs, a task which was assumed by the accountants in the foodstuffs department. This same principle was followed in the law of 1882 which divided the directorate that procured provisions from the department charged with storing, distributing and paying for the foodstuffs.

3 *Clothing* The decision to make uniform obligatory was taken in 1672 but it was not generally effective until 1690. Captains of units purchased the uniforms for their companies and were reimbursed by deductions from the soldiers' pay. Under Choiseul's reforms, this was taken over by the state but the royal stores merely supplied the necessary cloth. In 1788, a directorate of clothing was set up but the units still had to make up the material themselves. Not until 1796 did Petiet create a clothing service. Its work rooms were under the supervision of the war commissaries and the service also took over responsibility for the soldier's pack and web equipment.

Requisitioning was another task performed by the intendants. Previously, this had been a royal prerogative but it was widely employed during the wars of the Revolution and the Empire. After 1815, requisitioning of foodstuffs fell into disuse. However, since the Prussians regularly made recourse to requisitioning during the Franco-Prussian War, the French government reaffirmed the principle and laid down the manner in which it was to be executed by a law in 1877. In 1931, the law on the wartime organization of France extended its sphere of application.

The proliferating and complicated functions of the intendants necessitated training. Recruiting by examination was introduced in 1827. Captains in various branches of the army could offer themselves for examination as could administrative officers after 1882. A course of training was made compulsory in 1895 and this developed, in 1926, into the École Supérieure de l'Intendance. Initially, this was

housed in the Hôtel Royal des Invalides but it was moved to the École Militaire in 1956.

Beneath the intendants, there was a need for a subordinate level of administrative personnel. In 1788, the baking of bread was passed from private contractors to the army. Under the Empire, companies of civilian workers in governmental employment provided this service. Similar arrangements were extended by the Restoration to the hospital service in 1823, for foodstuffs in general in 1825 and for clothing in 1830. The administrative officers in charge of these departments were formed into a department in 1824 and into a corps in 1838. The three areas of responsibility of the administrative corps – hospitals, foodstuffs and clothing – have continued except that hospitals were detached to the army medical service in 1889. In 1855, a training course was instituted for the officers in the foodstuffs branch and this was developed in 1875 into the École d'administration militaire. This was accommodated in the Château de Vincennes until it moved to Montpellier after the Second World War. *See also* ADMINISTRATION, ARMY; FINANCES; INSPECTIONS; LOGISTICS; MEDICAL SERVICES; ORDNANCE; RATIONS; STAGING POSTS; TRANSPORT; UNIFORM; WEAPONS.

A. CORVISIER

FURTHER READING
D. C. Baxter, *Servants of the Sword: French intendants of the army, 1630–70* (Urbana, Ill., 1976); I. A. A. Thompson, *War and Government in Habsburg Spain, 1560–1620* (London, 1976); Geoffrey Parker, *The Army of Flanders and the Spanish Road, 1567–1659* (Cambridge, 1972); *Revue historique des armées* (October 1957 & January 1968).

Internationalism *See* PACIFISM

Invalids 'Invalids' or 'disabled' has been used as a term for soldiers who are incapable of continuing their active service on account of wounds, infirmity or the wear and tear of years, and who are without resources of their own on which to live. The idea of disability stems naturally from warfare and can be found in earliest antiquity. The history of the attitude towards disabled soldiers can be divided into four periods. During Antiquity, the soldier who had been wounded or who had become infirm was, on the majority of occasions, merely abandoned. Although there were exceptions, generally he had to fend for himself. In the Middle Ages up to the beginning of the seventeenth century, private charitable organizations, which were mostly inspired by Christian sympathies, provided some help to soldiers who were crippled or worn out with age. In the seventeenth and eighteenth centuries, monarchs assumed this function from individuals and founded royal establishments which served as places of refuge for their old and infirm soldiers and provided them with food and a decent mode of existence. From the nineteenth century onwards, national governments have taken over these institutions and partially replaced them with systems of pensions and retirement homes.

Ancient warfare seemed to recognize only two martial categories – the living and the dead. Depictions of battles do show wounded and maimed soldiers and even severed limbs but they also illustrate massacres of the wounded and, in the case of the Assyrians (seventh century BC), the infliction of horrifying tortures on prisoners. The relief on Trajan's Column in Rome (second century AD) of wounded soldiers having their wounds dressed and receiving attention is most unusual. Apart from a few exceptions, Antiquity never developed a system of aid to those disabled in war. In Athens, from the time of the laws of Pisistratus (sixth century BC), maimed soldiers were fed at the city's expense. More frequently, however, they were abandoned to their fate. These unfortunates sometimes suffered cruel treatment at the hands of the victors, especially at the end of the Peloponnesian War; 2,000 wounded and sick soldiers, who were abandoned by the Athenian Nicias, were immured in the salt mines by the Syracusans. Disabled Macedonian soldiers sometimes received gifts of land. Alexander assisted some of his soldiers who

had been maimed while prisoners of the Persians, and at the end of his campaigns in 324 BC he intended to furnish superannuated men with money and send them home. Under the Roman Republic, wounded citizens returned home after a war but the state made no provision for them. There may have been some state assistance under the Roman Empire but modern historians have not turned their attention to this subject.

In the medieval period, the fate of disabled soldiers depended on the initiatives of charitable Christians, even though their motive was as much to save souls as to heal bodies. The Crusades effectively placed an obligation on the Church to establish hospices for the benefit of the soldiers of Christ. The hospice of St John of Jerusalem and, later, those of the Knights of Rhodes and Malta, provided a pattern. In France, the same spirit of charity inspired the foundation, in 1260, by King Louis IX, of the Quinze-Vingts Hospice to house 300 blind knights whom he had brought back from the Holy Land. Conversely, although some succour was given to the Crusaders, those injured in baronial wars had to seek help through feudal connections, the traditions of chivalry or the membership of a family or a local community. During the Hundred Years' War, old soldiers, when wounded or sick, had no option but to follow the bands of looters and bandits, unless they themselves became the victims of such desperadoes, or to join the hordes of beggars who infested the towns. They then incurred fear and repugnance rather than pity.

Nevertheless, in France and the Holy Roman Empire, the monarch enjoyed a right to require an abbey to look after an *oblat*, also termed a lay monk or lay brother. The king made use of his powers in this respect for the benefit of old retainers, generally invalided or decrepit soldiers. These often rough and coarse men were incongruous in religious institutions and frequently sought to escape, preferring a vagabond existence. Abbots were equally glad to be rid of them.

By initiating the system of *mortes-payes* (soldiers sent, on a reduced scale of pay, to certain castles with vague assignments for defence and maintenance but, in reality, so that they could end their days there), Francis I opened the way for a new policy towards the invalids although its development in Europe was to be slow. From the sixteenth century, the stronger political position of monarchies and the growth of standing armies obliged rulers to assume these responsibilities from the Church and private charities, although the latter continued to function into the mid-seventeenth century. At the close of the fifteenth century, several powerful Venetian families had a building erected to house noblemen who were impoverished and no longer in a condition to go to war. In 1576, Nicolas Houël founded in Paris a 'Maison de la Charité Chrétienne' to help crippled soldiers and in 1656 a husband and wife named Berthelot had a house built to accommodate 50 crippled soldiers. In 1658, Count Strozzi founded a hospital in Bohemia entirely for the use of old soldiers who had been maimed or wounded, of whom there were large numbers after the Thirty Years' War.

It was in France that a monarchical government first took upon itself the responsibility for the fate of old, disabled soldiers, thus answering the entreaties of Blaise de Monluc on behalf of the 'poor cripples'. By the edicts of 1578 and 1585, Henry III put disabled soldiers under royal protection but he lacked the resources to give them positive assistance. Henry IV, when enjoying the benefits of peace and an uncontested authority, attempted to reserve for his veterans the house of Nicolas Houël, which had been placed under the king's control in 1604, but his death in 1610 put an end to the scheme. Louis XIII had no better success with the founding of an ambitious establishment at Bicêtre under the name of the 'Commanderie de Saint-Louis', which never fulfilled its aim, because of lack of money.

By an ordonnance of 26 February 1670, Louis XIV founded the 'Hôtel Royal des Invalides'. The scheme combined ambition, grandeur, vision and the fiscal means to make it effective. The construction of the building was entrusted to Libéral Bruant and its decoration to the best artists from Versailles. At the same time, military 'disability' was given a precise definition with the word 'disabled' being substituted for 'crippled'. Those admitted to the Hôtel Royal were aged or worn out, wounded or infirm soldiers, in addition to those with ten (later twenty) years of service. The large number of eligible men, coupled with the notion that they might be restored to health and the desire to preserve their self-respect by providing gainful employment, in accordance with the teaching of St Paul, led to the creation in 1690 of independent companies of 'disabled' soldiers. These were posted to frontier fortresses and interior castles. This was a reintroduction of the *mortes-payes* of Francis I. These companies continued until the Revolution. Two ordonnances, of 26 February and 30 November 1764, further assisted the old, disabled soldiers by giving them a modest pension which enabled them to return to civilian life outside the milieu of the Hôtel Royal. Unfortunately, this measure was hampered by the financial embarrassment of the crown and the number of abuses which had worked their way into the administration of the invalids.

Until the reign of Charles II, English military invalids were dependent on parish poor relief or, for the lucky few, a county pension. After Charles II had twice sent the Duke of Monmouth to inspect the Hôtel Royal and had secured the plans from Louvois, the Royal Hospital at Chelsea was started in 1682 and received its first pensioners two years later. Chelsea Hospital was over-subscribed before it had officially opened and 'in-pensioners' were given the chance of taking a pension and becoming 'out-pensioners'. To make room for the returning wounded from Flanders, four 'invalid companies' were organized from among the fitter out-pensioners in 1690. By 1697, there were 600 serving in the invalid companies. Based on a similar system to the Hôtel Royal and Chelsea Hospital, Kilmainham Hospital in Dublin was built during 1681 to house the old and unserviceable men from the Irish army. In the Holy Roman Empire, similar establishments were founded in Vienna by the Emperor Leopold I in 1697 for the

Kilmainham Hospital, Dublin, was opened in 1681 to accommodate old and infirm soldiers from the Irish army. It was modelled on the Hôtel Royal des Invalides of Louis XIV, which was built between 1670 and 1676 to the designs of Libéral Bruant. Chelsea Hospital was founded along similar lines in 1682. However, the first home for old and crippled soldiers had been established by the Spanish Army in Flanders at Halle ('the Garrison of Our Lady of Halle') in the early seventeenth century. In 1640 it housed 346 veterans.
(Irish Tourist Board)

Austrian invalids, by Charles VI at Pest in 1724 for the Hungarian pensioners and at Prague in 1728 for Bohemians and Moravians.

During the course of the eighteenth century, the major European states all provided similar arrangements in the form of pension systems and/or residential hospitals. In Prussia, a pension scheme was begun in 1707 for the benefit of soldiers no longer fit for duty and in 1748 the 'Invalidenhaus' was opened in Berlin. Here, 600 invalids could live with their wives. In 1730, Frederick William settled 480 invalids of the Guards on Werder Island in the River Havel. These measures were inadequate to deal with the massive casualties of the wars of Frederick the Great and the majority of Prussian invalids were left to beg. As early as 1684, an institution for disabled soldiers was created at Celle in Brunswick-Lüneburg. In Russia, after his visit to Paris in 1717, Peter the Great granted pensions to disabled soldiers. Initially, these pensioners were distributed among the various Russian religious communities but from 1764 they were assigned to residence in garrison towns and performed a role similar to the invalid companies in France and England. Catholic charities remained important in Spain and Portugal until well into the eighteenth century. Philip V of Spain founded an institution for disabled soldiers at Toro in 1717 but it was not opened until 1753. The last hospital to be created in the eighteenth century was the 'Asilo dos invalidos militares' at Runa in Portugal in 1792. In other countries, however, traditional systems remained in being; Sweden relied upon its rural communities both to provide soldiers and to care for them when disabled. Nevertheless, this did not prevent the establishment in 1647 of the 'Krigsmanhus' at Vadstena.

During the nineteenth century, the establishments dealing with the invalids took on a different shape for a number of reasons. In the first place, a clear distinction was drawn in France, Austria and Spain between the old soldiers who were completely incapacitated and the veterans who, though old, were still fit and could be expected to serve in a non-mobile role.

Second, the development of national conscript armies replaced or supplemented professional, regular armies, altering the relationship between the state and its armed forces. Third, disability and retirement pensions were extended to bring all old soldiers within an overall military welfare scheme; this reduced the relevance of the old hospitals and private charities. However, despite the growth of state welfare some of the hospitals continued to exist. The Chelsea Hospital continues its charitable work down to the present day as does the 'Asilo dos invalidos militares' at Runa. The Hôtel Royal declined during the nineteenth century and was put to other uses in 1904. However, the enormous French casualties of the First World War brought it back into being and it is now the headquarters of the 'Institution nationale des invalides'. It still takes in some pensioners who are crippled, in poor health, suffer 80 per cent disablement or are over sixty years of age. Since 1871, Louis XIV's building has been the home of the French Artillery Museum which became the Army Museum in 1945. Since the beginning of Louis XVI's reign, the Hôtel has been the host of the magnificent collection of relief models of French fortresses and fortifications. *See also* HONOURS AND AWARDS; MEDICAL SERVICES; PENSIONS; RECRUITMENT; VETERANS.

J.-P. BOIS
JOHN CHILDS

FURTHER READING
O. de Riencourt, *Les Militaires blessés et invalides, leur histoire, leur situation en France et à l'étranger* (2 vols, Paris, 1875); *Les Invalides. Trois siècles d'histoire* (Paris, Musée de l'Armée, 1974); C. G. T. Dean, *The Royal Hospital Chelsea* (London, 1949); David Ascoli, *A Village in Chelsea: an informal account of the Royal Hospital* (London, 1974).

Iphicrates (*c.*415–*c.*353 BC) This Athenian general occupied a pre-eminent place in the military history of Athens between 394 and 356 BC. He stands as a good example of the Athenian military leaders of the fourth century BC who were used to commanding troops of mercenaries rather than armies of citizens and who sometimes took liberties with the directives of the established authorities or ignored them altogether, and so became genuine *condottieri*. Iphicrates much enhanced the role of peltasts, lightly armed soldiers who had originally been introduced from Thrace as mercenaries, and whom he had several opportunities to command in his early career. In 390, using these troops, he achieved his most famous exploit by destroying a force of 600 Spartan hoplites in the Corinthian War. In 388 Iphicrates, operating on behalf of Athens in the Hellespont, destroyed a small force of Spartans and their allies near Abydos by using a surprise attack mounted by peltasts. After this he served as a mercenary commander for the kings of Thrace. The peltasts were armed with the *pelte*, a circular Thracian shield smaller than that of a hoplite, a long lance, and a sword twice the length of a hoplite sword. Trained with strict discipline, they fought like hoplites in close formation, but with greater mobility. Iphicrates is usually credited with these developments in the fighting techniques of peltasts, but this has perhaps been exaggerated and such features may be seen rather more as variants of the existing Thracian peltast techniques. Many cities made increasing use of peltasts in their armies without, however, renouncing the use of hoplites. Since these peltasts were most often mercenaries, their frequent use inevitably had repercussions on the state of mind of the Greek armies and their leaders. *See also* GREECE, ANCIENT; INFANTRY.

R. LONIS
B. CAMPBELL

FURTHER READING
J. K. Anderson, *Military Theory and Practice in the Age of Xenophon* (Berkeley, 1970); J. G. P. Best, *Thracian Peltasts and their Influence on Greek Warfare* (Groningen, 1969).

Iran The military history of Iran consists of brilliant passages interspersed by periods of eclipse. After the loss of the Persian Empire to Alexander the Great by Darius III, the last of the Achaemenids, the Seleucid dynasty (Greek descendants of Seleucus I (c.358–281 BC), one of Alexander the Great's generals) turned their attention westwards into Mesopotamia and towards Syria. Iran became a political and military backwater. During the third century BC, Iran was infiltrated by the Parthians, desert nomads from east of the Caspian Sea, and their king, Mithridates (170–138 BC), established control over the region. The Parthian army fought on horseback. Heavy cavalry sported a long lance, the 'Parthian shaft', and both riders and horses wore armour. Light cavalry were armed with the bow. This organized, disciplined and well-articulated army defeated a numerically superior Roman army under Crassus at Carrhae in 53 BC. The Roman heavy infantry were shot to pieces by the Parthian bowmen and then charged by the lancers. The Sassanian dynasty emerged from the Parthian Empire (AD 240–651) and re-established much of the Achaemenid Empire. Rome was defeated in AD 363 and between 613 and 620, Syria, Egypt and Asia Minor fell to Iran. The Battle of Qadisiya in 637 marked the end of the Sassanian period and Iran was conquered by invading Arabs and its religion was altered to Islam. In the eleventh century, Iran became a part of the Turkish Empire, contributing both regulars and mercenaries, principally bowmen, to the Turkish standing army. Iran was overrun by the Mongols in the twelfth and thirteenth centuries.

Under the Safavid dynasty (1501–1722), Iran recovered its independence through the Shi'ite religion, patriotic sentiment and a brilliant civilization. Shah Abbas the Great (1587–1629), aware of the difficulties in relying upon the loyalty of the tribes which constituted the sovereign's power base, created a new, royal standing army complete with a corps of artillery. Tribal contingents provided 30,000 men but Abbas supplemented them with mercenaries, mainly from Georgia, enlisting 10,000 cavalry and 12,000 infantry. Abbas tried to equip his army in the Western style, and in 1598 he took into his service two English gentlemen, Anthony and Robert Shirley, together with twenty-six of their companions, among whom was a cannon founder. The arsenal of Bander Abbas is reputed to have stocked 500 cannon and 6,000 muskets, obtained either through purchase or manufacture. Abbas also permitted the English East India Company to establish a factory at Isfahan. With his new army, Abbas drove the Ottoman Turks out of Kurdistan and Mesopotamia and the Ozbegs from northern Iran. The end of the Safavid dynasty in 1722 was marked by a further bout of Turkish and Russian conquest and Iran returned to instability. Her army was out-of-date, poorly trained, lacked modern weapons and was badly beaten by the Russians between 1797 and 1834. By the mid-nineteenth century, the levying of feudal forces was abandoned and a small, rudimentary regular army was founded. Throughout the nineteenth century, Iran was increasingly penetrated by Britain and Russia, ending with the division of the country into three zones in 1907, one British and one Russian with a small neutral buffer zone in between. Britain and Russia raised forces within their own spheres of influence. Persian Cossacks, commanded by Russian officers, came into existence in the north while the Persian Rifles under officers from the Indian Army controlled the south. Reza Khan was first a private and then an officer in the Persian Cossacks. Iran was invaded by Turkey, Russia and Britain during the First World War.

The accession of the Pahlavi dynasty in 1925 (Reza Shah) saw the creation of a modern, indigenous Persian army. Initially established at 40,000 men it had reached 200,000 by 1941, to which were added a small navy and an air force. Despite Reza Shah's policy of Westernization, he was unable to prevent the invasion and occupation of his country by Russia and Britain in 1941. Reza Shah went into exile. After the occupation (1941–6) the Iranians resisted socialist tendencies and managed to re-establish a centralized government and Muhammad Reza Shah was installed in 1953. Between 1953 and 1957, a repressive regime ensued during which political activity was suppressed. In 1963, Muhammad Reza Shah introduced the 'White Revolution' in which the Iranian society and economy were Westernized and modernized. Militarily, Muhammad Reza Shah also moved closer to the West, signing a military co-operation treaty with the United States in 1959. By 1965, Iran had an army of 200,000 largely composed of conscripts on two-year terms of service commanded by regular officers and NCOs. The air force consisted of 25 combat aircraft. The armed forces were privileged and pampered, enjoying good quarters, special shops, schools and sports facilities. As far as was possible, the armed forces were kept separate from civilian society. As the Shah came under pressure from the Islamic revolutionaries during 1978, he turned to the army for support and to form a government but it was desperately unpopular and unable to secure confidence. When the Shah was overthrown in 1979, he commanded 415,000 troops. By the time of the outbreak of the Iran–Iraq War (1980–8), Iran possessed 150,000 regular soldiers supported by 400,000 reserves. She had 1,740 tanks and 1,000 pieces of artillery. Her air forces consisted of 445 combat aircraft and 500 combat helicopters. The majority of her armaments were American. By the end of the war, her regular army consisted of 655,000 men reinforced by 650,000 'Revolutionary Guards', 1,575 tanks and 1,750 guns. The air force had been reduced to 90 combat aircraft and 341 combat helicopters. Having severed her ties with the United States and cancelled a number of outstanding weapons contracts, revolutionary Iran was militarily and diplomatically isolated, without access to spare parts and replacements. As the Gulf War against Iraq continued, her shortages of operational modern weapons became acute and she resorted to the tactics of massed infantry attacks, spurred on by Islamic fervour. Since 1988, Iran has begun to re-equip her armed forces through Third World sources and the international arms market. By 1991, her army had risen to 305,000 men (c.250,000 conscripts) supported by 350,000 reserves and c.700 main battle tanks. The air force had 213 combat aircraft but less than half the United States models were serviceable. The navy possessed 3 destroyers, 5 frigates and 42 coastal vessels. *See also* GREECE, ANCIENT; INDIA; INDIRECT WARFARE; IRAQ; MONGOLS.

A. CORVISIER
JOHN CHILDS

FURTHER READING
Herodotus, *The Histories*, tr. Aubrey de Selincourt (Harmondsworth, 1954); J. M. Abdulghani, *Iran and Iraq: the years of crisis* (London, 1984); *The Cambridge History of Iran*, eds J. A. Boyle et al. (8 vols, Cambridge, 1968ff); A. Ehteshami, G. Nonneman and C. Tripp, *War and Peace in the Gulf* (Reading, 1991).

Iraq   In 1967, Iraq had an army of 70,000 conscripts on two years' service. Her air force consisted of 170 combat aircraft. In 1980, the army had 200,000 regulars with 250,000 reserves and a further 250,000 in the paramilitary Popular Army. She had 2,500 battle tanks, 335 combat aircraft and 40 combat helicopters. In 1988, Iraq had the fourth largest army in the world composed of 955,000 troops supported by 650,000 reserves in the Popular Army. She possessed 4,500 battle tanks, 484 combat aircraft and 232 combat helicopters. After her defeat in the Gulf War of 1991, her army had been reduced to *c*.350,000 men, her main battle tanks to *c*.2,300, her combat aircraft to *c*.260 and her combat helicopters to 120.

Iraq, composed of three provinces of the Turkish Empire, emerged from the First World War as a quasi-independent state under British mandate in 1921. In the north in Mosul were the Kurds, descendants of the Medes, racially and linguistically different from the Arabs in the south. Kurdistan became vital in 1927 after the discovery of a major oil field in the Kirkuk region. An Iraqi army had been founded in 1921 along Western lines; the lower ranks were mostly Shi'ite while the officers were drawn from the former Ottoman officer corps and were predominately Sunni. However, it was dominated by British senior officers and British troops continued to garrison Iraq. During the 1920s, Iraqi nationalists vowed to form a genuinely national army which might be used to help expel the British. By 1936, 23,000 men served in the armed forces and a Military College had been established to train officers but, in that year, the army and air force assisted in the Bakr Sidqi coup. In 1941, the British overthrew the nationalist government of Rashid

Ali Gailani and Iraq was then used as a source of oil and as a staging post for the delivery of supplies to Russia. The British Military Mission left Iraq in 1948. In 1955, Turkey, Iran, Iraq, Pakistan and Britain signed a military alliance, the Middle East Treaty Organization (Baghdad Pact), which allowed Britain and America to maintain their influence over Iraq. Between 1952 and 1956, inspired by the Egyptian Revolution under Nasser, groups of 'Free Officers' organized themselves into revolutionary cells within the army. In a futile effort to buy its political loyalty, extensive privileges were granted to the army. Pensions were increased, special housing was provided for officers and whole streets in Baghdad were inhabited by retired and serving officers. However, despite this, in 1958 the pro-Western monarchy was overthrown by these nationalist republican army officers and Abdul Karim Qasim was made president. Western influence was expelled and Iraq became a genuinely independent state. She withdrew from the Baghdad Pact in 1959 and became non-aligned. In 1963, the pan-Arab Ba'ath Socialist Party overthrew Qasim but the Ba'athists fell out amongst themselves and the non-Ba'athist Abdul Salam Arif usurped power in November 1963. Elements of the army and the air force sided with both Qasim and the Ba'athists but the majority of the armed forces remained neutral and awaited the outcome. However, the army viewed the growth and development of the Ba'athist National Guard with growing jealousy and suspicion. Arif died in 1966 and was succeeded by his brother, Abdul Rahman. He was overthrown in 1968 by an alliance of Ba'athists, the army and air force. The Ba'athists rapidly tightened their grip on all aspects of the state, military and civil.

In 1971, Britain withdrew from east of Suez and both Britain and the United States determined to employ Iran as a bulwark against communism and Russian influence in the Gulf. Iraq responded, after the seizure of strategic islands in the Gulf by Iran, by signing a fifteen-year treaty of friendship and co-operation with Moscow in 1972. Iran replied by moving closer to the

United States, purchasing large quantities of American weapons using the huge funds created by the rise in oil prices in 1967 and 1973. Iraq saw herself as the leader of militant Arab nationalism confronting Iran, the stable monarchical gendarme of the Gulf. The two countries clashed repeatedly over the Shatt al Arab waterway and the Iranians gave constant support to Kurdish rebels in the north of Iraq. The realization that secessionist tendencies were spreading from Iraqi Kurds to Iranian Kurds, caused the two countries to initial the Algiers Accord in 1975 re-establishing more harmonious relations. Iraq was now free to spend her huge oil revenues on the modernization of the structure of the state, rather than on arms. However, the Iranian Revolution of 1979 presented Iraq with an ideal excuse for attacking Iran in order to solve the problem of the Shatt al Arab waterway. The resultant Gulf War (1980–8) ended in a partial defeat for Iraq with Iran occupying 920 square miles of Iraqi territory. In 1990, President Saddam Hussein renounced all claims to Iranian territory and to the Shatt al Arab as he prepared the ground for his seizure of Kuwait. Despite his inauguration of Kuwait as the 19th province of Iraq, a United Nations force, under US leadership, ousted the Iraqi army from Kuwait in 1991 and inflicted a severe defeat on Saddam Hussein. Under attack from US, British, French, Saudi and Italian airpower and land forces, Iraq lost the majority of its Soviet tanks and heavy equipment. *See also* GULF WAR; IRAN; ISRAEL, SINCE 1948.

JOHN CHILDS

FURTHER READING
Phebe Marr, *Modern History of Iraq* (Boulder, Col., 1985); Dilip Hiro, *Inside the Middle East* (London, 1982).

Irregular warfare *See* GUERILLA WARFARE; INDIRECT WARFARE; POPULAR WARFARE; RESISTANCE

Israel, early (to AD 135) Tribal settlement probably occurred in Canaan in the thirteenth century BC, historians dating the exodus from Egypt between 1450 BC and 1250 BC. A united kingdom of Israel was probably founded under King Saul in *c*.1020 BC but he was killed while fighting the Philistines, the traditional enemies of the Israelites. David assumed the throne in *c*.1000 BC and took Jerusalem as his capital. He was followed by Solomon, who expanded the frontiers and made Israel into a minor Middle Eastern power. This period of dominance only endured for about one hundred years but it was during this time that the Temple was built in Jerusalem. Israel was resisted by the Nabathites and, particularly, the Philistines to the south. The latter, who possibly originated from Crete, had also invaded Canaan at much the same time as the Israelites. The united kingdom of Israel broke up during the tenth century BC. Rehoboam, the son of Solomon, became king of the two tribes of Judah in the south and the remaining ten tribes formed the kingdom of Israel under Jeroboam (I Kings, 11–14). The two states were rarely at peace, either with each other or their neighbours. The Assyrians destroyed Israel in 721 BC and Judah in 701 BC, carrying much of their populations into slavery. The Babylonians, who had defeated Assyria, occupied Judah in 597–538 BC, deporting still more of its population. Israel and Judah (Palestine) were ruled by Persia from 538 BC but were annexed by Alexander the Great in 332 BC. During the sixth and fifth centuries BC many Jews returned from Babylon and rebuilt the Temple (516 BC) and the walls of Jerusalem (445 BC). Palestine was ruled by the Ptolemies (Macedonian kings of Egypt) in the third century BC and in 200 BC it passed under the control of the Seleucids (the Greek empire in Mesopotamia). Attempts by the Seleucid emperor Antiochus IV to repress Judaism resulted in a revolt by Judas Maccabaeus (167–160 BC). By 142 BC, the Seleucids had been expelled and Israel became an independent military power for the next eighty years. In 63 BC, Pompey took Jerusalem and by AD 6 the region had been annexed to Rome. A revolt (AD 66–73) ended in the Roman recapture of Jerusalem (AD 70) and the mass suicide of the defenders of Masada in AD 73. A major revolt occurred between AD 132 and 135 led by Simon Bar Cochba. It was defeated at Bethar, 6 miles south-west of Jerusalem.

Israel-Canaan-Judah stood on important trade routes, especially the caravan road from Egypt and the Levant to Mesopotamia. The region possessed a population which probably never exceeded one million people. The conquest of Canaan can be studied from the Bible but a new investigation has recently been made by Abraham Malamat in the context of the *Strategemata* of Frontinus (*c.*AD 30–104) and the *Stratagems* (AD 162) of Polyaenus. The tribes of Israel which had come from Egypt under Moses, regrouped in Canaan with members of their own people who had been left behind at the time of the resettlement in Egypt. They encountered vigorous resistance from fortified towns. The Israelites were poorly armed and organized, and when confronted by numerically superior professional soldiers equipped with effective weapons, including highly manoeuvreable two-wheeled chariots, they had to rely on stratagems and cunning. The first kings developed an army modelled on those of neighbouring states, 'For by wise counsel thou shalt make thy war; and in multitude of counsellors there is safety' (Proverbs, xxiv. 6). Solomon introduced a force of two-wheeled chariots and in 835 BC, during the reign of Ahab, Israel could put 2,000 chariots into the field. Judah organized a similar force. There was no cavalry, the army consisting of infantrymen armed with the spear, sword and bow to complement the chariot forces.

Troops were raised by quotas from the tribes and organized into subdivisions based on multiples of ten (10, 50, 100, 1,000). Early in the period, soldiers provided their own arms but, later, these were supplied from central armouries. The army was probably only raised in time of war. During peacetime, the frontiers were guarded and the fortifications garrisoned by mercenaries based around the chariot force. Sizeable towns were enclosed within walls and as the Israelites had no siege engines until the second century BC, sieges could only succeed through starvation or stratagems.

Before the town of Ai, Joshua divided his army into two sections. One group, having failed to take the town by siege, pretended to succumb to a sortie by the besieged garrison. They retreated, pursued by the besiegers. The second Israelite division, carefully concealed, proceeded to enter Ai unopposed. The retreating division then turned and fought while the Israelites in Ai sallied forth and took the garrison in the rear (Joshua, viii. 12–22). The Israelites were assiduous in gathering intelligence. Moses sent out twelve spies to infiltrate into besieged towns (Numbers, xiii. 17–21). Rahab, the harlot at Jericho, probably pro- vided the besiegers with both intelligence and a route into the city. Psychological man- oeuvres also played their part. Joshua's parading round Jericho once a day for six days and seven times on the seventh day was a stratagem which was later mentioned by Frontinus. Once the towns of Canaan had been conquered, warfare became defensive.

In open warfare, surprise was combined with stratagems. After a night march of between 15 and 18 miles from the Jordan Valley involving a climb of 1,000 metres, Joshua fell at dawn on the Amorite army which was defending Gibeon in the valley of Ajalon (Ayalon). He took advantage of a fierce rising sun to blind his enemies, forcing them to raise their shields to their eyes thus exposing their bodies to arrows and javelins: 'Sun, stand thou still upon Gibeon' (Joshua, x. 12). This stratagem was also common in Antiquity. Night operations were frequent. Gideon struck the Midianites with 300 crack raiders just at the moment when the guard was being changed 'at the beginning of the Middle Watch' (Judges, vii. 19). *See also* FRONTINUS; INDIRECT WARFARE; ISRAEL, SINCE 1948; MASADA; ROME.

A. CORVISIER
JOHN CHILDS

FURTHER READING
Abraham Malamat, 'Conduite de la guerre chez les Israélites à l'époque biblique', *Acta of the International Commission for Military History*, iii (Bucharest, 1978), pp. 115–23; C. Herzog and M. Gichon, *Battles of the Bible* (London, 1978); W. Keller, *The Bible as History, Revised* (London, 1980).

Israel, since 1948 Although 1,800 years separate the biblical from the modern state, Israelis are keen to emphasize their historical roots. The birth of the state of Israel was attended by acts of war, and its history has been marked by wars. From the Balfour Declaration of 1917, the settlers in the Jewish homeland of Palestine had to defend their lands against Arab raiders. The British refusal to permit an extension of immigration after 1945 brought armed resistance to the mandatory government from 1943 onwards. Before the Second World War, the Jews created an illegal armed force, the *Haganah*, of about 60,000 men, which developed its own shock troops, the *Palmach*, in 1941. Open hostilities between the British and the Jews broke out in 1945 with the men of the *Haganah* often being committed to the fighting by the more extreme political groupings, the *Irgun* and the Stern Gang.

Following the UN resolution (29 November 1947) to partition Palestine between the Jews and the Arabs, Britain relinquished her mandate on 15 May 1948. A few hours before the deadline, the Arab states of the Middle East unleashed a surprise attack on the new state. To general surprise, the Israelis held out in a series of battles. They captured Zefat and repulsed the powerful Arab Legion at the Battle of Jerusalem. Under this threat of extermination, the Jews reacted violently (Deir Yassin) and expelled 600,000 Arabs from Palestine.

Born into hostile surroundings and hampered by a low population and a weak economy, Israel found that she had 620 miles of frontier to defend. Also, the frontiers drawn by the United Nations made no military sense. Many of the centres of population were within artillery range of enemy states, Tel Aviv was only 12 minutes flying time from El Arish and 30 minutes from Cairo. Above all, the country could be snapped in two by an attack through her narrow, central 'waist', just to the north of Tel Aviv, which was only 10 miles wide. Israel could not defend herself in depth and she could not afford to fight on her own soil. All her military efforts had to be geared towards the offensive and, preferably, pre-emption. Also, the borders had to be rendered more defensible and this could only be achieved by seizing more territory from the Arabs. Her weak industrial base meant that she was dependent on imported arms and ammunition. She could only contemplate short wars. In this latter aim Israel has been assisted by the US, British and Soviet reluctance to see major wars develop in the fragile Middle East. Ceasefires have usually been arranged promptly. Because of her low population, Israel is highly sensitive to battle casualties. This is probably exacerbated by the Jewish history of persecution and the close-knit structure of the extended family. Even now, the prime minister is personally informed of all soldiers killed in action and each casualty has his/her photograph and obituary printed on the front page of the daily newspapers. This humane concern has created in Israel a mentality of 'metal not men' leading to a search for high-technology weapons capable of achieving maximum results with minimum risk to operatives. This has meant enormous imports, particularly from the United States, and the development of her own weapons industry. The annual military budget averages over one-third of total state expenditure.

The initial response after the victory in 1948–9 was the establishment of local defence based on villages and semi-militarized communes (*kibbutzim*). The second step was to organize Israel as a nation permanently in arms. Compulsory military service for all men and women has provided Israel with a great number of highly trained service personnel in relation to the size of its population. Basic training is followed by a two-, three- or four-year period of conscription, reinforced by annual periods of training in the reserve. Soldiers and officers have to be trained and motivated to move straight from civilian occupations into front-line units within a few hours. As Yigael Yadin, Israeli chief of staff between 1949 and 1952, said, 'every citizen is a soldier on eleven months' annual leave'. The Israeli Defence Forces have achieved a remarkable degree of efficiency without a rigid hierarchy or over-strict discipline. The old *Haganah* and *Palmach* principles of individual initiative have been preserved and there is considerable integration between rankers, NCOs and officers. Only the Swiss militia, although not under the pressure of the Israeli forces, comes close to emulation. In many ways, the Israeli army has become 'civilianized'. It is quite common for bank managers to serve under the command of their clerks and conscription has provided a homogeneity for the heterogeneous Israeli population. Its intelligence services (*Mossad*) are highly developed and certain of its units are trained to carry out long-distance operations (Entebbe, 1976).

The army showed its worth in the Sinai campaign during the Franco-British operation against Suez, destroying Egyptian forces and occupying the Sinai peninsula (29 October–5 November 1956). The Israelis used mobile forces to infiltrate around Egyptian positions, sever their communications and then defeat the disorganized forces. From 1956 to 1967, the Israeli army was kept on the alert by the danger of reprisal operations. The Six Day War (5–11 June 1967) confirmed Israel's crushing superiority over her adversaries. Pre-empting a general attack, in less than three hours the Israeli air force destroyed 85 per cent of the Egyptian air force thus ensuring total command of the air. The army advanced to the Suez Canal with minimal losses. As a result of this conflict, Israel occupied Sinai, the Golan Heights and the region between the 1948 border and the west bank of the River Jordan.

The Yom Kippur War (6–25 October 1973) was launched by substantial Egyptian and Syrian forces and surprised the Israeli general staff, who were let down by their intelligence service. However, despite an initial defeat on the Suez Canal and a desperate battle to retain the Golan Heights, the Israelis recovered their balance and ended the war just 63 miles from Cairo and 22 miles from Damascus. The Yom Kippur War had proved the resilience of the Israeli military structures and the high morale of the people. The peace treaty signed with Egypt on 26 March 1979, allowed Israel to evacuate Sinai except for

the Gaza Strip. Although now in a more comfortable strategic position, Israel has continued her policy of forward defence with the occupation of southern Lebanon in 1982 and the destruction of a Palestine Liberation Organization base in Tunisia in October 1985. However, whatever the military abilities and *esprit de corps* of the Israeli state, she is now approaching the point where military solutions to her relations with her neighbours are no longer sufficient and a political *modus vivendi* will have to be sought. The international sympathy extended to the Jews in general after 1945, and to the Israeli state in particular after 1948, has been partially forfeited through Israel's aggression and territorial acquisitions. In 1991, Israel reluctantly agreed to participate in a general Middle Eastern Peace Conference subject to American mediation.

In 1991, the Israeli Defence Forces numbered 141,000 men and women, of whom 110,000 were conscripts on 4 years' service for officers, 3 years' for men and 2 years' for unmarried women. In addition, there were 504,000 reservists. The army had an active strength of 104,000 expanding to 598,000 on mobilization, the navy possessed 9,000 (10,000 on mobilization) and the air force 28,000 (37,000 on mobilization) serving 591 combat aircraft. *See also* DAYAN; INDIRECT WARFARE; ISRAEL, EARLY; MILITIAS; MOBILIZATION; RECRUITMENT; SWITZERLAND.

A. CORVISIER
JOHN CHILDS

FURTHER READING
E. Luttwak and D. Horowitz, *The Israeli Army* (London, 1975); Y. Allon, *The Making of Israel's Army* (London, 1970); R. Ovendale, *The Origins of the Arab–Israeli Wars* (London, 1984); N. Lucas, *The Modern History of Israel* (London, 1974); F. H. Toase, 'The Israeli experience of armoured warfare', in *Armoured Warfare*, eds J. P. Harris and F. H. Toase (London, 1990), pp. 162–86.

Issus, Battle of (333 BC) This was a victory won by Alexander of Macedon over the Persian king, Darius. The battle took place in Cilicia, on the banks of the River Pinarus, in a narrow coastal plain, some distance from the town of Issus. Darius, whose army was numerically superior, occupied the battlefield before Alexander and drew up his battle line in a defensive position behind the river, with the cavalry on the right by the sea, the mercenary infantry in the centre, and the Persian infantry on the left approaching the foothills of the Amanus mountains. Alexander positioned the phalanx in the centre of his line with allied cavalry on his left and the Macedonian cavalry on his right, where he took command himself. Alexander led the advance across the river, aiming directly at the Persian king. Although the phalanx and the cavalry on his left wing were hard pressed, Alexander's attack was decisive. It was by forcing the Persian Royal Guard out of its positions and threatening the person of Darius, that Alexander compelled him to flee. From that point on, the Persian army ceased to resist effectively and a rout ensued. This battle did not decide Persia's fate, for Alexander chose first to capture the fortified towns of Phoenicia rather than to press on immediately into the heartland of the empire. *See also* ALEXANDER THE GREAT; GAUGAMELA; GRANICUS; GREECE, ANCIENT; HYDASPES.

R. LONIS
B. CAMPBELL

FURTHER READING
F. E. Adcock, *The Greek and Macedonian Art of War* (Berkeley, 1957); J. F. C. Fuller, *The Generalship of Alexander the Great* (New York, 1968); A. B. Bosworth, *Conquest and Empire: the reign of Alexander the Great* (Cambridge, 1988), pp. 56–62.

Italy Italy has, at several different points, played a major role in the development of the arts of war. Its Roman past, which is dealt with elsewhere in this volume, has been an inspiration to the whole of Europe, except perhaps for Eastern Europe, and has never been forgotten in Italy. Moreover, at various periods, Italy has seen intense military activity: by turns it served as a base for the crusading armies (Genoa and Venice), as a battleground in the fight against Islam (Sicily) and in resistance to the aims of the German emperors, and as the theatre of bloody struggles between states and city-states in the thirteenth and fourteenth centuries and then of the Habsburg–Valois Wars in which the French fought against the Spaniards and Imperialists. While the French and English were engaged in the Hundred Years' War, Italy was the testing ground for a particular military experiment, characterized by quite original forms of army organization (the *condotte*) and by research into military technique. The fact that terms of Italian origin – bastion, cartridge, fusilier, infantry, salvo, soldier, etc. – have passed into the international military language also bears witness to the intensity of this military past.

Italy was not the only breeding-ground for such companies of adventurers, but the *condotta* was the first well-organized form of the 'military enterprise' of the sixteenth and seventeenth centuries. From the 1320s onwards, such companies quickly became widespread as the ruling classes of the Italian city-states turned firmly towards the employment of professional fighting men. To provide for their defence, they preferred to call upon mercenaries recruited from among the inhabitants of other Italian or foreign states. They did not shrink from unleashing wars, but had them fought by professionals, thus affirming the superiority of intelligence and money. The urban militias, which were not much trusted, gradually disappeared. The *condotta* was a contract laying down reciprocal obligations: the term of engagement of the *condottiere*, the pay, number of soldiers, the oath to be taken, armament, sums allotted for the raising and maintenance of the company, etc. From 1340 to 1380, foreigners such as the famous John Hawkwood were the leading figures in this area. These men, who were unreliable, often passing from one camp to another when they received a better offer, frequently came to a tragic end. In the following generation, however, the *condottieri* became integrated into the structures of society. At Venice some of the fortresses were put in their charge. They became members of the Great Council (*Maggior*

Consiglio), were given public funerals and even had statues erected in their honour if they remained loyal (e.g. Colleoni). Some succeeded in acquiring states for themselves (e.g. Visconti, Sforza, etc.). In the fifteenth century, they belonged to a small number of families. In the end, foreigners came to represent only a small number of the *condottieri*, even among the ordinary soldiers. This system was to become the norm in most of the countries of Europe, either as the standard system (as in Germany) or as a complementary form of organization in the shape of companies of foreign soldiers in countries where there was a strong central power.

The *condotta* inspired a new structuring of troops. The company, which was self-administering and varied in numbers, had the lance as its basic unit. This was made up of a man-at-arms, a squire and a page, all on horseback. Five lances formed a post commanded by a corporal, ten made up an ensign under the command of a decurion, twenty-five a banner under a *bannerrerio*. The captain had command over all the banners. The company might, in some circumstances, include a small number of foot soldiers (*fanti*), musicians, a chancellor and marshals for discipline and justice. Though the infantry were equipped early on with hand culverins, the *condottieri*, who had acquired territorial possessions for themselves, did not keep up with improvements in military technique and the end of the Habsburg–Valois Wars in the second half of the sixteenth century marked their final decline.

However, Italy saw a brilliant revival of military thinking. From the end of the thirteenth century, in his *Liber recuperationis Terre sancte*, the Franciscan Fidenzio of Padua advocated heavy infantry formations of men armed with pikes, used in a 'wall' or a 'hedgehog', and light formations of archers and mounted crossbowmen. At the beginning of the next century, the Venetian, Torsello, in his *Liber secretorum fidelium crucis* dealt particularly with siege engines and stratagems drawn from ancient or contemporary history. Treatises of this kind became widespread throughout the whole of the West.

Of the military authors of the sixteenth century, pride of place probably goes to Machiavelli, whose *Discourse on the Art of War* (*Dell'arte della guerra*) was widely read. Torsello had drawn maps of the military theatres of operation in the Mediterranean. Military cartography really emerged in Italy in the fifteenth century, as can be seen from the map of Lombardy dating from around 1450 which is preserved in the *Bibliothèque nationale* in Paris and which shows roads with distances, stone or wooden bridges and fortifications. This intellectual effort received a further boost at the Renaissance with the renewed interest in the work of Vegetius and Frontinus. In the sixteenth century, academies spread throughout Italy where, alongside the martial arts, the elements of mathematics, fortification and general culture were taught. This example was soon followed in neighbouring countries, including France, where such courses were offered for the education of gentlemen. At the same time, the imagination of the Italian men of letters and artists led to an upsurge in the creation of new weapons, such as breech-loading cannon and gun-barrels grouped together in organ-pipe form. Leonardo da Vinci is a fine example of the imagination run riot in this way, though most often these efforts produced no practical results. Since techniques for manufacturing metals of sufficient strength had not yet been developed, these weapons were too dangerous for their users. However, alongside these ideas for the future, some lasting inventions were made, including grenades, rockets and rifled weapons.

It was principally their work in the field of fortification which brought the Italian engineers fame in the sixteenth and seventeenth centuries. From the fifteenth century, Italian writers were developing what was by then already the widespread idea that broad embankments should be introduced to protect walls against artillery fire (Leon Battista Alberti, *De re aedificatoria*, 1440–50; Averlino (Antonio Filarete), *Trattato de architettura*, c.1460). The bastion seems to have been an Italian invention, deriving either from the artillery tower or from the boulevard. It was first conceived by Giuliano da Sangallo in the early sixteenth century (and not Leonardo da Vinci, as has been asserted). The underlying cause was probably the sudden appearance of French artillery on the Italian scene. Between 1515 and 1540, a real transformation came about. Military architects became real engineers, skilled in calculations regarding ballistics and the resistance of materials. If we leave aside the speculations of such men as Francisco di Giorgio Martini and Leonardo da Vinci, Antonio da Sangallo at Civita Vecchia and Michele Sanmicheli in Venetia built the first modern fortifications, in a style that was not without its elegance. The Italian rulers took these men into their service and they supplanted the local masterbuilders.

As the focus of war shifted towards the Empire, France and the Netherlands, the Italian engineers responded to the calls they received from these countries. We find them in France from 1535–40 onwards, though there were fewer of them than has often been suggested, and they covered an astonishing amount of ground. They drew up plans for many fortresses, the building of which they would leave to local architects, returning to inspect the work in progress and to take delivery of the final constructions. Montreuil, Doullens, Vitry-le-François and the 'Fort Carré' at Antibes are evidence of their skill. In the eighteenth century, they inspired the emerging schools of fortification in the countries of Western Europe and continued to be an influence right up to the point where these reached maturity in France and Holland.

The seventeenth century saw a decline in military activity in Italy, part of which was dominated by Spain. The local nobility finally turned away from the profession of arms and almost everywhere warfare was conducted mainly by the 'civil' power. However, Italy did provide military leaders of great repute, such as Montecucoli, Piccolomini, Burlamachi, to a number of countries, including the Empire. Almost 10 per cent of the 'military entrepreneurs' in the Thirty Years' War mentioned by Fritz Redlich were Italian in origin. At Vienna, there were a great many Italians, including a number of military men. Lastly, there were Italian regiments in the armies of both Spain and France.

However, two states proved exceptional in deviating from this pattern in the seventeenth and eighteenth centuries. These were the Republic of Venice, which maintained troops for the defence of its Mediterranean possessions, and Piedmont, which in 1718 had become the Kingdom of Sardinia and whose territory was subject to frequent French invasions. To preserve its independence, its rulers deliberately turned it into a semi-military state which adopted the military structures of France. Thus a militia was formed (1701) which was reorganized in 1714 by Marshal Rhebinder, and was virtually a reserve line army. In 1734 one Piedmontese in fifteen of an age to serve was in the army, a ratio only surpassed by Prussia and Sweden. However, apart from the mountain troops (who were to become the *Alpini*), there was nothing particularly original about the military organization of Piedmont-Sardinia. From the French Revolution, northern Italy came under French or Austrian influence. It was not until the formation of the Kingdom of Italy, in which Piedmont played the major preparatory role, that there was a significant military revival in Italy.

After the first war of the Risorgimento (1848–9), which culminated in defeat at the first Battle of Custozza, Piedmont recruited French support for the second war in 1859. The bloody battles of Magenta and Solferino persuaded Napoleon III to force his ally to sue for peace, gaining Lombardy in the process; thereafter first the central Italian states and then, largely as a consequence of the success of Garibaldi's volunteers in the south in 1860, the Kingdom of the Two Sicilies accepted Piedmontese leadership. The Kingdom of Italy was proclaimed on 17 March 1861 and the Italian army formally came into existence on 4 May, its structure determined by the rapid process of amalgamation and the need to assimilate a variety of different armed forces. On 25 May 1861 the War Minister, General Manfredo Fanti, decreed that henceforth all units of the Italian army were to be composed of recruits from at least two different regions of Italy and to be stationed outside those regions. The main purposes of this system, which lasted until the First World War, were to diminish the dangers of regionalism and to make the army a more secure instrument for domestic use. To ensure Piedmontese predominance the officer corps was expanded by promoting often under-qualified Piedmontese non-commissioned officers; and while some senior officers of Garibaldi's army of the south were admitted to the new Italian army, the overwhelming majority were excluded. In the navy there were also clashes between Piedmontese officers and former members of the Neapolitan fleet which probably contributed to its poor performance in the war of 1866.

Although some southerners did achieve prominent positions in the Italian army, it remained essentially Piedmontese in character, preserving a fierce loyalty to the house of Savoy which was matched by the modest degree of professional accomplishment. The reverses it suffered in the war of 1866 – which included a second defeat at Custozza and the loss of the naval battle of Lissa – together with the successes of the Prussians in 1870–1, demonstrated the need to modernize the newly formed army. In 1867 a staff college, the Military Academy, was established at Turin, followed shortly afterwards by the Institute of Maritime Warfare; laws passed in 1872 and 1875 introduced a system of general conscription; and in 1882 the post of chief of the general staff was created. The army enjoyed a privileged position in Liberal Italy – between 1862 and 1913 it received 17.4 per cent of the national budget, the navy getting 6.3 per cent and all the remaining ministries having to share 22.8 per cent. Nevertheless, it still resembled its Piedmontese forefather rather more than its Prussian ideal: economic and political concerns dictated only partial conscription with many grounds for exemption (only abandoned in 1910), and the continuation of a law of 1853 reserving one-third of all promotions to a commission for non-commissioned officers affected the quality of the officer corps and the ranks adversely.

The Italian navy, under the energetic leadership of Vice-Admiral Saint Bon and Benedetto Brin, built a fleet of powerful modern warships in the 1870s and 1880s – a period when the Italian fleet ranked third in terms of tonnage behind Great Britain and France. By 1900, in part because of budgetary weakness, it had fallen to seventh place. However it was an Italian engineer, Colonel el Vittorio Cuniberti, who in 1903 produced the design of an all big-gun warship which subsequently resulted in the battleship *Dreadnought*.

In the years between unification and world war the army was used extensively inside Italy to suppress disorder (notably at Palermo in 1866 and Milan in 1898), in part because Italy lacked an adequate police system. After Italy joined Germany and Austria-Hungary to form the Triple Alliance in 1882, the army was also involved in discussions on combined operations; from 1888 plans were developed for Italian troops to operate on the Rhine against the French, though they remained somewhat sketchy and were never put into effect. The army also began a lengthy period of colonial warfare with the occupation of the port of Massowah on the Red Sea in 1885. Penetration of the hinterlands by the military led to a collision with Emperor Menelik of Ethiopia which finally resulted in Italian humiliation at the Battle of Adowa on 1 March 1896, when a combined Italian and native force of some 17,000 was smashed by an Ethiopian army numbering perhaps 125,000 men. The army was more successful in the Libyan war of 1911–12, wresting the provinces of Tripolitania and Cyrenaica from Turkey, but rapidly found itself entangled in a guerilla-type war with the Arab population which it was unable to win.

Italy entered the First World War in May 1915, mobilizing an army which numbered 31,000 officers and 1,058,000 men. Her armies, under the command of General Luigi Cadorna, were concentrated against the Austrians along the Isonzo River in the north-east. Believing that the only way to win was to exhaust Austrian manpower and material, Cadorna launched eleven major offensives along the Isonzo, in which Italian forces advanced a maximum of 18 miles and lost 900,000 casualties. A remote and authoritarian figure, Cadorna wielded command with considerable ferocity: 34,000 courts martial involved 1 in 12 of all front-line Italian troops, and 217 generals and 225 colonels were sacked for failing to come up to his requirements. On 24 October 1917 Italian forces were taken by surprise at the Battle of Caporetto. By the time the retreat had been halted on the Piave sixteen days later, the army had lost 30,000 dead and wounded and 280,000 taken prisoner. Under Cadorna's successor, General Alberto Diaz, the army husbanded its strength until the dying days of the war when it fought the Battle of Vittorio Veneto (27–30 October 1918). The Italian navy was never able to tempt its Austrian rival out to do battle, but from mid-1916 it had some success in penetrating Austrian naval bases along the eastern shore of the Adriatic with its MAS motor torpedo-boats, one of which sank the cruiser *Wien* in December 1917, and with human torpedoes, one of which sank the battleship *Viribus Unitis* at Pola on 1 November 1918. The nascent Italian air force amounted to only 72 aeroplanes in May 1915 but by the end of the war numbered 700 machines and made an important contribution to Italy's war effort.

Although the circumstances are still not entirely clear, the army undoubtedly acquiesced in Mussolini's advent to power in October 1922. After two years, the Duce abandoned any serious attempts to fascistize it, leaving it considerable internal autonomy. The army took the largest share of military expenditure, which amounted to 31 per cent of total budgets in 1923–31 and 25 per cent in 1931–5. Although it remained predominantly an infantry force, designed to fight either Yugoslavia or France, there was some experimentation with mechanization: a tank detachment was formed in 1923 and a tank regiment in 1927.

The Royal Italian Air Force, created in 1923, was much more politicized than either of the other services. Under Italo Balbo (1926–33) it became a show-piece of Fascism, concentrating on international competitions and exhibitions which culmin-

ated in Balbo's trans-Atlantic crossing in 1933. While these activities may have had a political value, they were carried out at the cost of developing an advanced modern air force and infrastructure: Balbo handed over 3,095 aeroplanes to his successor, of which only 911 were fully operational. The air force ostensibly followed the doctrines of General Giulio Douhet (1869–1930), modern Italy's best-known military thinker. Even before 1914 Douhet had grasped the potentiality of air power and in his best-known work, *Il dominio dell'aria*, published in 1921 (English translation, *The Command of the Air* published in 1942), he advocated pre-emptive strategic aerial strikes against an enemy's airfields and the use of explosives, incendiaries and gas against industrial and commercial establishments, transportation and centres of civilian population. Douhet's ideas had some influence abroad, particularly on 'Billy' Mitchell, and contributed to the American doctrine of strategic bombing; in Italy they were discarded by Balbo's successor, General Giuseppe Valle, in favour of the operational concept of air–land co-operation propounded by Amadeo Mecozzi.

Until 1935, when Mussolini revealed that he contemplated a war against Great Britain, the Italian navy was designed to fight a surface war against France. Although restricted by a lack of industrial capacity and shortages of raw materials, the navy developed a programme based on heavy cruisers in 1928. In 1936–7, under its head Admiral Domenico Cavagnari, it proposed the construction of a fleet of 8 battleships, 2 or 3 aircraft carriers and over 100 submarines to be ready to conduct Mediterranean and Oceanic operations by 1942–4. In one of his rare interventions in naval policy, Mussolini, under pressure from the air force, forbade the building of carriers. Operationally the navy proved somewhat backward: it shunned practice at night-fighting and went to war in 1940 lacking either radar or sonar.

The Italian army was in action overseas almost continually during the Fascist era. Libya, where Italian forces had retreated to footholds on the coast during the world war, was reconquered from 1922 by General Rodolfo Graziani in a ferocious and effective campaign culminating in the capture and execution of the Senussi chieftain El Mukhtar in September 1931, during which some 150,000 Arabs were killed. Italian Somalia was similarly pacified between 1923 and 1937. In October 1935 the Abyssinian war began with 218,000 Italian and native troops, backed by 112 tanks and 126 aeroplanes, facing some 300,000 Ethiopians. For the first three months the Fascist Party controlled the conduct of the campaign, which was leisurely and ineffective; thereafter the army took over, Marshal Pietro Badoglio entering the capital city, Addis Ababa, on 5 May 1936. The Italian victory owned much to air power, the use of gas and wireless interceptions. From December 1936 substantial Italian forces were involved in the Spanish Civil War: Italian air power played a large part in the Battle of Bilbao (April–June 1937–8), and Italian artillery contributed to Nationalist victories at the Battle of Teruel in 1937–8 and in the campaigns in Aragon and Valencia in 1938. Italian naval help, requested by Franco, consisted mainly of piracy by submarines until this ceased in September 1937.

Italy's armed forces were weakened by the campaigns in Abyssinia and Spain, and planned rearmament programmes for all three services were nowhere near completion when Mussolini hurried Italy into the Second World War on 10 June 1940 to take advantage of what he expected to be an imminent Anglo-French collapse. The army numbered 19,500 officers and 1,600,000 men (by the summer of 1943 it had swollen to over 3,000,000), and lacked modern artillery, tanks and motor vehicles. Thirty Italian divisions attacked France but made little headway before the armistice on 24 June, while Italian forces in Libya under Graziani advanced into Egypt and troops commanded by the Duke of Aosta occupied British Somaliland.

Mussolini's attack on Greece in October 1940 soon bogged down, and over the winter of 1940–1 Italian forces were driven out of Cyrenaica and Ethiopia fell to British forces.

Thereafter the 'parallel' war became the 'subaltern' war as Mussolini was forced to accept Hitler's leadership, not least because of Italy's dependence on German raw materials. Three Italian divisions were sent to the Eastern front in 1941 and another seven in 1942, along with the few modern heavy and anti-tank guns and over 16,000 motor vehicles; most of this force was lost in the Russian offensive of November 1942–February 1943. Some 40 Italian divisions were also locked up in France and the Balkans, where they fought a bitter partisan war. The Italian navy (comprising 6 battleships, 19 cruisers and 113 submarines) was conserved in 1940, when fuel was most abundant, committed to the defence of convoys at the end of 1941 and during the first half of 1942, and withheld again in 1942–3. Its strength was severely curtailed when Fleet Air Arm torpedo bombers disabled three battleships at Taranto (11–12 November 1940). Once again, human torpedoes had some success, damaging the British battleships *Queen Elizabeth* and *Valiant* in December 1941. The Italian air force found itself flying inferior machines and was able to have little effect on the course of operations.

On 8 September 1943 the armistice between Italy and the Allies was announced. Individual Italian units fought bravely but hopelessly against the Germans at Cefalonia, on the island of Leros and in Rome. Lacking orders, the army as a whole disintegrated; 650,000 soldiers were deported to Germany. Thereafter Italian forces made a contribution to the Allied Campaign which is often overlooked: an Italian Liberation Corps operated in the Adriatic sector and four more divisional-sized combat groups were used on the north-eastern front between January and April 1945.

In 1949 Italy became a founding member of NATO and two years later, in 1951, the West lifted restrictions on the size of her armed forces, although she was still not permitted to possess nuclear weapons. She committed herself to build a twelve division army – a size which was never attained – based on conscription, imposed in 1947 and which, since 1973, has entailed twelve months' service in the army and air force or eighteen months in the navy. For reasons of domestic politics no public statements were made about these forces' exact purpose. Their main roles, in collaboration with NATO, are the defence of the north-eastern frontier, the air defence of national territory and internal defence of that territory. Jupiter missiles were deployed in Italy in 1959 but withdrawn in 1962. Until the Gulf War (1991) Italian forces had been engaged in no military operations other than disaster relief. *See also* CAPORETTO; CERESOLE; CITADELS; DOUHET; ENGINEERS; EXPLOSIVES; FORTIFICATION; GENTILI; GLORY; ICONOGRAPHY; LAWS OF WAR; LISSA; MACHIAVELLI; MARIGNANO; MERCENARIES; MILITIAS; MINING AND MINES; MONTECUCOLI; NATIONALISM; NAVAL WARFARE; NAVIES; PAVIA; RAVENNA; ROME; SOLFERINO; TARANTO.

A. CORVISIER

R. LURAGHI

JOHN GOOCH

FURTHER READING
Philippe Contamine, *War in the Middle Ages*, tr. Michael Jones (London, 1984); Michael Mallett, *Mercenaries and Their Masters* (London, 1974); M. E. Mallett and J. R. Hale, *The Military Organisation of a Renaissance State: Venice, c.1400–1617* (Cambridge, 1984); John Gooch, *Army, State and Society in Italy, 1870–1914* (London, 1989); John Whittam, *The Politics of the Italian Army* (London, 1977); MacGregor Knox, *Mussolini Unleashed, 1939–1941* (Cambridge, 1982).

J

Japan The Japanese people developed from a mixture of the first inhabitants of the archipelago, the Ainu, who, over time, were pushed back to the north, the Malayo-Polynesians and the Turco-Mongol invaders who arrived between 1000 and 750 BC. In 660 BC, a state was formed on the island of Kyushu but it was not until the first century BC that this was extended into the north of Honshu and onto Hokkaido. An attack on Korea in the second century AD brought the Japanese into contact with Chinese civilization. These influences inspired the reforms of the seventh century, of which the most important were military. By this stage, the emperor was already surrounded by the *buke*, a military aristocracy. An army was created which had a standard organization based around a minister of war and military districts under the command of governors or *Daimyōs*. Men were compelled to perform military service, for which they had to equip themselves at their own expense, but they were only called up in time of war. The concurrent increase in population reduced the burden of this service so that it fell on only one man in four. These men, the forebears of the samurai, were exempt from statute labour and received a ration of rice.

At the end of the eighth century, the Emperor Kwammu created Japan's first royal standing army. The eleventh and twelfth centuries saw the soldier assume a greater social and political role. The *Daimyōs*, recruited from amongst the *buke*, came into rivalry with the landowners who purchased places in the Imperial Guard and defied the authority of the *buke* and that of the emperor himself. Even the Buddhist clergy took up arms, though this ran counter to their teachings of non-violence. In 1192, a *buke*, Yoritomo, was appointed Shogun (generalissimo) and formed a government parallel to that of the emperor which was known as the *bakufu*. The Shogun was more or less a 'mayor of the palace' and succeeded in delaying the development of feudalism in Japan for two centuries and prevented the Mongols of Kublai Khan from incorporating Japan into their empire. Once the Mongol danger had passed, the civil wars recommenced. Zen Buddhism, which preached self-control acquired by constant exposure to the harshest trials, stamped the Japanese with a marked and distinct military character. A code of honour, the *Yamato*, known as the *Bushido* after 1900, applied to all members of society. The samurai transformed themselves into a martial caste who were exempt from work but bound by a set of absolute rules: once given, their word was their bond; they obeyed only one master and were prepared to give their lives for him. This ethic was propagated by a group of marginal, masterless samurai, the *rōnin*. In its epic tales and drama, the *Nō* plays, Japanese literature glorified the military hero. At the same time, there was a prodigious expansion in weapons production. The mark of the samurai was the wearing of two swords and the emphasis of warfare was upon the blade weapon. The Japanese rejected firearms, although they had been acquired by the Mongols, until the sixteenth century when contact was made with the Portuguese.

Between 1500 and 1600, the development of feudalism led to the period of the Warlords when the weakest of the *Daimyōs* succumbed. In 1600, a single family dominated the Shōgunate and brought the remainder of the *Daimyōs* under its rule. Tokugawa Ieyasu (1542–1616) founded a dynasty of Shōguns which rebuilt the Japanese state and governed Japan in the name of the emperor for two and a half centuries. The *Yamato* acquired its final form and became accepted by the majority of the people. It was based on Buddhism, particularly in its Zen form, which taught both the quest for the absolute and the observance of the laws of this world, on Shinto with its loyalty to the sovereign and veneration for ancestors and, lastly, on Confucianism with its respect for hierarchy. Honesty, integrity, truthfulness, kindness towards the weak and defeated, courage and self-control were the duties of the samurai. If he failed to meet his obligations, he was obliged to commit ritual suicide, hara-kiri. Through its rejection of the outside world and the outlawing of any contact with Europeans, the social and military system became static. The Portuguese merchants and missionaries who had arrived via Macao were run out of the country in 1639. After 1642, only the Dutch were tolerated but they were restricted to the small island of Deshima where their continuation was rendered extremely difficult.

The Japanese army scarcely developed, as can be seen from the collections in the Stibbert Museum in Florence. Contact with the Western world was not resumed until 1854. The Meiji Revolution of 1868 set itself the goal of creating a modern army and Westernizing the country's technical and industrial structures so that Japan could preserve its own values. French military instructors were invited but, after 1870–1, they were supplemented by advisers from Germany; the pan-German ideology sounded a sympathetic note to the aspirations of the Japanese military. Within twenty years, Japan created a Western-style army and became a formidable military empire. The supreme command was answerable to the emperor alone and constantly intervened in politics to press through an expansionist policy. The officers were recruited from among the rural population and remained very close to their men, in spite of an absolute respect for rank, and were hostile to wealth, bourgeois values, commerce and industry.

Servicemen of all ranks were inspired by the spirit of sacrifice. In its ultimate form, this was expressed in the Kamikaze warriors, who were struck from the lists of the living and regarded as officially dead the moment that they accepted a no-return

mission. Moral superiority over the enemy was incontestable and the Japanese were ready to accept the heaviest losses. This sense of moral superiority caused the Japanese General Staff to start wars without the usual Western diplomatic preliminaries. The attacks on Port Arthur in 1904 and Pearl Harbor in 1941 were made without declarations of war. Given equal weaponry, the Japanese army was a match for any opponent during the Second World War but it did suffer from a number of weaknesses. There was a lack of formal education among the NCOs, though the junior officers were capable of covering for their subordinates. The rigidity of the military caste system and the strict hierarchy of rank rendered the higher direction of war stiff, formal, inflexible and unimaginative. Particularly during the Second World War, Japan undertook a strategy of expansion which was too ambitious for her very limited industrial capacity and was over-dependent on raw materials imported from conquered territories via long marine supply lines. In China, the Japanese army was neither trained nor equipped to deal with guerillas. The atom bomb dealt the Japanese army a fatal blow at a time when Japan was continuing its resistance despite the exhaustion of the country. It took all the authority of the emperor, who was regarded as divine, to bring the military to accept surrender. *See also* CHINA; ETHOS; GUADALCANAL; MIDWAY ISLAND; MORALE; MUKDEN; NAGUMO; NUCLEAR WAR; PEARL HARBOR; TOGO; TSUSHIMA; UNITED STATES; YAMAMOTO.

A. CORVISIER

FURTHER READING
E. H. Norman, *Soldier and Peasant in Japan* (New York, 1943); R. J. C. Butow, *Togo and the Coming of the War* (Princeton, 1961); Ian Nish, 'Japan, 1914–18', in *Military Effectiveness*, eds A. R. Millett and W. Murray (3 vols, Boston, 1988), i, 229–48; A. D. Cox, 'The effectiveness of the Japanese military establishment in the Second World War', ibid., iii, 1–44; W. G. Beasley, *Japanese Imperialism, 1894–1945* (Oxford, 1987).

Jemappes, Battle of (6 November 1792) The Austrians, who were besieging Lille, withdrew on the approach of a French army under Dumouriez, the victor of Valmy, and retired to winter quarters a few miles from the French frontier. With 40,000 men, Dumouriez attacked and defeated the Austrian force, 13,000 strong. This surprise victory enabled him to occupy a large part of Belgium. Jemappes is normally seen as the first application of Guibert's tactical theories, advocating a concentration of force and a sustained all-out offensive. *See also* FRANCE; GUIBERT; VALMY.

A. CORVISIER

FURTHER READING
Arthur Chuquet, *Jemappes et la Conquête de la Belgique*, vol. 4 of *Les Guerres de la Révolution* (Paris, 1890); C. de la Jonquière, *La Bataille de Jemappes* (Paris, 1902). For general background on the French republican armies, see: Alan Forrest, *Soldiers of the French Revolution* (Durham, NC, and London, 1990); John A. Lynn, *The Bayonets of the Republic: motivation and tactics in the army of revolutionary France 1791–94* (Urbana and Chicago, 1984); Samuel F. Scott, *The Response of the Royal Army to the French Revolution: the role and development of the line army 1787–93* (Oxford, 1978).

Jena and Auerstädt, Battles of (14 October 1806) By virtue of an extremely rapid strategic operation, Napoleon had succeeded in threatening communications between the Prussian army and Berlin. To remedy this situation, the Duke of Brunswick marched on Auerstädt with the greater part of his forces (63,000 men), while the Prince of Hohenlohe protected his rear with 51,000 men strung out between Jena and Weimar. Napoleon concentrated 80,000 men on Jena and attacked at dawn. By noon, Hohenlohe's troops were scattered. Meanwhile, some 15 miles to the north, at Auerstädt, Davout with 27,000 men resisted Brunswick's repeated assaults for six hours. The latter was killed during the action and King Frederick William III (1797–1840) took command. The news of the defeat at Jena demoralized the Prussians, and Davout counterattacked. Marching to the sound of the guns, Bernadotte, who up to this point had not been involved in the fighting, fell upon

the Prussian rear with 20,000 men. The Prussian army was annihilated: 25,000 men were killed or injured and a further 25,000 were taken prisoner. The French lost 8,000 men. These twin battles represented the tactical exploitation of an important strategic victory. However, it was the French pursuit to Berlin, and beyond to Lübeck and Stettin, which made Jena–Auerstädt so decisive. The shattering of the Prussian army, the creation of Frederick the Great and the embodiment of the state, was traumatic. Jena–Auerstädt provided Prussia with the springboard for reform, not only of its army but of all its leading institutions. *See also* AUSTERLITZ; DAVOUT; FRANCE; GERMANY; NAPOLEON; SCHARNHORST.

D. REICHEL
HEW STRACHAN

FURTHER READING
David Chandler, *The Campaigns of Napoleon* (London, 1967); F. L. Petre, *Napoleon's Conquest of Prussia* (London, 1907); D. Reichel, *Davout et l'art de la guerre* (Neuchâtel, 1975).

Joan of Arc *See* SAINTS, MILITARY

Joffre, Joseph Jacques Césaire (1852–1931) Born to a family of small vinegrowers, Joffre entered the École Polytechnique in 1869 and, a year later, was given command of a fort at Paris. An engineer, he embarked on a series of colonial postings in 1885 which included Formosa, Upper Tonkin, Timbuktu and Madagascar. Promoted to brigade command in 1900, Joffre was given the first in a series of important appointments in the war ministry in 1903, attaining the rank of major-general two years later. Despite his lack of staff training, his political neutrality probably secured his appointment in 1911 as chief of the general staff with responsibility for commanding the northern and eastern armies in the event of war. Accepting the prevailing military orthodoxy, he advocated the offensive and failed to appreciate the importance either of the generalized use of heavy artillery or of machine-guns. Having effectively lost the battle on France's frontiers in August 1914, he none the less proved himself a leader of great composure. A number of generals were replaced, a withdrawal carried out in good order and, taking advantage of the orientation of the French railway system (which made it easier to transfer units to the vicinity of Paris), Joffre effected the flanking manoeuvre suggested by Galliéni to exploit the gap which had opened between the German 1st and 2nd armies advancing east of the city. The resulting victory on the Marne (6–12 September) enabled the Allied forces to push the Germans back towards the Aisne and, in the subsequent 'race to the sea', Joffre's forces, including the British Expeditionary Force, successfully prevented the Germans breaking through to the Channel ports. However, in 1915 Joffre stubbornly pursued a policy of costly offensives such as those in Artois in May and Champagne in September in which a decisive breakthrough proved illusory. The equal failure of the Allied offensive on the Somme in 1916 and mounting criticism steadily undermined Joffre's once unassailable reputation as victor of the Marne. On 31 December 1916 he was compelled to relinquish his command for a meaningless appointment as the government's technical adviser from which he soon resigned. Retirement was sweetened by elevation to the rank of marshal of France. *See also* FRANCE; GALLIÉNI; MARNE.

A. CORVISIER

FURTHER READING
A. Goutard, 'L'énigma du plan d'opérations de Joffre en 1914', *Revue internationale d'histoire militaire*, xxx (1970); J. C. King, *Politicians and Generals* (New York, 1951); D. Porch, *The March to the Marne* (Cambridge, 1981).

Jomini, Antoine-Henri (1779–1869) Jomini has proved arguably the single most influential military theorist of the modern age. Clausewitz, the most obvious rival for this title, did not produce principles which could form the basis for military education; Jomini did, and his writings therefore

(Mansell Collection)

shaped the teaching in European military academies throughout the nineteenth century. Although Swiss by birth, Jomini received first-hand experience of the Napoleonic Wars by serving on Ney's staff from 1805. Rather than seeing war as chaotic and full of friction as Clausewitz did, Jomini emphasized its logic. His *Traité des grandes opérations militaires* (1804–11) embraced the campaigns of Frederick and Napoleon in Italy, and compared eighteenth-century warfare with revolutionary warfare. In 1813 he left France in order to enter Russian service. Of the prolific output which followed, Jomini's most important work was *Précis de l'art de la guerre* (1838). Influenced by his experience in Spain, Jomini acknowledged that war was a 'terrible and impassioned drama', but then aimed to impose system through the principles of strategy. The key to manoeuvre was the choice of the line of operations, in particular a line designed to cover the security of an army's base and, at the same time, to allow mass to be concentrated on the decisive point. Jomini distinguished between 'interior lines', the ability to occupy a central position between two converging armies and deal with each successively, and 'exterior lines' or envelopment. He saw the former as safer and preferable. Jomini became the interpreter of Napoleon for subsequent generations of soldiers, the man who had unlocked the secrets of the emperor's strategic genius. *See also* BÜLOW; CLAUSEWITZ; HAMLEY; NAPIER; NAPOLEON; STRATEGY; TACTICS; TRAINING.

HEW STRACHAN

FURTHER READING
John Alger, *Antoine-Henri Jomini: a bibliographic survey* (West Point, NJ, 1975); Ferdinand Lecomte, *Le général Jomini, sa vie et ses écrits* (Paris, 1860); Michael Howard, 'Jomini and the classical tradition', in *The Theory and Practice of War* (London, 1965); John Shy, 'Jomini', in *Makers of Modern Strategy*, ed Peter Paret (Oxford, 1986), pp. 143–85.

Josephus, Flavius (b. AD 37) Josephus was a Jewish priest from an aristocratic family that could claim royal blood, since his father's grandfather had married a princess of the Hasmonean rulers of Palestine. He was also a Pharisee and wrote extensively on Jewish history, religion and culture, notably in the *Antiquities of the Jews*, published in 93/4. Although his native languages were Aramaic and Hebrew, he could speak Greek, and in Judaea at this time the influence of Hellenistic culture was still relatively strong. Josephus went on an embassy to Rome in 64 and was prominent enough in Jerusalem to be chosen by the Sanhedrin to take charge of Galilee in the Jewish revolt from Roman rule which began in 66. But he was not in sympathy with the views of extreme Jewish nationalists and was sceptical of the revolt's chances of success. As a military commander he was mainly on the defensive and he employed a skilful stratagem to prevent the defection of the town of Tiberias from his command; he brought up a large fleet and then kept it so far away that it was impossible for the inhabitants to see that each ship was manned by only four men. In 67 Josephus organized the defence of Jotapata against the Roman commander Vespasian.

When he was eventually captured he won Vespasian's favour by predicting that he would become emperor. When this prophecy came true in 69 Josephus remained closely tied to the favour of the imperial family. He settled in Rome, became a Roman citizen and wrote a detailed history of the revolt, with a graphic description of the fall of Jerusalem in 70 to Vespasian's son Titus, and the capture of Masada by Flavius Silva in 72–3. This work, published between 75 and 79, probably incorporated material from the commentaries of Vespasian and Titus, and is an important source for the history of the Roman army on campaign in the first century AD. It contains Josephus' famous encomium on the organization, training, discipline and skill of the Roman legionaries (*Jewish War*, 3, 70–107). *See also* ISRAEL, EARLY; MASADA; ROME.

B. CAMPBELL

FURTHER READING
Josephus, *The Jewish War*, tr. G. A. Williamson, revised by E. M. Smallwood (Penguin, 1981); T. Rajak, *Josephus: the historian and his society* (London, 1983).

Journals *See* SERVICE PERIODICAL PUBLICATIONS

Jutland, Battle of (31 May 1916) Jutland was the only major naval battle fought in the First World War. Vice Admiral Scheer's German High Seas Fleet put to sea, and the British Grand Fleet, under Jellicoe, attempted to intercept it.

In the early afternoon contact was made between the British battle-cruiser force of six battle-cruisers and four battleships capable of 24 knots, under Beatty, and the German scouting group of five battle-cruisers under Hipper. Immediately, Hipper went about and drew the British towards his main body. During this first phase, the superiority of German fire and the weak armour of the British vessels brought about the destruction of the battle-cruisers *Indefatigable* and *Queen Mary*. At 16:30 Beatty found himself in sight of the High Seas Fleet, and altered course so as to cause the German Fleet in

HMS *Iron Duke* was the flagship of Admiral Sir John Jellicoe at the Battle of Jutland. It was typical of the post-Dreadnought battleships which comprised the core of the Royal Navy in both the First and Second World Wars. Completed in March 1914. Scrapped in 1946. Displacement: 25,000 tons. Length: 580 feet. Armament: 10×13.5 inch; 12×6 inch; 2×3 inch AA; 4×21 inch torpedo tubes. Armour: 12 inch belts around hull; 11 inch belts on sides and front of main turrets; 2.5 inch plating on decks. Speed: 21 knots.
(Mansell Collection)

its turn to steam towards the British main fleet coming from the north.

The two fleets met in the late afternoon in conditions of poor visibility. During this second phase, the German main body twice encountered the Grand Fleet, which was deployed in an arc crossing Scheer's 'T'. Scheer only escaped destruction by turning away into the mist, and by sending his battle-cruisers and destroyers on a so-called 'death ride'. During the night, several confused engagements took place in which the British destroyers sank the old battleship *Pommern*. At dawn, the two fleets were out of sight of each other, and the German fleet returned to its bases by way of Horns Reef, leaving the Grand Fleet at sea.

There were interminable discussions of the battle in the interwar years. Overall, the young German navy distinguished itself both by the accuracy of its fire and the quality of the construction of its ships. In all, the British lost three battle-cruisers, three armoured cruisers and eight destroyers, of a total of 112,000 tonnes, whereas the Germans lost only one battle-cruiser, one old battleship, four light cruisers and five destroyers, of 60,000 tonnes. On the other hand, Jellicoe achieved a tactical success, foiled by the mist. Strategically, the battle confirmed that a state of deadlock existed, as had been evident since the beginning of the war. If anything, it made the German command even more circumspect, and led it to resort again to all-out submarine warfare to break the Allied domination of the seas. *See also* FALKLAND ISLANDS; FISHER; NAVAL WARFARE; NAVIES.

P. MASSON

FURTHER READING

J. E. T. Harper, *The Truth about Jutland* (London, 1927); D. Macintyre, *Jutland* (London, 1957); Arthur J. Marder, *From Dreadnought to Scapa Flow* (London, 1966), vol. iii; *The Jellicoe Papers*, ed. A. T. Patterson (Navy Records Society, cviii, London, 1966; cxi, London, 1968); *The Beatty Papers*, ed. B. McL. Ranft (Navy Records Society, cxxviii, London, 1989; cxxxii, London, 1993).

K

Kadesh, Battle of (c.1300 BC) The Hittite empire in Anatolia frequently clashed with Egypt. The Hittite king, Muwatallish, encouraged Egypt's client rulers in Canaan and Syria to rebel against Egyptian domination. To put down this rebellion, Pharaoh Ramesses II led an army of c.20,000 men through Lebanon into Syria, while a force of 5,000 Canaanite mercenaries, the Ne'arim, advanced by a coastal route with orders to join Ramesses on the River Orontes around Kadesh. Ramesses' main force was arranged in four divisions which marched separately: Amon, Re, Ptah and Seth, names of Egyptian deities. The Hittite army, perhaps 16,000 strong and containing Syrian and Canaanite troops, spread false intelligence that it had withdrawn into Aleppo. Actually, it lay in ambush beyond the River Orontes near Kadesh. Ramesses with the Amon division encamped at Kadesh and waited for the other divisions and the Ne'arim to join him. Within a mile of Ramesses' camp, Re, the second division, was attacked and put to flight by the Hittite chariotry, which had forded the Orontes. The Hittites then set about the encamped Amon division and forced it to withdraw, but they delayed their pursuit in order to loot the Egyptian camp. This gave Ramesses sufficient time to attack at the head of the Ne'arim, just arrived from the coast, and these elite troops drove the Hittites back against the Orontes and routed them. The Egyptian success was completed by the timely arrival of the Ptah and Seth divisions. But the Hittite infantry beyond the river was not involved in the battle and Ramesses failed to take Kadesh itself. The outcome, therefore, was indecisive and shortly afterwards a peace treaty was concluded between Ramesses and Muwatallish. As a result of information contained on a surviving monument to Ramesses II, Kadesh is the first battle of the Bronze Age in the Near East about which we have some evidence on tactics and the organization of the armies. *See also* EGYPT, ANCIENT; HITTITES.

A. CORVISIER
JOHN CHILDS

FURTHER READING
O. R. Gurney, *The Hittites* (Harmondsworth, repr. 1966); Y. Yadin, *The Art of Warfare in Biblical Lands in the Light of Archaeological Discovery* (London, 1963); P. Montet, *Eternal Egypt* (London, 1964); J. Baines and J. Málek, *Atlas of Ancient Egypt* (Oxford, 1980).

Kahn, Hermann (1922–83) Kahn was a civilian analyst, first at the RAND Corporation (a civilian defence research institute with close ties to the US air force) in the late 1950s and 1960s and then later established the Hudson Institute. Although his background was in physics he established several key ideas and concepts in the field of strategic studies. He was one of the first analysts to attempt to set out what he believed would happen in a nuclear war. His analysis led him to two conclusions: first, that a nuclear war was survivable; second, that the United States should acquire a limited-war capability – and especially a first-strike capability – to enable it to survive. Kahn was attacked in many quarters for his rational and detached approach to the subject and was accused of lacking ethical values.

Kahn was also instrumental in developing the idea of 'escalation' in warfare. Kahn viewed it as a purposeful strategy in which the costs could be logically and rationally increased in order to encourage an enemy to disengage from the conflict. He developed the idea of an 'escalation ladder' ranging from Cold War at the bottom to Spasm War at the top. He also introduced the idea of 'thresholds'. These represented a significant escalation or step on the ladder such as moving to a state of nuclear war from no nuclear use. Kahn's ideas on escalation represented an attempt to introduce the basic rules and limitations of conflict to a nuclear age although they have been criticized for encouraging the belief that war (and nuclear war) is manageable. Such a concept also needs to be recognized by all parties to a conflict and there is no indication that the Soviet Union, at the time that Kahn was writing, operated within a similar strategic framework. *See also* NUCLEAR WARFARE; STRATEGY; WEAPONS.

DAVID WESTON

FURTHER READING
Hermann Kahn, *On Thermonuclear War* (Princeton, 1960); *Thinking about the Unthinkable* (London, 1962); *On Escalation* (London, 1965). For an examination of Kahn's place in the development of strategic thinking, see: Lawrence Freedman, *The Evolution of Nuclear Strategy* (London, 1981). For a criticism of Kahn and strategic theory in general, see: Philip Green, *Deadly Logic* (Ohio State, 1966); Anatol Rapaport, *Strategy and Conscience* (New York, 1964).

King, Ernest J. (1878–1956) Entering the US navy in 1897, King's ability soon became evident, and he served in the Atlantic Fleet on the staff of Admiral Henry T. Mayo (1856–1937), by whom he was much influenced. After the First World War he became associated for some time with submarines and indeed salved two after accidental loss. In 1926, however, he turned to the air and qualified as a pilot. He then commanded the *Wright* seaplane tender and, from 1930 to 1932, the new carrier *Lexington*, developing carrier tactics. After a period at the Naval War College, he was promoted Rear-Admiral and became chief of the Bureau of Aeronautics from 1933 to 1936. Command of the patrol planes followed, until he took over the Carrier Division in 1938, producing tactics for carriers working together. After serving as a member of the General Board, he was appointed to command the Atlantic Fleet in December 1940, his task

being to carry out the various stages of the move towards open assistance to Britain. In December 1941, he was called to Washington as Commander-in-Chief, United States Fleet, a post he soon after combined with that of Chief of Naval Operations. He therefore conducted all US naval operations until his retirement in December 1945. While he certainly recognized the importance of the Atlantic battle, he was determined to maintain pressure upon the Japanese, and so was regarded by many as being primarily concerned with the Pacific war. He saved much effort there by insisting on the by-passing or neutralization of many enemy bases rather than waste time on their capture. His rigid belief that the US navy must never be subordinated to, or even, apparently, learn from, others, caused friction, in the latter case leading to the massacre of shipping off the east coast of the United States between January and May 1942. Nevertheless, he set and maintained a very high standard. *See also* LEYTE GULF; MACARTHUR; MIDWAY ISLAND; NAVAL WARFARE; NAVIES; NIMITZ; PEARL HARBOR; UNITED STATES.

A. W. H. PEARSALL

FURTHER READING
T. B. Buell, *Master of Sea Power: a biography of Fleet Admiral Ernest J. King* (Boston, 1980); S. E. Morison, *History of the United States Naval Operations in World War II* (Boston, 1947–62); E. J. King and Walter M. Whitehill, *Fleet Admiral King: a naval record* (London, 1953).

Kinsale, siege of (September 1601–January 1602) **and Battle of** (24 December 1601) Kinsale was the scene both of the only Spanish military intervention in Ireland and of the battle that proved decisive for the Elizabethan conquest. The course of the 'Nine Years' War' (1594–1603) between the English crown and Hugh O'Neill, Earl of Tyrone, had seen the English garrison obtaining little success in penetrating Ulster, while Tyrone's resistance had inspired widespread rebellion throughout Ireland. This posed for the Lord Deputy in 1600–1, Charles Blount, Lord Mountjoy, the same dilemma that his predecessors had faced: whether to concentrate against Ulster and leave the southern rebellion alone, or disperse his men in the south and give Tyrone the initiative. The novelty of the Spanish intervention was the consequence of Philip II's abandoning of his earlier abstention from Ireland after the English attack on Cadiz in 1596. Long discussions led to a decision in 1601 to send 6,000 men together with arms for Tyrone with the intention of creating at least a diversion for the Siege of Ostend. The Spanish expedition was successful in evading English naval patrols, but it was partly dispersed by weather and the controversial decision was then taken to land Don Juan del Aguila with 3,400 men at Kinsale near Cork on 20 September 1601. Aguila immediately appealed to Tyrone for reinforcements and horses, but in the meantime Mountjoy and his subordinates moved quickly to contain him. By the end of October Mountjoy had some 7,000 men investing Kinsale and was beginning to reduce the Spanish outposts; by 23 November his siege battery (nine guns) was bombarding Kinsale itself. In the beginning of December a second Spanish convoy arrived with 600 reinforcements, but it was driven into Castlehaven where the troops were blockaded by English warships. More decisive was Tyrone's decision to aid Aguila. By 21 December Tyrone had brought nearly 7,000 men to the vicinity of Kinsale, and three days later (the 24th) he approached the English camp with the intention of combining with a Spanish sally. Mountjoy despatched his cavalry (c.500) and three regiments of infantry to hold him off. The Irish army halted behind a boggy stream; after a brief exchange of musketry the English cavalry advanced on the Irish centre; at their second charge the Irish horse, followed by the foot, dissolved in panic. Although the Irish suffered heavily in the pursuit, casualties on both sides in the battle were relatively few. On the following day Aguila did attempt a sally against the besiegers but this was beaten back. On learning of the Irish retreat, he sued for terms on 31 December. On 2 January 1602 the Spaniards surrendered and in March were evacuated to Spain. Tyrone's army retreated directly to Ulster, its morale shattered and with many of its arms abandoned on the field at Kinsale. Despite the alarm caused by the Spanish invasion, Kinsale gave Mountjoy an opportunity he might never have obtained otherwise, for Tyrone was drawn out of Ulster and into an encounter where the English had the advantage. It also revealed the difficulties of effective Spanish intervention; with English naval power still unchecked, all the Spaniards could accomplish was to disembark a small force and then withdraw, leaving the landing force to be bottled up. *See also* GREAT BRITAIN; OSTEND; SIEGES; SPAIN.

SIMON ADAMS

FURTHER READING
C. Falls, *Elizabeth's Irish Wars* (London, 1950); C. Falls, *Mountjoy: Elizabethan general* (London, 1955); J. J. Silke, *Kinsale: the Spanish intervention in Ireland at the end of the Elizabethan wars* (Liverpool, 1970).

Knights and chivalry Innumerable documents of all kinds dating from the eleventh to the fourteenth centuries AD emphasize the fundamental importance of the part played in contemporary wars by one particular class of participants. In Latin texts they were called *milites*, though, in the strict sense, this meant merely 'soldiers', or *equestres* ('horsemen'), while in manuscripts in vernacular languages they became *ritter*, *chevaliers*, *caballeros*, *cavalieri* or knights. Especially in pitched battles, these knights formed up several ranks deep and were grouped into tactical units termed battles, *échelles*, *convois*, etc.; they then charged with lances levelled or engaged in hand-to-hand combat. As their name implies, they generally fought mounted but, occasionally, for various tactical or technical reasons, they dismounted and fought on foot as heavy infantry. Although they usually faced other knights, their opponents might also be light cavalry, archers armed with longbows or crossbows, or foot soldiers carrying spears. However great their reputation and however predominant they might be, knights were always attended and supported by other types of fighting men, normally lighter horsemen and infantry employing missile weapons.

The fighting value of knights primarily depended on the quality of their warhorses (destriers), which had to be well-schooled yet mettlesome, fast yet strong. Great efforts were made to choose the most suitable animals and to acquire famous breeds, no matter how expensive. The development of the horseshoe (ninth century) helped to preserve the active life of the horse as well as greatly improved its ability to move along roads and over hard and rocky surfaces. From their earliest youth, knights were expected to undergo an exacting course of training in horsemanship and to maintain this standard by regular practice in all types of equestrian activity – tournaments, tilting, hunting. Control of the mount was assisted by the use of saddles and stirrups, which gave the rider all-round support, and of spurs. The wearing of gilded spurs became one of the distinguishing marks of the knight.

Fighting equipment during the period from the eleventh to the fourteenth centuries underwent some change. The principal offensive weapons were the wooden lance, tipped with either an iron point or a spear blade, and the straight sword. Defensive equipment was made from iron or steel, leather, skins, wood for the shield, and animal horn in order to provide adequate protection for the body of the knight and his horse. Protective steel armour became more complex, steadily reducing mobility, hindering bodily movement and increasing fatigue. However, considerable progress was made in the fourteenth and fifteenth centuries in producing light-weight armour which provided a high degree of protection while enabling the wearer to be fully at ease when mounted but also able to dismount without too much difficulty and fight on foot. Knights had to rehearse formation manoeuvres in close order – charging in line at speed, forming ranks about the commander and his flag, wheeling and turning about. Battles in the Middle Ages did not always consist of disorganized mêlées or hand-to-hand contests between isolated pairs of combatants.

It was an accepted necessity for every knight to be attended by at least one man, and often as many as five or six, complete with a corresponding number of horses. Each band accompanying a knight was referred to as a 'lance'. For example, in 1100 Robert II, Count of Flanders, promised to provide assistance to King Henry I of England to the tune of 1,000 knights each of whom would bring with him three horses. Later, the rules of the Templars stipulated a maximum of three horses for each brother-knight. In 1268, for the purposes of his Italian campaign, Charles, Count of Anjou, reckoned on each knight in his army having suitable armour, four horses and a squire (*armiger*) in attendance. In addition, the knight was to bring with him two retainers (*gardiones*) properly furnished with military accoutrements. The knight fought as a heavy cavalryman, his squire as a light horseman, and the retainers as infantry. Thus each knight represented a fighting unit which necessarily involved an initial investment followed by maintenance costs, both of which were high. Besides, from the eleventh to the fourteenth century, there was a tendency for the number of horses and retainers and for the cost of equipment to increase. Certainly, some counterbalancing effect was provided by the rise in European population with its consequent expansion of national resources and capacities and improvement in living standards. However, no army or society could multiply its number of knights indefinitely. In the twelfth and thirteenth centuries, the fielding of 2,000 or 3,000 knights indicated a powerful country which was mobilizing most of its military resources.

By 1100, the nomenclature of 'knight' was given to both armed retainers of a king, prince or nobleman and to vassals who held a piece of land, a manor or a fief of reasonable size. Two hundred years later, the great majority of knights were enfeoffed, or sub-enfeoffed, holding, at least in theory, land which was due a knight's, or hauberk's, fee. As the centuries went by, knights were increasingly absorbed into the nobility, the military and social elites tending to intermingle and become virtually identical. However, in England, the separation between knighthood and nobility endured.

During the same 200 years, the code of moral values which knights were expected to observe was enriched with new considerations. To discipline, courage and unswerving loyalty to the commander were added the protection of the weak and the poor, respect for non-combatants and their property, courtesy and the defence of the Church of God and Christianity against the forces of evil, especially the Infidel. The knight's sword was regarded as a symbol of strength placed at the service of justice. When the Crusades began in 1096, some knights made manifest the essential religiosity of their vows; the military and the religious life were no longer considered to be incompatible. It was in this context that the Order of the Templars was founded in about 1120, an organization which was to secure approval and eulogy from St Bernard of Clairvaux (1090–1153).

The traditional ceremony of the giving of weapons to the future knight acquired a new solemnity. His dubbing sometimes took the form of a liturgy during which the Church explained to the graduand knight the full details of that ideal code which he undertook to observe by his oath when he entered the 'order of chivalry'. The highest ranks of the social hierarchy gloried in laying claim to a reputation for chivalry. A whole corpus of literature extolled knights who displayed such virtues – the valiant who lived 'without fear and without reproach' – and sought to demonstrate that without them a society was doomed to destruction. 'A prince without knights has neither power nor authority, like a body without the use of arms or hands.' From the fourteenth century, some kings and princes exploited the mystique by forming orders of knighthood with restricted memberships (e.g. the Orders of the Garter, of the Golden Fleece, and of St Michael). However, by this time the ideal of knighthood was becoming more enfeebled and these attempts to revive it by exclusivity were not successful. At its height, knighthood was

a supranational principle which bound together different levels of lay aristrocracy by emphasizing the basic Christian duties of those whose social duty was to bear arms, even when they were on opposite sides in war. This method of attempting to limit the extent, damage and severity of war between Christians was partly entrusted to the heavenly guardian angels of knighthood, St George, St Michael and St Maurice.

Nevertheless, knighthood entailed costly obligations during war and an expensive style of life in peacetime. In the thirteenth century, changes in the concept of nobility made knighthood less indispensable even for those who aspired to nobility. By 1300, a large number of the heavy cavalry in armies were no longer really 'knights' who had taken vows but mounted 'sergeants', squires or, quite simply, men-at-arms. The decline of military knighthood in the later Middle Ages thus had two principal causes: because of expense and changing social values it was no longer necessary to be a knight in order to serve as a heavy cavalryman while cavalry itself was rivalled as a fighting force by other arms, particularly infantry and artillery. However, even by 1500, no substitute had appeared to replace the atrophied ideal of knighthood; various orders of military knighthood survived in Spain (the orders of Santiago, Alcántara and Montesa) and Portugal into the nineteenth century while the Hospitallers remained on Malta until 1798 and the Teutonic Knights were not dissolved in Germany until 1809 only to be reformed in Austria in 1834. Among both the nobility and persons of modest rank and wealth, the title of knight remained in demand; the former sought an enhancement of their military stature and prowess while the latter were not content to remain plain gentlemen or modest squires. In England, by the sixteenth century, knighthood was conferred for increasingly non-military services and became a mark of social and economic distinction as well as a political reward. *See also* ARMOUR, PERSONAL; CAVALRY; ETHOS; HONOURS AND AWARDS; FAMILIES; LAWS OF WAR; SOLDIERS AND SOCIETY.

P. CONTAMINE

FURTHER READING
Philippe Contamine, *War in the Middle Ages* (London, 1984); M. Keen, *Chivalry* (London, 1984); M. G. A. Vale, *War and Chivalry* (London, 1981); J. Gillingham, 'War and chivalry in the history of William the Marshal', in *Thirteenth Century Studies*, eds P. Coss and S. Lloyd, ii (1988).

Konev, Ivan Stepanovich (1897–1973) Konev was born of peasant stock in the village of Lodeino in Vologda province. He enlisted as a volunteer in 1916 and joined the artillery. During the civil war he was a political commissar, and was promoted to divisional command in 1920. In 1926, Konev attended the Military Academy and had regimental and divisional commands until 1934, when he was posted to the Frunze Military Academy. From 1938 to 1940, Konev commanded the Second Detached Red Banner Far Eastern Army against the Japanese, and was later transferred to command the Transbaikal Military District. At the outbreak of war, Konev distinguished himself as commander of the 19th Army at Smolensk. After this, he was Front Commander for, successively, the Western Front, the Kalinin Front, the Western Front again, the Northwestern Front, the Steppe Front, the Second Ukrainian Front and the First Ukrainian Front. Konev took a prominent part in the liberation of the Ukraine and the Vistula-Oder operation. His forces provided cover in the south for the capture of Berlin and joined up with the American forces on the Elbe at Torgau and reached Prague. Konev was made a marshal of the Soviet Union in 1944. From 1946 to 1950 he was supreme commander of the ground forces and then chief inspector of the Soviet Army. From 1952 to 1955 he headed the Carpathian Military District and then once more became supreme commander of the ground forces until 1956. For the next four years he was both supreme commander of the Warsaw Pact forces and First Deputy Minister of Defence. From 1952 onwards, Konev was a full member of the Central Committee of the Communist Party. His writings include *Zapiski komanduiushchevo frontom 1943–1944* (*Notes of a Front Commander*, Moscow, 1972). *See also* RUSSIA/USSR; SHAPOSHNIKOV; SOVIET MILITARY THEORISTS; STALIN; ZHUKOV.

A. CORVISIER
KEITH NEILSON

FURTHER READING
Stalin and his Generals, ed. Seweryn Bialer (New York, 1969); John Erickson, *The Road to Stalingrad* (London, 1975); John Erickson, *The Road to Berlin* (London, 1983).

(Mary Evans Picture Library)

Königgrätz, Battle of *See* SADOWA

Korean War (June 1950–July 1953) In post-1945 military history Korea occupies a unique position. Until the United Nations sanctioned the use of force against Iraq in 1990 the war in Korea was the only example of the United Nations committing itself to using military force against an aggressor. In both cases the UN forces were predominantly those of the United States and a US general the commander-in-chief but here many of the parallels end. The conduct and outcome of the two wars were very different.

The Korean peninsula was of little interest to the West until the end of the Second World War. The Potsdam Agreement between the Allies in July 1945 left Korea and Manchuria to be dealt with by the Soviet Red Army. The Americans, however, did not foresee the swift ending of the war in the Far East and did not anticipate the rapid progress of the Soviet forces through Manchuria. Soviet forces were able to occupy Korea north of the 38th parallel and to install a puppet government under Kim Il-Sung. Negotiations began to establish a single government while the Soviet Union continued to build up the North Korean Army. In 1947 the United Nations resolved that elections be held in spring 1948. The Soviet Union, however, refused to allow a UN commission access to the North and elections were only held in the South. Syngman Rhee was elected and the Republic of Korea was established. The North responded by proclaiming the People's Democratic Republic of Korea. In 1948 the Soviet Union withdrew its forces from the North leaving behind a strong North Korean Army.

In the South the US-backed regime of Syngman Rhee and the army of the Republic of Korea were not similarly supported. The army was supplied only with arms sufficient for border control duties and for the support of the police in an internal emergency. The US military presence was, furthermore, only token. It appeared to the North, therefore, that if challenged the South would be unlikely to be defended by the Americans. This perception was further supported by public statements that Korea was not 'very greatly important'. However, the US administration, under President Truman, had already agreed in private that any Soviet challenge, wherever in the world, would be met by the United States.

Then, on 25 June 1950, in a clear act of unprovoked aggression the North Korean Army of 135,000 men plus Soviet-supplied tanks, aircraft and artillery swept across the 38th parallel. Rhee's badly equipped army of 95,000 could do little to halt their progress. The next day the UN Security Council unanimously condemned the act and was soon to agree to provide military support to the South Koreans. This action was facilitated by the absence of the Soviet delegation at the UN. They had walked out in January 1950 in protest at the UN refusal to allow Communist China a seat in place of Nationalist China. The North Koreans were thus without their protector at the UN. It was a mistake that the Soviet Union was not to make again.

General Douglas MacArthur, the hero of the war against Japan and then the Supreme Commander in Tokyo, was appointed the Commander-in-Chief of the United Nations forces in Korea. While the decisions were being reached at the UN, however, the North Korean Army was moving quickly south brushing aside the South Korean Army and the small American force. The South Korean capital, Seoul, was taken. US forces were shipped from Japan but they were unable to stem the advance. The North Koreans used a method of warfare with which the Americans were unable to cope, massive human-wave charges – even using refugees as cover – and complete indifference to the taking of prisoners. By August they were in reach of Pusan on the south-east coast. It was here that the momentum of the invasion broke. The Pusan Perimeter held out for several weeks and a co-ordinated attack at the end of August was unable to break completely through the defence lines.

In the meantime MacArthur devised a plan that would wrest the initiative from the North Koreans and force them to pull back. He proposed an amphibious landing on the opposite coast at Inchon south-west of Seoul. The landing went ahead unopposed on 15 September; despite the fears of many leading generals; and by the end of the month Seoul had been retaken. Having forced the withdrawal of the North Korean forces in the south-east, MacArthur now wanted to push ahead across the 38th parallel and into North Korea itself. The US administration and their allies were uneasy about this extension of the UN war aims but nevertheless in October UN forces crossed the parallel. Some resistance was encountered but it was quickly subdued. The North Korean forces broke and fled north pursued by the US and South Korean forces. On 20 October the North Korean capital, Pyongyang, fell and victory seemed imminent. MacArthur wanted to push on to the Chinese border at the Yalu River. China now became increasingly alarmed at the prospect of US forces at her border. The United States was the main supporter of the Nationalist Chinese, and Communist China feared that the United States would now pursue this conflict by widening the scope of the war in Korea. By November some Chinese forces had been engaged on a small scale but then on 25 November the Chinese entered in force.

The human tide of the Chinese army of 300,000 overwhelmed the UN forces and the headlong rush north now became a rapid retreat south. The United States and its UN allies were once again forced south beyond the line of the 38th parallel. The Chinese forces, however, as they drove the UN forces out of North Korea also greatly extended their lines of supply to such an extent that they were heavily exposed to interdiction by the US air force. They were unable to continue the drive south and became over-extended.

Meanwhile, MacArthur began to overstep the bounds of his military authority and engage in political debate about the conduct of the war. He publicly campaigned for an extension of the war that included, if necessary, military victory over the Chinese, operations beyond the Yalu and the use of nuclear weapons. Truman and his political advisers, aware of the possibility of adverse reaction by the Allies

and fearful of Soviet intervention – either directly in the conflict or as a challenge elsewhere in the world – could not countenance MacArthur acting without political direction nor could they allow him to continue to campaign for a strategy that now ran contrary to American aims. The United States now saw that victory, in the sense of a united non-Communist Korea, could not be achieved. Their aim became to return to the status quo *ante bellum* and to get out of Korea without losing face. In April 1951 MacArthur was replaced by General Matthew Ridgway, who was to prove much more willing to act on the political directions of Washington.

Ridgway was able to revitalize the UN forces in Korea and they were even able to push north once again and go back beyond the 38th parallel. This time there was to be no race to the Yalu but instead an attempt to consolidate and hold ground around the line of the 38th parallel. This was helped by the arrival of more troops and the establishment of air superiority. The UN forces now consisted of troops from fifteen nations.

A point of stalemate had been reached. The Chinese and North Koreans were unable to push south against a better equipped UN force while the UN no longer had the political will to carry the war north. There were still attempts by the Chinese to push through. An offensive in April 1951 at points along the whole front saw the British 29th Brigade isolated in the centre near the Imjin River. They suffered 1,000 casualties, of which the Gloucesters counted for nearly 700. The UN forces were pushed back but again the Chinese were unable to maintain the momentum and the UN forces held. It was to be the last major push. Both sides were now more concerned to establish strong defence lines around the 38th parallel as the long peace talks began.

Many more lives were still to be lost as both sides continued to probe and send political signals to each other but essentially the war now became one of securing the best possible peace. The first talks took place in July 1951 in Communist-held territory but the Chinese attempted to portray them as a picture of UN capitulation. The next talks took place at Panmunjom on neutral ground. The peace talks lasted until July 1953 with discussion of the post-armistice exchange of prisoners being the most contentious issue.

The war lasted just over three years with the last two consisting of static trench warfare. Thirty-three thousand Americans were killed and 3,000 other UN soldiers (including 800 from the United King-dom); 107,000 Americans were wounded or missing and 16,000 other UN troops (3,000 from the United Kingdom). South Korean casualties have been estimated at 400,000 killed, North Korean 500,000 and Chinese 900,000. Korea remains bitterly divided.

Given US military and nuclear domin-ance it is unlikely that the Soviet Union would have intervened in the conflict had the UN crossed the Yalu but there was considerable risk of getting embroiled in a conflict from which it would have been difficult to withdraw. There was the sup-port for such an action neither at the UN nor among the American public. Mac-Arthur was out on a limb. He might have pulled off a tactical masterstroke with the Inchon landings but he was completely out of touch with the political dimensions of the conflict.

The conduct of the war was to show how badly the West coped, initially, with the 'people's' armies of Asia and in this sense it was a forerunner to Vietnam. This was, though, largely a conflict fought by Second World War methods. In the static period from June 1951 onwards the United Na-tions forces, with their better equipment and superiority in the air, were largely suc-cessful against a primitive Chinese army. *See also* CHINA; GULF WAR; MACARTHUR; UNITED STATES; VIETNAM.

DAVID WESTON

FURTHER READING
Bevin Alexander, *Korea: the lost war* (New York, 1986); Anthony Farrar-Hockley, *The British Part in the Korean War* (London, 1990); Rosemary Foot, *A Substitute for Victory: the politics of peacemaking* (Cornell University, 1990); Max Hastings, *The Korean War* (London, 1987); C. A. MacDonald, *Britain and the Kor-ean War* (Oxford, 1990); Matthew Ridgway, *The War in Korea* (London, 1967); R. Whelan, *Drawing the Line: the Korean War 1950–53* (London, 1990).

Kossovo, Battle of (20 June 1389) The sultan of the Ottoman Turks, Murad I (1359–89), succeeded his father Orhan and continued the policy of territorial expan-sion into the Balkan peninsula. He de-feated an army of 50,000 Serbs in 1366 and smashed 70,000 south Serbs under King Harmanli on the River Maritza in 1371. Further Ottoman victories obliged Bul-garia to recognize Turkish suzerainty in 1376 and, ten years later, after Murad had taken Nish, King Lazar Hrebeljanovich of Serbia was also forced to cede allegiance to Murad. However, internal problems in the Ottoman Empire presented Lazar with the opportunity to form a coalition which de-feated the Turks on the River Toplica in 1387. In the wake of this success, Croats, Bulgars, Albanians, Hungarians and Poles joined the league. Having dealt with the rebellious Bulgarians, Murad marched through Kustendil into Old Serbia until he met the army of the league on the Plain of Kossovo (Plain of the Blackbirds), 50 miles north of Uskub. While organizing his troops for battle, Murad was mortally wounded by a Serbian aristocrat, Milos Kobilic, who had gained access to the sultan by posing as a deserter. Murad's brother, Bayazid, took command of the 60,000 strong Turkish army. Lazar's force, supposedly numbering 100,000 men, was winning the ferocious action until Vuk Brancoviç, probably by prior arrange-ment, deserted to the Turks with 12,000 men late in the day. This proved decisive and the coalition army was routed and Lazar captured and beheaded. After Kossovo, the resistance of the Balkan states virtually collapsed and the Turks were left in control of the whole region.

Süleyman had reorganized the recruit-ment of the Ottoman armies between 1340 and 1350 during the reign of his father Orhan (1324–59). Although the janis-saries, recruited from among Christian prisoners of war, were present on the battlefield, it was the new heavy cavalry, the *sipahis*, who were largely responsible

429

for the victory at Kossovo. *See also* BYZANTIUM; CONSTANTINOPLE; MEHMET II; NICOPOLIS; OTTOMAN TURKS.

R. MANTRAN
JOHN CHILDS

FURTHER READING
Dorothy M. Vaughan, *Europe and the Turk: a pattern of alliances, 1350–1700* (Liverpool, 1954); Maximilian Braun, *Kosova. Die Schlacht auf dem Amselfelde in geschichtlicher und epischer Überlieferung* (Leipzig, 1937); L. Leger, 'La bataille de Kossovo et la chute de l'empire serbe', *Comptes Rendus de l'Academie d'Inscriptions et Belles-Lettres* (1916), pp. 533–43.

Kursk Salient, Battle of the (5–16 July 1943) The battle for the Kursk salient was the pivotal battle on the Eastern front in the Second World War. After the surrender at the beginning of February 1943 of the German forces encircled at Stalingrad, the German army regained the initiative in March with the recapture of Kharkov. As their next theatre of operations, the Germans chose the exposed salient at Kursk, planning to envelop it with a two-prong attack launched from Orel in the north and Kharkov in the south. To achieve this aim, the Germans gathered enormous amounts of *matériel*: nearly 3,000 tanks and some 1,800 aircraft. Unlike operations earlier in the war, *Operation Citadel*, as the attack on Kursk was named, did not achieve strategic surprise. The Soviet forces, as a result of espionage and the deciphering of German codes, were aware of both the time and location of the assault. In consequence, the Soviet positions were formidably prepared, with extensive earthworks and anti-tank traps. The Soviets also concentrated their mechanized forces: some 4,000 Soviet tanks took part in the battle making Kursk the largest tank engagement in the Second World War. The result of the battle, which involved more than two million men, was a stalemate. This marked the first time that the German blitzkrieg had been unable to penetrate Soviet defences, and the heavy losses in tanks that the Germans experienced at Kursk were never fully rectified while Soviet factories rapidly replaced the Red Army's losses. The battle for Kursk represented the last major German offensive in the East; the strategic initiative had finally passed to the Red Army. *See also* GUDERIAN; HITLER; MANSTEIN; RUSSIA/USSR; STALIN.

KEITH NEILSON

FURTHER READING
John Erickson, *The Road to Berlin* (London, 1983).

Kutuzov, Mikhail Ilarionovich (1745–1813) After a distinguished career as a student, including a period at the University of Strasbourg, Kutuzov, a highly educated artillery officer, fought in the Russian army in the wars with Poland and Turkey. He gave little thought to danger, being twice wounded in the head. Kutuzov was respected for his wide military knowledge and produced some tactical writings, notably on *jäger* evolutions. In 1794, he was appointed commandant of the Cadet Corps. As commander of the Russian troops at Austerlitz (1805) he was placed in an impossible position and advised strongly against giving battle. Unable to prevent his troops suffering a crushing defeat, Kutuzov was replaced. In 1812, when Napoleon was less than 130 miles from Moscow, public opinion forced Tsar Alexander I (1801–25) to give Kutuzov command of the army in place of Barclay de Tolly (1761–1818). He continued Tolly's strategy of retreat, trading space for time, but also managed to halt Napoleon temporarily by fighting at Borodino (7 September). His army unbroken, he took the decision to abandon Moscow, which was evacuated and partially burned, and regroup at Tarutino to the south-west covering the industrial region around Tula. He displayed great energy, unleashing irregular actions on the rear of the French army and reinforcing the troops who had remained on the flanks of the French advance in Latvia and in the south. The Russian army began to regain the numerical advantage. When Napoleon withdrew from

Moscow, Kutuzov forced him to employ the now devastated route by which he had advanced. Kutuzov continually harried the French withdrawal, fighting actions against Davout and Ney at Smolensk and against the French rearguards at the crossing of the Beresina. However, the French army was effectively destroyed without the need for major engagements. *See also* INDIRECT WARFARE; MOSCOW, RETREAT FROM; NAPOLEON; RUSSIA/USSR; SUVOROV.

A. CORVISIER

FURTHER READING
R. Parkinson, *The Fox of the North: the life of Kutuzov* (London, 1976).

L

La Hogue and Barfleur, Battles of (29 May–3 June 1692) The origins of the battles along the northern tip of the Cotentin peninsula lay in an attempt by the French to effect a landing in south-west England, in the vicinity of Torbay. Twelve thousand Irish troops plus an equal number of French were to be conveyed in 300 transports in an effort to overthrow William III and replace James II on the English throne. However, before this operation could take place, the French had to secure the naval command of the English Channel.

Against the Anglo-Dutch fleet of 99 ships under Edward Russell (1653–1727), the Comte de Tourville had only 44 plus 13 fireships. However, James II had led him to believe that one third of the English officers would desert to his side. Furthermore, Louis XIV sent a positive order to fight. Skilfully holding off the Allied van, Tourville was able to fight a stiff action in line and yet withdraw safely at dusk, although having sustained some damage. Twenty-seven French ships retired to Brest but fifteen were unable to weather Cape Barfleur before being caught by a fierce flood tide. Three of these took shelter off Cherbourg but were destroyed. The remaining twelve sought refuge at La Hogue, hoping to gain artillery protection from the assembled landing forces, but on 2–3 June they were all burned by the Allies. The invasion attempt was abandoned.

The consequences of this battle are the subject of a stubborn myth. Though the material losses were appreciable, loss of life was small and it did not have the strategic ramifications so frequently suggested, namely that Louis de Pontchartrain, the French minister of marine, abandoned fleet operations and fell back on commerce-raiding, the *guerre de course*. Indeed, in 1693, Pontchartrain's plan of revenge succeeded when Tourville seized a large part of the Anglo-Dutch Smyrna (Levant) Fleet off Lagos Bay in Portugal. It was the catastrophic harvest of 1694 and the enormity of France's financial problems which made it impossible to continue with fleet operations. Financial necessity lay behind the 'industrial' warfare, not the effect of La Hogue. *See also* BLOCKADES; COMMERCE-RAIDING; NAVAL WARFARE; NAVIES; SEIGNELAY.

J. MEYER
JOHN CHILDS

FURTHER READING
Philip Aubrey, *The Defeat of James Stuart's Armada, 1692* (Leicester, 1979); J. Ehrman, *The Navy in the War of William III* (London, 1953); E. H. Jenkins, *A History of the French Navy* (London, 1973); Geoffrey Symcox, *The Crisis of French Sea Power, 1688–97* (The Hague, 1974).

Landings *See* COMBINED OPERATIONS; EXPEDITIONS; OVERLORD

Language The need to make men concentrate on an intended goal and effective action has led the military to employ a brief, simple and direct language. The reputation of the Spartans for being sparing in their use of words has given us the word 'laconic' (from *Lakon*, meaning of Laconia, the region wherein Sparta lay and which it, at times, dominated). There are three aspects to military language: (1) the language of command used in battle and drill; (2) the spoken or written professional language of soldiers, especially their style and vocabulary; (3) the military speech, either delivered as a harangue before battle or committed to paper.

Commands in Battle, Manoeuvre and Drill It is difficult to know the exact words of command which have been used in history, or the manner in which they were given. Military writers have generally disdained to report them verbatim. Commands have to be simple and precise resulting in the performance of specific actions as conditioned reflexes. This is particularly the case for orders issued in battle, such as the order to charge, which may be replaced by bugle calls or drum rolls in order to reach troops who may be out of earshot on account of distance or the noise of battle.

Drill commands are more varied but are still precise. They are repeated tirelessly in the same order and in two stages: warning and execution. The end of the eighteenth century saw the development of expressions which have only been slightly changed in order to adapt them to the development of weapons and military technique. Commands have generally evolved from a single sentence, although some of these remain in use in the British army, towards a kind of cry which forcefully exaggerates the natural stress pattern of the language. This cry generally consists of a long syllable followed by a short syllable, or a long word succeeded by a short word – 'Atten – Tion'; 'Bayonets – Fix!' In French, German and English, the articles have disappeared. 'Carry your arms on the shoulder' has been reduced to 'Shoulder Arms' ('Portez armes'; 'Gewehr auf'). In some cases, verbs have become redundant – 'Stand at Attention' is now 'Attention' ('Garde à vous'); 'Rest your musket on the ground' has been reduced to 'Order Arms' ('Reposez armes'; 'Gewehr ab'). The lexical content no longer has any significance and orders of this kind can be readily understood by all members of multilingual forces – colonial troops, the Indian army, the Austro-Hungarian army and the Soviet army. In weapons drill, the path of development has run from a varied code of command which mirrored the complex operations involved in handling the early musket and rifle to the short, sharp orders which reflect the simplicity of operation of modern infantry weapons and tactics.

Military Language It is often possible to detect a military man by his spoken language, both in his vocabulary and manner of speaking. One of the most striking examples was the British 'cavalry accent' of the nineteenth century whose affected tones continued to be fashionable well into the twentieth century. The banter of the Royal Air Force during the Second World War was almost incomprehensible to civilians.

Concision is the essence of military language but it is also conditioned by the increasingly technical nature of the military art which requires a special vocabulary. Military men were the first to make extensive use of abbreviations, initials and acronyms. Gradually, from the late eighteenth century, the orders, ordinances and regulations which emanated from the civilian administration of the army grew more precise and brief, avoiding those nuances which had allowed a certain leeway in interpretation.

The parallel development of military science in different countries ensured the spread of linguistic borrowings from the most innovative states. In the fourteenth century the main source of martial words was Italian, followed by Spanish in the sixteenth century. French was the dominant military language in the seventeenth and eighteenth centuries, German in the later nineteenth and early twentieth centuries and English and American in the middle and later twentieth century. This has given rise to a tendency to employ an international vocabulary. Among modern navies, English predominates, whereas in the days of sail when navies were more dependent upon local navigational techniques, they had more varied vocabularies. There was a marked difference between the terminologies of the French Atlantic and Mediterranean fleets. French colonial armies have borrowed many everyday terms from Arabic and the languages of Indo-China, a process copied by the British Indian army, although these have rarely met with official approval.

In the twentieth century, military language has become familiar to a large section of the population through compulsory military service and, equally, as a result of clandestine armed struggles. Even peaceful movements and institutions talk of 'general mobilization', 'commando raids', and so on.

Military expression generally prefers brevity. The great historical sayings, whether authentic or *ex post facto*, are pithy. Some of these have become slogans such as MacMahon's 'J'y suis, j'y reste' – 'Here I am, here I stay' – at the Malakoff, or Wellington's 'Up Guards and at 'em' at Waterloo. Military speech also shows a fondness for lively terms which may, in the hands of practitioners like Patton and Stilwell, decline into profanity and coarseness. Today's fashion is more for black humour.

Military Speeches In contrast to the familiar tone of the camp, military speeches are intended to raise soldiers' spirits to the level required by the task at hand. We know little of harangues to the troops since those which have come down to us have been embellished in the process of writing. Caesar provides an early example. The language of such addresses varies according to the make-up of the troops – mercenaries were often promised the chance to pillage – the period and the cultural context. In Antiquity the main theme was the defence of the city. Harangues in the Middle Ages usually contained a reference to religion, Islam specializing in accounts of the heavenly fate awaiting those who died fighting for the faith. A form of speech that was both religious and military in character developed in the later centuries of the medieval period and during the Renaissance. The soldiers of the Spanish *tercios* heard some fine examples from their chaplains. Speeches of this kind were still used in the seventeenth and eighteenth centuries. An eighteenth-century chaplain exhorted the French Grenadiers, 'Children of glory, in spite of the boldness which is in your souls, humble yourselves before the Lord. He alone gives victory.' Many clergymen were less brief. Before Rocoux in 1746, a lieutenant-colonel interrupted the chaplain to say, 'Soldiers, the holy father wishes to tell you that there will be no salvation for cowards. Long live the King.'

The French Revolutionary Wars saw a flowering of military eloquence which borrowed the themes and phraseology of the Revolution. This could be heard not only on the eve of battle but also in the education sessions given by the political commissars which formed part of the soldiers' service training. These practices have reappeared in the twentieth century in those countries with totalitarian regimes.

When written, the military address takes on a literary form. The term *discours militaire* is used in the sixteenth century by Brantôme to refer to the type of dissertation constituted by his *Discours des grands capitaines français et étrangers* and his *Discours sur les colonels de l'infanterie en France*. The discipline of the *discours militaire* soon slipped into memoir and some military authors composed maxims. The object of the *discours* was to glorify the martial virtues – honour, loyalty, devotion to king, country and God, and the spirit of sacrifice. It often consisted of an analysis of case-studies and past situations and was generally normative in character. In Europe, the high-point of such writing occurred in the eighteenth century. In the twentieth century, this type of military writing has taken on a more militant, patriotic or ideological character. The question of military ethics which was addressed by the *discours* has found less and less expression. *See also* COMMAND; DISCIPLINE; GLORY.

A. CORVISIER

FURTHER READING
Although there is no general work in this field, material may be gleaned from memoirs, journals, etc. As an example of the establishment of an international military vocabulary, see C. M. Schulten, *Contribution à l'étude des termes militaires français en néerlandais, 1567–1625* (The Hague, 1966). There is some information on military speeches and harangues in John Keegan, *The Mask of Command* (London, 1987). On clerical addresses to the military, see J. R. Hale, 'Incitement to violence? English divines on the theme of war, 1578 to 1631', in J. R. Hale, *Renaissance War Studies* (London, 1983), pp. 487–517. For a modern compilation of military quotations, see Peter G. Tsouras, *Warriors' Words* (London, 1992).

La Rochelle, Siege of (November 1572–July 1573) La Rochelle did not become the capital of French Protestantism until the Second War of Religion (1567–8). During the First War (1562–3) the town had remained neutral, and it was only after a Huguenot coup in January 1568 that its allegiance was won. Its possible strategic importance was detected immediately by both the local royalist commander, Monluc, and the Huguenot leadership, who fled there on the outbreak of the Third War in September 1568. La Rochelle's site among salt marshes deep within a strongly Huguenot hinterland and its distance from the main royal naval bases made both a siege and an effective naval blockade difficult. The town also gave the Huguenots control over the salt pans of Brouage and enabled them to maintain communication with foreign allies by sea. La Rochelle was not directly threatened during the Third War (1568–70), but it was then extensively fortified (making it possibly the most heavily fortified town in France) and it provided both the Huguenots and their Dutch allies with a lucrative privateering base. In the Fourth War (1572–3), however, La Rochelle became the centre of Protestant resistance. Following the Massacre of St Bartholomew's Eve (23–4 August 1572) large numbers of Huguenots fled there and the town refused to accept a royal governor or pay its taxes. After failing to persuade the town to return to its allegiance in October, Charles IX formally declared war on 6 November. This 'war' was largely confined to the sieges of La Rochelle and Sancerre. The season and the distance from Paris meant that it was not until December that La Rochelle was invested and February 1573 that a substantial army was despatched under the command of the Dukes of Anjou and Alençon. The royalist army was, however, riven by internal dissension and the siege did not begin in earnest until a large contingent of Swiss arrived in April 1573. May and June saw a number of unsuccessful assaults and attempts to mine the walls; the sinking of blockships in the harbour mouth was no more effective. Like the contemporary sieges in the Netherlands, there was extensive popular participation (including women) in the defence. The town's defiance was sustained by the hope of English intervention, and by June and July, when this did not materialize and food shortages grew, morale began to decline. However, at the same time the crown decided to bring the war to an end for its own political reasons, and offered the necessary concessions (the Edict of Boulogne, July–August). La Rochelle was not again threatened until the great siege of 1627–8, when popular resistance was to some extent inspired by that of 1573. Yet the comparison between the two reveals that, for all the strength of its position and the commitment of the population, the town's ability to resist the military power of the crown in 1573 was to a large extent due to political dissension within the royalist army. *See also* FRANCE; LA ROCHELLE (1627–8); MONLUC; SIEGES.

SIMON ADAMS

FURTHER READING
There is no full-scale narrative of the siege in English. Recent brief accounts are found in M. P. Holt, *The Duke of Anjou and the Politique Struggle during the Wars of Religion* (Cambridge, 1986) and R. M. Kingdon, *Myths about the St Bartholomew's Day Massacres, 1572–1576* (Cambridge, Mass., 1988). For La Rochelle as a privateering base, see B. Dietz, 'The Huguenot and English corsairs during the Third Civil War in France, 1568–1570', *Proceedings of the Huguenot Society of London*, xix (1959), pp. 278–94.

La Rochelle, Siege of (August 1627–October 1628) Operations against the Huguenots, the French Protestants, who had risen in revolt had become concentrated around La Rochelle, one of the places of safety which had been granted to them by the Edict of Nantes in 1598. The inhabitants of La Rochelle had some support from English forces, which had temporarily occupied the Île de Ré. To avoid the Huguenots combining with the English by sea, Richelieu, who had taken control of operations alongside Louis XIII, ordered the engineer Métezeau to build a barrier across the entrance to the harbour. Two English relieving fleets were repulsed in May and September 1628. The town, beset by famine, surrendered on 29 October. It was a victory for tenacity and method, achieved with minimum losses to the besieging troops. *See also* FRANCE; RICHELIEU; SIEGES.

A. CORVISIER

FURTHER READING
David Parker, *La Rochelle and the French Monarchy* (London, 1980); T. Cogswell, 'Prelude to Ré: the Anglo-French struggle over La Rochelle, 1624–7', *History*, lxxi (1986), pp. 1–21; T. Cogswell, 'Foreign policy and parliament: the case of La Rochelle, 1625–6', *English Historical Review*, xcix (1984), pp. 241–67; S. J. Stearns, 'The Caroline military systems, 1625–1627: the expeditions to Cadiz and Ré' (University of California, Berkeley, PhD Dissertation, 1967).

Larrey, Dominique (1766–1842) Coming from a medical family, Larrey first studied at and was then assigned to the Hôpital de La Grave in Toulouse. At the age of twenty, he passed out top in the competitive examination for surgeon-majors in the army. He completed his education in Paris at the College of Surgeons. With the exception of one short campaign to protect the cod fishermen off Newfoundland in 1788, his wartime activities were entirely devoted to accompanying the Revolutionary and Imperial Armies of France to Italy, Egypt, Germany, Spain and Russia. He was wounded and taken prisoner at Waterloo. In peacetime, he practised and taught at Val-de-Grâce, the military hospital in Paris founded in 1796, and was surgeon-in-chief at both the Hôpital du Gros-Caillou and Les Invalides. Larrey was the most significant of a number of important French military doctors who cared for the wounded during this period. Also worthy of mention are Pierre François, Baron de Percy (1754–1825), the military surgeon and inspector-general of army medical services, and Nicolas Dufriche, Baron de Desgenettes (1762–1837), the physician and inspector-general of the medical services of the Grande Armée. To the very end of his life, Larrey demonstrated great technical skill, amputating a limb in two minutes, and was an effective organizer who, when chief surgeon to the Imperial Guard and inspector-general of the army medical services, constantly encountered and resolved formidable administrative problems. In disgrace under the Restoration, he returned to service in 1830 and undertook a mission of inspection to Algeria. Larrey introduced the 'flying ambulances' which provided the necessary equipment for surgical operations to be conducted in the field prior to the evacuation of the wounded to more distant hospitals. (Percy introduced the corps of stretcher bearers to bring the wounded to the advanced 'surgical waggons'.) In amputation, he developed the technique of retraction to create 'lambeaux circulaires' (rounded flaps of soft tissue) which reduced the risk of later infection in the stump. He also improved the thread used in sutures, developed better methods for extracting bullets from the chest, and wrote several treatises on military surgery. *See also* MEDICAL SERVICES.

A. CORVISIER

FURTHER READING
J. H. Dible, *Napoleon's Surgeon* (London, 1970); R. G. Richardson, *Larrey: surgeon to Napoleon's Imperial Guard* (London, 1974).

Law, military Since the first establishment of professional armies, the strongest have been those with the highest standards of discipline. Usually, this has been imposed through the army's own judicial system. Without appropriate penalties, acts of indiscipline might grow in number, eventually sowing sufficient seeds of disorder to weaken the armed forces to the point where they are vulnerable to defeat. Since an early stage in history, careful attention has been paid to suppressing such acts. In the modern world too, the primary justification for armies possessing powers of jurisdiction lies in the contribution which these can make towards preserving discipline, the foundation of the quality of any fighting force. In every age, those entrusted with command have made the maintenance of military discipline their constant concern.

Military Jurisdiction from Antiquity to the Early Middle Ages At the outset, a commander's jurisdictional powers were extensive. They comprised not only the right to punish, which was a natural part of the command function, but also that of making judicial decisions, resulting in the merging of the two prerogatives. This was the system that long remained in operation in the Roman armies, even under the Empire. Depending on the seriousness of the occurrence, the consul or tribune, with the centurions in attendance, heard the accused soldier's defence and then pronounced judgement. The decision, which was given before the assembled troops, was approved or applauded by them, except in instances where they were first given the opportunity to declare their collective opinion on the guilt of the accused. However, this appears to have been no more than a ritual reflecting the influence which a commander exercised over his men. In the *Annales* (I, ch. XLIV), Tacitus gives this description of the trial of the leaders of the mutiny of the legions in Germany (AD 14): 'They [the soldiers] dragged the mutineers in chains before the legate of Legion I, Gaius Caetronius, who pronounced judgement and sentence on each individual in the following manner. The legions were assembled with drawn swords, and the accused were displayed by a tribune on a raised platform; if there was a shout of "guilty", he was thrown down to them and slaughtered. And the soldiers took great pleasure in this massacre, since they felt they were absolving themselves.'

The establishment of professional armies and the recruitment of mercenaries coincided, during the second century AD, with the appearance of a judicial system peculiar to the military. It was separate both from the chain of command and from the ordinary processes of law. The *Digest* contains some provisions which relate to this system. It was retained by Constantine, improved by his successors and implemented by *magistri militum*.

These advances in judicial procedure were obliterated in the western part of the Roman Empire by the Barbarian invasions. Once again, the old confusion between the right to punish and the right to judge reappeared. As the celebrated story of the Soissons vase demonstrates, Clovis acted as both commander of his warriors and as their dispenser of justice. The feudal system did not put an end to this situation, which endured throughout the Middle Ages; a lord commanded his men at arms and passed sentence on them. As the feudal system declined and the authority of the nation-state was created, a better-organized system for the administration of justice, both military and civilian, came into existence.

Military Jurisdiction in France It is customary to quote the Edict of Montdidier, issued by Philip VI on 1 May 1347, which declared that the ordinary processes of law were no longer appropriate for dealing with the men at arms employed to guard castles, as the beginning of military jurisdiction in France. In fact, the basis of military jurisdiction was older, dating from the middle of the thirteenth century when the *Tribunal de la connétablie* appeared. As the commander of the king's army, the *connétable* naturally held, from the time of the creation of his post during the thirteenth century, jurisdiction over all the men at arms under his command. However, since his primary responsibility was the conduct of military operations, he was compelled to delegate his judicial functions to his *maréchaux* and other officers. All those who formed part of the king's army were subject, from that time onwards, to the court of justice of the *connétable*. Subsequently, to bring soldiers on campaign more closely within the jurisdiction to which they were answerable, the *connétable* specifically delegated his jurisdictional authority to the *prévôt*. This officer, who had originally been responsible for policing the army by seeking out delinquents and presenting them before the *Tribunal de la connétablie*, was also given the task of judging the offenders. This roving judge was named the *Grand Prévôt* but he later established himself permanently at the royal court and delegated his powers to lieutenants who assumed, under Louis XI (1461–83), the title of *prévôts provinciaux*. During the reign of Francis I (1515–47), they became known as *prévôts des maréchaux*. They travelled from 'garrison to garrison, the better to dispense justice to the military, and to maintain law and order'.

Originally, the *Tribunal de la connétablie* and the *prévôts* had to hear all cases in which men at arms stood accused, regardless of whether the offence was civilian or military. During the fifteenth century, and often subsequently, the monarchy was anxious to limit the peacetime scope of these courts in order to appease the grievances of the rural population, who complained ceaselessly about the pillage to which they were subjected. The civil judges, *baillis* and *sénéchaux*, had a reputation for being more determined than their military counterparts but it was not easy to persuade commanders to allow their soldiers to be tried before civilian courts. Gradually a *modus vivendi* was established. When on campaign, all offences committed by the soldiery were tried before military courts. In peacetime, civilian offences committed by soldiers were judged before civilian courts; purely military offences were dealt with by the *prévôts*.

This principle of a division of powers between civil and military jurisdictions was observed until the end of the *ancien régime*. When, under Louis XIV, courts martial were introduced, their establishment implied no deviation from the traditional practice since they were required to judge only the specifically military offences which had previously been assigned to the *prévôts des maréchaux*. The purpose of the courts martial was 'to maintain discipline within army units and to pass penal sentences on instances of misconduct of which commanders and soldiers might have been guilty, either during battle or when moving from place to place'. Generals, governors of provinces and commandants of specialist arms had the right to convene courts martial. In garrison, the fortress commandant, and, in the field, the brigade commander, presided over the court, which consisted of at least seven officers appointed by the convening authority. The preliminary work on a case coming before the court was carried out either by the fortress adjutant, in garrison, or the regimental adjutant, in the field.

The political upheaval that France began to experience in 1789 led to repercussions on the military judicial system in the following year. The law of 22 September–5 October 1790 introduced a new court martial which included a jury and whose competence was confined to exclusively military crimes. The hearing of cases concerning 'civilian offences' committed by military personnel, i.e. 'such as contravene the general law of the realm', was left to the ordinary judicial system. These arrangements were refashioned during the next two years (e.g. courts of summary jurisdiction, without a jury, were to be convened as required to handle the least serious military misdemeanours) and then set aside altogether in 1793 when military criminal courts were created on the scale of two per army. In January 1794, police courts of summary jurisdiction and disciplinary boards were added to these courts to deal with minor offences. Generals, however, in contradistinction from other military personnel, came within the jurisdiction of the Revolutionary Tribunal 'in order to obviate the effects of intrigue and of the influence which these officers might have on the courts attached to each army'. The counter-revolutionaries of Thermidor replaced the system with new military courts composed of three officers, three NCOs and three other ranks. A year later, the NCOs and other ranks were excluded when officers were on trial. The law of 13 Brumaire Year V (7 November 1796) marked the final stage in these rapid changes. It set up in every army division a standing court martial of seven members (six officers and one NCO) nominated by the general commanding the division. He also appointed a captain as *rapporteur*, responsible for carrying out the preliminary investigation of each case, and another captain to act as prosecutor ('representative of the executive').

This system endured until 1857 when the Code for the Judicial System of the Land Army was introduced; its naval counterpart followed in the following year. Basically, the 1796 system was unchanged except that the rank of the judges varied in accordance with the rank of the accused. However, the new Code expressly sanctioned 'jurisdiction over military personnel as such'; they were to be judged by the court martial for all offences, even infractions of the civilian law, except for those committed in peacetime in collusion with civilians. The severity of punishments was reduced. The Code of 1857 was well suited to the professional armed forces of the Second Empire and was not subjected to serious criticism until the end of the nineteenth century. However, since 1871 military service had been compulsory and a citizen army had replaced its professional predecessor. Though a system of justice that could award penalties through a special military court was readily acceptable to the latter, the former preferred the civilian penal system subject to those exceptions that emanated solely from the requirements of discipline. However, although the passions aroused by the Dreyfus Case proved influential in questioning the role of courts martial, the advent of the First World War interrupted the examination of draft proposals aimed at their elimination.

Investigation of the matter was resumed after the war, resulting, in 1928, in a new code for the army's judicial system whose provisions were extended to the air force in 1934. The code for the navy was issued in 1938. Military boards, presided over by a civilian magistrate, replaced courts martial. Their sphere of jurisdiction was limited to the offences specified in the code. However, on the eve of the Second World War, the scope was extended to cover contraventions of civilian law which were committed in the service, whether in a military establishment or in billets. After 1945, a movement towards amalgamation developed, leading to the merger of the army and navy military boards in 1953 and of the personnel of the army and navy judicial systems in 1956 and to a Code of Service Judicial Procedure applicable uniformly to the whole of the armed forces in 1965. The system was also brought into line with the administration of civilian justice. A second civilian magistrate was introduced alongside the civilian president and civilian magistrates were also permitted to perform service legal duties by acting as prosecutors and by carrying out preliminary investigations, duties previously executed only by service magistrates.

Over four decades the judicial powers of the service commanders had been greatly reduced. As long as the 1857 Code remained in operation, those powers remained extensive, with the military laying the accusation, mounting the investigation and deciding whether to send the accused to trial. In 1928, the corps of military judicial officers was created, independent of the command hierarchy; this became the corps of service magistrates in 1956. Although the command authorities decided which cases should be taken up, the corps was responsible for the necessary investigations and for the prosecution. Moreover, the military commanders lost the power to send an accused before the judgement board. On the other hand, they possessed the right of appeal ('the lodging of an objection') against the decision of the investigating magistrate. This right to lodge an objection was withdrawn by the 1965 Code. From that time, the sole prerogative remaining to the service command was the power to initiate proceedings. The reason behind the retention of this basic and traditional power was that the commander, who had sole responsibility for discipline, was best placed to assess whether the punishment already imposed on an offender was sufficient without recourse to further legal proceedings.

A minor section of public opinion, which had remained resolutely opposed to any departure from civilian law in the matter of punishment and which was assisted by the shift in political power in 1981, finally succeeded in making its views prevail. The law of 21 July 1982 abolished service judicial systems except where forces served outside French territory and where international agreements permitted no other solution. Responsibility was given to three judicial authorities which normally awarded penalties under ordinary law – a board of summary jurisdiction, an assize court and a court of appeal within each area – to hear cases that were specified under the Code of Service Judicial Procedure. At a stroke, command authorities lost their power to initiate proceedings since the public prosecutor decided whether to lay a case before one of these agencies. Nevertheless, in purely service offences (e.g. desertion, refusal to obey orders, etc.) or infractions of civilian law committed during the course of service activity – e.g. infractions which raised questions of discipline – it is the rule that the service authorities, when they have not themselves informed the public prosecutor about such cases, should be consulted by him on the way in which each instance ought to be treated. Thus, the service command has the opportunity to make its views fully known even if the actual decision of whether or not to proceed with a case rests with a civilian judicial agency. Leaving aside a few special points of procedure, service delinquents are now subject to the same rules as the civilian.

If war is declared, the service judicial systems, as they existed before 1982, would be re-established. They can also be resurrected in situations which, from a legal point of view, do not quite qualify as 'wartime' – states of siege, states of emergency, mobilization and states of readiness. In all these circumstances, the exigencies of discipline and of the country's defence would justify a return to a more appropriate military judicial system. However, there is an important limitation of practicality. How, after its disappearance in peacetime, could the service judicial system be reconstituted in wartime or other emergency? Perhaps further consideration should be given to the words of Georges Clemenceau – 'the military judicial system is the necessary consequence of that other necessity – the army.'

Other Countries During the post-medieval period, military legal systems were established in several European countries besides France and England. In Spain during the sixteenth century, and also in the Spanish Netherlands, there were several edicts of Charles V (1519–56) setting up *conseils de guerre* and appointing *auditeurs de camp*. These *conseils*, which were composed of officers, had two tasks: they passed judgement on military personnel who had committed grave offences and advised the command on the conduct of military operations. The *auditeurs* were officers with some experi-

ence of the law and were responsible for providing clarification and advice to the *conseils*. In 1586, twenty years after the appearance of the first military penal code, Alexander Farnese, Duke of Parma and Governor of the Spanish Netherlands, finally settled the duties of the *auditeurs* thus providing the Spanish army with its own legal arrangements. The system of *auditeurs* was copied in the Spanish Latin American colonies.

It was also adopted in Scandinavia. In 1621, Gustavus II Adolphus, King of Sweden (1611–32), issued a code of military law, largely inspired by the ideas of Grotius, laying out in detail the organization of the administration of military justice. Apart from a few minor modifications, this code remained in force until a revision was carried out at the end of the eighteenth century by King Gustavus IV (1792–1809).

However, not all countries which possess an army have developed or retained military judicial systems in peacetime. In modern Europe, Austria, Denmark, Sweden and Norway are in this position, though their armed forces are very small. The case of Germany, which has adopted the same policy, is more surprising because it has a relatively large army (*c*.500,000 men). Disciplinary tribunals, which can inflict punishments that differ little from those awarded by civilian courts, have replaced the court martial. However, all these countries have military judicial systems ready for inauguration in time of war. In fact, the vast majority of countries which have armies above a certain size have adopted military judicial systems; it is the natural corollary of the retention of substantial armed forces. After achieving independence during the 1960s, various African countries – Zaire, Algeria, the Cameroons, Gabon, the Ivory Coast, Malawi, Uganda, etc. – have provided their armed forces with military judicial systems usually modelled on those of the ex-colonial power.

In countries where military judicial systems exist, their scope varies considerably. One extreme form subjects a serviceman, whatever his offence, to military jurisdiction. This rule, which was the case in France under the Code of 1857, is currently practised in Russia and the other republics which previously formed the USSR, Belgium and the Netherlands. At the other extremity, military jurisdiction applies only to military offences. In between, the variety is considerable. If a general tendency can be identified it is the increase in the role of civilian lawyers at the expense of the military, a change that has been accompanied by a strengthening of the lawyers' independence.

M. GARREC

Great Britain The exact form and content of military jurisdiction varies from country to country and from time to time. Many of the main variables can be identified and illustrated by reviewing the British experience, as analysed by Peter Rowe in *Defence: the legal implications*. Modern British military law has developed out of the seventeenth-century struggle between the Crown and Parliament. The Bill of Rights (1689) stated that 'the raising or keeping a standing army within the kingdom in time of peace, unless it be with consent of Parliament, is against law.' In other words, Parliament and not the king controlled the raising and maintenance of the army in peacetime. The basic code of discipline for members of the army was first set out in the Mutiny Act (1689). Revised and re-enacted annually, except for a hiatus between 1697 and 1701, the Mutiny Act steadily increased the number of military offences and became a 'christmas tree' on which Parliament hung a multitude of regulations concerning the army: billeting, requisitioning of transport, false musters, etc. Nowadays, the lawful existence of the army, navy and air force depends upon the renewal every five years of an Armed Forces Act. This perpetuates Parliament's sovereignty over the military and military jurisdiction, which is the form that military subordination to political authority takes in Britain.

The Mutiny Act of 1689 allowed the military to try a limited range of offences and made available a variety of penalties, including capital punishment, which has still not been abolished in British military law though the most recent execution occurred in 1953. The modern system of courts martial developed together with the growing range of offences identified in successive Mutiny Acts. Most of the offences were specifically military, such as desertion, mutiny, absence without leave, malingering and neglect of duty. Offences against the ordinary common law have gradually been added to the competence of courts martial. Pragmatic adjustments have both avoided conflicts of jurisdiction between military and civilian courts and minimized involvement of the civilian system in the minutiae of military administration. Thus, a theft in the High Street will normally bring a soldier before the civilian courts whereas the same offence in barracks will be dealt with by a court martial. A soldier tried before a court martial cannot then be tried for the same offence in a civilian court.

Each court martial is established specifically for the trial which it is to hear. This allows the convening officer to summon the court at the most convenient time and place, a flexibility which fits neatly into operational military requirements. In recent years, still greater flexibility has been achieved by the gradual transfer of jurisdiction in lesser offences to a commanding officer, who is now permitted to deal summarily with many types of case. If a penalty involving loss of liberty or pay is in prospect then the accused can elect for trial by court martial.

There are two types of court martial. A *general* court martial consists of a president and at least four other officers who have held their commissions for at least three years. A *district* court martial comprises a president and two other officers who have held their commissions for at least two years. The *judge advocate* always assists a general court martial and may assist at a district court martial. This official is an independent, legally qualified person appointed by the Lord Chancellor and is not a member of the military command structure. He advises the court on points of law and procedure and sums up at the end of the case. Trials are normally conducted in open court with the same rules of evidence that apply in the civilian system, but the scope for appeal is greater. Although the soldier does not have the protection of trial by jury, there is no call from servicemen to alter the system.

As this review of the British experience makes plain, military jurisdiction is inseparably bound up with civil–military relations and the civilian law. The British case has been shaped by a long tradition of civilian control and pragmatic accommodations made possible by a largely harmonious relationship between the civil and the military authorities. It is to be expected that the detailed nature of a military jurisdiction will be more complex if it embodies a recent or formative history of civil–military conflict. *See also* CIVIL POWER, SUPPORT OF; DISCIPLINE; ESPRIT DE CORPS; ETHOS; GLORY; GROTIUS; HONOURS AND AWARDS; SOLDIERS AND SOCIETY.

BARRIE PASKINS

FURTHER READING
Pierre Huguenay, *Traité théorique et pratique du droit pénal et procédure pénale militaires* (Paris, 1933); Alain Picard, 'La justice au sein des forces armées' (unpublished thesis, University of Toulouse, 1980); R. Colas, 'Évolution et fondements des extensions de compétence des juridictions militaires', *Revue de science criminelle et de droit pénal comparé*, no. 2 (1969); *Revue de droit pénal militaire et de droit de la guerre*, xix (1980); *Rapport du VIIIe Congrès de la Société internationale de droit pénal militaire* (1981); Peter Rowe, *Defence: the legal implications* (London, 1987).

Lawrence, Thomas Edward (1888–1935) 'Lawrence of Arabia' made his first visit to the Middle East in 1909 while researching his Oxford undergraduate dissertation, later published in 1936 as *Crusader Castles*. He returned to Syria in 1911 as an archaeologist working under D. G. Hogarth, later participating in a joint archaeological and topographical expedition to the Sinai in early 1914. In October 1914 he joined the Geographical Section at the War Office and was then transferred to Military Intelligence in Cairo in December. Involved from the beginning in the negotiations leading to the Arab revolt against the Turks, Lawrence was sympathetic towards Arab self-determination. Joining Hogarth's newly established Arab Bureau in October 1916, Lawrence became effectively military adviser to the Arab forces during their campaign to disrupt the Hejaz railway and was particularly influential in subsequently shifting Arab forces north in August 1917 following their capture of the port of Akaba to support Allenby's advance into Syria. He was then part of the Arab delegation to the post-war Versailles conference at which their expectations were to be disappointed by previous Allied agreement to partition the Ottoman Empire. In 1921, during an Arab revolt in Mesopotamia which led to a degree of self-government both there and in Trans-Jordan, he was appointed an adviser to Churchill at the Colonial Office. However, a sense of disillusion undoubtedly contributed to his decision in 1922 to enlist in the Royal Air Force as an ordinary aircraftsman under the pseudonym of Ross, followed by similar service in the Tank Corps as a private under the pseudonym of Shaw from 1923 to 1925 and, in the RAF once more, from 1925 to 1935. Yet, at the same time, Lawrence also wished to cultivate a literary reputation and maintained a wide circle of influential contacts, his classic memoir, *Seven Pillars of Wisdom*, being published by private subscription in 1926 and in a popular abridged version as *Revolt in the Desert* in 1927. While Liddell Hart saw Lawrence's military achievements as ideally illustrative of his own concept of the 'indirect approach', Lawrence's memoirs and an article on guerilla warfare he contributed to *Encyclopaedia Britannica* in 1927 were elegant and influential expositions of the possibilities of guerilla conflict utilized in a political cause. Stressing the importance of secure base areas and the exploitation of space by small and highly mobile forces furnished with good intelligence, Lawrence also perceived the importance of popular support. Indeed, among his three defined functions of command – algebraical, biological and psychological – the last not only embraced the motivation of both guerilla and population but also the undermining of an opponent's morale. Lawrence finally retired from the RAF in February 1935 only to be fatally injured in a motorcycle accident three months later. *See also* INDIRECT WARFARE; LIDDELL HART; POPULAR WARFARE.

IAN F. W. BECKETT

FURTHER READING
Brian Holden-Reid, 'T. E. Lawrence and his biographers', in *The First World War and British Military History*, ed. Brian Bond (Oxford, 1991), pp. 227–60; Jeremy Wilson, *Lawrence of Arabia* (London, 1989); Jeremy Wilson, *T. E. Lawrence: a guide to printed and manuscript material* (Fordingbridge, 1990).

Laws of war The expression 'law', when used in connection with war, has frequently been the subject of differing, indeed completely opposed, interpretations. The earliest, which was still mentioned in the *Dictionnaire du Comité d'Officiers* (published in 1900), held that war is 'the triumph of brute force, used without restraint'. Its corollary is that victory confers absolute rights. Although long considered to be self-evident, this view was modified by various authors in Antiquity, and particularly by Christianity, as a result of its search for a distinction between just and unjust wars. In this way, the concept of the right to have recourse to arms in a just cause was established; but since the justice or otherwise of a cause was almost always controversial, attention turned to making wars, if they could not be prevented, less cruel. In the Middle Ages, the Church laid down the rules, while a code of good conduct among professional warriors was a product of the rise of 'chivalry'. The idea of regulations for war, as opposed to the primitive conception that it confers absolute rights, thus has ancient origins. It developed particularly in the sixteenth century and reached the point, at least in Western Europe, of the formulation of a framework of established practices covering the actual conduct of war, its occurrence being deemed inevitable, which was generally respected for two centuries (the eighteenth and the nineteenth). In the twentieth century, in spite of the establishment of international institutions, wars that have taken place outside Europe or were connected with revolutions or were struggles for colonial independence have often brought with them a reversion to ancient practices, which violate human rights.

There is justification for using the term 'laws of war' as soon as war takes place within a framework of rules, whether observed in practice or only recognized in theory, and of usages which are established between nations, and which apply to conduct in war between combatants, as well as between combatants and civilians. Although they belong to different fields of enquiry, the two interpretations of 'law' in connection with war (i.e. the right to have recourse to arms and the rules governing the conduct of war itself) will both be discussed here in the course of a chronological survey. This accordingly deals with the question of the relationship between war and international law, and with the general and particular practices of war, in the light of the development of military techniques and human attitudes. Before starting such a survey, it is useful to recall that one of the most powerful influences backing the 'laws of war' has been, over the centuries, the fear of reprisals.

The Ancient World
Even in primitive societies, war was not merely recourse to the use of physical force. It was unusual for it not to take on a nonmaterial aspect, if only in the form of invoking the support of occult, moral or religious forces. Ever since it brought organized groups of human beings into conflict with each other, war has been accompanied by rituals – for the opening of hostilities, the return of peace and, indeed, battle itself. The digging up of the tomahawk, and the smoking of the pipe of peace, determined among the North American Indians the commencement and the end of a state of war, which justified the use of practices generally condemned in peacetime. The leader decided, though only after discussion, on the issues of peace or war. Among many peoples of Antiquity, the enemy became a kind of tainted being, towards whom there no longer existed any obligations. Among the Greeks, this idea rested

on racial pride. Aristotle considered that the barbarians (i.e. non-Greeks) were destined to be the slaves of Greeks, and that any means could be employed to reduce them to that status. But wars between Greeks were also extremely cruel. The lives of prisoners belonged to the victor and they were sacrificed, unless it was in his interest to enslave them or exact a ransom for them. Among the more primitive peoples plunder, and among other peoples the appropriation of property, seemed legitimate, and were often the object of a war. Cicero declared that 'victory made profane everything that was most sacred to the Syracusans' (*Speeches* – prosecution of Verres). Yet the same Cicero, here following a number of Greek authors, asked himself what made a war just, and concluded that it was if it intended to restore a state of law and redress wrongs.

The idea of a just war appeared also in the Mosaic law. It said that war should be declared only for just causes, and that it is always just when fought against unbelievers. The victor is seen as the instrument of God's will, even when it was His chosen people who were to be chastised. The practices of war it recommends are as cruel as those of other peoples: 'And when the Lord thy God delivereth it [a city] into thine hand, thou shalt smite every male thereof with the edge of the sword . . . but the women, and the little ones, and the cattle . . . thou shalt take for a prey unto thyself.'

Christianity

Christianity's condemnation of the violence and injustice of war produced no immediate, radical changes in men's conception of it or in the practices they employed. The New Testament alludes more to relationships between individuals than to those between nations. Although, up to the eighth century, priests generally took the view that the profession of arms was incompatible with sanctity, civil communities fervently awarded that title to warriors.

The Concept of War   Christian thinking on the subject of war derives largely from St Augustine who, because he thought that complete peace was impossible in this world, admitted that it was permissible to make war for the sake of securing 'the tranquillity of good order' and justice, and he condemned war for gain and for the subjection of others. War had also to be declared and waged by a legitimate ruler, a condition which made the ruler an instrument in God's hand and freed those who carried out his orders from all responsibility.

The Barbarian invasions and the collapse of the Roman Empire increased the number of armed confrontations; hence, the reflections of Isidore of Seville on the *jus militare* (laws of war) and the *jus gentium* (laws universally accepted) remained in the sphere of academic studies. Nevertheless, for Barbarian kings who had been converted to Christianity, war tended to be looked upon as a divine judgement. Charlemagne's empire, which drew much of its inspiration from the Church, was not sufficiently strongly based to make the practices of the time conform to the principles of Christianity.

Christian thinking on war, which – during the conflicts of feudalism – did not penetrate beyond the monasteries, and which was compromised by the military activities of priests, showed renewed vigour from the year 1000 onwards. At the time when methods which tended to limit private wars were being established, and the authority of rules was being restored in principalities and kingdoms, there appeared the concept of the holy war. The jurists of Bologna rediscovered Roman law. A kind of code of war emerged; St Thomas Aquinas contributed to it on the spiritual plane, and St Louis on the practical. In his famous theory of the just war, St Thomas Aquinas excluded from the definition of 'war' revolts, civil and class conflicts and military action by private individuals or groups. War proper had to be declared by a competent authority, for a just cause and with a lawful intention. Before St Thomas, Rufinus defined the conditions of a just war with regard to (1) the person who declared it – who had to be the legitimate ruler; (2) those who took part – who had to be professional soldiers; and (3) the adversary – who had to be at fault. These ideas had sufficient influence for kings frequently to ask for surety from the Church before declaring war; such action was taken, for example, by Philip VI in 1336, Charles V in 1369 and Charles VII in 1449. Though the majority of authors thought, like St Thomas Aquinas, that the combatants should obey their ruler, Etienne Langdon believed that they should withdraw from an unjust war.

The Practices of War During the late summer of the Roman Empire, St Augustine could still add to his philosophical discourse on war the practical recommendation to avoid useless acts of violence, profanation of churches, and atrocities which displayed motivations other than those of justice. He still believed that the victor should not extort too cruel a retribution from the vanquished. The Merovingian period had to pass, and then the empire of Charlemagne to emerge, before St Augustine's recommendation had some chance of being heard. Up to the eleventh century, religious works that listed penances distinguished those murders of enemies which a commander had ordered from those committed without orders. A relative moderation seemed to come over the practices of war. For example, the massacre of prisoners or their enslavement appears to have been employed only in wars against the infidels, on the borders of Christian Europe. Even so, the appropriation of land belonging to private owners, despite becoming less frequent, still occurred in the Carolingian period and went on until shortly after the Norman Conquest of England, although such cases were the doings of kings.

Philippe Contamine noted that the period between 1000 and the twelfth century saw important innovations in the laws of war, which were inspired by a return to the distinction between violent action by private persons and war (*bellum*).

As part of an effort to arrest the spread of feudal wars, there appeared simultaneously peace movements and the birth of 'chivalry', together with changes in ideas and social values. At the same period, the Crusades provided Europeans with an outlet for their warlike activities and a justification for them. Several stages can be seen in this process. The first was the 'Peace of God', a movement which originated at the Council of Le Puy; this was convened by Bishop Guy d'Anjou in 975, and it enjoined on feudal lords the duty to respect the property of the Church and of peasants, when they lay outside their fiefs. The Council of Charroux (989) threatened looters and disturbers of the peace with excommunication. That at Verdun-sur-le-Doubs (1016) laid down an obligation to protect peasants whenever there was a real war. In 1038, there began the establishment of 'leagues of peace', which made it a duty for every believer over the age of 15 years to take up arms, in case of need, against disturbers of the peace. It is certain that the 'Peace of God' did cause some progress towards procuring immunity in wartime for peaceful members of the community and their possessions. These measures applied only to private wars, not to those which took place between principalities or states, but they had some influence on wars between states in which the whole body of vassals had been called out. For example, the once accepted practice of confiscating the property of those on the defeated side was reduced to one by which the victor state took over the feudal rights of the defeated, i.e. seizures were made in the lands held by the sovereign of the latter.

The 'Truce of God' made its appearance in 1027 in Roussillon. It forbade all warlike activity from Saturday evening at the ninth hour to Monday morning at prime. Later, similar prohibitions were applied to Advent, Christmas, Lent, Easter, Pentecost, feast days of the Virgin and their vigils and certain saints' days.

The Papacy and some monarchs encouraged movements of this kind. Nevertheless, the Vatican failed to achieve its ambition of securing a universal decision from sovereigns in favour of them. The same results attended the attempt to prohibit the use of the bow and crossbow among Christians (at the Lateran Council of 1139) on the grounds that these weapons made treacherous ambushes possible and were too deadly. On the other hand, the movement to militarize the

445

clergy was stopped, except in the case of the orders of monastic knights which were set up for participation in the Crusades.

The Church concerned itself equally with integrating into Christian thought the idea of 'knighthood', in the sense of enjoining and guaranteeing the protection of the weak and respect for the defeated. The Crusades gave rise to the idea of a mutual understanding among Christians, indeed of a universal peace, at least in the Christian world (as urged by Pierre Dubois), and even of a federation of states which, at the end of the fifteenth century, George of Podiebrad, King of Bohemia, and later Pope Paul II, invited Louis XI to form. Particular evidence for this is found in the cult of soldier saints. A body of excellent literary productions spread these ideas and encouraged the practice of 'chivalry'. References need only be made to Honoré Bonet's 'Tree of Battles' and Christine de Pisan's 'Book of Feats of Arms and of Chivalry'.

In the fourteenth century, however, social troubles brought about new conflicts and the evolution of the art of war compromised this attempt at its humanization. The revolts on the part of the inhabitants of Flemish cities or of the Hussites appeared to be just wars to those who started them, but the reverse to their adversaries – hence the initial massacres and the subsequent terrible repressions. Finally, it was the employment of mercenaries (rather than the introduction of artillery, which remained for a long time very ineffective) which changed the nature of war. In the fifteenth century, a distinction was drawn between 'decent warfare', waged by knights, and 'deadly warfare', as carried on by mercenaries, 'soldiers of fortune' of every kind, or by members of the populace with no respect for the rules of chivalry. The one ended in the taking of prisoners and the payment of ransoms, the other in massacres. Some wars of the fifteenth century, which had a national character and therefore involved the civilian community, exercised an influence similar to that of the Hundred Years' War. At the same period, the re-establishment of state authority put in kings' hands the means which encour-

aged them to take up again the idea of total war. The English kings, Louis XI, Charles the Bold, all gave orders for systematic destruction. Thus, there was some hint of a movement away from the Christian laws of war even before a renewal of sheer violence displayed itself during the Wars of Religion.

From Medieval to Institutionalized Warfare

The legacy of chivalry still maintained its influence in the sixteenth century, as was shown by the success of 'The Rose Bush of Battles' (written at the end of the fifteenth century), even though the book mentions developments in methods of war (artillery and the preponderance of infantry). Nevertheless, a 'secularization' of war appeared in the writings of Machiavelli, who reduced war to an act based on analyses of a situation and objective evaluation of the expected results. This outlook was shocking to many minds but it is noteworthy that, at the start of the sixteenth century, the economic aspects of war took on a new importance. For example, there was an increase in the measures taken against an enemy's trade. Merchants living in an enemy's territory were the object of persecutions, expulsions, confiscations, etc., except when self-interest dictated that the occupier leave them in peace or extort money from them in return for residence permits.

The Wars of Religion added a highly emotional aspect to conflicts. Since they were at the same time civil and foreign wars, and their battlefields ranged far and wide, they caused upheavals in a great number of areas. Psychological elements played a large part, with initial enthusiasm, panic, vengeance, self-interest and war-weariness all acting in turn. Certainly, the rules of war did not undergo any fundamental change, but they were frequently forgotten. As proof, numerous examples could be cited of massacres of communities who had defended themselves overlong, sackings of cities by troops who had not received their pay, etc., and particularly, the great increase in individual crimes on the part of hardened soldiers and also of civilians goaded beyond endurance.

Communities themselves, however, sometimes initiated truces to enable the tilling of their fields. However, the dreams of universal peace or of international institutions which proliferated in the sixteenth century, from Erasmus to Sully, in the seventeenth faded away in face of the necessity to recognize the immediate realities and the fact that states were strengthened by war. Also, leading statesmen like Richelieu sought, by a continual series of negotiations, to secure a political equilibrium that was advantageous to their own nation, and there was a renewal of thinking on the theme of the laws that were universally accepted (*jus gentium*), or rather, the laws regulating relations between nations (*jus inter gentes*), which were to become 'International Law' in Bentham's writings. Vitoria, Gentili and Grotius, in his famous *De jure belli ac pacis* (*Of the laws of war and peace*) of 1625, gave currency to those ideas which were to lead to war taking on an institutional character. But that process took a long period of time to complete.

In fact, during the Wars of Religion, the distinction between soldiers and civilians ceased to be drawn. In the middle of the century, there were examples of sovereigns ordering their civil populations to rush upon an invader, without troubling over the consequences to public order. The position was the same over the distinction between peace and a state of war. During the Thirty Years' War, 'concealed wars' were a frequent occurrence, as when the English supported the Protestants of La Rochelle who were in revolt, or when the French sent troops into the Valtelline, both entirely without a declaration of war. Louis XIV even succeeded in making limited annexations of territory ('reunions', as they were termed) in full peacetime. Conversely, negotiations went on openly during the course of hostilities.

It was not until the short period between wars (from 1697 to 1701) that Western Europe knew a complete cessation of armed struggle – the first for a very long while – with a period of what was certainly an armed peace, but nevertheless an effective one. Under the influence of statesmen like Louis XIV and Louvois, armies became more professional in character. The mobilization of civilians took a new form with the introduction of militias; uniform helped to mark the distinction between soldiers and civilians, and discipline was made stricter. The obligations of soldiers towards civilians, as well as of civilians in a military environment, could accordingly be more clearly defined, with civilians being forbidden to commit acts of violence and soldiers to fight among themselves.

Agreements concluded locally between combatants did not become more frequent but were better kept. Rules were made covering the lot of garrisons that had surrendered after an honourable defence, i.e. release on promising not to take up arms again during the campaign, or confinement in the victorious country. In the same way, there were more exchanges of prisoners. Regulations emerged for military occupations. There were even cases of 'contribution agreements' being signed, under which troops operating in a particular enemy region were to be supplied with the provisions which they required, in return for their being forbidden to pillage (e.g. the treaty of 1710 between the French and Dutch governments with regard to Artois). Observance of the letter of such agreements was very strict. For example, a court martial held by a Dutch regiment that was in captivity at Saumur condemned to death one of its soldiers, a German, for having been converted to Catholicism in contravention of his terms of engagement. On the other hand, political actions did not always show a respect for the 'laws that are universally accepted'. Frederick II incorporated the defeated Saxon army into his own, and Louis XV raised the militia in the Austrian Netherlands, which he was occupying.

For a short period, the French Revolutionary government imperilled the laws of war. By abolishing feudal rights in occupied countries, it did violence to the regulations and properties of communities, even when it worked under the cover of local leaders who had been put in power by its troops. These latter were encouraged to jettison established rules because the members of the Convention wished to give the war the look of a crusade for liberty. A decree of 26 May 1794 ordered enemy garrisons who refused calls to surrender to be put to the sword, though no commander was prepared to carry this out. On the other hand, civil war generally fell outside the laws of war, but it led only very infrequently to instances of extermination such as that in the Vendée.

The giving of an institutional form to war provided Western Europe with a period of at least two centuries during which belligerents observed reasonably well-ordered practices. In fact, not only did the first half of the nineteenth century retain the usages that had been established in the eighteenth, but from 1860 there were clear signs of a wish to define them more clearly. The first effort in this direction was the 'Instructions for the armies of the United States', drafted in 1863 by a committee of officers and the German jurist Lieber; these were applied during the American Civil War. From the time of the first Geneva Convention, attempts to humanize war moved from the unilateral or bilateral plane to the international.

It may be useful here to list various technical terms employed in the usages of war at the start of the twentieth century:

- Hostilities began in accordance with a regular ritual: recall of ambassadors; arrangements for partial, then general, mobilization; ultimatum with time given for reply (a procedure which was still respected by Britain and France in 1939).
- The return of peace was dealt with similarly: request for the conditions of an armistice; negotiations between military leaders and, eventually, between diplomats from both sides; establishment of an armistice; peace conference; signature of a treaty; exchange of instruments of ratification of the peace treaty; renewal of diplomatic relations.
- The warring parties: spontaneous taking up of arms was permitted in territories that were threatened, but not yet occupied, on condition that a visible and distinctive emblem was always worn and that fighting was overt.

- The modes of fighting included stratagems of war and surprise, but not acts of perfidy, such as the false use of flags of truce. Reprisals were allowed, but not in a spirit of vengeance, which was deemed to include both bombardments of cities (only artillery was involved in this period) and blockade.
- Espionage was condemned, but it was necessary to establish that a person had been caught in the act of spying, and then to give him a trial.
- Signed agreements between opposing military commanders, which established, for example, a suspension of hostilities, had to be executed and always observed, even if the situation had changed.
- Prisoners of war were required to obey the enemy's laws. In France, a regulation of 1895 laid down their living conditions and pay.
- The rules of military occupation. The invader took the place of the legal government, if that had been rendered incapable of carrying out its functions. For this, there had to be complete occupation of a country. The occupier had to announce his assumption of power by means of posters. He could forbid all contact on the part of inhabitants with their government, but could not impose on them obligations contrary to those which they had towards their own country. He was required to respect the beliefs and forms of worship of the occupied population, and their right to patriotism. He had the right to protect the safety of his troops, and to set up courts martial to deal with any attempts to endanger it. He could restore order, if that had been disturbed, but had to use the laws of the land for the purpose. If he made any change in these, he was obliged to give notice of the fact by posters. (In 1870–1, the German authorities published the official gazette in French.) The occupier could remove the governmental officials of occupied countries and make use of general, but not of local, tax proceeds for the purpose of carrying on the war. He could not sequester private funds that were

deposited in official banks. The inhabitants could be compelled to pay monetary contributions, but only at the discretion of the general commanding. The right to requisition was recognized, but pillage was forbidden. Submission to the occupier's orders in respect of requisitions was not counted as treason. The practice of taking hostages was tolerated, but they had to be treated as prisoners of war. Residents who were nationals of a foreign country were not exempted from the demands of the occupier, but it was often in his interest to take care not to offend them.

War at sea: a warship which had sunk an enemy vessel, whether another warship or a merchant ship, was morally bound to pick up the shipwrecked crew – which was clearly impossible in the case of submarine warfare. A country at war had the right to seize enemy ships docked in its harbours, though a period of grace was often given. In 1907, there was a proposal to regularize this practice but Britain, France and Japan opposed it. This period of grace should rightly have applied to ships which were on the high seas and were unaware of the outbreak of hostilities. Boscawen's outrageous attack in 1755 was an example of a British violation of this regulation. Neutral ships were, in principle, forbidden to carry war contraband; contravention justified the seizure of the merchandise in question but often involved that of the ship also, which led to numerous diplomatic incidents. Nevertheless, the list of goods considered to be contraband was, for practical purposes, at the discretion of the belligerents, and could include foodstuffs. Blockade of enemy coasts was permitted. Where naval action was concerned, economic considerations played a large part in the way in which the war was conducted, and practices varied according to circumstances.

The rules and usages detailed above were reasonably observed, to a greater or lesser degree, during the First World War.

The Twentieth Century: Condemnation of War, and the Internationalization and Violation of the Laws of War

Two world wars, the wars over colonial independence, the division of the world into two rival groups, but chiefly the power of new methods of destruction and the greatly increased importance of the ideological factor have completely revolutionized the conditions in which wars are fought. There have been efforts of a serious kind to secure international recognition of the laws of war and to establish more-precise rules (though these have soon been overtaken by events) which lead on to a formal condemnation of war. On the other hand, since open war has become more difficult, either because of this condemnation, or because of the apocalyptic possibilities that an outbreak brings into view, states have returned to the covert type, as practised, e.g., during the Thirty Years' War.

The Period of International Conferences

The earliest of these, which was initiated by Henri Dunant and drafted at Geneva in 1863, was the first convention to provide for the protection of soldiers who had been wounded or were ill, and for military hospitals, medical services and chaplains. From that point onwards, other conferences were held – at Geneva (1906, 1929, 1949), St Petersburg (1868, 1874), The Hague (1899, 1907). The victors in the two world wars established the League of Nations (1919, with its headquarters in Geneva), and the United Nations Organization (1945, New York).

In 1874, a conference, which was originally suggested by Russia, proposed a draft formulation of an international declaration on the laws and usages of war but negotiations on this, followed by a subsequent session in Brussels, proved abortive. Nevertheless, in 1880 the Institute of International Law was set up and published a manual setting out the general principles of the laws of war. The Geneva Convention of 1864 was followed by others which defined its terms more precisely and extended its application to prisoners of war – this last, in particular, as the result of a conference in 1929.

The rules governing resident enemy nationals have been modified in several respects. In 1914, Britain allowed resident enemy males a period of eight days after the declaration of war to leave her territory, but Germany and Austria-Hungary introduced some limitations. In 1939, Britain still gave Germans a period of grace (up to 9 September) but France, on account of fears that a 'fifth column' might have been infiltrated among the German refugees, adopted a selective policy. In accordance with the view taken of each individual case, German citizens in France were interned, placed under house arrest or left at liberty.

The Geneva conference of 1949 developed a type of multilateral agreement based on the rules already laid down for prisoners of war and designed to protect civil populations who were becoming more and more frequently involved in wars.

The introduction of new weapons provided occasions for various attempts at their regulation but these produced little effect. In 1868, a conference held at St Petersburg condemned the use of explosive or inflammable projectiles of less than a pound in weight. The Hague Conference of 1925, in a draft protocol, sought to secure immunity, in the event of air warfare, for civil populations, churches, hospitals and historic monuments, but this was not ratified. Chemical and bacteriological warfare were also prohibited; in this case, despite the use of defoliants, the prohibition has been, on the whole, better observed.

The rituals covering entry into a war and its conclusion have often been disturbed in the case of wars between European and non-European powers, since the latter's history has not included any contact with that development of the laws of war which had gone on in Europe since the eighteenth century. Thus, Japan began war without any declaration in 1904, with its attack on Port Arthur, and in 1941, with that on Pearl Harbor. In the same way, since Germany's surrender led to a partition of the country, no formal peace treaty could be signed with her. The war was officially ended by means of a simple announcement.

Condemnation of War The Hague Convention of 1899 affirmed that it was in the signatories' interest to avoid war. In that of 1907, nations were reminded of the principle that there must be a declaration before the start of any war. In addition, all belligerents were considered as equals, except in the case of rebellions or of hostilities outside a war. Also, the International Court at The Hague provided a means whereby law suits caused by the seizure of enemy property could be brought before an international court of justice.

These ideas developed further after 1918. In 1926, negotiations began between the Frenchman Aristide Briand and the American Frank B. Kellogg; these were to reach fruition in the 'Briand–Kellogg Pact', which outlawed aggressive war. It was signed in Paris by 14 countries, and subsequently ratified by 63. Its aim was to ensure the condemnation of an aggressor and the use against him of international sanctions. This was the case in regard to Italy (1935), Germany (1939) and North Korea (1950). The Pact also provided the legal basis for the 'Lease–Lend Act'. In a different field, reference can be made to the condemnation of war crimes by the International Tribunals of Nuremberg and Tokyo. These developments thus led to an abandonment of the concept of equality between belligerents.

In 1919, Germany had scarcely any chance to discuss the peace terms. The Germans were merely faced with an accomplished fact, and hence they nicknamed it a *Diktat*. This concept of unequal rights was to some degree given further currency when, in 1942, Roosevelt looked forward to the unconditional surrender of the enemy – terms which recalled those of the surrender of the Southerners at Appomattox in 1865 at the end of the American Civil War. The defeated enemy was looked upon as having rebelled against international law and thus lay outside the normal rules of war. He could not take part, on equal terms, in drawing up peace treaties, and he was not represented on the international tribunals set up to try war crimes.

It is true that since 1945, or rather since 1953, when the Korean War ended, no war, except those in the Falkland Islands and the

Persian Gulf, has assumed the traditional forms of open warfare. This has not prevented the existence of conflicts which, though apparently limited to this or that country, were really the nodal points of a more wide-ranging struggle between the superpowers, the USSR and the United States. Doubtless, condemnation of aggressive war has contributed to such limitation, but probably a much stronger influence has been the fear of the unpredictable consequences of a worldwide conflict in the atomic era.

Violations of the Laws of War Currently, it looks as if the impossibility of making war openly has given the signal to covert warfare – that is to say, in fact, to numerous violations of the laws of war as previously established.

The origin of twentieth-century examples of going to war without any declaration lies outside Europe. Colonial wars have been started in this way in so far as they were waged against countries which were not organized states in the European sense of the term. But, as has been seen, Japan acted in the same way. The most important factor influencing this tendency seems, indeed, to have been the recrudescence of ideological and people's wars. In 1918, Trotsky, in launching the keynote expression 'neither war nor peace', which astonished statesmen elsewhere, heralded – perhaps unconsciously – a new kind of relationship between nations.

The occupation of a large part of Europe by the German armies during the Second World War led to a large increase in examples of armed resistance on the part of the occupied populations. According to earlier usages, the practice of men without uniform acting as soldiers was to be condemned; in opposition to those, the Resistance revived, and extolled, the practice though, at the same time, by removing the distinction between soldiers and civilians, it provided a pretext for merciless repression and for the execution of hostages. It is obvious that the practice of the Ancient World, which had the aim of eliminating a race by systematic massacre, in whatever form, a practice which had been revived in the present century (Armenians, 1915–17; Jews in Nazi Germany) cannot be considered an act of war, and belongs to a different sphere, particularly since it can occur even in peacetime.

Previously, since the Wars of Religion, actions connected with armed struggle against an established authority had scarcely ever reached an international scale. Now, assisted, or inspired, by a foreign power, and by neighbouring states which adopt the guise of 'refuges' and serve as operational bases for those in revolt, they have proliferated with the wars over colonial independence, and with the political recognition given by certain countries to such movements; they have frequently been encouraged by the United Nations and by its condemnation of the colonial power. In this way, insurrections in the colonies have reached the rank of wars proper.

The practices which lie outside the normal laws of war, but which are accepted when they proceed from movements for colonial independence, have been employed, nevertheless, also in countries where the superpowers faced each other in a kind of masked war. The Lebanon and Central America provide recent examples. In order to act more effectively on public opinion in countries which enjoy free expression, various groups have not hesitated to perpetrate terrorist outrages, entirely outside 'the battlefields', in order to exert influence – with the help of the immense publicity given to such actions by the media – on the feelings of those living in peaceful regions. By striking at individuals completely unconnected with the conflict, terrorism causes the prevalence of an atmosphere of insecurity, which in turn leads to a feeling of helplessness. At the moment, international authorities have still not discovered, in the sphere of law, an appropriate answer to this exacerbated and cruel form of psychological warfare.

A. CORVISIER

The prestige of resistance to Nazi occupation during the Second World War and the moral impetus generated after 1945 by non-state military opponents of the European empires gave strength to the conviction that the humanitarian laws of war should be extended to include armed rebellions, insurgencies, 'wars of national liberation', etc. This was given legal form in the Additional Protocols of 1977. This theoretically revolutionary development has four especially interesting implications. First, guerillas are required to wear a uniform and to carry their arms openly. How this relates to the undoubted military right to resort to ambushes and surprise is uncertain. Second, the Additional Protocols are part of a far-reaching new idea of responsibility for, or under, the laws of war: states and other military organizations are required to instruct their personnel in the laws and customs of war; the individual soldier or guerilla is required to disobey manifestly illegal orders, i.e. such orders as a person who knows the laws and customs of war cannot but recognize as being illegal. The old absolution of subordinates from responsibility for their part in warfare, repudiated in the charter under which the Nuremberg trial was conducted, is thus subjected, in theory at least, to radical legal challenge. Third, the Additional Protocols, and especially the public sentiment of which they are a legal expression, exert a certain pressure on rebels as well as states to confine their military activity within certain limits. Certain kinds of indiscrimination are likely to be disowned (or countenanced only as regrettable necessities) by all but the most lawless of rebels. Finally, it is noteworthy that the modern reluctance of states to follow the traditional practice of *declaring* war against one another has a parallel in their reluctance to admit that they are engaged in *war* against such enemies as the IRA. It seems to be obscurely felt that recognizing the fact of war confers legitimacy on the opponent, and an organization such as the IRA is especially criticized when it resorts to those kinds of action which are most clearly condemned by the laws of war.

The war which was provoked by Iraq's invasion of Kuwait signalled the possibility of a new kind of approach to the international legitimation of war. Once the US was persuaded of the need to expel Iraq from Kuwait and to eliminate its future capacity for aggression, political considerations motivated resort to the UN. A series of strongly worded resolutions expressed agreement by all of the Permanent Members of the Security Council to actions including unspecified types of military measures. US policy was explicitly linked to these resolutions, and represented as drawing legitimacy from them. One could argue that this was the harbinger of a new internationalism in the decision to go to war. But the case is by no means conclusive. The United States and the United Kingdom said nothing to put an end to their right under Article 51 of the UN Charter to employ military force in self-defence should they deem this to be necessary. The very wide scope for sovereign decision, insisted upon when the Briand–Kellogg Pact was reported to the US Senate, was not compromised by the welcome which was given in Washington and London to the Security Council's readiness to share responsibility for countering Iraqi aggression.

The laws of war remain a paradoxical institution. Looked at in one way, they are the creation of the sovereign wills of independent states, subject to all of the pressures and contradictions of politics. From this point of view it is no surprise that the law condemns dumdum bullets (which expand on impact), while apparently permitting the Permanent Members of the UN Security Council to target the innocent inhabitants of one another's cities. Looked at in another way, the laws of war are a legal expression of the common conscience of mankind; from which viewpoint they can well be regarded as scandalously inadequate. *See also* ARMISTICES; BLOCKADES; CHEMICAL AND BIOLOGICAL WARFARE; CIVIL WAR; COLONIAL WARFARE; COMMERCE-RAIDING; CONVOYS; CULTURE, PROTECTION OF; DEPREDATIONS; DUNANT; ECONOMIC WARFARE; ETHOS; GENTILI; GROTIUS; GULF WAR; HOLY WAR; INTELLIGENCE; IRREGULAR WARFARE; LAW, MILITARY; LOSSES OF LIFE; MEDICAL SERVICES; NATIONALISM; NAVAL WARFARE; NEUTRALITY; NUCLEAR WARFARE; PEARL HARBOR; PENSIONS; POPULAR WARFARE; PRISONERS OF WAR; RESISTANCE; TERRORISM; VITORIA.

BARRIE PASKINS

FURTHER READING
R. Lonis, 'La guerre en Grèce', *Revue des études grecques* (July–December 1985); P. Contamine, *War in the Middle Ages* (London, 1984); G. Livet, *Guerre et paix de Machiavel à Hobbes* (Paris, 1972); Hugo Grotius, *De jure belli ac pacis* (1625), ed. J. B. Scott (2 vols, Oxford, 1913–25); Emerich de Vattel, *Le Droit des gens ou principes de la loi naturelle appliquée à la conduite et aux affaires des nations et des souverains* (1758), ed. Albert de Lapradelle (3 vols, Washington, 1916); Raymond Aron, *Peace and War: a theory of international relations* (London, 1967); M. Sibert, *Traité de droit international public* (Paris, 1951); N. Sing, *Nuclear Weapons and International Law* (New York, 1959); Geoffrey Best, *Humanity in Warfare* (London, 1980); Michael Glover, *The Velvet Glove: the decline and fall of moderation in war* (London, 1982); *Restraints on War: studies in the limitation of armed conflict*, ed. Michael Howard (Oxford, 1979); Quincy Wright, *A Study of War* (2nd edn, Chicago, 1965).

Leadership *See* COMMAND

Lee, Robert Edward (1807–70) Lee was the son of a soldier, an engineer and a graduate of West Point. In 1861 he would have been the Union's choice as its commander in the Civil War, but, as a Virginian, he joined the Confederates. Lee recognized that the Union's superiority in men and resources would overwhelm a purely defensive strategy. He therefore argued that operationally the Southern forces must attack, with speed, so as to force the Union forces to forfeit the initiative and concentrate. Jefferson Davis, the president of the Confederacy, whose adviser Lee was, preferred a purely defensive strategy, but the success of Lee's doctrine in Stonewall Jackson's Shenandoah campaign (April–May 1862) increased Lee's leverage and in June he took over command of the Army of North Virginia. Despite his inferior numbers, Lee cleared the threat first to Richmond and then to Virginia. However, these battles had already revealed the flaw in Lee's thinking: successive offensives, particularly frontal assaults without the element of surprise, invited losses which relatively were far harder to bear for the South than the North. After a brilliant defensive success at Chancellorsville (May 1863), Lee was at last able to carry the war into the North. His hope was to convince the North to recognize the South by achieving victories on the North's own territory. But his invasion of Pennsylvania was checked at Gettysburg (July 1863), and with it his army's offensive capacity was effectively broken. Lee fought on to 1865, exploiting field fortifications in defensive battles, but underestimating the threat to Southern resources presented by Sherman's campaign in the west. Arguably, Lee was a great operational commander confronted with an impossible task, the adaptation of inadequate means to a strategy that demanded more than battlefield success. *See also* ANTIETAM; GRANT; GETTYSBURG; SHERMAN; UNITED STATES.

HEW STRACHAN

FURTHER READING
Thomas L. Connelly, *The Marble Man: Robert E. Lee and his image in American society* (New York, 1977); Douglas Southall Freeman, *R. E. Lee: a biography* (New York, 1934–5).

Leicester, Robert Dudley, Earl of *See* DUDLEY, ROBERT

Leipzig, Battle of (also known as the Battle of the Nations) (16–19 October 1813) Before the converging offensive of the Allied armies on the French forces established in Saxony, Napoleon was unable to execute successful manoeuvres on interior lines, his lieutenants being beaten before he could reach them in order to mount counter-attacks. He therefore ordered his corps to concentrate, but the subsequent manoeuvre on the Prussian rear failed and Napoleon had to give battle simultaneously to Blücher's Prussians in the north and Schwarzenberg's Austro-Russians in the south. Napoleon initially attacked Schwarzenberg but the arrival of Bernadotte's army to the north-east left him with no exit from the battlefield except to the west through Leipzig and across the River Elster. On 18 October, the Allies launched a frontal attack, but Napoleon was able to withdraw towards Leipzig without his lines being broken. At this point, 30,000 men in the Saxon contingent fighting in the French army deserted; retreat was unavoidable. Blücher could not interrupt the well-conducted French withdrawal through Leipzig and over the Elster but the Lindenau bridge was blown up prematurely stranding 20,000 Frenchmen from the rearguard on the east bank. The French lost 60,000 out of the 200,000 men involved in the battle, along with 150 cannon and 500 waggons; the Allied casualties amounted to 60,000 out of 330,000. Altogether, the German campaign of 1813 had cost Napoleon over 500,000 men. France could no longer replace such losses, forcing Napoleon to abandon Germany. In 1814, the Allies were able to invade France. *See also* BLÜCHER; FRANCE; NAPOLEON; WATERLOO; WELLINGTON.

A. CORVISIER

FURTHER READING
David Chandler, *The Campaigns of Napoleon* (London, 1967); F. Lorraine Petre, *Napoleon's Last Campaign in Germany, 1813* (London, 1912).

Lenin, Nikolai (Vladimir Ilyich Ulyanov, known as) (1870–1924) A revolutionary leader best known for his political theories and action, Lenin has also exerted influence on the art of war in the twentieth century. In 1915 he annotated Clausewitz, whose influence he would later acknowledge in the elaboration of his insurrectionary strategy and the organization of the Soviet armed forces. He was a proponent of mass warfare and, though he did not condemn action by partisans, he refused to regard them as the country's main military force and moved to end their often disorganized activity by incorporating them into regular units. He contributed to the development of revolutionary guerilla warfare both through inspiring revolutionary strategists of anticolonial movements and through providing them with the organizational weapon of a highly centralized Communist Party system capable of forging the proletariat into an instrument of revolution. *See also* CLAUSEWITZ; INDIRECT WARFARE; POPULAR WARFARE; RUSSIA/USSR; SOVIET MILITARY THEORISTS; STALIN.

A. CORVISIER

FURTHER READING
L. Fischer, *The Life of Lenin* (London, 1964); B. C. Friedl, *Les Fondements théoriques de la guerre et de la paix en U.R.S.S. suivi des Cahiers de Lénine sur Clausewitz* (Paris, 1945); D. Shrub, *Lenin* (2nd edn, Harmondsworth, 1966); Condoleezza Rice, 'Soviet strategy', in *Makers of Modern Strategy*, ed. P. Paret (Oxford, 1986), pp. 648–76.

Leningrad, Siege of (21 August 1941– 27 January 1944) Two months after the German invasion of the Soviet Union, Nazi forces began the Siege of Leningrad. For the next two and a half years, the city was fought over bitterly since it had both symbolic value and was a key position, commanding the railway line to the ice-free port of Murmansk through which the Russians received Allied *matériel*. Determined to defend Leningrad, Stalin placed Georgii Zhukov in command of the city during the initial phase of the siege, and it was at Leningrad that Zhukov earned the first of his many honours. During the winter of 1941–2, Leningrad suffered badly from famine. The only line of supply for the city was across the frozen surface of Lake Ladoga. In the spring of 1942, the Germans renewed their offensive against Leningrad but were never able to effect a complete blockade of the city. The determined resistance of the people of Leningrad was essential to its successful defence; more than half a million citizens constructed barricades and defensive works, while women and children worked in the factories to produce war goods. From the late summer of 1942 until early 1944, the Leningrad front remained stable. On 15 January two Soviet army groups attacked, taking advantage of the frozen conditions and, by the end of the month, the Siege of Leningrad had ended. Leningrad paid a heavy price: estimates of the death toll range from 600,000 to 1.5 million. The valour of its citizens earned Leningrad the title of 'Hero City'. *See also* RUSSIA/USSR; ZHUKOV.

A. CORVISIER
KEITH NEILSON

FURTHER READING
John Erickson, *The Road to Stalingrad* (London, 1975); John Erickson, *The Road to Berlin* (London, 1983); Harrison Salisbury, *The 900 Days: the Siege of Leningrad* (New York, 1969).

Leo VI, 'the Wise' or 'the Philosopher', Emperor of Byzantium (886–912) Though he had never commanded troops in the field, in *c*.900 Leo VI wrote a significant and important treatise on Byzantine military practice and history, *Leonis Imperator Tactica: sive de re militari*. It was probably compiled by many hands although Leo personally wrote the section dealing with the recruitment and financing of the Arab armies and the ideology of the *Jihad*. The treatise described the nature and military methods of the various peoples and races who posed a threat to the Byzantine Empire. It also gave an account of the tactics, command structure, organization and armament of the contemporary Byzantine army, as well as traced their historical development. Leo appended to his treatise a number of eye-witness accounts by his father, Basil I (867–86), and his generals. The *Tactica* was a remarkable success in Europe in the period from the sixteenth to the eighteenth century and was translated into Latin, Italian, French, German and Hungarian. *See also* BYZANTIUM; WAGGON-LAAGER.

G. DAGRON

FURTHER READING
A. Dain, 'Les statégistes byzantines', *Travaux et Mémoires*, ii (1967).

Lepanto, Battle of (7 October 1571) Lepanto, the greatest and last of the Mediterranean galley battles of the sixteenth century, was the consequence of the Ottoman Sultan Selim II's decision in 1570 to seize Cyprus from the Venetians. Appeals from Venice for assistance to the Papacy and Philip II of Spain led to the assembly of a combined Christian fleet off Crete in September 1570. By the end of the month it had reached the Turkish coast but then news that Nicosia had surrendered (9 September) caused it to retire and disband. However, the continued resistance of the Venetian garrison of Famagusta during the winter of 1570–1 inspired the formation on 25 May 1571 of a more formal alliance (the Holy League) between Venice, the Papacy, Philip II and his Italian dominions and allies, and the Knights of St John. To relieve Famagusta another fleet under the command of Philip's half-brother Don Juan of Austria was to be assembled at Messina, but this fleet was not ready until September.

In the meantime the Ottoman fleet under Ali Pasha had entered the Adriatic to divert or intercept it. In late September the Christian fleet sailed to Corfu, where news was received of the surrender of Famagusta (4 August). On the look-out for the Ottomans, Don Juan cruised south in the first week of October, and on the 7th discovered the enemy fleet in the Gulf of Lepanto on the north shore of the Gulf of Corinth. Both admirals wanted a battle and both deployed their fleets off the coast in three divisions and a reserve, giving each an inshore and a seaward wing. The precise size of the fleets is debated, but the most reliable figures give the Christians 201 galleys and six Venetian galleasses and the Ottomans 210 galleys and 86 lighter galliots and fustas. Ali Pasha sought to use his greater numbers to envelop his enemy. The Ottoman inshore (right) wing was able to outflank the Christian (chiefly Venetian) left, but was then held. On the seaward flank the Christian right under Gian Andrea Doria countered the Ottoman left under Uluj Ali by extending southward, so that both wings were drawn away from the main battle. This occurred in the centre where Don Juan, as he had planned beforehand, took the offensive. His flagship attacked Ali Pasha's successfully; the Ottoman admiral was killed, and his death led to confusion and demoralization in his fleet. A belated attempt by Uluj Ali's wing to intervene in the main battle was beaten off by the Christian (largely Spanish) reserve, and Uluj Ali decided to retire with his surviving fifteen galleys. Only some 35 other Ottoman vessels also escaped, the remainder (*c.*240) were either sunk or captured, as against 12 Christian galleys sunk and 1 successfully captured.

The Christian victory has been attributed to the greater size of their galleys, their heavier armament (especially the Venetian galleasses), and the larger infantry complement (some 40,000 men) that they carried. The effect of Lepanto has been the subject of some debate. The Ottomans had no difficulty in replacing their ships, but the skilled manpower lost (35,000) may have been more decisive. Lepanto, following Malta, stopped the Ottoman advance west. Yet it did not lead to a successful Christian counter-offensive. Philip II's attention was directed increasingly towards the Netherlands and in 1574 the Venetians conceded the loss of Cyprus. The Spanish–Ottoman truce of 1578 divided the Mediterranean into eastern and western spheres of influence, which reflected the effective operating ranges of the respective galley fleets. For the remainder of the century warfare in the Mediterranean was conducted at the level of maritime guerillas rather than battle fleets. *See also* MALTA; NAVAL WARFARE; NAVIES; OTTOMAN TURKS.

SIMON ADAMS

FURTHER READING
M. H. Anderson, *Naval Wars in the Levant, 1559–1853* (Liverpool, 1953), pp. 26–54; J. F. Guilmartin, *Gunpowder and Galleys* (Cambridge, 1974), pp. 221–52; G. Parker and I. A. A. Thompson, 'Lepanto, 1571: the costs of victory', in G. Parker, *Spain and the Netherlands, 1559–1659: ten studies* (London, 1979), pp. 122–33; F. Braudel, *La Méditerranée et le monde méditerranéen à l'époque de Philippe II* (2nd edn, Paris, 1966), ii, 383–430.

Lettow-Vorbeck, Paul Emil von (1870–1964) One of history's most successful practitioners of guerilla warfare, Lettow-Vorbeck entered the Prussian army in 1891 and, following service in both the Boxer Rebellion in China (1900–1) and the Herero Revolt in German South-West

Lettow-Vorbeck, second from the right, photographed with German settlers at Moshi in German East Africa before the outbreak of war in 1914.
(Imperial War Museum, London)

Africa (1904–6), was posted to command the forces in German East Africa just prior to the Great War in the rank of lieutenant-colonel. With a few hundred Europeans and no more than a few thousand native *askaris*, he successfully inflicted severe blows on British, Imperial and Allied troops of whom some 300,000 were eventually ranged against him. Only when faced by such overwhelming odds was Lettow-Vorbeck driven from the colony in November 1917 but he then continued a war of harassment inside Mozambique and Northern Rhodesia. Indeed, he only formally surrendered on 25 November 1918 after hearing of the armistice in Europe. A masterful guerilla campaign cost the British alone some 63,220 casualties from battle and disease and an estimated £72 million. Returning to Germany in January 1919 Lettow-Vorbeck, who had been promoted major-general in autumn 1917, was soon leading a *frei korps* against Spartacists in Hamburg. Subsequently, he was court-martialled for his part in the 1920 Kapp *putsch* before dabbling in politics as a Reichstag deputy between 1929 and 1930. *See also* COLONIAL TROOPS; INDIRECT WARFARE.

IAN F. W. BECKETT

FURTHER READING
E. P. Hoyt, *Guerilla* (New York, 1981); B. Gardner, *German East* (London, 1963); L. Mosley, *Duel for Kilimanjaro* (London, 1963).

Leuctra, Battle of (371 BC) The Battle of Leuctra was won by Thebes against the forces of Sparta and her allies, who had invaded Boeotia. It provides a striking illustration of the talent of the Theban general Epaminondas who employed his famous 'diagonal' tactics. A characteristic of hoplite battles was that the two contending phalanxes of hoplites exerted continuous pressure until in the end the stronger phalanx broke the weaker. In practice the pressure exerted was never evenly spread over the whole front. The military leaders were in fact accustomed to placing their best troops on the right wing so as to drive in the enemy's left rapidly and thus outflank him. At Leuctra Epaminondas changed this practice, first by reinforcing his left wing, and second by deploying the rest of his line diagonally, so that he engaged the enemy only at the point chosen. Spartan attempts to outflank and encircle the Theban left wing were thwarted by its massed strength, especially the 'Sacred Band' under the command of Pelopidas, and the Theban cavalry. Eventually the Spartan right wing was driven in and its leaders, including King Cleombrotus, were killed, before the left wing, made up of Spartan allies, had even become involved in the action. The rout of the Spartans led the rest of the Peloponnesian army to flee in confusion. The Battle of Leuctra marked the end of Spartan military supremacy in Greece. It is true that Sparta had in fact been suffering since at least the end of the fifth century from an increasing shortage of manpower, but the military genius of Epaminondas struck the blow which finally revealed the decline of her military capacities. Thebes then exploited its military superiority by establishing hegemony in Greece. But this was short-lived and was terminated after the Battle of Mantinea in 362 BC. *See also* EPAMINONDAS; GREECE, ANCIENT; MANTINEA; SPARTA.

R. LONIS
B. CAMPBELL

FURTHER READING
J. Buckler, *The Theban Hegemony 371–362 BC* (Cambridge, Mass., 1980); J. K. Anderson, *Military Theory and Practice in the Age of Xenophon* (Berkeley, 1970).

Leuthen, Battle of (5 December 1757) Immediately after defeating the Franco-German forces of Soubise and Hildburghausen at Rossbach (5 November), Frederick II, with 36,000 men, moved against Daun's Austrian army of 80,000, which had taken Breslau. Established along a front more than 4 miles long, in an area of rolling hills, the Austrians had placed their reserves on their left in anticipation of an enveloping manoeuvre by Frederick, while their right took up a position protected by marshland. Frederick, taking advantage of the hills to hide his movements from enemy view, launched a surprise attack in oblique order, making a demonstration on the Austrian right which avoided the marshes. Deceived by this show of force, Daun transferred his reserves to his right wing, but Frederick made his main attack on the Austrian left. The Austrians, unable to realign their forces sufficiently, suffered almost 7,000 casualties, also losing 20,000 prisoners, 114 cannon and 51 colours. More than 6,000 Prussians were killed or wounded. Leuthen was probably Frederick's finest victory. Napoleon called it a 'masterpiece of manoeuvre and resolve'. *See also* FREDERICK II; GERMANY; ROSSBACH.

A. CORVISIER

FURTHER READING
C. Duffy, *Frederick the Great: a military life* (London, 1985); Thomas Carlyle, *History of Friedrich II of Prussia, called Frederick the Great* (6 vols, London, 1858–65) vol. 5; J. F. C. Fuller, 'The Battles of Rossbach and Leuthen, 1757', in *The Decisive Battles of the Western World* (London, 1955), ii, 192–215.

Leyte Gulf, Battle of (24–26 October 1944)   On 20 October 1944, MacArthur's forces began landing on Leyte in the Philippine archipelago under the protection of Halsey's Third Fleet. Faced with such a serious threat to a key position, the Japanese navy's Commander-in-Chief, Admiral Toyoda, decided to fight. The last group of Japanese aircraft carriers, under Admiral Ozawa, came from Japan to draw the main body of the American fleet northwards from Luzon, with the aim of allowing two groups of battleships and cruisers, under Kurita and Nishimura, coming from Singapore through the archipelago, to attack the amphibious fleet off the beaches.

The Japanese plan almost succeeded. On 24 October, after some effective aerial attacks from Halsey, Kurita seemed to be in retreat in the Mindanao Sea, while Nishimura's division was destroyed by gunfire in a night engagement with Old-endorf's battleships in the Surigao Strait. Believing all danger averted, Halsey steamed north at speed and engaged Ozawa's fleet. Kurita, however, doubled back during the night, passed through the San Bernardino Strait and (25 October) steered towards the landing fleet.

Halsey turned back, but he was 400 miles away. However, Sprague's threatened force of destroyers and escort carriers put up such a heroic resistance, and inflicted such losses, that Kurita again turned and withdrew. Meanwhile, Halsey was in action with Ozawa with great effect, sinking his four carriers. Altogether, Japan lost 3 battleships, 4 carriers, 10 cruisers and 9 destroyers, while American losses were only 3 escort carriers and 3 destroyers. The Imperial Japanese navy almost ceased to exist. One darker aspect was that the Japanese resorted for the first time to the desperate solution of kamikaze. *See also* GUADALCANAL; MACARTHUR; MIDWAY ISLAND; NIMITZ.

P. MASSON

FURTHER READING
M. Hamlin Cannon, *Leyte: the return to the Philippines* (Washington, 1954); St L. Falk, *Decision at Leyte* (New York, 1966); S. E. Morison, *History of the United States Naval Operations in World War II* (Boston, 1947–62); C. Vann Woodward, *The Battle for Leyte Gulf* (New York, 1947).

Liddell Hart, Sir Basil (1895–1970) Liddell Hart was one of the foremost British military intellectuals of his time. He joined the British army in 1914 when still a history student and ended the war with the rank of captain. After the First World War, Liddell Hart played an important role in the recasting of the tactical doctrine and training methods of the British army. He was an advocate of manoeuvre and deep penetration (the 'expanding torrent'), but was forced in 1924 to leave the army owing to illness. As the military correspondent of the *Daily Telegraph* and later of *The Times*, Liddell Hart was deeply involved in the public discussion of military affairs in the interwar period. He produced an expanding torrent of books (eight alone in the period from 1925 to 1930) to outline his views. Liddell Hart favoured deep strategic penetration by tanks accompanied by motorized infantry, along with close tank–aircraft collaboration. His ideas, which complemented those of Fuller, found a greater acceptance abroad than in Britain. In Germany, the future German tank commander, Heinz Guderian, was an early convert to Liddell Hart's views. In the 1930s, Liddell Hart advocated that Britain avoid any war on the Continent, since she was not militarily prepared. To support his view, he wrote his best-known book, *Strategy: the Indirect Approach*, which held that Britain had traditionally pursued a maritime, amphibious approach to European wars. Liddell Hart was an influential adviser to Duff Cooper and Hore-Belisha, successive British secretaries of state for war, in the period from 1935 to 1939. In 1939, Liddell Hart lost both his influence and his position with *The Times* for continuing to advocate coming to terms with Hitler. After the Second World War, he rebuilt his reputation and was influential in the debate about nuclear weapons. Liddell Hart was one of the first to argue that nuclear weapons made war unacceptable and that the strategy of massive retaliation was pointless. *See also* FULLER; GUDERIAN; STRATEGY; TACTICS; TANKS.

A. CORVISIER
KEITH NEILSON

FURTHER READING
Brian Bond, *Liddell Hart: a study of his military thought* (London, 1977); John J. Mearsheimer, *Liddell Hart and the Weight of History* (London, 1988).

Light cavalry *See* CAVALRY; DRAGOONS; HUSSARS

Limes *See* FRONTIERS, MILITARY; ROME

Lissa, Battle of (20 July 1866) On 16 July 1866, three weeks after the defeat at Custozza, the Italian government sought to take its revenge on Austria at sea. Over-

coming his hesitations, Admiral Persano steamed out of Ancona and unsuccessfully attacked the island of Lissa on the Dalmatian coast. The operation caused an Austrian response and on 20 July the two fleets came into contact. Boldly, Tegetthoff, at the head of a squadron of seven ironclads and a number of old wooden vessels, formed up in line abreast and rammed the Italian fleet, which contained ten modern ships. The Austrian tactics created a confused mêlée engulfed in thick smoke which ended in an Austrian victory. The ironclad *Palestro* blew up and the *Ferdinand Max*, Tegetthoff's flagship, rammed and sank the *Re d'Italia*. The Battle of Lissa had considerable consequences. The encounter seemed to confirm the superiority of 'line abreast' over 'line ahead' while the proponents of ramming saw in it a striking vindication of their theories. *See also* AUSTRIA; ITALY; NAVAL WARFARE; NAVIES; TSUSHIMA.

P. MASSON

FURTHER READING
Karl Gogg, *Österreichs Kriegsmarine, 1848–1918* (Salzburg, 1967); A. Frigdjung, *The Struggle for Naval Supremacy in Germany* (New York, 1966).

Lloyd, Henry Humphrey Evans, Major-General (*c*.1718–83) Despite Lloyd's prominence as the only British military writer, prior to the twentieth century, to have influenced European military thought, much of his life remains shrouded in mystery. Its outline is the stuff of legends. A Welshman who had been a Jesuit lay brother, he pursued a remarkable career in which he served French, Austrian, Russian, Prussian and British masters, not just as a military officer but also as a spy. His writings were varied, including both military and political themes. He saw military history as serving a didactic function and in his best-known work, *The History of the Late War in Germany between the King of Prussia and the Empress of Germany and her Allies* (1766), later expanded to include the so-called *Military Memoirs* (1781), he both criticized the generalship of Frederick the Great, which stimulated much debate, and attempted to lay down 'certain and fixed principles' of war. Lloyd derived much from French thinking. He drew on Montesquieu and had a clear affinity with Saxe. Although his own 'principles' of war largely dealt with the 'organization' of armies, and included an examination of such matters as moral qualities, his *History* was none the less instrumental in shifting the interest of military theorists away from these organizational aspects, focusing instead on the actual conduct of operations. Developments in cartography enabled military planners to visualize their projected operations in new ways through a range of graphic images, and Lloyd's concept of a 'line of operations', representing the communications of an army with its bases of supply, was one of the first and most useful. It was Lloyd's graphical representation that was novel rather than the notion itself. Lloyd's view of the importance and correct use of the 'line of operations', although it was later dismissed as an absurdity by practitioners like Napoleon, was to prove a fertile ground for graphical representations of military operations for future generations. Bülow transformed Lloyd's concept into the centrepiece of his new science of operations and Jomini said that he owed Lloyd his greatest intellectual debt. *See also* BOURCET; BÜLOW; CLAUSEWITZ; FOLARD; GUIBERT; JOMINI; SAXE; TEIL.

G. A. STEPPLER

FURTHER READING
Azar Gat, *The Origins of Military Thought from the Enlightenment to Clausewitz* (Oxford, 1989); Franco Venturi, 'Le aventure del generale Henry Lloyd', *Revista Storia Italiana*, xci (1979), pp. 369–433; Hew Strachan, *European Armies and the Conduct of War* (London, 1983); John Shy, 'Jomini', in *Makers of Modern Strategy from Machiavelli to the Nuclear Age*, ed. Peter Paret (Oxford, 1986), pp. 143–85.

Logistics 'Logistics' is possibly derived from the Greek *logisteuein* meaning 'to administer'. In Roman legions, the *logista* was the quartermaster. During the Middle Ages and the early modern period, the term 'logistics' took on a more general sense and came to designate the science of reasoning and mathematics. From the second half of the eighteenth century it can be found, though rarely, in works on the art of war. In the modern military world, 'logistics' is the science which seeks to plan for the joint influence of two factors – time and space – which have a major bearing on the tactical movements of troops.

At the beginning of the twentieth century, the manuals used in military schools in France confined the term *logistique* to the body of rules for ensuring that 'troops in the field can subsist, march and rest in the most orderly and secure manner'. During the two world wars, and especially between 1939 and 1945, the increased size of armies made logistics the major factor in assessing the feasibility of operations and of the decisions of commanders. In his book *Introduction à l'histoire militaire*, Eric Muraise has provided an up-to-date definition: 'logistics is the art of moving and servicing troops in accordance with the tactical and strategic requirements.' Logistics is therefore concerned with three main issues:

1 Maintenance/transport: ensuring that appropriate levels of equipment are maintained and that both the equipment and the troops are in good condition. These tasks are executed by the army service corps.
2 Selection/evacuation: the assessment, withdrawal and replacement of both personnel and equipment that are out of action.
3 Restoration to effective condition: repair services for equipment and medical services for casualties. This function requires bases and depots, some unprotected, some defended.

Until the beginning of the twentieth century, logistics covered little more than the supply of food and organizing the routes of march and billets. In the period when the number of soldiers was small and did not differ much from the density of the surrounding population, military provisioning did not need an organization that was capable of forward planning. Although the soldier was often irregularly paid, he was supposed to provide himself, from his pay, with foodstuffs from the local markets. The French army intendants, whose origins dated from the first quarter of the seventeenth century, limited themselves to fixing in advance, on the basis of the previous three days' prices in the market, the price of the bread, vegetables, meat and drink which constituted the soldiers' daily ration. By this means, it was hoped to balance supply with demand. During the French Wars of Religion, the continual devastations and the increasing size of armies made it extremely difficult to supply soldiers with the necessary foodstuffs through the free market. Unit commanders tried to establish, in advance, stores of corn and flour in future billeting and camping areas.

In 1572, a contract was concluded between the Comte de Lude, the royal lieutenant-general in Poitou, and Amaury Bourguignon, a merchant from Niort, and his associates, for the provision of food for the soldiers in the camp at La Rochelle. Right up to the eve of the French Revolution (1789), the monarchy abstained from establishing an organization for supplying food at its own expense. The most important aspect of logistics rested in the hands of private traders. Between 1672 and 1697, the Sephardic Jewish firm of Machado and Pereira supplied the Dutch, British and Spanish armies in the Low Countries. They provided a complete service: bread, flour, river transport, waggons, horses, storage, drivers and distribution. The Oppenheimer family looked after the affairs of the Imperial armies during the same period. Generally, the system worked well enough, although it was open to abuse by the contractors and the royal agents. Its main attraction was that under-funded and fairly primitive state governments did not have to administer large sections of military business. Further, as certain areas of Europe, especially the Low Countries, the Rhineland and northern Italy, grew expert in supplying the needs of foreign armies, so those regions became attractive theatres for international warfare.

Concurrent with state employment of private contractors was the practice of exacting 'contributions' from occupied populations. Tracts of land which were 'placed under contribution' had to pay heavy taxes, either in kind or in money, to the occupying army. Various unsuccessful attempts were made between 1672 and 1697 to render the harsh burden of contributions no more onerous than normal, peacetime taxation. The levying of contributions obliged armies to fight on the enemy's soil or in neutral lands; even partial occupation by an enemy army depredated the local economy and reduced the revenue of the government. During his first period in command of the Imperial armies in the Thirty Years' War, Wallenstein perfected this system. On orders from his generals, the inhabitants of occupied regions were compelled to pay huge sums which Wallenstein then deployed to produce the required supplies from his own estates in Bohemia. During the second half of the eighteenth century, more sophisticated governments commanding higher revenues brought military administration more fully under state control and audit. More centralized logistics improved the discipline of the troops – there was never much difference between collecting contributions and marauding – and so brought armies more closely under the political control and direction of the state.

Under Frederick the Great of Prussia, advance logistical arrangements became a regular aspect of military policy. On account of the militarized governmental system of Brandenburg-Prussia, Frederick was able to dispense with the need for private contractors. However, despite his dictum that 'it is unwise ever to launch out forward troops, and success is always more likely to be achieved in wars fought near one's own frontiers than in those wars where the army takes the risk of advancing too far', the Prussian army drew only a fraction of its food supplies from its own magazines. Frederick, like his contemporaries, supplied his army by stripping bare enemy territories, particularly those of Electoral Saxony. Armies, even in the middle and later eighteenth century, still lived off the land especially in searching for forage for the horses. However, it became less and less frequent for such organized pillages to have a devastating effect, not from any change in the soldiers' behaviour, but because agricultural production between 1630 and 1800 markedly improved especially through the cultivation of the potato.

Napoleon I, whose army, strategy and tactics remained similar to those of the time of Frederick the Great, developed the latter's system of logistics by extending the range of operations that could be supported from magazines. In 1807, he established a transport corps which served as a model to all contemporary armies. Provided that he could find good roads and navigable waterways, Napoleon was able to create lines of communication of several hundred miles in length. By delegating transport to a special command, Napoleon freed his fighting troops from some logistical concerns and so accelerated their speed of movement and flexibility. Contemporaries attributed the rapidity of the marches of the French armies to a revolutionary system of logistics but Napoleon simply developed existing methods and, in particular, used his improved lines of communication to exploit conquered territories. It could go hopelessly wrong. The Russian campaign of 1812 revealed the physical limits of the horse-drawn convoy and emphasized the necessity of advancing and retreating via different routes.

From the second half of the nineteenth century, the Industrial Revolution caused a profound, although not abrupt alteration in logistics. In 1870, 30 per cent of all army supplies consisted of equipment while the remaining 70 per cent was composed of foodstuffs and forage. In 1918, as much as 52 per cent of transport facilities was taken up by ammunition, engineer equipment and fuel; only 39 per cent was required for moving provisions. Finally, by 1943, just 6 per cent of the total capacity remained available for foodstuffs, medical supplies and the post. The mushrooming number of mechanized units with their density of firepower, demanded huge quantities of mechanical equipment, fuel and ammunition,

commodities which could not be found in enemy countries. In addition, battlefields became merely small sections of immensely larger operational zones; as the spatial range of operational logistics increased, its turn-round time and speed of action declined. The provisioning of the Prussian army in 1870 serves as an illustration.

Railway networks expanded transport capacity but the railway layout in 1870 was insufficiently dense and the stations were mostly located away from the front. In 1870, as in 1914, horse-drawn convoys provided the connecting link with the combat area; the speed of rail transport was negated by the pace of the horse. The Prussian troops who were besieging Paris employed the same methods, although in a more civilized form, as their ancestors in the time of Wallenstein. Thousands of soldiers helped to harvest the neighbouring fields and the country people sold them meat and vegetables in the markets at the camps. During the entire Franco-Prussian War, the average daily march of the army did not exceed 11½ miles, no more than the armies of the seventeenth and eighteenth centuries. Even so, the transport could not keep in touch with the marching units. Fortunately, the requirement for ammunition was still modest, a fact which prevents us from interpreting the Franco-Prussian War as a 'modern' type of conflict as logistics did not play a prominent role.

When preparing the Schlieffen Plan, the German General Staff failed to predict the logistical problems. The railways could not be extended along the armies' routes at the desired speed and horse-drawn convoys were less and less able to cover the increasing distances. As the food supplies dwindled, the German soldiers were forced to live off the French countryside. Trench warfare, with its more or less fixed combat zones, increased the difficulties arising from the capacity, rather than the speed, of transport. The huge expenditure of ammunition posed problems for the armaments industries in all the countries which participated in the First World War but these related to industrial production rather than logistics. The motorization of armies during the 1914–18 war also raised almost insurmountable obstacles. Not only were the early trucks no faster than a horse-drawn cart but motorization was valueless without an adequate production of fuel and rubber. This latter weakness became even more apparent during the Second World War. While the transport capacity of the Allies increased, the German armies, particularly after the loss of their sources of natural oil in 1944, had to resort to horse-pulled carriages, which restricted their operations and made supply more uncertain (e.g. the Ardennes Offensive in 1944). The Allied advance through France in 1944 demonstrated that motor columns could not supply their fighting units with sufficient fuel and ammunition at a range of 375 miles. The battles of encirclement at Demyansk in 1942, Stalingrad in 1942–3 and Bastogne in 1944 showed that a new era in logistics was beginning: air supply. Early attempts indicated that the transport aircraft of the Second World War could deliver no more than 20,000 tons a day, enough for a corps but insufficient to supply an army of more than 250,000 men at Stalingrad. The air bridge to Berlin in 1948–9 was a major breakthrough in the concept of air supply. At present, with the development of aircraft which can carry larger payloads, the proportion of long-distance military supplies which can be delivered by air has grown appreciably. *See also* ARSENALS; INTENDANTS; MEDICAL SERVICES; ORDNANCE; RATIONS; TRANSPORT; TRANSPORT, AIR; WEAPONS.

B. KROENER
JOHN CHILDS

FURTHER READING
D. W. Engels, *Alexander the Great and the Logistics of the Macedonian Army* (Berkeley, 1978); Martin van Creveld, *Supplying War: logistics from Wallenstein to Patton* (Cambridge, 1977); Fritz Redlich, *De Praeda Militari: looting and booty, 1500–1815* (Wiesbaden, 1956); G. Perjés, 'Army provisioning, logistics and strategy in the second half of the seventeenth century', *Acta Historica Academiae Scientarium Hungaricae*, xvi (1970), pp. 1–51; Roland G. Ruppenthal, *Logistical Support of the Armies* (2 vols, Washington, 1953–9).

Losses of life Apart from the aspects of morality and humanity, the problem of war

casualties has to be envisaged from two angles – the losses suffered by one's own side and those inflicted on the enemy. Military leaders have usually tried to limit the former but their attitude to the latter has often been equivocal. In certain periods of history, the defeat of the enemy implied the destruction of his fighting forces either with the tactical intention of ensuring a complete victory or the strategic aim of putting him out of action and preventing him from reopening hostilities. In the latter case, it is not just the enemy's soldiers who form the target but also the civilian population. Fatalities may also be inflicted by the use of terror tactics to bring about rapid capitulation. The question of losses in warfare has always preoccupied statesmen, concerned as they are about the effects of war on their countries.

In general, wars increase mortality levels but, as Gaston Bouthoul observes, the amount varies. The behaviour of combatants both on the field of battle and towards civilians is closely connected with the forms of violence current in a particular era. Behaviour may change during the different phases of a single conflict. The prolongation of hostilities may lead to a tacit code being agreed to limit the slaughter or to the emergence of a spirit of vengeance which adds to the killing. So far as the levels of loss are concerned, the actual outcome of the encounter is a determinant. Where an army is defeated on its own soil, the percentage of casualties is often higher. The distribution of casualties also varies. Generally, the victor loses only common soldiers, e.g. young men. For the vanquished, however, whose country has been invaded, ravaged and sometimes systematically destroyed, age and sex tend to lose their significance in the face of the murderous frenzy of the victorious enemy which, in primitive societies, was only limited by the enslavement of those who could be of service, an enslavement which sometimes took place after those males who were of an age to bear arms had been massacred (e.g. the Trojan War).

In Christian societies war is considered alongside plague and famine as one of three scourges inflicted upon humanity. *A peste, fame, belloque libera nos, Domine!* For a

463

Table 1 *Losses suffered in various battles*

| Battle | Date | Nationality | *Victors* | | % losses/ in action |
			In action	Losses	
Cannae	216 BC	Carthaginian	32,000	6,000 dead	18
Poitiers	1356	English	12,000	1,000 dead	8
Grandson	1476	Swiss	18,000	200 in total	1
Marignano	1515	French	35,000	5,000 dead	14
Ceresole	1544	French	12,000	2,000 dead	17
Lepanto	1571	Spanish	84,000	8,000 wounded	9.5
Lützen	1632	Swedish	18,000	10,000 (?)	56
Rocroi	1643	French	23,000	4,000 dead	16
Fleurus	1690	French	45,000	2,500 dead	6
Blenheim	1704	Imperial/ English	56,000	4,500 dead; 7,500 wounded	21
Poltava	1709	Russian	80,000	1,300 dead; 3,300 wounded	4
Malplaquet	1709	Imperial/ English/Dutch	110,000	6,500 dead; 14,000 wounded	19
Denain	1712	French	33,000	500 dead; 1,000 wounded	1.5
Fontenoy	1745	French	52,000	7,200 dead & wounded	19
Leuthen	1757	Prussian	36,000	6,100 dead & wounded	17
Austerlitz	1805	French	65,000	9,000 dead & wounded	15
Eylau	1807	French	75,000	18,000 dead & wounded	24
Wagram	1809	French	160,000	34,000 dead & wounded	21
Waterloo	1815	Coalition	120,000	22,000 dead & wounded	18
Solferino	1859	French/ Piedmontese	160,000	17,200 dead & wounded	11
Gettysburg	1863	American	115,000	3,110 dead; 14,500 wounded; 5,100 missing	19
Fröschwiller	1870	German	125,000	9,600 dead & wounded	8

long time little attention was paid to the fact that plague and famine, which were regarded as natural calamities, could be seen as secondary effects of the third. The focus was placed mainly on those who died on the field of battle or as a consequence of their wounds. The expression, 'fallen on the field of honour', even suggests the exclusion of the latter though they were of great numerical importance before the advance of medicine led to their reduction. J. Dupâquier is of the opinion that, for the seventeenth century, one should multiply the number of those who died on the battlefield by a factor of three to give an idea of the numbers who died from wounds received in battle, skirmishes and accidents. During the Franco-Prussian War (1870–1), it would still be necessary to apply a multiplication factor of two as the progress of prophylactic medicine had not kept up with the advances in surgery and a considerable number of successful amputations or extractions of projectiles resulted in death from gangrene and infection. During the 1914–18 war, the number of deaths ensuing within a short time as a result of wounds received was markedly reduced, producing a larger number of disabled ex-servicemen. The number of maimed veterans was itself diminished as surgery made progress during the Second World War.

Death from wounds was not, however, the only danger to threaten a soldier when not on the battlefield. The wars of the

Table 1   *cont.*

Nationality	In action	Defeated Killed and Wounded	Prisoners	% losses/ in action
Roman	65,000	60,000		92
French	35,000	2,500	2,600	7
Burgundian	15,000	1,000		6
Swiss/Italian	20,000	6,000		30
Imperial	19,000	6,000	3,200	31
Turkish	88,000	20,000	300	23
Imperial	20,000	12,000(?)		60
Spanish	27,000	7,000	8,000	26
English/Spanish/ Imperial	37,000	6,000	8,000	16
French/Bavarian	60,000	Total losses 38,000		
Swedish	20,000	9,000	11,000	45
French	80,000	4,500 dead; 8,000 wounded		16
Imperial	8,000	2,000	3,000	63
English/Hanoverian	50,000	7,500		15
Austrian	80,000	6,700	20,000	8
Austrian/Russian	83,000	Total losses 26,000		
Russian	83,000	25,000	3,000	30
Austrian	130,000	24,000	21,000	35
French	72,000	23,000	7,000	32
Austrian	160,000	22,000		14
Confederate	76,000	3,900 dead; 18,700 wounded 5,300 missing		36
French	46,500	10,760	6,200	23

twentieth century have certainly witnessed a decline in the number of soldiers killed by epidemics. As a result of the growth of armies from the sixteenth century onwards, contagions scythed down huge concentrations of men. 'I know of many more armies destroyed for want of bread and administration', said Richelieu, 'than by the efforts of the enemy armies.' Dupâquier estimates that the figure for total losses inflicted on soldiers by warfare is three times higher than the number of men lost by death from wounds, and thus roughly ten times greater than the figures for losses on the battlefield. A more detailed study is possible for France after 1716. Both in war and peace, military and civilian mortality was higher in winter than in summer. In general, eighteenth-

century military operations took place during the more clement weather. Thus in the Regiment of the Vivarais between 1716 and 1749, excess mortality due to warfare was 14.0 per cent in summer and 23.0 per cent in winter, omitting the epidemic of 1734 which struck down half the French army. This difference can be explained by the men being crowded into dirty and unhealthy billets in winter. Armies transmit their diseases to the civilian population. The vague expression, 'military fever', formed by extension from the term 'miliary fever' (a fever with a rash), was an indication of the impotence of the medical profession and the authorities in the face of populations being decimated in this manner. In the eighteenth century, the

465

Table 2   *Losses in the war of 1870–1*

	German army	French army
Men mobilized	914,000	c.900,000
Battlefield deaths	24,000	
Deaths from injuries sustained	29,000	139,000
Deaths from illness	12,000	
Missing	4,000	
Total losses	69,000	151,000
Losses as a percentage of numbers mobilized	7.6%	c.17%
Deaths from illness as a percentage of battlefield deaths and deaths from injuries	22.6%	
Men hospitalized:		
for wounds	129,000	131,000
for illness and exposure	?	328,000
Number of sick as a percentage of wounded		69.7%

mortality rate for soldiers in peacetime seems to have been more or less equivalent to that of the general population, around 3.5 per cent, but the individuals involved came from a relatively youthful social group, supposedly the most robust segment of the national population.

During the Franco-Prussian War, the total dead in the French army was probably three times the number of those who died on the battlefield and almost twice the number of those who succumbed to wounds. Such figures have now become exceptional, apart from in colonial and Third World wars, and were caused by the poor quality of the medical services. Over the same period, the German army reduced the proportion of soldiers dying from sickness to just a little above one in five of total deaths.

During the First World War, the proportions were reversed both as a result of the growing efficiency of weapons and the improvement in supplying the troops. In the French army, the proportion of men dying on the battlefield or from wounds received was 87 per cent of the total of dead, despite the 'pandemic' of Spanish 'flu in 1918. Military losses from illness have always had a great influence on the conduct of operations, at least until the seventeenth century in Western Europe and the eighteenth in Eastern Europe, and even later in wars in Asia and the colonies,

especially in the West Indies. This was even more markedly the case in navies where, until the nineteenth century, sickness frequently rendered entire fleets incapable of action.

Military casualties are only one element in the human losses occasioned by war. The populations within the actual theatres of war or those countries under enemy occupation are also affected to a greater or lesser degree. In ancient times, massacres were often accompanied by the mutilation of adult males or the reduction of the men to a condition of slavery which they would not long survive. Similar actions were not unknown in Roman history, such as the conquests of Sardinia, Carthage and the province of Asia. Some writers have gone so far as to suggest that two million died during the Roman conquest of Gaul, 36 per cent of the population.

Indisputably, wars of religion have been the most murderous for defeated peoples. Arabs, Turks and Crusaders put to the sword the inhabitants of towns which dared to resist. The same practice often occurred during the wars between the Catholics and the Protestants which ravaged much of Western and Central Europe between 1521 and 1648. However, the vividness of the impact of the Sack of Magdeburg in 1631 attests that in Western Europe such actions had become less common. In Eastern Europe, the same development took place

150 years later; the massacre at Ochakov in 1788 in the Russo-Turkish War has retained its notoriety as an increasingly infrequent example. Ideological conflicts, which often have a religious base, have assumed a similar character: the war in the Vendée (at least 400,000 deaths), the massacres in Armenia in 1915, in the Ukraine in 1917–18, the atrocities of the Nazis in Poland and Russia, those in Cambodia in 1975 and in Iran between 1978 and 1985. The only way of restraining armies from such massacres of the civilian population has been to distinguish clearly between military and civilian personnel. This distinction was made in the West in the mid-eighteenth century, when civilians were forbidden to bear arms and soldiers forbidden to make war on them. Frederick the Great was a leading exponent of this practical philosophy. However, this advance in international law has been compromised by the armed resistance of civilian populations and the consequent breakdown of the division between the civil and the military. This development reached its logical conclusion during the Second World War with civilian populations regarded as legitimate military targets by all belligerents.

Civilian populations also suffer from the indirect mortality rate produced by warfare. Where populations are put to flight, refugees may die from hunger or exhaustion. When local inhabitants abandon a region, fields lie fallow, leading to famine. This increases the occurrence of epidemics which are further encouraged by populations being herded together. As many as 80 per cent of the Indians of Southern and Central America were wiped out by diseases introduced by their Spanish conquerors. The Aboriginal population of Australia was similarly decimated by European bacilli. Closer to our own day, the Spanish 'flu of 1918–19 accounted for nearly 20 million deaths world-wide.

It is impossible to know exactly the total of human casualties occasioned by war. The use of administrative documents encounters the problems of definitions. For example, although those men taken to a hospital close to the battlefield shortly after an engagement and who die within the next month may be considered as dying from their wounds, it is difficult to say the same for those who die later. Conversely, men left wounded on the field who expire in captivity within a few days may be omitted from calculations altogether. Battle reports cautiously speak of men 'missing', among whom are included, in addition to the dead and prisoners, deserters and even men absent from their units before the action commenced. For obvious reasons, civilian casualties are even more difficult to establish. At best one might hope to assess the number of inhabitants who are present in a region quite a long time after a catastrophe, in order to be able to take into account the return of refugees, and compare this figure with that for the previous population. The surest way of assessing the overall casualty figures is to turn to historical demography and examine the age pyramids, searching for deficits within certain age groups. Age pyramids also reveal significant 'low-volume groups' resulting from a fall in the birth rate during wartime. In order to undertake such calculations, however, it is necessary to have at one's disposal precise registers of births and deaths. These did not appear in the West until the nineteenth century and later elsewhere.

The estimation of the direct casualties of war is fraught with difficulties, caused principally by unreliable data. Calculation on a battle by battle basis only makes sense when and where individual battles can be discerned (Table 1). In the Russo-Japanese War (1904–5) and the First World War the establishment of a seamless front redefined battle as a periodic heightening of almost continuous action. The precise battlefield, Verdun, the Somme, Passchendaele, had to be demarcated in time and space. During the Second World War, with the coming of air power and combined operations, the battlefield was no longer a strip of earth but a three-dimensional theatre in land, sea and air.

The wars of religion in sixteenth- and seventeeth-century Europe had been noted for their barbarism with the wounded being dispatched on the battlefield and disarmed men being massacred unless they could offer a ransom. Subsequently, despite the development of more-lethal weapons,

467

direct casualties did not increase as quickly as the size of armies. Admittedly, war killed more soldiers overall but, proportionately, the number of wounded rose more quickly, though in many cases they were only to be short-term survivors, and the number of prisoners of war jumped even more sharply. It seems to have been during the Thirty Years' War (1618–48) that the number of wounded began to overtake the number of fatalities. During the Nine Years' War (1688–97), the number of prisoners reached the same total as the dead and often that of the dead and wounded added together. In the eighteenth century, the percentage of casualties among the defeated tended to be close to that of the victors. The cause is probably to be found in the facts that the larger-scale mass battles left less scope for hand-to-hand fighting and that generals preferred to withdraw in good order rather than risk the destruction of their commands.

Furthermore, sieges, which were usually unfavourable to the defeated side, became less common, as did pursuits which often led to men being drowned (St Gotthard Abbey, 1664; Blenheim, 1704; and Denain, 1712). This tendency was reversed during the Napoleonic Wars. Losses grew very high once again, especially among the victorious forces, who often indulged in unbridled offensives. Drownings during retreats still played a role (Austerlitz, Friedland and the Beresina). In spite of the passions generated at Solferino, the war in Italy of 1859–60 was less costly in lives than the Crimean War (1854–6). In 1870–1, the difference in losses proportionate to the numbers of men can be explained by the inadequacy of the French army's medical services. Table 3 is based on the work of G. Bodart.

Table 3 *Casualties in battles*

Conflicts	Percentage of casualties in battle	
	Victor (%)	Defeated (%)
Wars of the sixteenth century	10	50
Thirty Years' War	15	30
Wars of Louis XIV	11	33
Wars of the eighteenth century	11	17
French Revolutionary Wars	9	16
Napoleonic Wars	15	20
1870–1	4	15
First World War	12	13
Second World War	15	15

Efforts have also been made to assess the effectiveness of armies by establishing a coefficient reflecting the losses of one adversary divided by the number of troops possessed by the other. The calculations carried out by E. Muraise give the following results for the Franco-Prussian War (1870–1):

Imperial Period	*Republican Period*
Germans: 8.5%	Germans: 9%
French: 14%	French: 3.3%

Armies composed of soldiers recently raised were less effective in battle, though they also had fewer losses, since the men were not able to stand their ground in difficult situations except where they had been combined with seasoned troops.

Thus, again in the Franco-Prussian War, while the German army lost 12.4 per cent of its soldiers in defeats, the French professional army lost 14.5 per cent while units of newly raised French troops lost only 6 per cent. However, Christopher Duffy has pointed out that during the mid-eighteenth century raw and untried troops often fought better than seasoned veterans. As a formation became more accustomed to combat, so its operational efficiency declined. A similar pattern was discernible in the British army during the Normandy campaign in 1944.

The proportion of killed to wounded during the nineteenth century was around 1:3.5. During the Franco-Prussian War it was 1:5.4 among the Germans but 1:2.4 if those who died from wounds are included. During the Russo-Japanese War, these ratios were respectively 1:4.7 and 1:1.8 in the army of Japan; the latter rate was exceptionally high due to episodes of great slaughter. Today, advances in surgery have reduced the contribution of deaths as a result of wounds within battlefield fatalities to less than 10 per cent.

Attempts have been made to calculate the ratios of deaths in action among the various branches of the armed forces. During the Napoleonic Wars, it was, for France, 1:22 among officers in the artillery, 1:23 in the navy, 1:29 in the infantry and 1:44 in the cavalry. The question of whether casualties varied between the various ranks has also been investigated. It would seem that the level of casualties can be expressed by a disymmetrical curve. The maximum number is situated at the level of captains and lieutenants, platoon and company commanders, in all wars from the seventeenth century to the present day.

The cost of warfare for France between 1635 and 1962, counting both military and civilian casualties, is indicated in Table 4.

It is possible to attempt a general assessment of mortality among the soldiery caused by war. However, the figures are vague and must be treated with care. J. Dupâquier estimates that the wars of the seventeeth century killed 2,300,000 soldiers in Europe, including 600,000 in 1618–59 and 700,000 during the War of the Spanish Succession, out of a total of between 10 and 12 million who bore arms, excluding territorial formations. This represents an excess mortality due to war of between 20 per cent and 25 per cent. Of the approximately 500 million people born in seventeenth-century Europe, the proportion of military-inspired deaths amounts to 0.5 per cent.

Estimating the losses to the civilian population is more difficult as they varied with the nature of the civilization and the type of war. In the seventeenth century, perhaps 2 per cent of the non-military European population perished through war, Germany having been particularly badly affected during the Thirty Years' War. The establishment of the laws of war and their institutionalization in the eighteenth and nineteenth centuries considerably reduced civilian casualties. According to G. Frumkin, civilian casualties represent no more than 5 per cent of the total losses during the First World War, at least on the Western Front, before rising to 52 per cent

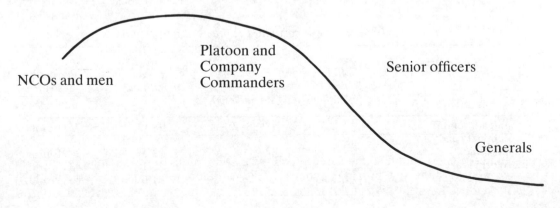

NCOs and men   Platoon and Company Commanders   Senior officers   Generals

Table 4   *French losses, 1635–1962*

Franco-Spanish War, 1635–59	380,000
Dutch War, 1672–8	120,000
Nine Years' War, 1688–97	160,000
War of Spanish Succession, 1702–14	500,000
War of Austrian Succession, 1742–7	140,000
Seven Years' War, 1756–63	175,000
Revolutionary Wars, 1792–1802	500,000
Napoleonic Wars, 1803–15	800,000
Crimean War, 1854–6	96,000
(+75,000 deaths from sickness)	
War in Italy, 1859–60	16,000
Franco-Prussian War, 1870–1	140,000
First World War, 1914–18	1,300,000
Second World War, 1939–45	210,000
War in Indo-China, 1946–54	65,000
Algerian War, 1954–62	23,000

for the whole of Europe in the Second World War. G. Bouthoul has made calculations for the wars that ravaged the planet between 1740 and 1974. He arrives at a figure of 85 million dead, 8.5 million of whom died in the First World War and 38 million in the Second. Out of 13,000,000,000 deaths within this period, this would mean 0.6 per cent being attributable to war, including direct and indirect civilian losses. The figures presented by R. E. and T. N. Dupuy, which include epiphenomena of the two world wars (the Soviet Revolution, the Armenian massacres, etc.), give higher figures for those two wars – 15,100,000 and 41,000,000 respectively, but they do not significantly alter the overall percentage.

A rational mind might infer that, since the murder of Abel, the percentage of human losses due to war has diminished in spite of the quasi-hyperbolic increase in the number of lives lost created by the spread of conflict across the planet. One should, however, note that after an appreciable diminution in Europe between 1700 and 1914, the twentieth century has been responsible for a marked rise in casualties caused by war (Table 5).

The involvement of civilians in war has led to some great catastrophes and these bald figures take no account of the human pain and suffering. *See also* DISCIPLINE; MEDICAL SERVICES; MORALE; PENSIONS; RECRUITMENT; SOLDIERS AND SOCIETY; TACTICS; VETERANS.

A. CORVISIER
JOHN CHILDS

Table 5   *Increasing war casualties in the twentieth century*

	Military deaths (in millions)	Civilian deaths (in millions)	Total (in millions)	Percentage of civilian deaths
Seventeenth century	2.3	8–10	10–12	75 (Europe)
Revolutionary and Napoleonic	2.5	1.0	3.5	30 (Europe)
First World War	8.5	6.6	15.1	43 (World)
Second World War	15.0	26.0	41.0	63 (World)

FURTHER READING
G. Bodart, *Losses of Life in Modern Wars: Austria-Hungary and France* (Oxford, 1916); G. Frumkin, *Population Changes in Europe, 1938–1947* (Moscow, 1972); S. Dumas and K. O. Vedel-Petersen, *Losses of Life Caused by War* (Oxford, 1923); J. B. Schechtman, *European Population Transfers, 1939–45* (New York, 1946); M. P. Gutmann, *War and Rural Life in the Early Modern Low Countries* (Princeton, 1980); E. A. Wrigley, *Population and History* (New York, 1969); F. Prinzing, *Epidemics Resulting from Wars*, ed. H. Westergaard (Oxford, 1916).

Louvois, François Michel Le Tellier, Marquis de (1641–91)   Louvois, the son of a family of Parisian *noblesse de robe*, was prepared for his future function as secretary of state for war by his father, Michel Le Tellier. He was a member of the Conseil du Roi from 1671 and became a devoted and diligent servant of Louis XIV, tirelessly visiting the sovereign's armies and military camps. He built up the largest, most efficiently supplied, most mobile and best equipped army in late seventeenth-century Europe; at its height it contained 380,000 men. He was responsible for the regulations which laid down the system of promotion; the organization of an artillery corps; the adoption of the socket bayonet; the creation of inspectors of infantry and cavalry; improved administrative checks on troops and officers; and the establishment of the Hôtel des Invalides for aged and disabled soldiers. With the aid of Vauban and Chamlay, he inspired Louis XIV's pursuit of the fortified 'Pré Carré', rational, defensible frontiers, which was achieved through warfare and aggressive diplomacy. This process, culminating in the annexation of Strasbourg in 1681, laid the basis for the frontiers of modern France. *See also* ADMINISTRATION, ARMY; CHAMLAY; FRANCE; VAUBAN.

A. CORVISIER
JOHN CHILDS

FURTHER READING
André Corvisier, *Louvois* (Paris, 1983); Camille Rousset, *Histoire de Louvois* (4 vols, Paris, 1886).

Ludendorff, Erich (1865–1937)   Son of an estate agent, Ludendorff entered the Berlin military academy in 1883. Twelve years later he joined the general staff which constituted the operational centre of the Prussian army. In 1908 he became head of the mobilization section and was instrumental in drafting the 1913 Army Bill, which sought to expand the army to meet the exigencies of the Schlieffen Plan. In the process, his political tactics in pressing for expansion proved unacceptable and he was tranferred to an infantry command at Düsseldorf. However, when war broke out he distinguished himself as deputy chief of staff to 2nd Army in seizing the Belgian fortress of Liège with only a brigade and was then appointed chief of staff to 8th Army in East Prussia on 22 August 1914 at the same time that Hindenburg was appointed to its command. While the resounding victory over the Russians at Tannenberg owed much to operational plans drawn up by Ludendorff's predecessor, Max Hoffmann, Hindenburg and Ludendorff proved a formidable team and enjoyed a series of spectacular successes on the Eastern Front. When Hindenburg replaced Falkenhayn as chief of the general staff on 28 August 1916, Ludendorff became First Quartermaster General and the real power within the 'silent dictatorship', which dominated both domestic and foreign policy-making. An advocate of total war demanding the absolute subordination of politics to military considerations, Ludendorff exerted an increasing and ultimately disastrous influence on the government of the Reich. In particular, his strategic errors during the great spring offensive of 1918 lost Germany the initiative in the west and Ludendorff himself collapsed with nervous exhaustion on 29 September 1918, resigning on 26 October. After the war he was associated with extreme right-wing politics and was actually the Nazi candidate for the presidency of the Weimar Republic in 1925. *See also* GERMANY;   HINDENBURG;   SCHLIEFFEN; TANNENBERG (1914).

B. KROENER
IAN F. W. BECKETT

FURTHER READING
Correlli Barnett, *The Swordbearers* (London, 1963); D. J. Goodspeed, *Ludendorff* (London, 1966); Martin Kitchen, *The Silent Dictatorship* (London, 1976); Roger Parkinson, *Tormented Warrior* (London, 1978).

Lützen, Battle of (16 November 1632) After a campaign during which Gustavus Adolphus's Swedish army and Wallenstein's Imperial force had manoeuvred to embarrass each other's logistics, during September Wallenstein moved north from around Nuremberg to threaten the territories of John George of Saxony, Sweden's ally. Although Gustavus had decided to exploit Wallenstein's march by advancing towards the Danube, news that Pappenheim was leading a second Imperial contingent in the direction of Saxony caused Gustavus to abandon his scheme and march northwards. Gustavus determined to fight the Imperial forces who were threatening his base areas in northern Germany.

On 14 November, Wallenstein concluded that the campaign was finished and began to dispatch his men into winter quarters. The next day he received reports from his patrols that the Swedes were marching rapidly towards his headquarters at Lützen, near Leipzig. Wallenstein could only recover *c.*19,000 of his men to face an equal number of Swedes. Wallenstein's right was anchored on the castle of Lützen but his left was 'in the air'; his centre lay in the hollow of a valley behind a sunken road which he lined with musketeers. Despite early morning fog, Gustavus discerned that the Imperial left was the weakest sector and led the Swedish cavalry in a sweeping attack which broke through the Imperial left and began to roll up the infantry *tercios* in the centre. Gustavus had reached the Imperial artillery when Pappenheim arrived on the battlefield and led his cavalry in a charge around the Swedish right which obliged Gustavus to break off his assault. Fog and smoke so obscured the battlefield that Gustavus could not see that Pappenheim had been killed and his attack had failed. Instead of exploiting his almost total victory over the Imperial left and centre, Gustavus launched an unsuccessful attack against the strong Imperial right near Lützen castle. When this attack faltered, Gustavus led a regiment of cavalry to retrieve the situation but was shot three times and killed. Bernhard of Saxe-Weimar assumed command of the Swedish army and launched a final attack which carried Lützen village. This steadied the front and both armies remained in their positions as dusk fell. Having lost some 12,000 men compared to Swedish casualties of 10,000, Wallenstein withdrew during the night abandoning his artillery and baggage. Although a confused and drawn battle, Lützen ended the run of Protestant successes which had followed the Swedish entry into the Thirty Years' War. Roughly equal in strength, the Protestant states and the Imperialists began to search for foreign assistance. *See also* BREITENFELD; GUSTAVUS II ADOLPHUS; INFANTRY; SWEDEN; TILLY; WALLENSTEIN.

A. CORVISIER
J. CHILDS

FURTHER READING
Geoffrey Parker, *The Thirty Years' War* (London, 1984); Michael Roberts, *Gustavus Adolphus* (2 vols, London, 1953–8); George Pagès, *The Thirty Years' War* (London, 1970).

Luxembourg, François-Henri de Montmorency, Duke of (1628–95) Luxembourg first campaigned under Condé in Catalonia in 1647 and in 1672 he served under the same commander as a lieutenant-general in the Franco-Dutch War (1672–8). He played a major role in the retreat from the Dutch Republic in 1673 and fought at Seneffe in 1674. He was made a Marshal of France on the death of Turenne in 1675 and was given the chief command of the French armies in Flanders in 1677. At the opening of the Nine Years' War (1688–97), the principal command in the Low Countries was given to d'Humières but his poor performance at Walcourt led to his recall and the appointment of Luxembourg in 1690. Luxembourg then commanded the French armies in the Low Countries until his death at Versailles early in 1695. Luxembourg was not an outstanding battlefield tactician – he was surprised by William III of Orange at St Dennis in 1678 and at Steenkirk in 1692 – but he was a master of strategic and tactical marching and manoeuvre. In positional warfare and the organization of supply, Luxembourg claimed few equals in the later seventeenth century. *See also* CONDÉ; LOUVOIS; MONTE-CUCOLI; TURENNE.

JOHN CHILDS

FURTHER READING
Le Chevalier de Beaurain, *Histoire militaire de Flandre depuis l'année 1690 jusqu'en 1694 inclusivement* (Paris, 1755); John Childs, *The Nine Years' War and the British Army, 1688–97* (Manchester, 1991); Général Camon, *Le maréchal de Luxembourg* (Paris, 1936).

Luxembourg, Siege of (January – 7 June 1684) As part of the campaign of 'reunions' which followed the Peace of Nijmegen in 1678, French troops had occupied most of the Duchy of Luxembourg by September 1680. In an effort to force the Governor of the Spanish Netherlands, the Marquis de Castañaga, to cede this territory to France, Luxembourg City was blockaded. Although this blockade was temporarily lifted during the Turkish invasion of Hungary and the ensuing Siege of Vienna in 1683, the Turkish defeat at the Kahlenberg saw the blockade resumed later in the same year. In desperation, Spain declared war on France and during the short conflict (1683–4), Luxembourg City was subjected to a formal siege.

The operation forms an excellent illustration of Vauban's methods and the customs of siege warfare. Under the command of Marshal François de Créqui, French troops tightened the blockade around the fortress during January and February. As the Spanish–Walloon garrison grew weaker from desertion and famine, a French covering army encamped close to Luxembourg while another corps executed a feint march towards Brussels. Between 28 April and 8 May, Vauban had lines of contravallation (*see* SIEGES) dug around the town before breaking ground and opening the trenches. By 27 May, the saps and parallels were sufficiently close to the covered way of a hornwork (*see* FORTIFICATION) to risk an assault. Mines tore a breach in the hornwork and this was the signal for the governor, the Comte de Chimay, to order his drummers to sound a parley so that he might request a suspension of hostilities until orders arrived from the King of Spain. However, fearing that the city might be sacked by a victorious but restless French army, Chimay shortly opened direct negotiations with Créqui. The terms of surrender, which preserved the security and liberty of both the garrison and inhabitants, were carefully drafted. On 7 June, the garrison marched out through the breach in the hornwork with the full honours of war – drums and trumpets playing, flags flying, bullet in mouth and matches lit. Chimay dismounted and saluted Créqui.

In the course of the Hispano-French War, France also captured Courtrai and Dixmuyde as well as bombarded other cities and towns in Flanders and invaded Catalonia. France's 'conquest' of Luxembourg and her other 'reunions' were recognized for twenty years by the Truce of Regensburg (Ratisbon) in August 1684. *See also* CHAMLAY; FORTIFICATION; LOUVOIS; SIEGES; VAUBAN; VIENNA, SIEGE OF.

A. CORVISIER
JOHN CHILDS

FURTHER READING
C. Duffy, *The Fortress in the Age of Vauban and Frederick the Great* (London, 1985); David Chandler, *The Art of War in the Age of Marlborough* (London, 1976); Georges Livet, 'Strasbourg, Metz et Luxembourg. Contribution à la politique extérieure de Louis XIV', *Actes du Colloque de Luxembourg* (1977).

Lyautey, Louis Hubert Gonzalve (1854–1934) Lyautey was probably the greatest, and certainly the best known, of France's colonial generals. Vain and ambitious, Catholic and royalist, a cavalryman caught in the malaise of the metropolitan French army after 1871, Lyautey was often at odds with his chosen profession. In 1891 his article on the social role of the officer, published in the *Revue des deux mondes*, arguing for the educational role of the army in the nation, vented his criticisms of his colleagues and their failure to attend to the needs of their men. In 1894 he was sent to Tonkin, where he became Galliéni's chief support and admirer. He followed Galliéni to Madagascar. In 1900, Lyautey published in the *Revue des deux mondes* an article on the colonial role of the army which has come to be regarded as the basic theoretical text on its subject. Basing himself on the precepts of Galliéni, Lyautey argued that an efficient and benevolent occupation must follow the attacking column, that the colonial soldier was settler and administrator as well as conqueror, that political action was more important than military. In 1903 he was sent to Morocco, whose pacification was to be the main achievement of his life's work, and whose commander-in-chief he was in 1912–16 and 1917–25. He proceeded slowly, likening his strategy's progressive nature to a spreading patch of oil. The reality of the conquest of Morocco was not as close to Lyautey's theory as he might have liked; in the last analysis French power rested on raids and conquests, rather than 'hearts and minds'. But during the First World War only small forces were required to maintain France's hold over its colony, and the success of the colonial generals in metropolitan France added further lustre to Lyautey's name. In 1917 he was briefly recalled to Paris to serve as minister of war. In 1921 he became a Marshal of France. *See also* BUGEAUD; COLONIAL TROOPS; FRANCE; GALLIÉNI.

HEW STRACHAN

FURTHER READING
André Le Reverend, *Lyautey* (Paris, 1983); André Maurois, *Marshal Lyautey* (London, 1931); Douglas Porch, *The Conquest of Morocco* (London, 1986).

M

MacArthur, Douglas (1880–1964) Mac-Arthur, the son of a distinguished soldier, graduated first in his class at West Point in 1903. He entered the army as an engineer and served as an aide to both his father and President Theodore Roosevelt. He served with bravery and distinction in the First World War and was promoted to brigadier general. From 1919 to 1922, MacArthur was superintendent at West Point where he modernized the curriculum. He was promoted to major general in 1925. Five years later MacArthur became Chief of Staff, a position he held until 1935. From 1935 to his retirement from the US army in 1937, MacArthur acted as military adviser to the government of the Philippines. In 1941, MacArthur was recalled to duty and made commander of the US army in the Far East. Forced to withdraw from the Philippines in March 1942 by the Japanese invasion, MacArthur fled to Australia, vowing that 'I shall return.' In April 1942, MacArthur was made Supreme Commander of the allied forces in the Southwest Pacific Theatre. From August 1942 to January 1943, MacArthur's forces defeated the Japanese in the Papuan campaign. MacArthur then went on the offensive, clearing the Japanese out of New Guinea from September 1943 to August 1944 by means of amphibious assaults utilizing air power. Late in 1944, his forces invaded Leyte and Mindoro in the Philippines, fulfilling his earlier vow. In December, MacArthur was promoted to General of the Army. A month later, MacArthur's 6th Army invaded Luzon. In April 1945, he was made commanding general of US Army forces in the Pacific and received the Japanese surrender in September. After the war, MacArthur oversaw the Allied occupation of Japan. In the summer of 1950, MacArthur was appointed commander-in-chief of the US and United Nations forces in Korea. He handily defeated the North Korean forces but suffered a disaster when caught unawares by Communist Chinese forces at the Yalu River in November 1950. While MacArthur managed to retrieve the position, he quarrelled with President Truman over the strategic aims of the war and was removed from his command in 1951. *See also* GUADALCANAL; KOREAN WAR; LEYTE GULF; NIMITZ; UNITED STATES.

A. CORVISIER
KEITH NEILSON

FURTHER READING
James D. Clayton, *The Years of MacArthur* (2 vols, Boston, 1970–5); John Gunther, *The Riddle of MacArthur* (New York, 1951).

Machiavelli, Niccolò (1469–1527) The significance of Machiavelli's military writings has been the subject of some debate. They were undoubtedly extensive; besides the *Art of War* and his proposals for the organization of the Florentine militia, commentaries on military affairs are also found in the *Discourses on Livy*, The Prince and the *History of Florence*. If they share a common theme it is Machiavelli's belief that political and military institutions were interdependent. Thus the collapse of the Italian states in the face of the foreign invasions after 1494 was the result of a degeneracy both political and military; the corruption of the *condottieri* mirrored that of the princes. However, Machiavelli's solutions were dictated by his dogmatic classicism. Since Rome had been the greatest of all states, serious military reform could only take the form of reviving Roman military organization, particularly the citizen militia of the Republic. This intellectual rigidity led him to dismiss almost entirely the tactical effects of firearms and artillery.

The only contemporary armies to win his praise were those that appeared to him to employ Roman tactics: the German, Swiss or Spanish infantry. In the case of the Spaniards he completely ignored their use of firearms and field entrenchments in the campaigns of Gonsalvo de Córdoba or at the Battle of Ravenna (1512). Similarly, he scorned the contemporary interest in the fortification of cities because this had not been Roman practice. Machiavelli's own influence on the organization of the Florentine militia during the restoration of the republic between 1506 and 1512 is still unclear, but the failure of the militia in the face of the Spanish army in 1512 did not cause him to revise his opinions. Machiavelli's tactical theories (whatever the value of his wider comments on the conduct of war) were therefore obsolete in his own lifetime. Nevertheless his posthumous reputation helped to shape the great debate between the 'ancients' and the 'moderns' which dominated military literature for the remainder of the century. It was against the background of the rigid theoretical position adopted by Machiavelli and other advocates of the 'ancients' that the 'experimental' military authors of the latter part of the century, Sir Roger Williams for example, advanced the case for revising infantry tactics around the use of firearms. *See also* CÓRDOBA; MERCENARIES; MILITIAS; RAVENNA; WILLIAMS.

SIMON ADAMS

FURTHER READING
C. Oman, *A History of the Art of War in the Sixteenth Century* (London, 1937), pp. 89–97; S. Angelo, *Machiavelli: a dissection* (London, 1969), pp. 129–57; J. R. Hale, 'To fortify or not to fortify? Machiavelli's contribution to the Renaissance debate', and 'War and public opinion in Renaissance Italy', in *Renaissance War Studies* (London, 1983), pp. 189–209, 359–87.

Magdeburg, Sack of (20 May 1631) The Protestant city and bishopric of Magdeburg revolted against Imperial rule in 1630 and allied with Sweden. A small Imperial force laid siege to the town but Gustavus Adolphus of Sweden, whose base area lay to the north in Pomerania, felt that the city was capable of prolonged resistance provided that the main Imperial army under Count Tilly did not intervene and assist the besiegers. In order to support Magdeburg, Gustavus would have been obliged to violate the neutrality of the Electors of Brandenburg and Saxony at a time when he required allies in Germany and could not afford to alienate powerful Protestant princes. Despite a series of manoeuvres designed to draw Tilly away from Magdeburg, the Imperial general joined the besieging force in March 1631 and captured the city by storm on 20 May. The city was looted and burned and out of 20,000 inhabitants only 5,000 survived the massacre. The severity of Tilly's treatment of Magdeburg resulted from the famine and privations which his men had suffered in the trenches and was also in revenge for the Swedish sack of Küstrin and Frankfurt-on-Oder. Egregious, even by the standards of the Thirty Years' War, the Sack of Magdeburg produced a widespread revulsion which did much to persuade wavering Protestant states to ally with Sweden. After the Peace of Westphalia in 1648, the memory of the fate of Magdeburg aided the movement towards a consolidation of the rules governing the honourable surrender of besieged towns and fortresses. *See also* DEPREDATIONS; ETHOS; GUSTAVUS II ADOLPHUS; LAWS OF WAR; SIEGES; SWEDEN; TILLY.

A. CORVISIER
JOHN CHILDS

FURTHER READING
C. V. Wedgwood, *The Thirty Years' War* (London, 1938); Georges Livet, *La Guerre de Trente ans* (Paris, 1963); Herbert Langer, *The Thirty Years' War* (Poole, 1980).

Maginot Line The Maginot Line is the name normally given to the system of fortifications built by France mainly in the period from 1929 to 1934. The line was named after André Maginot, the French Minister of War, although he died in 1932 before the line was completed. Portrayed in French propaganda as impregnable, the Maginot Line is often seen as a symbol of the defensive and passive mentality of the French army in the interwar period.

The First World War had been one of position, marked from the beginning by the occupation of a substantial part of France and the loss of some of her major industrial zones. In the years from 1923 to 1927, the task of elaborating a defensive plan that would protect the provinces won back from Germany and the Alpine frontier, all without incurring the heavy casualties that the French commitment to the offensive had caused in the First World War, fell to the Commission for the Defence of Frontiers. Its plan was put into operation by the Commission for the Organization of the Fortified Regions (*Commission d'Organisation des Régions fortifiées,* or CORF) in the period from 1928 to 1935 (or 1940 in the case of the south-east).

The strategic conception behind the Maginot Line was to create a complex set of fortifications in the Metz-Thionville and Basses-Vosges regions, together with defensive sectors that would close off the points at which it was possible to cross the Alps. An extension of the defensive works was also begun at Maubeuge. Gaps between the major fortifications were to be covered by field fortifications and planned inundations, areas which were to be flooded before the system came under assault in order to channel attackers into prescribed fields of fire. After 1935, the gaps were filled by casemates built in extended order without any overall plan. The aim of the Maginot Line was to create a prepared battlefield complete with anti-tank systems, outpost screens and main defensive positions that could provide artillery cover. In the 'new fronts' built after 1935, artillery cover was no longer offered.

The Maginot Line was built using reinforced concrete and armour plate. It featured gun turrets which could be retracted underground and observation and light-arms turrets. The casemate guns fired through funnel-shaped embrasures, which afforded maximum protection. In the large fortified complexes, all facilities – barracks,

Artillery turrets on the Maginot Line. On the assumption that the next war would be similar to the last, the interwar period (1919–39) witnessed an emphasis upon linear fortifications: the Belgian defences along the Albert Canal, the Czech defences in the Sudetenland, the German *Westwall*, and the Finnish Mannerheim Line across the Karelian Isthmus. This concept of the 'prepared battlefield' has perhaps been taken to its logical conclusion in modern Switzerland, where the design of all buildings and developments has to include prescribed military features.
(Topham)

power plants, magazines, etc. – of the fortifications were linked by tunnels built 75–100 feet underground. In the casemates, the latrines were on the lower level. An internal railway network and lifts for goods made for the easy and protected transportation of munitions and men. Special quick-firing artillery, together with a pre-calculated range-finding system, made it theoretically possible to destroy any target. This was aided by the fact that the individual forts had interlocking fields of fire. Each sector was also equipped with concrete shelters for the skirmishers sent out from the main fortifications, an underground cable signals network, a narrow-gauge railway system and heavy artillery on rails for distant defence.

Under fire, the fortifications in the Alps held up well, as did those of the 'old fronts' in the north-east, even when there were no skirmishers to support them. On the other hand, the small forts at La Ferté proved inadequate as early as 19 May 1940. In June, the major complex around Maubeuge also was unable to defend itself effectively. On the Rhine, the individual casemates, unsupported by major fortifications, fell. The 'jerry-built' casemates constructed either just before the war or during the 'phoney' war put up very little resistance. The enormous cost of the Maginot Line, in the order of 5 milliard francs for the CORF fortifications and between 3 and 4 milliard francs for those built later, was not justified by its results.

The Maginot Line had both its imitators and its competitors. The new Belgian fortifications consisted of concentrated defensive positions whose above-ground aspects were undefended, but which had entrances to the underground sections near the line of fire. The Czech fortifications, begun in 1936 but still unfinished in 1938, were based on improved versions of the Maginot Line.

The German fortifications (*Westwall*) on the French border (the so-called Siegfried Line) were fortifications in depth, inspired by those built on the Aisne in 1916–17. Beginning with anti-tank obstacles ('dragon's teeth'), the Siegfried Line consisted of a large number of combat shelters several miles in depth. These shelters, often unarmoured, were for the use of troops in the field. After playing a deterrent role in 1939–40, the Siegfried Line played a significant and active role in 1944–5. The German occupation of the pre-1914 French forts at Metz for example, held up General Patton's army for a month. The German fortifications along the Channel coast known as the Atlantic Wall were essentially linear defences without armoured gun positions. *See also* COASTAL DEFENCE; FORTIFICATION; FORTIFICATION, FIELD.

J.-M. GOENAGA

FURTHER READING
J.-Y. Mary, *La Ligne Maginot* (Metz, 1980); Judith M. Hughes, *To the Maginot Line: the politics of French military preparation in the 1920s* (Cambridge, Mass., 1971); Robert Young, *In Command of France: French foreign policy and military planning, 1933–40* (Cambridge, Mass., 1978).

Mahan, Alfred Thayer (1840–1914) Mahan entered the US navy in 1856, and during a creditable career, wrote *The Gulf and Inland Waters* as part of a naval history of the US Civil War. This led to his joining the staff of the newly founded Naval War College in 1885 with the object of producing a book as the basis of advanced study. This book was published in 1890, after which, by his extraordinarily high output, Mahan came to have immense influence in his own lifetime, extending far beyond the United States. His chief works are *The Influence of Sea Power upon History 1660–1783* (1890), *The Influence of Sea Power upon the French Revolution and Empire, 1793–1812* (1892) and his treatise *Naval Strategy* (1911). He is regarded as the first great theorist of war at sea. He sought first of all to determine the origins of maritime power (geographical position, economic and demographic conditions or mentalities), while at the same time advocating winning control of the seas by battle, a concept which entailed the condemnation of other policies regarded as merely secondary, such as commerce-raiding or the strategy of 'keeping the fleet in being'.

In spite of some lacunae, such as his not according sufficient importance to combined operations, and the confusion caused in the minds of certain military thinkers by the First World War, which was marked by the absence of a decisive battle, Mahan's thinking was generally confirmed by the 1939–45 conflict, and still dominates the whole of the literature devoted to maritime strategy and the role of the sea in military conflict. *See also* CASTEX; CORBETT; NAVAL WARFARE; NAVIES; STRATEGY.

P. MASSON

FURTHER READING
William E. Livezey, *Mahan on Sea Power* (Norman, Okl., 1947, repr. 1980); William D. Puleston, *The Life and Work of Alfred Thayer Mahan, U.S.N.* (New Haven, CT, 1939); Robert Seager and Doris Maguire, *The Letters and Papers of Alfred Thayer Mahan* (Annapolis, 1977).

Maintenance of order *See* CIVIL CONTRIBUTION OF ARMIES; CIVIL POWER, SUPPORT OF

Malazgirt, Battle of *See* MANZIKERT

Malplaquet, Battle of (11 September 1709) After the defeats of Blenheim (1704), Turin and Ramillies (1706), and Oudenarde (1708) had demonstrated the essential inferiority of the French commanders in the face of the Allied generals Marlborough and Eugene of Savoy, Villars was authorized by Louis XIV to seek battle to prevent the capture of Mons which was invested on 6 September. His movements covered by the thick woods to the south of Mons, on 7 September he feinted towards Boussu to the west of Mons before marching to the east and driving off a body of Allied cavalry. He then established his army on a well-entrenched front some three miles to the south-east of Mons in a gap in the woods just to the north of the small village of Malplaquet. The position, said Villars, was 'narrow enough to give the enemy a formidable task in forcing it but sufficiently well protected by woods on the flanks to prevent our being overlapped on the flank by superior numbers'. Marlborough and Eugene, who commanded 110,000 men against the 80,000 of Villars, repeated the dispositions which had brought them success at Blenheim and Ramillies. At daybreak on 11 September, despite rumours that on the previous day they had been thinking of an armistice, the Allies attacked.

The French had fortified the woods on either side of the 'Gap of Aulnois' which itself was blocked with entrenchments, redoubts and nearly eighty cannon. Marlborough and Eugene initiated the action without having properly reconnoitred the enemy positions. Instead of attempting to manoeuvre Villars from his strong position by wide flanking movements towards his rear, Marlborough decided to drive through the woods to assault the French flanks in an effort to oblige his opponent to denude his heavily defended centre. The broken terrain of the battlefield meant that the action dissolved into a series of infantry combats across the front which were difficult to co-ordinate. In the centre, repeated assaults by the Dutch infantry under the Prince of Orange (1687–1711) resulted in horrendous casualties which did much to wreck both the quality and the morale of the Dutch army. Under increasing pressure, Villars was slowly forced to shift troops from his centre to reinforce his threatened left wing. At this point, the French commander was badly wounded in the knee and command passed to the Duc de Boufflers (1644–1711). After the occupation of the redoubts in the French centre, the Allied cavalry advanced onto the plain south of the original French lines. Gradually increasing Allied weight on the French flanks forced them to break off the action and retreat. This obliged Boufflers to draw back the French centre after a cavalry action which had lasted for nearly two hours. The Allies also left the field of battle and returned to the investment of Mons.

Malplaquet was the most bloody battle of the age: the French lost 4,500 killed and 8,000 wounded, while the Allies had 6,500 killed and 14,000 wounded. This indecisive battle, although undistinguished from the tactical point of view, blocked the progress of the Allies towards France. After Malplaquet they had to content themselves with conducting siege operations against the fortresses comprising Vauban's 'iron frontier'. *See also* BLENHEIM; DENAIN; EUGENE OF SAVOY; MARLBOROUGH; RAMILLIES; VAUBAN; VILLARS.

A. CORVISIER
JOHN CHILDS

FURTHER READING
David Chandler, *Marlborough as Military Commander* (London, 1973), pp. 240–72; Maurice Sautai, *La bataille de Malplaquet, 1709* (Paris, 1904).

Malta, Siege of (May–September 1565) The destruction of the Spanish–Italian galley fleet off Djerba (Tunisia) in May 1560 allowed the Ottomans to attack at will in the central Mediterranean. Early in 1565 Süleyman I decided to capture Malta, home of the Knights of St John since the surrender of Rhodes in 1523, partly for strategic reasons, partly in response to recent attacks by ships belonging to the Order. In the spring a fleet of 200 galleys carrying some 36,000 fighting men assembled off the Greek coast, and on 18–20 May landed its army on Malta. To defend their main strongholds in the Grand Harbour the Knights could muster only about 2,500 professionals (including some recently arrived Spanish reinforcements) supported by 5,000 to 6,000 Maltese. The Ottomans were worried that their ships might be surprised at anchor (as had happened to the Spaniards at Djerba) by the fleet commanded by the viceroy of Sicily, Don García de Toledo, and in order to bring their fleet into the Grand Harbour concentrated their initial efforts on the isolated Fort St Elmo, which guarded its entrance. St Elmo resisted until 23 June, costing the Ottomans many lives and much precious ammunition. The siege of the main strongholds (the Birgu and the Sanglea) did not begin until 3 July, by which time further Christian reinforcements had reached Malta from Sicily. This siege lasted until 7 September, when news was received that García de Toledo's galleys were approaching. Worn out by several failed assaults and suffering from food shortages, the Ottoman commanders decided to evacuate their army, and by 11 September they had slipped away safely before the smaller Spanish fleet could arrive. The siege and the defence were conducted with the bitterness characteristic of warfare between Christians and Muslims, but for all their numerical superiority the Ottoman commanders faced a complex technical challenge in attempting so ambitious a siege so far from ntheir bases. The delay caused by the resistance of St Elmo has been generally considered the key to their defeat and this, as well as the failure of the main siege, has been attributed to their relative weakness in artillery. At the time much criticism was directed at García de Toledo for failing to intervene earlier but, in recent scholarship, his decision to employ his weaker fleet as a threat rather than risk an early defeat has received more credit. *See also* LEPANTO; NAVAL WARFARE; NAVIES; OTTOMAN TURKS; SIEGES.

SIMON ADAMS

FURTHER READING
R. C. Anderson, *Naval Wars in the Levant, 1559–1853* (Liverpool, 1953); E. Bradford, *The Great Siege* (London, 1961); F. Braudel, *La Méditerranée et le monde méditerranéen à l'époque de Philippe II* (2nd edn, Paris, 1966), ii, 318–29; J. F. Guilmartin, *Gunpowder and Galleys* (Cambridge, 1974), pp. 176–93.

Mannerheim, Carl Gustaf Emil, Baron von (1867–1951) Mannerheim was from a noble Swedish family which had emigrated to Finland. He joined the Russian Imperial Army in 1889 and fought in both the Russo-Japanese War and the First World War. When Finland declared herself independent in 1917, Mannerheim organized the Finnish White Guards, who, with the aid first of German and later Allied troops, defeated the Bolsheviks. Defeated in the presidential elections of 1919, Mannerheim lived an active, but quiet

(Hulton-Deutsch Collection)

civilian life until 1931. In that year he became head of the National Defence Council and was responsible for the strengthening of the defensive line (Mannerheim Line) across the Karelian Isthmus. During the Winter War with the Soviet Union (1939–40), Mannerheim conducted a defensive war in Karelia and held the enemy in check for three months. In 1941, Finland resumed the struggle against the Soviet Union (the Continuation War), but was unable to progress much beyond her 1918 borders. Mannerheim was appointed president to negotiate an armistice with the Soviet Union in 1944, and remained in that office until retiring due to ill health in 1946. *See also* FINLAND, SINCE 1809; RUSSO-FINNISH WAR.

A. CORVISIER
KEITH NEILSON

FURTHER READING
The Memoirs of Marshal Mannerheim (London, 1954); J. E. O. Screen, *Mannerheim: the years of preparation* (London, 1970).

Manoeuvre and manoeuvres A military unit is said to manoeuvre when it chooses or changes its formation or direction of movement. This can be determined by the terrain, the nature of the enemy and his strength or dispositions. The term is applied both to movements on the battlefield and to large-scale peacetime rehearsals and practices. Manoeuvre by a small unit is confined to a combination of 'fire and movement' with the aim of bringing it to grips with the enemy; one section pins down the opponent by fire and the assault section attacks.

The object of manoeuvre is to focus the offensive capabilities of troops in such a way that the task assigned is successfully accomplished. This involves deciding what role the various arms should play along a defensive front or on the axis of an offensive push. A manoeuvre must be centred on a careful plan which correctly positions the troops, delivers them, via appropriate movements, to the right place at the right time, and puts the enemy at a disadvantage.

Manoeuvre is seen in its most elementary form in the attack which is made on an enemy from two directions simultaneously, perhaps frontally and round a flank. From the sixteenth to the early eighteenth century, armies drew up for battle with their infantry in the centre, cavalry on each wing and artillery in front. Available troops were spaced evenly along the selected line. A development which appeared in the mid-eighteenth century was the 'staggered' or 'oblique' system employed by Frederick II of Brandenburg-Prussia, although it had already been used by Epaminondas in the fourth century BC. William III also adopted an oblique order at the Battle of Steenkirk in 1692. The system increased the strength of one wing at the expense of the rest of the battle line in order to achieve a breakthrough. Napoleon made this local concentration of force into a normal battle tactic. At Wagram in 1809, Napoleon realized a decisive concentration of force by massed artillery fire and by the retention of a powerful cavalry reserve for exploitation of the critical point of the battle. Spreading troops thinly and evenly over a long front can prove a positive assistance to an enemy's offensive manoeuvres. It explains why Villars was victorious at Denain in 1712 and why the German army broke through at Sedan in 1940. If this type of defensive deployment is used then it must be supported by powerful mobile reserves ready to seal off any breach and to counter-attack with turning movements. General Sharon and the Israeli army conducted such an operation after the Egyptians had crossed the Suez Canal in 1973. The essence of manoeuvre, both offensive and defensive, is to achieve a superiority of force at the decisive tactical or strategic point.

The forms of manoeuvre are conditioned by an army's own resources, the situation and state of the enemy – numbers, armament, morale – and the terrain, which needs to be carefully investigated. It is these factors which determine a commander's decision to employ either infantry or mechanized forces, or a combination, supported by artillery and/or aircraft. An able use of ground adds considerably to the potential of a defensive position – marshes are impassable to mechanized troops, escarpments make infantry advance difficult and positions on reverse slopes are protected from observed artillery fire. Ground can be made still more difficult for an enemy by the construction of artificial obstacles – mantraps, ditches, abatis, redoubts – which hamper the movement of the attacker but facilitate defensive counter-attack. An obstacle is doubly effective if it is covered by fire.

During peacetime, most armies throughout history have carried out training exercises in preparation for war – the Hittites even included day and night route marches. The first large-scale, modern manoeuvres which justify the title took place in France at the Pont de l'Arche camp in 1480 when Louis XI mustered the Picardy bands and instructed them in the Swiss exercise of the pike. Under Louis XIV, the practice developed. During the summer months, considerable forces of horse and infantry were assembled to carry out manoeuvres and mock battles together with simulated attacks on entrenched camps and fortified towns. These exercises lasted for several weeks. The training camps were suspended during the Regency but were reinstated in 1727 on the initiative of the Comte de Belle-Isle. He had noticed that two-thirds of the army had no experience of warfare and thought that 'it was essential to show units a representation of it before they experienced it in practice'. Every effort was made to produce as close a resemblance as possible to wartime situations. These training camps were also used as proving grounds for new tactical systems. After some of these had been tried out at the camps of 1753, significant changes were made in the infantry and cavalry instruction manuals. The camp at Vaussieux in 1778 provided the opportunity to compare the efficacy of the thin line with that of the deep column.

The British army started peacetime training camps and manoeuvres under Charles II and James II (1660–88) but these lapsed during the eighteenth century for reasons of economy. Frederick the Great of Prussia instituted manoeuvres for his army in 1743 and after the Seven Years' War (1756–63) they were conducted every spring and autumn. In 1911, the United States formed the 'Maneuver Division' to serve as a demonstration school for the main army.

Manoeuvres taught troops to change direction and formation on all types of terrain. After the mid-nineteenth century, when conscription became the norm in many European armies, reservists returned to the colours annually for three weeks of manoeuvres and exercises, usually in the autumn, after the harvest. Manoeuvres traditionally concluded with a review and a march past. Not only were manoeuvres schools of command for all officers from sergeants to generals but they provided the opportunity to test communications, transport, supply and mobilization procedures. Most manoeuvres consisted of mock battles with one side attacking and the other defending; umpires adjudged casualties and the success of operations. Officers also took part in manoeuvres without troops, the so-called 'staff rides', in which map exercises were supplemented by reconnaissances of the actual ground.

Manoeuvres continue to be part of the military system. However, the scale of modern forces and the range of modern weapons demand manoeuvres over huge areas of land. Manoeuvres combining all arms are therefore rare and usually manoeuvres test a specific aspect of tactics or logistics. Manoeuvres have been partially replaced by exercises without troops which supplement officers' training by facing them with a variety of imaginary tactical situations and give practice in combined operations. *See also* PROPERTY OWNED BY THE MILITARY; TACTICAL ORGANIZATION; TACTICS; TRAINING.

G. BODINIER
JOHN CHILDS

FURTHER READING
J. A. Houlding, *Fit for Service: the training of the British army, 1715–1795* (Oxford, 1981); R. S. Quimby, *The Background of Napoleonic Warfare* (New York, 1957, repr. 1973); Christopher Duffy, *The Army of Frederick the Great* (London, 1974).

Manpower *See* MOBILIZATION; NAVAL PERSONNEL; NUMERICAL STRENGTH; RECRUITMENT

Manstein, Erich von Lewinski von (1887–1973) Manstein, the son of an artillery officer, joined the German army in 1906. During the First World War he held staff positions, but was wounded in 1914. After the war, he served in a number of positions, rising by 1935 to Chief of the Operations Branch of the General Staff. A year later he became Deputy Chief of Staff, but in early 1938 he was given a minor post when Hitler purged the army of traditional elements. Despite this, Manstein was active in the occupation of the Sudetenland. In the Polish campaign of September–October 1939, Manstein served as von Rundstedt's Chief of Staff, a post he also held during the invasion of France. It was Manstein who suggested to Rundstedt that Army Group A attack through the Ardennes

forest, a move that ensured the German victory. During the invasion of the Soviet Union (*Operation Barbarossa*), Manstein initially commanded a Panzer Corps in Army Group North's drive on Leningrad. In September of 1941 he was transferred to the south and commanded the 11th Army in its attack on the Crimea. He was promoted to Field Marshal in 1942. Manstein was briefly transferred to the Siege of Leningrad, but in November 1942 was returned to the south to assist the German forces at Stalingrad. Despite his efforts to free von Paulus's 6th Army, it remained invested in the city but Manstein did manage to extricate the German units from the Caucasus. Manstein led a successful counter-attack against the Soviets at Kharkov in the spring of 1943, and commanded part of the German forces at Kursk in July. The stalemate at Kursk and the German retreats in the autumn of 1943 led Hitler to dismiss Manstein at the end of March 1944. In 1949, Manstein was sentenced for war crimes to eighteen years in prison, of which he served four. *See also* FRANCE, BATTLE OF; GERMANY; KURSK SALIENT; RUNDSTEDT.

B. KROENER
KEITH NEILSON

FURTHER READING
E. von Manstein, *Lost Victories* (Chicago, 1958); B. H. Liddell Hart, *The Other Side of the Hill* (London, 1948); Rüdiger von Manstein and Theodor Fuchs, *Manstein. Soldat im 20. Jahrhundert* (Munich, 1981).

Mantinea, Battle of (362 BC) This was the battle in which Epaminondas and the Theban army, attempting to secure dominance of the Peloponnese, met a force composed of Spartans, Peloponnesian allies, and Athenians which was protecting Mantinea. In order to repeat the manoeuvre he had used at Leuctra, Epaminondas first marched north-west towards the neighbouring hills to the right of his opponents and deceived them into thinking that he was preparing to make camp. He then approached the enemy line obliquely, having specially strengthened the left wing, which was under his personal command. His intention was to make a decisive breakthrough with his reinforced left wing, supported by cavalry. Epaminondas prevented his right wing from being outflanked by stationing a body of horse and light infantry ahead of his battle line. The Theban left wing broke through the Spartans and the Mantineans opposite but Epaminondas was killed and his army failed to exploit its initial success. The death of Epaminondas precipitated the decline of Theban hegemony. *See also* EPAMINONDAS; GREECE, ANCIENT; LEUCTRA; SPARTA.

B. CAMPBELL

FURTHER READING
J. Buckler, *The Theban Hegemony, 371–362 BC* (Cambridge, Mass., 1980); J. K. Anderson, *Military Theory and Practice in the Age of Xenophon* (Berkeley, 1970).

Manzikert, Battle of (19 August 1071)   In 1055, the Seljuk sultan Tughril Beg (1055–63) took the Abbasid capital of Baghdad. The Seljuk Turks then continued their expansion under Alp Arslan into the Levant and the eastern provinces of the Byzantine Empire in Asia Minor. After capturing the Armenian capital, Ani, in 1064, the Seljuks seized the majority of Armenia, which had only been held by a weak Byzantine garrison. The Byzantine emperor, Romanus IV Diogenes (1067–71), personally led the counter-offensive but his indisciplined army was mainly composed of mercenaries (Pechenegs, Oguz, Normans and Franks), certain elements of which deserted to the enemy. The Byzantines had learned how to deal with the lightly armed mounted bowmen who constituted the majority of the Seljuk army, having beaten Alp Arslan on two previous occasions; unmounted bowmen were always positioned close to the heavy cavalry, the army always covered its flanks and rear, and it always fought concentrated. Before Manzikert, Romanus had dispatched all his infantry to conduct a siege. The deciding battle took place near the modern Turkish town of Malazgirt, in mountainous country north of Lake Van Gölü.

Romanus advanced his army of heavy cavalry in a single line, supported by a strong rearguard. The Turks withdrew steadily but their mounted archers constantly harried the Byzantine flanks. Although human casualties were probably few, many Byzantine cavalrymen lost their mounts. The advance continued until dusk when Romanus ordered his army to return to camp. However, the flanks did not understand the signals and the army began to collapse in confusion. This was turned into chaos when Romanus, now separated from his rearguard and wings, continued to advance with his centre as the rearguard began to retreat towards the camp. The Turks attacked and defeated the separated and disorganized sections of the Byzantine army in detail. Virtually all of Romanus's army was killed or captured, with the exception of the rearguard. Ten years of war and civil war ensued in which the Seljuk Turks occupied virtually all of Asia Minor to create an empire which stretched from the Euphrates to the Sea of Marmora. Asia Minor became the Seljuk sultanate of Anatolia with its capital at Nicaea. Besides radically altering the balance of political, religious and human geography in Asia Minor and the eastern Mediterranean (the Seljuks captured Jerusalem at about the same time), Manzikert also led to the loss of Byzantium's main recruiting grounds, the collapse of its military institutions and their replacement by an increasing reliance upon mercenaries. *See also* BYZANTIUM; CAVALRY; INFANTRY; IRAN; MIDDLE EAST; OTTOMAN TURKS; TACTICAL ORGANIZATION.

R. MANTRAN
JOHN CHILDS

FURTHER READING
Alfred Friendly, *The Dreadful Day: the Battle of Manzikert, 1071* (London, 1981); J. C. Cheynet, 'Manzikert: une désastre militaire?', *Byzantium*, 1 (1980); M. Angold, *The Byzantine Empire, 1025–1204* (London, 1984).

Mao Tse-Tung (1893–1976) Mao was born into a peasant family in Hunan Province. He became a Marxist and played a central role in the civil wars between 1927 and 1949 which ended in the Communist Revolution in China. In 1931, with Russian support, he established a soviet republic in the Chinese interior and emerged, four years later, as leader of the Chinese Communist Party. Five major 'annihilation campaigns' by the Nationalist Kuomintang (KMT) between 1930 and 1934 finally succeeded in encircling the Communists in Kiangsi Province. However, in October 1934 Mao broke out with 120,000 followers and began the 'Long March' which ended one year later at Yenan in Shensi Province. Only 20,000 survived. When the Japanese attacked north China in 1937, the KMT under Chiang Kai-Shek theoretically united with Mao's Communists to resist the invader but they continued to fight each other as well. After the surrender of Japan, Mao's People's Liberation Army, with its greater manpower and secure bases, was able to defeat Chiang and the KMT, proclaiming the People's Republic of China in 1949.

Mao was a military theorist as well as a practitioner and summarized his ideas and experiences in *Strategic Problems of China's Revolutionary War*. He achieved a synthesis of traditional Chinese military methods with those of revolutionary warfare. Like Sun-Tzu and his successors, Mao believed that it was essential to impose one's will on the enemy by seizing the intitiative and forcing him to disperse his forces. Secrecy and deception were essential elements: 'The whole art of warfare is based upon deception.' Contrary to the theories of Russian and Western Marxist–Leninists, who believed that the urban working class was the source of revolution, Mao demonstrated that revolutionary warfare could be pursued by a rural peasantry.

The main aim of the 'struggle' was for the 'hearts and minds' of the masses, achievable by various forms of ideological conversion based on agrarian revolution. To achieve this end, Mao formulated three stages of 'protracted warfare'. The primary object of the first, guerilla warfare, was to impose a type of warfare upon the enemy which rendered ineffective his technical superiority. 'War among the masses', a new version of guerilla warfare, was most suitable for a people's war. The key element in guerilla warfare was flexibility – the ability of forces to disperse and disappear into the population yet be able to concentrate to hit specific targets or installations. Mao identified the second stage of warfare as one of equilibrium. As increasing numbers of enemy troops became engaged, the guerilla attacks behind enemy lines intensified. The third stage, 'mobile warfare', only occurred when the enemy had been sufficiently worn down for regular troops to launch an offensive in the field. Mao applied these ideas and principles to his campaigns against the KMT and the Japanese. His models inspired the theorists of anti-colonial warfare, the Vietnamese Ho Chi Minh and General Vo Giap being notably successful disciples. *See also* CHINA; GIAP; GUERILLA WARFARE; POPULAR WARFARE; SUN-TZU; VIETNAM.

DAVID WESTON
A. CORVISIER

FURTHER READING
J. R. Adelman, *Revolutionary Armies: the historical development of the Soviet and Chinese People's Liberation Armies* (Westport, Conn., 1980); S. B. Griffith, *The People's Liberation Army* (London, 1968); *Mao-Tse-tung on Guerilla Warfare*, ed. S. B. Griffith (New York, 1978); Mao Tse-tung, *On Guerilla Warfare*, tr. Anne Freemantle (New York, 1971).

Marathon, Battle of (490 BC) This was a battle at which the Athenians defeated the Persians during the first Persian invasion of Greece. A seaborne Persian expeditionary force landed in the Bay of Marathon in eastern Attica. About 9,000 Athenians, assisted by a contingent of about 600 from the small city of Plataea, marched out to meet them led by Callimachus the commander-in-chief, although one of the generals, Miltiades, is credited with the major role in the formulation of tactics. On the grounds that they had religious duties to fulfil, the Spartans delayed coming to their aid, in spite of an urgent appeal carried by the Athenian messenger Philippides or Pheidippides, who ran the 140 miles in 36 hours. After a delay of several days, the Athenians took advantage of the fact that the Persians were engaged in re-embarking part of their troops in order to make a direct assault upon Athens, and launched a surprise attack, closing at the double. This tactic disconcerted the enemy and gave them no opportunity to launch the usual barrage of fire from their bowmen, nor perhaps to unleash a cavalry attack, though it is not clear whether the Persian cavalry was still on land when the battle began. Miltiades' tactics were to extend his centre to cover the Persian line, while strengthening both wings. As the Persian troops forced back the Athenian centre, they were enveloped by the wings, which had routed the soldiers opposed to them. The Persians were driven back to the ships, leaving 6,400 dead; the Athenian dead numbered 192, including the commander-in-chief. After embarkation the Persian fleet sailed directly to Athens in the hope of finding the city unprotected. But the Athenian hoplites by forced marches got back in time, and the Persians sailed away. Although Marathon was only one engagement in the continuing Persian efforts to conquer Greece, it did mark the first setback to the expansion of the formidable Persian empire, and also greatly enhanced the prestige of Athens and the confidence of the people in the democracy. *See also* GREECE, ANCIENT; IRAN; PLATAEA; SALAMIS; THERMOPYLAE.

R. LONIS
B. CAMPBELL

FURTHER READING
N. G. L. Hammond, 'The campaign and battle of Marathon', *Journal of Historical Studies*, lxxxviii (1968), pp. 13–57; Y. Garlan, *War in the Ancient World: a Social History* (London, 1975); A. R. Burn, *Persia and the Greeks: the defence of the West, c.546–478 BC* (London, 1984), pp. 236–57.

Marches *See* STAGING POSTS

Maréchaussée *See* GENDARMERIE

Marengo, Battle of (14 June 1800) The Marengo campaign was, at the time, the most dramatic illustration yet of Napoleon's impact on the conduct of war – a plan of vast geographical sweep, an emphasis on extraordinarily rapid manoeuvre, and a disregard of the traditional restraints (in particular, terrain and fortifications) on the achievement of a quick victory. Although his success was used as evidence of Napoleon's genius, in reality it owed as much to good luck as to good judgement.

The Austrians had two armies, one on the upper Rhine watching Moreau, and the other, Melas's, confronting Masséna at Genoa. Napoleon raised a fresh army at Dijon and, calling on Moreau to join him, swept through the Alps. By occupying Milan, he cut the Austrians' communications to the north. But on 4 June Genoa fell to the Austrians and Napoleon now feared that, with access to the sea, they would not fight to regain their communications. Failing to realize that the Austrians were concentrating against his divided army, Napoleon was surprised by forces of twice his strength at Marengo on 14 June 1800. By the afternoon Napoleon was in retreat. But the Austrian pursuit was slow, Napoleon had time to regroup and – most importantly – Desaix's corps arrived on the battlefield in time. The Austrians were routed. *See also* NAPOLEON; RIVOLI.

HEW STRACHAN

FURTHER READING
David Chandler, *The Campaigns of Napoleon* (London, 1967); G. A. Furse, *1800: Marengo and Hohenlinden* (London, 1903).

Marignano (Lombardy), Battle of (13–14 September 1515) The victory of Marignano was the fruit of the first Italian campaign of Francis I, King of France, and inspired his life-long obsession with the

Duchy of Milan. In 1512–14 the French had been driven out of Italy by an alliance organized by the Papacy and an army largely supplied by the Swiss, under whose protection Maximilian Sforza had been restored to the Duchy of Milan. The new French king was determined to regain Milan and, having formed an alliance with Venice, made a rapid crossing of the Alps in August 1515. By early September he had established an entrenched camp near Milan with about 35,000 men (23,000 of them German *Landsknechte*) and a large artillery train to await his Venetian allies. Despite repeated French diplomatic efforts to win them over, the Swiss decided in an emotional mass meeting of their army in Milan on 13 September to remain loyal to the Sforza. Immediately afterwards they assembled in three large squares of 7,000–8,000 pikemen each and assaulted the French camp. The fighting halted at midnight and was resumed at dawn on the 14th, but by mid-morning rumours that the Venetians were approaching caused the Swiss to withdraw. Although none of the Swiss attacks on the French camp succeeded, they were only repulsed by very bloody fighting in which the French *gendarmerie* and artillery played a leading part. The casualties on both sides were considered horrific, though estimates vary from 5,000–6,000 to 16,000 each. Marignano destroyed the Swiss reputation for invincibility and they never again attempted to act as the arbiters of Italy. Francis, who considered that the importance of the victory lay as much in the restoring of French military pre-eminence as in the regaining of Milan, was none the less impressed by Swiss tenacity and ferocity and concentrated in future on winning their support. More subtle observers, however, attributed the defeat to the stupidity and arrogance of the Swiss, a verdict that the next decade was to confirm. *See also* ARTILLERY; FRANCE; INFANTRY; MERCENARIES; PAVIA; RAVENNA; SWITZERLAND.

SIMON ADAMS

FURTHER READING
Jean Jacquart, *François I*er (Paris, 1981); R. J. Knecht, *Francis I* (Cambridge, 1982); E. Hardy de Perini, *Batailles françaises* (6 vols, Paris, 1894–1908).

Marines   At all periods of history, navies have felt the need to possess troops of their own that are able to defend bases, maintain order aboard ship, provide skilled marksmen or gunners in battle, and carry out combined operations. Accordingly, in the fifth century BC, Athenian triremes had among their complement a dozen soldiers or *epibatai*, whose role was to ensure the capture of enemy ships with which they came to close quarters or to conduct combined operations along coasts, as can be seen in the course of the Peloponnesian War. This system was used on an increasing scale during the Hellenistic period and, during the Punic Wars, Roman ships contained a strong force of eighty legionaries whose task was to board the enemy.

In the Middle Ages, Byzantine, Arab and Italian galleys always held a high proportion of archers and crossbowmen (and, a little later, arquebusiers and gunners), intended for repulsing a possible attack by pirates or privateers or for taking part in a battle proper. The same is true of the complements of the improvised fleets that composed Northern navies. Alongside the true seamen there were to be found archers or crossbowmen and men at arms fully equipped for fighting in a style of battle closely approximating to engagements on land.

In the sixteenth century, owing to the development of artillery, soldiers played an increasing part in this sphere. When required, they joined in the deck work (such as putting stores aboard, manning the capstans). Aboard the *Henry Grâce à Dieu* in 1514, there were 300 sailors, 349 soldiers and some fifty gunners. During the whole of the period up to the French Revolution, the continuing shortage of seamen compelled the major fleets to have recourse to soldiers to make up crew numbers, in a proportion that might rise as high as 20–30 per cent.

Such constant calls on contingents from the army could only encourage the formation of a separate corps of naval soldiers which would be completely independent of land forces. In France, this departure encountered the strongest objections not only from the military but even from certain politicians who had little grasp of the exigencies of discipline aboard ship and the need to have at hand in peacetime forces experienced in combined operations. The first two regiments of marine infantry formed by Richelieu in 1627 and 1634 were accordingly short-lived. Colbert made a fresh attempt, but with no greater success. Louvois rapidly achieved the integration into the army of the two regiments created in 1669 (*Royal Marine* and *Amiral*). The navy sought to circumvent the difficulty by establishing a category of 'military guards' and by raising ninety independent companies of soldiers to provide vessels with fighting capacity and to maintain discipline on board.

In the middle of the eighteenth century, a new attempt was made to form a corps specifically intended for such tasks, but this too soon came to nothing. Planned as eight regiments, the corps was soon limited to a single large formation in 1774, prior to its reorganization as four regiments in 1792, and to its complete disappearance on 28 January 1794. At the close of the *ancien régime*, Bourgeois de Boyne had already conceived the idea of a military complement aboard deep-sea vessels; but the use of soldier conscripts for this purpose, under the First Empire, in no way amounted to the establishment of a real marine infantry. The creation of a marine battalion of the Guard paid lip-service to the need for a specific corps, and it too did not long survive.

The British Royal Navy was subject to the same exigencies but was more successful in dealing with them through the creation in 1664 of the Duke of York's Maritime Regiment of Foot, which led to the foundation of the Royal Marines in 1802. Wearing a red uniform, and enjoying the same ranks and scales of pay as the army, the Marines finally accounted for up to one quarter of the complements aboard the larger ships in wartime. They had three tasks: to maintain order on board, to work some of the guns and provide musketeers and boarding parties in action, and to act as landing units in the context of limited operations. This model of corps, which was adopted and developed by the Americans in 1775, remained in being into the twentieth century.

Since the French navy, during the post-Napoleonic period, found itself unable to arrange for a corps for its own use inside the army structure, it finally turned to the scheme of forming, within the fleet itself, a specialized branch – this being unconnected with the entirely different matter of the *infanterie de marine* which was assigned to colonial defence. The *décret* of 5 June 1856 accordingly established, with the setting up of a training battalion at Lorient, the special category of marine fusilier. These marine fusiliers took part, as landing units, in operations carried out under the Second Empire in China, Cochinchina and Mexico. In 1870–1, these companies fought on land (at Bazeilles), and were then grouped together under Vice-Admiral de la Roncière in Paris, where they manned six forts, two batteries and a flotilla on the Seine. At the same time – and within a quite different organizational structure – more than 30,000 sailors drawn from naval depots and crews were formed into battalions and fought in the armies of national defence, in which the *marsouins* became popular figures.

In 1871, the training battalion at Lorient was re-established and took part in colonial campaigns. In 1914, on account of the excess numbers provided by conscription of seamen, a brigade of marine fusiliers was formed and fought on the Yser under Admiral Ronarc'h. After suffering losses amounting to more than 6,500 men, the brigade was disbanded in 1915. All that was left was a battalion which was in action at Nieuport and Moulin de Laffaux in 1917.

From 1940 to 1945, various units of marine fusiliers participated in land battles. Their 1st regiment fought at Bir Hakeim, in Italy and in the Vosges, while Leclerc's 2nd Armoured Division contained a marine fusilier armoured regiment. The Kieffer commando, numbering 160 men, took part in the Normandy landings and in the clearing of the Scheldt estuary. Marine commandos also fought in Indo-China and Algeria, where a half-brigade of marine fusiliers was responsible from 1956 to 1962 for the Nemours sector.

After the Algerian War of Independence, a reorganization took place. The training establishment for marine fusiliers, which since 1945 had operated near Algiers in the Sirocco Centre, returned to Lorient. Aboard ship, the fusiliers still have responsibility for maintaining order and training in sports. They form the core of the landing forces when these go into action. On land, the marine fusilier commandos are used to stiffen guard companies looking after the security of bases. The most sizeable formation comprises the Jaubert, Trepel, de Penfentenyo, de Montfort and Hubert commandos, the last named being made up of men trained for operations in and under water.

Since the Second World War, the British Royal Marines have developed along the same lines. With numbers reaching nearly 8,000, their role as commandos has become preponderant especially as the number of large ships has been reduced. As the result of an extremely arduous training, the men in green berets are experienced in every kind of amphibious operation, and are particularly well equipped to deal with fighting in Arctic conditions. In the event of war, their assignment is to be ready to take part in the defence of NATO's northern flank. The Royal Marines showed their traditional effectiveness during the Falklands Campaign in 1982.

It is the American Marine Corps, however, which has had the most astounding development. Copied at the outset from the system in force in the British navy, this corps has seen a continuous growth in its responsibilities throughout the nineteenth and twentieth centuries, which have come to include security, a combat role, provision of landing companies, the guarding of bases, and interventions in territories outside the United States on the orders of the President of the United States and under the tactical control of the navy. In the service of the 'big stick' policy, the Marines have hence been engaged on several occasions in the Caribbean and in Central America.

In 1941, the Marine Corps had already reached a strength of nearly 20,000 men, who had undergone an intensive training and were divided into two divisions, stationed respectively on the east and west coasts. Owing to the war in the Pacific, it was to experience a spectacular expansion, rising by 1945 to six divisions and nearly 500,000 men. After the battles of attrition in Guadalcanal and the Solomon Islands, the Marines made up the spearhead of Nimitz's counter-offensive from Tarawa to Okinawa.

Directly after the war, they were to be found again in Korea, and later on in Vietnam, the Lebanon and the Caribbean. At present, the Marine Corps numbers 194,000 men, organized in three divisions supported by three air groups. It has 400 aircraft, 600 helicopters, 300 tanks and 450 amphibious craft. Two brigades, consisting of 33,000 men, in combination with the resources of the fleet, can currently be brought immediately into action. The Marine Corps enjoys an ever-wider autonomy and has tended to become the fourth branch of the US armed forces. All in all, it presents an imposing picture, as by far the largest of the thirty-six marine infantries to be found in the world, of which the smallest is probably that of Guatemala, which numbers only 200 men. *See also* COLONIAL TROOPS; COMBINED OPERATIONS; EXPEDITIONS; GUADALCANAL; INFANTRY; NAVAL PERSONNEL; NAVAL WARFARE; NAVIES.

P. MASSON

FURTHER READING
L. Edye, *The Historical Records of the Royal Marines* (2 vols, London 1893); Cyril Field, *Britain's Sea Soldiers* (2 vols, Liverpool, 1924); S. E. Morison, *History of the United States Naval Operations in World War II* (15 vols, Boston, 1947–62); W. D. Parker, *A Concise History of the United States Marine Corps, 1775–1969* (Washington DC, 1970); *Records of the United States Marine Corps*, ed. M. Johnson (Washington DC, 1970).

Marlborough, John Churchill, 1st Duke of (1650–1722) Under the patronage of James II, Marlborough entered the English army in 1667. He fought in Tangier (1668–70), at sea during the Third Anglo-Dutch War, with the French army in Flanders (1672–7) and against the Duke of Monmouth at Sedgemoor in 1685. At the Glorious Revolution he was instrumental in bringing part of the English army over to William III and, as a reward, he commanded the British corps in Flanders against the French in 1689, where he played a major role in the Battle of Walcourt. In 1690, he was commander-in-chief of the army in England and led an expedition to capture Cork and Kinsale during the Jacobite War in Ireland. Marlborough was dismissed from all his military and civilian offices in 1692 on suspicion of treachery and Jacobitism; he had allowed his avarice and greed to outrun his undoubted military and political abilities. After the death of Queen Mary in 1694, he was gradually allowed back into royal favour and was finally restored to political office in 1698. In 1701, William III appointed him to command the British forces in the Netherlands, and in 1702 Queen Anne and the Dutch commissioned Marlborough captain-general of the British army and commander-in-chief of the forces of the Grand Alliance in the War of the Spanish Succession. Commanding a polyglot army of British, Dutch and Germans, Marlborough enjoyed a string of victories against a weakened French army directed by mediocre generals: Blenheim in 1704, Ramillies in 1706, Oudenarde in 1708 and Malplaquet in 1709. His success was founded on a number of factors. In the first place, he inherited British and Dutch armies which had been trained, and had gained experience during the Nine Years' War (1688–97). Second, he combined the military leadership of the Grand Alliance with its political direction thus giving him some control over both strategy and policy. Third, his political alliance in England with Godolphin and Robert Harley gave him a secure platform and a base for patronage. Fourth, the French armed forces were in a poor condition after the long wars of Louis XIV. In the field, he was extremely skilled at deception and manoeuvre as witnessed by the forcing of the Lines of Brabant in 1705 and the piercing of the 'Ne Plus Ultra'

Lines in 1711. Marlborough also believed in the efficacy of battle, provided that the conditions were right, and his victories at Blenheim and Ramillies were among the few decisive battles of the eighteenth century. He lost his commissions on 31 December 1711 and went into exile until 1714. George I restored him as captain-general in 1714 but he suffered a severe stroke in 1716 which seriously affected his mental capacities.

Blenheim Palace, at Woodstock near Oxford, was built with funds voted by a grateful Parliament and now serves as a museum of Marlborough's career. Of especial interest are the wall tapestries which Marlborough commissioned to commemorate his victories in Flanders. *See also* BLENHEIM; DENAIN; EUGENE OF SAVOY; GREAT BRITAIN; MALPLAQUET; RAMILLIES.

JOHN CHILDS

FURTHER READING
David Chandler, *Marlborough as Military Commander* (London, 1973); I. F. Burton, *The Captain-General* (London, 1968); R. E. Scouller, *The Armies of Queen Anne* (Oxford, 1966).

Marne, Battle of the (6–12 September 1914) Despite having departed from the original concept of the Schlieffen Plan by strengthening his left wing at the expense of the right wing and then again doing so by sending further reinforcements to East Prussia after the war had actually begun, the German chief of staff, the younger Helmuth von Moltke, won the 'battle of the frontiers' in August 1914 and inflicted heavy casualties on the French armies. However, the logistic and other deficiencies of Schlieffen's plan became increasingly obvious the further the Germans advanced into Belgium and France and Moltke himself was unable to maintain contact with his field armies from his headquarters in Luxembourg. Meanwhile, Joffre was preparing a counter-attack, surreptitiously moving troops from east to west and forming two new armies (the 6th and 9th) from reservists. On 31 August von Kluck commanding the German 1st Army on the extreme right of the advance judged that the British Expeditionary Force and the French 5th Army were sufficiently weakened to allow him to encircle the latter by wheeling south-east and away from Paris, which it had originally been intended that he should outflank to the west. It would also enable contact to be maintained with von Bülow's 2nd Army whilst Kluck moved towards the Marne, which was reached on 2 September. On 4 September Joffre issued his historic order to halt the Allied retreat and ordered Maunoury's 6th Army to strike at Kluck's exposed western flank. Kluck riposted on 7 September by changing front once more but the military governor of Paris, Galliéni, quickly sent all available troops forward as reinforcements, most strikingly requisitioning the capital's taxis for the purpose. In fact, in meeting the new threat, Kluck had widened the gap that had opened between him and Bülow, whose own army was itself under attack by Foch's 9th Army. Moreover, the British were now advancing into the gap between the German armies. As the engagement became general along the whole front, Moltke's liaison officer, Lieutenant-Colonel Hentsch, who had been sent to the front with full powers, on 9 September gave Bülow the order to retreat. The Germans pulled back to the Aisne where they entrenched in positions from which they could not be dislodged, each side having suffered approximately 250,000 casualties on the Marne. On the one hand, the Allied strategic victory had been won through Moltke's indifferent generalship as compared to Joffre's composure. On the other, the ability of the French to use a railway system whose lines converged upon Paris also contrasted greatly with the enormous logistic gamble of Schlieffen's original plan. Moltke was replaced as chief of staff by von Falkenhayn on 14 September 1914. *See also* FOCH; FRANCE; GERMANY; JOFFRE; SCHLIEFFEN.

A. CORVISIER
IAN F. W. BECKETT

FURTHER READING
Correlli Barnett, *The Swordbearers* (London, 1963); Georges Blond, *The Marne* (London, 1965); H. Isselin, *The Battle of the Marne* (London, 1965).

Marriage *See* FAMILIES

Marshall, George Catlett (1880–1959) Marshall graduated from the Virginia Military Institute in 1901 and joined the army the following year. He attended the Infantry and Cavalry School and the Army Staff College. During the First World War he served as both a training and staff officer, rising to the rank of lieutenant-colonel. He helped to draw up the plans for the operation against Saint-Mihiel in September 1918. Marshall served as an aide to the commander of the American Expeditionary Force and later Chief of Staff, General Pershing, until 1924. Marshall held a number of posts, including five years as chief instructor at the Infantry School in Fort Benning, until 1938, when he was appointed first head of the War Plans Division and then Deputy Chief of Staff. In 1939, Marshall became Chief of Staff. Marshall oversaw the expansion of the US army from 60,000 men in 1939 to over one million in 1941 and then to three million in 1943. He was a consummate organizer who insisted on close co-operation and co-ordination between all branches of the army and between the American and British General Staffs. He served as an intimate adviser to President Franklin D. Roosevelt and accompanied the latter to most of the major conferences during the war. Marshall retired in November 1945 but was sent by President Truman to China on a special mission to attempt to end the civil war. In 1947, Truman appointed Marshall US Secretary of State, a position he held until January 1949. As Secretary of State, Marshall initiated the European Recovery Plan (Marshall Plan) and was instrumental in ensuring that a firm policy was taken by the West in the Berlin crisis of 1948–9. Stemming from Marshall's policy was the formation of NATO in 1949. Marshall served as US Secretary of Defense in 1950–1 and won the Nobel Peace Prize in 1953. *See also* EISENHOWER; OVERLORD; UNITED STATES.

A. CORVISIER
KEITH NEILSON

491

FURTHER READING
Forrest C. Pogue, *George C. Marshall* (3 vols, New York, 1963–73).

Marston Moor, Battle of (2 July 1644) Marston Moor was a major battle of the English Civil War (1642–6) fought a short distance to the west of the city of York. The army of King Charles I, under the command of his nephew Prince Rupert, consisted of 7,000 cavalry and 11,000 infantry, while the combined forces of the Scots and Parliament numbered 7,000 horsemen and 20,000 foot. The Parliamentarian army including the Scottish forces, had been attempting to besiege York but had withdrawn to a position near the village of Long Marston on the reported approach of Rupert's relief force from Shrewsbury. The command of the Parliamentarian army was divided between Sir Thomas Fairfax, the Earl of Leven and the Earl of Manchester. The Parliamentarian army advanced towards the Royalists but the right wing under Fairfax was charged and routed by the Royalist cavalry, exposing the right flank of the Scottish foot in the centre. On the Parliamentarian left, Oliver Cromwell and David Leslie charged with their horse and forced the Royalist right wing cavalry off the field. The situation was now thoroughly confused with both armies suffering enemy horsemen in their rear and around an exposed flank. Unluckily for the Royalists, Lord Goring, whose horsemen had shattered the Parliamentarian right, had not exploited his success but had wasted his time in plundering the Parliamentarian baggage train. In the gathering darkness, as the Parliamentarian infantry pressed against the Royalist foot in the centre, Cromwell led his cavalry around the rear of the Royalist centre and successfully attacked Goring's troopers as they filtered back onto the field. The remaining Royalist foot were now virtually surrounded. Night came to the rescue and many were able to escape, but a considerable number of the Marquis of Newcastle's 'Whitecoats' were cut down in a final stand. Marston Moor was a battle lost by Royalist mistakes rather than won by Parliamentary generalship. It sealed the fate of the Royalist garrison in York and secured Yorkshire and the north of England for Parliament. *See also* CROMWELL; GREAT BRITAIN.

A. CORVISIER
JOHN CHILDS

FURTHER READING
Peter Young, *Marston Moor, 1644* (Kineton, 1970); P. R. Newman, *The Battle of Marston Moor* (Chichester, 1981).

Martial law *See* CIVIL POWER, SUPPORT OF; LAW, MILITARY

Marx, Karl Heinrich (1818–83) The assumption underpinning Karl Marx's revolutionary theories was that eventually the Communists would need to seize power. The failure of the 1848 revolutions required socialists to study the art of conducting a successful insurrection. Much, therefore, of the journalistic output published between 1851 and 1861 in the *New York Daily Tribune*, and after 1861 in *Die Presse* of Vienna, was concerned with military matters. But, although published under Marx's name, most – if not all – of the technical military material was written by Engels. Marx, as an historian and economist, observed war from a broader, more political and more Clausewitzian perspective. He recognized that war, by needing to mobilize the support of the masses, could itself create a revolutionary opportunity and that the exploitation of that situation would itself require combat. *See also* CLAUSEWITZ; ENGELS; LENIN.

HEW STRACHAN

FURTHER READING
Sigmund Neumann, 'Engels and Marx: military concepts of the social revolutionaries', in *Makers of Modern Strategy*, ed. E. M. Earle (Princeton, 1943); *Marxism and the Science of War*, ed. Bernard Semmel (Oxford, 1981).

Masada, Siege of (AD 72–4) Masada is a rocky, isolated plateau rising 1,300 feet (400 metres) above the western shore of the Dead Sea in Israel. It had been established as a military post during the revolt of the Maccabees (168–142 BC), and was converted into a fortified palace by King Herod the Great (b.73 BC) during the Parthian invasion of 40 BC. Early in the first Jewish revolt against Rome (AD 66–73), around 1,000 Zealots under the command of Eleazar Ben Jair captured Masada from its Roman garrison and held out there for three years after the fall of Jerusalem in 70. The Roman commander Flavius Silva besieged Masada and did his utmost to reduce the fortress with the assistance of 7,000 troops. The Roman military operations are described in great detail by Josephus and archaeological investigation has revealed many of the siege works. Silva built eight camps around the hill and constructed a line of circumvallation and a huge earth ramp on which he mounted his artillery on a stone platform. After six months, the Romans breached the main wall of Masada and the garrison committed mass suicide rather than surrender. Just two women and five children remained alive. Masada became a symbol of Jewish national identity and heroism and modern Israeli officers go there to take their oaths of allegiance. *See also* ISRAEL, EARLY; JOSEPHUS; ROME; SIEGES.

A. CORVISIER
JOHN CHILDS

FURTHER READING
I. A. Richmond, 'The Roman siege-works of Masàda, Israel', *JRS*, iii (1962), pp. 142–55; M. Livneh and Z. Meschel, *Massada* (Tel Aviv, 1966); Y. Yadin, *Masada: Herod's fortress and the Zealots' last stand* (London, 1966); E. Schürer, *The History of the Jewish People in the Age of Jesus Christ (175 B.C. – A.D. 135)*, vol. 1, revised by G. Vermes and F. Millar (Edinburgh, 1973); E. M. Smallwood, *The Jews under Roman Rule* (Brill, 1976).

Matériel *See* ORDNANCE

Medals *See* HONOURS AND AWARDS

Medical services Military medicine is closely connected with health care in general. The former is both a specific aspect of the latter, since its aim is to heal men wounded in battle – which is not altogether unlike treating the victims of accidents – and also a major one, because from an early stage it had the task of keeping on the active list, and hence in good health, a considerable mass of men brought together by adventitious circumstances and at great cost, and who frequently had to endure hard living conditions.

The evolution of medical treatment in armies has been influenced by four factors which are to some extent interrelated – the development of the military art itself; the advances in science, especially in relation to medicine; the increasing influence of governmental administration; and the growth of compassion.

Historically, the number and nature of wounds have been determined by the mode of fighting. Cutting (edged) weapons made numerous wounds, which were spectacular but often superficial, while those inflicted by thrusting (pointed) ones, while less frequent, were deeper and more dangerous, the rapier, in particular, being a murderous weapon. Various forms of protective equipment – cuirasses, armour, mail coats, etc. – were of some value. However, the crossbow, which was condemned by religious authorities on its introduction, and firearms rendered any form of body protection far less efficacious, and increased the numbers of deaths from wounds. Among well-disciplined troops of the seventeenth and eighteenth centuries, 60 per cent of the wounds received by infantry in battle were on the left side of the body. Artillery and automatic weapons have forced individual soldiers or bodies of troops to seek natural forms of cover, the most elementary being the prone position; and a wider range of wounds has appeared caused by bullets, shell-bursts, bombs or falls of debris and shrapnel.

The main points of reference in the advance of medical science are the practice of amputation (curtailed for a while on account of a religious interdict in regard to operations that caused an effusion of blood), the invention in the sixteenth century of the tourniquet for stopping haemorrhages, the increasing skill of surgeons and the slow steps in the struggle against infection of wounds which lasted from the sixteenth to the nineteenth century, from the use of the red-hot iron to Pasteur's employment of antiseptics. In many fields, military surgeons and doctors have very often been in the van of progress, because they have had to deal with massive and unexpected demands which, except in the case of epidemics, have been on a different scale from those encountered in civilian settings. The prime need has always been for urgent action, all the more so since, for a long while, speed of treatment was the surest way of combating gangrene.

Governmental machinery and administrative systems developed rapidly when rulers assumed responsibility for the maintenance of their armies. After the Roman Empire began to use costly mercenaries in its legions, it developed a medical service for them. Later, the Spanish monarchy, followed by other European rulers, also paid doctors to work in their armies (sixteenth century). When armies of considerable size began to be raised by conscription, their medical services became a state responsibility. In Louis XIV's time, the quality of the medical services depended on the efficiency of the administration and the availability of finance. In the eighteenth and nineteenth centuries, on the other hand, military doctors tended to complain that the administrative authorities exercised too tight a control.

Perhaps the determining factors are the level of compassion and the value attached to life in each era. Over a long period, casualties of war received no greater attention than any others. The Greeks, who felt so strongly about harmonious physical development, described and treated wounds which could interfere with it. The Romans of the Republican era seem, on the contrary, if their authors are to be believed, to have stressed the primacy of qualities of character and to have displayed a rather ostentatious stoicism (as in such as Mucius Scaevola and Horatius Cocles). Christianity has always felt for the sufferings of humanity, without according any special place to soldiers. Throughout many centuries, which were times when epidemics cut wide swathes through civil communities, the demise of professional soldiers, whose death was less often by violence than by disease (the way in which most human beings died), attracted no special attention. Pictorial representations of Death leading mankind to the grave gave no prominence to soldiers. After the elimination of plague in Europe, three-quarters of a century more had to elapse before the feelings of men influenced by the Enlightenment began to be moved by the soldier's plight. Fontenoy (1745) is the first battle to be described as a charnel-house, although Malplaquet (1709) and many other engagements had been much bloodier. The passions aroused by the Revolution stifled for a time such incipient compassion, but it revived in Europe with the war in the Crimea (1854–6) and in Italy (1859–60). The losses at Solferino, which were relatively small in relation to the numbers engaged despite the advances in weaponry, excited public feelings much more than those of the First Empire, and started a current of opinion to which Henri Dunant gave expression by founding the Red Cross (1864). Such views gained further strength when armies were no longer made up solely of professional soldiers, but mostly of conscripts drawn from the general population. Care of the wounded was no longer viewed merely as a matter of economy on the state's part, but more than ever as a humane duty incumbent upon its wider responsibilities.

Various turning points in the history of military medicine, the principal ones being during the Renaissance (1400–1600) and between 1860 and 1890, can be seen as resulting from the interplay of these different factors.

From the Beginnings to the Renaissance No references can be found to the provision of special medical treatment for soldiers earlier than those in the *Iliad* concerning two doctors in the Greek army, Machaon and Podaleirius, and the Scythian depiction of a soldier bandaging a wounded comrade (fourth century BC). In the Bible, however (e.g. Numbers and Deuteronomy, fifteenth century BC), there are set out instructions aimed at combating infections in camps (removal of lepers and sufferers from dysentery, burying of excrement outside). In Greece, soldiers were among those treated by ordinary medical practitioners, but army doctors proper appeared when mercenaries began to be employed. Armies of the Roman Republic seem to have entrusted their wounded to the care of friendly or conquered cities. On the other hand, the armies of the Roman Empire had on their strength *medici legionis* (ten per legion) and *medici castrorum*, as well as *milites medici*. Overall, the Roman army probably had 1,000 doctors (i.e. a scale of 1 per 450 men); it seems also to have possessed permanent hospitals (*valetudinaria*).

The hospitals which were widely set up under Christian influence, particularly following the lead given by St Basil, made no distinction between soldiers and other men. The Byzantine armies, which were small in size and highly developed, had men acting as medical orderlies, on the scale of 8 or 10 per *tagma* (1,500–4,000), to collect the wounded in order to free soldiers from this task and to avoid breaking up the battle formation. The medical treatises composed by Alexander of Tralles and Paul of Aegina contain chapters dealing with armies. Some technical advances, like the first methods for stopping haemorrhages, were made in Moslem territories. The Seljuk army in the eleventh century possessed a field hospital complete with texts, instruments, medicines, doctors, orderlies and 200 Bactrian camels. The Crusades gave rise to the foundation of orders of hospitallers, such as the Order of St John of Jerusalem, composed originally of personnel dispensing medical care but who eventually were called upon to take up arms, and of several hospitals for the disabled (e.g. the Quinze-Vingts of Paris). The period from the fourteenth to the seventeenth century was marked by several waves of renewed enthusiasm for establishing hospitals (e.g. the Antonians), by the transfer of municipal hospitals from ecclesiastical to civil control and by the great charitable movement of which St Vincent de Paul has remained the symbol. Soldiers, who were more and more frequently professionals, began to enjoy the use of medical services which were specifically allocated to them.

From the Renaissance to the Turning Point in the Years 1860–90 In the fifteenth century, there were already in armies a number of surgeons who were paid out of sovereigns' finances, particularly in the state of Burgundy, and field hospitals appeared in Spain at the end of the *Reconquista*. The *tercio*, which derived from the reforms of Gonsalvo de Córdoba, included around 1560 one doctor and one surgeon for 2,200 men; they were attached to its headquarters, but the responsibility for the general health of the men lay with the captain, who maintained in his company at least one barber-surgeon. Temporary field hospitals appeared increasingly in the second half of the century (Landrecies, 1543, boasted 49 staff and 330 beds, etc.). Thanks to the initiative of Alexander Farnese, the establishment at Mechelen became in 1585 the first known permanent military hospital. Such hospitals were maintained by a deduction from military pay, the amounts at Mechelen being 10 reals for a captain, 5 for an ensign, 3 for a sergeant and one for the other soldiers.

In several countries, some doctors devoted themselves entirely to treating soldiers, the best-known being Ambroise Paré. A specifically military form of medicine slowly came into being. There was an increase in the number of amputations, since men preferred heroic remedies to a lingering death by infection. Anaesthesia was produced by means of alcohol, and cauterization by red-hot iron; the use of boiling oil was abandoned. Artificial limbs of metal, with a crude form of jointing, made their appearance. The speculative outlook of men of the Renaissance led them to invent amazing instruments, such as tubes for the extraction of musket balls. They hit on the scheme of adapting artillery waggons as transport for the wounded, but movement of the injured by water, being less subject to jolting, remained the preferred mode. A practice was adopted of putting into quarantine men suffering from fever, and especially those with venereal diseases.

Agreements between two sides at war

contained an increasing frequency of provisions for any wounded left in enemy hands at the time of surrender and for medical personnel, who were released without ransom when prisoners were exchanged. But, although war was beginning to acquire a set of accepted principles, there was no question of these applying to those fighting in partisan forces (such as Barbets and Camisards).

The growing instances of complaints about the lot of the wounded during the seventeenth century, and particularly in the eighteenth, did not mean that treatment had deteriorated but rather that the numbers involved had become larger and that feelings of compassion on their behalf had been aroused. This was particularly the case in respect of decrepit or crippled old soldiers, a small number of whom were grouped together as *mortes-payes* in the fortresses or as 'lay brothers' in abbeys. In 1554, Henry II of France decided to allocate the Saint-Jacques hospital at Haut-Pas to soldiers wounded in his service. Despite various attempts (*Maison de la Charité chrétienne* in the Faubourg St Michel, 1576; *Commanderie de St Louis* at Bicêtre, 1634) it was not until the foundation of Les Invalides by Louis XIV that at least several thousand soldiers could be assured of spending their last years in respectable circumstances. Les Invalides was imitated throughout Europe (e.g. Kilmainham Hospital, Dublin, 1681, and Royal Hospital, Chelsea, 1684). Seamen were not forgotten. They had the Chatham Chest, founded in England in 1588 with private funds, the *Caisse des Invalides de la Marine* in France (1673) and port hospitals (1689).

At the end of the seventeenth century, all European armies had surgeons on their strength. In France and England, they were part of the regimental headquarters but did not rank as commissioned officers. Captains sometimes took care to have among the soldiers in their companies a few who could act as 'barbers' and, if need arose, provide some first aid. It was noted that sick men disliked leaving their unit to go into hospital, because they found more human warmth in the former. Even so, an effort was made to establish military hospitals, and Vauban built a number in citadels and fortresses. They were modelled on the Hôtel des Invalides, which itself had borrowed much from the design of monasteries such as that at Saint-Gall. Attention was mainly concentrated on ensuring that the rooms had plenty of air, on putting in water points and lavatories and on arranging for adequate heating, but these medical considerations which were essentially concerned with physical hygiene were not supposed in any way to take second place to religious preoccupations.

The edict of January 1708, which established the first comprehensive army medical service, marked an important step forward. There has often been a reluctance to attribute any importance to this document on account of its financial aspect, in that it turned the doctors and surgeons who already worked in the king's army into state officials and even enabled such posts to be purchased. (This measure lost its financial bearing, however, in 1716, when the sale of medical posts was prohibited.) It is none the less true that this edict represented the starting-point for the development of medical services in the French army, and it was copied elsewhere. It established a medical inspectorate consisting of twelve doctors and surgeons, who were split up over four sectors – Flanders–Moselle, Moselle–Franche-Comté, Dauphiné–Provence, Roussillon–Guyenne. In each of these was located a medical inspector-general, a surgical inspector-general and a chief surgeon for corps and armies. Fifty hospitals which already existed in citadels and fortresses were then absorbed into the overall organization with, at the head of each, a chief doctor and a chief surgeon. Ultimately, 159 posts of chief surgeon were created in the ordinary units and in the corps of the royal household. The number of medical practitioners was thus about 300, a figure which was obviously small for an army of 300,000 men. Doctors and surgeons became medical officers, on an equal footing with each other, and enjoyed certain privileges, like other royal officers. They also enjoyed what was, at that period, the highly symbolic right of wearing a sword.

The growth of the French military medical

service in the eighteenth century is shown in its increase in numbers. In 1781, there were 724 medical officers, (86 doctors, 508 surgeons and 130 apothecaries), i.e. 1 per 250 men, and 90 fortress hospitals, of which the main ones – Lille, Metz and Strasbourg – became demonstration hospitals for teaching practitioners (1775). These now had a better knowledge of their subject, and were equipped with works of reference – the *Textbook of Military Medicine* (1772) and *Rules of Guidance on Soldiers' Hygiene* (1775) by Jean Colombier. In 1766, there appeared the first periodical publications dealing with military medicine (*Recueil d'observations de médecins militaires*) and in 1782, in particular, the *Journal de médecine militaire*.

The ordonnance of January 1747 set out the way in which military hospitals were to be run by the *commissaire des guerres* assigned to them for discipline, administration and finance. Medical officers complained unceasingly of this supervision which, though it freed them from numerous administrative tasks, made them subordinate to the management. The mobile hospitals that served the Rhine army during the Seven Years' War were operated as state-controlled enterprises, while the base hospitals were put out to contract. The contractors were accused of false statements in regard to provision of supplies. However, they received payments from the king only irregularly and, in 1760, the private company operating the fixed hospitals was declared bankrupt.

Emphasis should be given to the importance assumed by the naval medical service, which had to combat epidemics aboard ship, in particular, scurvy. On many points, the navy was in advance of the army. Training establishments for naval doctors were set up at Rochefort, Toulon and Brest between 1722 and 1740. In a different field, mention should also be made of Bourgelat's creation of veterinary schools at Lyons (1761) and Alfort (1765).

The scale of provision to Rochambeau's expeditionary force (1780) can be considered as marking the high point of military medicine under the *ancien régime*; there were, for a force numbering 6,000, 60 medical officers (i.e. 1 per 100 men), 100 medical orderlies and 17 administrative personnel. At the end of the eighteenth century, French military medicine enjoyed a high reputation in Europe. An unmistakable sign of its quality was that soldiers had to be extracted from hospitals to which they had gained admittance without proper reason. The epidemics which had proved deadly during the War of the Polish Succession seem to have been checked in the Seven Years' War. Those who contracted venereal disease (1 in 12 of the French Guards) were generally cured. Unfortunately, the severe financial cuts that the army suffered in 1788 had disastrous consequences.

In the English army, the provision of medical care had often been calamitous, but it improved slowly during the eighteenth century. Almost the only area where field hospitals were maintained to an appropriate standard was Flanders, where they benefited from being organized by private contractors. Surgeons were not highly esteemed, and some were found to prefer the command of a company to the exercise of their professional skills. As in France, a latent conflict made itself felt between the administrative personnel (commissioners for the sick and wounded) and the 'physicians, surgeons and apothecaries to the forces'. The medical organization in Frederick II's Prussian army was hardly any better. Making men fit again for active service at minimum cost took precedence over everything else, and the monarch had scant confidence in doctors. However, under the orders of the *Generalchirurgus* and the *Generalstabmedicus* were to be found *Regimentsfeldschere* and hospital *Feldschere* (in all, 1 per 200 men), as well as *Feldapotheke*. There was much variation in the standard of such personnel; they might come from the Berlin medical schools or be merely a personal choice of the colonel. As everywhere else, the commissioners and inspectors who handled the administration and supplies were accused of incompetence and dishonesty. During the Seven Years' War, the medical services of the Prussian army are said to have dealt with 220,000 sick and wounded; but during the War of the Bavarian Succession, the army apparently lost 40,000 men almost without an engagement being fought, and the survival rate of those who entered hospital was only one in five.

The wars of the Revolution and the Empire provided a stern test for the medical system of French armies. The organization which the *ancien régime* had bequeathed underwent constant modification. This succession of contradictory reforms did not prevent medical personnel from carrying out their task conscientiously under arduous conditions. In Egypt, there were 108 medical officers for 34,000 men (i.e. 1 per 315), and many of these officers died from epidemics. Under the Directory, the control exercised by the administrative services, on whom Napoleon placed great reliance, seems to have become firmer. Doctors-in-chief, surgeons-in-chief and pharmacists-in-chief, who were attached to the headquarters of each army, were responsible only for arranging the carrying out of medical treatment, and they appointed the necessary surgeons, on the scale of one chief surgeon per regiment and two surgeons per battalion. Some great names made their appearance, such as that of Desgenettes among the doctors, or of Larrey and Percy among the surgeons, but hospital surgeons, often picked from among students with inadequate qualifications, frequently made a poor showing. In addition, when the tempo of military operations slackened, Napoleon cut down the medical services. Nevertheless, in 1806, ambulance battalions were brought into being; these had six companies, each with sixteen ambulance vehicles, for the collection and transport of the wounded. Mobile hospitals which could divide up into ambulance sections, temporary second-line hospitals and permanent hospitals in rear areas, were particularly designed with a view to the offensive, but the system collapsed during the retreat from Moscow. According to statistics collected by Larrey, out of 22,000 wounded who were treated in 1813, it appears that 11 per cent died from their wounds, 16 per cent were totally disabled and 18 per cent partially, 30 per cent were cured and made fit for active service and 25 per cent were on the way to complete recovery. In France, the medical services of the navy were the major casualties of the Revolution and the Empire while, on the other hand, large advances were seen in those of the British navy.

The Restoration was a period of reconstruction. Teaching hospitals were reopened; the recruitment of medical officers was made subject to their possession of a diploma established by an ordonnance of 1824; and a corps of administrators of military hospitals was created. The number of officers holding the diploma rose in ten years from 900 to about 1,300 (1 per 250 men). This was due particularly to the effect of the conquest of Algeria, because there the French army found itself confronted by the problem of malaria. The Crimean War proved a severe test for all the countries that took part, and the medical services of the French army were judged to be inadequate. Hence, an effort was made to improve the training of medical officers by the creation in 1856, in association with the Faculty of Medicine at Strasbourg, of the *École impériale de Service de Santé*, entry to which was by competitive examination.

Medical Services from the American Civil War Modern military medicine evolved in the second half of the nineteenth century, when a new conception of the organization of medical services came to the fore during the American Civil War. At the same time, many countries adopted conscription, Pasteur initiated 'revolutionary' methods and increasing attention was given to hygiene in ordinary daily life.

The US army, whose numbers were raised from 15,000 to 1,200,000 in a very short time, had rapidly to improvise a medical service of a size never previously seen, in view of calls upon it that were all the greater with the increased destructive power of weapons, and because the army was composed of civilians who had been called up and needed to be provided with some benefits in return for the sacrifices they were making. It must be remembered that there were more wounded at Gettysburg (1863) than at Solferino (1859).

The Northern side in America tried at first to model its medical organization on those of Britain and France, but rapid action was needed for coping with an armed force that was five times larger. Hence, civilian medicine was put at the service of the army. The authorities gave doctors the means to organize medical services and left them an almost entirely free hand. Contrary to practice in European armies, the American medical officer was at once a doctor and in command of a group of men, and also dealt with their administration. A doctor who was head of a hospital or a field ambulance unit made his requisitions direct, either to the Treasury or to the Purveyor's Department, a supply function which came directly under the medical service and was administered by doctors, who were designated 'acting purveyors'. Normal commercial methods were used for obtaining supplies of pharmaceutical products, which were then placed in stores sited in strategically important cities, with overall administration being centred at Philadelphia.

The Northern army had, in total, one doctor of officer rank per 180–200 men, without counting storekeeping personnel or hospital stewards. In addition, 1,000 doctors served on short-term contracts. The whole of the medical service came under the Surgeon-General who was nominated by the President of the Republic, but was under the superintendence of the Federal government, one holder of the post, indeed, being cashiered. Every military department had its corresponding medical section, headed by a doctor as director, while medical inspectors kept a check on the execution of orders from higher levels. Medical services for the troops were deployed in accordance with the main organizational divisions within the army; an army corps, for example, had a doctor as director of medical affairs, and under him came a doctor-in-chief for each division, with a doctor, two assistant doctors and a hospital steward for each regiment. Every formation, from the corps to the regiment, had a field ambulance unit, and every army a permanent hospital. The evacuation of the wounded was carried out by large ambulance trains, which were organized at army corps level. They had extremely well-adapted carriages and also waggons of medical supplies with very fully equipped operating tables.

In 1863, there were some 300 hospitals containing 84,000 beds. They were, in fact, camps set up outside cities (like the temporary towns built in periods of plague), on a hill and near a railway line, and made of rapidly erected wooden constructions – which yet had to last for five years. They provided very hygienic environments (Chestnut Hill being an example) and had a large medical staff assisted by men belonging to the Invalid Corps. In addition, convalescent camps were established; these were virtually temporary towns, where men were gradually retrained as soldiers while they were being restored to full health. An instance was the camp at Fairfax, whose admissions totalled 170,000.

The situation in regard to general health in the Northern army was far superior to anything found in Europe at that period, despite the prevalence of fevers in the region bordering the Atlantic coast and botulism, a microbic infection caused by eating preserved food which has been too hastily prepared. In June 1863, the number of men who had received medical treatment amounted to 13.5 per cent of the total strength under arms (9.1 per cent in hospital, 4.4 per cent in the field); 11 per cent of them had been sick and 2.5 per cent wounded. From June 1862 to June 1863, the number of deaths in hospital fell to 3.9 per cent of men undergoing treatment. This excellent bill of health was apparently due, according to statements from French observers, to good organization certainly, but particularly to the almost complete absence of venereal diseases, the prohibition of alcoholic drinks, care over cleanliness and the wearing of flannel shirts. Mention must also be made of the remarkable work of the Sanitary Commission, set up in 1861 by the Reverend Ballows under the patronage of the Federal government, in distributing relief to the wounded and in establishing a corps of nurses.

This was the first effect of the sudden awareness which had been stirred after the war in Italy, and of which Henri Dunant had been the principal instigator. Societies providing relief to the wounded were set up over a period in numerous countries under the emblem of the Red Cross. In 1864, the countries which signed the Geneva Convention undertook to protect in wartime the wounded of either side. This convention was revised in 1907 and extended to cover the wounded in warfare at sea. Other conventions covered prisoners of war (1929) and civil populations (1949). At present, the Red Cross is represented at international level by the Red Cross International Committee, which is an independent committee composed of twenty-five Swiss citizens, with its headquarters in Geneva, and acting in wartime as an intermediary between the belligerents, the various national associations and the League of Red Cross Societies, an international federation which is made up of national associations, such as the British Red Cross. In Moslem countries, the Red Crescent has developed along similar lines.

The Red Cross has brought help to various military medical services and has created a current of sympathy in the minds of the general public towards the wounded, which in its turn has given support to advances in, and developments of, military medicine. The first important manifestation of the work of the Red Cross took place during the Franco-Prussian War, especially during the Siege of Paris, where numbers of 'American' ambulance vehicles made their appearance.

After the heavy toll of casualties in 1870–1, which was largely due to typhus, the Third Republic devoted great efforts to bettering the army and navy medical services. The school at Strasbourg was reestablished in a new form at Lyons in 1888, and in 1890 a medical school for the navy was set up at Bordeaux. A problem that remained to be settled was the relationship between the officers who administered military hospitals and the medical officers themselves. The example provided by the Americans and, in particular the prestige which medicine had acquired in the wake of Pasteur's discoveries, turned public opinion in favour of the latter. The army medical service became autonomous by the military law of 1889. In 1900, the establishment of the colonial army involved also that of a special medical service for overseas troops and this contributed greatly to advances in the treatment of tropical diseases and to the installation of hospitals and medical attendance centres in the colonies.

In the twentieth century, the organizational structure of medical services in the various armies became more and more alike, under the influence of practitioners and of the demands imposed by medical science itself. Despite the increase in size of armies and the invention of new weapons, the results achieved by military medicine and surgery since the American Civil War have been considerable. During the First World War, the number of deaths from sickness fell well below those from battle, and the men who died from wounds represented no more than two-fifths of the total of those killed outright. In the Second World War, there was also a reduction in the number of seriously maimed who were left permanently disabled. Among the reasons for these changes must be put the very real advances in surgery as well as of military medicine.

Hence, military doctors and surgeons gained a solidly established standing in armies. Medical personnel and military medicine provided soldiers with a kind of insurance. An example that can be cited is the fact that, since 1899, every soldier in the French army has been equipped with a packet of dressings for his own personal use. Experience has changed the way in which medical services do their work. During the First World War, the aim was to evacuate the wounded as quickly as possible, and this often resulted in deaths on the journey; today, a number of surgical units are pushed forward into the battle area, and surgeons operate at the earliest possible moment, prior to evacuating the wounded by helicopter. During the wars in Indo-China, medical units in this way shared in the life of the men engaged in battle and, by so doing, had a beneficial effect on their morale.

In general, military medicine and, perhaps even more, its naval counterpart, have shown themselves, ever since the eighteenth century, to be in the van of progress, and military medicine has, in particular, made a great contribution to the improvements of health and hygiene in countries of the Third World. *See also* ADMINISTRATION, ARMY; LARREY; LOSSES OF LIFE; MORALE; PENSIONS; ROME; VETERANS.

A. CORVISIER

FURTHER READING
Richard A. Gabriel and Karen S. Metz, *A History of Military Medicine* (2 vols, London, 1992); N. Cantlie, *A History of the Army Medical Department* (2 vols, Edinburgh, 1974); John Laffin, *Surgeons in the Field* (London, 1970); G. W. Adams, *Doctors in Blue: the medical history of the Union Army in the Civil War* (New York, 1952).

Mehmet II (1432–81) On his accession in 1451, the Ottoman sultan Mehmet II began a new phase of Ottoman expansion and conquest. He achieved lasting fame by the capture of Constantinople, the Byzantine capital, in May 1453, a victory which gained him the title of *Fatih* (the Conqueror). It had been preceded in 1452 by the construction of the fortress of Rumeli Hisari, known to the Byzantines as Boghaz-kesen, to cut the Bosphorus and isolate the city. The conquest of Constantinople was due to the overall superiority of the Ottoman military machine, which was the largest and best organized of the fifteenth century, especially the infantry, the navy and, above all, the artillery. The capture of Constantinople, followed by the conquest of Greece (1456–60) and Trebizond (1461), confirmed the Ottoman Empire as the successor of the Byzantine. In 1479, Mehmet attempted the conquest of Rhodes and invaded southern Italy, landing an expedition at Otranto. Equipped with their formidable army, in which the corps of janissaries played the leading role, the Ottomans continued to extend their territories for a further century. *See also* BYZANTIUM; CONSTANTINOPLE, FORTIFICATIONS OF; OTTOMAN TURKS.

R. MANTRAN

FURTHER READING
Steven Runciman, *The Fall of Constantinople,* *1453* (Cambridge, 1955); R. Mantran, *Histoire de la Turquie* (3rd edn, Paris, 1968).

Mercenaries Generally speaking, the term 'mercenary', which originally referred to a man working for money, has, since the eighteenth century, been applied almost exclusively to a particular class of soldier. Military mercenaries have been in existence for as long as there have been states of any size. The object of employing mercenaries is to complement or replace those armed forces raised from among a state's citizens or subjects by voluntary enlistment or conscription. Through contracts between rulers and the men in question, mercenaries may be employed who are particularly desirable on account of their skills or merely for their willingness to engage in a dangerous activity not highly regarded by 'civilians'. Thus the mercenary may fight in a cause which is not that of his own nation. During the medieval and early modern periods the profession of arms was considered to be among the most noble but, during the eighteenth century, it gradually acquired a more pejorative tone.

A fairly common accepted definition of the mercenary sees him as 'a man who, for money, fights in a cause which does not concern him'. This applies precisely to professional soldiers who sell their services to the highest bidder, changing army and side as it suits them, even when the war is at its height, justifying the pejorative character attached to their venality. Voltaire contributed to this image: 'A million regimented assassins running from one end of Europe to the other, engaging in murder and banditry in a disciplined fashion to earn his crust, since he has no more honest trade' (*Candide*). Many of these men did, however, show a certain sense of honour. The mercenary changed sides when he felt his contract had been broken, when the employer dismissed him because he had no further use for him, when the employer took too long to pay him or tried to employ him for tasks different from those originally agreed. In 1735, for example, some French hussars went over to Piedmont because the king, who had dissolved their regiment, offered them service as dragoons. Moreover, the mercenaries observed their contemporary code of war more readily than improvised troops because they appreciated the value of reciprocity.

Before the eighteenth century, the term 'mercenary' rarely bore a burden of opprobrium. And it was not used to refer to nobles, officers or engineers whose contracts were made directly with the sovereign rather than through a 'military enterpriser'. Not all mercenaries were strangers to the cause they served, even when they were paid to do so. This was the case with poverty-stricken nationals or refugees from religious, political or ideological persecution. Can one call a man a 'mercenary' who, in some foreign land, is serving a cause in which he believes and receives a wage that is all the higher for the fact that his services are greatly in demand? Where the services of a group of warriors or the entire male population are only called on in times of grave danger, paid professional soldiers are used in normal times to allow the rest of the men to pursue their civilian occupations. Moreover, professional soldiers often proved to be more effective. This was the concept which ultimately won acceptance in Ancient Greece, Rome and sixteenth-century Europe, in different forms. Considered first as a complement to the citizen army of Antiquity, then as a source of supplementary forces to the feudal army or the knights, mercenary service became the norm and compulsory service (militia service, then conscription combined with a system of drawing lots) came to be seen only as a way of providing those additional forces which voluntary service could not entirely supply.

There have been periods in which the system of employing mercenaries has undergone great developments and assumed new forms. Having initially been conceived to compensate for a population's lack of time, aptitude or enthusiasm to defend its city or state, it was known in the ancient East and in China. The mercenaries often came from foreign countries and formed ethnic corps. The Pharaohs of the Old and Middle Kingdoms used Libyan or Nubian archers and those of the New Kingdom employed Greek hoplites. In China, the Sung dynasty (960–1279) employed Huns and Mongols as auxiliaries. The Greek city-state had little regard for mercenaries. In the fifth century BC, however, the Athenians did entrust the policing of the city to Scythian archers, but the use of mercenaries spread in the fourth century BC on account of the pauperization produced by the social crisis and, more importantly, of the population shortage which afflicted its citizenry as a result both of losses in war and of inbreeding. Mercenaries acquired some respectability mainly as a result of the writings of Xenophon who, in narrating the adventure of the Ten Thousand (*Anabasis*), enunciated an ethics of the profession of arms.

The great empires employed mercenaries more than other states. The Persian army contained mercenary contingents from conquered countries. In their turn, the armies of Alexander and his succcessors included Aetolians, Cretans, Celts, Galatians, Egyptians, Syrians, and proletarians from the cities, the countryside and, particularly, the poor mountain areas, formed into ethnic corps with their own specific armaments and styles of fighting. It was thanks to their mercenaries that Alexander's generals (the *Diadochi*) were able to carve out kingdoms for themselves. They sought to win the loyalty of their men, or at least their leaders, by allotting lands to them (cleruchies), which were to become hereditary and which would allow them to merge into the local aristocracies.

Following the example of the merchant cities like Carthage, Rome itself had to have recourse to mercenaries from 213 BC onwards when it induced the *Celtiberi* to come over to its side from Hannibal's army. The introduction of mercenaries at Rome was, however, quite slow and cautious, in order to spare the city a revolt of mercenaries such as the one which had put Carthage in peril (241–238 BC). However, the army of the Roman Empire was composed of professionals who, although they were Roman citizens, were increasingly recruited from among the 'Barbarian' peoples, of whom the Germans had the best reputation. Rome subsequently took into its service tribes and then entire peoples, who settled in the Empire and saved it from the Mongol invasions (e.g. the Huns).

The Germanic invasions led to a decline in the use of mercenaries because the profession of arms was rewarded by grants of land. Thus, in a manner similar to the Greek and later the Byzantine worlds, there was a spread of military colonies in various different forms, and, later, of fiefs in the West, *fiefs de soudée* (i.e. lands given as pay) in the Holy Land, *timars* in the Ottoman Empire and later still the military *pomest'e* (domains) system in Russia. In the West there was a revival of the use of mercenaries during the Hundred Years' War which saw the development of the infantry. The *piétaille* (the body of foot soldiers), the auxiliary to the cavalry, was attracted by pay and opportunities for pillage. It did, however, prove somewhat difficult to handle and, when peace was restored, it sought to continue the war on its own account. These mercenaries were to be termed *soudards* (*soldoyer*), whereas the 'soldier' (from the Italian *soldato*) in the sixteenth century was regarded as noble in character.

There was a substantial development of the use of mercenaries in the sixteenth and seventeenth centuries with a considerable increase in the numbers of men involved (from 100,000 men to a million in Europe), which posed some difficulty for the fiscal systems of the period. However, modern states did attempt to impose some control on the employment of mercenaries. Where the central government was weak (Italy, the Empire), the princes and the city republics struck contracts with generals (*condottieri*, 'military enterprisers') who, either for a sum of money, or the ceding to them of the right to raise taxes or the granting of land or fiefs, undertook to raise, equip and command troops. An army was thus formed by a 'general enterpriser' who subcontracted to colonels, while these latter subcontracted to captains each of whom owned their own units. Some of the *condottieri*, who had become powerful, either endangered the states that employed them or succeeded in carving out principalities for themselves (Ludovico Sforza). This system reached its height in Italy at the beginning of the sixteenth century and in Germany during the Thirty Years' War, especially in the person of Emperor Ferdinand II's general, Wallenstein. In the stronger states (Spain, France and England), the ruler called on the services of mercenaries recruited by colonels and captains, but remained in overall charge of the undertaking. None the less, the system was subject to much abuse: corrupt administration by the officers, the presence of 'rolling stones' who passed from one army to another, enlisting in several different armies at the same time in order to receive advances against the *Handgeld* or *argent du roi* (bounty). The soldiers were usually nationals, but foreigners were also enlisted and the term mercenaries increasingly came to be applied only to them. Mercenary soldiering became an industry for some poor or overpopulated countries. A sort of international exchange rate had become established by the seventeenth century, corresponding to the value of – or the demands made by – the different mercenaries. Thus the Austrian came cheaper than the Walloon, the Spaniard or the Italian. On occasion, the Emperor sold off regiments after a campaign, though, in some cases, he had to buy them back again the following year. Switzerland provided a large number of soldiers to many European states, but these were grouped into regiments of a sort and were placed at the disposal of a foreign ruler through a treaty struck with the individual cantons (the so-called *régiments avoués*). In 1776, the Margrave of Hesse entered into an agreement with George III of England to provide 12,000 men to fight for him in America.

In the eighteenth century, the use of mercenaries was denounced on all sides and the French Revolution condemned the practice. Meanwhile the ideal of the nation emerged as a justification for voluntary enlistment. In the nineteenth century, with the creation of the Foreign Legion in 1831, the status of the mercenary was enhanced, even in France, through his affirmation of an ideal consisting of respect for his contract and sacrifice. The Legion saw itself as a breeding-ground of military virtue in a period when compulsory military service had become the norm.

After this point, the use of mercenaries in Europe declined, though it took on new forms in others parts of the world where countries vied for the services of European soldiers with a knowledge of the most recent military technology. Thus in the 1920s, the Chinese generals were to take White Russians into their service to instruct their armies and provide them with officers. Mercenaries with technical skills were particularly appreciated in the artillery and the engineers, as they would be, a little later, in air forces. In fact they often served with what was at least the tacit consent of their governments which reserved the right to forbid such practices or to repudiate the actions of these men. Thus the 'Flying Tigers' (nickname of the 'American Volunteer Group') under Major Claire Chennault served in China against the Japanese between 1937 and 1941. They received pay of 750 dollars a month plus a bonus for each plane shot down. More recently, mercenaries have acted as instructors and military advisers to various African factions in the local conflicts that have followed decolonization in that continent.

Since such conflicts have taken on an increasingly ideological character, sometimes becoming akin to civil wars, the same men may be termed either mercenaries or volunteers depending upon the position of the speaker. They play an important role in contemporary military confrontations but the number of mercenaries in the original sense of the term is becoming smaller and smaller. *See also* FOREIGNERS, SERVICE BY; GREECE, ANCIENT; RECRUITMENT; ROME; SWITZERLAND; WALLENSTEIN.

A. CORVISIER

FURTHER READING
Fritz Redlich, *The German Military Enterpriser and his Work Force* (2 vols, Wiesbaden, 1964–5); Michael Mallett, *Mercenaries and their Masters* (London, 1974); Rodney Atwood, *The Hessians* (Cambridge,1980).

Metz, Siege of (31 October 1552–5 January 1553)   If Mühlberg was the great triumph

of Charles V's later years, the Siege of Metz was the great disaster. The Imperial Free City was one of three bishoprics in Lorraine long claimed by the kings of France, and demanded by Henry II as the price of his alliance with the German princes against Charles V in January 1552. Metz was occupied by the French in April 1552 and the Duke of Guise appointed governor. The German revolt had taken Charles V completely by surprise, but by the summer of 1552 he had recovered, raised an army of 60,000, and by means of the 'Peace of Passau' had won over most of the princes. In September, rather than disband his army, he proposed the immediate recapture of Metz, partly to restore his prestige, partly for strategic reasons. The dangers of beginning a siege so late in the season were obvious, but against them Charles argued that the French fortifications would be stronger if they were given a further breathing space. The decisive point came when the Duke of Alba, who had begun investing the city with a small advanced guard in October, won over the Margrave Albert-Alcibiades of Brandenburg-Kulmbach, the last rebel prince, whose army of 15,000 could now be added to Charles's own. The siege began in earnest on 31 October and the Emperor himself arrived on 20 November. However, Guise, expecting an Imperial counter-stroke, had worked ruthlessly and effectively to improve both the outerworks and the inner fortifications. Moreover, Metz, situated at the juncture of the Moselle and the Seille, was vulnerable only on the south. Here the Imperial siege train of thirty-six cannon was concentrated, and by 24 November a breach had been made. The assault, however, collapsed in the face of Guise's inner entrenchments; further attempts to storm the breach were made during the first weeks of December but both they and the efforts to mine the ramparts were equally unsuccessful. By mid-December the Imperial army was suffering heavily from exposure and food shortages and, by Christmas, it was close to mutiny. Charles had been sustained by the hope of a miracle but, at the beginning of January 1553, he was finally persuaded to abandon the siege and strike camp. Like other Imperial disasters (the Algiers expedition of 1541, for example) the failure at Metz was the result of a gamble by Charles V that went wrong, compounded by his stubborn belief that divine providence would intervene on his behalf. On the other hand, his fear that postponing the siege until the following year would only give the French further time to improve their defences was also justified. The successful conduct of the defence made the reputation of Guise; without his efforts, Charles's assault in November might have succeeded. *See also* ALBA; GUISE; MÜHLBERG; PAVIA.

SIMON ADAMS

FURTHER READING
G. Zeller, *La Réunion de Metz à la France, 1552–1648* (Paris, 1926), i; K. Brandi, *The Emperor Charles V* (London, 1939), pp. 615–22; W. S. Maltby, *Alba: a biography of Fernando Alvarez de Toledo, 3rd Duke of Alba* (Berkeley and London, 1983), pp. 61–3.

Metz, Siege of (14 August–27 October 1870) Marshal François Bazaine, who had been appointed commander-in-chief of the main French army to survive the early reverses of the Franco-Prussian War, had established a position at Metz. He attempted to retreat, but the German 1st Army cut off his route to the south (Borny, 14 August) and the 2nd Army did likewise in the west (Mars-la-Tour, Rezonville, 16 August). On 18 August, at St-Privat, Moltke attacked Canrobert's 6th Corps, which resisted the onslaught but had to fall back towards Metz since it had received no support from Bazaine. Moltke besieged the entrenched camp at Metz while simultaneously preparing to march on Paris. On 27 October, after forty-four days of siege, famine made surrender inevitable: 173,000 men, the whole of their artillery and other *matériel* fell into German hands. The fighting had also cost the French 35,000 killed and wounded while the Germans had lost 40,000. Bazaine was later condemned by a court martial and his irresolute conduct had indeed been the cause of the disaster. *See also* FRANCE; GERMANY; MOLTKE; SEDAN.

A. CORVISIER

FURTHER READING
Michael Howard, *The Franco-Prussian War* (London, 1960); François Roth, *La Guerre de 70* (Paris, 1990); S. Audoin-Rouzeau, *1870: La France dans la guerre* (Paris, 1989).

Mexico *See* PRE-COLUMBIAN STATES OF AMERICA

Middle East For centuries, the Arab armies had to combine three elements that were, to some extent, contradictory: the methods of warfare and the warrior values of pre-Islamic Arabia, the justificatory thrust given to the 'war of the faithful' (*Jihad*) by the Islamic religion, and the development of a professional soldiery.

Within the framework of tribal structures, some of which are still in existence today, Arab societies were warrior communities with an undifferentiated military function. Every man capable of bearing arms fought and companies of soldiers were formed on the basis of divisions between or within tribes. In Arabia, the great camel-driving tribes protected or attacked the caravans of the merchant aristocracies which dominated the oasis towns. The bedouin raid was both a means of redistributing wealth and women and of ensuring the primacy of the nomads over the sedentary agriculturalists. Using lances, bows and swords, bedouin war parties mounted on camels and horses undertook large-scale raids. Their strategy was to maintain a long-distance threat from across the desert. Their tactics relied on surprise, encounters with these 'noble mounted brigands' involving fierce hand-to-hand fighting, the very 'stuff of romance'.

Because of the pressures from the economic and social movements induced by the propinquity of the two bordering empires, the Byzantine and the Sassanid Persian, Arabian tribal allegiances grew very close. Mohammed (*c*.570–632) challenged the domination of the aristocracy of his native city, Mecca, and surrounded himself with followers from various tribes or clans, bodies of volunteers which allowed him to form alliances with the Medinans who were hostile to the Meccans. Having risen to become leader of the 'city-community', which formed both a logistic and a strategic base, Mohammed conducted traditional-style raids over a wide area. However, he also learned how to defend a city (the 'Battle of the Ditch' in 627), recaptured Mecca by employing a subtle blend of war and diplomacy, and launched the first expeditions against the neighbouring empires.

The four legitimate caliphs, the *Rashidun* (632–61), continued this policy towards those peripheral populations which were experiencing fiscal and theological friction with the administrations of the Byzantine and Sassanid Empires. This led to the rapid augmentation of the Muslim armies to some tens of thousands of men. The soldiers were volunteers and often marched in tribal contingents, complete with their women and children; this often resulted in the partial relocation of population. It is difficult to assess the extent to which Arab expansion was military rather than demographic. From the beginning, the marches of the Arab armies constituted vast tribal movements or migrations and succeeded in ethnically and culturally Arabizing the whole of the plains, if not the mountains, from the Atlantic to the Taurus. In part, demographic superiority provided the impetus behind both the counter-Crusades (1096–1271) and the wars of anti-colonial liberation in the twentieth century.

In parallel with the conquests made under the second legitimate caliph, Omar (634–44), in Syria, Palestine, Persia and Egypt, and the conquests of Kabul, Bukhara and Samarkand under the first Umayyad caliph, Mu'awiya (661–80), and of the Indus and Spain under the sixth, Walid I (705–15), was forged the religious instrument with which these conquests were justified. This was the *Jihad fi Sabil Allah*, effort directed along the path of God, a phrase usually translated too narrowly as 'holy war'. Ritually, in a religious society perpetually suppressing the impure by the observance of sacred prescriptions (prayers, ablutions, fasting, etc.), the *Jihad* re-evokes the tension between blind faith and unbelief, rebellion and schism. If necessary, it demands combat between the *umma* (the Muslim community) and the infidels. The *Jihad* also creates a practical distinction between the *dar al-Islam* and the *dar al-Harb*: the world of Islam and the world of war. Seeking to achieve the Muslim (collective) order on earth represents the most favourable undertaking by which a person can gain his ultimate reward in heaven: Paradise, closeness to God.

However, there also arose internal wars dictated by the common interest (*h'urub al-masalih'*): the wars against the apostates and then against the militarily organized schismatics. From the beginnings of Muslim history, anti-caliphal revolts employed theological justifications as a cover for their dynastic, political or economic motives, calling for a *Jihad* against an unjust government, accusing it of having allowed the Muslim law (*shari'a*) to be corrupted. The *h'urub al-masalih'* was invoked to suppress the early form of total democracy even when this operated to the advantage of those newly converted by Kharijism. The pursuit of the common interest also led to the split between the Shi'ites, who postulated the charismatic value and right to power of the direct descendants of the prophet by his son-in-law 'Ali, and Sunni Islam. The division occurred after the Battle of Kerbala (680) at which the Umayyad army killed the last pretenders of the prophet's family.

The revolts of the Kharijites and Shi'ites, movements which themselves subdivided into a variety of sects and heresies, inspired numerous fragmentations of Islam over the following centuries. For example, the egalitarian revolts of the Qarmatians in the ninth century; the mystical warrior esotericism of the Ismailis (Septimanian Shi'ites), who fought against the Sunnis of the established dynasties (the Nizaris, nicknamed the *Hashishin* or Assassins, of the eleventh to thirteenth centuries established a transnational terrorism *avant la lettre* against the Muslim and Crusader governments in the Middle East and, at times, in Europe); and the *'ayyarun*, who were a kind of urban bandit fighting for justice in Iraq between the tenth and thirteenth centuries.

These traditions raised the problem of tyrannicidal terrorism which has assumed enormous proportions in contemporary history and is justified today by an appeal to social, ethical and anti-imperialist revolution.

A curious combination of antithetical social and religious factors accounted for the creation of most of the great Muslim dynasties and the consequent revival of the Arab armies. On the one hand stood the *jawad*, the military aristocrat, and the *shaykh*, the chief of the warrior tribe who was able to call upon thousands of sabres or guns. On the other was the theologian who assembled an army of scholars. Thus, the duality of Muslim power is embodied in both the Word of God and the material reality of force. This was the case for the Fatamids, the Almoravids and the Almohads. The warrior-theologian combination is unified in a doctrine which is rejected by orthodoxy but has powerful resonances among the people: the doctrine of the *Mahdi*. The *Mahdi* bursts onto the stage of history to renovate the impure century. With his weapons in hand and theological controversy reopened, he calls for the *Jihad*.

The *Jihad*, a powerful mode of legitimation, was rooted in social and economic history. The bedouin raid, or *Ghazwa*, was developed, within the perspective of Islam, to become a method by which to purify wealth (the laundering occurring as it passed from non-Muslim to Muslim hands in the form of booty) before its employment in the cause of Muslim expansion. In this way, the old warrior impulses of the bedouin civilization (*badawiya*), glory and plunder, were translated into a mode of warfare whose stirring moral principles effected the ethical transfiguration of the fighting man.

The accumulation of territories and wealth transformed the community of willing believers into organized empires. The warrior democracy which had reigned among the great nomadic tribes ensured a relative equilibrium between them based on mutual assistance. The fact that the desert and the steppes were not places of great wealth prevented any single tribe

from achieving predominance. Fighting side by side did, however, reinforce their *asabiya* (ethnically and genealogically based social cohesion). Where, for one reason or another (religious revival, the control of an agricultural region or a caravan route), one family or clan dominated a tribe, that tribe would gather together its forces and, through warfare, create a new dynasty. This had three main consequences. The first was a socio-political transformation: the transition from the initial warrior democracy to a military aristocracy and, subsequently, to a centralized monarchy, creating a tax system, a network of communications with the provinces, and an army (*jund*) in which the military function was officially recognized. Second, a military council was established (*diwan al jich*) which controlled and administered the army, recording the warriors in lists classified by family and tribe, organized campaigns and allotted shares in booty. The centralized monarchy and the *diwan al jich* led to the third main consequence, a geo-strategic shift. Where a new empire was founded, a capital city developed in the midst of its territory to provide a centralized base for the bureaucracy and a fortress to protect the dynasty and its institutions. This implied a movement of population into the capital.

However, the provincial towns which were emptied of their notables, scholars and craftsmen often stood in outlying parts of the empire and had to be defended from attack. Local militia organizations came into existence, but these had to be financed. A number of phenomena then combined to produce troublesome effects. Rivalries were fomented by the relatives of the sovereign and the chief members of the tribe. As a result, from the ninth century both were replaced by slaves who were elevated to high office and granted estates (the Mamluks in Egypt, the janissaries in the Ottoman Empire). The native cohesion of the tribal warriors was further weakened and softened by the luxury of a more urbanized and static lifestyle. This led to increasing demands for improved remuneration which necessitated higher taxes on trade to meet the growing cost of military wages. In turn, this led to more discontent and hence, in a vicious circle, to a need for more slaves and mercenaries.

For a while other military factors were able to mitigate the worst aspects of this decline in the armed forces.

In war, a powerful *esprit de corps* is only necessary to reinforce bonds of mutual affection. In a town this role is performed by the ramparts. A town does not therefore have as much need of men or of blood ties. The possession of a city by the opponents of a dynasty can, therefore, hold in check the spirit (*élan*) of a nation. Hence, a monarchy will ensure that it controls the cities situated on its territory.

In fact, 'a town's best defences are the neighbouring tribes who are alerted by the shouts and noise of battle and also, in mountain regions, steep paths' (Ibn Khaldun).

The embodiment of the military function within social institutions was always a problem. The dynasties used two types of social structure and thus two partially contradictory types of armed forces existed. The first of these was the tribe, or fraction of a tribe, which was a ready constituted military entity; it continued with its own style of life and was led into battle by its own natural leaders. The second was the armed band of paid soldiers or 'regiment', which could assume many forms. It might be a regular company of slaves or mercenaries, who could be non-Arabs, non-Muslims or newly converted Muslims; light, irregular units drummed up in time of peril; or contingents of volunteers.

This dichotomy was reflected in the methods of warfare adopted by the colonial armies. The main bodies of regular troops were preceded by a cloud of fighters whose task it was to sweep across an enemy's lands, terrorizing and plundering, and who, by so doing, collectively satisfied their own inclination to revolt. If necessary, the *goums* (light troops or skirmishers) of a tribe were launched against a rebel tribe. This produced distortions in strategy – the bedouin protected or attacked caravan routes or the paths taken by herdsmen and conducted raids or punitive expeditions, while the regular troops maintained order and fought in organized campaigns – and also in tactics where the bedouin fought in scattered groups over wide geographical areas executing guerilla actions against the enemy's communications and resources, while the regular troops fought concentrated employing the advantages of disciplined formations and incorporating into their fighting the military techniques of a variety of peoples: the Byzantines (siege engines, catapults, etc.), the Sassanids and Franks (heavy cavalry, fortification), and the Turks and Mongols (light cavalry armed with bows swarming across the theatre of operations).

It also produced ethical distortions. A hierarchy of those licensed to commit acts of violence was established. At the bottom was the *'askri* or *jundi*, the soldier, a mere instrument, whose role was to maintain public order. Next came the warrior aristocracy, tribal or 'corporatist', consisting of the military nobleman (*jawad*) or naval privateer chief (*rais*) and the armies or crews who fought on their expeditions. Finally, there was the *ghazi*, the volunteer who took up arms for the *Jihad*, the sacred struggle defined in religious law, whether it was in the time of offensive action or, after the great conquests, during the defensive period. After the tenth century, the Islamic *limes* (fortified frontiers), reaching from the Atlantic to Transoxiana, including both coastal and land borders, were defended by *ribats*, monastery-barracks which provided a home for those mounting guard against the infidel. The ardour of the frontier defenders was fuelled by numerous treatises on holy war which, unlike those written in the preceding period, were concerned not so much with institutional matters (the theory and practice of the politico-administrative organization of conquered lands) or with strategy (the theory of non-stop offensive) and tactics (archery, horsemanship, the use of mangonels – stone-throwing machines) as with religious apologetics and praise of warrior virtues, purveying a doctrine of military action which gave as much weight to the notion of self-sacrifice as to earthly victory. Each was a *mujahid*, a fighter in a holy war who, if he died on campaign, would become a *shahid* (martyr) and travel directly to paradise since, by absolute faith in God (*tawakkul*), he had given his life for the temporal success of the *umma*, a victory which demonstrated the judgment of God on the value of Islam.

Although political and ethical reservations surrounded the troops drawn from non-Arabic populations (Slavic, Circassian, Caspian, Tartar, Turkish, Kurdish, etc.) who were not initially Muslims, even after these populations had converted to Islam, they gave birth to some of the most prestigious figures in the Muslim pantheon. Among the most notable were the Kurd Salah ad-Din Yusuf ibn Ayyub (Saladin), who recaptured Jerusalem in 1187, and the Mamluk sultan of Egypt, Baybars (1223–77), who fought against the Frankish Crusade of Louis IX at Mansourah in 1250 and whose lieutenant, Sultan Qutuz halted the Mongol invasion of Hulegu at Ain Djalout in 1260. They took as their ideal the virtue of *futuwwa* which incorporated Islamic solidarity, the mystical symbolism of arms, spiritual elevation and chivalric honour.

This period also marks the high point of the art of war among the Arabs. There was unity of command, military discipline and religious unity, strategic mobility based on the network of fortresses captured from the Crusaders, an effective spy service and a large number of engines of war fed by arms manufactories. Only the Arabic navy, launched in the time of the third caliph, 'Uthman, failed to rise above the level of commerce-raiding. The Arab dynasties were, however, dismantled by the *Reconquista* in the West, and by the second Mongol invasion and the establishment of the Turkish empires, first the Seljuk then the Ottoman, in the East. The latter empire came to devour the whole of the Arab world, except for Morocco in the western Maghreb.

There then arose in the politically subjugated Arab world the idea that the *Jihad* could be kept alive as much by actions motivated by the desire for individual profit as by the actions of rulers. Arab and Malay pirates roamed the Indian Ocean, while Turkish and Barbary corsairs operated in the Mediterranean. The fight against the strongholds of Berber irredentism (which ultimately dissolved into tribal struggles) and the disputes in the Maghreb under Turkish governments also matched the new pattern of the *Jihad*, as did the semi-commercial, semi-missionary expeditions into Black Africa which fuelled the slave trade.

Saladin, who seized Egypt in 1169, included a corps of Kurdish, Turcomen and Arab slaves (Mamluks) among his forces. Thereafter, repeated importations of slaves, particularly from the Caucasus, fuelled the Egyptian army. The slave boys were educated and converted to Islam before being enrolled in the armed forces. In 1249, the Mamluk generals seized power. Egyptian society was divided into two sections: *ahl al-qalam* (people of the pen) who manned the huge bureaucracy, and *ahl as-sayf* (people of the sword), the Mamluks who ran the army and occupied the principal offices of state. The system of *iqta* (non-transmissible landed tenures) prevented the formation of a true feudal system and encouraged a fragmentation of power. In 1517, the Ottomans occupied Egypt which became a province of the Turkish Empire. The Mamluks remained as a distinct social group and enjoyed some success in infiltrating the Ottoman ruling class. By the seventeenth century, the Ottoman Mamluks had formed 'households', private forces of some hundreds or thousands of men, largely Circassian slaves or Egyptian recruits. Against the Ottoman governor (*wali*), who enjoyed the status of a *pasha* and ruled with the assistance of a council (*diwan*) and militias (*odjaks*) of different types composed of *azabs* and janissaries, were ranged these private armies of the Mamluk beys. As Ottoman government weakened, the authority of the Mamluks over much of the country was officially recognized in return for the guaranteed payment of taxes. When Napoleon Bonaparte invaded Egypt in 1798, he derived considerable advantage from the fragmentation of native political and military power.

The Arabic and Muslim military systems were destroyed at the beginning of the nineteenth century. Mehmet Ali in Egypt and the Ottoman Tanzimat reforms put an end to the system of military tenures; the Mamluks were massacred in 1811 and the janissaries in 1826, and both Egypt and the Ottoman Empire began to organize conscript armies on the Western European model. However, after the Young Turk Revolution (1908), efforts were made to politicize the Ottoman army. Almost one-third of the Ottoman troops were Arabs. In the spirit of the anti-panislamist and anti-Ottoman political and literary renaissance (*Nahda*), the Arab officers, especially the Mesopotamians, formed themselves into a military league and a number of them organized the tribal contingents that Sherif Hussein of Mecca sent, alongside the Allied forces, against the Turks during the First World War. In these actions, T. E. Lawrence and Faysal (1885–1933), King of Iraq from 1921, developed a new form of guerilla warfare combining the strategic mobility of the Arab raid with modern fire-power.

In the struggle against the European colonial conquerors, the chief role was still played by the tribal warrior who, in spite of his efforts to find a base for the thrust of the *Jihad* in modern forms of political and military organization (Abd el Kader in Algeria, Abd el Krim in Morocco), did not manage to create an independent state. The Sudanese *Mahdi* (1848–85) was, admittedly, more successful in this regard than Arabi Pasha in Egypt (1882). However, the peasant revolts (Palestinians, Druzes in 1860, Sanusis) ran out of steam while the colonial rulers established modern bureaucratic and economic institutions, played on tribal divisions and raised bodies of local troops which were increasingly accorded a 'regular' position in their armies. The 'African regiments' or 'native' troops fought with distinction in the colonial wars and on the battlefields of Europe. There were the *Turcos* in the French army in 1870–1, the French North African divisions in 1914–18 and 1939–45, the Moorish *Regulares* of Franco's revolt, as well as the Middle Eastern Arab units – the Arab Legion, the Camel Corps – associated with the British armed forces. This recruitment of regular forces created the 'native soldier' who was subject to long periods of service and, consequently, often found himself out of phase with his original milieu. A solid stratum of NCOs was produced, promoted from the ranks, in addition to a few career officers, generally the sons of prominent loyalists, who had gradually assimilated the methods and military ethos of the West.

However, a deep underlying desire for the material liberation and spiritual purification of Arab territory remained. The first signs of this emerged after 1918, mainly in the shape of urban riots (Cairo, Damascus, Constantine and Fez) and nationalist actions. Manifestation of nationalist sentiment had to assume these forms as the changes which had been wrought upon Arab society by the colonial powers had undermined the tradition of tribal revolts and combat by a volunteer soldiery and replaced it by militancy and terrorism. Gradually, diffuse action by the urban and peasant masses was melded together and fighting forces trained to conduct indirect and guerilla warfare after the manner pioneered by the Chinese and Vietnamese. These troops were divided into a hierarchy of cadets (*aspirants*), auxiliaries, militiamen and regular soldiers (the Algerian *katibas*).

These processes were codified in the notion of revolution (*thawra*), embracing a general denunciation of imperialism and colonialism, borrowing aspects of strategic and economic technique from Marxist-Leninism and cherishing hopes of reconstructing the Arab and Islamic community in its original democratic form. Revolutionary strategy did, however, revive the figure of the volunteer, the lone soldier (*fida'i*). The Muslim Brotherhood at Suez and the Palestinians, Algerians and Lebanese Shi'ites took up this old concept and, stripping it of the remaining vestiges of anarchist terrorism, transformed it into a code of instigatory and tactical action. It no longer represented self-sacrifice in an isolated death but integration into the collective struggle. Thus, in the great tradition of Arab-Muslim societies, the independence of the new states which emerged from the aftermath of the First World War was achieved more by groups of volunteers than by fighting forces grouped into regular military units. These independent states were, however, governed by administrations that were military in nature – on the 'classical' military model in the monarchies; 'revolutionary' in style, along the lines laid down by Mustapha Kemel and Reza Pahlavi, in Egypt (the 'Free Officers'), Iraq, Syria and Libya; and shaped by revolutionary war in Algeria.

The Arabic armies currently fall into two categories: those which seek to create a mix of the whole population (Algerian national service, the Yemeni example, the Libyan doctrine of the 'People's Army' which is supposed to draw together the military, as an organization, and the nation), and those armies drawn predominantly from certain categories of the population. This latter situation pertains in the surviving monarchies, where the armies are essentially recruited from the tribal areas 'up country', most notably in Jordan and Saudi Arabia and, to a lesser extent, in Morocco. However, this unbalanced recruitment is offset by the coexistence in these countries of several types of force, each of which represents a particular community or ideological tendency. (In these cases, it is the tension between these factions which presents, and sometimes settles, the central issue which the regime has to resolve.) Thus, a distinction is made between the army and paramilitary forces in Syria and Saudi Arabia, and even in Morocco, not to mention the fragmentation of the Palestinian and Lebanese forces into rival militias.

Historically, Arab general staffs do not yet seem capable of mastering the art of conducting large-scale warfare. Out of the five Arab (Egypt, Syria, Palestine Liberation Organization) wars against Israel, even that of 1973, the Egyptian campaigns in the Yemen, the governmental campaigns in Iraq against the Kurds and in Sudan against the southern forces, the Moroccan campaigns in the western Sahara, the Sultan of Oman's war in the Dhofar (aided by Iran and by British instructors), the Iraqi war against Iran, and the Algerian war of independence, no military victory has been produced. In this last conflict, which derived support both from the worldwide anti-colonialist movement and from a demographic resurgence, the *katibas* on the frontiers were more significant in focusing attention and winning diplomatic support than in battle.

The Arab armies were formed as their new nation-states were consolidating. However, these states were caught up in long-standing conflicts in which long periods of calm were punctuated by brief, savage campaigns. The periods of calm were long because even a war of attrition requires a relative balance between the rival military forces and relative equality in economic resources. Neither of these factors was possessed by the Arabs in relation to Israel. Inter-Arab wars were small-scale both in duration and in the nature of the operations. However, these minor offensive and tactical wars, the strategic objective of which is to prevent the enemy from finding psychological comfort in the hope of a true peace, are only possible where both sides can shelter behind a shield of deterrent defensive forces which will prevent escalation into full-scale war.

Technically, the Arab soldier is faced with a major contradiction. When war breaks out he loses *matériel* at such a rate that he has no chance of sustaining large-scale operations for a prolonged period: the lightning campaign bogs down and turns into a war of attrition. He suffers because he has not been able to establish armaments industries capable of producing modern weapons systems, heavy tanks and combat aircraft, a situation which does not help him to formulate coherent tactical doctrines; he is dependent on imported hardware. However, the rapid and widespread growth in the number of participants, both national and private, in the international trade im light and medium weapons and the development of a triangular market in heavy arms sales (United States, Europe and Russia/Commonwealth of Independent States) have allowed the Arab states to escape the logical consequences of this dependency. By alternating between national suppliers and employing private agencies wherever possible, they have avoided declining into the status of satellites. However the

511

limitations of the situation in which Arab countries have alternated between suppliers, and hence instructors, have forced the Arab armies to model their operational organization and drill regulations on those of their international quartermasters. Lastly, all Arab countries are within range of the strategic and tactical nuclear forces of the United States and Russia. Also, and this is the source of the most intensely bitter feelings, Israel and India are credited with possessing a virtual military nuclear capability. Of the Arab states, only Iraq seems within range of producing a nuclear weapon but her capacity has been much reduced by military action during and since the Gulf War of 1991.

Thus, at a level below full-scale war, i.e. short of recourse to combined air and land military campaigns, Arab strategic thinking has most often shifted to urban guerilla warfare, to what their opponents describe as terrorist strikes, and to the physical occupation of territory (western Sahara, Chad, southern Sudan, Kuwait). These are forms of action which threaten to destabilize regional, if not indeed international, balances of power. They also continue to pose the centuries-old dichotomy between the volunteer fighter and the soldier. *See also* AIN DJALOUT; BLACK AFRICA; BYZANTIUM; COLONIAL TROOPS; GULF WAR; HOLY WAR; IRAN; IRAQ; ISRAEL, EARLY; ISRAEL, SINCE 1948; LAWRENCE; NUR-AD-DIN; OTTOMAN TURKS; SALADIN; TERRORISM; YARMUK.

J.-P. CHARNAY
JOHN CHILDS

FURTHER READING
J.-P. Charnay, *Principes de stratégie arabe* (Paris, 1984); J.-P. Charnay, *L'Islam et la guerre. De la guerre juste à la révolution sainte* (Paris, 1986); *The Cambridge History of Islam*, eds P. M. Holt, A. K. S. Lamblin and B. Lewis (2 vols, Cambridge, 1970); David Pryce-Jones, *Closed Circle: an interpretation of the Arabs* (London, 1989); Majid Khadduri, *War and Peace in the Law of Islam* (Baltimore, 1955); Shaykh Abu Zahra, *The Concept of War in Islam* (Ministry of Waqfs, Cairo, n.d.); D. Ayalon, *Gunpowder and Firearms in the Mamluk Kingdom* (London, 1956).

Midway Island, Battle of (4–5 June 1942) The Battle of Midway Island was one of the major turning points not just of the war in the Pacific, but of the Second World War. In the spring of 1942, the Japanese were in a sound position. With only slight losses, Japan had captured the whole of South-East Asia and established a solid defensive perimeter in the central Pacific. At this point, the commander-in-chief of the Imperial Japanese Navy, Admiral Isoroku Yamamoto, planned a final operation to destroy what remained of the American fleet, particularly its aircraft carriers, and to seize the final piece in the Japanese outer defensive perimeter. A landing on Midway Island, within striking distance of Hawaii by air, seemed likely to achieve both these goals.

The plan, finalized on 5 May, involved the whole of the Japanese navy. On the morning of 4 June, under cover of a diversionary operation against the Aleutian Islands, three Japanese task forces converged on Midway: the landing fleet, Vice-Admiral Chuichi Nagumo's First Carrier Strike Force with four aircraft carriers, and the main fleet under Yamamoto. The Japanese high command was convinced that the American fleet was still at anchor at Pearl Harbor, that the landings would be unopposed, and that a naval battle would occur after the amphibious operation at Midway was complete. They were mistaken. Following the interception and deciphering of Japanese radio messages, Admiral Chester Nimitz, Commander-in-Chief US Pacific Fleet, had placed his three aircraft carriers north-east of Midway. To Nagumo's surprise, the decisive clash came about on the morning of 4 June. The battle was essentially one of carrier-based aircraft, although US aircraft from Midway did see action. The result was catastrophic for the Japanese. The Japanese aircraft carriers were caught with many of their aircraft, back from an initial strike against Midway, on deck. The result was that all four Japanese aircraft carriers were sunk, while the Americans lost only one, the *Yorktown*, to a combination of air and submarine attack. Seeing the disastrous turn of events, Yamamoto decided on 5 June to turn back, losing one further ship, a cruiser, in the course of his retreat.

The Battle of Midway Island was expensive for the Japanese. They had lost two-thirds of their first-line aircraft carriers, many of their best trained naval pilots and the strategic initiative. The naval balance between Japan and the United States in the Pacific had been restored. Nimitz now had sufficient naval power to ward off the next Japanese offensive: an attempt to take Guadalcanal in the Solomon Islands as a preliminary to an assault against Australia. *See also* GUADALCANAL; JAPAN; NAGUMO; NIMITZ; PEARL HARBOR; YAMAMOTO.

P. MASSON
KEITH NEILSON

FURTHER READING
Walter Lord, *Incredible Victory* (New York, 1967); A. J. Barker, *Midway: the turning point* (New York, 1971); E. B. Potter, *Nimitz* (Annapolis, 1976); Gordon W. Prange, *Miracle at Midway* (New York, 1982).

Militarism *See* SOLDIERS AND SOCIETY; TRAINING

Military districts From Antiquity, armies have required some degree of regional organization in order to muster and equip troops. In Ancient Egypt, the existing local governorships (*nomes*) acted as the basis for military administration. Armies that were composed of citizens and were raised for a short duration required points at which to assemble. The territories of Athens and Sparta were divided into districts for this purpose as was the territory of Rome in the earliest stage of its history.

With the advent of standing armies, the main concern was the selection of areas suitable for the maintenance of units. In the early Roman Imperial period, each legion, composed of professional soldiers, was assigned to a specific province or group of provinces. Under the later Empire, military districts assumed a permanent character relevant to the tasks allotted to the troops they contained. Frontier troops (*limitanei*) were assigned the defence of well-defined sectors, particularly in regions where forti-fied lines (*limites*) had been constructed. The legions which constituted the mobile part of the army were established in permanent camps (*castra*). The Roman system of military districts was carefully integrated with the road network. This type of organization reached its apogee under the Byzantine Empire where the territory was split according to a systematic grid into military districts (*themes*), commanded by a *strategos*. This system developed in two directions. The *themes* increased in number (there were thirteen in the seventh century and thirty in the tenth) and became smaller with each advance in martial technique. Second, they gradually coalesced with the administrative regions of the Empire, which were arranged according to geographical criteria.

In the West, the conquering barbarian armies had merely to concern themselves with the mustering of forces and it was not until the emergence of Charlemagne's empire that there reappeared army units which stayed basically in one location. The counts who acted as the sovereign's agents were both military commanders and civil governors. Along the vulnerable frontiers, formal military districts called *marches* were entrusted to *marquises*. As the Carolingian Empire decayed, the counts and marquises grew more independent and their military and administrative districts were gradually converted into fiefs. Feudalism was basically a military system and fiefs can be considered as military districts, even though there were also ecclesiastical and urban fiefs.

With the revival of centralized monarchies, sovereigns delegated some of their military powers to agents – bailiffs, seneschals, sheriffs and vogte. In France, bailiffs and seneschals remained in charge of the general call-up until it was abolished and, in England, the sheriffs organized the local militia. At the close of the Middle Ages, the districts controlled by these officials gradually passed into the hands of more organized governmental authorities which had a distinctly military function.

In France, where Francis I had remodelled the system, there were, in Louis XIV's time, twelve major governorships-general bearing the names of provinces or areas roughly according with their physical and historical boundaries; governorships-general of lesser importance; and, finally, individual governorships covering a town and its immediate surroundings. An ordonnance of 1776 curtailed this variety by introducing a systematic arrangement whereby the number of governorships-general 1st class was fixed at eighteen and 2nd class at twenty-one; 114 individual governorships were retained and divided into three categories corresponding to their importance. Governors' emoluments were scaled in accordance with this hierarchy. The governor was the military commander of the province acting in the name of the king. He would step aside only if an army commander was operating within his jurisdiction. Nevertheless, he was far from having complete responsibility for everything concerning the army. The task of dealing with the upkeep of troops stationed in the province, or passing through it, fell to the intendant of the province, or rather of the *généralité*, an official who first made his appearance in the time of Louis XIII. The intendants were also responsible for the mustering and maintenance of the royal militia (1688) and for settling differences between the civilian and the military communities. The *généralité* was originally a fiscal district. The artillery and engineering services were also allocated districts which were assimilated either with the governorships or with the *généralités*.

The boundaries of those districts, which were concerned with technical branches, could admit of some modification. Others had a close connection with the lives of the population and could be changed only with difficulty. This was the case with recruitment districts for the navy and the coastguard service and with militia districts. The countries bordering the Ottoman Empire were shaped by the establishment of militarized border zones and by the outlines of their military districts. In Sweden, the modern military districts still bear the imprint of the *Indelta* established by Charles XI in 1682. Indeed, it was Sweden which first introduced the modern concept of the military district. Sweden was divided into eight military districts in 1617–18, each raising several regiments, and this was further modified by the *Indelningsverket* of 1682 which split all of Sweden and Finland into military districts, each of the larger ones responsible for raising an infantry regiment or regiments of 1,200 men. Smaller districts raised a specified number of companies.

During the eighteenth century, the Swedish model of the military district was adopted and refined by many European states. Between 1727 and 1735, Frederick William I of Brandenburg-Prussia established a cantonal system for recruiting his army. Each regiment was assigned a permanent geographical region, centred on its depot town (*standort*), from where it drew its native conscripts. The infantry, cavalry, engineers and artillery could use the same cantons or their cantons could overlap as the physical requirements for each service were different. During the 1740s, the cantonal system was extended into Silesia and after 1763 it was further improved through the registration of all male births. Although the cantonal system came to an end with Prussia's collapse in 1806, the Prussian and German armies of the nineteenth and twentieth centuries were organized around the military district for recruiting and maintenance. Frederick II of Hesse-Kassel adopted the Prussian cantonal system in 1762. The hereditary lands of the Austrian Empire were organized into cantons in 1781 followed by Hungary and the Tyrol in 1784. Towards the close of the eighteenth century, the alterations in army articulation led to the adoption of the division. Gradually, European states adjusted their military districts to accommodate the new formation. By 1791, France had been divided into 21 military districts supporting 17 'territorial divisions'. In 1879, corps districts were superimposed on the divisional districts, each corps containing a number of territorial divisions. The corps and divisions roughly equated with the field formations which would be created at mobilization. In 1868, the army of Prussia and the North German Confederation was organized into twelve corps districts with a single divisional district in Hesse. By 1914, the German Empire contained twenty-four corps districts each responsible for raising and training one active and one reserve corps. During war, additional districts were frequently superimposed on these peacetime structures: operational sectors, fronts and commands. Between 1939 and 1945, Great Britain was divided into six military commands and two military districts (London and Northern Ireland). The commands were further split into areas, each corresponding to an army corps.

During the War of 1812, the United States was divided into nine military districts, each under a general officer. The districts were grouped into two divisions, the Northern and the Southern. In the aftermath of the Civil War, the ten reconstructed southern states were organized into ten military districts, each commanded by a general officer who was also responsible for civil government and administration. By 1869, the army of the United States was arrayed in 255 military posts, administered by eight staff departments and eleven military districts under the headquarters of three territorial divisions – the Atlantic, the Pacific and the Missouri.

England's military districts were synonymous with the county or shire. From the reign of Elizabeth I, the militia was organized on a county basis and coastal counties could be taxed to provide shipping for their own defence. Since its foundation in 1660, the English army has recruited on a county and territorial basis but this was not formalized until the army reforms of Edward Cardwell in 1870–1. England and Wales were divided into sixty-six administrative brigade districts, corresponding, as far as was possible, with the existing county boundaries. Two regular battalions, two militia battalions and the volunteers were attached to each district.

In 1945, the Soviet Union was divided into twenty-one military districts, each commanded by a marshal or a senior general, which varied considerably in size depending upon population and strategic location. The districts called up and trained conscripts, including those for the navy and the air force, raised new formations in time of war, supervised military schools and commanded all transport and economic resources.

However, the Soviet military district, like the German, French and the British model, was not an operational command; it merely raised and trained corps, divisions, brigades, regiments and battalions before they were dispatched to operational commands. *See also* ADMINISTRATION, ARMY; ADMINISTRATION, NAVAL; BYZANTIUM; COASTAL DEFENCE; FORTIFICATION; FRONTIERS, MILITARY; MOBILIZATION; NAVAL PERSONNEL; OTTOMAN TURKS; PROPERTY OWNED BY THE MILITARY; RECRUITMENT; ROME.

A. CORVISIER
JOHN CHILDS

FURTHER READING
G. E. Rothenberg, *The Austrian Military Border in Croatia, 1522–1747* (Urbana, Ill., 1960); G. E. Rothenberg, *The Military Border in Croatia, 1740–1881* (Chicago, 1966).

Military law *See* LAW, MILITARY

Military restrictions on use of land Military restrictions on the use of land initially derived from the defensive requirements of fortresses and later came to be applied to national defence. By the mid-seventeenth century, there were few significant towns and cities in Western Europe which were not fortified in the style of the 'trace italienne'. In order to secure a clear defensive field of fire for the garrison, the development of suburbs or any buildings beyond the glacis was subject to severe restrictions. In France, laws established three zones. Within the first, which was 275 yards wide, no buildings of any kind were permitted; in the second, 530 yards wide, no masonry buildings were allowed; while in the third, 1,060 yards wide, authority had to be obtained for the constructions of paths, embankments, roads, dumps of rubble, etc. Exceptions were granted in particular areas which 'were not normally used for firing practice' subject to the proviso that all such developments would be demolished without compensation when the fortress was placed on a war footing. Prussia and Piedmont emulated French regulations. In 1871, a law in the German Empire set out new rules which widened the zones up to 3,250 yards reflecting the

515

improved ranges of rifled artillery. In Italy, a new system of regulations was introduced in 1930.

Fortified towns were thus corsetted within a broad band of fortifications, separated from their suburbs by a distance of nearly 2 miles. Land became scarce and expensive within the towns while the suburbs tended to develop as distinct villages and satellites. In the mid-nineteenth century, the continuous fortifications were gradually replaced by rings of detached forts. Henri Brialmont refortified Liège, Namur and Antwerp. His forts at Liège were mostly buried underground at a distance of 4 km from one another and 8 km from the city centre. Urban development was free to breath. The demolished belts of fortifications became pleasant parks and open spaces for the enjoyment of the citizenry as in Maastricht, Paris or Vienna.

In the twentieth century, frontier zones and fortified zones such as the Maginot Line or the Mareth Line have continued to demand fields of fire and have placed restrictions on developments within a distance of 9 km. Restrictions have also been placed upon air space with civilian overflying of the fortifications strictly prohibited. Switzerland imposes military requirements on all building, both private and public. Bridges have to contain special demolition chambers, schools and all places of work have to provide nuclear fall-out shelters, fields of fire before established artillery positions have to be kept clear and all new roads must be built with military aspects in mind. During the Second World War, civilian access was prohibited to all British beaches and a zone up to 5½ miles inland.

Firing ranges and military training grounds may be either permanent or temporary (used only for a few days or weeks a year). In the latter case, the owner is entitled to claim compensation. Some firing ranges, as at Hythe or Foulness, have danger zones stretching out to sea and their use is subject to prior notice to shipping. Aircraft bombing ranges are marked on aircraft charts and there are designated corridors of air space which can be used by military aircraft for low flying.

Stores of explosives, weapons development sites and weapons research establishments and manufacturing facilities also require safety zones. According to the output of the factories or the storage capacity of the dumps, an uninhabited belt must surround the sites and limitations are placed on the number of rooms and density of living accommodation within the adjacent 2.5 acres. *See also* ARSENALS; BASES, AIR FORCE; BASES, NAVAL; COASTAL DEFENCE; FORTIFICATION; PROPERTY OWNED BY THE MILITARY.

J.-M. GOENAGA
JOHN CHILDS

FURTHER READING
John Childs, *Armies and Warfare in Europe, 1648–1789* (Manchester, 1982); C. Bertout, *Le Domaine militaire* (Paris, 1909); John McPhee, *The Swiss Army* (London, 1985).

Militias Technically, a militia can be any form of military force but it is usually defined as a body of armed men raised from among the civilian population to supplement the regular troops. A militia is both traditional and territorial. By extension, the term can be applied to paramilitary organizations. Prior to the eighteenth century in Europe, militias had their origins in the obligations to perform military service which arose from Germanic institutions. Under these arrangements, free men had to respond to the call of the king for periods fixed by custom and had to provide their own equipment. In fact, from the twelfth century onwards, the term was restricted to the units created by those towns and cities which, in return for their loyalty to the sovereign, had obtained the right to conduct their own administration and thus bore the onus of organizing their own policing and defence. These were the 'urban militias' which grouped together, either by locality or guild, all the male inhabitants capable of bearing arms under the command of municipal officials and magistrates. Under the *ancien régime*, the urban militia of Bordeaux consisted of six regiments, each under the command of one of the six *jurats*, roughly equivalent to an English alderman. By this time, only the urban militias in Italy and the Holy Roman

Empire played a significant military role. In 1302, for example, the combined militias from the Flemish cities inflicted a defeat on the French army at Courtrai. In centralized kingdoms, the militias were often called on to provide contingents for the royal army, as, for example, in France at the Battle of Bouvines in 1214.

Faced with the rising cost of armaments and soldiers and the need to centralize the military forces of the kingdom, the French crown partly disarmed the urban militias after the Fronde (1648–53). They were restricted to policing operations and, in some cases, to employment as army auxiliaries in frontier towns, particularly during sieges. By the eighteenth century, the role of urban militias had become minor indeed. The tasks of manning police posts and mounting patrols were tedious and unpleasant and most burghers paid substitutes to perform their duties. Only in those towns which had established small companies of elite burgher guards, 'gardes bourgeoises', which bore a variety of titles – 'companies of archers' (Edinburgh), 'companies of crossbowmen', 'town guards' or 'companies of the watch' (Amsterdam) – did the volunteers carry out their own duties in return for certain privileges. In France, the concept of a militia reappeared in 1789 in the form of the National Guard.

Apart from the urban militias, there were other forms of traditional militias under the *ancien régime* in France. The Provincial Militias mainly belonged to the frontier provinces, Béarn and Boulogne for example, and men were grouped by parishes under the command of leading local magnates. Finally, the need to defend the shores of France led to the formation of coastal militias which were first centrally organized by Francis I who instructed all his male subjects between the ages of 16 and 60 to form a 'watch'. From the reign of Louis XIV onwards, the most able-bodied men in the coastal regions were arranged into 'detached companies' whose task was to oppose enemy landings on the coasts, or to deter such attempts.

It was on the basis of the duty of the subject to perform military service that Louis XIV and Louvois formed the idea in 1688 of creating Royal Militias which were intended as auxiliaries to the regular army and as a reserve army of potential recruits. Bachelors and married men without children were made to draw lots and those who drew the unlucky numbers became militiamen. The militias were dissolved when peace returned in 1714 but they were reformed in 1726 to become a standing reserve that was drawn on in time of war to bring the regular cadres up to full strength through the mechanism of 'incorporation', the forerunner of what is today called 'amalgame'. This constituted a step towards conscription and the subject is dealt with below in the entry on RECRUITMENT, where the transformation of militias in other countries, such as Sweden (*Indelta*) and Prussia (*Kantonsystem*), is discussed.

In other countries, the militia remained a territorial armed force which did not fight outside the national borders. English county militias refused to operate outside the boundaries of their own shires. The parliamentary statute of 1558 restated the martial obligations of all freeholders of between 16 and 60 years of age. These men had to provide their own equipment and were divided into cavalry and infantry according to their landed status. The lord-lieutenant commanded the militia of a county assisted by a number of deputy-lieutenants. The gentry provided the officers. In the sxteenth century, there were one million names on the militia roles out of a population of four million, but less than 100,000 men were trained. In spite of the basic organization, the reality was less impressive. Barons had the right to retain county militiamen on their estates in their own service and these men formed contingents who only fought in the militia under the command of their lord. Towns with royal charters enjoyed similar privileges. In 1573, it was felt necessary to form the best of the militiamen into 'trained bands', whose members received pay for days spent in training and on active service. This militia was on alert between 1588 and 1598 but it was not tested in war. After the end of the Spanish War in 1604, the militia went into a steady decline despite Stuart projects for creating an 'exact militia' or a 'select militia'. After 1660, the militia became a political pawn between Parliament and the King in the quest for the control of the armed forces. The sole exeption to the atrophy of the English militia was the London Trained Bands who provided the core of Parliament's army during the English Civil War (1642–6) and were both more numerous and better trained than their comrades in the shires.

The English militia was effectively re-founded in 1757; its numbers were limited and chosen by drawing lots. The 'New Milita', which became a permanent force in 1769, was at its height in the period between 1775 and 1802. During the nineteenth century, all British males between 17 and 45 years of age were still theoretically required to perform military service but militias only existed in a few counties and these were paid forces, manned from among the youngest men chosen by lot. Each man selected enjoyed the option of providing a substitute. Duties were not onerous, the men serving only for a few days over a five-year term. The mounted Yeomanry, which provided rural policing, also faded from view during the early nineteenth century. As in all times of national emergency, the English militia was reactivated in 1940 in the form of the Local Defence Volunteers, better known as the Home Guard.

The European powers transplanted the militia system into their colonies. It made its appearance in Virginia in 1623 and spread into the other British colonies in North America with the exception of Pennsylvania where the model of the Trained Bands was copied. No social class was excluded although Indians and slaves were naturally not part of the organization. In French Canada, the example of the Provincial Militias in France was imitated. They were constantly on the alert and served as a back-up to the regular 'Compagnies franches de la marine' and the regiments sent from France. During the eighteenth century, French Canada was probably the country with the greatest proportion of its men under arms. The captains of the militia played a substantial role in the civil administration, the police force and the legal system. The same was true in the French territories in the West Indies, particularly Santo Domingo where it also fell to the militia to keep order among a population of varied racial origin. The militia council served as an intermediary between the governor and the inhabitants, setting in place a kind of 'militia democracy' which thwarted the attempts of the French government to militarize the island militia. The British West Indian islands all adopted militias similar to the county models with compulsory service for all white colonists and the leading planters acting as officers. Throughout the seventeenth and eighteenth centuries, they were reasonably successful in defending their colonies and in attacking French and Spanish possessions.

The colonial militias played some part in gaining independence for their countries. In 1775, the militias of the thirteen British colonies in North America listed some 500,000 men, or one-third of the entire population, though only a fraction of these numbers were effective and experienced. These militiamen harboured a hostility towards the British regular army and most joined the rebellion in 1775. However, they were loath to engage in long campaigns or to fight outside their own colonies and the war effort of the American rebels came to depend more and more on the regular, 'Continental' army created by George Washington. The militias of Spanish America, which were established in 1775, played a similar role in the battles for independence fought by the states of Latin America.

Once the United States had secured its freedom from Britain in 1783, the Federal government became concerned by the risk of a military dictatorship and reduced the strength of the militias which remained under the control of each state. They were involved to a certain degree in the Anglo-American War of 1812–14, and during the American Civil War both sides used the militias as reserves. During the remainder of the nineteenth century, the state militias went into a steep decline as the frontier pushed steadily to the west and the Federal army assumed responsibility for the battle against the Indians. Only the officers remained to command a few units charged with the maintenance of law and order in a country where the possession of firearms was legal. These units, which were under the control of the state governors, acted as a rapid intervention force. In theory, every male citizen between the ages of 18 and 45 was a militiaman, except for priests, ministers, schoolteachers, judges, lawyers and sailors. Around 1840, the militias began to admit some immigrants. By 1877, most states had followed the lead of New York and renamed their militias the National Guard. The 'Dick Act' of 1903 restated the obligation to universal male military membership of the militia, 'the Reserve Militia', but designated the National Guard regiments, 'the Organized Militia' and it took the decision to form the National Guard into a reserve for the Federal army. National Guardsmen could join the regular army by voluntary enlistment and National Guard formations could enter into Federal service as formed units. Some 80,000 National Guardsmen amalgamated with the Federal forces during the First World War. Today, the number of Reserve Militiamen in the United States stands at around 1 million but the form of their organization varies from state to state. These bodies act as auxiliaries to the Federal army in border and coastal areas. Their main task is the maintenance of law and order and relief work during natural catastrophes and other disasters.

France possessed a similar type of arrangement during the Revolution and the period known as the 'censitary monarchy' (after 1842) when the force was called the National Guard, the term 'militia' being generally reviled on account of memories of the Royal Militias of the *ancien régime*. Towards the end of his reign, Napoleon I attempted to turn the National Guard into an auxiliary force for the regular army. Under the July Monarchy, these paramilitary formations, largely recruited from among the middle classes, played a part in putting down riots right up to the Revolution of 1848. The *Garde Nationale Mobile*, established by the 'Loi Niel' in 1868, was the last example in France of the concept of an auxiliary army drawn from the whole male population. The 'Loi Militaire' of 1872 sounded the death-knell for military institutions of this type.

The Swiss militia was an organization of a quite different sort. The Federal Pact of 1815 forbade the formation of a permanent army and only provided for martial institutions in so far as they were intended to defend Switzerland's neutrality. The cantonal militias of the pre-1789 period were reformed on an entirely new basis. Their role was to provide contingents for the Federal army which would be equipped and maintained by the separate cantons. The Federal General Staff was composed of officers appointed by the Federal Executive (the *Conseil Fédéral* or the *Bundesrat*). By the constitution of 1874, the army came under the immediate control of the Confederation and citizens were incorporated into it directly. Between the ages of 20 and 44, all able-bodied Swiss males have to serve initially in the *Auszug* or *Élite* and then in the *Landsturm* or *Réserve* and no substitution is permitted. After a short spell of basic training, the Swiss militiamen have to undergo annual spells of instruction for varying lengths of time depending on their rank. The Swiss air force and navy are also run on the militia principle.

In imitation of the arrangements in the former Soviet Union, the term 'militia' was adopted in the 'peoples' democracies' to describe the army intervention forces in the service of the state. This role bore no relation to the function of the traditional people's militias in Western Europe. The Vichy regime in France revived the name 'Milice' for its armed political police force. *See also* FRANCE; GREAT BRITAIN; RECRUITMENT; SCHWENDI; SWITZERLAND; UNITED STATES.

A. CORVISIER
JOHN CHILDS

FURTHER READING
André Corvisier, *Armies and Societies in Europe, 1494–1789* (Bloomington, Ind., 1979); Lindsay Boynton, *The Elizabethan Militia, 1558–1638* (London, 1967); J. R. Western, *The English Militia in the Eighteenth Century: the story of a political issue* (London, 1965); John McPhee, *The Swiss Army* (London, 1985); J.

Dan Hill, *The Minute Man in Peace and War: a history of the National Guard* (Harrisburg, 1963).

Mining and mines Mining is one of the oldest methods of attacking fixed fortifications. It was perhaps through mining that Jericho was captured by Joshua, and the Jews made use of the technique against the armies of Vespasian in AD 72. Since then, mining has become a regular feature of siege warfare. Before the employment of gunpowder and explosives, mining basically consisted of digging a tunnel, or gallery, which passed underneath the wall or rampart under assault. In rare cases, the gallery might surface within the main body of the fortress enabling the attackers to achieve a surprise break-in. Generally, however, the mine created a cavity beneath the foundations of the wall. The wall was supported by timber pit-props and the cavity filled with inflammable material. When the fire was lit, the props burned away and the wall collapsed. Occasionally, the miners worked directly at the base of the wall protected by 'tortoises' of metal shields or portable metal and wooden roofs called 'mantelets'. When mines had been detected, either by vibration or from underground 'listening galleries', the defenders dug a countermine to intercept that of the attackers. Then either the attacking mine was collapsed about the ears of the assaulting miners or a subterranean skirmish occurred. In order to achieve efficient combustion, adequate ventilation had to be provided within the mine and use was made of a number of the techniques employed by civilian coal and metal ore miners.

Ordinary gunpowder – a mixture of charcoal, sulphur and saltpetre – appeared in Western Europe around 1250 and was first used in mining by the Italians towards the end of the fifteenth century. A charge of gunpowder was positioned in the cavity beneath the foundations of the wall in place of the inflammable pit-props and combustible materials. The first attempts – at Orense in 1468, Malaga and Sarzanello in 1487 – did not fully produce the desired effect, because the explosions were not properly directed. Simply placing a gunpowder charge in an open chamber connected directly to a long tunnel, dissipated the explosion. The solution is customarily attributed to Francesco di Giorgio Martini of Sienna who, in a treatise dating from 1495, included a drawing of a zig-zagged final section of tunnel. This permitted efficient 'tamping'. The charge was placed in the tip of a small, 'bayonet-shaped' chamber and the tunnel was zig-zagged over the final few yards. The gunpowder was packed tightly in a 'plug', fronted by a wooden support through which passed the fuses enclosed in leather 'sausages'. The whole force of the explosion could now be directed at the foundations of the wall. The first effective use of explosive mines was by the Spaniard, Pedro Navarro, at the Castle of Uovo at Naples in 1503. In the same year, a fellow countryman, Ramirez, who had built the fortress of Salses in Roussillon, inflicted heavy losses on the French by exploding counter-mines which had been laid in advance during the construction of the fortress. Further improvements were made during the sixteenth century. Giuliano da Sangallo built into his fortresses listening galleries at ditch level and connected them to the beginnings of tunnels for counter-mines. Mines were detected by ripples on water rather than by the drumskins and pebbles which had been used at Rhodes in 1522. Mine galleries were better directed, with fewer ending below the wrong place. Gunpowder rendered counter-mines more effective and charges called *camouflets* (literally, something which stifles) were employed to blow in attacking mines. Sieges came to be conducted on two levels: on the surface by sappers attempting to install batteries on the covered way, and underground by miners, both parties trying to breach the walls. Following Errard de Bar-le-Duc (1594), Antoine de Ville (1628) advocated the building of a continuous gallery beneath the scarp of a fortress from which counter-mines could be constructed. In 1703, Vauban wrote that the defenders should dig mines under the covered way so that attackers could be blown up if they tried to dominate the counterscarp. During the 28-month period from 1657 to 1659, in the course of the Turkish siege of Candia in Crete, the Turks dug 1,364 mine tunnels, one of which contained a charge of 18,000 lb of powder.

In the eighteenth century, Bélidor, an instructor at the École d'artillerie at La Fère, made advances in the theory of explosives. In 1729, he penned the *Nouvelle théorie de la science des mines* and in 1732 and 1753 he conducted experiments which were resumed in 1754 by Simon Lefebvre, an engineer in the service of the King of Prussia. He showed that counter-mines containing a very high charge could destroy the mines of the besiegers at a considerable distance. During the Prussian siege of Schweidnitz in Silesia in 1762, Lefebvre conducted the assault and Jean-Baptiste Gribeauval was the engineer in charge of the Austrian defence. The attack was directed against the Jauernicker Fort which was equipped with counter-mines. Mines were dug from the first parallel but a combination of Prussian inexperience, spirited sorties by the garrison and the detonation of counter-mines drove Lefebvre into a state of nervous collapse. Eventually, a mine was sprung under the ramparts of the Jauernicker Fort, but its surrender on 9 October after a siege of sixty-three days was principally occasioned by a lucky mortar bomb which blew up the main magazine. Mines were extensively employed in the sieges of the Revolutionary and Napoleonic Wars, most notably during the inch-by-inch struggle for Saragossa in 1808–9. The Siege of Sebastopol (1854–5) during the Crimean War was a battle between the French and Russian miners, the latter commanded by Eduard Ivanovich Todleben. Mines and counter-mines were dug on a daily basis and the Russians laid additional galleries some 18 yards below their main tunnels to protect them from French countermines. At the Siege of Port Arthur between May 1904 and January 1905, the Japanese ensured the fall of the stronghold when, using modern explosives, they destroyed the counter-scarp casemates blocking off the entrance to the ditches around the forts. The invention of dynamite by Alfred Nobel in 1867 and the development of trinitrotoluene

(TNT) have added enormously to the efficacy of mining.

The experimental use of explosive mines in open country appeared during the Russo-Japanese War (1904–5). The First World War, in which trench warfare witnessed a return to many of the methods of seventeenth- and eighteenth-century siege operations, saw a widespread and spectacular employment of mines. The British attack at Messines in 1917 was preceded by the detonation of eighteen mines containing a total of 600 tons of explosives at the end of 8,000 yards of tunnelling. All along the Western Front, mining and countermining were regular pastimes. Galleries were begun from the second line of trenches with the main tunnel often being doubled by additional galleries to serve as substitutes or to deceive the enemy. Galleries were protected by tunnels excavated at a lower level and sophisticated listening systems. During their withdrawal to the Hindenburg Line in 1917 and their general retreat in 1918, the Germans transformed the mine from an underground to a surface weapon in the form of the anti-personnel mine.

The Second World War saw the development and perfection of the light, man-portable anti-tank and anti-personnel mine resting on the surface of the earth. Minefields covered defensive positions, channelled potential attackers onto the defenders' pre-positioned guns and 'refused' sections of the front. Minefields were laid according to precise plans with roads through them to allow for counter-attack and to enable them to be lifted when no longer required. So long as mines had metal casings, detection was by magnetic detectors, the 'frying pan'. More sophisticated mines enclosed in wood, glass or plastic containers were less easy to discover and often prodding with the bayonet proved the only sure method. For the invasion of Normandy in 1944, the Allies invented a range of specialized armoured vehicles which were equipped with heavy rollers and flailing chains on their bows to clear a path through the German coastal minefields. In 'double firing', a fake mine concealed a real one, which exploded when the dummy was lifted. Anti-personnel devices underwent considerable improvement during the wars in Korea and Vietnam, especially with the invention of the bouncing mine which, when triggered by a trip-wire, sprung up to waist-height before detonating. This improved the range and effectiveness of its fragmentation. Another mine set off by trip-wire or remote control is the Claymore which showers metal balls within an arc of 60 degrees. It is used principally in ambushes and prepared defensive positions. Anti-tank mines, although first conceived in 1917, were brought to a higher state of sophistication in 1935 with the German Tellermine. Anti-tank mines are heavier than the anti-personnel variety as they have to destroy caterpillar tracks or smash the underbellies of armoured vehicles, whereas the anti-personnel mine only needs to deliver an incapacitating wound to the foot or the lower leg. The sweeping of anti-tank mines can be rendered more dangerous by mixing them among anti-personnel devices. The majority of modern mines are plastic and can be broadcast by helicopter, from vehicles, by artillery and by rocket-dispenser (the British Ranger system). Unfortunately, the mine is an indiscriminate weapon and, once laid, is difficult and time-consuming to clear. Large areas of Europe and North Africa remain uninhabitable on account of mines extant from the Second World War and since 1945 the cheapness and effectiveness of mines have led to their widespread adoption throughout the world. The Falkland Islands and Afghanistan are riddled with minefields, as are parts of Angola, southern Africa, Vietnam and Cambodia. Anti-personnel mines continue to cause large numbers of civilian casualties long after a war has been concluded.

Land forces have used 'river' or 'drifting' mines, inspired by their maritime counterparts, to hinder river crossings. Anti-aircraft defences have used aerial mines hung on wires from tethered balloons to guard against dive-bombing and low-level attack. During the Second World War, mines in the form of prepared demolition charges were employ-ed to destroy bridges, railway lines and buildings. Some countries, particularly post-war Switzerland, have built chambers for demolition mines into their strategically important railway and road tunnels and bridges in order to obstruct an invasion of their country. *See also* ENGINEERS; EXPLOSIVES; NAVAL WARFARE; PROPELLANTS; SIEGES; TODLEBEN; WEAPONS.

J.-M. GOENAGA
JOHN CHILDS

FURTHER READING
Simon Pepper, 'The underground siege', *Fort*, x (1982), pp. 31–8; C. Duffy, *The Fortress in the Age of Vauban and Frederick the Great* (London, 1985); P. R. Courtney-Green, *Ammunition for the Land Battle* (London, 1991), pp. 171–84.

Mitchell, William ('Billy') (1879–1936) Mitchell was an officer in the US Army Signal Corps who had served in Cuba and the Philippines before his appointment to the army's general staff in 1913. He had already predicted that the air would eventually become a theatre of military operations and that aircraft would be used as bombers, fighters and for long-range reconnaissance as well as in the more obvious role of spotting for the artillery.

Mitchell left the general staff for the fledgling aviation section of the Signal Corps in 1915. Sent to France just before the United States entered the First World War, he was in a position to study aerial operations up to that time and to influence the recommendations sent by the French government to Washington on how the United States should develop its aviation industry and air force. Appointed chief of the air service [US] Army in January 1918, he gathered together and commanded nearly 1,500 US and Allied aircraft to gain air superiority over the front during the US army's St Mihiel offensive and then experimented with strategic bombing in the Meuse–Argonne offensive.

Knowing the cost of army support operations and the as yet unreached potential of bombing forces, Mitchell became a crusader for air power, an independent air force and strategic bombing when he returned to the United States after the war – opinions which soon incurred the hostility of the army, the navy, and the government. He finally went too far when, in September 1925, he accused the US Navy of 'incompetency, criminal negligence and almost treasonable administration' following the crash of its dirigible *Shenandoah*. Mitchell was court-martialled and resigned from the army but he continued to develop his ideas regarding the cardinal importance of strategic bombing and the growing threat from Japanese expansion in the Pacific.

Mitchell had supporters in the air service, officers like Henry H. (Hap) Arnold, Carl (Tooey) Spaatz and Ira Eaker, who agreed with his ideas on bombing but, for a number of years, they were out of favour because of Mitchell's stand. By the late 1930s, however, the advocates of strategic bombing had a great deal to do with the writing of the US air war plans – and in terms of doctrine and equipment the US army air forces were reasonably well prepared for the bomber offensive in which they would eventually take part. *See also* AIRCRAFT, BOMBER; AVIATION; UNITED STATES.

P. FACON
STEPHEN J. HARRIS

FURTHER READING

Alfred T. Hurley, *Billy Mitchell: crusader for air power* (New York, 1964); Dewitt S. Copp, *A Few Great Captains: the men and events that shaped the development of US air power* (Garden City, NY, 1980).

Mobilization This operation usually coincides with or slightly precedes a declaration of war. An army, navy or air force is put on a war footing by calling reserves to the colours and providing the equipment required to take the field. Mobilization can be partial or total but it must be meticulously planned. Every staff, unit and establishment maintains a regularly updated check-list of all the steps to be taken, day by day and even hour by hour. Mobilization must be distinguished from the levying of additional troops in wartime.

After the reforms of the *Indelningsverket* (1682–91), Charles XI of Sweden designed a mobilization plan to enable his essentially territorial army to be concentrated and mustered in the shortest possible time. Under the direction of Erik Dahlberg and Rutger von Ascheberg, new military roads were built in the south and west of Sweden, and along all the roads which were to be used for mobilization new inns were constructed and some existing inns were rebuilt at different locations to serve as staging posts for the troops. Maps were made of all provinces and, at their triennial musters, careful note was taken of how long it took each company to muster and march to its rendezvous. On the basis of these calculations, precise mobilization timetables were prepared. By the death of Charles XI in 1697, the master mobilization plan was housed in the College of War and every regimental colonel and captain possessed a map and detailed orders on how, where and when his unit was to move when the mobilization occurred. In March 1700, Charles XII put the plan into operation and the Swedish army smoothly assembled for war with Russia.

The Swedish model set the pattern for modern mobilizations, particularly in Brandenburg-Prussia. During the mid-nineteenth century, efficiency was improved by the electric telegraph and the railway. The earliest 'modern' mobilization occurred in Prussia in 1870. Young Prussian males were conscripted to serve for two years in the infantry or three years in the cavalry or the artillery. Subsequently, until reaching the age of 32, they were placed in the first reserve of the *Landwehr* where they were called up for two periods of annual training. Between 32 and 40 they entered the second reserve. They could still be mobilized between the ages of 40 and 50 and, in that event, were given the task of guarding the home territory and ensuring its internal security. Thanks to her mobilization system, Prussia could raise a total armed force of 954,000 men when the peacetime army numbered only 300,000. From a population which amounted to just half that of France, Prussia could raise twice as many soldiers. In addition, since mobilization took only seven days to complete, Prussian war plans assumed that the troops would be formed up and ready to fight within nineteen days. At the end of that time in France, even those units which were already serving were still dispersed and lacking equipment while the reserves had not yet rejoined their regiments.

Napoleon III wished to create a copy of the Prussian system in France but was unable to secure its adoption. The law drafted by Marshal Niel, dated 1 February 1868, brought into being an initial period of conscription of five years, followed by four years in the reserve, in addition to the creation of a mobile defence force consisting of conscripts who had drawn 'unlucky numbers'. Owing to lack of time and money and the need to avoid upsetting the civilian population, the latter received virtually no training. When war was declared in 1870, mobilization consisted of recalling 50,000 reservists and putting on an active footing 13,300 'unlucky numbers' in the mobile defence force who had managed four or five months of their periods of service. The classes of 1869 and 1870 were called up in full and 31,000 volunteers enlisted for the duration of the war. The imperial government raised a 12th and 13th army corps and the succeeding government of national defence established a further fourteen new army corps. On 2 November 1870, the government of national defence called up all men under 40 who were fit for service, a step which brought the numbers mobilized to one million. In addition, there were 400 units of *francs-tireurs* totalling 80,000 men. However, the French efforts suffered from poor training, bad organization and mediocre leadership and proved incapable of halting the Prussian invasion or of defending Paris.

France learned from the defeat of 1870 and adopted the Prussian model in 1872, establishing a five-year term of conscription and a fifteen year period in the reserves, four of these being served in the reserve proper, five in the 'home army' and six in the home army reserve. All of the reserve was formed into theoretical peacetime units based on the subdivision for the infantry and the region for the other arms. When mobilization was decreed, the units of the home army could be assigned to the defence of fortresses, coasts, strategic points and lines of communication but they might also be formed into field brigades, divisions and corps. Unfortunately, the law of 1872 allowed numerous exemptions and young men who drew a 'lucky number' or who were graduates completed only one full year of service. It was not until 21 March 1905 that military service was made universal and compulsory, an obligation which applied equally to all male citizens. The length of full-time service was cut to two years followed by a period of 23 years in the reserve; in 1913, full-time service was raised to three years and that in the reserve to 24 (Table 1).

In August 1914, Germany possessed, in addition to 25 army corps of soldiers on full-time service, a further 14 composed of the reserve army and the *Ersatz-Reserve*. This gave a total of 98 divisions plus 14

Table 1 *Length of liability for French military service (years)*

	Army proper	Reserve proper	Home army	Home army reserve	Total
27 July 1872	5	4	5	6	20
15 July 1889	3	7	6	9	25
10 July 1892	3	10	6	6	25
21 March 1905	2	11	6	6	25
7 August 1913	3	10	7	7	27

brigades of the *Landwehr*. The Austro-Hungarian Empire had fewer reserves and produced only 59 divisions and 25 mixed brigades. France put into the field 57 divisions from the regular army, 25 from the regular reserve and 12 from the home army. From a population that was less than half that of Germany, France raised more than four million men in August 1914, just 30 per cent less than her adversary. On 18 August, the day on which French forces had formed up at their appointed stations, 2,700,000 men were ready for operations, 680,000 were at depots, 235,000 were serving overseas, 200,000 from the home army were guarding lines of communication and 65,000 were at sea. During the course of the 1914–18 war, eight million Frenchmen were called up for military service and 800,000 were categorized as in 'reserved occupations' and worked in armaments factories. The Russian army's infantry divisions numbered 55 with a further 35 in reserve; the cavalry comprised 20 regular divisions and 20 reserve. Since Britain had no compulsory military service, she could field only 170,000 men. Her territorial army was a volunteer reserve of 315,000 men charged with the defence of the British Isles. Belgium raised 7 divisions and Serbia 11.

Between 1875 and 1884, because of the greater rapidity with which the Germans could bring their forces together and the lack of a fortified border with Germany, French mobilization Plans I to VII envisaged that their own troops would assemble well back from the frontier in order to cope with a sudden attack. Between 1887 and 1897, frontier fortifications were built and an alliance signed with Russia. In the light of the new situation, French plans took on a decidedly offensive aspect and provided for troops to be moved close to the frontier before assuming their positions. Following the establishment in Germany of an advance guard, French troop dispositions for a delaying action were included in Plan XIV and repeated in Plan XV, dated March 1903, which also took into account the possibility of British hostility. Plan XVI was subjected to lively criticism on the grounds that it did not cover the frontier with Belgium. Plan XVII in 1913, drafted by Joffre, was based on the supposition of a German invasion of Belgium and provided for moving forces as close as possible to the frontier to deliver a double-pronged offensive.

The successive French governments which came to power after 1919 drew lessons from the 1914–18 conflict and decided, from the moment that peace was declared, to plan for the future economic mobilization of the country. However, the law giving execution to this concept was not passed until 11 July 1938. The plan for military mobilization described procedures for bringing units to a state of readiness (e.g. places of assembly, dates for completion) and provided for the various systems of transport and the logistic arrangements required for its accomplishment (e.g. requisitioning, supplies). It was to be executed via the military districts through the agency of their recruiting offices which were responsible for the paperwork connected with soldiers who had been released from full-time service. These offices were to send out the instructions to report to 252 mobilization centres. These had been set up in 1928 and released the regular army from the task of administering the mobilization machinery.

Table 2   *Length of liability for French military service (years)*

	Army proper	Liability to recall	1st reserve	2nd reserve	Total
1 April 1923	1⁶/12	2	16⁶/12	8	28
31 March 1928	1	3	16	8	28
17 March 1936	2	3	16	8	29

On 1 April 1923, the duration of full-time conscript service was reduced to eighteen months, although the total period of liability for military service remained at 27 years. To compensate for the lack of numbers resulting from the reduction in full-time service, it was established that a period of two years' liability to immediate recall should follow release at the end of eighteen months. Men aged less than 40 were placed in the first reserve, those at or over that age in the second. Full-time conscript service was reduced to one year on 31 March 1928 but again raised to two on 17 March 1936.

Between 1919 and 1939, ten successive war plans were produced. Up to 1929 these were offensive in character; after that date they became defensive. In consequence, operational plans became mere mobilization plans and the anxiety to anticipate every possibility led to dispersion of effort. To cope with the increase in German military potential, recourse was made to such expedients as strengthening the full-time army during periods of 'political tension' and putting it into position as a covering force whose task was the protection of the mobilization of the remainder of the armed forces (Plan B). A special feature of Plan C, May 1931, was the creation of units specially designed to serve in fortresses. Plan D, 1933, provided for an extension of the fortifications and an improvement in the covering arrangements by recalling, before general mobilization, the men of the first reserve, since the full-time army comprised just 20 per cent of the covering force. The aim of Plan E, which took two years to draft and came into effect on 19 January 1938, was to defend the territory between the Moselle and Basle, no offensive action being envisaged unless circumstances permitted. However, Plan E did cater for an offensive operation, albeit of a very limited nature, to relieve possible pressure on Polish forces. It also took into account the situation which might have arisen from Italian neutrality or hostility and made provision for an offensive against northern Italy. It also scheduled the positioning of troops in the Pyrenees and Morocco to counter any Spanish threat and in Tunisia to oppose Italian aggression. Plan F, which

was supposed to come into force at the end of 1939, differed little from Plan E but emphasized the possibility of a German attack through Switzerland. Plan F decreed the immediate mobilization of the fortress troops and the covering force was to move into position between days 1 and 6; mobilization was to be completed on day 12 and all units were to be assembled and in their designated positions on day 22. Apart from the general mobilization, the system included provision for partial mobilization in the south-east and in the Pyrenees. Sixty per cent of the other ranks and 74 per cent of the officers and NCOs on the wartime strength of the A series divisions were reservists, and in the training divisions these percentages were 95.7 and 82. The large units in the B series had a very small nucleus from the regular army but they were not intended to go into action immediately.

Mobilization in September 1939 was achieved in eighteen days. It required the use of 9,400 trains, compared with 5,000 in 1914, and the road transport represented the equivalent of a further 2,300 trains. The numbers mobilized in 35 regular and 51 reserve divisions reached 4,600,000 in September 1939, those serving full-time on that date numbering only 670,000, and 5,000,000 on 1 May 1940. The number of men in reserved occupations rose between these two dates from 670,000 to 1,600,000. Germany raised 53 regular and 53 reserve divisions in 1939; Poland 30 full-time and 9 reserve; and Britain 5 regular and 5 reserve. After the defeat in 1940, the struggle against the Axis was continued along three lines. In Vichy France, officers working in secret made preparations for a mobilization whose object was to multiply by three the numbers allowed in the army under the terms of the armistice but this plan was brought to nothing by the German occupation of the free zone in 1942. In French North Africa a real mobilization was successfully achieved; the numbers called up for service reached 633,000, of whom three-fifths were indigenous. These troops fought as the Free French in Italy, Africa, France and northwest Europe. The resistance movement carried out partial mobilizations, such as those in Vercors and St Marcel.

The appearance of the nuclear threat after 1945 called into question the desirability of mobilizing mass armies. Although the principle of mobilization is still observed in France, the numbers due to be called up are just a quarter of those in 1939 and the men concerned are only those 'liable for instant recall' and the youngest classes. However, they are capable of achieving a state of readiness in a much shorter time as the covering force is scheduled to be in position within 48 hours. It is now also possible to stagger recalls through the 'warning order' system set out in the 1959 ordonnance on defence organization. The percentage of reserve personnel in the three army corps is small but it would reach 80 per cent in the affiliated units to be brought into being on mobilization.

The length of military service was raised to eighteen months on 30 November 1950 but, during the Algerian War, contingents were retained beyond the legal time limit and others were recalled. Full-time conscript service was reduced to sixteen months on 15 October 1963, and to one year on 10 July 1970.

The new French mobilization plan of 1978 adopted the principle of 'affiliation' – making use of full-time formations to bring reserve units of the home army to a state of readiness. These reserve units can then amalgamate with larger formations. To a considerable extent, the units of the regular army have assumed the functions of the mobilization centres and they are also charged with training the reserves to an operational condition. The modern British army also utilizes 'affiliation' by reinforcing regular formations with reserve units from the volunteer territorial army.

If mobilization and reserves play a decreasing part in the armies of the major powers, they retain their importance for a small country like Israel which is under threat from forces very much larger than its own and is compelled to summon all its resources to repel the danger. In 1920, the *Haganah*, a secret army, was formed to protect the Jewish population of Palestine. It emerged from the shadows in 1948 to defend Israeli territory from an invasion by the armies of five Arab powers. A spontaneous mobilization allowed Israel to raise a combat force of 120,000, including both men and women, from a population of 600,000. In the longer term, Israel adopted the Swiss model. The small number of regular military men that Israel possessed were employed as instructors and the nuclei of staffs. A long period of military service, three years for men and two for unmarried women, makes it possible to produce units of high operational quality. To maintain this standard there are frequent call-ups of reservists lasting for between 60 and 80 days with combat formations and 40 in support units. Liability for service continues until the age of 45 in the first reserve, i.e. the reservist's own unit, and until 54 in the second reserve. The Israeli Defence Forces, which numbered 141,000 men and women in 1991, could reach a total of 645,000 on calling reserves to the colours. Mobilization is carried out by telephone and through code words put out on national radio and television. Recruitment works on a territorial basis within a framework of brigades in which a skeleton cadre handles the card

Table 3 *Length of liability for French military service (years)*

	Army proper	Liability to recall	1st reserve	2nd reserve	Total
30 November 1950	$1^6/12$	3	16	$7^6/12$	28
15 October 1963	$1^4/12$	3	16	$7^6/12$	$27^{10}/12$
10 July 1970	1	4	12	—	17

indexes and keeps the weapons and equipment in good order. The reservist keeps his or her uniform at home.

The Swiss army exemplifies the type that only exists on mobilization. The regular armed forces are limited to an air force containing 150 pilots and a body of army instructors (620 officers and 890 NCOs). Military service for men is compulsory, those with physical disabilities being placed in administrative positions. Exemption is rare and, when granted, incurs a tax as does any permitted absence from reserve training. Thirty-seven thousand conscripts are brought onto the strength every year. On mobilization, the Swiss army could reach a total of 625,000 from a population of 6,500,000. Mobilization can be effected in 48 hours. Conscripts complete seven weeks' basic training and are then recalled to duty for a total of 330 days until the age of 50. Beyond this age, reservists serve ten years in the civil defence forces. *See also* ISRAEL, SINCE 1948; MILITIAS; NUMERICAL STRENGTH; PLANNING/PLANS; RECRUITMENT; SWEDEN.

G. BODINIER
JOHN CHILDS

FURTHER READING
The War Plans of the Great Powers, 1880–1914, ed. P. M. Kennedy (London, 1979); John Gooch, *The Plans of War: The General Staff and British military strategy, c.1900–1916* (London, 1974); Albert Seaton, *The German Army, 1933–45* (London, 1982); John McPhee, *The Swiss Army: La Place de la Concorde Suisse* (London, 1985); E. Luttwak and D. Horowitz, *The Israeli Army* (London, 1975).

Moltke, Helmuth von (1800–91) Moltke, although born and brought up a Dane, was the key figure in shaping the Prussian general staff and its doctrine, making it the model for all armies in modern Europe. When he was appointed chief of the general staff in 1857, that body had achieved its technical independence of the Ministry of War but it had not transformed its status into effective power. That came in the wake of the Danish war of 1864. In 1866 the chief of the general staff was given the right of direct communication with the army's field commanders and, in 1883, that of immediate access to the Kaiser. Thus the general staff established its freedom from political control. Moltke recognized the impact of the railway on strategy and therefore emphasized the need for the prior planning of military operations in peacetime. The victories over Austria in 1866 and France in 1870–1, achieved in short order and with decisive success, ensured Moltke's personal prestige. But his approach to operations remained flexible. He recognized that strategy was a system of expedients and that a plan would not survive the first contact with an enemy. His instructions to his field commanders were therefore no more than guidelines or directives. By creating a common body of doctrine within the general staff, he was able to delegate to junior commanders, secure in the knowledge that they would conform to his leading ideas. This combination of technological advance and intellectual application allowed him to keep his army divided, not massed, aiming at convergence on the battlefield itself. Thus he could put larger forces into the field; thus too he could make envelopment his leading operational idea. Moltke remained chief of the general staff until 1887. His successors rendered dogmatic that which had been creative. *See also* GENERAL STAFF; GERMANY; METZ (1870); NAPIER; PARIS, SIEGE OF; SADOWA; SCHLIEFFEN.

HEW STRACHAN

FURTHER READING
H. von Moltke, *Militarische Werke* (Berlin, 1892–1912); E. Kessel, *Moltke* (Stuttgart, 1957); G. Ritter, *The Sword and the Sceptre* (London, 1970–2); *Moltke's Military Correspondence, 1870–1871*, ed. Spenser Wilkinson (Oxford, 1923, repr. Aldershot, 1991).

Mongols Genghis Khan was one of history's greatest military leaders. Having unified the nomadic Mongol tribes, over a period of some twenty years he proceeded to create a vast empire subjugating northern and western China (1206–17), then destroying the Khwarizmian Turkic Empire of 'Ala ad-Din Muhammad, consisting of Turkestan and Iran (1218–21), and ultimately pushing as far as the Indus, the Caucasus, the Black Sea and southern Russia. The latter campaigns were mainly conducted by his lieutenants, Soubotai and Jebe. Under Genghis Khan's successor, Ogedai, the Mongols penetrated into Central Europe, crushing a Polish–Lithuanian army at Liegnitz in Silesia (9 April 1241). They were close to both Vienna and Venice when the death of Ogedai caused them to be recalled into Asia. Meanwhile, Hulegu, some of whose forces had been defeated by the Mamluks of Egypt at Ain Djalout (1260), occupied Syria and Anatolia while, under Kublai Khan, the Mongols completed the conquest of China and attacked Annam, Japan and Java. The Mongol Empire broke up during the thirteenth century but under the command of a leader of Tatar origin, Tamerlain (Timur Lenk), the Mongols reconstructed an empire which stretched from central and western Asia into southern Russia. Having defeated the Ottoman Turkish sultan, Bayazid I (1389–1403), at Ankara in 1402, Tamerlain was preparing to attack China when he died in 1405. Southern Russia and Turkestan were to remain under the domination of the Khan of the Golden Horde until political authority fragmented the Samarkand regime into a series of khanates during the fifteenth century. Most of these khanates were reduced by the princes of Muscovy during the sixteenth century, particularly Ivan IV 'the Terrible' (1547–84). Only the Khanate of the Crimea and the Kuban survived until it was finally annexed by Russia in 1783.

A sweeping engulfment by a barbarian 'horde' was the usual description provided by contemporary chroniclers within the vanquished lands. In fact, the Turkic word 'horde' actually meant a troop, a clan or a camp. At the most, Genghis fielded only 240,000 men against Muhammad while the Mongols who invaded Europe numbered perhaps 150,000. Normally, a Mongol army consisted of between 30,000 and 50,000 men. More convincingly, the Mongol victories have been attributed to terror. The Mongols systematically massacred all opponents; the blazing pyramids of severed heads were not a myth. However, the principal reason for the Mongols' irresistible conquests was the quality of their martial organization. Genghis Khan imposed simple but effective military structures on his tribes, which already had considerable fighting abilities, and he also learned and absorbed technical lessons from the peoples whom he defeated.

Genghis Khan's Mongols were those tribes which had not been tempted to settle in northern China or Iran but had continued to follow a harsh, nomadic style of life in Inner Mongolia, a region with a particularly inhospitable climate – frozen winters, torrid summers and violent winds. They were hardy people, living on horseback from early childhood in order to tend their herds, their warrior skills honed by hunting and incessant inter-tribal warfare. The Mongols were abstemious and indefatigable men, capable of riding 125 miles in a day. They were rough-hewn and mostly lacked abstract spiritual values; they knew no moral code other than honour, courage, comradeship and loyalty to their master and community. They regarded the army as the principal manifestation of their race and society.

It would appear that the Mongol leaders (the khans) took the inspiration for their military organization from the Chinese administration, just as their craftsmen copied Chinese methods of working tempered steel. Genghis Khan derived support from his great vassals (the *noyans*) to whom, after each conquest, he distributed a variety of fief consisting of lands and groups of inhabitants. However, in order to reduce the risk of revolts, he stored the main weapons of war in arsenals and surrounded himself with an especially devoted personal guard. The social hierarchy was arranged as a simple pyramid on the decimal system: family to clan, clan to tribe, and tribe to group of tribes. Each family tent (*yourt* or *gers*) had to supply one or two men for military service. Ten horsemen made up an *arban* and ten *arbans*, at the level of the clan, composed a *jaghun* (100 men). Ten *jaghuns* constituted a *minghan* (1,000 men), a kind of regiment, commanded by a 'valiant' warrior of the tribe, the *baghatur*. Ten *minghans* formed a *tumen* (10,000 men), and an army usually consisted of two or three *tumen* (20–30,000 men). Thus the *tumen*, commanded by a *noyan*, and the armies were formed from groups of tribes thereby utilizing the cohesion of the social structure as the basis for the military hierarchy.

The Mongols were all horsemen, rendering their armies exceptionally mobile and manoeuvrable. Forty per cent of their forces consisted of heavy cavalry protected by a cuirass of lacquered leather or chain mail and a helmet, and armed with a lance. The horses also wore protective coats of leather. The heavy cavalry was the shock weapon. The light cavalry, 60 per cent of the forces, was only protected by a helmet. Every man, both heavy and light cavalry, carried two bows, one for fighting on foot, the other for mounted combat, together with two quivers. Extra supplies of arrows were brought up by chariot. The light cavalry executed reconnaissance, formed screens to conceal the movements of the heavy horse, intervened to support the former with missile fire, and pursued the beaten enemy. All soldiers had more than one horse, enabling them to change mounts during the course of a battle. In action, the Mongols wore shirts of very heavy silk; when a soldier was struck by an arrow, the shirt also entered his flesh but was not usually pierced. The projectile could thus be removed from the body simply by pulling on the material, an art in which Chinese surgeons excelled. Supply of the troops was made easy by the fact that they drank mare's milk.

Discipline and training reached levels of sophistication unknown in other contemporary armies. The rank and file were drilled in silence relying upon commands given by black and white flags in daytime and by flaming arrows at night. The Mongol army was thus maintained in a high state of readiness and combat efficiency. Campaigns generally opened with the rapid advance of the *tumen* on a wide front, mounted orderlies providing liaison between them. If one of the *tumen* encountered weak forces, it crushed them. Should the enemy forces prove too strong, the *tumen* either gathered its forces behind a mobile screen of light cavalry or combined with its neighbouring *tumen* to bring maximum force to bear. In battle, the heavy cavalry, manoeuvring behind the light cavalry, sought to outflank the enemy and, for preference, attacked from the rear. Often, the attacking column feigned a retreat in order to mount fresh horses. The heavy cavalry would only strike its decisive blow once the enemy had been halted by a diversionary frontal attack.

Away from the steppes, when attacking regions of high population density, fortified towns or the Great Wall of China, the Mongols had to acquire the military skills of sedentary peoples. Genghis Khan therefore formed a corps of engineers, who were mainly Chinese, and acquired a powerful and mobile artillery consisting of all the known ballistic machines of the age complete with the full range of projectiles, including incendiaries. Once his artillery had breached fortifications, the assault was launched by dismounted cavalry usually advancing behind a screen of prisoners. At Liegnitz, it seems that the Mongols used rockets or asphyxiating smoke bombs.

Surprise was a vital element in Mongol tactics. Their troops could travel 45 miles in a day. They took advantage of winter conditions to move over frozen rivers and marshlands. Surprise was also a product of co-ordination, and this implies that the Mongols possessed a genuine general staff. With the aid of his advisers, the khan prepared his campaigns most carefully. He had an intensive complex of spies in the trading caravans and among merchants in towns. It was sometimes the case that the Mongols knew the theatre of operations better than the generals of the states they were invading. The campaign against Muhammad of Khwarizm required two years of preparatory work – reconnoitring the march routes, setting in place a network of emissaries whose role was to sap the enemy's morale through diplomacy and propaganda, drawing up a list of roads and staging posts, and assembling more than 200,000 men. The leaders of the *tumen* were given very precise objectives but were then allowed considerable operational freedom. The mounted orderlies who passed orders and information at great speed enabled the leader to grasp the situation quickly and ensured unity of command. Once a territory had been reduced, Genghis Khan superimposed on the existing administration of the subjugated lands a Mongol administration designed to maintain order and extract the resources necessary to prosecute war.

Tamerlain (Timur Lenk), who was not a Mongol but a Transoxianan Turk, revived the methods of Genghis Khan and relied heavily on the propaganda and psychological effect generated by the maximum use of terror. He raised the soldier's equipment to such a level that each man became virtually self-sufficient with two horses, bows, sabres, his personal possessions contained in a leather bag, an inflatable skin for crossing rivers, axe, saw, awl and sewing needle. The Mongols camped in eighteen-man tents. The evolution of a monetary economy allowed Tamerlain to pay his men in cash once every six months. A man's wage was equal to the value of his horses, while the remuneration of the officers was steeply graduated. Individual pillage was punishable by death but, when permission was given, booty belonged to the soldier who had seized it.

Armies of this quality and organization outclassed all contemporary rivals as long as they were commanded by leaders of outstanding ability. Leaving aside the problems created by their own internal divisions, it seems that the long-term decline of the Mongols was due to the coming of firearms, the employment of which demanded different fighting qualities and tactical organization, an emphasis on infantry at the expense of cavalry, and the possession of urbanized industrial regions. *See also* AIN DJALOUT; ANKARA; CAVALRY; GENGHIS KHAN; HULEGU; INDIRECT WARFARE; TAMERLAIN.

A. CORVISIER

FURTHER READING
David Morgan, *The Mongols* (Oxford, 1986); J. J. Saunders, *The History of the Mongol Conquests* (London, 1971); René Grousset, *The Empire of the Steppes: a history of Central Asia* (New Brunswick, 1970); J. F. Fletcher, 'The Mongols: ecological and social perspectives', *Harvard Journal of Asiatic Studies*, xlvi (1986).

Monluc, Blaise de Lasseran-Massencome, Seigneur de (*c*.1501–77) If best known as the author of the most vivid military memoirs of the sixteenth century, Monluc was also a virtual archetype of the contemporary officer. A younger son from the impoverished lesser nobility of Gascony, he followed a career pattern similar to those of Roger Williams and Lazarus von Schwendi. A youthful appointment as a page to the Duke of Lorraine and then as an archer in Lorraine's company established an attachment to the house of Lorraine which culminated in his association with the clientele of François, Duke of Guise. Monluc took part in most of the major campaigns of the reign of Francis I (1515–47) including those of La Bicocca, Pavia, Ceresole and Boulogne. However, it was only in the reign of Henry II (1547–59) that his career blossomed through a combination of royal favour and the patronage of Guise. In July 1554 he was given the command of the French troops sent to aid Sienna, which had revolted from Florence and Charles V in 1552. Although he was forced to surrender on 21 April 1555, Monluc's conduct of the defence of that city was widely praised. In reward (and through the help of Guise) he was appointed Colonel-General of the French Infantry in 1558 and in this capacity served with Guise at the sieges of Thionville and Arlon later that year. The outbreak of civil dissension in France following the death of Henry II in 1559 placed his loyalties under great strain. Although not initially personally antagonistic to Protestantism, Monluc was also very much a Guise client, losing his colonel-generalcy following the expulsion of the Guise from the court in 1561. By 1562 he had become bitterly hostile to the Huguenots. During the First War of Religion (1562–3) he was appointed Lieutenant of Guienne, an office he held for the remainder of the decade; and which made him the leader of the Royalist and Catholic cause in south-west France. Monluc's brutal repression of the Huguenots attracted the fierce enmity of his opponents and he was dismissed from his lieutenancy after the reconciliation between the crown and the Huguenots at the Peace of St Germain in 1570. He was, however, restored to favour in the wake of the revival of Guise influence at court in 1572 and in 1574 was created a Marshal of France.

His famous *Commentaires* were the product of his enforced retirement in 1570–1. Although they reveal some classical influence, they were more the product of the contemporary French vogue for memoir-writing and, in part, a memoir of services to the crown. Moreover, since Monluc considered war primarily an occasion for the individual to win honour and advancement, his memoirs were less didactic than the works of Schwendi or Williams, and very much a personal narrative of his own rise through the ranks. The accounts of battles and campaigns are not always reliable but the anecdotes and reminiscences still sparkle, a reflection of Monluc's contemporary reputation (like Williams again) for loquacity and braggadocio. Although his career spanned the period of the adoption of the arquebus by the French infantry, he showed little interest in technical matters and it is clear that, like many of his contemporaries, he accepted firearms with minimal enthusiasm. *See also* BICOCCA; BOULOGNE; CERESOLE; GUISE; PAVIA; SCHWENDI; WILLIAMS.

SIMON ADAMS

FURTHER READING
The standard edition of the *Commentaires* is that edited by Paul Courteault (Bibliothèque de la Pléiade, Paris, 1964). More accessible to an English readership is the abridgement, *Blaise de Monluc: The Habsburg–Valois Wars and the French Wars of Religion*, ed. Ian Roy (London, 1971).

Monongahela, Battle of the (9 July 1755) This defeat of a small Anglo-American force under the British major-general Edward Braddock on the banks of the Monongahela River (near present-day Pittsburg, Ohio) has derived its notoriety from its supposed symbolic significance, rather than from its immediate military importance. After a long and fatiguing march through the wilderness, the object of which was to curtail French 'encroachments' by ejecting them from Fort Duquesne, Braddock's force of about 1,300 effectives (of whom perhaps 40 per cent were Americans) was decisively beaten by an inferior Franco-Canadian and Indian force, numbering no more than 900, 66 per cent of whom were Indians. In a forest encounter, which took both sides by surprise, Braddock's marching column was quickly enveloped and then decimated over a 2–3-hour period by a largely unseen foe who relied on individual fire and concealment. France gained a momentary advantage on the American frontier but the lasting significance of the battle was in the interpretation given to the manner of Braddock's futile response to his assailants. The clash was soon seen as one between Old and New World ideas, between a practical, flexible and imaginative North American approach to warfare and a European one which was rigid, stale and completely inappropriate. Regardless of how much this ignored the full circumstances of the action, the defeat became a seedbed for many enduring myths of American superiority and British ineptitude. The result has long been to obscure the fact that 'what is called guerilla warfare' was itself well known in eighteenth-century Europe and, that by drawing on that experience, the British army soon showed itself not only adaptable to New World conditions (developing looser tactics with greater emphasis on aimed fire, and providing training specifically for 'the Service of the Woods'), but even a superior practitioner of the very tactics which had overwhelmed Braddock. *See also* COLONIAL TROOPS; GREAT BRITAIN; QUEBEC; UNITED STATES.

G. A. STEPPLER

FURTHER READING
Daniel J. Beattie, 'The adaptation of the British army to the wilderness, 1755–63', in *Adapting to Conditions: war and society in the eighteenth century*, ed. Maartin Ultee (Alabama, 1986), pp. 56–83; Douglas S. Freeman, *George Washington: a biography* (7 vols, London and New York, 1948–57), vol. 2, *Young Washington*; lawrence H. Gipson, *The British Empire before the American Revolution* (15 vols, New York, 1946–70), vol. 6, *The Years of Defeat*,

1754–1757; Paul E. Kopperman, *Braddock at the Monongahela* (Pittsburg, 1977); Stanley Pargellis, 'Braddock's defeat', *American Historical Review*, xli (1936), pp. 253–69; Peter E. Russell, 'Redcoats in the wilderness: British officers and irregular warfare in Europe and America, 1740 to 1760', *William and Mary Quarterly*, xxxv (1978), pp. 629–52; R. L. Yaple, 'Braddock's defeat: the theories and a reconsideration', *Journal of the Society for Army Historical Research*, xlvi (1968), pp. 194–201.

Montecucoli, Raimondo (1609–80) Entering the service of the Habsburgs in 1625, Montecucoli fought in both the Thirty Years' War (1618–48) and against the Swedes (1657–60). Promoted to field marshal in 1658, he defeated the Turks at the Abbey of St Gotthard in 1664 and commanded the Imperial army in Germany (1672–5) during the Franco-Dutch War (1672–8). From 1664, he was president of the Austrian *Hofkriegsrat*. Montecucoli was a skilful and prudent general who offered battle only when there was no alternative or when the odds were heavily in favour of a successful outcome. Generally, he favoured manoeuvre in order to achieve strategic objectives. Taking his inspiration from the examples of Ancient Greece and Rome, he aimed to use his wings to encircle an enemy and came to adopt a linear battlefield formation rather than the square and phalanx. Influenced by Gustavus Adolphus, against whom he had fought at Breitenfeld and Lützen, Montecucoli stressed the importance of freedom of action, the principle of economy of force and sought better co-operation between arms. His most important work was the establishment of an Austrian standing army complete with a modern logistical organization based upon the French model of Le Tellier and Louvois. *See also* AUSTRIA; ITALY; ST GOTTHARD ABBEY; TACTICS; TURENNE.

J. NOUZILLE

FURTHER READING
Raimondo Montecucoli, *Mémoires de Montecucoli* (3 vols, Wettstein, 1742); Thomas Barker, *The Military Intellectual and Battle: Raimondo Montecucoli and the Thirty Years' War* (Albany, NY, 1975).

Montgomery, Bernard Law (1887–1976)
The son of a bishop, Montgomery graduated from Sandhurst and joined the army in 1908. Montgomery served in the First World War in France. Between the wars, he both attended and taught in the Staff College at Camberley. In the 1930s, Montgomery spent much of his time in India and Egypt. In 1939, he was given command of the 3rd Division, which formed part of the British Expeditionary Force (BEF) to the Continent. The 3rd Division was evacuated from Dunkirk in May and June 1940. For the next two years, Montgomery helped train the expanding British army. In August 1942, Montgomery was given command of the 8th Army in Egypt. In October and November 1942, Montgomery defeated Rommel's *Afrika Korps* in the Battle of El Alamein and pursued the defeated Germans across North Africa. Montgomery was in charge of the British forces that invaded Sicily in July 1943, and later led the British forces in Italy in 1943. Montgomery did not get along well with Patton, the commander of the US troops in the invasion of Sicily. Montgomery was the commander of the British forces in the invasion of France, and his strategic ideas clashed with those of the supreme commander of the Allied forces, Eisenhower, who preferred an advance on a broad front to Montgomery's concept of a single thrust into Germany. At the Battle of the Bulge in December 1944 and January 1945, Montgomery and Patton once again collided, as the former was given temporary command of some US forces in order to stem the German advance. After the war, Montgomery was the British member of the Allied Control Council in Germany from 1945 to 1946. In the latter year, he became Chief of the Imperial General Staff and, in 1951, the Deputy Supreme Commander of the NATO forces in Europe. Montgomery was an egotistical, prickly, tactless and difficult colleague but an original thinker of high intelligence. He fully appreciated the weaknesses in the personnel, training, morale and equipment of the British army during the Second World War and did his best to adapt his methods to achieve the maximum mitigation. Above all, he

533

believed in complete preparation and meticulous detail in planning and training. He preferred setpiece operations, where his overwhelming dominance in artillery and air power could be brought to bear, rather than fluid manoeuvre where his troops were at a disadvantage compared to the German army. His one departure from this principle was at Arnhem in 1944 which resulted in his single major operational failure. The publication of Montgomery's *Memoirs* in 1958 gave rise to heated controversy centring on Montgomery's seemingly wilful misrepresentation of many of his operations, especially Alamein and *Overlord*. *See also* BRADLEY; BROOKE; EISENHOWER; EL ALAMEIN; NORMANDY; OVERLORD; PATTON.

A. CORVISIER
KEITH NEILSON
JOHN CHILDS

FURTHER READING
Nigel Hamilton, *Monty* (3 vols, London, 1981–6); Richard Lamb, *Montgomery in Europe, 1943–1945* (London, 1983); *Montgomery and the Eighth Army*, ed. Stephen Brooks (London, 1991).

Morale Although the French term 'le moral' only appeared as a noun in the second half of the eighteenth century (Buffon), in the general sense of the 'totality of our moral faculties' or the more particular sense of 'firmness in the face of danger, fatigue and difficulties', military authorities had appreciated the importance of morale long before and had identified the main problems. The word 'morale' did not enter English usage until the 1830s. Morale has many aspects: individual and group morale; the morale of men in battle, in the field and in barracks; and the principal physical, affective and moral factors involved whether positive or negative and of internal or external origin. However, for a considerable period, attention focused solely on the motivation of fighting men, concentrating on their honour and discipline, which were viewed as the paramount sources of unit cohesion. The interest paid to psychological factors during the Enlightenment made it possible to cast light on the crises of morale which had grown more frequent with the coming of standing armies and quartering in barracks.

Motivation From Herodotus onwards, historians have emphasized the importance of motivation, contrasting, for example, the patriotism of Greek warriors defending their city or even the whole of Ancient Greece with the lack of motivation displayed among the contingents brought together by the rulers of the Persian Empire. During the Spartan supremacy, legend told how, in the dark days of the Second Messenian War (seventh century BC), the poet and general Tyrtaeus had raised the morale of his men by exalting firmness of spirit in difficult moments, scorn for death and love of country in elegies, songs and marches. However, armies can draw their cohesion from other sentiments such as the sense of superiority felt by Alexander's soldiers and the Roman army. Barbarian peoples drew strength from attachment to their leaders and, with the coming of feudalism, this was reinforced by respect for the oath and a sense of honour. The most common motivation was fervent commitment to a shared faith in the face of enemies regarded as heretics or evil fiends. Muslims, for whom death in battle represented entry into the paradise of Allah, were more highly motivated than their opponents, a factor which explains the rapidity and extraordinary success of the *Jihad*, or Holy War, in the seventh and eighth centuries. It also assists comprehension of the apparently suicidal offensives of Ayatollah Khomeini's army against the better equipped Iraqi forces during the war of 1980–8. In a similar fashion, the Christian knights were motivated by the Crusades. We find the same state of mind in all religious wars, at least at their beginnings. It was partially a religious motivation which fired the Spanish troops in the sixteenth century, who confidently saw themselves as champions of the Catholic faith. On the Protestant side, the soldiers of Gustavus Adolphus were exhorted to self-sacrifice by their chaplains. We find the same ardour among the men who fought at Malplaquet or Valmy, armed with the desire to repel the invader, among the armies of the

Vendée or the poilus of 1914, or again among the Bolshevik armies of 1918–20 and the troops who undertook Mao Tse-Tung's 'Long March'. In most of these cases, leaving aside the exceptional circumstances of 1914, we are talking mainly of volunteers, even though volunteering for military service can sometimes be less than spontaneous and enthusiastic.

By contrast, it has often been claimed that mercenaries showed no disinterested motivation. If this had been the case, mercenary armies would have collapsed whenever the suffering and privation outweighed the glory and gain. Not just their professional loyalties but a feeling of superiority over the civil population – 'civilians' as they would be called from the nineteenth century onwards – retained men in the ranks. Honour, *esprit de corps* and camaraderie also played their parts. 'A man is only a soldier', wrote Bugeaud, 'when he no longer feels homesick and has come to regard the flag of the regiment as his village church tower.' This was particularly true of small mercenary companies, the core element of which was often composed of men with a loyalty to the captain and formed by local, even seigneurial, recruitment. During the early modern period, desertion was the bane of most armies. However, although it was a substantial problem often related to brittle morale, it was often the work of 'rolling stones' or *billardeurs* who made a virtual profession out of moving from unit to unit and even from army to army.

The raising of conscript armies can only be envisaged where a sufficient consensus exists around the idea of fatherland or nation. The upkeep of these armies creates obligations towards the citizens on the part of the state and demands that attention be paid to making future soldiers aware of the need for military service and the defence of the homeland. Thus the problem of morale takes on wider dimensions than in countries which rely upon professional, regular armies.

Crises of Morale We should distinguish between phenomena of panic, which are relatively frequent but limited, from the collapses that sometimes afflict armies and which have more general, though partly similar, causes. In the latter condition, technical factors are often cited – being outclassed by the number or quality of opposing weapons – as well as human factors like the lack of training. Failures of leadership, through the creation of scapegoats, is cited more often than the demoralization of the men, since it is dangerous to insist on this latter reason when trying to regain control over the same troops. However, this idea is never absent from the discussion since, from its beginnings, the art of warfare has included the objective of demoralizing the enemy while protecting one's own army from the identical hazard. The Homeric insults exchanged before battle by warriors in ancient times bear witness to this, as do the war cries and battle yells with which soldiers still seek to terrify their opponents. The humiliation of prisoners and the massacring of the wounded are intended to spread terror and break the morale of the enemy. Propaganda is a more sophisticated form of this tactic which has now matured into modern psychological warfare.

Concomitant with the growth of permanent armies was the need to maintain morale in uncomfortable winter quarters and peacetime garrisons. Towards the end of the eighteenth century, the appearance of a new malady was observed in garrisons – homesickness. The well-known song, *Der Schweizer*, tells of the sad fate of a Swiss soldier garrisoned at Strasbourg who, having heard an air from his native mountains wafting across the Rhine, cannot resist his longing for his homeland, deserts and is shot by firing-squad. In the second phase of the illness, and doctors recognized it as such, men lost their appetites and slipped into lassitude. Men from mountainous regions and those isolated by their dialects were particular sufferers. It seems to have been less common in regionally recruited units although if homesickness did strike such a formation then it became virulently contagious. In fact, the appearance of homesickness was related to a number of factors, including the increasing tendency to quarter soldiers in barracks and the

535

adoption of the Prussian model of severe discipline in a number of European armies. Desertion, which was often the ideal remedy, was now more difficult and some sufferers resorted to suicide. The only solution, apart from showing concern and kindness, was to grant the victim a period of leave although there were limits as to how often this could be done. The problem seems to have diminished in France during the Revolution and the First Empire with the return of active service to occupy men's minds, the increase in enthusiasm for war and the more frequent opportunities for desertion.

When universal compulsory military service was introduced, the soldier's condition was transformed. Patriotic sentiment encouraged men to accept their common fate and morale was often lower among those men excluded from military service. Nevertheless, for frailer spirits conscription represented a great hardship and, during the First World War, it became a severe trial as the conflict dragged on. The term *cafard*, dating from the 1880s, is applied to the state of boredom and world-weariness which does not necessarily lead to rebellion. In peacetime, *cafard* mainly affects recruits in their early days. At the beginning of military service, the transition from civilian to military status, separation from family and the restrictions on individual liberty imposed by military discipline, together with the harsh introduction to military life through basic training and an unfamiliar collective style of living, frequently seem difficult to bear. Some react badly to the realization that they might have to kill. For the majority, growing accustomed to the life and feeling the need to fit in with the rest prove stronger than their discomfort, though this can produce a certain detachment in some men which is not always the best guarantee of high morale in difficult times.

The 1914–18 war was an ordeal for soldiers and civilians. The latter could become a source of demoralization to the armed forces and vice versa. Belligerents sought to undermine the morale of both their enemy's troops and his civilians. The crisis of 1917 stemmed from a combination of extreme weariness among the soldiers, privation and pacifist propaganda. It struck Russia first where it resulted in revolution and the disintegration of the army. France too experienced this crisis of morale, but all participating armies were afflicted to some extent. By contrast, the French collapse of 1940 was caused, after the inactivity of the previous winter, by the fact that the French troops were outclassed by the German army. It began as a local panic on the Sedan sector where the Germans had concentrated their spearheads for a breakthrough and then spread to a considerable number of formations despite combat in a number of other sectors of the front. The organization of resistance and the campaign of 1944–5 showed to what degree the factors influencing the morale of an army are conjunctural in character.

Combating Crises of Morale Leaders attentive to the state of their men did not wait for the establishment of psychological services to realize that the maintenance of morale requires both negative and positive measures. Where military discipline was pushed to extremes, it led to the men being more frightened of their officers than of the enemy with, in some cases, disastrous results. During the Seven Years' War (1756–63), the Prussian army had proportionately more deserters than the Austrian or French army, though it is true that many of them had been forcibly recruited. Good material conditions are vital in creating good morale. Some leaders, like Turenne, showed especial concern for the well-being of their troops, ensuring, as far as was possible, that they received plentiful, regular and healthy rations and that they were properly billeted. Such leaders also took care that their men were not exhausted by long and pointless marches but were never left idle. It is particularly important to give the men confidence in themselves and in their leaders through good relations between officers and soldiers and the maintenance of physical fitness.

Keeping up soldiers' motivation remains the essential factor. Except where appeal was made to religious sentiments or to ideology, motivating the men – recalling their duty to their sovereign, fatherland, corps or comrades, or stressing martial honour – was done through military speeches which, during the Renaissance, often reached the level of a literary form (Monluc, La Noue, etc.). The officers of the *tercios* regularly employed speeches, often delivering them at meal times, thus imitating the monastic practice of readings in the refectory. In a more banal way, songs, which were intended to keep the soldiers in high spirits, played a great role in all armies and particularly in Europe from the mid-sixteenth century. Songs became prominent towards the end of the eighteenth century, and not just in the French Revolutionary armies, and also after 1871 in the 'armed peace'. In France during this latter period, most sentimental or satirical songs, being inspired by a revanchist spirit, contained a patriotic verse. Military ceremonies are designed to impress the men and reviews are intended to give them confidence through the size of crowds which gather to watch. Smart uniforms also contribute to morale. General mobilizations are particularly testing. In France in 1914, with a short war expected, no measures were taken to prevent the men from becoming bored and miserable. Gradually, mail had to be organized between the soldiers and their families along with regular leave and entertainments for the men in their billets, such as theatre, film shows and concert parties. In Britain, the morale of the recruits of 1914 was partly evaporated by the chaotic conditions and lack of preparedness which awaited them in the depots. The experience of the 1914 mobilization was to be of value in the early days of the Second World War. Captivity is likely to be the greatest trial of morale, particularly when this involves being held by enemies who practise brain-washing, such as the Chinese in Korea and the North Vietnamese.

Among the factors intended to maintain soldiers' morale and that of their families is propaganda, the aim of which is to convince men of the rightness of their cause and to prevent them from yielding to the enemy's counter-propaganda. Since the beginning of the seventeenth century such psycho-logical warfare has been carried on in pamphlets and lampoons but it became more significant with the advent of radio. Exaggerating the enemy's losses and saying nothing of one's own or playing them down, selectively reporting news and, as a corollary, establishing a censorship of the press and the mail are practices common to all states at war. The feeding of optimistic news to the public during the First World War, which was denounced by the pacifists, was a factor in the Allied victory but it also played its part in the disciplined conduct of the German troops in defeat. The development of political ideologies since 1917 has led to troops being inspired by a degree of fanaticism, partially re-creating the states of mind seen in the earlier holy wars and wars of religion. *See also* ESPRIT DE CORPS; GLORY; HONOURS AND AWARDS; NATIONALISM; PANIC; PSYCHOLOGICAL WARFARE OPERATIONS: RECRUITMENT.

A. CORVISIER
JOHN CHILDS

FURTHER READING
John Keegan, *The Face of Battle* (London, 1976); John Baynes, *Morale: a study of men and courage* (London, 1967); F. M. Richardson, *Fighting Spirit: a study of psychological factors in war* (London, 1978); Christopher Duffy, *The Military Experience in the Age of Reason* (London, 1987); Richard Holmes, *The Firing Line* (London, 1985).

Morat, Battle of *See* MURTEN

Moscow, Battle of (30 September 1941–20 April 1942) In September 1941, Hitler decided to launch an attack (*Operation Taifun*) against Moscow. Army Group Centre, under the command of Field Marshal von Bock, was given this task, while Army Group North established the blockade of Leningrad and Army Group South continued to drive into the Ukraine. The strength of the German army was much diminished, but the initial thrust towards Moscow was successful, prompting Stalin to assign General Zhukov to the defence of the capital. The German advance slowed in the second half of October as a result of the autumn rains and the breakdown of equipment. However, the final phase of the offensive against Moscow, begun on 15 November, resulted in Army Group Centre being within 40 km of Moscow by the end of the month. While the Germans moved forward, Zhukov was busy mobilizing his forces: new armies were raised in the interior and troops were transferred from the Far East. The Soviet defence was aided by the weather. By the beginning of December, the temperature had fallen to −40 degrees, largely immobilizing the German troops who did not have winter equipment. On 6 December, Zhukov began his counter-attack. By the end of December, the German forces were driven back to the positions that they had held on 15 November. This defeat prompted Hitler to assume personal control of the German army on 19 December; Bock had been replaced by von Kluge as commander of Army Group Centre two days earlier. Hitler insisted that there be no further retreat, and the Germans fought a remarkable defensive action which stabilized the front by mid-January 1942. The two exhausted armies remained in their positions until the spring. Moscow had been saved, and the battle for the city marked the first significant check for Hitler and the blitzkrieg. *See also* GERMANY; RUSSIA/USSR; STALIN; ZHUKOV.

A. CORVISIER
KEITH NEILSON

FURTHER READING
John Erickson, *The Road to Stalingrad* (London, 1975); Albert Seaton, *The Battle for Moscow, 1941–1942* (London, 1973).

Moscow, retreat from (19 October–8 December 1812) Napoleon entered Moscow on 14 September. The city had been partially destroyed by fire and on 19 October Napoleon gave the order to retreat. The road to the south-west had been barred by Kutuzov at Maloyaroslavetz (14 October) and he had no alternative but to withdraw along the devastated route by which he had advanced. Snow began to fall on 4 November but, contrary to the legend of 'General Winter', the temperature remained relatively clement until December (better than in Poland in 1807 and Castile in 1808). However, the starving troops had insufficient ammunition to contend with constant harassment from the Russian troops and partisans and had abandoned their baggage. They were vulnerable to typhus and found the cold difficult to bear. Napoleon managed to break through when the Russians barred his way at Krasnoi (16–17 November) and then to cross the Beresina (26–28 November), which was cluttered with drifting ice. Only 10,000 out of the 90,000 men who had left Moscow successfully reached the west bank of the Beresina. The exhausted Russians abandoned the pursuit at the Niemen. Napoleon's *Grand Armée* had lost 300,000 men and the Russians 250,000. *See also* FRANCE; KUTUZOV; NAPOLEON; RUSSIA/USSR.

A. CORVISIER

FURTHER READING
D. G. Chandler, *The Campaigns of Napoleon* (London, 1967); E. Tarle, *Napoleon's Invasion of Russia, 1812* (Oxford, 1942); R. F. Delderfield, *The Retreat from Moscow* (New York, 1967).

Mühlberg (Saxony), Battle of (24 April 1547) Charles V's defeat of the Schmalkaldic League at the Battle of Mühlberg was both the first major battle fought by Spanish troops in northern Europe and the greatest success for the Habsburg military system after Pavia. It was also a victory that owed as much to political as to military circumstances. A contest between the Emperor and the alliance of Lutheran princes and cities had been in the offing since the creation of the League in 1531, but it was only in 1546 that, having recently made peace with Francis I, Charles decided to resolve the religious division in the Holy Roman Empire by force. He proceeded carefully to win over certain Protestant princes and to obtain assistance from the German Catholics. In the summer of 1546, while he was assembling his army, the League, led by the

Elector John Frederick of Saxony, moved first and opened hostilities on 14 August. Charles's preparations were not complete, but the League's attempts to invade the Austrian duchies were thwarted by a skilful defensive campaign conducted by the Duke of Alba along the Danube in the autumn of 1546. At the same time Duke Maurice of Saxony, who had been won over by the Emperor, invaded the Electorate and forced John Frederick to retreat. By early 1547 Charles had both completed the assembly of an army of 30,000 Spanish, Italian, Netherlandish and German troops and forced a number of League members into neutrality. In April he advanced into Saxony, catching John Frederick, who had remained curiously indecisive during the first months of 1547, with his army dispersed. Having only some 15,000 men with him the Elector was retiring on his capital, Wittenberg, when Charles's scouts encountered his outposts near Mühlberg on the Elbe. The Elector had assumed that the Elbe could not be crossed but Charles was informed of a nearby ford and decided to use it in conjunction with a bridge made from boats collected along the river bank. Early on the morning of 24 April the crossing began, Spanish skirmishers driving off the Saxon outposts by means of the new long-range musket. The Elector did not attempt to defend the river line but commenced a hasty retreat towards Wittenberg. However, he was pursued too closely by Charles's cavalry and was forced to make a stand. The superior Imperial cavalry swept the opposing horse from the field before attacking the Saxon foot from the flanks. Under this pressure the Saxon infantry collapsed and dispersed. The ease of the final Imperial victory was a result of careful preparation. Charles's success in reducing the number of his opponents while concentrating his own forces left John Frederick practically isolated. Charles was thus able to deploy a massive numerical superiority at the decisive moment while the bold seizure of the crossing of the Elbe by the Spanish infantry gave him the crucial tactical advantage. *See also* ALBA; METZ (1552–3); PAVIA.

SIMON ADAMS

FURTHER READING
C. Oman, *A History of the Art of War in the Sixteenth Century* (London, 1937), pp. 244–53; K. Brandi, *The Emperor Charles V* (London, 1939), pp. 549–68; W. S. Maltby, *Alba: a biography of Fernando Alvarez de Toledo, 3rd Duke of Alba* (Berkeley and London, 1983), pp. 61–3.

Mukden, Battle of (21 February–10 March 1905)   One of the most significant battles of the Russo-Japanese war, Mukden saw around 310,000 Russians commanded by General Aleksei Kuropatkin confront almost as many Japanese under the command of General Iwao Oyama along a front of some 40 miles in a series of 'reciprocal and alternating outflanking manoeuvres' until neither had any more reserves available. On 6 March General Maresuke Nogi's Japanese 3rd Army extended its area of operations to encircle the Russian right wing. To counter this, Kuropatkin took troops from his own centre but then had to retreat to avoid his centre being overrun in turn. Despite their undeniable offensive spirit, the Japanese nevertheless failed to achieve an overwhelming victory against determined Russian resistance. The Japanese suffered more than 70,000 casualties and the Russians almost 100,000, the battle proving the effectiveness of machine-guns in defensive action and of artillery in the offensive. However, the same lessons were not really learned by Western armies until the Balkan Wars. *See also* INFANTRY; JAPAN; RUSSIA/USSR.

A. CORVISIER

FURTHER READING
R. Connaughton, *The War of the Rising Sun and the Tumbling Bear* (London, 1988); D. Walder, *The Short Victorious War* (London, 1973).

Murten, Battle of (22 June 1476)   Making light of the defeat he had suffered at the hands of the Swiss at Grandson on 2 March, Duke Charles the Bold of Burgundy again invaded the Swiss Confederation and laid siege to the town of Murten or Morat. As the Swiss desperately raised their levies,

Murten, under the governorship of Adrian von Bubenberg, an old friend of Charles the Bold, put up an unexpectedly stout resistance enabling the Swiss army to arrive by forced marches. Some contingents marched for 36 hours before going straight into action. Charles's army was divided into three sections, none of which could rapidly come to the assistance of either of its neighbours. He also failed to reconnoitre with his light troops and the rapid approach of the Swiss caught him completely by surprise. Having waited for 6 hours yet still ignorant of the location of his enemy, Charles sent his main body back to camp leaving a few thousand men to man the field fortifications and palisades. The Swiss, under cover of Murten Wood, marched across the front of the Burgundian left and centre in the knowledge that if they beat the Burgundian right then the Burgundian centre and left would be trapped in their positions around Murten. Assaulting the palisades of the Burgundian right, the Swiss phalanxes drove the defenders down the hill into the path of the main body which was marching to their support from the camp. Acting vigorously, the Swiss smashed the Burgundians in detail before pursuing the fugitives towards Avenches. The 6,000 Italian infantry who had been besieging Murten were trapped and scarcely a man escaped. At Murten, the Swiss added skilful generalship to the customary power and fighting qualities of their infantry phalanxes. In the following year, the Swiss invaded Lorraine and killed Charles the Bold at the Battle of Nancy. *See also* CHARLES THE BOLD; GRANDSON; INFANTRY; SWITZERLAND.

D. REICHEL
JOHN CHILDS

FURTHER READING
Richard Vaughan, *Charles the Bold* (London, 1973).

Museums, military The most widely recognized function of a museum is the collection, conservation and interpretation of artefacts for the benefit of the public. The earliest military collections were probably trophies captured in war which were amassed and paraded before an audience prior to storage, often at a site of religious significance. A practice possibly as old as this tradition of displaying captured enemy equipment is the exaltation of the victorious general by preserving relics in association with his tomb. This concept of the military commander as hero may also be witnessed in museums of 'the revolution' or 'national liberation'.

Although the spoils of war and the need for examples to emulate have provided two of the ingredients of military museums down the centuries, of equal importance, certainly in post-medieval Europe, has been the development of armouries both as functional groups of weapons in their own right to which interested visitors could gain access and as the basis of collections subsequently located in national museums where, over time, the military–historical interest has become subordinated to that of the decorative arts. Perhaps the best example is the Royal Armouries in the Tower of London; its nucleus is the personal armour of the kings of England and it has been open to visitors since the fifteenth century. Among the substantial number of armouries which have formed the bases for military museums are those of Madrid, Stockholm and the Kremlin in Moscow.

The need for technical instruction, especially in the operation of artillery, provided an added impetus. More modern museums often disguise old collections; although the *Musée de l'Armée* in Paris was created in 1905 one of its component parts was the *Musée d'Artillerie* established in 1684. Similar cases can be found in Italy, Spain and Russia. Even the West Point Museum in the United States, founded in 1854, which included in its remit a requirement to house trophies of the American Revolution, the War of 1812 and the Mexican War, was created to assist in ordnance instruction at the Military Academy.

A particular contribution to the development of military museums in the nineteenth century was the establishment in the United Kingdom of the Royal

In 1489, the public were permitted to view the arms and armour in the **Royal Armouries** housed in the keep of the Tower of London. The Royal Armouries is probably the oldest military museum in the world. It continues to house its main collection in the Tower but now additionally hosts an artillery museum at Portsmouth and is building a new museum in Leeds.

(Drawing by Don Pottinger)

United Services Institution Museum. It had a strong didactic bias. Many of its more significant items were ultimately passed to the National Army Museum in Chelsea, established by royal charter in 1960, and which by 1990 had redefined its role as a social history museum of the British army. The emergence of regimental and corps museums in the decades following the re-organization of the British army in 1870–1 gave the United Kingdom probably more military museums than any other country. The linking of regiments with their localities gave rise to the classic museum of this type, its strength lying in relics of campaigns and past members of the unit. The local connection determined that many such collections would become associated with town and county museums, especially in the second half of the twentieth century. Of those retaining their separate identity, the Royal Artillery, Tank and Army Flying Museums have been recognized as possessing collections of national importance.

The need to assimilate the concept of total war in the twentieth century resulted in an Act of Parliament in 1920 which founded the Imperial War Museum. Its original brief was to record the British military endeavours of the Great War but this was extended to cover the Second World War and, in due course, the vast subject of conflict in the twentieth century, civil as well as military, the latter on a tri-service basis. The need to communicate sacrifice as well as to interpret conflict is perhaps best exemplified in the Australian War Memorial at Canberra. Other momentous events in the twentieth century have stimulated the initiation of museums – the Central Museum of the USSR Armed Forces, the title by which it was known in 1965, was formed in 1919 to mark the role of the army in the Bolshevik Revolution of 1917 and its subsequent history.

One of the most significant trends in the development of military museums in the twentieth century has been 'battlefield interpretation' and the construction of site museums. Much of the credit must lie with the US National Parks Service which pioneered work in this field. There has been a slower response in the United Kingdom, although the Culloden battlefield has been successfully interpreted by the Scottish National Trust and much effort has been put into the conservation of historic buildings such as the barracks at Berwick-on-Tweed and Fort George, near Inverness, Scotland, which is still an active army garrison. In Europe, important preservation schemes have been launched, not least to secure the survival of parts of the Great War trench system in north-eastern France. Public interest has meant that museums have been established to interpret a number of Second World War sites, including the 'D' Day landings and the Arnhem campaign.

Many naval museums – in Copenhagen, St Petersburg and Karlskrona in Sweden – have their origins in collections of model ships. Others were established in Spain and Norway during the nineteenth century. In the United Kingdom a Royal Naval Museum was created on the centenary of the Battle of Trafalgar in 1905 whilst the National Maritime Museum at Greenwich, equipped with a broader remit, was opened in 1937. Dockyard heritage projects, such as those at Portsmouth and Chatham, have extended the interpretative options and into the former complex has gone the Mary Rose, Henry VIII's flagship which was successfully raised from the seabed in 1982. The precedent for the Mary Rose project was the raising, salvaging and placing into a museum in 1964 in Stockholm of the Vasa which had capsized on its maiden voyage in 1628. These modern archaeological exercises were pre-dated by attempts to preserve ships before they were scrapped. Perhaps the earliest was Elizabeth I's instruction that the Golden Hinde, Sir Francis Drake's flagship on his circumnavigation of the globe, should be preserved at Deptford; apparently it survived for about a century before disintegrating. Such a fate, however, did not befall the USS Constitution nor the light cruiser Aurora which menaced the Winter Palace in St Petersburg during the Bolshevik Revolution. In the United Kingdom the most important preserved ships include HMS Victory, still in commission, HMS Warrior, and HMS Belfast, now moored in the Thames forming part of the Imperial War Museum. The Submarine,

Fleet Air Arm and Royal Marines Museums mark their distinctive contributions to the Senior Service.

The fact that the history of military flying is closely connected with the history of flight itself is reflected in air force museums. The establishment of the RAF Museum at Hendon in 1963 covers the history of the Royal Flying Corps, the Royal Naval Air Service and the Royal Air Force, the third being formed by the amalgamation of its two predecessors in 1918. Many countries have set up similar institutions. One of the most impressive museums of military aviation in the world is the vast collection at the US Air Force Museum in the Wright-Patterson Air Force Base.

Military museums have enjoyed a long and honourable past having demonstrated resilience in the face of occasional neglect and ideological abuse. The best have applied rigorous intellectual standards to collecting, conserving, documenting and interpreting original objects from this crucial area of human activity. *See also* CULTURE, PROTECTION OF; GLORY; HONOURS AND AWARDS; ICONOGRAPHY; VEXILLOLOGY.

IAN G. ROBERTSON

FURTHER READING
Terence Wise, *A Guide to Military Museums* (7th edn, Hemel Hempstead, 1992); *The Tower: its buildings and its institutions*, ed. John Charlton (London, 1978); Jean-Marcel Humbert, *The Hôtel des Invalides*, vol. 2: *The Army Museum* (Paris, 1986).

Music, military At a very early date military music took on the role of inspiring fear in the enemy, transmitting orders or signals, keeping a body of soldiers marching in step or urging it on into battle and, lastly, enhancing military prestige. We may sum up these objectives under two heads: (1) to assist in the carrying out of military activities; (2) to contribute to ensuring the high morale of the combatants.

1 In ancient times, among the Spartans the Pyrrhic dance played a part in the soldiers' physical training. The Roman army used numerous instruments of the time to indicate parades, striking camp, retreats, a visit from the leader, battle, etc.

2 Inspiring fear in the enemy was the objective sought by the trumpets at the siege of Jericho and the same goal was achieved by a great many of the Barbarian peoples such as the Gauls and the Germans by banging their weapons on their shields. Plutarch wrote that 'nothing is more appropriate than music for carrying men on to great actions and particularly for exciting in them the degree of courage necessary to brave the dangers of war.' It has long been recognized as indispensable to build up the courage of the warrior and inure him to the dangers of war. The Spartans sang the 'Song of Castor' when charging and they accorded an important role to Tyrtaeus who, by his elegies and marching songs, had given them renewed courage in the Messenian wars.

It seems that military music rendered greater service to the infantry than to the cavalry, for the beating of the horses' hooves, particularly after the appearance of horseshoes (ninth century), may drown out the sound of the instruments. Some writers see this as the possible cause for the decline of military music in the Middle Ages, when it was maintained only in chivalric ceremonies. The Crusades are said to have brought the introduction of drums and cymbals into the West and created the conditions for a revival of military music. Cesare Borgia's armies had particularly brilliant musicians, while the German towns acquired drum and trumpet bands. The cavalry adopted the trumpet, whereas the infantry kept simply to the drum, which was used to set the marching rhythm. The fife spread throughout Europe among foot troops after 1540, whilst the Scottish mercenaries introduced bagpipes. Francis I authorized the use of a fife and a drum for each company of foot.

In the seventeenth century, drum and bugle calls were established for the various troop movements. Generally the military administration, in the case of Louvois or the administrators of the Spanish *tercios*, took particular interest in the instruments which gave the signals for drill: the

543

trumpets and kettle-drums of the cavalry, the drums and fifes of the infantry and only awarded pay to a small number of men playing these instruments. Contact with court music through the sovereign's household regiments brought in various different instruments, including cornets, trombones, bassoons and even oboes, and indeed violins, as the leaders determined.

Harmonic military music developed in the eighteenth century, first in Germany, then in Britain and later in France, particularly with the encouragement of Maurice de Saxe, as expressed in his *Rêveries* (1757). In France, the example came from the foreign regiments in the king's service. An ordonnance of 1764 allotted sixteen musicians to the *Gardes françaises* and in 1766 another two fifes and one clarinet per infantry battalion were attached to the staff of the regiment. Following the creation and suppression of various units, the French infantry in 1788 possessed eight musicians and one director of music per regiment. In fact, everything depended on the colonel. The musicians attached to the regimental staff were classed as non-combatants and were engaged by the colonel and the administrative council of the corps for one year or two. They were badly paid and often poor in quality. J.-J. Rousseau wrote that in France not one trumpet sounded in tune, which seems somewhat exaggerated. The musicians, even in the Prussian army, showed great reluctance to take part in battles. In France, except during the Revolution, the military authorities showed a certain reticence where military bands were concerned. Out of a concern to maintain the fighting power of the corps, ordonnances forbade musicians from being included among the soldiers, though these were often disregarded. Saint-Germain considered military bands a useless luxury and Bonaparte suppressed them in the cavalry, arguing that the cost of twenty regimental bands would make it possible to raise a twenty-first regiment. It is true that many colonels wanted these musicians to be very colourful. For many, indeed, the chief function of the regimental band was to entertain the soldiers at the evening tattoo.

However, military bands came to assume an increasingly important role in public ceremonies and contributed to the prestige of the army among the population. Here, the Romantic movement also played its part, with Berlioz for example conducting the *Marche des Francs-juges* – later to become the *Marche hongroise* – marching ahead of the musicians and beating time wtih a sabre. From Russia came the (passing) fashion for 'gunpowder music', music accompanied by cannon shots. During the Restoration, the military band consolidated its existence in France as in other countries. In 1838, the French army included 2,725 musicians, or 1 musician for every 117 men. The status of these musicians only came to be clarified rather slowly. Their professional training most often took place before they entered the service, but already in its school for the 'children of the regiment', the *Gardes françaises* trained instrumentalists. In 1789, they had Sarette as their conductor and they were to form the basis for the band of the *Garde nationale* and later of a free school which would contribute to the creation of the *Conservatoire de Musique* in November 1793.

The character of military music varies according to the goals pursued. The drum-rolls and bugle-calls heard on the parade-ground or those used to set the tempo of military life are designed to seize the attention, even by strident or indeed discordant sounds. Lully and, following him, Philidor did, however, compose rhythms and melodies of genuine musical value. What may properly be called a musical code emerged in the reign of Louis XIV and acquired a formal structure in France around 1750. In the nineteenth century, this acquired a certain sobriety which is, on occasion, quite moving (the last post), though most often rudimentary. However, at the beginning of the twentieth century, the number of bugle calls increased, particularly in the technical arms, reaching a high point in the navy. After the Second World War, mechanization in the air force, the navy and, later, in the army tended to see the number of bugle-calls and drum-rolls fall off and often dictated their replacement by a code of signals by siren.

Harmonic military music has followed the development of its secular and sacred counterparts. In the Middle Ages it had some connections with religious music. In 1270, Saint Louis's musicians played the *Veni Creator* before setting sail at Aigues-Mortes for the crusades. And later, at least during Lent, the Vendeans were to make the *Vexilla Regis* a genuine marching song. However, in the sixteenth century, it was to court ceremony and particularly to tournaments that military music was to turn for its themes. In the following century, it would turn to opera. It was thus a long time before military music assumed the rhythmic, martial character which became the norm in the nineteenth century. Handel in England, Keiser in Germany and Pugnani in Italy did, however, compose marches. We must, however, note that Frederick II's army was proud of its 'silent' cadenced step, assisted only by the clicking of heels. The rhythm of that step was slow and would remain so in the armies in which the soldier was required to sing while marching or again in those where a tiring form of parade step was practised (goose-step in the German and Russian armies, slow march in the British). In France, the pace of marching increased under the July Monarchy, perhaps under the influence of the colonial campaigns, except in the Foreign Legion.

The success of military bands in the nineteenth century increased the number of marching airs. At first each of the arms, then each of the regiments wanted its own march. Tunes were borrowed initially from fashionable melodies, often taken from operas. Apart from the rhythm, there are evident similarities between *La Galette de Saint-Cyr* or *L'Artilleur de Metz* and Bellini's Chorus from *I Puritani* (1834) or between the *Marche des Chasseurs* and the *Choeur des Ouvriers* of 1848. It must be admitted, however, that in France the increase in the number of regimental marches did nothing to raise the standard of their musical quality. However, marches like the *Marche des soldats de Turenne* (Lully), *Les Dragons de Noailles*, the *Marche consulaire*, the *Dessauer Marsch*, *Der gute Kamerad*, *Prince Eugene's March* and the *Radetzky March* have become part of the world's musical heritage.

The words attached to these marches, whether inspired by events or heroes, have rarely enriched the poetic heritage, but they have played a substantial part in the formation of patriotic sentiment, just as the rude words which soldiers often attached to their bugle calls have played their part in leaving men with fond memories of the days in the barrack-rooms of their national service. *See also* ETHOS; MORALE; TRAINING.

A. CORVISIER

FURTHER READING
L. S. Winstock, *Songs and Music of the Redcoats. A history of the war music of the British army, 1642–1902* (London, 1970); M. B. Leslie, *Battle Hymns of the British and Indian armies, 1695–1914* (London, 1970).

Musselburgh *See* PINKIE

Musters *See* INSPECTIONS; INTENDANTS; LOGISTICS

N

Nagumo, Chuichi (1887–1944) After joining the Imperial Navy in 1908, Nagumo became a specialist in torpedoes, and then participated in forming the Japanese fleet air arm. He showed ability and leadership and, after serving on the Naval General Staff and on that of the Combined Fleet, he rose to flag rank, commanding first a destroyer squadron and then the First Carrier Strike Force. With the latter he conducted the attack on Pearl Harbor (7 December 1941) and later the attack on Ceylon (5–9 April 1942). At the Battle of Midway Island, however, poor intelligence led to his carriers being attacked while landing their aircraft, all four being sunk. Nevertheless, he continued to command the remaining Japanese carriers in the Battles of the Eastern Solomons (24 August 1942) and Santa Cruz (26 October 1942), achieving some success despite great losses of pilots and aircraft. He was relieved by Ozawa in November 1942 and later became the naval commander on the crucial island of Saipan, but was unable to prevent the Americans landing there. On the island's fall, he committed suicide. *See also* JAPAN; MIDWAY ISLAND; PEARL HARBOR; TOGO; YAMAMOTO.

A. CORVISIER
A. W. H. PEARSALL

FURTHER READING
M. Fuchida and M. Okumiya, *Midway* (London, 1957); S. E. Morison, *History of the United States Naval Operations in World War II* (Boston, 1947–62).

Napier, Sir William (1785–1860) Napier can claim to be the father of British military history, the six volumes of his *History of the War in the Peninsula* (1828–40) being not only of profound historiographical importance but also a foundation for professional self-regard in the British army. Napier came from an Anglo-Irish family.

He served first in the 52nd Light Infantry and, throughout the Peninsular War, with the 43rd Light Infantry. These were the regiments whose tactical role made them a model for the army as a whole, and whose discipline was based on emulation rather than repression. Napier was particularly influenced by Sir John Moore, their mentor. A wound received in the Peninsula effectively ended Napier's active career, although he reached the rank of major-general and was Lieutenant-Governor of Guernsey from 1841 to 1847. Napier's account of the Peninsular War shows an indebtedness to Jomini, although it does not itself explicitly set out any military theory. It condemns the guerillas specifically and the Spanish in general, and it glorifies the deeds of the British infantry. Its focus is on battles and tactics. A staunch Whig and an admirer of Napoleon, his history aroused considerable con-

(Mansell Collection)

troversy, a debate Napier entered with vehemence. He proved similarly trenchant in his defence of his brother, Charles, the conqueror of Sind in 1843 and commander-in-chief in India (1849–50). Despite its contentiousness, Napier's history proved definitive for almost a century. *See also* JOMINI; NAPOLEON; TRAINING.

HEW STRACHAN

FURTHER READING
H. A. Bruce, *The Life of General Sir William Napier* (London, 1864); Jay Luvaas, *The Education of an Army* (London, 1965); Priscilla Napier, *The Sword Dance: Lady Sarah Lennox and the Napiers* (London, 1971); Priscilla Napier, *Revolution and the Napier Brothers, 1820–1840* (London, 1973).

Napoleon (1769–1821) Napoleon believed that the art of war was essentially a question of practical execution and his place among innovators is therefore modest. His indisputable military genius does, however, place him in the front rank of strategists and tacticians. A graduate of the École de Guerre, he drew with extraordinary felicity on the experience of his predecessors (Villars, Frederick the Great) and the fund of eighteenth-century French military thinking on the offensive (Folard, Guibert). He also made good use of the recent restructuring of the army into divisions, the new equipment developed in France (the model 1777 musket and Gribeauval's cannon), and the improved maps which were being produced in many parts of Europe.

He had the capacity to judge a situation swiftly before committing his forces wholeheartedly, often at a high cost in lives, while also concentrating his artillery. In this way, he usually caught his enemies by surprise and was able to make use of their supply depots. It was only possible to beat him after he had undertaken a wild act of folly – the march on Moscow (1812) – resulting in the formation of a general anti-French alliance (1813). After the defeat at Leipzig in the 'Battle of the Nations' (1813), the disproportion of the forces and the war-weariness of the French population made it impossible for Napoleon to exploit the normal patriotic urge to defend national territory. Although he fought a masterly campaign in eastern France (1814), he could not prevent a general collapse and the fall of Paris. The analysis of his operations, most notably by Clausewitz and Jomini, became a subject of military scholarship throughout the nineteenth and twentieth centuries. *See also* AUSTERLITZ; BLOCKADES; CARTOGRAPHY; CLAUSEWITZ; DAVOUT; FIREARMS; JENA AND AUERSTÄDT; JOMINI; KUTUZOV; LEIPZIG; MOSCOW, RETREAT FROM; NAVAL WARFARE; TACTICAL ORGANIZATION; WATERLOO; WELLINGTON.

A. CORVISIER

FURTHER READING
D. G. Chandler, *The Campaigns of Napoleon* (London, 1967); Jean Delmas and P. Lesouef, *Napoléon chef de guerre* (3 vols, Paris, 1969).

Narses (d.567) Narses, a eunuch, was a Persarmenian general of the Byzantine emperor Justinian I (527–65). He was sent with an army to Italy in 538 but he failed to co-operate with Belisarius and was withdrawn in the following year. Despite his advanced age and lack of military experience, this court favourite was again sent to Italy in 550 where he assumed the supreme command. At Taginae (552) in central Italy, Narses's Byzantine army of 15,000 encountered the Ostrogothic army of King Totila. The two armies went into line of battle across a shallow valley. Narses formed his heavy infantry into a phalanx to block the foot of the valley, ordering some of his heavy cavalry to dismount and join the infantry. Over 4,000 archers were massed on either flank with the remaining heavy cavalry in their rear. The Ostrogoths placed their heavy cavalry in front of their infantry and charged. They were unable to break through the Byzantine infantry and stood halted before the infantry line receiving showers of arrows from the flanks. Narses then ordered his infantry to press forward while his heavy cavalry attacked from either wing. The Ostrogothic cavalry retreated but became entangled with their own foot soldiers. King Totila was mortally wounded. The victory at Taginae led to the recapture of Rome in 553 and the return of Italy to Byzantine control. At the Mons Lactarius (Vesuvius) in 553, Narses defeated and killed Totila's successor, Teias. In 554, at Casilinum, Narses fought a raiding army of Franks under the Alamanni dukes, Buccelin and Lothar. Narses outnumbered the Franks, his battle-line overlapping the wings of the Frankish army. The Frankish heavy infantry attacked in a column and although they broke through the first two lines of Byzantine heavy infantry, they were halted before the third and final line by fire from the Byzantine bowmen and horse-archers positioned on the flanks. Unable to advance and subjected to hails of arrows, the Frankish column lost cohesion, presenting the opportunity for the Byzantine heavy cavalry to charge and inflict severe casualties. For the remaining thirteen years of his life, Narses administered the government of Italy. *See also* BELISARIUS; BYZANTIUM; CAVALRY; INFANTRY; ROME.

JOHN CHILDS

FURTHER READING
Procopius, *The Gothic War*, in *Procopius*, tr. H. B. Dewing (7 vols, Cambridge, Mass., 1914–40, repr. 1961–2); L. H. Fauber, *Narses, Hammer of the Goths* (New York, 1990).

Narva, Battle of (20 November 1700) After an arduous march along boggy roads, the army of the young Charles XII of Sweden arrived at Narva, a port in Swedish Estonia, on 13 November 1700. There were 10,500 effectives. Since 4 October, the town and fortress had been besieged by a force of around 40,000 Russians led by Tsar Peter I. The poor quality Muscovite artillery, under the command of the Saxon von Hallart, had barely made an impression on Narva's defences. Learning of the arrival of the Swedish vanguard and of Charles himself, who had recently defeated the Danes, Peter decided to leave his army to fetch reinforcements from Novgorod. His intention was to trap the Swedes between the two corps.

After discussions with Karl Gustav Rehnskjold, Charles decided to mount the swiftest possible attack against the long line of contravallation which curved around the town for 7,200 metres, both ends resting on the banks of the Narva River. The only route by which Peter's troops could return to Russian territory was a raft bridge across the river near Kamperholm to the northeast. There were too few Swedes to make a methodical attack on a wide front against the double line of trenches. Instead, the king decided to break through on either side of the main Russian camp, which was under the command of the courtier Prince Yury Trubetzkoi, using two deep shock columns of infantry with fixed bayonets. The assault was launched at 2.00 p.m., the left column, complete with Charles and his halberdiers, being commanded by Rehnskjold and the right by Otto Vellingk. The artillery of Grand Master Johan Sjobald was divided into two supporting batteries. The cavalry were ordered to charge through the breaches.

The Duke de Croy, the Walloon commander of the Russian army, was taken by surprise, his German staff finding liaison difficult with the Russian officers. A snowstorm concealed the Swedish advance and blinded the Russians. Throwing fascines (bundles of long sticks) into the ditches, Charles's infantry stormed the trenches; the Russian right began to withdraw across the Kamperholm bridge which collapsed under the weight. Only the Semionovski and Preobrazhenski regiments offered resistance from behind a barricade of waggons. The Russian line was broken into three sections under the converging fire of the Swedish columns. In the evening, the remains of the Russian right surrendered although the left wing, commanded by the wounded General Weide, did not submit until the following dawn.

The whole of the Russian camp, with 145 cannon, 151 colours, 20 standards, the war chest and the entire stock of ammunition, fell to Charles. The Russians lost 10,000 men while the Swedish casualties amounted to just 31 officers and 650 men killed and 1,200 wounded. Charles only took the general officers prisoner; the officers, non-commissioned officers and men were disarmed and led down to the river which they crossed by the repaired bridge. To contemporaries, this victory seemed to verge on the supernatural and the Russians denounced it as the work of Finnish sorcery. From it, Folard drew the conclusion that the column was the superior tactical formation and declared Charles XII to be the greatest captain in history. However, in the words of Peter the Great himself, although the Swedes would continue to defeat the Russians for many years, they would also teach the Russians how to defeat them in their turn. Narva provided the spur for the rapid modernization of the Russian army leading to the victory over the Swedes at Poltava in 1709. *See also* CHARLES XII; PETER I; POLTAVA; RUSSIA/USSR; SWEDEN.

C. NORDMANN
JOHN CHILDS

FURTHER READING
C. Duffy, *Russia's Military Way to the West* (London, 1981); R. Hatton, *Charles XII of Sweden* (London, 1968); Gustavus Adlerfeld, *The Military History of Charles XII, King of Sweden* (3 vols, London, 1740).

Nassau, Prince Maurice of Orange-Nassau (1567–1625) Prince Maurice of Orange-Nassau was appointed president of the council of state of what was to become the Republic of the United Provinces in 1584, the same year in which his father, William the Silent, had been assassinated. In 1585, the provincial estates of Holland and Zeeland offered him the office of stadholder, to be followed in 1587 by those of Utrecht, Gelderland and Overyssel. Simultaneously, he became captain-general of the Dutch armed forces. In conjunction with his cousin, William-Louis of Nassau (1560–1620), stadholder in Friesland and Groningen, he succeeded in introducing many reforms into the army. These were partly based on the lessons he had drawn from studying the classical authors, particularly Vegetius, Aelian, Frontinus and Emperor Leo VI of Byzantium. He reduced his disparate artillery to four basic calibres; reorganized his logistics; made his infantry more manoeuvrable by splitting the large regiments, or *tercios*, into smaller battalions of 580 men; and he introduced a system of drill and discipline which became the model for most European armies. In 1599, the entire Dutch field army was re-equipped with weapons of the same size and calibre. He was supported in his efforts by the advocate of Holland, Johan van Oldenbarneveldt, who occupied a key post in the new republic. Maurice had some very competent officers serving in his entourage whose roles have not yet been fully studied. As a consequence, it is very difficult to determine the precise extent to which he was personally responsible for the reforms. He maintained warm relations with the humanist Justus Lipsius, the mathematician Simon Stevin and the engraver Jacob de Gheyn. The latter translated Maurice's new infantry drill into a series of pictorial representations, *Wapenhandlingen van roers, musquetten ende spiessen* (Amsterdam, 1607), which was quickly followed by English, German, French and Danish editions. In the decade 1590–1600, Maurice obtained a series of brilliant military successes including the conquest of Geertruidenberg (1593) and the victory at the Battle of Nieuport (1600) which consolidated his international reputation. During the Twelve Years' Truce (1609–21), a conflict over religion occurred within the Republic in which Maurice was opposed by Oldenbarneveldt. He was able to put an end to these disturbances by calling on the loyalty of the army. Oldenbarneveldt was condemned to death and executed in 1619. This unfortunate affair somewhat damaged Maurice's reputation. Maurice aged rapidly in his later years and was unable to demonstrate his military skills after the truce; the banner was handed to his half-brother, Frederick Henry (1584–1647). *See also* GUSTAVUS II ADOLPHUS; INFANTRY; NETHERLANDS; NIEUPORT; OSTEND; SIEGES; STEVIN.

C. M. SCHULTEN
JOHN CHILDS

FURTHER READING
B. H. Nickle, *The Military Reforms of Prince Maurice of Orange* (Ann Arbor, Mich., 1981); H. H. Rowen, *The Princes of Orange*

(Cambridge, 1988); H. Amersfoort and P. H. Kamphuis, *Je Maintiendrai: a concise history of the Dutch army* (The Hague, 1985).

Nationalism This entry only covers the question of nationalism in so far as it relates to military history. At first sight, it may seem that national sentiment gives an added dimension and, often, a greater degree of violence to wars between states. For a French writer, it would have been easier to attempt to define nationalism or patriotism around the year 1880, at a point when a variety of elements and some occasionally contradictory notions were coalescing around the idea that the fatherland had received a bad battering. These ideas had acquired the status of a universally accepted dogma and Maurras was able to speak of 'Revenge, queen of France'.

In current usage, the terms 'fatherland' and 'nation' are often used interchangeably when referring to the reality of different states as they exist and are recognized by the international community, such as France, for example, even though some of these states may be regarded as heteroclite, if not indeed artificial constructions. Without any further qualification, patriotism and nationalism might simply be taken to mean attachment to the state of which one is a national. Below, we shall examine to what degree these notions actually correspond to cultural or emotional realities.

'Fatherland' and 'nation' are not, however, synonymous. The word 'Fatherland' carries an emotional charge which, beyond the mere sense of the land of one's ancestors, evokes the idea of the place where they lived and normally where they lie buried, the land where one is born and has one's being. 'One's fatherland is what one loves,' wrote Fustel de Coulanges. '"Nation" refers to the community of people who normally live in a country' (E. Renan, *Qu'est-ce qu'une nation?*, 1882). Today, we tend to see the nation, if not the fatherland, as an idea rather than a concrete reality to be distinguished from clans, tribes and social classes. It is an entity revealed only by the feelings one has for it and the attitudes to which it gives rise. The idea is present in the images and ideas which in-dividuals have of the entity they collectively constitute. It might therefore be regarded as a myth (G. Burdeau). And yet, is German *Volkstum* a myth?

In fact, the idea of fatherland also implies that of the community to whom the country legitimately belongs and the idea of nation that of the country which belongs to it legitimately if not legally. That is why in order to study these two such closely connected notions, after looking at their various component elements, as currently understood, we should examine the various roles which have been accorded to them, in so far as onomastics and literature may allow us to glimpse these (and certain forms of silence may also be regarded as source material here), together with their political and ideological connotations, the two sets of facts not necessarily covering identical ground. It is only by undertaking such a task that we may attempt to explain the strife and crises which give rise to conflicts. It is also necessary to take into account the forms of state, whether unitary or federal, within which the fatherlands and nations are found and, lastly, the problems posed by cases where the boundaries of states and nations do not coincide.

It should be noted that fatherland and nation are relatively recent terms in so far as a large part of their content is concerned. Let us leave aside the sense momentarily accorded to the word 'patriot' in 1789, when it meant a person committed to the public good. In Antiquity, both attachment to 'the city' and to the cultural world were found, for example in Greece, where, though they were often rivals, the city-states recognized that they belonged to a single world distinct from the 'Barbarian' lands. No matter where he was, the Roman citizen always bore that particular title with pride. Strangely, the Middle Ages were to have no similar vocabulary, even when the importance of separate states had been re-established. The French term *pays* expressed both the sense of the Latin word *pagus* and that of *patria*. The word 'nation' (from Latin *natus*, born), which appeared in the twelfth century, denoted birth or extraction, without any specific reference to territory and was applied to groups who differed in terms of their language (the different contingents of crusaders in the Holy Land, for example), the different ethnic corps in the service of a single ruler, the groups formed by students of common origin within a university (the four 'nations' of the University of Paris). It was not until the sixteenth century that the word *patrie* (fatherland) appeared in France. Until then, *patria* was a term in ecclesiastical language with two senses, the first temporal, *patria consuetudinis* (its current meaning), and the second spiritual, *patria communis* (meaning Christianity).

However, as Marc Bloch has shown, national feeling was in existence long before the terms used to express it today. 'France' was referred to as though no other fatherland or nation existed and the Revolutionaries would refer to 'the Nation' when they meant the French nation. At least from the thirteenth century, the term France has contained, albeit in a confused way, the ideas which were later to be expressed in terms of fatherland and nation. The Salic law, which is referred to from the fourteenth century onwards, is one of the expressions of that French nationalism which rejects all foreign rulers. In the short term, France paid for that principle with the terrible crisis brought about by the Hundred Years' War. However, it was later to mean that she avoided fighting wars of succession. A multinational state established on either side of the Channel may have been conceivable in the twelfth century, but this was no longer the case by the fourteenth.

The formation of the kingdoms of France and England as states by the French and English royal houses and the Hundred Years' War, which exacerbated national sentiment in the two countries, were the essential facts leading to the birth of the two nations. In France, Joan of Arc was very soon seen as a miraculous saviour sent by God. Charles of Orléans and, more importantly, Villon and Gringore, expressed their sense of Frenchness even though neither of the terms 'fatherland' and 'nation' was available to them. For them, France was a person, the mother of all who were born there and, consequently, of all those who made it a community. It also came to be seen as the mother of the most highly regarded qualities of civilization: 'France, mother of the Arts, of Arms and Laws, long have you nourished me with the milk of your breast,' wrote J. Du Bellay who was one of the first to employ the word *patrie*.

The bases of nationhood are varied and many are not indispensable. One may find juridical bases – such as freedom in the sense of independence (the principle of nationalities) – which are recognized at the international level; and material bases such as location, frontiers and territorial space, though these are sometimes subject to change (as in the case of Poland) or by no means closely related to geographical realities. All in all, natural frontiers are quite rare, even in groups of islands. Though it plays a very important role, cultural unity is not always indispensable as is demonstrated by the United States. The same is true – indeed more so – at the level of economic realities. Since medieval times, France has been praised for the diversity of its production, a feature which derived from its various different local economies and styles of life. It is complementarity of resources which then becomes a factor of national unity and this is developed by improving the routes of communication. None of these components is sufficient nor even necessary for the formation of a nation. Though many nations are built on a linguistic or religious community, Switzerland offers an example of a nation that is not united in either sphere. Conversely, it is not necessary for a solid state to be formed for an intellectual, literary, academic or scholarly community to exist. The Holy Roman Empire had more or less the same educational system and a unified intellectual life throughout its territory in spite of the division into different religions and states.

The most important factor ultimately seems to be collective memory, the memory of suffering endured together or past glories whose memory is kept alive by symbols (the flag), monuments, commemorative ceremonies and what is taught in schools. A living nation is a nation that has created a past for itself and is now chiefly occupied with its future. This 'primacy of culture' means that a nation may exist without a juridical basis and that, alongside nation-states, nations do exist that are not independent (e.g. Tibet) and may indeed be divided between several different states (Armenia, the Palestinians, the Kurds). In the former type, the future is seen initially in terms of maintaining the nation's existence. For nations which do not currently enjoy independence, the future consists in winning or regaining it, even if that independence is to all intents and purposes mythical. In this case, independence takes precedence over all other aspirations. Almost always added to this is the hope of a better future: regaining past political grandeur, rising to a higher economic level, exercising greater influence, etc.

The most difficult aspirations to satisfy are those of the nations which have been divided between several different states, as was the case with Poland between 1795 and 1918, or of Armenia and the Kurds, and this is so even when attention is momentarily directed towards one of the parts of their territories which is being treated less well than the others.

The question of the 'human scale' arises where the fatherland – and also the nation – is concerned. Fatherland: the land of one's forefathers. In ancient times, this corresponded more generally to one's country, *Gau* or *pays* (*pagus*), a geographical unit grouped around a small town, which holds a market and acts as a primary administrative centre. The sense of belonging and attachment to one's homeland are defined against what is 'foreign', which is itself characterized in terms of traditional stereotypes. Distinctions are made between various degrees of foreignness. The 'outsider' or 'off-comer' is a member of another nation. The scale varies with the degree of organization of political government and the ease of travel between different areas. The 'provinces' are, in most cases, products of the actions of the great feudal princes and do not always represent geographical units (e.g. Normandy). The feudal monarchies were made up of more or less unified groupings of territories with a high degree of political unity and developing administrative unity. By contrast, the Empire developed into a territorial entity centring on the Germanic world which, in spite of clear juridical boundaries, included within it extra-national marginal areas (Lotharingia, the Netherlands, northern Italy). This situation enabled cluster-states (*États-nébuleuses*) to form, such as those of the house of Habsburg. The Habsburg state brought together different nations, some of which were nation-states, and a variety of territories, whether or not these were members of the Empire; the only link between these lands was a common sovereign. It was quite rare for these associations to give rise to a common nation, though this did occur in the Iberian peninsula where the kingdom of Spain was born out of the fusion of the crowns of Castile and Aragon with the Catholic kings (a period of common sovereignty stretching over sixty years was not, however, sufficient to bring Portugal and Spain together in a lasting bond) and in Great Britain, which was formed in 1707 after a century of common rulers.

National sentiment crystallized around the sovereign. The name of the king was known to all his subjects, since it was spoken in the prayers of the religious services and his effigy was to be found on the coin of the realm. It was in his name that justice was meted out (at least in the supreme court of the kingdom) and it was the ruler who called out the whole body of vassals. As monarchical rule evolved, it became increasingly more common for national unity to emerge where a common danger was perceived. In actual fact, only the intellectuals – i.e. in this case mainly the clergy – could have a fairly precise view of what the unity of a kingdom meant, but they were also motivated by a sense of belonging to a wider, supra-national community – Christendom or Islam.

The revolutionaries of 1789 and, in their wake, the French Republican historians of the nineteenth century, sincerely believed that nationhood implied unity of legislation and the same law for all, whereas, under the *ancien régime*, 'one law' meant common observance of the various laws and customary rights of the peoples of the realm. It is, however, a fact that equality before the law constitutes a very powerful mobilizing principle for attachment to the nation. 'One faith, one king, one law' was an axiom of the French *ancien régime*. Yet the *ancien régime* nation coped very well with diversity, with remnants of a 'personal' jurisprudence subsisting in the division of society into orders and corporations subject to different statutes or privileges (clergy, nobles, royal officers, city burgesses and also 'peoples' living under the customary law of their provinces). Mirabeau's oft-repeated remark that *ancien régime* France was an 'unconstituted aggregate of disunited peoples' is a terrible misrepresentation. Under the customary Constitution of the *ancien régime*, uniformity was not essential to the unity of the nation. It became so progressively after the reign of Louis XIV and, in 1789, the 'peoples' were so little disunited that, as soon as they were given the opportunity, they swept away all that differentiated them in terms of legislation, without however disowning their individual characteristics. The very prudent centralizing work of the monarchy and the progress made in communications and education (one third of the French population were literate in the sixteenth century and the figure rose to more than half at the end of Louis XIV's reign) had relegated attachment to local diversity to the status of a mere argument against a government that had become unpopular for reasons other than its policy of patient unification.

It took the blundering actions of the Convention to produce an opposition movement calling itself federalist, which took the form of open or clandestine armed revolts. Chief among these was the revolt in the Vendée, though that particular rising had more profound causes. We might note that most uprisings, acts of open or clandestine armed resistance against a central power, have felt a pressure to appeal to the reflexes of old attachments to the native heath. This was the case in France during the Fronde, the revolt of the Camisards and the rising in the Vendée. The same tendency was seen again in resistance against the Prussian invaders of 1870–1 and against the occupying forces in 1940–4.

For many years, the various *pays* have been seen in France as the building blocks of several mosaics, or geographical (e.g. Beauce), economic and administrative (e.g. *départements*). The fragmentation of *ancien régime* Germany still left intact the memory of the *Gau* (*pagus*), a notion which the Hitler regime skilfully exploited to complete the unification of Germany, even if it did not always follow the old boundaries exactly in doing so. In the countries of the Mediterranean, the old, powerful urban structures retained their influence. Unification respected the primacy of the town and city.

Together with the locality, the *pays* constituted the very basis of patriotism in its most emotive dimension. However, a common sovereignty, a certain administrative uniformity, communications, the education system and, lastly, the media have contributed to a confusion between fatherland and nation in the expression of national sentiment. After religious feelings, the fatherland/nation complex has been the most powerful mobilizing force in history. Moreover, along the frontiers between the differing religious confessions, attachment to a religion is often one of the components of national sentiment (in Poland, for example).

National feeling may be a unifying factor, in spite of religious or political differences (Switzerland, Third Republic France), and even, though less often, in spite of linguistic differences (Switzerland). It provided such a degree of motivation that the bodies of men of Brittany, the Auvergne and Corsica, for example, are found in great numbers in the military cemeteries of northern and eastern France, the most magnificent sacrifice made to the nation.

The fatherland/nation complex may also exist outside the state. There existed a sense of German nationhood even if it was not openly expressed at the time of the *Pax westphalica* and Italy was never completely reduced to a mere 'geographical expression'. The awareness that one is different from one's (sometime dominant) neighbours has often preserved an emotional potential that is capable of stirring a divided or subjugated people. The ultimate effect of the partitioning of Poland can be seen merely to have been a reinforcement of Polish national sentiment. Sooner or later, most peoples have succeeded in creating a national state, though there are still some exceptions (Armenians, Kurds, Palestinians).

However, individual national heritages may retain a certain degree of vigour. Most of the world's states at the present time have been formed by progressive annexations or additions. This has involved several processes, including that of dynastic fusion. Though this succeeded in Spain and Great Britain, it has not always been successful. In Scandinavia, in spite of some common features such as a common religion, the union of Sweden and Norway did not survive, on account of the size of the country and the diversity of its population. The Habsburgs failed to create a common national sentiment, in spite of shared economic interests, on account of the extent of their territories, which accentuated the cultural differences, and the disappearance of the Turkish threat.

In the case of France, a higher principle, the Frankish monarchy, invested with a holiness conferred upon it in the coronation ceremony, existed before the nation. It was the Frankish monarchy which made the formation of the kingdom of France possible by the attachment to the crown and to the royal domain of most of the lands accorded to *Francia occidentalis* by the Treaty of Verdun and, subsequently, by the addition of other, neighbouring territories by a transference of sovereignty, usually after campaigns of conquest.

Where this 'higher principle' had grown too weak (as happened in the case of the Holy Roman Empire, whose influence was less strong than local loyalties) or where it did not exist, states assumed a federal form: the Swiss cantons, the United Provinces (which became the Netherlands), the thirteen colonies of America, which became the United States, and even the German Empire in 1870 all affirmed their national unity while still retaining local particularisms. This did not always occur without a crisis (the War of the Sonderbund in Switzerland, the American Civil War, the Austro-Prussian War of 1866).

The sense of a common heritage may come under threat, at least on some counts when a religious or ideological difference arises, as was the case in Europe in the sixteenth century and has been so in the contemporary period. Let us take the case of France. Following the Wars of Religion, 'Good Frenchmen' and 'Good Catholics' were ranged in opposition on account of the one group putting the interests of the Church first, while the other gave first consideration to the interests of France. Yet both groups were as patriotic as they were steadfast in their faith. The Protestants were only persecuted by Louis XIV because, though they were Frenchmen body and soul, they seemed to be placing themselves outside the law that was common to the whole nation.

The Revolution was another occasion of great strife. As in the Wars of Religion (including the Camisard rising), above and beyond the mere request for immediate defence from persecution, the call for foreign assistance was made with the intention of saving France from a particular conception of the national community. During the Revolution, the *émigrés* offered the Allies nothing in return for their assistance. From such trials as these, national feeling generally emerges strengthened. If the Restoration was sometimes reluctant to employ the word 'nation', this is explained by the use that had been made of it by the revolutionaries. In practice, however, that regime was as nationalistic as all the preceding ones since 1793. National sentiment remains strong so long as the idea of a common heritage retains primacy over that of the different local heritages. Marc Bloch used to say that to understand the continuity of national sentiment in France, one had to take into account both the emotions aroused by the coronation of its kings and the feelings stirred by the *Fête de la Fédération*.

There remain those instances in which the fatherland and nation are not exactly identical, as is the case with most colonial lands. Europeans whose families had left their own countries several generations before to settle in distant countries, populated by people whose civilization was, at least in technological terms, originally somewhat behind their own, became attached to the land which they had cultivated and which had become their fatherland without for all that ceasing to feel they were members of their nation, whether or not mixed marriages had been possible. In the eighteenth century, for the American or 'island' creoles, the French Canadians, the settlers in the thirteen British colonies of America or the Russian settlers in Asia, the fatherland was the country where they had been born and the nation the community to which they belonged – and the metropolis was the most vivid expression of that community. This was still the case with the *Pieds noirs* in Algeria, even when they were only French by adoption. The feeling was practically the same whether the autochthonous populations had been eliminated, as was virtually the case in Anglo-Saxon America and the West Indies, or whether they had survived, reaching higher population levels after the initial crisis on account of advances in medical treatment and the development of food resources, as in Latin America or Southern Africa, or again where the original population was boosted by the introduction of a coloured labour force as in the sugar-producing islands. None the less, even though distance has been conquered and the media now bring them more closely than ever into contact with the metropolis, a point is reached when a crisis may occur.

In fact, the former USSR offered almost the only modern example of a state which succeeded, for a time, in assimilating its colonies, thanks to a politically unitary but administratively federal constitution, to the demographic reserves of settlers and, above all, to exceptional geographical conditions in which the colonized territories formed a territorially continuous block with the metropolis. However, it is now apparent that seventy years of imposed unity and political uniformity were not sufficient to eradicate a sense of nation and fatherland in the constituent republics of the USSR. On the contrary, with the weakening of central authority in the metropolis, the nationalism in the Baltic states, in the Ukraine and in the Trans-Caucasus has re-emerged with exceptional virility. A similar process, whereby an apparent assimilation of colonies and client states fell apart, occurred with the collapse of the Austro-Hungarian Empire in 1918.

Distance and different geographical conditions have caused most fatherland/nation associations between distant territories to founder. No 'native question' lay at the origin of the independence of the United States or that of Canada and Australia. Similarly, the independence of the Spanish and Portuguese American colonies was the work of the Creoles, not of the Amerindians. The sense of a fatherland brought the sense of nationhood in its wake. Independence was gained either by wars which, in Latin America, cemented a new sense of nationhood or, in the case of the British dominions, by gradually becoming distanced from the metropolis politically. In both cases, there was a revolt by the settlers against a metropolis considered too possessive.

The phenomenon of decolonization carried out to the advantage of those peoples who were in place when the Europeans arrived or the coloured people who were subsequently settled there, as in Haiti, was quite different. That was the product of revolts assisted – if not indeed stirred up – by foreign powers: ideological, material or armed aid provided to non-European populations who reacted against a situation of subordination or social inequality, made more sensitive by an increasing demographic disproportion between the ethnic groups, and who rejected the form of social or cultural advancement proposed by the colonial power. The anti-colonial wars have created new states, though not always new nations. They have, however, given birth to, or developed, national feelings, though not without exacerbating the national sentiments of the Europeans against whom they were directed.

For many years, wars had as their official causes dynastic quarrels or rivalries between ruling houses, though these were often an expression of oppositions between nations, which were exploited by the sovereigns. The American and French revolutions gave war a national aspect. Wars between sovereign peoples do, however, lead rather quickly to total warfare. The scale of the world wars and the destruction they wrought produced reactions which were expressed in the formation of the League of Nations and later the United Nations. By their very titles, these organizations affirm the existence of nationhood. In actual fact, they tend to limit certain manifestations of nationhood. However, the peace imposed among the old nations was not total. A negative consequence of the condemnation of total warfare has been an increase in the number of extra-European states and wars for territorial conquest from which the great powers have by no means been absent.

Nationalism, which is a graft upon the body of ordinary national feelings, is an attitude not easily amenable to academic inquiry. The term, which is often used polemically, appeared in England at the beginning and in France at the end of the eighteenth century. In France, nationalism first referred to excesses of national feeling (chauvinism), then to doctrinal or practical excesses among groups standing for the defence of national values and interests above all, movements now generally classified as being on the right of the political spectrum, though in the last century they were seen as left-wing. Nationalism is generally in favour of a unitary state. Naturally, the nationalism of subjugated peoples differs from that of dominant ones. Today, public opinion tends to praise the former and condemn the latter. As Raoul Girardet remarks, 'If we take into account the different attitudes towards society, we are led to distinguish between a nationalism of satisfaction and euphoria and a nationalism of uneasiness and anxiety', a conservative nationalism and a nationalism of revolt. Lastly, as nationalism tends to take into itself the full range of values which a society regards as its own, it may take different forms depending upon the cultural area concerned.

Nationalism still constitutes one of the themes most capable of mobilizing people's energies, particularly when allied with a religion or an ideology. *See also* ETHOS; FRONTIERS; GLORY; MORALE; MUSEUMS; PACIFISM; SOLDIERS AND SOCIETY; SYMBOLISM.

A. CORVISIER

FURTHER READING
A Vagts, *A History of Militarism* (New York, 1959); Eric Carlton, *War and Ideology* (London, 1990); M. Walzer, *Just and Unjust Wars* (Harmondsworth, 1977); *Nations without a State: ethnic minorities in Western Europe*, ed. C. R. Foster (New York, 1980); Hans Kohn, *The Idea of Nationalism* (New York, 1958); F. H. Hinsley, *Nationalism and the International System* (London, 1973).

Naval personnel (recruitment and training) Throughout history, until a quite recent date, navies have encountered difficulties over the recruitment of personnel. The requirement for crews exceeded the capacity of seafaring communities to supply them, and the harshness of life on board aroused a profound aversion for naval service. In order to compensate for inadequate numbers of volunteers, all navies have had to have recourse to systems of more or less compulsory enrolment and to a whole range of expedients.

In Mediterranean countries, such difficulties became apparent in Antiquity and in the Middle Ages. But, contrary to a belief that has been slow to die, the galley crews consisted, in fact, of free men, whether citizens doing a spell of service or mercenaries. Navies resorted to using slaves in exceptional circumstances only. In addition, they were normally given their freedom before being taken aboard. There is a particularly clear illustration of this point in fifth- and fourth-century Athens, at a period when the very life of the city was dependent on the sea. The triremes were manned by free men. It fell, however, entirely to citizens of the poorest classes (*thetes*) to make up the crews, since they had insufficient money to be able to buy the expensive equipment of the hoplites. From Pericles' time, as one aspect of a vast social policy which was regarded as the best bulwark of democracy, the oarsmen even began to receive pay.

In face of the increasing needs, this source of recruits often proved inadequate. Certainly, in peacetime, the Athenian navy was limited to a constantly mobile squadron of limited size, consisting of around twenty triremes used for training and for policing the sea routes. But, in time of war, the fleet could number 200 ships, each requiring 170 oarsmen. During the second Persian war, which was settled by the Greek victory at Salamis, the numbers in the Athenian crews ultimately reached 34,000, a huge figure for a citizen population of military age that did not exceed 40,000.

Hence Athens, like the majority of other Greek cities, such as Corcyra or Corinth, had to have recourse to makeshift solutions. From the end of the fifth century onwards, metics, i.e. aliens, were enlisted, and a call was made upon contingents provided by the allied cities of the Delian League. In the case of major operations, such as the Sicilian expedition during the Peloponnesian War, wealthy citizens for whom the normal course would have been to fight as hoplites were mobilized for service on the galleys. The Athenian fleet also made use of mercenaries, though the number of these is unknown.

During the Peloponnesian War, these mercenaries seem to have been used, however, on a particularly large scale. Their help was one of the major prizes that each side had to play for in the war. Since Sparta and her allies had to create a fleet, they sought, on the advice of the Corinthians, to seduce these mercenaries into deserting to them by the use of subsidies provided by the Persian king or of borrowings from the treasuries of the temples at Olympia and Delphi. Despite this increasing recourse to paid crews, who in all probability came from that remarkable breeding-ground of seafarers formed by the Aegean archipelago, the Athenian fleet was no less of an exceptional and surprising phenomenon, which ran counter to one of the most prevalent beliefs of Antiquity. The fact is that the sailor of that period was very often an object of contempt. He seemed a being on the fringes of society, an outsider with no real native land.

The sailor came generally from the poorest classes, and thus belonged socially to the proletariat. He represented an element which was disturbing to the stability of societies based firmly on a class of small landed proprietors. In so far as he acted as the instrument of large-scale imperial trade or as a participant in common piracy, the sailor seemed the agent of a complex economic network which posed a fatal threat to the future of cities where stability rested on self-governing independence and on a territory protected by the gods, with clearly defined boundaries. The seafarer even put himself outside the sphere where the laws of religion could operate. He took the risk of disappearing at sea, which meant that the last honours could not be paid to his body.

There is a simple explanation for the prestige accorded to Athenian sailors. On the morrow of the victory at Salamis, they were seen as the saviours of the city. Subsequently, they became the guarantors of its prosperity and its influence. They came to put the hoplites, and even those who had earlier fought at Marathon, in the shade. Aristophanes tells us of a compliment which came into fashion, 'he's the best man with the oar'. But, following the defeat of Athens, and in the immediate aftermath of the Peloponnesian War, the whole subject became a matter of renewed debate. Moralists like Isocrates condemned the maritime orientation which proponents like Themistocles or Pericles had given to the city. A reaction set in; military service, it was held, should be confined to those citizens who preserved the sacred type of relationship with the soil. The small proprietor, who in war became the hoplite, constituted the model fighting man.

This contempt for sailors helped to aggravate, at the end of the fourth century, the long-standing problems of recruitment. The Athenian trierarchs, who had the formidable task of commissioning the triremes out of their own pockets, complained about the *thetes'* lack of willingness and constant desertions. The use of mercenaries, which tended to become general practice throughout the Greek world, just as much in armies as in navies, was the principal reason for such defections. The same situation seems, in fact, to have prevailed in the Hellenistic era also. In order to man large-scale fleets, the Ptolemies, and the Macedonians as well, recruited mercenaries in Asia Minor and on the coasts of the Aegean. The Rhodian fleet, which was small in size but of excellent quality, seems however to have provided a notable exception. As in Athens of the fifth century, service in the fleet was looked upon as an honour, and by far the larger part of the crews was made up of citizens.

Though the predominant component of fleets in the eastern Mediterranean was either citizens or mercenaries, Rome had recourse to an original solution of the perpetual problem of recruiting crews, at the time when the Punic Wars required the formation of a powerful navy. There too, the conscription of prisoners, convicts and slaves was not contemplated. The sea had little attraction for the Romans, who turned for their naval manpower, with the exception of high-grade command staff, to the cities of Magna Graecia, such as Tarentum, and particularly to the allied Italian cities – so much so that the latter finally bore the revealing title of *socii navales* (maritime allies).

A fact which is, to say the least, surprising is that the crews, whose total numbers were considerable (of the order of 30,000 or more), were formed in record time and by means of rapid and sophisticated training methods. By far the great majority of the recruits came from country districts and had never seen the sea. Hence, preliminary training with the oar took place on land, aboard replicas of galleys. With these improvised crews, however, the Romans succeeded in gaining victory over the Carthaginian squadrons.

The continual problem of recruitment for the fleets of the Ancient World is not to be attributed solely to the relatively small size of seafaring communities, the fears inspired by the sea or reasons of a religious order.

The size of the losses that occurred in naval battles played a part also. On a number of occasions – whether at Salamis, Mylae, Cape Ecnomus or the Aegates Islands – whole fleets disappeared. Storms too took a heavy toll. It was from such a cause that, on the morrow of the victory at Cape Ecnomus in 256 BC, the Roman fleet, in mid-summer and off the Sicilian coast, suffered a terrible disaster. Out of 464 ships, 80 alone escaped unscathed from the experience. The total of dead, including the Carthaginian prisoners, amounted to nearly 100,000. Two years later, another Roman fleet was engulfed by a similar catastrophe.

The establishment of the Roman Empire meant that there was an extraordinary cessation of naval warfare in the Mediterranean for nearly five centuries. Pompeius had suppressed piracy there; but to prevent its recrudescence Rome kept some light squadrons for policing purposes based at Alexandria, Ravenna or Misenum. There too, this fleet suffered from the Roman dislike of the sea, and it did not enjoy the same prestige as the army. Whereas, until the third century AD, the legions accepted citizens only, enlistment in the fleet only provided a means of obtaining citizenship after twenty-six or twenty-eight years' service. Recruits were no longer drawn from Italy proper but from among the inhabitants of provinces with a seafaring tradition. Thus, in the fleet could be found Greeks, Phoenicians, Egyptians and even slaves.

In the medieval period, at least up to the fifteenth century, there was no major change in the general make-up of crews. Certainly, we know little about the complements of the Byzantine and Arab fleets, at the moment when war in the Mediterranean broke out again with renewed vigour from the seventh century onwards. On the other hand, we are much better informed about those who normally manned the fleets of the Italian cities. The oarsmen who served aboard the galleys of Genoa, Pisa or Venice, or again, those of Marseilles or Barcelona, were free men, and in no sense slaves. Most frequently, it was the same men who formed the crews of the large trading galleys and the vessels designed for battle. They were not held in very high regard, and were drawn from the poorest classes of the population. On board, they ranked below everyone else – after the captain, the officers, the steersman, the crossbowmen, whose task was defence against pirates or pre-boarding fire when attacking, and skilled sailors assigned to handling the sails, which were furled in battle.

The oarsmen received pay. They were entitled to a locker of their own, a mattress, a provision of water and firewood, and of flour and biscuits, as well as of meat and dried fish. Although they were not chained, these men still endured particularly harsh conditions. They passed their entire time – work, meals and sleep – on their bench. Opportunities to land were infrequent. It is true that the living conditions of the other crew members were hardly such as to excite a great deal of envy.

Nevertheless, some cities enforced a real military type of service. In grave situations, the Venetian government carried out a mobilization. The heads of the sixty parishes in the city were given the task of taking a census of all able-bodied men between the ages of 20 and 60, who were then put into groups numbering a dozen each. Names were then drawn by lot in each of these groups, and this established an order in which any particular man would be called up. Despite the rigorous constraints, these crews of oarsmen, the *galeotti* or the *menu gent* (to use Martino da Canale's expression) showed a genuine enthusiasm when their turn to serve came.

In short, even in the fifteenth century, the crews of the Christian powers were composed, if not of volunteers, at least of free men. They were Italians *di buona voglia* or Spanish *buenas boyas*. Contrary to a belief which remains widely held, the Turks themselves, even immediately after the capture of Constantinople, had recourse only exceptionally to impressed personnel or to slaves. A system of short-term regular service allowed them to meet the requirement for large complements. The provinces of Anatolia and of Europe had to provide a certain number of oarsmen, on the scale of one from every 20 or 30 men.

families. Many came from Serbia or Bulgaria, and knew nothing of the sea. This system confirms a point which had been noted in Antiquity. Unlike sailing ships, the galley was very well suited to recruits who came from areas in the interior of a country. It was relatively easy to learn how to handle an oar, and one experienced man only was needed for training the rest.

From the middle of the sixteenth century this type of recruiting began to lose its effectiveness. For that, there were a number of reasons. The size of the conflicts between the Ottoman Empire and the Christian powers resulted in a spectacular expansion in fleets. At the end of the sixteenth century, the squadrons of Christian galleys, as well as those of the Moslems, required almost 200,000 oarsmen, a huge figure if account is taken of the relatively small numbers of men in the seafaring communities. This increase in crew totals is also explained by changes that took place in the galley itself. The desire to make it more powerful was accompanied by a considerable increase in its tonnage and in the size of its complement. This drive for greater power in galleys brought about a serious decline in living conditions on board, and consequently, by that token alone, a reduction in those wishing to enlist.

This decline in conditions was not merely a result of overcrowding with men and gear. At the close of the Middle Ages, the fighting vessel followed the same course of development as the trading ship. The captain, officers, sailors and oarsmen ceased to form a group of comrades. The captain's authority became absolute and discipline increasingly strict, while corporal punishments made their appearance. In addition, the large nations, finding themselves faced with the burden of increasing expenditure, reduced pay scales and rations, and thus caused a rise in the rate of occurrence of mutinies and desertions.

Thenceforth, members of the indigenous population alone were ready to serve aboard the galleys. Methods of recruiting contained an increasing element of compulsion. In Venice, in the fifteenth century, mobilization by parishes already had to be replaced by service arranged through the medium of the tightly knit guilds of artisans and shopkeepers. This system too proved inadequate and, in the following century, conscription was finally applied to the Dalmatians, the Cretans and even communities in inland territories. In 1522, those just named had to provide 6,000 men.

In the mid-sixteenth century, Venice took the final step. Finding that enlistment of volunteers and conscripts did not produce adequate numbers, she had to make use of men deprived of their civil rights, that is, slaves obtained during raids in the Adriatic and convicted criminals. This expedient was first used in 1545, and some expressed satisfaction over it. Placed in command of the first galley crewed by galley-slaves, Christoforo da Canale took the view that *forzati* governed by fear were much more obedient and effective than free men. The adoption of the new method of recruitment probably explains the practice that came into common use of rowing *a scaloccio*, i.e. with a single bank of oars and 5 to 7 men to an oar.

Other Mediterranean countries took to acting in the same way. The expedient of using galley-slaves was next employed in Spain before spreading to Genoa, the Papal States and the Knights of Malta. There was a similar development within the Ottoman Empire. As early as the mid-sixteenth century, out of a fleet of 130 galleys, no more than 60 were crewed by Moslems receiving regular pay, while 40 were rowed by slaves and 30 by defectors, that is, Christians who had gone over to Islam.

This practice caused privateering, which had been endemic in the Mediterranean since the fall of the Roman Empire, to become even more widespread. Slave markets became established at Majorca, Genoa, Livorno, Malta and Crete. This privateering was not restricted in scope to the age-old conflict between Christians and Moslems. All the Mediterranean cities took part to their reciprocal detriment. Commerce-raiding became one of Malta's principal activities. The Grand Duke of Tuscany went so far as to create a special religio-military Order, the Knights of St Stephen, to procure the prisoners who were required for his galleys.

At the end of the sixteenth century, the changeover was complete. The galley crews contained no more than a tiny minority of volunteers, for the most part drawn from the destitute and the drop-outs. The large majority consisted of slaves – prisoners of war or men captured at sea or picked up in raids along coastlines. They were chained to their benches, with shaven heads and wearing the red coat and cap which were the marks of slavery and disgrace. In the seventeeth century, the costliness and rarity of slaves led to the breaking of the final barrier. To make up the numbers, the major countries fell back on convicted criminals, heretics, beggars and vagrants, who were considered to belong to classes that constituted a danger to society. Previously, the galley had only been a place in which men were compelled to serve; now it became a focus of repression. This type of recruiting went on until the fleets of galleys progressively disappeared in the eighteenth century.

Problems of the same kind made their appearance in the case of early fleets of the northern seas. At the rare periods when French kings like Philip Augustus or Charles V made an effort to set on foot a naval policy, coupled with an early form of dockyard, (*Le Clos des Galées*, near Rouen), it already proved extremely difficult to recruit crews. During the Hundred Years' War, an effort was made, through a general levy, to mobilize all 'sailors and men whose business was connected with the sea'. On the eve of the Battle of Sluys, this system, with its declaration of impressment, was applicable to the whole Channel coast from Cherbourg to Boulogne. This type of recruiting was dishonoured at the outset by features which subsequently tended to become its regular concomitants. There was no doubt that it resulted in serious poverty for the families of sailors who had to give up all their normal business of fishing or coastal trade. Pay was low, issued at irregular intervals and not all of the men received it. Hence, desertions were common. Want led men to dubious methods of escaping service, and these soon became an established custom. Therefore, foreign sailors, preferably Genoese, were enlisted and, from the fifteenth century onwards, criminals were enrolled as crew members, despite protests from local authorities.

Contrary to a still widely believed myth, England also suffered from the same difficulties. Certainly, there existed an established custom under which the king could have a navy at his disposal in time of need. The Cinque Ports of the south-east had to provide a contingent of ships and sailors. This system, however, proved highly inadequate. From the outset of the Hundred Years' War, the monarch had to revert to impressment, i.e. an enforced enrolment which, as is recorded, was used for the first time in 1337, by an Order in Council authorizing the admiral, Sir John de Ros, to requisition ships of more than 30 tons with their crews.

This system also met straightaway with strong opposition; desertions were numerous, and attempts were made to check this scourge by increasingly severe punishments. Although at the outset the penalties did not exceed one year's imprisonment, in the fifteenth century they finally included the death sentence. A writ of Richard II's underlines the necessity for exemplary punishments 'given that sailors, after being enlisted and retained for the king's service at sea and for the defence of the realm, and after having received an advance of pay, have taken the step of quitting their duties, without authority from the admirals or their subordinates, to the very great peril of the king and the realm.' At the same time, impressment provoked complaints in the Commons, who deplored the detriment suffered by the merchant fleet, which ran the risk of being immobilized as soon as enlistment in the navy reached a sizeable level.

At the end of the medieval era, such enlistments could sometimes involve practically the whole of the seafaring population. This point is even clearer in the sixteenth century, with the commissioning of the commerce-raiders used against Spain by Drake, Frobisher and Hawkins, and particularly at the time of the crisis caused by the Spanish Armada. In 1588, mobilization took 195 ships and 14,385 sailors out of a total seafaring population estimated at 17,000. Commissioning on this scale, how-

ever, remained in force for a short time only, and the seriousness of the danger rendered it tolerable.

Meanwhile, from the fourteenth century onwards, complements of fighting ships began to assume a modern character. They were not confined to professional seamen, but comprised a whole range of specialists – master axemen, caulkers, coopers, and even barbers and musicians. They also contained a high proportion of soldiers, whose task was to board the enemy in battle and to operate the earliest firearms (such as arquebuses and cannon); from the fifteenth century onwards, the sides and superstructures of carracks, and later of galleons, which were the ancestors of ships of the line, bristled with these weapons. In case of need, the soldiers took part in the 'jobs on deck', such as stowing gear, working the capstans, etc. Aboard the *Henry Grâce à Dieu* in 1514, there were 300 sailors, 349 soldiers and some 50 gunners. In 1588, the *Ark Royal* had on board 125 soldiers and 300 sailors. The proportions were of the same order in other navies. At the same time, the ranking order aboard ships became much more sharply defined. A corps of petty officers with disciplinary responsibilities called in France *caserniers* or *quarteniers*, made their appearance. The old feeling of comradeship among equals of the twelfth and thirteenth centuries had disappeared.

It was from the seventeenth century onwards, with the appearance of regular navies and the development of major European wars, that recruitment truly became a terrible tyranny weighing on the seafaring population, particularly since every new war exacted a ruthless toll of casualties. The Royal Navy's strength amounted to 50,000 men in 1714, 65,000 in 1762 and 107,000 in 1783; this had sunk to 7,000 in 1715, 15,000 in 1775 and 13,000 in 1786.

In all countries, with the exception of the United Provinces, at least during the seventeenth century, the number of volunteers was inadequate, and there was a general reluctance to serve aboard warships. Louis XIV was continually expressing his regret over 'the almost insurmountable loathing that seafaring men felt towards serving in his ships'. The causes of this aversion were the harsh life aboard, the savage and arbitrary discipline, the lengthy periods spent uninterruptedly at sea, the dangers of shipwreck and sickness, and the way in which families who had been left behind sank into poverty. In the majority of navies, pay was not issued until the end of a voyage, and adjustments of accounts dragged on for long periods, with delays lasting several months or sometimes several years. In the minds of a sailor's family, his service aboard a warship was synonymous with financial hardship for them. That could turn into tragedy if he were posted as a deserter, reported missing or taken prisoner.

The bad reputation of navies was also related to the arbitary form of recruitment. There were two opposing methods – the system of classes used in France and the type of impressment which was traditional in England. Devised by Colbert, developed by Seignelay, and subsequently modified on many occasions, the system of classes provided for a census and classification of all sailors, and instituted a liability to be required for service on the king's ships for one year in every three or four. Coastal areas were divided into 80 *quartiers* or *circonscriptions*, each under a classifications officer, who was responsible for watching the movements of seafaring men and for organizing levies of them. During the year when they were due for service, these men were not allowed to go aboard a fishing boat or trading vessel or even to change their place of residence. In return for this constraint, which bore a partial resemblance to conscript service proper, they gained a certain number of advantages – exemption from having soldiers billeted on them, from *tutelle* and *curatelle* and from the duties of any official post. During their period at sea, any legal proceedings in which they were concerned were suspended. Pay was given to sailors assigned to a ship, and half-pay to those who remained ashore.

The system also contained a novel feature, which was a forerunner of social security measures and pension funds. By means of a deduction of 2 per cent from the pay of all the personnel in the royal fleet, a naval fund was able to grant a pension to those who had been crippled and disabled in the king's service, and this was extended from the start of the eighteenth century to sailors in privateers and in the merchant service. The *ordonnance* of Castries in 1784 caused this pension to be given also to old sailors over the age of 60.

This scheme for recruiting, though cogent on paper, held in store some very severe disappointments. In the minds of its originators, it would reconcile the needs of the fisheries, the mercantile marine and the navy. In practice, it did nothing of the kind. Owing to the relatively small numbers to be found in coastal communities – the figure varied between 50,000 and 60,000, and this contained a high percentage of men whose work was on land – and, from the time of the War of the League of Augsburg, to the importance of large complements, it was necessary in reality to have recourse to a disguised impressment, i.e. to call up all seafaring personnel and to keep on board men who should have been released.

In 1691, when the great naval force was raised, the whole seafaring population of the Atlantic seaboard was conscripted. These levies were intended for the crews of ships on long-distance cruises, whose return was scheduled for March, as well as for those who should have embarked for Ireland and Canada. An appeal for men was also addressed to the colonists in Newfoundland. When manpower had to be collected for large crews in the eighteenth century, which generally formed up at Brest, the levies affected the whole seafaring population of France, and – amazingly – parties of sailors could be seen converging on Brittany, not only from the direction of Charente or the Basque country, but from the Channel coasts, from Languedoc and Provence. Thousands of men were thus forced, before the winter was over, to make a journey of several hundred miles. The parties sometimes numbered as many as 1,000 men. In charge of them were some naval officers and guards.

The authorities tried to make these exhausting journeys easier. The officers had to attend to the quality of foodstuffs (i.e. the bread, meat and wine). As was customary at that period, maximum use was made of waterways for movement. The sailors from Normandy, Picardy and Flanders were directed to the Loire, and embarked at Briare or Blois. Those from Languedoc started from Agde on the *Canal des Deux Mers*. The men from Provence, after going up the Rhône, took a boat on the Loire at Roanne.

Despite such examples of forethought, the system was made hateful by the length of the journeys, of which at best a major part had to be made on foot, the arbitrary nature of the levies, the unpunctuality in the issue of pay, the breaking of home ties and the reduction to poverty of the families left behind. Hence, men tried to put themselves beyond its reach by all possible means. Some attempted to pass themselves off as sick but desertion was certainly the commonest method of escape. The Basques were particularly hostile to the system and crossed into Spain; those from Provence went to Italy and the men from Dunkirk left for Ostend, Nieuport or Amsterdam. Those from upper Normandy, from Le Havre or Dieppe tried to reach England or the Austrian-held Low Countries. Other methods were attempted, such as pretending to be foreigners, with the help of false passports, or getting hold of the certificate which was given to sailors who had been paid off. Some hid in the interior, for preference in marshy or mountainous areas, as being difficult of access. Others sought to disappear in the heavily populated districts of major ports.

At every period when there was a call for large numbers of crews, the naval watch, who were the *gendarmes maritimes* of the period, devoted themselves to hunting down defaulters. The authorities were extremely angry that the sailors who had escaped benefited from the collusion of all levels of society. Practically all the seaboard communities felt an aversion for the levies, the sole exception being, it seems, the Bretons, since service in the fleet ultimately offered a lifeline to a community that habitually lived in extreme poverty. However, desertions remained relatively few in number, of the order of about 5 per cent,

with quite marked differences between regions. The most refractory areas were the Dunkirk district and the island of Levant. Despite terrifying threats, punitive sanctions for such offences were, in fact, relatively light; and condemnation to the galleys – a punishment often employed in the army – was rare in the navy. In addition, there were regular amnesties. Such relative indulgence is partly attributable to the scarcity of sailors. Besides, the authorities were aware that some of the blame lay with themselves. They had a bad conscience in regard to a system which had come to be seen as a terrible form of slavery.

In England, the impressment system was entirely different. Characteristically of the British, it was based on an ancient custom dating from medieval times. The king reserved to himself the right to call on the seafaring community to serve aboard his ships if ever danger threatened the country. Under the command of naval officers duly detailed for the task, press-gangs – squads armed with cudgels – worked through the streets of ports, visited taverns and proceeded, sometimes brutally, to round up and conscript all the sailors they found. For this work, the press-gangs were awarded bonuses. Here too, this style of recruiting produced disastrous results; it was its arbitrary nature which caused it to be hated, and which contributed to lowering the high standing of the Royal Navy. Its randomness was shown by the way in which the burden fell mostly on particular regions. In theory, all coastal populations were liable to impressment; in practice, the press-gangs preferred to work, in order to avoid expensive journeys, near large naval bases, that is, on the southern coasts or in the south-east of England. In 1776, at the outbreak of war with America, out of 21,000 men collected by the press-gangs, more than one-third came from the Thames area. The numbers drawn from distant ports like Dublin, Liverpool, Bristol or Newcastle seem relatively small, when account is taken of the size of their seafaring populations.

In theory, exemption was granted, for various reasons, to certain categories of seamen, such as foreigners, apprentices, those who fished for cod off Greenland or for herring in the North Sea during the season, whalers, Thames watermen and men transporting coal by sea from Newcastle to London. Impressment also covered, again in theory, sailors aged from 18 to 35 only. In fact, such rules were constantly broken, and the courts were bombarded with complaints from men who were entitled to exemption.

The press-gangs could not always easily distinguish between genuine sailors and landsmen; in any event, certain categories of the latter whose skills were linked with the sea, such as carpenters or caulkers, and which could perfectly well be turned to account on board, could legally be impressed, provided that they were aged between 18 and 35. The press-gangs worked not only in ports or in fishing villages, but on the high seas. They boarded ocean-going ships returning to England, and enlisted the topmen, who were much sought after. For a number of sailors, particularly those who had families to support, this mishap was a real catastrophe. The man found himself separated, for an interminable period, from his wife and children. He could not draw his pay personally and, in order to secure its payment to his family, he had to entrust the task to someone unknown to him.

One final element contributed yet further towards arousing hatred for the system. When they had barely been enlisted, the unfortunate sailors were herded, under conditions bordering on imprisonment, into the 'press-rooms' of old taverns, like those of the 'White Swan' or the 'Cock and Runner' in the heart of London. After a day or two, the men were transferred aboard tenders, that is, hulks anchored in the roads; these were of various sizes, and might have been those of a modest schooner or of an old ship of the line. Inside these floating prisons, they were guarded like criminals by soldiers with fixed bayonets.

In the eighteenth century, impressment came under almost universal condemnation, as is proved by the success of a pamphlet entitled 'The Sailor's Advocate'. The main points in its argument were that the system stood condemned on grounds of morality and commercial interest alike; it was unjust and damaged the business of shipowners and merchants; it was contrary to the rights of the individual, and went against the principles of Magna Carta and of the Bill of Rights; it spawned an army of petty tyrants, who had no hesitation in using their cudgels to knock on the head anyone attempting to frustrate their intentions. But though condemnation was unanimous, no one knew how to replace a system which was indispensable to the country's survival. Thomas Corbett, the Secretary of the Admiralty, recognized this in 1745, by his admission that 'it is impossible to imperil national security just because some personal sensibilities suffer hurt'.

Men tried every possible means of avoiding impressment. They barricaded themselves in their homes, hid in the interior of the country, and tried to escape abroad, to obtain false certificates of exemption, to pass themselves off as sick and even to disable themselves physically. Some even sought, though without much success, to bribe the men in the press-gangs. Still, in time of war or of international tension, a sword of Damocles was permanently suspended over the members of the coastal population.

Despite the continuous use of such high-handed methods, both systems – the French as much as the British – proved inadequate. The French navy suffered permanently from a deficiency of manpower. The Royal Navy's case was no better. The requirements of the two large fleets exceeded by a large margin the number of sailors that their countries could produce, even where the Britain of the end of the eighteenth century was concerned. In any event, impressment – like the system of classes – could not go beyond a certain point. It was out of the question completely to paralyse the fishing fleets, coastal shipping and, particularly, large-scale overseas trade, since it was this last that furnished the cabinet in London with the sinews of war. The taxes levied on the income from foreign trade allowed the British government to finance its military effort, and to provide generous subsidies to its allies on the Continent.

Shortfalls in numbers were inevitable even at the outbreak of war and, as the war continued, they became aggravated through losses in battle and from sickness and desertion. In this last respect, the British fleet was even more seriously affected than the French. During major wars, desertions reached considerable proportions, numbering 75,000 during the Seven Years' War alone, 42,000 during the American War of Independence, 42,000 again during the first phase (1793–1802) of the conflict in the period of the Revolutionary Wars. Nearly 16,000 of these deserters then took service on American trading ships, which were constantly liable to be stopped by British frigates and searched. This policy was to lead to the war with America of 1812.

Chronic shortfalls in numbers and a constant drain on manpower forced both of these major fleets to have recourse to expedients. These contributed towards discrediting still further the normal systems of recruiting and increased men's reluctance to serve aboard warships. The expedients naturally centred on the enlistment of men from the interior of the country. One of the most common makeshifts consisted in putting soldiers aboard, as was done in the case of French ships; in 1778, there were 2,000 in d'Orvilliers' fleet. This improvised system probably reached its climax during the War of American Independence. The deficit in numbers was at that time vast – of the order of 30,000 men in 1780, when the full total required was 72,000. The authorities tried numerous makeshift solutions to the problem of obtaining gun crews or men for work on deck, for which special skills were not required. A campaign conducted throughout the whole of France to recruit 'volunteers' produced nearly 10,000 men, who were attracted by the large bonuses offered. But, in the event, personnel so collected proved difficult to use, since they consisted in large part of the sickly, the vagrant and the dissolute. From the very outset, this group was ravaged by desertions.

Once again, the system of classes was extended to the Loire, the Garonne and their tributaries. Through fears about the likely reaction of the respective populations, the basins of the Seine and the Rhône were not included, although the measure was put forward as a fair contribution by the communities of the interior, on the grounds that they enjoyed all the benefits produced by the fishing industry and overseas trade. This attempt to extend the system encountered an extreme reluctance and 'the insubordinate attitude of the sailors'.

As a last resort, the authorities turned to the 'provincial soldiers' serving in the militias on garrison duty in the interior of the country. The result was very modest – 1,300 men who were looked upon as the dregs of the battalions. It proved necessary to make a call, in addition, on all the resources of the militia, with the special proviso that the draw by lot should apply only to short men, standing 5 feet tall or less; the rest remained at the army's disposal. In line with what tended to become standard practice, other elements too – beggars, the destitute and inmates of workhouses – were enrolled, and then packed off under strong guard to the ports. Despite all such expedients, the shortfalls continued.

In Great Britain, the range of improvised solutions was just as varied. There too, soldiers were put aboard ships. In 1664, that system was given an institutional status by the creation of a regiment of marines. One of the most original supplementary methods of recruiting was the work of the Marine Society. Founded in 1756, at the start of the Seven Years' War, by the philanthropist Jonas Hanway, with the backing of the king and of admirals like Anson and Boscawen, its purpose was to collect the destitute and, in particular, the young waifs and strays of major cities such as London, prior to training them for service in the navy or the merchant service, in accordance with the requirements of the situation. The additional numbers which this scheme provided still proved insufficient. Hence, in 1743, in the midst of the War of the Austrian Succession, impressment was finally applied officially to landsmen aged from 20 to 35 who had no experience whatsoever of seafaring work, but who could be useful for handling the guns or for some work on deck. The Royal

Navy also accepted those known as 'the Lord Mayor's men'. These were minor delinquents, who signed on for a period of service as a way of expunging a conviction, and who were sent aboard ships by London magistrates for disorderly conduct in the street or for disturbing the peace at night.

All in all, the effort brought in a singularly composite collection of recruits, and one which would seem unlikely to inspire great confidence. A good proportion of the men served unwillingly and had, for the most part, no experience of a seaman's work. But this was not as serious a drawback as might be supposed. A vessel formed a many sided entity and – however paradoxical this might appear – it required no more than a minority of real seamen who could go aloft and handle the sails. It provided a sufficient spread of tasks to allow the useful employment of men from diverse backgrounds, even if they had previously never seen the sea.

There were, in fact, three main categories of seamen proper. Those experienced in long-distance voyages formed a sort of 'aristocracy', though of a somewhat capricious disposition; they were, to some extent, a group with no fixed national allegiance, and they frequently took the opportunity to desert. They could read and write well, but were superstitious and far along the road to divorce from any form of Christian belief. Without any settled family, but with a woman in every port of call, a very high percentage of them suffered from venereal disease. Secondly, the deep-sea fishermen, whether from towns (Yarmouth, Dunkirk, Texel, Flushing, Boulogne, Dieppe, Le Havre, St Malo, etc.) or from rural districts (like the whole of the St Brieuc Bay) were looked upon by experts and politicians as providing the nurturing environment for naval crews, and this was why the fishing grounds off Newfoundland and St-Pierre-et-Miquelon were thought of such importance. These fishermen were very religious, though there was a much wider spread of Christian belief in some geographical areas – the two Basque countries and the parts of the sea coast of Brittany where there were no ports – than elsewhere. They enjoyed a very stable

family life and had a high birth-rate. Few of them could read or write, but they were used to facing the stormiest seas; yet they scarcely made up, in France as in Britain, more than 30 per cent of the total. Finally, the short-distance sailors comprised those occupied in small-scale cargo trade or inshore fishing; they were often part-peasant, part-fisherman, and their seamanlike qualities should certainly not be overestimated. In addition, there were the mixed group of landsmen from various different parts.

The most highly prized seamen in fighting fleets were naturally the topmen, who were skilled in working aloft, that is, at climbing in the rigging and in furling or spreading the sails in all weathers. These men received a special rate of pay, and were recruited from sailors experienced in ocean-going ships or deep-sea fishing or off-shore cargo work. On the other hand, the low-paid sailors who were used entirely for deck work – stowing gear, operating the capstans, helping with the guns – were drawn from short-range coastal shipping. They worked alongside the apprentices, the deck boys, the soldiers and drop-outs of every kind.

A British 100-gun vessel thus had a highly diversified complement. Out of an overall total of 839, the officers, their servants and the specialist personnel numbered 291. The remaining 548 could be divided into three categories. The first was made up of able seamen, who were termed forecastle men (because they were berthed forward) or topmen, who were skilled at working aloft in the rigging. There were only 219 of these, split into three sections, because of the normal three-mast design of warships. The other categories consisted of ordinary seamen or landsmen who made up the afterguard (i.e. were berthed aft) and the waisters (berthed in the middle of the ship). Both of these latter were employed on deck work and on helping with the guns. In all, a ship of the line, of the period before the Revolution, needed only 15 per cent of its complement to be highly skilled seamen. The major part of the crew was occupied with the guns, deck work and maintenance.

But the whole, none the less, consisted of a strange collection of humanity. In it could be seen the gulfs that divided society at the period, with the officers coming from the highest classes and with a sound scientific training, with staunch petty officers, all old professional sailors and devoted to duty, and with a peculiarly heterogeneous collection of men under them. The main body of the crews was, indeed, of an extreme diversity. They contained all ages between 10 and 55, and even beyond. Unmarried men rubbed shoulders with heads of families and widowers.

Some French ships were real towers of Babel. A certain percentage of foreign nationals proper, whose numbers varied from time to time, could speak French. But, except in their case, French remained, to the end of the eighteenth century and even into the following one, a totally foreign language for the immense majority of men from Brittany, Flanders, Provence and the Basque country. The same situation was true in Britain in relation to the Scots, the Welsh and even more to the Irish. The mode of recruiting also played a part in producing crews of such diversity. On the one hand, there were those who had enlisted voluntarily, and on the other, those who had been forcibly impressed, the apprentices, the deck boys and the whole gamut of landsmen – soldiers, artisans, minor delinquents or real criminals.

This odd mixture helped to strengthen the rather unflattering image of the sailor, whose style of behaviour seemed aggressively at variance with that of the settled classes of society – peasants, craftsmen, bourgeoisie and nobility. To the great majority of his contemporaries, the sailor serving in the navy or the mercantile marine gave the impression of a creature on the fringes of society, notable alike for his brutality, his inordinate appetite for drink and women, and his refusal to observe the most basic precepts of Christian morality. In every country, sailors were the target of very uncomplimentary epithets. These 'brutes in human form', with their 'loutish' temperament, had the reputation of being 'rebellious, undisciplined, mutinous and dissolute'. They constituted, in the general view, 'the scum of the earth'.

Hence, since the authorities were determined to prevent these heterogeneous and restive crews from fragmenting, an iron discipline seemed to be justified. But such an approach served only to aggravate the harshness of life aboard and the reluctance to endure naval service, and also caused the appearance of one of those vicious circles to which disciplinary methods of the past were subject. Although designed to prevent insubordination and failures to perform duties, rigorous discipline, in fact, increased the risk of mutiny. Above all, it caused greater numbers to desert, and – by that very circumstance – obliged the naval authorities to impress men in more arbitrary and onerous ways than before.

There were also problems over recruiting and training officers, although these were of quite a different nature. Actually, little is known about them at all during Antiquity, with the exception of certain inscriptions mentioning naval officers of Rhodes or Rome, though sources of information become more plentiful in the medieval period. Italian navies seem to have experienced no difficulty in recruiting, and young scions of the aristocracy looked upon service aboard the galleys as an honour.

The situation seems to have been very different in the northern seas, at least up to the fifteenth century. 'Warships' were not specifically built as such, but were merely improvised, and they were commanded by officers of the merchant fleet, by privateer captains or by just plain pirates. One such was the famous Eustache le Moine who served the French king, and who, having been captured by the English in the Battle of Dover in 1217, was beheaded on the bulwark of his ship. At the outset, knights viewed war at sea with contempt; fighting there was considered 'inappropriate', a situation where one could do battle only on foot, like an ordinary villein.

Later, a change came about. On the eve of the Battle of Sluys, Edward III made ready to 'joust' with the opposing ships. The poet Eustache Deschamps had no longer any feeling of contempt for naval officers, as shown by his words, 'Fine are the knights of the sea'. Alphonse the Wise, King of Castille, gave voice to the same attitude when he said, 'Ships are the mounts of those who move on the sea, as

567

horses are of those who move on land.' At the close of the Middle Ages, there was no longer anything dishonourable in fighting on foot, if one rode the waves aboard ship.

The specific features of the naval officer, however, really come into view only in the sixteenth and particularly the seventeenth century, with the appearance of regular corps which remained in being even in peacetime. He had to unite in himself a twofold ability – both that of the fighting man and of the sailor. While this combination might seem commonplace enough, it proved difficult to find in the right proportions, and history can show some odd departures from the ideal. In the early days of the Royal Navy, at the time of Cromwell, the Stuarts and even William III, the English naval officer was first and foremost a soldier, and most of the major commanders, like Monck, Blake and Prince Rupert, came from the army. On the other hand, their Dutch counterparts came from the merchant service, and were principally sailors. During the course of the wars in the second half of the seventeenth century, some instances of the two abilities in combination began to appear. Without losing his qualities as a sailor, the Dutchman became more and more of a soldier, as seen in the case of De Ruyter, while the Briton, while not abandoning his training in military tactical methods, gave pride of place to skills that were, strictly speaking, naval. This trend has continued right up to the present time.

A similar variety of orientation was revealed in the field of training. Until the end of the nineteenth century, the British officer's training concentrated very heavily on practical aspects, while that of the French officer seemed much more theoretical; the studies he was required to make of the effect of hull shapes, of ballistics and particularly of the calculation of bearings at sea, all seemed to justify the use of mathematics as the basis of this training. For the same reason as the engineers, and even more the artillery, the French navy at the close of the *ancien régime* was looked upon as a scientific arm. This type of scientific training was also introduced into the colleges for the 'naval guards', who owed their formation to Louis XIV.

The social origin of naval officers seems to have differed according to country. This might be the well-off classes, like the English gentry, or the Dutch bourgeoisie, or even the real nobility, as can be seen in France, Spain and Italy. Such social requirements could, however, be varied. Under Louis XIV, the companies of naval guards admitted non-nobles; and, at that period, well-known privateersmen reached the summit of the naval hierarchy. On the eve of the Revolution, some doubt enshrouded the recruitment of naval cadets, who belonged in theory to the highest ranks of the nobility. Social origin may have perhaps contributed to the opposition noticeable within the French officer corps between the 'reds', of noble descent, and the 'blues', commoners with a background in the merchant service. There too, caution is required, the more so since this opposition was deliberately magnified, at the start of the Revolution, by some officers who wanted to stand well by inventing, or claiming, a non-noble origin. In reality, the 'blue' officers who had come from the merchant service were recruited for wartime requirements and put in command of auxiliary ships that were part of the naval 'small fry'. The majority of them were demobilized the moment that peace came, when the navy entered into a state of 'organized neglect'. The situation described could throw up disagreements and bitterness, without going as far as overt hostility.

The Franco-Spanish practice of drawing officers exclusively from the nobility was the cause, however, of other difficulties. A major aspect of them was that inborn trait of a nobleman, an inability to accept orders from above. It was reinforced by the fact that the captain was 'after God, the sole master aboard ship'. This lack of discipline and spirit of rivalry could be found at the highest levels. The senior commanders got on very badly with each other. Suffren was hated by the officers of his ships, and d'Estaing was shunned by the whole of the officer corps, just as de Grasse was after the Battle of the Saints. The 'naval guards' behaved in Brest as if they were in an occupied territory – a state of affairs not unconnected with the revolutionary attitude of the bourgeoisie there. The situation was the same in Toulon. On the eve of the Revolution, there was a move to recruit from a wider field. In 1786, non-noble volunteers could be appointed as naval sub-lieutenants – a rank which had been specially created – after serving for six years. The Revolution, when it came, found an officer corps that was undergoing a process of major change.

These problems did not arise exclusively in the French and Spanish navies; they can be found in the Royal Navy of the eighteenth century. Violent altercations broke out between admirals on the day following certain battles, like Ushant or the Virginia Capes. The penalties for failure were, however, very heavy. After the fall of Minorca and an indecisive battle in 1756, Admiral Byng was executed by firing squad. This was the origin of the celebrated remark of Voltaire, 'in this country, we like to shoot an admiral from time to time, to encourage the others'. It was not until the wars of the Revolution and the Empire that a genuine harmony was established within the corps of British naval officers.

During the course of this long drawn out conflict, the traditional method of recruiting crews, with all its disadvantages, was employed in its most extreme form. To keep up the numbers, which attained the record level of 140,000 in 1812, the Royal Navy had to turn to fresh expedients. Despite a considerable increase in enlistment bonuses (which rose from £5 to £70), those who joined voluntarily represented less than 25 per cent of the total strength. Although applied in a draconian fashion, only 50 per cent was supplied by impressment. Hence, it proved necessary to fall back on foreigners and on the celebrated 'quota-men', who were used solely for work with the guns or for tasks on deck which required none of the skills of the real sailor.

Under this system, a certain number of recruits had to be provided by the British counties, which used the opportunity to get rid of dubious characters and to send off to the ports men who had been condemned to degrading punishments; the latter's 'enlistment bonus' was a kind of release on bail.

Two other circumstances allowed the Royal Navy to keep its crews up to strength – a fall in the number of desertions, following a relative relaxation of discipline, and a reduction of deaths from disease, thanks to the conquest of scurvy.

The situation of the French navy, which was in the grip of a terrible political and social crisis from 1791 onwards, was even worse. In the ports there was a succession of mutinies, while emigration took its toll of the officer corps, which found itself exposed to suspicion on the part of enthusiastic patriots. By draconian methods, i.e. by using every means of naval impressment, which had replaced the system of classes, the Convention, under the leadership of the 'Mountain', succeeded for a short while in rectifying the situation and in meeting the squadrons' requirements in crews. But, from 1796 onwards, the system began to break down, particularly since the traditional regions for recruits – the west and the south-east – had gone over to the counter-revolution.

Under the Empire, enlistments failed equally to come up to the numbers needed for the fleet, which Napoleon tried to reconstruct after Trafalgar – all the more so because the defeats suffered by the French privateers had led to a fresh drain on the seafaring population and an influx of prisoners into Britain. Hence, it was necessary on this occasion too, to increase the number of expedients employed; these included putting conscripts from the regions of the interior into the category of 'crews of ocean-going ships', resorting to the mobilization of all the inhabitants of the seafaring nations of the Empire (Italians, Dutch citizens of the Hanseatic towns), and enrolling in addition 'allies' such as the Danes. This system resulted in composite crews which could only with difficulty be blended into homogeneous units, and was the root cause of the desertions and cases of insubordination which grew in number from 1812 onwards.

During the first half of the nineteenth century, the old method of recruitment continued in operation in all navies, although mitigated to some slight degree by the absence of major conflicts at sea. In

France, *inscription* for the navy applied to all men aged between 18 and 50, whether sailors, port workers or lightermen, and was always an object of loathing, as pointed out by Admiral Jurien de la Gravière. The threat of being compulsorily enlisted hung permanently over these men, and the selections were arbitrary. In theory, periods of service were supposed not to exceed three years. In practice, they lasted as long as four or five, where distant stations were concerned or when there was a state of international tension.

During the Algerian expedition, the Mediterranean crisis of 1840–1 or the Crimean War, the system based on *inscription* proved incapable of supplying the required numbers, and the authorities were forced to revert to a disguised impressment, as in the worst days of the *ancien régime*, and to the habitual range of expedients, i.e. enlisting vagrants, the destitute and inmates of workhouses, or even taking aboard military conscripts, who were put on to 'furling the sails while still wearing a knapsack'. This form of mobilization was of doubtful value in terms of the quality of men that it produced, and its traditional results also made their appearance – disorganization of maritime trade and fishing, anger among the seafaring communities and, of course, desertions. These last numbered over 10,000 in 1845.

In the main, the British were in very much the same situation. The system of impressment, in theory, remained in being. It was, however, no longer used, but merely kept in reserve, during those periods when large complements were not needed. Being well aware how disgraceful such a system was generally felt to be, the Admiralty was reluctant to put it back into practice, even at the time of the Crimean War. The Baltic squadron was, therefore, urged to enlist Scandinavians, in order to make up its numbers. Throughout the war, there was a continuing shortfall in crew strengths, and it was very reasonable for the Second Sea Lord to ask himself what the situation would have been if Great Britain had had to face a real naval war.

Even so, the Crimean War did consti-

tute a turning point. It heralded a revolution in naval affairs, which was marked by the appearance of the 'ironclad' while still to come were the torpedo-boat and the submarine; and these developments were to mean a complete change in recruiting. With the introduction of steam propulsion, the increasing complexity of weapon systems and the progressive disappearance of sails, there was less and less place aboard for personnel whose only equipment was a maritime background. The numbers of such men declined, and they gradually disappeared in the face of qualified seamen who were the product of technical training establishments.

In the light of this radical change in the composition of crews, the old distinction between topmen, skilled at working aloft, and the rest of the personnel, restricted to helping with the guns and deck tasks, faded away. It was replaced by a different division, within the body of the ship itself, between the men in the engine-room, down in the depths of the hull, and the sailors on the decks above them, who were mainly, and in an increasing proportion, specialists – helmsmen, gunners, torpedo men, riflemen and, at a slightly later stage, electricians and radio operators. In this way, the ship became like an industrial plant – a point to which Engels drew attention – and the traditional sailor who had come from the world of fishing or merchant shipping no longer played more than a minor role aboard. He became the sailor categorized as 'non-spec.', and was relegated to the task of stowing gear and stores. This situation is entirely different from that which existed in land forces. In 1914, 50 per cent of the personnel of the German navy were specialists, while for the army the figure was 12 per cent. The percentages were the same in the British and French fleets.

Changes in methods of recruiting went hand-in-hand with those in the composition of crews. In France, the navy made less and less use of the system of *inscription*, which deservedly went into a decline and disappeared completely in 1927. In 1907, the number of *inscrits* in crews still represented 50 per cent of the total, but this had dropped by 20 per cent by 1914 and to 6 per cent by 1939. In complete contrast with the past, crews were no longer recruited from among seafaring men or seaboard communities. They were mainly made up of men from the interior, who were the product of the industrial centres. At a time when obligatory military service became a general practice in the majority of modern states, the broadening of the field from which recruits could be drawn allowed certain countries, like Germany and Russia, to overcome the handicap of a reduced seafaring population and still provide themselves with powerful navies.

There was another important circumstance which represented a complete break with the past – there was no lack of volunteers. This was due to the continuous improvement in living conditions aboard ship, even though the vessel became like an industrial plant and remained an instrument of battle. From the middle of the nineteenth century, ships were heated by steam, and, a little later, by electricity. Traditional maritime illnesses were reduced in incidence, and then eliminated, as shown by such examples as scurvy, typhus and yellow fever. Voyages were made shorter. The routes of voyages became more regular, and there were more opportunities for relaxation ashore. The harshness of discipline was progressively reduced. In France, under the Second Republic, corporal punishment was completely abolished. In England, the Naval Discipline Act of 1866, which replaced that of 1749, conveyed a new note of leniency. In 1871, the whip was prohibited in peacetime, and eight years later, in wartime also. The cat-o'-nine-tails disappeared too, though without having been officially abolished.

All of these circumstances drew men into the navy. And there was a further difference in that enlistments were especially numerous in wartime. This fact received ample confirmation in the two world wars. Navies were reputed – a supposition frequently proved false – to be less exposed to danger than land armies, and provided living conditions definitely superior to those of infantrymen, which had remained largely unchanged. During the early years of the Second World War, the German submarine fleet contained a higher percentage of volunteers than the army.

The change in the calibre of man employed in navies was also revealed in his attitude. The volunteer or the conscript from inland who already had some experience of a civilian trade was less tolerant even of a milder discipline than his predecessors in sailing ships. He also felt greater dissatisfaction over the length of tours of duty and how long he was away from home. Having become accustomed early in life to the routine of factory work and to the means by which workers put forward their demands, he entered the navy with a potentially confrontational attitude which could come to the surface in the form of mutinies. In the course of, or immediately after, the First World War, service mutinies took place in all the major navies, including those considered to have been on the winning side.

A change, though of an entirely different kind, took place in the officer corps too, and this can be noted in the French navy in the Restoration period. The corps acquired a homogeneous nature which it had never previously known. As a result of departures, postings to the retired list and promotions, the political divisions which had been produced by the Revolution lost their sharpness. More important still was that officers were no longer subject to the deplorable atmosphere of cliquism and denigration which had poisoned the navy under the *ancien régime*. There was an end to the jealousy, vanity and perpetual rancour which were so damaging to harmonious staff relations, and which had contributed to a number of disasters. The principles implicit in a hierarchy of ranks were no longer called into question, and obedience to orders, over which there had been so much wrangling under the monarchy, and even under the Revolution and the Empire, became one of the essential driving forces of service life. In this aspect, the French navy was slow in coming into line with the Royal Navy, where this change took place in the era of men like Jervis and Nelson.

On the other hand, there was continual criticism of the training of the French naval officer, which was considered to be too theoretical. From the time of the Restoration until the middle of the century, there was no great change in the arrangements whereby entry to the naval training college (situated first at Angoulême, and later in the Brest roads, aboard a disarmed warship) was by examination, and the young officer first joined a ship after two years of study.

Some of the more prominent naval personalities, like the Prince de Joinville, Admiral Jurien de la Gravière or Bouvet (who commanded a fleet squadron), deplored a system of training which was much too theoretical, and which gave an almost exclusive prominence to the exact sciences and mathematics, at the cost of practical exercises. These latter were confined entirely to the Brest roads, and were of doubtful value. Their first real contact with the sea came only at the conclusion of their studies, in the form of a trip along the Brittany coasts which offered the attractions of a pleasure cruise.

The senior French officers mentioned above considered that it would be preferable to adopt a system similar to that of the Royal Navy, which was much more pragmatic and closer to real life. The midshipmen joined a ship at the age of thirteen and, in the course of long voyages, received a training which was both theoretical and practical. After examinations to monitor progress and a regular weeding-out of the less able candidates, only the most strongly committed were retained. At the age of seventeen, with the rank of sub-lieutenant, the young officers were in a position to exercise command in the full sense. In spite

In 1729 the Royal Naval Academy was founded at Portsmouth to educate forty 'young gentlemen'. The term 'naval cadet' was introduced in 1840 when the establishment moved to a training ship in Portsmouth harbour. In 1904 it came ashore into new buildings as the Royal Naval College at Dartmouth, Devon. In 1955, it was renamed Britannia Royal Naval College.
(Courtesy of Britannia Royal Naval College, Crown Copyright)

of the establishment of the naval college at Dartmouth, at the beginning of the twentieth century, the British training programme retained its practical bent and the officers of the Royal Navy always enjoyed the benefit of a dual training, which combined the expertise of the soldier with that of the sailor.

The French navy was by no means the only navy to have a training programme which was too theoretical, and in which navigational skill was sacrificed in favour of the acquisition of theoretical knowledge and skill in the use of weapons. At the end of the nineteenth century, Mahan noted that the same phenomenon existed in the navies of all the continental countries. In fact, the officers of the Russian navy, who were skilled in military techniques and in the handling of artillery, showed a reluctance to confront an enemy in the open sea. The same trait, which had already been observed during the Crimean War, manifested itself again during the Russo-Japanese War and in the two world wars. The young German navy suffered from the same defect. Shortly before 1914, the British naval attaché in Berlin noted that the imperial fleet never really went out on the high seas, but was continually carrying out exercises in sheltered German waters, with a precision that was very Prussian. The officers looked more like 'soldiers at sea' than sailors.

But whether or not his training emphasized the military or naval aspects, the officer could still not avoid being affected by fresh developments in warships. He too became a specialist. In view of technical changes, navies soon divided into three branches: surface ships, naval air arm and submarines. Within these branches, new specialized sections developed – gunnery, navigation, torpedoes, signals, radar, etc. On account of this growing technical emphasis, the naval officer tended to become isolated from his colleagues in other branches of the armed services. That specialization was the basis for a remark which Marshal Foch once made jokingly: 'You sailors, you're nothing but a bunch of locksmiths.'

Such isolation can occur in spheres other than the technical one; it has often appeared in fields that border on the political, especially in continental countries, where the part that the sea can play has rarely been clearly understood. The naval officer corps has then acquired the reputation of being a caste of 'aristocrats', or even of 'reactionaries'. This view was widely held about both the officers of the German navy and those of the French navy, and it was encapsulated in references to the service by that most expressive nickname, 'la Royale'. The existence of this caste, if there really was one, was not the outcome of its members' social origins. In the period of steam, just as in that of sail, British naval officers were recruited mainly from among the sons of officers – who did not necessarily come from families noted for their wealth or high birth – or of the clergy or of modest landowners. The situation was the same in the French navy of the nineteenth century. The scions of noble families were the exceptions, the majority of the officers coming from a military background or from the middle classes. In the German navy of 1914, out of 142 cadets only 24 were from the nobility, while 42 came from military circles. The others were sons of landowners, pastors, university professors, small industrialists and businessmen. Such recruits were far less aristocratic than those who became officers in the army.

A naval officer's isolation stems, in fact, from the demands of his work. His life is spent aboard ship, alone at sea or as a unit in a squadron, or else in ports, whose activities and interests are directed not inland, but towards the open sea. Professionally and geographically, he is cut off from the rest of the country and of its population to a far higher degree than the army officer, posted to garrisons situated in the heart of the mainland.

Even though the haughtiness of the officers of the *ancien régime* had vanished, a sense of superiority vis-à-vis petty officers, and particularly engineer officers, who were from humbler backgrounds and who had received a different – and exclusively technical – training, continued for a long while. In navies at the end of the nineteenth century and during the first half of the twentieth, engineer officers formed a separate group. Even though they were admitted to the wardroom, they were excluded from clubs and from social life ashore. They felt themselves, therefore, to be closer to the petty officers than did the deck officers. On the eve of the First World War, in Germany, unlike Great Britain, this segregation was made even more rigid. The training establishments were asked to recruit their candidates only from among those from very humble families.

This kind of segregation is progressively vanishing in the majority of the major fleets in the course of the second half of the twentieth century. There is coming into being an officer corps which does not suffer from such divisions, and which offers wide opportunities to petty officers for promotion into its ranks via special training establishments. It is none the less still true that the naval officer has to possess a threefold proficiency; he must be at once a sailor, a technician and a fighting man.

The change that can be seen to have taken place in naval vessels in less than one generation is on the same scale. The fighting ship of today enjoys air-conditioning; the lower decks are clean, even if not completely sound-insulated. In the period between the two world wars, the adoption of oil-firing for the engines had already led to the disappearance of stokers. The introduction of automation has meant a considerable reduction in the number of artificers, whose remaining responsibilities are increasingly concentrated on individual repairs and regular maintenance.

Living conditions also have been greatly improved. Hammocks have disappeared and have been replaced by bunks. More recreation facilities have been installed, such as cafeterias, libraries and games rooms. Thanks to the video recorder, crews can enjoy ship's television and cinema shows. Drinking water is freely available, and the sailors have a whole range of facilities – launderettes, hairdressers, NAAFI, post office, etc. Plentiful meals are served in the messroom and in the cafeterias at tables for four or six. Even life aboard nuclear submarines is entirely different in quality from that in vessels of the immediate postwar period.

This improvement has contributed to the completion of a change which began a century ago. There are a sufficient number of men volunteering for service to deal with a whole range of specialized functions, after passing through the training establishments. Navies thus provide a profession. In France, the number of men conscripted in 1985 did not exceed 25 per cent of the total entrants. The US and British fleets are recruited entirely from volunteers. The Soviet Union conscripted the large majority of its crews, who served for a period of three years. The navies of some Western countries have now taken the ultimate revolutionary step of experimenting with having women aboard.

The ease with which recruits are secured is also explained by other factors. At the end of fifteen years' service, and already entitled to a pension, specialists can then go back into civilian life and readapt. The escape from everyday surroundings, and the voyages to far-off places, play a part too in attracting men. 'If you enjoy cruises, join the navy.' This recruiting poster for the US navy speaks volumes, and is sufficient on its own to demonstrate how immensely long the road is that has been travelled since the days of the navy under sail, when the ship fairly closely resembled a floating prison.
See also ADMINISTRATION, NAVAL; BLOCKADES; COLBERT; COMMERCE-RAIDING; CONVOYS; MARINES; NAVAL WARFARE; NAVIES; PENSIONS; RECRUITMENT; TRAINING.

J. MEYER
P. MASSON

FURTHER READING
H. Ahrweiler, *Byzance et la mer. La marine de guerre, la politique et les institutions maritimes de Byzance aux VIIe–XVe siècles* (Paris, 1966); J. Aman, *Les Officiers bleus dans la marine française* (Geneva, 1977); J. D. Davies, *Officers and Tarpaulins: the officers and men of the Restoration navy* (Oxford, 1991); Christopher Lloyd, *The British Seaman* (London, 1969); Philippe Masson, *Servitude et grandeur des gens de mer* (Paris, 1986); Michel Mollat, *La Vie quotidienne des gens de mer en Atlantique, IXe–XVIe siècles* (Paris, 1983); Nicholas Rodger, *The Wooden World* (London, 1986); J. Rouge, *La Marine*

dans l'Antiquité (Paris, 1975); M. Vigie, *Les Galèriens du roi* (Paris, 1985); John Winton, *Hurrah for the Life of a Sailor!* (London, 1977).

Naval stores In the seventeenth and eighteenth centuries, naval needs for timber, sailcloth, hemp, pitch, tar and linseed were enormous: no maritime nation could satisfy them without resorting to the Baltic supply. The Baltic trade played the same role, relatively speaking, as the Near Eastern oil monopoly does in our own time. Naval administrations had to be more closely involved in the purchase of these stores than in later periods, owing to the quantities required by the state. Holland and England depended almost wholly on such imports, and naval domination was therefore a question of life and death for them. Both France and Britain could meet some of their needs from their own forests, but intensive exploitation in the past meant that there were not enough large pieces of timber which were needed for the structure of a ship. Spain was reduced to using woods from the north-west, hence her recourse to exotic woods and the importance of Havana as a shipbuilding centre. Calabria and Dalmatia were available as sources, but quality was another problem – Pyrenean conifers produced masts which were very brittle. Costs of transport also influenced the trade towards northern Europe. The river system of the north European plain allowed great trees to be moved very easily, while in the French mountains a system of roads had first to be built, and land transport generally was poor. Finally, we can add to these drawbacks the imperatives of the market. Riga was the great centre of distribution, but the market was organized on sale by sample, and by lots. British effectiveness at sea derived in part from the tactic of 'blockade by prior purchase'; her greater needs gave power to obtain the best lots, and reduction of the purchasing power of others. She was never able to prevent French timber imports, as French convoys running along the coast under batteries could usually get through, but at great extra cost and with much delay, leading indeed to the development of internal waterways.

All navies kept watching for new supplies of timber; master shipbuilders and commercial spies were sent to examine possibilities. Home production was encouraged; the British Admiralty sought alternative sources in North America. Only the advent of the iron ship ended this pressing problem; no such serious matter replaced it. *See also* ADMINISTRATION, NAVAL; BASES, NAVAL; BLOCKADES; CONVOYS; DOCKYARDS.

J. MEYER

FURTHER READING
R. G. Albion, *Forests and Seapower* (Harvard, 1926, repr. Hamden, Conn., 1965); P. W. Bamford, *Forests and French Sea Power, 1660–1789* (Toronto, 1956).

Naval warfare Warfare at sea is marked by characteristics of a very special kind. It takes place on an uninhabited, neutral element, no part of which can be either occupied or lost. Its strategy is aimed at the control of sea routes in the interests of trade, commerce-raiding or mere piracy, or again, of combined operations, which can be on widely differing scales.

In Antiquity, this strategy reached a remarkably high level of development. In the Egypto-Homeric period, the purpose of the earliest fighting ships was to prevent pillaging of coastal areas by the 'sea people'. From the beginning of the Greek classical period, Greek cities maintained what can be properly called navies, which were intended for carrying out or repulsing small-scale raids or large amphibious operations. The era of great sea battles, carried out with the help of carefully prepared tactics, began in the fifth century BC. The Battle of Salamis (480 BC) marked the thwarting of a huge combined operation aimed at the subjugation of Greece; the destruction of the armada of the Persians led to their defeat in the following year at Plataea, and to their evacuation of Greece. Simultaneously, the Battle of Mycale allowed the Greeks to undertake the liberation of their cities in Asia Minor.

During the Peloponnesian War, Athens used her supremacy at sea to carry out repeated raids on her enemies' coasts, and large scale operations like the Sicilian expedition. At the same time, she strove to exercise control over all Greek seaborne commerce. During the First Punic War, the maritime supremacy which the Romans had gained, and kept, as a result of the Battles of Mylae (260 BC), Cape Ecnomus (256) and Drepanum (249) and the Aegates Islands (241) was aimed at isolating Sicily and making feasible a landing in Africa. This latter scheme was still premature and was brought to a halt by the disaster suffered by Regulus.

Far too little attention has been paid to a fundamental aspect of the Second Punic War. Since he lacked command of the sea, Hannibal could not reach Italy from Spain except by an interminable journey through territory that had hardly been explored, via the Pyrenees, the south of Gaul and the Alps. Despite resounding victories, his final failure can be put down as much to his inability to communicate abroad and receive reinforcements as to Roman staying power and the loyalty of the Italian cities. And it was the sea which made possible a conclusion to a conflict that had seemed unending. When he heard of Scipio's landing in Africa, Hannibal succeeded, by an exceptional stroke of good fortune, in returning there also; but he suffered at Zama in 202 BC the defeat which foreshadowed the complete destruction of the Punic city in 146 BC. Later, at the moment when the Roman republican system was in its death throes, the Battle of Actium (31 BC) opened up the East to Octavian and proved the prelude to the downfall of Antonius and Cleopatra. Throughout the whole Imperial period, Rome kept in the *Mare Nostrum* merely some light squadrons, whose task was to prevent any recrudescence of piracy which had been rendered completely quiescent by Pompey's masterly operation of 67 BC, and was indeed to remain so for more than five centuries.

During this whole period, a considerable range of types of ship and of tactics was employed. Greeks, Rhodians and Romans preferred light vessels (biremes, triremes), while ships of large tonnage (quadriremes, quinqueremes) were widely employed in Hellenistic navies. Battle at sea took the form of using the impact of a ship's ram, a method invented by the Ionians at the start of the fifth century BC, and culminating in the *diekplous*, which was practised in the heyday of classical Greece. The triremes were stationed in line abreast, and the aim was to break through the enemy line. A circular formation, on the other hand, with the rams pointing outwards, could be adopted as a defensive manoeuvre; it is recorded, indeed, that it was employed at Arginusae. But, in view of the risks inherent in the battle of impact, in which the rammer could easily become the rammed, naval battles during the Hellenistic period tended more and more to take the form of coming alongside an enemy ship and storming it; this attack was very often preceded by fire from catapults and ballistas, in the shape of bolts, blocks of stone or blazing missiles. This method was assisted, in Roman naval practice, by the use of the *corvus*, a gangway which could be lowered and which, since it was fitted with hooks, made possible an assault by a company of legionaries. But, contrary to the views of Polybius, this kind of assault did not rule out the need for ability in manoeuvring ships.

After the fall of the Roman Empire, there was a recrudescence of naval warfare in the Mediterranean, once again often in association with combined operations, whether these were connected with attempts by Justinian to restore the Roman Empire, or with Arab conquests, Ottoman expansion in the Mediterranean or attacks on Barbary coast bases or pirates' haunts. Whatever the type of vessel employed – Byzantine *dromon* or heavy galley of the sixteenth century – naval tactics reflected more and more closely those of battles on land. Fleets faced each other in line abreast, with a centre and two wings, one of the latter normally keeping close in to a coast, as seen in descriptions of such battles as Preveza (1538) or Lepanto (1571). The decisive stroke was to break through the centre or turn one of the flanks. The battle came down none the less to a series of single combats between galleys. Boarding always brought the engagement to an end, and it was preceded by missiles from catapults and arrows from bows and bolts from crossbows, as well as – from the middle of the fifteenth century – by fire from three to five cannon sited forward as chase-guns.

As early as the Battle of Lepanto, the galley had begun to appear outdated. This type of ship, which had dominated the Mediterranean since Antiquity, found itself outclassed by the warship with which large navies were now equipped. Its decline in importance was all the greater in that it was really fit only for use in enclosed seas, such as the Mediterranean, the Red Sea, the Baltic or the Caribbean. In spite of attempts to save it by increasing its tonnage, it gradually faded away during the seventeenth century, and disappeared entirely as an active fighting ship in the middle of the next. It continued to be used only as an auxiliary vessel or for ceremonial purposes. When the last battle between galleys took place – in fact, in the Baltic between the Russians and Swedes in 1808 – it seemed as if the past had come momentarily to life.

The ship of the line, which became the spearhead of sailing navies, was created by Northerners' sea forces, although it was a very long time before they had a real fighting ship as such. Apart from the special case of the Veneti, the Vikings never had a warship and naval tactics worthy of the name. Even though the *drakkar* made an excellent boat for raids, it possessed no armament for making an attack. If a battle at sea did occur, like the one reported at Nissa in 1062 between Norwegians and Danes, the boats crowded alongside each other, and their fully armed crews fought to board and capture those of the other side. Hence the battle became a confused mêlée.

The situation had scarcely changed in the Middle Ages, even though a certain degree of strategy was evident, as seen in accounts of the conflicts between Denmark and the Hanseatic League or France and England at the start of the thirteenth century. The matter at issue was always the command of the narrow seas, like the Straits of Denmark or the English Channel. The encounters brought into play fleets that had merely been put together for the occasion, and which belonged to private confederations like that of the Cinque Ports near Dover; the ships were improvisations based on *cogghes*, i.e. ordinary merchant ships. With very few exceptions – one being the Battle of Dover in 1217, where an English squadron, by operating to windward, succeeded in catching up with, and engaging, a French convoy – tactics were always rudimentary. There was no idea of manoeuvre, and fleets were stationary, with ships pressed closely alongside each other. Starting with a hail of arrows from bows and bolts from crossbows, the engagement was like a land battle, or rather, an assault on a fortress. It brought into action men-at-arms accoutred from head to foot.

This is what is recorded of the Battle of Sluys (1340), where the French ships were closely packed and made fast to each other, thus looking like a 'huge forest'. The victory of Edward III was, in no sense, the result of superiority in manoeuvre but was due to the use of a 'secret weapon', the large yew bow which was to be seen again at Crécy and Agincourt. Hails of arrows caused a massacre among the French crews and made it easy for the English to board and capture all the ships. Despite the crudeness of such tactics, the strategic aim was achieved; as master of the sea, Edward III was now in a position to commence operations in France.

It was not, however, until the end of the fifteenth century, and the beginning of the sixteenth, that the fleets of Western countries at last possessed real warships and used them with naval tactics worthy of the name. A good example of these new style vessels, which were also suitable for lengthy ocean voyages, were the Portuguese carracks, with their imposing superstructures bristling with light cannon. Vasco da Gama adopted for the first time a formation in line ahead and, thanks to the greater fire power and accuracy of his ships' guns, he routed a Moslem fleet off the Malabar coast. Some years later, these ships also demonstrated their superiority over Chinese junks. It was in carracks, or in ships developed from them, that the Normans, the Basques, the English 'sea dogs' like Drake, Hawkins and Frobisher, and very soon, the Dutch, allured by the riches of the new empires, set off to attack the Spanish and Portuguese sea routes. They did not hesitate to practise a form of commerce-raiding that bordered on plain piracy. Their opponents were obliged to increase their ships' armament, to build up chains of bases and to start a system of escorted convoys. War at sea took on a new dimension with this requirement to protect the lines of communication.

The ravages caused by the English were no longer confined to the Caribbean but extended also to the Pacific. The support given by Elizabeth I to the revolt in the Netherlands, and the Protestant attacks on the Flanders route, led to a break between England and Spain and prompted Philip II in 1588 to undertake the venture of the 'invincible Armada', that is, a landing in England in liaison with the Duke of Parma's army. The failure of one of history's most grandiose operations was not, in reality, due to the English naval forces' harassing of the Armada in the Channel. Despite the expenditure of considerable amounts of ammunition, losses on either side were small, owing to the

weakness of the cannon used. The issue was, in fact, decided by a night attack with fire ships off Gravelines, and by a sudden change of wind which pushed the Armada into the North Sea; it had no hope of withdrawing down the Channel, and was forced to attempt a return voyage round the north of Britain, which proved disastrous. A factor that reappears continually until the mid-nineteenth century also played a significant part in success or failure at this dawn of modern naval strategy. This was disease. Vasco da Gama and the English 'sea dogs' experienced on their ships scurvy, which was unknown to sailors of Antiquity and the Middle Ages. Hawkins could speak of 100,000 deaths from this cause in the Elizabethan era. Scurvy contributed to the disaster of the invincible Armada. Other diseases followed, including typhus and yellow fever. On the morrow of the battle in 1588, the English vessels were ravaged by a terrible wave of poisoning, probably linked with beer that had gone bad. Despite being victorious, the

A 28-gun frigate of the Royal Navy c.1790. Although many varieties of smaller sailing vessel had been described as 'frigates', after 1760 the word was applied solely to fully rigged, three masted, single gun-decked men-of-war. Armed with between 24 and 50 guns, these fast vessels were used for cruising, patrolling and reconnaissance.
(National Maritime Museum, Greenwich)

English fleet would have been unable to give battle a second time.

It was in the second half of the seventeenth century that warfare at sea assumed its full dimensions. It is easy to explain the reasons. Major nation-states like England, the United Provinces, France and Spain now possessed permanent fleets which were provided with arsenals, a more or less forcible system of recruiting, like the British press-gang or the French call-up of age classes, and a corps of officers made up of real sailors. These fleets were composed of ships with two or three decks, which possessed a powerful complement of cannon made of bronze or cast iron and very effective at short range. Confrontations over colonies, religious conflicts and the desire to maintain a balance of power in Europe or, on the other hand, to establish by force a continental supremacy, explain the range and the relentlessness of the wars at sea.

These conflicts were marked by the introduction of new tactics, whose effects were to be felt right up to the middle of the nineteenth century. During their first war with Holland (1652–4) the English adopted the line ahead formation, instead of the line abreast system, which had been inherited from the galley period and resulted in engagements that were merely confused and frequently without any definite result. With the new formation, and by use of the increasingly improved signal-books, the commander-in-chief had better control of his fleet. This meant that all ships' captains had to be involved in the battle as a matter of course. In addition, the line ahead formation ensured that guns distributed along the ships' sides had the maximum effect. In a few years, the new formation was adopted by all major navies.

During its early period of use, the line ahead system also allowed great flexibility and encircling manoeuvres. At the Battle of the Texel, on 21 August 1673, the English tried to pass round the head of the Dutch fleet, while de Ruyter attempted to ward off this manoeuvre by attacks with groups of ships on his enemy's centre and rearguard. At Beachy Head on 10 July 1690, after having begun the engagement in line parallel to his opponent's, Tourville succeeded in rounding the Anglo-Dutch van and forcing it to retire. To secure victory, some admirals not only used their ships' gunfire, but brought into play fireships, or even galleys, when they were attacking squadrons at anchor. Yet, at the start of the eighteenth century, this tactical system became ossified and institutionalized and gave rise to that celebrated formalism which affected every navy. Out of prudence, and also from concern to avoid the risk of encircling movements, attempts to make concentrated attacks were increasingly severely frowned upon, or even strictly forbidden. Battle instructions like those issued by the Duke of York, or treatises on tactics such as those of P. Hoste (1696), Bigot de Morogues (1763) or Bourdé de la Villehuet (1765), laid down rigid rules for the line ahead formation and for fire discipline, with court martial as the penalty for contravention. From Velez Malaga (1704) to Minorca (1756), and even well beyond, the majority of battles were limited to endless evolutions to take advantage of the wind, followed by an unprofitable exchange of fire, at a respectful distance, between two perfectly straight lines of ships. This formalism was particularly prevalent in the French and Spanish navies, where it was made a rule to engage in battle with their ships to leeward of the enemy, that is, so that they could always break off the engagement and retire at will. On the other hand, the British could sometimes show a more offensive spirit. Thus, they frequently adopted the 'to windward' position, which meant that their line was driven towards the enemy's. Their admirals exploited, when opportunity offered, a loophole in their instructions, by carrying out a 'general chase', whenever the enemy weakened or started to withdraw; each ship then had orders to catch up with, and engage, its nearest opponent. The system provided the Royal Navy with its major successes, whether at Finisterre (1747) or at Quiberon Bay and Lagos (1759). But, most frequently, as can be seen from descriptions of the Battle of Chesapeake Bay (1781), which decided the war with America, the British too remained slaves to the traditional formation.

The problems caused by this formalism were further increased by the indiscipline and lack of offensive spirit shown by too many of the admirals and ships' commanders. These factors provide an explanation for the desertion of two ships at Lagos, the break-up of Conflans's squadron at the Battle of Quiberon Bay, and the failure of some of Suffren's plans through the wavering behaviour of his officers. This kind of indiscipline led to painful incidents, as can be seen during the British war with America. After the Battle of Ushant (1778), the British admirals Keppel and Palliser fought a legal case against each other. On the morrow of the Battle of Chesapeake Bay, a violent altercation took place between the admirals Graves and Hood. De Grasse sent for trial several of his ship commanders whom he considered guilty of not having supported him during the Battle of the Saints (1782).

This formalism arose also from the limited nature of the battles of the eighteenth century, in which no strong passions were involved and admirals were asked, in the majority of cases, to operate with the greatest caution, and not to jeopardize the forces entrusted to them. The system turned into what is, in fact, a denial of the basic principles of strategy. It reached the point of admitting that success in an encounter was a matter of having superior forces which obliged an enemy to refuse, or break off, combat; and that it was possible to carry out large-scale operations – such as sea-borne landings or convoy protection – without having to join battle. Some tried to free themselves from this restraint, like Rodney, who succeeded in breaking his opponent's line at the Battle of the Saints, or Suffren, whose tactics were to seek to overwhelm the enemy's rear. But such successes still remained limited, because of a lack of understanding or drive on the part of subordinates coupled with the inability of the system of signals to convey the admiral's desires when circumstances were unusual.

The astounding successes of the Royal Navy between 1793 and 1815 may be explained by the quality of British guns, the use of carronades which fired grapeshot across decks, the exceptionally high standard of training of the gunners, and the systematic employment of a murderous fire into enemy ships' hulls. Fired at point-blank range, the cannon balls pierced the ships' sides and played havoc among their gun crews, by hurling deadly splinters of wood in all directions. Another reason for these victories was a tactical innovation. This was to move in from the windward side and, in two parallel columns, to attack the enemy line in such a way as to overwhelm it and destroy its centre and rearguard before the leading ships had had time to intervene. But this method's success was also due to a remarkable mutual rapport. British admirals like Jervis and Nelson never ceased to emphasize *esprit de corps*, comradeship and the removal of any kind of jealousy between their ships' commanders. It was this psychological preparation that gave birth to the 'band of brothers' of the Battle of the Nile. The increasing weakness and disorganization of the Spanish and, particularly, of the French navy – the latter being a victim of the crisis caused by the Revolution – were further reasons for the British triumphs. But another factor also now came into play. Sharp differences of ideology meant that hatred appeared in the context of real battles also. That explains the *furia britannica*, but also the behaviour of their enemy. The pattern of previous wars was not repeated. The French and Spanish did not give in; they spurned evasion or flight. They accepted battle; despite their inferiority, they offered, as seen at Trafalgar, a desperate passive resistance, and maintained it to a suicidal degree.

As a result of these unending and repeated conflicts of the modern era, a difference of approach became apparent between the mainly maritime powers, such as the Netherlands and Great Britain, which gave pride of place to the naval arm, and the largely continental ones, like Spain or France, where the navy suffered long periods of eclipse owing to the burden imposed by European land wars, or to lack of interest on the part of rulers and the general public. France was in a position on two occasions only to meet Britain on equal terms. These were at the beginning of the Nine Years' War (1688–97) and during the American War of Independence (1775–83), when she was no longer burdened with European concerns, and was joined by two minor navies of the period, those of the Netherlands and Spain.

During these conflicts, two kinds of strategy took shape. Writing at the very end of the nineteenth century, Mahan analysed the motive forces behind them. For the predominantly maritime powers, control of the sea, won by close action or strict blockade, had various aims. These were to ensure the defence of the national territory, to render it safe from invasion and to turn it into a place of refuge; and, in addition, to ensure the protection of its own seaborne commerce, while facilitating the destruction of the enemy's. But, in the context of the great European conflicts of the seventeenth and eighteenth centuries, a maritime power's sphere of action ranged still wider. It took a hand in the continental struggle by means of subsidies ('St George's cavalry') and transporting military forces, the scale of whose activities could be very varied. Thus, the list of interventions by British troops covers raids of a limited nature on an enemy coast, as seen during the Seven Years' War, the dispatch of expeditionary forces or even large armies, in pursuit of the continental doctrine of Marlborough, or even the opening up of an entirely separate theatre of operations, as shown in the war in Spain from 1808 to 1814.

Lastly, the British army, for the same reason as the Royal Navy, formed one of the cornerstones of British power throughout the whole of this period. Britain could exercise her military might with maximum effectiveness only in so far as she was linked with one or more allies on the Continent. Otherwise, the struggle between 'the trouble-maker' on the Continent and the maritime power became like that of the elephant and the whale, both finding themselves reciprocally powerless.

The inferior naval power, as was often France's case, possessed a considerably more restricted range of options. She could make play just with the 'existence of a fleet', and immobilize sizeable enemy forces by the mere presence of squadrons shut up in roadsteads. She could also make use of commerce-raiding, employing both service and private vessels, so as to counterbalance her own loss of commerce and oblige the enemy to expend a huge effort in protecting his own trade routes. On the other hand, she was barred from one sphere – that of combined operations. The examples of Choiseul and Napoleon demonstrated that all attempts at raids on the heartland of an enemy power, even with the help of surprise or under cover of winter, resulted in tragic disappointment, like those at Quiberon Bay and Trafalgar.

During the naval *détente* of the nineteenth century the absence of major conflicts at sea offered no opportunity of using the whole range of naval strategy. Major naval battles were exceptional events; there is little that is worthy of note except Navarino (1827), with the annihilation of the Turco-Egyptian fleet by British, Russian and French squadrons, and also Lissa (1866), which has remained famous because the Austrian flagship sank the *Re d'Italia* by ramming her. No fleet engagement of great importance took place during the European interventions in Latin America, the Opium Wars, the Crimean War, the American Civil War, the Franco-German conflict of 1870–1, or Courbet's operations against China. During these limited conflicts, naval action was restricted to commerce-raiding, blockade, bombardment or support of troops engaged on land.

The major event of the period is to be found in the technical changes in fighting ships that stemmed from the industrial revolution. With the introduction of steam power, armour plating, the explosive shell and the torpedo, ships of the line, frigates and corvettes made way for battleships, cruisers, destroyers and torpedo boats, while the submarine was still to come. These changes were bound to cause an upheaval in current thinking on tactics. Thanks to its flexibility and ease of manoeuvre, there seemed some likelihood that the steamship might make ramming feasible once again in sea battles. Basing themselves on the lessons of the encounter

581

between the *Merrimac* and the *Monitor* in 1862 or the Battle of Lissa, a number of naval men became obsessed with the idea of ramming in battle, and asserted their firm belief in a revival of this naval tactic of Antiquity. The line ahead formation seemed doomed to give way to battle in line abreast.

In fact, even before the end of the century, this wave of opinion in favour of the ram was rapidly losing strength. Naval exercises demonstrated that the risks incurred in battle by using this means were as great for the rammer as for the rammed. The advances made in rapid-firing guns, using armour-piercing shells, rendered battle at close quarters increasingly hazardous. In view of the lessons learned from the Battle of the Yalu River (1894) between the Chinese and the Japanese, there was a return to the doctrine of the artillery duel at long range and the line ahead formation. British tactical theory had, indeed, never moved away from it, since there had been a persistent scepticism about the advantages of the ram.

Another technical innovation, the self-powered torpedo, led at almost the same moment to a further change in tactical doctrine, which finally proved both costly and disastrous. According to the views of the 'Jeune École', which had a dominant influence on French naval policy from 1880 to 1900, the right strategy was for large flotillas of torpedo-boats to break the close British blockade, and then for commerce-raiding to be prosecuted on an unexpectedly large scale, thus simultaneously endangering Britain's control of the sea. At the time of the Fashoda crisis in 1898, it had to be recognized that this was a completely blind alley. The improvements in the defensive armament of battleships, and the appearance of destroyers or anti-torpedo boats, reduced to a marked degree the torpedo boat's advantages. By one of history's ironies, this type of ship was not to disappear. It survived merely as an auxiliary of the battleship in the fight against the submarine and, a little later, the aircraft.

Despite the technical changes, a reversion to conservative ideas appeared, therefore, to be in evidence at the very beginning

of the twentieth century. There was the same tendency over strategy. The conflicts in the Far East, with the wars carried on by Japan against China (1894–5) and against Russia (1904–5), seemed to confirm Mahan's teaching to the hilt. Once control of the sea had been secured by battle, it would ensure freedom of communication and ability to support the forces operating on the mainland, as had been proved by the example of the Japanese armies in Korea and Manchuria.

The war of 1914–18, though ultimately reverting to traditional methods, none the less produced doubts in some minds; these came into view subsequently in such works as the *Theories stratégiques* of Castex. Contrary to all expectations, 'the battle' did not take place; all that happened was a chaotic and inconclusive encounter, occurring late in the war, between British and German forces off Jutland on 31 May 1916. For the duration of the war, the Central Powers' squadrons were content to play the part of 'potentially active fleets' while the Allied navies kept watch on them from a distance. This situation in which the Royal Navy found itself was, therefore, one which had been well known to it in the seventeenth and eighteenth centuries.

The lack of offensive action by their opponents still meant that the Allies possessed control of the sea. Certainly, this control did not extend everywhere. The Entente Powers could not secure mastery of the Baltic and the Black Sea, and lack of it contributed to the isolation of Russia, which was one of the major factors in the war. The control was also relative. In 1915, and from the start of 1917 until the Armistice, the Allies encountered a type of warfare that consisted of commerce destruction of a revolutionary kind and unprecedented extent. During a good part of the war, the Franco-British navies, therefore, found themselves dealing with the anti-submarine battle and the protection of lines of communication. It was a duty that they carried out with success, despite the huge U-boat effort deployed by the Germans.

There were no spectacular results at sea but the role of that element was no less important, although it must be seen in the context of a struggle whose issue could naturally be decided only on land. Freedom of communications allowed the Entente Powers to use the huge resources of their colonies and of neutral countries, in particular the United States, while maintaining an increasingly strict blockade in regard to the Central Powers which contributed to the deterioration of civilians' and troops' morale. Control of the sea also allowed increasingly large forces of British troops to play a part in the Western theatre of operations, in the period before the appearance of a great American army, whose assistance – in terms of war supplies and morale – proved decisive in 1918. There was one dark cloud. The failure in the Dardanelles seemed to spell the doom of any large-scale amphibious operations.

The Second World War only confirmed the decisive part played by sea power. It was control of the sea that secured Britain against a German landing in the summer of 1940, after the fall of France. It should not be forgotten, in fact, that the German aim, in the first phase of the Battle of Britain, was to give the *Luftwaffe* air superiority, so that it could attack and destroy the flotillas of destroyers which guarded the Channel in order to resist any enemy combined operation.

In the Western theatre, the battle at sea was once again over control of communications, more especially since the Germans, lacking large surface ships, could not meet the British Home Fleet in direct combat, and since the Italian navy, apart from rare sorties, was content to play the part of being 'potentially active'.

This struggle for the control of communications took place in two sectors. In the Atlantic, the Allies could, by mobilizing considerable resources, respond to the threat from aircraft, surface ships and particularly U-boats. Victory there was not won until the spring of 1943 and, despite its final failure, this commerce destruction had had the result of delaying for long months the development of Allied strategy, which came to depend upon the availability of merchant and landing ships.

In the Mediterranean, it was the British who, using Malta as a base, waged war against Axis communications between Italy and Africa before succeeding in liaison with the Americans, in isolating Tunisia completely, and thus hastening the surrender of the German and Italian forces there in May 1943.

By means of their control of the sea, which had been completely secured in 1943, the Allies were in a position to make use of a well-established formula, though on a scale that had never previously been seen. A series of combined operations – in North Africa, Sicily, Italy, Normandy and Provence – made possible a return to the continent of Europe, and the re-establishment of that western front which had disappeared in 1940 with the defeat of France. A whole series of factors had a part in ensuring the success of these seaborne landings, in which the fate of whole armies was involved – control of the sea, air superiority, fleets of motorized landing-craft and deception plans.

There too, the experience of the past was repeated. This strategy relied for success on the existence of a continental ally with certain natural advantages. From 1941 onwards, the Soviet Union, which was holding down the bulk of the *Wehrmacht*, became the pivot of the maritime powers' strategy. Its fundamental role explains, in large part, the political concessions accorded to Stalin, and the considerable material assistance transported to the USSR via the Arctic Ocean, the Persian Gulf and the Pacific Ocean – yet another example of tradition being followed.

In the Western theatre, the Second World War brought into action the whole range of sea power. There was, however, one notable exception. By contrast with 1914–18, the blockade proved to be quite ineffective, owing to the policy of self-sufficiency pursued by the Third Reich and to its ability after 1940 to exploit the whole of Europe. In order to weaken the German economy and morale, the Allies were forced to put an intensive effort into strategic bombing.

In the Pacific, the battle seemed even more in accord with Mahan's theories. Control of the sea, gained by the attack on Pearl Harbor and the annihilation of the Allied naval forces off Malaysia and

Indonesia, allowed the Japanese to carry out successfully a remarkable series of combined operations and to occupy all of South-East Asia. After the turning point had come with the Battle of Midway Island, and with the occupation of Guadalcanal and the rest of the Solomon Islands, it was still by naval battles, together with intensive submarine warfare, that the United States reached the position of being able to carry out a victorious counter-offensive aimed at the Japanese archipelago. The victories of the Marianas Islands and Leyte provided scope for the attacks on Guam, Saipan, the Philippines and Okinawa. The successful investment of Japan in the spring of 1945 went hand in hand with devastating bombing raids, which disorganized the economy, and with a blockade achieved by the destruction of the Japanese merchant fleet.

Thus, the Second World War displays all aspects of naval power, against the background of yet further technical changes. From the outset of the conflict, the surface ship had to adapt to the threat from the air, whose seriousness had been greatly underestimated. Combat fleets had therefore to incorporate aircraft as a means of both attack and defence, and the battleship, which had still been looked upon in 1939–40 as the 'capital ship' was relegated to an undeniably important, but secondary, role below the aircraft carrier, which became the main fighting ship.

From 1942 onwards, the combat fleets took the shape of powerful 'task-forces', composed of aircraft carriers, ringed by battleships, cruisers and destroyers, whose role was to ensure close protection against enemy surface ships, aircraft or submarines. Thus, the line ahead formation became a thing of the past. Henceforth, as shown by the engagements in May and June 1942 in the Coral Sea and off Midway Island, naval battles took place 'below the horizon'. Confrontation was through the agency of groups of aircraft carrying torpedoes or using dive-bombing tactics, and operating at distances of 100–200 miles. Engagements in which ships used their surface guns took place only at night, and became progressively rarer. There was

another change which concerned the submarine. In 1944, the single form of propulsion had not yet been introduced, submarines having to be equipped with both diesel and electric motors, but thanks to the snorkel, this type of vessel no longer had to come repeatedly to the surface, and began to escape from the aircraft, which had become its most dangerous enemy.

Finally, and contrary to previous wars, the fighting fleets' offensive action was not limited to the range of their guns and to a narrow strip of coastline. At the end of the war, the American aircraft carriers were in a position, thanks to the squadrons of aircraft that they carried, to mount raids in depth throughout the whole Japanese archipelago. The war in Korea provided similar examples, as later that in Vietnam was to do also, of massive operations by naval air forces. That day was long past when – to quote a remark of Nelson's – a sailor who carries out an attack on land is a lunatic.

Since 1945, the capabilities of navies have not ceased to grow. For a small group of leading powers, the Soviet Union, the United States, Great Britain, France and China, strategic nuclear submarines, armed with ballistic missiles, have come more and more to constitute one of the major components of their forces of deterrence, and are now in a position to reach any point on the earth's surface.

Apart from the deterrents, however, navies are still the preferred method for dealing with most types of crisis. Though a naval force may seem to take relatively too long before it can intervene, it must be remembered, on the other hand, that movement at sea is not subject to any restrictions of a political or technical kind. The sheer size of the resources that can be brought into play by this means is considerable, as seen in the Falklands campaign (1982), where 500,000 tons of military supplies were transported by sea, as against a mere 6,000 by air. There are other advantages too. There are very subtle gradations in the scale of forms that naval intervention can take. On a modest level, naval forces can show a presence, provide friendly support or can undertake limited action within the context of a localized conflict. On a larger scale, their action can take the form of a blockade like that of Cuba in 1962, or of a combined operation carried out at long range, of which the Falklands Campaign has in recent years given an example. In this type of operation, a fleet provides a perfect instrument for bringing to bear an instant task-force of the kind maintained today by France and the United States. By means of aircraft carriers, modern navies also have the capacity for action over a range of 600 miles, and thus are able to cover the fringes of continents, where 80 per cent of the world's population is concentrated.

Until 1991, in the event of an East–West confrontation, the US navy, by the use of the groups of heavy aircraft carriers which represent a considerable offensive potential, expected not only to neutralize the Soviet naval forces, which were the world's second largest, but to carry out operations on the rear of the Warsaw Pact troops, in the Norwegian, Barents and Okhotsk Seas, within the framework of a strategy that had the normal aim of attacking anywhere on an enemy's perimeter. Such operations would not have excluded attacks on sea communications; these could have been carried out by nuclear submarines whose capacities are infinitely greater than those of the type used in the Second World War.

These operations could have brought nuclear weapons into play, with material and psychological consequences that would have been less serious than on land, since no populations would be involved. Whatever the uncertainties of the future, these scenarios show that the task of developing major fleets involves dealing with a particularly wide span of requirements, which range from forces of deterrence to formations which can provide a presence or make an intervention. They prove too that in half a century naval power has moved beyond the narrow bounds that Mahan traced for it. As envisaged in the light of modern strategy naval forces are no longer confined to the support of war economies or of armies engaged in operational theatres. Today the sea can attack the land directly and can challenge the continental masses. *See also* BASES, NAVAL; BLOCKADES; COMMERCE-RAIDING; CONVOYS; LOSSES OF LIFE; NAVAL PERSONNEL; NAVIES.

CASTEX; COLBERT; CORBETT; DÖNITZ; DRAKE; GRASSE DE TILLY; MAHAN; NAGUMO; NELSON; RAEDER; RODNEY; RUYTER; SEIGNELAY; SUFFREN; SURCOUF; TIRPITZ; TOGO; YAMAMOTO.

ACTIUM; ATLANTIC, BATTLE OF THE; FALKLANDS WAR; GUADALCANAL; JUTLAND; LA HOGUE AND BARFLEUR; LEPANTO; LEYTE GULF; LISSA; MIDWAY ISLAND; PEARL HARBOR; SALAMIS; TRAFALGAR; TSUSHIMA.

P. MASSON
J. MEYER

FURTHER READING
Julian S. Corbett, *England in the Seven Years' War: a study in combined strategy* (2 vols, London, 1907); Hervé Coutau-Bégarie, *La Puissance Maritime. Castex et la stratégie navale* (Paris, 1985); Alfred T. Mahan, *The Influence of Sea Power upon History* (London, 1890); Philippe Masson, *Histoire des batailles navales, de la voile aux missiles* (Paris, 1983); Philippe Masson, *De la mer et de sa stratégie* (Paris, 1986); H. Pemsel, *Atlas of Naval Warfare* (London, 1977); E. B. Potter and C. W. Nimitz, *Sea Power, a Naval History* (New York, 1960); Clark G. Reynolds, *Command of the Sea* (London & New York, 1976).

Navies Throughout history, the warship represents a compromise, which it attempts to reconcile with varying degrees of success, between range of action, living conditions aboard, protection and offensive capacity, regardless of whether the last is provided by a ram, ballistic weapons, cannon, torpedoes, aircraft or missiles. Fighting ships also have a ranking order of importance, which is determined by their ability to perform given tasks or by the appearance of new weapons. In fleets of the past, frigates and corvettes acted as scouts for the main squadrons, carried out liaison duties, lent aid to vessels in difficulties or undertook the repetition of signals. During the First World War, battleships did not go to sea except with an escort of destroyers, whose task was to repulse, or forestall, attacks by torpedo-boats or submarines. Aircraft carriers of contemporary navies require a surrounding screen of vessels designed for battle against aircraft and submarines.

From Antiquity until the nineteenth century, two types of vessel formed the backbone of navies, depending on the particular geographical area – the galley, of Mediterranean origin, and the ocean-going sailing ship, which, however, made a late entrance on the scene. The galley's history was, in fact, a strange one. Its existence, in various forms, was immensely prolonged, and extended over nearly two millennia. In the Mediterranean, and in certain narrow seas, it was the dominant fighting ship throughout Antiquity and the Middle Ages, and its career came to an end only at the dawn of the modern era.

It was with the Phoenicians that the first galleys made their appearance. They were long and narrow, with oars as their primary means of propulsion, and were fitted with a projecting keel, strengthened at the bow end with sheets of bronze. With the Greeks, the success of this type of ship was confirmed. The ram was first used on the *pentekonteres* (a galley with 50 oarsmen, 25 on each side), before being employed as the major weapon of the bireme, which appeared in the seventh century BC, and of the trireme, whose origin dates from the middle of the following century; the latter proved to be a remarkable technical success, and was still found even in the time of the Roman Empire. The dimensions of the dockyard at Zea, in the Piraeus, show that an Athenian trireme of the fifth century BC must have measured about 125 feet long and 16 feet wide and had a draught of around 3 feet. The crew consisted of 170 oarsmen, 13 sailors whose task was to handle the sails, 7 officers and a dozen *epibatai* (soldiers forming a landing or boarding section).

In view of the lack of precision in the literary sources, the division of the oarsmen into three 'banks', supposedly one above the other, has been the subject of heated debate in the world of scholarship. The most convincing explanatory theory is that of the British historian Morrison, whose solution involves an *apostis*, or outer gallery for the third 'bank' of oarsmen.

Whatever may be the truth here, biremes and triremes were certainly designed solely with a view to making a ramming attack – a peculiarly difficult technique and, in addition, a hazardous one, which demanded an exceptional skill in manoeuvre, if only to prevent the would-be rammer from being rammed. Hence, it cannot be a matter for surprise that, in the Hellenistic period, this method of attack gave way to that of boarding, which might or might not be preceded by missiles from ballistic weapons. Even though the major part of the Macedonian and Ptolemaic navies still consisted of triremes, such a tactical trend undoubtedly contributed to the appearance of ships of large tonnage, even indeed gigantic vessels, with 6, 12 or even 20 or 30 'banks' of oarsmen. According to Athenaeus and Plutarch, the record seems to belong to a monster with two hulls – a kind of catamaran – which was constructed at the end of the third century BC, on the orders of Ptolemy IV. This *tessarakontores*, which was over 400 feet long, had 40 rows of oarsmen, that is, 4,000 men, without counting the 2,850 soldiers and 400 sailors. These enormous ships have been the subject of academic dispute. But, in fact, there can no longer be any question of supposing that it was the 'banks' of oarsmen that were increased in number. The only solution is to accept that there was a larger number of men to each oar. Apart from their improved seaworthiness, these large vessels could be equipped with a powerful armament based on ballistas and catapults. Hence, attack by ramming gave place to boarding of an enemy ship, preceded by missile fire.

During the Punic Wars, the Romans also employed boarding, using triremes or quadriremes modelled on those of the Syracusans. This system of attack was aided by a technical innovation named the *corvus*, a hinged gangway fitted with grappling irons, and intended for dropping on an enemy ship's deck, thus allowing an assault by a formed-up body of legionaries. As Polybius has pointed out, what one sees here is an assimilation to fighting on land, a situation in which the Roman soldier felt fully confident. But, contrary to a belief which dies hard, the use of such tactics in no way prevented the Romans from showing a considerable ability in manoeuvring their ships; indeed, the truth was quite the reverse.

The Roman Empire set itself against the pursuit of sheer size in its naval vessels, thus exemplifying a trend of thought that can be observed occurring on many occasions in subsequent history. At Actium, the victory of Agrippa's fleet was due principally to light ships with one or two 'banks' of oarsmen and capable of hurling incendiary missiles, while making a ramming attack. Thanks to their ease in manoeuvre, these small ships operating in packs outclassed the heavy vessels of Antonius and Cleopatra. During the five centuries of the *pax romana*, the imperial navy employed, with the exception of a few giant ships kept for prestige purposes, chiefly the light and fast 'Liburnians' which had one or two 'banks' of oarsmen. They were responsible for policing the seas, putting down piracy and guarding the vital lines of communication.

After the fall of the Empire in the West, and the reversion to an unremitting war at sea between Constantinople and the Arab world, it was the Byzantine *dromon* which seems to have provided a successful compromise between combat effectiveness and manoeuvrability. It was relatively light and rapid, with 50 oars on each side divided into two 'banks' one above the other. It was fitted with a ram above the water line. But the purpose of this ram was no longer to destroy the enemy ship, but to assist boarding, the attack being preceded by the shooting of missiles, and particularly by the use of a weapon that has been overdramatized. This was 'Greek Fire', forced through tubes, i.e. acting as flamethrowers, or placed in jars and thrown by catapult on to the decks of enemy ships.

From the twelfth century onwards, the galleys employed by Italian cities were descended from this type of ship. The only innovations of note were in the method of propulsion. When the *alla sensile* method of rowing was adopted, in the fourteenth century, three oarsmen using the same bench, which was set at an angle to the ship's side, pulled three separate oars. In the sixteenth century, this arrangement gave way to rowing *a scaloccio*, with several men, from 5 to 7 in number, pulling a single oar only. During the whole of the medieval period, the galley remained the principal fighting ship in the Mediterranean, the Black Sea and the Red Sea. It was exactly suited to the specific navigational conditions associated with the absence of regular tides, winds and currents. Also, quite apart from naval engagements as such, the galley lent itself admirably to combined operations, to the defence of ports or to attacks on them, as well as to the battle for the control of shipping routes.

Sea battles came more and more to resemble encounters on land, as can be seen from such examples as those of Preveza and Lepanto. The normal practice was for the two fleets to face each other in line, with one flank close to, and hence protected by, a coastline. The skill of admirals consisted in making a breakthrough in the centre, or an encircling movement round the enemy's seaward flank. Tactics differed little from those employed since Antiquity, even though ships' armament, from the middle of the fifteenth century, included three or five cannon, sited forwards for bow fire. Boarding – preceded by bombardment from these cannon, together with fire from small arms, such as bows, crossbows and arquebuses – was always the ultimate aim in a battle, which was then settled by hand-to-hand fighting. To make the assault easier, the ram was given up and replaced by a triangular platform.

At the close of the sixteenth century and at the outset of the seventeenth, the galley underwent – just when it was on the eve of its decline – its final stage of development. Increase in firepower found expression in an appreciable rise in the galley's tonnage and crew numbers. Normally, a vessel measured about 150 feet long, 18 feet wide and drew from 6 to 9 feet of water. It carried two lateen sails, which were extremely difficult to manage, and 25 pairs of oars pulled by 250 oarsmen. The complement also included 120 sailors for handling and steering the ship, and a boarding unit of 50 soldiers. Certain prestige vessels carried still more. At Lepanto, Don Juan's *Real* had 400 oarsmen and 400 men armed with the arquebus. In fact, ships became terribly encumbered. Every increase of 50 per cent in tonnage involved a rise of 100 per cent in crew numbers, and it was doubtful whether any advantage accrued. In return for a limited increase in their armament of cannon, galleys lost their traditional qualities of speed, lightness and manoeuvrability, and became heavy ships which handled poorly and had a small cruising range.

These points can be observed even more clearly in the case of the galleasses. Their motive power was supplied by oars, with sails only as an accessory, and they were equipped with cannon firing laterally, as well as with others pointing forward. At Lepanto, they acted in a defensive role, and contributed to the breaking up of the Ottoman galleys' attacks. But, in general use, these hybrid ships, which were heavy, had little maneouvrability and, lastly, could muster only a limited firepower, proved singularly disappointing. Like the galleys, they showed themselves ultimately unable to rival the ship of the line, which came into being in northern seas.

Nevertheless, the real fighting ship was extremely slow to make an appearance in northern fleets. Apart from the remarkable vessels used for their raids, the Vikings never possessed warships proper, and were ignorant of all naval tactics worthy of the name. The situation was almost exactly the same in the Middle Ages. During the conflicts in which the Hanseatic League was opposed to Denmark, or England to France, the battles were fought by what were nothing more than improvised ships adapted from cargo boats, broad-beamed vessels or 'cogghes' provisionally fitted for the occasion with two timber platforms raised above the prow and the poop. From the end of the fourteenth century, these superstructures became permanent features and an integral part of the hull; mounted on them were culverins, light breech-loading cannon of forged iron. A three-masted rig evolved, and they were thus the progenitors of the huge Portuguese carracks which were still in use in the Indian Ocean in the seventeenth century.

By that time, the ship of the line was the backbone of the major European fleets. It represented the conjuncture, or rather, the amalgamation of the galleon, an English type of merchant vessel, with carefully designed hull shape and graceful lines but shorn of the huge 'castles' of the carracks, and a modern armament comprising large muzzle-loading pieces in bronze or cast iron. In place of the astonishing collection of light guns with which the 'castles' had bristled, the armament was distributed along both sides of the ship, on two or three decks, and firing through ports. Following a general standardization, ships of the eighteenth century used 8-, 12-, 24- or 36-pounder pieces, the heaviest naturally being employed in the lowest tier of guns. Constructed between 1635 and 1638, the *Sovereign of the Seas* of 104 guns, copied in France with *La Couronne* of 70 guns, provided the prototype of this new type of vessel, which revealed its effectiveness in the first Anglo-Dutch War of 1652-4. Its success started a real arms race involving all the major countries.

Throughout the seventeenth century, the warship proved its superiority over galleys, even if the latter were operating in large numbers. In 1684, the 50-gun French ship *Le Bon*, commanded by Count de Relingue, crushed, during the course of a five-hour engagement, an attack by 35 Spanish galleys. In July 1702, however, the galley registered its final success, in the North Sea. Six of them, commanded by La Pailleterie, succeeded in the capture by boarding of the Dutch ship *La Licorne*. But this ultimate victory was due to exceptional circumstances. The Dutch ship had only a scratch crew, and was immobilized by a flat calm.

At the beginning of the century of the Enlightenment, in fact, the galley was no longer any match for the ship of the line, which handled well and whose firepower, in particular, was immeasurably superior. The galley still lingered on in existence for quite a long period, but as no more than an auxiliary vessel. Although they helped in Vivonne's victory before Palermo in 1676, their use resulted in an almost complete fiasco in the Channel during Tourville's foray of 1690. They were already outdated in the Mediterranean and when a number were moved to the Channel along the

Rhône, the Saône, the Burgundy canal and the Seine, they proved completely unable to cope with seas that were subject to tides, winds and violent currents. Apart from a few operations where seaborne landings were involved or in defence of coastline fortresses, galleys were soon used only for towing ships that were entering or leaving harbour, except when employed as a display vessel for transporting important personages. France abolished its galley units in 1748. Venice stubbornly held on to a few until the loss of her independence. In the Baltic, oared craft were retained for use within the numerous islands of the Finnish archipelago, but when the last battle with galleys took place in 1808 between the Russians and the Swedes, the event had all the appearance of an anachronism.

Until its disappearance in the middle of the nineteenth century, the ship of the line was continually being improved. Following a general trend, efforts were directed towards increasing its firepower, and hence, its tonnage, while also introducing better designs of hull or distribution of sail. On several occasions, both in France and in England, there were official regulations laying down a classification of ships by the number of their guns, which ranged from 50 to 100, or even 118 or 120. One of the most celebrated of the French three-deckers was the *États de Bourgogne*. Launched in 1780, this magnificent ship was still sailing in 1842, under the name of *Océan*, and had to be broken up only in 1855. Apart from these giants, of which Nelson's *Victory* is one of the most famous examples, major fleets showed a preference for ships of more modest proportions. At the end of the eighteenth century, the ships that were in most general use were the Spanish two-deckers of 70 guns and the French and British types of 74 and 80. The French ships designed by Sané were considered the most successful, while the British vessels, which were the first to have their hulls copper-sheathed, maintained their sailing qualities better in tropical waters.

Thanks to such a process of development, ships' armament also improved continuously. Their guns gained in accuracy and range, reaching about 500 yards, though they were really effective only at distances ten times less. Ships' sailing qualities also became better. Hulls were made longer and slimmer, with the beam being equal to about 30 per cent of the length overall. There was also a greater standardization in navies, through the reduction in the number of 'classes' or 'rankings' of ships, in the interests of securing roughly comparable speeds, so that, as La Luzerne emphasized, 'in whatever wind they are sailing, they can have more or less the same forward speed, the same broadside (i.e. the same firepower) and the capacity to wear the same amount of canvas'.

A fleet of 'one-off' ships constructed by master shipwrights – practical men working with hereditary know-how and by experience, based on secrets handed down in the family – gave place to small batches, whose design was laid down by higher authority, and which were produced by naval shipbuilding engineers (the Paris college was founded in 1750). In theory, these ships were 'standard'; in practice, it proved impossible to achieve line production of ships. On the other hand, the principle did operate in the manufacture of a certain number of components, such as blocks turned out by steam-powered machinery in the years 1770–90, or even more, of guns cast in solid bronze and bored by steam power, as is recorded to have been done at Indret. There was a considerable advance in the performance of these large sailing ships. In the middle of the eighteenth century, it was still unusual to speak of a vessel which was capable of maintaining for long a speed of more than 3–4 knots. Around 1790, that had become commonplace, and it was no longer abnormal to come across speeds of 9–10 knots being kept up for distances approaching 1,200 miles. Alongside this development, their carrying capacity in munitions, food and water – which was one of the weak points in seventeenth-century ships – rose to a level where they could be self-sufficient for 5–6 months (except, obviously, for water), thus making the most distant seas of the world accessible to whole squadrons and putting all the oceans henceforth within reach of European might. Defoe already foresaw this at the beginning of the eighteenth century in the second part of *Robinson Crusoe*.

These ships were, however, very fragile. The hull, being of a living substance like wood, was liable to warp and ships – particularly frigates, which were designed for high speeds – became 'hogged', and showed a partial loss of performance. The wood used, particularly in wartime when the construction rate was highest, was often of very poor quality. A ship was normally expected to last for about fifteen years. In fact, losses in battle and by shipwreck, and still more, the large number of ships that were completely defective, meant that those which had proved themselves to be 'good sailers' were kept going as long as possible. Occasionally, they reached ages of 40 or 50; but it could be questioned whether they were still the same ships. Repairs were followed by remodelling, and remodelling by reconstruction. The results showed up in financial terms. If one takes the cost of a 50-gun ship, around 1789–90, as £100,000, between five and ten times more, depending on the durability and quality of the vessel, was needed for its maintenance. Politicians, who looked at the initial construction cost only, failed to understand this point, as can be seen in Choiseul's case.

In the eighteenth and early nineteenth centuries, fighting ships were divided into three main categories:

1 Ships of the line, intended for major battles.
2 Frigates, fast-sailing, chiefly meant at the outset for scouting and communication at a distance, but – thanks to their increasingly heavy armament – becoming suited to a real operational role.
3 Corvettes and similar types of vessel (e.g. xebecs in the Mediterranean) which were lighter and intended for coastal convoys and related tasks.

Here can be seen a general trend towards the change in thinking about 'power' in ships. Two decked vessels of 50 and 64 guns were dropped, and replaced by fast, yet still heavily gunned, single-decked frigates like the *Constellation* and *Constitution*, which are carefully preserved in the United States

and still provide good examples of the type. As a backing to this powerful nucleus there was a host of naval 'small fry' – brigs and sloops, launches, gunboats (though fire-ships became rarer) – and also a large-sized service and maintenance fleet, including store ships (with special ones for masts), old ships of the line more or less completely disarmed so as to be used as troop transports or, with upper decks removed, as harbour pontoons, lighters and coasting luggers, cargo boats, etc. Thus, the French fleet of 1790 consisted of 241 vessels in service, classified as follows: 70 ships of the line (2 of 118 guns, 5 of 110, 8 of 80, 54 of 74 and 1 of 64); 65 frigates (15 of 18 guns and 50 of 12); 19 corvettes (8 of 8 guns and 11 of 6); 29 brigs and sloops of 6 or 4 guns; 7 gunboats of 24 or 18 guns; 12 transports and 19 lighters – both unarmed – of 100 to 400 tons. To these should be added another 20 ships of the line and 16 frigates which were under construction.

The Royal Navy, which was much stronger, put the accent on the numerical superiority of its ships of the line, though it did not fail to include a support group of increasingly heavily armed frigates. At a time when, in the three major opposing navies (of Britain, France and Spain), the big ships represented 30–33 per cent of the total number, the other sizeable navies (of Russia, Denmark, Holland and Sweden) cut down the small craft. Navies of the third rank (of which that of the Two Sicilies was, until 1860, one of the most modern) had several heavy ships and some fast vessels intended for the battle against piracy.

Alongside these standing navies were fleets that could be considered ancillary, the main ones being those of the three major East India companies. Their ships, which were armed as a matter of necessity, were often designed as a compromise between a warship and a merchant vessel, and hence frequently combined the disadvantages of both. The spectacular shipwreck of the Spanish *San Pedro* (64 guns) in 1785 on the coast of Spain with a cargo of Peruvian silver, gold and copper, worth considerably more than 10 million French livres, illustrated the danger of this type of compromise. The *Compagnie des Indes*, after having bought their ships first from Hamburg in the 1720s, and then from London, finally relied upon their own yards. At the time of the Seven Years' War, the *Contrôle Générale* instructed the company to adopt the 64-gun ship as their standard and, when their business was wound up, any examples of that type were absorbed into the navy. The obligation to build a fleet of warships was the main reason for the failure of the French company. The British company, by adopting from the East such materials as teak and some native methods of construction (i.e. straighter sides) showed itself capable of innovation, thanks to the naval architect Chapman, who later served in the Swedish navy.

Changes involve constant recourse to development in new directions. As the pre-eminently technical arm of the fighting services, a navy provides encouragement to technical research, and gives rise to inventions and innovations, though these, in their turn, sometimes run counter to views that are obstinate mental fixtures. For this reason, the major fleets constituted, before the era of the Industrial Revolution, one of the areas where the period showed its greatest dynamism, and which was in the forefront of progress, whether one looks at the methods employed or the personnel engaged in the work.

From the time of Louis XIV, all work in connection with ships necessarily had a mathematical basis. The French hulls of the eighteenth century were so much admired and copied that the 'working drawings' which are currently the best preserved are to be found either at Greenwich or Copenhagen. The race between France and England to develop chronometers, with the aim of being able to calculate longitude, provided one of the forces motivating the application of scientific research and of advances in craftmanship. The major navies compiled vast collections of maps, of which the French cartographies of the seventeenth century represent one of the most famous examples. Sails – a sphere in which the British and the buccaneers excelled – were, on the other hand, a matter for individual initiative, based on experience of the behaviour of the 'old ladies', that is, the

ships. Every captain had, more or less, his own rig. Naval guns, which were very heavy, constituted – together with anchors, a subject that posed difficult problems – one of the incentives both to scientific experiment and to metallurgical development.

Because ships and their equipment were highly susceptible to wear and tear, the fleets needed constant maintenance, as well as the products of an increasingly developed technology. For example, the sheathing of wooden hulls entailed the use of sheet copper, which England alone manufactured. Enormous quantities of timber were required. The masts were imported from Scandinavia, or, more exactly, from the market in Riga, where rigorous management guaranteed a constant level of quality; the same was true of flax and especially hemp. Oak came from all round the Baltic (from such ports as Lübeck, Rostock, Stettin and Dantzig). But the supply of large size timber from Polish forests became exhausted. If the average size of French ships in the decade 1780–90 was set at 80 guns, it was because French forests could supply suitable material in reasonable quantities only for that size and below. In wartime, however, there was no option but to fall back on whatever supplies might be available locally, even if of inferior quality. An example of such material is provided by the masts of pine which came from the Pyrenees; they tended to fracture because after a year their resin dried out. Corsican pine was more highly regarded. In Britain, experiments were made with fir and larch for masts, as well as timber from North America, but for hulls only teak reached the standard of British oak. These deficiencies could be overcome by accumulating stocks, provided that finance was available. Forests near naval ports were reserved for use in periods of war. But the open market was dominated by British buyers, who carried out what amounted, in fact, to a blockade, by sweeping the board of huge quantities of best quality timber.

A warship therefore represented an extremely complex compromise between, among other things, the constraints imposed by the need to be an efficient fighting unit, the current stage of scientific and technical advance, construction and maintenance costs and the availability of raw material and finished products, this last factor itself involving the options of self-sufficiency or dependence on world markets. A warship was still based, nevertheless, at the end of the eighteenth century, on the combination of wooden hull – sail as the motive element – and crew of men; in theory, there had been no change of system. But, beneath the outward appearance, there had silently taken place an enormous advance – one that was even more marked in design than in constructional techniques. An 80-gun ship exemplified a huge improvement over a vessel of the mid-seventeenth century. This change had occurred as the result of a host of minor innovations, often too small to be noticed.

In the middle of the nineteenth century, the ship of the line reached its acme, and major fleets did not resist the temptation to opt for vast size and to build huge three-deckers of 4,000 tons, like the French 120-gun *Valmy*. But this trend was then on the eve of a re-examination, enforced by the appearance of steam power and the explosive shell. Experiments carried out on the *Triomphant* in 1817, and the overcoming of the forts of St Jean d'Ulloa by Baudin's squadron in 1838, underlined the destructive effects of explosive shells on hulls and walls.

The Crimean War, which was the first major conflict of the industrial era, removed any final doubts. On 30 November 1853, the Russian Black Sea fleet destroyed seven Ottoman frigates in the roads of Sinope and, on 17 October 1854, the Franco-British squadron suffered severe damage during the attack on Sebastopol. Wooden ships did not stand up to the new projectiles, and some form of protection became essential, as also did steam propulsion. Hence, directly after that war, in 1856, the ship of the line, after its two centuries of existence, made way for the 'ironclad', of which the first examples were frigates – the French *Gloire* and the British *Warrior* and *Black Prince*. The superiority of the new type of ship was decisively established by three features – propulsion

by steam-driven propeller, an armament of rifled guns firing explosive shells and a protective belt of armour round the vital parts. During the years that followed, a constant increase in ships' tonnage resulted from the battle for supremacy between guns and armour. The growing weight of guns, on account of the huge increases in calibre, together with the need to protect those who operated them, meant a limitation in their numbers and an end to positioning them along a ship's sides. There was a changeover to the system of putting guns in casemates or redoubts, and later in turrets, when it became essential to give the heavy armament a wide arc of fire, a possibility which had been opened up by the complete disappearance of masts.

Around 1890, the design of the armoured ship seemed to have settled down to a standard form. Its displacement was 15,000 tons and its speed 15 knots. Owing to the use of nickel steel, which provided a favourable ratio of resistance to thickness, the armour consisted of a belt right round the sides, together with an armoured deck which ensured the protection of the engines and the magazines. The bridge and the gun turrets also had a strong protection. With the development in metallurgy and the introduction of slow-burning propellants, it proved possible to produce lighter, if longer, guns and still have an armament with long range and high initial velocity. The main armament consisted of four 12-inch guns in two turrets, firing armour-piercing shells, and 10–12 6-inch guns using projectiles of high explosive capacity.

Also carried were light, quick-firing guns, intended for dealing with torpedo-boats. In fact, the armoured ship of the end of the nineteenth century took its place, under the name of 'battleship', in a new ranking order, which also contained fast, well-armed, lightly protected 'cruisers' of 4,000–10,000 tons, designed for scouting duties with squadrons, for the battle against commerce-raiders and for the protection of convoys, and 'torpedo-boats' and 'torpedo-boat destroyers'. During the last quarter of the century, the torpedo-boat of 100–200 tons enjoyed a quite extraordinary vogue among a certain number of nations, such as

Russia, the Scandinavian countries and, particularly, France, where it served as the origin of the theories of the 'Jeune École'.

The successful self-propelled torpedo was introduced by the British engineer Whitehead in 1876, and its performance was rapidly improved subsequently. Making use of this weapon, the torpedo-boat showed itself to be the deadly enemy of the battleship, when it could operate under cover of darkness and near coastlines, particularly in connection with blockade operations. The 'poisoned device', 'the steel spindle' as it was sometimes called, seemed to spell the doom of the giant ship. In actual fact, the threat to the battleship was countered by giving it a defensive equipment, which included searchlights, rapid-firing cannon and steel nets. It was also protected by destroyers (i.e. anti-torpedo-boats) of 800–1,000 tons, armed with light guns and torpedoes as well.

All navies went on building torpedo-boats or destroyers up to the period immediately after the Second World War. The race for extra tonnage affected them too. In 1939, a torpedo-boat had a displacement of 1,500 tons, and some destroyers were just touching 3,000. Their use of the torpedo became more and more unusual. Destroyers became the jack-of-all-trades of navies, and were given mainly such duties as the protection of squadrons or convoys against enemy aircraft or submarines.

Meanwhile, the battleship reached its definitive form in the shape of the British *Dreadnought* in 1906. On the eve of the First World War, however, there was a fresh impetus, maximum tonnages increasing from 17,000 to 24,000. With the adoption of systems of centralized fire direction, the main armament was restricted to a single calibre within the range 11–15 inch, depending on the ship concerned. The main task of the secondary armament, with guns of 3–6 inches, was to break up attacks by torpedo-boats. The Royal Navy and the German navy made use of the battle-cruiser, which had the same armament and tonnage as the battleship, but a lesser amount of protective armour to allow a higher speed, which made the type very

suitable for the role of scouting and for sinking light cruisers or battleships.

Between the two world wars, the ship of the line underwent no fundamental change, or rather, what happened was an amalgamation of the battleship and the battle-cruiser. Areas of progress were the improvement in fire control, with the adoption of remote operation, and the strengthening of armour and armament against enemy aircraft and submarines. Ship performance was increased, with speeds of the order of 30 knots in place of the 22 of the battleships of 1914, but progress also meant larger tonnages, which ranged from 35,000 to 45,000 tons, and higher cost. Major navies, therefore, contented themselves with short runs of sister ships, or one-off super-battleships like the German *Bismarck*, the American *New Jersey* or the Japanese *Yamato*.

Just at the moment when the battleship reached a remarkable peak of perfection, it found itself reduced to the position of an auxiliary, albeit a highly valuable one, of the aircraft carrier, to which it could give the backing of a considerably intensified anti-aircraft armament, not to mention support fire during amphibious operations. Indeed, from the outset, the Second World War showed the huge offensive power that the aircraft equipped with armour-piercing bombs or torpedoes could bring to bear against the surface ship. But, given the speed and turning capacity of ships and the relatively small target that they presented, these weapons achieved full effectiveness only when used by fast, manoeuvrable and compact single-engined aircraft operating as dive-bombers or attacking at wave height. Such aircraft's small flight radius limited their employment over water, except in the case of narrow and enclosed seas. Mobile take-off platforms were needed for use as bases for operations, maintenance and re-fuelling – in a word, aircraft carriers. From 1941–2, this type of vessel became the capital ship of modern navies, with the American *Essex* type of 27,000 tons or the *Independence* type of 14,000 tons being able to put into the air 50–100 aircraft.

Aircraft carriers represent the apex of a new ranking order. Within the framework of task-forces, and in conjunction with a fleet train of repair and supply vessels, they are provided with an entourage of fast battleships, cruisers and destroyers, whose task is to ensure their protection against surface craft, aircraft and, in particular, submarines. Since the Second World War, in fact, navies have had increasingly to take account of the submarine, which provides the opportunity for the torpedo to be used with maximum effectiveness. In the course of the two world wars, this craft has proved itself to be a remarkable instrument in the attack on merchant shipping and a deadly weapon in battle.

However, until the beginning of the 1950s, the submarine suffered from a congenital weakness and deserved, in actual fact, the name of 'submersible' only. Certainly, it had the invaluable capacity of being able to slip away into hiding in the depths of the sea; but, since it remained dependent on two methods of propulsion, diesel on the surface, electric motors submerged, its movements when submerged, which were bound up with the capacity of the batteries, were extremely limited and deprived it of the major part of its offensive power. To counteract this weakness, Admiral Dönitz initiated, during the Second World War, the system of the night attack by a submarine 'pack' on the surface. The submarine thus became a torpedo-boat which was fast and difficult to see. Despite the introduction in Germany, in 1944, of high-performance craft, equipped with the *schnorkel*, it was not until 1955, and the entry into service of the American *Nautilus* powered by nuclear reactor, that the submarine in the full sense at last made its appearance.

The advent of the single-engine submarine was in line with the fresh change which navies underwent after 1945. The key factors in this change were nuclear energy, missiles and electronics. In the range of options that are open at present, the heavy aircraft carrier equipped with catapults still constitutes the capital ship of surface fleets. Large vessels of 90,000 tons, like the *Nimitz*, *Eisenhower*, *Vinson* and *Enterprise* display an exceptional capacity. They have on board about 100 aircraft like the Tomcat fighter, the Hornet and Phantom bombers,

the Hawkeye reconnaissance and lookout machine, the Prowler electronic warfare aircraft or Sea King helicopter. These aircraft carriers can play a part in wars of limited scope or, on the other hand, direct deep into enemy territory bombers carrying missiles with nuclear warheads or atomic bombs, all within the context of the extreme complexities of electronic warfare. These ships cannot, however, rely entirely for their protection on the aircraft which they carry. They require at all times an entourage of support vessels, such as cruisers, destroyers and frigates, to match a whole range of threats which did not fail to appear as the aircraft carrier's power increased. Aircraft still remain, as the Falklands Campaign (1982) demonstrated, one of the most dangerous enemies of the surface ship. They can attack flying at sea level, or by means of homing missiles, whether or not fitted with nuclear warheads, and the types of aircraft that deliver them may be light machines, of the Étendard type, or heavy bombers like the Backfire, with a wide radius of action.

Since the spectacular sinking of the Israeli destroyer *Eliath* by a Russian-made Styx missile launched from an ordinary MTB, the majority of surface ships have been equipped with similar surface-to-surface weapons. There is a very wide range – the Swedish Saab, the American Harpoon, the French Exocet, etc. Self-guided, i.e. equipped with positive self-steering, they give a range of 25–180 miles, provided that they can lock on to a beam pinpointing their target. The American cruise missile Tomahawk, originally designed for attacking ground targets, is equally suitable for use against naval ones.

But the most serious threat comes from the submarine. Though examples of the conventional type with diesel/electric propulsion are still built, it remains true that they cannot compare with the nuclear-powered submarine. The latter is under no compulsion ever to use the surface. It has a high speed which is often greater than that of the general run of surface vessels, and a radius of action which, for practical purposes, is limited only by its crew's endurance. Large navies of today maintain two types of these nuclear-powered craft. Missile-launching nuclear submarines form, on account of their ability to move unobserved, the major weapon of the forces of deterrence. The most recent American examples – those of the *Ohio* type – have a displacement, when fully submerged, of over 18,700 tons, and can launch 16–24 missiles with a range of 4,000 nautical miles, and with an accuracy on target of the order of 500 yards. Each missile is also fitted with 8–14 warheads, all capable of independent, guided trajectories. Hence, a single submarine lurking in the depths of the Indian Ocean can hold the threat of 128–336 nuclear warheads over its enemy. The second category comprises nuclear submarines intended for attacks on ships. Of smaller tonnage than nuclear missile-launching submarines, they can attain speeds of over 40 knots and dive to depths of more than 250 fathoms. They are equipped with a formidable armament, consisting of both wire-guided or homing torpedoes and underwater-to-surface missiles of the Sub Harpoon or Exocet SM39 type. With a range of 35 miles, three times greater than that of torpedoes, and covering the distance in 3 minutes rather than 20, these devices increase considerably the variety of the submarine's modes of attack, and provide it with a weapon whose performance equals that of its sound-monitoring equipment.

It is hardly necessary to emphasize that this latter type of submarine provides opportunities in attack that belong to a different world from that of its predecessor. They are rivals of the missile-launching nuclear submarine, and have some advantages over it, since – in the case of the latter – continual efforts need to be made to improve the accuracy and range of its missiles, thereby increasing the volume of research work. They are naturally suitable for attacks on ships at sea. With their missiles, they can engage large ships at distances of 35–45 miles, or even 330 miles, if they can lock on to a beam pinpointing their target. Attacks on vital shipping routes always form one of their basic tasks; and to this classic role can now be added the entirely new one of attacks on targets sited inland, by means of underwater-to-surface or, alternatively, cruise missiles.

The increasing size of the missile threat explains the interest shown in intelligence gathered by observation satellites, by radio interception, and by the use of radar aircraft on long-range watch or of nuclear-powered attack submarines carrying out passive monitoring in liaison with surface vessels. At the same time, there has been continual improvement in the whole range of defensive missiles. For the battle against heavy bombers, the Americans have the SM1 or SM2MR, with a range of 90 miles and an altitude of 13 miles.

The most critical aspect of naval warfare today remains the battle against the submarine. Despite the improvement in sonar, the use of underwater-to-surface missiles and of helicopters employing submerged sound-detection equipment or homing torpedoes, the struggle is still finely balanced. The US navy approaches the problem on a strategic level, with surveillance being carried on across the world's oceans through networks of hydrophones, whether stationary and laid in channels through which submarines have to pass, e.g. on the GIUK line (i.e. Greenland–Iceland–United Kingdom), or towed by ships.

This battle against missiles introduced, in fact, an entirely new factor into warfare at sea. A major necessity is still to seek and destroy the missile-bearer, whether ship, aircraft carrier or submarine. But to this traditional aspect has now been added another which is, frankly, revolutionary. Although in the past there was never any question of destroying the bullet, shell or torpedo, new weapons systems, based on short-range missiles or multiple-barrel quick-firing cannon, such as the American Vulcan-Phalanx, aim at knocking out the missile itself.

The variety of weapons systems, the wealth of incoming intelligence and the extremely rapid manner in which situations can develop, necessitate a highly developed integration of all data, and involve equipment like the French Senit or the American NTDS, which provides round the clock an overall view of the tactical situation, and indicates the appropriate measures for warding off a threat. On a higher level, the American JITDS (Joint Integrated Tactical Data System) incorporates all the tactical information in a comprehensive view, which also takes in the data arising from action carried out by the air and land forces. In line with this approach, naval operations are now envisaged as taking place only within the context of a complex array of electronic counter-measures designed to jam enemy signals traffic, radar or missile guidance systems. Operations by aircraft carrying out attacks deep into enemy territory would be preceded, and accompanied, by counter-measures put out by specially equipped aircraft, such as the American naval air arm's Intruder, Prowler and Hawkeye.

Factors like these serve to underline another aspect of modern navies which imposes limits on development, both in terms of quantity and quality, and that is their cost and complexity. In contradistinction to what was seen in 1914, in 1939, and even as late as 1950, navies are no longer all of the same pattern. For example, the US navy alone is in a position to have a string of heavy aircraft carriers equipped with catapults and which can put into the air a full range of combat aircraft. Although seeking to emulate the Americans, the Russian navy cannot yet compare in naval air power. While awaiting its first aircraft carrier proper, which is in process of completion, the Russian navy contents itself for the moment with smaller types from which only helicopters or aircraft of the Forger type with their short take-off can operate.

For technical and, above all, financial reasons, the majority of secondary navies do not seek to have more than the simpler type of aircraft carrier. Since taking out of commission, in 1979, its last large aircraft carrier, the *Ark Royal*, the Royal Navy relies on three ships of the *Invincible* class, whose Sea Harriers proved their effectiveness in the Falklands. These are of moderate tonnage (16,000 t) and have a straight deck, with 'ski-jump' but without angled take-off/landing or catapults. Spain is preparing to equip herself with a ship of this class in the shape of the *Canarias*. The French navy alone of these secondary navies retains in service two full-sized aircraft carriers, whose replacement by nuclear-powered types is planned for the end of the twentieth century.

In the sphere of nuclear submarines, it is only a few navies that are in a position to have in service the most advanced types. Five powers, the United States, Russia, Great Britain, France and China possess missile-launching nuclear-powered submarines, though naturally in very differing numbers. The same is true of nuclear-powered submarines of the attack type. The first two of the navies just mentioned have several dozen nuclear-powered submarines while the Royal Navy possesses thirteen, France two only, since she did not begin to build vessels of this class until very recently, and China one.

Developed from the landing ships of 1939–45, the USS *Saipan* (LHA-2) is one of five *Tarawa*-class amphibious assault ships, specially designed to support combined operations by the US Rapid Deployment Force. It has a displacement of 39,300 tons and a maximum speed of 24 knots. It can carry and deploy c.30 helicopters or STOL and VTOL aircraft, has storage for 200 vehicles and accommodation for 2,000 troops and 900 crew. Tank and infantry landing craft and amphibious vehicles sail directly from its two docking wells.
(Beken of Cowes)

In sum, the US navy alone has currently in service a complete range of all the combat vessels, and one that provides, in each category, the highest level of striking power and effectiveness. Thus, it has 127 nuclear-powered submarines, 37 of the missile-launching and 90 of the attack type; 14 heavy aircraft carriers (of which 4 are nuclear-powered); 4 *Iowa* class 45,000 ton battleships, which have been updated and equipped with a complete armament of missiles; 31 missile-launching cruisers and 135 anti-submarine vessels. These ships total 2.5 million tons, and to them must be added the further 1.5 million tons of a fleet designed for use in combined operations and for logistic back-up.

Despite its relatively recent origins, the Russian navy can stand comparison today with the American, even though it is not a replica of it and some of its ships are of a novel kind. It has in service 2.5 million tons of combat ships and 500,000 tons of logistic back-up vessels.

Two big groups make up the dominating features of this navy, and the outline of a third is beginning to take shape. In the first place, Russia possesses the world's leading submarine fleet, numbering more than 380. It is true that 100 of these are old, with conventional systems of propulsion and only a limited operational range. But the fleet includes also 66 nuclear-powered missile-launching submarines and 125 nuclear-powered attack submarines. In number, it exceeds that of the United States. The second group consists of about 100 large surface ships, which can carry out a wide variety of tasks and are equipped with a range of surface-to-surface missiles; the latest of these give a range of 330 miles and have beam guidance systems. There is an extremely complete defensive armament also, designed to deal with the air and submarine threat. Notable among the most advanced ships are the cruisers *Kresta II*, *Krivak* and *Kara*, and also the nuclear-powered 23,000 ton *Kirov*.

Light aircraft carriers have long been given low priority, and those in service are still limited to the *Moskva* and *Leningrad*, which carry helicopters, and to four 'large anti-submarine cruisers' of the *Kiev* class. In line with Soviet naval thinking during the 1970s, they are hybrid or, rather, dual-purpose ships, furnished with an almost complete range of weapons. Apart from surface-to-surface and sea-to-air missiles, they have helicopters and about a dozen short take-off aircraft. These ships are, therefore, flexible in use, well suited to the battle against surface ships and submarines, and able to ensure air cover over a relatively restricted area. They are, on the other hand, not suited to delivering air attacks at a distance. Consequently, the Russian navy is turning to the construction of genuine aircraft carriers, copied from American models, which possess both offensive and defensive capabilities.

Europe's decline as a power has meant that its navies could not escape curtailment, and they can no longer stand comparison with those of the United States or Russia. In 1914, the fleets of Great Britain, Germany, France, the Scandinavian countries, Italy and Spain represented three-quarters of the world's tonnage of fighting ships. In 1939, the figure was still 60 per cent. Today, it is only 15 per cent. But, because of its inventive genius and high industrial standard, Europe remains able to design and manufacture top quality war equipment, which is often in the vanguard of technical progress.

It remains true, nevertheless, that Western navies experience increasing difficulty over keeping in service fleets of a size commensurate with the extent of their vital interests. Many countries are now content with fleets of restricted size, and smaller than their economic potential would warrant, but which are adequate for subsidiary tasks, within the context of the defence of the sea approaches to Western Europe. This would be the position of the northern countries' fleets, which would operate in the North Sea or the Baltic, and the Italian and Spanish ones which would do the same in the Mediterranean. Despite the reduced size of these fleets, they would nevertheless constitute, if occasion arose, a worthwhile supplement to the US navy.

Two countries do, however, possess appreciable fleets, even if they cannot today aspire to anything more than secondary roles. They are Great Britain and France, which maintain navies that have comparable features and are in the forefront of technical progress. They both have a force of light aircraft carriers, which would be useful in such eventualities as anti-submarine warfare or a requirement to participate in an overseas operation. Both countries have built up a deterrent force, based on nuclear-powered missile-launching submarines, and they have also other submarines of the nuclear-powered attack type. They maintain, in addition, a surface fleet, made up of destroyers, frigates and corvettes, all armed with missiles. Great Britain has, too, an excellent auxiliary force for logistic back-up, which allows its navy to operate anywhere in the world.

In the Far East, the situation of Japan is comparable with that of many European navies. Within the framework of a policy of 'self-defence' and of the protection of vital lines of communication, the Japanese government has made important strides in rearmament, based on ships capable of operating well outside home waters – frigates, corvettes and submarines – while not neglecting to build up a naval air force. The collective tonnage of this navy is currently 200,000 tons, i.e. similar to that of France. As far as its employment and equipment are concerned, however, this fleet forms merely an adjunct to the US navy.

Lastly, there is a further factor in the world situation which is produced by the rejuvenation of the navies of the major Latin-American countries and of India, and by the proliferation of small fleets. Certain countries, such as Indonesia, Iraq, Saudi Arabia, Libya and Algeria are showing themselves to have large-scale ambitions in this field. This policy on their part is assisted by the appearance of a new generation of fighting ships, which have a high offensive capacity, coupled with limited tonnage and a relatively modest cost. Among these are numbered high-performance conventional submarines and, in particular, light vessels, such as patrol boats, corvettes and MTBs, equipped with surface-to-surface missiles and helicopters and capable of posing a threat to major fighting ships in coastal waters or enclosed seas.

This development springs from the progressive independence of such countries, the growth in the number of areas that are subjects of dispute, and the appropriation of large areas of the world's seas against the background of a new attitude to 'territorial waters'. In certain sensitive areas, like the Mediterranean or the Persian Gulf, the build-up of these fleets constitutes a disturbing and destabilizing influence, whether viewed in the light of a possible North–South confrontation, or as a factor in East–West opposition. *See also* BASES, NAVAL; BLOCKADES; COMMERCE-RAIDING; CONVOYS; DOCKYARDS; DÖNITZ; NAVAL WARFARE.

P. MASSON

FURTHER READING
H. Ahrweiler, *Byzance et la mer. La marine de guerre, la politique, et les institutions maritimes de Byzance aux VIIe–XVe siècles* (Paris, 1966); S. Breyer, *Battleships and Battlecruisers, 1905–1970* (London, 1973); Donald Macintyre, *Aircraft Carrier* (London, 1968); Donald Macintyre and Basil Bathe, *The Man-of-War* (London, 1968); J. Rougé, *La Marine dans l'Antiquité* (Paris, 1975).

Nelson, Horatio, 1st Viscount, Duke of Brontë (1758–1805) Nelson joined the Royal Navy at the age of twelve, and came into prominence from the beginning of the wars of 1793–1815. He distinguished himself at the Siege of Calvi in Corsica, where he lost an eye, and in 1795 he captured the *Ça Ira*. At the Battle of St Vincent (14 February 1797) his initiative in turning to prevent two parts of the Spanish force joining contributed greatly to the success. He lost his right arm in 1798 in an attack on Tenerife. By now a Rear-Admiral, he was sent in pursuit of the French expedition to Egypt, and caught up with Brueys' fleet and destroyed it in a daring night attack (Battle of the Nile, 1 August 1798). His reputation stood very high, as this was the first great victory of the European coalition; after it, the King of Naples made Nelson Duke of Brontë, and this was also where his romantic adventure with Lady Hamilton began.

In 1801, by virtue of a famous act of disobedience, Nelson played a crucial role in the defeat of the Danish fleet at Copenhagen (2 April 1801) and broke up the Armed Neutrality. It was, however, in the campaign of 1805 that he demonstrated his prowess to the full. He first pursued Villeneuve's fleet from Toulon to the West Indies and back, before blockading it at Cadiz and destroying it at Trafalgar (21 October 1805), where he met his death.

Britain then provided a magnificent funeral for the man she already considered, quite rightly, as her greatest sailor. Nelson, who had remarkable command of strategy, was also an astute tactician. He managed to free himself totally from the formalism of the eighteenth century and fight battles of destruction. The 'Trafalgar memorandum', with its prescription for attack in two columns, remains a model of its kind. Nelson also showed a tremendous feeling for the importance of friendship and comradeship. He managed to create remarkable harmony among his captains, the so-called 'band of brothers'. His campaigns were to play a major role in the formation of Mahan's ideas at the end of the nineteenth century. *See also* GREAT BRITAIN; MAHAN; NAVAL WARFARE; NAVIES; TRAFALGAR.

P. MASSON

FURTHER READING
Carola Oman, *Nelson* (London, 1947).

Netherlands, The   At different times, the armed forces of the Netherlands have been known as those of the States-General, of the Batavian Republic (1795–1806), of the Kingdom of Holland (1806–10) and of the Netherlands (since 1813). Despite this, there has been continuity in Dutch military development due to the defensive role which the army has played (except for its participation in Napoleon's career of conquest) and to the restriction of naval activities to the protection of colonies and seaborne commerce.

In 1568, the seventeen provinces of the Spanish Netherlands began a series of revolts against the overlordship of Philip II of Spain. Under the leadership of William 'the Silent' of Nassau, Prince of Orange, the seven northern provinces finally revoked Spanish authority by forming the Union of Utrecht in 1579. The Seven or United Provinces, also known as the Dutch Republic, adopted the old Spanish forms of government and military organization, including the office of *stadhouder*. The *stadhouders* had been the royal governors of the provinces but under the Dutch Republic they became responsible for each province's armed forces. Five or six of the provincial *stadhouderates* were usually concentrated in the hands of the reigning Prince of Orange. William the Silent began to organize the Dutch armed forces, a task which his son, Maurice of Nassau, continued after his father's assassination in 1584. The States-General of the United Provinces, the representative assembly, attempted to discover another 'lord' to replace the King of Spain but after the Duke of Anjou, the Earl of Leicester and Elizabeth I of England had proved inadequate or unavailable, the States-General assumed the government after 1588. The commander of the armies of the States-General was the Captain-General, a post usually occupied by the ruling Prince of Orange although his authority was severely circumscribed by the presence in the field of representatives of the States-General, the 'field deputies'. Responsiblity for creating a military navy lay with the rich coastal provinces of Holland and Zeeland in the person of the Grand Pensionary of Holland.

Between 1590 and 1609, the United Provinces were a testing ground for a new version of the military art, to which the title of the 'Nassau Doctrine' might be given. In the face of the invincible Spanish *tercio*, the 10,000 regular soldiers which had been raised by the States-General to replace the city militias and the guerilla bands, could not hold their own on the open plains of Brabant. On the other hand, in Holland and Zeeland the incursions of the sea and the numerous peat bogs created a marshy terrain on which the *tercio* could not adopt its normal formation. The small amounts of firm ground could be literally packed with Dutch troops thus negating the Spanish army's advantage of superior numbers. Maurice of Nassau and his advisers realized that the most useful method was to split the Dutch forces into smaller and more mobile units in order to hold the towns and the dykes. The 'Nassau Doctrine' was indebted to the high level of scientific and cultural endeavour within the United Provinces, to a reading of Roman military writers, to the contribution of Italian engineers who provided the foundations of a Dutch school of fortification which employed expanses of water to defend the approaches to fortresses, but, above all, to the adaption of tactics to suit the terrain.

In the first decade of the seventeenth century, the Netherlands played a major part in the development of military science in Europe. Indeed, since there was a cessation of warfare elsewhere, the war between Spain and the United Provinces attracted numerous mercenaries and visitors. As the campaigns involved only limited movement within a confined theatre, gentlemen who had come from all over Europe were able to observe operations from the numerous towns, few restrictions being placed upon them. Dutch leadership in printing allowed reflections on the experiences of war to be circulated widely. This helps to explain the fame of Jacob de Gheyn's engravings, first published in 1607 and frequently reproduced in military manuals, and also the influence which the 'Nassau Doctrine' exerted upon the military academy at Sedan, founded in 1609 by the Duke de Bouillon, Maurice of Nassau's brother-in-law, on the *Kriegs und Ritterschule* at Siegen, established in 1617 by John VII of Nassau, as well as on Gustavus Adolphus, Wallenstein, Turenne and even Montecucoli. Subsequently, when involved in the Thirty Years' War (1618–48) and the wars of Louis XIV, the United Provinces played a lesser part in military innovation. Coehoorn (1641–1704), the engineer and expert on fortifications, was the only Dutch soldier of the later seventeenth century to achieve European renown.

The Dutch navy was no less important. Some evidence suggests that it probably originated during the fifteenth century. Maximilian of Austria's ordinance of 1480 deals with an organization which had been, since about 1450, under the command of an admiral. The town of Veere on the island of Walcheren was used as the naval base.

Other historians have traced the origins of the Dutch navy to the beginning of the Eighty Years' War against Spain (1567–1648) when the 'Sea Beggars' were conducting their privateering campaign against Spanish shipping. This ill-disciplined band of irregulars caused William the Silent a great deal of trouble but was indispensable. With the establishment of the Dutch Republic, a more sophisticated organization was set up in 1597. The *stadhouder* of Holland was the admiral-in-chief. In the event of there being no *stadhouder*, the function was exercised *de jure* by the States-General and *de facto* by the Grand Pensionary of Holland. This explains the great and beneficial influence which Johann de Witt (1625–72) exercised on the navy during his tenure of the latter office.

The administration of the navy was in the hands of five naval headquarters (admiralties) – Zeeland (at Middelburg), the Maas (at Rotterdam), Holland (alternatively at Hoorn and Enkhuisen), Friesland (first at Dokkum and then at Harlingen) and Amsterdam which soon became dominant. The strength of the Dutch navy was proved by its major victories. The capture of the Spanish treasure fleet in 1620 by Piet Hein secured a fabulous amount of plunder and the success of Tromp at the Battle of the Downs in 1639 ended Spanish preponderance at sea. The struggle for naval supremacy between England and the Dutch Republic involved three wars (1652–4, 1665–7 and 1672–4), during the course of which the Dutch admiral de Ruyter (1607–76) distinguished himself and the United Provinces retained their colonial empire.

The Dutch army of the seventeenth century needed to be large, over 100,000 men between 1694 and 1697, in order to combat the power of France. However, the population of the United Provinces was only 1.8 million and so much of the Dutch army was composed of foreign mercenaries hired on long-term contracts. Swiss regiments served in both peace- and wartime until 1828, an Anglo-Scottish Brigade of six regiments served until 1688 and a Scottish Brigade served until 1782. There were also considerable numbers of Germans and, after 1685, French Huguenots. Much of the officer corps was also of foreign extraction. The Franco-Dutch War (1672–8) dealt some heavy blows to the United Provinces. The lightning invasion by Louis XIV's armies in 1672 was only arrested by opening the dykes and creating the inundations of the 'Water Line'. Subsequently, the United Provinces participated in wars within the shelter of various coalitions. Her effort reached its peak during the Nine Years' War (1688–97) but declined during the War of the Spanish Succession (1702–14). Although the United Provinces were involved in the War of the Austrian Succession (1742–8), they played no part in the Seven Years' War (1756–63). A weakening economy and the huge expense involved in renewing many of the sea dykes forced the United Provinces to remain aloof from European war and to concentrate on the defence of her territories and colonies. Developments in her army followed the models of France and Prussia (as in the reforms of 1771–2 and the establishment of artillery schools in 1789).

The French invasion of 1795 put an end to the old system. A central committee, a kind of Naval Ministry, replaced the five admiralties. The land forces were reorganized along French lines and renamed the troops of the Batavian Republic (later changed to Holland). They fought in the campaigns of the French Revolution and the Empire as far afield as Spain and Russia where Captain Benthien's bridging unit distinguished itself at the crossing of the Beresina in 1812.

Having recovered its independence, the kingdom of the Netherlands (which included Belgium until 1830) took part in the Battle of Waterloo on the side of the Allies. Thenceforth, Dutch military activity was entirely given over to the maintenance of the state's neutrality, which it succeeded in preserving from 1831 to 1940, and to the protection of its colonial empire. The thorniest problem was the question of conscription which had proved highly unpopular when introduced in 1810 during French occupation. In principle, the nineteenth-century Dutch army was a regular force of

volunteers. It numbered 40,000 in 1840 and 20,000 in 1850. At these strengths, voluntary enlistment supported by a militia was adequate. However, in the wake of the Franco-Prussian War (1870–1) and the arming of France and Germany, the Dutch army rose to 50,000 in 1875, 75,000 in 1890 and 200,000 in 1914. These expansions could only be achieved by conscription. It was not a total conscription. Those liable were balloted and the unlucky were allowed to provide substitutes although this privilege was abolished in 1898. Balloting continued until 1938. The larger army was needed to garrison fortifications. Ever since the 'Water Line' of 1672, the Dutch had developed a system of fixed fortifications and planned inundations to protect the heartland of the country, culminating with the Fortress Act of 1874. This created a fortified zone, 'Fortress Holland', comprising the northern and southern sections of Holland and a portion of Utrecht. A general staff was established in 1870.

The Dutch army was mobilized in 1914–18 and again in 1940. However, by 1940 its equipment was obsolete; the Germans invaded on 10 May and the army surrendered on 15 May. The Royal Netherlands Army lost 2,200 men killed and 2,700 wounded. Two thousand civilians lost their lives during the short campaign. The Dutch government in exile continued the struggle with the Axis Powers, particularly against the Japanese; Admiral Doorman's vessels took part in the Battle of the Java Sea (27 February 1942). From 1945 to 1950, the Netherlands armed forces were involved in the war of decolonization in Indo-China. Having joined NATO in 1949, the Netherlands reorganized its army along US lines and in 1953 it established an independent air force. Their current task, in the event of war, is to safeguard the lines of communication between the NATO forces in Germany and the Dutch North Sea ports. In 1991, the Dutch army contained 64,100 men, 40,500 of whom were conscripts serving between 12 and 15 months, with a further 16,600 in the navy and 16,000 in the air force. In addition, there were 152,400 reservists up to a maximum age of 45. The air force contains

117 combat aircraft (101 American F16s and 16 F27s). *See also* BELGIUM; BREDA; COEHOORN; COLONIAL WARFARE; DEPREDATIONS; FORTIFICATION; GROTIUS; NASSAU; NAVAL PERSONNEL; NAVAL WARFARE; NAVIES; NIEUPORT; RUYTER; STEVIN.

C. M. SCHULTEN

JOHN CHILDS

FURTHER READING
H. Amersfoort and P. H. Kamphuis, *Je Maintiendrai: a concise history of the Dutch army* (The Hague, 1985); *Revue Internationale d'Histoire Militaire*, no. 58 (The Hague, 1984): this is a collection of articles and bibliographies, in English, on the military history of the Netherlands.

Neutrality As J. Charpentier observes, neutrality, implying abstention and impartiality in the face of a conflict, seems to reflect a liberal, *laissez-faire* attitude. It may also be prompted by other considerations: a wait-and-see attitude, which consists in awaiting the outcome of a military confrontation before declaring one's own position, or the primacy accorded to one's own national interest. This latter consideration, when allied to a desire for peace, may suggest isolationism as the most advisable course (as was the case with the United States in relation to conflict in Europe before 1917) when the war does not concern one's own nation directly. For a country weakened by its own internal difficulties (as was the case with Spain in the Second World War) or eager not to compromise a unique strategic position (as in the case of Turkey between 1939 and 1945), it may alternatively suggest not coming to the aid of one's allies. A country may also decide on neutrality on the basis of a calculation which consists in leaving one's opponents to exhaust themselves so that one may profit from their temporary incapacity to pursue other political objectives (Soviet neutrality in 1939–40 enabled the USSR to recapture the territories lost in 1918) or take advantage of their weak economic situation to capture their markets.

Neutrality may be adopted as a permanent position. In that case, it is normally the result of an attitude decided upon by a state (usually a small state) or of a consensus among its larger neighbours. The diocese of Liège thus enjoyed a kind of permanent neutrality in the sixteenth and early seventeenth centuries. The Europe which came out of the Congress of Vienna (1815) saw the proclamation of the permanent neutrality of Switzerland and the beginning of a period of Swedish neutrality. Such neutrality may be guaranteed by an international pact (as in the case of Switzerland in 1815 or Belgium in 1839). Depending on the situation, it may lead the neutral country to disarm, as Denmark did between 1866 and 1940 or, on the contrary, to make efforts to equip itself with powerful armed forces (Switzerland, Sweden).

Neutrality obliges the nation that has chosen it to avoid pursuing warlike policies or entering a system of alliances which may lead to war. The ways in which it has been achieved have, however, been varied. Until the eighteenth century, the *Transitus inoxius* or, in other words, the right of a belligerent army to pass through a neutral state, was accepted so long as it was not accompanied by acts of war. The Spanish armies passed legitimately through Franche-Comté, a possession of the King of Spain, without thereby violating the neutrality of that province, which had been agreed between Francis I and Charles V. The Spanish and French armies passed through the diocese of Liège which had been established on the Meuse and which became a veritable invasion route. The powers involved could also agree to a portion of a state's territory being treated as neutral. As has already been mentioned, this was the case with Franche-Comté before 1635 and also with the Straits after 1841 or the Suez Canal between 1869 and 1956. This provision did not prevent the state which owned the territory from maintaining armed forces there and, in case of war, taking sides and allowing the armed forces of its allies to pass through.

Occasional neutrality does not necessarily signify indifference. It may be 'benevolent' towards one of the belligerents, making it possible to help one of these indirectly without committing acts of war. This attitude is particularly likely to be of consequence in naval warfare. War at sea, involving blockades and searches for war *matériel* or 'strategic supplies' destined for the enemy's stores, brings with it the need for the belligerents to examine cargoes carried by ships flying the flag of a neutral state ('right of visitation'). To counter these practices, which the British fleet employed during the American War of Independence, a 'League of Neutrals' was formed, comprising Russia, Sweden, Denmark and Prussia. During the First World War, the German fleet sank neutral ships suspected of transporting arms and foodstuffs for the countries of the Triple Entente, thus bringing about American entry into the war in 1917.

Armed neutrality is practised by a state which wishes to limit the conflict or exert pressure on one of the belligerents or on another state which might be tempted to intervene. This policy was followed on several occasions by Austria, Russia and Prussia during conflicts which saw two of these powers ranged against each other. A war between two states or a civil war may divide a group of nations which help one or other side by sending arms or instructors, or by permitting their nationals to go and fight on one particular side or by sending troops who are allegedly volunteers. This is what occurred during the Spanish Civil War (1936–9). Their interests at a particular moment may cause governments to sign non-intervention pacts of varying degrees of effectiveness.

The creation of the United Nations Organization brought about new developments in the meaning of neutrality. Since, in theory, aggression was condemned, neutrality seemed fated to disappear. States were not supposed to remain neutral toward an aggressor. On the other hand, were they to be expected to render assistance to the victim of the aggression? In fact, since the difference between a state of war and a state of peace had become blurred, neutrality lost its meaning, to be replaced by tacit agreements limiting intervention. Another concept emerged as significant, namely that of non-alignment. The Bandung Conference of 1955 encouraged the states of the Third World to stand

aside from the rivalry between the two superpowers in order to profit from that rivalry by pursuing decolonization through playing one off against the other. This did not prevent the world from dividing into two camps.

In time of war, the neutrals play an essential role by maintaining the possibilities of contact between the belligerents – offering them their 'good offices' – and by enabling humanitarian actions to be carried out, mainly through the Red Cross, which assists in repatriating wounded non-combatants or applying the conventions relating to prisoners of war, etc. Moreover, the neutral states where nationals of the warring countries have an opportunity to meet provide an ideal theatre for espionage and the most varied kinds of intrigue. See also ALLIANCES; BLOCKADES; COMMERCE-RAIDING; CONVOYS; LAWS OF WAR.

A. CORVISIER

FURTHER READING
Roderick Ogley, *The Theory and Practice of Neutrality in the Twentieth Century* (London, 1970); Yoram Dinstein, *War, Aggression and Self-defence* (Cambridge, 1988); H. Lauterpacht, *Neutrality and Collective Security* (London, 1936).

New Zealand There are many similarities between Australian and New Zealand military history, and forces from both have served together in all of their twentieth-century conflicts. Although ANZAC thus has a military reality, it should be stressed that there are some important differences.

The white (*pakeha*) settlement of New Zealand faced a major threat in the nineteenth century from the indigenous Maori people. A settled agricultural society with a strong martial tradition and highly developed warrior caste, the Maoris vigorously opposed white encroachment on their lands, fighting two major wars against them in the 1840s and 1860s. The latter, in particular, forced the colonial government to raise large forces of its own to supplement the British garrison. These were among the fiercest colonial conflicts faced by Victorian Englishmen, for the Maoris proved highly adaptable in their military methods, easily absorbing firearms into their tactical system and negating the effect of European artillery and numerical strength through the construction of modified *pa* (redoubts).

New Zealand faced many of the same problems as the other dominions in dealing with the demands of Imperial defence. With a small, ethnically homogeneous white population and largely agriculturally-based economy – both heavily oriented towards Britain – it was more difficult for New Zealand to indulge in the displays of independent action more characteristic of Australia and Canada. New Zealand sent 6,495 men in ten contingents to fight the Boers in South Africa, proportionately a much larger contribution than Australia's. Before 1914 British models of territorial military organization were followed, organized by a British officer, Major General Sir Alexander Godley, and the government paid the cost of providing a Dreadnought, HMS *New Zealand*, for the Royal Navy.

Combined with Australian forces as a result of pre-war planning, the 1st New Zealand Expeditionary Force (NZEF) under Godley sailed to Egypt in 1914 and took part in the Gallipoli campaign, before being split like its Australian counterpart; the New Zealand Infantry Division went to France in 1916 while the mounted rifle regiments fought in the Middle East. Losses in France were heavy – in twenty-three days in September 1916 the division suffered 7,000 casualties on the Somme – and this led to the introduction of conscription for overseas service in November 1916. More than 100,000 New Zealanders served overseas, suffering a 58 per cent casualty rate.

The Second NZEF, again commanded by a British officer, Bernard Freyberg, went to the Middle East in 1940 and first saw action in the Greek and Crete campaigns the following year. The 2nd NZ division fought in the Mediterranean theatre throughout the war, taking a leading and costly part in the Italian campaign, notably at Cassino. The 3rd Division of two brigades, raised in May 1942, fought

alongside the Americans in the Solomons before being disbanded in October 1944 in the face of manpower pressures. Once again, over 100,000 served overseas, losing 6,839 dead and 16,543 wounded.

New Zealand contributed small contingents to the Korean War, Malayan Emergency, Konfrontasi and Vietnam, sometimes in combination with Australian units. While there was some anti-war activism during the Vietnam period, it lacked the heat and divisiveness of the Australian case because only regulars were sent overseas. Since 1984 New Zealand has pursued an increasingly isolationist stance in defence issues, having withdrawn from the ANZUS [Australia–New Zealand–United States] Treaty after refusing access to New Zealand ports for nuclear-propelled or capable US warships. *See also* AUSTRALIA; COLONIAL WARFARE; GREAT BRITAIN.

JEFFREY GREY

FURTHER READING
James Belich, *The New Zealand Wars and the Victorian Interpretation of Racial Conflict* (Auckland, 1986); Ian McGibbon, *The Path to Gallipoli: defending New Zealand, 1840–1915* (Wellington, 1991); *Blue-Water Rationale: the naval defence of New Zealand, 1914–1942* (Wellington, 1981); Christopher Pugsley, *On the Fringe of Hell: New Zealanders and military discipline in the First World War* (Auckland, 1991); John McLeod, *Myth and Reality: the New Zealand soldier in World War Two* (Auckland, 1986).

Nicephorus II Phocas (912–69) The arrogant, ascetic and monkish Nicephorus Phocas was a leading Byzantine military aristocrat who came to the imperial throne in 963 through a marriage of political convenience with the dowager Empress Theophano, the second wife of Romanus II (959–63). As Domesticus of the Scholarii of the East (commander-in-chief), he captured Candia after an eight-month siege (960–1), completing the reconquest of Crete later in the same year. During this time, his brother Leo Phocas had defeated Emir Saif of Aleppo in central Asia Minor. Returning from Crete, Nicephorus assumed

Leo's command and prosecuted the war of reconquest in the east. In 962, he recaptured much of Cilicia and raided into Tarsus and Syria. Although Nicephorus ascended the throne in Constantinople in the following year, he continued with his wars of expansion. In 965, Nicephorus, with his brother Leo and John Tzimeskes, later Emperor John I Tzimeskes (969–76), captured Tarsus while the fleet took Cyprus. Nicephorus was successfully campaigning towards Antioch at the time of his death in 969; the city, along with Aleppo, fell to Byzantine forces in 970. However, Nicephorus was not uniformly successful in all aspects of his reign. His nephew, Manuel, failed to recapture Crete in 964 and Nicephorus made an enemy of the Church by his attack on monastic wealth and property and by his insistence that soldiers who fell in battle with the infidel should be sanctified as martyrs. His policies towards Emperor Otto the Great and Bulgaria involved Byzantium in simultaneous wars in Italy and Bulgaria. He was murdered in a palace coup.

Nicephorus either personally composed or had written on his behalf two treatises on warfare. One dealt with guerilla warfare against the Arabs in the mountains of Asia Minor and the other described the campaigns of Nicephorus himself, particularly those against the Bulgarians (968–9). Not only did Nicephorus contribute to the reconquest of Byzantine lands previously lost to the Arabs and Saracens, but he enlarged the recruiting base of the Byzantine army in Anatolia and developed the heavy, armoured cavalry (cataphracts). *See also* BYZANTIUM; HOLY WAR; LEO VI.

G. DAGRON
JOHN CHILDS

FURTHER READING
G. Schlumberger, *Un Empereur byzantin au Xe siècle. Nicéphore Phokas* (2nd edn, Paris, 1923); G. Ostrogorsky, *History of the Byzantine State* (3rd edn, Oxford, 1968).

Nicopolis, Battle of (25 September 1396) Realizing the Ottoman danger to Hungary, King Sigismund, who was also Count of Luxembourg and Elector of Brandenburg, appealed to Western sovereigns to mount a crusade. Supported by Pope Boniface IX, Sigismund was able to secure a substantial force of French knights commanded by the Count of Nevers, the son of Duke Philip of Burgundy. English, Poles, Germans, Italians, Hungarians, Wallachians and Knights Hospitallers from the island of Rhodes also answered the papal summons. Venice provided shipping. The French contingent was the largest, about 1,000 knights with 1,500 additional troops, and the whole army numbered around 10,000 horsemen. By the time they reached Nicopolis, casualties and garrison duties had reduced this total to *c*.7,500.

The Crusaders marched along the Danube, supplied by a river flotilla. Sigismund talked of freeing the Balkans from the Turk and even of retaking the Holy Land. The army crossed the Danube at the Iron Gate and advanced into Bulgaria taking towns and cities in an effort to draw Sultan Bayazid I (1389–1403) away from his positions near Constantinople. Vidin surrendered without delay and Rahowa after just five days, but Nicopolis was still holding out after sixteen days when the presence of an Ottoman relief army was noticed. Bayazid had marched so rapidly to Nicopolis that he had taken the Crusaders completely by surprise.

Bayazid's army of 11–12,000 men occupied a plateau 3 or 4 miles from Nicopolis. The janissaries were stationed in the centre, their position fortified by stakes and palisades, while light horsemen armed with bows skirmished to their front. The French insisted on the right to open the action despite the fact that Sigismund's Hungarians, with their mounted archers, were far better suited to initiating the battle. To reach the plateau from the Danube valley, the French knights had to negotiate a narrow defile before deploying. Without waiting for the rest of the army, the French knights charged and dispersed the Ottoman light horse. However, they were halted before the central redoubt of the janissaries, where they were subjected to heavy arrow fire. Bayazid then led forward his *sipahis*, who had been hidden from view behind a hill, and quickly surrounded the confused and disorganized French. By the time Sigismund led the remainder of his mounted men up the defile and into action, the French were already beaten. Blocked against the broad Danube, the closed city of Nicopolis whose garrison sortied in their rear, and the Ottoman army, the Crusaders were defeated in detail. Nevers was captured but Sigismund escaped by boat.

After the disaster at Nicopolis, Constantinople might have fallen to Bayazid's forces but for the invasion of Anatolia by Tamerlain and the Mongols of the Golden Horde. The ensuing Battle of Ankara in 1402 saved the Byzantine capital for a further fifty years. *See also* ANKARA; BYZANTIUM; CONSTANTINOPLE; HOLY WAR; KOSSOVO; MONGOLS; OTTOMAN TURKS; TAMERLAIN.

JOHN CHILDS

FURTHER READING
A. S. Atiya, *The Crusade of Nicopolis* (London, 1934); G. Kling, *Die Schlacht bei Nicopolis im Jahre 1396* (Berlin, 1906).

Nieuport, Battle of (2 July 1600) With the exception of the engagement at Turnhout (24 January 1597), when Maurice of Nassau surprised four regiments of Spanish infantry on the march and routed them with a cavalry charge, prior to Nieuport the latter stages of the Dutch Revolt were dominated by siege warfare. The unexpected battle was the result of the controversial decision of the States-General to exploit the mutiny of the Spanish Army of Flanders in 1599 by taking the offensive against the Spaniards' privateering bases in Nieuport and Dunkirk. On 19 June 1600 Maurice embarked the Dutch field army (14,000 foot and 1,600 horse) at Flushing (Vlissingen) with the intention of invading Flanders by sea. However, two days of adverse winds led to a change of plan: instead the army sailed up the Scheldt to Sas van Gent (21 June) and then marched overland, skirting Bruges and mopping up the Spanish redoubts investing Ostend, the last Dutch garrison in Flanders, en route.

By 1 July Maurice had invested the harbour of Nieuport where he was joined by the Dutch fleet. The Dutch had already suffered a disappointment in discovering that the army's arrival did not inspire a popular revolt against the Spaniards but worse news arrived on that same day. The enemy offensive had enabled Archduke Albert, the governor-general of the Netherlands, to rally the mutineers and, on 29 June, some 10,000 foot and 2,000 horse assembled at Ghent. On 1 July Albert surprised the Dutch garrisons of the redoubts surrounding Ostend and was thus well placed to cut off Maurice's retreat. Maurice responded by sending Count Ernest of Nassau with two regiments of foot and some horse to hold the bridge over the Yperlé at Leffinghem while the army reassembled and, at the same time, ordered the fleet to leave Nieuport harbour at high tide on the next day. Ernest of Nassau reached Leffinghem early in the morning of 2 July only to find the Spaniards crossing the bridge; when the Spaniards attacked, his regiments panicked and fled to Ostend. Buoyed up by this success, and then the sight later in the morning of the Dutch ships leaving Nieuport, which suggested that Maurice was trying to evacuate his army by sea, the Spanish council of war persuaded Albert to attack immediately. By 13.30 the two armies had deployed along the beach but the incoming tide and enfilade fire from Dutch warships (as at Gravelines and Pinkie) caused Albert to shift inland into the dunes. The redeployment disorganized both armies and the actual battle was confused. Although the Dutch cavalry drove off the attacking Spanish horse, the advance of the Spanish foot against Sir Francis Vere's English regiments, which formed the Dutch advanced guard, was more successful. Both sides fed fresh infantry into the fight but the entry of the Archduke's reserve nearly proved decisive as the Dutch battle line then collapsed. However, the exhaustion of the Spanish infantry, who had been on the march for nearly twelve hours, prevented them from exploiting the Dutch retreat. Maurice threw in his Anglo-Dutch cavalry reserve and, this time, the Spanish line dissolved in a rout, pursued by the Dutch horsemen as far as Leffinghem bridge. Dutch losses (including the engagement in the morning) were in the region of 2,000 men, the Spanish at least 4,000. In ordering the attack, the Archduke's mistake had been to overlook the state of his infantry. For the notoriously cautious Maurice, however, the near-disaster was a confirmation of his existing doubts and he immediately withdrew his army, refusing, in future, to undertake further offensives. *See also* GRAVELINES; INFANTRY; NASSAU; NETHERLANDS; OSTEND; PINKIE; SPAIN.

SIMON ADAMS

FURTHER READING
The most accessible accounts of Nieuport are found in J. L. Motley, *History of the United Provinces* (London, 1876 edn), iv, 1–51; C. Oman, *A History of the Art of War in the Sixteenth Century* (London, 1937), pp. 584–603.

Nieuwpoort, Battle of   *See* NIEUPORT

Nimitz, Chester William (1885–1966) Nimitz, born in Texas, was the son of a master mariner. After entering the US navy in 1903, he served largely in submarines, rising to be chief of staff to Captain Robison, the commander of submarines in the Atlantic fleet. He held various surface ship appointments until Admiral Robison, when Commander-in-Chief, US Fleet, asked for him as assistant chief of staff. After commanding a submarine division, he commanded the cruiser *Augusta* in 1933, followed by a period as assistant chief of the Bureau of Navigation in 1935. He reached flag rank with the command first of a cruiser division and then one of battleships, before returning to the Bureau as chief in 1939. After the Pearl Harbor disaster, he was selected to be Commander-in-Chief, Pacific Fleet, with the rank of Admiral, a post he held with much success until the end of the war, directing the vast campaigns by which Japan was eventually defeated. After the war he succeeded King as Chief of Naval Operations (1945–7). Nimitz's obvious ability was accompanied by realism

and foresight, as well as by a kindness and accessibility which enabled him not only to restore the confidence of the fleet after Pearl Harbor, but to continue to draw the best from his subordinates. *See also* GUADALCANAL; JAPAN; KING; LEYTE GULF; MACARTHUR; MIDWAY ISLAND; PEARL HARBOR; UNITED STATES.

A. W. H. PEARSALL

FURTHER READING
E. B. Potter, *Nimitz* (Annapolis, 1976).

Normandy, Battle of (26 July–19 August 1944) The Battle of Normandy was the Allied effort to ensure that their initial landings on the beaches of Normandy became a full-scale invasion of the Continent. As Montgomery's 21st Army Group attacked in the east around Caen, the Americans, starting out from the vast bridgehead created by *Operation Overlord* and preceded by carpet bombing, broke through the German front towards Coutances (*Operation Cobra*). Patton's 3rd Army poured through the breach made at Avranches on 31 July, and struck out towards the Loire, before turning back towards Le Mans. On 6 August, von Kluge launched a German counter-attack from Mortain, aimed at capturing Avranches in order to cut off Patton's advancing army and then to isolate the landing ports by striking back toward the north. This thrust, of which Allied signals intelligence had given forewarning, was halted by Bradley's US forces and British aerial attacks. On 8 August, an attack by the Canadian 1st Army towards Falaise raised the possibility of enveloping the defending German forces. Patton's forces moved from the south towards Argentan, but part of Kluge's forces, taking advantage of a lack of co-ordination between the Allies, was able to escape from the Falaise pocket before it finally closed on 20 August. Nevertheless, the Germans had lost 10,000 dead, 50,000 prisoners and substantial amounts of equipment, while the Americans had 19,000 dead and wounded. With the second Allied invasion of France, which occurred on 15 August between Cannes and Toulon, the German armies were in retreat everywhere. The pursuit now began. *See also* EISENHOWER; MONTGOMERY; OVERLORD; PATTON.

A. CORVISIER

FURTHER READING
Carlo D'Este, *Decision in Normandy* (New York, 1983); John Keegan, *Six Armies in Normandy* (London, 1982).

Northern Ireland Since 1969 British troops have been deployed on British territory against terrorist organizations in the small province of Northern Ireland. In the past twenty years the death toll has reached nearly 3,000. At its height in 1972 there were 482 deaths and over 20,000 British troops deployed in a province of only 1½ million people. Since then both the death levels and the number of troops deployed have been considerably reduced but the capabilities of the largest terrorist organization, the Provisional Irish Republican Army, remain formidable. However, an upsurge in violence early in 1992 resulted in a temporary augmentation in the number of troops.

The present-day campaign of the IRA has deep historical roots. English dominance dates from the twelfth century and since that time successive English rulers have attempted to stamp their mark on Ireland. In the sixteenth century land in Ulster was confiscated from its occupiers and given to Scots and English Protestants – known as 'Plantations'. In this way the seeds of the modern conflict were planted as the Protestants quickly became mixed with the established ruling classes and came into conflict with dispossessed Catholics. Attempts by the Catholics to regain their lands led to several massacres by soldiers of Cromwell's army in 1649. In 1689 came the unsuccessful siege of Londonderry by the Catholic army of James II and the following year his defeat at the hands of his Protestant successor, William of Orange, at the Battle of the Boyne. Recurrent crop failures throughout the eighteenth and nineteenth centuries led to massive emigration particularly to the United States.

Inequality was a hallmark of Irish life.

Numerous sectarian groups sprang up both to attack and defend against opposing groups as well as to try to cope with oppressive landlords. The first 'modern' revolutionary movement was established by Wolfe Tone between 1796 and 1798. He hoped to gain support from both sides of the religious divide, and although he had middle-class backing he was unable to draw on any lower-class support. The next movement to try to gain independence for Ireland was the Irish Republican Brotherhood in Dublin and the Fenian Brotherhood in New York. Both advocated violence as a means of achieving independence but an attempted uprising in 1867 came to nothing. The next bout of violence was led by James Connolly, a labour organizer. He was prominent in the 1916 uprising and commanded the Republican forces in Dublin. Like the other leaders he was executed for his part in the rising. The organization that took part in the 1916 uprising was formed in 1913 as the Irish National Volunteers but soon became the Irish Republican Army. Despite the failure of the uprising it provided a stimulus to the paramilitary groups and to the independence political party, Sinn Fein.

In the elections immediately following the First World War, Sinn Fein won 73 of the 105 Irish seats in the British parliament. In early 1919 Sinn Fein adopted a provisional constitution and issued a Declaration of Independence. This 'Dail Eirann' and the nascent Irish Republican Army now represented an alternative political structure for Ireland. The British responded by augmenting the Royal Irish Constabulary. In the north the Unionists now saw that it might be expedient to accept two governments in Ireland in order to maintain the union for the Protestant counties of the north. In 1920 the British government passed an Act authorizing two governments in Ireland. Sinn Fein ignored the move and pressed on with its guerilla campaign. The first Northern Ireland parliament opened in 1921. At the end of 1921 steps were taken to bring the 'war' to a close and a treaty was signed by the Irish provisional government and the British. The Irish Free State came into being as a dependent legislature of the United Kingdom. Civil war in southern Ireland broke out between 'pro-treaty' and 'anti-treaty' forces. The IRA and the 'anti-treaty' supporters were finally defeated by the Free State in 1923.

In the north, despite attempts to integrate the minority Catholic community into the governmental structures of Northern Ireland, it quickly became a 'Protestant parliament for a Protestant people'. Much of the border area and parts of Belfast were, however, strongly Catholic. Overall the Catholic community constituted one third of the population of the north but it was largely excluded from governing the province and was discriminated against in a variety of fields particularly in housing and jobs. The IRA and Sinn Fein were now spent forces and although sporadic campaigns were launched in 1939–40 on mainland Britain and in the 'Border Campaign' of the late 1950s they were unable to command widespread support and soon fizzled out.

In the 1960s the Republican movement increasingly shifted to the Left and away from the traditional 'physical force' policy and also became involved in the Civil Rights movement in the north. The Civil Rights Campaign reached a climax in 1969. Demonstrations and marches by Civil Rights groups campaigning for changes in housing law and against employment discrimination and gerrymandering were attacked by Protestant groups and the overwhelmingly Protestant police force, the RUC, and in particular by the part-time force, the 'B' Specials. The Ulster Volunteer Force, a Protestant paramilitary organization, also grew dramatically. The most serious violence occurred in August – the 'marching season' – and the police were unable to contain it. The army which had already been guarding sensitive establishments was called in to assist the civil authorities maintain order on the streets of Londonderry and then in Belfast. The army was initially seen as the defender of the Catholic communities and this was reinforced by the decision to disband the 'B' Specials. This presumed status did not last long, however. The army's attempts at creating 'peace-lines' to keep the communities apart allowed the IRA to rebuild within these areas and portray themselves as the 'defenders' of the community, and also once the British army assumed responsibility for security, they could claim that the traditional enemy was once again in control.

The IRA was split, however, between the 'Officials' who espoused Marxist doctrine and wanted a united socialist Ireland and were opposed to violence between Protestant and Catholic workers, and the Provisionals who were of the traditional physical force republican background. Some shootings by the Provisionals did occur during 1970 but the first British soldier to be killed was shot in February 1971. As the Provisionals became more active, so the response of the authorities increased. In August 1970 internment was introduced and 300 people arrested, but this only served to increase the level of violence and the support for the Provisionals. Their strategy became established. First, they targeted members of the security forces and second, they waged an economic war against the infrastructure of the north. By 1972 the campaign had escalated to such an extent that there were over 20,000 British troops in the north. The Provisionals' campaign received boosts such as 'Bloody Sunday' in January when thirteen civilians were killed by the army. The campaign of violence appeared to pay dividends as well when Stormont was suspended in March and talks were held with Provisional leaders in July.

The intensity of the campaign also meant that it could not continue indefinitely. As it became more and more obvious that it was to be a long drawn out struggle, the leadership of the provisional IRA began to adopt a terrorist 'cell' system rather than the more traditional army structures. These were known as Active Service Units and consisted of 2–4 people. The Provisional IRA were still capable of large-scale operations but began to rely more on operations requiring small numbers of highly trained personnel. As the intensity of the campaign lessened the authorities were able to reduce the manpower to levels below 10,000 and British policy has been one of reducing

British army involvement in areas other than the border area and bringing the RUC to the fore as much in an effort to introduce 'normal' policing as to provide an Ulster solution to an Ulster problem. The hated 'B' Specials were disbanded and in their place the Ulster Defence Regiment was established, a part-time element of the British army. Although less provocative than the 'B' Specials, they were still viewed by many as armed Loyalists. In the Defence Review of 1991 it was decided that the UDR was to go and would be amalgamated with the Royal Irish Rangers in an attempt to reduce still further dominance by Loyalists within its ranks.

There have been further splits in the ranks of the Republicans. The Irish Republican Socialist Party was a splinter group of Official Sinn Fein. It formed its own armed wing, the People's Liberation Army, which later became the Irish National Liberation Army (INLA). They hoped to attract those Republicans disaffected by the Provisionals' move into politics and emphasized the purely physical force element of republicanism. They operated extensively in the late 1970s and early 1980s but have themselves been riven by internal strife and a further group has broken away from them calling themselves the Irish People's Liberation Organization (IPLO). This group does not command widespread support but does advocate assassination of Loyalists as well as attacks on security forces personnel.

The terrorist campaign since 1971 has involved a number of strands and has seen the terrorists develop a wide variety of techniques. The primary target of the Provisionals remains members of the Security Forces but they have also attacked economic targets bringing Belfast to a standstill, particularly in the early days, and have assassinated prominent people as well as politicians. There have also been sporadic campaigns on the British mainland and they have achieved spectacular successes such as bombing the hotel used by the Conservative Party at the Brighton Conference in 1986 and firing a mortar bomb at 10 Downing Street in 1991. The terrorists recognize clearly the publicity value of such attacks. They have also been able to extend their theatre of operations to Germany and Holland where attacks have been made on British army personnel. They are believed to possess a vast array of weaponry, ranging from AK-47 rifles to M-60 heavy machine-guns and simple surface-to-air missile systems. From an initial reliance on home-made explosives, they are now using quantities of commercial Semtex explosive and their own mortar designs have developed from simple tubes and bombs to weapons capable of being aimed with a great degree of accuracy. In a campaign that has been raging for over twenty years the Provisional terrorist is now among the most professional and well equipped in the world.

The Loyalist community has responded to Republican terrorism with terrorism of its own. There are a number of organizations involved such as the Ulster Freedom Fighters, the Ulster Volunteer Force and the Ulster Defence Association. Most Loyalist violence has been sectarian in nature assassinating known Republican activists or sometimes murdering Catholics at random. One of the most notorious groups were the 'Shankill Butchers' who carried out numerous sectarian murders throughout the 1970s. The membership of the Loyalist organizations is believed to be extensive and there have been many accusations of links with the security forces, especially the UDR. Their range of weaponry is unlikely to be as wide as the Provisionals' but they are believed to have access to considerable quantities of arms.

The Republican terrorists have also been involved in a number of political campaigns. Following the phasing out of Special Category Status (which in effect had recognized political status) in 1976 there have been a number of prison protests culminating in the 1981 hunger strike campaign which resulted in ten deaths and the election of a hunger striker to the Westminster Parliament. Sinn Fein candidates have also stood in local council elections and in European elections. In West Belfast Gerry Adams, the Sinn Fein leader, was the elected member of parliament. The British government since 1972, however, has resisted direct talks with terrorists. Since Stormont was prorogued there have been a number of attempts to introduce some measure of local political accountability in the province and a variety of conventions and assemblies have been designed but there has been no satisfactory devolution of power and authority continues to reside with the Westminster parliament. There have also been international developments. It is recognized that Eire should have a voice in events in the northeast corner of the island and the Anglo-Irish Accord provides a framework for such involvement as well as for increased cross-border co-operation between the security forces. Such developments have not been viewed with enthusiasm by the Loyalist community.

The struggle in Northern Ireland now seems to have developed a life of its own. A political solution continues to flounder against the demands of the two communities while the terrorist organizations have remained undefeated although kept in limited check by the security forces. In Britain there appears to be no resolve by any political party to attempt to face the problem and in Eire there is no real desire to contemplate integration with recalcitrant Loyalists and a fear of the historical skeletons that militant republicanism might release. It is improbable that violence will achieve its desired ends but the pressures generated by the past make it appear as though the future holds only continued violence. *See also* CIVIL POWER, SUPPORT OF; CIVIL WAR; GREAT BRITAIN; GUERILLA WARFARE; INDIRECT WARFARE; POPULAR WARFARE; TERRORISM.

DAVID WESTON

FURTHER READING
The literature on Northern Ireland is extensive but often highly partisan. Below are listed some secondary sources from a variety of backgrounds: David Barzilay, *The British Army in Ulster* (4 vols, Belfast, 1973–81); J. Bowyer Bell, *The Secret Army* (New York, 1979); Patrick Bishop and Eamonn Maillie, *The Provisional IRA* (London, 1987); David Boulton, *The UVF, 1966–73* (Dublin, 1973); Tim Pat Coogan, *The IRA* (London, 1980); Martin Dillon, *The Dirty War* (London, 1989); Desmond Hamill, *Pig in the Middle: the army in Northern Ireland, 1969–84* (London, 1985); David Miller, *Queen's Rebels: Ulster Loyalism in historical perspective* (Dublin, 1978); A. T. Q. Stewart, *The Narrow Ground: roots of conflict in Ulster* (London, 1989).

Northumberland, Duke of *See* DUDLEY, JOHN

Nuclear testing *See* DISARMAMENT; NUCLEAR WARFARE

Nuclear warfare The use of the two nuclear bombs at Hiroshima on 6 August 1945 and at Nagasaki on 9 August took the history of warfare into a new phase.

Research into atomic fission had been underway before 1939 but political upheavals in Europe and then the war itself brought the majority of the scientists involved to Britain and the United States. In 1942 the United States, fearful of the development of the atom bomb in Germany, established the Manhattan Project, a top secret plan to develop and build the first nuclear device. The Manhattan Project brought together all the scientists then involved in atomic fission so that their work could be directed and controlled centrally. By 1945 the Manhattan Project had produced three devices; the first was used in an experimental test at Alamogordo, New Mexico, the second, 'Little Boy', a uranium device was used at Hiroshima, and the third, 'Fat Man', a plutonium device like that used at Alamogordo, was employed at Nagasaki. 'Little Boy' was a 'gun-type' weapon with a detonating mechanism which shot one piece of enriched uranium into another in order to create a super-critical mass and an explosion. 'Fat Man' used a different mechanism, the 'implosion method', with a ring of 64 detonators shooting segments of plutonium together in order to obtain critical mass.

At Hiroshima about 80,000 were killed with many more dying in the following days from radiation sickness. The number of identified victims at the Hiroshima Cenotaph is 138,890 (1986). At Nagasaki

40,000 died at the time of the explosion with the death toll rising in later years to nearly 50,000. The impact of the dropping of the bomb was so great that Japan considered surrender as soon as the first was dropped.

After the war, research continued in the United States and in the USSR, often with the aid of German scientists, and it led to the manufacture of fission bombs with a yield of several hundred kilotons. The development of fusion devices (the hydrogen bomb) made possible weapons of truly mass destruction with yields of around 100 megatons ('Little Man' and 'Fat Boy' were both around 14 kilotons). Where fission weapons rely on the energy released when heavy nuclei split (by using either the 'gun shot' method or 'implosion') fusion weapons rely on the energy released when the lightest atoms combine to form the heavier atoms. This requires very high temperatures, but sufficiently high temperatures can be reached when the heaviest isotopes of hydrogen are used together with the heat generated by the explosion of a fission device. Hence the term 'thermonuclear'. There is no known critical size for the fusionable material, the amounts of the reacting isotopes determine the size of the eventual explosion. Such a weapon is of little value in a military sense and the nuclear powers have oriented themselves towards the establishment of nuclear arsenals consisting of large numbers of bombs of 'limited' power. There has been an increasing tendency for warhead sizes to decrease as developments in missile technology have meant that the number of warheads could be increased. The land-based Titan II missile, first deployed in 1963, had a single warhead with a yield of 9,000 kt; the MX missile, first deployed in 1986, carried ten warheads each with a yield of 335 kt (each one still over 20 times more powerful than those used at Hiroshima and Nagasaki).

A nuclear weapon consists of two parts: a warhead carrying the nuclear explosive and the detonation system and the vehicle that carries it to its target. The nuclear weapon operates chiefly by light flash, shock and blast effects, thermal or seismic effects, direct radiation, radioactive contamination and electro-magnetic disturbances. The use of such a weapon presupposes the design and establishment of a weapons system – the means of delivery.

A distinction can be made between strategic and tactical nuclear weapons. Strategic nuclear weapons are used for long-distance attack against 'strategic' targets such as the enemy's cities and own missile force and are launched from the silos in which they are stored or from aircraft or submarines. In the United States the responsibility for strategic missiles is split between the land-based ICBMs, a bomber force (the B-52 and the B-1) and a sea-based missile force of which the most recent is the Trident II. The cruise missile, which can be launched from land, sea or air, can be viewed as a strategic weapon although it can also be used against tactical targets and can be equipped with chemical or conventional warheads. The Soviet Union deployed a far larger number of its strategic warheads on land but also had aircraft capable of launching nuclear strikes against Western Europe such as the Backfire Bomber. It also possessed a sea-based strategic force. Recent developments in the former Soviet Union and the devolution of responsibility to the republics raises questions over control of the strategic nuclear force but it seems likely that they will still fall under some sort of central authority. In France the air force has responsibility for its land-based nuclear force located in silos in Provence and the navy for control of its submarine-launched missiles. The strategic forces of the United Kingdom are sea-based using US missile technology. China possesses a small number of land-based ICBMs of the heavy single-warhead variety.

Technical advances in missile construction have made it possible to diversify nuclear weapons in terms of point of launch (ground, sea or air) and definition of target (strategic, tactical or battlefield). The shift from single warheads to multiple warheads and to multiple and independently targeted warheads has blurred many of the distinctions between strategic and tactical weapons. Many of the latest improvements have been made in the field of anti-missile technology. Besides having multiple independently targeted warheads many systems also contain decoys as they attempt to blind or saturate defence and detection systems. Miniaturization has benefited the field of tactical weapons such as the development of nuclear artillery – Lance (US/NATO) and Pluton (FR) – and cruise missile technology.

The nuclear weapon was initially thought of as a super-gun. In 1980 basing the assessment on the number of experimental explosions detected, the relative league table of the nuclear powers was as follows: United States and USSR, followed by France, Great Britain and China. However, the use of nuclear weapons was feared in case reprisals should unleash a process of incalculable reciprocal destruction. The idea therefore soon took root that the threat of use constituted the best possible deterrent. However, the existence of nuclear weapons has not prevented the development of conflict in zones considered marginal by the superpowers, but it has encouraged the tacit establishment of thresholds which international tension must not overstep. Thus, a certain interdependence has come about between the nuclear powers, particularly between the United States and the USSR. At the end of the 1960s this led them to declare their opposition to the proliferation of nuclear weapons and to begin negotiations to control them. The Non-Proliferation Treaty aimed at stopping the spread of nuclear weapons was signed in 1968, although a number of significant states refused to sign the NPT, such as India, China, Israel, Pakistan, Cuba, Brazil, Argentina and South Africa. Shortly afterwards the SALT (Strategic Arms Limitation Talks) process began; SALT 1 in 1972 fixed the number of ICBMs and SLBMs on each side. In 1979 SALT 2 was signed, although not ratified by the US Congress, to try to limit the total number of delivery vehicles (although in practice it increased the total number of warheads because of the increased use of MIRV technology). These talks have been followed by agreements to reduce the number of nuclear weapons in Europe and most recently the Strategic Arms Reduction Talks (START) Agreement aimed at cutting the number of strategic armaments.

While tensions between the United States and Russia appear to have lessened sufficiently for some progress to be made in the reduction of the nuclear stockpile (the Bush–Yeltsin agreement in January 1993) the problem of nuclear warfare is likely to remain. There are a number of countries in the world that appear likely to develop nuclear devices before the end of the century. It is already widely believed that Israel possesses a nuclear arsenal and Iraq has made efforts in the past to obtain the technology and will probably do so again. India already possesses nuclear weapons and Pakistan is recently believed to have acquired the technology. There are several other states believed to be attempting to gain nuclear status such as North and South Korea, Taiwan, Syria, Iran, Brazil and Argentina. Terrorist use also cannot be ignored. While the danger of nuclear warfare between the superpowers may diminish, it is still too early to rule out their use elsewhere in the world. *See also* BEAUFRE; BRAUN; DETERRENCE; DISARMAMENT; KAHN; STRATEGY; TERRORISM.

A. CORVISIER
DAVID WESTON

FURTHER READING
Michael Armine, *The Great Decision: the secret history of the atomic bomb* (New York, 1959); Herbert Feis, *The Atomic Bomb and the End of World War II* (Princeton, 1966); Lawrence Freedman, *The Evolution of Nuclear Strategy* (London, 1981); Norman Moss, *The Men Who Play God: the story of the hydrogen bomb* (London, 1970); R. Nield, *How to Make your Mind up about the Bomb* (London, 1970); Andrew J. Pierre, *Nuclear Politics: the British experience with an independent strategic force* (London, 1972); Report of the Secretary-General of the UN, *Nuclear Weapons* (London, 1981); also publications by the Stockholm International Peace Research Institute (SIPRI) on weapon types, stockpiles and nuclear treaties.

Numerical strength One of the key aspects of warfare is numerical strength. Superiority in numbers has always been considered one of the factors that leads to victory, though on many occasions it obviously has to yield place to fighting quality. Political and military leaders have always sought to maximize numbers. In 1793, Carnot recommended that an attack should not be made with a superiority of less than six to one, and – during the Siege of Paris in 1870–1 – there were those who still entertained the dream of breaking out in a 'gigantic surge'. Much attention has been given to the collecting together of as many troops as possible, whether in the form of seeking allies or of concentrating the maximum number of men on the point which is to be attacked or is under threat.

Numerical strength depends, in large part, on the structure of any given society and on various factors in the situation in which its army is likely to be used. It needs to be analysed on several levels: (1) the number of men called up during a conflict (actual figures and figures of the theoretically available; ratio of total numbers raised to total population), and the number of men under arms simultaneously – in other words, the military potential in terms of manpower; (2) the number of men in an operational army; (3) the number of men engaged in a battle. There must, in addition, be taken into consideration the proportion of fighting troops in an army to those who are only in support. Various factors affect the question of numbers:

The Nature of the Population For the purpose of comparing the war efforts of different countries in varying circumstances one must accept the rough estimate which gives the number of men of the correct age and fitness to bear arms as a quarter of the total population, except in cases where there are castes or orders of warriors.

Populous nations can more readily muster large numbers. This is naturally so in the case of empires, because they cover large areas of territory and involve vassals and allies. The Persian empire probably maintained an army of two hundred thousand, the Mongol empire of Genghis Khan 200,000, the Chinese empire under the Sung dynasty more than 500,000, the Great Empire of Napoleon, with its allies, in 1812,

nearly one million, the USSR and the Warsaw Pact countries four million. The USSR alone mobilized twenty million men between 1941 and 1945. Such numbers of men actually raised are not always in the same ratio to total population. It would even seem that the percentage mobilized increases as the size of population decreases. Thinly populated states, if they do not wish to resign themselves to a subject status, have to accept heavier sacrifices than others. For example, at the period of the Persian wars, Athens maintained under arms one man in four, but the real figure is much higher if resident foreigners and slaves, who were mobilized only in exceptional circumstances, are excluded from the calculation. Obviously, the Persian empire's proportion was much lower. During the American Civil War, the North mobilized in total (though not all at the same time) one man in three, and the South, which was less populous, one in two; and the ratio was as high as 1 : 1.25, if whites only are counted. During the First World War, the ratio of men mobilized to men of military age was 1 : 1.4 in Germany, and 1 : 1.2 in France, which had a lower density of population. If the figure used is that of men serving at the same time, the maximum number on the Northern side in the American Civil War was 1,100,000, or 1 : 6, on the Southern 600,000, or 1 : 2.5. When the same type of calculation is applied to the German and French armies of the First World War, the results are, respectively, 1 : 2.8 and 1 : 2.4.

Spatial Extent of Territory When large, it interferes with the mobilization of men belonging to widely separated communities, and whose presence in their respective regions is often essential for dealing with an emergency. Conversely, mobilization is easier in countries which are small and compact, with a high density of population.

Resources Needed for the Maintenance of Armies A distinction has to be drawn between different modes of maintaining armed men. In warrior societies (e.g. the Gallic, the Germanic), free men were under an obligation to serve as soldiers, and had to arrange for their own maintenance.

Therefore, the numbers mobilized came very close to the total of men of military age, but obviously they took up arms, and were used, only at very irregular intervals. Maintenance by a *condottiere* was bound up with the principles of mercenary warfare. It all depended on the financial resources of the 'war magnate' (the *condottiere*'s employer), who gave him the sums agreed in the contract for a force of the size to be used. Maintenance by the state began when the sovereign kept men under arms for a time longer than that established by custom. In modern nations, members of armies, whether regulars or conscripts, have their maintenance completely assured. The numerical strength of the army depends, therefore, on the financial resources of the state. It is political and economic realities that settle the way in which such principles are put into practice.

Political Factors In ancient empires, armies consisted partly of soldiers belonging to the dominant race, and partly of contingents provided by vassal or subject peoples. In ancient city-states, the numerical strength of their armies was limited by the number of citizens, and the severe drop in population of the fourth and third centuries BC naturally reduced that strength. In the course of two centuries, the Spartan hoplites (heavy infantry) declined in number from 8,000 to 2,000, since membership of the warrior caste was not open to the other inhabitants of Laconia. This drop in the indigenous potential led to the employment of mercenaries. Rome of the Republican period called on a high proportion of its citizens for armed service. At the time of the Second Punic War, no less than 750,000 were called to arms out of a population of 3,500,000, i.e. 1 : 4.5 but, in fact, not more than 200,000 were mobilized at any one time, or 1 : 18. In the case of the Barbarians (e.g. the Germanic invaders), contemporary writers give figures from which it appears that one-third of their population was in arms – an obvious exaggeration, unless they were including adolescents and the aged, whose military roles would have been of a restricted character. Gaul, a huge country with a population of some six million, is said to have called on half a million men to take up arms against Caesar, but could, in fact, mobilize only 90,000. The societies produced by the feudal system confined military service, in principle, to the 'second order' of society ('those who fight'), the nobility, which provided its own equipment. The numbers available for military service declined, despite efforts to supplement them by calls on the urban militia. This decline was less a result of the closed nature of the second order than for other reasons which are examined later in this article. From the thirteenth century onwards, recourse was made to professionals. The introduction of professional soldiers contributed to the lessening in numbers of armed forces for various reasons:

1 The professional is inherently more efficient than the citizen-soldier, unless the latter belongs to a military caste. The employment of professional soldiers often goes hand-in-hand with the quest for quality rather than for large numbers.
2 Professional forces are costly and, for that reason, incompatible with the idea of mass armies.

In the Roman Empire, Augustus reduced the army, which had become a professional force, to 300,000 men, i.e. 1 : 30 of those of an age to bear arms out of a population of *c*.40,000,000. From *c*.50,000,000 inhabitants the later Empire employed 450,000 soldiers, among whom there were a certain number of Barbarian origin. It appears that the Byzantine Empire maintained under arms not more than 1 : 40 or 1 : 50 of those of military age. At the start of the Hundred Years' War, the proportion of men under arms was 1 : 50 of the total French population, and 1 : 20 of the English. The military censuses carried out in Castille at the end of the fifteenth century covered 1.2 million men, or a quarter of the population. In fact, the king obtained from that area merely a few tens of thousands of soldiers (50,000 for the Siege of Granada). The formidable *tercios* were even smaller. In the later seventeenth century, numbers in armies began to grow, and the establishment in Europe, during Louis XIV's reign, of militias as a kind of reserve to line units, made it possible to maintain under arms, on average, 1 man in 25, a ratio which reached 1 : 8 in Prussia and Sweden. When conscription was introduced it permitted mobilizations on a scale limited only by economic and technical factors.

Economic Factors These came into play in countries with a settled population, where there was a need to leave at work that number of men which was essential for the subsistence of the community, and for the maintenance of the army. Societies with a system of castes or of orders met this requirement. Non-citizens or non-nobles were called to arms only when great danger threatened. The same was true of societies with racial segregation; during the American Civil War, the South could mobilize a higher percentage of the whites, because the economy rested on black labour. During the First World War, after several months of hostilities, a large number of workers, especially the oldest whose civilian employment was in agriculture, had to be returned to that work as 'special postings'. Economic warfare often leads to blockades, and because of that, also to a requirement to increase the domestic production of certain commodities. Numbers, however, vary also in accordance with the maintenance costs of an army. The cost per fighting man rises as military techniques develop.

Technical Factors and Techniques of War There have been several developments in military technique which have brought about changes in the number and types of soldiers in armies.

The development of cavalry was one of the first. The Mediterranean countries, the Chinese paddy-fields or mountains are not suitable areas for the deployment of cavalry. In Athens, horsemen represented only 1/20th of the numerical strength, and in Rome they were 1/15th of the legion. The proportion increased as wars of conquest brought Mediterranean countries into contact with states which had extensive flat terrain. In Alexander's army, the cavalry

numbered 1/7th of the total, and its importance grew equally in the Roman army of the later Empire, when combating invasions by people from the steppes. The Battle of Adrianople (AD 378) is considered to have been a major turning point in the development of cavalry, owing to the appearance there of *cataphractes*, armour made of metal scales sewn onto leather tunics. This covered the horseman more fully and yet allowed him freer bodily movement. Two other new devices allowed cavalry to reinforce the progress it had already made – the iron stirrup, introduced about AD 600, which gave the rider a more secure seat and increased the power of impact when charging; and the iron horseshoe (ninth century), which allowed the cavalryman to reduce the number of horses he needed since it was no longer necessary to let mounts rest for long periods in order to avoid over-rapid wear of their hooves on hard ground. These developments produced a relative decline in infantry forces, which became an arm that complemented or accompanied cavalry. In this way, cavalry quite often represented over half an army's numbers. Cavalry, however, requires – besides horses and harness – the employment of armed attendants and non-combatant artisans. While the Greek hoplite needed only one attendant, the cavalryman required at least three to help him. Cavalry was, therefore, a costly arm, which could never be mobilized in very large numbers; the biggest armies of the Middle Ages contained only some tens of thousands of men.

Advances in methods of siege warfare, together with the use of the infantry pike and firearms at the close of the Middle Ages, reduced the role of cavalry, but also reduced the total numbers under arms. Until the middle of the seventeenth century, the cost of firearms was high as production capacity was limited. During the Thirty Years' War, the total numbers under arms in the service of each of the main participants exceeded 100,000, at the cost, however, of heavy financial sacrifices. Under Louis XIV, difficulties over the production of armaments were progressively surmounted. During the War of the

Spanish Succession, with the regular troops (400,000 men, 1 in 18 of the population), the coastguard, local militias and the fleet, the number of men under arms in France exceptionally bordered on 600,000, or 1 in 12 of those of military age. In Year II, the count was 1 in 9. The rise of coal-fired smelting in the nineteenth century allowed that proportion to be attained regularly. The Franco-Prussian War of 1870–1 saw 1 German in 18 opposed to 1 Frenchman in 30 in the opening phase, rising to 1 in 15 without counting the National Guards, during the Siege of Paris. After the high point in mobilization achieved in certain nations during the First World War (the French figure was 6 million out of a theoretically possible 8.5 million), a drop was noticeable in the Second World War, owing to the more important part played by economic and technical requirements. It can also be seen that, in parallel, the proportion of actual combatants in the total numerical strength of armies continued to decline; it fell, indeed, on average, to a level of the order of 1 in 10, and less still in the case of armoured or air forces, because of the increase of personnel concerned with equipment, logistics and administration.

In Antiquity, if allowance is made for exaggerations in the figures put forward by Herodotus, it would appear that the Persian armies did not exceed c.200,000 men. The maximum strength attained by the Roman army was probably 50,000 to defend an empire of c.2,500,000 square miles. At certain periods, the Chinese Empire is said to have reached the figure of 11,000,000 men under arms. Genghis Khan's Mongols probably never attained a total of more than 240,000 men and the Ottomans about the same. Charlemagne is reported to have counted on mobilizing 130,000 men, with 15–20,000 of them being cavalry. It may be that more than 100,000 men left for the First Crusade, but Jerusalem was captured by only about 10,000. The military orders numbered from 5,000 to 10,000 fighting men, of whom 1,500 were mounted knights. In the fifteenth century, the principal sovereigns had only several thousands of soldiers. The 100,000 mark, probably reached by all the armies of Philip II of Spain taken together, was not really passed by France until 1635. In Asia, a fall in total numbers can be seen when the use of firearms became widespread – this trend occurring about two centuries later than in Europe. From the end of the seventeenth century, the mastery of the use of firearms, the advances in industrial production and the widespread employment of militias created numbers which until then had been exceptional. In particular, the divergence between peacetime and wartime numbers was reduced, in most European countries, to 1 : 1.5, except in two instances already noticed – in France, during the War of the Spanish Succession and the Revolutionary and Napoleonic Wars. The numbers in Year II were five times higher than those of the period immediately prior to the Revolution. It was in the American Civil War that the figure of one million men was first reached by a belligerent. But during the world wars, armies rose far beyond that point. At the present time, owing to the wide diffusion of automatic weapons, a marked reduction has taken place. The appearance of nuclear weapons has increased that tendency. The forces of deterrence require only a few handfuls of men.

The numbers marshalled for particular military operations are dependent on the scope which the prospective theatres offer for manoeuvre and for maintenance and supply. In desert steppes and, again, in countries with broken terrain, an invader cannot make use of his full potential, as shown by the Persians in Greece, or the Spanish and French in Holland. Switzerland has been invaded only rarely, and then by very small forces. Even though an army's subsistence may be assured by pillage or requisition, the resources of the country in which it is operating will impose some limit on its numbers. That is why, over a long period, the policy of 'scorched earth' has been considered effective in stopping an enemy, at least temporarily, from securing a footing in a region. If an invader wished to maintain troops in numbers that were too great for a country's capacities, he had to bring in his own means of subsistence and, for that purpose, to

617

arrange for warehouses, to assemble stocks and to establish a distribution network for foodstuffs and munitions (in current terminology, logistics). For a long while, these problems prevented, or caused difficulties for, winter operations of any size, and for the subsistence of armies that were at a distance from their base. It was like the case of the horse that has to transport its own forage; it cannot travel far. A miracle of modern technical capacity was the advance of the Allied armies in 1944 experiencing no shortage of petrol until after they had driven nearly 400 miles, and then only because they had moved faster than anticipated. In the case of overseas operations, the problem naturally presents itself in a different form. Long-distance operations require the assistance, both on land and at sea, of allies or neutrals, to secure safe passage on the journey, or when replenishing stocks. Even with help of this kind, the Crusader forces, or the French or Spanish armies during their wars in Italy, rarely numbered more than 50,000 men. The same is true of the general run of colonial wars. The figure of 100,000 men was not regularly exceeded, until the Napoleonic Wars. At the dawn of the twentieth century, the Boer War and the Russo-Japanese War were the occasion of transporting large armies overseas, but the figure of a million was not surpassed until the Second World War.

The numbers that armies commit to battle depend on the scope that any given terrain provides for manoeuvre, as well as on logistical considerations. Moreover, the nature of the ground plays a certain part. Large confrontations take place in open country, with the smallest changes of level in the ground being used either as a strong point or – before the days of aviation – to conceal movement. The Pratzen plateau stands only a few score feet above the Austerlitz marshland, and is not inaccessible. It appears that the battle where the tactic of using the weight of frontal assault reached its apogee was Malplaquet (1709), where the Anglo-Dutch force of 110,000 men was aligned on a front 3 miles wide. The use of the 'division' as the basis of an army's organization, which began

during the Seven Years' War, allowed a commander to articulate large armies, and thus temporarily to concentrate in a sudden encounter battle and bring to bear more than 100,000 men. There were 160,000 French and 130,000 Austrians at Wagram, 160,000 at Solferino and 220,000 at Sadowa. The 1914–18 war saw the advent of that series of major battles whose aim was a breakthrough (or the attrition of enemy forces) on some particular sector of a huge front – Verdun, the Somme, Stalingrad, Kursk, Korea – with more than half a million men being engaged. Are such encounters still conceivable today? Modern armaments allow, in theory, a reduction in the numbers engaged. The attack or defence of the Gap of Aulnois (Boussu), which was the key to the Battle of Malplaquet (1709), would now require only a few hundred modern soldiers.

The numerical size of forces is, perhaps, not quite so important today as it was at the start of the twentieth century. The quality and killing power of modern weapons systems mean that an infantry battalion now possesses the firepower of a division of the Second World War. Also, the development of chemical, biological and nuclear weapons together with more sophisticated conventional weapons like cluster bombs and helicopter gunships has rendered armies composed of mass infantry highly vulnerable. However, up to the end of the Cold War in 1990, the balance of forces between NATO and the Warsaw Pact continued to be expressed in comparative numerical strengths. In the less technically developed armies of the Third World, numerical strength has remained an important factor in assessing military capability. Vietnam has the world's third largest army; Libya, with a population of 3,500,000 inhabitants, maintains an army of 73,000 regulars; Iraq possessed in 1988 the fourth largest army in the world, 955,000 men. Despite the highly efficient modern weapons, their maintenance and logistic support require large numbers of trained personnel. Also, difficulties in recruitment and the improvement in lifestyle mean that soldiers in Western armies demand a high standard of living, even in the field, which can only be met by employing large numbers of soldiers on non-combatant services. *See also* LOGISTICS; LOSSES OF LIFE; MOBILIZATION; RECRUITMENT; TACTICAL ORGANIZATION.

A. CORVISIER
JOHN CHILDS

FURTHER READING
Archer Jones, *The Art of War in the Western World* (Oxford, 1989); *The Military Balance* (published annually by the International Institute for Strategic Studies, London).

Nur-ad-Din (1117–74) Also known as Nur-ed-Din (Nureddin), Nur-al-Din and Nour-ad-Din, Nur-ad-Din, the second son of Zangi, the *atabeg* of Mosul, was chosen to succeed his father in the government of northern Syria in 1146 in the rank of emir of Aleppo. In that same year he took Edessa from the Franks, thus precipitating the unsuccessful Second Crusade (1147–8). Having beaten Raymond of Poitiers, Prince of Antioch, at Fons Muratus (Fountain of Murad) in 1149, he seized both Harim and Afamiya to extend his control into southern Syria. Subsequently, while maintaining his pressure on the Crusader States, particularly the County of Tripoli (Damascus fell in 1154), he endeavoured to control Egypt. With the assistance of Shirkuh and Saladin this was largely achieved by 1168, despite the efforts of the King of Jerusalem, Amalric I. The death of the Fatimid Caliph of Egypt in 1171 eliminated the last of the opposition; the Frankish states in the Holy Land were now encircled. It was one of Nur-ad-Din's achievements to have realized Muslim unity against the Franks, manifested in his revival of the spirit of Holy War, the *Jihad*; moreover he was seen as the restorer of Sunni Muslim orthodoxy. His actions prepared the ground for his successor, Saladin. Nur-ad-Din was respected by both allies and enemies, Christian and Muslim, as a wise, pious and just ruler. *See also* HOLY WAR; SALADIN.

R. MANTRAN

FURTHER READING
H. E. Mayer, *The Crusades* (2nd edn, Oxford, 1988); Steven Runciman, *A History of the Crusades* (3 vols, London, 1951–5); E. Sivan, *L'Islam et la croisade* (Paris, 1968).

O

Obligations and duties All societies need to defend themselves against possible enemies and to make preparations in anticipation of an attack. There has never been a tribe, a city or a state lacking some fixed arrangements, however rudimentary, for military action; of necessity, these imply common duties on all members of that society. Duties vary in accordance with the gravity of the danger and with the structure of the society. Generally, liability for military service rests on men whose age and physical condition fit them to bear arms. However, when extreme peril threatens, the aged, children, men whose religious functions normally preclude them from martial obligations, and even women may share in the work of defence or actually take part in combat. Such instances tend to occur during sieges, civil wars and in resistance to an occupying power, although in these situations the term 'duty' can only be applied in the moral sense. Operations in defence of a home territory need to be distinguished from those conducted outside it. In the latter case, the participants are exclusively men who have committed themselves fully, whether as a lifetime's profession or just for a limited period, to the business of fighting. There is, first of all, a need to establish the distinction between 'duty', when considered in the context of defence, and armed service.

The term 'duty', when applied to defence, can have several definitions. It may mean the obligation to undertake armed service in person, with or without a stipulation to provide the necessary equipment; to supply one or more fully accoutred men; to participate in auxiliary military work; to make a contribution in kind to the upkeep of soldiers; or to pay a monetary tax.

Personal armed service, whether full-time or temporary, normally falls only on men capable of bearing arms, implying physical fitness and a certain age range. In primitive societies, physical strength alone determined the beginning and end of the obligation to military service but in later societies, such as the Gauls and the Germans, apprenticeship to arms began at puberty. When mention is made by ancient writers of a precise age – from 20 to 50 for the Persians, up to 60 in Sparta – the allusion must be to apparent age only as no accurate system of birth registration existed. In Athens, young men of 18 were required to perform garrison duty but could not participate in battle until the age of 20. King Servius Tullius of Rome (578–535 BC) fixed the limits for bearing arms at between 17 and 46 and under the Byzantine Empire the age for entry into military service varied from 16 to 20. In the Middle Ages, young men had a duty to take up military service at an early age if they occupied high positions in the social order, reflecting the responsibilities of their rank. According to Philippe Contamine, pages were admitted into the *compagnes d'ordonnance*, a creation of Charles VII, between the ages of 13 and 17. The Statute of Winchester (1285) laid down militia service for all able-bodied males between the ages of 16 and 60. In France, at the age of 16 in 1693 and 18 after 1765, young men were compelled to serve in the militia, individual liability being decided by lot. The *levée en masse* of 1793 was directed at men between 18 and 25. Britain accepted volunteers over the age of 19 between 1914 and 1916. During the Second World War the age of entry into military service was steadily lowered by advancing the dates of call-up, the German *Werwolfe* of 1945 being no more than adolescents. In postwar Europe, young British men had to enter the National Service between the ages of 18 and 21 and, after 1970, French conscripts could choose any age between 18 and 21 for their entry into the armed forces.

As a general rule, all men who perform personal armed service have been granted dispensation from other obligations relating to their country's defence. In some societies, the mere fact of liability for armed service, even if the man was not actually called up, exempted both him and his family from other obligations. During the era when fighting men provided their own equipment, personal military service took many forms. In most countries, up to the mid-sixteenth century when firearms came to be adopted in Western Europe, free men had both to serve and to equip themselves, their financial resources determining the type of unit they could join. In Athens, citizens might serve in the cavalry, the heavy infantry (hoplites), the light infantry or, in the case of the poorest, as oarsmen in the navy. 'Knights' enjoyed a leading position in the social hierarchy. Other systems, such as that instituted by Charlemagne, equated the 'quantity' of a man's required military contribution with the size of his landed property. Large landowners had to serve in person accompanied by as many men, whom they also had to equip, as the extent of their farming interests or the number of their manors seemed to justify. Small landowners were allowed to pool their resources to equip and maintain a single fighting man. The army of the feudal state, when raised by the king, brought together the *ban* and the *arrière-ban*, the vassals and sub-vassals, who were organized in accordance with their feudal connections, for a period of unpaid service generally limited to 40 days in any one year. Beyond that time, if they agreed to continue in service, the king had to maintain them at his own expense. When a sovereign granted a charter of privilege to a town it usually entailed an obligation on the civic authorities to guarantee the defence of their metropolis by maintaining their walls and providing men for the *ban* and *arrière-ban* in the form of a militia. The only other possible form of military service was by voluntary enlistment and those so joining had to be paid.

Between 1066 and the reign of Edward I (1272–1307), the holder of every 'knight's fee' in England was obliged to serve the king in full armour on horseback for 40 days in any one year. Substantial landowners who possessed several 'knight's fees' had to provide deputies. This meant that the king always had available a force of heavy cavalry to repel an invasion or put down an insurrection. The system was unpopular and made long campaigning and fighting overseas difficult. By the time of Edward I, the feudal host had all but been replaced by a system of indentures, or contracts. Knights agreed with the king how long they were to serve, how much they were to be paid and how many men they were to raise. In effect, all soldiers became stipendiaries of the crown leading to a better disciplined army and a more orderly chain of command and subordination. The principle of military obligation on all able-bodied male members of society was continued through the militia.

After the period of indentured or contracted armies, the growth in the size of armed forces and in the scale of European warfare during the sixteenth and seventeenth centuries witnessed a partial return to the principle of military obligation. This concept has remained in vogue to the present day. In Sweden, Charles XI created in 1682 the *Indelta* system, which linked military service with entitlement to a grant of land. In France, from the time of Louis XIV, the state assumed responsibility for paying seafarers who were called up for service aboard the royal ships under the *classement* system and those subjects required to serve in the militia (formed in 1688 and nominated by lot after 1693). During the seventeenth century, 'Europe swarmed with militias'. A further step was taken by Frederick William I of Prussia in 1733 with the establishment of the *Kantonsystem*. All male peasants in the recruiting canton had to be registered at the age of ten (*obligat*) and, when they became adult, joined their units for eighteen months to two years' service. After that they returned to civilian life but remained liable to call-up in time of war and had to undergo two or three months' reserve training every year over a period of thirty to forty years.

621

The Prussian system, partially copied by Austria-Hungary in 1781, foreshadowed the French conscription which followed the *levée en masse* of 1793. This was originally based on the law put forward by Jourdan in 1798 and modified in 1818. Not until the military laws of the Third Republic, passed in 1872, 1884 and 1905, did military service become compulsory for all citizens. At first, the conscript's period of service was determined by governmental policies or by the mechanics of the system (long-term service for those who drew an unlucky number in the ballot). Later, when service became obligatory for all, full-time service was restricted to two or three years depending on the army's needs. Men released at the end of their conscript service entered the reserve and were liable to recall until they reached a certain age, usually 48, but more for officers and NCOs. Apart from the conscripts and volunteers already with the colours, there were three other categories in the armed forces, namely, in descending order of age: the reserve of the army proper, whose members had to undergo regular periods of training, the home army and the home army reserve. Today, developments in the methods of warfare have reduced the likelihood of reservists being recalled.

Though most countries of continental Europe have established systems of conscription comparable with that of France, some nations have prescribed this form of service only in time of war. To face other emergencies, the United States and Britain employ forms of militia, the National Guard and the Territorial Army, to support the regular army. Switzerland has set up a novel form of militia based on a universal but short initial service supplemented by annual periods of training.

It has always been recognized that the calling-up of a large number of men for military service imposes a severe penalty on the life of a nation. Consequently, both militias and conscription systems have frequently made provision for exemptions from service in peacetime. These may be based on family considerations (e.g. not more than one brother to serve at a time) or on a desire not to disturb the social and economic structure. Even during hostilities, men whose work is essential to the nation, on economic or technical grounds, may be classified as in 'reserved occupations'.

Obligations relating to the army, apart from armed service, come under the headings of requisition and taxation. Armies across the centuries have made use of peasants and their waggons to labour on fortifications and transport supplies. In addition, they have called upon the populations of towns to billet soldiers. Although the quartering of troops on private householders diminished during the eighteenth century to be replaced by taxation to provide barracks, British civilians were ordered to billet troops during the Second World War. However, the burden which weighed most heavily on those who did not perform military service was taxation. The 'taille', originally a wartime tax, was first levied in France in 1357 and with the growth of standing armies and the scale of warfare during the sixteenth and seventeenth centuries most European governments imposed heavy taxation on their populations to meet rising military costs.

The system by which liability for military service has been determined has always been bound up with the structure of society. During Antiquity, military service was incumbent on free men or citizens, foreigners and slaves being excluded on principle. The practice of arms was closely linked with the notions of liberty and honour. However, whenever a degree of security against outside danger was achieved, the number of warriors tended to diminish as men returned to their peacetime occupations. Defence was left in the hands of those committed to the pursuit of arms. A class system arose in which various orders of warriors became endowed with a special status which eventually turned them into nobilities and quasi-nobilities, the order of knighthood being the supreme example of the latter category. This trend reached its extreme in India where marriage outside one's caste was not just misalliance but sacrilege. Defence and warfare grew into the specialized occupation of well-defined social groups. The creation of large armies under government control tended to modify this arrangement and the military nobilities ceased to possess the monopoly of arms. In emergencies, a call had to be made to commoners, as in Rome during the second century BC or in France after the fourteenth century. Nobilities retained their privileges but no longer had sole responsibility for their country's defence. Nevertheless, they still claimed the duties of command on the justification that arms was their profession. During the seventeenth and eighteenth centuries, nobles comprised the majority of the officer corps in European armies. These claims were partly pushed aside in France after 1789 but the Prussian, Austro-Hungarian and Russian armies remained dominated by the aristocracy until the coming of conscription and the organization of mass armies.

The extent to which liability actually affects a population varies with the type of society and its epoch. Few men escape personal service in primitive societies or in some modern ones. In France, among men of an age to bear arms, 1 in every 12 was a soldier in 1714; the proportion among the nobility was 1 : 3. The general figure was 1 : 9 in 1793; 1 : 12 in 1913; 4 : 5 in August 1914, either in fighting units or auxiliary services. In England during the Nine Years' War (1688–97), 1 : 7 men of an age to bear arms served in the army. In modern Israel, where military service extends to women, the ratio is 1 : 5. Apart from personal military service, taxation has most affected societies. In peacetime during Louis XIV's reign, half the annual revenues were spent on military budgets. This had declined to a third in 1789, remained at this proportion in 1939 but declined to a tenth in 1983. In Russia under Peter the Great during the Great Northern War, 64 per cent of his annual revenues were spent on the army and the navy. *See also* BILLETING; FINANCES; MILITIAS; MOBILIZATION; MORALE; NUMERICAL STRENGTH; RECRUITMENT; RESERVES; SCHWENDI.

A. CORVISIER
JOHN CHILDS

FURTHER READING
J. R. Hale, *War and Society in Renaissance Europe, 1450–1620* (London, 1985); M. S. Anderson, *War and Society in Europe of the Old Regime, 1618–1789* (London, 1988); André Corvisier, *Armies and Societies in Europe, 1494–1789* (Bloomington, Ind., 1979); John Childs, *Armies and Warfare in Europe, 1648–1789* (Manchester, 1982); Denis Hayes, *Conscription Conflict: the conflict of ideas in the struggle for and against military conscription in Britain between 1901 and 1939* (London, 1949).

Occupation *See* CULTURE, PROTECTION OF; LAWS OF WAR

Officers, naval *See* NAVAL PERSONNEL

Onasander Onasander was a Greek living in the Roman empire in the first century AD who, according to tradition, wrote a commentary on Plato's *Republic*. He also produced a treatise on the duties of a military commander, addressed to Quintus Veranius, consul of AD 49, who died in office as governor of Britain, probably in 58. Onasander concentrates on the importance of strength of character and moral uprightness in the commander, while providing common-sense advice on how to organize an army: marching order, encampment, the use of scouts and intelligence reports, deception of the enemy, pursuit of defeated forces, concealed retreat, military psychology, troop formations and the deployment of reserves, sieges, stratagems and leadership by personal example. Onasander aimed to give practical instruction, and his work, which was popular in Antiquity and the Renaissance and with soldiers of later ages, should not be dismissed as merely antiquarian and commonplace. At a time of slow technological development in warfare when there was no formal training for commanders, military textbooks including examples taken from past engagements were part of the preparation of men for generalship. *See also* AENEAS TACTICUS; ARRIAN; FRONTINUS; ON MILITARY MATTERS; VEGETIUS RENATUS.

B. CAMPBELL

FURTHER READING
Aeneas Tacticus, Asclepiodotus, Onasander, (Loeb Classical Library, Harvard, 1923).

On Military Matters (*De Rebus Bellicis*) This short, anonymous treatise addressed to the reigning emperors probably dates from the second half of the fourth century AD. The author, who was not a professional soldier, deals with a number of miscellaneous points which he claims will bring great benefits to the empire. A large part of the work is concerned with technical military devices: two catapults, three models of scythed chariots, a moveable defensive screen, a reinforced shield, two javelins with special features, a portable bridge, a warship driven by paddles rotated by oxen, and a protective coat to be worn underneath armour. A number of illustrations accompany these suggestions. It is likely that the treatise is a compilation drawn from a number of sources, rather than a profession of the original ideas of the author; the mobile catapult described in the treatise bears a close resemblance to the *cheiroballistra* of Heron. However, the author's imagination may also have played a part, and some of the mechanical devices seem impracticable for warfare. His purpose was probably not primarily to deal with the consequences of any shortage of manpower for the army, but to highlight the financial pressures on the empire's taxpayers, which arose partly through the need to maintain a large military establishment. The treatise is important both as a comment on government and administration in the late empire, and also as an expression of continuing interest in technological innovations for the army. *See also* HERON; PHILON OF BYZANTIUM.

B. CAMPBELL

FURTHER READING
E. A. Thompson, *A Roman Reformer and Inventor* (Oxford, 1952); B. A. R. International Series 63 (Oxford, 1979): Part 1, *Aspects of the De Rebus Bellicis*, papers edited by M. W. C. Hassall; Part 2, the text, ed. R. Ireland; A. E. Astin, 'Observations on the *De Rebus Bellicis*', *Collection Latomus*, clxxx (1983), pp. 388–439.

Ordnance The Ordnance, which was originally a non-combatant sevice but later became an operational arm, supplies to army units all types of weaponry, bridging, signals and detection equipment, transport, ammunition, explosives, helicopters, etc. In some countries, it can also be responsible for maintaining the equipment in working order.

United States The United States Ordnance Department was created on the eve of war in 1812 and was charged with the construction of artillery carriages and equipment, inspecting ordnance and maintaining records. In 1821, the Ordnance was amalgamated with the artillery and assumed responsibility for the manufacture of artillery. During the twentieth century, the Ordnance Department has extended its activities into the design and manufacture of tanks and self-propelled guns.

France The French Ordnance Department was not formed until 1940, when the artillery (the fighting arm) was separated from the service sector (the Ordnance). Until that date, the French artillery had been responsible for manufacture, service and operation in the field. The Ordnance also took over some service and storage institutions belonging to the engineers and signallers in 1968 and 1969, respectively.

Great Britain The English (British from 1707) Ordnance Office emerged from the royal household during the fifteenth century and grew into a department of state during the mid-sixteenth century. From this date, it became the central supply service for the British armed forces, even supplying cannon to the Royal Navy. It was responsible for the manufacture and design of artillery, swords, hand-guns and all associated equipment. The Ordnance Office was also in charge of all fortifications, garrisons and engineering services within the British Isles. Camp equipment (after 1685) and uniform also came under the Master-General of the Ordnance and barracks were added later in the eighteenth century. During the Crimean War, the Master-General and the Board of Ordnance were abolished in 1855 and their work was distributed among a Directorate of Stores, a Directorate of Contracts, an Inspectorate of Fortifications, a Directorate of the Royal

Artillery and a Directorate of Naval Artillery. In 1863 a Barrack Department was created. This proved too disparate and inefficient, and in 1870 a Surveyor-General of Ordnance was appointed to supervise all the supply services of the army – artillery, transport and stores. In 1887, the navy was made responsible for its own ordnance. In 1899, the Director of Ordnance was also made responsible for army clothing and for munitions factories. In 1904, the post of Master-General of the Ordnance was revived to take care of artillery and fortifications. He was responsible for manufacturing ordnance, arms, ammunition and equipment, mostly from the Royal Ordnance Factories. Nevertheless, there remained areas of overlap with the functions of the Army Service Corps under the Quartermaster-General.

During the First World War, many of the functions of the Ordnance Department were assumed by the Ministry of Munitions, created in 1915. A Director-General of Munitions Production was established in 1936 and he was moved into the Ministry of Supply in 1939. In 1940, a Cabinet Committee (Defence Committee, Supply) under the chairmanship of the prime minister took overall charge. In 1971, the research, development and production of armaments were placed under a civilian politician, the Minister for Defence Procurement, with responsibility for all three services. The Master-General of the Ordnance currently presides over the army side of the Procurement Executive.

As the Ordnance Department became simply an agency for the design, manufacture and supply of weaponry, the function of distribution and maintenance passed to the Royal Army Ordnance Corps which was founded in 1865. At the same time, transport, barracks, military stores and the commissariat were grouped into the Army Service Corps. By the time of the Second World War, the Royal Army Service Corps was responsible for barracks and quarters and for supplying the soldier with his daily needs – food, gasoline, lubricants and blankets. The Royal Army Ordnance Corps was responsible for procuring and issuing all ordnance and ordnance stores –

armaments, ammunition, all armoured fighting vehicles; radio, electrical and optical equipment; clothing; and general stores. In 1942, the repair of vehicles and other electrical and mechanical equipment passed to the newly formed Royal Electrical and Mechanical Engineers. *See also* ARSENALS; ARTILLERY; ENGINEERS; FIREARMS; SIGNALS; WEAPONS.

J.-M. GOENAGA
JOHN CHILDS

FURTHER READING
A. Forbes, *A History of the Army Ordnance Services* (3 vols, London, 1929); O. F. G. Hogg, *The Royal Arsenal* (2 vols, Oxford, 1963); N. Skentelberry, *Arrows to Atom Bombs: a history of the Ordnance Board* (London, 1975).

Orhan *See* OTTOMAN TURKS

Orléans, Siege of (1428–9)   Adverse reaction to the Treaty of Troyes (1420) sparked off partisan warfare in those areas of France occupied by the English, especially Normandy. However, the French field forces were heavily defeated by the English and the Burgundians at Cravant in 1423 and by the Duke of Bedford at Verneuil in 1424. In desperation, Charles VII of France (1422–61) allied with Duke John V of Brittany, but John was routed by Bedford at St James, near Avranches, in 1426. The English and Burgundians then proceeded to attack the heart of Charles VII's remaining lands. The Earl of Shrewsbury took Laval in Maine in 1426 and, in 1428, the Earl of Salisbury laid siege to Orléans in order to gain a crossing of the Loire before advancing on Berry.

Orléans was a large, populous and well-fortified city. The English first attacked the Bastille des Tourelles, a twin-towered masonry work which protected the southern end of the bridge over the Loire. Salisbury was mortally wounded during the successful storming of the Bastille, the Earl of Suffolk succeeding to the command. Suffolk invested Orléans with seven wooden forts on the northern side and a further four to the south. However, Suffolk had insufficient men to blockade the eastern side of the city and a trickle of supplies continued to enter Orléans although never enough to eliminate the danger of starvation. The field army of Charles VII attempted to interrupt the food and supply convoys of the English. On 12 February 1429, a convoy of 300 waggons under the command of Sir John Fastolf was attacked at Rouvray to the north of Orléans. He formed his waggons into a laager in the Hussite manner and defeated his assailants in the 'Battle of the Herrings'. Orléans had now become a symbol of French resistance and nationalism as manifested by numerous peasant risings in the English occupied territories. The arrival of Joan of Arc at Chinon provided the leadership and inspiration for a French revival. On 27 April 1429, she set out for Orléans with a convoy of supplies escorted by between 3,000 and 4,000 armed men. Receiving considerable assistance and advice from professional soldiers, Joan entered Orléans on 29 April. The English besiegers were now so reduced in number that they were locked inside their forts and the French were able to enter and leave Orléans virtually at will. Between 4 and 7 May, Joan and the French attacked and captured a number of the English forts causing the siege to be lifted on 8 May. Under Joan's guidance, the French retook the line of the Loire before recapturing Châlons and Rheims, where Charles VII was formally crowned on 18 July 1429. *See also* AGINCOURT; SAINTS, MILITARY; SIEGES; WAGGON-LAAGER.

P. CONTAMINE
JOHN CHILDS

FURTHER READING

M. G. A. Vale, *Charles VII* (London, 1974); A. H. Burne, *The Agincourt War* (London, 1956).

Ostend, Siege of (5 July 1601–20 September 1604) The great struggle for Ostend – a siege that contempories termed the new Siege of Troy – was the focal point of the final stage of the Dutch Revolt. The loss of Sluys in 1587 had left Ostend the last Dutch

outpost on the Flemish coast. Together with its symbolic value, its retention was also desired by Elizabeth I, and from 1585 there had always been an English contingent in the garrison. Despite the fact that it had been isolated on land since 1587, Ostend was not without its strong points. Since its two harbours opened directly onto the sea and the Spaniards lacked the shipping to mount a blockade, the Dutch were able to replenish and reinforce it without effective hindrance. Thanks to the estuarial waters that formed its harbours and the sand dunes on which it was built, its complex ring of fortifications was difficult to destroy by bombardment. The North Sea weather made winter operations largely impossible. Lastly, owing to the strategic situation in the Netherlands and two major mutinies in the Army of Flanders between 1600 and 1605, Archduke Albert of Habsburg, the Spanish governor-general, was unable to concentrate sufficient men for an effective siege. He undertook the siege at the request of the States of Flanders who had been alarmed by the Battle of Nieuport in 1600, and offered him a subsidy for the reduction of Ostend. He began on 5 July 1601, with an army of 20,000 against a garrison of about 6,000, commanded initially by Sir Francis Vere. The Spanish siege battery of fifty-nine cannon fired what contemporaries considered the incredible number of 1,000 rounds a day during the autumn, but only slow progress was made and a major assault on 7 January 1602 was repulsed. The Dutch were able to keep the garrison up to strength by the regular rotation of units, but the expense incurred led the States-General to press Maurice of Nassau to relieve the town. However, Maurice, made cautious by Nieuport, refused to invade Flanders directly and chose instead a diversionary operation along the Rhine. This led to the capture of Grave (18 September 1602), which, in conjunction with the mutiny, kept the Spanish investing force too low to mount an assault. In an attempt to cut Ostend's sea communications the Spaniards sent a flotilla of galleys to Flanders in 1602, but it was intercepted by Dutch warships and its commander, Federico Spinola, killed. In 1603 Maurice mounted another diversionary operation, the Siege of 's Hertogenbosch. A second major Spanish assault on Ostend on 13 April 1603 failed, and the siege was only revived when Federico Spinola's brother Ambrosio offered to conduct it at his own expense. Spinola took command in October 1603, but it was not until the spring of 1604 that the weather permitted him to make progress. A bitter struggle for the outerworks took place between April and June 1604, during which five Dutch governors were killed in succession. Domestic pressure on Maurice to halt Spinola's progress led him to propose the siege of Sluys, which would either relieve Ostend or provide a more useful replacement. This siege began in July, and, after an attempt by Spinola to break it failed, Sluys surrendered on 18 August 1604. By this stage, however, the Ostend garrison held only a small portion of the works, and when it became clear that Maurice would not proceed further, the last Dutch governor, Daniel van Hertaing, Heer van Marquette, sued for terms on 20 September 1604. Given that both sides were equally skilled and determined, and that the Spaniards did not possess the decisive weapon in sieges – starvation – Ostend could only become a struggle of attrition. The number of lives lost during the course of the siege remains unknown, though contemporaries talked in terms of 100,000 men. The successful conclusion made Spinola's reputation and boosted the morale of the Army of Flanders, but the siege exhausted both sides. Its length also demonstrated one of the key aspects of the strategy of the Netherlands wars. Whatever the overall strengths of the opposing armies, garrisons absorbed such a large proportion that both sides could only muster field armies of between 5,000 and 20,000 men. An operation on the scale of Ostend would soak up all their deployable resources which, in turn, could easily be reduced below the effective level by a mutiny or a diversion. *See also* BELGIUM; GARRISONS; KINSALE; NASSAU; NETHERLANDS; NIEUPORT; SIEGES.

SIMON ADAMS

FURTHER READING
The most accessible narrative account is still that found in J. L. Motley, *History of the United Provinces* (London, 1876 edn), iv. However, the place of the siege in Dutch strategy is discussed at length in Jan de Tex, *Oldenbarneveldt* (Cambridge, 1973), i; and, more briefly, in Spanish strategy by G. Parker, *The Army of Flanders and the Spanish Road, 1567–1659* (Cambridge, 1972), pp. 249–50.

Ottoman Turks The Ottoman state originated in a Turkoman tribe which the Seljuk sultans established, along with other tribes, on the Byzantine frontier in Asia Minor. At the point when the Seljuk Empire declined, which coincided with the deterioration of the power of Byzantium, these tribes began the gradual conquest of the old Greek territories. They were fired with a dynamic religious spirit and strengthened by the presence of militant confraternities, such as the *gazis*, of which the first Ottomans were members.

After settling the eastern parts of Bithynia, Bey Osman I (1280–1324), who gave the dynasty its name (*Osmanli* – Ottoman), and his son, Orhan (1324–59), made their conquests using the traditional military organization consisting essentially of Turkish cavalrymen under the leadership of the various tribal and clan chiefs commanded by the bey and other members of his family. Orhan soon discovered that undisciplined nomads, although useful in the initial act of conquest, were incompatible with the need to settle and institutionalize occupied territories. He accordingly founded a separate, professional, paid army, loyal to himself. The new, regular infantry were called *yaya*, grouped into tens, hundreds and thousands, while their mounted counterparts were *müsellems* organized into troops of thirty men. Both Christian and Muslim Turks were employed initially but the latter soon became prevalent. Although technically salaried, the troops usually received lands in lieu of pay. Gradually, the Turkoman tribes were pushed towards the frontier and employed as irregular shock troops, with the terms *akinci* (raider) for the horsemen and *deli* (fanatic) or *azab* for the infantry replacing the nomenclature of *gazi*. They operated in advance of the regular troops, raiding into Greece, Hungary and even as far as Austria.

Between 1340 and 1350, Süleyman Pasa (1316–58), the son of Orhan, carried out a reorganization of his father's army. This was made necessary by the poor quality of the existing soldiers and the fact that their first loyalty was to their commander rather than to the sultan. Building on the old Seljuk system of training young slaves, the new soldiers were 'slaves of the Porte' (*kapikullari*), men who came into the sultan's possession as his *pençik*, or one-fifth share of all plunder captured from the enemy. These young men were educated in the Turkish language and culture, converted to Islam, and trained as soldiers. The infantry were known as *yeni çeri* (new troops), janissaries to Europeans, while the cavalry were called *sipahis*. The *yayas* and *müsellems* were relegated to garrison and rear area duties leaving the janissaries and *sipahis* to execute the conquests. The system was regularized by the *pençik kanun* (law of one-fifth) embodied in 1362 or 1363.

The territories conquered by the Ottomans were divided into fiefs, *timars*, and given to military commanders in return for services. As the commanders of the *yayas* and *müsellems* acquired *timars* and became *timariots*, the treasury passed to them responsibility for the troops' payment and support. In effect, the central government decentralized the *yayas* and *müsellems* thereby creating a territorial militia. The cavalry of the *kapikullari*, principally the *sipahis*, were also transferred to *timariots*. It became the responsibility of the *timariots* to make good use of their lands ensuring that they provided the revenues stipulated by the state and, when necessary, supplied a number of armed soldiers proportionate to the revenue of the *timar* at the rate of one equipped soldier (*djebeli*) for every 3,000 *aspres* of revenue. Gradually, the *timariots* came to be known as *sipahis* and formed the *timariot* cavalry which was organized into companies (*beuluks*) under the command of a *soubashi*. The *beuluks* were grouped into regiments (*alay*) commanded by *alay beyi* and then into brigades (*sancak* or *liva* – standard or banner) under the direction of *sancak beyi*. Several *sancaks* were commanded by the two governors-general,

beylerbeyis (bey of beys), who ruled the provinces (*eyalets*) of Anatolia and Rumelia.

Around 1380, Murad I (1359–89) refined the military system by converting the *kapikullari* into his own, personal troops, independent of the *yayas* and *müsellems* of the provincial army. By the *devsirme*, or forced levy system, a fixed number of Christian boys aged between eight and sixteen were rounded up at the rate of one child per family in the European provinces of the Ottoman Empire. The villages in which this recruitment took place were designated on a rota basis throughout Bulgaria, Serbia and Greece, then in Albania and Bosnia and later in Hungary and the islands of the Aegean. The round-up normally occurred every two or three years and only a few hundred individuals were concerned. After being taken to Anatolia, where they were converted to Turkish customs and to Islam, they were transferred to the Palace of Gallipoli where they formed the group of *adjemioghlan* (foreign children). Depending on their particular abilities, they were either assigned to the corps of *itchoghlan* (children of the interior) who served in the royal household guard, or to the corps of janissaries or the cavalry where they gradually supplanted soldiers who had been recruited from among Christian prisoners. Around 1390, there were about 10,000 *kapikulu* divided equally between the infantry (janissaries) and the cavalry (*kapikulu süvarileri*). The pay of the janissaries and the cavalry came directly from the state treasury. By 1500, the term *sipahi* referred exclusively to the *timariot*, feudal cavalry in the provinces. Bayazid II (1481–1512) extended the *devsirme* system to the Christians of Anatolia.

The janissaries were led by an *aga*, appointed by the sultan, who could play an important role in affairs of state. His two deputies were the *koul kahya* (chief quartermaster) and the *segban bashie*. A dozen officers comprised the general staff. The janissaries were divided into four divisions (*jemaat*, *beuluk*, *seimen* and *adjemioghlan*) which were split into 229 *ortas* (battalions), which varied in strength from fewer than 100 to more than 500 men. Each *orta* was commanded by a *corbaci*. The *ortas* were subdivided into *odas* (barrack rooms) each commanded by an *odabaci*. Each large formation of janissaries was directed by an *aga* who was answerable to a commander-in-chief, the *aga* of the janissaries.

The *kapikulu süvarileri*, generally known as *sipâh* (horsemen) or *bölük halki* (regiment men), were divided into six regiments and enjoyed higher pay than the janissaries. The first two regiments were the *ulufeciyân* (salaried men), split into right and left, formed during the reign of Murat I; the third and fourth were the *gureba* (foreigners), again organized into a regiment of the right and one of the left, composed of Muslim mercenaries; and the final two regiments, the *silâhtars* (weapon bearers) and the *sipahi oglan* (*sipahi* children), were raised during the reign of Mehmet I (1413–21). The *silâhtars* and the *sipahi oglan* were the elite of the cavalry, guarding the sultan in battle and acting as the vanguard on campaign. Their soldiers came from among those of the *itchoghlan* who were not quite good enough for palace service, children of existing cavalrymen in the six regiments, other Muslims, mostly Arabs, Persians and Kurds, and janissaries who had distinguished themselves in battle. By 1600, there were 6,000 *bölük halki*, rising to 20,844 in 1700 and 22,169 early in the eighteenth century.

Towards the end of the fourteenth century an artillery corps was created – Murad I possessed gunpowder artillery at the Battle of Kossovo in 1389. Gunners were recruited from among the *adjemioghlan*, but the origin of the technical personnel is unknown. Defeats by the Mamluks in eastern Anatolia led Bayazid II (1481–1512) to equip the janissaries with handguns, probably arquebuses, and to develop a more mobile field artillery. During the fifteenth century, the corps of *cebeci* (armourers) was created to manufacture, repair and transport the janissaries' firearms. Its foundry and barracks were located at Tophane in Istanbul. Murat II (1421–51) organized a cannon corps (*topçu ocagi*), later reformed by Bayezit II,

charged with manufacturing ordnance and operating the guns at sieges and in battle. The cannon corps had 1,100 men in 1574 and 5,000 by 1700. Mehmet II (1451–81) introduced a cannon-waggon corps (*top arabaci*) to transport arms and ammunition on campaign; its headquarters and waggon factory were also at Tophane. Mehmet further created a corps of miners and sappers (*lagimciyan*) and a mortar corps (*humbaraciyan*) to manufacture and operate mortars, grenades and bombs both on land and at sea.

During the last quarter of the fifteenth century, the Ottoman army comprised 10–12,000 janissaries, 8,000 regular cavalry, 600 ordnance troops, and around 40,000 *timariot sipahis*, making, in total, some 60,000 men. In the sixteenth century, after the expeditions and conquests achieved by Selim I (1512–20) and Süleyman the Magnificent (1520–66), the expansion of the Ottoman Empire made it easy to create new *timars* leading to an increase in the number of *timariot* soldiers. At the end of the sixteenth century however, the halt to new conquests and internal difficulties put an end to the growth of the *timars*, while the regular forces increased in number. There were 20,700 regular soldiers in 1510, 27,000 in 1560 and 48,000 in 1595. These figures included, respectively, 12,000, 13,300 and 26,000 janissaries; 7,000, 11,200 and 17,000 cavalry; 500, 800 and 3,000 *cebeci*; and 1,200, 1,200 and 1,300 gunners. We know that there were 37,521 holders of *timars* in 1527, 28,000 of whom were *sipahis* who, with their men-at-arms (*cebelis*), formed a force of 70–80,000 men. Alongside these there were also fortress soldiers, fortress *timariots* (around 10,000) and the various service troops and specialist corps. In total, around 1600 the Ottoman Empire could probably call upon the services of 100,000 troops.

Up to and including the reign of Süleyman the Magnificent, the sultan himself commanded the army in the field although he sometimes delegated this power to the Grand Vizier. Military campaigns took place between April and September/October; the late autumn and winter were devoted to preparing for the next year's expeditions. The campaigns were constructed around the main routes across Anatolia and Rumelia where logistical bases were established in key towns: Erzurum on the road to Iran and Azerbaijan; Diyarbakir and, later, Mosul and Aleppo, on the road to Syria. In Europe, Adrianople (Edirne) was the starting-point for Balkan expeditions, supported by Sofia, Nis and Belgrade; further north were the bases of the Danubian region – Ismailia, Silistra and Ruschuk; finally, Salonica stood on the route into Greece and Albania. During marches strict discipline had to be observed and each corps occupied its specified place. In battle, the Ottomans relied on an essentially defensive posture usually described by Europeans as 'the Turkish crescent'. The sultan with his cavalry (*bölük halki*) and janissaries occupied a central redoubt defended by earthworks, palisades and artillery. On the right (Rumelia) and left (Anatolia) stood the *sipahi* cavalry and the *yaya* and *azab* infantry. Usually, the basic tactic was to employ the *akinci* light cavalry to draw the enemy into an attack. The janissaries then fought the main part of the action from their defensive positions before the sultan's standard. This remained the pattern of Ottoman warfare until the eighteenth century. Up to the middle of the sixteenth century, the Ottomans gained a series of important victories and conquests, during which time they were considered virtually invincible, on account of their discipline, methodical organization, high quality weaponry and skilful leadership.

Even before the end of the sixteenth century this conquering dynamism was waning, arising from a relaxation in discipline and a desire to take advantage of the gains which had been made. Not only were Ottoman troops no longer winning victories but conflict broke out between janissaries and *sipahis* (1622). Lastly, a clear weakening of the Ottoman government brought about a change in the *timar* system: the holders transformed their *timars* into their own private property which they could hand down to their heirs, an irreversible development which gave birth to a landed aristocracy which was to play an important

political role during the seventeenth and eighteenth centuries. Effectively, the *timar* holders turned their backs on their military obligations and the feudal army rapidly declined. To preserve its military power, the Ottoman government intensified recruitment, not through the *devsirme* system, but by enlisting Christians and Muslims – deserters, mercenaries, underage boys – from Anatolia and Rumelia. The number of these soldiers rose from 48,000 in 1595 to 66,300 in 1609. It stood at 70,900 in 1630, 85,000 in 1652, 61,300 in 1660, 95,000 in 1669, 87,300 in 1690 and 59,000 in 1702 following the Peace of Carlowitz. Two-thirds of these numbers were composed of janissaries. The actual corps of janissaries was hugely expanded, reaching 200,000 by 1750, as men purchased the privileges attached to membership of the corps but hired inferior substitutes to undertake their military duties. As the *timariot* army dwindled, the janissaries and other *kapikulu* corps took over provincial garrison and occupation duties serving under local commanders, further weakening the concept of a professional force at the sole disposal of the sultan. The changing nature of warfare was also responsible for these changes. As the Ottoman boundaries solidified during the early seventeenth century, the predominantly cavalry army was no longer needed. Infantry was now at a premium to garrison fortifications. Across Europe, the seventeenth century saw the gradual demise of the emphasis on cavalry in favour of the musket-armed infantryman. The rise in the numbers of troops caused serious financial problems which the political leaders attempted to solve by increasing taxation although this led to revolts, particularly in Anatolia. The results of this decline were seen in the last two decades of the seventeenth century when, after the failure to capture Vienna in 1683, the Turks were evicted from Hungary by the Habsburgs (1683–99).

Grand Vizier Hüseyin Pasha (1644–1702) set about reforming the Ottoman army after the Peace of Carlowitz in 1699. The janissary corps, which had grown to 70,000 during the war although only

10,000 actually served, was cut to 34,000 fighting men and the artillery corps was reduced from 6,000 to 1,200. The *sipahis* were again required to provide sufficient armed retainers when required and the authority of *sancak beys* was re-established. The reign of Mahmut I (1730–54) saw a second bout of military reform after the appointment of the French nobleman, Claude-Alexandre, Comte de Bonneval (1675–1747), as technical adviser. Although his attempts to re-organize the janissaries along Western European lines failed, Bonneval did have some success in modernizing the artillery, engineering and other technical services. Baron François de Tott (1730–93), a Hungarian, created a modern artillery corps for the Turks in 1774 plus a school of mathematics and a new cannon foundry. Selim III (1789–1807) introduced examinations and inspections for officers and removed many incompetents. The corps of janissaries was reduced to 30,000 and a beginning was made in introducing them to modern firearms. However, although Selim's reforms only achieved limited success with the janissaries and the *sipahis*, the artillery, engineering, and transport and technical branches were brought thoroughly up to date and commanded by young Ottoman officers trained by Frenchmen and Hungarians. Finally, despairing of reforming the janissaries yet fearful of arousing their political opposition, Selim abandoned his attempts at reform and created a brand-new infantry force to supplant them – the *nizam-i cedit* (new order). The corps was trained, clothed, drilled and disciplined in the European manner and adopted European tactics and weaponry under the direction of experts from France, Germany and England. It was financed by a new series of revenues. Recruits came from Turkish peasants in Anatolia and the corps was housed in barracks overlooking the Bosphorus at Levend Çiftlik near Istanbul. The first regiment was created in 1794, a second in 1799 and a third in 1801. The corps contained 2,536 men and 27 officers in 1797 but 9,263 men and 27 officers in 1801. The introduction of conscription in Anatolia in

1802 enabled the *nizam-i cedit* to expand to 22,685 men with 1,590 officers by 1807. Along with the reformed artillery and the foundation of technical schools and modern foundries for cannon and manufactories for small arms, Selim produced the bases for the complete modernization and westernization of the Ottoman army. The fall of Selim III brought the instant reversal of all his reforms but the abolition of the janissaries in 1826 allowed Mahmut II (1808–39) to reform the army along the precedent of the *nazim-i cedit*. The new *Mansure* army possessed infantry regiments divided into three battalions, each of which comprised eight companies. Recruits were provided through forced levies and conscription. This reform was paralleled in the cavalry and in the feudal militia where the basic unit became the infantry battalion of 889 men. The latter developed into a reserve militia after 1833. From this point, the Ottoman Turks ceased to follow an independent military development and adopted the Western European pattern even though the state failed to develop the necessary infrastructure.

The final *timars* were abolished in 1831. Under the influence of Prussian advisers (including the young Helmuth von Moltke in 1835–9 and Colmar von der Goltz in 1886–97), the Ottoman army was fixed in 1843 at a strength of 150,000 in the first line with 90,000 reserves, the soldiers being chosen by lot through a system of conscription and serving for five years. The Ottoman army was the first in Europe to be organized into permanent brigades, divisions, corps and military districts. One of the weaknesses of the army was a lack of trained and educated officers. To remedy this shortcoming, a Military Academy was opened in 1834 and a Staff College in 1849, a Military Medical School was founded, and the Naval and Military Engineering Schools from the eighteenth century were further developed. At a more fundamental level, special military secondary schools were established after 1855 and, by 1897, there were twenty-nine such schools attended by 8,250 pupils.

Although the Ottoman army resembled

the Prussian and German armies in its tactics, weaponry, organization and training and could give a good account of itself in action (Plevna, 1877, and Gallipoli, 1915), the economic and social weakness of the Ottoman state undermined the efforts of its armed forces leading to political and military collapse in 1918.

The Navy Because Ottoman conquest and expansion relied principally on land campaigns, the Ottoman navy was initially relegated to guarding the coasts and transporting soldiers. The navy was thus slower to develop but finally grew to maturity during the later sixteenth century. However, its institutions did not possess the *sui generis* qualities of the Ottoman army and from the earliest beginnings the navy was heavily dependent upon the practices of the Italian naval powers, particularly Genoa and Venice. The commander of the navy, the *derya bey* (bey of the sea), sometimes called *kaptan* after the Italian *capitano*, was granted permanent *timars* in Gallipoli and Algiers to provide funds for shipbuilding and the maintenance of the navy. The *kaptan* later became the grand admiral (*kaptan-i derya*) and administered his service through the Imperial Dockyard, an umbrella organization which co-ordinated the work of several dockyards throughout the Ottoman Empire. Each vessel was commanded by a captain (*reis*) but larger ships were commanded by a *hassa reis* who held a *timar* from which to provide a crew and necessary funds. Not until the late seventeenth century was a structure of command interposed between the grand admiral and the individual ship captains. Crews were found from the coastal provinces, including Greeks, Dalmatians, Albanians and Turks, to whom the name *levent* was applied. These seamen served in lieu of taxes or in return for salaries. The oarsmen (*kürekçiler*) were prisoners of war or criminals.

Oar-powered ships were called *çektiri* and classified according to the number of oar-benches. *Kirlangiç* (frigates) had between ten and seventeen benches with two to three men per oar and also carried a crew of 70–80 *levents* and officers. Brigantines (*pergende*) had 18 benches, galliots (*kalite* or *kalyota*) between 19 and 24 with a total complement of 250 men. Galleys (*kadirga*) had 25 benches accommodating 200 oarsmen; a further 150 *levents* and officers completed the crew. Large galleys (*bastarde*) had 500 oarsmen plus 300 soldiers and sailors. Some sail-powered ships were also employed: the two-masted *agripar* with 40 cannon; the two- or three-masted *barça* (barque) with 65–70 cannon; and various three-masted vessels, the largest carrying 110 cannon and a crew of 1,000 men.

During the 1690s, the Ottoman navy changed from oar-powered to sail-powered ships and introduced a new command structure. The fleet was divided into squadrons, each under a *derya bey*, who supervised training and victualling. A rear admiral (*kapudane*), a vice-admiral (*patrona*) and a staff admiral (*riyale*) assisted the grand admiral. Merit was made the basis for promotion, pensions and full wages were introduced for both officers and men and a special naval branch of the artillery corps was created. This modernization was speeded up during the first decade of the eighteenth century. Between 1774 and 1784, Gazi Hassan Pasha re-modernized the Turkish fleet. With the assistance of British and French technical experts, he introduced up-to-date ship designs, built new dockyards in the Aegean, the Golden Horn and the Black Sea, and developed de Tott's school of mathematics into a naval engineering school. In 1784, the Turkish fleet consisted of twenty-two ships of the line and fifteen frigates. Gazi Hassan's successor, Küçük Hüseyin Pasha (1792–1803) continued this process including the foundation of a system of conscription in the Aegean coastal provinces. Despite the crushing defeat at Navarino (1827), the Turkish navy continued on its path of Western development throughout the remainder of the nineteenth century. *See also* AIN DJALOUT; ANKARA; BYZANTIUM; CAVALRY; CONSTANTINOPLE; DARDANELLES; DORYLAEUM; HATTIN; HULEGU; IRAN; KOSSOVO; MANZIKERT; MEHMET II; MONGOLS; NICOPOLIS; NUR-AD-DIN; SALADIN; VIENNA; YARMUK; ZENTA.

R. MANTRAN
JOHN CHILDS

FURTHER READING

Robert Mantran, *Histoire de la Turquie* (3rd edn, Paris, 1968); *A History of the Ottoman Empire*, ed. M. A. Cook (Cambridge, 1976); H. Inalcik, 'Ottoman methods of conquest', *Studia Islamica*, ii (1954); S. T. Christensen, 'The heathen order of battle', in *Violence and the Absolutist State*, ed. S. T. Christensen (Copenhagen, 1990), pp. 75–138; S. J. and E. K. Shaw, *History of the Ottoman Empire and Modern Turkey, 1280–1975* (2 vols, Cambridge, 1976–7); David B. Ralston, *Importing the European Army: the introduction of European military techniques and institutions into the extra-European world, 1600–1914* (Chicago, 1990), pp. 43–78.

Overlord (Normandy landings) (6 June–18 July 1944)   *Overlord* was the code name of the Allied landings in Normandy which began on 6 June 1944. The date for the invasion of Western Europe by a cross-Channel attack was initially set for 1 May 1944 at the Trident Conference, held in Washington on 12–25 May 1943. This conference, which was attended by Roosevelt, Churchill and the Allied chiefs of staff, was the culmination of earlier discussions for invasion, all of which had suffered from differences between British and American strategical ideas. Preliminary planning for *Overlord* was carried out under a British officer, Lieutenant-General Sir Frederick Morgan, who established a combined British–American body, Chief of Staff to the Supreme Allied Commander, to co-ordinate and plan the effort. After the Tehran Conference in November 1943, overall command of the invasion was given to an American general, Eisenhower. Eisenhower came to London early in 1944, and Morgan became his deputy chief of staff. Taking into consideration earlier Allied experiences with amphibious landings – including the Dieppe raid (19 August 1942), North Africa (8 November 1942), Sicily (9 July 1943), Salerno (9 September 1943) and Anzio (22 January 1944) – plans were made for landing five divisions along a 40-mile front. Naval and air support were to be put under the control of two British officers, Admiral Sir Bertram Ramsay and Air Chief Marshal Sir Arthur Tedder. Such an undertaking demanded a considerable degree of logistical support: troops had to be carried in landing craft, some of which had to be diverted from the Mediterranean, floating harbours (mulberries) had to be installed on the French coast and sunken pipelines (PLUTO – pipelines under the ocean) laid across the Channel. The Germans had built a defensive system (Atlantic Wall) which ran all along the coasts of Western Europe and was particularly dense along the Channel coast. The total air superiority of the Allies enabled them, by driving off German reconnaissance aircraft, to ensure that preparations were carried on in secret. An elaborate deception campaign was also mounted which left the Germans in doubt as to the ultimate objective. The German communication routes were harassed by constant bombing, a task in which the French resistance also played its part through repeated acts of sabotage. Five points on the Normandy coast between the Orne and the Cotentin were chosen for the landings. The British were given three beaches – codenamed Gold, Juno and Sword – while the Americans had two – Omaha and Utah. The overall control of the ground forces was given to Montgomery. On 6 June 1944 some 176,000 men, transported in 4,000 ships landed under the protective fire of 600 warships. They were preceded by three airborne divisions.

Somewhat paradoxically, while Eisenhower, at the head of a coalition, had real powers, Hitler had divided up authority between von Rundstedt, the commander of the Western Front, and Rommel, the commander of coastal defences, while the German navy was under the command of Dönitz, the *Luftwaffe* under Goering, intelligence under Himmler's SS, and fortifications under the *Organisation Todt*. Further, the military commanders of the Netherlands, Belgium and France retained control of the administration.

Believing, due to the Allies' efforts at deception, that the principal Allied objective would be the Pas-de-Calais, Hitler was slow to send reinforcements to Rundstedt and Rommel. By 12 June, the units that had landed had joined up and formed a solid bridgehead and supplies were flowing ashore from the artificial harbour at Arromanches. By 17 June nearly 500,000 men and 90,000 vehicles had come ashore. However, the Allies made progress only with difficulty, as the Germans made good use of the natural obstacle presented by the Normandy hedgerows. The Allies' advance was halted outside Caen, but they made better progress in the Cotentin, where Cherbourg surrendered after a five-day siege (27 June). The port could not, however, be brought back into operation until 7 August. On 13 July, the British captured Caen, which had resisted for a month, and the Americans took a ruined St Lô on the 18th. The Allies lost 122,000 men in the operation, while the Germans lost 114,000, including 41,000 taken prisoner. The success of *Overlord* is attributable to the close all-arms co-operation, the smooth functioning of the Anglo-American command structure and the unprecedented logistical build-up. *See also* COMBINED OPERATIONS; EISENHOWER; MARSHALL; MONTGOMERY; NORMANDY; PATTON.

A. CORVISIER
KEITH NEILSON

FURTHER READING
F. H. Hinsley et al., *British Intelligence in the Second World War: its influence on strategy and operations* (3 vols, London, 1979–84); Carlo D'Este, *Decision in Normandy* (New York, 1983); John Keegan, *Six Armies in Normandy* (London, 1982).

P

Pacifism The natural and legitimate desire for peace has inspired a variety of currents of thinking, the traces of which can be found as far back as Classical Antiquity, particularly in Aristophanes (d. *c*.385 BC) (*The Acharnians*, *The Peace*, *Lysistrata*). The two terms 'pacifism' and 'internationalism', which appeared at the end of the nineteenth century and between which Marcel Merle feels it difficult to distinguish, stand at the termination of long processes of intellectual development running, through Christianity or utopianism on the one hand, and natural or positive law on the other, over two millennia. Pacifism may range from the dream of universal peace to the desire for peace at any price; internationalism extends from the pacifist dream of union between all peoples without national distinction to the union of men fighting for a common cause against enemies perceived as forming another international which is hostile to peace (the 'holy alliance' of peoples against the holy alliance of kings, the proletarian international against the international of capitalist interests).

The strict point of view of military history permits us to regard the study of these various strands and attitudes as a single complex, though we shall also seek to bring out the differences between them. In Ancient Greece, a number of thinkers expressed the desire to introduce into relations between states legal rules inspired by those prevailing within the various city-states. Certain forms of worship and the administration of common temples (Delphi, etc.) gave birth to the Amphictionies which issued decrees (sacred truces) intended to limit wars, at least between brother peoples. Similarly, medieval Christian theologians and jurists tried to define and impose rules, generally taking natural law as their starting point. Appeal was frequently made to natural law in the work of

Vitoria (*c*.1492–1546) and the Spanish theologians, and of Gentili (1552–1608) and Grotius (1583–1645). It was found that the content of natural law was problematic because of disagreements about the character of the state of nature: whereas Pufendorf (1632–94) and Burlamaqui saw this latter as peaceful, Hobbes (1588–1679) and Locke (1632–1704) saw it as a barbarous condition. However, Wolff (1679–1754) and Vattel (1714–67) in the eighteenth century showed the issue to be still more complex by arguing that states could not be governed by the same rules as individuals. Despite the advances made by positive law, the reference to natural law still inspired the Jesuit Taparelli in *Essai théorique de droit naturel* (1841–3) and, in the twentieth century, the papal encyclical *Pacem in terris* (1963).

Another current emerged at the end of the fifteenth century with Pierre Dubois and G. de Podiebrad. This was a school of utopian writers who presented, in an imaginary future, both a critique of the present and plans for an ideal society. The leading exponents of utopianism were Thomas More (1478–1535) in *Utopia* (1516), Campanella (1568–1639) and, later, Sully (1559–1641), William Penn (1644–1718) and the abbé de Saint-Pierre (1658–1743). In fact, it was the critique of war rather than plans for bringing about a future state of peace which inspired most of the pacifists. La Bruyère (1645–96) and Fénelon (1651–1715) were *moralistes* who saw war as an absolute evil created by the unleashing of the worst instincts of human nature. The Enlightenment philosophers followed their lead though with some variations, such as Voltaire's scepticism, the utilitarianism of David Hume and Jeremy Bentham and Bernardin de Saint-Pierre's sentimentalism, which was to be the foundation of the Romantic school's attitude towards war right down to Tolstoy's total pacifism and Mahatma Gandhi's (1869–1948) theory of non-violence. In spite of certain fundamental differences, the quest for peace through progress and the quest for peace through revolution may be regarded as continuations of this particular train of thought.

The success of the theories of positive law in the nineteenth century opened other avenues for envisaging the future. Whereas, from the end of the seventeenth century onwards, the main hopes for peace had resided in the establishment of a balance of power, at the end of the nineteenth, two schools of thought, which were concerned to distance themselves from utopianism, sought ways to achieve peace. Federalism, the school of Proudhon's disciples, saw the creation of a federation of peoples as a way of reducing the threat of war, while 'Solidarism' sought to bring about *de facto* cases of international solidarity leading, by way of agreements between states, to a system of *de jure* solidarity established by the arbitration of a tribunal. This latter movement, whose most famous representative was Léon Bourgeois (1851–1925), inspired the Hague Conventions of 1896 and 1907 as well as the League of Nations.

The aim of Federalism was either the removal of economic frontiers (examples might be the German *Zollverein* (1834), which pre-dated Pierre Proudhon (1809–65), and the European Economic Community of 1952, or the reduction of the importance of political frontiers (Aristide Briand, 1862–1932). There were, however, frequently discrepancies between the ends and the means. It took the impact of the Second World War for these various trends to coalesce in the formation of the United Nations Organization in 1945. The increase in the number of democratic regimes, even though they were very varied in nature, imposed democratic ideology as the framework for such basic documents as the United Nations Charter or the Universal Declaration of Human Rights, which tended to orient states towards arrangements likely to remove certain causes of conflict. However, these efforts encountered an increase in the number of appeals made to the right of self-determination which, by 'Balkanizing' certain parts of the world, created new problems.

These various pacifist currents may have a demobilizing effect on individuals, except where they mobilize them to resist all forms of nationalism, inspiring anti-militarism or even opposition to the armed forces of the homeland. Such resistance may be passive, as in the case of conscientious objectors who refuse to perform military service, an attitude with deep historical roots, i.e. the Christian martyrs in the pagan Roman Empire. Although Christianity recognized a duty to bear arms, the earlier pacifist attitudes resurfaced in a number of Protestant sects, most notably the Quakers and the Anabaptists. More generally, non-violence was raised to the status of a theory by Gandhi, who saw it as the weapon of the weak.

However, it has proved possible for pacifism to be diverted into violence, declaring war on war, or to be virtually hijacked by internationalist revolutionary movements. First sabotage, then terrorism, became the preferred weapons of these movements. These techniques acquired effectiveness through both the cycle of provocation and repression and the oxygen of publicity and amplification provided by the media.

One of the indirect results of pacifism is the degree of favour presently enjoyed by fully professional armies which can be attributed to latent anti-militarism. Compulsory military service has disappeared from a number of states where it had been, in many cases, only grudgingly accepted. Where military service does rest on a solid tradition, rather than giving weapons to men who are reluctant to use them or who might even be ready to turn them against their own country's institutions, governments have chosen to accept the right to conscientious objection by creating a form of civilian national service, which is a little longer than the military form, and by increasingly entrusting the main military tasks to units composed of specially trained volunteers. This neatly dovetails with current developments in the art of warfare.
See also GENTILI; GROTIUS; LAWS OF WAR;

MORALE; NATIONALISM; NUMERICAL STRENGTH; RECRUITMENT; SOLDIERS AND SOCIETY; VATTEL; VITORIA.

A. CORVISIER

FURTHER READING
Sydney D. Bailey, *War and Conscience in the Nuclear Age* (London, 1987); Wolf Mendl, *Prophets and Reconcilers: reflections on the Quaker peace testimony* (London, 1974); J. Y. Yoder, *Nevertheless: the varieties of religious pacifism* (Scottdale, PA, 1971); Marcel, Merle *Pacifisme et internationalisme, XVIIe–XXe siècles* (Paris, 1966); Jean Rabault, *L'Antimilitarisme en France, 1810–1875: faits et documents* (Paris, 1975).

Pagan, Blaise François, comte de (1604–65) *See* FORTIFICATION

Paixhans, Henri-Joseph (1783–1854) Paixhans was a French artilleryman who had a major influence on the development of heavy artillery. Finding himself unemployed after service in the Napoleonic Wars, he published books on heavy artillery in 1815, on its effects on sea power in 1822 and 1825, and on its consequences for the defence of France and Paris in 1830 and 1834. Paixhans reckoned that guns in static positions could employ a large mass with reduced velocity, and so fire shells rather than solid shot. Shells could therefore be fired at long ranges and flat trajectories, rather than be restricted to field guns or to mortars and howitzers. From the mid-1820s onwards France and Britain, following Paixhans' principles, developed a whole new series of heavy large-calibre guns, for both sea service and coastal defence. Shell fire proved as capable of penetrating wooden ships as did solid shot, and furthermore broke up within the hull, so causing further damage. The iron-clad vessel was thus the consequence of Paixhans' development. *See also* ARTILLERY; FRANCE; GUNFIRE; NAVIES.

HEW STRACHAN

FURTHER READING
Howard Douglas, *A Treatise on Naval Gunnery* (London, 1851); *Nouvelle biographie générale* (Paris, 1862), xxxix.

Pakistan The state of Pakistan was founded in 1947 when the Indian subcontinent was granted independence from British rule. It consisted of two territories with East Pakistan on the Bay of Bengal separated by over 1,000 miles from West Pakistan. The only factor common to both territories was the Muslim religion. Muslims had been under-represented in the Imperial Indian Army so that when the Pakistani armed forces were created at independence the highest ranking officer was a solitary major-general. Initially, the army was 150,000 strong, mainly recruited from Punjabi peasantry. The modern army has over 500,000 soldiers, plus an equal number of reserves, while a further 20,000 serve in the navy and 45,000 in the air force. The army has 2,000 main battle tanks, the navy possesses six submarines and thirteen principal surface ships, while the air force flies 327 combat aircraft.

The dominating issue of Pakistani foreign and defence policy has been its relationship with India, especially concerning the status of Jammu and Kashmir. This has resulted in a number of conflicts, the first occurring immediately after independence. Kashmir was ruled by a Hindu family but the majority of the population was Muslim. In western Kashmir, fighting broke out against the Mahahrajah, and Azad (Free) Kashmir was declared with the backing of Pakistan. The Mahahrajah, appealed to India which responded by sending troops leading to fighting between regular Pakistani forces, the Indian army and the Azad Kashmiri rebels. A truce was finally agreed at the end of 1948 by the two British generals who were the chiefs of staff of the Indian and Pakistani armies. Early in the following year, a UN ceasefire line was established (the Line of Control) dividing Kashmir into Indian and Pakistani sectors, the latter containing 700,000 people out of a total population of four million.

With the onset of the Cold War, Pakistan was courted by the United States and received material aid. In 1954 she became a signatory of two regional alliances – the

South-East Asian Treaty Organization (SEATO) and the Central Asian Treaty Organization (CENTRO). Internally, the military became increasingly involved in politics and came into power in 1958 through a coup led by General Ayub. Martial law was retained until 1962 although the military remained formally in control of the state until 1969.

In the meantime, the Kashmir question had again come to the fore. After her defeat by China in 1962, India began to reorganize and re-arm her forces. Although this alarmed the Pakistanis, it also gave them the opportunity to extend their hold over Kashmir. A number of small incidents along the Line of Control during early 1965 were followed by infiltration by Pakistani irregular units and the engagement of regular forces in August. The Pakistani armoured units included modern US Patton M-60 tanks and the air force flew US F104 Sabres. The Indian army possessed some British Centurions but most of her tanks were either light or of Second World War vintage while her only high-performance aircraft were a few Soviet MIG-21s. International pressure from the United Nations but, more particularly, the British and US decision to cut military supplies, brought about a ceasefire. Having each suffered about 3,000 fatal casualties, both sides agreed to return to their pre-August positions.

Growing demands in East Pakistan for greater independence from West Pakistan largely resulted from the need for good relations with India which the government of General Ayub, with its Kashmir policy, could not provide. Ayub was replaced in 1969 by General Yahia Khan and elections were arranged for 1970. The Awami League, an organization that campaigned for a degree of independence for East Pakistan, won a majority in the National Assembly. General Yahia postponed indefinitely the opening of the Assembly leading to riots in East Pakistan, the declaration of martial law and the deployment of more troops. India supported Mukti Bahini, the militant wing of the Awami League, and to counter this Pakistan once more threatened the Line of Control in Kashmir and even

attacked Indian airfields in early December 1971. India retaliated but this encouraged Azad Kashmiri irregulars to attack Indian positions along the Line of Control. These attacks gave Indira Gandhi, the Indian prime minster, the justification she needed to attack Pakistani army units in East Pakistan. The Indian army was now much better equipped with Russian T-55 and T-56 tanks as well as the home-produced Vickers Vijayanta tank, a Centurion derivative. The Pakistani units in the East had only light tanks. While the Pakistani armoured troops in the Kashmir with their Pattons were able to hold their own, the light forces in the East were no match for the superior Indian armour and aircraft. On 6 December 1971 Mrs Gandhi announced that India recognized the independence of Bangladesh and the Pakistani soldiers in the East surrendered on 15 December.

Since then there have been no major clashes along the border in Kashmir although there have been many incidents and tension remains high. However, the Pakistani military have been heavily involved in domestic politics and there have been periods of martial law in 1970–3 and 1977–89. In addition, a number of internal security problems have arisen, notably in Baluchistan. Pakistan is no longer a member of SEATO and the US arms embargo has pushed Pakistan more towards the Chinese, with whom they have been co-operating on research and development, procurement and technology transfer. The Pakistani army currently has a number of Chinese T-69 tanks. The Soviet invasion of Afghanistan restored some US aid and arms although Pakistan's reluctance to abandon her nuclear projects has forfeited much US goodwill especially since the ending of the Cold War has reduced the United States' need to secure regional allies against the Soviet Union.

The continuing struggle of the Mujaheddin against government forces in Afghanistan has created major security problems. In 1987 it was estimated that there were over three million Afghan refugees in Pakistan and, at one time, there were over 100 different resistance organizations operating from Peshawar. Soviet/

Afghan forces violated Pakistani air space and pursued the Mujaheddin across the border. Pakistani villages were also bombed. General Zia ul-Haq was unable to adopt a neutral stance as he was pressurized, particularly by the United States, by those interests which wished to funnel aid to the Afghan rebels through Pakistan. Since the Soviet withdrawal, these difficulties have lessened but the use of Pakistani territory as a safe refuge continues.

The resumption of civilian rule in 1989 with the election of Benazir Bhutto, and her replacement in August 1990 by Nawaz Sharif, has led to no reduction in the strength of the military. In 1990, Miss Bhutto gave way to the military's demands for an acceleration of the nuclear programme. Neither India nor Pakistan is a signatory of the Nuclear Non-Proliferation Treaty. India tested a device in 1974 and both countries have nuclear research facilities. It has been estimated that Pakistan might have sufficient fissionable material to manufacture up to seven devices. The air force possesses the capability to deliver early generation nuclear weapons and there have been a number of tests of missile systems. India and Pakistan recently signed a treaty undertaking not to attack each other's nuclear facilities. The Jammu and Kashmir region remains a permanent source of tension between the two countries and the likely flash-point for any future conflict.

Although the population of Bangladesh is the same as that of Pakistan (115,000,000), her armed forces are much smaller reflecting both her poverty and her reliance upon India's support and protection. In 1991, her army numbered 93,000 men and was equipped with 50 main battle tanks and 40 light tanks. Her navy (7,500 men) operated four frigates and 35 coastal craft while her air force (6,000 men) flew 85 combat aircraft. In addition, 55,000 men served in the paramilitary border and internal security guards and in the armed police. See also CHINA; DISARMAMENT; INDIA; NUCLEAR WARFARE.

DAVID WESTON

FURTHER READING
Russell Brines, *The Indo-Pakistan Conflict* (London, 1968); Stephen P. Cohen, 'Pakistan army, society and security', *Asian Affairs* (Summer 1983); E. H. Dar, 'The Pakistan army in the 1980s', *Army Quarterly and Defence Journal*, cxiv (1984); B. M. Kaul, *Confrontation with Pakistan* (Delhi, 1971); Fazal Muqueem Khan, *The Story of the Pakistani Army* (Oxford, 1963); D. K. Palit, *The Lightning Campaign: the Indo-Pakistan war, 1971* (Salisbury, 1972).

Panic Panic is a sudden, uncontrollable fear or alarm which can quickly become infectious. It can affect soldiers and civilians. Its cause appears to be a feeling of helplessness and does not affect just those who have fired their last round. In fact, it occurs when ammunition is still available, but it accompanies an impression – whether true or false – of being abandoned, surrounded or overwhelmed or, in any event, of the situation being hopeless. Panic may paralyse, or may induce bewildered flight. It inhibits readiness for self-sacrifice and feelings of honour and loyalty to a unit; it can also engender senseless, indeed suicidal, behaviour. Such lack of self-control may be momentary; there have been many instances where units carried away by panic have been rallied and re-formed. Such feelings can be brought under control by an *esprit de corps* such as, for example, encouraged the soldiers of the Burgundian regiment to stand fast at Malplaquet (1709), while in the same brigade the Alsatian regiment scattered. Besides, enemy pressure will be less intense in some places during a battle than in others. The Duc de Boufflers remarked, when speaking of Dettingen (1743), that those regiments 'which did not make a charge are those which may be considered to have acted wisely, since they had no cause for breaking up in disarray'. If localized, a panic does not seriously endanger the success of a battle or a campaign, as shown by such examples as Fontenoy (1745), the bridge of Arcola (1796) and Bertrix (1914). If it is general, then the whole battle could be forfeit in a very short time as at Killiecrankie in 1689.

Panic in a regular, professional army is relatively rare and is often concealed in official reports. On the morrow of Arcola, no mention was made of the 'unspeakable cowardice' of the troops, although attested by Sulkowski, one of Bonaparte's aides-de-camp, and by a number of other witnesses. After Dettingen, the Minister of War intercepted all letters at the frontier. When it became impossible to deny the wholesale failure, Noailles, the commander-in-chief, in an open letter to the king, laid the blame on the poor performance of the militia and the recruits. Subsequently, he directed the storm of criticism on to the French Guards. Only a study of the secret correspondence between Noailles and Louis XV reveals that the most famous units of the royal household had 'behaved as badly' as the rest. After Minden (1759), which was a far more serious defeat, hardly any criticism arose, since there the soldiers had fought fiercely. The historian has, therefore, to use great care over the construction he puts on occurrences where silence has always been considered expedient, otherwise there is a danger of unjustly fastening long-lasting discredit on *corps d'élite*, which naturally were given the more dangerous positions in battle. When collapse spreads through a whole army, there can be a feeling that national honour has been tarnished, as occurred in France over Rossbach (1757) or in Italy after Caporetto (1917).

In their panic, soldiers try to get to safety by any means – if necessary, by jumping into water. The 'ducks of the Main' acted like that at Dettingen, accepting the danger of drowning, as did also Napoleon's grenadiers in the Alpone and the French at the Beresina in 1812. But flight is only the final manifestation of panic. Generally speaking, it shows itself first as a state of mental disarray; even chance occurrences make men unable to carry out movements either collectively or individually in the manner they have learned during training, or just to behave as they have done previously in other battles. In the eighteenth century, officers recognized the symptoms when they saw their mounted men unable to manoeuvre, or their infantrymen hastening to fire their weapons before they were even within range of the enemy.

The figures of losses and the study of wounds can be illuminating. A regiment or an army seized by panic will, in fact, leave on the battlefield more prisoners than wounded or killed. Officers and, indeed, NCOs too, more often master their fear; when deserted by their rank and file, they pay a very high price for their steadfastness. At Dettingen, one officer in six was killed in the French Guards, but fewer than one soldier in fifteen. A grenadier is said to have written to his wife: 'we took to flight; if our officers had done the same, far fewer of them would have been killed.' The way in which units in those days were drawn up for battle meant that infantrymen were likely to be wounded on the left side of their bodies, which they presented to the enemy when firing or when levelling their bayonets in the regulation position for awaiting an attack. Cavalrymen, on the other hand, would normally be struck by sword strokes on their right side. The description of the wounds suffered by 411 of those engaged at Malplaquet (1709), and who were placed in Les Invalides, allows the conclusion that the majority of them were at their proper stations, and that the panic was restricted to a few regiments.

Explanation of instances of panic is a much harder task than their mere description, if only because, on the morrow of a defeat, a general may be doing no more than advancing lame excuses, when he blames, for example, the poor quality of the recruits he has received. Surprise appears to be a determining factor in many cases. It can be caused by the unexpected courage of an enemy whom troops have not met in battle for a long while. In 1743, for example, at Dettingen, the French believed that they could break through the Anglo-Hanoverian dispositions by shock tactics in a sudden assault – a short-cut procedure which had succeeded against the Austrians in 1734 and 1742. It was a lamentable failure when it came up against the fire-power and sang-froid of the British infantry. The large-scale employment of new weapons by one side only can produce disarray among its enemy. The gunners and infantry who occupied the heights of Bulson and the woods of the Marfée, near Sedan, on 13 May 1940, were deafened by the screams of the Stukas, which had complete control of the air. They became victims of an illusion, and imagined that the

German tanks had already crossed the River Meuse, when in fact they were still on the right bank.

Surroundings which seem full of threats and are impenetrable to the eye are apt to lead to fatal mistakes. The collective madness which gripped Dillon's column near Lille, on 29 April 1792, was doubtless made worse by the fact that it was night-time. Nothing else could explain why the bolting of a few horses in the rearguard should lead to a murderous stampede. Even more seasoned troops can be subject to panic when they find themselves without protection among hedges or woods which conceal the enemy's movements from them, and where they run the risk of having their retreat cut off. At Malplaquet, thickets and gulleys partitioned the battlefield; at Dettingen, the French unwisely took up position with a deep ditch behind them; at Bertrix, it was in the midst of a forest that a German division made a surprise attack on the front and rear of the artillery units of the 17th Corps.

Human factors must not be overlooked. The regiments of the 33rd Infantry Division, which was routed at Bertrix, were raised from garrisons in Aquitaine. Possibly the behaviour of the soldiers should be put down to the environment from which they came, and which (according to Colonel J. Defrasne) 'did not particularly predispose them to standing up to an ordeal'; or they may have felt that the north-east frontier was too remote from their 'homeland'. In the pre-Revolutionary period, the blame was more frequently laid on lifestyle rather than on region of origin. The French Guards failed to stand fast on several occasions, and opinion was that this was because most of them were not trained soldiers, but workmen, worn out and corrupted by residence in Paris. Another view was that becoming used to victory perhaps blunted their courage; it was because the soldiers of Year V had become accustomed to sacking Italy that they forgot love of country and glory at Arcola. More frequently, panic can be explained by a lack of psychological and physical training, made worse by under-nourishment and, especially, by repulsion at the experience of the sight, sound and smell of suffering and death, and of bodily contact with them. Neither Dillon's soldiers nor the Rouen *gardes mobiles*, who were put to flight at Buchy in 1870, had any real experience of war; both were, in addition, hungry.

In the end, men will risk their lives only if they have confidence in their leader. The great commanders of the sixteenth century made a habit of issuing, before a battle, a solemn challenge in a swashbuckling speech, intended to show the community between the general and his soldiers in the face of danger. The soldiers who behaved like heroes under the command of Maurice de Saxe or Löwendahl must have been much the same men who had fled under Noailles two years previously. An unnecessary order to retreat, given by a general who was suspected of betraying the Revolutionary cause, was enough to trigger a panic in Dillon's column. Many British soldiers who advanced into enfilading French artillery fire at Fontenoy in 1745 fled in panic before the charge of the Highlanders at Falkirk early in 1746. Later that year, they successfully resisted the Highland charge at Culloden. The first effective use of gas by the Germans, at Ypres in 1915, caused total panic and the disintegration of two French divisions creating a 4½-mile gap in the front. By 1916, both the British and the French had learned how to deal with the new weapon. Familiarity with the enemy – knowing what to expect – was as important as confident, professional leadership.

Technical advances have considerably increased the number of those who could be subject to attacks of panic in the twentieth century; at the same time, they have reduced the role of topographical conditions and human factors. The effects of 'total war', with bombing from the air and the use of chemical weapons, magnified alike by propaganda, can bear directly on the whole of a population. This type of warfare does not restrict itself to damaging an enemy's armed strength; it seeks also to foster a feeling of insecurity and misery which will lead to irrational behaviour, such as instances of mass exodus by civilians or the overthrow of a legitimate government accused of being unable to defend the country. *See also* COMMAND; ESPRIT DE

641

CORPS; ETHOS; GLORY; LANGUAGE; LOSSES OF
LIFE; MORALE; VEXILLOLOGY.

J. CHAGNIOT
JOHN CHILDS

FURTHER READING
E. Dinter, *Hero or Coward. Pressures facing the
soldier in battle* (London, 1985); John Keegan,
The Face of Battle (London, 1976); Christopher
Duffy, *The Military Experience in the Age of
Reason* (London, 1987); M. Dixon, *The Psychology of Military Incompetence* (London, 1976).

Parachute troops The use of parachutes
stretches far back into history. As early as
1306, Chinese acrobats attached to parachutes jumped off towers. At the same time
as the first flights with early forms of
balloons, experiments using animals were
carried out with rigid parachutes.
Jacques-André Garnerin, the first real
parachutist, who jumped from a balloon on
22 October 1797, advocated the use of
parachutes for military purposes. Parachute demonstrations were given throughout the nineteenth century and, at its close,
a German named Kathe Paulus made the
first jump with a folded parachute.

With the increasing frequency of aircraft
accidents, the parachute became an object
of great interest as a safety measure. The
first jump from an aircraft took place in
1912. But air crews during the First World
War, apart from those of Germany at the
end of the conflict, were not equipped with
parachutes. On the other hand, parachutes
were adopted by observers in the French
balloon corps at the end of 1915, and by the
British and German balloonists in 1916.
During the First World War, the Italians,
and later the Germans, dropped by parachute a few soldiers on special missions.

The first airborne operation proper was
carried out by the Soviet Union on 2 August
1930. Several Soviet paratroop battalions
were formed in 1932 and, during the 1934
manoeuvres, 1,500 paratroops were
dropped. Other nations quickly followed
suit. On 1 April 1935, Goering formed the
first German paratroop unit. On 2 October
1936, France decided to form two groups of
airborne infantry, and these were raised on

1 April 1937. Italy formed her first airborne
unit in 1938; the British and Americans did
not follow suit until 1940.

At the time of the occupation of the
Sudetenland, the Germans had contingency plans for an airborne operation.
Nazi paratroop units were dropped on
Denmark and Norway in the spring of 1940,
demonstrating the value of such troops. On
10 May 1940, during the German invasion
of Belgium, glider-transported paratroops
seized the two bridges over the Albert
Canal and a key position – Fort Eben-
Emael – while in Holland 4,000 paratroops
captured bridges and airfields. These successful actions played a valuable part in
ensuring the success of the German offensive.

The effectiveness of paratroops against
limited objectives at considerable distances
from the fighting front encouraged the
Allies to use them on an equally large scale.
Prompted by David Stirling, the Allies
created, at the end of 1941, the Special Air
Service (SAS), which destroyed 400 German and Italian aircraft in Libya in the
following year. The SAS was later used
throughout Europe.

Paratroops were particularly used in the
Second World War for raids in depth.
Typical episodes of this sort were those
mounted against the Japanese in Burma by
Wingate (British) and Merrill (American).
These raids had as their object attacks on
lines of communication and depots, capturing or destroying airfields, the carrying
out of sabotage (like the destruction of
the Brunéval radar station on 27 February
1942) and helping guerilla operations in the
enemy's rear echelons (as was frequently
done by the Soviets). Paratroops have also
been used on missions with a political
purpose, like Otto Skorzeny's daring
snatch of Mussolini from captivity on 12
September 1943.

Paratroops also were used in large-scale
operations, of which the German major-
general Kurt Student was an advocate. But
Student's paratroops suffered heavy losses
when they occupied Crete in May 1941, and
Hitler subsequently gave up employing
them in large formations. The Americans
did not, however, and utilized paratroops

extensively in combined operations. This was particularly evident at the Normandy landings, where two US and one British division of paratroops were employed. The largest airborne operation of the Second World War was at Arnhem in Holland in September 1944. This operation featured 35,000 paratroops, but it failed and over 13,000 paratroops were either killed, wounded or missing. Subsequently, there was a return to operations of smaller scope. These were often more productive; a particularly successful example was the establishment of a Rhine bridgehead on 25 March 1945. Serious losses in paratroop operations resulted often when the troops were dropped in error either close to enemy defences or onto inhospitable terrain.

In the conflicts of the second half of the twentieth century, the large-scale use of paratroops has been given up, particularly in conventional wars. In the Korean War, for example, paratroops were only dropped once. But paratroops proved particularly well suited for employment in wars of decolonization due to their mobility and rapidity of deployment. In Indo-China, French paratroops were used to extricate or reinforce outpost garrisons and, utilizing the element of surprise, to retake towns that had fallen into enemy hands. Some examples of this were *Operation Lea* in the Langson-Caobang area and the destruction of an enemy base on 9 November 1952 when 1,500 weapons and 250 tons of ammunition were captured (this latter operation was successfully repeated at Langson in July 1953). Paratroops did not always act alone in Indo-China; they also co-operated with other army units. In October 1951, while two mixed groups advanced against Colonial Highway No. 6 and the Black River, three French parachute battalions dropped on Hoe Binh and captured it. On 25 November 1953, when French army units took Dien Bien Phu, paratroops comprised 40 per cent of the total numbers employed, and they were reinforced by six further paratroop battalions during the course of the battle.

The glory gained by the effectiveness and heroism of the French paratroopers at Dien Bien Phu led to their becoming the spearhead of the French army in Algeria. Their reputation rose even higher after the Suez actions on 5 and 6 November 1956, at which time the employment of helicopters led to a transformation in the use of paratroops. Only one large airborne operation took place during the Algerian War, and that was in November 1957 when paratroops were dropped at Timimoun in the Sahara. As in Korea, paratroops in Algeria were chiefly used as a general reserve, and as specialists for short and intense engagements. However, they were competent to deal with any kind of assignment including the task of wiping out terrorism in Algiers in 1957.

During the Vietnam War, American paratroop units, carried by helicopter, were used intensively. Because this type of operation had the advantage of putting the fighting troops down with greater accuracy and of bringing them immediately to grips with the enemy, it began to be employed widely. The Israelis used these tactics during both the Six Day War in June 1967 and the Yom Kippur War in October 1973. The Egyptians parachuted commandos behind the Israeli lines on the Suez Canal.

Although the parachuting of equipment and supplies retains its tactical value, the dropping of paratroops has been, in general, replaced by landing troops by air. However, in some circumstances, the use of paratroops remains the only feasible mode of action, especially when the objectives are far from the take-off bases. Good examples of this were the dropping of Belgian paratroops at Stanleyville in 1964 and Kolwezi in 1978 in order to rescue Europeans taken hostage by the Congolese.

Even though the dropping of paratroops has tended to disappear as a tactical method, all countries have kept, or have provided themselves with, airborne units. Small powers maintain a company, a battalion or a regiment of paratroops, medium ones a brigade or a division, while the United States has two airborne divisions and the Soviet Union had seven. In every country, paratroops constitute a *corps d'élite*; their exploits during the Second World War and in other conflicts have become legend and have given paratroops a particular aura.

The special assignments which they are given require novel types of organization and of unit structure. Operations require meticulous preparation, and command during action is widely decentralized, which means that a great deal is left to individual initiative. Hence, these units often provide a haven for strong, nonconformist personalities like Lord Lovat or Bigeard. Trained for every type of action in which his branch of the army engages – and every branch has its paratroop units – the 'para' is conscious that he is a member of an elite, of a higher category akin to medieval knights and select formations in the past.

In order to build up the 'para spirit' in paratroop units, training concentrates on developing the penchant for taking risks, for effort, for daring, even recklessness, and for stretching capacities to their limit. Along with cultivating this particular outlook, paratroop units are distinguished from other units by special uniforms and often by a contempt for certain so-called 'bourgeois values'. The participation of paratroops in conspiracies and coups d'état has earned them the steadfast enmity of many who view the paratroops as opponents of Western, democratic values.

Paratroops and their world, therefore, constitute a kind of 'order', with its own vocabulary and rite of initiation – the first jump. For many, after the fear that accompanies the first jump, parachuting becomes an exciting activity in itself. Following jumps with automatic opening, that is, where the parachute cover is pulled off by a strap on exit from the aeroplane, a further step is to make jumps with a parachute that opens only when the wearer so wishes, thus allowing free fall. Parachuting has become a competitive sport, and various shapes of parachute have been developed which allow greater accuracy in reaching the desired point of landing. *See also* AIRBORNE TROOPS; AVIATION; COMBINED OPERATIONS; INFANTRY; MARINES; TRANSPORT, AIR.

G. BODINIER
KEITH NEILSON

FURTHER READING
Histoire mondiale des parachutistes, ed. Pierre Sergent (Paris, 1974); Michael Hickey, *Out of the Sky: a history of airborne warfare* (London, 1979).

Paris, Siege of (19 September 1870–28 January 1871) On 19 September 1870, the Chief of the Prussian General Staff, Helmuth von Moltke, invested Paris. The city was defended by a system of fortifications comprising a continuous *enceinte* of two lines supplemented by advanced detached forts. The garrison comprised numerous *ad hoc* formations plus the *gardes mobiles*, assisted by the National Guard. Moltke had to conduct two important sieges simultaneously – Paris and Metz. His lines of communication were threatened by the *francs-tireurs* while Léon Gambetta's (1838–82) hastily improvised armies, of little value despite their courage but continually expanding as stragglers and deserters returned to duty, tried to interrupt his operations. Moltke did not let himself be distracted from the most important business, the Siege of Paris, especially after the government of the Republic issued a proclamation on 4 September in which it announced its refusal to leave the capital city. Just when the armies of the Republic started to function more effectively, the surrender of Metz (27 October) released enough German troops to counter all the attempts to relieve Paris. Three unsuccessful sorties were made by the Governor of Paris, General Louis Trochu: at Bougival-Montretout (29–30 November), at Champigny (21 December), and at Le Bourget (19 January 1871). The Germans bombarded the city in an attempt to establish a psychological advantage but without effect. Starvation eventually caused the capitulation of Paris. All soldiers and the *gardes mobiles* were taken prisoner while the National Guard were allowed to retain their arms in order to fulfil necessary police duties. On 1 March, the German army made a triumphal entry into Paris. The Siege of Paris had cost the French armed forces many more killed and wounded than the German army in addition to exceptionally high civilian casualties. The presence of a government within a besieged city was thenceforth forbidden.

The Siege of Paris also demonstrated that the siege remained an effective military and political strategy in the age of modern industrial warfare. This lesson was to be repeated at Port Arthur (1904–5), Stalingrad (1942–3), Leningrad (1941–4), Saigon (1975), and Sarajevo (1992–). *See also* ARTILLERY; FORTIFICATION; FRANCE; GERMANY; MOLTKE; SIEGES.

A. CORVISIER

FURTHER READING

Michael Howard, *The Franco-Prussian War* (London, 1960); Alistair Horne, *The Fall of Paris: the Siege and the Commune, 1870–1* (London, 1965).

Parma and Plasencia, Alexander Farnese, 3rd Duke of (1545–92) Captain-general of the Army of Flanders from 1578 to 1592, the Duke of Parma was the son of Octavio Farnese and Philip II's half-sister Margaret. He was unique among Spanish commanders of the sixteenth century in being both an Italian prince and a member of the royal family. This gave him an unusual political and moral ascendancy over the multinational army, but it also inspired suspicions of his own dynastic ambitions and partiality for Italians.

Parma's military career began in the retinue of his cousin Don Juan of Austria at Lepanto, and he followed him to the Netherlands in 1577. On Don Juan's death on 1 October 1578 he succeeded him as captain-general. His overall appraisal of the strategy needed to defeat the Dutch Revolt differed little from that made by the Duke of Alba earlier in the 1570s, but he possessed a far greater political sensitivity. Although the diversion of Philip II's resources to the conquest of Portugal between 1578 and 1583 reduced his army to little more than a garrison, Parma was remarkably successful in winning back the Catholic nobility. In 1584–5 he rapidly regained the key cities of Flanders and Brabant through a mixture of shrewd exploitation of the dissensions among the rebels and well-planned sieges. But, after his greatest achievement, the surrender of Antwerp in August 1585, following a year-long investment, his ability to maintain the momentum of the reconquest was crippled by English intervention and diversions ordered by Philip II, most notably the preparation of the enterprise against England. The Armada campaign of 1588 remains the most controversial episode of Parma's career, and accusations that he had deliberately failed to co-operate with the fleet dogged his last years.

In 1590 Parma was ordered again to divert the Army of Flanders from the reconquest of the Netherlands: this time to relieve the Catholic garrison of Paris in the French Civil War. Parma's conduct of this campaign and a second to relieve Rouen in 1592 (in which he sustained the wound from which he died) were masterpieces of sixteenth-century generalship and the Spanish school of strategy. In both cases he accomplished his strategic purpose by a combination of manoeuvre and the offensive use of field entrenchments that completely foiled Henry IV's attempts to force him into a disadvantageous battle. Parma's widely recognized stature as a commander owed much to his versatility; his employment of strategic deception, careful observation and rapid exploitation of his enemy's weak points, together with well-organized sieges and a combination of shock tactics and entrenched firepower, made the best of the professional skills of his army. He possessed only a limited influence over Philip II's grand strategy, however, and therefore was forced to fight campaigns in which he had little ultimate confidence. *See also* ALBA; ANTWERP; ARMADA; LEPANTO; NASSAU; NETHERLANDS; SPAIN.

SIMON ADAMS

FURTHER READING

L. Van der Essen, *Alexandre Farnèse, duc de Parme, gouverneur général des Pays-Bas* (5 vols, Brussels, 1933–9); G. Parker, *The Army of Flanders and the Spanish Road, 1567–1659* (Cambridge, 1972). For Parma in 1588, see also, H. O'Donnell y Duque de Estrada, *La fuerza de desembarco de la Gran Armada contra Inglaterra (1588)* (Serie Gran Armada V, Madrid, 1989); H. O'Donnell et al., *Los Sucesos de Flandes de 1588 en relacion con la empresa de Inglaterra* (Serie Gran Armada III, Madrid, 1988); F.

Riaño Lozano, *Los medios navales de Alejandro Farnesio (1587–1588)* (Serie Gran Armada VII, Madrid, 1989).

Passchendaele   *See* YPRES, BATTLES OF

Patton, George S., Jr (1885–1945)

Patton was the leading US tank commander in the Second World War. He was born in California and attended both the Virginia Military Institute and the US Military Academy at West Point from which he graduated in 1909. Patton entered the cavalry, and eventually taught at the cavalry school in Fort Riley, Kansas. In 1916, he was part of the Punitive Expedition to Mexico, in which campaign he saw combat. In 1917, Patton became part of the US Expeditionary Force in Europe, where he became a tank commander. Patton was promoted to colonel during the First World War, but reverted to captain after the war ended as a result of the reductions in the US army. During the interwar period, Patton published articles dealing with tank tactics and taught in various army schools. In 1938, he was again promoted to colonel. In 1941, Patton was given command of the 2nd Armoured Division, and in the following year he was placed in charge of the 1st Armoured Corps. In November 1942, Patton led the US forces that invaded Africa. The following April, he was given command of the 7th Army as it prepared to invade Sicily. The Sicily campaign was Patton's triumph, but revealed some of his more unpleasant traits. After capturing both Palermo and Messina with rapid movements of his forces, Patton was left as part of the occupying force in Sicily as a result of his striking two hospitalized soldiers whom he suspected of malingering. Patton thus missed the Italian campaign and his career was not rehabilitated until 1944 when he was given command of the US 3rd Army during *Operation Overlord* and the Battle of Normandy. Patton's troops exploited the breakout into Brittany (*Operation Cobra*), and by November they had reached the Saar. In December 1944 and January 1945, Patton helped defeat the German counter-attack in the Ardennes, the so-called 'Battle of the Bulge'. When the Allied forces renewed the offensive, Patton was particularly effective. In March and April, his forces advanced 30 miles a day in the dash for Kassel. Patton's wish to drive on to Prague was not granted because that city was in the zone recognized as a Soviet area of operations. In September 1945, Patton was relieved of his command because of his refusal to prohibit former Nazis from holding positions in the organizations set up under the Occupation. In December 1945, Patton died as a result of injuries sustained in an automobile accident. *See also* BRADLEY; EISENHOWER; MONTGOMERY; NORMANDY; OVERLORD; UNITED STATES.

KEITH NEILSON

FURTHER READING
Martin Blumenson, *The Many Faces of George S. Patton, Jr* (Colorado Springs, 1972); Hubert Essame, *Patton: a study in command* (New York, 1974).

Pavia (Lombardy), Battle of (24 February 1525)

Pavia is both the most famous and the most complex and confusing of the battles of the Italian wars of the early sixteenth century. Following the repulse of an Imperialist invasion of Provence at the Siege of Marseilles in September 1524, Francis I decided to exploit his advantage by a rapid invasion of Italy. At the end of October he laid siege to Pavia. However, the stout defence by its garrison of 6,000 Spaniards and Germans under Antonio de Leyva forced Francis to maintain the investment into the new year. An Imperialist relieving army was quickly assembled under Charles de Lannoy and the Marquis of Pescara and by the end of January 1525 they had forced the French into an entrenched camp. Throughout Europe this was regarded as a decisive contest of endurance. However, Francis then made two controversial detachments of substantial contingents from his army and, on 23 February, the Imperialists decided to mount a night attack on the French camp. There is some evidence that Francis had received a warning of this and had drawn out his troops, but the foggy morning of the 24th saw a confused encounter battle begin in the walled park of a country house. Francis attempted to crush the Imperialists by a charge of the *gendarmerie* of the *maison du roi*, but they in turn were surprised at short range by a relatively small unit of 1,000 Spanish arquebusiers. The massacre of the *maison du roi* and the capture of the king led to the collapse and rout of the French army (particularly the large Swiss contingent) by noon that day. Reinforcements and detachments on both sides make the numbers involved particularly difficult to compute, but in January 1525 the Imperialists comprised 22,000 foot and *c*.2,500 horse and the French between 24,000 and 26,000 foot and upwards of 6,000 horse. The capture of Francis I gave the battle an unusual political significance, but the whole campaign was close run. If the slaughter of what amounted to the core of the French court reinforced the lesson of La Bicocca, Francis's widely criticized conduct of both the campaign and the battle suggests that simple bad generalship was equally important. *See also* BICOCCA; FRANCE; SPAIN.

SIMON ADAMS

FURTHER READING
Jean Giono, *Le Désastre de Pavie* (Paris, 1963); R. J. Knecht, *Francis I* (1982).

Pearl Harbor (7 December 1941) The Japanese airborne attack of 7 December 1941 against the US fleet anchored at Pearl Harbor began the Pacific phase of the Second World War. The surprise nature of the assault has resulted in Pearl Harbor's becoming a symbol of the need for a nation to be prepared for war in time of peace.

During the summer of 1941, amidst the worsening diplomatic relations between the United States and Japan, Admiral Isoroku Yamamoto, the commander-in-chief of the Imperial Japanese Navy, announced a plan for a surprise strike of carrier-based aircraft against the US Pacific Fleet stationed at Pearl Harbor in Hawaii. Should the Japanese destroy the bulk of the US Fleet, Japan would be able to garner a substantial empire in South-East Asia while the United States was powerless to interfere.

While diplomatic negotiations between Japan and the United States were still going on in Washington, the Japanese strike force – six aircraft carriers, two battleships, three cruisers, nine destroyers and a number of supply ships – assembled secretly in the Kuriles. This force, commanded by Vice-Admiral Chuichi Nagumo, set out for Pearl Harbor on 26 November. On 5 December, a final message from Tokyo authorized the attack on Hawaii. The attack, carried out by two successive waves of dive bombers and torpedo planes, took place on the morning of Sunday, 7 December. For the loss of 29 aircraft and five midget submarines the Japanese achieved a spectacular success: 8 battleships were either sunk or damaged, 3 cruisers were seriously damaged, and 160 aircraft were destroyed on the ground. The Japanese lost fewer than 100 men, while American killed, wounded and missing amounted to about 4,500.

The Japanese success was considerable, but incomplete. The three aircraft carriers of the US Pacific Fleet were not in Pearl Harbor at the time and thus escaped damage. Nagumo decided against launching a third attack on the installations (particularly the oil reserves) at Pearl Harbor with the result that they remained largely intact, allowing the US fleet both to fuel and to repair itself relatively quickly. The major miscalculation by the Japanese was political. The 'date which will live in infamy', as President Franklin Roosevelt termed the attack on Pearl Harbor, produced an extraordinary wave of anger and indignation in the United States, sweeping aside the isolationist sentiment that had been prevalent until that time. Japan thus found itself fighting a total war against the United States instead of a limited war leading to a negotiated settlement of Japanese–American differences. Contrary to the belief held by many, Roosevelt was not aware of an impending Japanese attack on Pearl Harbor, although last-minute information about Japanese intentions might have induced the US military to place the base on the alert. *See also* JAPAN; NAGUMO; NAVAL WARFARE; UNITED STATES; YAMAMOTO.

P. MASSON
KEITH NEILSON

FURTHER READING

Walter Lord, *The Day of Infamy* (New York, 1957); Roberta Wohlstetter, *Pearl Harbor: warning and decision* (Stanford, 1962); John Toland, *Pearl Harbor and its Aftermath* (New York, 1982); Gordon W. Prange, *At Dawn We Slept* (New York, 1981).

Peltasts *See* GREECE, ANCIENT; INFANTRY; IPHICRATES

Pensions While oriental empires furnished pensions to old soldiers to keep them from mutiny, the Greek city-states cared for the children of those who had died in battle and granted pensions to men disabled in war. Certain civic employments were reserved for disabled veterans. During the Middle Ages, they were permitted to beg on the public highway, a pension having become an exceptional favour granted by a sovereign to his most faithful servants following long service or disability. A monarch sometimes undertook to provide a living for a man who, after service into which he had voluntarily entered and for which he had received pay, had become unable to subsist without help. However, the man's wages had been the monarch's sole legal obligation towards his servant. The only factors that could influence a monarch to award pensions as an act of grace were the charitable impulses instilled by Christianity, a sense of humility, a concern to present an image of magnanimity – which was another way of demonstrating royal power – and the wish to take some precautions against the threat to himself inherent in the discontent of men who had been reduced to want and then abandoned without succour. Latter-day social developments have undermined the sovereign–servant relationship and replaced it with a reciprocity of duties which are binding on both the citizen and the state. The former is required to serve while the latter has an obligation to provide compensation, in the form of a disability pension, for wounds or other injury received in that service. A disability pension is designed to provide the soldier or conscript with the same level of livelihood that would have been his by right at the termination of his normal period of engagement. Military retirement pensions after long service fall within the principle that the state is required to provide for the old age of those who have served it during the active years of their lives. Whereas formerly a man might have benefited from an act of grace, he now receives that provision by right and legislation merely defines the conditions within which that right is exercised.

French kings and Holy Roman Emperors exploited the tradition of charity which lay at the heart of Christianity. By arranging residence in abbeys for old soldiers whom age and wounds had rendered unfit for further active service, the abbots were made responsible for maintaining these burdensome 'lay monks' as one of the Church's natural duties. Later, when monarchs set up residential establishments for their retired servants, the religious houses whose annual revenues exceeded 1,000 livres were required to provide pensions for the 'lay monks'. In France, these were paid up to 1789.

The impoverishment of the Church caused by the Reformation forced Protestant countries to find alternative methods of providing for veterans. In 1593, 1597 and 1601, the English Parliament passed statutes to help disabled soldiers and sailors, largely to reduce the threat of vagrancy and crime. Each parish had to levy a weekly rate of between 2d and 10d to create a county fund from which the justices of the peace could issue pensions. In 1588, the 'Chatham Chest' was established into which all serving seamen paid 6d a month, the resulting fund being administered by the Navy Board. Kilmainham Hospital was founded in Dublin in 1680, a sick-bay was opened in Plymouth for men of the Royal Navy in 1681 and Chelsea Hospital received its first pensioner in 1684. By 1690, with Chelsea Hospital full, disabled veterans were allowed to live outside the Hospital but draw a small monetary pension. The Royal Palace at Greenwich was turned into a hospital for naval pensioners in 1692. Both Chelsea and Greenwich were maintained by stoppages from the pay of all soldiers and sailors.

The Hôtel des Invalides had been founded in Paris in 1670 and in 1684 the Duke of Brunswick-Lüneburg established a hospital for military invalids in Celle. In 1707, Frederick I of Brandenburg-Prussia set up a pension scheme for his disabled soldiers since there was no hospital in which to house them. For the same reason, Tsar Peter the Great instituted pensions in 1722. In the Austro-Hungarian army, the German and Austrian veterans were accommodated in the 'Armenhaus' in Vienna, the Bohemians and Moravians in Prague, the Hungarians in the invalid house in Pest, and the Netherlanders in Limburg. These institutions were maintained partly by state funds and partly by stoppages from army pay. Inmates received a small pension plus free accommodation and food, but after 1750 invalids who could not be housed in the various establishments were granted monetary pensions. In America, from as early as 1636 Plymouth Colony supported men who had been maimed fighting the Indians, and this was copied in Virginia after 1644. The individual colonies, or states, paid disability pensions to their soldiers during the War of Independence and these were extended into federal pensions for all disabled military and naval personnel after 1789.

Louis XIV established pensions for the Protestant members of the Swiss Guard in 1710 as they could not be admitted to the Catholic Hôtel des Invalides. In 1764, disability pensions were introduced for all soldiers who preferred to reside in their own homes rather than enter an institution. Retirement pensions for some soldiers in every regiment were established in 1762 and in 1771, under the name *vétérance*, long-service pensions were available to all soldiers who had completed 24 years in the army. The pension was larger than army pay. In France, the first modern pension law dates from 22 August 1790 and it clearly stated the bases of the new rights: the state had an obligation to reward services to society if the citizen had suffered disability or served for 30 years in the defence of his country. The law established a minimum military retirement age of 50. For every year of service above the statutory 30, the retirement pension was increased. This was extended in 1793 and 1794 to the granting of disability pensions according to the gravity of the injuries or infirmity. In 1831, retirement pensions were granted to NCOs and other ranks after 25 years and to officers after 30 years and disability pensions were divided into six classes according to the nature of the injuries. Retirement ages were also introduced – 47 for NCOs and 62 for brigadiers. In 1919, the numerous casualties from the First World War caused a revision and disability pensions were made dependent on rank and the nature of the injuries suffered. The law applied to all soldiers, sailors, airmen, widows, orphans, parents and civilian victims of war. Members of the Resistance and the French Forces of the Interior were added after 1945. A law of 1948 set retirement for officers after 30 years of service and for NCOs and other ranks at 25 years.

Disabled and invalided British soldiers were granted a pension after 1806 if they had served for 14 or 21 years. By 1829, there were 85,756 men on the pension list. In that year, length of service rather than disability was made the basic criterion for the award of a pension. After 21 years' service in the infantry or 24 in the cavalry, the discharged man received a pension of one shilling a day with additions for wounds and rank. The US navy established a Naval Home in Philadelphia in 1811 although it was not completed until 1833. In 1851, the National Soldiers Home was opened in Washington DC and ten additional branches were in existence by 1917 along with thirty other state institutions for veterans. A Veterans' Administration was set up in 1930 which supervised the introduction of life insurance for service personnel and facilities for training, educating and rehabilitating veterans.

Finally, mention must be made of the important welfare work undertaken by charities. The semi-official Royal Patriotic Fund was set up in Britain during the Crimean War to assist disabled soldiers, and this was made into a corporation at the time of the Second Boer War. Parliament then entrusted various funds to its management for the benefit of service families.

Private associations – the Soldiers' and Sailors' Families Association and the Soldiers and Sailors Help Society – supplemented state assistance via Chelsea Hospital, the Greenwich Commissioners and the Royal Patriotic Fund. Since 1918, the tradition of private charity has continued with the work of such institutions as Lord Roberts' Workshops for the disabled. Veterans' associations – the British Legion and the Royal Air Force Association – also play a benevolent role. *See also* FAMILIES; INVALIDS; LOSSES OF LIFE; ROME; SOLDIERS AND SOCIETY; VETERANS.

J.-P. BOIS

JOHN CHILDS

FURTHER READING
R. Salomon, *Les Pensions militaires* (Paris, 1962); R. Hargreaves, 'In the discard', *Army Quarterly*, lxxxii (1961), pp. 70–80; E. T. Devine, *Disabled Soldiers and Sailors: pensions and training* (New York, 1919); W. H. Glasson, *Federal Military Pensions in the United States* (New York, 1918).

Periodicals *See* SERVICE PERIODICAL PUBLICATIONS

Pershing, John Joseph (1860–1948) After graduating from West Point in 1886, Pershing had a varied early career embracing a period as professor of military science at the University of Nebraska and three tours of duty in the Philippines, where he displayed a particular understanding of indigenous Moro culture. His nickname, 'Black Jack', derived from earlier service with a negro cavalry company. Nevertheless, he had still attained only the rank of captain when in 1906 – possibly through the influence of his father-in-law, who was chairman of the Senate military affairs committee – he came to the attention of President Theodore Roosevelt who, pushing aside normal rules of seniority, had him promoted brigadier-general over 862 other officers. Pershing conducted the 'punitive' expedition into Mexico in pursuit of Pancho Villa between March 1916 and February 1917 before being given command of the US Expeditionary Force in Europe. He rapidly established the organization necessary to maintain and make operational a US army whose independence he succeeded in preserving from Allied direction. His units played a prominent role in the Saint Mihiel and Meuse- Argonne offensives between September and November 1918, although his conduct of the 'open warfare' he had advocated appeared unduly cautious. It was the first time Americans had fought on such a scale at such a distance from the United States and a large proportion of their Second World War commanders were to gain initial battle experience under Pershing's command: in this regard he may be seen as a founder of the modern US army. After the war he served as chief of staff from 1921 to 1924 and as chairman of the Battle Monuments Commission. His memoirs, published in 1931, were awarded a Pulitzer Prize. *See also* UNITED STATES.

A. CORVISIER

IAN F. W. BECKETT

FURTHER READING
E. M. Coffman, *The War to End All Wars: the American military experience in World War One* (New York, 1968); J. Pershing, *My Experiences in the World War* (2 vols, New York, 1931); D. Smythe, *Guerilla Warrior* (New York, 1973); F. E. Vandiver, *Black Jack* (2 vols, College Station, 1973).

Persia *See* IRAN

Pétain, Henri Philippe Benoni Omer (1856–1951) After graduating from the military academy of Saint-Cyr in 1878, Pétain served on the Italian frontier and attended the École de Guerre, where he was to be an instructor between 1901 and 1907. He emerged as a man of independent mind through his advocacy of the power of the defensive, which ran counter to the prevailing orthodoxy of the offensive. Indeed, he was removed to a command in Brittany and, when the First World War began, he was an elderly colonel in temporary brigade command. However, the war showed him to be an active but calm and cautious leader and, after doing well at Guise in August 1914, he was not only quickly confirmed in his brigade command but also rapidly promoted to a division in September, a corps in October and to the 2nd Army in May 1915. He was entrusted with command of the Verdun sector on 25 February 1916 at a point when it seemed the Germans were seeking to wear down the French where they stood. He reorganized the defence and moved up men, weapons, munitions and supplies in spite of the precarious nature of the lines of communication. On 19 April 1916 he was appointed to the central group of armies and also served briefly as chief of the general staff before replacing Nivelle as commander-in-chief of the northern and north-eastern armies on 15 May 1917 in the wake of the mutinies following Nivelle's disastrous offensive. Pétain gave his soldiers renewed confidence by improving administration and the leave system and also gave up the policy of mounting costly offensives in order to await the arrival of US forces. In 1918, when he wished to withdraw his armies to the south in face of the German spring offensive, the Clemenceau government preferred Foch as Allied supreme commander. Created a marshal of France in December 1918, he was vice-president of the Conseil Supérieur de la Guerre from 1919 to 1931 and also head of the short-lived Conseil Supérieur de la Défense Nationale. Backing the construction of the Maginot Line, he also successfully suppressed Abd el-Krim's rising in Morocco in 1925–6. Recalled from retirement, he served as Minister of War in 1934 and went as ambassador to Spain in 1939 only to be recalled once more in May 1940 as deputy prime minister in Reynaud's reconstituted government. This ushered in the most controversial phase of his career. On 16 June he replaced Reynaud as prime minister and swiftly arranged an armistice which resulted in his heading an authoritarian government over the non-occupied zone of France centred on Vichy. The Germans subsequently occupied Vichy France in November 1942 and carried Pétain himself off to Germany in August 1944

but it was inevitable that his considerable power over an often brutal regime would provoke retribution. Accordingly, the provisional government of a now liberated France sentenced Pétain to death in 1945 although this was then commuted to life imprisonment on the Île de Yeu. *See also* FOCH; FRANCE; VERDUN.

A. CORVISIER
IAN F. W. BECKETT

FURTHER READING
M. Ferro, *Pétain* (Paris, 1987); R. Griffiths, *Marshal Pétain* (London, 1970); H. R. Lottman, *Pétain: Hero or traitor?* (New York, 1985); G. Pédroncini, *Pétain, Général en Chef, 1917–18* (Paris, 1974).

Peter I, 'the Great', Emperor of Russia (1672–1725) As Emperor of Russia from 1682 to 1725, this reformer created a westernized Russian army although the degree of originality and innovation has often been exaggerated. The freshness lay in the scale of his efforts, together with the determination and energy with which he pursued his task. There were several stages in the process. In 1699, after brutally eliminating the power of the *Streltsy*, a force originally raised by Ivan the Terrible (1533–84) but which had grown ineffective, Peter decreed a system of national recruitment. This was based on the old sixteenth-century method of raising one man from every twenty-five households on the estates of clerical landlords and from groups of between thirty and fifty households on the lands of secular lords. Volunteers were also encouraged. The new levies served for life and, with the aid of foreign instructors, were formed into regiments equipped in the Western manner. When put to the test against Sweden at the Battle of Narva in 1700, this young and inexperienced army proved inflexible and brittle. This reverse gave rise to a series of measures. In 1705, a more systematic form of conscription was introduced among the peasantry, one man being summoned from every twenty households. In the first year, this raised $c.44,000$ men. Particular attention was paid to officer training in order to reduce reliance upon mercenaries (one-third of Peter's officers were hired foreigners, mostly Scots, Austrians and Germans). The Preobrazhenski and Semenovski Guards regiments were devoted to instructing cadets, and schools for artillery, engineering and medical officers were established around 1712. Officers were drawn from the gentry as well as the aristocracy but, after 1721, a commission conferred nobility. Peter ensured that his soldiers were well equipped and trained for the realities of battle. Special attention was paid to the artillery, a Russian speciality since the reign of Ivan the Terrible. Under the grandmaster of artillery, James Bruss (Bruce) (b. 1670), a soldier of Scottish ancestry, a central corps of artillery was created in addition to a regimental artillery of two guns per infantry and cavalry regiment, the latter forming a genuine horse artillery. After the defeat of the Swedish army at Poltava in 1709, Peter continued to develop his military establishment which, at the time of his death, probably numbered around 130,000 field troops, 68,000 garrison troops, plus a number of special (Cossack) and foreign (Kalmyk) corps, a total of c.250,000 men. Sixty-four per cent of Peter's annual revenues (8,500,000 roubles) were spent on his army and navy. The tactical, organizational and strategic doctrine of the new army was laid down in Peter's *Rules of Combat* (1708) and the *Military Code* (1716). These were mostly culled from or inspired by Dutch, Swedish, German and, above all, French regulations. He stressed the need for discipline as well as the essential cohesion that must exist between officers and men. His strategy, which reflected the lessons he had drawn from his earlier failures against Sweden and the Turks, was based on a precise appreciation of a situation, careful preparation and a recognition of the need for manoeuvre. The thinking of Russian generals at the end of the eighteenth century was still influenced by Peter's teachings. A War College, based on the Swedish model, was established between 1718 and 1720 to administer the armed forces. The first president was Alexander Menshikov (1673–1728) and the College organized promotion, the granting of leave, military justice and law, procurement of weapons and equipment, camps, quarters, routes of march, and finance. Later, it initiated commissions of reform (1730–1, 1754–7, 1762 and 1763–5).

Three Russian fleets were developed during Peter's reign, on the Sea of Azov, the Caspian and the Baltic. The latter was the most important and its first major vessel was the 28-gun frigate *Shtandart* which was launched in 1703. The first ship of the line was built in 1712, the *Poltava*, and by the end of the Great Northern War in 1721, the Baltic fleet possessed 124 Russian-built vessels and 55 captured from the Swedes. The new city of St Petersburg (founded in 1703) housed the principal dockyard while Kronstadt Island served as the main base. Learning from the usefulness of oared galleys in the Sea of Azov, the Russian Baltic fleet operated over 400 of these vessels in the war against Sweden. *See also* CHARLES XII; NAVIES; POLTAVA; RUSSIA/USSR; SUVOROV; SWEDEN.

A. CORVISIER
G. A. STEPPLER
JOHN CHILDS

FURTHER READING
M. S. Anderson, *Peter the Great* (London, 1978); Christopher Duffy, *Russia's Military Way to the West: origins and nature of Russian military power, 1700–1800* (London, 1981); John L. H. Keep, *Soldiers of the Tsar: army and society in Russia, 1462–1874* (Oxford, 1985); Richard Hellie, 'Warfare, changing military technology, and the evolution of Muscovite society', in *The Tools of War*, ed. John A. Lynn (Urbana and Chicago, 1990), pp. 74–99.

Philippi, Battles of (42 BC) A city in eastern Macedonia on the Via Egnatia where in the civil war after the murder of Caesar, two of the triumvirs, Antony (Antonius) and Octavian, defeated Brutus and Cassius, who aimed to restore the traditional form of senatorial government. Antony and Octavian encamped on the road itself with a marsh on their right wing. Antony first attempted to outflank the enemy by secretly building a causeway through the marsh, but Cassius discovered what he was up to and built a cross wall to intercept this road. A battle ensued from these skirmishes and after a hard struggle, since both sides had well-trained legionaries, Octavian on the left wing was defeated by Brutus, who captured the camp; but on the right wing Antony drove back Cassius, who committed suicide though the outcome of the whole engagement was indecisive. During the next three weeks Antony succeeded in turning Brutus's southern flank and, in order to prevent complete encirclement, Brutus lengthened his line. Cajoled by his officers into offering battle a second time he was defeated by Antony, who fully exploited the experience of Caesar's old soldiers, many of whom were serving in his legions. The Battles of Philippi ensured that the triumvirs would control the Roman world and opened the way to the final conflict between Antony and Octavian. *See also* ACTIUM; ROME.

B. CAMPBELL

FURTHER READING
Appian,*Civil Wars*, 4, 105–29, Loeb Classical Library (Harvard, 1979); L. J. F. Keppie, *The Making of the Roman Army: from republic to empire* (London, 1984), pp. 119–22.

Philon of Byzantium This Greek writer who lived in Byzantium at the end of the third century BC, produced under the title of 'A Treatise on Mechanics', a general scientific work whose surviving parts deal mainly with war catapults, fortifications and the defence of cities. Philon asserts that his descriptions are based on techniques actually employed by master craftsmen to whom he had spoken at Rhodes and Alexandria, which were the two main centres in the Hellenistic period for the manufacture of siege equipment. His study on the defence of cities won great renown in Antiquity, and the Roman architect Vitruvius expresses a high opinion of it in his *De Architectura*. It appears also in the majority of those collections of works on siege technique which were compiled from the tenth century AD onwards by non-specialists in military affairs. Because of this, Philon's work continued to be influential until comparatively late. *See also* GREECE, ANCIENT; HERON.

R. LONIS

FURTHER READING
Y. Garlan, *War in the Ancient World; a Social History* (London, 1975); E. W. Marsden, *Greek and Roman Artillery* (2 vols, Oxford, 1969–71).

Pinkie or Musselburgh (Lothian), Battle of (10 September 1547) The last major Anglo-Scottish battle of the sixteenth century, Pinkie was the consequence of Edward Seymour, Duke of Somerset's, resumption of Henry VIII's campaign to obtain the marriage of Edward VI and Mary, Queen of Scots by force. The English army marched north from Newcastle on 28 August 1547. It comprised between 14,000 and 16,000 men, mainly shire levies armed with bows and bills (as at Flodden), but with an artillery train of 15 pieces, 800 horse and foot arquebusiers and some 4,000 heavy and light horse. By 8 September Somerset had encamped at Longniddry on the Forth, where he was joined by the fleet. To oppose the invasion, the Governor of Scotland, James Hamilton, Earl of Arran, had summoned a national levy to assemble at Edinburgh. From this he mobilized an army of 23–25,000, which then took up a defensive position on the western bank of the River Esk in front of the town of Musselburgh. Apart from some 4,000 Highland archers and 1,500 light horse, the Scottish army was composed almost entirely of pikemen. There was an artillery train, but apparently no arquebusiers. On 8 September Somerset sent some of his cavalry to reconnoitre a possible crossing further up the Esk; a brief fight with the Scottish horse ensued, and, as a result, most of the Scottish cavalry was eliminated before the main battle. Somerset then decided to advance to the mouth of the Esk, plant his artillery and assault the Scottish left under cover of a cross-fire from those guns and the cannon of the fleet. As the English army advanced by its right on the 10th, Arran mistook the manoeuvre for the beginning of a retreat and decided to attack. As the Scots crossed the Esk, the English fleet opened fire, throwing the Scots left wing into disorder. As they retired upstream out of range, the Scottish army was compressed into a single mass. Somerset, taken by surprise by the

653

unexpected Scottish advance, sent in his cavalry to disrupt it and give his foot time to deploy. The English cavalry attacks were beaten off with serious losses, but the Scottish advance was halted, and the English artillery, arquebusiers and bowmen found the pike mass an easy target. A withdrawal out of range was ordered, but under the increasing volume of fire it became a full-scale retreat, and the Scottish army, harried by the English cavalry, dissolved in a flight to Edinburgh. English casualties, almost entirely from among the horse, were in the region of 200 to 500; the Scottish are more difficult to compute, but some 10,000 dead is generally agreed, with a further 1,500 prisoners.

Contemporaries unanimously blamed the disaster on Arran's misjudgement in attacking, and compared it to James IV's equally catastrophic decision at Flodden. Sir Charles Oman has suggested that Somerset's tactics of countering the pike mass with cavalry and artillery were inspired by those employed at Marignano. Both armies were composed mainly of traditionally armed militia, but the English artillery and the professional contingents of arquebusiers and cavalry gave Somerset the decisive edge. *See also* FLODDEN; GREAT BRITAIN; MARIGNANO; SEYMOUR.

SIMON ADAMS

FURTHER READING
The basic modern accounts are those of Sir Charles Oman, 'The Battle of Pinkie, Sept. 10 1547', *Archaeological Journal*, xc (1933), pp. 1–18, and *A History of the Art of War in the Sixteenth Century* (London, 1937), pp. 350–7. See also W. K. Jordan, *Edward VI: the young king* (London, 1968). A number of eyewitness narratives exist; the most accessible is W. Patten, *The Expedition into Scotland*, reprinted in *Tudor Tracts*, ed. A. F. Pollard (London, 1903).

Piracy *See* COMMERCE-RAIDING

Planning/plans Plans are prepared by governments and military leaders in order to be ready for the conduct of operations. There are three basic types of plans:

1 War plans, dealing with the strategy, aims and circumstances of a possible conflict.
2 Campaign plans, concerning the operations to be conducted during a particular phase of a conflict in a given theatre of war.
3 Connected plans, relating to particular aspects of the preparations for war.

1. The war plan provides an appreciation of the various courses open to the enemy and of the likely support by allies, sets out the aim, decides on the means of achieving this and determines the broad lines of required action. It should also evaluate the chances of success and predict both the enemy's probable responses and the main changes that might occur in the overall situation. The adoption of a war plan rests entirely with the government, which makes its decision on the basis of a draft submitted by the general staff, the chief of which is in a position to call for all the information he requires.

War plans were produced throughout Antiquity but usually only dealt with aims. Nevertheless, Pericles is described as having drawn up a more detailed plan at the time of the Peloponnesian War. The advent of artillery fortifications in the sixteenth century and the concomitant rise to importance of the military engineer resulted in broader and more varied war plans. The development of detailed planning also arose from the desire to wage short, decisive wars. One of the earliest examples was the preparation by Louis XIV and Louvois for the Dutch War in 1672 which was conceived as a lightning operation. Napoleon's plans, on the other hand, were as much campaign plans as war plans since he was engaged in practically continuous warfare. Among the most celebrated plans was that of Moltke, produced in the winter of 1868–9, which was carried out almost to the letter in 1870–1. The Schlieffen Plan for Germany's war with France and Russia, which envisaged the invasion of Belgium, failed because of some mistakes committed during its execution, some unwise adjustments and unforeseen problems with logistics and the endurance of troops.

Taken up afresh and adapted to the different circumstances of 1940, it achieved complete success.

2. The campaign plan should be based on a detailed study of all the relevant factors; the aims, including the predicted aims of the enemy, an evaluation of the forces facing one another, reserves, morale, battle tactics and geographical features. Once again, it was the sixteenth century which saw the first coherent campaign plans. Maurice of Nassau and Montecucoli further improved the science of systematic planning. Under Louis XIV and Louvois, campaign plans were carefully elaborated and, after a series of difficulties that occurred over instructions in 1673–4, their execution was closely monitored. Indeed, during the Nine Years' War (1688–97), this monitoring from the court seriously impaired the freedom of French commanders in the field. Strategy came to be controlled by governmental authorities – the *Hofkriegsrat* in Vienna or the Secretaries of State in Westminster. In the eighteenth century, Frederick the Great of Prussia escaped from these shackles, as did Napoleon later, whose plans merged the political assessment of the situation with the necessary operational strategy. Government control of strategy tends to inhibit generals from displaying initiative. At the end of the eighteenth century, Guibert called for more latitude to be given to the army commander in his conduct of operations. The growth of technological and total war in the nineteenth and twentieth centuries has further eroded the decision-making authority of the battlefield commander and enhanced the centralization of war control within the government.

3. Connected plans made their appearance with the increase in the size of armies and the use of reserves. The mobilization plan lists all the measures to be taken when mobilization is about to be, or has been, ordered. It is drawn up by the chief of the general staff and the Minister for War with the object of translating the army from a peacetime to a wartime footing. All units covered by the mobilization plan receive instructions on the action which they are individually required to take. This may entail partial or general mobilization, the former comprising such steps as the recall of reservists or the placing of frontier troops on a war footing, and the latter a total call-up. The mobilization plan is altered every time that modifications are made in army organization, on receipt of credible intelligence of foreign developments and when the political situation changes. Between 1875 and 1913, the French general staff produced seventeen mobilization plans.

Mobilization is followed by the moving of units into their appointed positions. In general, the positioning plan is intimately associated with the mobilization plan and deals with the moving of troops: distances, routes and capacities and varieties of transport. The transport plan, a necessary accompaniment to the positioning plan, takes on particular importance and complexity in the case of overseas and combined operations.

Operational plans detail precise and limited military operations. *See also* COMMAND; GENERAL STAFF; INTELLIGENCE; MOBILIZATION; SCHLIEFFEN; STRATEGY.

A. CORVISIER
JOHN CHILDS

FURTHER READING
M. S. Watson, *Chief of Staff: pre-war plans and preparations* (Washington, 1950); John Gooch, *The Plans of War: the General Staff and British military strategy, c.1900–1916* (London, 1974); *The War Plans of the Great Powers, 1880–1914*, ed. P. M. Kennedy (London, 1979); Gerhard Ritter, *The Schlieffen Plan* (London, 1958).

Plassey, Battle of (23 June 1757) Robert Clive (1725–74), having been sent from Madras to restore the British East India Company's fortunes in Bengal, recaptured Calcutta in December 1756 from the forces of Siraj-ud-Dawlah, the Nawab of Bengal, Orissa and Bihar. The following March Clive seized the French post at Chandernagore and, in June 1757, hoping to take advantage of a conspiracy among the Nawab's supporters, marched north with a force of 1,100 Europeans, 2,100 sepoys and 10 cannon. At Plassey he confronted the Nawab's entire army, said to be 50,000 strong with 53 cannon (four of which were crewed by French gunners), in an entrenched camp. At dawn on 23 June the Nawab's forces emerged from their entrenchments and deployed in a wide encircling movement. A lengthy cannonade ensued, but the Nawab's forces failed to press home an attack, the fire of their artillery slackening noticeably after a heavy rainstorm soaked their powder. A cavalry charge by the Nawab's most trusted general was beaten off by Clive's artillery and about 2 o'clock the Nawab's forces were seen to be withdrawing. Following up quickly, the small British force eventually succeeded in penetrating the Nawab's entrenchments and putting his army to flight. British losses were trifling. A better served artillery, resolute leadership, superior discipline and high morale had been essential to Clive's victory, but the final outcome had turned on the lack of determination in an enemy whose leaders were at odds with each other. If the battle was not an example of great military skill, it was one of great consequence, for the new position acquired by the British East India Company as a result has marked Plassey as the beginning of British domination in India. *See also* COLONIAL TROOPS; GREAT BRITAIN; INDIA.

G. A. STEPPLER

FURTHER READING
Michael Edwardes, *The Battle of Plassey* (London, 1963); Sir George Forrest, *The Life of Clive* (2 vols, London, 1918); J. F. C. Fuller, 'The Battle of Plassey, 1757', in *The Decisive Battles of the Western World* (London, 1955), ii, 221–42; James P. Lawford, *Britain's Army in India* (London, 1978).

Plataea, Battle of (479 BC)   Plataea was the site of the Greek victory over the Persian army during the second invasion of Greece. In the previous year Xerxes' fleet had been defeated at Salamis and the king had returned to Asia, leaving an army of perhaps about 70,000 men under the command of Mardonius, one of his generals. In the spring of 479 BC Mardonius set up his camp on a plain not far from Plataea, a city in Boeotia. He was confronted by a Greek army which, according to Herodotus, consisted of 38,700 hoplites and a substantial body of light armed troops, including 35,000 helots fighting alongside the Spartans. The commander-in-chief of the Greeks was Pausanias, the regent for the young son of King Leonidas, who had been killed at Thermopylae.

Twelve days were spent in manoeuvring for position during which the Greeks suffered heavily from attacks by the Persian cavalry until its commander, Masistius, was killed. Eventually, Pausanias ordered the Greek army to move to a new position during the night in what was probably a well-planned move; but a rapid Persian advance at dawn prevented the accomplishment of the plan and the Spartans were left isolated on the right wing facing Mardonius with his best Persian troops, while on the left the Athenians faced those Greeks who were fighting on the Persian side, especially the Thebans. The rest of the Greek line had become separated from the wings. The battle was won by the training and discipline of the Spartans, who distinguished themselves in the battle by crushing the Persian line and killing Mardonius, and by the Greek hoplites' superiority in discipline, weapons and armour over their less well-organized and more lightly equipped opponents. The 8,000 hoplites of Athens also played an important role by holding the left wing firm against the Thebans. The Battle of Plataea finally liberated Greece from the threat of Persian domination and confirmed the effectiveness of the phalanx formation, though it also exhibited one weakness of Greek armies, in the lack of strong cavalry support, which was to persist until the time of Alexander of Macedon. *See also* GREECE, ANCIENT; IRAN; MARATHON; SALAMIS; THERMOPYLAE.

R. LONIS
B. CAMPBELL

FURTHER READING
P. W. Wallace, 'The final battle of Plataea', *Studies in Attic Epigraphy, Hesperia*, supplement 19 (Princeton, 1982); C. Hignett, *Xerxes' Invasion of Greece* (Oxford, 1963), pp. 289–344; P. Connolly, *Greece and Rome at War* (London, 1981), pp. 29–36; A. R. Burn, *Persia and the Greeks: the defence of the West, c.546–478 BC* (London, 1984), pp. 508–46.

Turkish breech-loading field guns firing from behind earthwork fortifications during the Russian Siege of Plevna, 1877. Despite the powerful combination of Turkish weaponry, especially the Peabody-Martini and Winchester Model 1866 rifles, and field fortifications, the Russian infantry initially attacked in massed columns. Later, they adopted smaller and more flexible formations. The final assault on Plevna was preceded by a four-day artillery bombardment. Plevna also demonstrated the superiority of the howitzer over the field gun for attacking troops protected by field fortifications.
(Mary Evans Picture Library)

Plevna, Siege of (1877) Plevna was the site of the major action of the Russo-Turkish war of 1877–8; it also provided evidence of the advantages given to the defence by the development of firepower. In June 1877 the Russians crossed the Danube and penetrated the Turkish Balkan defences. However, they were slow to exploit their success. Omar Pasha garrisoned Plevna with 30,000 men so as to threaten the Russian right flank. Three times, on 20 July, 30 July and 11 September, the Russians assaulted the town but were repulsed with heavy losses. In the final assault they enjoyed a threefold superiority in artillery. But the attacks were ill-coordinated, and mounted frontally and in close order. Todleben, the hero of the defence of Sebastopol, was brought up to direct the siege operations. His solution was to cut Plevna's communications with Sofia and starve the Turks out. On 10 December the garrison surrendered. The Russians, now joined by Romania, Serbia and Montenegro, were able to bring the war to a speedy conclusion. *See also*

FIREARMS; INFANTRY; RUSSIA/USSR; SIEGES; TODLEBEN.

HEW STRACHAN

FURTHER READING
Rupert Furneaux, *The Siege of Plevna* (London, 1958); F. V. Greene, *The Russian Army and its Campaigns in Turkey in 1877–1878* (London, n.d.).

Poitiers, or Tours, Battle of (25 October 732) This famous battle probably took place on Saturday 25 October 732 at Moussais on the old Roman road between Poitiers and Tours. Initially setting out to discipline Othman ben abi Neza, a rebellious Muslim ruler whose lands lay to the north of the Pyrenees, the governor of Muslim Spain, Abd-ar-Rahman, developed his campaign into a grand raid through Aquitaine. Eudo, the Duke of Aquitaine, was defeated near Bordeaux and Abd-ar-Rahman then split his army into several columns, crossed the Dordogne and invested Poitiers. Leaving some of his troops to besiege the city, Abdar-Rahman pressed

657

on towards Tours in order to sack the church of St Martin. Having returned from campaigning on the Danube, Charles Martel, the mayor of the palace to the Merovingian king Theodoric IV, crossed the Loire, probably at Orléans, with a large army and forced Abd-ar-Rahman back towards Poitiers. The armies faced each other for a week as Charles Martel waited to gather reinforcements.

The 'Saracen' army was basically composed of horsemen armed with the lance and the sword. It was poorly disciplined and incapable of sustained defence and its principal tactic was the wild cavalry charge, rendered particularly efficacious by the use of the stirrup. The Frankish army, probably composed of contingents from various 'European' races, was also primitive in organization and discipline. However, it was basically an infantry force consisting of the heavily armed and armoured private host of the general and more lightly equipped militia. The small number of heavy cavalry fought dismounted as heavy infantry. Both armies lived off the land and could only retain cohesion as long as supplies endured. Knowing that the Saracens would launch a furious cavalry charge, Charles Martel drew his infantry into a large phalanx which resisted repeated Saracen attacks. Abd-ar-Rahman was killed at some stage in the fighting. Towards evening, Eudo and his Aquitainians assaulted the Saracen camp, which contained the bulk of the plunder, obliging the Saracen army to withdraw. The unmounted Franks were unable to pursue the Saracen force as it retreated over the Pyrenees. The Battle of Poitiers ended the large-scale Saracen raiding into Gaul and encouraged the Franks to develop their cavalry by adopting the stirrup. After 740, Charles drove the remaining Muslims from the Rhône valley bringing all of Gaul under his personal rule. The Battle of Poitiers halted the Muslim expansion into Western Europe in the same way that the successful defence of Constantinople by Leo the Isaurian in 717–18 had blocked Muslim aggression in the East. *See also* CAVALRY; CHARLEMAGNE; INFANTRY.

P. CONTAMINE
JOHN CHILDS

FURTHER READING
Philippe Contamine, *War in the Middle Ages*, tr. Michael Jones (London, 1984); B. S. Bachrach, 'Military organisation in Aquitaine under the early Carolingians', *Speculum*, xlix (1974); L. T. White, *Medieval Technology and Social Change* (Oxford, 1962).

Poland Both the general and military histories of Poland have been conditioned by the absence of natural frontiers in the east and the west. The country has been a meeting place for eastern and western influences, frequently acting as a relay station in either direction. Poland has also been shaped by a national consciousness, based around the Catholic religion, which was awakened at an early date through a sense of distinctness from Russian Orthodoxy. After some hesitation in the sixteenth century, Poland rejected the Reformation, partly because of its association with her Germanic enemies. Except during the period of foreign domination (1795–1918), Poland has been involved in more foreign wars than most other European countries, fighting successively, if not simultaneously, against all her neighbours. Although Poland was spared major religious civil wars, she fell prey to numerous internal conflicts which, until the eighteenth century, were feudal in character before becoming more nationalistic.

Although Polish national consciousness has historically leaned more towards the West than the East, in military affairs the two influences have been more evenly balanced. The Kingdom of Poland, founded at the end of the tenth century by Mieszko I, saw a short-lived expansion under Boleslaw I, the Brave (992–1025), in which Brandenburg, Lusatia, Saxony, Bohemia, Moravia, Slovakia and Ruthenia were absorbed. It then fragmented into principalities, and Poland was unable to prevent the colonization of the Baltic coast by the Teutonic Knights or the invasions of the Mongols. Under Casimir III (mid-fourteenth century), the reconstituted Polish state turned its attention towards Ruthenia. The Jagiellion dynasty (1386–1572) was in a stronger position to pursue these ambitions after its alliance with the Grand Duchy of Lithuania (1385), which, at that date, stretched as far as the Ukraine. Poland-Lithuania halted German expansion at the Battle of Tannenberg in 1410. Poland and Lithuania were formally united in 1569.

The introduction of an elective monarchy (effectively from 1572) passed real control of the Polish Republic to the diet (*Sejm*) and the provincial diets (*sejmiki*), which then proceeded to emasculate themselves by a voting system which required unanimity (*liberum veto*, 1573). As Poland entered a long period of decline she had to sustain almost constant wars against the Turks, Muscovy and Sweden. In the eighteenth century, Poland fell victim to Russia, Prussia and Austria who successively partitioned her territories in 1772, 1793 (without Austria) and 1795. Between 1807 and 1813, Napoleon reduced Poland to the Grand Duchy of Warsaw. The Kingdom of Poland was reconstituted in 1815 and granted the larger part of her historic lands. She was placed under the protection of Russia but lost her independence after the Revolution of 1831–2. Poland was not reborn until 1918.

In the period from the sixteenth to the end of the eighteenth century, Poland was one of the most militarized societies in Europe. The petty nobility (*szlachta*) comprised 12 per cent of the total population in 1773, the majority impoverished. The few rich and powerful magnates patronized their lesser brethren to form private armies which far outnumbered any forces the king could assemble. By ancient custom the magnates enjoyed the right to form sworn confederations to oppose and apprehend any wrongdoer, a situation which resulted in law and order being maintained by the private armies of the most important aristocrats rather than by the monarch. During the Great Northern War (1700–21), between 1733 and 1735, from 1767 to 1768, and in 1791 and 1792 these confederations conducted full-blown civil wars which gave Poland's enemies ample opportunity for intervention. State service was unpopular and the nobility assisted the government only in times of national emergency. After the war against the Turks from 1683 to 1699, it became difficult to persuade the nobility to fight on foreign soil.

During the tenth and eleventh centuries, Poland's huge and indefensible frontiers were open to attack from all directions. While the tribal host provided the manpower, defence was based around the royal fortress (*grod*) and much use was made of inundations and patrols to channel attackers towards these garrisons. Peasants were exempted from military service in the twelfth century, except in the defence of their homes, and their labour was used to support a force of mounted knights. As a consequence, heavy cavalry dominated the Polish feudal army and the proportion of infantry steadily declined. After 1320, all landholders had to present themselves for military service complete with arms, armour, horses and retinue. The feudal host was raised by a *levée en masse* (*pospolite ruszenie*) and organized around tribal or clan regiments led by the great families whilst the lesser nobility, towns and royal officials commanded district regiments. In 1340, Poland could field a force of 11–12,000 knights, rising to 18,000 by 1450. The feudal levy was inefficient and unsuitable for campaigning outside Poland. It had largely died out by 1500 and the lords paid a money tax in lieu of their physical service in the field but it remained in legal force until the country's collapse in 1795. A permanent force of 2,000 men was established in the 1490s for the defence of Red Ruthenia.

In 1563, a quarter tax on all income derived by leaseholders from crown estates provided money for a standing army of *c*.4,000 knights. Military finance thus rested in the hands of the barons and not in the person of the elected monarch. Towns also sent contingents and after 1578 the royal lands provided 'selective infantry'. This was a peasant militia; the 'twentieth field' or the 'select field' on royal estates was reserved for a peasant who owed six months' annual military service as a musketeer in return for freedom from serfdom and other duties. He was paid and supported by the remaining nineteen families who did not have to serve. The new standing army was brought to a high professional standard by Jan Tarnowski (1488–1561). Not only did he develop horse artillery, military discipline and a medical service, but he adapted the

Hussite *wagenburg* from the supply train (*see* WAGGON-LAAGER). The large, six-horsed ammunition waggons could be chained together into a circular laager providing a defensive location in the flat and featureless steppe. The resulting army was composed of 75 per cent cavalry and only 25 per cent infantry, an imbalance which rendered it incapable of serious opposition to Russian, Swedish, Prussian and Austrian forces.

Stephen Batory (1575–87) introduced reforms and established a mixed force of foreign mercenaries and native volunteers but the nobility regarded a standing army as an instrument of absolutism which might be used to strip away their privileges. Consequently they ensured that the crown was starved of military funds and that the small Crown Army (*starosty*) was confined to frontier defence and never allowed to grow sufficiently to bolster monarchical authority. By the early seventeenth century, the peacetime standing army numbered 12,000 but this could be quadrupled in wartime. The granting of cash for martial purposes was further curtailed in 1652, and by 1700 it was apparent that Poland could not compete in the same military league as her neighbours. When John III Sobieski (1674–96) raised an army to help lift the Siege of Vienna in 1683, his 25,000 men were slowly accumulated from feudal noble cavalry, foreign mercenaries and the Crown Army. In 1717, the *Sejm* established the Crown Army at 24,000 men (18,000 from Poland and 6,000 from Lithuania), not enough to defend the country or to interfere in internal politics. It was dispersed in garrisons along Poland's borders.

The organization of the Cossack bands which emerged on the eastern marches of Poland was markedly different. The Cossacks existed on the fringes of civilized society and lived by raiding into Poland, Lithuania and Muscovy. With a political centre, the *Sich* (or *Sech*) on the Dnieper, elected leaders (*atamans* or *hetmans*) and a way of life based on war and hunting, these groups formed federations, occasionally fought each other, multiplied with the aid of the Muscovite state and pushed eastwards, first from the Dnieper to the Don, then to the Urals. They had a certain influence on the cavalry techniques of Central Europe. The Zaporozhian or *Sich* Cossacks were politically and militarily free, although some served in the Polish *starosty* as individuals. A number of Cossack volunteers were registered by the Polish state after 1578 and formed into bands under their own *atamans*. Their task was to protect the Polish frontier with Muscovy and the Turks. Cossacks also formed military units (*vataha*) which entered the Crown Army.

A Polish army was conscripted by Napoleon in the Grand Duchy of Warsaw but it was dissolved after the retreat from Moscow in 1812. The Polish army of the Kingdom of Poland, which had been raised by the Tsar, was disbanded in 1832. From that year, Poles served as mercenaries, conscripts and volunteers in the Russian, Austrian, Prussian and later German armies, as well as in West European services. During the First World War, Poles fought for both the Entente and the Central Powers.

With French assistance, the Polish army was hastily re-formed in 1918. This was largely the work of Marshal Joseph Pilsudski who had covertly created a Polish Nationalist Army after the German–Austrian conquest of Poland in 1915 and 1916. In November 1918, the Polish army amounted to just 24 battalions, 3 squadrons of cavalry and 5 batteries. By January 1919, this had risen to 110,000 men and within one year to 600,000. However, the forces suffered from over-rapid expansion and were poorly equipped and inadequately trained. In 1919, Pilsudski attacked the Soviet Union in an attempt to regain the 1772 boundaries of Poland and, at the Battle of Warsaw in 1920, the Polish army defeated the Russian counter-offensive. Between 1920 and 1939, Poland's standing army of 350,000 was insufficient to defend a land frontier of 3,290 miles. Despite the rapid mobilization of reserves which raised her armed forces to over one million men, the Polish army with 150 tanks, 400 modern aircraft and 40 divisions was no match for the *Wehrmacht* in 1939. However, under the terms of the agreement with France and England, the Polish army was intended to hold the Germans for just two weeks by which time her allies were supposed to have launched an attack with 70 divisions in the west. The Polish army achieved this objective.

A Polish émigré army was formed first in France, then later in England, by the government in exile under General Sikorski. Another émigré force, the Anders Army, recruited from among Polish prisoners of war in the Soviet Union, fought in the Middle East and in Italy, while resistance was organized within Poland by the *Armia krajowa* (Home Army) and, after 1942, by the *Armia ludowa* (People's Army) formed by the Communist Party. Between 1943 and 1945, Polish resistance efforts were hampered by rivalry between the Home Army, which was supported by the London government in exile, and the Soviet sponsored People's Army. The Home Army was destroyed in the Warsaw Rising of 1944. After the German defeat in 1945, Poland passed into the Soviet sphere of influence and joined the Warsaw Pact. Her army was organized on the Soviet model.

The Polish army was fixed at 400,000 in 1948 but by 1955 it was the second largest army in the Warsaw Pact. In 1977, Poland possessed 404,000 men and 605,000 reservists, a mixture of volunteer professionals and national servicemen on two-year enlistments. The army had 15 divisions, 3,800 tanks and 4,200 armoured vehicles. The air force boasted 745 combat aircraft. There was a small navy of 25 missile-carrying fast patrol boats. *See also* MONGOLS; OTTOMAN TURKS; RUSSIA/USSR; SWEDEN; TANNENBERG (1410).

A. CORVISIER
JOHN CHILDS

FURTHER READING
East Central European War and Society in the Pre-Revolutionary Eighteenth Century, eds G. E. Rothenberg, B. K. Király and P. F. Sugar (New York, 1982), pp. 165–252; D. Stone, 'Patriotism and professionalism in the Polish army in the 18th century', in *Studies in History and Politics*, iii (Lennoxville, Quebec, 1983–4); Norman Davies, *God's Playground: a history of Poland* (2 vols, Oxford, 1981); P. Longworth, *The Cossacks* (London, 1969).

Police *See* GENDARMERIE

Poltava, Battle of (27 June 1709)   Charles XII of Sweden failed to defeat the Russian armies of Peter the Great decisively during the summer of 1708 (the Battles of Holovzin and Dobroe). An attempt in September to advance towards Moscow through the province of Severia had to be abandoned in the face of the Russian 'scorched earth' policy. Instead, Charles marched into the Ukraine to link up with the Dnieper Cossacks under their *hetman* (elected leader), Mazeppa, in order to winter his troops ready for a fresh attack towards Moscow in 1709. Already reduced from 44,000 to 25,000 men, Charles was relying on meeting up with Lewenhaupt's corps of 12,500 men which was trekking south with a supply train from Livonia. Peter overtook Lewenhaupt at Lesnaya (28 September 1708) and inflicted such a severe reverse that only 7,000 Swedes eventually struggled into Charles's camp. During the winter, the 30,000 Swedes and 8,000 Cossacks attempted to extend their base area ready for a march on Moscow. In April 1709, Charles laid siege to the small fortress of Poltava in order to open the road to Moscow through Kharkov and Kursk as well as cover a possible line of retreat towards the Crimea. A Russian army of c.42,000 men and 102 cannon under the personal command of Peter advanced to relieve the besieged town.

Peter crossed the River Vorskla and established an entrenched camp to the north of Poltava which he additionally protected by nine redoubts arrayed in a 'T' formation. Although many of his forces were tied down besieging Poltava leaving a field army of only c.25,000 men, Charles determined to attack before the Russian position grew any stronger. Commanding from a litter, having been wounded in the foot on 16 June, Charles attacked the Russian field fortifications at 2.00 a.m. on 27 June 1709. The Swedish columns attacked through the line of redoubts and eventually reached the ditch of the Russian entrenched camp but they were so reduced by artillery fire and musketry from the Russian redoubts that barely 5,000 formed a single line for the final assault. Peter led 24,000 Russians and 70 guns out of the camp and formed a double line of battle. Although the Swedes moved forward at 9.00 a.m. they were rapidly overwhelmed when the Russian lines began a general advance. Charles managed to escape across the River Bug into Turkish territory and was effectively interned until 1714, while Lewenhaupt surrendered the survivors to Menshikov at Perevolochna on 30 June. The Swedish army had been totally destroyed – c.9,000 dead and c.11,000 prisoners.

Poltava confirmed the considerable progress which Peter the Great's army had made since its defeat at Narva in 1700. It also reinvigorated the alliance of Saxony– Poland, Hanover, Prussia, Russia and Denmark to demolish Sweden's Baltic Empire, an aim which was largely accomplished by the Treaty of Nystad in 1721. The logistical problems of maintaining an army over interminable distances along with the over-reaching ambition of their leader had been the undoing of the Swedes. The same combination of factors was to prove fatal to subsequent western invaders of Russian lands in 1812 and 1941. *See also* CHARLES XII; FORTIFICATION, FIELD; MOSCOW, BATTLE OF; MOSCOW, RETREAT FROM; NARVA; PETER I; RUSSIA/USSR; SWEDEN.

G. A. STEPPLER
JOHN CHILDS

FURTHER READING
Christopher Duffy, *Russia's Military Way to the West: origins and nature of Russian military power, 1700–1800* (London, 1981), pp. 17–26; R. M. Hatton, *Charles XII of Sweden* (London, 1968); John Adair, 'Poltava', in *Great Military Battles*, ed. Cyril Falls (London, 1964), pp. 42–9; F. G. Bengtsson, *The Life of Charles XII, King of Sweden* (London, 1960); Peter England, *The Battle of Poltava* (London, 1992).

Polybius (*c*.200–after 118 BC) The Greek historian Polybius came from a leading family in Megalopolis, a Greek city which was a member of the Achaean League in the third and second centuries BC, and which was intimately connected with Greek political and military affairs during the period when Rome was beginning her expansion eastwards. He was deported to Rome after the Battle of Pydna in 168, and this period of detention enabled him to develop a friendship with Scipio Aemilianus, later nicknamed 'Africanus the Younger', and to become a member of his circle of acquaintances. Polybius' personal experience of war and politics and in particular of the Roman political situation, coupled with a power of critical analysis, provided him with the inspiration for an outstanding work, which is the source of his reputation as one of the greatest historians of Antiquity. Indeed, it is to him that we owe the best account both of the Punic Wars and of the events which took place in Greece at the end of the third and the beginning of the second century BC. Polybius enjoyed during his lifetime a high reputation for military expertise, on account of the excellent training which he had received in that field. His interest in the military arts is indicated by his book on *Tactics*, now lost. In addition, his historical work contains many accounts of battles that are remarkable for their precision and clarity. Moreover, he has an extremely valuable description of the organization, marching line, discipline, weaponry and camp building techniques of the Roman army of his day. Polybius doubtless intended that his work to some extent should have a didactic purpose, in the provision of guidance for political and military leaders. Later ages were under no misapprehension about the value of Polybius; his work was among the favourite reading of various sovereigns, for example, Frederick II of Prussia, and it was widely discussed by eighteenth-century writers on military theory, such as Folard. *See also* FOLARD; FREDERICK II; GREECE, ANCIENT; ROME; SCIPIO AEMILIANUS.

R. LONIS
B. CAMPBELL

FURTHER READING
F. W. Walbank, *A Historical Commentary on Polybius* (3 vols, Oxford, 1957–79); F. W. Walbank, *Polybius* (Berkeley and London, 1972).

Popular warfare The active participation of populations in warfare has occurred in all historical periods: inhabitants of besieged towns, feudal 'aids', resistance movements, conscription, etc. It became more systematically organized during the Hundred Years' War between England and France. The ordonnance of 1357 placed an obligation upon the French people to contribute to the defence of the realm against the English invader and there was no shortage of examples of such armed resistance (*Le Grand Ferré*, the *compagnons des Vaux de Vire*, etc.). The monarchy of the *ancien régime* often repeated its injunctions to the population that they must 'rush upon' invaders, until the late seventeenth century when advances in international law and military conduct made such practices more difficult to accept and less effective. Frederick the Great of Prussia forbade his civilians to participate in warfare and punished offenders. However, with its mass levies, the French Revolution proclaimed the mobilization of the whole population in the defence of the country. Ironically, the principal manifestations of popular warfare during the Revolutionary and Napoleonic Wars occurred against French armies: German *Schnapans* who were involved in the war in the Netherlands, *guerilleros* in the Peninsular War and partisans during Napoleon's invasion of Russia. Other sources of popular warfare are civil wars and wars of religion, especially the religious conflicts of the sixteenth and seventeenth centuries in Germany, France and the Netherlands. Popular warfare also occurs in risings against oppressive and foreign regimes: the Dutch Revolt against Spain, the American War of Independence, the struggles in nineteenth-century Latin America and modern anti-colonial wars.

Popular warfare is distinct from the regular variety which pits formally constituted armies in the service of states against one another. Depending upon their circumstances, governments and institutions have either condemned or advocated popular warfare. The German General Staff, having denounced every act of resistance against German occupation forces between 1939 and 1944, attempted to promote popular resistance in 1945 when Germany was invaded. This was in conformity with the directive of Frederick William III in 1813: 'One does not need to wear a uniform to rush on the enemy. The battle to which the nation is called sanctifies all means.' To the Russians in 1812 and between 1941 and 1944, popular war was 'patriotic'. The most elaborate theories of popular warfare emanate from Marxist thinkers and practitioners, Lenin and Mao Tse-Tung, who have related it to social revolution.

Clausewitz referred to wars conducted with the participation of the population as 'people's wars'. Today, with the proliferation of wars connected with political and social revolution, military theorists prefer the term 'revolutionary war'. Politicians tend to reserve the term 'revolutionary war' for those conflicts which have as their objective either the transformation of the political and/or social structures of a country or the imposition of such a transformation on their enemies. The expression 'subversive war' is used to describe a struggle against the established authorities inside one particular territory or region of a state, usually with the support of some, if not all, of the inhabitants. There exist just as many examples of popular wars fired by conservative as by revolutionary ideals – the revolts during the 'General Crisis' in early modern Europe, the war in the Cévennes (1702–10) and Pugachev's Rebellion in Russia (1773– 4). There are also cases where the revolutionary and the conservative entwine, as in the revolts of the Netherlands and the United States against governments felt to be alien and oppressive.

Muraise's study serves as a guide. Popular warfare may use the techniques of regular warfare. This was the case with the Catholic and Royal army of the Vendeans, with Gambetta's armies in 1870–1 and, in a sense, with the institutionalized underground in the Vercors. However, this has rarely been successful. Popular warfare is more naturally associated with irregular warfare. For this to function, safe havens are required and the ultimate safe haven is to be found in the collaboration of the population to the extent that it becomes impossible to distinguish 'whether the civilian is a neutral, a sympathizer or an enemy; everyone is suspect'. The Spaniards, clearing areas and practising guerilla warfare against the French, provided the first systematic example of the links between popular and irregular warfare. There are hardly any examples of revolutionary warfare being successful by itself. Enforced secrecy and the formation of parallel networks whose members must necessarily have no knowledge of one another to escape repression, lead the combatants to organize themselves in quasi-feudal structures which sometimes disperse their efforts. Moreover, the successes of popular warfare have often been due ultimately to the decisive intervention of a regular war for which they have laid the foundations. Popular forces are incapable of fighting a regular war from their own resources. In order to fight such a war, they generally have to call upon foreign aid, which entails the danger that the objectives of the war become modified. There is seldom agreement between resistance fighters within a country and those who have had to take refuge abroad, while relations with states supporting the war and pursuing their own individual goals at the same time are even more difficult. The failure of the landings at Quiberon (1795) is an illustration of this. The Vendeans and the émigrés were incapable of co-ordinating their actions and the English re-embarked alone. To weld together such disparate elements, a faith or ideology of extraordinary force is needed.

It is often necessary, at some point, to establish close collaboration between popular and regular warfare. Wellington understood this very well when he set up his logistical and strategic base at Torres Vedras in 1810 surrounded by a countryside that had been ravaged by its inhabitants to prevent the French from finding subsistence. He thus achieved harmony between the concentration required by regular warfare and the dispersion needed in irregular or popular warfare. The French were faced with a dilemma: either to concentrate their forces to fight the British but abandon the countryside to guerilla warfare, or to disperse into posts throughout the area to counter the guerillas but risk being defeated in detail by the British forces. Foreign aid often manifests itself in the form of sanctuaries where, away from the war zone, clandestine troops can train on foreign soil or rebuild their forces. The Swiss canton of Vaud performed this role for a certain number of Camisards who subsequently made their way back to the Cévennes through Savoy, which was neutral, and the Dauphiné, where there were Protestant communities. There is no shortage of contemporary examples.

The object of popular warfare is first to win over the people in order to conquer or liberate the country. If popular support does not exist, or disappears, the resistance fighters have to live by exacting subsistence from the population and must seek to counterbalance the weight of established authorities by means of terror. In either case, popular or revolutionary warfare has two dimensions: the military and the politico-administrative. In the fight against popular warfare there are two phases: conquest followed by reconquest or pacification. In the first instance, the population are treated as enemies. In the second, the object is to divide them by taking severe measures against those caught red-handed but exercising clemency towards those who defect to the side of the government. The Cévennes War offered Muraise an opportunity to distinguish between several phases. After the incubation period (1685–1702) came the failure of the royal forces in direct warfare. This was followed by repression carried out by Maréchal de Montrevel. He broke down the open resistance of the Camisards but increased their determination. Then came pacification, conducted by Villars and the Intendant Basville: the leaders who surrendered were dealt with leniently but, at the same time, the 'infested' cantons were encircled and the loyal population were organized into self-defence groups (small Catholic militias) both for self-protection and to control the area. (The same technique would be used by the French 'Territorial Units' during the Algerian War.) The situation was finally resolved after the failure of the final Anglo-Dutch operations (landings at Agde and Sète) which removed the last hopes of the Camisards. During the Boer War (1899–1902), the British were to revive the methods of Villars and Basville. The British also forcibly removed local populations, a technique later used by the Greek government which cleared the Pindus mountain range of its inhabitants during the Communist rising of 1945–9, and by the French during the Algerian War when 12 per cent of the population were displaced. Whereas in the last two cases the people were resettled elsewhere, during the Boer War the British detained their enemies in concentration camps.

The essential dimension of popular war is the time expended in attrition, both physical and psychological. It is often more wasteful of human lives than regular warfare. Muraise is confident that revolutionary warfare cannot last for more than seven or eight years. After that point, reduced to despair, the partisans tend to attempt suicidal direct operations, unless their enemy has grown weary and anxious to negotiate. This explains why, in cases where they have not had sufficient success, the staffs of popular movements prefer to abandon a particular region and open a front elsewhere, a move which delays the moment of decision. *See also* CIVIL WAR; CLAUSEWITZ; DEPREDATIONS; GUERILLA WARFARE; HOLY WAR; INDIRECT WARFARE; LAWS OF WAR; LOSSES OF LIFE; MAO TSE-TUNG; RESISTANCE; SPAIN; STRATEGY; SUN-TZU.

A. CORVISIER

FURTHER READING

E. Muraise, *Introduction à l'histoire militaire* (Paris, 1964); Otto Heilbrunn, *Partisan Warfare* (London, 1962); R. B. Asprey, *War in the Shadows* (London, 1975); Walter Laqueur, *Guerilla* (London, 1977).

Pre-Columbian states of America The Pre-Columbian states provide an almost unique example of a large segment of humanity which, after total isolation, saw its civilization immediately and irremediably doomed by its first contact with other peoples. It only took a matter of years for a few handfuls of *conquistadores* to conquer the Aztec and Inca empires with the help of the crushing superiority of European armaments. They were assisted in this by the form of organization of those states, which were federations of diverse peoples. Other peoples, because of the inhospitable character of the regions they occupied or the backwardness of their civilizations by comparison with these empires, or the lack of interest initially shown in them by the Europeans, resisted for longer: thus the Maya of Yucatan resisted until 1697, the North American Indians and the Araucanians of southern Chile until the end of the nineteenth century. These two last-mentioned had time to adopt certain European innovations such as horses and firearms which, combined with their tradiional modes of combat and the vast size of the countries where they lived a semi-nomadic life, made them formidable opponents for many years. However, in a general way, nothing or hardly anything would in the end remain of the military art of the American Indians, except those notions which belong to the general principles of warfare.

The military art of the American Indians is characterized both by a highly elaborate organization of their states and by a level of technology so low that most of them were living in stone age conditions. Though they share numerous similar characteristics, particularly the absence of a sea-going fleet, the cases of the Aztecs and the Incas have to be considered separately.

The Aztecs After being established by armed force in the mid-fourteenth century, the Aztec Empire succeeded in bringing together in a federation a certain number of cities and kingdoms covering more or less the present territory of Mexico, in which the emperor placed military governors. The civilization of the Aztecs was a synthesis of the preceding civilizations which the peoples of the Mexican plateau (Zapotecs, Toltecs) or the coastal regions (Maya) had developed.

The Aztecs were a warrior people. Huitzilopochtli was both the god of war and the god of Tenochtitlan (present-day Mexico City). Warriors in fact constituted the most important social order since, in the form of prisoners of war, they provided the priests with the victims who were offered to the gods as sacrifices, in order to ensure the normal operation of the cycles of nature. Every male citizen of Tenochtitlan was born a warrior and received military training. His head remained shaven until the point when, having captured a prisoner, he became an *iyac*. If he went a number of years without achieving some exploit, he was considered unworthy to be a warrior and had to become a worker. By contrast, once he had captured or killed four enemy soldiers, he became a *tecuhtli*, and a military career in which he could achieve command, as well as acquire a share in the revenue from taxes, was then opened up to him. Warriors received a very thorough training in the use of weapons and physical fitness. Their ideal was self-control, scorn for death and the acceptance of total sacrifice.

The Aztec army was commanded by the emperor, aided by a number of dignitaries. The companies of warriors were split up into divisions and subdivisions, as were the allied armies, but there was little specialization among the men. Originally, recruitment of warriors and their leaders was relatively open, but at the point when the Europeans burst upon the scene, a warrior aristocracy was in the process of forming, the emperor's power was diminished and the bonds with the subject peoples were also weakening.

From a technical point of view, the Aztecs were very backward by comparison with the Europeans, possessing neither horses, wheels, iron nor gunpowder. The Aztec warrior was protected only by a kind of breastplate made of cotton padding and by a helmet of fabric or wood. He carried a round shield made of wood or plaited reeds. His offensive weapons consisted of swords, lances, wooden javelins with obsidian blades or heads, bows, slings and blowpipes. His clothing and protective armour were covered in brightly coloured decoration – from reeds, feathers, stone and gold – which played an important role. Orders were given by shrill whistles.

War always began at the end of a process of unsuccessful negotiations, according to a ritual which allowed it to be seen as the judgment of the gods, but the conduct of warfare was not governed by rules, victory being the sole objective. Battle began with the use of missile weapons, followed by hand-to-hand fighting in serried ranks to the sound of wind or percussion instruments making a noise designed to strike fear into the enemy. The objective was more to take prisoners than to kill; men equipped with ropes therefore stood back from the fighting waiting to tie up enemy soldiers who had been struck to the ground. Siege warfare was not unknown. The Aztecs used rafts to cross the marshes behind which towns were built for their protection and they attacked the ramparts with the aid of ladders. The destruction of the temple of the defeated people was seen as registering the judgment of the gods and gave the victor the right to annihilate his adversary. He was prepared to surrender this right, however, in return for compensation: the subjection of the defeated people and the payment of tribute or the performance of tribute labour. The prisoners were honoured before being sacrificed, consentingly, to the gods of the victors in a strictly ordained ritual. The Aztecs saw such sacrifices as indispensable and this led, when there was no war, to their organizing a kind of tournament between tribes, so that the prisoners required to propitiate the gods could be obtained. These ritual mass sacrifices gave the deeply Christian Spanish conquerors a further motivation for fighting a pitiless war against the Aztecs and destroying their civilization (1519–40).

The Incas On the Andean plateaux, at very high altitude, to the north-west of Lake Titicaca, an empire had been built up by the Quechua people. That empire was to extend as far as the Amazonian forest and would border on the Pacific Ocean from Colombia to the north of Chile. The society was divided into two orders, a kind of nobility, the 'Incas', who were charged with a divine mission, and the relatively passive mass of the people.

Under the authority of the emperor, the Inca, whose residence was at Cuzco and who was regarded as a living god, there had developed a state born of conquest, whose highly elaborate administration was based upon the use of the *quipu*, an object made up of knotted strings (a 'knot-string record'), whose meaning had the value of a written document. The emperor's authority rested on fortified towns such as Paramunca and Canete, which were in many cases built by a people – the Chimu – whose particular hour of glory was past. These fortress towns consisted of terraces which were reached by means of flights of steps, separated one from another by cyclopean ramparts. These towns in the mountains with their 'staircase' construction and also rope bridges, were connected together by a network of roads on which messengers operated. There were runners placed at relay points (*Chozas*) who carried oral messages or *quipus*. A system of bonfires completed the signalling system which could transmit a message over more than 125 miles in a day. This form of organization had enabled the Incas to establish a kind of state communism. The Inca provided clothing for all and equipment for his warriors. He also maintained supply depots along the roads.

The noble order was subjected to a harsh process of education. The young nobles learned to understand the *quipus* and were then subjected to a series of ordeals, which began with fasts, sacred dances and ritual sacrifices and continued in the form of a mountain run (which was still a great trial in spite of their being acclimatized to the altitude), simulated combat, archery and slinging contests and trials of endurance to test their resistance to blows, fatigue and danger. Lastly, they also had to make weapons. Those who triumphed received insignia from the Inca: diadems of feathers, metal breastplates and enormous ear-rings.

The Incas did not have a standing army. Apart from the nobles, warriors were raised in the provinces whenever necessary to form companies of the line, where the men were grouped in tens, hundreds, five hundreds, thousands and five thousands. Lastly, the subject peoples provided men who fought as auxiliaries under Inca command.

The Incas used metal: copper, silver and gold. Their armour consisted of leather breastplates, cuirasses of cotton padding, wooden or wickerwork shields and the leaders wore wooden helmets. All these were decorated with designs and feathers.

Their weapons were wooden sabres fitted with copper blades, lances, spears, heavy axes or clubs. As missile weapons, they used the bow, which was generally a weapon of the auxiliaries, the sling, the true national weapon, and lastly the *ayllos* (*bolas*) made up of three balls strung together with little cords which was spun around the head and thrown at the enemy.

As among the Aztecs, the onset of war was always preceded by negotiations whose objective was to persuade the enemy not to offer resistance. Military operations began with a campaign of espionage and propaganda. Battle commenced with the use of the missile weapons and this was followed by the use of shock weapons. Battles were often decisive, since waverers on one side were often led to rally to the other. The resistance of the various towns did, however, set some limits upon their effects. The conquest of the Inca empire occurred as quickly as that of the Aztec empire (1532–6). *See also* SPAIN.

A. CORVISIER

FURTHER READING
J. Collier, *The Indians of the Americas* (New York, 1956); *The Americas on the Eve of Discovery*, ed. H. Driver (New York, 1964); Brian Fagan, *The Aztecs* (Oxford, 1984); H. Innes, *The Conquistadores* (London, 1969); John Hemming, *The Conquest of the Incas* (London, 1970).

Press, military *See* SERVICE PERIODICAL PUBLICATIONS

Prisoners of war   In ancient warfare it was customary for the lives of the defeated and the captured to be at the mercy of the victor. Vanquished troops who were wounded or surrounded were likely to be massacred on the battlefield. However, there were occasions when, usually for reasons of religion or propaganda, the death of captives was postponed. This was the case among peoples who practised ritual cannabalism believing that the consumption of a part of the enemy's body (the heart or the brain) could instil his warlike

667

qualities. The 'head shrinkers' of Borneo displayed their trophies on the thresholds of their houses to publicize their conquests and as late as 1389 the tower of skulls beside the battlefield of Kossovo served as a monument to the victor. Massacre, captivity or ritual death was the fate of both captured soldiers and civilian populations, especially civic leaders.

Once nations came under a central authority, there was a rapid change in the position of prisoners of war; they now belonged to the state and not to the warrior who had taken them captive. A ruler could keep them alive to adorn his triumph, as with the Romans or Aztecs, and then have them executed (as Vercingetorix was beheaded eight years after his surrender) or reduce them to slavery. Very soon, those who wielded power had to weigh the effect of the terror which they could inspire by the massacre of prisoners against the risk of suffering reciprocal treatment. As a result of a considerable development of more humane attitudes, the massacre of prisoners away from the battlefield became far less common, unless they failed to fulfil their undertakings. Even so, the victor often did not take prisoners ('no quarter!'), either because the fighting men had been provoked to the extent of losing all self-control, or because the vanquished had resisted too stubbornly (had sold their lives dearly), or had contravened the usages of war. The same result also occurred when towns were taken by storm. The matter rested entirely on the victor's summing up of the situation. In fact, the victorious commander sometimes ordered the defeated to be massacred because he considered that he could not cope with the danger which too large a number of prisoners would present to his rear (Agincourt, 1415), or because he was unable to feed them without depriving his own soldiers of some of their rations. In Western Europe there were several massacres of this kind during the Thirty Years' War and in Eastern Europe even up to the eighteenth century in the Russo-Turkish wars. Nevertheless, from the moment the victor spared his prisoners' lives, he had the right to require the latter to fulfil any conditions he

specified. This same view was still stated in Grotius's *De jure belli ec pacis* (lib. III, cap. VII), which appeared in 1625.

Also in Antiquity there were instances where, though the lives of the defeated were spared, the victor had them mutilated as a warning to others before letting them go (as when Caesar ordered the right hands of the defenders of Uxellodunum to be cut off) or condemning them to slavery. In the most fortunate instances, the latter might mean that they became household slaves, but very frequently they were merely sold in the markets. The large number of prisoners taken from warrior nations by the Romans caused a slump in prices, and the expression 'Sardinians for sale' (*Sardi Venales*) was used to describe merchandise of little value.

The various stages in the improvement of the treatment of prisoners of war cannot be assigned exact dates. These varied in accordance with the order in which regions became 'civilized', and the same developments reappeared, although at differing periods, depending on the evolution in each country of principles of ethics, humane attitudes and practical morality, as well as the course of their individual histories. Thus, Christianity could moderate the barbarity of some practices where wars between Christian nations were concerned. It has been in wars between peoples belonging to different civilizations that the fewest prisoners of war have been taken (e.g. the Moslem conquest; the capture of Jerusalem in 1096 and of Constantinople in 1453; the conquest of America), or where the lot of those taken prisoner has been the most severe. A distinction must be drawn between the case of besieged forces and of those defeated on the open field of battle. The besieged who surrendered could negotiate their terms and arrange for their lives to be spared or even to avoid captivity – if the victor gave his consent – by undertaking not to serve again against the victors. A body of soldiers surrounded on the battlefield could be induced to capitulate. In most instances, however, surrender in battle put the defeated at the mercy of the victor and, in general, it was not until after Christian ideas had become widely diffused that the latter would be ready to encumber himself with wounded prisoners.

It was at an early date that the prisoner of war took on the character of hostage; his life could, therefore, depend on the carrying out of written or tacit agreements between the belligerents and be subject to the principle of reciprocity. Capture established the victor's rights over the conquered and the latter could regain his freedom only by offering some acceptable compensation in the form of a ransom reflecting his wealth, social rank and political importance. At the period when it was still current practice to massacre the defeated, individuals of great distinction or those who had been able to win the esteem of the victor could escape this fate (e.g. John the Fearless at Nicopolis in 1396). The capture of military commanders, and even more, of sovereigns, was clearly a great prize. The release of the latter was usually made the subject of a treaty whose terms were always demanding, most generally accompanied by the cession of territories and the handing over of hostages in order to guarantee the performance of the treaty's provisions (e.g. the Treaty of Calais signed by John the Good in 1360 after his capture at Poitiers, or that of Madrid by Francis I in 1526 after the Battle of Pavia). In the case of other leading individuals, their release was covered by a private treaty, to which their family became a party having been required to stand surety. If the sovereign himself desired to recover the services of a particular general, he paid the ransom, as Charles V did for du Guesclin. Negotiations like these also occurred at lower levels. Hence, war became an opportunity for making money. In the 'warfare within the rules' in which the mounted knights of the fourteenth and fifteenth centuries engaged (as opposed to the 'all-out warfare' of the foot soldiers), few were killed, many were ransomed and, on the whole, captivities were short. As for the ordinary soldiery, they could hardly hope to buy their freedom or even to have their lives spared, except by offering, on the battlefield, whatever possessions they had with them – usually the fruits of plunder – or else by ransom. Nevertheless, in as much as they had taken service with a captain, it was up to the latter to ransom his men. Indeed, he did so whenever it was possible, since it was more advantageous for him to ransom an experienced soldier, and one of whose loyalty he would thus be assured, than to find himself a new recruit.

The trend towards a system of regular payment to troops, particularly foot soldiers, and the frequency of wars in the sixteenth and seventeenth centuries, led to the establishment of a 'ransom tariff', which was generally equal to the prisoner's pay for one month. The captains, however, did not always have the cash needed for such ransoms, and the prisoners were then freed from their obligation towards them; hence, they could take service with the victor, their enlistment bonus, however, being waived and retained in lieu of ransom. There were also occasions where opposing sides exchanged prisoners. Monarchs who were at war realized the importance of this question of prisoners, and hence began to conclude agreements with each other over exchanges. The first known example of such an agreement appears to have been settled between the kings of France and Spain in 1553, and was followed by others, an increase in their number occurring during the Thirty Years' War. The main points in these agreements were: (1) a guarantee given by monarchs to enter into special negotiations in respect of generals and other leading figures; (2) an exchange between enemy armies of officers and soldiers, on the basis of man for man of similar rank; (3) a ransom equal to the value of one month's pay to be handed over for the release of every extra man held by one of the sides; and (4) the prisoners to remain the responsibility of their own sovereign during their period of captivity, it being his obligation to reimburse those who had borne the expense of their upkeep. In theory, monarchs sent accredited officers to their enemies charged with the task of ensuring the proper execution of the agreements.

What actually happened was that the men were dispatched to towns which acted as centres where their units could be split up. Thus, a party of Spanish prisoners taken by the French at Rocroi (1643) went to Rouen, where they were divided into small groups and then sent to castles in the cities of Normandy. These cities had to keep them under surveillance by making use of the citizen militia, to provide for them and to incur such costs in advance, until the French king could reimburse them – which he could do only when the money arrived from Spain. Hence, the system operated somwhat irregularly. It was, in addition, common practice, before prisoners were taken to their place of captivity, for attempts to be made to influence them, particularly if they were of foreign nationality; every army dealt with its own nationals separately either with the object of condemning them for their treason or of 'salvaging' them. The others were invited to enlist in the ranks of the victors and many did so without any qualms of conscience or with the aim of discovering a better opportunity to escape. Prisoners who had been 'salvaged' did not benefit from any particular attention, and they often lost their seniority. In all cases, officers and soldiers were separated, in order to break up the chain of command. Officers pledged their word not to escape and enjoyed complete freedom of movement; sometimes, they were even allowed to go home, on condition of not rejoining their army. During the Thirty Years' War, the system worked about as well as could be expected; it lapsed when supplies of money were lacking, and when too many cases of escape led to the suspension of treaties of exchange. The length of time that had elapsed since capture did not always have any influence on release, and some men remained prisoners for ten years or more.

This system, which also covered naval personnel, became sufficiently well established in the eighteenth century to allow the bilateral treaties concluded at the opening of hostilities to be considered as valid throughout the ensuing campaigns. Military captivity did not generally last long. In the case of surrenders, the captive units remained in being under the control of their headquarters; the Brussels garrison was thus treated when it surrendered to the French in 1746. Normally, prisoners were housed far away from frontiers – Austrians in the south or centre of France, French in Transylvania or on British hulks. These accepted practices were rarely breached except, for example, by Frederick II of Prussia, who put Saxon prisoners forcibly into his own army in 1756, and made up from French prisoners taken in the Seven Years' War some *Freibataillonen Französischer Deserteuren* which, incidentally, proved a severe disappointment to him.

Development was slower in Eastern Europe. Nevertheless, in Hungary a system came into being whereby volunteers agreed to take the place of Habsburg subjects who had become prisoners of war, and to accept captivity in their stead.

The situation of prisoners of war was not altered in any important respect by the wars of the Revolutionary period or of the Empire. The law of 20 June 1792 stated that prisoners of war would be placed under the protection of the nation, and a decree of 25 May 1793 laid down that no prisoner would be compelled to serve the state which had captured him. Exchanges were accepted as permissible, but on a man-for-man basis only and not in return for money. In fact, the system of exchanges worked badly with Britain and Spain, and some prisoners remained for a long period away from their own country. Dartmoor Prison was built to house French prisoners of war. Some also settled down in the country which had made them a prisoner.

After 1815, there was an improvement in the situation of prisoners of war, at least in Europe, and particularly for those who were wounded. An agreement signed at Geneva on 22 August 1864, and ratified in 1868, defined a victor's duties. Chaplains and medical personnel were to count as non-combatants and were not to be made prisoners of war. These stipulations were still too recent to be applied in every detail to some 300,000 prisoners of war in 1870–1. The number of prisoners increased during the two world wars, and particularly in the latter. Conditions governing captivity had, however, been defined by the Hague Conferences of 1899 and 1907, which established a code of conduct. Certain improvements were added in 1929 and 1949 with amendments in 1975, but it was during the 1914–18 war that the current system of military captivity was actually brought into being. In line with a procedure which the British had used during the Boer War and which aroused rather strong feelings at the time, camps were to be set up, surrounded by barbed wire and provided with barrack hutments. Prisoners were to wear a uniform marked on the back with letters showing their status. A distinction was made in Germany between officers' and other ranks' camps, which were termed respectively *Oflage* and *Stalage*. Other ranks only could be compelled to work, either in a factory near the camps, in small parties under armed guard, or singly in farming operations. The length of these conflicts made the captivity more burdensome. Some prisoners were sent to the mines, of which the salt mines were the most feared. There were special camps for prisoners who had tried to escape. However, the Germans generally treated the British and US prisoners of war according to the Geneva Conventions because of the danger of retaliation against the numerous Germans in Allied captivity. Where retaliation was not feared, as in the cases of Russian prisoners and occupied countries, Germany failed to observe the Geneva Conventions.

The subject of prisoners of war appeared in an extreme form during the Second World War. In 1940, the German army captured 2,000,000 Frenchmen and, in 1941, 3,000,000 Russian soldiers. Various circumstances made the lot of prisoners still harder; Allied captives were sent far away from the Reich's western frontiers, and German prisoners of the Russians often went to Siberia. The Americans suffered from having forced on them the rations of the Japanese soldier, which were lower in calories and different from those to which they were accustomed. The German government made political capital out of the large number of men whom they had captured and who served as hostages in their hands. Thus, it forced the Vichy government to pay in the form of concessions for the release of medical personnel, the sick and wounded and the oldest pris-

oners. In 1943 it conceived the scheme of freeing prisoners in return for the supply of (more or less) voluntary workers – though any hopes raised by this were soon disappointed since, shortly afterwards, a system was established under which Frenchmen were compelled to go to Germany and work in factories. On the other hand, some prisoners were able to secure the status of 'free worker' in the place of captivity. All Allied prisoners in German captivity had been freed by the spring of 1945, whilst those in the hands of the Japanese had been released by the end of that year. The majority of German and Japanese prisoners who had been captured by the Western Allies were released during 1946 and 1947.

An aspect of captivity in the Soviet Union was the attempt to convert prisoners to communism ('brain-washing'), a practice that frequently recurred during wars of decolonization, particularly those in Indo-China, and in Korea (1950–3). The North Vietnamese denied the rights of the Geneva Conventions to American prisoners of war during the conflict in Vietnam while Iraq ignored the Conventions during the Gulf War of 1991. It must be noted finally that the speed of an enemy advance has not always allowed prisoners of war to be evacuated to rear areas, and that some command headquarters have, on occasion, not abstained from massacring them (e.g. Katyn).

From the seventeenth to the mid-twentieth century, captured partisans have been unprotected by the rules of war, and have usually been shot. The current growth of this type of warfare has meant that it is not always possible to distinguish them from soldiers proper, and attitudes towards them are undergoing some degree of adjustment. *See also* ETHOS; GROTIUS; LAWS OF WAR; ROME; VATTEL.

A. CORVISIER

FURTHER READING
Geoffrey Best, *Humanity in Warfare* (London, 1980); G. I. A. D. Draper, *The Red Cross Conventions* (London, 1958); S. D. Bailey, *Prohibitions and Restraints in War* (Oxford, 1972); *The Hague Peace Conferences of 1899 and 1907*, ed. J. B. Scott (2 vols, New York, 1972); *Restraints on War*, ed. Michael Howard (Oxford, 1979).

Privateering *See* COMMERCE-RAIDING

Promotion, army Promotion in the army is normally a process of selecting men who are thought capable of assuming larger responsibilities than those with which they have previously been charged, but it can also be used as a reward for services already rendered. The former principle tends to lead to advancement through selection (merit), the latter by length of service (seniority), although influence, nepotism and purchase have also played their parts. Non-commissioned officers are usually appointed and promoted within their regiment or branch on the recommendation of commissioned officers.

Most modern armies operate a peacetime promotion system based partly on merit, as demonstrated in competitive examinations, and partly on seniority. Peacetime promotion is generally slow and predictable, although every effort is now made to establish definite career patterns for young officers. In wartime, promotion can be rapid and pay little or no regard to seniority, able and enterprising officers being pushed into senior commands at great speed. Very often, this is achieved by the use of temporary or acting rank; an efficient lieutenant-colonel might well find himself advanced to the rank of temporary major-general commanding a division although only receiving pay for his substantive rank. This method, which was much used, and abused, by the British army during the Second World War, reduced costs, put competent officers into appropriate commands, and did not interfere with established patterns of seniority.

In the English New Model Army (1645–60) it was possible for rankers to achieve commissions, particularly in regiments destined for foreign service. Among officers, promotion was 'by merit, tempered to some extent by seniority' (C. H. Firth, *Cromwell's Army* (London, 1962), p. 49). However, officers had to pay to the state a fee on receiving their commissions. After the Restoration of Charles II in 1660, a personal and venal system of promotion by purchase operated within regiments until its abolition in 1871. Although much

decried, the purchase system ensured that the British army remained a decentralized collection of regiments, an important factor in a country which viewed the military with the height of suspicion. It also provided retiring officers with a lump sum. In effect, the purchase system was a means by which officers invested in their own military careers. On entering the army, a new officer paid a sum of money directly to the officer who was leaving the service. When the new officer eventually received promotion, he did not sell his initial commission but paid the monetary difference between the value of his old commission and that of his new one directly to the officer whose retirement was creating the vacancy. Other officers who received promotion because of that retirement also paid the difference in value between their old and new places, all of this money going to make up the full value of the commission of the retiring officer. If a captaincy was worth £1,800, a lieutenancy £700 and an ensigncy £450, then the retiring captain's gratuity of £1,800 was composed of the lieutenant paying him £1,100 for his promotion, the ensign £250 for his elevation plus £450 from the new ensign.

Purchase did, of course, demand strict promotion by seniority and ensured that commissions could only be secured by the wealthy. The price of commissions in established standing regiments was high but cheaper commissions could be obtained in regiments raised for a war but liable to disbandment on the return of peace. Numerous attempts were made to abolish purchase – 1689, 1693, 1694 – and an oath denying purchase was even included in the annual Mutiny Act after 1695 but to no avail. Various efforts were also made to regulate the prices of commissions, notably in 1854, but market values were usually dominant. When purchase was abolished in 1871, 6,938 officers had vested rights which had to be bought by the government at the regulated prices.

After 1871, officers were appointed to their first commissions after a competitive examination in non-professional subjects. Within three years, the 2nd lieutenant had to pass an examination for promotion to 1st lieutenant; after five years he had to take the examination for advancement to the rank of captain. A final examination enabled the captain to be considered for field rank. In 1877, compulsory retirement was introduced for officers and pensions were provided. However, the abolition of purchase made little difference to the British officer class as the social expenses of army life were so high that only the wealthy could contemplate taking commissions. The huge expansion of the army in 1914 and 1939 and the introduction of conscription in 1916 and 1938 did much to remedy this situation. The officer corps had to accept thousands of young men into wartime commissions, and promotion on merit rather than seniority was essential. The retention of conscription until 1960 continued this trend. After 1960, the system of competitive examinations was retained although in any peacetime army, a measure of promotion by seniority is essential for the maintenance of domestic harmony within regiments.

During the *ancien régime*, Prussia, Austria, Russia and Sweden promoted their officers on merit although within a system of regimental seniority. Prussia favoured an exclusively aristocratic officer corps but the majority of states permitted promoted rankers, commoners and bourgeoisie into their lower ranks, especially during time of war. The French army operated a dual system. Certain regimental ranks were available without purchase in order to favour meritorious but poor nobles as well as promoted rankers, while the higher and more prestigious ranks were reserved for puchase and became the preserve of the wealthy nobility.

In the army of the United States before the Civil War, promotion was by seniority within regiments and staff departments. In 1861, all candidates for commissions in the Union Army had to appear for examination before an efficiency board and a retirement scheme for incompetent officers was introduced at the same time. Examinations for all ranks below that of major were established in 1890 along with promotion by seniority within each arm, corps or staff department rather than within the regiment. Compulsory retirement at the age of sixty-four assisted the flow of promotions. *See also* HIERARCHY; NAVAL PERSONNEL; SOLDIERS AND SOCIETY; TRAINING.

J. CHAGNIOT
JOHN CHILDS

FURTHER READING
Anthony Bruce, *The Purchase System in the British Army, 1660–1871* (London, 1980); André Corvisier, *Armies and Societies in Europe, 1494–1789* (Bloomington, Ind., 1979).

Propaganda *See* PSYCHOLOGICAL WARFARE OPERATIONS

Propellants Gun and rocket propellants do not explode but burn to produce an even and progressive emission of gas. The emitted gases then drive the projectile along the barrel.

Greek Fire, probably first used by the Byzantines during the Siege of Constantinople (AD 673–8), was a combustible mixture of uncertain composition (probably saltpetre, sulphur and naphtha) delivered through a tube or pipe, or by catapult and hand-bomb. It was much used in naval warfare and for the defence of towns against ships and assault towers until the thirteenth century.

Gunpowder was the major invention which transformed warfare. Originating in China in AD c.700, gunpowder came into use in the West towards the middle of the thirteenth century probably through the work of Roger Bacon (c.1214–92) and Albertus Magnus (c.1200–80). Gunpowder was used to demolish fortifications before 1500 and was employed as a propellant in guns by 1320. Between 1548 and 1572, the bed of the River Niemen was dredged with gunpowder explosions and Gaspar Weindl introduced gunpowder into mineral mining in 1627. It was first used in England as a blasting agent in the Cornish tin and copper mines in 1689 by the elder Thomas Esply.

It was initially composed of 41 per cent saltpetre (potassium nitrate), 30 per cent sulphur and 29 per cent charcoal, the ingredients being impure. The modern proportions are 75:10:15. The constituents were ground separately into fine powders and then mixed in a dry state. This 'black powder' was employed both as a blasting explosive in grenades, shells and mining and as a propellant for rockets, cannon balls, shells and bullets from artillery pieces and hand-guns. After the mixture had been tamped into the breech of a gun, it became hard and difficult to ignite. When ignition was achieved, the powder burned unevenly producing a relatively weak explosion. An additional problem with this 'serpentine' was its tendency to separate out into its component parts when subjected to vibration. This meant that the powder had to be remixed after long storage or transportation, a dangerous business as the powder was sensitive to friction. Serpentine was difficult to keep dry because saltpetre is hygroscopic.

Early in the fifteenth century, the three components of gunpowder were mixed wet and the resulting 'cake' was then broken up and passed through a sieve to achieve grains of an equal size. The regular-shaped grains did not pack as tightly as the old serpentine powder, allowing more air space and a faster and more even combustion. The new 'corned' or granulated powder attracted less atmospheric moisture, did not separate out when transported, and did not foul barrels so heavily. Its higher explosive power allowed metal cannon balls to be substituted for stone and was a more suitable propellant for hand-guns. Mealed powder or 'pulverin' was a very fine powder used for priming and flares. During the sixteenth and seventeenth centuries, the quality of gunpowder was further refined by increasing the proportion of saltpetre relative to the sulphur and charcoal: 6:1:1 by 1700. In Britain, saltpetre was obtained by digging beneath dunghills but, in the later seventeenth century, it was imported from countries where it could be obtained in its natural state. Towards the end of the eighteenth century, the Royal Gunpowder Factory was established at Waltham Abbey to the north of London, on the site of an old sixteenth-century powder mill, to manufacture high quality powder in the proportions 75:10:15 by the employment of Congreve's Machine which produced grains of a uniform size.

The explosive qualities of fulminates of silver and mercury had been known since the seventeenth century. Alexander John Forsyth invented the percussion method of igniting the charge in muskets and rifles in 1807 using fulminate of mercury and potassium chlorate and this was refined into the percussion cap by Joshua Shaw in 1816. The percussion cap was adopted by the British army in 1838.

Guncotton (nitrocellulose) was developed between 1838 and 1845. Cotton, treated with nitric and sulphuric acids, created a powerful explosive, but the initial material was unstable. During the 1860s guncotton was purified but it produced an explosion too violent for use as a propellant, although it was useful as a filler for shells. Instead, several experiments were made to improve the quality of gunpowder by compressing the damp powder into various shapes. The object was to retard the speed of the explosion so that the shot was given a long, slow push out of the barrel rather than a sudden acceleration; every grain of powder had to burn in order to release all possible explosive gases. In 1846, the Italian Ascanio Sobrero discovered nitroglycerine and in 1867 Alfred B. Nobel of Sweden introduced dynamite (basically stabilized nitroglycerine).

In 1884, Paul Vieille patented a nitrocellulose powder (nitrocellulose dissolved in ether and alcohol) which was both powerful and smokeless. This was adopted in France under the name 'B' Powder but was more generally known as single base powder. Nobel invented ballistite in 1888, another smokeless powder (45 per cent nitrocellulose and 55 per cent nitroglycerine), which became more widely known as 'double base' powder. When acetone was used to dissolve both the nitroglycerine and the nitrocellulose, the result was cordite, developed by Alfred Abel in 1889. Cordite acquired its name because it was hardened into a long, thin rope or cord. Used in the 0·303 inch rifle, cordite increased muzzle velocity from the 1,800 feet per second achieved with compressed black powder to 2,000 feet per second and later to 2,440 feet per second when used with a lighter, pointed bullet. In addition to providing propulsion of high power, cordite was stable and smokeless. During the First World War, variants of nitroglycerine and nitrocellulose powder (carbamite in Germany and Austria) were the basic propellants for both infantry small arms and artillery. After 1918, the nitroglycerine in double-base powder was replaced as a solvent for nitrocellulose by nitrodiglycol (DGDN) to produce G Powder, which burns at a lower heat thus reducing wear on rifle and cannon bores. Using double-base powder, a rifle barrel can fire between 15,000 and 17,000 rounds. After smokeless powder came flashless powder, which was achieved by adding nitroguanidine to double-base powders (GUDOL in Germany) to form triple-base powder. Modern artillery continues to employ variants of triple-base powders. Modern tank guns employ high energy propellants (equal proportions of RDX (*see* EXPLOSIVES) nitrocellulose, nitroglycerine and nitroguanidine) to achieve very high muzzle velocities for kinetic energy armour piercing ammunition. Black powder remains in use in some sporting guns.

Rocket projectiles were also propelled by double-base powders or black powder. More recently, rocket projectiles have been powered by perchlorate mixtures, usually based on ammonium, or a combination of rubber and ammonium nitrate. Guided missiles and rockets employ solid or liquid fuel motors, following the examples set by the German V-1 flying bomb and V-2 rocket. The V-1 was powered by a petrol and compressed air ram jet whilst the V-2 had a rocket motor fuelled by alcohol and liquid oxygen. *See also* ARTILLERY; EXPLOSIVES; FIREARMS.

J.-M. GOENAGA
JOHN CHILDS

FURTHER READING
T. Urbanski, *The Chemistry and Technology of Explosives* (3 vols, Oxford, 1964–7); M. A. Cook, *The Science of High Explosives* (New York, 1966); A. Bailey and S. G. Murray, *Explosives, Propellants and Pyrotechnics* (London, 1989); P. R. Courtney-Green, *Ammunition for the Land Battle* (London, 1991); S. Fordham, *High Explosives and Propellants* (2nd edn, Oxford, 1980).

Property owned by the military The military have always required land reserved for their own special purposes. Since the Ancient Greeks and Romans, soldiers have needed parade grounds, housing and space for fixed fortifications. After 1363, English village greens were turned over to the compulsory practice of archery on holy days, but the military appetite for land did not significantly increase until the early modern period with the advent of gunpowder weapons and artillery fortifications. In 1537, the Guild of St George, later the Artillery Company, was founded to develop the 'science and feate of shooting' with hand-guns and bows in the Artillery Gardens on Bishopsgate, London. The Artillery Company was revived in 1610 and established a 'Military Garden' in St Martin's Fields in the same year, whilst a 'Military Yard' was founded in Westminster in 1635 and a 'Martial Yard' in Southwark. Similar military institutions, with their own plots of land, were founded in Colchester, Bury St Edmunds, Norwich, Bristol, Gloucester, Great Yarmouth, Derby, Coventry and Ipswich during the 1620s. By 1669, the Artillery Ground near Spitalfields was regularly used by the Ordnance Office for proofing and weapon trials.

Medieval castles were usually owned by members of the aristocracy, apart from those in the possession of the reigning sovereign (e.g. the Tower of London). Towns were responsible for the erection and maintenance of their own walls and fortifications, although citadels might belong to a local noble or to the ruler. However, with the necessity for artillery fortifications in the sixteenth and seventeenth centuries, and the development of the notion of a linear frontier, the crown became both the builder and owner of fortifications. In most cases, the crown owned and maintained the military installations in a fortified town while the civil and religious buildings remained under municipal and ecclesiastical control. In France, by 1715, the fortifications around a town were, indisputably, crown property. This was confirmed by a law of 1790. The fortifications of Berwick-upon-Tweed

(1558–70) and those at the major ports and dockyards of Hull, Harwich, Sheerness, Tilbury, Portsmouth and Plymouth followed this pattern. In France, the Netherlands, northern Italy and Germany, the greater size and number of artillery fortifications made the military greed for land far greater than in Britain.

Areas for training became more important after the introduction of a standing army in Britain after 1660, although the ditches and areas of restricted land within the field of fire of fortifications had long been used for butts, drill and gunnery practice. Blackheath and Hounslow Heath were used frequently between 1660 and 1714. During the Seven Years' War (1756–63), the American War of Independence (1775–83) and the Revolutionary and Napoleonic Wars, training camps became regular features on the British landscape – Bromeswell Heath in Suffolk, Coxheath near Maidstone, Colchester, Newbury, Dorchester, Salisbury, Barham Downs, Shorncliffe and Blandford – stretching along the southern and eastern coasts to guard against invasion. Although these were only temporary, wartime camps on rented ground, they became semi-permanent venues for the army with trenches, drains and latrines excavated, and hedges and superfluous buildings removed. In 1778, an acre could be hired for £6 and a battalion of foot required 10.5 acres; compensation was paid for damage. The French army assembled in large training camps (Vaussieux in Normandy, 1778), while the Prussian army of Frederick the Great concentrated in large training camps for review, inspection and training every spring and autumn.

The housing of soldiers gradually became a direct concern of government during the eighteenth century, necessitating the acquisition of land for the construction of barracks and supporting installations. Some progress was made towards accommodating the French army in barracks during the reign of Louis XIV but the high cost brought the programme to a premature halt and it was not resumed until after 1763. The British army was moved into municipal barracks, a responsibility of the Board of Ordnance, between 1792 and 1858. Similarly, the Prussian and Austrian armies were transferred from billets to barracks between 1763 and 1800. The nineteenth century witnessed the development of long-range rifled artillery and small arms and the mass-conscript army. Both required governments to purchase or rent large tracts of agricultural or waste land for use as ranges, depots and camps in addition to land for fixed fortifications, barracks, installations for support services and offices for the administration. The British School of Musketry was opened at Hythe in 1853, the School of Gunnery at Shoeburyness in 1859, the first wooden barracks were built at Aldershot in 1855, and Tidworth Camp on Salisbury Plain was founded in 1902. The French state purchased or rented unproductive land as firing ranges and permanent camps after 1818, Châlons-sur-Marne being the initial establishment. There are currently twelve such national camps in France, the smallest at Valdahon (7,500 acres) and the largest at Canjuers (87,000 acres).

The United Kingdom contains approximately 56,000,000 acres of land. By 1938, the Ministry of Defence owned either the freehold or the leasehold or had purchased 'rights' to 225,000 of these acres. Between 1939 and 1945, the Ministry of Defence extended its claims to 11,500,000 acres, 20 per cent of the total land area, including the entire coastline. After the Second World War, the retention of conscription until 1960 and the longer range of weapons meant that more land was required than before 1939. In 1947, the Ministry decided to retain 1,027,000 acres, approximately 2 per cent of the land available. Although the number of troops in Britain fell dramatically after 1960, the Ministry of Defence only released 279,200 acres between 1947 and 1971, principally because of the growing range of weaponry and the loss of training grounds overseas. In October 1972, the military occupied 747,000 acres, half of which was the preserve of the army. Training areas and ranges took up 512,000 acres, the remainder being divided between offices, depots, bases, airfields, dockyards, barracks, Royal Ordnance factories and other nationalized defence industries, research and development centres, colleges, schools, hospitals, prisons and fortifications. Unfortunately, 114,331 acres lay within National Parks or along 'heritage' coasts; a further 91,000 acres were on Salisbury Plain. The public had access to one third of Ministry of Defence land but much of the remainder was let for agriculture as training only took place at certain periods of the year – in 1992, it was reported that most land owned or rented by the Ministry of Defence was only used by the military for 20 per cent of the time – access was totally prohibited only to firing ranges and impact areas. Under pressure from the growing movement for the preservation of the environment, the Ministry released 32,700 acres in 1974, but despite continued assaults from a number of environmental pressure groups and semi-official government agencies like English Heritage, the Nature Conservancy Council and the Countryside Commission, no significant tracts of land have since been released by the Ministry of Defence. Indeed, in 1985 the Ministry of Defence reported that the British military needed an additional 2,000,000 acres; between 1985 and 1989, 600,000 acres were actually acquired in Britain, Europe and North America. The Ministry of Defence also rents training grounds overseas, in particular the 750 square miles at Suffield, Alberta, Canada, as well as hires the temporary use of some of the training areas of the United States armed forces. At the time of writing, it appears that the Russian Revolution of 1991 has caused such a decrease in international tension that many defence installations in Great Britain might well be closed in the near future. In addition to the physical use of land within National Parks for military purposes, regions like the Yorkshire Dales are employed by the RAF for regular low-flying exercises. Noise pollution is a major problem. A certain amount of air space is reserved for military flying, particularly over maritime bombing ranges. The Navy exercises at sea but can interrupt merchant shipping lanes and interfere with fishing.

Submarines, in particular, pose a grave danger to inshore fishing craft.

The United States, France and the Soviet Union (until 1991) also required large areas for the testing of nuclear warheads. Initially, these were tested at altitude over the American and Australian deserts, or over remote Pacific islands; there were twenty-three US tests over Bikini Atoll between 1946 and 1958 while the hydrogen bomb was first tested above Eniwetok Atoll in 1952. Intense radioactive fallout from the first Bikini 'shot' descended on an area of 7,000 square miles. Following the Nuclear Test Ban Treaty in 1963, tests have been confined to deep underground chambers. However, China and France ignored the treaty and continued to conduct atmospheric tests.

Whereas Britain has approximately 1.2 per cent of its total land owned or rented by the military, the proportion in the United States is much lower. In 1962, the Federal Department of Defense occupied 28,003,071 acres (16,287,181 acres owned and 11,715,890 acres rented or leased), 50 per cent of the total land area of Great Britain. Altogether, the Federal authorities owned 770,796,843 acres. In 1963, the Department of Defense 'controlled' 30,200,000 acres, of which 26,800,000 acres were in the United States, 200,000 acres in United States 'possessions', and 3,200,000 in foreign countries (i.e. bases in the Philippines, NATO countries, Thule in Greenland, etc.). Within the United States, 55.6 per cent of the 26,800,000 acres were situated on lands in the public domain, i.e. Federally owned lands in public use – national parks, reservations, etc. The Corps of Engineers acts as the real estate agent for the US army and air force, while the Bureau of Yards and Docks serves in a similar capacity for the navy and the marine corps.

The real estate of the French armed forces amounted to 642,000 acres in 1954 but had contracted to c.500,000 by 1990. In addition, the French have a number of training grounds in their former overseas colonies (Polynesia, Antilles, Chad, etc., as well as occupation forces in Germany). As in Britain and the United States, much of the land is owned by the state, particularly that which contains fortifications and defence works, while the rest is leased or rented from the civilian land market. The property is divided into six categories: 'A' – administrative premises, both for central and local commands; 'C' – permanent installations providing accommodation and facilities for the troops, together with training establishments and police complexes; 'D' – defence works and sites (fortifications, air force and naval bases, sites for ground-to-ground ballistic missiles); 'H' – accommodation for officers and NCOs, buildings used by welfare services; 'S' – permanent industrial and support installations, including arsenals, stores, hospitals, etc.; 'T' – tactical exercise areas, firing ranges. In France, the *gendarmerie* (100,000 men and women) is treated as a branch of the armed forces and police buildings were added to the military estate in 1935. Urban areas contain 7 per cent of the property of the French armed forces, the remaining 93 per cent lying in rural regions.

Although navies and air forces are essentially systems of transport as well as combat services, the land forces have usually relied upon the public communications networks of roads, railways, rivers and canals. The German, Russian, Austrian and French railways in the nineteenth century were all built with the needs of mobilization in mind, as were the German *Autobahnen* during the 1930s. Similarly, the *Autobahnen* in modern Germany are ready for instant mutation into a military road network. However, it is rare for an army to own a transport system, apart from private roads and railways on its own bases and training areas. The Royal Military Canal, built in 1798 to link Shorncliffe to Winchelsea and to provide a tactical barrier to an invading French army, was an exception. See also ARSENALS; BARRACKS; BASES, AIR FORCE; BASES, NAVAL; FORTIFICATION; MILITARY RESTRICTIONS ON USE OF LAND; ORDNANCE; TRANSPORT.

J.-M. GOENAGA
JOHN CHILDS

FURTHER READING

C. Bertout, *Le Domaine militaire* (Paris, 1909); *Defense Management*, ed. Stephen Enke (Englewood Cliffs, NJ, 1967); Ministry of Defence, *Report of the Defence Lands Committee, 1971–73* (London, 1973).

Provisions *See* LOGISTICS; RATIONS; STAGING POSTS; TRANSPORT

Prussia *See* GERMANY

Psychological warfare operations Sometimes known as 'combat propaganda' and more usually associated with wartime, psychological operations, or PSY OPS, have also acquired a significant role in the era of the Cold War and of modern peacetime international relations in general. PSY OPS have been defined by NATO as: 'Planned psychological activities in peace and war directed to enemy, friendly and neutral audiences in order to influence attitudes and behaviour affecting the achievement of political and military objectives.' Psychological warfare, however, is a much more specific branch of this activity, being war propaganda directed at enemy audiences (combat personnel, civilians and leadership) designed principally to serve the purposes of those manipulating the information and opinions, usually the undermining of morale and the inducement of surrender, insurrection or disruption.

Because of its modern association with 'dirty tricks' and the manipulation of the human mind, psychological warfare is often regarded as a somewhat sinister activity which somehow seduces the human soul into doing something it would not otherwise do. Yet in reality, psychological warfare is designed to save lives by persuading the enemy to lay down his arms or withdraw his support from the war effort. It can utilize a variety of techniques, including fear, fact or fiction, but what is most effective is propaganda based on military realities or likelihoods or, in other words, on propaganda which is rooted in factual or identifiable lines of argument. Moreover, it can take essentially three forms: black, white and grey. Black propaganda emanates from a disguised source or purports to emanate from a source other than the true one. White propaganda is disseminated openly by clearly identifiable sources. Grey propaganda fails specifically to identify any source.

During the Gulf War of 1991, a variety of psychological warfare techniques were employed against the Iraqis, ranging from the dropping of almost 30 million leaflets (60 for every Iraqi soldier believed to be in theatre) inducing troops to 'Cease Resistance and Be Safe', to black propaganda radio broadcasts emanating from unknown sources inciting the population of Iraq to overthrow Saddam Hussein. The most celebrated single known incident to have emerged from this war occurred when a special operations squadron of the US air force dropped leaflets declaring: 'Tomorrow if you don't surrender we're going to drop on you the largest conventional weapon in the world.' That night, on schedule, a BLU-82 ('Daisy Cutter') 15,000 lb bomb was dropped, to be followed the next day by more leaflets stating: 'You have just been hit with the largest conventional bomb in the world. More on the way.'

As this example illustrates, the most effective form of psychological warfare is that which is conducted hand in hand with military operations. This has been recognized as an effective adjunct to warfare since the Ancient World, whether it was Joshua outside the walls of Jericho or the appeals of commanders such as Alexander the Great or Julius Caesar to their troops prior to battle. The rapid transformation of communications technology may, however, have revolutionized the employment of psychological warfare techniques, but many of the methods have remained the same. In the case of *Operation Just Cause* in 1989, for example, the Americans borrowed from Joshua by playing incessant rock music to the besieged Panamanian leader, Noriega, in an effort to drive him out of his bastion.

Siege warfare in the ancient and medieval periods made psychological operations an essential ingredient in the starving out and subjugation of cities. The advent of printing in the fifteenth century revolutionized the means of communicating and persuading enemy forces and civilians. Religion was frequently used as a propaganda device, with Eternal Life being dangled as the carrot, and Eternal Damnation the stick. The narrowing of the gap between soldier and civilian, through the Thirty Years' War and through the American War of Independence and the French Revolutionary Wars, led to the increased employment of printed pamphlets and visual devices such as prints and cartoons in an attempt to undermine civilian support for military operations. But in reality it is only with the advent of total war in the twentieth century, in which the gap between soldier and civilian has been narrowed substantially, that psychological warfare has been extended scientifically as a 'fourth arm' of attack. During the First and Second World Wars in particular, dropping 'bits of bumpf' by balloon and aeroplane became a tried and tested method of influencing enemy morale. The British, in particular, developed a reputation for the effective deployment of this weapon, although General Wilson had first considered this in 1915 to be 'a minor matter – the thing was to kill Germans'. By 1918, however, the War Office and the Department of Enemy Propaganda at Crewe House had developed a highly sophisticated organization, which General Ludendorff described as the Ministry for the Destruction of German Confidence. Enemy testimony to the effectiveness of British propaganda continued after the war with Adolf Hitler devoting two admiring chapters of *Mein Kampf* to the subject and the following statement: 'Our soldiers learned to think the way the enemy wanted them to think . . . We were hypnotized as a rabbit by a snake.'

Great care must be taken with such statements, especially since they were used by certain disaffected elements within Germany as 'proof' that the German armies had not been defeated on the field of battle but rather had been forced to submit due to 'a stab-in-the-back' on the part of a collapsed civilian morale that had been fostered by superlative British propaganda. Even so, rudimentary interrogation techniques were employed in 1918 in order to ascertain why growing numbers of German soldiers began to surrender or simply go home, and many testified that their decision had been made after reading Allied leaflets. Although it is well known that prisoners of war often say what they think their captors want to hear, the experiment was considered to have been sufficiently successful for it to be tried on a much greater scale in the Second World War.

By 1939–45, the medium of radio was added to the psychological warfare armoury and it was used to great effect in the British Political Warfare Executive's attempts to undermine morale inside wartime Germany and to sustain resistance within occupied Europe. The Germans tried their own version against the British with the broadcasts of William 'Lord Haw Haw' Joyce but, once again, it was the British who perfected the art of black radio propaganda with Sefton Delmer's secret 'Research Units' transmitting disaffection and rumours, apparently from within occupied Europe itself although in fact from Britain. Greatly helped by the entry of the United States into the war and the arrival of the high-powered Aspidistra transmitter, such broadcasts were widely listened to inside Germany and the object of frustrated admiration by no less a figure than Joseph Goebbels himself.

In fact it was the Americans who also brought with them a new scientific and organizational approach to the conduct of psychological warfare in conjunction with military operations and this became most apparent in the preparations for *Operation Overlord* in 1944. Throughout the entire planning process for D-Day, a massive deception campaign code-named *Fortitude* was devised in an elaborate attempt to make the Germans believe that the landings would take place other than in Normandy – and it worked. In the 1944 Standing Directive for Psychological Warfare against members of the German Armed Forces it was stated that 'psychological warfare is not a magic substitute for physical battle, but an auxiliary to it. By

attacking the fighting morale of the enemy, it aims at: (a) reducing the cost of the physical battle, and (b) rendering the enemy easier to handle after surrender.'

With the development of the Cold War in the post-1945 period, PSY OPS assumed a prominence in international relations unprecedented in history. The Cold War was, after all, the continuation of warfare by other means, including propaganda, espionage, intelligence and counter-espionage activity, and the threat of global annihilation. It was an ideological struggle between two diametrically opposed political systems which both recognized the importance of words as an alternative to weapons of mass destruction. 'Traditional' PSY OPS techniques continued to be used in 'hot wars' in Korea, Suez and Vietnam but it was the global struggle for hearts and minds between two warring ideologies which prompted the employment of new, often hidden, techniques of persuasion conducted by such organizations as the CIA and KGB. It was President Eisenhower's profound belief in 1953 that 'the Cold War must have some objective, otherwise it would be senseless. It is conducted in the belief that if there is no war, if two systems of government are allowed to live side by side, that ours, because of its greater appeal to men everywhere, to mankind, in the long run will win out.' By 1990, when President Bush was pronouncing his New World Order, he would no doubt have discovered that President Gorbachev would have to concede that Ike's words had indeed proved prophetic. *See also* INDIRECT WARFARE; INTELLIGENCE; LANGUAGE; OVERLORD; POPULAR WARFARE; SECRECY.

PHILIP M. TAYLOR

FURTHER READING
Philip M. Taylor, *Munitions of the Mind: war propaganda from the ancient world to the nuclear age* (Wellingborough, 1990); C. Roetter, *Psychological Warfare* (London, 1974); D. Lerner, *Psychological Warfare against Nazi Germany* (Cambridge, Mass., 1971); T. H. Qualter, *Propaganda and Psychological Warfare* (New York, 1962).

Publications *See* SERVICE PERIODICAL PUBLICATIONS

Q

Qadesh, Battle of *See* KADESH

Quartermaster-general *See* GENERAL STAFF

Quarters *See* BARRACKS; BILLETING

Quebec, Battle of the Plains of Abraham
(13 September 1759)   On 27 June 1759, a
youthful British major-general, James
Wolfe, landed on the Île d'Orléans near
Quebec, with 9,000 regular soldiers who
had been brought by flotilla from
Louisbourg. Built partly on a rocky outcrop
overlooking the St Lawrence River and its
tributary, the Saint Charles, Quebec was
defended by the Marquis de Montcalm
(1712–59) with *c*.14,000 French regulars
and militiamen and some 1,200 Indians.
For two months Wolfe tried to breach the
defences below the city before discovering
upstream above Quebec, in the cliffs overhanging the St Lawrence, a path which
Montcalm had left inadequately guarded as
he thought it inaccessible. On the night of
12 September, Wolfe sent a battalion of
light infantry up the path, followed by the
greater part of his army. By early morning
they were formed in battle order just outside the city on a piece of relatively open
ground known as the Plains of Abraham.
Montcalm attacked in haste, without waiting to concentrate all his available forces or
a large part of his artillery. The superiority
of the British musketry broke the French
attack and forced the survivors back into
Quebec. Both Wolfe and Montcalm fell in
the action. Quebec surrendered on 18 September leading, in the following year, to the
fall of French Canada.

The capture of Quebec affords an excellent example of a successful amphibious
operation. Full co-operation between the
army and navy was essential to the success
of the final British plan. Although the
army's victory on the Plains of Abraham
precipitated the capture of the city, it was
the mobility provided by the British fleet
that enabled Wolfe to make the most
effective use of his numerically inferior
force. The superior discipline and training
of the British regulars were quickly proven
in the main engagement, but the success of
Montcalm's Canadians in harassing the left
flank of the British line pointed to a
vulnerability which might have been better
exploited. Wolfe's light infantry dealt with
this threat but the British position was
extremely precarious and the surrender of
the city was by no means a certainty. *See
also* COMBINED OPERATIONS; EXPEDITIONS;
FRANCE; GREAT BRITAIN; WOLFE; YORKTOWN
CAMPAIGN.

A. CORVISIER
G. A. STEPPLER

FURTHER READING
A. G. Doughty and G. W. Parmelee, *The Siege
of Quebec and the Battle of the Plains of
Abraham* (6 vols, Quebec, 1901); W. J. Eccles,
'The battle for Quebec: a reappraisal', in *Essays
on New France* (Toronto, 1987), pp. 125–33;
Duncan Grinnell-Milne, *Mad, is he? The char-
acter and achievement of James Wolfe* (London,
1963); Lawrence H. Gipson, *The British Empire
before the American Revolution* (15 vols, New
York, 1946–70), vii; Francis Parkman,
Montcalm and Wolfe (Boston, 1884); C. P.
Stacey, *Quebec, 1759* (Toronto, 1959).

Quiberon Bay, Battle of (21 November
1759)   A French landing corps under the
command of the Duke of Aiguillon assembled near the Gulf de Morbihan ready
for transportation to Ireland. A second
army, under Chevert, intended to cross the
Straits of Dover. To support these operations, the Toulon fleet was ordered to join

the Brest fleet. The former, under de la Clue, was sighted passing Gibraltar by the British Mediterranean fleet under Edward Boscawen and a chase action ensued which ended off Lagos in Portugal with five of the twelve French vessels lost, five taking refuge in Cadiz while two reached Rochefort. This setback put the whole scheme in jeopardy while Sir Edward Hawke's (1705–81) strict blockade of Brest caused further delay. Eventually, Admiral de Conflans managed to leave Brest with twenty-one vessels on 14 November heading for Quiberon Bay. Hawke followed and pursued Conflans right into Quiberon Bay though a gale was rising and the waters were dangerous even if well known to the British. Six French ships were sunk, six took shelter in the Vilaine estuary and eight made Rochefort. Two British ships were lost on the rocks.

While the French defeat was primarily due to the unnecessarily complicated initial plan, their fleet was ill-manned owing to sickness which had been introduced via the returning squadron of Dubois de la Motte. However, Hawke was an extremely bold and adventurous commander who, having found his foe, was prepared to risk his ships in perilous conditions in order to achieve a decision. The battle was a major factor in deciding the outcome of the Seven Years' War. *See also* BLOCKADES; HAWKE; NAVAL WARFARE; NAVIES.

J. MEYER
A. W. H. PEARSALL

FURTHER READING
Ruddock F. Mackay, *Admiral Hawke* (Oxford, 1965); Geoffrey J. Marcus, *Quiberon Bay* (London, 1960).

Quiberon Bay, landings of émigrés at (27 June–22 July 1795) In the summer of 1795, the British government dispatched a force of French émigrés and recently recanted Republican prisoners of war, under Commodore John Warren and the Counts de Puisaye and d'Hervilly, in an attempt to reopen a front in the west (in Brittany) against revolutionary France. An initial party of 3,500 men, later joined by a further 1,500, were landed on the Quiberon peninsula. Much was expected from a rising of the local Royalists, 'les Chouans', but full co-operation foundered on the hesitation of the landing forces, poor liaison and a general mistrust of Puisaye. General Hoche acted vigorously against the landings and the venture was soon abandoned. Less than half of the original landing force re-embarked, some 6,000 (of whom 748 were executed) surrendering to the Republican troops. The later British landings at den Helder in 1799 profited from the lessons learned at Quiberon Bay. *See also* COMBINED OPERATIONS; EXPEDITIONS; INDIRECT WARFARE.

A. CORVISIER
G. A. STEPPLER

FURTHER READING
Charles Robert, *Expédition des émigrés à Quiberon, 1795* (Paris, 1899); John Ehrman, *The Younger Pitt* (2 vols, London, 1969–83), ii *The Reluctant Transition*; E. Gabory, *La Révolution et la Vendée* (3 vols, Paris, 1925–8); Ch. L. Chassin, *Les Pacifications de l'Ouest, 1794–1801* (3 vols, Paris, 1896–9).

R

Raeder Erich (1876–1960) Raeder became an officer in the Imperial German Navy in 1897 and rose rapidly to higher ranks in a brilliant career. During the First World War, he fought in the Battles of Dogger Bank and Jutland before commanding the cruiser *Köln*, and then becoming head of the central section of the Naval Ministry. He wrote the official history of German overseas cruiser warfare 1914–18. Promoted rear-admiral in 1922, he became vice-admiral in 1928, and Commander-in-Chief of the *Kriegsmarine* the same year. Raeder tended to underestimate the role of aircraft and submarines, and undertook the creation of an imposing surface fleet, built around a large number of capital ships (Plan Z). The war interrupted this programme. Nevertheless, he also revived the U-boat fleet.

During the conflict, increasingly acute differences of opinion set Raeder against Hitler. The grand admiral was unable to persuade the Führer to focus his strategy on the Mediterranean. Furthermore, the part played by capital ships turned out to be disappointing, submarines taking the chief role in the Battle of the Atlantic. Following a far from glorious engagement in the Barents Sea on 31 December 1942, Hitler wished to pay off the big ships. Raeder resigned, but became Inspector-General of the Navy for the rest of the war. He stood trial at Nuremberg and was condemned to life imprisonment, though he was released in 1955 on account of his age and health. *See also* ATLANTIC, BATTLE OF THE; DÖNITZ; GERMANY; HITLER; JUTLAND.

B. KROENER

FURTHER READING
Erich Raeder, *Struggle for the Sea* (London, 1959).

Raids, coastal *See* COMBINED OPERATIONS; EXPEDITIONS

Railways *See* TRANSPORT

Ramillies, Battle of (23 May 1706) The action at Ramillies, 35 miles south-east of Brussels, between the Allied army of the Duke of Marlborough and the French commanded by Marshal Villeroi (1644–1730), offers a prime example of what could be achieved by good generalship in the eighteenth century. The encounter came unexpectedly when the French marshal, under explicit orders from Louis XIV, emerged from behind the River Dyle to take offensive action. The time and place of the clash surprised both participants as they had miscalculated the distance separating them. Both armies were confident of success and well matched in overall numbers, with *c*.60,000 men on either side, and in their proportions of infantry and cavalry. The French deployed on rising ground in a concave line nearly 4 miles long, their left wing covered by marshy ground. Marlborough proceeded to attack this position from a deployment made within its arc, on a shorter, convex front, a situation he employed to good effect during the battle. An initial assault on the French left succeeded in attracting Villeroi's full attention and he drew troops from his centre and right to contain the threat. Subsequently, making use of dead ground and of his shorter interior communications, Marlborough was able to redeploy sufficiently to achieve a breakthrough in his opponent's weakened centre and right wing. The battle was notable not only for Marlborough's generalship during the action itself, in particular his skilful employment of dead ground, but also for the rapid exploitation of victory. Having suffered over 13,000 casualties, the French were immediately subjected to a vigorous pursuit. In the following weeks, their disarray

683

was pressed to maximum advantage until they were virtually expelled from the Spanish Netherlands and their own frontier was placed in jeopardy. Marlborough's tactical decisions both during and after the battle emphasized the importance placed upon cavalry. The battle also illustrated the advantage to be gained by a commander of superior moral strength willing to attack a strongly posted opponent even though encountered unexpectedly. By seizing the initiative, Marlborough forced his enemy into merely responding to his blows. A similar situation was to arise at Oudenarde in 1708. *See also* BLENHEIM; DENAIN; EUGENE OF SAVOY; MALPLAQUET; MARLBOROUGH; VILLARS.

G. A. STEPPLER

FURTHER READING
C. T. Atkinson, *Marlborough and the Rise of the British Army* (London, 1921); Hilaire Belloc, *The Tactics and Strategy of the Great Duke of Marlborough* (London, 1933); D. G. Chandler, *Marlborough as Military Commander* (London, 1973); Frank Taylor, *The Wars of Marlborough* (2 vols, Oxford, 1921).

Ranks *See* HIERARCHY

Raphia, Battle of (217 BC) This battle, at which the King of Egypt, Ptolemy IV Philopator, won a victory over the ruler of the Seleucid kingdom of Asia, Antiochus III, marked an important turning point in the recruitment of soldiers who made up the armies of the Hellenistic kingdoms. Until then, the Greek Kings of Egypt had barely utilized their indigenous subjects in the military machine. They relied mainly upon Macedonian and Greek soldiers whom they recruited either from among the colonists settled on parcels of land provided by the king, or from among the mercenaries for whom they paid high prices in the marketplaces of the Mediterranean. To these were added Libyans, Gauls, Thracians and others, depending upon the need for specialized units. The most distinguished arm was the phalanx of heavy infantry and this was made up exclusively of Graeco-Macedonians. However, on the eve of the Battle of Raphia, the King of Egypt decided for the first time to enlist Egyptians in the phalanx in large numbers. According to the figures given by the historian Polybius, there were 20,000 native Egyptians fighting in this unit. It is unclear whether there was another, Graeco-Macedonian phalanx alongside this phalanx of Egyptians or whether, as is more likely, the Egyptians composed almost the whole of the phalanx of 25,000 men arrayed against the Seleucid infantry at the decisive moment. Ptolemy's left wing was routed by a combined assault of cavalry and elephants led by Antiochus himself; but while Antiochus continued the pursuit, Ptolemy rallied his forces and launched a counter-attack by means of his phalanx in the centre, which crushed the Seleucid infantry and decided the battle. The innovation of using Egyptian troops and their courageous performance had important consequences both on the military level, in the rapid Egyptianization of the Ptolemaic army, and on the political level, in the emergence of an awareness on the part of the native Egyptians of the force they represented within the Greek kingdom of Egypt. *See also* EGYPT, ANCIENT; GREECE, ANCIENT.

R. LONIS
B. CAMPBELL

FURTHER READING
Y. Garlan, *War in the Ancient World: a Social History* (London, 1975).

Rations Until the seventeenth century, the question of food supplies received scant attention from armies, except in the case of fortresses in danger of siege. In contrast, victualling has always been a priority for navies. Armed forces were relatively small and lived off the country. Some forward logistical planning was essential in long-range operations like the Crusades. The Spaniards achieved a high level of efficiency during the later sixteenth century. A daily bread ration of between 1½ and 2 lb was established for the Army of Flanders during the 1590s, financed by deductions from pay, while the Spanish navy achieved a sophisticated level of logistics in the preparation of large war fleets. Rations are only used to feed troops who are on the march or otherwise unable to find fresh food for themselves. Whenever possible, army quartermasters prefer to furnish their men with fresh produce purchased from local markets.

During the Thirty Years' War, during which armies were obliged to operate in already devastated landscapes, steps had to be taken to establish magazines of food to supply the soldiers on campaign. In order to maintain discipline and prevent soldiers from plundering, armies adopted the methods of supply organization and food preservation employed by navies. Food was supplied to troops on campaign by civilian contractors, commercial firms which undertook to provide bread for the men, fodder for the horses and a complete system of transport and distribution. All that the military had to provide was a corps of inspectors and accountants to ensure that the contractors did not embezzle the state or its troops. Foodstuffs were preserved by salting, in the case of meat and fish, or baking hard biscuit, which might keep for twelve months in the correct conditions, instead of bread. These arrangements only applied during a campaign; in winter quarters or in peacetime, soldiers were expected to fend for themselves from their own pay.

The introduction of daily rations allocated a specific amount of food to the soldier and fodder to his mount. In the period up to 1789, the number of rations issued to an individual took no account of dietary requirements or the amount of physical energy expended but depended upon rank. The early modern soldier on campaign consumed c.1,700 calories and 40 g of protein a day. In the 1930s, a soldier on garrison duty was reckoned to need between 3,200 and 3,500 calories a day, rising to 3,800 calories and 160 g of protein when in action. British soldiers on active service during the 1690s received daily a single 1 lb loaf of rye bread, or 1 lb of hard biscuit, at a cost of 1¼d. This sum was deducted from their daily pay. Prussian and Austrian troops during the Seven Years'

War (1756–63) received a free bread or biscuit ration of 2 lb a day. All armies expected their men to supplement their diets from the regimental sutlers, or provisioners, local markets and by foraging.

More variety was gradually introduced into the military diet towards the end of the eighteenth century. On 4 November 1775, the Continental Congress in America established a uniform ration for the Continental Army.

A ration should consist of the following kind and quality of provisions: 1 lb. beef, or 0.75 lb. pork or 1 lb. salt fish per day; 1 lb. bread or flour per day; 3 pints of peas or beans per week, or vegetables equivalent; 1 pint of milk per man per day; 1 half pint of rice, or one pint of Indian meal, per man per week; 1 quart of spruce beer or cider per man per day, or nine gallons of molasses, per company of 100 men per week; 3 lbs. candles to 100 men per week, for guards; 24 lbs. soft, or 8 lbs. hard soap, for 100 men per week.

During the nineteenth century, two important changes occurred: the cost of rations was no longer stopped from a soldier's pay and rations were increased when and where soldiers expended more energy. In France, after 1876, four categories of rations were specified – for peacetime, on manoeuvres, 'normal' field duty and 'extra' field duty. In the Russian and Austro-Hungarian armies, the issue of bread and biscuit was reduced in wartime but the amount of meat was increased. In the German and French armies, the bread and alcoholic drink ration remained the same in periods of activity, but the issue of biscuit, dried vegetables, meat, sugar and coffee was raised considerably. In Central and Eastern Europe, rye bread continued to be the military staple, although France and Britain changed to wheat flour.

Considerable advances in the victualling of troops were made during the American Civil War. Desiccated vegetables, 'desecrated' according to the Union troops, and canned meat were extensively employed. Because the processes of canning were not fully understood, botulism and other forms of food poisoning made their appearance. By 1900, the US army relied heavily on canned corned beef on overseas expeditions and this became one of the staples of the British army ration during the First World War. In the Second World War, the American K rations were widely emulated. Modern techniques of sterilizing and freeze-drying meat, vegetables and fruit have removed most of the problems of feeding mobile troops. Since 1945, the system has been adopted of providing troops with combat rations, consisting of a light package of small bulk containing food sufficient to provide three meals for one day ready to be served cold or hot. *See also* ADMINISTRATION, ARMY; ADMINISTRATION, NAVAL; LOGISTICS; ROME; STAGING POSTS; TRANSPORT.

J. CHAGNIOT
JOHN CHILDS

FURTHER READING
Martin van Creveld, *Supplying War: logistics from Wallenstein to Patton* (Cambridge, 1977); G. Perjés, 'Army provisioning, logistics and strategy in the second half of the seventeenth century', *Acta Historica Academiae Scientiarum Hungaricae*, xvi (1970), pp. 1–51.

Ravenna (Romagna), Battle of (11 April 1512) The bloodiest single battle of the Italian wars, Ravenna was the scene of the first major French attempt to counter the tactics developed by Gonsalvo de Córdoba. In 1511 the Pope (Julius II) formed an alliance with Ferdinand of Aragon and the Swiss to drive the French out of the Duchy of Milan. The French commander in Milan, Gaston de Foix, Duke of Nemours, was able initially to exploit his interior lines to fend off the uncoordinated thrusts of the allies, but in the spring of 1512 he decided to force the commander of the main Spanish–Papal army, the viceroy of Naples, Ramon de Cardona, into a decisive battle by investing Ravenna. Cardona, whose army numbered only 16,000 to Nemours' 23,000, sought to break the siege by threatening Nemours' supply line. However, on the advice of his engineer, Pedro

Navarro, that the position would be impregnable once entrenched, he dug in his army between the River Ronco and a marsh near the French camp on 10 April. Nemours, who had now obtained what he wanted, mounted a direct attack on the following day with most of his army, leaving only 2,000 men to mask the city. His answer to Cardona's entrenchments was a heavy bombardment of the stationary enemy by his large train of fifty-four cannon. The bombardment had little effect on the allied infantry, but Cardona's cavalry, who were stationed on the wings and without shelter, suffered heavily. To escape the artillery fire, they charged the French horse, but were defeated and driven from the field. Believing that the defeat of the cavalry had demoralized the allied infantry, Nemours then launched a series of assaults on the entrenchments with his French and German foot. These assaults, however, were repulsed with severe loss and only the return of their cavalry in the rear of the entrenchments secured the French victory. The encircled allied infantry suffered horrifically and allied casualties reached between 9,000 and 12,000 out of an army of under 16,000. However, French casualties were in the region of 4,000 (among them Nemours himself), chiefly suffered by the infantry in the course of their assaults on the allied entrenchments. For the French, Ravenna was a pyrrhic victory; if the combination of superior artillery and manoeuvre provided an answer to Spanish defensive tactics, the losses suffered by their infantry showed that entrenchments still had to be treated with caution. *See also* ARTILLERY; CÓRDOBA; FRANCE; INFANTRY; SPAIN.

SIMON ADAMS

FURTHER READING
C. Oman, *A History of the Art of War in the Sixteenth Century* (London, 1937), pp. 130–50.

Reconnaissance *See* AIRCRAFT, RECONNAISSANCE; CAVALRY; INTELLIGENCE

Recruitment, air force *See* AVIATION

Recruitment, land forces Recruitment for armies has always been conditioned by men's natural inclination and capabilities, as well as by their numbers, since it is not always easy to match military requirements with the human resources available. When armies need more men than those available with a vocation for arms, this is likely to restrict their scope for operations; although the contrary – more warriors than required – can also cause problems. Here, therefore, is a major issue which political entities – whether peoples, tribes or states – have solved in accordance with their defence needs or political ambitions, while taking into account, to a greater or lesser degree, the moral and social values of their societies. The conditions of service and its duration raise a further question. Over the course of history, the aim of recruitment has continually shifted between the two poles of a small army of long-service volunteers, which leads to a regular, professional army, and of a large number of short-service conscripts. It is possible, in the light of these basic considerations, to identify three major modes of recruitment which, with sundry variations, have succeeded each other: reliance on military orders or classes, on volunteers and on conscription.

In Antiquity, the bearing of arms was generally the prerogative of a particular social class. It was restricted to free men and only in dire need were those of inferior status, such as foreigners, serfs or even slaves, called upon to serve. There were two different situations depending on whether men provided their own arms and equipment or received these from the king, or from their city. The first case seems to have been the most common in tribal societies or in primitive kingdoms. All free men able to bear arms, except priests and some artisans who were essential for the making of weapons, were warriors or, at least, were ready to take up weapons at any moment. This situation occurred in societies where the division of occupation had not reached an advanced stage, such as nomadic or mountain races. Where the number of warriors became too large for the military needs of a particular society, it tended to feel the attraction of raiding

expeditions outside its own territory, or provided mercenaries to neighbouring empires which lacked sufficient loyal fighting men, but had the means to pay for the upkeep of foreign soldiers. The second case occurred in states which possessed an advanced political and administrative system, like the ancient empires of the Middle East.

Egypt during the period of the Old and Middle Kingdoms seems not to have had a standing army. When need arose, the pharaoh applied to his local officials (nomarchs) who provided him with ready equipped contingents, though exact knowledge is lacking about the way in which these were recruited. The arrival of the Indo-Europeans (around 1900 BC) seems to have disrupted the recruitment of armies in the ancient Middle East. In the Hittite Empire, which reached its height in the fourteenth century BC, there was a class of lords, termed 'nobles of Hatti', who accompanied the king to war and commanded the contingents which they supplied. Conquered or subject peoples had also to provide troops. Other nations copied this example. Egypt, under the New Kingdom (Ramesses II, thirteenth century BC), possessed a standing army made up both of nationals, who were provided with grants of land and who tended to become a privileged social class on which all recruitment was based, and of foreign mercenary units which, however, retained their independence. In the Assyrian army, there were national and subject peoples side by side. By the close of the Assyrian period of dominance, the king was in a position to call up practically all the able-bodied men in the tribes, and had in being nothing less than a conscription system among conquered peoples (seventh century BC).

It appears that social distinctions between members of armies occurred very early in history. This was quite understandable when men bore the cost of their own equipment, since that practice led to differences in armour and weapons. The more well-to-do wore heavy armour and became the assault troops, while the poorer men formed the light units. The introduction of the horse by the Indo-Europeans worked in the same direction. This gradation in accoutrements, which turned into one of prestige, was reflected in a social hierarchy, and that linkage seems to have been retained, even when states provided the equipment. The aristocrats composed the cavalry, the other free men the heavy infantry, serfs and dependants the light infantry, and lastly, foreigners were formed into ethnic units, which were differently equipped. The Persian army seems to have combined all forms of recruitment then known.

Ancient Greece shows several examples of warrior aristocracies – descendants of the Indo-European conquerors – of which the most famous was the force formed by the citizens of Sparta. They had originally been granted equal-sized plots of land. The eldest sons were soldiers by right of birth and the younger sons who found themselves unable to pay their share of the common meals suffered demotion to an inferior class. The citizens, or 'equals', as they were called, wore in battle the heavy equipment of the hoplite, and they had no occupation except that of arms. The other inhabitants, who had a lower status, and were known as *perioikoi*, served – depending on their level of affluence – as hoplites or as light infantry (peltasts), while the slaves (helots) were also used as the latter. In Athens, the city required from its citizens services that varied with their wealth. There were four classes, based on levels of property ownership. The richest (the *pentakosiomedimnoi*) fitted out, and commanded, the warships or served in the cavalry. Next in order came the *hippeis*, also serving in the cavalry, then the *zeugitai*, armed as hoplites, while the poorest (*thetes*) became light infantry or rowed the triremes. Foreigners (metics) were on occasion required to serve as hoplites. While serving, all received pay. When grave danger threatened, Greek cities sometimes called on slaves, but it was difficult to arm them without granting them their freedom. The recruitment of citizens operated in its fullest form in the fifth century BC, but losses in war and reductions in the birthrate – the number of the Spartan 'equals' fell from 8,000 to 2,000 – as well as a decline in civic spirit, rendered the system unworkable. From the fourth century BC compulsory service was gradually abandoned, and mercenaries were increasingly called upon to fill the gap.

The Macedonian army's history is a summary of this development. At the outset, Macedonia provided mercenaries who served abroad. Then, when she had acquired a well-established political system, she formed, for the king's service, an army of free men organized in the phalanx and in squadrons of cavalry, to which were attached contingents from her allied cities. Later, after Alexander's conquests, the Macedonians were spread across the empire, or in the states which were its successors, and having been rewarded by grants of land no longer provided forces of any size to armies whose modes of recruitment came more and more to resemble those of the Persian army.

Rome was to follow a similar process. In early times, the free men (citizens) provided their own equipment, and served in wartime in accordance with their wealth and age, as *hastati*, lightly armed, as *principes* or as *triarii*, a reserve of men heavily armed, with the richest forming a relatively small force of cavalry, and all of them being combined in formed units (legions). Members of the *plebs* were not compelled to serve. In fact, only part of the male population performed armed service. When the men of service age were assembled in the *comitia centuriata*, the officers chose those whom they wanted to take into the field. In 230 BC, there were 273,000 citizens out of a total of one million Romans, but of the former, only some 50,000 were mobilized. The remainder of the army was recruited from among the allied peoples in Italy. Nevertheless, the length of wars exhausted the middle classes and large numbers of Romans arranged to be exempted from military service which took them further and further away from their home base; just as in fourth-century Greece, the central body of citizens had abandoned their military role. A call had to be made to the *proletarii*, and their equipment was provided by the state. In *c.* 107 BC, Marius opened the army fully to them and, from that time, the Roman legions, which had become regular units, were made up of professional soldiers drawn from the poorest classes. The Roman army had also to employ foreign mercenaries, who retained their own types of arms and equipment.

In the Imperial period, the army was recruited mainly from men in the provinces who were granted citizenship and were rewarded with grants of land. It seems that Rome maintained 350,000 legionaries on long-term service, which represents, for a population of about 50 million, an average annual intake of 25,000–35,000 men. There were, in addition, auxiliary units (*numeri*), which tended to lose their racial character, on account of admixtures of personnel and changes of station; their members were given citizenship at the end of their service. With the increase of dangers on the frontiers, Rome had to maintain an army of 500,000 soldiers, but volunteers came forward in insufficient numbers, and the method of recruitment was changed. Since soldiers had been granted the right to marry, the state imposed on them an obligation that applied to their families. Their children (*ex castris*) were compelled to become soldiers, except in the event of physical disability. A fall in the birthrate, however, destroyed the hopes which had been placed on this system. The state then attempted to make the supply of recruits a charge on landed property, and proprietors had not only to supply, but also to equip, such men. Since those who were subject to this burden sought to use it as a means of removing undesirables from their estates, the results proved disappointing. For want of anything better, the state took into its service Barbarians whom it had settled on imperial territory as colonists, and even whole tribes to whom it had given the title of allies (*foederati*); these retained their own commanders and their own style of arms and equipment. Thus, Rome introduced into the West the system used by warrior peoples of the Middle East, and the German invasions caused its sudden extension. In the Barbarian kingdoms which superseded the Empire, the basis of recruitment was the obligation placed on every free man able to fight to respond to his king's call and to serve for the duration of a campaign, while providing his own equipment and being responsible for his own maintenance. Despite very wide differences of practice between various countries, military service tended to be organized around the most powerful men.

Among peoples with a fixed habitat, land forms the best reward for military service. Hence, in the empires of Antiquity, army service tended to be linked with land ownership and assume a hereditary character. From the second century BC, there was a slow development, though frequently interrupted by internal troubles and invasions, towards the formation of aristocracies, whose members were both landowners and warriors, and which were destined to provide, first, Barbarian kings, and then the Carolingian empire, with fully equipped soldiers in numbers proportional to their manors (feudal units of agricultural property) occupied by free men. The establishment of certain contractual legal relationships between men, which were the basis of the feudal system, brought with it a distinction between free men proper, whose obligation in regard to military service was limited, and vassals, who were maintained by the large landowner and by imperial officials (counts), and upon whom calls for service were continually being made. The latter were brought together in *champs de mai*, and had to give three months service a year. These customs prompted the formation of private armies by a hereditary group ('the fighting men') which owed the king a service (*ost*) that was limited in time (forty days a year) and in radius of action. In turn, this service provided those who were bound by its obligations with a special status – one that was destined to evolve into that of a nobility.

Obviously, a nobility that proclaimed the vocation of arms as its unique possession could never by itself provide all the fighting men required, but the nobles formed the backbone of armies and they took with them as infantry the men who owed them service. When monarchical rule became re-established in the West, the feudal *ost*

689

produced by the ban and arrière-ban proved inadequate, even when reinforced by the urban militias, and mercenaries began once again to be employed. Forces centred round a nobility still played a part during the French Wars of Religion, but the *ban* and *arrière-ban* – rendered out of date by the development of new weapons and poorly organized – fell into disuse at the end of the seventeenth century. Although, from the fourteenth century onwards, the number of nobles who took no part in affairs of arms increased, and a new non-military nobility (*noblesse de la robe*) made its appearance, there remained a general conviction up to the end of the *ancien régime* that the nobility was the military class, and as such, it claimed the monopoly of membership of privileged units of the royal household troops and of the position of officer in the army. It can be estimated, for example, that the nobility provided Louis XIV with one man in three who was able to bear arms, while the rest of the population produced only one in twelve. Such an effort, however, remained an exception and, during the eighteenth century, there was a variation from at least one in two in Prussia to one in ten in France in the numbers of the nobility taking up military service.

It has already been mentioned that voluntary enlistment became a normal practice at several times from Antiquity onwards among both nationals and foreigners, most often in the form of mercenary service. Quite frequently, it was regarded as the ideal form of military recruitment, whereas the placing on a citizen body of the obligation to serve in wartime or a regular conscription system was considered merely as a method to fill the gaps left by an inadequate supply of mercenaries. Depending on circumstances, voluntary enlistment can be prompted by vocational interest, spontaneous support for a cause or the desire for a contract of employment, the latter encouraging a trade in soldiers (*Soldatenhandel*) and the establishment of recruit markets. It was rare for voluntary enlistment not to be accompanied by the payment of a bounty. It was thus subject to the law of supply and demand, which could operate on the psychological and moral plane, as well as the economic. Family traditions also played a part, exactly as they do in the choice of any calling. In other words, the factors affecting voluntary enlistment are many and varied.

The increase in the size of armies in the fourteenth century, which was largely in terms of foot soldiers, provided very little attraction to the nobility. As wars between states replaced private wars, the combatants were separated from their homes by greater distances, thus lengthening campaigns. For that reason it became essential to call on mercenaries. Hence, units of a particular nationality reappeared, e.g. Genoese crossbowmen, German or Swiss *Landsknechte*, German *Reiter*, Croatian cavalrymen and Gascon adventurers, and – since wars went on indefinitely – more and more cosmopolitan groups were employed. It was the golden age in the West of war as a business, whether it involved whole armies raised by a general at the request of a 'war lord', as in Italy or in the Holy Roman Empire, or merely regiments and companies in situations where a king retained control of his armies.

As far as the men were concerned, the procedures for recruiting remained the same. The captain received, together with his commission, an authorization to recruit which set out the conditions, area and places where he could operate, the location and date at which he was to hand over his recruits to the regiment and the sum of money made available to him for the number of men required (*Wartegeld*). In certain instances, the king supervised these operations. The recruiting officers then had to approach the provincial or urban authorities, who were required to provide him with men selected from among those whose names appeared on the registers listing all who were liable for service. This system produced the *tercio* in Spain during the sixteenth century. It was not so in France, where Francis I's experiment with provincial legions in 1534 was a failure. The scheme was revived by Richelieu in 1635, but the towns merely used it to rid themselves of undesirables. In extreme circumstances, the authorities assisted the process of recruiting by press-gang methods, which consisted of shutting the gates of a city and then recruiting all the men who could not afford to purchase their release. It even happened that inmates of prisons were enlisted. During the War of the Spanish Succession, the French king commuted sentences to the galleys into military service.

Most frequently, the recruiting officer enjoyed a certain freedom of action. He could have the assistance of any sergeants or soldiers that he wanted. Recruiting became a matter of such moment that a captain was often valued more for his ability to produce good recruits than for his abilities as a fighting soldier. The contract that was arranged between a captain and his recruit was most commonly oral. There was a difference between the German and French methods, in which the recruit received half the bonus money (*Handgeld* or the king's silver) so that he could make his way to the assembly area, with the other half being paid on his arrival at the unit, and the Dutch system, in which the recruiting officer billeted and fed the recruit during the journey, in order to keep a closer watch on him. To the official bonus there was added a further sum which was settled by negotiation, based more on a man's height and sturdiness than on his abilities, since experience might hide a dishonourable military past. There was a ritual celebration of enlistment, part of which was the gesture of drinking the king's health. On arrival at the unit, the soldier had to swear an oath of loyalty to the king, after he had listened to the text of the 'Articles of war' or the ordonnance. The next step was to put him officially on the strength of the unit, if he fulfilled the required conditions (minimum age of 16 and height of at least 5 feet 4 inches in the French infantry, and 5 feet 8 inches in the cavalry). The soldier's name was then placed on the company's nominal roll (enrolment), and he took part in the next inspection parade in front of the *commissaire des guerres*. British recruits underwent a similar procedure except that, after 1693, new soldiers had their enlistment attested before a justice of the peace to make sure that they had not been enlisted against their will.

This procedure was the same for all men who enlisted, but different circumstances could greatly change the psychological atmosphere in which it took place. Very often recruiting was carried on quite outside the sphere of any regulations stipulated by the state. What was sometimes a mere trade in recruits could take on the guise of the assembling of troops by a feudal lord. A captain, either directly or through the agency of relatives or friends, might recruit in his own domains or his own region men who preferred to serve under a commander whom they knew and with compatriots speaking the same dialect. Connections like these led to excellent results, but produced insufficient numbers when the requirements were on a large scale. Then the recruiting officers betook themselves to towns, usually on market days, 'beat the drum' and engaged young men who were unemployed, had no family or were experiencing difficulties with their parents. When there was a shortage of volunteers, they tried to dupe young men, made them drink the king's health and went to the extent of using force, shutting them away, for example, in sweated training camps from which they could only emerge as soldiers. In the 'job of recruiting', apart from the differing degrees of attraction to military service that men might feel, the general economic situation played a large part. The size of the enlistment bonus varied in line with these factors. Similarly, the pressures imposed by recruiting officers were strongest at the time of the considerable increase in the size of armies during the Dutch War (1672–8) and the War of the Spanish Succession (1702–14). Despite efforts to stop abuses, Louvois had to admit that 'when the king needs men, that is not the time to examine whether they were enrolled in due form'. On the other hand, recruiting became easy during the 1693–4 economic crisis and especially in 1709–12, when the combined effect of patriotic emotions and economic depression came into play. Some recruits were seeking one thing only – bread. A curtailing of the recruiting officers' abuse of their authority and a lessening of interest in the military calling led to an increase of the engagement bonus in the eighteenth century, despite an attempt to fix a maximum figure for this (which in 1730 was 60 livres). For the same reason, the man who wished to buy himself out had to pay a higher and higher sum of money or, preferably, to provide two replacements.

Voluntary service meant that those who enlisted were characterized by a particular regional and sociological character. Generally speaking, a large number of men joined up in places where troops were stationed and particularly in frontier provinces, but the large cities, for their part, produced only the misfits from the influx produced by rural depopulation. In France, at the end of the eighteenth century, though two-thirds of the soldiers were born in the countryside, half of them enlisted in Paris, which became the principal market for recruits, in parallel with its famous scrap-iron market. Casual labourers, city artisans suffering from frequent unemployment, discontented younger sons and young gentlemen of an adventurous temper were proportionally more numerous than the countrymen, though certainly some men joined because they felt a genuine calling. Even so, it looked as if the nation was tending progressively to draw its recruits from among men who came from the northern and eastern provinces and from the lowest classes of society.

At the end of the eighteenth century, it became difficult to secure sufficient volunteers for the army. Various attempts were made to organize recruiting on a national scale; one of the outcomes in France was the formation of regiments of volunteers (1765), but these did not produce the hoped-for results, and quite rapidly disappeared. The Revolution rescued voluntary enlistment, by emphasizing its patriotic character. Early on, the idea that men should be induced to enter military service by financial means was condemned, and voluntary engagement, in theory without any enlistment bonus, was regarded as the only way in which recruits should be obtained. It proved necessary none the less to make, first, a selective call-up, and then a *levée en masse*. Later the Jourdan Law introduced a system of conscription. A

nationwide network of enrolment offices was set up, and these had also the task of enlisting volunteers. Although conscription was progressively established in a number of European countries, it did not cause the demise of voluntary enlistment; that still continued to provide men who joined entirely of their own volition, as well as replacements paid for by conscripts who had drawn an unlucky number, until the drawing of lots and the replacement option were abolished. Even Britain came close to introducing a limited form of conscription in 1803.

As earlier, so in modern times, voluntary engagements have reflected both a vocation for military life and the current economic and psychological circumstances (the latter, for example, often producing enlistments for the duration of a war). The length of service for which men have enlisted has varied in different periods and countries. Re-enlistments after initial military service have constituted a variably sized portion of full-time armed forces. In France, in 1984, 37 per cent of army, 62 per cent of air force and 73 per cent of naval personnel were regulars. Also in France, the introduction of compulsory service in 1872 retained alongside it some forms of voluntary enlistment that did not lead to membership of the regular army as a profession. For example, there was the voluntary engagement for one year (1872–1902), which was actually a favour done to young men who were still pursuing their education; up till 1889 they had to pay 1,500 francs and served for one year instead of five. Also, it was made possible for men, on reaching the age of 18, to anticipate the call-up, and they were then permitted to choose their regiment. Currently, the term 'volunteer' is often abused, as when used to describe soldiers sent by certain states to take part unofficially in the wars of other countries.

Although the term 'military conscription' made its appearance some years before the Revolution, and had been given official currency by the Jourdan Law of 1798, this form of recruiting had older roots, since it implies the choosing of men from among those in suitable physical condition, and whose names appear on a list that has previously been prepared. This method of calling men to arms had already been exemplified in the registers used for the *ban* and *arrière-ban* at the end of the Middle Ages. When conscription is applied to the whole population, an administrative organization of some size is required for its operation. Hence, it is not surprising that it appeared – under other names – in France only in the second half of the seventeenth century (registers of the naval classes, 1669; of the royal militia, 1688), in Sweden in 1682 (*Indelningsverket*) and in Prussia in 1733 (*Kantonsystem*), among other examples. A feature that is common to these old forms of conscription is that the obligation to serve is shared out among different sections of the population.

The *Indelningsverket* which Charles XI established was part of a more general reform. The recovery of crown property from the nobility allowed soldiers to be given grants of land – a desirable possession in a rural country where a monetary economy was still in its infancy. The kingdom was divided up into cantons, some with the task of recruiting a regiment, and others, with smaller territories, a company. One militiaman was raised from each group of farming properties or *rote*. The various proprietors of a *rote* had to hand over to the militiaman a plot of ground, which those who were not required for military service cultivated for him while he was away on campaign. Thus Sweden was covered with what amounted to a grid of *rotars* – in fact, military villages as depicted in a military survey map of the kingdom.

In France, the royal militia was put on a war footing from 1688 to 1697, from 1702 to 1714 and from 1726 onwards; the name was changed to provincial regiments in 1771. The king called up for six years a determinate number of men (the figure being 60,000 during the wars of the eighteenth century), divided out among *généralités* and *subdélégations*, and finally among parishes, in proportion to the number of unmarried men which they contained. After 1693, the militiamen were chosen by lot from among those liable for service – men over 18 years of age, at least 5 feet in height and not exempt on medical grounds (suffering from

disability), for family reasons (only son), because of the nature of their employment (servants of local clergy or gentry) or, particularly after 1754, on account of their economic situation (sons of small farmers with more than four ploughing teams or paying a poll tax of more than 20 livres). The officers were recruited from the country gentry. In peacetime, the militia companies were assembled for a few days each year for drilling. They formed battalions which, in wartime, were sent to frontier garrison towns as replacements for regular units. Volunteers from these battalions were used to make good the losses in regular regiments (a process termed 'bringing on to the regular strength'). During the War of the Spanish Succession, militia battalions were attached to those regular regiments which consisted of a single battalion. This was nothing less than compulsory military service. Selection by lot was very much disliked. Hence, it was applied only fleetingly in towns (in 1743), and rural communities continually attempted to circumvent it, particularly by means of joint contribution. This involved the collection by those liable for militia service of a sum destined for the purchase of a volunteer. The banning of this practice by the king often led, just at the time of the drawing of lots, to flight by those liable for service, who took up work as servants to local clergy or to gentry, quit the country for a while or married. Although the militia was no longer called up after 1782, the *cahiers de doléances* of 1789 were almost unanimous in denouncing selection by lot. Nevertheless, the French militia system was copied in Europe.

In 1733, Prussia created an original and much more demanding system, the *Kantonsystem*. Boys were enrolled at the age of 10 (*obligats*) and had to wear a distinctive badge. At the age of 20, they were called to their regiment for a one and a half- or two-year period and, subsequently, had to serve for two or three months a year over a period of thirty to forty years, as long as they remained able-bodied. In wartime, the *Kantonists* were mobilized as full-time soldiers. Recruitment was on a regional basis. A regiment drew its members from a *Kanton* of 5,000 hearths. The militarization of the nobility and of the peasantry contributed to the creation of a Prussian nation. The domains of the landowners and the military companies began to exercise a certain influence on each other. The local squires introduced military discipline on their land and so prepared their men for service. The system of recruitment used by the state borrowed from the old feudal model. Those who were exempt were the owners of large-scale agricultural properties and their heirs, the serfs (*Kossäte*), foreigners who had been induced to come into the country as smallholders and those living in the eastern provinces. The proportion of *Kantonists* reached two-thirds in the army of the 'Sergeant-King' and a half in that of Frederick II, which meant that 14 per cent of the adult male population (i.e. one in seven) were then compelled to perform military service.

A more modern form of conscription made its appearance in Austria in 1781 under Joseph II. In France, on the proposal of Dubois-Crancé, the Constituent Assembly accepted the principle that every Frenchman had a duty to serve in his country's defence, though without defining the ways in which that duty would be performed. Hence in 1793, 300,000 men were called up, and subsequently there was a *levée en masse*. These measures were not employed subsequently, and the Revolutionary army tended to become a regular force, but difficulties arose over keeping up the large numerical strength that it required. The Jourdan Law of 1798 established conscription for men aged between 20 and 25, who were divided into five age classes and were called up in accordance with need, starting with the youngest. This law ensured the supply of recruits for the army of the Empire reasonably well. Conscription was abolished in 1814, but reinstated in 1818 by the Gouvion-Saint-Cyr Law, in order to make up for the deficiencies in voluntary enlistment. The intake required by the army was decided yearly, and the *cantons* had each to supply their share. The young men in the class that had been called up went to the main town of their *canton*, where the drawing of lots determined which of them had to do a seven-year term of military service. They were allowed, however, to produce a replacement in substitution. There were, too, insurance policies which could be arranged; these were drawn in the name of a boy when young and provided cover against the risk of drawing an unlucky number. By means of paying an annual premium, a young conscript received, if that moment of misfortune arrived, the money needed to purchase a replacement. Nevertheless, conscripts were responsible for their replacement, and still had to serve in person if he became physically unfit or deserted.

In European countries at war against France in the Revolutionary period, there were at first considerable misgivings over conscription, since it seemed unwise to arm the people. Napoleon's expansionist ambitions, and the limitations that had at that time been prescribed on the army's numbers, led Prussia to adopt conscription after Jena (in the form of the short-service *Krümper* system), together with the social consequences that it implied – the abolition of bond service and the opening of officer rank to commoners. A number of other countries acted similarly in the course of the nineteenth century. It had, in any event, become clear that the barracks could be an extension of school and foster a spirit of patriotism. Features common to the nineteenth-century military legislation in Europe were the reduction in the length of service from seven to three, or even two, years, the recruiting of a large proportion of those due in any year for service by abolition of the drawing of lots and by a reduction of exemptions granted on grounds of particular types of employment, professional duties (e.g. clerics, teachers) or even family responsibilities.

In France too, after the 1870–1 defeat, the drawing of lots did no more than determine length of service (five years or six months) – the younger sons of soldiers being required to serve for six months only – and voluntary enlistment for one year was introduced in 1872 (see above). Selection by lot was abolished in 1889, but service became an equal obligation for all only in 1905. Young men had to serve for two years, and then belonged to the reserve of the army proper up to the age of 34, after which they passed into the home army from 34 to 40 and finally into the reserve of the home army until they were 46. The obligation to serve now fell without distinction on all, except for those suffering from physical disability. After appearing before a medical examination board, conscripts were either declared fit for service or – for reasons of physical disabilities – had their entry postponed for a year or were declared exempt. Once taken on the strength, they were posted to a fighting unit or to an auxiliary service, depending on their physical capacities. In European countries, the burden of military service was greater or less, depending on a nation's defence requirements in relation to the size of the population. In order to deal with the consequences of a fall in the birthrate, military service was lengthened in France from two to three years in 1913, and exemptions on health grounds were proportionately fewer than in Germany. Hence, on the eve of the First World War, France called up 1 in 52 of her inhabitants to produce an army of 780,000, while Germany's figure was 850,000 from 1 in 76. During the war, France mobilized 8 million men, i.e. 1 in 5 of the population. Even Great Britain, which had been reluctant to do so, introduced compulsory military service from 1916 to 1919.

Between the two world wars, the duration of service depended on the political situation at the time; in France, it was 18 months in 1923, a year in 1928, two years in 1936. During the Second World War, almost all the belligerent powers had recourse to obligatory military service but, except in the extreme case of Germany in 1945, mobilized relatively fewer men than during the First World War, on account of the needs of industry for labour. Since then, the increasing cost of armaments and their specialized character have led countries to lower the numerical strength of their forces, whether by reducing the duration of service or by opting for professional armies composed of specialists. The United States abandoned conscription in 1973, and Great Britain in 1960, but other countries chose composite solutions to the problem, depending on their national traditions and views on defence (e.g. varying lengths of service in different arms in the USSR, longer voluntary service in France). *See also* FINANCES; FOREIGNERS, SERVICE BY; GREECE, ANCIENT; INFANTRY; MERCENARIES; MOBILIZATION; NAVAL PERSONNEL; NUMERICAL STRENGTH; RESERVES; ROME; SPARTA; SWEDEN; TACTICAL ORGANIZATION; TRAINING.

A. CORVISIER

FURTHER READING
John Childs, *Armies and Warfare in Europe, 1648–1789* (Manchester, 1982); André Corvisier, *Armies and Societies in Europe, 1494–1789* (Bloomington, Ind., 1979); P. Contamine, *War in the Middle Ages* (London, 1984); G. A. Craig, *The Politics of the Prussian Army* (New York, 1964).

Recruitment, naval   *See* NAVAL PERSONNEL

Religious wars   *See* HOLY WARS

Reserves   In field operations, commanders may hold a reserve of troops to commit in an emergency or to exploit success. Reserves can range in size from a platoon forming a reserve for a company to a division or even a corps acting as the reserve of an army group. Within the organizational structure of armed forces, reserves comprise trained soldiers who have served their term with the colours and have returned to civilian life but who remain under an obligation to resume military service during a mobilization.

Operational Reserves   These are the portions of a fighting force which a commander retains under his own control ready for the most appropriate employment in a situation. There are *strategic reserves* and *tactical reserves*.

In the eighteenth century, the *strategic reserve* varied in size and functioned in the rear of armies which were engaged in operations. It protected lines of communication and dealt with emergencies. In 1806, Clausewitz criticized strategic reserves which played no useful role until after a battle; during the Jena and Auerstädt campaign, the Prussians had kept 15,000 men inactive in the strategic reserve. Jomini, on the other hand, thought them indispensable for occupying strategic points, guarding depots and covering possible retreats. In order not to weaken the field army by tying down regular soldiers to the strategic reserve, a scheme was devised during the seventeenth century for forming special units which could act, should occasion arise, as a strategic reserve. The garrison battalions under Louis XIV and the French militia after 1688 were the products, bodies which could be called upon to participate in field operations if stiffened by regular regiments. The English militia and invalid companies provided a similar service, taking over garrison and security duties to free regular soldiers for the field armies. During the Seven Years' War, the War of American Independence and the Napoleonic Wars, Britain again resorted to the formation of volunteer militias to act as a strategic reserve for the defence of the British Isles. This principle has continued into the twentieth century with the formation of the Local Defence Volunteers (Home Guard) in 1940.

In large theatres of war, commanders frequently retain a body of first-line troops which moves in concert with the main field army ready to assist in operations. In this case, strategic reserves are barely distinguishable from tactical reserves.

Tactical reserves are that section of a force which a commander needs to keep uncommitted in order to clinch victory, deal with a setback or cover a withdrawal. Perhaps the earliest use of a reserve in battle was by Hannibal at Cannae in 216 BC. During the Roman Republic, the legion formed three lines. The *hastati* opened the battle, the *principes*, the shock troops, formed the second line, whilst the *triarii*, older veterans, were the third line forming a reserve which could be brought forward in moments of crisis. Julius Caesar employed a fourth line of heavy infantry as a reserve at the Battle of Pharsalus in 48 BC. Little use was made of tactical reserves during the Middle Ages but they returned to fashion with the adoption of linear tactics during the seventeenth century. Commanders retained a force, usually of cavalry, to deliver the decisive blow. Condé's victory at Rocroi in 1643 was founded on the possession of a reserve. The extension of linear tactics in the eighteenth century saw commanders forming second and third lines of infantry battalions to act as reserves to plug gaps in the first, or main, battle line. The introduction of the divisional system after 1760 permitted armies better articulation through organization into manageable groups containing all arms. During the French Revolutionary and Napoleonic Wars, the divisional system allowed a commander to retain some divisions, or a corps, in a central reserve to exploit any opportunity. Under Napoleon, the tactical reserve became the instrument of victory. Hence, unlike the strategic reserve, the tactical reserve was often composed of the best troops, such as the Imperial Guard. The positioning of the tactical reserve during a battle became a matter of the utmost importance.

Reserves in the Organization of Armed Forces The function of this class of reserves is to ease the transition of an army from a peacetime to a wartime footing. Up to the mid-seventeenth century, it was considered sufficient on the outbreak of war to increase the army's strength by calling for volunteers either from the general public or from militias. Louvois built up trained reserves by arranging for regiments which had been retained in peacetime to employ 'supernumerary' officers, or *reformadoes*. These officers had previously commanded units which had been disbanded and, when war began again, their task was to train and command the new troops. In 1697, the English army adopted the half-pay system, in which disbanded officers were given half their establishment pay as a retainer. When war broke out again, they were re-engaged on full pay to command the new levies. During the eighteenth century, the English army stationed as many as 12,000 troops in Ireland to serve as a reserve. The French Royal Militia, founded in 1688, was used to replace regular regiments in garrisons and as a source of drafts to make up losses amongst the professional army.

The introduction of conscription and fixed-term military service led to a new principle governing reserves. The British Army Enlistment Act of 1870 stated that regular soldiers were to enlist for twelve years, six years with the colours and six with the reserve. It was hoped that this would produce a reserve of 80,000 trained men. In 1908, the British established the Territorial Army as their main reserve supported by a special reserve to provide replacements for the regular army. Germany, France and most major European states during the nineteenth century adopted systems of universal conscription whereby a recruit served for two or three years with the colours and then entered the reserve. In wartime, the reservist returned to the colours. They spent two or three years with the regular army and then entered the first reserve which provided replacements and reinforcements for the regular army. He then served for a further period in the *Landwehr*, a territorial army designed to fight shoulder-to-shoulder with the regular army in time of war. *See also* HIERARCHY; MILITIAS; MOBILIZATION; NUMERICAL STRENGTH; RECRUITMENT; STRATEGY; TACTICAL ORGANIZATION; TACTICS.

A. CORVISIER
JOHN CHILDS

FURTHER READING

G. A. Craig, *The Politics of the Prussian Army* (New York, 1964); E. M. Spiers, *Haldane: an army reformer* (Edinburgh, 1980); *The War Plans of the Great Powers, 1880–1914*, ed. P. M. Kennedy (London, 1980).

Resistance Resistance, which is the action of morally or physically opposing an established authority with the aim of rendering its decisions ineffective, takes many forms, running from what is known as passive resistance to insurrection and guerilla warfare. Though today the term is most often used to refer to the operations carried out against German occupation during the Second World War, resistance has been practised down the ages by individuals and groups fighting against an invader or a government in conflict with their patriotism, faith or political ideas. These resistance fighters have been known variously as partisans, irregulars or guerilla fighters. In Gaul, between 54 and 50 BC, Vercingetorix led the resistance against the Roman forces of occupation before being defeated by Caesar. The Hebrews also put up resistance to Roman occupation, rising in revolt in AD 66–73 and 132–5 (this latter being the insurrection of Bar Cochba). During the Hundred Years' War, the English were subjected to guerilla action in France. Le Grand Ferré fought with great distinction in that conflict in 1358 and du Guesclin exhausted the enemy by fighting a series of harassing actions. In the Balkans, between the fifteenth and twentieth centuries, the Christian populations have shown their opposition to Ottoman rule in revolts and guerilla warfare conducted by the *Haiduks*. To defend their faith, the Vaudois of the Alpine valleys fought the troops of the Duke of Savoy and Louis XIV, while the Calvinists of the Cévennes, or 'Camisards', resisted the French Royal Army from 1702 to 1710. During the French Revolution, federalist risings broke out in sixty *départements* as a show of resistance against the Robespierre government. Between 1793 and 1796 and again in 1799–1800, the peasants of the Vendée, of Loire-Atlantique and of Maine-et-Loire rose against the government and resisted the efforts of the Republican armies to put down their revolt. Movements of resistance against foreign occupation are particularly in evidence after the end of the eighteenth century. The peasants of Transylvania rose up against the Habsburgs in 1784–5 under the leadership of the Romanian patriot Vasily Horia. In Serbia, Karageorge (George Petrovic or 'Black George') organized the resistance against the Turks before leading the insurrection of 1804–8. In Spain, between 1808 and 1813, the population put up violent resistance against French occupation, particularly in Seville, Madrid and Saragossa, inflicting heavy losses on the Imperial army. In Austria in 1809, Andreas Hofer called upon the

Tyroleans to fight against the Bavarian invader and then against the French army. In Russia, General Davydov, commanding the 1st Regiment of Cossack Partisans, harassed Napoleon's troops in 1812. In 1821, he published his 'Essay on the Theory of Partisan Warfare'. In 1814, French partisans harassed the Allied troops – particularly in Alsace and the Vosges. In 1821, Alexander Ypsilantis attempted to incite the Christians of the Ottoman Empire to revolt. The Greeks did rebel and resisted the Turks until 1827, before obtaining independence for their country in 1832. During the Franco-Prussian War (1870–1), units of *francs-tireurs* and partisans were raised to fight against the enemy's rear. The occupation of Bosnia-Herzegovina by Austria in 1878 ran up against sharp resistance from the Muslim population and violent actions continued in Herzegovina throughout 1881–2. In Macedonia the internal Macedonian revolutionary organization had recourse to terrorism after 1894 in its efforts to shake off the Turkish yoke and the *comitadji* created insecurity in the province. Serbia encouraged the Christian populations of Bosnia-Herzegovina to resist the Austrians and backed the resistance in Macedonia, to which country she sent irregulars (chetniks). In South Africa, from 1900 to 1902, the Boers resisted the British by means of guerilla action. General Kitchener riposted by burning farms, destroying food reserves and interning women and children in concentration camps, where 25,000 died. During the 1914–18 war, there were a great many acts of resistance in the occupied territories, either in the form of attempts to gain intelligence for the Allies, assistance rendered to escaped prisoners or refusal to carry out the enemy's orders. In occupied Serbia, a resistance movement led by Kosta Milanovic-Plecanac started an insurrection in the Toplica mountains in 1917 and carried out operations against the Austro-German forces and the Bulgarians. In 1919–20, Soviet partisans organized resistance behind the lines of the White armies. In Palestine, the Palestinian Nationalist Movement, created in 1920, called upon the Arabs to resist Jewish immigration, caused rioting and organized a genuine guerilla war against the British until 1937.

It was, however, during the Second World War that the resistance to occupying forces assumed relatively large proportions, both in the occupied territories and inside the Axis countries themselves. German occupation gave rise to national and ideological resistance, both passive and violent. Passive resistance took the form of the distribution of clandestine leaflets and news sheets, of strikes, manufacturing go-slows and the refusal to perform forced labour. Active resistance was effected through the organization of escape chains, the formation of intelligence and operational networks, the carrying out of attacks or acts of sabotage and the creation of armed groups in the towns and bands of *maquisards* in areas where the conditions were right for guerilla activity. In the beginning, the resistance movements, which were motivated by patriotism and a spirit of revenge, were apolitical. They were poorly armed and inexperienced and suffered heavy losses. After the German attack on the USSR, all the European Communist parties became involved in the struggle against the occupying forces. The clandestine forces in Europe were, however, divided into two groups. The Communists advocated immediate action to make the popular masses rise up, while the other resistance fighters wanted to organize for a rising that would be co-ordinated with the action of the Allied armies. The characteristics of the resistance movements were different in Western and Eastern Europe and in the Axis countries. In the West, the resistance was dependent upon the Allies – and mainly upon Great Britain, which saw it as an auxiliary force that could weaken the Axis powers. In the Netherlands, where the terrain was not propitious for guerilla action, resistance was, until 1944, mainly intellectual and moral in character. In Belgium, the secret army ran intelligence and escape networks, but did not create a *maquis* in the Ardennes until 1944. In Norway, resistance took the form of intelligence networks and networks of commando groups whose task it was to carry out strikes on German installations. In France, it developed first in the Occupied Zone, then later in the Free Zone. General de Gaulle sought both to bring the resistance forces under his own authority and to have the Allies recognize him as leader of the Resistance. To this end, he sent Jean Moulin to France in 1942 to co-ordinate the actions of the resistance movements, certain of which, such as 'Alliance', were directly attached to the British 'Special Services' (SOE). The three major movements in the southern zone came together to form the *Mouvements unis de la Résistance* and General Delestraint became the commander-in-chief of the Secret Army. The National Council of the Resistance was formed on 27 May 1943, and the French National Liberation Committee (CFLN) was also set up at Algiers. In the spring of 1944, the 'French Forces of the Interior' were formed by merging the Secret Army, the Army Resistance Organization and the *Francs-tireurs* and Partisans under the leadership of General Koenig. The Resistance played an active role in the liberation of France and in setting in place new institutions after the 'collaborators', both political and administrative, had been removed. In Eastern Europe, where the Germans had carried out large-scale population movements and massive exterminations, resistance assumed a more popular character and showed itself more in violent actions than passive defiance. In Czechoslovakia, armed groups did not appear until May in Bohemia-Moravia while the Slovakian resistance bands launched the insurrection of August 1944 and operated in liaison with the Red Army. In Poland, from 1940 onwards, the resistance carried out a great number of acts of sabotage on lines of communication. While the army of General Anders fought alongside the Allies, General Tadeusz Komorowski, who was known as General Bór, organized the Home Army and General Berling led the Communist partisans. On 1 August 1944, General Bór launched the Warsaw rising, which the Soviet army allowed to be crushed. In April–May 1943, the Jews of the Warsaw ghetto had risen against the Germans. In

Yugoslavia, the resistance was led from 1941 onwards by Colonel Mihailovich and his chetniks and by Tito's 'partisans'. The split between the two movements became irreversible in December 1941. Favouring a federal Yugoslavia, Tito created a national liberation army and occupied vast stretches of mountain territory where he set up a new Communist administration. After inflicting quite heavy losses on the Axis forces, Tito liberated his country alone and exterminated the Yugoslavian Royalist resistance. Though Yugoslavia lost 10 per cent of its population in the war, the Yugoslav resistance had kept fifteen German divisions pinned down in the country throughout the war. In Greece, resistance groups formed in the mountains from the autumn of 1941 onwards. Greek resistance was essentially divided between two movements: the Greek Democratic National Army (EDES) of General Zervas, which was monarchistic and anglophile, and the National Popular Liberation Army (ELAS), which was Communist. In September 1943, ELAS attacked the non-Communist resistance groups, and EDES was only able to maintain itself thanks to the intervention of the Allies. After the German troops withdrew, a new civil war broke out in Greece. With the support of the USSR and Yugoslavia, General Markos created a government of Free Greece, but he was abandoned by the Soviet Union in 1949 and the Communist resistance was defeated.

In the USSR, Stalin's radio broadcast to the nation on 3 July 1941 called for scorched earth tactics and all-out resistance. Bands of partisans took to the woods and marshlands, while the High Command of the Red Army sent out – or parachuted in – officers to organize the resistance. A veteran of the civil war was placed in charge of the partisan groups. A partisan general staff was created in Moscow and training schools in Moscow, Leningrad and Stalingrad provided courses in guerilla warfare. The partisans sowed a sense of insecurity behind the lines of the enemy armies, carrying out long distance raids, keeping up the resistance of the population and operating in liaison with the Red Army. To combat them, the Germans employed the so-called *Jagdkommandos*. The Soviet partisans inflicted severe losses on the German army. In the Axis countries, resistance first became organized in Italy in September 1943. In Germany, it was confined to networks passing on secret information and to the plot of 20 July 1944, which ended in total failure.

The lessons of resistance in Europe and China became the inspiration for the theorists of revolutionary warfare, and guerilla techniques were employed in the wars in Indo-China, Algeria, Afghanistan and Latin America, as well as in the Middle East and Africa. *See also* FRANCE; GIAP; GUERILLA WARFARE; GUESCLIN; INDIRECT WARFARE; LAWS OF WAR; MAO TSE-TUNG; MORALE; POPULAR WARFARE; SPAIN; SUN-TZU; VIETNAM.

J. NOUZILLE

FURTHER READING
H. Michel, *Les Mouvements clandestins en Europe, 1938–1945* (3rd edn, Paris, 1974); Matthew Cooper, *The Phantom War* (London, 1979); *Civilian Resistance as a National Defence*, ed. Adam Roberts (Harmondsworth, 1969); R. B. Asprey, *War in the Shadows* (London, 1975); Walter Laqueur, *Guerilla* (London, 1977); Otto Heilbrunn, *Partisan Warfare* (London, 1962).

Retirement *See* INVALIDS; PENSIONS; VETERANS

Reviews *See* INSPECTIONS; MANOEUVRE AND MANOEUVRES; MUSIC; TRAINING

Revolutionary warfare *See* GUERILLA WARFARE; INDIRECT WARFARE; POPULAR WARFARE; RESISTANCE

Richard I, the 'Lionheart' (1157–99) Richard I was King of England from 1189–1199, during which time he spent only five months in his kingdom. He was the very model of the chivalric warrior, a prudent and cautious general but also a bold knight who won the allegiance of his troops by his courageous exploits and his careful logis-

tical preparations. After becoming leader of the Third Crusade (1189–92), he captured Acre in 1191 and defeated Saladin on several occasions (Arsouf, 1191, Jaffa, 1192) but without ever managing to capture Jerusalem. On his journey homeward from the Holy Land in 1192, he was captured in Vienna and held prisoner by the Holy Roman Emperor Henry VI until ransomed in 1194. He then proceeded to defend the Angevin lands in France against King Philip II Augustus (1180–1223), on whom he inflicted a number of defeats (e.g. Fréteval in 1194). Château-Gaillard on the Seine, which his engineers constructed in eighteen months between 1196 and 1198, represents a high point in the achievement of medieval fortification in Western Europe. *See also* CHÂTEAU-GAILLARD; GREAT BRITAIN; HOLY WAR; KNIGHTS AND CHIVALRY; SALADIN.

A. CORVISIER

FURTHER READING
John Gillingham, *Richard the Lionheart* (2nd edn, London, 1989); John Gillingham, 'Richard I and the science of war in the Middle Ages', in *War and Government in the Middle Ages*, eds J. Gillingham and J. C. Holt (Woodbridge, 1984); R. C. Smail, *Crusading Warfare, 1097–1193* (Cambridge, 1956).

Richelieu, Armand Jean du Plessis, Cardinal and duc de (1585–1642) This prelate, who became chief minister to Louis XIII of France in 1624, occupies an important place in military history. He viewed war as the chief activity of the state. In order to ensure peace, he attempted to loosen the Habsburg ring around the borders of France. Initially, he occupied the Habsburg forces by 'covert war', principally through the sponsorship and support of the Swedes in Germany. When 'open war' became necessary after 1635, he raised the strength of the French armed forces from *c*.30,000 to over 150,000 in that same year, augmenting them to 250,000 in 1640. Since he had only limited confidence in the existing French military institutions, he increased the absolute powers of the state to provide for the war effort thereby invoking a good deal of domestic opposition from all sections of French society. His dictum that 'there were in history more armies which had perished for want of bread and administration than from the efforts of enemy armies', led to the imposition of heavy sacrifices on the French population and a stricter discipline upon the army through the medium of civilian intendants. Richelieu pursued a cautious land strategy. He aimed to hold the 'gates of the kingdom' both to protect France from invasion and to enable French armies to debouch into the Spanish Netherlands, Germany and northern Italy. By contrast, his maritime schemes were more adventurous but he lacked the means for their implementation. Richelieu was at the heart of the military revival of France during the seventeenth century and his pioneering work was further developed by Michel Le Tellier, Louvois and Louis XIV. The model of monarchical absolutism established by Richelieu was imitated by many European rulers during the later seventeenth century. *See also* FRANCE; INTENDANTS; LA ROCHELLE (1627–8); LOGISTICS; LOUVOIS.

A. CORVISIER
JOHN CHILDS

FURTHER READING
R. J. Bonney, *Political Change under Richelieu and Mazarin* (Oxford, 1978); W. F. Church, *Richelieu and Reason of State* (Princeton, 1972).

Rivoli, Battle of (14 January 1797) This battle was part of the cycle of operations that took place around Mantua, a fortified city held by the Austrians and besieged by the French, during Napoleon's first Italian campaign. Twenty-five miles to the north of Mantua, Alvintzi's Austrian army pushed a French division back into a narrow corridor between Lake Garda and the Adige. To support it, Napoleon brought several elements of his army to converge on the heights of Rivoli. Alvintzi, advancing in five columns, outflanked the French, but his assaults on both wings of Napoleon's position were repelled by the timely arrival of reinforcements led by Masséna and Rey, who, thanks to divisional organization, were able to manoeuvre against the Austrians to great effect. The pursuit,

which was mounted immediately, prevented the enemy forces from re-forming. *See also* COMMAND; FRANCE; NAPOLEON; TACTICAL ORGANIZATION.

A. CORVISIER

FURTHER READING
D. G. Chandler, *The Campaigns of Napoleon* (New York, 1967); G. Fabry, *Campagne de l'armée d'Italie, 1796–1797* (Paris, 1900–2).

Roads *See* TRANSPORT

Robins, Benjamin (1707–51) If, during the eighteenth century, there was relatively little of note contributed from Britain to the general evolution of the military art and sciences, there was a clear exception in the case of Benjamin Robins, a mathematician and engineer who made a noteworthy contribution to the advancement of gunnery. Born into a poor Quaker family, Benjamin Robins showed an exceptional mathematical ability at an early age and on leaving school came to London where, in 1727, he was admitted to the Royal Society. An active young man with varied interests, he at first taught pure and applied mathematics and physical science, eventually giving up teaching to become a practising engineer, while also establishing something of a reputation as a political pamphleteer and writer. Although his engineering work was of a civil nature, he soon developed a keen interest in the principles of gunnery and in fortifications, travelling to Flanders to study fortifications and conducting numerous experiments on gunpowder and the resistance of air to swift and slow motions. In 1742 he published his best known and most influential work, *New Principles of Gunnery*, which was translated into German (1745) and French (1751). Despite an unsuccessful attempt in 1741 to secure an appointment as Professor of Fortification at the new Royal Military Academy, his experiments continued under the patronage of Lord Anson. In 1747 he was invited by the Prince of Orange to assist in the defence of Bergen-op-Zoom, and two years later accepted a military engineering

701

appointment in India, a decision which cost him his life. In July 1751 he died at Fort St David, Madras.

In a very few years Robins made an important contribution to the study of ballistics. From the very invention of gunpowder, the laws governing its force, and the motion of projectiles, had been subjects of speculation. The shape of a projectile's trajectory had been established only theoretically (first by Tartaglia in the 1530s) but, being unproved by actual experiment, the effect of air resistance was not considered. Through experiment Robins demonstrated the validity of the relevant mathematical theories advanced by Sir Isaac Newton in the 1680s and for the first time revealed the great force exerted by the resistance of the air to bodies passing through it. He worked on the theoretical principles of the rifle and in his study of trajectories in smooth bore barrels revealed defects which later gunmakers came to consider as his most important contribution to the science of gunnery. The ballistic pendulum, which he invented to measure the velocity of shot, continued in use, with refinements, into the early twentieth century. *See also* ARTILLERY; BÉLIDOR.

G. A. STEPPLER

FURTHER READING
Benjamin Robins, *New Principles of Gunnery* (London, 1742; repr., with new introduction by W. S. Curtis, Richmond, 1972); R. H. Vetch, 'Robins, Benjamin', *Dictionary of National Biography* (London, 1895), xlviii, 434–6.

Rocroi, Battle of (19 May 1643) The Spanish Army of Flanders, led by Francisco de Melo, was besieging Rocroi, a small fortified town at the head of the road leading to Paris via the valley of the River Oise. Rocroi occupied a plateau between the Oise and the Meuse, 35 km north-west of Charleville-Mézières. Rather than simply advance to rescue the small French garrison, the 22-year-old Duc d'Enghien, the future Prince of Condé, decided to bring the Spanish invading army to battle. The Rocroi plateau could only be approached via a wooded defile but the march of the 17,000 French infantry and 6,000 horse on 18 May 1643 was uncontested by

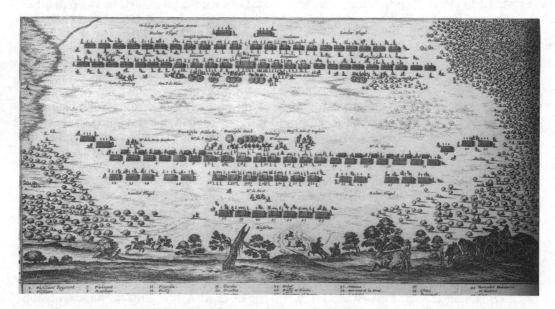

This near contemporary representation of the Battle of Rocroi shows the confined battlefield and Condé's cavalry and infantry reserve.
(Hulton-Deutsch Collection)

Melo's 19,000 foot and 8,000 cavalry. The Maréchal François de l'Hôpital immediately launched a premature cavalry attack which was beaten back by the veteran Spaniards. Both armies drew up their infantry in two lines with their cavalry on the flanks, but Enghien placed a reserve of horse and foot to the rear of his second line. In all probability, this reserve was intended to watch for and cover the expected arrival of 6,000 Spanish reinforcements.

Enghien reopened the battle at dawn on 19 May with all his cavalry. On the right, Enghien swept away the Spanish horse and turned to attack the left flank of the Spanish infantry. However, on the French left, the cavalry were beaten by the Spaniards and the victorious horsemen assaulted the left wing of Enghien's infantry in combination with the infantry *tercios*. Intervention by the French reserve prevented the total defeat of the French infantry of the left-centre but Enghien, realizing the danger, brought the French horse around the back of the Spanish centre and attacked the successful Spanish cavalry in the rear. Once the enemy horse had been defeated, Enghien concentrated on the Spanish infantry. Musketeers and artillery opened gaps in the Spanish phalanxes which were then exploited by the cavalry. After three assaults, the Spaniards surrendered. The French lost 4,000 men while the Spaniards had 7,000 casualties and 8,000 taken prisoner. Rocroi, a victory gained by a tactical turning manoeuvre and the shock action of cavalry, ended the threat of an invasion of France by the Army of Flanders. It also demonstrated the decisive role of cavalry as the offensive arm in mid-seventeenth century warfare. *See also* CAVALRY; CONDÉ; FRANCE; INFANTRY; SPAIN; TACTICS.

A. CORVISIER
JOHN CHILDS

FURTHER READING
Great Military Battles, ed. Cyril Falls (London, 1964); G. Mongrédien, *Le Grand Condé* (Paris, 1959); C. V. Wedgwood, *The Thirty Years' War* (London, 1938).

Rodney, George Brydges Rodney, 1st Baron (1719–92) The son of a captain of marines, Rodney won rapid promotion. He first fought in the War of the Austrian Succession, being prominent at Hawke's action of 14 October 1747. He became Governor of Newfoundland in 1748 (a post always held by a naval officer). During the Seven Years' War, he took part in the unsuccessful Rochefort expedition (1757), and then, having reached flag rank in 1759, commanded the force which bombarded Le Havre in 1759 and another fleet which occupied Martinique, St Lucia, St Vincent and Grenada in 1760–1. He became a full admiral in 1771, but, having got into debt, he was obliged to seek refuge in France until 1779. Returning to Britain, he was appointed to command the Leeward Islands fleet. On the way out he won an outstanding success against the Spanish squadron of Don Juan de Langara off Cape St Vincent (10 January 1780), and relieved Gibraltar. In the West Indies, he fought three indecisive battles against de Guichen. His reputation was assured by victory at the Battle of the Saints (12 April 1782), where he defeated de Grasse. Apart from the good gunnery and intensive use of the carronade by the English, the victory was due to the tactics employed by Rodney, who seized an opportunity to break through the French line, thus cutting off and concentrating on a part of the French fleet, and avoiding the actions in line which had proved so indecisive. *See also* GRASSE DE TILLY; NAVAL WARFARE; NAVIES; NELSON; QUIBERON BAY, BATTLE OF.

J. MEYER

FURTHER READING
David Spinney, *Rodney* (London, 1969).

Rohan, Henri, Duke of (1579–1638) *See* TACTICS

Rome The army always played a leading part in the history of ancient Rome, which traditionally was founded in 753 BC and continued until the deposition of Romulus Augustulus in AD 476, the date conventionally considered to mark the end of the empire in the west. In the early regal period the army consisted of the nobles grouped round their chief; as more soldiers were needed, a wider cross-section of the citizen body was included in the levy (*legio*); the nobility then constituted a small force of cavalry, the *equites*. King Servius Tullius (*c*. 580–530) supposedly divided the citizens into six groups on the basis of wealth, an arrangement that had a military as well as a political relevance in that wealth determined the weaponry a man could provide for himself. The *equites* were set apart as the richest group who made up the cavalry; there were five other groups, and then the *capite censi* (literally, 'registered by a head count'), who had no property and were excluded from military service. So, from the start military service was a duty and responsibility for Roman citizens, but also a kind of privilege.

After the establishment of a Republic towards the end of the sixth century BC, Rome continued with this system, which produced an army of some 4,000 men who were armed like Greek hoplites and fought in a phalanx. In the early fourth century after Rome's defeat by the invading Gauls, the phalanx was modified into a more flexible formation by the creation of smaller units (maniples, 60 or 120 men) which could be manoeuvred independently. Moreover, an oval shield was adopted in place of the circular hoplite shield, and some soldiers were equipped with a javelin (*pilum*) instead of a thrusting spear (*hasta*), and a sword. The word 'legion' was now used to describe a body or division of troops. By 311 the Roman army normally consisted of four legions. They were commanded by the chief magistrates, the consuls. The usual formation probably involved three battle lines – the *hastati* at the front, then the *principes*, and finally the *triarii*, who were the most experienced men. These developments gave the Romans an advantage over those who still relied on the old phalanx and opened the way to their domination of the Mediterranean world. Throughout this period Rome's levies were supported by troops contributed by the Italian communities who were allies or subjects; these units served under their own local commanders, and a number of them were grouped together in larger contingents, which were equivalent in size to the legions, and were commanded by Roman officers. In addition, foreign mercenaries such as archers from Crete were occasionally employed.

The Punic Wars contributed to a number of changes in Roman military practice. There was increased military activity; for example, at the end of the second war in 201 there were sixteen legions in service. Therefore more men were called up and they served for longer. The need for more recruits seems to have led to a reduction in the property qualification and the creation of a body of lightly armed soldiers (*velites*) who could not afford extensive defensive armour. Polybius in his description of the Roman military establishment probably refers to the army that emerged from the Punic Wars. The size of a legion varied between 4,200 and 5,000 men; each year a selection was made of those of military age (17–46) who were liable to military service according to the property qualification. A man could be required to spend up to six years in continuous service, and after this to be available for enlistment up to a total of sixteen years; for a cavalryman the maximum length of service was ten years. All soldiers received a daily allowance for maintenance and equipment. In the battle formation of the legion, the *velites* served as a screen of lightly armed troops; then the *hastati* and *principes*, who were chosen on the basis of age and experience, composed the next two ranks and were armed with an oval shield, two throwing spears (one being lighter than the other), and a two-edged Spanish sword; finally came the *triarii*, the most experienced of the soldiers, armed with the thrusting spear (*hasta*), and sword. These names were retained for traditional reasons, although they were no longer a description of the real system. All three ranks were equipped with metal cuirass, helmet and greaves, and 300 cavalrymen were attached to each legion.

With the *velites* in front, the infantry advanced in three lines, each having ten maniples which were drawn up with intervening gaps. The gaps in the front line were covered by the second line and so on, but it is possible that, as the legionaries approached the enemy, the gaps were closed up by extension of the line or some other method. First the *velites* hurled their light javelins before retreating through the ranks. Then the battle was taken up by the *hastati*, who threw their javelins and closed with their swords; if they did not break through, they retired through the *principes*, who now moved up to attack; if this failed the *triarii* with their thrusting spears moved forward in a final effort to defeat the enemy. The arrangement of the legion in maniples (120–200 men) gave a measure of flexibility, enabling the troops to be regrouped or reinforced as the developing circumstances of a battle demanded, and perhaps encouraged the deployment of reserves. Cavalry and contingents of infantry from Rome's allies were usually deployed on the wings. On campaign at the end of a day's march, a legion always constructed a fortified camp with a square layout, straight streets intersecting at right angles, and carefully arranged quarters for the officers and men, so that each unit had a tent in an assigned location. Every Roman army or detachment was therefore protected against surprise attacks in hostile territory. The army was commanded by magistrates, either consuls or praetors, or men whose tenure of responsibility had been prolonged as proconsuls or propraetors. The senior officers were the military tribunes, six in each legion, mainly of equestrian status (the second most prestigious social group), though some were the sons of senators; they were supposed to have served at least five years in the army. The tribunes came to have responsibility for the command of individual legions, perhaps in groups of two in rotation. However, the early second century saw the development of the position of *legatus*, who was generally a more experienced senator appointed by the Senate after consultation with the commanding officer, and who assumed greater responsibilities in army command; in some cases he could be given the leadership of troops in a semi-independent command.

As Rome acquired overseas provinces, some of which required a constant military presence, so the need to keep troops in service increased. Legions remained permanently in being and extra levies were required. Since recruiting officers and magistrates preferred experienced men, some were required to serve continuously for a long time; moreover, men who had served tended to be called up again. There was increasing trouble over the levy in the second century BC and a decline in the property qualification for military service. At all times volunteers were accepted. Against this background the experienced C. Marius was appointed to the staff of Metellus, who was commanding the Roman forces in Africa against the local prince Jugurtha. Partly by exploiting discontent at the conduct of the war, Marius was elected consul and given the command in Africa (107 BC). Although he was responsible for a number of changes in the organization of the Roman army, these were not revolutionary in themselves but rather assisted the development of trends already established. Marius enlisted volunteers from those with no property (*capite censi*), and arranged for them to be equipped at the state's expense, in accordance with the legislation of Gaius Gracchus. Recruits swore to serve for a specific period, probably sixteen years, and since, as before, all soldiers received pay, gradually a more professional outlook emerged in the army. However, conscription was still used when required. Marius is credited with the change in the tactical structure of the legion from maniple to the cohort; there were ten cohorts in a legion, each containing six centuries of 80 men, commanded by a centurion. Consequently, there were at least 4,800 men in a legion, though the first cohort may have been larger, and with other support troops and 300 cavalry, the total was over *c.*6,000. In battle four cohorts were drawn up in the first rank, with three in each of the two remaining ranks; the cohort had greater stability, strength, and cohesion than the maniple, which however was retained for administrative purposes. It is possible that this was an evolutionary change and that both formations existed as alternatives for a time. With the appearance of the cohort in a more important role, the significance of the centurions as junior officers increased, and there was a system of promotion to the post of chief centurion. It was perhaps at this point that the eagle was adopted as the symbol of the legion, personifying its permanent existence; when the legion was on campaign the eagle was carried by the *aquilifer* and to lose it in battle was considered a great disgrace. Marius also modified the design of the javelin (*pilum*), by substituting a wooden pin for one of the two iron bolts which attached the iron tip to the wooden shaft. This meant that on impact the *pilum* bent and so could not be thrown back by the enemy. All soldiers in the legion were now uniformly equipped and the thrusting spear (*hasta*) was abandoned. Marius apparently insisted that the legionaries should carry with them in their packs all the materials needed to make them self-sufficient in the field; traditionally they were called Marius' mules.

After the Social War (91–87 BC), which resulted in victory for Rome over her Italian allies but also the granting of Roman citizenship to the Italians, there was a great reservoir of citizens upon which to draw for military service. By 49 BC about 172,000 Italians were under arms. The army became increasingly embroiled in the political struggles in Rome, since the actions of Marius had serious long-term consequences which he had neither intended nor foreseen. Soldiers tended to be loyal to the commander who had recruited them; instead of the army of the Roman state, there was a succession of armies owing allegiance primarily to their respective generals. Moreover, when the professional soldier retired he expected a gratuity, either in cash or, more frequently, in land. Since the state did not recognize this responsibility, a commander tended to organize the provision of allotments of land to his veterans, who would be suitably grateful. Consequently, the personal relationship between general and army was strengthened and this made possible the use of the army for political purposes. Leading figures often exploited popular support to obtain repeated military commands, which they then used to increase their personal power and build up the number of their political adherents, especially among their discharged soldiery.

These developments were all the more dangerous in that there was no distinction between military and civil posts in the Roman idea of office-holding. The same man could hold great political posts and military commands. In 88 BC Sulla set the precedent of using his army to march on Rome and seize control. Thereafter politics often became a trial of strength between ambitious generals commanding armies personally loyal to them, regardless of how they represented their stance politically. During his governorship of Gaul, Caesar increased his army from four to twelve legions and doubled legionary pay in 49 BC before defeating Pompey and the supporters of senatorial government and making himself dictator. After his murder in 44 BC, instability and prolonged civil war ensued until Caesar's grandnephew Octavian established himself as master of the Roman world, and was granted the name Augustus in 27 BC, by which the first emperor is usually known.

Augustus proceeded to organize the army as a bulwark not only to the empire but also to his personal political position. After the Battle of Actium in 31 BC there were about sixty legions in service. He immediately pensioned off large numbers of troops, establishing twenty-eight veteran colonies in Italy for his own men, and settlements in the provinces for the defeated soldiers. Augustus' policy, which was not revolutionary, but rather a development of the practices of the past century, was to meet all the military requirements of the empire from a standing, professional army, so that there was no need to raise any special levies. This army was eventually settled at twenty-eight legions permanently in service, although three were lost in AD 9 in the military disaster of Quinctilius Varus in Germany and not replaced. Military service was a career, and by AD 5 terms of service had been finalized; legionaries, who were all Roman citizens, served for 20 years and probably 5 years in the reserves for an annual salary of 900 *sesterces* and a discharge gratuity either in land or money, worth about 13½ times a year's pay. In AD 6 the military treasury was established to pay legionaries' discharge benefits; it was funded by a large grant from Augustus and thereafter by taxes on legacies and auctions. Augustus was responsible for two further innovations. In 27 BC he had created the Praetorian Guard as his personal bodyguard consisting of nine cohorts with probably 500 men in each, although only three cohorts were quartered in Rome at any one time; this elite unit, which had its origins not so much in the small guard which had attended upon the headquarters of army commanders in the Republic, as in the large personal bodyguards of the military dynasts, had superior pay and service conditions to the rest of the army and emphasized the monarchical character of Augustus' rule. In addition, the emperor kept a special squad of German bodyguards. Secondly, it had been the practice in the later Republic to use foreign and conquered peoples for specialist troops, such as slingers, archers, and cavalry. Augustus now incorporated soldiers of this kind into the formal structure of the army as auxiliaries (*auxilia*); they were non-citizens who served originally in ethnic units of cavalry or infantry (500 or 1,000 strong) recruited from their local area; they enlisted perhaps for twenty-five years with lower rates of pay and, by the end of Augustus' reign, were as numerous as the legionaries.

Under Augustus' auspices the army embarked on a series of conquests which confirmed Roman control of provinces previously acquired but neglected, and also added new territory. By the third century AD there were thirty-three legions, which, along with auxiliary troops, were stationed in nineteen of the provinces as a permanent garrison. When necessary, legions or legionary detachments (*vexillationes*) could be transferred to other areas in an emergency. The garrisons were supplemented in some regions by forts and continuous defensive walls which served to protect Roman interests and facilitate control. The empire remained militarily active and over a period of 150 years three major new provinces – Britain, Dacia, and northern Mesopotamia – were annexed.

Augustus had placed great emphasis on his personal association with the army, and his successors developed the theme of the troops' loyalty to the emperor, expressed by the oath they took to value his safety above that of all others, by the religious observances made in celebration of him, and by the presence of the emperor's portrait in every camp. The emperor himself was careful to perform his role as commander-in-chief, by addressing the soldiers formally whenever he could (*adlocutio*), by conducting himself as a 'fellow-soldier' (*commilito*) when present with the troops (Trajan described them as 'my most excellent and loyal fellow-soldiers'), by accumulating military honours and distinctions which marked him out as a great leader, and by ensuring the pay and benefits of the army. Increasingly emperors took charge of campaigns in person, and military success could bring political advantages, as Claudius demonstrated by his annexation of Britain. A loyal army made an emperor more secure against usurpation, and at the accession of a new emperor the demonstrable support of the troops was of paramount importance. The Roman emperor ruled as an autocrat backed up by an army tied in personal loyalty to him rather than to the Roman state, and his control was such that this produced relatively stable government for over 250 years.

The senior command structure of the army recalled the practice of the Republic. Those provinces containing a garrison of several legions and *auxilia* (with the sole exception of Egypt whose governor was of equestrian rank) were governed by senators of consular rank, who were non-specialist, non-professional commanders, many of whom had had little military experience before assuming their post, and who rarely held a senior command for more than three years. Traditionally, it was a senator's duty to serve the state in whatever capacity it demanded, as administrator, judge, priest and army commander. Moreover, the arrangement suited emperors who were themselves senators and who did not wish to encounter the possible political threat posed by a high command or cadre of senior officers.

Individual legions were commanded by legates of praetorian rank, who in provinces containing only one legion were also governors. In addition, there were six military tribunes, one of whom was a senator, the rest being of equestrian status. The *praefectus castrorum*, who probably ranked above the five equestrian tribunes, was often an ex-chief centurion whose job was to administer the details of camp life. Next in rank was the chief centurion (*primus pilus*), who commanded the first century of the first cohort, which was organized differently from the other cohorts. It had five centuries of probably 160 men in each and so had a complement of 800 instead of the 480 in the other nine cohorts, and was regarded as the leading cohort. There was a system of promotion for the 59 centurions in a legion, with the centurions of the first cohort (*primi ordines*) being the most senior. Centurions were in the main enlisted legionaries of long service or men transferred from the Praetorian Guard; experienced and knowledgeable, they provided consistency and continuity in a command structure lacking professional officers. Below the centurions there were many junior posts in the legion's administration or in specialist tasks. The total complement of a legion was between 5,000 and 6,000 men, including 120 legionary cavalry. Arms and armour remained largely unchanged from the Republic, the offensive weapons being two javelins of different weight, the Spanish sword and a dagger; armour consisted of a bronze helmet, an iron cuirass in a series of segments stitched onto a leather base, and a curving rectangular shield. During the first century AD the period of legionary service became standarized at 25 years, and legionary pay, which had been increased by Domitian, could be supplemented by occasional cash handouts from the emperor. In addition, soldiers enjoyed certain legal privileges which were not extended to the rest of the population. Conscription was employed in the provinces, though not normally in Italy; in any event the proportion of volunteers probably increased, especially towards the end of the second century as service conditions improved. For the poor man enlistment in the army offered a chance to attain a status above that to which he could normally aspire. The most striking change in the composition of the legions was the decline in the number of Italians, so that by the time of Hadrian the legions consisted almost entirely of Roman citizens from the provinces. This was undoubtedly connected with the tendency towards local recruiting as the legions acquired permanent bases in the provinces. Italians presumably did not want to serve far from Italy. Moreover, those sons of legionaries who had been born from a union with a non-Roman woman and who were therefore not citizens, were enticed to join the army by the offer of citizenship on enlistment.

The *auxilia* provided the army's light infantry and cavalry, and the number of their units, both infantry cohorts and cavalry *alae*, steadily increased; in the main they contained 480–500 men, though some had 800–1,000, and all were commanded by men of equestrian rank. A hierarchy of command developed in which the prefecture of a cohort was held first, then the military tribuneship of a legion, and finally the prefecture of an *ala*. The *auxilia* gradually lost their ethnic character as fresh recruits were accepted from areas outside the original area of enlistment.

At the end of their 25 years' service, auxiliaries were granted Roman citizenship for themselves and their children born in service, and also for children born subsequently. By the mid-second century the distinction between legionaries and auxiliaries had become less significant as more citizens chose to serve in the *auxilia*.

In the garrison of Rome, by the end of the first century AD, there were ten cohorts of Praetorian Guardsmen, probably now with 1,000 men in each, still largely recruited from Italians, with special service conditions, and based in a camp in Rome. The Guard was commanded by two Praetorian Prefects of equestrian rank. In the late first century an elite cavalry unit was added to the Guard – the *equites singulares Augusti*. As a police force there were three urban cohorts, each 1,000 strong, recruited from Italians and commanded by tribunes of equestrian rank. They were responsible to the Prefect of the City, who was of senatorial rank. The capital's forces were completed by 7,000 *Vigiles*, recruited from freedmen and organized in seven cohorts under the command of tribunes who had seen service as chief centurions; they acted as a fire brigade and were responsible to the Prefect of the *Vigiles*, who was of equestrian rank.

In the field the army was supported by well-organized artillery; according to Vegetius a large engine designed to fling heavy rocks was attached to each legionary cohort; there were also lighter catapults like large crossbows, which fired iron bolts; they were mounted on carts pulled by oxen and one was assigned to each century. They could be used as mobile field guns on the battlefield or as siege guns. The Romans were skilled in deploying this artillery in combination with battering rams, siege towers, ramps and circumvallation, in order to eliminate all places of refuge for the enemy, as for example in the Sieges of Jerusalem and Masada in the Jewish revolt (AD 66–74) and the storming of Maiden Castle in Dorset in AD 44, where the Roman artillery fire drove the defenders from the ramparts.

All recruits underwent a rigorous programme of physical training, marching, swimming, practice of sword skills with wooden weapons, target practice with javelins, and manoeuvres in battle-line formations. The discipline of the army was in principle strict with severe penalties in law for desertion, cowardice and dereliction of duty. On the other hand, there were numerous military decorations awarded by the emperor for valour in the field. The best possible provision was made for sick and wounded soldiers. In each legionary camp there was a hospital which was designed to ensure good insulation and minimal noise. Doctors, along with medical orderlies and dressers, were apparently assigned to all branches of the Roman armed forces, and specialist medical instruments to deal with wounds have been found. The importance of hygiene and general cleanliness was recognized and great attention was given to adequate bathing and latrine facilities.

Although the army was the glory of the Roman military establishment, Augustus had also created an imperial fleet with bases in Italy at Misenum and Ravenna. Subsequently, further detachments were established, for example, on the Rhine and the Danube and in the English Channel. The sailors were recruited from non-Romans in the provinces of the empire and were treated like the *auxilia* on discharge. Slaves were not employed in any part of the Roman armed forces. The fleets, however, did not have an important role in the defence of the empire, and Rome's control of the Mediterranean depended largely on her domination of the lands around its shores.

The army had a significant social and economic role in the life of the empire. The soldiers based in permanent camps were important consumers of foodstuffs. It has been conjectured that 300,000 troops would consume 100,000 tonnes of wheat a year. Some of this was provided by the local population in the form of taxes, but some could doubtless be sold to the camps. Moreover, the soldiers attracted many camp followers, and although not permitted to marry, formed liaisons with local women, who often came to live in settlements (*canabae*) attached to military camps. All this helped to foster the local market. The people could sell to soldiers, who had money to spend, or exchange goods for surplus objects made in the camp, such as bricks or tiles. At Carnuntum (modern Petronell in Austria), founded as a legionary base on the bank of the Danube in the first century AD, the *canabae* developed into a sizeable urban community with its own administration and amphitheatre. After discharge, many soldiers were settled individually, or sometimes in groups in veteran colonies close to where they had served. Veterans and their families provided additional consumers needing a market and other services; they brought money with them and could often attract imperial interest and benevolence. Centurions in particular were very well-off and in a position to become town councillors and bestow benefactions on a community. Veteran colonies helped to foster the security and urban development of an area since they required either a new town or extra buildings in an existing settlement. For example, Thamugadi (modern

Timgad in Algeria), which was founded by Trajan in AD 100 as a colony for veterans from the *III Augustan* legion in north Africa, became a flourishing community, which, despite its regimented lay-out on the model of a Roman military camp, had all the amenities of civilized town life including a theatre, a library and extensive bathing facilities. Furthermore, the settlement of veteran colonies and the extension of citizenship to soldiers' children and discharged auxiliaries may have assisted the Romanization of the empire. However, the army's involvement in the social and economic life of the empire had a less appealing aspect. The presence of large numbers of soldiers, permanently stationed in the provinces, or in transit, contributed significantly to the oppression of the civilian population, especially those who lived along major roads. Soldiers used their role and privileged status to rob, abuse and intimidate civilians, and emperors made frequent but unsuccessful attempts to curb this.

In the third century, despite serious political dislocation, there were several developments in military practice. The Emperor Gallienus (AD 253–68) introduced an independent cavalry unit to help deal with the threat of barbarian cavalry incursions into the western provinces, and increased the use of detachments from larger units. The role of senators as army commanders was restricted. Gallienus initially may have had no policy of removing senators from military responsibilities in the provinces, but he was prepared to use and promote men of equestrian rank as the situation demanded, and did not feel constrained by the old traditions of senatorial appointments. By 268 Gallienus had effectively decided that equestrians should command the bulk of Rome's armies. The equestrians so employed tended to be schooled in military affairs and had often been promoted from the ranks of experienced centurions and senior centurions. Diocletian (AD 284–305) provided a period of stability in which further military reorganization took place. He increased the number of legions to the extent that the manpower of the army would have been doubled if the legion had retained its traditional complement of men, though this is disputed. He also developed the use of a mobile field army, which consisted of contingents drawn from various parts of the army, and which was attached to his person, able to move round the empire quickly and respond to any strategic requirement. But Diocletian preserved the traditional emphasis on troops permanently stationed in individual provinces; fortifications were strengthened and a number of forts were built whose purpose was perhaps not primarily to provide a defensive line, but to protect communications by roads and rivers, ensure internal security, and enhance the possibilities both for defence and counter-attack. Constantine (AD 306–37) increased the size of the mobile field army (*Comitatenses*), which, in status and emoluments, was distinguished from the troops permanently stationed in the provinces, who served as a static covering force (*Ripenses, Limitanei*). In addition, the Praetorian Guard was abolished in 312 and the task of protecting the emperor given to the *Protectores*, and the *Scholae Palatinae* which Constantine reorganized and developed. However, the organization of the troops in the provinces was largely unchanged and their command was entrusted to *Duces*, each of whom was responsible for a section of the frontier. The recruitment into the army of entire peoples from outside the empire increased; they settled in Roman territory under their national commanders, and when the empire in the west collapsed some established independent barbarian kingdoms.

The Roman army pointed the way to the development of modern armies. With over 400,000 men, it was the largest professional army before the nineteenth century, and in the Ancient World surpassed all rivals in its high degree of organization, training, and discipline, in its concept of regular pay, bonuses and superannuation, and in its recognition of the essential importance of good equipment, logistics, ordnance, and technical and engineering support. At the height of their empire, the Romans succeeded in building an army recruited almost entirely from outside Italy, the privileged home of the imperial power, and welding it into one of the most effective, durable, and well-integrated military machines in history. *See also* ACTIUM; ADRIANOPLE; ALESIA; ARRIAN; ARTILLERY; ATTILA; BELISARIUS; BLADE WEAPONS; BRITAIN, CONQUEST OF; BYZANTIUM; CAESAR; CAMPS; CANNAE; CARTHAGE; CEREMONIES; CYNOSCEPHALAE; FORTIFICATION; FRONTIERS; FRONTINUS; GREECE, ANCIENT; HANNIBAL; HONOURS AND AWARDS; INFANTRY; JOSEPHUS; MASADA; MERCENARIES; NAVAL WARFARE; NAVIES; ONASANDER; ON MILITARY MATTERS; PENSIONS; PHILIPPI; POLYBIUS; SCIPIO AEMILIANUS; SCIPIO AFRICANUS; SIEGES; TACTICAL ORGANIZATION; TRAJAN; VEGETIUS RENATUS; VETERANS; VEXILLOLOGY; ZAMA.

JOËL LE GALL
B. CAMPBELL

FURTHER READING
G. L. Cheesman, *The Auxilia of the Roman Imperial Army* (Oxford, 1914, repr., 1971); H. M. D. Parker, *The Roman Legions* (Oxford, 1928; revised, 1958); C. G. Starr, *The Roman Imperial Navy 31 BC–AD 324* (Cambridge, 1960); A. H. M. Jones, *The Later Roman Empire 284–602* (Oxford, 1964), pp. 607–86; J. Harmand, *L'Armée et le soldat à Rome de 107 à 50 avant notre ère* (Paris, 1967); G. R. Watson, *The Roman Soldier* (London, 1969); M. Grant, *The Army of the Caesars* (London, 1974); E. Galba, *Republican Rome: the army and the allies* (translation, Oxford, 1976), pp. 1–69; E. N. Luttwak, *The Grand Strategy of the Roman Empire* (Baltimore and London, 1976); P. Connolly, *Greece and Rome at War* (London, 1981); V. A. Maxfield, *The Military Decorations of the Roman Army* (London, 1981); J. B. Campbell, *The Emperor and the Roman Army 31 BC–AD 235* (Oxford, 1984); L. J. F. Keppie, *The Making of the Roman Army: from republic to empire* (London, 1984); F. Lepper and S. Frere, *Trajan's Column* (Gloucester, 1988); G. Webster, *The Roman Imperial Army* (Totowa, NJ, 1985); Y. Le Bohec, *L'Armée romaine sous le haut-empire* (Paris, 1989).

Rommel, Erwin (1891–1944) Rommel is the best known of the field marshals of the Third Reich, and enjoys an unparalleled reputation. Rommel served in the First World War and was decorated for bravery. During the interwar period he held minor posts until 1933, when he became military instructor to the Nazis' paramilitary force, the *Sturmabteilung* (SA). Rommel gained Hitler's attention and was attached to Hitler's headquarters during the Polish campaign. He commanded a tank division (7th Panzer), nicknamed 'the Ghost Division' because of the speed of its manoeuvre, during the campaign in France. In 1941, Rommel was given command of the *Afrika Korps*. His daring leadership and flair for manoeuvre allowed Rommel to force the British back to Egypt. By the autumn of 1942, Rommel had pushed beyond his supply lines and his German forces were defeated at El Alamein. Rommel was obliged to retreat to Tunisia from where, in poor health, he was recalled to Germany. In January 1944, Rommel was given command of Army Group B in France in the expectation of an Allied invasion. Rommel preferred to meet this invasion on the beaches, in opposition to the belief of the front commander, Rundstedt, who favoured a defence in depth. Rommel became disillusioned with Hitler's military leadership when the latter did not permit German forces to be withdrawn to defensible positions after the Normandy invasions. While Rommel did not take an active role in the July plot against Hitler, he was sympathetic to the idea of removing Hitler from power. This resulted in Rommel's being offered suicide as an honourable alternative to arrest. He chose the former and took poison on 14 October 1944. *See also* EL ALAMEIN; FRANCE, BATTLE OF; GERMANY; OVERLORD; RUNDSTEDT; TANKS.

B. KROENER
KEITH NEILSON

FURTHER READING
R. Lewin, *Rommel as Military Commander* (Princeton, 1968); *The Rommel Papers*, ed. B. H. Liddell Hart (London, 1953); David Irving, *The Trail of the Fox* (London, 1977).

Rossbach (Saxony), Battle of (5 November 1757) After the defeat at Kolin (18 June 1757) by the Austrians, and at Gross-Jägersdorf by the Russians (30 July 1757), Prussia was invaded by Austrian, German, Russian, Swedish and French armies who converged upon Berlin. With 21,000 men, Frederick II decided to face the 64,000 Franco-German troops under the command of Soubise and Hildburghausen, near Leipzig. His two opponents planned to envelop the Prussian left flank with 40,000 men, but Frederick, guessing their intentions, used the cover offered by several hills to turn his infantry and artillery about, in order to launch a surprise attack while his cavalry descended on the enemy's flank, creating confusion. The main Prussian attack was then carried out in echelon (oblique order). In an hour and a half, the Allies lost 8,000 men, the Prussians 500. The battle had a considerable impact on France where it remained a symbol of military unpreparedness and prompted the French government to undertake a reform of its army along Prussian lines. *See also* FRANCE; FREDERICK II; GERMANY; LEUTHEN.

A. CORVISIER

FURTHER READING
W. Elze, *Friedrich der Grosse* (Berlin, 1936); C. Duffy, *Frederick the Great: a military life* (London, 1985); Thomas Carlyle, *History of Friedrich II of Prussia, called Frederick the Great* (6 vols, London, 1858–65) vol. 5; J. F. C. Fuller, 'The Battles of Rossbach and Leuthen, 1757', in *The Decisive Battles of the Western World* (London, 1955), ii, 192–215.

Routes of march   *See* STAGING POSTS

Rundstedt, Karl Rudolf Gerd von (1875–1953) Rundstedt came from an aristocratic Prussian military family. A graduate of the Military Academy and General Staff College, Rundstedt served in the General Staff in the First World War. He was prominent in developing new infantry tactics in the 1920s. From 1933 to 1938, Rundstedt commanded the 1st Army Group, but was forced to retire by Hitler in 1938 when the latter eliminated many traditional elements from the General Staff. He was recalled to service in 1939 and took part in the Polish campaign, his forces capturing Cracow and Lodz. In the campaign against France, Rundstedt commanded Army Group A. He gained assent for the views of his Chief of Staff, von Manstein, who advocated striking through the Ardennes, thus ensuring the defeat of France. In 1941, Rundstedt was given command of Army Group South for the invasion of the Soviet Union (*Operation Barbarossa*). Army Group South was completely successful in taking the Ukraine and the Crimea. Rundstedt opposed the offensive against Moscow, and resigned his post at the end of November in protest about the way that the campaign in the East had been handled. On 1 March 1942, Rundstedt was made Commander-in-Chief of all the German forces on the west coast of Europe. Rundstedt did not believe in fixed defences and planned to defend France with a war of manoeuvre and movement. Rundstedt failed to prevent a successful Allied landing at Normandy in June 1944 and was relieved of his command on 6 July. The failure of his successor to stop the Allied advance resulted in Rundstedt's being reinstated as Commander-in-Chief in the West. Rundstedt played a subordinate role in the German Ardennes offensive. He resigned in March 1945. *See also* FRANCE, BATTLE OF; GERMANY; MANSTEIN; NORMANDY; OVERLORD; ROMMEL; TANKS.

A. CORVISIER
KEITH NEILSON

FURTHER READING
G. Blumentritt, *Von Rundstedt: the soldier and the man* (London, 1952); J. Wheeler-Bennett, *The Nemesis of Power* (London, 1953).

Russia/USSR   The military history of Russia is dominated by two great watersheds: the Europeanization of the army by Tsar Aleksei Mikhailovich (1645–76) and the formation of the Red Army at the end of the First World War. Both instances represent the establishment of institutions with a certain degree of originality which served as models for other countries. Three main phases can be identified.

From the Origins to Modern Russia In their search for continuity, Soviet historians tended to push further and further back into history the point at which some of the permanent traits of their army were formed. Long before AD 862, which for many years was regarded as the official date for the appearance of the Russian state, the populations of the great plains of Eastern Europe were confronted by a succession of invasions from different quarters. The history of ancient Russia contains the names of many celebrated warriors: Svyatoslav (late tenth century), Alexander Nevsky (mid-thirteenth century) and Dmitri Donskoi (second half of the fourteenth century). However, ancient Russia did not produce any original military systems since, as circumstances demanded, it adapted the techniques of its enemies: the Byzantines, the Varangians (of Scandinavian origin), Poles, Lithuanians, Teutonic Knights, the Turkic Pechenegs and Polovtsians, and, particularly, the Mongol horsemen who overwhelmed the country in the thirteenth century and exerted pressure down to the sixteenth century. Anchored in an attachment to the soil and the Orthodox religion, facing Western Christianity on one frontier and the Asiatic world on the other, Russia acquired a wholly new importance under Ivan IV, the Terrible (1533–84), who, in 1547, took the title of Tsar (emperor). He expanded Muscovy into Turkic lands by annexing the Kazan and Astrakhan on the middle and lower Volga. This was the first major Russian incursion into non-Slavic lands and split the Turkic world in two. Ivan the Terrible was also the creator of a semi-regular army with his institutionalization of the infantry arquebusiers (*streltsy*) in the 1550s.

Cavalry service had already been linked by Ivan III (1462–1505) to the possession of land during the last quarter of the fifteenth century. *Pomest'e*, areas of land farmed by anything from a handful to several hundred peasant households, were allotted to men-at-arms to support them in kind for their cavalry service to the state. Ivan IV developed this system. The code of laws (*Sudebnik*) of 1556 recorded categories of 'service men' divided into three ranks or *chin*: the *boyars* of the court and other members of the upper service class who provided officers; the middle service class who were granted *pomestiyes*, amounting to some 25,000 cavalrymen by the 1650s; and the members of the lowest service class who received an annual salary and served as arquebusiers (*streltsy*) and then, in the seventeenth century, musketeers, artillerymen and other military forces. The linchpin was the cavalry, half of which served in the spring and early summer and the remainder in the late summer and autumn. Ivan IV also took Tartars into his service and paid a great deal of attention to artillery, especially very heavy cannon. His army continued to be Asiatic in character, both in its dress and fighting methods.

After the death of Ivan IV, the army descended into stagnation and corruption. By 1649, the men of the middle *chin* obtained hereditary rights to their *pomestiyes* and formed a closed social group anxious to defend their privileges against the peasants who had become their serfs. To an extent, they also lost their martial vocation. In their turn, the *streltsy* became an obsolescent, privileged corporation, occupied more with maintaining public order, as a constabulary, or rebelling, than with fighting wars. In 1630, in preparation for the Smolensk War (1632–4), 'new formation' regiments were created commanded by foreign mercenaries and often manned by foreign troops as well. Half of the 34,000 men in the Russian army at Smolensk were of the 'new formation' regiments trained in Western linear tactics, recruited in north-west Europe. Beginning in 1647, a number of native 'new formation' regiments were raised by a crude method of conscription in which each group of households was obliged to provide a soldier. Foreigners were still hired but only to officer the 'new formation' regiments. These 'new formation' regiments served in the Thirteen Years' War (1654–67) which annexed Kiev and much of the Ukraine to Muscovy. Around the time that he effectively came to power in 1689, Peter the Great (1682–1725) formed two new regiments on the Western model, the Preobrazhenski and the Semionvski Guards. He wanted to marginalize the *streltsy* by forcing them to man the frontier garrisons but, taking advantage of Peter's first journey to the West, they revolted. First, Peter had them decimated, then abolished. He proceeded to order a general levy of soldiers throughout the empire whom he proposed to equip and train on Western European lines.

The Imperial Armed Forces from 1699 to 1917 Peter the Great's military plans were realized only gradually and were not immediately effective. After the defeat at Narva by Charles XII of Sweden (1700), he was victorious over the Swedes at Poltava in 1709, largely on account of serious strategic and tactical errors committed by Charles, but he blundered into a reverse by the Turks on the River Pruth in 1711. Peter was not discouraged and in 1721 ended the Great Northern War as a member of a coalition that was victorious over Sweden. One of the fruits of the Treaty of Nystad (1721) was the acquisition for Russia of a window on to the Baltic.

Peter the Great was driven by the cult of efficiency and therefore selected his collaborators from all ranks of society, employing the criterion of ability. Alexander Menshikov (1673–1728), the cavalry commander, was of peasant origin and James Bruss (Bruce) (b. 1670), grandmaster of the artillery, was of Scottish extraction. He did not hesitate to penalize failure cruelly, without consideration of rank. Officers were subject to capital punishment and, indeed, flogging with the knout and exile to Siberia. The military regulations of 1716, which he largely composed himself, constituted a military testament. They were a synthesis of German, Dutch, Swedish and, most especially, French practices, adapted to Russian conditions through the experience of his earlier misfortunes.

The levy of 1699 had been carried out on the basis of the so-called 'households' system, the elders (*starosty*) choosing the sturdiest man from each group of twenty-five households on the estates of clerical landlords and from groups of between thirty and fifty on the lands of secular lords. This was refined in 1705 when one man was summoned from every twenty households. In the last years of his reign, and certainly from 1721, the date of the first modern population census, a new recruitment system was set in place. In 1726, the levy raised one man per 250 male inhabitants registered in the census (this was increased to one per 121 male inhabitants in 1747); the men were enrolled by district and province, each district having to support one regiment. Soldiers served for life. Officer training was one of Peter the Great's principal concerns and he called on the services of foreigners as instructors though he did not form them into special corps. In *c*.1712, he opened schools for artillery and engineering officers and for military surgeons.

The creation of the first Russian ocean-going fleet was a logical development from the seventeenth-century flotillas which had plied the Black Sea and the Western Dvina River down to Riga. Russia's initial maritime access had been through the White Sea ports of Kholmogory, founded in the 1550s, and Archangel, established in 1584. In 1703, Peter the Great began the construction of the town and port of St Petersburg on lands reclaimed from the shores of the Baltic. Calling on the services of mainly Dutch technical experts, he transformed it into a major harbour complete with extensive naval dockyards. These measures enabled Russia to become a more significant naval power during the second half of the eighteenth century.

The Russian army continued to develop under Peter the Great's successors. It suffered occasional setbacks and vigorous bouts of reform were periodically required to counter the repeated appearance of stagnation. These improvements were executed by energetic leaders like Marshal Burchard von Münnich (1725–41) and Peter Shuvalov (1753–62), usually inspired by the Prussian example, which, during the reigns of Peter III (1761–2) and Paul I (1796–1801), was sometimes slavishly imitated particularly over matters of uniform.

The development of society affected the composition of the army. As the aristocracy was Westernized, it rose to a position of power. The choice of recruits passed from the control of the communities of residents into the hands of the great landowning nobles. At the end of the eighteenth century, the provincial governors, whose interests were allied to those of the aristocracy, took over the process. The 1766 general instruction on the levying of recruits made provision for exemptions which the nobles could apply to the serfs they found most useful. Taking men into the army meant tearing them away from their villages for ever, since service was for life; the reduction in the period of conscription to twenty-five years in 1793 made little practical difference. Soldiers who became unfit were taken into monasteries, until Catherine II (1762–96) established garrisons for their accommodation in 1764. The departure of the recruits frequently gave rise to distressing scenes; sometimes, recruits had to be chained during the journey to their regimental depot. On arrival, the conscript was shaved, given a haircut and dressed in a uniform modelled on that of Western armies, though adapted to the Russian climate (boots and a more ample tunic). He was then taken in hand by Orthodox priests, veterans nicknamed 'uncles', and his officers.

The Corps of Noble Cadets was formed in 1730 to undertake the training of officers and this was followed by the foundation of the Military Cadet School in 1766, though the Preobrazhenski and Semionovski Guards remained the main training institutions for future officers. Under the *chin* system, the officers were mostly members of the gentry or non-hereditary nobles to whom the army offered a limited chance of social advancement. The army had assumed a prime position in the nation. Even civil servants were compelled to wear uniform. The armed forces were, however, isolated from society by the long service periods, their accommodation in barracks, and by their constabulary role in the maintenance of public order.

Technically, the Russian army continued to show certain weaknesses during the eighteenth century. Armaments, although abundant in quantity thanks to the workshops in the Urals, failed to keep pace with Western technological developments until Peter Shuvalov secured permission to establish commissions to examine various reform projects, bearing particularly on the artillery and the engineers. As a consequence, the artillery was separated into regimental, army and heavy branches, calibres and types were rationalized and some original designs (the *unicorn*) adopted; the 'Shuvalov howitzer' (1757) proved to be an excellent field weapon. In the same year, an engineering corps was formed divided into companies of sappers, pontoneers and artisans. One of the main failings of the Russian army was its slowness. The cavalry remained mediocre in quality, though this was partially remedied by the inclusion of Tatar and Cossack units, the latter being reorganized into regiments before making their debut on the battlefields of Western Europe. First companies, then battalions and finally a corps of *chasseurs* were formed under Catherine II. The many wars in which the Russian army fought during the second half of the eighteenth century, under the direction of some remarkable leaders like A. V. Suvorov (1729–1800), provided a thorough training in varied fighting conditions (e.g. the Italian, Netherlandish and Swiss campaigns of 1799). During the wars against the Napoleonic Empire, the Russian army distinguished itself more by dogged determination and endurance than by its technical qualities.

When peace returned in 1815, the army was afflicted by a crisis of morale. In a plan to improve recruitment and discipline, Alexander I (1801–25), misguided by the notorious A. A. Arakcheev, created military colonies which were entrusted with training recruits. Villages were arranged into groups to provide conscripts to act as reserves for line battalions and the boys in those designated villages were compelled to wear uniform from the age of eight while the soldiers accommodated therein could be detailed to work on the land. These reforms aroused much discontent as they took insufficient account of social and economic realities. The peasants felt that they were being turned into soldiers while the soldiers thought they were being translated into serfs. This, and numerous other factors, caused mutinies within the army. Constitutionally minded officers seized on the pretext of the succession to

715

Alexander I to revolt (the Decembrist Rising, 1825). After the military colonies had rebelled, they were abolished (1831).

During the nineteenth century, the Russian army expanded to a substantial size: officially it contained 1,300,000 men but only 700,000 were actually in service and barely 30,000 of these were properly armed and trained. Against well-known and predictable enemies, like Turkey and Persia, the army fought well but its weaknesses were revealed in the Crimean War (1854–6). After the Peace of Paris, the Russian army was reorganized by a commission including D. A. Milyutin, who was subsequently appointed Minister of War. The period of service was reduced to fifteen years, twelve of which were to be spent on active service. This was developed by the great military regulation of 1874, directed by Milyutin, the last of Alexander II's (1855–81) epoch-making attempts at reform. A system of conscription, based on the Prussian model, was introduced in which the term was further reduced to six years on active service and nine years in the reserve for the land forces, and seven and three years respectively, in the navy. The efficacy of the reform was weakened by exempting more than half of the potential recruits.

In spite of assistance and financial aid from France after 1893, the technical quality of the Russian army remained generally inferior to that of Western formations. Access to officer rank had been considerably widened and, after the abolition of the Council for National Defence in 1908, the High Command had been subordinated to the Ministry of War. During the Russo-Japanese War (1904–5), and particularly during the period of Russia's involvement in the First World War (1914–17), the Russian people were called upon to make a tremendous contribution to the war effort. Twelve million men were mobilized, including almost four million combatants, but they were poorly supplied, not always well employed, and sometimes not employed at all. Morale suffered constant blows and, in the rear areas, the army disintegrated.

The Russian navy had won itself a posi-tion of some honour at the end of the eighteenth century (the victory at Chesme, 1770). However, it could not overcome the obstacles created by the scattered nature of its coastal areas, and its weaknesses were revealed in the defeat by the Japanese at Tsushima in 1905. Having been treated poorly, the navy played a leading role in the October Revolution of 1917 (the cruiser *Aurora*).

The Soviet Army Directive no. 1 issued by the Petrograd Soviet in March 1917 called for the formation of soldiers' committees, the abandonment of external marks of respect to officers and for officers to be placed under the control of their troops. The destruction of the imperial army by the soviets of workers and soldiers and the anti-militarist tendencies of many of the revolutionaries meant that the resurrection of a powerful army ready for renewed sacrifice seemed thoroughly improbable. The civil war, however, revealed the degree of attention that had been paid to military problems by some of those new Russian leaders who had previously been exiled. At the time of the October Revolution, the Red Guard had been formed, composed of volunteers from among the revolutionaries, mostly soldiers from the old army. In these new units, ranks disappeared and the officers were elected by the men. L. D. Trotsky, who presided over the Military Revolutionary Committee, which, after the Provisional Government had fled to Moscow, had been created by the Petrograd Soviet to defend the city against an anticipated German attack, attempted to give these units a structure. However, the dissolving and disintegrating Russian state found the Red Guard inadequate to grapple with the secession of non-Russian peoples, offensives by the German armies which seized many of the country's food and mineral resources in the Ukraine, and the insurrections led by the White generals. Once the Bolsheviks were in power, they created the 'Red Army of Workers and Peasants' (28 January 1918) and introduced compulsory military training (22 April). In contrast to the Whites, who wanted to reconquer the whole of the former Russian territories, the Bolsheviks adopted a more pragmatic approach. While explicitly drawing on the military theories of Friedrich Engels (1820–95), they called upon the services of a great number of officers from the old imperial army, including General A. A. Brusilov, who declared, 'The country is sick and I can see no other remedy than the Red Flag.' The extraordinary energy of the Supreme War Council, over which Trotsky presided, and the divisions amongst their adversaries, allowed the Bolsheviks to bring the situation under control during 1920 and, at the cost of concessions over administration to non-Russian peoples, to found a new state, the USSR, in 1922.

In 1923, M. V. Frunze replaced Trotsky at the head of the Supreme War Council; he created the military academy which bears his name. His work was continued by M. N. Tukhachevsky, who was assisted by B. M. Shaposhnikov and V. I. Chuikov. The army quickly became, once more, the source of the country's resilience, the guarantee of its independence and was intimately associated with the life of the nation; Lenin wrote, 'every institution of Soviet Russia should always accord primacy to the army.' From the 1930s, the slogan, 'For our Soviet Motherland' replaced the Tsarist motto, 'For the Faith, the Tsar and the Motherland', while, on flags, the five-pointed star ousted the cross. A military hierarchy was re-established complete with decorations and the outward marks of rank. The 'People's Commissars' were continued after the Revolution but they had changed into emissaries of the government rather than delegates of the troops; the soldiers' committees ceased to play any further role. The army had been re-unified and Russian was restored as the single language of command. For both foreign and domestic consumption and propaganda, until the end of the 1980s the anniversary of the October Revolution was celebrated by a gigantic military parade through Red Square in Moscow. At least until the Stalinist purges of 1936–9, the ex-imperial officers who had joined the Red Army formed one of its chief strengths. However, despite the purges, a new gen-

eration arose composed of soldiers from the First World War who had joined the Communist Party, worked hard in the military academies and won rapid promotion. This generation provided most of the Soviet military leaders during the Great Patriotic War (1941–5). Emphasis was placed upon the training of the individual soldier and the need for protecting the army's rear. The teaching of Suvorov was constantly repeated – 'The front is everywhere!'

Both the first Five Year Plan (1928–33), which concentrated upon heavy industry, and the second, which covered a wider range of production, accorded an important place to armaments. To the pursuit of quantity was added the search for quality. The Soviet army prepared itself for mass warfare and for a war of movement. The artillery was substantially increased and the cavalry, tanks and air force were developed. Partisans had played a prominent role during the civil war and the general staff carried out research into irregular warfare. However, these efforts seemed to have been wiped out by the purges of 1937–9. Marshal Tukhachevsky, almost two-thirds of the generals, and, in all, some 33,000–40,000 officers were either imprisoned or shot. As a result of Stalin's destruction of his own officer corps (the executions continued into the first half of 1941), the Soviet army was 'headless' at the time of Hitler's invasion in June 1941. The war in Finland and the devastation wrought by the German blitzkrieg, demonstrated the tactical inferiority of the Soviet army and the absence of leadership. Invasion did, however, enable the moral force of the Soviet people to manifest itself while the armed forces rapidly learned how to combat German tactics. By the winter of 1942–3, the Soviet army had turned again to the offensive doctrines of the earlier 1930s and, combined with modern, mass-produced weaponry and extensive Anglo-American aid, was able to launch an almost continuous offensive as far as Berlin. The USSR ended the war in a position of great political and military strength within Europe. After 1945, the evocation of the Great Patriotic War was a source of energy for the Soviet people and propaganda for its government.

Though materially weakened by the war, the USSR strove after 1945 to catch up with the technological lead of the United States, most notably by equipping itself with nuclear weapons in 1949. It even succeeded in overtaking in some sectors, especially space technology (*Sputnik*, 1957, first man in space, 1961). Before its dissolution in 1991, the Soviet Union possessed the largest army in the world in terms of the number of soldiers (over 1,400,000 in 1990) and the quantity of armaments (e.g. 54,400 main battle tanks in 1990). Its improved continental situation encouraged the development of a powerful navy which became the world's second largest after that of the United States. It was especially strong in submarines (317 modern vessels in 1990, including 66 carrying strategic nuclear missiles). Making skilful use of ideological warfare, the Soviet Union lent support to anti-colonial and Marxist movements which enabled it to establish important naval bases in Asia and Africa and, despite being thwarted in its ambitions in Cuba in 1962, it gained a temporary foothold in the Western Hemisphere. However, as the army became increasingly an instrument of Soviet foreign policy, its history was linked to that of nuclear deterrence and to the history of attempts to destabilize the enemy.

A. CORVISIER

Albert and Joan Seaton, *The Soviet Army: 1918 to the present* (London, 1986), paint a very different picture from that depicted in this article. They accuse both the Tsarist and the Soviet armies of being pale imitations of Prussian and German practice, right up to the end of the Great Patriotic War. Soviet strategic and tactical thinking and doctrine are portrayed as derivative and confused through their adherence to Marxist ideology and the necessities of domestic power politics. Not until the 1950s do they detect a coherence in strategic thought, which became reflected in the tactical doctrine and equipment of the armed forces. The Seatons accuse many Western historians and observers of being the victims of Soviet propaganda.

JOHN CHILDS

See also CIVIL WAR; COLONIAL WARFARE; DETERRENCE; DISARMAMENT; HIERARCHY; INDIRECT WARFARE; LOGISTICS; MANPOWER; MONGOLS; NAVAL PERSONNEL; NAVAL WARFARE; NAVIES; NUCLEAR WARFARE; POPULAR WARFARE; PSYCHOLOGICAL WARFARE OPERATIONS; RECRUITMENT; RESISTANCE; SOVIET MILITARY THEORISTS.

BRUSILOV; DRAGOMIROV; ENGELS; KONEV; KUTUSOV; LENIN; MARX; PETER I; SHAPOSHNIKOV; SOKOLOVSKY; SUVOROV; STALIN; TROTSKY; ZHUKOV.

AUSTERLITZ; KURSK SALIENT; LENINGRAD; MOSCOW, BATTLE OF; MOSCOW, RETREAT FROM; MUKDEN; NARVA; POLTAVA; STALINGRAD; RUSSO-FINNISH WAR; TSUSHIMA.

FURTHER READING
John S. Curtiss, *The Russian Army under Nicholas I* (Durham, NC, 1965); L. Raymond, *How Russia Makes War: Soviet military doctrine* (London, 1954); Richard Hellie, *Enserfment and military change in Muscovy* (Chicago, 1971); John L. H. Keep, *Soldiers of the Tsar: army and society in Russia, 1462–1874* (Oxford, 1985); Philip A. Bayer, *The Evolution of the Soviet General Staff, 1917–1941* (New York, 1987); *The Soviet Army*, ed. B. H. Liddell Hart (London, 1956); David B. Ralston, *Importing the European Army: the introduction of European military techniques and institutions into the extra-European world, 1600–1914* (Chicago, 1990), chapter 2; Christopher Duffy, *Russia's Military Way to the West: origins and nature of Russian military power, 1700–1800* (London, 1981).

Russo-Finnish War (1939–40)   The Soviet Union invaded Finland on 30 November 1939 after failing to persuade the Finnish government to give up territory demanded to enhance the security of Leningrad. A period of negotiations and rising tension was accompanied by the Finnish mobilization (described as 'special manoeuvres') on 7–11 October of 300,000 men and women. This gave the army (nine divisions – including two in reserve – and some independent battalions) time to settle into its defensive positions. This was vital above all for the 120,000 men on the Karelian Isthmus, where the main defences were sited. Soon to be known after the commander-in-chief

In the east of Finland, in temperatures of –40°C, the 163rd Division of the Soviet army, poorly equipped to combat the climate and the forested terrain, was surprised near the village of Suomussalmi by a division of the Finnish army. The 44th Motorized Division advanced to relieve the 163rd but it was trapped on a forest road by Finnish troops and defeated in detail. The surrounded 163rd Division was annihilated. The Finns lost 900 killed and 1,800 wounded while the Soviet casualties amounted to 27,500 men killed in action or frozen to death, 1,300 prisoners, 50 tanks and all their artillery. Although this Polar battle did little to influence the development of warfare, it demonstrated the need for troops to be properly equipped for Arctic warfare and gave the German General Staff an exaggerated notion of the weakness of the Soviet army.
(Topham)

– Field Marshal Gustaf Mannerheim – as thc Mannerheim Line, these defences comprised a combination of concrete strong points and field works.

The Red Army deployed 28–9 divisions and several tank brigades for the attack on Finland, with 200,000 men on the Isthmus, 130,000 north-east of Lake Ladoga (opposed by 40,000 Finns) and 65,000 on the long frontier to the Arctic Ocean (against 16,000 Finns). The Soviets quickly reached the Mannerheim Line but failed to break through in fierce fighting between 16 and 19 December. More dangerous to the Finns were Soviet offensives north of Ladoga and in the 'waist' of Finland. The first was stopped by 10 December and

broken up with heavy losses between 27 December and 5 January; a Soviet division was destroyed at Tolvajärvi in mid-December. The most spectacular Finnish victory was at Suomussalmi (in the 'waist') where two Soviet divisions in succession were destroyed between 11 December and 6 January. The lightly armed Finns, mobile on skis, had the advantage in the northern forests over the mechanized and road-bound Russians during a particularly severe winter with temperatures falling to −40° Celsius. These victories boosted Finnish morale.

The Soviet command reorganized and retrained, and strengthened their forces against Finland to 45 divisions, 25 on the

Isthmus, where they began a renewed offensive, with massive artillery support, on 1 February. They broke through the Mannerheim Line at Summa on 13 February, the Finns having to withdraw on 15 February to an intermediate position, and on 27 February to their rear position covering Viipuri. The severe winter now helped the Soviets by allowing tanks to cross the ice of the Gulf of Viipuri from 4 March, outflanking the Finnish defences and threatening their communications. Britain and France offered Finland military intervention but it would be too little and too late. While the army still held out, therefore, Finland signed the Peace of Moscow on 12 March 1940, ceding extensive territory to the Soviet Union.

The Finnish army began the war short of men, uniforms, artillery ammunition and equipment, particularly field and anti-tank artillery, tanks and aircraft. The Finnish defence, lacking artillery support, was worn down by heavy casualties and, by the end of the war, had become increasingly improvised. Nevertheless, the Finnish army fought outstandingly well, denied the Soviet Union an expected easy conquest, and forced it to negotiate. The Soviet military performance, initially poor, improved significantly, though losses in prestige, *matériel* and men were severe. Finnish war dead numbered 25,000; Soviet losses were perhaps eight times as great. *See also* FINLAND, SINCE 1809; RUSSIA/USSR.

J. E. O. SCREEN

FURTHER READING
Allen F. Chew, *The White Death: the epic of the Soviet–Finnish winter war* (East Lansing, Michigan, 1971); Thomas Ries, *Cold Will: the defence of Finland* (London, 1988); Anthony F. Upton, *Finland, 1939–1940* (London, 1974).

Ruyter, Michael Adrianszoon de (1607–76) After entering the Dutch merchant service at the age of eleven, de Ruyter, the son of a brewer's drayman, rose rapidly in rank to become a naval captain in 1637. Reverting to the mercantile marine in 1643 and having accumulated an honest fortune, he retired in 1651. Recalled when the First Anglo-Dutch War (1652–4) broke out, he fought with distinction under Maarten Tromp (1598–1653). As Vice-Admiral of Holland, he subsequently commanded squadrons in the Mediterranean and the fleet sent to the Sound in 1660. The declaration of war against England in 1665 found de Ruyter in Africa defending Dutch trading stations. In 1666 he defeated George Monck (1608–70) in the Four Days' Battle, only to be beaten himself off the North Foreland on St James's Day. In June 1667, however, de Ruyter surprised the depleted English defences, capturing Sheerness. He then sailed up the Medway and burned or captured ships at Chatham, including the *Royal Charles*. This success led to the signing of the Treaty of Breda (21 July 1667), a settlement more favourable to the English than the outcome of the war warranted. When England, allied to France by the Treaty of Dover (1670), attacked at the beginning of the Third Anglo–Dutch War (1672–4), de Ruyter held the allies at Solebay (28 May 1672) and obtained two successes at Schoonveldt (28 May and 4 June 1673) and at the Texel (21 August 1673). When England dropped out of the war in 1674, the States-General sent de Ruyter to the Mediterranean to support their ally, Spain, but he was mortally wounded at the Battle of Augusta. De Ruyter has been described as the greatest sailor of his age. He was the creator of the Dutch navy which defied English maritime supremacy for almost two decades and dealt a severe blow to Colbert's young French navy. *See also* COLBERT; GREAT BRITAIN; NAVAL WARFARE; NAVIES; NETHERLANDS.

J. MEYER
A. W. H. PEARSALL

FURTHER READING
R. C. Anderson, *Journals and Narratives of the Third Dutch War* (Navy Records Society, lxxxvi, London, 1946); P. J. Blok, *The Life of Admiral de Ruyter*, tr. G. J. Renier (London, 1933); P. G. Rogers, *The Dutch in the Medway* (London, 1970).

S

Sadowa, or Königgrätz, Battle of (3 July 1866) This decisive victory by the Prussians over the Austrians was preceded by a remarkable strategic operation conducted by Moltke, based upon the convergence of the 1st Army, 2nd Army and the Army of the Elbe which had been spread over a front of 200 miles. This operation, made possible by the extensive use of railways and the electric telegraph, was sustained by leaving a margin of initiative to the corps and army commanders who marched with their troops. The Austrian commander, Benedek, gathered his forces into a single army and seemed more concerned with supplies than with hostilities. At Sadowa, in northern Bohemia, 220,000 Prussians were ranged against 190,000 Austrians and 25,000 Saxons. As a consequence of a breakdown in telegraphic communications, the Army of the Elbe did not sufficiently stretch out its front, and also blocked the passage of the 1st Army, and the 2nd Army failed to attack at the appointed hour. Benedek took advantage of this confusion to launch a violent assault supported by artillery but held back his cavalry. When the 2nd Army finally arrived on the battlefield and counter-attacked, the superiority of Prussian firepower turned the situation around. The Austrians escaped rout by a skilful withdrawal but lost 25,000 killed and wounded and 20,000 men taken prisoner, while the Prussian casualties amounted to 10,000 dead and injured. Sadowa was the fruit of excellent technical preparation but it nevertheless demonstrated the difficulties involved in concentrating a very large number of troops on the battlefield, a feat which demanded precise co-ordination and timetabling. In a campaign of seven weeks, Austria forfeited her leadership of the German states and Prussia laid the foundation for German unification in 1871. *See also* AUSTRIA; COM-MAND; GENERAL STAFF; GERMANY; MOLTKE; SIGNAL COMMUNICATION; TRANSPORT.

A. CORVISIER
HEW STRACHAN

FURTHER READING
Jean Colin, *Les Grandes batailles de l'histoire* (Paris, 1915); Gordon A. Craig, *The Battle of Königgrätz: Prussia's victory over Austria, 1866* (Philadelphia, 1964); Martin van Creveld, *Command in War* (Cambridge, Mass., 1985), pp. 103–47.

Sailors *See* NAVAL PERSONNEL

St Gotthard Abbey, Battle of (1 August 1664) The Turks declared war on Austria–Hungary in April 1663 but their armies moved very slowly and did not invade Hungary until the following spring. Montecucoli, the Imperial commander-in-chief, intended to assemble his scattered forces in late April but he did not achieve his concentration of 30,000 men until mid-July. By this time, the Turkish army of 50,000 under the Grand Vizier Ahmed Köprülü was threatening both Graz and Vienna. Montecucoli intercepted the Turks at Kormend on the River Raab and covered their advance. Here, he was joined by a French expeditionary force of 6,000 commanded by Jean de Coligny. On 1 August, the Turks began crossing the Raab near the Abbey of St Gotthard but Montecucoli was unable to intervene immediately because Coligny and the Margrave Leopold of Baden-Baden, commanding the Imperial contingents, had difficulty in co-ordination. The Imperial army was thrown back from the river into a region of woodland. Here, as the Turks rallied for a fresh assault, Montecucoli brought his forces together into three lines and persuaded Coligny and

Baden-Baden to launch a joint attack. The Turks fled back to the river in panic, many drowning. Köprülü, unable to bring the rest of his army over the river, abandoned his campaign and peace was signed between Leopold I and the Turks at Vasvár just ten days after the battle. *See also* AUSTRIA; MONTECUCOLI; OTTOMAN TURKS; VIENNA, SIEGE OF.

J. NOUZILLE

JOHN CHILDS

FURTHER READING

K. Peball, *Die Schlacht bei St. Gotthard Magersdorf, 1664* (Vienna, 1964); T. M. Barker, *Double Eagle and Crescent* (Albany, 1967).

St Quentin, Battle of (10 August 1557) St Quentin was the first battle of the reign of Philip II and the most important of the last phase of the Habsburg–Valois Wars. This phase was the result of the collapse of the Truce of Vaucelles (February 1556) following a French expedition to Italy led by the Duke of Guise to support the Pope against the Duke of Alba at the end of 1556. Full-scale hostilities broke out in early 1557. Philip II decided to retaliate by an invasion of northern France from the Netherlands and, after a major financial effort, an army of 45,000 was assembled under the command of the governor general of the Netherlands, Emanuel-Philibert, Duke of Savoy. To provide the young king with an easy victory Savoy in turn decided to besiege St Quentin. His advance in July 1557 took the French northern commander, Anne, the Constable Montmorency, by surprise, for he had deployed his 20,000-odd men (most of the French army being with Guise in Italy) for the defence of the Champagne. Montmorency had time only to rush a small reinforcement commanded by his nephew, the Admiral Coligny, into the town on 2 August; however, he was determined to assist Coligny further. St Quentin lay on the northern bank of the Somme and the marshy river valley prevented Savoy from investing the town completely. Believing that there were sufficient paths through the marshes to send further reinforcements into the town and that the nearest ford in the river was too small to permit Savoy to transfer troops to the south bank with speed, thus giving him ample time to escape should Savoy try to intercept him, Montmorency advanced to the Somme. The French reached the river in the early hours of 10 August but then found first that they could not get through the marshes and, next, that the Habsburg cavalry was able to cross the ford in strength. Montmorency ordered a retreat, drawing out his horse to shield the retiring infantry, but the larger force of Habsburg cavalry rode right through the French horse, capturing Montmorency himself. They then caught the French infantry in column of route who, after a brief resistance, either surrendered or dispersed. Only about a third of the French army managed to escape, while Habsburg casualties were no more than a hundred. St Quentin was now doomed, but Coligny did not surrender until after a full-scale and bloody assault on the 27th. Ironically, the dramatic and unexpected victory caused Philip considerable embarrassment, for, although nothing now stood between him and Paris, financial constraints had forced him to plan only for a limited siege, not a longer campaign. He was thus obliged to disband his army in September as previously planned without proceeding further. If Montmorency's miscalculations and Habsburg numerical superiority were the keys to the victory, it nevertheless showed that in the right conditions cavalry could still be the decisive weapon. The overthrow of the French horse was in part caused by the adoption of the wheel-lock pistol by the Habsburg cavalry; St Quentin therefore initiated a vogue for arming cavalry with pistols that lasted for the remainder of the century. *See also* ALBA; CAVALRY; FIREARMS; GRAVELINES; GUISE.

SIMON ADAMS

FURTHER READING

C. Oman, *A History of the Art of War in the Sixteenth Century* (London, 1937), pp. 254–66; F. Lot, *Recherches sur les effectifs des armées françaises des guerres d'Italie aux Guerres de Religion, 1494–1562* (Paris, 1962). For the strategic context, see M. J. Rodríguez-Salgado,

The Changing Face of Empire: Charles V, Philip II and Habsburg authority, 1551–1559 (Cambridge, 1988), pp. 169–79. An eyewitness account can be found in the *Memoirs* of Sir James Melville of Halhill (Edinburgh, 1827; and abridged by Gordon Donaldson for the Folio Society, 1969).

Saints, military Many religions have reserved a special place in the afterlife for warriors who have fallen in battle. This remains true of modern Islam and provided motivation for the Iranian armies during the Iran–Iraq War (1980–8). However, within the Christian religion, the notion of sainthood now seems incompatible with the profession of arms.

Together with the Book of Revelation, which introduces St Michael as the first warrior against evil, the Gospels did not exclude soldiers from religious experience, as in the cases of the centurion who described himself as unworthy to receive the Lord and the soldier on Calvary who declared that Jesus was the son of God. The Early Church counted among its numbers a great many soldiers martyred for their faith; St Sebastian and St Maurice of the Theban Legion are perhaps the most famous. Others, such as St Martin of Tours, also preached the gospel. Their conversion did, however, generally result in the abandonment of the military life. They were not specially invoked in the West to guarantee success on the battlefield, except where they became the patron saints of nations like St George in England or St Maurice in Piedmont, a privilege they shared with non-military saints such as St James (Santiago) in Spain or St Denis in France. Their names were emblazoned on the soldiers' banners and shouted in rallying cries. St George replaced Edward the Confessor as the patron saint of England during the reign of Edward III, who founded the Order of the Garter under his patronage in *c.*1349. Quasi-professional qualifications have been attributed to saints in certain armies – St Barbara is generally regarded as the patron saint of the engineers and the artillery whilst the Virgin Mary is the patron saint of the Italian *carabinieri*.

Some saints, usually monarchs, earned their status through converting enemies of the faith by force of arms. Among their number are Constantine, Clovis and Charlemagne. The instances of Joan of Arc and Alexander Nevsky are more exceptional. They did not spread the gospel but their missions were regarded as divine within the context of a just war. Joan of Arc (1412–31) aroused sufficient enthusiasm in Charles VII to be entrusted with a role in his armies but also sufficient scepticism for him to abandon her once events began to turn to her disfavour. Joan's enemies feared her to the extent that they burned her as a witch but she was later rehabilitated by the Church. Joan is of interest to military historians on two counts. First of all, for her campaigns. It seems that, acting on the advice of Jean d'Aulon, she not only exercised a moral influence on the French troops but also suggested a number of strategic initiatives, which were often contested, but which usually advocated a constant offensive to take advantage of the disarray and weariness of the enemy. After her martyrdom, she became the symbol of the defence of France and emphasized the importance of morale. The legend of Joan of Arc was partially eclipsed from the time of the French Wars of Religion until the eighteenth century. This was probably because she was too closely associated with the Valois kings. It was not until the writings of Voltaire and, more especially, of Michelet, who saw her as a child of the common people, and the national disaster of 1870 that France once again came to revere her memory. She was beatified in 1909 and canonized in 1920. *See also* CHAPLAINS; MORALE; ORLEANS.

A. CORVISIER
JOHN CHILDS

FURTHER READING
D. H. Farmer, *The Oxford Dictionary of Saints* (Oxford, 1978).

Saladin (1137–93) On the death of Shirkuh, the Kurdish commander of the troops of Nur-ad-Din, his nephew, Salah ad-Din Yusuf ibn Ayyub (Saladin), succeeded him. He made Egypt his main base for operations against the Crusaders although, after the death of Nur-ad-Din in 1174, he was also able to establish his authority over Syria. He proceeded to reorganize his army, which included Turkoman, Turkish and Kurdish cavalry (*askari*), an infantry militia (*adjnad al-halka*), and Bedouin auxiliaries and Mamluks under the direction of feudal emirs. From 1181 he fought battles against both minor Muslim emirs and Christian leaders, such as Renaud de Châtillon, Prince of Antioch. The Frankish army of Guy de Lusignan was badly beaten at Hattin, near Lake Tiberias (Sea of Galilee), on 4 July 1187. As a consequence, Saladin was able to take virtually all the ports on the Palestinian coast and recapture Jerusalem on 2 October. Only Acre escaped Muslim conquest although a later agreement returned some of the coastal strongholds to the Franks and gave them right of access to the sanctuaries of the Holy Land.

In the eyes of the Muslims, Saladin is the leader who not only won back their sacred territories and restored their military prestige but also contributed to the re-establishment of Muslim unity, continuing the work of Nur-ad-Din. However, his achievements did not endure. *See also* HATTIN; HOLY WAR; NUR-AD-DIN; RICHARD I.

R. MANTRAN

FURTHER READING
R. C. Smail, *Crusading Warfare, 1097–1193* (Cambridge, 1956); P. M. Holt, 'Saladin and his admirers', *Bulletin of the School of Oriental and African Studies*, xlvi (1983); H. A. R. Gibb, 'The armies of Saladin', *Cahiers d'histoire égyptienne*, series 3, fasc. 4 (1951), pp. 304–20.

Salamis, Battle of (480 BC) This was a naval battle in which the Greeks won a victory over the Persian fleet of King Xerxes during the second Persian invasion of Greece. Much was at stake in the battle, since the Persian army, having opened up the Greek defences at Thermopylae, had invaded Attica and taken Athens and the Greek armies had been compelled to fall back into the Peloponnese. The Persian fleet, though damaged by a violent storm and weakened by losses inflicted by the Greeks at the indecisive Battle of Artemision, continued its steady advance. The Greeks therefore had to stop the Persian naval forces if they were to avoid annihilation. The Greek fleet of about 300 ships lay at anchor in the narrow channel separating the island of Salamis from the mainland; the Persian fleet, which was rather larger, was anchored in the bay of Phaleron to the south of Athens, watching the entry to the channel and awaiting the emergence of the Greeks in order to engage in battle. For Xerxes, Salamis itself was an important military objective since the Athenian government was now based there. But his fleet was no longer strong enough to permit the detachment of a squadron to launch a simultaneous attack on the Peloponnese. According to tradition, Themistocles, who was commanding the Athenian contingent, tricked Xerxes into thinking that the Greeks were planning to flee, in order to provoke a battle in the narrows of the channel. Encumbered by the number of ships and the difficulty in manoeuvring in the narrow space, the Persian fleet was caught in a pincer movement as the Greek wings closed in; a further Greek squadron attacked the Persians in the flank and completed the rout. The ships which did escape destruction managed only with great difficulty to get out of the channel. At the same time a contingent of Greek hoplites landed at Psyttaleia, an island in the channel, and took control, preventing the shipwrecked Persians from taking refuge there. The Greek victory was due in large part to Themistocles' command of tactics and his exploitation of the narrow waters and the swell which strong south winds created in the channel. Salamis was hailed by the Greeks as one of the greatest victories in their history and the Athenians, who had played the main part, long regarded it as a glorious achievement. Xerxes abandoned the idea of pursuing a naval campaign and withdrew to Asia with what remained of his fleet. *See also* GREECE, ANCIENT; IRAN; MARATHON; PLATAEA; THERMOPYLAE.

R. LONIS
B. CAMPBELL

FURTHER READING
Y. Garland, *War in the Ancient World: a Social History* (London, 1975); C. Hignett, *Xerxes' Invasion of Greece* (Oxford, 1963), pp. 193–239; W. K. Pritchett, 'Salamis revisited', *Studies in Ancient Greek Topography Part I* (University of California Publications: Classical studies, Berkeley, 1965), i, 94–102; A. R. Burn, *Persia and the Greeks: the defence of the West, c. 546–478 BC* (London, 1984), pp. 423–75.

Saldern, Friedrich Christoph von, Lieutenant-General (1719–85) As an outstanding Prussian tactician who later turned to writing, von Saldern was of great importance in spreading Prussian tactical ideas through the armies of late eighteenth-century Europe. Having entered the army of Frederick William I (1713–40) as an ensign, at the age of sixteen, he first attracted royal attention on account of his great height. Subsequently, his distinguished service during the Seven Years' War (1756–63) secured rapid promotion to the rank of major-general. Frederick the Great considered his tactical ability to be without equal and, from 1763 until his death in 1785, he served as Inspector-General for the Magdeburg Infantry Inspection. His published thoughts on tactics – *Taktik der Infanterie* (1784) and *Taktische Grundsätz* (1786) – though in part criticized as impractical, were soon translated (into English in 1787). In Britain, his evolutions were copied directly by some regiments and his thoughts were influential in the formulation of the British tactical *Rules and Regulations* of 1792, the adoption of which was seen by many contemporaries as finally making complete the Prussianization of the British service. *See also* FREDERICK II; GERMANY; GREAT BRITAIN; INFANTRY; TACTICS.

G. A. STEPPLER

FURTHER READING
C. D. Kuster, *Characterzüge des Preussischen General-Lieutenants von Saldern* (Berlin, 1793); Curt von Priesdorff, *Saldern, der Exerziermeister des Grossen Königs* (Hamburg, 1943); *Biographie Universelle: ancienne et moderne* (Paris, c.1864), xxxvii.

Saragossa, Siege of, (20 December 1808–20 February 1809) After invading Spain in March 1808, the French had, in vain, laid siege to this important city, which was central to Spanish communications. However, the Spaniards had organized resistance (Baylen, 19 July) and aid had been received from Britain. On his arrival in Spain, Napoleon forced Sir John Moore's British army to retreat to Corunna before besieging Saragossa for a second time. After six weeks of repeated assaults, the French broke through the outer defences but they had to conquer the city house by house. For three weeks, the people put up desperate resistance despite famine, sickness and bombardment. The Siege of Saragossa has remained the symbol of popular armed resistance and of the horrors of a war fought beyond the observance of normal conventions. *See also* GUERILLA WARFARE; INDIRECT WARFARE; NAPOLEON; POPULAR WARFARE; RESISTANCE; SIEGES; SPAIN.

A. CORVISIER

FURTHER READING
David Gates, *The Spanish Ulcer* (London, 1986); Alphonse Grasset, *La Guerre d'Espagne* (2 vols, Paris, 1914–39).

Saratoga (Burgoyne's campaign) (June–October 1777) Lieutenant-General John Burgoyne's (1722–97) 'Expedition from Canada' into northern New York was a crucial turning point in the American Revolutionary War. His defeat led to the active intervention of France on the side of the American rebels thus transforming a colonial rebellion into a world-wide conflict. The problems experienced by Burgoyne during his campaign were characteristic of those encountered by eighteenth- and early nineteenth-century military operations conducted in the interior of the North American continent.

Burgoyne's intention was to march from Canada a distance of 200 miles to Albany, situated about 100 miles north of New York City on the Hudson River, to cut off New England from the other American colonies.

He then intended to subdue New England with or without assistance from the forces of Lieutenant-General Sir William Howe (1729–1814) stationed in New York City. Burgoyne's expedition consisted of a mixed force of 7,200 German and British regulars, a large artillery train of fifty-two pieces, and supporting detachments of American loyalists, Canadians and Indians. A smaller force advancing towards Albany along the Mohawk River was intended to provide further support. His regulars were well trained and had made efforts to adapt both their tactics and their dress to suit local conditions. Training and tactics, however, would not determine the outcome of the campaign, which, from its inception, was entirely dominated by logistics. Although small by European standards, Burgoyne's corps had to be sustained in a wilderness over distances of hundreds of miles. The immense logistical effort required to support an offensive meant that operations could only follow navigable water routes.

Burgoyne met with success early in July, capturing Fort Ticonderoga and defeating its retreating defenders, but thereafter his progress slowed dramatically coming to a standstill at Fort Edward where he was obliged to halt to accumulate supplies ready for the final push to Albany. His long and vulnerable supply line to Canada made this a tedious and time-consuming business and also diminished his fighting forces through the need to detach troops for its protection. While he delayed, his enemies recovered from their reverses and gathered to oppose him in strength. Imperceptibly, the balance shifted. In August, the Mohawk column was turned back and Burgoyne's supply difficulties led directly to his first defeat when a strong foraging detachment and its support were decisively beaten at Bennington. Finally, in September, with about 5,000 effectives, Burgoyne pushed on towards Albany but in two battles (19 September and 7 October) he was unable to dislodge an enemy corps of over 12,000 men which blocked his path at Stillwater on the Hudson, near Saratoga. In Burgoyne's rear, American troops had cut his communications with Canada; he was now encircled. An attempted relief from New York City failed and on 17 October Burgoyne surrendered.

Burgoyne anticipated, but badly underestimated, the problems he would face. Even simple communications between the various British commands in North America and with London proved extremely unreliable, important letters being delayed or failing to arrive. Initiative was required from the commanders in the field but they often lacked certain knowledge of each other's real circumstances and intentions. For Burgoyne, such problems might not necessarily have proved fatal had it not been for the grave miscalculations about the sentiments of the local people and the ability of the Americans to create a force, separate from Washington's field army, of sufficient size to stop and then overwhelm him. Howe, with the majority of his troops, had left New York in July to campaign against Philadelphia. In the recriminations which followed Burgoyne's defeat, Howe and Lord George Germain (1716–85), the secretary of state for the colonies, were much criticized for failing to ensure direct support for Burgoyne, but the truth would seem to be that even Burgoyne did not think that he really needed such help, until it was too late. When George Washington heard of Howe's departure from New York for the Chesapeake he could scarcely believe the news. Unlike his opponents, Washington immediately realized the scale of the predicament into which Burgoyne was entangling himself as he advanced, every step weakening his fighting power and inviting ultimate defeat. See also MONONGAHELA; UNITED STATES; WASHINGTON; YORKTOWN CAMPAIGN.

G. A. STEPPLER

FURTHER READING
George Athan Billias, 'John Burgoyne: ambitious general', in *George Washington's Opponents*, ed. G. A. Billias (New York, 1969), pp. 142–92; R. Arthur Bowler, *Logistics and the Failure of the British Army in America, 1775–1783* (Princeton, 1975); Richard J. Hargrove, *General John Burgoyne* (London, 1983); Piers G. Mackesy, *The War for America, 1775–1783* (London, 1964); M. M. Mintz, *The Generals of Saratoga* (New Haven, CT, 1990);

Hoffman Nickerson, *The Turning Point of the Revolution, or Burgoyne in America* (Boston and New York, 1928); William B. Willcox, 'Too many cooks: British planning before Saratoga', *Journal of British Studies*, ii (1962), pp. 56–90.

Saxe, Maurice, Count de (1696–1750) The natural son of Frederick Augustus of Saxony, later Augustus II, King of Poland, Saxe received his baptism of fire in 1709 at the age of twelve while serving with the Imperialists at Malplaquet. In 1719, after fighting with Prince Eugene's army at the Siege of Belgrade (1717), he joined the French army as the colonel of a German regiment, rising to *maréchal de camp* in 1720 and lieutenant-general in 1733. During the War of the Austrian Succession (1742–8), he achieved fame as the commander of the main French armies in the Low Countries, achieving victories at Fontenoy (1745), Rocoux (1746) and Lauffeld (1747). In 1747 he was granted the exceptional title of Marshal of France.

Although Maurice de Saxe was basically a practical soldier, he did not neglect academic study. In 1732 he wrote his *Rêveries ou Mémoires sur l'Art de la Guerre* and, shortly before his death, *L'Esprit des Lois de la Tactique*. Both were published posthumously. *Rêveries* was frequently reprinted, and was translated into English and German, but Saxe never became an established authority in France. From a wealth of experience acquired in a variety of operational theatres, Saxe thought it especially necessary to take account of different national temperaments and military qualities. The 'sublime' part of war, he said, had neither rules, principles nor certainty. He advocated a five-year period of obligatory military service, pressed for the development of artillery, and recommended operational armies of a size sufficiently limited to be commanded effectively by a single general. Officers needed to train their men in rapid manoeuvres. The commander had to observe the enemy, threaten him with feigned attacks and take advantage of his errors. Campaigns were to begin with a number of actions designed to weaken the adversary. Once a decisive result had been achieved, there was to be an unstinting pursuit. If Saxe revealed himself as a disciple of Montecucoli and Turenne, he nevertheless adapted to changes in the military art. He insisted on close co-operation between the different arms, urging the creation of mixed units and the development of light troops whose task was to reconnoitre, disorganize the enemy's dispositions and pursue. He expressed a preference for 'indirect warfare'. Saxe exerted an influence on Guibert and was much admired by Napoleon. *See also* BELGRADE; EUGENE OF SAVOY; FONTENOY; GUIBERT; INDIRECT WARFARE; NAPOLEON.

A. CORVISIER
G. A. STEPPLER

FURTHER READING
J. L. A. Colin, *Les Campagnes du Maréchal de Saxe* (3 vols, Paris, 1901–6); B. H. Liddell Hart, *Great Captains Unveiled* (London, 1927); Maurice de Saxe, 'My reveries upon the art of war', ed. and tr. Thomas R. Phillips, in *Roots of Strategy*, ed. Thomas R. Phillips (London, 1943), pp. 95–162; John Manchip White, *Marshal of France. The life and times of Maurice, Comte de Saxe, 1696–1750* (London, 1962); René G. E. (Saint René) Tallandier, *Maurice de Saxe: étude historique d'après les documents des Archives de Dresde* (Paris, 1865).

Scharnhorst, Gerhard von (1755–1813) As Director of the War Academy in Berlin, this Hanoverian in the Prussian service exercised a great influence over his disciples, amongst whom was Karl von Clausewitz. After the defeat of Prussia by Napoleon at Jena–Auerstädt (1806), in which campaign he had been chief of staff to the Duke of Brunswick, Scharnhorst was appointed to chair the Commission for Military Reform (July 1807). In order not to break the terms of the Treaty of Tilsit (1807) which had limited the Prussian army to 42,000 men, Scharnhorst and his colleagues, August von Gneisenau and Karl von Grolmann, introduced short periods of service for recruits to build up a trained reserve. In keeping with French revolutionary ideas, he sought to create a bond, under the overall protection of the monarchy,

(Mansell Collection)

between army and nation. To achieve this goal, he established a system of obligatory military service and a national militia (the *Landwehr*), supported by volunteer riflemen (the *Jäger*). In constant conflict with the ruling classes, particularly the Prussian nobility, which feared for its privileges, he strove to weed out the poorer commanders and professionalize the officer corps by facilitating access to non-nobles. The reformers founded a series of schools for officer candidates, culminating in the revitalized Superior War Academy (*Oberkriegscollegium*). Military administration was organized under a Ministry of War divided into two branches, one handling general matters and the other responsible for finance and supply. Scharnhorst also brought together a General Staff to define common doctrine thus permitting a decentralization of command. When Prussia returned to war with Napoleon in 1813, Scharnhorst served as chief of staff to Blücher. He was wounded at the Battle of Lützen and died from his injuries on 8 June 1813. For the armed forces of Germany, Scharnhorst remains the symbol of the first attempts at a proto-democratic modernization of the Prussian army. *See also* BLÜCHER; CLAUSEWITZ;

GENERAL STAFF; GERMANY; RECRUITMENT; TRAINING.

B. KROENER
JOHN CHILDS

FURTHER READING
W. O. Shanahan, *Prussian Military Reforms, 1786–1813* (New York, 1945); Peter Paret, *Yorck and the Era of Prussian Reform, 1807–1815* (Princeton, 1966).

Schlieffen, Alfred, Graf von (1833–1913) Following initial service in the Prussian army as a one-year volunteer in 1853, the majority of Schlieffen's subsequent career was spent in staff appointments although he did command the 1st Guard Uhlans from 1876 to 1884. Accordingly, his view of war was that of a theoretician and technician rather than a practitioner. He rejected Clausewitzian 'friction' for the belief that rigid adherence to operational objectives and timetables would maintain the initiative for the attacker. Schlieffen's neglect of the moral factor met with some criticism from within the German military establishment, notably from von Bernhardi and von der Goltz, but, as head of the historical section of the German General Staff from 1884 to 1891 and Chief of the General Staff from 1891 to 1906, Schlieffen was the dominant influence.

As Chief of Staff, he was the architect of the 'Schlieffen Plan' in response to the alliance of France and Russia, which threatened Germany with a war on two fronts. He drew on the example of Frederick the Great in choosing to strike a decisive pre-emptive blow at the most dangerous of Germany's likely enemies. In fact, the plan bequeathed to Schlieffen's successor, the younger Moltke, was no more than the culmination of a series of operational drafts, Schlieffen having overseen the preparation of forty-nine variants for action against Russia or France or both. Prior to his appointment, Russia had been regarded as the greater danger but, by 1894, Schlieffen's attention had turned to France. A keen student of military history, Schlieffen was greatly influenced by Delbrück's account of Hannibal's victory at Cannae. By 1897, what was later to be described by Liddell Hart as 'a giant revolving door' was taking shape. It envisaged a massive enveloping movement through neutral Belgium and the Netherlands to outflank French frontier fortifications, sweep west of Paris and push the French back against the Jura and the Swiss border. The younger Moltke greatly modified the plan before its implementation in 1914 in recognition of some of its manifold shortcomings: Schlieffen's failure to take probable enemy reactions into account, the fact that the troops required existed only on paper and the sheer logistical impossibilities which demanded enormous physical exertions from the infantrymen involved on the flanks of the great envelopment. In 1914, Moltke was unable to make even a diluted version of the plan work. He deleted the invasion of the Netherlands but he retained Schlieffen's insistence that political considerations must be subordinated to military necessity even though this risked British intervention through the violation of Belgian neutrality. Schlieffen's determination to wage preventative war created an enduring legacy in Germany although, ironically, his 'retirement', which was due to an alleged riding accident, was announced on 1 January 1906 after he had pushed too hard for such a war against France during the first Moroccan crisis. *See also* BERNHARDI; CANNAE; CLAUSEWITZ; DELBRÜCK; GERMANY; MARNE; PLANNING/ PLANS; STRATEGY.

IAN F. W. BECKETT

FURTHER READING
A. Bucholz, *Moltke, Schlieffen and Prussian War Planning* (Warwick, 1990); G. Ritter, *The Schlieffen Plan* (2nd edn, Westport, 1979); G. Ritter, *The Sword and the Sceptre* (London, 1972), ii; G. E. Rothenberg, 'Moltke, Schlieffen and the doctrine of strategic envelopment', in *Makers of Modern Strategy*, ed. Peter Paret (Oxford, 1986), pp. 296–325.

Schwendi, Lazarus, Freiherr von (*c.*1522–84) Lazarus von Schwendi was the leading German officer and military commentator of the mid-sixteenth century, though much of his contemporary reputation stemmed from his political activities. He was a member of the lesser nobility of Swabia, a social rank similar to that of Monluc or Roger Williams. In the 1540s he entered the service of Charles V and during the War of the Schmalkaldic League he was employed first as a diplomat and then as the commander of a regiment raised in Austria for the Mühlberg campaign of 1547. He was the Imperial commissioner at the Siege of Magdeburg in 1550–1 and he may have served in the Imperial army in Hungary between 1553 and 1560. In 1557 Schwendi raised and commanded the German cavalry employed by Philip II during the St Quentin campaign and later at Gravelines in 1558. After the Peace of Câteau-Cambrésis in 1559 his political role became more important. Although he remained a Catholic and a pensioner of Philip II, he was strongly Erasmian in sympathy and had grown increasingly hostile to Spanish influence within the Holy Roman Empire. He was thus a leading supporter of the German religious peace and encouraged the Austrian Habsburgs to follow a more German and independent policy, particularly towards the Dutch Revolt. In December 1564, Maximilian II appointed him Captain-General of the Imperial army in Hungary. During 1565 Schwendi was able to exploit the Ottoman absorption in the Siege of Malta to take the offensive against their Hungarian clients. In 1566–7 he conducted the successful defence of his conquests against the Ottoman counter-attack. After the Habsburg–Ottoman peace of 1568 Schwendi resigned his command and, at his own request, spent his remaining years in retirement.

This period, however, saw the production of his major military writings: the *Kriegsdiscurs* (written in 1570–1 but not published until 1593–4), his proposals for a militia (1577), and his advice on conducting war against the Turks. Schwendi's primary concern was the creation of a disciplined German national militia, based on an obligation of universal military service, which would provide an effective Imperial army for defence against the Ottomans or other foreign invaders. He also sought to prohibit mercenary service outside the Empire. Although political tension between the princes and the emperor prevented the adoption of Schwendi's scheme for an

Imperial army, versions of his militia proposals were taken up by a number of German princes. Moreover, the range of his acquaintances (which included William I of Orange, the Count of Egmont, and the Earl of Leicester, who sent his nephew, Philip Sidney, to visit him in 1574) gave his ideas a wider currency and made him one of the pioneers of the concept of a national army based on patriotic duty. *See also* DUDLEY, ROBERT; GRAVELINES; MALTA; MILITIAS; MONLUC; MÜHLBERG; OBLIGATIONS AND DUTIES; ST QUENTIN; WILLIAMS.

SIMON ADAMS

FURTHER READING
There is little on Schwendi in English. The main modern study is E. von Frauenholz, *Lazarus von Schwendi, der erste deutsche Verkünder de allgemein Wehrpflict* (Hamburg, 1939). Some discussion of his military theories can be found in G. Oestreich, *Neostoicism and the Early Modern State* (Cambridge, 1982).

Scipio Aemilianus (185/4–129 BC) Publius Cornelius Scipio Aemilianus was the son of L. Aemilius Paullus, but had been adopted by P. Scipio, the son of Scipio Africanus. As a military tribune he distinguished himself in the Third Punic War against Carthage, begun by Rome in 149 BC. This campaign had reached a stalemate because of the desperate resistance of the Carthaginians and the incapacity of the Roman generals. Although he was under the required age, Aemilianus was elected consul and given the task of ending the war. He took Carthage in 146 after a long, hard siege which ended in six days and nights of fighting within the city itself. Scipio returned to Rome to celebrate a splendid triumph. He was elected consul a second time for the year 134, although this was contrary to the law, and entrusted with the mission of ending the wars against the Spanish city of Numantia, which had been successfully leading Celtiberian resistance to Rome and had often repulsed sieges. This time Scipio starved the town by surrounding it with a continuous contravallation; after heroic resistance the last defenders had to surrender and the city was totally destroyed in 133. Scipio was

granted a second triumph and assumed the name 'Numantinus'. A sound general and efficient organizer who could be ruthless towards his enemies, Scipio was also a cultured man; he was at the centre of a circle of friends who enjoyed literature and philosophy, and he befriended Polybius. He was closely involved in the political struggles in Rome against the reforming tribune of the people, Tiberius Gracchus, and when Scipio died suddenly in 129, there were stories, probably false, that he had been murdered. His career was also significant in that he exploited the popularity gained by his military success to hold political office in defiance of the usual legal conventions. *See also* CARTHAGE; POLYBIUS; ROME; SCIPIO AFRICANUS; SIEGES.

JOËL LE GALL
B. CAMPBELL

FURTHER READING
A. E. Astin, *Scipio Aemilianus* (Oxford, 1967).

Scipio Africanus (236–184/3 BC) Publius Cornelius Scipio, nicknamed 'Africanus the Elder', was the outstanding general of the Second Punic War. When barely twenty-four years of age, he had put himself forward as commander of the Roman armies who were fighting the Carthaginians in Spain where his father and uncle had just been defeated and killed. Shortly after his arrival he captured Carthago Nova (modern-day Cartagena), his opponents' main base. Then in 208 he defeated Hasdrubal Barca at Baecula by using his light-armed troops as a defensive screen while the legionaries attacked on both flanks. These innovatory tactics exploited the flexibility of the manipular organization of the legions. Scipio could not prevent Hasdrubal leaving Spain to rejoin his brother Hannibal in Italy but in 206 he defeated Hasdrubal Gisgo and the remaining Carthaginian forces at the Battle of Ilipa, again by employing a complicated outflanking manoeuvre. This battle secured Roman control of Spain. He was appointed consul in 205 although contrary to convention for he had not yet been praetor. By calling for volunteers he increased his army to about 30,000 and carried the war into Africa where he landed in the spring of 204 in the neighbourhood of Utica and won some success. This forced the Carthaginians to recall Hannibal from Italy but Scipio won a decisive victory over him at Zama in 202. Scipio celebrated a magnificent triumph and the name 'Africanus' was conferred upon him. Later Scipio was attached as legate to his brother Lucius Cornelius Scipio when the latter was sent to fight against the Seleucid king Antiochus III the Great, but little is known of the role he played in that campaign, which culminated in the victory of Magnesia in 189. Scipio was an outstanding general whose well-conceived tactics, based on the manoeuvrability of the legions and surprise outflanking attacks, made the army a more effective instrument and contributed to Rome's advance to eventual supremacy in the Mediterranean world. He was also an inspirational leader who commanded the respect of his troops and who was adept at winning by diplomacy the goodwill of the leaders and populations who had initially supported the enemies of Rome. *See also* CARTHAGE; HANNIBAL; ROME; SCIPIO AEMILIANUS; ZAMA.

JOËL LE GALL
B. CAMPBELL

FURTHER READING
H. H. Scullard, *Scipio Africanus: soldier and statesman* (London, 1970).

Seamen *See* NAVAL PERSONNEL

Sebastopol, Siege of (1854–5) Sebastopol, the site of Russia's main naval base in the Black Sea, became the focus of operations in the Crimean War. Although called a siege, the British and French investment of the city was mounted from the south and was never complete. In reality the Russian defences were the base of operations for their field army, and the type of attritional trench warfare which followed was more characteristic of the First World War than of eighteenth-century setpiece attacks according to the principles of Vauban. By 25 September 1854, 67,000 British, French and Turkish troops had assembled south of the city, following the Battle of Alma. Only small Russian land forces (7,000 men) and the Russian fleet defended the city, while a Russian field army conducted limited offensive operations (the Battles of Balaclava and Inkerman) against the allies. Between 17 October 1854 and 5 September 1855 the allies mounted six so-called bombardments: for the last they had over 800 guns in battery. The Russian defences were progressively strengthened and deepened, not least through the efforts of Todleben. On 8 September 1855, the allies finally captured the Malakoff, the centre of the southern defences, and the Russians fell back to the northern side. Total Russian losses have been put at 102,000 men, to 71,000 allied. *See also* FORTIFICATION, FIELD; PLEVNA; SIEGES; TODLEBEN.

HEW STRACHAN

FURTHER READING
E. B. Hamley, *The Story of the Campaign of Sebastopol* (Edinburgh, 1855); H. D. Jones, *Journal of the Operations Conducted by the Corps of Royal Engineers* (London, 1859); A. W. Kinglake, *The Invasion of the Crimea* (Edinburgh, 1863–87).

Secrecy The notion of secrecy is not exclusive to military activity. It is also found in politics, business and particularly in diplomacy. It is a desire to surprise potential enemies which prompts a country to maintain secrets. Conversely, if that country is not itself to be caught unawares, it must also seek out all possible information about potential opponents. Thus secrecy becomes a defence against espionage; secrecy and information-gathering form an indivisible whole. It is in the interests of each country to preserve secrecy regarding its intentions and preparations and to pierce the shield of secrecy surrounding the intentions and preparations of a real or possible opponent.

Secrecy is of particular importance in the communication of orders, instructions or information. It became apparent at a very early stage that, since spoken words leave no trace, it was preferable to use oral communication, so long as there were no witnesses, and this explains the use of secret rendezvous. Often the transmission of

731

information was carried out by employing an agreed code of gestures to indicate which of a set of pre-arranged options was to be chosen or by agreed signs which did not even require a meeting to take place. Both of these were effective so long as the codes were not leaked to the enemy. Examples of this type can be found in the Old Testament and in Classical times. The transmission of a complex order does, however, require guarantees of authenticity and some degree of detail. It is thus often necessary to leave a material record of such a message which has to be made unintelligible to any third party. Since Classical times, men have employed the subterfuge of displacing the letters of the alphabet within a message. In Ancient Greece, rudimentary machines were employed to simplify the encoding and decoding of such messages. The Spartans used a machine called a *scytale*. This consisted of a wooden roller (or staff) around which was wound a thin strip of parchment. The parchment was wound obliquely and the message was written across the edges of the strip. The letters and signs were thus broken and could only be reconstituted by winding the strip around an identical staff. Julius Caesar also used a displaced alphabet, while Aeneas Tacticus sent messages by means of a disc etched with 24 notches which corresponded to numbers. These were joined together by a thread. The receiver unravelled this thread and wrote down the numbers uncovered, which corresponded to letters in a pre-arranged code. Pliny the Elder alludes to the use of secret ink bearing the name 'sympathetic'.

Though generally neglected in the Middle Ages, the use of ciphers or cryptography was re-adopted in Renaissance Italy. Generals and diplomats used dictionaries containing around 600 words or expressions which were conveyed by groups of figures. Most of these procedures fall into two categories: transposition or substitution. The elements serving as a base are known as the 'keying elements'. The message is then encoded using a grid. The Italian Girolamo Cardan devised the 're-volving grid', which can only be used if one knows the letter – or later the word – which serves as a key. The system was perfected by Blaise de Vignère who, in the sixteenth century, developed a square which offered the possibility of choosing between twenty-six alphabets, each offset in relation to the others.

After its encouragement by Richelieu, cryptography reached a high level during Louis XIV's reign. Rossignol made a great reputation for himself at the Siege of La Rochelle by decoding the cipher used by the besieged forces and then by developing what was to become the 'Great Code of Louis XIV', which was in reality a whole set of codes in which each word was replaced by a group of three figures with keys that varied according to circumstances and were changed when the code was deciphered. Louis XIV's secret services even used codes which they knew to have been 'cracked' to give out false information. Forms of address were not put into code since the ease with which these could be deciphered enabled the enemy to break the cipher. It is known that during the Second World War a German code was cracked because an officer had been so unwise as to encode the formula 'Heil Hitler'. The last elements of Louis XIV's code were only deciphered in 1907 by Major Bazeries. Cryptography played a major role up to the French Revolution, but Napoleon made little use of it, preferring the surprise created by rapidity of operations to time-consuming secrecy. The German General Staff adopted the same attitude in the hours preceding the attack on France of 10 May 1940.

During the nineteenth century, however, secrecy once again assumed great importance. It is well known how, through an indiscretion by the French newspaper *Le Temps*, Moltke was informed in 1870 of the route of march of MacMahon's army. Technical advances gave the use of secret communications a new lease of life. Documents were classified according to a scale of confidentiality: 'Top secret', 'Defence secret', etc. The composition of invisible inks also improved, making them easier to use, more dependable and irreversible. In the twentieth century, photographic techniques have also become available: latent images (two photographs superimposed, the one entirely run-of-the-mill, the other to be developed according to secret processes), microdots, and holography by the use of lasers, though this is very expensive. Cryptography also progressed, adopting more sophisticated codes, the addition of 'superencipherment' and new encoding machines or 'converters'.

In 1867, Wheatstone developed a converter consisting of two concentric discs. One contained the letters of the alphabet in their normal order, the other in a random order. Movement from the one to the other was by means of hands similar to those of a watch. In 1891, Major Bazeries invented a more sophisticated apparatus made up of twenty discs, with the letters of the alphabet in random order, threaded on to a cylinder. The message was composed using the various discs in a pre-set order. Skilful codebreakers did, however, manage to decipher messages compiled on machines of this type.

During the First World War, by listening in to German radio posts and breaking their codes, the Allies were able to read their order of battle and movements and to intercept important messages, such as the one from Moltke giving the order to his troops to march on Paris. The German code was again deciphered during the Marne offensive of May–June 1918 by Georges Painvin. Intelligence was thus gained regarding where the offensive was to be launched and troops were accordingly transferred from other sectors to reinforce the threatened zone.

From 1920 onwards, the Germans, Swedes and Americans created converters which made it possible to automate what had previously been the manual work of encoding. Shortly before 1939, the French army adopted the Swedish *Hagelin C 36* machine which printed groups of five letters and had an infinite range of combinations that made the decipherment of messages practically impossible. The similar German ENIGMA machine, developed from a commercial design, proved fallible during the Second World War being penetrated by the British (the 'ULTRA' source).

More recently, developments in computing have enabled a significant revival in coding. IBM has perfected a method of encoding computer data, the *Data Encryption System* (DES), which is difficult to crack. There are others: the 'public key system' based on 'non-reversible' functions, the 'products of two prime numbers system' and the 'rucksack system' (filled with stones satisfying certain inequalities). However, up to the time of writing there is no code that cannot be broken.

Perhaps the nearest to an unbreakable code is also one of the simplest, 'the one-time pad'. A letter or number code is used once only for one message – the sender and receiver then tear off their code sheet from the pad and destroy it. The next code on the pad is entirely different and will be employed for the next communication. Progress in decipherment has followed the advances made in encoding. 'Code-breaking' computers have been developed and a number of (mainly American) mathematicians (Stanford, Hifield, etc.) have acquired considerable reputations in the field.

Secrecy has sometimes been condemned on moral grounds. Thus in 1929, the American Secretary of State Stimson abolished (for a very short period) his country's deciphering bureau. It does, however, seem impossible to go against what is generally regarded as a political necessity.

The rise of liberal democracies in the Western world in the nineteenth and twentieth centuries has been an obstacle to the pursuit of military secrecy, especially in wartime. During the First World War, governments responded by bombarding their populations with inaccurate propaganda instead of news, a trend which continued during the Second World War. Official war correspondents were heavily controlled and their reports censored. However, with the arrival of television, video and satellite broadcasting it has become more difficult for governments to deny their populations access to up-to-date and reasonably reliable news about developments in war. Despite the efforts of the US government, live television reporting from the battlefields of Vietnam was a prime reason for the growth of anti-war sentiment in the United States. The efforts at censorship and propaganda of the British ministry of defence during the Falklands War (1982) were anachronistic and pedestrian compared with the reports and film footage from war correspondents with the British task force. In the Gulf War of 1991 between the UN forces and Iraq, almost perpetual news broadcasting from the theatre of war was almost certainly at variance with the desire of the United States, British and Saudi governments to maintain operational secrecy. The development of high-definition photography from satellites and high-flying aircraft since 1960, along with sophisticated electronic intelligence gathering, has also rendered the preservation of secrecy more difficult. *See also* AENEAS TACTICUS; COMMAND; INTELLIGENCE; SIGNAL COMMUNICATION.

J. ALLEMAND
JOHN CHILDS

FURTHER READING
Christopher Andrew, *Secret Service: the making of the British intelligence community* (London, 1985); Peter Calvocoressi, *Top Secret Ultra* (London, 1980); Ronald Lewin, *Ultra goes to War* (London, 1978); David Kahn, *The Codebreakers* (London, 1967); G. Mattingly, *Renaissance Diplomacy* (Boston, 1955); *Codebreaking and Signals Intelligence*, ed. Christopher Andrew (London, 1986).

Sedan, Battle of (2 September 1870) Marshal Patrice MacMahon's army of 120,000 men left Châlons-sur-Marne to help Marshal François Bazaine break out through the German blockade around Metz. However, since the press had divulged the manoeuvre, the choice of the northern route suggested to Moltke the idea of cutting off MacMahon's rear and then blocking a possible path of retreat towards the north. Consequently, the French, with a force of 200,000 Germans ranged against them, were encircled in a loop of the Meuse at Sedan, a position dominated by German artillery dug in on the surrounding heights. The French twice had to change commanders, as MacMahon had been wounded, and the presence of the Emperor Napoleon III proved a further distraction. In these conditions, the French army was unable to break out and Napoleon surrendered with 83,000 men. The French also lost 17,000 dead and wounded, while the German casualties amounted to 9,000 men. This battle, which removed a complete French army from the conflict, contributed greatly to the German victory in the Franco-Prussian War. It also led to serious efforts to reform the French army after 1871 by adopting German methods of mass conscription. Sedan has remained a symbol of unpreparedness and incompetence. *See also* FRANCE; GERMANY; METZ (1870); MOLTKE; NUMERICAL STRENGTH; RECRUITMENT.

A. CORVISIER

FURTHER READING
Michael Howard, *The Franco-Prussian War* (London, 1960); François Roth, *La Guerre de 70* (Paris, 1990); *Moltke's Military Correspondence, 1870–1871*, ed. Spenser Wilkinson (Oxford, 1923, repr. Aldershot, 1991).

Seignelay, Jean-Baptiste Colbert, Marquis de (1651–90) The son of Colbert, Seignelay received an almost princely education which was both theoretical and practical (voyages to Genoa, Venice, the Dutch Republic and England) and highly apposite to a future secretary of state for the French navy. Succeeding his father in this office in 1683, Seignelay fully deployed the naval instrument which had been created. Between 1683 and 1688, the French navy dominated the Mediterranean. In the early years of the Nine Years' War (1688–97), the French navy reached its zenith defeating the Anglo-Dutch fleet off Beachy Head in 1690. Overworked and worn out, Seignelay died a few weeks after the battle. His demise heralded a period of strategic uncertainty in French naval affairs.

Seignelay's administration of the navy was markedly different to that of his illustrious father. He was not concerned with the development of the institutions and infrastructure necessary to create mercantile and military sea power but merely with the political and martial prestige which it could enhance. Like his successors, Seignelay was a user of French fleets rather than a creative administrator. He master-minded the bombardment of Genoa in 1684 and was in favour of the decision to invade Germany in 1688. *See also* BEACHY HEAD; COLBERT; FRANCE; LA HOGUE AND BARFLEUR; NAVAL WARFARE; NAVIES.

J. MEYER
JOHN CHILDS

FURTHER READING
Geoffrey Symcox, *The Crisis of French Sea Power, 1688–1697* (The Hague, 1974).

Seré de Rivières, Raymond-Adolphe (1815–95) *See* FORTIFICATION

Service periodical publications Service periodical publications appear at regular intervals and are specifically intended for members of the armed forces and civilians with either an amateur or a professional interest in military affairs (academics, civil servants, etc.). Periodicals dealing with service issues have often been produced by commercial publishers with the agreement of and subventions from government ministries.

The series of newsbooks and newspapers from the English Civil Wars and Interregnum (1642–60) might be considered forerunners of service periodical publications although they were devoted to news and propaganda rather than debate about military issues and an investigation of military history. Almanacs of state affairs during the seventeenth century often contained military information. Edward Chamberlayne's series of compendia, *Angliae Notitia, or the Present State of England* (1671, 1679, 1684), listed regiments, garrisons and military office holders. The *Gentleman's Magazine* (1731–1907) carried much military information although it was directed at a wider audience. However, Marc Martin has shown that the authentic service periodical publication originated in France. 'Army lists', in the form of annuals or directories, were produced in several European countries in the middle of the eighteenth century. The earliest seems to have been Lemau de la Jaisse's *Carte gén-*

érale du militaire de France (1733), followed by the *English Army List* in 1740 and the *État militaire de la France* of Roussel (1758–89). These provided lists of commissioned officers and described the composition of units. However, the first service journal seems to have been the *Encyclopédie Militaire*, which ran from January 1770 to November 1771. It was a well-informed publication, written in a severe and didactic style, designed for military practitioners rather than theorists. Its aim was to awaken French officers to a realization of the military effort required to erase the memories of the reverses suffered during the Seven Years' War (1756–63). The *Encyclopédie Militaire* was an initiative of Choiseul and did not long survive his fall; 45 per cent of army regiments subscribed. Similarly, it was Vergennes who instigated the production of the *Journal militaire et politique*.

Germany also witnessed a flowering of the service periodical during the Enlightenment. Georg Dietrich von Gröben initiated the *Kriegsbibliothek* in 1755 which was published in twenty-three issues until 1784. During the decade of the 1780s, a number of periodicals appeared in Germany: the *Kriegserisches Wochenblatt* (Berlin, 1778), *Der Soldat* (Hamburg, 1779–80), and the *Militärische Taschenbuch* (Leipzig, 1780). The future reformer of the Prussian army, Gerhard von Scharnhorst, produced a number of influential military journals which enjoyed wide circulation among hundreds of army officers within German-speaking lands: *Militär Bibliothek* (1782–4), *Bibliothek für Offiziere* (1785) and *Neues Militärisches Journal* (1788–93 and 1797–1805). Most of this extensive military literature was mainly concerned with discussion of the great doctrinal issues emanating from France.

The majority of service journals in the eighteenth century were short-lived. They frequently changed their names or took the title of a publication which had died even though there was no connection between them. Among the journals bearing the title *Journal militaire* there was one which was produced by the monks of the Order of

735

Charity; it was supported by the government and stressed moral and historical rather than professional aspects. Alongside these appeared more specialized journals, like the *Journal de Marine* (started in 1766), or the very official *Journal de médecine militaire* (1782–9), which was circulated free to 600 medical officers.

During the French Revolutionary period, service periodicals enjoyed an efflorescence. Where journals had been, at most, monthlies, they now became weeklies, or even dailies, although with fewer pages. Alongside official publications like the *Mémorial des corps administratifs, municipaux, judiciaires et militaires* (1790), or those which drew their inspiration from particular individuals, such as *La Cocarde militaire*, with which Lafayette was closely connected, there appeared from the outbreak of war a second generation, which had its heyday in 1793, and which was composed of numerous short-lived army journals with such varied titles as *L'Argus de l'armée du Nord* (of Girondin persuasion), the *Journal de l'armée des Pyrénées orientales* (Jacobin), etc. These contained orders and communiqués issued by military commanders and revolutionary and patriotic propaganda in the form of exhortations and addresses to soldiers. Carnot's journal, *La Soirée du camp*, whose first number appeared on the eve of 9th Thermidor, represented a new departure in that it was intended for professional soldiers rather than citizen-conscripts. Under the Directory, Carnot still publicized his views through the *Journal des Défenseurs de la Patrie*, while the army journals became the mouthpieces of generals, among them Bonaparte, who arranged for the appearance of M. A. Jullien's *Le Courrier de l'armée d'Italie* and Regnault de Saint-Jean-d'Angely's *La France vue de l'armée d'Italie* and, later, of *Le Courrier de l'Égypte*, all of which were aimed at promoting his policies.

B. C. Gournay's *Journal militaire*, which, to some extent, continued the traditions of the *Journal militaire* of the *ancien régime*, deserves a special mention on account of its longevity. Taking from the outset a cautious attitude towards the Revolution, it mainly printed official announcements and contained little news, a policy which ensured its survival. After receiving financial assistance from the Convention, it achieved a national circulation. From 1796, under the section entitled 'Miscellania', it published the proclamations of the Directory. In 1798, monetary difficulties forced it into Bonaparte's hands, who reconstituted it into an official organ. In 1842 it became the *Journal militaire officiel* and although it was controlled by and in receipt of financial help from the Ministry of War, it remained in private hands. In 1886, the Ministry started the *Bulletin officiel du ministère de la guerre*, which became the *Bulletin officiel des armées* in 1965. It is circulated free to the various authorities and departments concerned with military administration, its contents being entirely confined to the official texts of legislation. The *Journal militaire*, however, continued in existence for some time though the epithet 'officiel' was dropped from its title. The current journal, like its now extinct predecessor, is divided into a section dealing with regulations, intended for service files, and a supplement containing lists of promotions, appointments, etc.

Alongside these official publications may be listed other periodicals of a more technical character. Among them were the *Journal des Sciences militaires*, started by Correard in 1825, which became the *Revue militaire française* in 1886 and, after frequent interruptions, finally closed in 1936; *Le Spectateur militaire, recueil de science, d'art et d'histoire militaire* (1826–1914); the *Revue de la Défense nationale*, which was founded in 1939, ceased publication from 1940 to 1945, but now continues to provide its readers with information on major national questions of a military, economic, politico-military and economic-scientific nature; and also *Stratégie*, which has been appearing since 1964. *La Revue maritime* was founded in 1847, though it had started life in 1817 as the *Annales maritimes et coloniales* but dropped the latter subject when the Ministry for Colonies was established in 1896. *Forces aériennes françaises* began its career as *Revue de l'Armée de l'air* in 1929. Finally, the *Revue des Troupes coloniales*, first published in 1902, became the *Tropiques, Revue des Troupes coloniales* in 1947.

The years around 1887 saw the appearance of various military reviews, partly instigated by General Boulanger – *Revue d'Infanterie, Revue de Cavalerie, Revue du Génie militaire*, and *Revue de l'Intendance militaire* – which, in general, ceased publication after 1920. The *Mémorial de l'artillerie française*, which began life in 1824, is still published today. The *Revue du Corps de santé* and the *Revue de l'Aumônerie militaire* are still in existence.

Numerous bulletins have been published by ex-servicemen's associations which act as yearbooks recording the past and present exploits of the unit. Some are concerned with a military academy, like *Le Casoar de la Saint-Cyrienne*, the *Revue prytanéenne* or the *Bulletin de la Réunion des officiers ORSEM* (staff officers of the reserve). Others deal with specific corps or units – *Le Cor de chasse*, or *Normandie en avant*, published by the veterans of the 9th infantry regiment.

English service journals have followed a similar pattern of development to their French counterparts. The French Revolutionary and Napoleonic Wars stimulated professional military periodicals – the *Soldier's Pocket Magazine* (1798), the *British Military Library* (1798–1801), the *Military Panorama or the Officer's Companion* (1812–14), and the *Royal Military Calendar*. Most of these publications died after 1815, except for the *Military Register* (1814–22), but in 1827 one of the most significant and influential British journals was founded, the *Naval and Military Magazine*. From 1829 to 1843 it was known as the *United Service Journal*, then as *Colburn's United Service Magazine* (1943–90) then again as the *United Service Magazine* from 1890 to 1920. In the latter year it was incorporated into the *Army Quarterly*, which became the *Army Quarterly and Defence Journal* in 1970. By the twentieth century, this publication had ceased to be the vehicle for crusading army reformers and had lapsed into non-academic military history. The torch of military debate and pioneering ideas was taken up by the *Journal of the Royal United Service Institution*, founded in

1857 and now published quarterly. Another journal close to army reform was the *Broad Arrow* (1868–1917), which had absorbed the *Naval and Military Gazette* (1833–86) in 1886 and merged with the *Army and Navy Gazette* (1860–1921) in 1917.

British military history has been well served during the twentieth century. The *Army Quarterly* has played an important role but the principal publication has been the *Journal of the Society for Army Historical Research* (1921–). The Naval Records Society has produced many volumes of printed manuscript sources relating to the Royal Navy, and the foundation of the Army Records Society in 1984 promises a similar service for the army. The expansion of British universities in the 1960s resulted in some (very limited) interest in military history amongst professional, academic historians. As a result some military history can be found in the pages of the major academic historical journals – the *English Historical Review*, the *American Historical Review*, *History*, the *Cambridge Historical Journal* (the *Historical Journal* after 1957), the *Journal of Modern History*, the *Bulletin of the Institute of Historical Research* (*Historical Research* after 1989) and *History Today*. The National Army Museum has produced a yearbook since 1984, *Army Museum*. On a wider plane, the *Revue internationale d'Histoire militaire* was launched in 1939 as the journal of the international working party on comparative military history, an affiliate of the International Committee for Historical Research. The same body is also involved in the preparation of the *Bibliographie internationale d'Histoire militaire* which was started in Switzerland in 1978. Commercial publishers have contributed to service periodicals, particularly *Brasseys Defence Yearbook* and the annual series devoted to military equipment by MacDonald-Janes. Mention should also be made of the *Military Balance*, a yearbook listing the known strengths of the world's armed forces produced by the Stockholm International Peace Research Institute.

In 1878 General William T. Sherman gave his blessing to the establishment of the Military Service Institution of the United

States, modelled on the Royal United Service Institution in London, to promote writing and debate on military science and history. The *Journal of the Military Service Institution of the United States* was inaugurated in the same year. In 1879, the *United Service Journal* began publication, supplemented by the *Cavalry Journal* in 1888 and the *Journal of the United States Artillery* in 1892.

The public press has also contributed to the dissemination of military ideas and debate. The London *Daily Telegraph* was an important instrument in the campaign to reform the British army during the 1920s and 1930s, especially when B. H. Liddell Hart served as defence correspondent. *See also* LIDDELL HART; TRAINING.

A. CORVISIER
JOHN CHILDS

FURTHER READING
Union List of Foreign Military Periodicals, eds P. H. Spence and H. J. Hopewell (Maxwell, Al., 1957); *British Union Catalogue of Periodicals*, ed. J. D. Stewart (4 vols, London, 1955–8) – *Supplements* (London, 1962–); Marc Martin, *Les Origines de la presse militaire en France à la fin de l'Ancien Régime et sous la Révolution (1770–1799)* (Vincennes, 1975).

Services, armed forces However rudimentary the organization of an army, it soon discovers the need to estimate the foodstuffs and war supplies that it will require and to make arrangements for them to be provided. In the armies of the city-states and the Middle Ages the men who were summoned to arms had to bring their own food to last several days after which time their maintenance became the responsibility of the sovereign. They also had to furnish their own weapons and accoutrements. It was a different matter if the state hired mercenaries. They had to be supplied by the sovereign unless they had been engaged through the services of a *condottiere* who supplied fighting forces on contract and therefore undertook their maintenance himself. The maxim that 'war provides for itself' eliminated the need to make detailed arrangements for the provision of foodstuffs. Pillage, and later the system of contribution and requisition, was sufficient.

The provision of weapons could not be dealt with in the same way. As weaponry became more complex, costly and standardized, the responsibility for its supply passed to rulers, or *condottieri*. Examples of weapons stores, presumably belonging to the state, can be found in Egyptian and Assyrian bas-reliefs from as early as the second millennium BC. Actual examples have been excavated in Crete. The assumption of the central supply of weapons automatically created the need for a service organization to deal with their storage, maintenance and issue. Navies were greatly ahead of land forces as they had to prepare in advance all the requirements of a fleet. The complex naval dockyards at Carthage in the third century BC were an outstanding example of a naval service organization, a model copied by the Venetian arsenal in the early modern period. However, land campaigns in which long distances had to be covered imposed similar demands. In the fourteenth century, the Turks arranged convoys for taking food to the frontiers of their empire. In Western Europe, this type of forward planning came to maturity in the fifteenth century, especially in the case of England, and by the beginning of the sixteenth century it had become one of the long-term considerations of strategists and statesmen. The Spanish army in the Netherlands had the most highly developed supply service.

Frederick the Great wrote that 'the art of winning wars is hamstrung if unaccompanied by the art of organizing subsistence.' In relation to armies, this maxim soon became too restricted as the competence of services was extended to cover everything that gave an army the capacity to fight. There also appeared a necessary distinction between general services – those executed or directed by the general staff, including inspections – and the specialized services, to which the epithet 'subordinate' was appended in the nineteenth century, dealing with administration, food supplies, recruiting, military medicine, remounts, veterinary works, legal affairs, baggage trains, transport, telegraphy and signals, ammunition, engineering, construction, arsenals, etc. These subordinate services all required specialist personnel and were progressively given a military style of organization.

Each of these services usually consisted of a headquarters with offshoots which operated as independent detachments or as units attached to major fighting formations. The British army developed a system of central corps – transport, medical, ordnance, signals, artillery and engineers – which sent units to serve the main fighting branches in the field. Since 1939, particularly in the US army, the service element has grown to an enormous size and now constitutes 90 per cent of a modern army. *See also* ADMINISTRATION, ARMY; ADMINISTRATION, NAVAL; ARSENALS; ARTILLERY; DEPREDATIONS; DOCKYARDS; INTENDANTS; MEDICAL SERVICES; NAVAL STORES; ORDNANCE; RATIONS; SIGNAL COMMUNICATION; TRANSPORT; WEAPONS.

A. CORVISIER
JOHN CHILDS

FURTHER READING
C. C. King, *The British Army and Auxiliary Forces* (2 vols, London, 1892–7).

Seymour, Edward, Duke of Somerset (1506–51) Although Somerset owed his rise to the peerage to his sister Jane's marriage to Henry VIII, he established himself during the years 1542–6 as the most successful and innovative of English commanders. His initial military experience was gained in the invasions of France of the 1520s, but it is not known whether he made a serious study of warfare. His first major appointments came in the border campaigns against Scotland in 1542 and 1543. In May 1544 he commanded the amphibious attack on Edinburgh, the most technically competent of all the Henrician military expeditions. In 1545 and 1546 he served at Boulogne and on the Borders. However, it was after he became Lord Protector to Edward VI in 1547 that the most important (and controversial) phase of his military career began. Determined to continue Henry's policy of imposing the marriage of Edward VI to Mary, Queen of Scots by force, he invaded Scotland in the summer of 1547 and won the Battle of Pinkie. His victory then encouraged him to implement a strategy that he had first formulated in the later years of Henry VIII's reign. Political success in Scotland was to be obtained by the planting of garrisons, supplied by sea, which would win over the population without the expense of maintaining a field army there. Over the winter of 1547–8 ten garrisons were established either on the Borders or along the Forth and Tay estuaries, with a central fortress at Haddington (East Lothian). These were Italianate bastioned artillery fortifications, generally earthworks but in some instances incorporating existing Scottish castles. However, Somerset's strategy was a gamble on Scottish inexperience in conducting sieges; once French military assistance was sent to Scotland (first in 1548 and then more substantially in 1549) its weakness was exposed. Naval supply of the estuarial garrisons proved difficult and after Haddington was invested in 1548 a relief army was necessary. However, the troops assembled for this force were diverted to the repression of the major popular uprisings in England in 1549, in the course of which Somerset himself was overthrown. Haddington was evacuated in September 1549, and the remaining garrisons were surrendered in 1551 following the Treaty of Boulogne. Despite its failure, this offensive use of the new fortifications showed both strategic imagination and tactical flair and justifies considering Somerset a pioneer of the military revolution in England. *See also* BOULOGNE; CITADELS; DUDLEY, JOHN; GARRISONS; GREAT BRITAIN; PINKIE.

SIMON ADAMS

FURTHER READING
M. Merriman, 'The fortresses in Scotland, 1547–1550', in *The History of the King's Works*, ed. H. M. Colvin (London, 1982), iv, 694–726; M. L. Bush, *The Government Policy of Protector Somerset* (London, 1969); W. K. Jordan,

Edward VI: the young king (London, 1968). A contemporary account of the 1544 expedition, *The Late expedition in Scotland*, is reprinted in *Tudor Tracts*, ed. A. F. Pollard (London, 1903).

Shaposhnikov, Boris Mikhailovich (1882–1945)   Shaposhnikov was born at Zlatoust. He joined the Tsarist army in 1901 and graduated from the Moscow Military School in 1903. After serving in the infantry, he attended the General Staff Academy from 1907 to 1910. During the First World War, Shaposhnikov served on the Caucasian front as a staff officer, reaching the rank of colonel by 1917. Shaposhnikov was sympathetic to the revolution, and joined the Red Army as a volunteer in May 1918. During the Civil War, he was an important figure in drawing up operational plans for the Red Army and was particularly involved in the campaign against Poland in 1920. He was Deputy Chief of Staff of the Red Army in 1921–5 and, successively, commander of the Leningrad (1925–7) and Moscow (1927–8) Military Districts. In 1928, Shaposhnikov became Chief of the Staff of the Red Army, a position he held until 1931. In 1930 he joined the Communist Party. Briefly demoted due to his acknowledgement of Trotsky's important role in the Civil War, Shaposhnikov became the head of the Frunze Military Academy in 1932, a position he held until 1935. From 1935 to 1937 he served as commander of the Leningrad Military District and was appointed Chief of the General Staff in May of the latter year. Shaposhnikov was responsible for the planning of the attack on Poland in 1939. In 1940 he became a marshal of the Soviet Union. He advocated a policy of defence in depth along the Soviet border with Nazi Germany, but his ideas were not acted upon. Due to ill-health, Shaposhnikov was not on active duty from August 1940 to early 1941, but resumed his post in February. He continued as Chief of the General Staff (and, from the outbreak of war, as Deputy Commissar for Defence) until forced to retire for health reasons in November 1942. Until his death in 1945, Shaposhnikov served as head of the Historical Section at the Voroshilov General Staff Academy. Shaposhnikov was a military intellectual of some note. He published a three-volume study, *Mozg armii* (Moscow, 1927–9), outlining the role of the general staff in future wars. His work owed much to the ideas of Clausewitz and won wide favour within the Red Army. Shaposhnikov's lectures at the Frunze Military Academy were attended by high-ranking Party members, and he was held in high regard by Stalin. *See also* RUSSIA/USSR; SOVIET MILITARY THEORISTS; TROTSKY.

KEITH NEILSON

FURTHER READING
John Erickson, *The Soviet High Command* (London, 1962); Condoleezza Rice, 'The making of Soviet strategy', in *Makers of Modern Strategy*, ed. Peter Paret (Princeton, 1986), pp. 648–76.

Sherman, William Tecumseh (1820–91) Although he became one of the most famous and controversial generals of the American Civil War, Sherman's initial military career was undistinguished. After the Mexican War, he resigned in 1853 to go into banking and then the law. In 1861, although he was not without sympathies for the Confederacy, he opted to serve the Union, arguing that if there was to be war it must be over as soon as possible. He served at Bull Run as a brigadier, and in 1862–3 took part in Grant's Vicksburg campaign, becoming a corps commander in January 1863. In September Grant was appointed to the supreme command in the west, and Sherman took over the army of Tennessee. In March 1864, Grant's move to the chief Union command left the path open for Sherman as his successor in the west. Grant's campaign in the east, pinning down major Southern forces, allowed Sherman freedom of movement in the west. In May Sherman led 100,000 men on Atlanta, which he captured on 1 September. In the autumn his men marched through Georgia, from Atlanta to the sea, feeding off the land as they went. Sherman's campaign was waged against the Confederate states as a whole, not simply their army, destroying their resources and breaking the will of the civilian population. In February 1865, he turned north through the Carolinas, and in April the Confederates surrendered. In 1869, Sherman once again succeeded Grant, this time as commander-in-chief of the US army, a post he held until 1883. His tenure of office was marked by clashes with the secretary of war as to their respective responsibilities, by the establishment of post-graduate special-to-arms schools, notably Fort Leavenworth, and by the ruthless suppression of the Indians on lines similar to those of the Georgia campaign. Sherman was a man of nervous temperament and sensitive to criticism; but his strategic thought, with his argument that war was hell and could not be moderated, particularly when applied to his own people, was bound to be controversial in its modernism. *See also* GRANT; UNITED STATES; UPTON.

HEW STRACHAN

FURTHER READING
B. H. Liddell Hart, *Sherman: soldier, realist, American* (New York, 1929); James Reston, *Sherman and Vietnam* (New York, 1985); W. T. Sherman, *Memoirs of W. T. Sherman* (New York, 1887).

Ships *See* NAVIES

Shrapnel, Henry Scrope (1761–1842) Shrapnel was commissioned into the Royal Regiment of Artillery in July 1779 and served during the latter years of the American War of Independence in the Newfoundland garrison. He early displayed a keen technical interest in his profession and, on returning to England in 1784, commenced experiments on projectiles and other devices.

Garrison duty in Gibraltar and the West Indies preceded his only spell of active service, with the Duke of York's expedition to Flanders in 1793. Thereafter his postings in the United Kingdom enabled him to resume his experiments, which resulted in the introduction to the British artillery service of 'spherical case shot' in 1803.

Multiple projectile artillery rounds for anti-personnel use had been in service on land and at sea from at least the sixteenth century. Case shot, a soldered sheet metal canister containing musket balls, which burst on emerging from the gun's muzzle, had been in use since the early eighteenth century. Common shells, hollow, powder-filled, cast iron spheres with a fuse, had been used since the early seventeenth century, and had become very familiar when fired from mortars during siege operations. Great Britain and most other European nations, though not the French, quickly appreciated the battlefield potential of shells, and made small versions suitable for firing from guns and howitzers. While the common shell of mortar or gun calibre could certainly be used to destroy buildings, its fragmentation effect made it a potent anti-personnel weapon.

The effectiveness of case shot was restricted by its short range, about 350–400 yards, and by the fact that its hitting power was derived exclusively from the impetus of its initial propulsion out of the cannon. The common shell's effectiveness was limited by the unreliability of its fuse and by the fact that it burst after landing, and sometimes harmlessly, having buried itself in the ground.

Shrapnel's invention, which, simply stated, was to add balls of various calibres to the charge inside a common shell, encapsulated four advantages:

1   increased range by retaining the balls within a substantial casing during the period of their flight;
2   the potential of airburst, in that by judicious shortening of the fuse the shell could be made to explode above and in front of the target;
3   greater hitting power, in that the cannon's discharge carried the projectile to the target and, on arrival, the bursting of the shell projected the components of the weapon into the target;
4   increased lethality, by adding the balls contained within the shell to the fragments of the casing produced by the bursting charge.

Although requiring considerable skill to achieve maximum effect the Shrapnel shell was widely adopted after its use by the British in the Peninsular war, though the French army was unable to manufacture a useable version until 1836.

Shrapnel received steady promotion, achieving the regimental rank of lieutenant-colonel by 1804. He served throughout the Napoleonic Wars as First Inspector of Artillery at the Royal Arsenal, Woolwich attaining his army colonelcy in 1813.

Despite being refused an invention reward for his shell by the Board of Ordnance in 1813, he received a government pension in the following year of £1,200 per annum supplementary to his salary. This however was taken to be a reward for all his inventions and improvements, not merely his shell. It also had the effect of denying him command of a battalion as he was seen to have been provided for and therefore to require no further patronage.

He retired from the Active List in 1825 disappointed at his lack of advancement; he received his last promotion, to lieutenant-general, in 1837 and died in 1842. His family successfully petitioned the War Office to change the name of his shell from 'spherical case shot' to 'Shrapnel shell' in 1852, a title which it had always borne in all other armies.

A collection of his papers, which have not to date received the attention due to them, is housed in the National Archive of Canada. *See also* ARTILLERY; EXPLOSIVES; GUNFIRE; ROBINS.

A. CORMACK

FURTHER READING
B. P. Hughes, *Firepower: weapons effectiveness on the battlefield, 1630–1850* (London, 1974); *JSAHR*, ii (1923–4), pp. 148–50; J. Campana, *L'Artillerie de campagne, 1792–1901* (Paris and Nancy, 1901).

Sieges Siege warfare is the art of capturing fortresses by means of a total or partial blockade followed by a systematic reduction. That reduction can be induced by a series of assaults, a single assault, the spread of disease or starvation. The techniques of defending fortresses are also contained within siege warfare. Early theorists distinguished it from the other branches of warfare – strategy, tactics and fortification – and called it 'poliorcetics'. Fortification and siege warfare have an obvious relationship, the former creating artificial or developing natural obstacles while the latter seeks their negation.

Amid the city-states of the Ancient World, siege warfare was of primary importance with the capture of a city entailing its total submission, the enslavement of its inhabitants or even their massacre. With the appearance of larger nation-states between the fifteenth and the nineteenth centuries, sieges continued to be as important as battles in the field. During the Russo-Japanese War and the First World War, the techniques of siege warfare were used in open country.

Before the invention of artillery using an explosive propellant, the basic technique of defence consisted of building a wall as high as possible to overlook the attackers. The defenders discharged their missiles – arrows, stones, boiling oil – either directly to their front on a flat trajectory or at high elevation to take the attackers in the flank. The attackers tried to counteract the disadvantage of height by achieving a position which overlooked the defenders. To this end an earthen ramp was constructed, which the Romans called an *agger*, along which could be pushed a wooden tower, termed *heleopolis* by the Greeks, and which was later employed by the Crusaders. This siege tower was protected against incendiaries by a covering of raw hides from freshly flayed animals. The tower supported marksmen to neutralize defenders on the ramparts, siege artillery and men-at-arms who advanced across a drawbridge attached to the tower and so secured a foothold on the wall. The defenders could also be forced to vacate sections of the wall by missiles from catapults and ballistas, the latter being capable of high-trajectory fire.

One of the first improvements in the defence was a ditch in front of the wall which prevented the siege tower from being pushed too close. To overcome this obstacle, the attackers filled the ditch with earth and fascines of brushwood, often at the cost of considerable casualties. In the fourteenth century, the Mongols employed on this work the inhabitants of towns which they had earlier captured. Another method was to scale the wall by ladders. One man can only handle a simple ladder up to a length of around 26 feet; in the Middle Ages the wall could be as high as 65 feet. Large, extending ladders were invented which supported three or four men abreast. For an assault by ladder to succeed, the defenders had to be neutralized by long- and medium-range fire. Generally, the attackers were assisted by the fact that the average castle garrison contained only a very few soldiers with a professional expertise in defensive techniques.

Where it proved impossible to 'top' the wall, attempts were made to destroy it. The ballistic armament, in the form of catapults and mangonels, hurled stones weighing from 110 to 220 lb sufficient to shake and batter masonry walls. The defence responded by strengthening the wall. Megalithic constructions, seen in Mycenae, Peru and Jerusalem, adopted a double stone wall infilled with rubble, while the Gauls created a shock-absorbing wall by interposing layers of wood between earth and stone. The simplest form of attack on massive walls was the ram, basically a tree trunk reinforced at its extremity by a head of bronze or iron. The ram and its operators had to be protected by a portable wooden shed, with a pitched roof to deflect stones and incendiary devices, which moved on wheels or rollers. A variant on the ram was the drill, which had a sharp, pointed head designed to pierce holes through walls.

If the ram and drill proved ineffective, miners were summoned. They dug a hole under the foundations while supporting the wall on wooden props. The hole was then filled with flammable material, which was set on fire. The wooden struts burned through and the section of wall collapsed creating a breach vulnerable to infantry assault. There were occasions when the attackers invited the defenders to examine the mine to induce surrender, as at Margat in Palestine in the twelfth century. Norm-

ally, the defenders did not remain passive. The noise made by miners enabled them to locate the threat and dig counter-mines to continue the struggle underground. Traces of such a battle between miners in the fifth century have been discovered at Dura-Europus in Syria. Where water was used as a defence, in the form of rivers or moats, its value could be negated by diversion (e.g. by Cyrus at Babylon), by filling the water course with earth or fascines of brushwood or, possibly, by crossing in light boats. The defenders could flood mine galleries or wash away any preparations for an assault, provided that they possessed a sufficient head of water. Surprise attacks, relying on sheer force without any form of preparation, were uncommon.

Besiegers had to prepare their positions carefully because the defenders rarely stood passively behind their fortifications. The attackers often had to protect their works and camps from attacks by the besieged with ditches, walls and redoubts. At Alesia in 52 BC, Caesar created a complete double ring of field fortifications. The inner ring, the lines of contravallation, protected the besiegers against sallies from the surrounded camp of Vercingetorix, while the outer ring, the lines of circumvallation, guarded against a field force operating in support of the besieged. A similar technique was employed by Silva at Masada in AD 72–3. Hunger and thirst were formidable weapons and caused many capitulations. However, attackers could find themselves facing the same difficulties, especially if the defenders had adopted a 'scorched earth' policy, and might be forced to withdraw. The fact that armies conducting a siege were relatively large exacerbated problems with their food supplies.

Artillery using an explosive propellant, after taking a long time to realize its full military potential, brought a fundamental change to the construction of defensive walls and fortifications. The tall, medieval wall was highly vulnerable to metal cannon balls and so the wall was drastically reduced in height and backed with a solid mass of earth to increase its resistance. These were known as ramparts. Unfortunately, the new, lower ramparts did not give the defenders the chance to fire at the attackers from long range and the defenders could only command the ditch to their immediate front. The answer was to build a series of outworks inside and beyond the ditch which pushed the attacking artillery back into the countryside, so reducing its effectiveness, and extended the physical range of the defence. Bastions at intervals along the ramparts enabled the defenders to enfilade attackers. To be effective against ramparts, artillery had to fire at a range of between 50 and 100 metres. The object of the attack was now to move the cannon close to the wall and then proceed to cut into the rampart both vertically and horizontally. The masonry revetment of the rampart was 4 to 6 metres thick and was sufficient to hold the backfilling in place provided that it had been well tamped. If it had not, it crumbled leaving a breach through which an assault could be made into the fortress. In order to position the batteries for this pounding of the wall, the attackers had to make a circuitous approach. At a distance of some 500 metres from the fortress they dug a broad trench, widened at intervals into redoubts which contained cannon for counter-battery fire against the ramparts and bastions. From this first parallel they moved forward, sapping zig-zagged trenches towards a second and third parallel. The chosen alignment aimed to avoid enfilade fire from the bastions, ravelins and other defensive works. The third parallel was the base for an infantry assault which, if successful, would gain command of the covered way in front of the ditch. The next step was to mine through the counterscarp, breaking down its revetment, and to position the heavy batteries scheduled for the demolition of the wall. All of this had to be conducted under fire from the defenders stationed in orillons and masked flanking emplacements. Mining was also employed at this final stage, explosives coming into use in this subterranean warfare at the end of the sixteenth century. Ricochet fire provided a means of eliminating the defenders' cannon, which were usually protected by traverses. All of these procedures were brought to a high level of efficiency by Vauban.

By the eighteenth century, sieges had become ritualized. In the siege diaries which they were required to keep, French fortress commanders reckoned on a period of 50 days, or rather nights, for the whole series of operations. It was accepted that a fortress could be surrendered with the honours of war once there was a breach in the wall through which the enemy could enter. Cases of unconditional surrender hardly ever occurred since the fate of prisoners of war was unenviable. Terms could be negotiated. The defending troops might be allowed to withdraw into the citadel, as was the case with Boufflers at Namur and Lille, or they might undertake to surrender if not relieved within a specific time. The practice of contravallation continued but circumvallation virtually disappeared, although it occasionally resurfaced, as at Belgrade in 1717. The attackers had their camp, parallels and trenches which were set out in the particular sector chosen for assault and their safety was assured by the presence of a covering field army. All of these commitments meant that the attackers needed five times as many men as the defenders. During the eighteenth century, there was a greater understanding of the science of ballistics which, together with improvements in the manufacture of cannon, allowed guns to destroy walls while firing at ranges of between 200 and 300 metres. However, this led to no important modifications in either the ceremony of sieges or the principles of fortification design.

In the nineteenth century, the explosive shell reduced the effectiveness of protective earthworks. By 1840, the precision attained with both low and high trajectory artillery fire sounded the death-knell for the spacious fortresses of the previous century. The new and favoured design was a polygon containing casemates in the counterscarp for flanking. The methods of besiegers remained basically unaltered, as seen at Antwerp in 1832 and Sebastopol in 1853. One important new feature was the change in the numbers employed by the attackers and the defenders – at the Sieges of Paris and Metz in 1870–1 they were roughly equal. At the end of the nineteenth century, the introduction of the high explosive shell resulted in the use of reinforced concrete in fortifications. Siege methods retained their classic form with forward movement being effected by means of trenches or mines, as at Port Arthur in the Russo-Japanese War, and Przemysl and Novo-Georgievsk in the First World War. However, sieges were rare. Fortresses, Liège in 1914 or Verdun in 1916, were attacked and defended almost entirely by artillery. Also, the trench warfare on the Western Front between 1914 and 1918 extended the methods previously used only in sieges to the whole theatre of operations. Even during the Second World War, isolated sieges occurred – the US defence of Bastogne in 1944 was an example – but the *raison d'être* had disappeared although it has temporarily re-emerged in Indo-China at Dien Bien Phu in 1954, the US strategy of fire-bases during the Vietnam War and in some Third World conflicts. The growth of huge urban conglomerations suggests that some future wars might well be fought inside cities, a trend of which the Battle of Stalingrad in 1942–3 provided a preliminary glimpse. *See also* ARTILLERY; ENGINEERS; FORTIFICATION; MINING AND MINES; WEAPONS.

AENEAS TACTICUS; COEHOORN; DEMETRIUS POLIORCETES; VAUBAN; VEGETIUS RENATUS.

ALESIA; BREDA; CARTHAGE; CHÂTEAU-GAILLARD; CONSTANTINOPLE; LENINGRAD; LUXEMBOURG; MASADA; METZ (1552–3); METZ (1870); ORLÉANS; PARIS; SARAGOSSA; SEBASTOPOL; VIENNA.

J. M. GOENAGA
JOHN CHILDS

FURTHER READING
Peter Connolly, *Greece and Rome at War* (London, 1981); J. W. Wright, 'Sieges and customs of war at the opening of the 18th century', *American Historical Review*, xxxix (1933–4), pp. 629–44; Christopher Duffy, *Siege Warfare: the fortress in the early modern world, 1494–1660* (London, 1979); Christopher Duffy, *The Fortress in the Age of Vauban and Frederick the Great* (London, 1985).

Signal communications The function of signals is to transmit a communication from one point to another while protecting it from interception by the enemy. Signals, the nervous system of an army, make it possible for a commander to receive information and to give orders. From Antiquity to the Industrial Revolution, the methods of transmitting signals over short distances and on the battlefield scarcely altered – written or oral instructions delivered at the speed of a man on foot or on horseback. A runner brought the news of Marathon in 490 BC and mounted messengers delivered orders to Marlborough's and Napoleon's regiments. There was more variety in the means of long-distance communication. The caliphs of Baghdad employed pigeons, as did Genghis Khan and, as an outcome of the Crusades, pigeon breeding and training were started in Western Europe. Pigeons were used during the First World War and even in the recent wars in Indo-China and Algeria. The Greeks also developed a system of communication by means of torches, each letter of a message represented by a number in accordance with a code which could be changed daily. The Persians, Carthaginians and the Gauls employed fire or beacon signals. The Romans developed an optical telegraph which consisted of 3,000 towers equipped with lamps, and the Emperor Augustus introduced the *cursus publicus*, carriages driving from station to station along strategic roads. Alerts in connection with coastal defence were relayed by similar methods; the English relied on a network of fire beacons in the sixteenth and seventeenth centuries. The insurgents of the Vendée employed windmills whose arms, when stopped in a particular position, provided rudimentary messages. However, these methods could only relay crude, simple messages in one direction only. As was the case with short-range communication, detailed, long-distance communication relied upon a written message delivered by a man on horseback.

In 1794, Claude Chappe invented a semaphore whose arms could be placed in several different positions, each combination corresponding to a letter or a word. The signals were observed by telescope. A message could be passed along the 16 stations between Paris and Lille in 2 minutes and the 116 stations between Paris and Toulon could relay a message in 20 minutes. Under the Empire, a network of 534 stations covered the whole of France but although messages could be enciphered, Napoleon made little use of it for military purposes. It could be useful along fixed lines of communication, as between the British Admiralty in London and Portsmouth, but once an army was on the march it soon departed from the rigid lines of semaphore stations.

The electric telegraph was made possible by the invention of the electro-magnet. Following development carried out simultaneously by Sir Charles Wheatstone (1802–75) in England and Samuel F. B. Morse (1791–1872) in America, the first telegraphic line was installed between Washington DC and Baltimore in 1843. The adoption of Morse's code of dots and dashes enabled the telegraph to make great strides. The telegraph was first used for military purposes by British and French engineers during the Crimean War (1854–6). Although the telegraph was employed extensively during the American Civil War and by the Prussians in their wars with Austria (1866) and France (1870–1) it remained, like the Chappe semaphore, a system more suited to long-distance fixed communication than for the relay of messages and orders over short distances or on the battlefield. Telegraph lines were vulnerable, as when the Prussians cut the lines out of Paris in 1871, and they could not be erected at the speed of marching and manoeuvring armies. Armies continued to use flags, messengers and, during the Boer War, heliographs which utilized the play of sunlight on mirrors to flash messages in Morse Code.

Although the telephone was patented by Alexander Graham Bell in 1875–7, it was not used militarily until the Spanish–American War of 1898. The field telephone became an essential signalling system for all armies during the First World War and it was especially useful in linking headquarters and for passing instructions to artillery batteries but it suffered from the same vulnerability as the telegraph. While it excelled for communications over long distances and between stationary headquarters, telephone wires could not survive artillery bombardments and it proved of very limited value for tactical command. The solution was discovered in radio or wireless.

The French and the Germans experimented with radio in 1914 and in February 1915 the British employed two-way wireless in an aircraft for artillery spotting. The set weighed 75 lb but this was reduced to 20 lb later in the year. By 1918, continuous wave wireless sets were in wide use by the French and the British in aircraft, in tanks and armoured cars and at the front. By 1917, a field set could be transported and operated by three men. During the First World War, valve radios replaced those working on the spark principle. Once radio had been made secure by the use of codes, it came to replace the telephone and the telegraph as the means by which to control and command troops on the battlefield. The armoured warfare and motorization of the Second World War would have been impossible without the installation of a light-weight and reliable radio in every fighting vehicle. There were numerous other advances in signalling methods between 1939 and 1945. Radio was extended into radar and radio guidance techniques for ships and aircraft, and the telephone lines also drove teleprinters. Because of the insecurity of radio (the British ULTRA intelligence derived from cracking the German ENIGMA code, and the American MAGIC originated from breaking the Japanese codes), long-distance communication in all countries came to rely on the telephone and teleprinter, both made more secure by 'Scrambler' mechanisms. At the front, radio allowed commanders to retain tactical control over their troops, a vital concern as weapons became more powerful and units fought in wider and more dispersed formations. Radio also permitted a more flexible approach to command and allowed the commanders of smaller units to exercise greater tactical initiative. However, better communications permitted and encouraged politicians and war leaders to exercise a greater control over daily operations at the front. Hitler, Stalin and Churchill are the most obvious examples.

Since 1945, communications have undergone a second revolution with the advent of the computer and the satellite. The huge worldwide communications network of the US National Military Command System and Defence Satellite Communications System, the latter based on the eight satellite MILSTAR, allows the President and the Secretary of Defense to exercise operational command over the US armed forces at all levels, at all times and in all parts of the world. Modern communications have permitted the national leader to resume the medieval role of war chief, although in a more indirect form. The systems include AUTOVON, an automatic telephone voice network; an automatic data network, AUTODIN, which transmits data worldwide; and AUTOSEVOCOM, which provides encoded telephone services. Satellites also provide secure communications between battlefield commanders and their subordinates. High-frequency radios for battalions and companies are made evermore jam-resistant and the day is not far removed when every individual infantryman will possess his own, personal radio set operating on a satellite link. Most communications are now via satellite and line-of-sight microwave relays. Armies are steadily abandoning land lines and are reducing their reliance on HF and VHF radios, except for communications with very mobile units. Short-range radios are being made more secure by the adoption of frequency-hopping techniques which automatically and regularly alter the frequency of transmissions. The aim is to make battlefield communications more secure against jamming and interference and also more mobile.

Signals formations are also responsible for intercepting and disrupting enemy communications. Before the twentieth century, this task amounted to no more than protecting one's own messengers while attempting to capture those of the enemy. Spies were widely employed. The Germans managed to use the thermionic valve to listen in to British field telephone conversations in 1915 and the early use of radio was retarded because of the need to encode all transmissions. During the Second World War, radio direction finding (RDF) could locate traffic from hostile transmitters thus making it possible to capture them, if they were 'underground stations', or to direct on them a bombardment from artillery or aircraft in the knowledge that radios were usually situated close to command posts. Some units specialize in 'jamming' enemy transmissions and others listen to hostile conversations since, even if they cannot always be deciphered, they can provide a partial identification of the enemy order of battle. This can be turned on its head and used as a deception ploy. In *Operation Fortitude* in 1944, the Allies created the illusion, solely through the production of bogus radio traffic, that the 1st United States Army Group was in south-east England. Since 1945, the whole field of electronic warfare has expanded to cover a range of jamming and interception techniques which has had to progress as fast as the developments in communications themselves. *See also* COMMAND; ENGINEERS; INTELLIGENCE; SECRECY; STRATEGY; VEXILLOLOGY.

G. BODINIER
JOHN CHILDS

FURTHER READING
R. F. H. Nalder, *The Royal Corps of Signals: a history of its antecedents and development, c.1800–1955* (London, 1958); Martin van Creveld, *Command in War* (Cambridge, Mass., 1985); E. L. Woods, *A History of Tactical Communications* (Orlando, Fla., 1945); S. Nalder, *Signals in the Second World War* (London, 1953); Frank Barnaby, *The Automated Battlefield* (Oxford, 1987).

Size of armed forces *See* NUMERICAL STRENGTH

Skagerrak, Battle of *See* JUTLAND

Society *See* SOLDIERS AND SOCIETY

Sokolovsky, Vasili Danilovich (1897–1968) Sokolovsky was one of the Soviet Union's leading military officers as well as an important military thinker. He was born into a peasant family in Grodno province and educated at a school for training teachers. In 1918, he volunteered for the Red Army and, after minimal training, rose to command a brigade during the civil war. In 1921, Sokolovsky graduated from the Red Army Academy. After a posting to Central Asia, Sokolovsky returned to European Russia where he held a number of posts, eventually rising to the position of chief of staff in a military district. In the shuffling of personnel after the Soviet débâcle in the Winter War against Finland, Sokolovsky was promoted to lieutenant-general (June 1940). In February 1941, Sokolovsky became deputy chief of the Soviet General Staff. During the war against Nazi Germany, Sokolovsky held a number of important commands: chief of staff of the Western Front, commander of the Western Front, chief of staff of the 1st Ukrainian Front and deputy commander of the 1st Belorussian Front under Marshal Zhukov. In 1946, Sokolovsky succeeded the latter as head of the Soviet forces in East Germany, a post he held until 1949. In that year, Sokolovsky became First Deputy Minister of the Soviet Armed Forces. Three years later he was also made chief of the Soviet General Staff. For five years, beginning in 1955, Sokolovsky was both chief of the general staff and First Deputy Minister of Defence. In 1960 he became Inspector-General of the Ministry of Defence Inspectors and presided over a collective of high-ranking officers who produced the work *Military Strategy* (1962). This book was an exposition of Soviet military doctrine during the Khrushchev era, most famous for its integration of nuclear weapons into the framework of Marxism-Leninism. *Military Strategy* reconsidered the thesis of the inevitability of war between capitalism and socialism in order to bring it into line with Khrushchev's concept of peaceful coexistence. But the book also rejected the Western concept of deterrence, arguing that nuclear war was not so catastrophic as to make war no longer a legitimate instrument of policy. The third edition (1968) adjusted military doctrine to the dictates of the Brezhnev era. Though widely disseminated within the USSR, *Military Strategy* has

been seen as a 'message' for Western consumption. *See also* NUCLEAR WARFARE; RUSSIA/USSR; SOVIET MILITARY THEORISTS; STALIN; ZHUKOV.

J.-P. CHARNAY
KEITH NEILSON

FURTHER READING
V. D. Sokolovskiy, *Soviet Military Strategy*, ed. H. F. Scott (New York, 1975); V. D. Sokolovskii, *Razgrom nemetsko-fashistskikh voisk pod Moskvoi* (Moscow, 1964).

Soldiers and society   The soldier's place in society and in the nation is determined by a large number of factors. His position is moral as he bears arms and is legally permitted to use violence; political and social, through methods of recruitment; moral and technical through the differing types of warfare; and finally circumstantial, whether the soldier is at peace or war. If the soldier occupies a leading place in society, that may represent only an unconscious facet of a nation's ethos and does not necessarily imply the existence of militarist tendencies. These may, on the contrary, develop when the pre-eminence of the soldier is disputed. The remainder of this article therefore considers the questions linked to the soldier's place in society under three heads: the moral and social aspects, the political, and lastly, the technical.

Moral and Social Aspects   In primitive societies, all men, to a greater or lesser extent, are warriors. It is the condition of a group's freedom, or even survival. The Indo-European experience has been, in general, that of a tripartite society composed of priests, warriors and workers though this has taken various forms. Very frequently, a man's possession of free status and his bearing of arms in battle have been indissolubly linked. This necessarily gives pre-eminence to the fighting man, whether the warriors make up one of the most highly regarded castes, as in India, or whether the status of being a free citizen entails membership of a standing army, as in Sparta, or the taking up of arms on mobilization, or in case of danger, as in the other Greek cities.

In Germanic societies, the social hierarchy was based on the closeness, or otherwise, of an individual's association with arms. The warriors formed an aristocracy, and among the workers, the most highly regarded were those who made weapons. Priests had to be classed separately, whether they occupied an official position, as in Rome, or had a private status, as in Germany. The coming of Christianity continued these social distinctions. The elect nature of the priesthood and its celibacy made its members an entirely separate section of society and this left the warriors as an internally competitive group which gradually, through the expedient of acquiring possession of land, divided into an hereditary aristocracy and commoners. Until well on in the eighteenth century generally throughout Europe the nobility remained the social group which the ambitious aspired to join, and the profession of arms thus retained a leading place among social values. Mercantile nations (like England and Holland) partially abandoned this outlook during the seventeenth century.

Nevertheless, and in spite of such an attitude, social realities were different. At least since the sixteenth century, many nobles directed their attention to commerce and the development of their properties, a process made easier as many no longer traced their descent from knightly ancestors. From the fourteenth century, in France the increase in the range of monarchs' activities led to the creation of a 'nobility of the gown', and later, of an administrative class of nobles, membership of which implied no military career, though they sent some of their sons into the army in order to assimilate themselves to the more prestigious 'nobility of the sword'. In the eighteenth century, even though scarcely one nobleman in five was serving, or had served, in the army, they were all intent on recalling the military occasions on which their family had distinguished itself. The reverse side of this situation was that the taste for, and admiration of, the profession of arms were not the exclusive prerogative of the nobility. Ability to defend oneself was a safeguard of freedom. The inhabitants of towns felt particularly strongly about this. Besides, the defence of the realm obliged all men able to bear arms to attack invaders. The general draft, which was not a call on noblemen only, was still used in certain localities during the eighteenth century, despite its increasing ineffectiveness. Civilian militias took on a military demeanour and adopted the wearing of a sword; the latter was, in theory, the preserve of the nobility, but was envied, and indeed, encroached upon, by many of the ambitious young, right up to the eighteenth century. In the same way, the practice of duelling was by no means confined to the nobility. The civil wars occasioned by religious disputes and by the temporary weakening of the power of kings (1560–1660) fostered the taste for arms. After the Christian virtues, military ones seemed the most admirable. It is, therefore, in the case of Europe, hard to discern the presence of two different societies – the military and the civil. Arms had a preferential place in the scale of social values. There was no need to wear the dress of a military man in order to prove oneself as such. Even though, in France, the king ceased, until 1750, to confer titles of nobility for military service, such service was always mentioned in letters patent. From the seventeenth century, however, England and Holland moved away from this view of society.

The rise of monarchies that were closer to being administrative organizations (such as those of Spain and France), the establishment of regular armies composed of professional soldiers, the developments in military techniques which entailed increasingly purposeful training, the practice of housing troops in barracks, which became a common practice in the eighteenth century, all produced, within society as a whole, a military community which grew more and more isolated from its parent society. In the second half of the seventeenth century, a sharper distinction can be drawn between soldiers and civilians, and war became an affair mainly for professionals. During the same period, there was a change in the hierarchy of social values on lines similar to those which had already occurred in mercantile countries. The pursuit of earthly happiness and the search for whatever could be socially beneficial, meant that those who moved into the foremost rank of society were thinkers, inventors, creators of wealth, contractors, merchants and manufacturers. The soldier became the technical expert in ensuring security and peace as the necessary conditions for other human activities. In addition, he saw his status further enhanced thanks to the improved behaviour of troops and their progressive separation from the civil population. Moreover, he gained on the political level part of what he had lost on the social. A soldier (Belle-Isle) became Minister of War for the first time in France in 1758 and large numbers of army and navy officers sat in the British parliament.

The French Revolution temporarily arrested this development, by starting in Europe a period of twenty-two years of practically continuous warfare. Certainly, it proved essential to reduce to the more viable level of 730,000 the French army strength which, in 1793, had stood at one million; even so, that figure provides proof of a successful war effort, and it had a real effect on the moral plane. The prestige given by victories, and then the dictatorship of a soldier for fourteen years, confirmed the leading place of the military man in the Napoleonic empire, as indeed also in the countries which had to defend themselves against it.

From 1815 to 1870, the soldier passed relatively into the background of French society, but the defeat of 1870–1 restored him to a position of considerable importance. On the one hand, for opponents and partisans alike of the new political regime, the army – looked up to like 'the ark of the covenant' – became once again the best means of serving the country. On the other hand, compulsory military service, which later became almost universal, together with the moral and psychological training provided by the normal educational curriculum, shaped the French to the point of being able to accept the sacrifice of one man in eight during the Great War. At the period of the 'settlement of accounts', however, it was a leading role in a moral sense, but not in a political one, that the military in France possessed. In many other parts of the Continent too, the military were traditionally very strong. It was so in Prussia, where the 'canton system' placed its stamp on the whole of society from the reign of Frederick William I onwards. In the eighteenth century, the enlightened despots often had a military background, giving their societies a martial tinge; in Prussia, Austria and Russia in the eighteenth century, even civil officials wore a uniform. In Germany, both in the time of the Second Reich and in that of the Third, ceremonies readily assumed a military hue. Fascism attempted to influence society in the same direction, with its watchwords 'Believe, Obey, Fight'. For their part, colonial countries have also experienced the primacy of the military, often imposed on them by colonizing powers. Today we are witnessing a marked decline in the soldier's status in society. In Western countries, uniforms are nothing more than working clothes, to be taken off as soon as possible, and in France, conscripts receive only fatigue dress. However, in the Third World, Africa and the Middle East, many dictators assume military dress to identify with their armed forces.

Political Aspects 'Cedant arma togae' – this maxim of Cicero's does not always apply in societies which enjoy the rule of law. Yet, on the other hand, it may do so in societies which give the foremost place to military values, even though civil and military power are concentrated in the same hands, as in the case of European monarchs before 1789. In fact, arms did not yield to the toga until quite a late stage in human history. Even if one omits barbarian states where the king was essentially the leader in war ('the first king was a successful warrior'), it remains true that public office in the Ancient World frequently combined political and military power. This was the case with that of the 'strategos' at Athens, at least in the fifth century BC, and also with the Roman curule magistracies (those of consul and praetor). The normal career through the higher offices of state took in military responsibilities, and arms yielded place to the toga only on the territory of the Roman state proper. Governors of provinces possessed combined military and civil authority. In the second and third centuries AD, even though the imperial (i.e. the praetorian) guard enforced the choice of emperors, and also assassinated them, the Roman imperial system was clearly more favourable to civil than military authority. The memory left by the Roman Empire was one of a state where the rule of law prevailed, and where the predominant element was civilian.

The period of the great invasions, and the setting up of the feudal system, meant that political power returned to armies and their leaders but the major feudal lords, and later the feudal monarchs, sought to refurbish the links with the Roman tradition, which were passed on through the teachings of the Church. The king was at once the dispenser of justice and the leader in war. At the time of his coronation, he received, with the sceptre, which symbolized his sovereignty, the hand of justice, since it was his duty to cause harmony to reign among all his subjects, and the sword, to show that he was required to preserve the security of the realm against all external dangers.

During the Renaissance, the military role of the sovereign was considerably enhanced, until the moment when the capture of Francis I made apparent the danger inherent in the king's personal presence on the battlefield. This did not mean, however, that the king could not continue to direct his armies, at least as far as their overall strategy was concerned, from his palace study. Philip II of Spain did so, and subsequently Louis XIV also, when he was growing old. During the same era, artists of the baroque school, and later of the classical, represented the king as a warrior. The evolution of a monarchy with judicial functions into one that had more and more of an administrative character changed nothing with regard to the place of the military in politics.

The philosophy of the Enlightenment, on the other hand, started a general European development which varied from country to country. In Western Europe, sovereigns ceased to claim to be military figures. The sole purpose of paintings which showed them wearing armour was to demonstrate that they retained military authority, even if they never actually commanded their armies. Louis XVI declined to be represented in this way. On the other hand, in monarchies which were examples of enlightened despotism, the military character of the sovereign was emphasized, even if the ruler were a woman (Catherine the Great of Russia), or if he wished to be shown also as a legislator (like Joseph II of Austria).

In France, the wars of the Revolutionary period not only restored the military to the highest level in the social scale but ended the subordination of military to political power. Government, as exercised by the Committee of Public Safety, had been a war dictatorship, in which the preponderance lay with political power. Its complexion changed after the 18th Brumaire (9 November 1799), when the two types of power were united in a military dictatorship. Despite efforts that were made, particularly at the end of the Second Empire, the Bonapartist tradition always carried with it an authoritarian political slant, often with an accompanying militarist tinge. Particularly in the states that arose out of the decolonization process in Latin America in the nineteenth century, and in Africa and Asia in the twentieth, military dictatorships multiplied. The *caudillos* of the nineteenth century, like modern military dictators, justified their seizures of power by the need to suppress subversive elements and proclaimed the priority of civil over military power. They promised the early establishment of a constitutional regime, following free elections, and with it the end of what would be merely a provisional dictatorship. However, circumstances frequently led to the postponement of such an outcome.

The liberal regimes of the nineteenth century distrusted armies and military commanders – an attitude which, in England, went back to Cromwell and in France, to the First Empire. They emphasized the subordination of military to political authority, even though their armies relied very little on conscription and could be considered professional forces. In France, soldiers were kept out of politics, and were even denied the right to vote, from the time of the Second Empire until 1945. This followed from the principle that the army was an instrument in the government's hands and, as such, should have no political ambitions of its own. The same proved true of liberal democracies of the twentieth century, in which traditional left-wing views were hostile to professional armies, and showed a preference for conscript forces, as having a more national character and less inclination to initiate a coup d'état. Nevertheless, the political outlook that is antagonistic to the idea of armies having influence often becomes infected with a fundamental anti-militarism which is closely related to the pacifist sentiments that are aroused by compulsory military service and by the apocalyptic prospects of modern warfare.

Since they were kept out of politics, and themselves abstained from entering it, twentieth-century armies could act in this sphere only as a pressure group, working for the preservation of defence interests – in particular, for an increase in, or at least the maintenance at the same level of, the grants allocated to the army in the national budget. They have done this through contacts with politicians and industrialists, and also through various organizations, such as ex-soldiers' associations.

Directly after the First World War, however, these associations ('Fasci' in Italy, the 'Stahlhelm' in Germany) provided leverage that helped in the setting-up of dictatorships – totalitarian regimes in which military and political power went hand-in-hand. Even so, the preponderant influence still rested with those exercising political power. The crisis in 1937–8, when Hitler and the general staff of the *Wehrmacht* were in opposition, ended with the dictator gaining the upper hand. For their part, the 'people's' democracies have not hesitated to call on the army for help in ensuring the consolidation of their power, and also for imposing their system on other countries. Lenin, Stalin, Mao Tse-Tung and Fidel Castro all maintained the status of the armed forces in their countries, but took good care to ensure that these remained under political control (e.g. the purge of generals in the USSR in 1937–9).

It is obvious, however, that in wartime technical necessities have the effect of much reducing dissimilarities in the practices of regimes with differing political systems.

Technical Aspects These arise from the requirements of standing armies which are equipped with increasingly large-scale and costly weaponry. Thanks to Louvois, Louis XIV could maintain a force of 400,000 men in wartime – that is, one-twelfth to one-eighteenth of the adult male population of France. The major portion of numerous industries – metallurgical, textile, leather, etc. – worked for the army, which became their main client. Agriculture and cattle-rearing had equally to make their contribution. Further, owing to its possession of fortified places and various establishments, the army occupied a large area of terrain. The situation soon became similar in all countries. Supplies to the army lay at the heart of the economic system. The general staffs of the army and the navy are consulted on the organization of the country's infrastructure, with particular reference to the transport system. Two examples from 1935 can be quoted: the French general staff delayed the electrification of French railways in the east of the country, whilst the German general staff pressed for the construction of motorways.

Ministries of war have become self-contained worlds, with their own supply agencies in a number of fields. Moreover, co-ordinated action is not easily secured in such matters, since the land, sea and air forces are frequently at odds with each other. In some countries, they may have views which differ from those of the regime currently in power. To avoid friction of this kind, certain countries have set up independent armament departments (Germany, France, Canada), or agencies to deal with matters affecting all three services (United States and Great Britain). Inspectorates are assuming considerable importance.

The army, or navy, is required to maintain close links with developments in its country's infrastructure, with scientific research, with the civil authorities (in order to organize the civil defence which may be needed in wartime) and – in military dictatorships or people's democracies – with the police, in the interests of the struggle against subversion. It was in the United States that armed forces first made research contracts with industrial laboratories or with universities, while at the same time binding them to maintain military standards of secrecy. Countries in Europe adopted this method in the 1960s. There are now what can be described as military–industrial complexes. Armed forces' contracts with industry represent on average 10–12 per cent of the national budget. In particular, the leading clients of the aeronautical industry are the armed forces (which provided 50 per cent of its contracts in the United States around 1970, and generally 70 per cent in European countries). The links between the armed forces and industry find expression in the fact that retired generals are chairmen of boards of industrial concerns, whether nationalized or not, a practice that is common in the United States. These military–industrial complexes necessarily keep in contact with the political authorities.

In every country, war means that the military assume the leading role, and that the work of the nation has to be adapted to the necessities of the struggle. In wartime, liberal Western democracies temporarily sacrifice many of their civic freedoms and rights (British Defence of the Realm Act 1914). Certainly, politicians decide on overall strategy, but they cannot do so without prior consideration in which the military has taken part. Since this is a sphere which involves very serious responsibilities, governments accept their own technical inadequacy and willingly leave to the military the task of preparation for and the general conduct of war, while still retaining for themselves the authority to replace unsuccessful military commanders (e.g. Nivelle in 1917, Gamelin in 1940) and to call on others who seem capable of turning the situation around (Foch in 1918, Weygand in 1940). It is noteworthy that, from 1916 to 1918, the German general staff exercised nothing less than a dictatorship over their country, by the expedient of pleading the technical needs of the war. In countries where a president holds the chief office, he can, assisted by a circle of military advisers, more easily take charge of the conduct of a war, in much the same way as monarchs did in the past. In the case of a localized conflict in a distant country, like the Korean War, President Truman removed General MacArthur from his command when actions taken by the latter were in danger of running contrary to the overall policy laid down by political authority. The same is true of totalitarian regimes or people's democracies; whether political authority rests with one person or a group, it is there that responsibility lies for military policy and the overall conduct of the war.

What is true of wars of the conventional type, in which military commanders retain a certain independence of action, is not necessarily so in the context of a possible nuclear conflict. Nuclear escalation is clearly part of the political 'game'. Those who govern have to reflect on the likely price of victory and the cost of defeat. Technical progress has, in fact, restored the primacy of the power of politicians over that of the military. Also, intellectuals are now making an appearance as military advisers to governments – for example, strategic study groups have been set up in the universities of Princeton and Harvard, and defence study centres in France and Great Britain. On the other hand, realizing that the army alone could maintain order in the event of a nuclear war, its officers are seeking a deeper understanding of the world in which they operate, partly through a broader education. In this way, the military and civilians are being drawn closer together, by the very fact of their relationships to a current state of civilization where technical expertise is of the essence. Even so, it seems clear that, in many countries, if a balance is to be re-established between military and political power, a good number of moral values will first need to be rediscovered. *See also* BARRACKS; BILLETING; CIVIL CONTRIBUTION OF ARMIES; CIVIL POWER, SUPPORT OF; ETHOS; GERMANY; KNIGHTS AND CHIVALRY; MOBILIZATION; MORALE; RECRUITMENT; SPARTA; TRAINING.

A. CORVISIER

FURTHER READING
A. Corvisier, *Armies and Societies in Europe, 1494–1789* (Bloomington, Ind., 1979); John Childs, *Armies and Warfare in Europe, 1648–1789* (Manchester, 1982); A. Vagts, *A History of Militarism* (New York, 1959); Karl Demeter, *The German Officer Corps in State and Society, 1650–1945* (London, 1965); S. P. Huntingdon, *The Soldier and the State: the theory and politics of civil–military relations* (New York, 1964).

Solferino (Mantua), Battle of (24 June 1859) This battle saw 160,000 Austrians ranged against a similar number of French and Piedmontese soldiers. Since both high commands virtually lost control of their troops, the successful outcome was due to the *élan* of the Franco-Piedmontese soldiers and the vigour of their corps commanders. Benedek saved the Austrian army from total rout. The Austrians lost 22,000 men, the Franco-Piedmontese 17,200. Apart from the political consequences, this bloody encounter (1) contributed to stirring public opinion and enabled Dunant to undertake the creation of the Red Cross, and (2) promoted an effort on the part of the military, especially in Prussia, to ensure better co-ordination between the actions of army corps. *See also* AUSTRIA; DISARMAMENT; DUNANT; FRANCE; LAWS OF WAR; SADOWA.

A. CORVISIER

FURTHER READING
K. K. Generalstabsbüreau für Kriegsgeschichte, *Der Krieg in Italien, 1859* (3 vols, Vienna, 1872); Carlo Mariani, *La Guerra dell' indipendenza italiana dal 1848 a 1870, Storia politica e militare* (3 vols, Turin, 1882–3).

Somerset, Duke of, *See* SEYMOUR, EDWARD

South America *See* PRE-COLUMBIAN STATES OF AMERICA

Soviet military theorists When the Bolsheviks seized power in Russia in October 1917, their notion that war, politics, revolution and society were indivisible was encouraged by the work of Clausewitz. Initially, the bourgeois and oppressive institution of a standing army was anathema to the Bolsheviks, who believed that revolution would be spread by the spontaneous uprising of the international proletariat. However, the enforced Peace of Brest-Litovsk in 1918 marked a distinct change in Lenin's attitude; socialism had to be consolidated in Russia before any thought could be given to worldwide revolution. The pressures of the civil war (1918–22) enabled Trotsky, the commissar for war, to replace the loosely organized workers' formations with a disciplined standing army under central command. Indeed, so great was the emergency of the civil war, that the Red Army reverted to many of the expedients of its Tsarist predecessor – impressment, conscription – as well as the employment of nearly 50,000 former Tsarist officers, euphemistically termed 'specialists'. Having reneged on communist principles which favoured a volunteer militia ('the working class armed'), the Bolsheviks proceeded to politicize and control their standing army to prevent it becoming a force for counter-revolution, a distinct possibility given the predominance of ex-Tsarist officers over the new 'Red Commanders'. The system of military commissars helped to maintain loyalty.

By attacking Poland in 1920, Mikhail Nikolaievich Tukhachevsky (1893–1937), a former Tsarist lieutenant, made the important political statement that the socialist revolution could be exported by military conquest through the agency of the Red Army. Defeat before Warsaw (13–25 August 1920) ended Tukhachevsky's scheme and the Bolsheviks became more introspective, concentrating on the defence of Russia's borders and the completion of the internal socialist revolution. Between the end of the civil war in 1922 and 1924, there was an intense debate between Trotsky and the Red Commanders under the leadership of S. I. Gusev and Mikhail Vasilyevich Frunze (1885–1925). Trotsky was pragmatic,

M. V. Frunze in 1920 (*centre*) with two Marshals of the Soviet Union, (*left*) K. Y. Voroshilov (1881–1961) and (*right*) S. M. Budenny (1883–1973).
(Camera Press)

accepting the services of the 'specialists' and recognizing that both the civil war and future external wars could only be fought by professional armed forces assisted by a territorial militia. Above all, Trotsky realized that the Red Army was too weak for offensive operations and would have to concentrate on the defensive. By 1924, Trotsky had organized the army into 42 territorial and 29 regular divisions. Gusev and Frunze feared that a peasant territorial militia led by 'specialists' was incapable of offensive action as well as provided a recipe for counter-revolution. In 1921, Gusev advocated linking political ideology and the Red Army into a 'unified organism' which would conduct offensive operations through manoeuvre, the method which had proved successful during the civil war, to counter the inevitable 'imperialist' counter-attack on Russia. Gusev also attacked the territorial militia, arguing that socialism required a standing army recruited from the proletariat. Frunze called for the complete mobilization of the state for total war,

following Engels's theory of 'mass warfare'. Like Gusev, Frunze rejected the territorial militia on the grounds that it was a 'peasant' formation and peasants were politically unreliable. Peasants were also defensively minded whereas the civil war had been won by manoeuvre and the offence, particularly by the cavalry. Only the proletariat was politically reliable and able to act consistently as offensive troops; therefore, Frunze favoured a cadre army rather than a militia. Frunze also foresaw that technology would play an increasing role in war, even though he was unable to reconcile the contradiction between his advocacy of 'mass warfare' and a professional cadre army.

In the face of Trotsky's blistering attack arguing that rigidity of doctrine was absurd in a time of great upheaval, Frunze retreated admitting that military doctrine should be a guide not a dogma. Gradually, as Trotsky's political position weakened, Frunze's views gained wider support, especially from Tukhachevsky and Boris

755

Shaposhnikov (1882–1945). Trotsky was opposed to the offensive as the First World War had shown that rigid adherence to this doctrine had frequently resulted in catastrophe; wars had to be fought according to what was possible, necessary and practical. However, the dynamic of Marxism was one of political offensive. Frunze never clearly stated whether he was referring to a political offensive coupled with an adaptable and expedient military strategy or whether he wanted the dogma of the military offensive applied in all circumstances. In 1923, Trotsky was ousted as war commissar by Frunze, only for the latter to die within two years, but not before he had launched the Red Army on the road towards mechanization and motorization. He was succeeded as commissar for defence by Stalin's associate and former Red Commander, Klimenty Yefremovich Voroshilov (1881–1961).

Josef Stalin's dictum of 'revolution in one country' finally determined that the defence of Russia and her revolution against all enemies, internal and external, was to be the strategic orthodoxy. Trotsky argued that denying the worldwide revolutionary drive of Marxism would create an introverted, repressive and coercive regime of which a dictatorship was the corollary. However, Stalin's views prevailed and were consistent with Frunze's ideas of 'mass warfare' and total mobilization of the state. Deputy Boris Shaposhnikov and Tukhachevsky (Chief of Staff, 1925–8; deputy commissar of defence, 1931–7) began planning the mobilization of the entire Russian economy for war. Tukhachevsky, in particular, stressed the need for industrialization to meet the needs of war and the ultilization of Russia's vast territories for the strategic dispersal of key industries. For his outspoken views and attacks on the defence commissar, Voroshilov, Tukhachevsky was banished to the Leningrad command in 1927 but was brought back into favour in 1931 to coordinate the re-equipment and re-arming of the Red Army. During the 1930s, Russia clung to her strategy of offensive warfare through manoeuvre but she improved her internal transport and communications and organized her whole society and economy

for war. The paradox of a strategic offensive within the framework of a politically and militarily defensive war was maintained.

Having determined the basic strategic doctrine, after 1927 the Red Army turned its attention to the conduct of operations in the field. In 1928, the head of the operations administration of the Red Army, V. Triandifilov, advocated deep penetrations to break the opposing front followed by 'successive operations' to prevent the enemy from regrouping and rallying. This, it was stated, would lead to encirclement and crushing victory. The keys were speed, mobility and operations in depth. Tukhachevsky organized the Red Army to operate in combined-arms teams with motorized infantry, tanks, self-propelled artillery and paratroopers, supported by an air force trained in ground attack and deep interdiction. Voroshilov and A. A. Svechin disagreed with Tukhachevsky, arguing for the necessity of defensive operations and more linear tactics, which could best be met by the tanks supporting the infantry and artillery rather than concentrating on elite tank and motorized divisions especially for the breakthrough battle and subsequent exploitation. Although Tukhachevsky's views remained dominant, a considerable amount of the new Russian armour was diverted to infantry and cavalry support. This debate within the Red Army took place against a background of similar controversies in the majority of European armies. By 1935, the Red Army possessed 7,000 tanks and 100,000 lorries and manufactured nearly 10,000 aircraft per year. Tactically and operationally, it was the most advanced and mechanized army in the world. Between 1936 and 1939 this position was forfeited. Beset by fears of conspiracy among the former Tsarist officers, many of whom were suspected of pro-German leanings, Stalin eliminated Tukhachevsky and 35 per cent of the Russian officer corps in the years from 1937 to 1939. Second, the Russian experiences in the Spanish Civil War undermined Tukhachevsky's doctrine of mechanization by demonstrating that the tank was not a decisive weapon in its own right but was better employed as a support to infantry and artillery after the manner of the British and French tactics in 1917 and 1918.

Voroshilov, Simeon Konstantinovich Timoshenko (1895–1970) and the exponents of defensive and positional warfare attempted to refound the Red Army in the wake of Stalin's purges but they had insufficient time to prevent defeats in battle by Finland (1939–40) and Germany in 1941 and 1942. Stalin assumed total command of Russia's war effort from 1941 to 1945 but ultimate victory after Stalingrad in 1943 was based upon the mobilization of the state for war, the fact that wartime conditions brought new and talented commanders to the fore, the army learning from experience and the practices of its enemies, and the development of its ability to fight defensively in depth, especially in 1942. After Stalingrad, the Red Army was able to revert to its 1936 doctrine of offensive manoeuvre.

The success of Tukhachevsky's basic doctrine when put into effect between 1943 and 1945 ensured that it remained at the heart of Russian postwar strategic thinking. Combined-arms operations, deep penetrations, surprise, manoeuvre and the offensive remained central. Similarly, the total mobilization of the state for war continued to be the pillar of the defensive political strategy, especially since the advent of thermonuclear weapons offered the ultimate defence against capitalist attack. Indeed, surrounded by her shield of satellite states in Eastern Europe, the nuclear bomb was the only weapon which could attack the Soviet Union. In order to preserve the revolution, the major economic and social effort of the state was committed to its military defence. Having suffered a surprise attack in 1941, the Soviet Union maintained a high level of conventional forces many of whom were stationed in the satellite states of Eastern and Central Europe as a buffer to protect 'Mother Russia'.

At the time of writing, the Revolution of 1991 has witnessed the break-up of the Soviet Union into a number of quasi-independent states, each having subsumed its own national elements from the old Red Army, navy and air force. No strategic or military theory has yet emerged from the new republics and no decision has yet been reached about the command of the nuclear arsenal. *See also* CLAUSEWITZ; LENIN; NUCLEAR WARFARE; RUSSIA/USSR; SHAPOSHNIKOV; STALIN; TROTSKY; ZHUKOV.

JOHN CHILDS

FURTHER READING
Condoleezza Rice, 'The making of Soviet strategy', in *Makers of Modern Strategy*, ed. Peter Paret (Oxford, 1986), pp. 648–76; John Erickson, *The Soviet High Command* (London, 1962); Malcolm Mackintosh, *Juggernaut. A history of the Soviet armed forces* (London, 1967); Albert and Joan Seaton, *The Soviet Army* (London, 1986).

Spain Spain has distinct military characteristics, the product of a certain style of military action, which became the foundation of a rich and unique tradition. Both by its length (197–133 BC) and its brutality (the Siege of Numantia, 133 BC), the Roman conquest reveals certain specific features of Iberian warfare. However, the causes of Spain's military particularism derive principally from the eight centuries of the *Reconquista* (711–1492) when the country was recovered from Muslim occupation. From the *Reconquista*, through the War of Independence from France (1808–14), to the nationalist uprising (1936–9), the people of Spain have always been the heart and soul of the struggle.

The Crucible of the Reconquista A high degree of popular participation differentiated the war of reconquest from the 'classic' feudal warfare of the Christian West. Pushed back into their Asturian stronghold, the Christian military leaders were forced, both by the importance of frontier fighting and the shortage of men, to call on the common people as a key instrument in the struggle for liberation. The monumental code, *Las Siete Partidas* (thirteenth century), of King Alphonso X 'the Learned' provides eloquent testimony to this development. The *Reconquista* led to a militarization of all aspects of life in the reclaimed territories. This phenomenon, which developed over centuries, produced a warrior spirit in Spain.

The *Reconquista* also delayed and then attenuated feudalism. Although the feudal system was able to develop in the vast liberated zones created by the receding frontier, particularly after the spectacular advance which followed the victory at Las Navas de Tolosa (1212), the sovereigns always retained the option of calling upon contingents of veteran foot soldiers (*milicias concejiles*) and an exceptional popular cavalry (*caballería villana*). The formal and courtly style of warfare depicted in Jean de Breuil's *Jouvencel* was unthinkable in Spain, where the necessary conditions never existed.

Reconquista, Holy War and Crusades Certain other characteristics of the *Reconquista* also need emphasis. Unlike other so-called holy wars, the *Reconquista* was not essentially conducted in pursuit of any divine purpose. The Christian armies were initially motivated by the desire to regain the territory needed to guarantee the independence of their community. The objective sought was not redemption through a martyr's death in battle, nor the conversion of the enemies of the Lord, even though his name was evoked both to justify the struggle and to assist in achieving a favourable outcome.

According to the typology established by René Grousset, the medieval crusade was closely identified with the seigneurial conception of existence. Thus the crusade bears only an indirect relation to the spirit of the *Reconquista* where men who were already free were fighting to achieve the complete liberation of the whole of *Hispania*. With hindsight, the *Reconquista* can be seen as a model for the formation of a nation-state by means of a series of persistent 'guerilla' campaigns. This constant irregular warfare was interspersed with great formal campaigns organized by kings and princes.

The Emergence of the Hidalgo From the crucible of the *Reconquista* emerged the *hidalgo*, the 'son of something', who slowly came to be separated from the people in arms. The *hidalgo* is closely associated with the military glory of Spain. He is a highly controversial figure whom French hispanists, Marcel Bataillon at their head, have been wrong to treat solely in terms of his conception of honour. The proliferation of the *hidalguía* throughout the Iberian peninsula emphasizes the *hidalgo's* militant origin and his close association with the people as a whole. This lower stratum of the nobility formed the base of the military system which dominated Europe at the beginning of the modern age. Since he generally also possessed limited economic means, the *hidalgo*, detached from material concerns, saw himself as embodying the old Christian ideal. He was viscerally opposed to the immoral opulence of the *converso* (converted Jew) and, subsequently, to the meritless ostentation of a bureaucracy preoccupied with acquiring titles of nobility from the Habsburg monarchs.

The Crisis of the Medieval Military System The Habsburg–Valois Wars in Italy (1494–1525) produced a crisis in the 'classic' forms of medieval warfare. In Spain, the slow and painstaking conquest of the Kingdom of Granada had contributed to forging a highly trained infantry which was expert in skirmishing and in the use of terrain. Organized by the Castilian state through the ordinance of 1495 on the general arming of the people and the ordinance of February 1496 which created a militia, the model for the formation of the new infantry was inspired by the example of the Swiss peasant-soldiers. Eventually, the Spanish infantry outclassed their mentors. The Spanish army, which already enjoyed a solid moral discipline, was subjected in Italy to an equally solid military discipline. Employed as the instrument of a superior strategy, the Spanish infantry conquered the phalanxes of the Swiss who were, ultimately, mere mercenaries. In the service of more realistic political objectives, the Spanish armies also overcame the French.

The Military Genius of Gonsalvo de Córdoba The military means by which the Spaniards triumphed in Italy had been built in Castile, in the heart of the Iberian peninsula. Spain, a poor country which had grown ambitious, sent to the Kingdom of Naples troops composed mainly from that *hidalguía* which had been depleted during the *Reconquista*. In Italy, with his back to the sea, Gonsalvo de Córdoba was forced to employ all his creativity and make the best possible use of his limited resources. During the second Neapolitan campaign, his victory at Cerignola (April 1503) may well be regarded as the point at which the military tactics of the Renaissance era reached maturity. Fabrizio Colonna, Machiavelli's mouthpiece in his *De re militari*, speaks with awe of this stroke of genius. That meticulous judge, Hans Delbrück, confirms this assessment. For Piero Pieri, a new phase in the art of war was born at Cerignola. Going further, he argued that during the operations on the Garigliano (autumn–winter 1503), the Spanish general demonstrated the highest attainment of the military art by his ability to harmonize resources with capabilities, something which proved beyond the commanders of Louis XII (1498–1515).

The Genesis of the Tercio However, Córdoba's greatest achievement lay in his appreciation of the deficiences displayed by his infantry when faced with soldiers operating in solid phalanxes, like the German *Landsknechte* or the Swiss pikemen. He was able to draw the lessons from his defeat at the Battle of Seminara (April 1495), where his troops had turned and fled the moment that the Swiss infantry in Charles VIII's (1483–98) army had lowered their pikes. During his second campaign, as soon as Córdoba was able to secure the services of a corps of *Landsknechte* (2,500 men), he allowed the Spanish soldiers to fight in the manner that best suited them: as *tirailleurs*, or skirmishers. Thus, while the Spanish infantry in Italy were 'domesticating' the individual, hand-held firearm, the monarchs of Castile were imposing the model of the Swiss pikemen in order to counter this manifest weakness in the nation's armed forces (*cédula* of January 1503). The positive experience of the War of Roussillon (September–October 1503) led to the creation in 1504 of the 'ordinance infantry' which preceded the

creation of the *tercios*. The whole system was supervised by an up-to-date and efficient military administration (Grand Ordinance of July 1503). The resulting transitional period of the *coronelias* allowed the organizational and experimental foundations to mature for over thirty years.

The Tercio: a Technostructure On his return in November 1536 from the victorious expedition to Tunis, Charles V announced an ordinance at Genoa which reorganized the Spanish standing army, at that time spread throughout Italy, into a number of *tercios*. They were composed of professional volunteers recruited through an administrative machinery established by the state. The *tercio* was originally divided into twelve companies of 250 men, each of which was subdivided into 10 *esquadras* (sections) of 25 men. The *tercios* were managed according to precise administrative procedures. The monthly pay included a number of distinctly modern features: a deduction was made from the basic wage for medical insurance but the soldier could earn additional money via a long-service allowance, a technical skill bonus, plus any general emoluments paid to his unit. Every *tercio* had its own commissariat, law officers and health service (a physician, a surgeon, an apothecary and ten barbers). The formidable combat efficiency of this infantry was founded on a weapons system which combined blade weapons (the pike) and firearms (the arquebus). The *tercio* thus achieved an effective synthesis of the dichotomy of infantry armament (blade and gunpowder weapons) which had developed with the advent of hand-held firearms during the fifteenth century. The tactics which permitted this weapons system to function were based on *escuadróns*, *ad hoc* groupings of soldiers constituted on the bases of requirement and availability. The fundamental tactical difference between the *tercio* and the Swiss phalanx lay in the former's greater articulation which allowed it to organize flexible sub-groups and its soldiers to engage in individual combat. Once again, this can be partially attributed to the experience gained during the *Reconquista*.

Finally, from the late fourteenth to the mid-seventeenth century, Spain achieved a remarkable mastery of military logistics. Her major battle was against distance. Despite the slowness of the official decision-making machinery, an exceptional administrative apparatus enabled Spain to compensate for numerical inferiority by the astonishing mobility of her armies and armadas.

The Tercio: a Microsociety The *tercios* were intervention forces usually based away from the Iberian peninsula. The material life of the soldiers thus depended on both positive factors (a favourable exchange rate) and negative factors (a foreign, if not indeed hostile, environment). Theoretically less burdened with family responsibilities and benefiting from the price differential resulting from the inflation caused by the flow of gold and silver into Spain from the Indies, the *infant* of the *tercios* definitely enjoyed a more advantageous economic situation than his compatriots in Spain. Although supplemented by occasional income from booty, these economic advantages were frequently eroded by an extravagant lifestyle. Most of these men came from the modest *hidalguía* and such circumstances suited them well, as did the strict discipline within the service. The whole arrangement was based on certain social, political and religious values which evolved into a creed as Spanish interventionism in European and African affairs accelerated throughout the sixteenth century: God and the Church of Rome, the king and the nation, and the honour of the individual. Unfortunately, Spain's extraordinary military success led to the exaggeration of this moral code until the point was reached where it poisoned the attitudes of the soldiers. Eventually, they came to regard themselves as superior to everyone.

The result was predictable: a diminishing degree of contact with the population at large contrasted with an intense and introverted social life among the men. Fraternity governed relationships within the *tercio* while the officers practised paternalism towards their soldiers. These relationships were all-embracing, offering some compensation to men isolated abroad and cut-off from normal civilian life. Gradually, from the end of the sixteenth century, a degree of mutual incomprehension arose between a military society that was scattered to the four corners of Europe and the parent society in Spain. This sensation was exacerbated by an awareness of the disproportion between the sacrifices made by the *tercios* on behalf of Spain and their seeming abandonment by the mother country. When, in the seventeenth century, Spain no longer enjoyed the economic resources to ensure its soldiers a minimum standard of material well-being, the best of her sons left the ranks of the *tercios*. Following a long period of decline, the *tercio* disappeared with the arrival of the Bourbon dynasty (1700). The new military practices which they introduced, based on the French armies of Louis XIV, were fundamentally alien to the Spanish people.

The Navy The reputation of the *tercios* has often led to the achievements of Spain's other armed forces being overlooked. Throughout the sixteenth and seventeenth centuries, the Spanish navy operated in many and varied theatres, in terms both of distance and of other particular techniques required and applied. Within an overall imperial framework, there were local responses to local needs. More or less autonomous squadrons operated in clearly differentiated zones: Sicily, Naples, the Levant (the 'Spanish squadron'), the Cantabrian zone, Flanders, the Indies, *Barlovento*, the Pacific (Southern Seas) and the Philippines. The unification of all these elements into a royal navy was not achieved until 1757 (with the integration of the Philippines squadron).

Following the example of the Portuguese, a preoccupation with science played a central role in naval activities as is shown by the publication throughout the empire of treatises on navigation and shipbuilding, e.g. Garcia de Palacio, *Instrucción nautica* (Mexico City, 1587). The navy enjoyed a similar level of bureaucratic efficiency to that of the army. Spanish naval administration was highly advanced and initiated and refined a number of measures before they were adopted by other countries: a system of maritime classes (registers of seamen) (Guipúzcoa, 1607); shipbuilding ordinances (1613, 1618); naval ordinance (1633), etc.

Colonization It is one of the paradoxes of Spain's acquisition of empire that no state armed forces were sent to fight against the American Indians although a dozen lancers from the Castilian Guard accompanied Christopher Columbus on his first voyage; their mounts were left on the island of Hispaniola. According to Jacques Lafaye, the conquest of South America was achieved by adventurers or adventurous sons of the people (*brazo popular*). The chief feature of Spanish colonization was its effectiveness. For three centuries, Pierre Chaunu has written, the administration of the Empire succeeded in keeping its territories intact against all the European maritime powers which, since the end of the sixteenth century, were distinctly superior to Spain at sea. Spanish colonization cannot be compared with the forms of European colonial expansion that occurred in Africa, India and the Far East during the nineteenth century. Spanish America was a series of kingdoms incorporated into the crown, lands inhabited by free and prosperous people until the coming of independence and liberalism in the early and mid-nineteenth century. There was practically no army in Latin America as there were practically no enemies.

The War of Independence and Guerilla Warfare It took the invasion of Napoleon's armies to revive Spain's popular military tradition through the outbreak of widespread guerilla warfare. As a form of armed struggle, guerilla warfare predates this period (e.g. to counter the French invasion of Catalonia between 1694 and 1697). However, the extent of guerilla action in the War of Independence went well beyond anything previously seen, reaching quite extraordinary proportions. It was the destruction of the regular armies in 1808 – disbanded but not crushed – which was the immediate cause of the appearance of guerilla warfare. The 'guerillas' consisted of civilians and groups of soldiers disbanded or seconded from the regular army. For both elements, guerilla warfare meant popular participation in a national rising against occupying forces. This method of conducting warfare was akin to total war and Spain became a nation in arms. Although the Napoleonic war machine had conquered most of the major armies of Europe, it had not previously encountered a people in arms.

Organized Guerilla Warfare The first *reglamento* regarding guerilla warfare was published in December 1808 (*Reglamento de partidas y cuadrillas*), but provincial juntas had already anticipated this by granting amnesties to attract outlaws whose knowledge of local terrain was vital. Shortly after, as a result of the widespread and rapid expansion of guerilla warfare, the legal position was further modified in the *Instrucción para el corso terrestre* of April 1809. The object of this *instrucción* was to legalize irregular warfare by adopting the analogy of commerce-raiding at sea. The text of the decree concentrated particularly on clarifying the relations between the guerilla fighters and the civil and military authorities. It clearly indicated the military objectives: to sabotage supply lines, intercept communications, destroy munitions depots, harass the enemy in order to keep him in an exhausting state of permanent alarm, and demoralize him by spreading false information. Finally, in July 1811, the *Reglamento para las partidas de guerilla*, adopted at Cadiz, gave a more general definition of the term 'guerilla'.

The Effectiveness of Guerilla Warfare Guerilla warfare functions in two dimensions: time and space. It transforms geographic space into a factor permanently hostile to the occupying army compelling it to accept dispersion, casualties and damage to its morale. The organization of the *guerillero* bands was based on small groups; in practice they never contained more than about one hundred men. They were lightly armed and possessed good and effective cavalry. Free of impedimenta, these bands had neither quartermasters nor supply services. They thus achieved maximum mobility, which enabled them to launch surprise attacks under optimum conditions. The guerilla war had important military consequences and this struggle of the unorthodox and weak against the orthodox and strong contributed immensely to the success of the War of Independence. However, its effect on the overall military situation must not be exaggerated. Had it not been for the British expeditionary corps and the Portuguese forces under Wellington, supported by the remnants of the Spanish regular army, conducting formal and systematic campaigns, the armies of France would not have been defeated in Spain. The principal achievements of the guerillas occurred when their activities were co-ordinated with the movements and operations of the regular forces.

The Pronunciamiento Following the War of Independence, particularly in the period after the return of constitutionalism in 1820, the struggle between absolutism, militarism, conservatism and emergent liberalism gave rise to numerous types of political conflict in most of which the armed forces were involved. Indeed, as Charles Esdaile has written, 'the chief legacy of the War of Independence was thus to afflict Spain with an army that not only possessed a tradition of political interventionism, but equated its own interests with the national good.' The subsequent popularity which the term *pronunciamiento* has enjoyed has contributed to writers making false analogies. The *pronunciamiento* possesses very specific features which have been analysed with great skill by Miguel Alonso Baquer. The *pronunciamiento* must be clearly distinguished from those other forms of internal conflict in which an attempt is made to gain power with the participation of the armed forces. The *pronunciamiento* is distinct also in the style of its action rather than in its ideological content. It is characterized by the low level of activity among its participants. It is a strategic mode of action, preferring indirect, complex and conspiratorial methods to an overt and direct approach.

The Spanish Typology In the typically Spanish *pronunciamiento*, the participants tend to await a favourable outcome rather than force the pace of events. It is an act of concealed force where a highly formalized procedure is designed to give the impression that reason will suffice. The objective is to convince rather than to overpower. From the military point of view, it really has no professional military content but, instead, substitutes intellectual force and moral courage. In practice, this type of conflict is usually manifested in a rebellion of the high command, fomented by political groups convinced that the officers' action will lead to political reforms without a disturbance of the public peace. During contemporary Spanish history, there have been liberal, royalist and militarist *pronunciamientos*. However, the phenomenon is sufficiently complex to include under its umbrella any situation in which a military man shows his disagreement with the government in power while also hinting at a possible armed intervention. There can only be a *pronunciamiento* where criticisms of the rulers are accompanied by a blatant intention to act with troops. Thus there has to be a rising against the authorities in order to force them to yield power. These authorities must then be supplanted by elements from within the new power group. In other words, there must be a rebellion within the precise definition accorded to this word in Spanish military law.

The Spanish Civil War (1936–9) The principal military event of the twentieth century in Spain has been the Civil War. Once again, one of the dominant features was that popular fighting spirit which runs throughout Spanish military history. The national rising of 18 July 1936, which regarded itself as a legitimate revolt, marked the beginning of a counter-revolution against a dictatorial minority that had taken hold of the levers of power and was leading the country towards socialism. The national army, which was 'popular' in the noblest sense of that word, transformed itself into a vehicle for this 'social action' of liberation. During that war, as had been the case throughout most of its long military history,

Spain provided an example of a struggle intensely sustained by a strong-willed, tenacious and determined people.

However, the wars and conflicts in which this spirit has been manifested have never descended into anarchy. The Spanish warrior spirit was channelled into a constructive force very early in its history by a brilliant and deceptively efficient administration. This passionate fighting spirit (*Reconquista*, War of Independence, Civil War), which gradually evolved into a military tradition, always recognized the comcomitant need for the reasoned analysis of military problems and formal military organization (*tercio*, organized guerilla warfare). The Spanish military style has a popular foundation which stands as a guarantee of the country's freedom. *See also* ADMINISTRATION, ARMY; ADMINISTRATION, NAVAL; ALBA; ARMADA; BELGIUM; CHAPLAINS; COLONIAL TROOPS; COMBINED OPERATIONS; CÓRDOBA; ENGINEERS; ETHOS; EXPEDITIONS; GLORY; INFANTRY; INTENDANTS; LEPANTO; LOGISTICS; MORALE; NAVAL WARFARE; NAVIES; NETHERLANDS; PARMA; RAVENNA; ROCROI; SARAGOSSA; SIEGES; STAGING POSTS; STRATEGY; TACTICS; VITORIA.

R. QUATREFAGES
JOHN CHILDS

FURTHER READING
René Quatrefages, *Los Tercios* (Madrid, 1983); I. A. A. Thompson, *War and Government in Habsburg Spain, 1560–1620* (London, 1976); Geoffrey Parker, *The Army of Flanders and the Spanish Road, 1567–1659* (Cambridge, 1972); Charles J. Esdaile, *The Spanish Army in the Peninsular War* (Manchester, 1988); E. Christiansen, *The Origins of Military Power in Spain, 1800–1854* (Oxford, 1967); Hugh Thomas, *The Spanish Civil War* (London, 1961); *Armed Forces and Society in Spain, Past and Present*, eds R. Bañón Martínez and Thomas M. Barker (Boulder, Col., 1988).

Spanish Armada *See* ARMADA

Sparta Sparta, founded around the tenth century BC, was the chief settlement of Laconia in the southern Peloponnese. As the Spartans extended their influence over neighbouring peoples they enslaved their defeated enemies, who became helots, that is, virtual slaves of the Spartan state. They were allocated to individual masters but remained state property. At the end of the eighth century Sparta conquered the rich land of Messenia in the south-west Peloponnese and acquired a large number of helots from the defeated Messenians. The Spartans were outnumbered by these helots, whose sporadic revolts were a menace to the security of the state. In addition, throughout Laconia there were other communities subordinate to Sparta but with limited local autonomy, the inhabitants of which were called *perioikoi* and were expected to provide soldiers to assist the Spartan army. The Spartan citizen was in a unique position since he was the absentee landlord of land worked by others and therefore could devote much of his time to training for war. At some time, perhaps in the early seventh century, Sparta underwent a social reorganization, traditionally ascribed to Lycurgus. The *agoge* was a system of military training in which young children were taken from their parents and brought up as the responsibility of the state so as to foster courage, fortitude, competitiveness and discipline. At the age of thirty the Spartan was admitted to the assembly of the people. By this stage he may already have been admitted to a military *syssition*, a select group of equals with whom he ate and trained, and alongside whom he fought in battle. The Spartans persevered with this system and their devotion to military excellence, becoming increasingly insular and austere and rigorous in the conduct of everyday life when other Greek communities were responding to more civilized influences. Doubtless fear of the helots played a part. In any event, the additional training, discipline and comradeship of the Spartan hoplites gave them a distinct advantage over soldiers of other communities. By the late sixth century they had acquired a reputation for invincibility in infantry battles, and the other Greeks readily accepted Sparta as the supreme commander of the Greek military effort against the Persian invasion in 480–479 BC. The splendid resistance of the Spartan king Leonidas and his small band of soldiers at Thermopylae confirmed the image of Spartan military prowess. The Battle of Plataea in 479 which delivered Greece from the invaders was won largely by the discipline and military skill of the 5,000 Spartan hoplites, who faced the best Persian troops.

Down to the early fourth century BC the Spartans could not be defeated on land in hoplite warfare (with the exception of the famous incident at Pylos, where the Athenians managed to trap a small Spartan force and compel it to surrender), and developed their power through the leadership of a group of states in the Peloponnese which owed them allegiance and provided many of the troops for the campaigns they led. Greeks respected and feared Spartan military capabilities and also marvelled at the stability of Sparta's system of government, a peculiar combination of monarchy, aristocracy and democracy. In the Peloponnesian War, in which Sparta and her allies fought the Athenians (431–404 BC), since their superiority on land proved unable to secure victory, the Spartans eventually broke the stalemate by adventurously developing a naval competence and defeating Athens at sea. Military excellence therefore brought Sparta a dominant position in the Greek world after 404, but she lacked the political skill to exploit it and alienated many of her erstwhile supporters by her high-handed and oppressive actions, despite the effective military leadership of her king, Agesilaos. Moreover, the Spartans still relied on the traditional methods of the hoplite phalanx, and proved unable to counter the new tactics employed by the Theban leader Epaminondas at the Battle of Leuctra (371 BC). This crushing defeat need not have permanently broken Spartan power, but because the Spartans had become so unpopular, revolts against their dominance broke out throughout the Peloponnese and the Messenians successfully seized their freedom and founded Messenia anew. Sparta had further contributed to her own downfall by her narrow social system which excluded all outsiders

and led eventually to a significant decline during the fifth century in the numbers of true-born Spartans available for military service. From the mid-fourth century BC Sparta lapsed into increasing obscurity but the tradition of her toughness and hardihood has had an important influence on European thought and remains in the English language with the adjectives 'spartan' and 'laconic'. *See also* EPAMINONDAS; GREECE, ANCIENT; LEUCTRA; MANTINEA; MARATHON; PLATAEA; SALAMIS; THERMOPYLAE.

B. CAMPBELL

FURTHER READING
E. Rawson, *The Spartan Tradition in European Thought* (Oxford, 1969); W. G. Forrest, *A History of Sparta, 950–192 BC* (London, 1980); P. Cartledge, *Sparta and Lakonia, a Regional History 1300–362 BC* (London, 1979); J. F. Lazenby, *The Spartan Army* (Warminster, 1985); P. Cartledge, *Agesilaos and the Crisis of Sparta* (London, 1987).

Speech and speeches *See* LANGUAGE

Spinoza, Benedict de (1632–77) Spinoza was an unorthodox Dutch Jewish philosopher of the seventeenth century who subjected the dualism of René Descartes (1596–1650) to boldly speculative reinterpretation. One of the main reasons for continued interest in his work is that he was one of the most systematic initiators of a thoroughly naturalistic understanding of the world, dispensing with the religious assumptions characteristic of medieval thought. He equated God with Nature, and argued that the true good for man lay in contemplating Divine Nature. Not surprisingly, this lofty doctrine led him to regard ordinary human life as being driven by passion rather than reason. The instinctual aim of each individual human being was, he thought, self-preservation, but human beings tend to be bad at this because passion prevents them from thinking clearly, and must be expected to continue doing so. In his political writings, the stark duality between (rare) reason and (everyday) passion leads to an explanation of war and the state which emphasizes individual human nature rather than the state or the inter-state system. *See also* GENTILI; GROTIUS; LAWS OF WAR; VATTEL; VITORIA.

BARRIE PASKINS

FURTHER READING
Kenneth Waltz, *Man, the State and War* (New York, 1959).

Staff *See* GENERAL STAFF

Staging posts During her Eighty Years' War (1567–1648) with the rebellious provinces of the Netherlands, Spain made extensive military use of an existing system of roads and staging posts between the Low Countries and Italy. The route stretched through Lombardy, Savoy, Franche-Comté, Lorraine and Luxembourg, enabling troops to be sent from the ports of northern Italy to the Spanish Army of Flanders. In Franche-Comté, the 'Spanish Road' consisted of four parallel tracks, the choice of which depended on climatic conditions and the need to avoid obstacles. To feed her troops in transit on the 'Spanish Road', Spain developed the system of étapes, 'staples' or staging posts. Such centres, where merchants could meet their customers and store, sell and distribute merchandise, had long been in use in civilian commerce but they were adapted to military use in the mid-sixteenth century. By an ordonnance of 1544, the French military took over the administration of étapes and in 1551 a chain of étapes was created to supply the passage of French troops through the Maurienne valley into Italy. In 1623, the Spanish army en route along the 'Spanish Road' established a chain of étapes.

Apart from greater efficiency, étapes removed the burden of troops billeting on private householders during a march. By designating certain towns to serve as étapes, the French developed the necessary infrastructure of stores, provisions, communications, barracks and quarters along the principal internal roads regularly employed by the army as it marched to the frontiers or tramped from one internal garrison to another. After 1623, the French established four main lines of military communication: Brittany to Marseilles; Normandy to Languedoc; Picardy to Bayonne; and Saintonge to Bresse. By the eighteenth century, most of the main French roads were equipped with étapes, civilian contractors providing the foodstuffs and fodder. In 1778, the Comte de Saint-Germain took the business out of the hands of private contractors and formed a state-owned company to supply the étapes. This became the basis for Napoleon Bonaparte's supply system which depended more on magazines than étapes. With the advent of railways for troop transport in the mid-nineteenth century, the étapes system declined in importance although it did not disappear until after 1870. *See also* BARRACKS; BILLETING; INTENDANTS; LOGISTICS; RATIONS; TRANSPORT.

B. KROENER
JOHN CHILDS

FURTHER READING
G. Parker, *The Army of Flanders and the Spanish Road* (Cambridge, 1972); C. C. Sturgill, 'Changing garrisons: the French system of étapes', *Canadian Journal of History*, xx (1985), pp. 193–201.

Stalin, Josef Vissarionovich Dzhugashvili, known as (1879–1953) Stalin was born in Gori, Georgia. He was educated for the priesthood but was expelled from the seminary for his political views. Stalin was twice exiled to Siberia, escaping on both occasions. From 1914 to 1916 he was imprisoned. In 1917, Stalin was prominent in the revolution and became Commissar for Nationalities. Stalin established a modest military reputation during the civil war for his efforts in the defence of Tsaritsyn (later renamed Stalingrad). After the death of Lenin in 1924, Stalin defeated Trotsky in the struggle for the succession, becoming undisputed leader of the Communist Party around 1928. During the 1930s, Stalin promoted the growth of the Red Army, but decapitated it by the 'purges' that either killed or removed most of its leaders in

1937–9. Fearing that the West was attempting to divert Hitler against the Soviet Union, Stalin signed the Nazi–Soviet Non-Aggression Pact on 23 August 1939. Stalin attempted to secure the Soviet Union's frontiers by initiating a war with Finland in November 1940, but this merely exposed the weaknesses of the Red Army. As a result of the poor showing of the Red Army, Stalin initiated a number of reforms, and promoted several commanders, including Zhukov, to key posts. Ignoring warnings provided to him both by his own intelligence sources and by Churchill, Stalin was caught unawares by the German attack of 22 June 1941. After an initial period of wavering, Stalin took supreme control of the Soviet war effort, appointing himself Commissar for War, taking the rank of general (1943) and later generalissimo (1945). For the most part, Stalin took the military advice of such people as Shaposhnikov and gave his generals their head. The war effort was co-ordinated by a collective body, the *Stavka Glavnovo Komandovaniia* (High Command Headquarters) headed by Stalin. He paid particular attention to appointments and moved capable men like Zhukov to the fronts where they were most needed. Stalin maintained Soviet war production at the highest possible levels and inculcated a sense of patriotism and national military values within the country. His efforts to do this included the removal of political commissars within the army in 1942 and the relaxation of the restrictions formerly placed on the Orthodox Church. During the war, Stalin proved a hard-nosed negotiator at the Allied conferences held at Teheran (1943) and Yalta (1945). After the war, Stalin made certain that none of his generals would be a threat to his leadership by appointing them to minor posts. At the same time, to counter the military strength of the West and to ensure that the Soviet Union achieved nuclear parity with the United States, Stalin launched a policy of re-armament. He also strengthened the grip of the Soviet Union on the Eastern European countries that the Red Army had liberated from the Germans during the war, using the Soviet military presence in these countries to set up puppet governments subservient to Moscow. In June 1948, Stalin precipitated the Cold War by quarrelling with the Western Allies about the way in which the occupation of Germany should be handled. He died in March 1953. *See also* KONEV; LENINGRAD; MOSCOW, BATTLE OF; RUSSIA/USSR; SHAPOSHNIKOV; SOVIET MILITARY THEORISTS; TROTSKY; ZHUKOV.

A. CORVISIER
KEITH NEILSON

FURTHER READING
John Erickson, *The Soviet High Command* (London, 1962); John Erickson, *The Road to Stalingrad* (London, 1975); John Erickson, *The Road to Berlin* (London, 1983); Adam Ulam, *Stalin: the man and his era* (London, 1974).

Stalingrad, Battle of (24 August 1942–2 February 1943) The German summer offensive of 1942 had as its goals the capture of Rostov, Stalingrad and the oil fields of the Caucasus. The early success of the offensive led Hitler to order on 13 July that the latter two objectives should be pursued simultaneously. On 23 August, the German 6th Army, under the command of von Paulus, reached Stalingrad and the battle for the city began. This conflict was one of the most bitter in modern history. The city was so damaged by the German attack that the streets were largely impassable to vehicles. Street-to-street and house-to-house fighting became the standard, and Soviet resistance was unparalleled in its ferocity and endurance. Meanwhile, other German forces continued onwards towards the Caucasus, ensuring that the northern flank of the German advance was only weakly held. On 19 November, the Red Army took advantage of this situation and launched a major counter-attack, which Zhukov had planned in September, designed to trap both the German forces at Stalingrad and those in the Caucasus. While the forces in the Caucasus were eventually able to extricate themselves from this encirclement, Hitler was convinced that a retreat from Stalingrad was out of the question. Drawing on his experience at the end of the 1941 campaign, and persuaded that the *Luftwaffe* could supply the 6th Army from the air, Hitler ordered von Paulus to stand fast. In December, German forces attempted to fight their way through to the embattled 6th Army, but were unable to link up with von Paulus's force. The fate of the German forces at Stalingrad was sealed. On 30 January 1943, von Paulus and his staff surrendered, and on 2 February the last German soldiers capitulated. The Germans had lost in all 300,000 men. Stalingrad was a bitter blow to the Germans. It marked the first major defeat for Hitler's army, giving new hope to the Soviet forces. While the German army was able to regain the strategic initiative in 1943, Stalingrad was important both in a strategic and symbolic sense. The victory of the Soviet forces was due to the over-extension of the German army, the heroic resistance of the Soviet forces and the skill of the Soviet high command, who cleverly took advantage of the situation. *See also* KURSK SALIENT; MANSTEIN; RUSSIA/USSR; ZHUKOV.

A. CORVISIER
KEITH NEILSON

FURTHER READING
Earl F. Ziemke, *Stalingrad to Berlin, the German Defeat in the East* (Washington, 1968); John Erickson, *The Road to Stalingrad* (London, 1975).

Standards *See* VEXILLOLOGY

Stevin, Simon (1548–1620) This Flemish mathematician, scientist and civil and military engineer was born in Bruges. Until 1570 he worked as a merchant's clerk in Antwerp before travelling extensively in Germany, Poland and Norway. He then settled in Holland and took up a teaching position at Leiden University; one of his students was Prince Maurice of Orange-Nassau, stadholder of the United Provinces after 1584. As a mathematician, Stevin helped to standardize the use of decimal fractions, ideas which he published in *La Thiende* (1585) and *La Disme* (1585). He made important contributions to the science of fluid mechanics and as-

(University of Leiden)

sisted in the refutation of the Aristotelian notion that heavier bodies fall faster than lighter bodies. After about 1590, Prince Maurice frequently consulted Stevin on matters relating to fortification and castrametation. He is mentioned as quartermaster-general and engineer of the Dutch army in 1592 and additionally held the post of commissioner of the public water works. Stevin planned entrenched camps and drew up instructions for the building of fortifications and the conduct of sieges. More importantly, Stevin designed the series of sluices and inundations which became the basis of Holland's 'Water Line'. His ideas were encapsulated in *Sterctenbouwing* (1594), in which he advocated a number of mathematical rules for the design of fortifications. This book was the theoretical expression of the 'Old Netherlands' System' of fortification whose principal exponent was Adriaen Anthonisz. Stevin frequently attended at sieges to advise on the methods of attack.

In 1600, Stevin and Prince Maurice established an embryonic school of military engineering at the University of Leiden. Lectures were delivered in Dutch rather than Latin. Stevin inspired many military engineers, especially A. Freitag and M. Dögen; the nineteenth-century Belgian engineer Henri Brialmont was profoundly influenced by Stevin's work. *See also* BREDA, SIEGE OF; COEHOORN; ENGINEERS; FORTIFICATION; NASSAU; NETHERLANDS; SIEGES; VAUBAN.

C. M. SCHULTEN
JOHN CHILDS

FURTHER READING
R. Depau, *Simon Stevin* (Brussels, 1942); Eduard Jan Dijsterhuis, *Simon Stevin: science in the Netherlands around 1600* (The Hague, 1970); *The Principal Works of Simon Stevin*, ed. W. H. Schukking (Amsterdam, 1964), iv, *The Art of War*.

Strategic arms limitation *See* DISARMAMENT; LAWS OF WAR; NUCLEAR WARFARE

Strategy The word 'strategy' derives from two Greek words – *stratos*/army and *agein*/to lead. It means the tactical and logistical control of a military operation. Therefore, it has generally been identified with the art of generalship, following the example of the Athenians who termed their military commander *strategos*. This word was again used with this meaning in the early period of the Roman Empire, around the first century AD, by Onasander, a philosopher of the Platonic school. But the Greeks themselves frequently designated the art of war ('military affairs') by the word 'tactics' (*taktika* sc. *techne*, i.e. the art of arranging, of putting into position). So did such writers as Polybius, Aeneas Tacticus and Aelianus Tacticus (this last being the author of a *Taktike theoria*). The word applied to the more specialized art of besieging cities was *poliorcetics*, from two Greek words meaning 'city' and 'art of capture'. The word 'strategy' found no greater favour with the Romans; Vegetius entitled his famous treatise *Epitoma rei militaris*. The Byzantines also preferred to use the word 'tactics' for the art of war and though the Emperor Maurice (assassinated in AD 602) still called his work on the subject *Strategikon*, Leo VI (AD 886–912) devoted his volume to military organization and tactics and gave it the title of *Treatise on Tactical Systems*. The last great Byzantine compilation on military matters – the work of Nicephorus Phocas – also went under the heading of 'tactics'. Similarly, although Polyaenus and Frontinus certainly spoke of 'stratagems', in the sense of schemes of various types designed to deceive an enemy in war, the word 'strategy' found little place in Western European languages of Graeco-Roman descent, except in its ancient Athenian sense or with a rather restricted meaning.

Spanish and Italian authors of the Renaissance, such as Machiavelli, dealt with the 'art of war', and writers of the succeeding classical period used the word 'tactics' in the sense defined by Furetière as the 'science of marshalling troops for battle and of manoeuvring them'. Together with the 'science of fortification', 'small-scale' and 'major' tactics were held to constitute the whole 'art of war'. Yet the best minds believed that, from among the tangle of causes and effects, of traditional wisdom and fresh discoveries, it was possible to elicit, by reasoning or intuition, some rules or principles which could be used as guidance for further studies, and to set out in a systematic treatise the whole expanse of knowledge on the subject, while at the same time providing a guide for practical action. In other words, the hope was to evolve a coherent theory which went beyond rule-of-thumb practice or that sudden flash of brilliant intuition on the battlefield so highly regarded by proponents of the theory of an innate faculty of generalship, and viewed by them as the point where war 'touches the sublime'.

In 1749, Puységur noted that a military theory (or, to use more modern terminology, a formulation of mathematical precision) had been worked out only for fortification, and for attacking and defending fortresses (cf. the work of Italian and Dutch engineers and Vauban). To this list were gradually added artillery, mines and then, thanks to Puységur himself, the moving and supplying of armed forces. Authors as dissimilar as Folard or Mesnil-Durand, who were advocates of formations in depth, and Guibert, who supported the thin, continuous line as used by Frederick the Great, asserted the need to apply the same kind of thinking to marches and orders of battle. In short, they wished to formulate a theory – alongside that of elementary 'minor tactics' relating to the engagement in battle of various types of unit – of 'major tactics', as the science and analysis of the calculable relationships between masses of men, movements, positions, time and space. 'Major tactics', when defined in this way, was no longer regarded as forming merely one aspect of warfare, but as the very basis of the art. Politics remained, so Guibert thought, 'the great and sublime science of guiding individual interests so that they contribute to the general good'. Not only was politics a science that reviews all possible relationships between all relevant factors, but also the art of balancing and reconciling them, together with a determination to bring them into line with each other and to fix their respective bounds.

At the end of the eighteenth century and the beginning of the nineteenth, the word 'strategy' became commonly accepted in its modern sense. 'Making war is a matter of reflection, combination of ideas, foresight, reasoning in depth and use of available means. Some of these means are direct, others indirect; these latter are so numerous that they comprise practically everything known to man. In order to formulate plans, strategy studies the relationships between time, positions, means and different interests, and takes every factor into account . . . which is the province of dialectics, that is to say, of reasoning, which is the highest faculty of the mind.' In fact, Joly de Maizeroy goes on, 'although pure dialectics represents the intellectual activity of the highest faculty, it is nevertheless based on elementary theory'. He defined tactics as 'the concept of the position of a given formation of soldiers in relation to that of other formations that make up an army, of their movements, their actions and

their interconnections. Tactics is a science dealing with magnitudes and ratios' (a point of view particularly favoured by the geometrical school of thought). But under the influence of the supporters of the rival geographical school, definitions began to stress military and topographical aspects at the expense of the more general ones drawn from logical reasoning and combinatory analysis. The Archduke Charles of Habsburg wrote: 'Strategy is the science of war: it produces the overall plans, and it takes into its hands and decides on the general course of military enterprises; it is, in strict terms, the science of the commander-in-chief. Tactics is the art of war: it teaches the way in which major military projects should be put into execution. Every formation commander must possess this art.'

The way in which the Revolutionaries, such as Carnot and Napoleon, used the relationships between large bodies of men, movement and firepower, and the introduction into the debate, by the German school of such theorists as Berenhorst and Clausewitz, of the moral qualities of a nation and the possibility of choosing the degree of violence to be employed in the prosecution of war, lent support to this distinction between strategy and tactics; hence, it remained in use until the Second World War and gave rise to a number of definitions based on the concept of two levels. One of these definitions drew a distinction between the political authorities, the commander-in-chief and subordinate commanders in their ranking order, with each higher level providing the objectives for the actions of the one below. Another differentiated between the two types of action with reference to their objects – that of strategy being the preparation of forces and their movement into position (i.e. to arrange with what, when and where to fight), and of tactics the prosecution of the battle (i.e. the conduct of the actual fighting).

Numerous writers have pronounced on the nature of strategy. According to Bülow, it was 'the science of the movement of troops, when outside the range of the enemy'; the totality of 'operations which span the theatre of war as a whole' (Jomini);

769

that part of the art of war which relates to 'general movements executed out of sight of the enemy and prior to the battle' (Marmont); 'the art of moving one's forces across the theatre of operations in such a way as to bring them on to the battlefield in close-knit formation' (Guibert). Admiral Castex summarized these views, while at the same time showing his support for them, in the concise formulation: 'Strategy's sphere stops short of the battlefield and continues beyond it.'

These writers respectively describe tactics as 'the science of movements carried out in the face of the enemy'; or 'the manoeuvring of an army on the day of battle, engagements, the pitching of camp and the various formations in which to lead troops in the attack'; or 'the art of handling troops on the battlefield and of making them march in good order'; or 'the art, when on the battlefield, of bringing the whole weight of one's forces to bear on a vital point'; or, according to another inclusive formulation from Castex: 'During an operation, tactics come into play from the time that fighting begins and until it ceases.'

All of this can be summarized in the following definition by Rüstow: 'Strategy is the art of commanding armies. It comprises the art of fighting battles, of moving forces and of resting.' Or, according to the definition given by the Littré dictionary, which shows the senses in which words were understood at the start of the nineteenth century, it is 'the art of drafting a plan of campaign, of directing the movement of an army towards vital or strategic points, and of picking out the places where, in the course of battles, the greatest weight of men must be brought to bear to ensure success.' Tactics, according to the same authority, is 'the art of fighting battles and of using the three main arms – infantry, cavalry and artillery – on terrain and in positions that are favourable to them.'

These many definitions have given rise to a huge amount of controversy in regard to their inclusions and exclusions, their pleonasms and tautologies, and the academic issue of whether strategy and tactics are arts or sciences. They have also left unanswered three basic questions. The

first centred on the preparation of an army – the instrument of war – in peacetime and on its relationship with conscription (involving a nation in arms and general mobilization), and with the civil administration and the economic system.

The second was the effect of the industrial revolution on war, which was becoming increasingly dependent on the products of manufacturing industry owing to the importance of firepower and mobility, whether powered by steam (in railway trains, ships) or petrol-driven (motor transport, aircraft, tanks). As a result, the idea of 'logistics' came to the fore. This expression at first denoted the task of arranging the movement of marching formations and of putting troops into billets and camps, hence its possible derivation from *logis* (lodging). Jomini extends logistics from a 'science of detail' to 'practically the whole of the science of staff work', in the sense of 'bringing to bear . . . on the vital points in the operational area formations . . . which have started out from widely separated places'. Littré defines logistics as 'that part of the military art whose object is to study the ways and means of bringing troops who have been mobilized, together with their equipment and transport, from their camps and garrison stations to forming up areas, and from there to the theatre of operations, with the maximum speed. Logistics provides the basis for strategy.' The greater supplies of ammunition necessitated by the increase in firepower and the complexity of equipment employed during major conflicts overseas (Abyssinian War, Sino-Japanese War, Second World War) have transformed it into one of the main aspects of strategy. Certain linguists now connect it etymologically with the Greek words *logistikon/logistike*, i.e. the faculty of reasoning and formulating practical calculations.

The third and final problem concerns the reciprocal relationships between politics, strategy and tactics, and the degree of their mutual subordination or otherwise. Clausewitz produced the imposing pronouncement: 'By the expression "direct destruction [of the enemy forces]" are to be understood tactical successes. They alone can lead to major strategic successes . . . and thus have a preponderant influence on the course of a war.' Accordingly, 'victory – that is to say, tactical success – is merely a first step, a means from the viewpoint of strategy, whose aim and object – which, moreover, are set by politics – are mastery of those aspects of the situation which it is thought will lead directly to peace', since 'war is merely a continuation of politics by other means.'

But alongside such views, there was also an intensification of revolutionary ideas and upheavals, and a condemnation of 'bourgeois military science' as excessively limited. This lay behind Lenin's inversion of Clausewitz's dictum in his remark that 'politics is a continuation of war by other means'. Hence, there were instances of the theories of strategy being turned upside down, in a way similar to what Marx and Engels had done in the case of the Hegelian dialectic, when they gave it a political and economic orientation in their aim to predict theoretically an intensification of industrial production which might result in the corollary of revolts on the part of the urban proletariat. This reversal of strategic concepts received illustration in the controversy between Trotsky and Stalin over continuous worldwide revolution or revolution in one country first. It is also evident in Mao Tse-Tung's synthesis of the wisdom of the ancient Chinese art of war, as described by Sun-Tzu. For Mao, the aim of strategy was to exploit the enemy's internal contradictions whilst eradicating those of one's own side. In the application of this doctrine to Vietnam and South America, the revolutionary's mode of existence among his own people needed to be like that of 'a fish in water'. To Guevara, strategy was 'analysis of objectives to be attained in the overall military situation and the measures needed for attaining them'. Since the period of decolonization, such ideas have been the cause of revolutionary and subversive wars, guerilla and terrorist movements and, as their counterpart, counter-revolutionary psychological warfare.

For the Marxist school in general and the Soviet one in particular, strategy remains, nevertheless, one of the branches of 'military science' and, because its theory must always be brought into line with its practice, its substance varies and takes its tone from developments in the nature of wars, but its 'laws are objective and apply impartially to both camps' (Sokolovsky).

As a result of all these phenomena, the word 'strategy' underwent a semantic change, and came to mean the totality of the actions and the institutional structures of a given society when confronted with the problems posed by the attitudes of enemies and tensions manifesting themselves in varying degrees of violence. Hence, the Robert dictionary, which reflects linguistic usage of about thirty years ago, defines strategy as the 'aspect of military science which is concerned with the overall direction of war and the organization of national defence: major operations, the drafting of plans of attack and defence that take account of the number of men available, logistics, industrial potential, salient geographic, diplomatic and political factors, etc.'.

This definition is, broadly speaking, analogous to the concept of 'national defence', in the form which it took between the First and Second World Wars, and as it figured in publications dealing with national organization in time of war or of danger from violent conflict, and with preparations for such conflicts and with the wartime economy. In short, it is in line with the idea of total war which came to the fore, as Ludendorff wrote, with the appearance of conflicts based on industrial potential and spanning the globe, and with the rise of worldwide revolutionary movements.

What is striking, however, about this new definition is its composite and heterogeneous nature. It can, nevertheless, be noted that it is still centred on the military aspect *per se*, although it takes account of the way in which it is influenced by extra-military factors. It no longer emphasizes, like Littré, the decisive character of strategic action, and it specifies the disparate factors which it has to mould into a composite whole. It is summed up in the Anglo-Saxon concept of 'grand strategy' as 'the most effective application of the art via all the powers possessed by the state'.

It reflected a huge change in the way in which the word was understood. Until the 1950s, strategy constituted one component only of the entire range of military action: it was no more than one of the major 'aspects' which war embraced. But today, as a result of the proliferation of the factors which it has to co-ordinate, and because the nuclear deterrent appears to have prevented (at least temporarily) the starting of major wars, a radical change has taken place in the relationship between strategy and war – it has, indeed, been inverted. Strategy now embraces war, which has become, as compared with other, more inclusive types of conflict, no more than a limited phenomenon, even if it is in the form of the hypothetical – and perhaps terminal – nuclear cataclysm.

Thus, the content of the concept of strategy has undergone modification throughout history. At the outset, it was the art of directing operations and of positioning and manoeuvring bodies of troops, as distinct from dealing in detail with the way in which battles were conducted. Later, it came to include a succession of technical factors which allowed a commander to extend the range of his control, in terms of time and space, over those who carried out his orders, and subsequently, aspects of logistics too. It now embraces psychological, socio-economic and even political and ideological factors, deployed to ensure the most effective development of national power.

This general shift of strategy away from the battlefield allows the old 'art of war' to extend into new fields. Over and above the conventional ones like 'strategic geography', geostrategy and geopolitics, the 'art of war' now takes into account geodesy, geosociology, demography as a function of ecology, economic development and the mass media. It is also concerned with the conquest of underwater and cosmic spaces and it seeks to co-ordinate the activities of society as a whole, and all the productive energy and strength of the nation or to integrate those of any social group that is disaffected.

The leading figure is, as a result, doubly removed. He is increasingly separated, in a physical sense, from the various theatres of war and from those operating in them, the constraints that limit his range of action now being merely a function of the present state of technology, instead of the old ones imposed by spatial and temporal separation; and strategy becomes a logical exercise carried out with intellectual representations of objects (troops, terrain, armaments, etc.), and not with these objects themselves. Accordingly, types of action and procedures which would once have been classed as strategic have been demoted to the level of tactics, while a distinction is now drawn, within the broad conception of strategy, between various types of plan (i.e. overall, general, specific, operational and those concerned with the methods of employment of particular forms of armament).

In fact, a significant modification has occurred in the dictionary treatment of the word. The sense of strategy just mentioned, as disengaged from actual battle and reduced to an ordered plan and a succession of 'moves', was previously represented by the word 'tactics' in its figurative sense, which Littré defined as 'course followed, means used, for success' and the Robert dictionary as 'the set of means employed in co-ordinated fashion to arrive at a result'. Thus 'strategy' has tended to hand over its purely military or war-related aspects to 'tactics' and the latter to lose its most general meaning to the word 'strategy'.

A similar critical analysis can be applied to strategies which seem, at first sight, to be highly futuristic. The observer who adopts the viewpoint of strategy *stricto sensu* (i.e. who bases himself on principles that can be detached from direct connection with military preparations and policies and from accepted theories regarding the use of various combinations of force) can see that it is (relatively) simpler to produce a rational basis for strategies of deterrence than for strategies involving conventional warfare; for, once it is accepted that the world is divided into areas of (relative) immunity and the opposite – a state of affairs which is the outcome of the operation of psychological factors, of the constraints of politics, history, geography, etc. and of emotional preferences based on the belief that there are 'vital interests' which can be readily perceived – the plans of strategies of deterrence bring into play elements that are smaller in number and less heterogeneous in nature (i.e. some thousands of warheads and delivery systems) than those which would be involved in conflicts between entire national populations in arms, backed by total mobilization in the demographic, ideological and economic senses. They also offer opportunities for quantification and negotiation and hence for combinative logic and simpler mathematical tools (e.g. game theory), whose use is assisted by computers, for the taking of decisions, and by electronic warfare in the conduct of operations.

Thus strategy can no longer be defined as 'the set of dispositions and measures to be taken, precautions to be observed etc., in conducting an army into the presence of the enemy', but becomes an art of decision-making. Beaufre produced a general, abstract formulation for strategy, writing that it was 'the art of the dialectic of wills, employing force to settle their differences'. And though Raymond Aron was still holding to classical ideas when he said, 'let us agree to call the conduct of the totality of military operations strategy and the conduct of relations with other political entities diplomacy . . . both being subordinate to politics', he later proposed a definition which brought in the differing conceptions of the world that were in play: 'By strategy I mean long-term objectives and the view of history which makes the choice of these intelligible; by tactics, I mean the day-to-day reactions, the putting together of measures to achieve aims which have already been fixed.' In this way, he re-opened the old controversy between the 'doctrinaires' who asserted the possibility of establishing a system of general application (to a given historical epoch) and the empiricists who affirmed that every human group is the vehicle of a history, an economy, a culture, etc. and must produce its own strategy from within itself. The problem, however, disappears in part if a distinction is drawn between the strategic courses which clearly have a specific relationship to the basic philosophical principles and political objectives of the group, and the intended modes of action, which must be of a kind common to a number of groups because they are dependent on technical possibilities that happen to exist at a particular period.

Consequently, strategy may be defined as 'the function which, by use of rational principles, organizes and directs the whole of the forces (resources and systems, not all of these being fully or constantly mobilized) of social entities with their various negative or positive attitudes, which are more or less intense and between which there is no necessary correlation or reciprocal equivalence.' And tactics can be defined as 'reification of one's enemy/convergence with one's ally through mastery of the natural (physical), psychological and social milieu.' The need to co-ordinate spheres of responsibility, disciplines and techniques, which are much more numerous than was previously the case, and to establish methods of analysis which can deal with a multiplicity of factors, means that the classic (conventional) plans of campaign, orders of battle and ideas drawn from peacetime manoeuvres have to be abandoned and the age-old principles of warfare – freedom of action, initiative, concentration of force, economy of effort, destruction of the opponent's organized formations, supremacy of psychological factors, etc. – are relegated to the mere status of 'guidelines'.

An accurate distinction thus has to be drawn between the various 'levels' of strategy, since this makes it easier, at the present time, to 'categorize' them, with their similarities and differences, while at the same time introducing new content. It is the aim in setting out these 'levels' to separate the processes of planning and decision-making from executive tasks at the technical level. A 'total' or 'strato-political' strategy, in the case of a given political entity, would bring together, alongside a classic military strategy (itself subdivided into specific forms – e.g. land, naval, air, space, revolutionary), economic, financial, psycho-political, etc. strategies. Each strategy would be divided into 'general' (study of the objectives laid down by higher levels and formation of a plan for attaining them) and 'operational' strategies (establishing a doctrine capable of serving for a reasonable period on the use of technical and tactical methods; and conduct of operations). In short, this mode of sectionalizing the subject should allow, in particular, more rapid changes from one form of strategy, which has 'got stuck', to another which will enable freedom of action to be regained.

The division of strategy in this way fits in with another widely accepted distinction, between the strategy of deterrence, the direct type of strategy (use of force) and the indirect (combination of a limited form of constraint with a wide-ranging psycho-sociological offensive), whether or not the last two are linked with 'strategies of action' or with tactics that avoid the use of force. This distinction could break down because of the difficulty in determining the exact line where an indirect type of strategy turns into a direct one, and vice versa. It might be reformulated as follows: direct strategy would be the type characterized by the use of effective force, whatever might be its strength or nature – from terrorism to major warfare – and whatever the other forms of action employed; and indirect strategy would cover policies based on operations of deterrence or persuasion, by whatever means – the threat of nuclear or other weapons (e.g. chemical, biological), and the use of the mass media, large-scale population transfers, economic strategy, etc. But even within each specialized strategy, this distinction between direct and indirect aspects tends to reappear.

Thus the modern definition of strategy is an outcome of an analysis of the policies that come into play when armies confront one another; it derives from the battlefield. However, the extension of its content and the enlargement of the prizes it offers have brought in their train a multiplication of the areas in which it is applied (e.g. the economic, social, literary, cultural). The very success of the concept of strategy has led to its devaluation. *See also* CARTOGRAPHY; CHEMICAL AND BIOLOGICAL WARFARE; CIVIL WAR; COMMAND; DETERRENCE; ECONOMIC WARFARE; INDIRECT WARFARE; LOGISTICS; NAVAL WARFARE; NUCLEAR WARFARE; PLANNING; POPULAR WARFARE; WEAPONS.

BÜLOW; CASTEX; CHAMLAY; CHARLES OF HABSBURG; CLAUSEWITZ; CORBETT; DOUHET; FREDERICK II; FRONTINUS; GAMBIEZ; GUIBERT; HANNIBAL; JOMINI; LENIN; LIDDELL HART; MACHIAVELLI; MANSTEIN; MAO TSE-TUNG; NAPOLEON; NICEPHORUS II PHOCAS; ONASANDER; ROMMEL; RUNDSTEDT; SCHLIEFFEN; SHAPOSHNIKOV; SOKOLOVSKY; SUN-TZU; TIRPITZ; VILLARS; WELLINGTON; YAMAMOTO.

J.-P. CHARNAY

FURTHER READING
Philippe Contamine, *War in the Middle Ages* (London, 1984); D. G. Chandler, *The Atlas of Military Strategy: the art, theory and practice of war* (London, 1980); B. H. Liddell Hart, *Strategy* (2nd edn, New York, 1967); J. Baylis, K. Booth, J. Garnett and P. Williams, *Contemporary Strategy* (2 vols, London, 1987).

Strategy, air *See* AVIATION; COMBINED OPERATIONS; STRATEGY

Strategy, naval *See* COMBINED OPERATIONS; NAVAL WARFARE; NAVIES; STRATEGY

Suffren, Pierre André, bailli de Saint-Tropez (1726–88) After an active early career, in which he was twice captured, Suffren obtained some fame commanding a xebec (a three-masted vessel) in efforts against Barbary piracy. During the American War of Independence, he achieved the destruction of five English frigates at Newport (Rhode Island) in 1778, took part in the Battle of Grenada and the action at Savannah in 1779, and in the capture of a convoy in 1780.

Sent to the East Indies in 1781, with five ships of the line and two frigates, he dealt a serious blow at a parallel British squadron at Porto Praya (16 April 1781), thus saving the Cape. In 1782–3 he fought five actions with the British squadron under Hughes – Sadras (17 February 1782), Provedien (12 April 1782), Negapatam (6 July 1782),

Trincomalee (3 September 1782) and Cuddalore (17 June 1783). All were indecisive, though he attempted to cut through the enemy line. He showed great resource in keeping his force ready for action, but was ill-supported by some of his captains. Nevertheless, his sparkling campaign earned him a permanent place in the history of the French navy. *See also* FRANCE; GRASSE DE TILLY; NAVAL WARFARE; NAVIES.

J. MEYER

FURTHER READING
P. Masson, *Histoire de la marine française* (Paris, 1981–3); Herbert W. Richmond, *The Navy in India, 1763–1783* (London, 1931).

Sun-Tzu (fourth century BC) Sun-Tzu was a general in ancient China who is thought to have served in the army of the king of Wu (Nanking). He was the author of one of the first military treatises, *The Art of War* (*Ping-fa*), a document which may have been written between 400 and 320 BC during the period of the 'Warring States', or, more precisely, at the point when the character of warfare was undergoing a change from a 'chivalric' to a 'realistic' style in which the sole criterion was efficiency. In pursuit of this efficiency, Sun-Tzu advocated the use of espionage. He urged that the 'net' of agents, whom he divided into five separate categories which are similar to those recognized today, should be spread wide and that these agents should be handled with humanity but firmness. In Sun-Tzu's view, 'the whole art of war rests on deception'. *See also* CHINA; INDIRECT WARFARE; INTELLIGENCE; MAO TSE-TUNG.

J. ALLEMAND

FURTHER READING
S. B. Griffith, *Sun-Tzu, The Art of War* (New York and Oxford, 1963).

Suomussalmi, Battle of *See* RUSSO-FINNISH WAR

Supply *See* BARRACKS; BILLETING; INTENDANTS; LOGISTICS; RATIONS; SERVICES; STAGING POSTS

Surcouf, Robert (1773–1827) Surcouf, who was related to the Trouins, went to sea in merchant vessels at an early age. After sailing to Port-Louis (Mauritius) as a lieutenant on a corvette, he took command there in 1795 of the *Émilie*, which conducted a successful campaign against the British in the Bay of Bengal. He was sent back to France after a dispute with the governor of the Mascarene Islands, but he returned to Mauritius in 1798. As a privateer, first in the *Clarisse* and then, in 1800, in the *Confiance*, he successfully raided commercial shipping throughout the Indian Ocean. Surcouf sailed to France after the Peace of Amiens and fitted out several privateers at St Malo. In 1807, he returned to commerce-raiding in the Indian Ocean in person commanding the *Revenant* which took sixteen prizes. Although he retired from the sea in 1808, he owned and invested in privateers until 1815 when he transferred his interests to peacetime commerce. In a period when the French regular navy, which had lost so many officers and ships, saw defeat pile upon defeat, when French sea-borne trade was virtually wiped out and commerce-raiding in general had proved a failure, Surcouf was one of the few French privateers to make significant captures. He also demonstrated the utility of the French bases in the Mascarene Islands. He owes his fame, which has been enhanced by the fact that he operated in distant seas, to the contrast between his exceptional achievements and the failings of the Revolutionary and Imperial navies. *See also* BLOCKADES; COMMERCE-RAIDING; NAVAL PERSONNEL; NAVAL WARFARE; NAVIES.

J. MEYER

FURTHER READING
P.Masson, *Histoire de la marine française* (Paris, 1981–3); E. Taillemite, *Dictionnaire des marins français* (Paris, 1983).

Surrender A surrender is a treaty by which one of the contracting parties delivers himself over to the enemy, either unconditionally or under the terms of an agreement, but always on the tacit or declared condition that his life will be spared; the purpose is for both sides to lay down their arms, either temporarily or permanently.

Surrenders are generally associated with siege warfare: a surrender is the treaty which a fortified place (a town, stronghold or fortress) negotiates with a besieging army to bring the fighting to an end. According to the terms of the surrender, the garrison is permitted to withdraw, generally with all the honours of war. In the seventeenth century, foot soldiers were allowed to come out under arms, 'bullets in mouth and matches lit' (i.e. ready to fire), and preceded by their colours, which the enemy was not permitted to seize. In Flanders, the agreement usually specified the place to which the capitulating garrison was to retreat, and it was escorted all the way there by the enemy cavalry.

Since a surrender is a negotiated settlement, the defenders can secure a number of advantages from the victor. Thus when Bois-le-Duc ('s Hertogenbosch) capitulated in 1629 to the Prince of Orange, after a siege which had lasted the entire summer, the inhabitants obtained concessions from the Dutch on everything they desired, except on the one essential point of religion. The Catholic clergy were exiled to the Spanish Low Countries and the Catholic churches became Protestant. But whatever the stipulations laid down, surrender offered one major advantage to the civilian population: a town which capitulated was spared from being sacked, that is, from three days of systematic pillage. This was the reward the troops expected to be granted after they had stormed a town and which the general-in-chief could not refuse, whatever his personal sentiments. Authorized pillage was evidently used as a pretext for the worst possible acts of violence and could bring about the temporary ruin of a city, as in the cases of Antwerp in 1576 and Rome in 1527. But for the troops to be granted this privilege, the town had to be considered to have been captured by storm, generally after the ramparts had been breached. This demanded considerable effort on the part of the besieging army and caused a high level of casualties among the assailants without automatically producing a successful outcome. Thus during the Siege of Vienna in 1683, the terrified burghers put repeated pressure on the governor, Starhemberg, to negotiate a capitulation with the Grand Vizier, Kara Mustafa, so that they might be spared the horrors of pillage and slavery.

In his *Mémoires sur la guerre*, Turenne makes no secret of the fact that the local townspeople were as much potential enemies of the garrison as the besieging army. They were to be distrusted and controlled by terror; if it was discovered that they intended to rebel, in order to precipitate a favourable surrender, they should be 'warned that the four corners of the town would be set on fire and that they would be put to the sword'; it was therefore necessary to have spies among the civilian population who could identify the troublemakers so that such extreme measures might be avoided. Citadels or strongholds were constructed to allow the town to surrender whilst the besieging army had to undertake a second operation against the citadel. This happened in Turin on several occasions, at Bonn in 1689 and at Namur in 1692 and 1695. This was also why Louis XIV, after he had taken Lille and Strasbourg, for example, instructed Vauban to construct impenetrable strongholds so that he could strengthen the town's defences and keep a sharp eye on a population whose loyalty could not be guaranteed.

Surrenders were conducted according to a certain ritual. It was the defenders who took the decision to surrender. Turenne recommended that the local governor first assemble the war council, that he examine the situation with his officers and then, in collaboration with the townspeople, draw up a report of everything they lacked – the major problem generally being shortages of provisions and ammunition, although sorties and battles on the counterscarp might, in addition, have reduced the number of men in the garrison. The report had to be signed by all the authorities. Only then could the governor 'sound a parley', which announced to the enemy that the defenders were prepared to negotiate a capitulation. Sometimes it was agreed to surrender at a certain future date: they would surrender the town after a week if assistance had not arrived by that time.

Surrender may occur at any stage of a properly conducted siege or on the termination of a blockade. An example of an extremely brief siege is the Siege of Strasbourg in 1681. Once the French soldiers, 30,000 in total, had surrounded the town, the magistrate lost no time in negotiating with Louvois, in spite of the opposition of its inhabitants, who were determined to resist, come what may. But the patricians were aware that the garrison was extremely weak, the citizen militia could not be trusted, and the Emperor would never be able to send help in time. So the magistrate proposed a treaty to Louvois, which was discussed point by point at Illkirch, accepted, and ratified on 30 September. Louis XIV was able to extend his protectorate over the free town without there being a single fatality, so great was the demoralizing effect on the local people of the surprise attack. The capitulation of Mainz in 1793 was another extreme example. The solidly entrenched French Republican army was allowed to leave with all its weapons and equipment; the only condition laid down by the Austrians was that Hoche's troops should cease to fight the Allies, an arrangement which provided the Committee of Public Safety with a seasoned army which it then engaged to fight the Vendean insurrectionists.

Except in exceptional cases, surrender agreements are ratified by the sovereign governments involved. Thus the Brussels garrison which surrendered to Maurice de Saxe on the 21 February 1746, after being disarmed (though its officers retained the right to carry their swords), was billeted in the Saumur region by the King of France. It remained under the command of its officers and subject to its own internal regulations.

History also provides examples of surrenders in the open field such as that of the Romans at the Caudine Forks (321 BC). Surrenders of this nature are always less readily accepted by the sovereign of the defeated side than surrenders in enclosed spaces. Thus the King of England did not properly endorse the surrender by the Duke of Cumberland's army at Klosterzeven in 1757, and Napoleon con-demned Dupont's surrender at Baylen in 1808. Sometimes the victor refuses to meet the terms agreed in the case of men he considers to be traitors (Quiberon 1795). Not all agreements governing the withdrawal of an army from a theatre of operations have the humiliating character of a surrender. Witness, for example, the Alkmaar Convention (1799) signed by the Duke of York, who had landed in Holland, or the agreement made by Napoleon's Egyptian army in 1802.

Military regulations have tended to limit the practice of surrender to those circumstances in which the possibility of withdrawal, and the hope of assistance, provisions and munitions, have been exhausted. The Imperial decree of 1 May 1812 specified the circumstances of surrender and also dictated the form surrender agreements must take, seeking to reduce the duration of the truce agreed for the discussion of the conditions to between twelve and fifteen hours. It stipulated that there should be no distinction in the way generals, officers and soldiers were treated. However, it became common practice in the nineteenth century to separate officers and troops, and the fate of soldiers who surrendered came increasingly to resemble the general conditions of prisoners of war. On various occasions, leaders who have capitulated have been accused of not exhausting all possible means of combat. The most famous prosecution on these grounds was brought against Marshal François Bazaine for surrendering Metz in 1870. In certain cases, the surrender of a state's capital city indicates acknowledgement of defeat. This was the case with Paris in 1814, 1815 and 1871, something which may be explained by the excessive centralization of France. Finally, the Second World War was terminated by the unconditional surrender of the state in Germany and Japan.

J. BÉRENGER

Readers of the *Iliad* will remember a less orderly and less predictable precursor of surrender: a defeated or unnerved hero grasps the knees of his opponent and pleads for life. According to some estimates, such capitulations had about a 50 per cent success rate in Homer's epic, the others suffering immediate slaughter for which the text shows no sign of reproaching the killers. In modern times the slavery into which surrender was formerly apt to deliver the defeated has been repudiated both as a system and more recently as an informal practice. The cruel terms dictated to Germany after the armistice in 1918 were criticized at the time for their imprudence as well as their harshness. After Germany's unconditional surrender in 1945 there was no question in the Western Allied sectors of countenancing any analogue of the sixteenth- and seventeenth-century pillaging discussed above. After the brief war which expelled Iraq from Kuwait (1991) some went so far as to feel that the United States and its allies had a special responsibility for the well-being of the Iraqi people to mitigate their sufferings under the continuing rule of Saddam Hussein.

The authority to surrender may be exercised at any level of military or politico-military command but a commander can only surrender that which lies within his authority. For example, an officer cannot be presumed to have authority to agree to the permanent cession of territory, or that the troops who surrender will never again bear arms against the forces of the opposing state. According to some theories of 'citizen defence' the state may and should forbid its subjects to surrender under any circumstances. It is argued that this might be a powerful deterrent to an opponent who would fear the indefinite hostility of an indomitable people for whom the armed struggle was eternal. It is questionable, however, whether a state can have the authority to bind its subjects so far beyond its power to protect them that it can require them to fight a hopeless war, or to be exterminated, rather than surrender.

BARRIE PASKINS

See also ARMISTICES; CITADELS; LAWS OF WAR; PRISONERS OF WAR; SIEGES.

FURTHER READING
Adam Roberts, *Nations in Arms: the theory and practice of territorial defence* (London, 1976); Michael Walzer, *Just and Unjust Wars* (London, 1980); Morris Greenspan, *The Modern Law of Land Warfare* (Berkeley, CA, 1959); G. Livet, *Guerre et paix de Machiavel à Hobbes* (Paris, 1972).

Suvorov, Alexander Vasilievich (1729–1800) This Russian field marshal, who entered the army as a common soldier in c.1745, rose through the ranks by application to his military vocation and his fine qualities as a leader. During fifty years he fought in all Russia's wars against Turkey, Prussia and Poland, winning numerous victories. After a short period in which he had fallen into disgrace, he was recalled in 1799 to command the Austro-Russian army operating in Italy. Given the task of occupying Switzerland, he demonstrated a ready adaptability to a theatre of war that was unfamiliar to his troops. His crossing of the Saint-Gotthard pass was a remarkable achievement. Isolated by the defeat of the other Allied armies, he succeeded in escaping from the grasp of the French by a no less remarkable retreat in 1800. Leading by example and enjoying the total confidence of his men, Suvorov engaged in lightning attacks which surprised the enemy. He influenced succeeding generations and the Soviet army was to rediscover his teaching, adopting for its own use his slogan that 'a lost battle is one you believed to be lost'. See also RUSSIA/USSR.

A. CORVISIER

FURTHER READING
Christopher Duffy, *Russia's Military Way to the West: origins and nature of Russian military power, 1700–1800* (London, 1981); Philip Longworth, *The Art of Victory: the life and achievements of Generalissimo Suvorov, 1729–1800* (London, 1965); Piers Mackesy, *War without Victory: the downfall of Pitt, 1799–1802* (Oxford, 1984); K. Osipov, *Alexander Suvorov* (London, c.1943).

Sweden In spite of its geographical isolation and its small population, Sweden imposed itself upon Europe in the century between 1618 and 1718. During this period, warfare became almost a national industry and many of the Swedish expedients and innovations were copied and developed by

Brandenburg-Prussia, the great European military power of the eighteenth and nineteenth centuries. The loss of Finland to Russia in 1809, confirmed by the Congress of Vienna in 1814, marked the end of Sweden's international authority even though she ruled Norway from 1814 to 1905. She adopted a defence policy of armed neutrality suited to her particular needs and the protection of her civilians. From its origins in the sixteenth century, the Swedish army expressed a degree of nationalism in marked contrast to the armies of its opponents.

The standing army was born under Gustav I Vasa at the Assembly (*Riksdag*) of Vasteras in 1544 which decreed the raising of militias by a form of conscription (*utskrivning*). The male peasants of military age (18–40) were registered in a *rote* (military district) and then divided into 'files' of ten or twenty men, each 'file' producing one man for the infantry. Any man who was prepared to do duty on horseback was exempted from taxation on his lands. Once nobility had become hereditary, the number of cavalrymen to be provided by an aristocrat depended on the size of his estates. The nobleman was not obliged to serve himself but could pay for a substitute.

Gustav II Adolf (Gustavus Adolphus, 1611–32) employed the existing methods of recruitment to produce the soldiers for his wars in Poland and Germany, extending the period of service to thirty years. In 1632, he replaced the parish 'files' with groups of farms, enabling the authorities to calculate precisely the number of potential recruits. The state paid each infantry conscript a wage but the group of farms from which he was drawn was expected to put aside a plot of land for the subsistence of the soldier and his family. Theoretically, the standing army would cease to be an economic deadweight within the country in peacetime and the state would possess the cheapest possible army. Unfortunately, peasant farmers proved remarkably reluctant to give away valuable land and the system was only operable on estates owned by the crown. This was a diminishing resource as more and more royal lands were donated to the nobility. Nevertheless, the idea was to provide the basis for the reforms of Karl XI (Charles XI). Gustavus's cavalry was still provided by the nobility and their substitutes but there were insufficient for the demands of the Thirty Years' War. Anyone willing to provide a trooper, complete with horse and equipment, was granted exemption from taxation on his lands. In 1634, these methods were designed to produce a Swedish army of 30,000 foot and 8,000 cavalry. This was supplemented by up to 50,000 mercenaries, mainly German and Scottish. The College of War was created in 1634 and continued in existence until 1865. It was the central administrative organ of the army, a combination of War Ministry and general staff, responsible for recruitment, mobilization, weapons and equipment.

In tactics, Gustavus Adolphus followed the reforms of Maurice of Nassau. He adopted a linear formation for the infantry and increased the number of musketeers in relation to pikemen making the two weapons mutually supporting within each company. Cavalry were trained to charge rather than caracole. The quality of firearms was improved and light, portable field artillery supported the infantry. These changes were made possible by the development of the Swedish iron and steel industry which had been modernized by the Dutch entrepreneur Louis de Geer and other Walloon immigrants. By the 1630s, Sweden no longer had to import armaments. After Gustavus Aldophus was killed at the Battle of Lützen in 1632, the College of War took over the administration and direction of the army, which, in 1648, was camped on a Baltic Empire. Karl X Gustav (1654–60) conquered Sweden's own southern provinces as far as Sund (1660).

In order to restore the diminution of royal power that had been suffered under the regencies which preceded the majorities of Christina (1632–54) and Charles XI (1660–97), the crown embarked upon the recovery of royal lands which had been alienated to the nobility. The *Reduktion* of 1655 was followed by the Great *Reduktion* of 1680. Once this had been executed, Charles XI possessed the territorial basis

779

for his major reform of the Swedish army, the *Indelningsverket* (allotment system). This was a standardization and extension of the earlier system of Gustavus Adolphus. It commenced in 1682 and was completed by 1691. Each province was instructed to maintain a regiment, or regiments, of 1,200 infantry. The military farms were grouped into pairs, 'files', each 'file' providing one recruit, usually by the hire of a substitute. These were not difficult to find as the recruit received a bounty, food, clothing and subsistence. The soldier was normally granted a plot of land and a cottage on the 'file' and he was expected to work as an agricultural labourer in peacetime. In wartime, his family remained in the 'file' cottage. If he fell in battle, the 'file' had to find a replacement, a heavy charge during the Great Northern War. Commissioners ensured that the burdens were shared equally among the 'files'. Recruitment of the cavalry was unaltered. Anyone offering to provide an equipped horseman was granted exemption from taxation on his lands, and his farm (*rusthåll*) was excluded from the 'file' system. The cavalry-substitute (*sventjänare*) usually lived in a cottage on the farm of the *rusthållare* and worked as a labourer.

The same principles were applied to the officers and non-commissioned officers. They drew their pay from the taxation of allotted farms situated within their regimental regions. Officers had to live near their men to supervise training, discipline and administration. If no existing house was available, then a special house was built to a standard specification. By 1700, there were 3,000 officers' houses in Sweden and 500 in Finland. The *Indelningsverket* created eleven cavalry regiments (11,000 men) and twenty-three infantry regiments (30,000 men). The *Indelningsverket* was not applied in the Baltic Empire outside Sweden and Finland; here, the frontier was guarded by 25,000 mercenaries. The resultant army was national and coherent, linked by regional ties and the Lutheran faith. Soldiers and officers were state employees. Officers were trained by cadetship in the Life Guards and were encouraged to seek experience in foreign armies.

In order for this basically territorial army to concentrate for war, a complex mobilization plan was created which involved the building of new roads and staging posts.

Karl XII (Charles XII, 1697–1718) put his father's military reforms to the test in the Great Northern War (1700–21). He imitated the strategic-economic notions of Gustavus Adolphus that 'war should support war', wars had to be fought overseas so that occupied and enemy states could provide the financial resources and commodities for the maintenance of the army. In this manner, war would not prove too onerous for Sweden, which lacked both density of population and natural resources. Tactically, Charles's methods differed little from those of other European states. His infantry formed in four ranks but they were offensively-minded and trained to charge home after firing one or two volleys. Charles also instructed his regiments in the use of column rather than line to attack vital points or to reinforce weak points (Narva, Holofzin). His cavalry were trained to charge in three ranks, knee-to-knee, and gallop from a distance of c.150 metres. They discharged their pistols at 30–40 metres and continued home with the sabre. Charles disregarded field artillery, relying on the musket, bayonet and sword and this cost him dearly at Poltava (1709) where 23,000 Swedes with four pieces of artillery were crushed by 40,000 Russians equipped with 132 guns. After the death of Charles XII in Norway in 1718, the Peace of Nystad in 1721 brought 'Sweden's Age of Greatness' to a close.

By the end of the Great Northern War, the social composition of the officer class had undergone great changes. Whereas in 1700, 58.1 per cent of the officers came from the established or recent nobility, in 1720–1, 66 per cent of the officers were of non-noble origin. The severe losses suffered by the military nobility had laid the ground for a remarkable degree of social mobility. However, with Sweden having lost its external possessions, invaded Finland was unable to mount opposition against the devastating incursions of the Russians in 1720–1. From the military point of view, the 'Age of Liberty' (1718–72) was an age of uncertainties and foreign interference. The number of officers was reduced as was the proportion of commoners. The wars of Finland against Russia (1741–3) and subsequently of Pomerania against Prussia (1757–62) revealed the decline of the Swedish forces and the damage done to the military staffs by party politics. Gustavian enlightened despotism (1772–92) only remedied these failings in part, the new Russo-Swedish conflict of 1788–90 ending in an inconclusive peace. Once again war enabled the commoners to rise from 22 per cent of the total number of officers in 1780 to 35 per cent in 1793 (14 per cent of the higher officer ranks).

The abortive attempt to create a territorial army, the *lantvärnet* of 1808–9, doubled the strength of the army and increased the number of non-noble officers, but was unable to prevent the loss of Finland. After 1815, the armed forces were weakened; the recruitment of officers became subject to rigid considerations of social rank; there were no more mercenaries; and the period of service was reduced to 30 days until the 1901 reform, which combined the conscripts (one year of service performed over a 3–5-year period) with 40,000 professional soldiers forming a melting-pot for an army of 400,000 potentially mobilizable men which deterred any aggression in 1914 and 1940. The wave of pacifism of 1918–36 came near to sweeping all this away, but an awareness of the rising danger led to increased military efforts, including the creation of an independent air force (1926) which, after 1945, became the spearhead of Sweden's defences. The democratization of officer and NCO posts gained considerably in pace between 1900 and 1970 (67.4 per cent to 97.1 per cent of non-nobles), but the percentage of aristocrats nevertheless remains greater in the army than in Swedish society as a whole.

Although a firmly non-aligned nation 35,000 Swedes did serve in the campaign to liberate Finland in 1919 and 7,000 fought in the winter campaign of 1939–40. Sweden decided voluntarily to forgo nuclear weapons. Units and observers (30,000 volunteers) have taken part in almost twenty UN peace-keeping operations in Cyprus, the Middle East and Zaire. Its aim is to protect its neutrality by conventional methods within the framework of an overall defence plan and, until 1991, to contribute to the maintenance of peace in Scandinavia between the two superpower blocs. Men and women of between 16 and 65 take part in civil defence operations. The annual contingent called up for compulsory military service (men between the ages of 18 and 47) numbers 36,500 in 1,500 bases, and 110,000 reservists are called up each year. If mobilized, the military defence force would contain 800,000 men and the civil defence organization 200,000 men and 300,000 female auxiliaries. Expenditure on defence represents between 3 and 4 per cent of GNP.

In general, Swedish weaponry is modern ('S' tank; Bantam, Hawk, Red-Eye and RB-70 ground-to-air missiles). The army contains 43,500 men (35,000 conscripts on service of between 7.5 and 15 months), supported by 550,000 reservists. Rapid fire 155 mm guns and 2,000 TOW anti-tank guns were ordered in 1983. Ninety per cent of this weaponry is produced in Sweden. The 470 combat aircraft, mostly *Viggen*, *Daken* and *Saab*, grouped in 6 support, 3 reconnaissance, 13 interception and 2 transport squadrons constitute an instrument of instant intervention, the Swedish air force comprising some 9,500 men including 4,500 conscripts. There is a small coastal defence navy (12,000 men including 6,300 conscripts) operating 7 submarines and 31 missile craft. The Swedish arms industry employs 30,000 people. One-third of the defence budget is devoted to research, development and the acquisition of new equipment. Since 1972, the security of Sweden's own borders has been the responsibility of the Secretariat for Security Policy (SSLP) of the Defence Ministry: Sweden's is therefore an active neutrality. The country's shelters can cater for just over five million people; three million gas masks have been stockpiled, as have a range of raw materials (coal, oil, textiles, salt) and medicines. Plans for the evacuation of towns and cities have been drawn up with great care. Modern Sweden is proud of its military past and intends to ensure its preservation and to defend its free and prosperous society, and to do so, if need be, by guerilla warfare, for which its forests would be well suited. Its army is thus closely tied to the political and social life of the nation. *See also* BREITENFELD; CHARLES XI; CHARLES XII; FINLAND, SINCE 1809; GUSTAVUS II ADOLPHUS; LÜTZEN; MOBILIZATION; NARVA; POLTAVA; RECRUITMENT.

C. NORDMANN
JOHN CHILDS

FURTHER READING
Michael Roberts, *Gustavus Adolphus* (2 vols, London, 1953–8); Ragnild Hatton, *Charles XII* (London, 1968); G. Artéus, Ulf Olsson and K. Strömberg-Back, 'The influence of the armed forces on the transformation of society in Sweden, 1600–1945', *Commission Internationale d'Histoire Militaire*, Acta no. 5 (Bucharest, 1981); G. Andolf, 'The social origins of the Swedish officer corps during the twentieth century', *Revue Internationale d'Histoire Militaire*, lvii (1984); R. R. Bohme, *The Defence Policy of the Scandinavian Countries, 1918–1945* (Stockholm, 1979); Alf Åberg, 'The Swedish Army, from Lützen to Narva', in *Sweden's Age of Greatness, 1632–1718*, ed. Michael Roberts (London, 1973), pp. 265–87.

Switzerland Both Caesar and Tacitus have testified to the military character of the Helvetii and the Rhaeti. In 107 BC, during a foray outside its own frontiers, a Swiss formation defeated at Agen a Roman army commanded by the consul Cassius Longinus and forced it to pass under the yoke. On the other hand, in 58 BC Caesar defeated the Helvetii at Bibracte (12 miles from Autun) and forced them to return to their own country, which was then placed under Roman rule. In AD 69, the Helvetii made an attempt at rebellion; the XXI legion (*Rapax*) crushed their resistance without too much difficulty. Tacitus remarks that the Rhaeti, for their part, provided an *ala*, an auxiliary cavalry unit, for the Roman army.

Invasion by the Alamanni and the Burgundians caused the country to take on some of the characteristics of these two ethnic groups whose territory, broadly speaking, covered the upper basins of the Rhine and the Rhône. During the Middle Ages, the Holy Roman Empire took on, to some degree, the mantle of the old Roman Empire and, with it, the latter's policy of keeping control over the passes through the line of the Alps. The forest cantons (or Waldstätten) of Uri, Schwyz and Unterwald occupied the mountain area in which the St Gotthard pass was the key to north–south communications and to the strategically important east–west route in the central region of the Alps. At the time of the Mongol invasion of eastern Europe, the St Gotthard route became the centre of an important development, doubtless because thought had already been given to the possible establishment of a safe area for people and property in the north Italian redoubt. In order that they should take responsibility for guarding this strategic route, the forest cantons received, in 1231, their first charters of freedom and the right to bear arms. When the danger abated and there was talk of abolishing these privileges, the Confederates signed a pact of mutual assistance (1291) and took an oath no longer to tolerate foreign judges in their territory and to expel them, if necessary, by force of arms. It was, in fact, on this essentially military basis that Switzerland was founded. In 1315, in order to bring the 'rebels' into line, Duke Leopold of Austria, at the head of the elite of his knights, advanced into the Schwyz canton. The Confederates, who may perhaps have made their strength appear to the enemy to be less than it was in reality, counter-attacked with means that were better suited to the terrain – improvised obstacles (produced by setting off an avalanche of rocks and tree-trunks) and the halberd (a cut-and-thrust weapon). Caught by surprise in a defile where it had no room to manoeuvre, Leopold's army was almost completely destroyed. The name of Switzerland (derived from Schwyz) made its first appearance in history. In this battle at Morgaten can be seen all the elements which were, in the future, to characterize Swiss military thinking – the prime importance accorded to infantry as shock troops, use of terrain and obstacles, the hardiness of citizen soldiers and, on the strategic plane, keeping the enemy in uncertainty about the time, place and tactics of battle.

Despite this initial victory, the independence of the cantons was far from assured. At that point they received highly important, and very timely, help in the shape of an alliance with several cities, among them Berne, Lucerne and Zurich, the last two being the northern 'bridgeheads' of the St Gotthard route. This complementary union of city, countryside and mountain represented a political development whose importance did not escape the Habsburg rulers, since they saw in it a serious threat to the feudal order. They opened an attack on the vulnerable point in the Swiss position where Berne's territory projected towards the west. The steadfastness of the Berne militia and the use by the Swiss leadership of an infantry reserve enabled them to win a pitched battle at Laupen (1339). Valuable time was thus gained, allowing the young Confederation to built up its strength and to provide itself with its first legal constitution. Strengthened by the accession of the cantons of Zug and Glarus to the alliance, Switzerland assumed the form of a communal league. The Habsburgs refused to accept the existence of this new state and sought to isolate it as a prelude to crushing it. Drawing lessons from previous campaigns, they equipped their knights with long pikes and sought battle at Sempach (1386). It appears that the Confederates adopted a triangular formation, with the aim of breaking the force of the assault. As usual, they hurled themselves at the enemy in order to come to hand-to-hand combat as soon as possible. At the outset, the battle did not go in their favour, since the serried array of pikes held by well-armoured knights resisted their assault. Then, for reasons which have never been properly established – whether it was the heat of the day proving overpowering to men in armour or the tenacity of the Confederates, some of whom charged forward and grasped a number of pikes allowing them to be plunged into their own bodies* – the Swiss were able to regain the initiative. Panic seized the Imperial troops; Duke Leopold III was killed. After a century of fighting, the Swiss had won their

* This is a reference to the legendary deed of Arnold von Winkelried.

freedom – *de facto* only, and not *de jure*, since the Habsburgs refused to recognize it. In view of the threat from their powerful neighbours, Swiss independence rested on force of arms.

The fifteenth century was an age of conquest, in the course of which the Swiss established a double defensive belt round the central redoubt. In the west, Freiburg joined the Confederation and an alliance was formed with the canton of Valais, the bulwark of the St Gotthard pass. In the north, the League received the adherence of Solothurn (1481), Basle and Schaffhausen (1501). In the east, the citizens of Appenzell lent their aid (1513), and Grisons, another bulwark, became an ally. In the south, the Levantina valley was won from the Milanese by conquest. The military expertise of the Swiss reached its peak at the end of the fifteenth century and the beginning of the sixteenth. The experience of two centuries had allowed them to acquire a profound understanding of the business of arms. Martial skills were bred into the nation through sports for young people and community festivals. Many an official ceremony bore a military imprint and thus contributed to the formation of a military outlook. A further factor was that war was the only 'industry' capable of absorbing the excess population.

In 1474, Louis XI of France stirred up the differences between the Swiss and the Burgundians. In his turn, Duke Charles of Burgundy engaged in a punitive expedition against the Swiss, who defeated him on three occasions, at Grandson and Murten (1476) and at Nancy (1477). On each occasion, the charges of the Burgundian cavalry broke on the bristling pikes of the Swiss, who had rediscovered the secret of the Greek phalanx. After absorbing the enemy assault, the Swiss infantrymen counterattacked the enemy ranks until they succeeded in breaching them. During the second phase, the halberdiers stormed into the breach, paving the way in turn for men armed with short swords and daggers whose aim was to secure victory in a hand-to-hand battle. This reinstatement of infantry as the premier arm gave the Confederates military supremacy in the heart of Europe for several decades. Their forays into the plains of Italy, and into Swabia, Alsace or Savoy, were equally successful. But though their tactical superiority won them Machiavelli's admiration, which he expressed in his *Dialogues on the Art of War*, it was not supported by an equivalent political ability. Stresses and strains which caused opposition between the cantons began to come into the open. In alliance with the Pope, the Swiss conquered the Duchy of Milan at the Battle of Novara (1513), but lost it after being defeated at Marignano (1515), where their infantry, despite performing prodigies of valour, was worsted by the cannon of Galliot de Genouillac, Francis I's Grand Master of artillery.

In 1516, a permanent peace was signed between the Confederates and the King of France; firepower (with its financial and industrial basis) had triumphed over the infantry assault. The Swiss military forces then began to pursue a new course. As specialists in infantry warfare, they were now prepared to put their power in the assault at the disposal of those who contracted to make use of it. France, in 1496, was the first country to do so, employing up to a dozen Swiss regiments. The Confederates' infantry thus became associated with the majority of the French army's major actions, as allies fighting under their own flag and not, as has so often been alleged, under the equivocal title of mercenaries. The Swiss were present at Malplaquet (1709) and Denain (1712). At Fontenoy (1745) the Swiss Guards and Courten's Valais regiment faced the assault by the British square column with the greatest resolution. At Rossbach (1757), the Swiss covered the retreat of Soubise, their behaviour under fire earning them Frederick II's praise. At the Beresina (1812) were to be found the pontoon bridging unit from Tessin under General Eblé and Swiss battalions who did not hesitate to sacrifice themselves in order to hold the bridgehead.

The Confederates were found also in the service of other countries. The Spaniards engaged Swiss instructors at the end of the fifteenth century to teach them the use of square formations. The handling of the pike by a formed body of troops was not an easy matter and the manoeuvring of infantry had become a task for professionals. The Swiss tactics were adopted by the Spaniards and helped to bring into being the *tercio*, whose musket and arquebus fire lengthened, in a sense, the 'range' of the pike. But Spain was not alone in this; there were Swiss troops in the service of the United Kingdom until 1856, Naples until 1859, and the Netherlands until 1828. In addition, numerous Swiss military men and experts enlisted in foreign armies. Lefort, the Genevan admiral and friend of Peter the Great, made a decisive contribution to the creation of the latter's fleet. General Jomini, for his part, served in succession the French emperor and three Russian tsars. Military service of this type in foreign lands, during more than three and a half centuries, gave the Confederates a number of advantages which a territorial expansion would probably not have provided: (1) Swiss territory hardly suffered from war throughout this period; (2) service in regiments fostered the social integration of the Swiss, whom otherwise everything tended to divide (different racial backgrounds and languages, different religions, very varied geographical habitats); (3) Switzerland became acquainted with the most varied aspects of the world, thanks to her soldiers who had fought in every quarter. Far from being closed to outside influences, the country threw herself open to them and sought to elicit from them a balanced formula.

The nineteenth century and the rise of nationalism in many countries gradually brought to an end the old Confederation's vocation of military service in Europe. The sacrifice of the Swiss Guard at the Tuileries on 10 August 1792 and the loss of more than 80,000 men on the battlefields of the Empire (among them Baylen, where the Schwyz general Reding led Swiss and Spanish irregulars against Dupont's French corps, in which Confederates were also serving), all conduced to the ending of 'foreign service'. The Congress of Vienna in 1815 gave official recognition to the perpetual neutrality of Switzerland and this marked the beginning of a new phase for her military system. In 1817, there was revived the ancient tradition of the militia, the principle of which had always been maintained by the independent cantons. On several occasions, these forces were brought to a state of readiness to ensure the country's neutrality (in 1831, 1848, 1856, 1870–1). In 1847, however, an extremely serious crisis brought its unity into question, when the Catholic cantons threatened the Confederation with what amounted to a secession. Thanks to the genius of General Dufour, who had previously been in French service, it proved possible to ward off civil war proper at the outset and to remove the threat of it altogether, after a few brief engagements. A spirit of tolerance, inherited from the old regiments, allowed those who for a moment had been opponents to rediscover a common language. In 1874, a law was published setting out a new military system, under which service was compulsory for all male citizens. The old custom by which the citizen-soldier kept his own weapon and ammunition at his home in token of readiness for almost immediate mobilization, was retained. From 1914 to 1918 and from 1939 to 1945, the Swiss army was mobilized to resist any use of its territory by the belligerents. The militia system allowed the country on each occasion to mobilize more than half a million men; it would have been impossible to reach such a figure with a professional army. Currently, the Swiss can mobilize 625,000 men, 565,000 in the army and 60,000 in the air force, which flies 289 combat aircraft. The navy comprises eleven patrol boats on the Alpine lakes. In Switzerland, the army unit is the repository of the military attitude of the nation and it is there that the meaning of the vocation of arms is largely instilled. The Swiss people have remained deeply attached to their democratic traditions and have kept a defence system with which they feel identified. As far as the army is concerned, it always considers the individual soldier to be the best 'weapons system', but it also seeks to form a coherent military theory from the rival doctrines and currents of ideas to be found outside its frontiers. *See also* FORE-IGNERS, SERVICE BY; GRANDSON; INFANTRY; JOMINI; MARIGNANO; MERCENARIES; MILITIAS; MOBILIZATION; MURTEN; RECRUITMENT.

D. REICHEL

FURTHER READING
Commissariat Central des Guerres, *Histoire militaire de la Suisse* (4 vols, Berne, 1915–21); John McPhee, *The Swiss Army* (London, 1985).

Symbolism, military Military symbolism is the generic name for that class of objects by which military personnel display their membership of the army as a whole or of one of its parts. The sources for the study of military symbolism are to be found in the origin and history of objects which have become symbols and through the investigation of why these objects have acquired a symbolic value. The enquirer who looks at the subject from these points of view can draw a distinction between objects designed from the outset with solely a symbolic purpose and those intended to be used for practical ends in military life but which have subsequently acquired a symbolic character with, or without, loss of their original function. The field of military symbolism covers various categories of symbols, some of which are common to other disciplines. Likewise, some symbols can belong simultaneously to several categories. Military symbols can be divided into six major categories, i.e. weapons, vexillological emblems, uniforms, devices, insignia/badges and national markings.

Weapons
Certain weapons that are carried on parade have today merely a symbolic character. An example is the sabre or sword, which is the symbol of an officer. Another instance is the halberd carried by the French sailor who does guard duty outside an admiral's office door. The same is true of the axes carried by the sappers at the head of columns in certain French regiments (e.g. the engineers, the Foreign Legion).

Vexillological Emblems
In common parlance these are called flags and can be divided into three classes. Flags

and standards compose the highest-ranking class, since they symbolize both the country and the character of the formations which carry them. Napoleon established a rule, which still remains in force in France today, according to which a unit must contain at least 1,200 foot soldiers to have the right to a flag or 800 mounted men for a standard. By tradition, this rule is waived in the case of military academies.

Formations which do not meet the requirements for the grant of a flag or standard can have a pennon, which merely symbolizes the nature of the formation to which it is given. Pennons form, in order of ranking, the intermediate class of emblems.

The class of lowest standing is composed of emblems whose symbolic value is more or less incidental. In this class are found especially pennons denoting commanders, buglers' banners and drummers' aprons.

Uniforms

Uniform is the main way in which a soldier is recognized. It distinguishes the military man from the civilian, the member of a regular fighting force from the *franc-tireur* and the soldier of one country from that of another.

Uniform is characterized by its cut, material, colours and, in particular, by its accessories. Uniform's main accessories are shoulder ornaments (epaulettes, *contre-épaulettes*, straps, ties, loops, knots), tabs (on collar, chest or arm), sleeve decorations, waistbands and belts of special designs, and ornamental additions to trousers (double or single stripe, piping and braid). Another accessory of military uniform is the button, usually of gilded or silver-plated metal. Their domed outer surfaces are sometimes smooth, but usually stamped with a device.

War memorials for victims of the Second World War were less grandiose than those erected after 1918. The American Military Cemetery at Madingley, near Cambridge, is beautifully landscaped into a hillside. It contains the graves of 3,811 United States servicemen who were based in Great Britain, while the roll of honour contains the names of a further 5,125 whose final resting places are unknown. In the chapel is a mural depicting the European theatre of operations.
(Roger Scruton)

Devices

A device is a motif, or a design comprising motifs, that forms the traditional representation of a particular military group. In general, the fighting arms use a straight-forward motif (grenade, anchor, stylized representation of flight, hunting horn, cannon, etc.), and the services made-up ones (the best-known being the lance and snake of the medical service and the crossed flags of the Signallers). Devices are reproduced on other accessories of uniforms, either embroidered on the cloth or embossed on metal accessories or cap badges. They may be painted on buildings and equipment, or depicted on other symbols, in particular emblems.

Insignia/Badges

Insignia/badges are small items, or representations of such, and are worn as a means of recognition or as a mark of distinction. Six kinds may be mentioned, as follows:

Insignia of Decorations These consist of crosses and medals hung on ribbons of characteristic colours. When military uniform is worn, and depending on circumstances, the insignia of decorations may be worn either complete (with the decoration hanging from its ribbon) or merely in the form of small strips of the ribbons. The general heading of military symbolism covers both decorations that are purely military (Military Medal, Victoria Cross, etc.) and those which can be awarded in either a military or civilian context (such as the George Cross).

Alongside the normal run of insignia there exist in the army some of a special kind, namely those of collective decorations, which take the form of shoulder lanyards worn by all members of the unit so honoured.

Badges of Rank These serve to indicate the place in the military hierarchy occupied by the various individual rank holders. They are normally worn on the uniform and appear in addition on other objects, such as commanders' pennants and plaques on generals' cars.

Insignia of Function Those who fulfil certain tasks wear insignia that denote their function. In certain cases, these insignia are the same as devices, or more or less repeat their motifs. Many insignia of function consist of plain brassards or of an item of uniform, e.g. the red hats of the military police. Insignia of function are, as a rule, worn only on duty.

Badges of Specialists Specialist personnel may wear particular badges. They are normally of a type called 'allusive' because they represent a tool or an instrument which is characteristic of the specialist ability in question (e.g. lyre of the musicians or the crossed axes of the sappers). Since they denote a permanent capacity, such badges are worn on all occasions.

Badges of Placings or Competitive Successes These are rewards given to soldiers who achieve a good result in certain competitions. Like the preceding ones, these badges are often of the 'allusive' type. An example is when they represent the weapon (or its ammunition) in the shooting/firing of which the soldier has distinguished himself (the crossed guns of the marksman).

Unit Badges These are very frequently heraldic in style, of restrained design and in good taste, and recall the principal traditions of the unit concerned. For this reason, they are also termed 'evocative badges'. In exceptional cases, a unit that is completely without traditions will turn to the memory of other glories when designing its badges. Unit badges will normally be worn on the uniform, either in the form of a piece of printed or embroidered cloth or of an enamelled or completely metallic brooch.

National Markings

Markings in national colours can be carried on buildings in a military area, on warships, on aircraft and aircraft carriers, as well as on land vehicles. In the same fashion as similar markings used by other governmental authorities, they symbolize state property as opposed to that of private individuals. In the sphere of international relations (war being merely one special instance of these), they serve to differentiate the property of one nation from that of another. The main ways of denoting nationality are standards, roundels, signboards and inscriptions. *See also* CEREMONIES; ESPRIT DE CORPS; ETHOS; GLORY; HONOURS AND AWARDS; ICONOGRAPHY; LANGUAGE; MORALE; UNIFORM; VEXILLOLOGY.

J. DE LASSALLE

FURTHER READING
W. W. May, W. Y. Carman and J. Tanner, *Badges and Insignia of the British Armed Services* (London, 1974).

T

Tactical organization Modern armies are organized into 'units' (platoons, companies and battalions) and 'formations' (regiments, brigades, divisions, corps, armies and army groups). Units of the same size sometimes have different names depending upon the particular branch of the service – 'company' in the infantry, 'squadron' in the cavalry or armoured forces and 'battery' in the artillery are all equivalent commands under a captain or major. The numerical strength of units has varied over the past 500 years. A company contained 1,000 men at the beginning of the sixteenth century, sometimes less than fifty in 1700 and around 150 in 1990. The Soviet army (up to 1991) did not have corps but subordinated its divisions directly to the level of army, the equivalent of a corps in Western forces. Similarly, the Soviets referred to the army group as a 'front'. In the German land forces of the Second World War, corps and army groups were only battle headquarters and did not possess administrative functions; these were reserved to divisions and armies amongst the higher formations. Similarly, *ad hoc* formations like battlegroups composed of elements from several different arms do not function as administrative entities.

The tactical organization of a particular land force is determined by its weaponry, by the number of men it contains and, to a lesser extent, by the weapons of its opponents. Weaponry decides the basic pattern of deployment and the degree of articulation required within units while numbers dictate the size, variety and hierarchy of formations. Infantry units have always tended to be much larger than their cavalry equivalents because of the difficulties of controlling large bodies of horsemen without a heavily subdivided structure of command. From the *ile* of Ancient Greece to the troop of the seventeenth, eighteenth and nineteenth centuries, the basic cavalry unit has remained between 50 and 100 men, whereas the essential infantry unit has varied according to the prevailing weapons – from the Greek phalanx of 4,096 men, through the 500-man battalion of the early modern period to the present-day battalion of between 400 and 1,000 men.

The heavy infantry of the Ancient World was armed with the pike or spear which could only prove effective in the offensive if delivered with the weight of massed numbers. Missile weapons and cavalry were not widely employed; battles were decided by the clash of heavy infantry. The Egyptian army of the 'New Period', the Assyrians, the Greeks and the Romans all adopted variations of the phalanx. The Egyptian heavy infantry was arrayed in a massive phalanx of 10,000 men, 100 men wide and 100 men deep, its flanks protected by chariots. The Greek and Macedonian phalanx was smaller, 4,096 men, with subdivisions providing a degree of manoeuvrability on the battlefield. Initially composed of 30 maniples, each of two centuries, the Roman legion was reorganized by Gaius Marius (*c.*157–85 BC). The maniple was abandoned and the legion was divided into 10 cohorts, each containing 6 centuries of 80 men. This gave the Roman legion far greater articulation and tactical flexibility than either its Egyptian or Greek predecessors, a necessity as the Romans faced a variety of enemies who employed different combinations of weapons and tactics, from the heavy infantry of the Gauls to the Parthian mounted archers. Light infantry, the Greek peltasts and the Roman *velites*, were organized in smaller units outside the main phalanx. Towards the end of the Roman Empire in the West, the legion evolved into a unit of 1,000 men, mostly armed with the bow and the spear in response to the horsed Barbarian invaders.

In the east, the army of the Byzantine Empire had to repel frequent raiders and invaders, many of whom employed light cavalry tactics. Defence required hitting power plus mobility. The Byzantine forces were accordingly based around the heavy, armoured cavalryman armed with the bow, equipped for both the charge in battle and stand-off missile action. By adopting a ternary arrangement, the Byzantine *meros* consisted of 3,000 cavalrymen, divided into 3 *moiras* each of 3 *tagmai*. There was also a mixed *tagma* of 1,300 cavalry and 4,000 infantry. In the seventh century AD, these formations came under the command of military districts, *themes*, each of which was split into 2 or 3 *turmai* (5,000 men). The *turma* was divided into 5 *banda* (1,000 men), the *banda* into 5 *pentarchies* (200 men), the *pentarchies* into 5 *pentekontarchies* (40 men), and the *pentekontarchies* into 4 *dekarchies* (10 men). Because they also relied upon cavalry, the Mongols employed a similar, highly flexible structure based on the decimal system. The major formation was the *tumen* of 10,000 men, split into the *minghan* of 1,000, the *jaghun* of 100 and the *arban* of 10.

Systematic articulation among both the cavalry and the infantry largely disappeared in Western Europe following the demise of the Roman Empire in the late fifth century AD. As battles were largely decided by the clash of heavy, armoured horsemen, the emphasis was placed upon individual combat and personal fighting qualities. The cavalry charged *en masse* while the infantry formed up in unarticulated bodies. The emergence of gunpowder weapons in the fourteenth century signalled the end of the dominance of the heavy cavalryman; infantry, the troops who operated the new guns, could now defeat cavalry. Initially, the Swiss phalanx returned to the principles of the Roman legion – massed heavy infantry – in order to combat cavalry although the new missile weapons were incorporated within the system. Similarly, Gonsalvo de Córdoba's reorganization of the Spanish infantry in 1505 was based on Greek and Roman models. He grouped the existing companies into twenty *colunelas* (later *coronelías*) under the overall command of a colonel-general. In 1534, this system was superseded by the *tercio*, which was again modelled on the Roman legion. Both the Swissphalanx and the Spanish *tercio* were essentially heavy infantry units designed to give weight to the 'push of pike' and to present a solid mass against cavalry attack, although they also included missile weapons. However, gunpowder weapons rendered the large squares vulnerable to both musketry and artillery. Also, as the number of hand gunners increased, the phalanx became decreasingly suitable as a tactical device because only a few of its own arquebuses and muskets could be brought to bear at any one time. By the 1590s, the *tercio* was no longer a monolithic block but had been broken down into a number of sub-sections. The French under Henry IV, Maurice of Nassau's Dutch forces and the Swedish armies of Gustavus Adolphus extended this process by thinning the phalanxes into smaller, more linear units, five to six ranks deep, with the pikes in the centre and the arquebusiers or musketeers on either flank. Instead of a phalanx of 3,000 men, the new battalions numbered around 500. During the last decades of the seventeenth and the opening years of the eighteenth centuries, the battalions abandoned the matchlock musket and the pike in favour of the flintlock musket tipped with a bayonet. In order to deliver the maximum weight of fire, infantrymen stood in three or four ranks, shoulder-to-shoulder, the battalions butted onto one another in a long line so as to avoid presenting flanks to the enemy. Each battalion contained between 8 and 16 companies for administrative and disciplinary purposes and platoons for the organization of volley fire but the battalion fought as a single tactical entity. For ease of command in battle, between 3 and 6 battalions were grouped into brigades. For administrative purposes, cavalry were assembled into regiments (300–400 men), each of between 6 and 8 troops, but the principal tactical unit was the squadron of between 100 and 150 men, usually formed by combining 2 or 3 troops.

The linear battalion remained the basic infantry unit until the development of the rifled, breech-loading gun in the mid-nineteenth century. Within the phalanx, the legion and the linear battalion, the infantrymen had served as building blocks of the corporate edifice; there was little or no scope for independent action. From the mid-nineteenth century to the present day, infantry has steadily abandoned mass action in favour of increased articulation within units leading to greater emphasis on individual initiative and independence. In a modern army, instead of the battalion acting as the principal tactical unit, that function has now been assumed by the company, the platoon and the 'fire cell'. In order to shield the infantry from long-range, accurate rifles, artillery and, later, tactical nuclear weapons, the linear battalion, as a tactical unit, dispersed into smaller and smaller groups relying on cover and 'fire and movement'. Minor tactics became the responsibility of the smallest units commanded by commissioned officers – the company and the platoon – the most that could be managed by one man on the extended battlefield. The increased weight of fire produced by the new rifles also reduced the need for volley firing; individual aimed fire was the method by which to maximize the capabilities of the rifles, while machine-guns gave one soldier the firepower of several men armed with manually operated weapons. The general adoption of automatic weapons during the First World War, altered the centre of tactical gravity to the squad and the section, sub-units under the command of NCOs. The 'fire cell' of the British infantry became a section of ten men grouped around a light machine-gun and commanded by a corporal. Since the Second World War, the augmented firepower of the infantry has continued to place the tactical emphasis on the squad and the section although the introduction of light-weight radios during the Second World War restored the ability of platoon, company and battalion commanders

to exercise some tactical control over their men in action.

Until the middle of the eighteenth century, there was little systematic subdivision of forces into formations. The brigade was only an *ad hoc* structure and, basically, the infantry battalion and the cavalry regiment were the highest organized bodies. During campaigns, armies marched in two wings, corresponding to the first and second lines of battle, and all regiments and battalions were assigned to a wing at the opening of a campaign. Armies of the seventeenth and eighteenth centuries also marched in a number of columns, but neither the wings nor the columns were permanent formations possessing fixed establishments. In 1759, the Duc de Broglie introduced the division into the French army. It was abolished in 1778 but reinstated ten years later. Initially, the French divisions were formations of 5,000–6,000 men, containing infantry, cavalry, artillery and some supply services under the command of a general officer. These miniature armies could fight independently, often against superior odds, and provided commanders with enhanced tactical and strategic flexibility. However, Napoleon discovered that the division was too weak and between 1802 and 1804 he developed the corps, which usually numbered between 9,000 and 21,000 men (2–5 divisions). Divisions were retained, but were made into discrete cavalry and infantry formations, while the corps, which contained infantry and cavalry divisions plus artillery, was sufficiently strong to fight for long periods against greater numbers. The Austrian army adopted the corps structure before 1805 as did the British army during the Peninsular War. After 1868, Germany, France and Britain used the corps of two divisions as the basic peacetime military district but, in war, the constitution of the corps was more flexible and might contain between 2 and 6 divisions.

Divisions grouped into corps proved adequate to cope with the numbers involved in the Napoleonic Wars but they were insufficient to deal with the mass conscript armies of the American Civil

War, the Franco-Prussian War and the First World War. The 'army' was used by Moltke in the Austro-Prussian War in 1866. He divided his forces into three armies, one of five corps, one of two corps and the Army of the Elbe of a single reinforced corps. For the Franco-Prussian War of 1870–1, Moltke divided his invasion forces into four armies. During the First World War, all nations employed the army as a formation to control a varying number of corps, anywhere between two and six, but as the number of armies grew so the general staffs found it convenient to bring the armies under another level of command, the army group. This, the highest formation, controlled between two and five armies. A similar pattern of formations has remained in place since the Second World War. However, corps, army and army group are temporary, *ad hoc* formations, often no more than battle headquarters, assigned to control varying numbers and types of subordinate formations. The highest formation with a fixed table of organization and strength is the division, although corps and army headquarters often have integral artillery. The British infantry division in 1914 contained 19,000 men (12,000 infantrymen, 4,000 gunners and 3,000 support troops), divided into three brigades, each of three battalions. It also possessed its own artillery of 30 guns and 24 machine-guns.

Until the interwar period, there existed only cavalry and infantry divisions. However, the advent of the internal combustion engine and the evolution of the tank brought a more complex picture in the Second World War. Marching infantry divisions remained in existence, particularly in the German and Soviet armies, but there were also motorized infantry divisions (infantry riding in lorries), mechanized infantry divisions (tanks plus infantry transported in armoured, cross-country carriers) and armoured divisions (all arms formations of tanks, mechanized infantry, artillery and supporting arms). Increasingly, all divisions came to include some units of armoured fighting vehicles. The British infantry division of 1942 contained 16,764 men and 757 officers. It consisted of one tank brigade of three battalions, and two infantry brigades each of three battalions, plus artillery and supporting services. The armoured division contained one infantry brigade of three battalions, one armoured brigade of three tank battalions, an armoured car regiment, artillery and supporting services, a total of 13,943 men and 732 officers.

In the Soviet and Warsaw Pact armies (up to 1990–1), the division was relatively small and most of the supporting services were gathered at army and front level. Since 1945, the British army has tended to concentrate on the brigade as the organic formation which contains its own services and support. The modern brigade is the smallest formation capable of independent operations and can be either an all-arms team (an armoured brigade may include two battalions of tanks plus one battalion of mechanized infantry with the proportions reversed for a mechanized infantry brigade) or composed of a single element (i.e. three battalions of infantry) with supporting artillery and services. Brigades are attached to divisions as and when required. In the pre-1945 German army and in the pre-1991 Soviet army, brigades and regiments were virtually synonymous.

Most armies have also formed specialist divisions for particular tasks – mountain divisions, airborne divisions (parachute and glider troops) and air mobile divisions (helicopters). The majority of armies have adopted either a triangular (three brigades/regiments) or a rectangular (four brigades/regiments) structure. Experience has shown that divisions with just two brigades are too weak and unbalanced. During the 1950s, the United States introduced a five-brigade 'Pentomic' division but reverted to the three-brigade ROAD (Reorganized Objective Army Division) in the next decade. However, between 1982 and 1987, the United States again altered its division to place more emphasis on the brigade as the organic formation. The new 'Division 86', five mechanized infantry battalions and five tank battalions in its infantry form (16,597 men) and six tank and four mechanized infantry battalions in its armoured version (16,295 men), has enlarged battalions plus an air cavalry combat brigade. The Soviet army (up to 1991) had a rectangular structure with three tank brigades and one motorized infantry brigade in its armoured divisions (11,470 men) and three motorized infantry brigades and one tank brigade in its motorized rifle divisions (12,695 men). The modern French division (1982) is closer to a British or US brigade in size, consisting of four small regiments (7,000 men). German armoured and infantry divisions are large, 21,500 men, while the British division, when constituted, possesses 14,000 men. Chinese armoured divisions contain 9,900 men while their infantry formations have 13,400. *See also* ADMINISTRATION, ARMY; ARTILLERY; BLADE WEAPONS; BYZANTIUM; CAVALRY; FIREARMS; GREECE, ANCIENT; GUSTAVUS II ADOLPHUS; INFANTRY; MILITARY DISTRICTS; MONGOLS; NASSAU; NETHERLANDS; ROME; SPAIN; SWITZERLAND; TACTICS; WEAPONS.

JOHN CHILDS

FURTHER READING
Archer Jones, *The Art of War in the Western World* (Oxford, 1989).

Tactics Tactics is the very general term used for dispositions made by a commander in preparation for battle and the measures which he takes during the engagement. The practical application of tactics depends as much on acquired knowledge as on innate skill. That knowledge concerns the factors involved in warfare, both human (in the sense of men's psychological, religio-ideo-logical and sociological attitudes) and technical (weapons, equipment, logistics, etc.). The art of the tactician comes into play at the point beyond which his acquired knowledge cannot take him, that is, when he becomes immersed in the atmosphere of uncertainty that characterizes warfare. The results of direct observation, which normally form the basis for any intelligent action, and reliable items of intelligence, are just what are often lacking when a commander prepares for battle. Hence, the tactician has to garner indications which will allow him to formulate a certain number of hypotheses in regard to the possible intentions of the enemy. The ability to interpret such indications during the course of the

action would be inconceivable without a mastery of the professional military skills or a development of those special faculties which allow a commander to divine what lies behind the outward appearance that an enemy presents.

During the course of history, military professional skills have developed against a background of four factors which have remained basic: (1) *uncertainty* arising from inadequate information, which leads a tactician to put together mixed troop formations that have the versatility to cope with all eventualities. In the course of the action, a military commander, even though the information which he has may be imperfect, will take the initiative with the aim of reducing his own area of uncertainty, while increasing that of his opponent; (2) the use of missile weapons – later to become *firepower* – for action at a distance, with the object of minimizing one's own casualties. As a counter to enemy fire, armies have turned to protective armour, defensive dispositions, fortifications, use of ground and rapid movement; (3) *manoeuvre*, by which a commander can, where possible without disclosing his intentions to the enemy, change the direction, point, moment and speed of his attack; (4) the *assault*, whose object is to effect the physical destruction of the enemy, or to paralyse his will to resist by a threat so menacing that he looks upon his own position as hopeless.

Tactics form a highly characteristic expression of civilizations or societies, whatever their nature, and always appear in the shape of a combination in space and time of these four elements. Study of numerous examples leads to the conclusion that the circumstances of no two battles are exactly similar, even though they may be in many respects analogous, each has a character of its own, shaped by all the factors which have determined its outcome. It is true that efforts have been made, in the interests of simplifying the teaching of tactics, to classify battles into a certain number of 'types', but it is precisely in the breaking free from these theoretical categories, which seek to confine it, that military genius manifests itself. In this connection, it should be mentioned that wars which continue over a long period often have the effect of producing a convergence of the tactical ideas of the opposing sides, so that they end by having a number of characteristics in common. This clearly occurred in Western Europe during the Second World War.

The development of tactics has been marked by a series of successive accretions, fresh introductions and parameters which have exercised an influence on the basic factors mentioned above. Hunting and hand-to-hand combat were the predecessors of more organized forms using missiles and assault. Hunting scenes are certainly the earliest of which pictorial representations exist, those of battle appearing only later. The Sumerians, who date from around 3000 BC, were the first to have left written testimony of an organized body of troops. A phalanx of infantrymen, equipped with helmets, spears and shields and disposed in rectilinear form, on the lines of their cities, formed the main bulwark. Battle chariots, whose occupants were armed with bows and arrows, used this mass as a pivot for their manoeuvres.

In their tactics, the Assyrians boldly placed the accent on assault by the cavalry. They developed the latter to a level of excellence which has rarely been equalled in the course of history. The cavalryman formed a genuine 'multi-purpose weapon', long before that term had been invented. He and his mount were as one, and he used his long bow with great skill from all directions, prior to dispatching his opponent with spear thrusts. Such tactics had a psychological dimension also, in that the murderous reputation which these warriors acquired inspired terror in their adversaries.

The Egyptian chariots were lighter than the Assyrian, and this allowed them to elude an enemy, and to give greater importance to manoeuvre. The Persians, for their part, added the weight of massed numbers to the tactical procedures developed by their forerunners. The Israelites were the first to contribute a military theory; the Book of Joshua reads like a treatise on the subject. As a consequence of the Assyrians' very harshly exercised domination, this theory began to acquire a religious aspect, which was original in the sense that it looked upon the fighting man as being responsible to God and not merely to other men.

In answer to the threat posed by Darius' massed phalanx, the Greeks discovered the advantages of tactics based on the separation of a force into organized groups – articulation. At Marathon, the Athenian general Miltiades made no attempt to stand up to the frontal attack by the Persians; he concealed from their observation the division of the major part of his force into two main bodies, allowed his enemies to launch their effort against a thin screen spread out between, and then made his own decisive assault on their flanks. (In later categorizations of tactical methods, this was termed a double envelopment.) In this field, the Greeks were the great inventors and it was they who gave to the art of positioning and manoeuvring troops the appelation of 'tactics' (from the verb *tassein*, or, in Attic, *tattein*, which means, in this context, to dispose a body of soldiers). The Roman contribution was to turn these Greek innovations into a connected system, by incorporating them into the structure of the legion. Consisting of 4,000–6,000 men, this was the archetype of the modern division – a real tactical formation of all arms. In normal Roman practice, the battle was opened by a screen of *velites*, light troops whose object was to mislead the enemy as to the real strength of the commander's forces and his intentions. During this initial phase, the aim was to force the opponent to expend his efforts prematurely, in the form, for example, of a hail of arrows which had little effect on the legionaries' shields. Then the *velites* withdrew, giving the enemy the impression that he had secured an initial success. Behind the *velites*, and disposed in chequer-board formation, were the Roman centuries, ready to deploy at the last moment in accordance with the results of the scouting carried out by the *velites*. When the Roman line was about 30 yards from the enemy ranks, the legionaries launched against it a first 'salvo' with the heavy *pilum* (a javelin which could penetrate up to an inch into solid oak). A more carefully aimed 'salvo' with the second *pilum* supplemented the first. The third phase of the attack consisted of hand-to-hand fighting with the short sword. In cases of emergency, the *triarii* (literally, the third rank), who consisted of the veterans, came into action to restore the position or to cover a withdrawal. When the professional skill of the Romans in tactics fell into decay and army discipline – which provided the legion with all its effectiveness in battle – suffered a decline, the Western Empire collapsed, while the Eastern Empire, where Greek military thinking remained a living force, succeeded in resisting the barbarian assaults for a whole millennium.

At the beginning of the Middle Ages, there took place a recrudescence of earlier forms of combat. Where territory was concerned, the feudal period was marked by the advent of larger-scale, more organized systems, and the warfare of the time mirrored this process. One development was the form of tactics based on a force of knights, unbalanced though this proved to be. Alongside such changes, the Arabs made use of ideas produced by the Israelite 'intelligentsia' throughout the Mediterranean basin, and grafted onto it a simplified military theory derived from that of the Jews of Antiquity. The extra dimension given to the military qualities of Islamic combatants by the religious factor was the stimulus leading to the creation, within Christendom, of the military religious orders. The blows dealt by the Mongols, who penetrated as far as Silesia (1241) and whose mode of fighting was almost the same as that of the Assyrians, had the effect of reminding the Christian side that no tactics are effective which do not make use of an adequate weight of numbers – given the nature of the Christians' circumstances these could only be provided in the form of infantry.

It has already been noted that the Eastern Empire was able to put up a longer resistance to barbarian attacks and suffered less damage from invasions. In fact, Byzantium acted as the repository for the military theory of Antiquity and for the riches of Greek tactical innovation. Men of the fifteenth century discovered them afresh, just at the time when the firearm was making its presence felt on the battlefield. The development of tactics from the sixteenth to the nineteenth century was shaped by the struggle for supremacy between firepower and the assault. Since firepower imposed a heavier financial burden than assault troops, political authorities strove practically without intermission to replace artillery, with its costly technology, by the weight of cavalry or the dash of infantry, which imposed less of a load on peacetime budgets. (A blind eye was deliberately turned to the fact that such economies were fallacious, with the real payment always being made in terms of excessive losses of men in battle.)

After much trial and error, the Spaniards took advantage of the tactical innovations of the Swiss (massed pikemen, who could be used as a solid phalanx or in separate groups) and of the Italians (firearm technology), and produced the *tercio* system (*tercio* = (literally) one third of the fighting force), a combined formation within which, for the first time, hand-to-hand weapons were integrated with firearms. The regiment, which is the direct descendant of the *tercio*, remained, from the seventeenth century onwards, the basic formation used in battle (whether in close order as a column of attack or in extended order/line). The way in which tactics have evolved from the Renaissance to the present has been determined by the developments of every type in technology and ideology which have imprinted their characteristics. The most important among such developments has unquestionably been in 'firepower', i.e. the delivery at long range of weapons of the classical explosive type or of a nuclear, chemical and biological nature, together with all the means of so doing, such as explosive propellants, aircraft, missiles and laser/electronic beams.

If challenged once again to exercise his art, the modern tactician has to give overriding attention to the following principles: (1) *Husbanding of human resources*: an enemy artillery preparation or nuclear strike should not cause a force to lose in killed or wounded more than 6 to 10 per cent. The force must, therefore, be protected by concrete, ruins (deliberately produced, if necessary) or natural rock – and also by movement and dispersion. (It may be worth mentioning here that Frederick II's reason for adopting the oblique formation was to put part of his forces out of range of his enemy's volley fire. It is possible to envisage a modern 'oblique order' designed to cope with the threat from overhead, and in which only a part of a force would be exposed to the enemy bombardment.) (2) The *speed* with which orders must be given. In every war, the time factor shows afresh its exacting nature, and the period which battle allows a commander for his reactions to the situation becomes ever shorter. (3) The importance assumed by the *individual fighting man* as a 'multi-purpose weapon'. Confronted by the enemy's massed weight of numbers and by the thermonuclear weapon, the soldier, as long as he escapes death, can retain his attacking potential, provided that he has been suitably trained. (It has been stated, in this context, that a guerilla is at one and the same time a combatant and a commander, is difficult to lay hands on, and creates a feeling of insecurity by rapid changes of position and by carrying out attacks, whose effects can be considerable, against vulnerable installations or key personalities. But the comment must be made, in regard to him, that, without a very well-developed infrastructure and an intelligence service equipped with all the necessary means – which could be likened to the ground organization which an air force must have to guide its aircraft to their objectives – it is difficult to see how a guerilla could fit into the tactical movements of a combined force of all arms which alone can deliver the decisive blow.) The fighting man's training seems, in short, to be the factor that underlies all tactical effectiveness, because that alone can put him in the proper state of mind to take, when the moment comes, well-considered steps which will surprise the enemy, and which will give the engagement, when conducted in this manner, its aspect of originality. A tactical success, which arduous effort has imposed on a situation that, in itself, lacked any form, ranks, in the art of war, as a genuine example of creativity. *See also* CHEMICAL AND BIOLOGICAL WARFARE; CIVIL WAR; ECONOMIC WARFARE; GREECE, ANCIENT; INDIRECT WARFARE; INTELLIGENCE; MANOEUVRE AND MANOEUVRES; NAVAL WARFARE; POPULAR WARFARE; ROME; SECRECY; SIGNAL COMMUNICATION; TACTICAL ORGANIZATION WEAPONS.

AIRCRAFT; ARTILLERY; AVIATION; CAVALRY; INFANTRY.

AENEAS TACTICUS; CHARLES OF HABSBURG; CHARLES V, DUKE OF LORRAINE; CHARLES XII; CLAUSEWITZ; DAVOUT; EDWARD, PRINCE OF WALES; EUGENE OF SAVOY; FOCH; FOLARD; FREDERICK II; GRANDMAISON; GUESCLIN; GUIBERT; GUSTAVUS II ADOLPHUS; HANNIBAL; JOMINI; MARLBOROUGH; MONLUC; MONTECUCOLI; NAPOLEON; NASSAU; NELSON; ROMMEL; RUYTER; SAXE; SUFFREN; SUN-TZU; SUVOROV; VILLARS; WELLINGTON; XENOPHON.

D. REICHEL

FURTHER READING
Archer Jones, *The Art of War in the Western World* (Oxford, 1989).

Tactics, air   *See* AVIATION

Tactics, naval   *See* NAVAL WARFARE

Taginae, Battle of   *See* NARSES

Tamerlain or Timur Lenk (1336–1405) Timur Lenk (Turkish – 'Timur the Lame', hence Tamerlain, Tamerlane or Tamburlaine in English), was a Transoxianan Turk born at Kesh in Turkestan, supposedly descended in the female line from Genghis Khan. In 1369 he took advantage of a period of internal unrest to ascend the throne of the Golden Horde in Samarkand to become one of the greatest of the Mongol khans. At the height of his conquests, he dominated territories stretching from India to Asia Minor and the extent of his successes has caused him to be compared with Genghis Khan. By 1386, Timur Lenk had conquered Persia, Georgia and Armenia while Mongol columns had marched as far north as Moscow. He then turned his attention southwards and conquered northern India and Delhi in 1398, founding a sultanate which became the basis of the Moghul Empire. In 1399, he cut a path of destruction to Aleppo before heading for Egypt via Jerusalem but a swarm of locusts destroyed the forage, obliging him to move northwards. After seizing Baghdad and Damascus, Timur Lenk marched into Asia Minor having beaten the Ottoman Turks under Bayazid I (1389–1403) at Ankara (Angora) in 1402. He advanced across most of Asia Minor, sacking Nicaea, Gemlik and Smyrna before returning to Samarkand in order to prepare for an invasion of China. However, he died in his capital city before this expedition could be realized.

Timur Lenk combined the Mongol nomadic–military traditions with the religion and law of Islam. His dominance was achieved through military strength, utter ruthlessness and outstanding cruelty to all those, both soldiers and civilians, unfortunate enough to stand in the path of his armies. Principally, his cruelty was directed at Christians and those who followed a different branch of Islam. His successes were achieved by terror as much as by victory on the battlefield. However, his conquests were ephemeral. They were dispersed in time and space and could never be brought together into a cohesive empire. Timur Lenk lacked constructive political ideas and the territories over which he attempted to rule suffered from political disunity and cultural diversity. *See also* ANKARA; BYZANTIUM; GENGHIS KHAN; MONGOLS; OTTOMAN TURKS.

R. MANTRAN
JOHN CHILDS

FURTHER READING
David Morgan, *The Mongols* (Oxford, 1986); René Grousset, *The Empire of the Steppes: a history of Central Asia* (New Brunswick, 1970); J. J. Saunders, *The History of the Mongol Conquests* (London, 1971); H. Hookman, *Tamburlaine the Conqueror* (London, 1962).

Tanks Though war chariots appeared near the end of the fourth millennium BC, we have to wait until 1482 before Leonardo da Vinci wrote to Ludovico Sforza ('the Moor'): 'I shall produce unassailable, covered chariots which will enter the enemy lines with their artillery and will break through any troop formations, however numerous they may be. The infantry will be able to follow, without losses or obstacle.' Three aspects of the tank appear in this text: mobility, firepower and protection. This project, like so many of da Vinci's ideas, had to remain on the drawing board and await the coming of the internal combustion engine that allowed the required weight-to-power ratio to be achieved.

The armoured car, mounted on wheels and equipped with a moving turret, appeared at the beginning of the twentieth century. In that vehicle, mobility won out over armament and protection. While the Irishman Richard Lovell Edgeworth (1744–1817) had designed a wooden caterpillar track in 1770, his invention was not exploited until the years just preceding the First World War, and then it was used on civil engineering vehicles and farm tractors.

During the First World War, after the French retreat, the 'miracle' of the Marne and the 'race for the sea', operations bogged down on the Western Front. There then began a war of position and attrition, which was to last until July 1918. This strategy, which offered no clear end to the war, posed a challenge to the inventors of new weapons and tactics.

In order that infantry might advance without excessive losses across the ploughed-up terrain that extended from their own trenches to those of the enemy, the British and French each looked at armoured vehicles with caterpillar tracks that might be capable of engaging at close range those enemy positions that had resisted artillery preparatory bombardments. In France, the future General Estienne turned towards this so-called 'assault artillery'.

In Britain, the first research was undertaken by the Royal Navy; hence the terminology used in armoured units (turrets, crews, and so on). Thanks to the support of Winston Churchill, the First Lord of the Admiralty, the prototypes, which were tested from September 1915 onwards, gave way to the first 'tank', thirty of which were to be found on the Somme in September 1916. As there was a space of only fourteen months between drawing up

A pre-production model (XM–1) of the United States Abrams M–1 main battle tank. The first production models were accepted by the United States Army in 1980. Crew: 4. Armament: 1 × 105 mm gun, with laser range-finder and computerized fire control, 3 × 7.62 mm machine-guns, one mounted coaxially with the main armament. Armour: classified but of composite type. Length: 26 feet (hull), 32 feet (including gun). Combat weight: 120,250 lb. Power plant: 1 × Avco Lycoming AGT– 1500 gas turbine. Road speed: 45 mph. Range: 310 miles. An improved model, M–1A1, is now in production armed with a 120 mm smooth bore gun.
(M.A.R.S.)

the first plans for the tanks and their use in the field, there were understandable deficiencies both in the tanks and in their crews. In France, it required all the energy of Colonel Estienne and the support of General Joffre to put 130 so-called 'assault cannons' into action at Chemin des Dames in April 1917.

The British and French vehicles, too few in number to be decisive, suffered terrifying losses, and were therefore unable to create strategic surprise. These failures made the Germans sceptical as to the worth of tanks and in 1918 they had only some sixty of them. In contrast, French industry pushed ahead and launched a lighter tank, the Renault FT, the first vehicle to include a fully revolving turret. Several thousand of these were produced before the end of the war. Fuller, the chief of staff of the British Tank Corps, envisaged a massive use of tanks for the 1919 campaign that was never fought. The defeat of Germany, however, cannot be explained by the emergence of the tank, which was still none too reliable by the end of the war.

After 1918, Britain opted for armoured

vehicles that would perform the traditional roles of the cavalry. In view of Britain's military commitments during the interwar period, her army commanders favoured tanks designed to meet the conditions of colonial warfare, even though these requirements were likely to be markedly different from those encounted in the European theatre. In May 1940, the British army had only one armoured division and 300 tanks. Estienne and Fuller, who had stressed the strategic role of the new weapon, were forgotten. In France, armoured vehicles served mainly as infantry support. Colonel de Gaulle criticized this doctrine, but he was not listened to, although in 1938 the authorities decreed the formation of 'armour-plated divisions' (*divisions cuirassées*). In May 1940 there were three such divisions. Conservatism and inadequate funding explain the lack of armoured divisions in the armies of the democracies. The Polish forces fell in with French military thinking, while Moscow, after promising experiments in the early 1930s, decided to abandon all-armour formations after the Spanish Civil War.

Whereas in France, 3,000 tanks were divided evenly among 100 battalions, in Germany tanks were organized into ten divisions. Although the Versailles Treaty forbade the Weimar Republic to possess tanks, officers like Guderian read the writings of the British tank enthusiasts, Fuller and Liddell Hart. The Germans experimented with tank-traps and secretly tested some of their equipment in the Soviet Union in the 1920s. This was the genesis of the blitzkrieg concept and the *Panzerdivisionen*, the latter the large combined-arms units which were extremely mobile and independent of the infantry, and whose role it was to break through or outflank the enemy in close co-operation with the *Luftwaffe*. This preparatory work, begun well before the Nazis came to power, explains why the armoured formations of the Third Reich developed at such a rapid pace.

Shock tactics, the tank–aircraft combination and flexibility of command are a few of the reasons for the initial triumphs of the *Wehrmacht* in the Second World War. On 10 May 1940, German armoured forces were no greater in either number or quality than those of the French army, though, on the other hand, the latter did suffer from gross deficiencies in military aviation. The enemies of the Reich subsequently adopted its tactics. By 1942, mechanized warfare was already different from its manifestation early in the war. Before sending in tanks to breach enemy lines, carefully co-ordinated air and artillery strikes were used. Advances in anti-tank weapons meant that the infantry had to support the armoured echelon more closely. With the coming of an unfavourable balance of forces, the *Wehrmacht* was forced to adopt a defensive strategy. Its mechanized formations learned to riposte or to launch counter-attacks aimed at stabilizing sectors held by the infantry, although this practice became increasingly hazardous as the enemy consolidated its air superiority.

The belligerents developed vehicles that had higher levels of performance and were better armed. The 88 mm gun of the German Tiger tank fired its shells at an initial speed of 1,100 metres per second. The Tiger's weight reached 57 tonnes, some 22 tonnes

more than the US Sherman tank of which 49,000 were produced. The Americans, who were the great exponents of standardization and mass production, assembled the Sherman tank in 30 minutes from prefabricated sections, and sheer weight of numbers made up for the relative weakness of its gun and armour. Armoured vehicles also became more varied, the better to fulfil their specialized roles. There were tanks for straightforward mechanized battle, tank-destroyers, which were in fact mobile anti-tank guns, tracked or half-tracked transporters, reconnaissance vehicles either with wheels or caterpillar tracks, recovery vehicles and engineering vehicles. Power–weight ratios and armour were improved; the Sherman's gun platform was partially stabilized, and amphibious armoured cars or vehicles equipped with snorkels were built which were able to drive straight across rivers or streams. The modern tank dates from the Second World War. In spite of its high cost, the modern tank remains vulnerable because it is the product of a compromise between protection, armament, speed, operational range and cost.

The advent of weapons of mass destruction, and in particular of battlefield nuclear weapons, gives added importance to all categories of armoured vehicles that provide good protection against blast, intense heat and gamma radiation. In their airtight compartments, the crews are also protected from the effects of chemical weapons. On the other hand, traditional armour is ineffectual against neutron bombs. Against this latter weapon, the light atoms found in the ceramics or plastics of multi-layered armour provide better protection. Armoured vehicles also make poor targets. By virtue of their mobility, armoured divisions can remain dispersed until the moment that they are sent into action, which means that they are unlikely to attract a nuclear strike. Finally, only tracked vehicles have the capability of traversing terrain devastated by nuclear weapons.

These facts explain why all units whose role it is to work in conjunction with tanks must possess vehicles which provide similar nuclear–bacteriological–chemical protection. In this mode we find troop transports or armoured personnel carriers, which are often amphibious; armoured howitzers, mobile anti-aircraft guns, bridge-layers, engineer vehicles and armoured tactical nuclear missile carriers.

The Yom Kippur War of 1973, during which the belligerents suffered enormous losses of tanks, threw most preconceptions about the role of the tank into question. It seemed that ground-to-air and anti-tank missiles were going to dominate battlefields and that the preponderant role of the tank and aircraft was coming to an end. In fact, the actual situation was quite different. What had occurred was that the Israeli army, which had excessive faith in the virtues of blitzkrieg, initially had been surprised by the massive deployment of missiles against its air and armoured forces. Rather than make the blitzkrieg obsolete, missiles simply underlined the need for close collaboration between all arms in order to neutralize them. With the support of artillery and air power, mechanized infantry can destroy these missiles, which lack mobility, before the tanks make their assault.

There have been other challenges to the tank. Since the Vietnam War, the helicopter has continued to grow in importance. With its high mobility and its missiles, which can have a range of up to 2½ miles, the helicopter is so formidable that it has led some to contend that tanks are now obsolete. This is, however, a dangerous prediction. In the current state of technology, the helicopter is unable to carry a large-calibre gun, which is the most effective anti-tank weapon. Bad weather and darkness also prevent the helicopter from operating normally, and its armour, where it has any, remains limited due to weight restrictions.

The function of the tank remains what it has been since 1916, to provide tactical mobility on the battlefield for a heavy artillery weapon and its operators. Nor is the tank likely to become a missile-firing platform. Four factors explain why the heavy gun, with a calibre ranging between 105 and 120 mm, remains its main weapon. A vehicle- or hand-launched missile takes several seconds to reach its target and needs to be guided during flight; a missile is much more expensive than a shell; the tank gun is well-suited to fighting at a distance of 2,200–2,700 yards, the common fighting range in Europe; and the fin-stabilized armour-piercing shell makes the heavy gun even more effective. Other technological advances make the tank likely to remain an important battlefield weapon. Multi-layered armour systems have increased the protection of the tank, while guidance systems (which are, in fact, micro-computers) and laser range-finders ensure a hit on the enemy at the first attempt, whether the tank is moving or stationary. At night, infra-red vision equipment and image-intensifying sights create the equivalent of daylight visibility. On roads, the tank can reach speeds approaching 45 miles per hour and it has a range of over 300 miles. Though ever more sophisticated microprocessors, electronics and computer systems are required for its operation, its crew is not about to be replaced by machines.

Along with the other armoured vehicles that either accompany or support it, the tank remains an indispensable weapon and seems likely to do so for at least the next twenty-five years. Its role and appearance may be altered due to changes in doctrine or advances in technology, but the basic value of an armoured weapons platform seems unchallenged. *See also* ARMOUR PLATE; ARTILLERY; AVIATION; CAMBRAI; CAVALRY; ESTIENNE; FRANCE, BATTLE OF; FULLER; GERMANY; GUDERIAN; ISRAEL, SINCE 1948; LIDDELL HART; ROMMEL; WAGGON-LAAGER.

H. DE WECK

FURTHER READING
Hervé de Weck, *Les Blindés: des origines à nos jours* (Lausanne, 1982); H. D. Crow, *British Armoured Fighting Vehicles 1919–40* (Windsor, 1970); John Weeks, *Men against Tanks: a history of anti-tank warfare* (Newton Abbot, 1975); B. Liddell Hart, *The Tanks* (2 vols, New York, 1959).

Tannenberg, or Grünwald, Battle of (15 July 1410)   Originally an order of German Hospitallers in the Holy Land, by the beginning of the fourteenth century the

Teutonic Knights had become based in Prussia with their headquarters at Marienburg. Here they continued their crusading to Christianize the Baltic region while simultaneously creating a well-administered, expanding and energetic state. In 1409, the ill-judged diplomacy of Grandmaster Ulrich von Jungingen created an alliance of Poland and Lithuania. In the summer of 1410, an army of 25,000 Poles, Lithuanians, Russians, Tatars and Bohemian mercenaries under Jan Ziska, commanded by King Ladislas II Jagiellio of Poland and his cousin, Witold, Grand Duke of Lithuania, invaded Prussia. Ulrich probably intended to assume the defensive as his troops were relatively strong in missile weapons and artillery. The Teutonic army took a position behind the River Drewenz, a tributary of the Vistula, with its right on the forest of Grünwald and the left resting on the village of Tannenberg. Ulrich had about 11,000 men: 3,850 heavy cavalry, 3,000 esquires or lighter horse, and 4,000 mounted archers and crossbowmen. The small body of infantry was stationed behind the German line in a waggon-fort. The details of the action are far from clear although it appears that a thunderstorm occurred before the battle which dampened the powder and rendered unusable the cannon of the Teutonic Knights. The German archers and crossbowmen successfully 'softened up' the lightly armed Lithuanians on the left leaving them vulnerable to the charge of the heavy cavalry which swept the Lithuanians from the field. However, on the centre and right, the contest was fierce and the action dissolved into a series of bitter mêlées. Eventually, the Poles and Lithuanians pressed into the gap left by the previous charge of the heavy cavalry and the German army was virtually surrounded. Ulrich desperately flung his remaining knights against the enemy centre in the hope of capturing King Ladislas but he was cut down along with the majority of his horsemen. The Poles then stormed the infantry defending the waggon-fort. Besides the Grandmaster, over 200 members of the Teutonic Order were killed along with thousands of their soldiers. The battle ended the expansionist policies of the Teutonic Order and marked the beginning of its political and military decline. *See also* GERMANY; POLAND; WAGGON-LAAGER.

JOHN CHILDS

FURTHER READING
Geoffrey Evans, *Tannenberg, 1410:1914* (London, 1960); Joseph Jakstas, 'The Battle of Tannenberg', *Baltic Review*, xx (1960), pp. 18–37; Constantine Jurgela, *Tannenberg, 15 July 1410* (New York, 1961).

Tannenberg, Battle of (26–30 August 1914) With the advance of the Russian 1st and 2nd Armies towards East Prussia, General Max von Prittwitz ordered his German 8th Army to retreat after failing to turn back the Russians at Gumbinnen on 20 August 1914. Prittwitz was then convinced by his staff, not least Colonel Max Hoffmann, that he could exploit superior communications to defeat Alexander Samsonov's 2nd Army before Paul Rennenkampf could effectively intervene with the 1st Army. However, unaware of the change of mood, German Supreme Headquarters (OHL), which was extremely nervous of the situation in the east while the Schlieffen Plan was still unfolding in the west, dismissed von Prittwitz and brought General Paul von Hindenburg out of retirement to command 8th Army with Major-General Erich Ludendorff as his chief of staff. Arriving on 23 August, Hindenburg and Ludendorff endorsed Hoffmann's plan to transfer 8th Army to the southern frontier of East Prussia with only a cavalry division being left to mask Rennenkampf. Having achieved a rough parity with Samsonov, who had betrayed his positions through lack of wireless security, the Germans commenced a double envelopment of the Russian army on 26 August. Within four days, the 2nd Army had suffered 70,000 casualties with at least a further 75,000 taken prisoner and Samsonov had committed suicide. German losses were barely 15,000 and 8th Army was then turned north to achieve an equally impressive victory over Rennenkampf around the Masurian Lakes in September 1914. The reputations of Hindenburg and Ludendorff were assured. *See also* HINDENBURG; LUDEN-DORFF; SCHLIEFFEN; TANNENBERG (1410).

IAN F. W. BECKETT

FURTHER READING
M. Hoffmann, *Tannenberg wie es wirklich war* (Berlin, 1926); Sir E. Ironside, *Tannenberg* (Edinburgh, 1933); N. Stone, *The Eastern Front, 1914–1917* (London, 1975); D. E. Showalter, *Tannenberg: clash of empires* (Hampden, Conn., 1991).

Taranto, Battle of (11–12 November 1940)   The entry of Italy into the Second World War placed the British Mediterranean fleet in an inferior position. However, after some months, and after one inconclusive action off Calabria (9 July 1940), it became clear that although Italian intentions at sea were defensive, their powerful fleet would remain a constant menace. Cunningham, in command of the British fleet, therefore adopted a plan proposed against the German fleet in 1918, to attack the enemy fleet in its base at Taranto by aircraft. The arrival of the new carrier *Illustrious* gave him the means.

After a long-range air reconnaissance, one of the first of its kind, had shown the detailed disposition of the Italian fleet, the attacking force of twenty Swordfish aircraft took off in the evening of 11 November, in two groups. Avoiding strong gun defences from ships and shore and a balloon barrage, the torpedo bombers managed to inflict severe damage on three battleships, all of which were out of action for long periods. The dive bombers caused damage to other ships and to the shore base. Only two aircraft were lost.

While Cunningham thus asserted British naval predominance in the Mediterranean, the attack provided a model which was followed by Yamamoto at Pearl Harbor (7 December 1941). In addition, it probably contributed to the German decision to intervene in the Mediterranean theatre. *See also* CUNNINGHAM; ITALY; NAVAL WARFARE; NAVIES; PEARL HARBOR.

A. W. H. PEARSALL

FURTHER READING
Donald Macintyre, *The Aircraft Carrier* (London, 1968); Don Newton and A. Cecil Hampshire, *Taranto* (London, 1974); B. B. Schofield, *The Attack on Taranto* (London, 1973).

Teil, Jean, Chevalier du (1738–1820) Through his writings, this French artillery officer and theorist made an important contribution to the development of an enhanced role for field artillery in battle, though it must be said that his ideas were not as original as has often been claimed, his fame resting largely on his assumed influence upon Napoleon. Although an officer of the *ancien régime* who had begun his career at a very early age in 1747, du Teil embraced the French Revolution of 1789 and continued to receive appointments and promotions in the Republican armies. He was suspended for several years on account of the arrest and execution (1794) of his elder brother and fellow artillery officer, Baron Jean-Pierre du Teil, but did not finally retire until 1813. Both the du Teil brothers would seem to have been influential in shaping the tactical ideas of Napoleon who, as a young officer, came under their tutelage at Auxonne in 1788–9. Jean du Teil insisted on a much greater number of guns and on their organization into highly mobile, massed batteries capable of effecting a decisive result at the point of attack by concentrating their fire on the enemy's troops rather than on counter-battery fire against the enemy's guns. Du Teil's theories owed much to Guibert who, in turn, had drawn on the thoughts of various artillery officers, most notably Du Puget. Such theories finally became reality in the armies of Napoleon. *See also* ARTILLERY; GUIBERT; NAPOLEON.

G. A. STEPPLER

FURTHER READING
B. H. Liddell Hart, *The Ghost of Napoleon* (London, 1933); Matti Lauerma, *L'Artillerie de campagne française pendant les guerres de la Révolution* (Helsinki, 1956); Joseph du Teil, *Napoléon et les Généraux du Teil* (Paris, 1897); R. S. Quimby, *The Background of Napoleonic Warfare* (New York, 1957).

Terrorism   The terms 'terrorist' and

'terrorism' provoke a mixed response; to some people acts of terrorism are a legitimate means of attacking an oppressor, to others the perpetrator is no more than a common criminal. An introduction to the topic, therefore, needs to address the questions of definition, organizations and techniques if there is to be any analysis of a phenomenon which, although predating the Second World War, is very much a feature of contemporary political conflict.

Political terrorism has been defined as the deliberate creation of a state of terror which involves either the use or the threat of the use of force in an attempt to influence groups or individuals for political purposes. This excludes terrorism for criminal purposes although modern developments in the nature of political terrorism in some parts of the world have blurred the boundaries between the strictly political and the strictly criminal.

Terrorism involves several components: it tends to be indiscriminate (although it may have specific targets it is the nature of the threat that is indiscriminate); its effects are out of proportion to the physical results and it appears unpredictable and arbitrary. It is also marked by a sense of amorality; the terrorists operate outside the accepted moral codes of society – the means are viewed as being justified by the ends. These components make it the ideal 'weapon' of small or weak groups. They are able to extract the maximum amount of influence from the minimum expenditure of force.

Terrorism differs from guerilla warfare in that the guerilla recognizes some of the conventions of warfare, particularly those that differentiate between the civilian and the armed combatant. Terrorism recognizes no such distinction although the boundary is not fixed; many terrorist groups have developed into guerilla bands while many guerilla organizations have carried out acts which may properly be defined as those of terrorism.

A number of types of terrorist organization have been proposed by a number of authors to help understand the nature of political terrorism. The main sub-groups are revolutionary terrorism, state terrorism and international terrorism.

Revolutionary Terrorism The primary aim of the revolutionary terrorist is the destabilization of the state and the replacement of the ruling regime. Terrorist activity may only be part of the process to undermine and overthrow the incumbent powers. Mao Tse-Tung, for example, viewed revolutionary terrorism as the initial stage in the revolution that would end in a conventional confrontation.

Two sub-groups of revolutionary terrorism have been identified: (1) terrorism in an attempt to overthrow a domestic regime; (2) terrorism to gain liberation from foreign rule.

In the first sub-group we can include organizations that existed in late nineteenth- and early twentieth-century Tsarist Russia. Groups such as the 'Battle Organization' carried out selective assassinations of Tsarist officials. More recent examples have been the Viet Cong operations against South Vietnamese villages and hamlets, which included attacks against local officials and those that supported the South Vietnamese regime. Asian organizations continue to follow the Maoist model. The Tamil Tigers' struggle for an independent Tamil state in northern Sri Lanka has included terrorist activities (such as the bombing of a bus station in 1987 which killed 127 civilians and the assassination of Rajiv Gandhi in 1991) as well as more conventional military activity against the Sri Lankan armed forces and the Indian peace-keeping force deployed in 1989. In South America a reactionary form of anti-state terrorism appears to be developing. In Peru a rural-based organization known as Sendero Luminoso (The Shining Path) has been terrorizing villages since 1980 and is believed to have been responsible for some 15,000 deaths. Its support comes primarily from the Amerindian population and its 'philosophy' looks back to a Peru based on the co-operative agricultural system of the Incas.

In Europe the principal terrorist organizations have been the IRA and ETA. The IRA have been waging a campaign of terrorism against British 'occupation' of Northern Ireland whilst ETA has been

The Provisional IRA's 'Barrack Buster' mortar. This large tube can launch a bomb containing several hundred pounds of explosives a considerable distance. It is usually mounted, like this example, in the back of a hijacked van. A hole is cut in the roof to permit the exit of the bomb.
('MODUK')

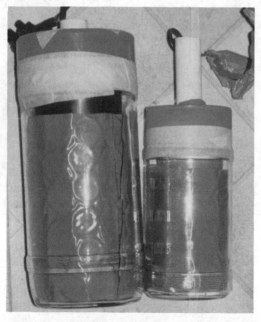

Typical 'coffee jar' grenades of the Provisional IRA: a pound or a half pound of explosives designed to explode either on impact or by a time-fuse. These examples have coins taped around the explosives to act as shrapnel.
('MODUK')

campaigning for an independent Basque territory in northern Spain. The IRA (and the Loyalist counter-terrorist organizations) have accounted for nearly 3,000 deaths since 1968 and have launched operations not only in Northern Ireland but also in mainland Britain and on the Continent. The terrorist campaign in the Basque region has been responsible for about 800 deaths – three-quarters of these by ETA.

Terrorism as a means of liberation was an important element of the decolonization process. Britain has faced terrorist activity in Ireland, Palestine, Kenya, Malaya, Cyprus and Aden; France in Indo-China and Algeria; Portugal in Angola and Mozambique. The organizations that developed in these countries were very different. In Kenya the terrorist organization, the Mau Mau, was largely based on tribal lines, while in Algeria the French authorities were faced with terrorist activity by both Algerian nationalists (FLN) and the white settlers (OAS). In Palestine the Zionist terrorist groups Irgun Zvai Leumi and the Stern Gang (a fanatical offshoot of Irgun) were primarily urban-based groups. The Irgun was largely modelled on the Irish Republican Army with a right-wing nationalist ideology. Both groups had a paramilitary structure, but whereas the IRA, in their struggle against British forces in the 1918–21 period, concentrated on military and police targets, the Irgun was less discriminate and planted bombs in Arab marketplaces and on buses, claiming revenge for Arab attacks on Jewish settlers.

State Terrorism   Terrorism as practised by the state falls into two distinct sub-groups. The first is repression by the state. The second is terrorism sponsored by a state and occurring outside its borders.

Repressive terrorism can occur as the state's response to revolutionary terrorism and indeed may be the aim of the revolutionary terrorist group as it attempts to undermine the support and legitimacy of the domestic regime. This was the experience of Uruguay in 1972 where a terrorist campaign by the Montoneros provoked a right-wing counter-terrorist backlash and in Turkey in 1980 where the high level of terrorist killings provoked a military coup. Repressive state terrorism has also been associated with the French Revolutionary period, the Stalinist period in the Soviet Union and more recently with the Argentinian 'Dirty War' of the late 1970s when people were killed or went missing at the hands of the military authorities. Repressive state terrorism may be associated with any regime using terrorism in order to quell opposition to its policies.

Sovereign states may often view it as in their interests to patronize and encourage terrorist groups as a means of undermining and attacking their enemies. Where it differs from supporting partisan groups in enemy territory during wartime is in the nature of the target. Partisan and guerilla organizations during the Second World War focused on the military (or that part of the infrastructure such as railways or the defence industry utilized by the military) although non-combatants could be, and were, killed and injured. Terrorist organizations focus on non-combatants. Although the military may also be targeted the aim is to instil a state of terror throughout the population and not necessarily to aid military victory. Into this category comes much of contemporary terrorism particularly in the Middle East.

Groups such as the Palestine Liberation Organization and Islamic Jihad are heavily financed and equipped by Arab states. The PLO is the richest terrorist organization in the world. Its assets have been estimated at $5 billion and its annual income at $1.25 billion. There are numerous splinter groups, however, partly as the result of their support from a number of states. Lebanon has also been a fruitful area for state-sponsored terrorist groups. Iran, Syria, Libya and Iraq all have their own groups operating there. Iran, for example, supported Hizbollah during its campaign of kidnapping Westerners in Beirut and attacking Western embassies and military bases where one of the key tactics was the 'suicide' attack.

International Terrorism The funding of terrorist groups by states for operations in a third country is one facet of international terrorism but the distinctive feature of the modern world is the way in which technology has enabled all terrorist groups, including those aiming at the revolutionary overthrow of domestic regimes, to give their campaigns an international dimension.

International revolutionary groups such as the PLO and the Islamic Jihad may be state-supported but they operate on an international scale. Splinter groups of the PLO, like Black September, have organized operations such as the killings of eleven Israeli athletes at the Munich Olympic Games. Airline hijackings also illustrate the international dimension of terrorism. One example of many was the hijacking of a TWA flight from Athens to Beirut in 1985. The flight carried mainly US citizens. The hijackers were a Shia fundamentalist group based in Lebanon and backed by Syria and their target was the release of Shia prisoners held by Israel. Modern developments in technology and especially in media communications make these operations highly attractive to terrorist groups anxious to attract worldwide publicity to their cause.

The ease and influence of modern communications also make it possible for the very small international terrorist groups to function on the world stage. These groups, which include the Baader–Meinhof Gang, the Japanese Red Army and the Red Army Faction, are very small and often drawn from student groups and the children of the privileged and influential. They preach world revolution but their support is often minimal.

The Japanese Red Army illustrate how well such groups can operate in the international arena. The JRA receive financial support from Arab states and have bases in North Korea and the Middle East. In 1972 they killed 26 passengers at Lod airport in Israel (16 of those killed were Puerto Rican). In 1973 they hijacked a plane taking off from Amsterdam airport. In 1974 they set fire to oil installations in Singapore. They have also carried out operations in France, Stockholm, Kuala Lumpur, Jakarta, Naples and have been sighted in many other cities scattered around the globe.

The growth of terrorism in the international arena is due primarily to two factors.

First, the nature of modern technology. There have been dramatic developments in weaponry, particularly in powerful, virtually undetectable explosives such as Semtex and electronic devices to control explosives. The growth of modern communications and media have provided the terrorist groups with innumerable opportunities for publicity. Second, the nature of the international system, which is based on the notion of sovereign states, has brought about great difficulties in dealing with sub-state actors who behave as though they were sovereign states, such as the PLO which has been granted a representative at the United Nations. There are also a vast array of targets that represent the 'state' for the international terrorist to attack. Finally, the problem of jurisdiction can be exploited as illustrated by the hijacking of planes and ships; it is often unclear who has responsibility for security.

Modern criminal terrorism has also moved closer to political terrorism particularly concerning the international drugs trade. This is most marked in Colombia where the size of the drugs industry is so large that it has far-reaching political consequences. Drugs trafficking is worth $80 billion a year to Colombia. The murder rate in Medellin in the centre of the cocaine producing areas is the highest in the world. Terrorist groups operating in Colombia are financed and supported by the drugs cartels. The largest of these, the Armed Revolutionary Forces of Colombia (FARC), has been involved in attacks on foreign companies and officials. It also has an open political organization, the Patriotic Front (UP), that receives funding from the drug 'barons'. Crime in general has proved a lucrative means of funding a terrorist organization. The IRA have been involved in a number of criminal activities. A large amount of cash has been raised by imposing 'revolutionary' taxes on local businesses and their employees. It has been estimated that at least £15 million a year is raised this way.

Terrorism is a fundamental problem for the advanced industrial democracies. Technological advances have made it even easier for very small groups to have a physical impact out of all proportion to their level of support. Coping with such small terrorist cells remains a difficult problem for a democratic state aiming to defeat the terrorist yet maintain the freedom and rights that are expected in a modern state. It is a problem that can be expected to be around for many years to come. The brief typology outlined above provides many examples of the vast array of organizations that exist and the range of tactics and techniques that are available to them. *See also* COLONIAL WARFARE; GUERILLA WARFARE; INDIRECT WARFARE; POPULAR WARFARE.

DAVID WESTON

FURTHER READING
Richard Clutterbuck, *Terrorism and Guerrilla Warfare: forecasts and remedies* (London, 1990); Christopher Dobson and R. Payne, *War Without End* (London, 1986); Donald Hanle, *Terrorism: the newest face of warfare* (London, 1989); Peter Janke, *Guerrilla and Terrorist Organisations: a world directory* (London, 1983); Walter Laqueur, *The Age of Terrorism* (London, 1987); Paul Wilkinson, *Political Terrorism* (London, 1974); Paul Wilkinson, *Terrorism and The Liberal State* (London, 1986).

Thermopylae, Battle of (480 BC)   This was a battle in which a force of about 7,000 Greek soldiers, commanded by Leonidas, King of Sparta, attempted to halt the progress of the Persian army led by King Xerxes during the second Persian invasion of Greece in 480–479 BC. Thermopylae is a narrow pass situated between sea and mountains on the eastern coast of Greece. The Persian army, which had invaded Greece from the north and was marching towards Attica, was forced to pass through it, while Xerxes' fleet pressed southward, following the coast. The Greeks, who positioned themselves in the pass, could not hope to contain the huge Persian invasion force for long. They were engaged either in a holding action, hoping that a Greek victory would come at sea to repulse the invasion, or in an operation aimed at stiffening the resolve of the cities of central Greece, which were always ready to defect to the enemy, by choosing a line of defence further north than the Isthmus of Corinth. For some days the Persian army was held up at Thermopylae, since its repeated assaults were unable to break down the Greek resistance, until a Persian detachment, guided by a local man who knew a path through the mountains, set out to dislodge the force guarding this route, reach behind the Greek position, and attack it from the rear. Forewarned of the arrival of the enemy, Leonidas sent home the bulk of the Greek contingents, in order to avoid the needless destruction of the hoplites, who would have been vulnerable to Persian cavalry if the enemy had broken through at once. He confronted the Persians with a battalion of 300 Spartans, and around 700 Thespians and 400 Thebans who agreed to stay with him. These men showed great courage, fighting to the very last man. Though the operation had little effect in military terms, Thermopylae remained a symbol of the heroic resistance of the Spartans and their leader Leonidas, and of Greek defiance of the Persians. *See also* GREECE, ANCIENT; IRAN; MARATHON; PLATAEA; SALAMIS; SPARTA.

R. LONIS

FURTHER READING
Y. Garland, *War in the Ancient World: a Social History* (London, 1975); C. Hignett, *Xerxes' Invasion of Greece* (Oxford, 1963), pp. 105–48; P. Connolly, *Greece and Rome at War* (London, 1981), pp. 13–24; A. R. Burn, *Persia and the Greeks: the defence of the West, c.546–478 BC* (London, 1984), pp. 406–22.

Tilly, Johann Tserclaes, Graf von (1559–1632) Tilly, who was born in the Castle of Tilly in Brabant, served with the Spanish Army of Flanders (1585–1600) and with the Austrian forces (1600–08). In 1610, he became commander of the armies of the Catholic League. He defeated Frederick V, Elector Palatine, at the Battle of the White Mountain in Bohemia (1620). He campaigned successfully in Germany during the 1620s, forcing Denmark from the Thirty Years' War through his victory at Lutter (1626). In 1630 he succeeded Wallenstein as commander of the Imperial armies as well as those of the Catholic League. He campaigned against Gustavus Adolphus of Sweden in 1631, but his army was responsible for the Sack of Magdeburg (1631) and was later badly defeated at Breitenfeld (1631). Tilly was mortally wounded in the action at Rain during the crossing of the River Lech in Bavaria in 1632. Neither a tactical nor an organizational innovator, Tilly was a highly competent professional commander, representative of the military entrepreneurs of the mid-seventeenth century. *See also* AUSTRIA; BREITENFELD; GERMANY; GUSTAVUS II ADOLPHUS; MAGDEBURG, SACK OF; MERCENARIES; WALLENSTEIN.

A. CORVISIER
JOHN CHILDS

FURTHER READING
Onno Klopp, *Tilly im Dreissigjahrigen Krieg* (2 vols, rev. edn, Paderborn, 1891–6); Fritz Redlich, *The German Military Enterpriser and his Work Force* (2 vols, Wiesbaden, 1964–5).

Timur Lenk *See* TAMERLAIN

Tirpitz, Alfred von (1849–1930) After entering the Prussian navy in 1865, Tirpitz quickly showed talent. Specializing in torpedoes, he rose through a series of important appointments, such as Chief of Staff to the High Command and commander of the Far Eastern squadron, before being elevated to secretary of state (minister) for the navy in 1897. His views were already known, and he became the creator of a navy which formed an integral part of overall German policy. If the Reich was not to decline in importance, he believed, then it had to acquire all the attributes of a great maritime power. This meant colonies, a merchant navy, and a high seas fleet. Though he could not rule out the risk of a British pre-emptive strike, Tirpitz succeeded in bringing William II, public opinion and the Reichstag round to his point of view, and the elements of German naval power were methodically created by the two navy laws of 1898 and 1900. Tirpitz remained in his post to see, in 1914, Germany possessing the second largest fleet in the world. As the war progressed, however, he saw with increasing impatience the restrictive instructions issued by the Kaiser regarding the use of the High Seas Fleet and the tentativeness and clumsiness of the early stages of submarine warfare. He gradually fell out of favour and resigned in March 1916. *See also* GERMANY; JUTLAND; NAVAL WARFARE; NAVIES.

P. MASSON
A. W. H. PEARSALL

FURTHER READING
Michael Salewski, *Tirpitz, Aufstieg, Macht, Scheitern* (Göttingen, 1979); Jonathan Steinberg, *Yesterday's Deterrent* (London, 1965); Alfred von Tirpitz, *My Memoirs* (London, n.d., *c.*1920).

Todleben, Eduard Ivanovich (1818–84) Todleben was a Russian engineer, to whose skill was attributed the success of the defence of Sebastopol in the Crimean War. He joined the Russian army in 1836 and served in the Caucasus in 1848–9. Sent in August 1854 to help with the construction of Sebastopol's defences against French and British attack, he was at first ill received. But after the Battle of Alma, when the siege began in earnest, Todleben's skill proved vital compensation for Russian numerical inferiority. His use of ground and his siting of guns to produce concentrated fields of fire were the traditional skills of his department. More novel was the extensive use of earthworks rather than masonry, producing a style of war more redolent of the First World War than of the formalized siege operations of Vauban. From 1863 to 1867 Todleben had overall responsibility for Russia's military engineers and for the country's fixed defences. In 1877 he was summoned to redeem the Russian army from its difficulties in the Siege of Plevna. In 1879 he was appointed to the State Council and became chief of the military district of Odessa. *See also* PLEVNA; RUSSIA/USSR; SEBASTOPOL; SIEGES.

HEW STRACHAN

FURTHER READING
Albert Seaton, *The Crimean War: a Russian chronicle* (London, 1977); E. Todleben, *Défense de Sebastopol* (St Petersburg, 1863); *Modern Encyclopaedia of Russian and Soviet History*, ed. Joseph L. Wieczynski (Gulf Breeze, Fl., 1985), xxxix.

Togo, Heihachiro (1847–1934) Togo joined the Japanese navy in 1864, his training including a period at HMS *Worcester*. Later, he oversaw the building of the *Fuso* on the Thames. The Sino-Japanese War gave him an opportunity to show his mettle as a sailor and as a tactician. He played a personal role at the opening of hostilities, when as captain of the cruiser *Naniwa*, he sent to the bottom the British steamship *Kowshing*, conveying Chinese troops to Korea. Later he fought at the decisive Battle of the Yalu river (17 September 1894). However, it was the war against Russia which enabled him to display his talents to the full, as Commander-in-Chief of the Japanese Fleet. First, he conducted a successful blockade of Port Arthur, which secured the lines of communication between Japan and the mainland for the army operating against Russia. He then frustrated an attempt by the Russian Asiatic fleet to escape from Port Arthur in the action of 10 August 1904. On 27–8 May 1905, he won a brilliant victory over the Russian Baltic fleet at the Battle of Tsushima, thus settling the outcome of the war. Following this battle, Togo was regarded as the modern Nelson and he enjoyed a remarkable reputation. His flagship, the *Mikasa*, is still preserved with great reverence, and at the attack on Pearl Harbor, Nagumo was to use the signal for attack, 'Z', which Togo had employed at Tsushima. *See also* JAPAN; TSUSHIMA.

P. MASSON

FURTHER READING
Robert Butow, *Togo and the Coming of the War* (Princeton, 1961).

Torres Vedras, Lines of (Portugal) (1810) While commanding the British forces in Portugal, Wellington created a line of fortified redoubts and earthworks to the north of Lisbon, in order to avoid being forced to re-embark. Composed of three lines of field fortifications stretching over 30 miles between the Tagus and the coast, the system was known as the Lines of Torres Vedras. It was armed with 600 cannon and the area to the front was completely cleared of supplies and shelter. Wellington withdrew into Torres Vedras on 10 October 1810 and Marshal André Masséna attacked on 14 October. One month later, on 15 November, Masséna withdrew, his forces exhausted by the problems of supply and the attacks of the *guerilleros*. This initiative enabled Wellington to operate on the Portuguese frontier without too many risks during 1811 and then to take the offensive early in 1812. The Torres Vedras Lines were often spoken of thereafter as a model for the construction of a redoubt where troops could be held in waiting ready to launch an offensive at a later date. *See also* FORTIFICATION, FIELD; GREAT BRITAIN; WELLINGTON.

A. CORVISIER
JOHN CHILDS

FURTHER READING
David Gates, *The Spanish Ulcer* (London, 1986); Charles Oman, *History of the Peninsular War* (Oxford, 1902–22).

Tours, Battle of *See* POITIERS

Traditions, military *See* ESPRIT DE CORPS; ETHOS; GLORY; HONOURS AND AWARDS; ICONOGRAPHY; MORALE; MUSEUMS; MUSIC; SYMBOLISM; VEXILLOLOGY

Trafalgar, Battle of (21 October 1805) On 25 May 1804, Napoleon abandoned the idea of a surprise crossing of the Straits of Dover by the Boulogne flotilla without the support of a fleet. He revived the old *ancien régime* plan of bringing together the Toulon, Brest and Spanish fleets to gain temporary superiority in the Channel. On paper, these forces should have been equal to the task but the calculation was purely numerical. The Spanish navy had always been short of seamen; since 1792, its timber supplies from the Baltic had been cut off, and it had not cast a single naval cannon.

The French fleet had been disrupted by a medical disaster and the effects of the Revolution. The death of Admiral La Touche-Tréville (20 August 1804) led Napoleon to place Villeneuve in command of the Toulon squadron.

The plan was for the Toulon squadron to draw the British fleet towards the West Indies before hastening back to combine with the Brest fleet. It was hoped that the Channel would then be clear. The British, however, had adopted their now customary policy of close blockade of Brest, which rendered the escape of the Brest fleet problematic. The British Mediterranean fleet under Nelson could not, however, so readily close Toulon. When Villeneuve sailed, Nelson thought he was making for Egypt, and so lost time in searching to the eastward. The poor state of the French ships and crews rendered their voyage slow; even though Nelson only had half as many ships as Villeneuve, he rapidly recovered his balance. As soon as Nelson's arrival in the West Indies was announced, Villeneuve had only one thought: to get back to France. Nelson followed. Off Cape Finisterre, on 22 July 1805, Villeneuve encountered a British fleet under Sir Robert Calder, stationed there to intercept him. Though the battle, fought in heavy fog, resulted only in the loss of two Spanish ships, Villeneuve realized that he could only turn south. He reached Cadiz after disembarking 2,000 sick men at Vigo, and was then blockaded. Nelson returned home.

The Cadiz blockaders were soon reinforced and Nelson rejoined them on 28 September. The French strategic plan had failed. Moreover, France was threatened by a coalition on land, so Napoleon was determined that his fleet should make a further effort. Although a countermanding order arrived too late, the Franco-Spanish fleet left Cadiz on 20 October. Next day, as it sailed in a concave line, Nelson attacked, having explained to his 'band of brothers' his tactics, involving a formation of two columns, the second under the command of Collingwood, in order to break the enemy line into segments. The result was a massacre. Thirteen French and nine

Spanish ships were lost, either sunk, foundered, burnt or captured that day or when a detached portion of the Franco-Spanish fleet was later seized. French losses of men were enormous, the British comparatively light except for the death of Nelson.

The Allies, with worn-out ships, unskilled crews and poor officers, had not proved equal to the genius of Nelson, the level of understanding between his captains, the extreme effectiveness of his 'lethal fire' and the experience of the British seamen. By building new ships, the Napoleonic navy was able to restore the number of vessels to former levels (France had more than 100 ships of the line in 1813). However, isolated in small groups, blockaded in port, without great leaders and with little sea experience for the crews, the French navy simply played the role of a 'fleet in being', tying down considerable British forces by its mere existence. *See also* BLOCKADES; NAPOLEON; NAVAL WARFARE; NAVIES; NELSON.

J. MEYER
A. W. H. PEARSALL

FURTHER READING
Julian S. Corbett, *The Campaign of Trafalgar* (London, 1910); Dudley Pope, *Decision at Trafalgar* (Philadelphia, 1960); Oliver Warner, *Trafalgar* (London, 1966).

Training Soldiers require a highly specific vocational training. War is the best school but, in peacetime, contrived exercises which attempt to accustom men to wartime situations must suffice. Modern electronics and computers permit simulations of actual battle but they are expensive and cannot reproduce the psychological and physical ordeal of combat. Since one of the cardinal principles of the military profession is that life might have to be sacrificed, training to produce courage, self-discipline and good morale has a high priority. Physical fitness is essential for a soldier. More recently, the introduction of sophisticated weapons systems and communications networks has demanded a higher level of technical expertise.

A distinction needs to be drawn between the various types of military instruction.

Schooling in the use of weapons – swordsmanship, musketry – can occur outside the armed forces. Within the army, the training of the other ranks differs from that of officers. Social factors strongly influence the varieties of training. Family traditions, or the membership of a class that has a military vocation, such as the nobility, or of a warrior caste can provide the bases of military training within a general social ethos. A parallel between a social and a military hierarchy was a feature of the *ancien régime* and has not entirely disappeared in the twentieth century. In most states, military training is closely associated with the current forms and expectations of civilian education. The moral and spiritual characteristics which produce a readiness for self-sacrifice may be common to all the male members of a particular society as a result of the prevailing religion or ideology. Similarly, the concept of honour fostered by European aristocracies in the early modern period served as a model for the military. These factors all affect the evolution of military drill, military instruction and lessons in theory and practice. Neither must the part played by historical events be overlooked. Though victories have often resulted in complacency (Prussia after the Seven Years' War and France following the First World War), they have also produced imitation of the successful methods. Defeats have often caused major reforms and advances in training (Cannae for Rome; Agincourt, Rossbach and Sedan for France; the Boer War for Britain; and Jena–Auerstädt for Prussia). However, it is the socio-cultural and moral climate that characterizes the two basic systems of military training – learning by experience and being taught in a military school.

Learning by Experience At one time, learning by experience was the only way of acquiring an acquaintance with military practices but it was inadequate for learning about military theory. However, the latter was not thought indispensable for officers until the nineteenth century. There are three basic methods of learning by experience: (1) the voluntary acquisition of knowledge in a family or social context, with or

810

without any wish to join the army, which was common in societies where fighting qualities were highly regarded; (2) learning by experience in army units, either voluntarily or compulsorily at the beginning of military service; (3) learning how to become an officer as a cadet or volunteer on attachment to a unit.

1 Exercise in the martial arts, long considered a privilege of the aristocracy, has frequently been taught alongside other forms of physical education. Instructors were employed in the houses of noble families and in public establishments to cater for members of the urban population, notably in Ancient Greece and Rome. Physical fitness for combat was based on a triad of skills – riding, wrestling and swordsmanship – plus the frequent addition of dancing. In Sparta, the period of military training (*agoge*) consisted of gymnastic exercises and the handling of weapons. It was followed, up to the age of 30, by a communal form of existence (*syssitia*). In both Greece and Rome, instruction in elementary arithmetic, geometry and physics was available which was useful for those likely to occupy positions of command. After a long hiatus, tuition in such subjects reemerged in the Jesuit colleges and Protestant academies of early modern Europe, with the addition of courses in fortification. Throughout the whole of nineteenth-century Europe, the establishments providing secondary education (the *lycée* in France, the *gymnasium* in Germanic countries and the public schools in England) gave their pupils a training which fitted them for a possible career as an officer. Moral training was taken for granted as a function of the family but was reinforced by the content of nearly all school courses in the choice of texts for Latin and Greek translation and the subjects for essays and in religious instruction.

It is unusual for ordinary soldiers to be prepared from infancy for the military profession, except in societies which contain military castes, e.g. Sparta, or the Ottoman Empire where some Christian children were removed from their families to be made into elite foot soldiers, the janissaries. Except in the case of families with a military tradition, entry into the army occurs because of conscription or an unpredictable act of voluntary engagement. In these circumstances men have no special preparation for the soldier's life except through the moral and physical training acquired in schools and by example in countries with large military establishments. However, children's games of mock warfare involving hand-to-hand struggles with rudimentary weapons are more formative than might be supposed.

The creation of urban militias in Western Europe, dating from the twelfth century, implied some degree of training in the handling of weapons. The fifteenth century witnessed a spread of training in the use of arms in Switzerland and Scotland as a preparation for engagement in the service of a local lord, a canton or a foreign monarch. In England, in the fourteenth century, the king encouraged archery and, in France, Charles VI forbade all public sporting contests except shooting with the bow and the crossbow (1384). However, the danger that widespread training might assist rebellion caused a change of mind. After the French Wars of Religion and the Fronde, the monarchy took steps to disarm the population and, with the developments in firearms, weapons of war ceased to be generally available to the public. Only the practice of swordsmanship remained in civilian favour, especially amongst those of gentle birth.

2 It was thus in their units that soldiers learned their trade. The recruits were taken in hand by corporals or experienced soldiers and taught the basics of weapons handling, drill movements and discipline. They then took their place in the ranks and files alongside veterans who taught them endurance and *esprit de corps* through exercises and mock battles. In various cities of Ancient Greece where military service was compulsory, this training occupied a year and was completed in villages situated on the frontiers. Except in the event of an invasion, young men could not be employed against an enemy until their period of training had finished.

In mercenary units, the length of training varied according to circumstances, at least until the eighteenth century. Recruits who had already seen service were particularly valued, a trend which fuelled the tide of desertion. In the sixteenth century, the Spanish *tercio* provided a model of how to train men. The *bisoño* (novice) was initially employed as a page under the command of senior non-commissioned officers and the tutelage of seasoned soldiers. This system created bonds between the old and the new soldiers. Training took place in garrisons, in winter quarters and in camp where there was practice in the use of weapons, in unit drill movements, skirmishes and mock battles. Sports – running, riding and wrestling – were also encouraged. Exhortations delivered by officers and martial ceremonies were aimed at developing morale. The army of Gustavus Adolphus and Cromwell's New Model Army took their example for the developing of morale from the *tercio*. The preferred time for recruitment was October and November when the troops were entering winter quarters. The higher the ratio of recruits to trained men, however, the more the quality of this type of training was affected, newly raised regiments being particularly unsuitable. It was in the army of Frederick William I of Prussia that the most rigorous training was introduced. Through drill, it aimed to produce automatic responses in the soldier. The example was copied elsewhere, particularly in Russia and Hesse-Kassel.

At various times, the military and civil authorities have turned their minds to organizing exercise in the martial arts from adolescence in order to prepare men for military service. In this way, military service could be institutionalized and more widely diffused amongst a society. Countries which were constantly under threat of attack, like colonies, often developed this form of training. During the reign of Louis XIV, in the French colonies in the Windward Isles, males were registered as militiamen from the age of twelve or fourteen. After the Franco-Prussian War, there was a scheme in France for establishing 'school battalions'. Teaching was given in schools on the use of weapons and young boys from the age of ten practised rudimentary drill with dummy wooden rifles (1882). This initiative was abandoned after about ten

years because of the disturbances it caused to family life; training had to be done on Sundays at the time of Mass and there arose a fear that children might become less obedient to their parents. Jules Ferry had intended to make this arrangement a school of republicanism and its political character was subsequently the inspiration of the *Balilla Fascista* in Italy and the *Hitler Jugend* in Germany. There were distinctly martial undertones to the Boy Scout movement, founded by Baden-Powell in 1908. In 1907, the Officers' Training Corps (OTC) was created in England with a senior division in universities and a junior branch, the Combined Cadet Force (CCF), in public schools. These institutions provided pre-training with the intention of easing the passage of young men into reserve commissions with the regular forces and commissions in the Territorial Army. Naval and air sections were added later. As the War Secretary, Haldane, said, 'the spirit of militarism already runs fairly high both in the public schools and at the universities. What we propose to do . . . is to turn to them and ask them to help us by putting their militarism to some good purpose.' Aside from political considerations, several types of military pre-training appeared after the First World War with the object of maintaining the military spirit. They were either, as in Germany, substitutes for a military service which had been forbidden by the peace treaty of 1919 or, as in France, means of assisting in the training of an army when the period of conscription had been reduced. For young men, the attraction lay in being able to choose the arm of the service to which they would be posted.

The training of soldiers in manoeuvre became the object of study very early in history, particularly in the cases of the Macedonian phalanx and the Roman legion. It appears that training in manoeuvre was brought to a level of excellence at Byzantium by the Emperor Leo VI 'the Wise', whose *Treatise on Tactics* (c.AD 900) remained an inspiration to military theorists in the early modern period. At the end of the sixteenth century, tactics were taught in the *tercio* with the aid of works based on the advances in geometry made during the Renaissance. The improvements in military training during the seventeenth and eighteenth centuries culminated in the 'Prussian style' of Frederick the Great, which became the universally adopted model until the French Revolutionary Wars. In the period immediately before the French Revolution, military thinkers classified planned movements by troops under the following heads – drill by individuals, drill by units, regimental manoeuvres and army manoeuvres. These distinctions have survived although under different labels.

Military thinkers also speculated about the way in which men could best be prepared for combat by training and mock battles. In principle, once the initial instruction (basic training) was complete, the remainder of the time in both first line and reserve service was devoted to this type of training. In the Roman army, mock battles, reproducing those of the Trojan War, were important. The Spanish experiments of the sixteenth century were extended by Louvois, who organized large-scale camps and troop concentrations in order to carry out manoeuvres (e.g. the camp at Bouquenom in 1683). This practice spread and was pursued with fresh vigour at the end of the eighteenth century (e.g. the camp at Vaussieux in 1778). The English adopted the system and between 1685 and 1688 there were peacetime summer camps on Hounslow Heath, near London, where numerous regiments were concentrated for mass exercises and mock battles. In the eighteenth century, the British army tended to exercise and camp *en masse* only during wartime. Frederick the Great began mass autumn manoeuvres for the Prussian army in 1743, bringing together no less than 44,000 men at Spandau in 1753. After the Franco-Prussian War, the manoeuvres of the major armies became international events. Even if the main object of such manoeuvres is the training of the higher command, they also have some value in training the rank and file.

Until the eighteenth century, non-commissioned officers received no special training. They were simply chosen from among those soldiers who seemed best able to fill the positions, literacy and numeracy frequently being two of the criteria. The *Gardes françaises* gave their non-commissioned officers some training within the regiment during the eighteenth century. When conscription was introduced, the men selected to be non-commissioned officers received a special course of instruction following their basic training.

3 For a long time, the training of officers was also carried out in the units themselves. However, a distinction must be drawn between officers who had risen from the ranks and young men whose birth gave them an automatic entry into the officer corps. The former moved up the various levels of non-commissioned rank and attained a commission only after many years of service. Above all, they were professionals, shaped by experience, but equipped with a very limited knowledge of military theory. The latter went into the field at a very tender age in the company of their father, or a close relative, who was usually a captain. In the seventeenth and eighteenth centuries, it was not unusual to find children of twelve years of age in army camps. These were the cadets. They served as soldiers but without any contract and without pay, waiting for an ensign's or a cornet's commission to fall vacant. The generally held view was that there was no better form of training for future commanders. The colonels took a great interest in these young men whose advancement would assist the cohesion of the regiment through ties of family, friendship and gratitude.

Kings employed their household units in the same manner. Louis XIV sought to make them nurseries of officers for his whole army. A period of service in the musketeers often led to a lieutenancy and this practice was extended to the Life Guards in 1664. During the War of the Spanish Succession, soldiers who had distinguished themselves were taken out of their units to serve for two years in the Life Guards, after which time they were returned to their regiments as lieutenants. The king's regiment (1663) played the same role, as did the *Gardes françaises* after 1716. Peter the Great of Russia followed this example with the St Petersburg Preobrazhenski and Semionovski regiments, the Swedish Life Guard was a training formation for aristocratic cadets and the English Life Guard was an officer seminary. However, as military science developed, it became clear that officers lacked training in theory. Initial efforts were made to provide this in specialized units and, subsequently, recourse was made to the establishment of military colleges.

Cadet Companies and Military Colleges
Military colleges evolved through several stages. During the Renaissance, military academies first appeared in Italy and then spread throughout Europe. The use of weapons, riding, drawing and a modest amount of mathematics were the usual subjects. Academies that were kept in Paris by Pluvinel under Henry IV and by Bernardi under Louis XIV proved attractive to the nobility. Having flourished during the first half of the seventeenth century, such establishments fell upon hard times and only three survived into the eighteenth century. However, the pages belonging to the *Grande Écurie du Roi* (the Royal Mews) constituted a kind of academy for young members of the higher nobility. The 'Royal Academy', founded by the Fouberts in London in 1679, finally closed in 1833.

At the end of the sixteenth century it was realized that future officers required some knowledge of theory. La Noue expressed this view in his *Treatise on Military Policy* (1587). The notion spread in Protestant circles, particularly in the House of Orange. In 1606, the Duc de Bouillon founded the Military Training Academy at Sedan, the first attempt at a military college. Among its graduates was Herman von Schomberg. In 1618, Maurice of Hesse founded the military college at Kassel and, in 1617, John VII of Nassau set up the *Kriegs und Ritterschule* (School of War and Knighthood) at Siegen. In the Catholic countries, Wallenstein created military colleges at Friedland and Gilschin, and Richelieu opened in the Temple district of Paris a college where the courses included surveying and a little history and geography. Mazarin gave a good deal of thought to having a military education provided at the College of the Four Nations, but it was obstructed by the University of Paris.

The Thirty Years' War put an end to many of these early endeavours but gave birth to other experiments. It was perhaps the Great Elector of Brandenburg-Prussia who had the idea of assembling the cadets who were serving with regiments into a single company stationed alongside the Knights' College at Kolberg (1653). Similar cadet companies were copied in various states but lacked the nourishment of adequate finance. In Prussia, cadet companies were also attached to old-established regiments. In 1682, Louvois copied the Great Elector's scheme and created nine cadet companies, of 400–500 men each, in fortresses, while Colbert set up companies of midshipmen. The cadet companies, whose overall strength was to reach 7,000, disappeared on Louvois's death in 1691; they were expensive and no one could decide whether to commit them to battle and risk losing the flower of the nation's youth or whether to keep so many courageous young men out of action. A fresh and more modest attempt was made in six garrison towns in 1726 but it was abandoned at the outbreak of the War of the Polish Succession in 1733. On the other hand, a cadet company for the colonies was continued at Rochefort from 1730 to 1761 and was then re-established on the Île de Ré in 1779.

Nevertheless, the need for a college became pressing in the technical branches of the service. In 1679, an artillery college was attached to the Royal Corps of Artillery. At the end of the seventeenth century, Vauban put forward a scheme for a college to train the king's engineers, with the cadets being admitted by examination, but it came to nothing. In Russia, where there was a dearth of technical training facilities for Peter the Great's new army, colleges were established for the artillery, the engineers and the army medical service around 1712. The Holy Roman Emperor created, in 1717, an *Ingenieurakademie*. In France, an experiment was made with a special college for the artillery at La Fère in

1719 (transferred to Bapaume in 1759), but preference was given to schools set alongside each unit, a process which was started in 1722 and extended in 1772. The college of Mézières, opened in 1749, provided training for engineers at one centre. This was pre-dated by the Royal Military Academy at Woolwich (1741), which trained both artillery and engineering officers. The idea of setting up colleges was extended to other branches of the service. Although some officers had a good classical education, others could not read or write correctly, a state of affairs which seemed increasingly regrettable to the Age of Enlightenment. The revival of the college scheme was assisted by the desire to allow impoverished noblemen to retain their opportunity to acquire commissions by equipping them to resist the pressures from young men of the middle class who were, generally, better educated.

In 1720, Frederick William I of Prussia grouped his cadet companies into a cadet corps college at Stolpe. Later colleges were formed at Potsdam, Kulm and, finally, Berlin. This experiment was imitated with the corps of noble cadets in Russia (1720) and in Saxony with the cadet centre in Dresden. In France, one of the Pâris brothers made a similar proposal, but without success, and the Comte de Lussan also tried to broaden the training given in academies by founding the *École de Mars* in 1738. Finally, in 1751, under pressure from Madame de Pompadour and Pâris-Duverney, Louis XV founded the Royal Military College (*École Royale Militaire*), which was intended to take in 500 noblemen. The success of this imposing establishment demonstrated the arrival of a new outlook on the part of military families; in the Age of Enlightenment they began to open their minds to education. The programme of studies included French grammar, Latin, German, Italian, mathematics appropriate for a soldier, drawing, logic as a preparation for geometry, the laws of war and the military ordonnances, dancing, swordsmanship, riding and some notions of tactical theory and troop manoeuvres. As the students entered with varied educational attainments, an introductory military college was opened at La Flèche in 1764. In 1769, the students were separated into graded classes and the teaching of Latin and Italian was abandoned.

In 1776, the Comte de Saint-Germain abolished the *École Militaire* and replaced it with a network of royal military colleges whose object was to provide the king with army officers and high-level civil administrators. These were set up in abbeys at Sorèze, Brienne, Thiron, Beaumont-en-Auge, Pontleroy, Rebais, Vendôme, Effiat, Tournon and Pont-à-Mousson. Students entered at the ages of eight or nine and courses lasted for six years. The educational plan was in conformity with the new outlook, combining physical, moral and intellectual training. The courses covered religion, French, Latin, German, history, geography, mathematics, drawing, ethics and logic. The best students, chosen by a national examination, became members of the corps of noble cadets which was housed in the buildings of the Military College, while the remainder served as noble cadets in regiments. This system, which gave Bonaparte the opportunity to enter the Royal Military College in Paris, was spoiled by the closure of the latter in 1788. Nevertheless, the Paris Military College had been used as a model by Austria (Academy of Wiener-Neustadt, 1752), whose students received their preparatory training at the Theresianum in La Favorita, by Russia with its military college for cadets, by Bavaria, Naples and, finally, by England, with its Royal Military College at High Wycombe in 1799.

Enlightened minds showed as much concern for the training of non-commissioned officers and soldiers. In the *Gardes françaises*, there was a depot for the training of recruits, who stayed there for forty days, and also for corporals and sergeants. Entry to the depot was granted, at the age of ten, to the sons of soldiers without means; there were as many as 120 pupils. The idea of bringing up children for the army was old (the *castrenses* of the later Roman Empire and the janissaries of the Ottoman Empire). It reappeared in the eighteenth century as a supposed panacea to solve the problems posed by the requirements of the army and by state charitable assistance. Whereas the ordinary soldier could be illiterate, during the seventeenth and eighteenth centuries non-commissioned officers were required to be both literate and numerate. In 1662, a schoolmaster was appointed to the British garrison of Madras and in 1675 two teachers were assigned to the garrison of Tangier. Their principal task was to educate the soldiers and non-commissioned officers but they also held classes for the children of the soldiers. Many British regiments instigated schools for both men and children during the eighteenth century, entrusting the work to a senior non-commissioned officer. The Grenadier Guards established a regimental school in 1762 and this had become general practice in Britain by 1800. In 1812, regimental schools were brought onto the official establishment. A corps of army schoolmistresses was formed in 1840 and of schoolmasters in 1846, infant schools were founded in 1850 and the Army Education Corps was created in 1920. Gradually, after the introduction of compulsory state education for all children (1870), army schools became exclusively concerned with teaching the children of soldiers rather than the men themselves. The motives behind army schools were ambiguous. There was an altruism to educate young people but there was also the hope that educated army children would themselves enter the ranks and improve the quality of personnel. Up to 1769, regimental education in Austria was in the hands of the chaplains but after the introduction of compulsory elementary education for all children in the Austrian hereditary lands after 1774, the army followed suit and established army schools. A corps of soldier-schoolmasters was established at the same time. Again, the motives were to provide a reservoir of potential non-commissioned officers and educate future recruits. Karl-Eugen of Württemberg established the *Karlsschule* in 1771 for 300 sons of titled officers and bourgeois soldiers. The Potsdam Military Orphanage provided a military education for its inmates. In 1801, the Royal Military Asylum at Chelsea was established to educate military orphans. A school for military orphans was founded in Paris in 1773, and at Liancourt in 1786 a school was opened for 100 children of soldier-pensioners.

By the end of the eighteenth century, the principle of military colleges had been well founded. As far as France is concerned, their history is marked by two important dates – 1802 and 1884. The *École Militaire* was re-established at Fontainebleau in 1802, and moved to Saint-Cyr in 1808 where it remained as the *École Militaire Spécialisée* until its transfer to Coëtquidan in 1947. A whole organization was set up to prepare students for the college. The military Prytaneum, opened first at Saint-Cyr and moved to La Flèche in 1808, was designed to collect young men from all over the Empire. It was closed down in 1814 but re-created under a succession of different names until it re-assumed the role of the old military college at La Flèche. At first reserved for the sons of officers, it was opened progressively to the sons of other ranks. Non-service channels for attaining military rank remained open. The *Lycées* (1882) revived the spirit of the old military colleges. The most important institution was the Central College of Public Works (1794), which became the *École Polytechnique* in 1795 and was militarized in 1804. It has, along with Saint-Cyr, the highest prestige of all French military colleges and was the model for West Point. The Royal Military College which had been founded at High Wycombe to provide staff officers for the British army was divided into two sections in 1801. The senior branch trained serving officers, moving to Farnham in 1813 and to Camberley as the Staff College in 1858. The junior branch went to Great Marlow in 1802 and to Sandhurst in 1812. The Royal Military Academy at Woolwich and the Royal Military College at Sandhurst amalgamated in 1947 to become the Royal Military Academy. The US Military Academy at West Point was founded in 1802, initially to train engineering and artillery officers. In 1910, the Army War College was founded to train staff officers.

The United States also introduced a system of postgraduate schools beyond West Point which trained officers in the techniques of particular branches of the army and equipped them for higher command. This method ensured a unified doctrine in all branches throughout the army, and commenced after 1868. In 1910 these were reorganized into the Army School of the Line (infantry and cavalry), the Signal School, the Army Field Engineer School, and the Army Field Service and Correspondence School for Medical Officers, all at Fort Leavenworth. There was also the Mounted School at Fort Riley, the Coast Artillery school at Fort Monroe, and the Engineer School and the Medical School in Washington DC. Since the Second World War, the United States has developed inter-service colleges to facilitate combined operations. For the British army, with its regimental tradition and organization, a system of service schools was an excellent method of guaranteeing that the independent regiments followed a standard doctrine in tactics, administration and attitude. A School of Musketry was founded at Hythe in 1853 and an Infantry Battle School at Barnard Castle in 1942. These were amalgamated into a School of Infantry, based at Warminster, in 1945. A School of Gunnery was created at Shoeburyness in 1859, moving to Larkhill in 1919 as the School of Artillery. An Army Signal School opened at Aldershot in 1905 and moved to Catterick in 1924–5 following the inauguration of the Royal Corps of Signals in 1920. An Armoured Fighting Vehicle School was established at Bovington. France also developed specialist schools during the nineteenth century: for the artillery and engineers at Metz (Fontainebleau after 1870), for the cavalry at Saumur, for the infantry at Saint-Maixent (Montpellier after 1967), and a college for the administrative branches in 1977. Despite attempts during the eighteenth and early nineteenth centuries, a French staff college was not permanent until the establishment of the Senior War College in 1890. An inter-service element was added in 1936 with the foundation of the Centre for Military Studies and the Institute of Senior Studies on National Defence.

The pattern of training has now assumed a standardized form common to most armies. Recruits receive 'basic' training for several weeks to learn physical endurance, group identity and weapon handling. They are then assigned to a branch of the service before joining their units for 'team' training as well as instruction in technical subjects – electronics, radar, signalling, etc. Officers first receive their basic training in colleges and academies and then join their units. Courses at specialist unit and command schools and colleges are associated with each level of promotion. The more able are sent to staff colleges in preparation for advancement to the highest ranks. *See also* FAMILIES; GREECE, ANCIENT; MANOEUVRE AND MANOEUVRES; MORALE; NAVAL PERSONNEL; RECRUITMENT; ROME; SPARTA.

A. CORVISIER
JOHN CHILDS

FURTHER READING
Ann Hyland, *Training the Roman Cavalry: from Arrian's Ars Tactica* (Stroud, 1993); Brian Bond, *The Victorian Army and the Staff College, 1854–1914* (London, 1972); John Smyth, *Sandhurst* (London, 1961); J. A. Houlding, *Fit for Service: the training of the British army, 1715–1795* (Oxford, 1981); N. T. St John Williams, *Tommy Atkins' Children* (London, 1971); F. B. Artz, *The Development of Technical Education in France, 1500–1850* (Cambridge, Mass., 1966).

Training, naval *See* NAVAL PERSONNEL

Trajan (Marcus Ulpius Traianus) (AD 53–117) Trajan, the Roman emperor (98–117), was a native of Italica in Spain, and had demonstrated an interest in military affairs by serving as military tribune for ten consecutive years, a post which senators normally held for one year. Subsequently he commanded a legion in Spain and was consul in 91 before becoming governor of Upper Germany in 97, when he was adopted by Nerva as his successor. Trajan attempted to revive the tradition of conquest, intermitted since the annexation of Britain by Claudius.

The Dacians, who occupied almost all the territory of present-day Romania, under their king Decebalus, had fought a series of campaigns (AD 85–9) against Domitian and, although defeated, had gained a favourable peace treaty. It could be claimed that they represented a threat to the Roman provinces of Pannonia and Moesia along the River Danube. Trajan resumed the offensive and conducted two wars against them in 101–2 and 105–6, which ended with the capture of the capital Sarmizegethusa and the suicide of Decebalus himself. Dacia became a Roman province. An important source of information for the wars is the Column of Trajan, a monument 100 feet high set up in the forum built by the emperor in Rome; the column's surface is in the form of a ribbon about 3 feet wide on which are carved reliefs depicting the military operations. Although it is difficult to say precisely what most of the scenes represent in the war, they give a vivid picture of the equipment and methods of the Roman army on campaign in the second century AD.

In 114 Trajan attacked the Parthians, who were the rulers of Iran and Mesopotamia, and who controlled the only sophisticated empire on the borders of Roman territory. However, during the previous 150 years relations between the two empires had been regulated by a diplomatic rapport which entailed the avoidance of large-scale conflict. Trajan, probably to enhance his personal glory, upset this balance by annexing Armenia, which lay between the two empires on the upper Euphrates, and then by invading Mesopotamia, where he won some victories as the Parthians retreated before him. The emperor captured the Parthian capital Ctesiphon and reached the Persian Gulf, but his success was illusory. Serious uprisings occurred in the captured territory to the army's rear and a major insurrection of the Jews in the eastern provinces spread to Mesopotamia in 116. Trajan may have intended to resume the offensive, but he died suddenly at Selinus in Cilicia in early August 117. Hadrian did not attempt to retain his predecessor's conquests in the east. *See also* IRAN; ROME.

B. CAMPBELL

FURTHER READING
F. A. Lepper, *Trajan's Parthian War* (Oxford, 1948); L. Rossi, *Trajan's Column and the Dacian Wars* (London, 1971); F. Lepper and S. Frere, *Trajan's Column* (Gloucester, 1988).

Transport Until the eighteenth century, the weight of horse fodder needed by an army outstripped that of supplies to the men. A soldier's total requirements were 3½ lb per day, including his drink, and that of a horse 20 lb, without counting its intake of water. The introduction of firearms and the internal combustion engine (with its need for fuel) caused a huge increase in weight. In the middle of the eighteenth century, the average daily scale of maintenance for a man and for a horse which needed to be provided by army transport was 9 lb, in 1870 it rose (per day in action) to 17½ lb (30 per cent in hardware and 70 per cent in provisions), in 1918 it was 28½ lb (39 per cent foodstuffs and forage, 19 per cent ammunition, 42 per cent hardware and fuel), in 1943 66 lb (5 per cent provisions, 48 per cent ammunition, 25 per cent fuel and the remainder hardware and other equipment) and in 1960 154 lb. A Roman legion required *c*.50 tons a month; in 1870, a division needed *c*.50 tons per day, and in 1944 1,200 tons.

In the armies of Antiquity, transport was only employed to convey the equipment for camps, arrows and spare weapons, and also the sick and wounded. Generally, pack animals were used and, more rarely, carts. The Greek hoplite and cavalryman carried just their weapons; foodstuffs and the remainder of their gear were carried by servants (*skeuophoroi*) and pack animals. In the Spartan army, *hypaspistai* carried the equipment of those whom they served, and also had the task of removing the wounded from the battlefield. But the Greeks had the ability to produce excellently designed means of transportation. For the attack on the Persians in the Hellespont, Alcibiades arranged for the construction of landing craft carrying forty men each, which could be run aground and which were fitted with a dropping bow door. The cavalry too had specially designed boats.

When the numbers of men raised for armies increased and when conflicts took place in poor countries, or far from centres which could supply provisions, use was made of convoys for carrying foodstuffs. Alexander the Great took with him more than a month's supply of food in 2,500 waggons. His army numbered 35,000 infantry and 5,000 cavalry; each cavalryman had one pack animal and infantrymen one between six. Since a convoy of this magnitude was very cumbersome, Alexander kept close to the coastline as he continued his advance so that he could be supplied by his fleet, and later was kept supplied by numbers of small boats on the Euphrates and the Indus.

The Roman legionary carried, apart from his weapons and armour, equipment which consisted of some camp gear, together with a mess tin and his food, contained in a leather sack that he originally carried at the end of a staff (*aerumnula*). Marius later replaced this by a spear. He sometimes took with him fifteen days' supply of food, his daily rations consisting of 1¾ lb of flour, 6 oz of salt pork and ¾ oz of cheese. Complete with his equipment and weapons, he could be carrying a total weight of around 90 lb. On the march, the average daily stage was about 18 miles but the Romans also made use of convoys composed of draught animals and two- or four-wheeled carts which carried thirty days' supplies of food, 60–100 of such carts being required for a legion. Under the Empire, transport services were established which, when supplemented by local requisition, allowed the weight carried by the infantryman to be reduced to about 55 lb.

The Gauls and the barbarian races who invaded the Roman Empire were accompanied by waggons which carried their equipment, their foodstuffs and their plunder. The Carolingian army used waggons, called *basternes*, lined with well-sewn skins which enabled them to go through water courses without damage to their contents. The men who were not used as combatants, because their revenues were not of the required level, and the peasants from land belonging to the Church, were made responsible for driving and escorting the convoys. During the subsequent centuries, landed property belonging to the Church had to continue to provide carts,

and under Charles the Fair the communes were obliged to contribute. In feudal armies, transport systems were rudimentary; battlefields were often only a short distance from where the opposing forces had set out, and the troops normally lived off the country. On the other hand, the Crusades gave rise to the development of large-scale arrangements for supply and transport which were mostly entrusted to the Italian maritime republics; the sole exception was the expedition by pilgrims under the leadership of Peter the Hermit, and their demise was due to the neglect of just such a provision. In 1249, St Louis bought from the Genoese flat-bottomed sailing ships, whose prows opened to allow both personnel and equipment to be put ashore onto a beach. Thanks to the use of the horse-collar, a horse at this period could pull a load of a ton, compared with 4 cwt in Antiquity and half a ton in the Byzantine era.

With the appearance of regular armies, efforts were made to provide troops with means of transport that were both specialized and standardized. Every fighting man could bring with him only the prescribed number of servants and pack animals. Convoys were systematically marshalled and were assigned a place within the general disposition of a force. The ordonnances of Charles the Bold laid down that, when an army was arranged in column, the soldiers marched at the head, followed by the light artillery, the tents and the baggage, and after these came the waggons of foodstuffs and military supplies. If the soldiers moved in two columns, the waggons were put in between; if in three, the convoy was divided into two sections travelling in the intervals. On the battlefield, the enemy's baggage, although guarded, was frequently the favourite target of the soldiers, some of whom, on occasion, turned aside from their principal task in order to plunder without concerning themselves unduly about the success or failure of the rest of the army (Marston Moor, 1644).

Henry IV of France's army contained 20 convoy captains, 4,000 horses, 1,000 waggoners and 600 waggons. In the seventeenth century, the system of statute

819

service was replaced by that of requisition, but this still did not make possible any standardization of waggons and also bore heavily on the peasantry. Transport arrangements were improved by the conclusions of deals with contractors, the use of arsenals in which military supplies were stored and the establishment within the country of routes along which staging posts were located at intervals. When Louvois was minister of war, a system of mobile stores was introduced, but these were heavy and, in addition, better suited to siege warfare than to wars of movement. The means of transport assembled by contractors were dispersed as soon as there was peace, and the task of getting them together again at the outbreak of hostilities inevitably meant delays which were detrimental to the smooth progress of operations. This system revealed its weaknesses during the Seven Years' War, and Choiseul then replaced it by a company in which the state had an interest but contractors were again employed a few years later, after this unsuccessful attempt at direct management of the transport forces. When on campaign each company had two pack horses for transporting its camp equipment, and each regiment a cart to carry supplies of spares and replacements, a vehicle for the baker and the butcher, and another for the sutler; others who also provided canteen services were allowed to bring pack horses. The colonel and surgeon also were allowed a cart. Officers and senior NCOs had pack horses in numbers proportional to their rank, from one for the *adjudant* to sixteen for the colonel. In all, a regiment took with it 300 pack or draught horses. The retinues of generals were often excessively large, and both their extravagance and the degree of hindrance which they caused led to numerous criticisms. Accordingly, ministers of war sought to reduce their size by bringing them within the scope of regulations. The British army fighting the rebels in the American War of Independence hired all its transport complete with civilian drivers and horses. Each foot regiment was assigned five waggons to convey its equipment, food and baggage. The army required about 900 waggons a year. Through-

out the early modern period, especially in Flanders, Germany and northern Italy, water transport by barge and bilander, a small Dutch or Flemish sailing vessel mainly used on inland waterways, was utilized wherever possible.

At the outset of the French Revolution, the contract system had to be supplemented by requisitioning because of the size of the army's requirements. The combined arrangements were placed under the authority of *commissaires des guerres*. On 6 March 1795, the waggon trains were divided into five categories – foodstuffs, camp equipment, hospitals, artillery, depots. On 11 April 1796, the personnel driving the waggons were brought within the military hierarchical system and made subject to military laws and regulations. Napoleon was dissatisfied with the contract system, and progressively militarized army transport, with the establishment of a train for the artillery in 1803, for the engineers in 1806 and for supplies in 1807. But wheeled transport was not employed exclusively, rivers being mainly used wherever feasible. The troops might move either on foot or in vehicles. Each waggon could carry 10–12 men a distance of 24–30 miles a day. The vehicles used were drawn by four horses and could carry over one ton of military stores or foodstuffs.

The military potential of railways was realized as early as the 1830s. In 1846, the Russians moved a corps of 14,500 men from Hradisch to Cracow, a distance of 200 miles, in two days. Four years later, the Austrians conveyed 75,000 from Hungary and Vienna to Bohemia. In France, in 1851, a committee drew up regulations covering the military use of railways. In 1861, the Prussian government issued a code of practice to be used for the transport of large numbers of soldiers. In 1867, the Prussians modified this in the light of the lessons of the war of 1866. The use of these regulations allowed them to concentrate their troops rapidly in 1870 – 1,300 trains transported 550,000 men, 150,000 horses and 1,500 pieces of artillery. This excellent use of railways contributed greatly to their victory. Railways were widely employed in the American Civil War, and a railway corps was formed in the United States. However, both the Union and Confederate armies became over-reliant on railways for their supplies and dared not campaign more than a few miles from the vulnerable railroads.

In France, Marshal Niel set up a central committee for railways, but his efforts did not have time to come to fruition. The government drew lessons from the war of 1870–1 and established both a special railways section at general staff level and a higher military committee for railways. In 1889, a military railway service was created, and this brought into being the system which was in force in 1914, and which continued into recent times with only slight modifications. A distinction needs to be made between 'mobilization' transport, whose purpose was to bring together at mobilization centres, by short routes from many different directions, resources of every kind, human and material, and 'concentration' transport, which in August 1914 carried ready equipped formations, often from a long distance, to the operational areas of the five French armies by the use of ten railway lines. While the operation of concentrating forces was taking place, supplies of food to the troops were ensured by trains going to stores sited at nine regulating stations. After operations had begun, transport routes became the lines of communication. The railway made it possible for supply centres to be positioned a long way behind the front, and allowed considerable flexibility over bringing forward replenishments. It had another advantage also; the armies were no longer, as in the past, encumbered with heavy convoys which they were obliged to protect. The railway system was also judiciously supplemented by the use of motor vehicles and waterways. From 1915 to 1918, the tonnage transported by these latter rose from 670,000 to 1,200,000 tons. In August 1914, troops were put into their allotted positions with remarkable precision, in accordance with the plan that had been settled in advance and within the specified time. In sixteen days, 1,200,000 men, nearly 400,000 horses and 800,000 vehicles had been transported; 4,035 troop trains and 243 supply trains passed through the regulating stations. During the whole war, 100,000 trains moved 60 million men and 1 million horses. From 100 to 200 trains were used daily. A division consumed daily 1,000 tons of supplies, i.e. the equivalent of two train loads.

When the Allies landed in Normandy in June 1944, the French rail network had been in large part destroyed by Allied air bombardment and by the work of the resistance movement; a third of the air raids carried out between May and July 1944 had the railways as their objective. 3,200 constructional works (bridges, viaducts, tunnels) had been demolished and over 2,000 miles of railway line destroyed, as well as 15 major marshalling yards and half the rolling stock. The network was progressively put back into working order as fast as the front moved forward. The Americans had a Military Railway Service with them, made up of personnel drawn from their home railways. The basic formation consisted of a headquarter company, a maintenance company, a company in charge of depots and an operating company; 30,000 men belonging to this service landed in France. From 1942 onwards, railway material was sent to Britain in Liberty ships, which had been specially fitted out for this purpose. More than 2,000 locomotives and 30,000 railway waggons were landed on the Continent.

During the three months immediately subsequent to the landing, supplies had to be maintained by trucks. The mud and the poor quality of the roads quickly reduced their capabilities but, fortunately, on 11 July, the railway began to function. It subsequently played a vital role because trucks were unable to keep up with the speed of the army's advance despite the initiation of the 'Red Ball' system. On 21 August 1944 the inter-Allied railway committee was created charged with keeping the high command informed about the capabilities of the French railway network. From October 1944 to May 1945, the railways transported 48 per cent of all supplies compared with 45 per cent carried by road, and 7 per cent by water.

Until logistics were freed by the railway and the internal combustion engine, armies

821

tended to rely on waterways for bulk transport despite the implicit limitations which this imposed upon strategy. Regions of Europe which possessed abundant natural and artificial waterways – the Low Countries, Germany and northern Italy – were able to support larger armies than those regions not so abundantly supplied. Consequently, major international wars tended to be fought in these theatres. Particularly in the Netherlands, military operations revolved around the domination of 'river lines'. Numerous rulers have built canals or improved the navigation of rivers for military purposes. Six thousand conscripted labourers commenced the excavation of a military canal in 793 to link the Altmühl River with the main European river system to enable Charlemagne's battle fleet to operate on inland waterways. The project was never completed although the *Fossa Carolina* remains visible. Frederick the Great of Prussia built a series of east–west canals both to improve internal trade and communications between his scattered lands but also to provide lines of military communication for the supply of his army in probable theatres of war: the Plauer and Finow Canals (1746) and the Bromberg Canal (1776) linked the Elbe with the Oder while the Warthe and the Netze Canals joined the Oder and the Vistula. Frederick also built the Mietzel–Floss Canal in 1740, the new Oder Canal in 1753, the Templin–Werbellin–Ruppin Canal (1766) and the Johannisburg Canal (1766). In 1780, the Ruhr was made navigable by the construction of locks. In wartime, a special corps of military barges supplemented requisitioned civilian vessels. The Royal Military Canal was cut in southern England in 1798 to link Shorncliffe with Winchelsea both to provide transport and to form a tactical barrier to an invading French army. All military waterways perform this dual function. Naturally, overseas expeditions and combined operations are almost wholly dependent on shipping for the majority of their transport although air transport has assumed a higher profile. Between 1940 and 1945, American ships alone carried 268 million tons across the Atlantic while the Berlin air bridge in 1949 carried 5,000 tons a day.

As important as the railway was the military adoption of the internal combustion engine. The First World War witnessed the large-scale use of trucks and lorries to convey both troops and stores, the French resistance at Verdun in 1916 being largely dependent on the supply line of the *voie sacrée* down which poured a daily average of one truck every 14 seconds. However, although the transport services between the front line and the rail-heads of the British and US armies were fully motorized by 1944, the German and, to a lesser extent, the Russian forces continued to make extensive use of horse-drawn waggons. Since 1945, all armies have adopted motorized transport in conjuction with railways and, increasingly, fixed-wing aircraft and helicopters. *See also* CONVOYS; FALKLANDS WAR; LOGISTICS; RATIONS; STAGING POSTS; TRANSPORT, AIR; VERDUN.

G. BODINIER
JOHN CHILDS

FURTHER READING
Martin van Creveld, *Supplying War* (Cambridge, 1977); J. W. Fortescue, *The Early History of Transport and Supply* (London, 1928); D. Bishop and W. J. K. Davies, *Railways and War before 1918* (London, 1972); Dennis Showalter, *Railroads and Rifles* (Hamden, Conn., 1975); I. V. Hogg and J. S. Weeks, *The Illustrated Encyclopaedia of Military Vehicles* (London, 1980).

Transport, air The idea of using aircraft for the purpose of military transport emerged and was accepted later than most other roles because, in the early days of aviation, the technology was simply not available to allow aeroplanes to carry reasonable payloads over worthwhile ranges.

Although the American General William Mitchell conceived a plan in October 1918 to carry and then parachute part of an infantry division behind the German lines in the Metz region, and the British used aircraft in Iraq in 1923 to carry troops to restore order following a Kurdish revolt, it was not until the late 1930s that it became practicable to use transport aircraft in a military role in a systematic fashion. The Nationalist forces in the Spanish Civil War, for example, moved 14,000 men and 500 tons of material from Morocco to the Iberian peninsula between July and October 1936, and the Italians supplied their forward columns in Ethiopia by air. Given their interest in developing airborne forces the Soviets produced a large fleet of transport planes.

The *Luftwaffe* had created one transport squadron before the outbreak of the Second World War. Its role was initially limited to carrying troops into battle, something which was done very effectively during the early German campaigns in Norway and Western Europe, but before the end of the blitzkrieg phase of the Second World War aircraft were also being used to carry supplies. After the Crete campaign of May 1941, when their parachute forces suffered severe casualties, the Germans never again attempted airborne operations, but air transport grew in importance as air bridges were 'built' to supply beleaguered and isolated garrisons like those at Demyansk and Stalingrad, or in Tunisia after the Allied landings of November 1942.

In Britain, the development of air transport had its origin in the need to ferry mainly bomber aircraft by air from the United States and Canada to the United Kingdom after the defeat of France. The 'Atlantic Ferrying Organization' gave rise to the Royal Air Force's Ferry Command in July 1941 but almost from its inception light-weight but essential war material (often medical supplies) was carried as well. For their part, the Americans created a 'Ferrying Command' which soon became a fully-fledged transport organization and was, in June 1942, succeeded by Air Transport Command. The RAF formed its Transport Command in May 1943. The fortunes of war and the global nature of the Second World War meant that air transport featured prominently in every Allied campaign. Supplies were flown to China over the Himalayan 'hump', and air transport kept Allied armies in Burma in the field. Airborne forces were landed in Normandy ahead of the amphibious assault

on D-Day (6 June 1944), were an integral part of the unsuccessful attempt by Field Marshal Montgomery to turn the German flank by taking Arnhem in September 1944, and took part in the assault crossing of the Rhine in March 1945. With very large aircraft with huge load-carrying capacities now a reality, air transport had become a normal and routine part of war, and the carrying of men and material into battle by air was seen as a way of increasing mobility, achieving surprise and maintaining far flung garrisons which might be cut off by land. The French strategy in Indo-China was based in part on the potential of air supply, the establishing of an outpost garrison at Dien Bien Phu being but one example.

Still, the most dramatic example of air transport at this time was unquestionably the Berlin Airlift, which was mounted by the Western Allies after the Soviets cut off all land access to West Berlin between June 1948 and May 1949, and which kept the Western presence alive in the former German capital. Since then there have been many other major airlifts which have affected regional balances of power. The Americans and Soviets alike replaced the equipment lost by their respective Middle East allies in the Yom Kippur War of 1973, the former providing Israel with electronic equipment and aircraft for on-site assembly, the latter giving Egypt and Syria missiles, anti-tank weapons and spare parts as well as replacement fighters. In 1975, the Soviets transported a Cuban expeditionary force by air to Angola, and their rapid intervention in Afghanistan was made possible only by the creation of an air bridge between the USSR and Kabul. By the same token, air transport was crucial to the American build-up in Vietnam.

Used initially for reconnaissance and rescue work, large and powerful helicopters added a new dimension to warfare in the 1960s – creating, in effect, the three-dimensional land battle. Capable of carrying troops and supplies over enemy-held areas, and able to land them almost anywhere, they were the foundation of the 'vertical envelopment' tactics devised and used by the Americans in Vietnam and which have been repeated in every major conflict since. *See also* AIRBORNE TROOPS; AVIATION; LOGISTICS; TRANSPORT.

P. FACON and A. TEYSSIER
STEPHEN J. HARRIS

FURTHER READING
C. Christienne, P. Lissarague, A. Degardin, P. Facon, P. Biffotot and M. Hodier, *Histoire de l'aviation militaire française* (Paris, 1980); James L. Stokesbury, *A Short History of Airpower* (New York, 1986).

Trenchard, Hugh (1873–1956) Trenchard entered the British army through the militia, which offered the easiest route to a commission, and on his second try was appointed a subaltern in the Royal Scots Fusiliers. He saw service in India, in South Africa during the Boer War, and in Nigeria before returning to England and, in 1912, transferring to the Royal Flying Corps. At the outbreak of the First World War he was appointed to command the RFC's Military Wing at Farnborough, where he was responsible for producing squadrons for service at the front and defending Britain against attack by German airships. He was offered command of the RFC's First Wing in France in the autumn of 1914 and was then appointed General Officer Commanding the Royal Flying Corps in August 1915. This gave Trenchard the opportunity to put into effect the ideas he had developed about tactical bombing and army support and, perhaps even more important, the need to fight in strength for air supremacy – an offensive strategy which cost lives and was criticized by airmen and politicians alike but from which Trenchard never shrank. Named Chief of the Air Staff (CAS) in 1917, Trenchard was not yet an advocate of either strategic bombing or of an independent Royal Air Force, believing it was the airman's first duty to support the army in the field, and he did not support the creation of a separate RAF on 1 April 1918. His resignation as CAS was accepted soon afterward, but later in the year he was – ironically – appointed to command the Independent Air Force in France and was thereby responsible for overseeing plans to employ this embryonic Bomber Command on strategic bombing operations against German industrial targets. When the war was over, however, he commented that the operations of his command were a 'gigantic waste of effort and personnel'. Yet once he was named CAS again in 1919, Trenchard fought long and hard against the British army and Royal Navy to protect the RAF's independence, and in doing so he not only fully embraced the theory that strategic bombing might well be decisive in the next war because, unlike armies and navies, air forces could attack the enemy nation and its war economy directly, but also argued that developing a powerful bombing force was the most cost-effective way to guarantee Britain's security and its continuing influence in the world. Trenchard won his fight to preserve the Royal Air Force as an independent service, and when he retired in 1929 he was already known as the Father of the RAF. So influential had he been, in fact, that his advice was sought on how to manage the war against Hitler. Consistent with the advice he had been giving since 1919, his recommendation was to intensify the strategic bombing of Germany. *See also* AIRCRAFT; AVIATION; DOUHET; GREAT BRITAIN; MITCHELL.

STEPHEN J. HARRIS
P. FACON

FURTHER READING
Andrew Boyle, *Trenchard: man of vision* (London, 1962); Denis Richards and Hilary A. Saunders, *Royal Air Force* (3 vols, London, 1953–4); John Terraine, *The Right of the Line: the Royal Air Force in the European war, 1939–1945* (London, 1985); H. R. Allen, *The Legacy of Lord Trenchard* (London, 1972).

Trotsky, Leon (1879–1940) Trotsky was born Lev Davidovich Bronstein of Jewish parents in the southern Ukraine. Trotsky attended school in Odessa and in Nikolaev, where he became involved in revolutionary activities. Imprisoned in 1898 for these efforts, Trotsky became a Marxist while incarcerated. Exiled to Siberia in 1900, he escaped and subsequently fled abroad to London. There he joined Lenin and other Russian revolutionaries in producing *Iskra*, the Russian Marxist newspaper. When the

Russian Social Democratic Party split into Bolshevik and Menshevik wings, Trotsky chose the latter, a move that separated him from Lenin until 1917. Trotsky returned to Russia during the revolution of 1905, where he was arrested and exiled to Siberia for life as a result of his activities. Trotsky again escaped, and spent the next seven years mostly in Vienna. He covered the Balkan Wars in 1912–13 as a war correspondent, an occupation that he took up again during the First World War. In 1916, the French authorities expelled him for his anti-war activities, and Trotsky fled to America. In 1917, he returned to Russia, where he played a major role in the Bolshevik revolution, temporarily patching up his relations with Lenin. Trotsky was responsible for the negotiations with the Germans that led to the Treaty of Brest-Litovsk. At this point, Trotsky was made Commissar for War, and was the man who founded the Red Army. Trotsky's leadership was instrumental in the Bolshevik victories during the Civil War, but he failed to establish his own position within the Bolshevik hierarchy. This failure, and his personal arrogance towards many of his colleagues, led to the collapse of his authority after Lenin's death in 1924 and, finally, his dismissal as Commissar for War in 1925. In the struggle to succeed Lenin, Trotsky proved to be no match for Stalin. In 1927, Trotsky was expelled from the Central Committee, the following year he was exiled to Alma Ata and in 1929 expelled from the Soviet Union. Trotsky spent his exile in Constantinople (1929–33), in Paris (1933–5), in Oslo (1935–6), and, finally, in Mexico City (1937–40), writing various historical and political works and involving himself in Russian émigré politics. In May of 1940, Trotsky was assassinated by a Soviet agent. *See also* LENIN; RUSSIA/USSR; SOVIET MILITARY THEORISTS; STALIN.

KEITH NEILSON

FURTHER READING
Isaac Deutscher, *Trotsky* (3 vols, New York, 1954–63); Baruch Knei-Paz, *The Social and Political Thought of Leon Trotsky* (Oxford, 1979); John Erickson, *The Soviet High Command* (London, 1962).

Truces *See* ARMISTICES

Tsushima, Battle of (27–28 May 1905) In the late nineteenth century, Russian ambitions in the Far East clashed with those of Japan. War broke out in 1904, and went badly for Russia. The Russian Baltic Fleet, under Rozhdestvensky, was dispatched to restore the position. After a long and arduous voyage, the fleet met the waiting Japanese Fleet, under Togo, at the mouth of the Straits of Tsushima. A running battle followed, as the Russian line continued, though with some evasive turns, to make for Vladivostok. Japanese gunfire concentrated on the head of the line was effective; night torpedo-boat attacks accounted for other ships. Out of 8 Russian battleships, 6 were sunk and the other 2 captured. Of 37 other vessels, 22 were lost, 6 surrendered and 6 were interned in neutral ports. Only 1 cruiser and 2 destroyers managed to reach Vladivostok.

The impact of the battle was enormous and Tsushima may properly be compared with the Battle of Trafalgar fought a century earlier. On the tactical level, the battle rehabilitated the use of the 'line ahead' formation and concentration of fire. It also demonstrated the superiority of heavy artillery and persuaded Lord Fisher in Britain to build the *Dreadnought* type of all-heavy-gun ship. It further proved the value of torpedo-boats, especially against disunited and damaged vessels.

The strategic consequences were no less important. It put an end to the Tsarist government's hopes of a Far Eastern empire and brought Japan into the ranks of the great powers. *See also* FISHER; JAPAN; NAVAL WARFARE; NAVIES; RUSSIA/USSR; TOGO.

P. MASSON
A. W. H. PEARSALL

FURTHER READING
Robert Butow, *Togo and the Coming of the War* (Princeton, 1961); Richard Hough, *The Fleet that Had to Die* (London, 1958).

Tukhachevsky *See* SOVIET MILITARY THEORISTS

Tunis, Siege of (June–July 1535) The Siege of Tunis was the first offensive operation conducted by Charles V against the Ottomans in the Mediterranean. Although it was in part a response to growing demands from Spain and Italy for the Emperor to take action against the Ottoman expansion into the central and western Mediterranean in the 1520s and early 1530s, the immediate cause was the seizure of the city by Khaireddin Barbarossa in August 1534. The expelled sultan fled to Charles and offered an alliance if he would restore him. Charles was then at peace in Europe and saw this as an opportunity to make a major demonstration of strength. A large fleet drawn from Spain and Portugal was assembled at Barcelona in the spring of 1535; in May it sailed to Sardinia where it rendezvoused with an Italian contingent. The combined fleet (100 galleys and 300 transports), under the command of Andrea Doria, then made a quick passage to North Africa and on 15 June began landing an army of 25,000 men near the fortress of La Goletta which commanded the harbour of Tunis. After three weeks of bombardment La Goletta was stormed on 14 July. The army then moved overland against Tunis itself, a riskier proposition as Barbarossa had determined to fight for the control of the principal wells en route. However, the Christian cavalry proved superior and the defeat of Barbarossa's army (20 July) inspired a revolt in the city. Barbarossa's flight to Algiers (21 July) and the destruction of his fleet in the harbour concluded the victory. Although assisted considerably by a local ally and the failure of Constantinople to intervene, the siege was nevertheless an impressive demonstration of Imperial strength against a common enemy that did much to reconcile Italian opinion to Habsburg domination of the peninsula. The revival of hostilities with France in 1536 prevented Charles from following up his success but the memory encouraged him to attempt a similar operation against Algiers in 1541. This was mounted late in the year (possibly to inhibit Ottoman intervention, and certainly against Doria's advice), and although the army landed safely on 23 October, a storm

the following night destroyed much of the fleet and forced Charles to evacuate his men one week later. The scale of these expeditions was immense, far larger than the *Gran Armada* of 1588. The difficulty and expense of mounting these combined operations, given the other pressures on Charles's resources, explain why, despite his own commitment and the popularity of such campaigns in Spain and Italy, the Imperial counter-offensive in the Mediterranean was so limited. *See also* ANDREA DORIA; ARMADA; COMBINED OPERATIONS; NAVAL WARFARE; OTTOMAN TURKS; SIEGES; SPAIN.

SIMON ADAMS

FURTHER READING
C. Oman, *A History of the Art of War in the Sixteenth Century* (London, 1937), pp. 685–702; K. Brandi, *The Emperor Charles V* (London, 1939), pp. 365–8, 453–7; J. F. Guilmartin, *Gunpowder and Galleys: changing technology and Mediterranean warfare at sea in the sixteenth century* (Cambridge, 1974), p. 78; W. S. Maltby, *Alba: a biography of Fernando Alvarez de Toledo, 3rd Duke of Alba* (Berkeley and London, 1983), pp. 29–32.

Turenne, Henri de la Tour d'Auvergne, Vicomte de (1611–75) Turenne was the second son of the Duke de Bouillon and related to the house of Orange-Nassau. He first served as a volunteer in the Netherlands under Maurice of Nassau in 1625 and assumed command of a French regiment of foot in 1630. There followed a second period in Dutch service from 1632 to 1635 after which he returned permanently to the French army. Two successful campaigns in Italy in 1639 and 1640 assured his reputation and he commanded the French armies in Germany from 1643 to 1648, defeating the Bavarians at Zusmarshausen in 1648. In 1658, he beat the insurgent Prince of Condé at the Battle of the Dunes. Although a Protestant, he was created Marshal of France in 1643 and Marshal General in 1660.

He was trained in the Nassau style, a scientific and realistic approach to warfare. His *Mémoires* merely recount in a matter-of-fact way the various actions in which he was involved and, being a reserved if not a secretive man, he left no didactic work to posterity. He was a circumspect and calculating tactician who believed military intelligence to be of the utmost importance. Unhindered by preconceptions, he quickly assessed a situation and then acted with despatch. In order to reduce desertion and provide a greater freedom of action he emphasized adequate logistics and supply. In his view, it was wise to occupy hostile territory to hamper the enemy's recruitment and logistics. He also preferred to hold the countryside where he could keep his forces concentrated rather than disperse them to defend fortified towns. After 1665, he had a better army at his disposal and developed more offensive methods. In 1672, he was appointed to command the French armies in the secondary theatre in Germany and his superb campaigns were a model of the art of warfare by manoeuvre, especially his march around the Vosges in the winter of 1674–5. He was killed by a cannon ball at the opening of the Battle of Sasbach on 27 July 1675. *See also* CONDÉ; FRANCE; MONTE-CUCOLI; NASSAU.

A. CORVISIER
JOHN CHILDS

FURTHER READING
Jean Bérenger, *Turenne* (Paris, 1987); M. Weygand, *Turenne* (London, 1930).

Turkey   *See* OTTOMAN TURKS

Turnhout, Battle of   *See* NIEUPORT

U

Uniform The adoption and development of a standard form of dress for troops represent responses to a complex of economic, technical and psychological pressures which have been intertwined throughout history. Since Classical times, the manufacture of protective armour in accordance with contemporary norms brought with it that uniformity of silhouette which we know today, for example, from Roman bas-reliefs. Until the end of the Middle Ages, tactics based on the frontal assault meant that any confusion between friend and foe was hardly likely to occur. A few banners were enough to identify the leaders on the battlefield and make it easy to follow them. The subsequent emergence of hand guns, the development of tactics involving manoeuvre and skirmishing and the growing use of mercenaries in the service of the highest bidder rendered identifying marks essential, whether these took the form of over-jackets, sashes or, more simply, armlets or even twigs cut from trees.

The abundance and magnificence of such distinguishing marks very soon became a matter of prestige for the sovereign or princes to whom the troops belonged. From the middle of the fifteenth century, the *compagnies d'ordonnance* of the King of France were each dressed in the same colour, chosen by their captain. At the beginning of the seventeenth century, the royal household troops were lavishly attired in order to impress the monarch's subjects and foreign visitors. This tradition has been carried on by the Imperial and Royal Guards and, down to our own day, by the Republican Guards. It was also regarded as desirable that troops who had the task of maintaining public order should have prestige, which doubtless explains the impressive uniforms and tall plumes of the troops of the Holy Alliance in the mid-nineteenth century or the gold braid indicative of an elite formation inherited from the *maréchaussée* of the *ancien régime* by the current French *gendarmes*.

The motivation which, around 1670, caused the sovereigns of Europe to provide the whole of their armies with a uniform seems to have been of a quite different order. It became apparent to them at that point that savings were to be made by providing the soldier with clothing rather than including a cash payment for this purpose in the amounts given to the captains and colonels to cover his pay. In France, this concern for economy shows through in the choice of an unbleached white cloth (i.e. *écru* or grey cloth) for making the infantry's jerkins. In England, the New Model Army of 1645 was the first to adopt a uniform. After 1660, there was considerable rivalry among colonels concerning the elegance of the dress of their regiments, a contest conducted at the soldiers' expense as they paid for their own clothing through deductions from pay. A series of regulations between 1721 and 1751 gradually brought uniformity and common sense to the design of British uniforms.

It was not until the eighteenth century that uniforms assumed a symbolic value. The tunic of the *Volontaires* during the French Revolution bears the three colours of the nation and, if the caricatures of the period are to be believed, the soldiers of the Republic remained attached to that attire even when it was in tatters. The white of the Austrians, the red of the British and the green of the Russians also became symbols. The soldier of the nineteenth and early twentieth centuries, proud of a uniform which, on occasion, won him success with the ladies, strove to wear it with elegance. He also knew that his countrymen regarded him with affection, if not indeed respect, if he belonged to one of the crack units. This fine uniforms will be the guards of honour greeting dignitaries at airports. *See also* ADMINISTRATION, ARMY; CAVALRY; INFANTRY; NAVAL PERSONNEL; RECRUITMENT; SYMBOLISM.

F. BUTTNER

FURTHER READING
Brian Lyndon, 'Military dress and uniformity, 1680–1720', *JSAHR*, liv (1976), pp. 108–20; C. C. P. Lawson, *A History of the Uniforms of the British Army* (5 vols, London, 1940–67); *Battledress. The uniforms of the world's great armies, 1700 to the present*, ed. I. T. Schick (London, 1978); *Index to Military Costume Prints, 1500–1914*, ed. R. G. Thurburn (London, 1972).

Uniforms of the infantry of the army of Württemberg, 1724–38: (*from the left*) private, officer, drummer, sergeant.
(Mary Evans Picture Library)

state of mind gave rise to the irrational attachment French public opinion developed for the soldier's red breeches. Even Jean Jaurès in July 1914 was to oppose the abandonment of that item of apparel, though admittedly he did so for financial reasons.

From the end of the nineteenth century, however, the perfecting of smokeless propellants raised the question of the visibility of uniforms on the battlefield and in all countries bright colours were abandoned. Khaki, *feldgrau*, the French 'bleu horizon' and other neutral colours were universally adopted. The appearance on the scene of aircraft, tanks and parachutes, the diversity of theatres of operation and the volume of American aid to the Allied armies in the Second World War led to the soldier's clothing coming to differ from civilian dress not only in its colour but also in its make-up. Battledress now has nothing whatever in common with walking-out dress, which itself is less worn in a society where all communities avoid features that might mark them apart. The time has perhaps come when the only troops to wear

United States The origins of the American military tradition germinated in Great Britain and were firmly transplanted in the seventeenth century. The sheer distance of the United States from the European great power system accorded her a substantial measure of protection from intervention in US affairs. The American military tradition was therefore largely governed by isolationism. Geography, as Marcus Cunliffe has reminded us, was of supreme importance because 'isolationism as an emotion derived from isolationism as a fact'. In 1897 the Secretary of the Navy J. D. Long declared, 'Our remoteness from foreign powers, the genius of our institutions, and the devotion of our people to education, commerce, and industry, rather than to any policy that involves military entanglements, make war to be thought of only as a last resort in defence of our rights, and our military and naval establishments as a police force for the preservation of order and never for aggression.' The second governing factor was anti-militarism, the profound suspicion Americans entertained for standing armies. This was inherited from the British and yet exacerbated by the behaviour of the British army before and during the American Revolution. Democracy, the 'palladium' of liberty, needed to be defended from the depredations of the soldiery and the dangers of military dictatorship. The career of Oliver Cromwell offered up an awful warning. Therefore, armies were kept small, placed firmly under civilian control, and Congress followed Parliament's example by regulating military finances.

A dual system was constructed which reflected both American remoteness from the centre of great power conflict in Europe and a deep-seated suspicion of professional soldiers. It comprised both a regular army (based on the regiments of the 'Continentals' during the American Revolution, under the direction of the Continental Congress Line – long service combat troops, mainly infantry) and militia. The militia system grew from an English model. The Anglo-Saxon 'fyrd' and the Plantagenet 'Assize of Arms' were its antecedents. The first militia laws were passed in Massachusetts in 1631 and in Virginia in 1623. Both required their men to attend periodic drills and bring along their own weapons. During the next 200 years this legislation underwent very little modification.

The militia tradition was also bolstered by its contribution to a number of nationalistic myths. The first was the myth of superb marksmanship. There were few Americans, declared Charles Lee, 'who wish a distance less than two hundred yards or a larger object than an orange; every shot is fatal.' The second was the agrarian myth. Americans had an inherent love of the soil. Yeoman farmers would rise 'spontaneously' to defend their liberty and property in a loosely organized body like the militia. And, finally, class barriers were of no account in the militia; it was a stout barrier against any group of 'aristocrats' subverting democracy. 'The sword shall not be put in the hands of any but those who have an interest in the community,' declared Josiah Quincy. ' . . . Such are a well-regulated militia composed of freeholders, citizens and husbandmen who take up arms to preserve their property as individuals.' Although these myths were not utterly devoid of foundation, their true significance lies in their contribution to the expanding folklore of American nationalism. This accounts for a passionate American attachment to the militia system and its exposed place in American political rhetoric, irrespective of its true military value, which in truth, was not great.

The major battles of the Revolutionary War were fought by a combination of militia and Continental units. The performance of the former was mixed; it fought best in an irregular capacity. As Sir John Fortescue observed, it 'could never be counted on by its friends but equally never ignored by its enemies'. In harrying Lord Cornwallis's army in South Carolina during the 1781 campaign the militia made a not insignificant contribution to the American victory. The concept of a people in arms had been seen to work. This feeling, combined with the period of financial weakness that followed the Revolutionary War, persuaded Congress to leave the colonial militia structure largely intact. The Militia Act 1792 affirmed the validity of earlier legislation. All white males between the ages of 18 and 45 were liable for enrolment and provided their own firearms and ammunition. The Act was in no sense a watershed but represented a confirmation of all that preceded it. There was little attempt to introduce uniformity. The suppression of the Whiskey Insurrection in 1794 revealed the militia system as inefficient but provided no pressing reason to change it.

The main components of the American military tradition were designed to suggest that the United States only acted *defensively*. This was the view taken of both the War of 1812–15 and the Mexican War of 1846–8 (although doubts were expressed about the latter case). Yet notwithstanding strong anti-military sentiment, as expressed in Andrew Jackson's inaugural address of 1829, which considered 'standing armies as dangerous to free governments', the short but violent history of the United States showed that not only was she born in war but that the martial spirit was a basic ingredient of American patriotism. The regular army's institutions, although in embryonic form, were slowly nourished. The foundation of the US Military academy at West Point in 1802 indicated that its regular officer corps would be leavened by a measure of professional education. Yet the regular army in that year was tiny, 2,873 strong of whom 175 were officers. Before 1861 the US army was involved in a number of minor conflicts with Indian tribes, the

Seminole War (1817–18), the Black Hawk War (1832), the Florida War (1835–41). These conflicts and the two foreign wars were fought under a dual system in which the regular units were deployed by the side of freshly raised (and untrained) volunteer forces. Raised in the volunteer tradition of militia soldiering, they (unlike the militia) could be used outside their local recruiting areas. Consequently, they could be disbanded once the war was over. Hence there was no need for a large military planning structure and staffs.

Such was the position on the eve of the American Civil War (1861–5). This tremendous conflict, for which both sides were utterly unprepared, was the first great industrialized war of the modern age. Yet though 2.5 million civilians joined the colours in the North (1 in 12 of the total population) and 1.6 million (or 1 in 3 of the white male population) in the South, the military system by which these enormous numbers were raised (a much higher proportion than the *levée en masse* in France in Year II of the Revolution, 1 in 36) was not modern but chaotic and archaic. The volunteer units were separated from the regular army (much of which remained on the Western frontier policing Indian reservations). They were untrained; non-commissioned officers were novices and easily overawed by the men in their charge; rates of desertion were staggeringly high. This system bore little resemblance to the modern notion of conscription. Southern soldiers fighting in their own states were initially better motivated and better commanded than their Northern counterparts. This was sometimes put down to the claim (frequently based on dubious evidence) that the South was the only region of the United States which enjoyed a military tradition. But the North compensated for these deficiencies by a high level of technological and logistical superiority, especially after Ulysses S. Grant was appointed general-in-chief in 1864.

The Civil War, it has been claimed, illustrates two prime features of the American approach to warfare. First, that Americans fight wars with a massive material preponderance; and second, that once engaged in a conflict, Americans show a tendency to fight to the finish, and justify their ruthlessness by crusading zeal. Both these generalizations require some qualification. In the first instance, it is the *moral* factor that features prominently in both the Virginia and Tennessee campaigns. Troops attacked with reckless abandon, and were proud of their capacity to withstand enemy fire. They did not prepare cautiously for an advance behind intense artillery barrages. Even in Grant's operations against Lee in Virginia, which is a textbook model of an attritional campaign, Grant pitted the staying power of his infantry (rather than their firepower) against the firepower of Confederates (and sent his artillery to the rear). During the Battle of the Wilderness (4–6 May 1864) Grant issued orders for the commander of the Army of the Potomac, General George G. Meade, to 'pitch in to Lee's army' whenever the opportunity presented itself. In the second instance it is true that after the issue of the Preliminary Emancipation Proclamation in September 1862 following the Antietam Campaign, the Civil War developed into something resembling a punitive (rather than a 'total') war. None the less, this was unexpected and unlooked for and generally unwanted. Northerners were disillusioned because the war was not short. They sought a justification for the massive expenditure of lives and money. It had been a general assumption in 1861 that the war would be short – and concluded in one dramatic and brief campaign. In 1861, as in all the wars of the United States, the universal expectation had been that the war would be short and won decisively.

A decisive victory over the Confederacy was eventually achieved in April 1865. The defeated Confederate generals were determined to bring the war to an end while the conflict remained regular and before extensive partisan operations began to disrupt further the battered social fabric of the South. Both champions of professional and those of volunteer soldiering claimed that the experience of the Civil War upheld their case. Since 1776, John A. Logan declared in his *Volunteer Soldier of America* (1887), 'the volunteer soldiers have constituted the prime military power of the Government'. Scattered in its frontier outposts and prone to nepotism (the famous 7th Cavalry, commanded by Lieutenant-Colonel G. A. Custer was dominated by members of the Custer family), the regular army developed a somewhat inward-looking, bitter ideology of its own. Its main author was Brevet Major-General Emory Upton. In his treatise *The Military Policy of the United States* (1904), which relied heavily on an analysis of 1861–2, Upton argued that all the military woes in America's previous wars could be laid at the door of raw volunteer soldiers. This was an exaggeration. There was little in the military history of the United States in the last half of the nineteenth century which would have justified the retention of a large, expensive regular army and a general staff designed along Prussian lines. In 1867–77 military forces were stationed in the former Confederate States to enforce the Reconstruction Acts; soldiers were employed to intervene in strikes, such as the 1877 rail strike; and until 1890 the army was engaged in the 950 skirmishes which constituted the Indian 'wars'. The 1890s witnessed a revival of militia activity in the guise of the National Guard. By 1892 it was 100,000 strong, with recruits drawn mainly from the middle class. In the years 1877–1903 the National Guard was deployed over 700 times. Even the regulars resembled a constabulary. 'In reality, the Army is now a gendarmerie – a national police,' claimed a colonel in 1895. The US army was 28,000 strong in 1897 and did not merit a mention in the German General Staff survey of world armies. Yet such a small force suited American requirements, for the United States did not face imminent invasion.

The projection of American influence was largely the product of the growth of naval power. This began in earnest in the 1890s. The Secretary of the Navy Benjamin F. Tracey was of the opinion that the 'sea will be the future seat of empire. And we shall rule it as certainly as the sun doth rise!' A. T. Mahan was the apostle of this kind of thinking. His *The Influence of Sea Power upon History, 1660–1783* (1890) was the most celebrated work of strategic theory written by an American before the nuclear age. The Spanish–American War of 1898 was primarily a naval conflict in the first instance. The navy had long studied the possibility of war with Spain; Cuba was blockaded, Puerto Rico and the Philippines were seized. Sea power was decisive. By comparison, the army's mobilization was chaotic. Whereas 100,000 men was the figure estimated for the war, 11,108 officers and 263,609 men were raised combining regulars and state and federal volunteers (such as the famous 'Rough Riders'). The acquisition of colonial territories brought problems as well as responsibilities. General Arthur MacArthur directed an increasingly brutal guerilla war against Filipino insurgents in northern Luzon (1899–1902).

The Spanish–American War confirmed the United States as a great power. The size of her military forces grew commensurately. Whereas in 1899 she had 36 battleships and heavy cruisers (costing $64 million), by 1916 she had 77 large ships (costing $153 million); $229 million was spent on the army and the National Guard in 1916 compared with $183 million in 1899. The size of American battleships increased from 10,000–15,000 tons in 1900 to 31,000 tons in 1914, equipped with ten or twelve 12 or 14 inch guns. Secretary Long introduced a General Board to co-ordinate planning and procurement. The army, too, sought, after the administrative blunders of 1898, to improve its structure and command system. The reforming Secretary of War Elihu Root (1899–1904) aimed to improve the professionalism of the US army. The rank of general-in-chief was abolished by the General Staff Act 1903, a Chief of Staff was created, rotating every four years, directing a staff of 45 officers, and a War College was established. Although restricted to co-ordinating planning, the expertise of this tiny group increased significantly. The deployment of 5,000 regulars to Cuba in 1906 was an immense advance over the confusion of 1898. Some muddle still prevailed when regular forces were dispatched to the Mexican frontier in 1911, but a marked improvement was demonstrated when troops were deployed in 1913 to deal with Pancho Villa. The National Guard was also rationalized. Under the Dick Act 1903, and a further Act of 1908, the Guard received moneys in proportion to the number of men it trained, and went to war as formed units, not as replacements for regular formations.

Many of the sinews used to stretch US military muscles in the First World War, therefore, were in place well before 1917. None the less the lack of 'preparedness' of the United States to fight (or deter) a major war became a major political issue in the years immediately before 1916. This was the first time that an issue of what later became known as 'national security' affected domestic politics in any significant way. Such lobbying paved the way for the passage of the National Defense Act 1916, which provided for the expansion of the army, and the Naval Act of the same year, which sought a 'Navy second to none' with ten new battleships, 16 cruisers and 50 destroyers. Although they had gone some way towards rectifying an organizational problem, the pre-1917 reforms did nothing to address a fundamental problem which would recur in 1941: that the security of the United States ultimately rested on its ability to mount a distant intervention outside the Western Hemisphere to rectify the balance of power in Europe. Thus the 'isolationist' case was not only outmoded but irrelevant. If the United States was to secure a rectification of the balance of power, then building up US military power in Europe became one of General John J. Pershing's prime aims in 1917. He would not allow it to be frittered away by piecemeal infusion of US units into British or French armies. In this Pershing succeeded. During the Meuse-Argonne battles, 600,000 men and 4,000 guns were launched into what was the greatest single operation in American military history. By November 1918 1.3 million Americans had served on the Western Front in 29 divisions. In anything other than managerial terms, however, American operations cannot be considered impressive; the troops were only engaged for 200 days, casualties were 50,280 killed and over 200,000 wounded, far fewer than the British casualties in the Somme battles alone.

In the years immediately after 1918 the United States experienced the revulsion against all things military which swept the Western world. Given her traditions this meant a rejection of intervention in European affairs and a return to 'isolationism'. The United States could secure her strategic goals without adding to her military power; indeed, again she relied on her potential. The army reverted to a small, introverted, frontier constabulary some 140,000 strong. Although the 1916 naval programme was confirmed in the Naval Act of 1919, by 1920 insufficient money had been voted to sustain it, and in the Washington Naval Conference of 1921–2, the United States accepted virtual parity with the Royal Navy (18 battleships to 20 British; Japan was permitted 10). The only area which witnessed vitality was in the air. Here the activities of Brigadier-General 'Billy' Mitchell were seminal; he is the only other theorist of signal importance produced by the United States before 1945. Mitchell argued for an independent air force liberated from the restraints of ground (army) control. In 1925 the Morrow Board rejected Mitchell's claim (a decision coinciding with his court martial for insubordination). In 1926 the Air Corps Act established a force of 1,514 officers and 16,000 men and 1,800 aircraft under the command of the Army Chief of Staff. Naval aviation was integrated more closely into the mainstream of maritime affairs. The main function of the Air Corps was coastal defence. There was an increasing tendency to assume (as did President Franklin D. Roosevelt) that naval and air forces could deter an aggressor; but they could supply no answer to the question of what would happen if the United States was *attacked*.

The Japanese aerial assault on Pearl Harbor in December 1941 thus forced the United States to repeat her improvised mobilization of 1917–18. This time, however, she was not allowed to repeat the experience unmolested and a number of humiliating defeats, notably the loss of the Philippines, were visited upon American arms. The collapse of France in 1940 had alerted her to the danger of allowing a military dictatorship to gain an undisputed *imperium* over the resources of a European super-state. In July and September 1940 Congress passed the 'Two Ocean Navy' Acts, which doubled the size of the fleet; by December 1940 the Army Air Corps was expanded to 84 groups and 7,800 combat aircraft. The size of the army was increased to 1.2 million men by the summer of 1941. US forces, therefore, were not totally unprepared. But such rapid expansion led to many organizational and training difficulties. With the exception of the Chief of Staff, George C. Marshall, George S. Patton and Douglas MacArthur, the great majority of senior US officers had not seen a shot fired in anger. The strategy decided on was 'Germany First'. Once more the US feat in the Second World War was a triumph of managerial and organizational skill. With Great Britain, the United States forged the most intimate and efficient alliance yet organized by two nation-states engaged in war. The United States produced such a wealth of military equipment that it was sufficient not only to equip her own forces in a war that straddled the globe, but those of the British Commonwealth, the Free French and (in terms of trucks and jeeps) those of the Soviet Union as well. Yet in terms of her population and resources, compared with the sacrifices of her allies, the United States did not find this a costly conflict. The great bulk of the German army was committed to the Russian front and thus the great burden of wearing it down was avoided. The United States mobilized 88 divisions and lacked a strategic reserve. Her territory remained inviolate. American warmaking nevertheless emphasized destruction. President Roosevelt at the Casablanca Conference in January 1943 demanded the 'Unconditional Surrender' of the Axis powers. But just enough American resources were mobilized to achieve this aim and no more.

Though perhaps not great in numbers by comparison with her total population, the logistic demands of US forces in the field were stupendous. Allied vehicles, numbering 250,000, consumed 7,000 tons of petroleum per day; an infantry division required one ton of supplies per man per month; the needs of an armoured division were five times as great. In the Pacific the great wealth of material plenty smashed the Japanese empire. The submarine force sank 60 per cent of the Japanese merchant fleet and 30 per cent of its surface fleet. In June 1944 the US 5th Fleet utterly defeated the Japanese in the Battle of the Philippine Sea: Task Force 58 of four carrier task groups, consisting of 15 carriers and their escorts, destroyed what remained of Japanese naval aviation, shooting down 480 aircraft for the loss of 130 aircraft; the amphibious forces (523 ships, 127,000 troops) seized Saipan, Tinian and Guam in the Marianas. These islands formed the base for launching B-29 bomber raids against Japan. This was a scale of fighting power that even the desperate kamikaze suicide tactics (first encountered at the Battle of Leyte Gulf in October 1944) could not resist.

The avalanche of destruction reached a climax in 1945 with the fire bomb raids on Japanese cities (on 9–10 March 84,000 people were killed) and the dropping of the two atomic bombs on Hiroshima and Nagasaki. The surrender of Germany and Japan confirmed that the United States was the world's greatest power. She had a monopoly of a new and devastating weapon; one third of the world's total manufacturing output and merchant shipping were in her possession. She had been forced to break her isolation to rectify an imbalance in the European (and East Asian) balance of power. The spread of communism to Central Europe, China and North Korea which accompanied the advance of Soviet arms, forced the United States to maintain an overseas military structure. Communism was perceived as an all-embracing, monolithic, ideological and strategic threat to the United States which warranted a massive build-up not just of conventional arms (which was sustained into the late 1980s) but of nuclear weapons after the Soviet Union exploded its first nuclear device in 1949. Under the Truman presidency the concept of 'containment' of communism was established, underpinned by a series of interlocking alliances drawn together by John Foster Dulles during the Eisenhower administration in the 1950s.

The overwhelming conventional superiority of the Red Army (and after 1949 of the People's Liberation Army of China) was deterred by the strategic nuclear doctrine of massive retaliation. The resulting militarization of American society – the apotheosis of the 'military–industrial complex' – was criticized not only by C. Wright Mills in his famous book, *The Power Elite* (1959), but in President Eisenhower's farewell address in 1961.

Superpower status seemed to bring a change to the US military tradition. Standing armies, navies and air forces were permitted in peacetime on a huge scale (the army alone was 1,025,778 strong in 1956). For the first time Americans became world leaders in strategic thought, especially that devoted to nuclear strategy. Academics such as Bernard Brodie, Hermann Kahn and Thomas Schelling were immensely influential. The Japanese attack on Pearl Harbor had come as a tremendous psychological shock, and much effort was exerted to prevent the Soviet Union (especially once it had acquired inter-continental ballistic missiles [ICBMs]) launching a surprise attack on the continental United States – something that had been inconceivable before 1918. 'National security' became an overriding preoccupation in American political life. In 1960, and again in 1980, the central issue was the fear that the United States was 'losing' the Cold War. Indeed, John F. Kennedy's famous inaugural address in January 1961 made no mention of domestic affairs.

Despite the colossal sums spent on defence – most particularly in two waves under Kennedy (1961–3) and Ronald Reagan (1981–9) – fears concerning the effects of this militarization were greatly exaggerated. Deterrence was a triumphant success. Only on one occasion – during the Cuban Missile Crisis of October 1962 – did it appear likely that open war would break out with the Soviet Union. The United States fought only two 'limited' wars against communism, both in East Asia, Korea (1950–3) and in Vietnam (1965–73). The reaction against the indecisiveness of the latter spawned a brief 'hippy' counter-culture among the young which rejected all 'militaristic' forms. The Vietnam War was the first war which the United States had 'lost'. It took almost a decade for her self-confidence to recover and, in the meantime, the Soviet Union had secured 'parity' with her in the nuclear arms race and in the construction of naval warships. This competition, combined with the massive Reagan reconstruction of the American armed forces (which had been foreshadowed in the Carter years), and the Strategic Defense Initiative (SDI), which sought to furnish a defence against ICBM attack by employing satellite-based weapons in space, bankrupted Soviet communism. By 1991 the great communist superpower had collapsed, leaving the United States triumphant on the world scene as an undisputed world policeman. Recalcitrant Third World states, like Iraq in the Gulf War (1991), were punished if they broke international law and attempted to destroy US client-states, such as Kuwait. Yet we may conclude that the years of *pax Americana* of 1945–91 go against the grain of the US military tradition. They may appear as an aberration. Without a major threat the traditional elements of isolationism (which throughout this period was voiced in the Senate), suspicion of standing armies and preoccupation with the defence of the continental United States, may again resurface and dominate US policy. Her leaders no longer enjoy the economic paramountcy of the Eisenhower–Kennedy years. Future presidents, as they enter the gates at 1600 Pennsylvania Avenue, may have to contemplate devoting less time to foreign policy and military affairs now that the Cold War has been won. *See also* ANTIETAM; BRADLEY; EISENHOWER; GETTYSBURG; GRANT; KAHN; KOREAN WAR; LEE; LEYTE GULF; MAHAN; MARSHALL; MIDWAY ISLAND; MILITIAS; MITCHELL; NIMITZ; NUCLEAR WARFARE; OVERLORD; PATTON; PEARL HARBOR; PENSIONS; UPTON; VETERANS; VIETNAM; WASHINGTON.

C. STURGILL
BRIAN HOLDEN REID

FURTHER READING
Allan R. Millett and Peter Maslowski, *For the Common Defense: a military history of the United States of America* (New York, 1984); Russell F. Weigley, *The American Way of War* (New York, 1973); Marcus Cunliffe, *Soldiers and Civilians: the martial spirit in America, 1775–1865* (London, 1969); Bruce Collins, 'The Southern military tradition, 1812–61', in *American Studies: essays in honour of Marcus Cunliffe*, eds Brian Holden Reid and John White (London, 1991); D. Clayton James, 'American and Japanese strategies in the Pacific war', in *The Makers of Modern Strategy: from Machiavelli to the nuclear age*, ed. Peter Paret (Princeton, 1986).

Units *See* TACTICAL ORGANIZATION

Upton, Emory (1839–81) Upton, the major advocate of German systems in US military organization, had an outstanding career in the American Civil War. Graduating from West Point in 1861, he entered the artillery, and found himself a brevet major-general in 1865. He had experience with infantry and cavalry as well as artillery; he was present at many of the war's major actions. He returned to West Point to begin his digestion of the lessons (and particularly, as he saw it, mistakes) of the fighting. In 1867 he published a revised system of infantry tactics. Securing the support of Sherman, he was appointed in 1875 to a commission to propose reforms derived from a study of foreign armies. The results of his two-year tour abroad were *The Armies of Asia and Europe* (1878) and *The Military Policy of the United States* (published, thanks to the intervention of Elihu Root, in 1904). Upton attacked the American idea of the citizen army, criticized the lack of military experience inherent in civilian political control and praised the professionalism of German organization; like others impressed by Germany he saw the ingredients of success more in organization than in strategy. In 1881 he took his own life. *See also* SHERMAN; UNITED STATES.

HEW STRACHAN

FURTHER READING
S. E. Ambrose, *Upton and the Army* (Baton Rouge, La, 1964); Allan R. Millett and Peter Maslowski, *For the Common Defense* (New York, 1984); Walter Millis ed., *American Military Thought* (Indianapolis, 1966).

V

Vallière, Florent-Jean de (1667–1759) Vallière entered the artillery in 1685 when it still retained much of the civilian organization which had originated in the sixteenth century. The administrative grades of the service were known as *commissaires* (Commissioners) and were appointed by the Grand Master of the Artillery. Within three years of his cadetship Vallière had become a Supernumerary (probationary) Commissioner (*commissaire extraordinaire*), and in 1692 he was confirmed as a *commissaire de l'artillerie*. His duties in administration and gunnery were supplemented by service in the military mining branch – a vital activity of siege warfare – and by 1699 he owned the most senior of the four companies of miners. He published a brief treatise on the defence of fortresses by the use of counter-mines which remained in use as a textbook until the end of the eighteenth century.

In 1713, Vallière commanded the artillery at the Siege of Le Quesnoy where he distinguished himself by his skilful positioning of the batteries; with only 30 guns he dismounted or suppressed all 84 enemy pieces facing the attack trenches. During his career he participated in more than 60 sieges and 10 battles.

By 1720, Vallière held the rank of *maréchal-de-camp* and the appointment of Captain-General of Miners and, on the reorganization of the Corps of Royal Artillery, he became its first Colonel-Inspector. Six years later he was appointed Director-General of the Battalions and Schools of the Artillery, Lieutenant General of the King's Artillery and Governor of Aire-sur-la-Lys.

He is chiefly remembered as the originator of the Ordonnance of 7 October 1732 in which he sought to standardize the principal element of artillery equipments, namely the barrels of cannon and mortars.

Only guns of 24, 16, 12, 8 and 4 lb, mortars of 13 and 9 inches and a 16-inch stone-throwing mortar were permitted to be cast for the army's artillery. All these weapons were of bronze.

The object of this reform was to reduce the variety of equipments in service. The official series of 1666, based partly on French and partly on Spanish types, included 33-, 24-, 16-, 12-, 8- and 4-pounders, the last two in long and short variants. However, other complete sets of natures deriving from the German and Spanish provinces recently acquired by France were used in parallel with the 1666 series, and there were also oddities such as double- and treble-barrelled pieces as well as 'newly invented' chambered guns. Mortars were just as diverse as cannon for, although their calibres were fewer, 18, 12½, 12 and 8 inches, the volume of their powder chambers also varied, as range was controlled not by elevation of the mortar, but by the quantity of charge propelling the shell.

The design of Vallière's guns was firmly rooted in the tactical usages of the late seventeenth century. Though his barrels were shorter and a little lighter than those of the 1666 series they could still be classified as artillery of position intended, even in the lighter natures, to be fired from platforms behind earthworks. As such they were ideal for siege warfare, and they gave creditable performances in the field at Fontenoy and Dettingen. However, when faced with the need to manoeuvre and the greater rates of fire of the Frederican battlefield they were unable to respond satisfactorily. Rates of fire were increased by setting aside the official method of loading loose powder with a ladle and replacing it with paper or cloth powder cartridges, but manoeuvrability was not so easily improved. Vallière's reforms make absolutely no mention of gun carriages and it is clear that they remained essentially those in use in 1666, as indeed they had to, for the proportions of the barrels had scarcely changed. Le Blond records that it took an eight-horse team to move an 8-pounder and four horses to move a 4-pounder, but this was not usually across country and never at more than walking pace. Add to this the fact that the draught service was composed of impressed civilians or reluctant contract carters and it is clear that once positioned the guns were almost immoveable.

The chosen solution to this problem was taken from a misapplication of Prussian and Austrian practice whereby each infantry battalion was provided with a light gun, usually a 4-pounder. Maréchal de Saxe initiated this attached artillery in 1743 and it was formally introduced by an Ordonnance of 20 January 1757. As the Vallière 4-pounders were deemed unsuitable for this role various out-of-series types were cast to meet the requirement. These in turn proved to be insufficiently powerful but, once accepted by the infantry, objection was raised to withdrawing them. While the battalions were thereby encumbered with these reassuring, if unsatisfactory pieces, the impetus for the reform of the artillery itself was retarded by this partial solution.

Vallière's guns therefore have been condemned as deficient *per se*, whereas their failings actually derived from unforeseeable tactical changes which rendered them obsolescent sooner than expected. The perception of their failure was enhanced by the unsuitable response made to the problem of mobility and it was compounded by the reluctance of Vallière's son, who in the manner of France under the *ancien régime* had inherited his father's appointments and offices, to permit the latter's work to be replaced.

The introduction of Gribeauval's system brought about the necessary changes, though even he was unable to improve upon Vallière's 16- and 24-pounders and retained them. *See also* ARTILLERY; BÉLIDOR; GRIBEAUVAL; ROBINS; SHRAPNEL.

A. CORMACK

FURTHER READING
P. Surirey de St Rémy, *Mémoires d'Artillerie* (3rd edn, 3 vols, Paris, 1745) contains the Ordonnance of 7 October 1732; H. O. De Scheel, *Treatise on Artillery* (repr. Museum Restoration Service, Bloomfield, Canada, 1984); *Carnet de la Sabretache*, special number on artillery (Paris, 1977); Général Susane, *Histoire de l'artillerie française* (Paris, 1874); I. Favé, *Historie et tactique des trois armes, et plus particulièrement l'artillerie de campagne* (Paris, 1845).

Valmy, Battle of (20 September 1792) Seeking to put an end to the Revolution, the allied armies of Prussia and Austria, consisting of a very small number of troops (73,000 men in all), invaded France after she had declared war. The French forces, disrupted both by a great number of officers having joined the Emigration and by the political agitation, had, from the very beginning of the war, seemed inclined to panic. Longwy and Verdun had surrendered to the Duke of Brunswick's Prussians without a fight. After joining forces, the French generals Dumouriez and Kellermann positioned themselves, with their 52,000 men, to the rear of the Prussian army (34,000 men) and an artillery duel began. The Duke of Brunswick, although he had not committed his main force, seeing that the French did not succumb to panic, that there was dysentery among his own army and that winter would soon be approaching, decided to withdraw, judging the operation a failure. This minor engagement had a considerable psychological significance. It proved to the allied coalition that the French would defend themselves. Historians have seen Valmy both as the last victory of the army of the *ancien régime* (with its structures and armaments renovated) and as the first victory of the Revolution, for though there was little participation by the Volunteers, the regular troops demonstrated their attachment to the Revolutionary cause. *See also* FRANCE; JEMAPPES.

A. CORVISIER

FURTHER READING
Valmy: la démocratie en armes, ed. Jean-Paul

Bertaud (Paris, 1970); Arthur Chuquet, *Valmy*, vol. 2 of *Les Guerres de la Révolution* (Paris, 1886 96); J. F. C. Fuller, 'The cannonade of Valmy, 1792', in *The Decisive Battles of the Western World* (London, 1955), ii, 346–69; E. Hublot, *Valmy, ou la défence de la nation par les armes* (Paris, 1987).

Vattel, Emerich de (1714–67) Vattel's *Law of Nations* was published in 1758. Succinct and attractively written in French rather than Latin, it was accepted as perhaps the most authoritative treatise on its subject until 1914. Vattel argued that states are equal and that the prime duty of each is national survival. The need to preserve oneself against aggressors did not, however, preclude the possibility of improvements beyond the mere struggle for survival, because it was open to states to enter into voluntary agreements with one another to limit their conflicts and to promote co-operation. Vattel was strongly opposed to the tendency for war to become punitive. He pointed out that every belligerent considers itself to be just and its opponent unjust, and that the consequence is pointless savagery; it was better, he thought, to accept that war can be just on *both* sides. Vattel was in no doubt that states could, and often did, transgress their obligations, but he doubted that the natural law thus violated could be enforced or vindicated by war. Vattel's teaching about the relation between a state and its subjects was such as to calm a troubled conscience. The sovereign should be obeyed for 'what would be the consequence if, at every step of the sovereign, the subjects were at liberty to weigh the justice of his reasons, and refuse to march to a war which might to them appear unjust?' (III, IX, 186). Because they are thus bound to obey, subjects are not to be required to make good the damage caused by unjust war. The overall thrust of Vattel's *Law of Nations* is towards moderation and a sort of rough justice which derives from the equality of states. His careful reasoning remains an important stimulus to thought about how the destructive potential of international conflict can be kept within reasonable bounds. *See also* GENTILI; GROTIUS; LAWS OF WAR; SPINOZA; VITORIA.

BARRIE PASKINS

FURTHER READING
Emerich de Vattel, *Le Droit des gens ou principes de la loi naturelle*, ed. Albert de Lapradelle (3 vols, Washington DC, 1916); F. S. Ruddy, *The Background of Emmerich de Vattel's Le Droit des gens* (Dobbs Ferry, Oceana, 1974); *The Reason of States*, ed. Michael Donelan (London, 1978).

Vauban, Sébastien Le Prestre de (1633–1707) Vauban's ability was recognized by Mazarin in 1653 at the Siege of St Ménehould during the Fronde. In 1655, he was appointed Ingénieur Ordinaire du Roi and he was instructed in military engineering by the Chevalier de Clerville. He participated in and directed a considerable number of siege operations during the War of Devolution (1667–8), the Franco-Dutch War (1672–8), the Nine Years' War (1688–97) and the War of the Spanish Succession (1702–14). He was appointed Commissary General of Fortifications in 1678, lieutenant-general in 1688 and he became the first officer from the Corps of Engineers to be awarded a baton as Marshal of France (1705).

In 1701 he wrote a *Traité de l'attaque des places* which was based on his observations and experience. He advocated attacking fortresses at their weak points by constructing a series of 'parallel trenches' connected to one another by zig-zagged saps. He particularly stressed the need to adapt attacking methods to the terrain. Since the mounting of a siege required the deployment of sizeable forces (five times the number of the besieged garrison), the strategic decision could only be taken by the king, assisted by advice from his council and principal officers.

He also wrote a *Traité de défense des places* (1706). He took as his starting point the system of the Comte de Pagan. This he steadily improved through his 'Three Systems'. The First System followed the system of regular polygonal *enceintes* defended by bastions at each angle. The Second System (Belfort and Besançon) saw the curtains between the bastions lengthened and the bastions replaced by smaller, tower bastions covered by detached bastions in the ditch. The Third

System (Neuf-Brisach) developed the Second by altering the shape of the curtain to accommodate more cannon and by increasing the size of the detached works.

He built 33 fortresses and improved or rebuilt a further 300 along the coasts and frontiers of France. In 1673, he offered to rationalize and 'square off' Louis XIV's kingdom to achieve a more defensible frontier. This was partially achieved at the Peace of Nijmegen in 1678. He was also a strong advocate of the policy of 'Réunions' between 1678 and 1684 by which the eastern and north-eastern French frontiers were further strengthened. By 1688 he had organized the 'iron frontier' around France, the crowning glory of which was the double line of fortresses covering Paris. He did, however, have to abandon the idea of fortifying the capital, which he had visualized as an entrenched camp between two *enceintes*, a concept which was revived in 1840.

Vauban left extensive writings, none of which was published in his lifetime. He was the foremost military engineer of the later seventeenth century and was held in high regard throughout Western Europe. Vauban was also interested in civil engineering and did much to advance reform in the French army, particularly over the welfare of troops, the recognition of the engineers as an independent branch of the armed forces, and the adoption of the flintlock musket and socket bayonet. *See also* COEHOORN; FORTIFICATION; ENGINEERS; LUXEMBOURG, SIEGE OF; SIEGES.

A. CORVISIER
JOHN CHILDS

FURTHER READING
Henry Guerlac, 'Vauban: the impact of science on war', in *Makers of Modern Strategy*, ed. Peter Paret (Oxford, 1986), pp. 64–90; C. Duffy, *The Fortress in the Age of Vauban and Frederick the Great* (London, 1985); R. Blomfield, *Sébastien Le Prestre de Vauban, 1633–1707* (London, 1938, repr. 1971); Anne Blanchard, *Vauban* (Paris, 1987).

Vegetius Renatus, Flavius The *Epitoma rei militaris* of Vegetius is the only treatise on the Roman art of war that has survived intact. The work was written after AD 383 and was perhaps addressed to Emperor Theodosius the Great. Vegetius was not himself a military commander and his work is a collection of material from many authorities and historical periods, without any systematic chronological order. Nevertheless, much of it relates to the army of the first two centuries AD and it has some value as an analysis of fieldcraft and the commander's duties. The treatise consists of four books dealing with: the recruit, army organization, tactics and strategy, fortifications and naval warfare. Vegetius stresses the importance of sustaining discipline and morale in preparations for battle, of maintaining order and vigilant readiness in enemy territory, of laying out a camp, of planning a campaign carefully, of arranging tactical deployment to suit the situation, of not forcing a defeated enemy to fight to the last man, of conducting a retreat in good order and of using stratagems. He ends with a series of aphorisms which, 'tested by different ages and proved by constant experience, have been passed down by distinguished writers'. The *Epitoma rei militaris* was extremely influential among military men in the Middle Ages and the Renaissance, and his aphorisms are still quoted today, for example by the British army in recruiting advertisements: 'Those who wish to preserve the peace must prepare for war.' *See also* AENEAS TACTICUS; ARRIAN; FRONTINUS; JOSEPHUS; ONASANDER; ON MILITARY MATTERS; ROME.

B. CAMPBELL

FURTHER READING
Latin text in the Teubner series (Leipzig, 1885); English translation by J. Clark (1767) in *Roots of Strategy*, ed. T. R. Phillips (London, 1943); G. R. Watson, *The Roman Soldier* (London, 1969); T. D. Barnes, 'The date of Vegetius', *Phoenix*, xxxiii (1979), pp. 254–7.

Vehicles, armoured *See* TANKS

Verdun, Battle of (21 February–18 December 1916) At the beginning of 1916 the chief of the German General staff, Falkenhayn, appears to have sought a battle of attrition in the Verdun salient. Whatever his precise aim, this was the result since the French were to defend it desperately as both a key fortified frontier zone and a symbol. After a nine-hour bombardment of unprecedented intensity, the German 5th Army attacked on an 8-mile-wide front on 21 February. The lack of armament in the surrounding forts and the loss of the largest – Fort Douaumont – on 25 February proved almost fatal to the French, but Joffre resolved to hold Verdun and entrusted its defence to Pétain's 2nd Army on 26 February. Having reached their initial objective of the east bank of the Meuse, the German advance came to a halt but was renewed on 29 February in an attempt to seize the west bank. Pétain reorganized the defence of the sector, providing artillery, establishing the relatively rapid 'Noria' rotation system and ensuring that material and munitions could be brought in by lorry along the one road that had remained open – the 38-mile *voie sacrée* between Bar-le-Duc and Verdun. Two German offensives towards the Mort Homme feature were halted on 6 March and 9 April but Nivelle, who succeeded Pétain on 19 April when the latter was appointed commander of the central group of armies, had to face repeated assaults during June. The fall of Fort Vaux on 7 June made the situation difficult but, against Pétain's advice, Joffre refused to abandon altogether the east bank of the Meuse. However, Brusilov's offensive on the Eastern Front forced the Germans to withdraw fifteen divisions from the Verdun sector while the escalation of the British offensive on the Somme also sucked in German reserves. Subsequently, Mangin's II Corps recaptured Douaumont on 24 October and Vaux on 2 November, and by December, when Nivelle was promoted to commander-in-chief, the French had regained almost all the positions held on 21 February. Falkenhayn's plans had not succeeded and he himself had been dismissed in August but the French had lost at least 270,000 men killed and the Germans 240,000. Moreover, the psychological effect was considerable, Verdun remaining a symbol of defensive battle taken to the extremities of suffering and willpower. From a technical point of view, Verdun saw perhaps the first systematic use of automobiles for transporting men and equipment, one lorry passing along the *voie sacrée* every 14 seconds; the first use by the Germans of phosgene on the Western Front and their experimentation with infiltration tactics; and the use by Nivelle of a rolling artillery barrage. *See also* ARTILLERY; FRANCE; GERMANY; INFANTRY; JOFFRE; PÉTAIN.

A. CORVISIER
IAN F. W. BECKETT

FURTHER READING
Jacques-Henri Léfèbvre, *Verdun: la plus grande bataille de l'histoire* (Paris, 1960); Alistair Horne, *The Price of Glory: Verdun, 1916* (London, 1962); Georges Blond, *Verdun* (London, 1965); G. Werth, *Verdun: Die Schlacht und der Mythos* (Bergisch Gladbach, 1979).

Veterans The veteran is an old soldier who has been discharged from the army. However, the term is very general and sometimes refers to corps made up of battle-hardened soldiers, seasoned by age and length of service, or quite simply to older soldiers, if they have fought in at least one – and possibly several – campaigns. Historically, the word has also been given extremely precise, though sometimes very varied, meanings.

Roman Period The word 'veteran' in the Latin language (from *vetus*, *veteris*, old) only had a vague meaning under the Republic. The army, which was made up of non-proletarian citizens, was called up at the beginning of each campaign and the soldiers returned home after the war. The veteran only really makes his appearance after Marius' reforms (*c.*107 BC), which extended the recruitment of legionaries to include the proletarians and thus created a standing army comprising a class of men living from war, fighting for booty and more devoted to their generals than to the Republic. At the end of the hostilities, the general had to reward his troops for their

841

loyalty and provide them with a source of income. He distributed lands to his veterans who thus became *coloni*. Marius, Pompey and Caesar all acted in this way. When organizing the Imperial army, Augustus took his inspiration from his predecessors and established an official veteran status. Veterans (*veterani*) had to have served for at least sixteen years if they were soldiers in the Praetorian Guard, twenty years if they had been legionaries and twenty-five years if they had been in the auxiliary corps. They could remain in the army, serving under the title of *vexilarii* (standard bearers) or return to civilian life. As pension they received a sum of money and a certain number of privileges (for example, the freedom of the city of Rome for soldiers from the auxiliary troops). They sometimes received an individual grant of land; more often they were settled in large numbers on the territory of a provincial town. Even more frequently, or at least more spectacularly, they might be given the task of founding a new colony, for example that of Fréjus (*Forum Julii*) in the

time of Augustus. It soon became customary to create such colonies on the frontiers of the Empire, both to romanize these distant regions and to defend them. Examples of this are Cologne (*Colonia Claudia Agrippinensium*) in the time of Claudius, or Timgad (*Colonia Marciana Trajana Thamugadi*) in Trajan's day. The difficulties which beset the Empire from the third century onwards brought about the decline and subsequently the disappearance of this institution.

Modern Period   In 1697, Huguenot veterans from the British armies of William III were settled in a military colony at Portarlington in Ireland. The veteran reappeared in the French army by an order of 1771, which granted a *haute-paye*, a uniform and an honorary medal to soldiers who had served for 24 years (3 terms), irrespective of age. It was thus both a pension and a form of public recognition. The *veteran's medal*, which was sewn on to the left breast of the man's coat, took the form of an oval patch of cloth, either red or

The *Stahlhelm*, 'the Steel Helmet', was one of numerous right-wing veterans' associations which sprang up in Europe after the demobilizations in 1918–19. They continued the bonds of comradeship formed at the front and opposed the spread of socialism. The best known was perhaps the *Fasci di Combattimento*, led by Benito Mussolini. The *Stahlhelm* was the paramilitary wing of the German Nationalist Party (DNVP) until amalgamation with the Nazi *SA* (*Sturmabteilung*) in September/ October 1933.
(Weimar Archive)

matching the colour of the trim of his uniform, bearing two crossed copper-coloured swords. The creation of this pension scheme put an end to vacillation in royal policy towards old soldiers, but it did not settle the general question of the fate of all former servicemen, who had not all served for such a long period. Moreover, the monarchy did not have the financial means to carry out its policy. In 1776, without abolishing the veteran's medal, the Comte de Saint-Germain replaced the *haute-paye* and the other pensions (invalidity and retirement) by a single military pension. In 1790, the law on state pensions abolished the category of veteran.

Contemporary Period The term was immediately taken up again as a name for the 100 companies (12 of gunners and 88 of fusiliers), each comprising 50 men, which were created by the Law of 16 May 1792. Their full title was *Compagnies de vétérans nationaux* (Companies of National Veterans). These companies, which were set up in the administrative capitals of *départements* and on the coasts, replaced the old *compagnies détachées* of the Royal Hôtel des Invalides, but performed the same function. They were intended not so much to play a military role (e.g. the guarding of a fortress) as to make provision for the last years of those disabled or exhausted soldiers who could not live without assistance, but who could neither be accommodated by the tiny Hôtel des Invalides nor granted a pension by a Republican state beset by financial crisis. The revolutionary wars created such a level of need that the corps of national veterans was increased by 15,000 men by a Law of Fructidor Year V. A plan was even considered for placing one such veteran in each commune in the role of rural policeman (*garde champêtre*). Reduced to 13,860 and subsequently to 11,500 men during the Consulate, the corps of veterans continued to exist under the Empire, during which time they were known as 'imperial veterans'. It was still made up of men who had served for at least 24 years or had been wounded in the course of their service or in war.

For a time, Napoleon planned a revival of the ancient idea of 'the veteran' and the old myth of the marriage of the old soldier and the land, by setting up retired soldiers in military colonies within newly conquered territories. These colonies, known as 'veteran camps', would presumably have consolidated the military conquest by asserting a French presence and would have been a way of harnessing these old soldiers to useful ends, since they would presumably have developed the lands placed in their charge. After twenty-five years, the land would become the property of the veteran or his heirs. Two such camps were actually established between 1804 and 1806, one at Alexandria in Piedmont, the other at Jülich in the Rhineland. In theory, both were meant to comprise 405 veterans and their families, who were to be housed within an area bounded by a crenelated outer wall! Both attempts failed and these short-lived camps disappeared in 1814. The institution was not revived in France but in the nineteenth century, the Austro-Hungarian Empire built similar camps on its borders, with the particular aim of asserting Austro-Hungarian influence among the minority nationalities who made up the Empire.

The old companies of veterans were reorganized in 1814, and in 1818 became the *Compagnies de canonniers et fusiliers sédentaires* (Companies of non-mobile gunners and fusiliers). As under the *ancien régime*, they maintained garrisons on the frontiers. However, having been rendered increasingly unnecessary by the introduction of pensions, these companies were reduced after 1848 and under the Second Empire; they were finally abolished by the Law of 1875. The only company to survive beyond this date was the 'Non-mobile Gunners of the Département du Nord', which was in existence until 1892.

The Gouvion-Saint-Cyr Law (1818) had taken up the term 'veteran' again to describe those NCOs and other ranks who had completed their service, but were required to serve six years in the territorial army in time of war. This use of the term disappeared in 1824. At that very moment, territorial service made its appearance in a comparable form within the Prussian army, though it did so under another name.

The word 'veteran' has therefore been applied to cover a wide range of situations. It has always been used to refer to a soldier whose quality – and the confidence that can still be placed in him – is attested by his age and length of service, and whose old age is recognized by the military administration. Emptied of its traditional content, the word is now used in civilian contexts in which all that remains is the notion of length of service or seniority. Only the British and North American armies have retained the word in its precise meaning. In the US army, the term veteran is applied to all ex-servicemen, irrespective of length of service or any disablement. *See also* FRONTIERS; INVALIDS; PENSIONS; ROME.

J.-P. BOIS

FURTHER READING
David Ascoli, *A Village in Chelsea* (London, 1974); W. Walker, *The Veteran Comes Back* (New York, 1944).

Vexillology This neologism, from the Latin *vexillum*, a military standard, means the study of flags and objects which possess a similar symbolic purpose. The oldest symbols seem to have been small bunches of greenery placed on top of poles. According to Diodorus Siculus, the Egyptians appear to have been the first to distinguish military formations by the effigies of animals and there is biblical testimony to the use of this practice by the twelve tribes of Israel, the Old Testament referring to 'ensigns'. These figures, later replaced by pieces of embroidered cloth, were lion cubs, stags, eagles and children, frequently embellished by religious inscriptions. Similar customs were followed by the Greeks – the owl or the olive denoted the Athenians while the letter alpha or lambda represented the Spartans. The symbol of the Persian king was an eagle with outspread wings mounted on the tip of a spear. Roman legions, cohorts and centuries had their *vexilli*, those of the centuries bearing their own number, the number of the

cohort to which they belonged and the number of the legion. The emperor was accompanied by the *labarum*, which acted as a national symbol. It consisted of a horizontal cross staff attached to a spear from which hung a red cloth bearing the image of an eagle. Constantine had a red silk banner decorated with a cross. The Byzantine Empire adopted the double-headed eagle, symbolizing the Roman Empires of the east and the west, and this was later adopted by the Holy Roman Empire and the Austro-Hungarian monarchy. Flags appeared under the Shang dynasty in China (*c*.1122 BC) and in ancient India where they were used in signalling. It was supposedly the Saracens who initiated the practice of attaching the leading edge of a cloth to a staff so that it floated freely outwards in the wind. However, the Bayeux Tapestry shows a variety of flags: streamers on the lances of knights, *vexilli* and oriflammes at the mastheads of Duke William's ships, and further flags identifying the positions of King Harold and Duke William during the Battle of Hastings. The flag was clearly common in Europe long before the Crusades and such a simple device must have derived from numerous different sources.

The history of the symbols of the earliest French kings is obscure. The oldest references speak of the Merovingian monarchs being accompanied by St Martin's cope or mantle. A seal dating from 1205 depicts a gonfalon with three streamers, and it was probably blue in colour. A ninth-century mosaic in the church of St John Lateran in Rome shows Charlemagne's oriflamme with a red background decorated by six roses and with three points. The oriflamme came to be called *Montjoie*, said to be the Emperor's battle-cry. The oriflamme of St Denis was the badge of the Bishop of Paris, and was plain red with five points. Because of its similarity to the Emperor's oriflamme, the two were combined into the *Montjoie St Denis*, first used as a battle standard by Louis VI in 1124. Up to the beginning of the fifteenth century, each declaration of war was accompanied by the ritual unfurling of this oriflamme at St Denis. Carried in four crusades and seventeen wars, the oriflamme was raised for the final time in 1465. Throughout the Middle Ages, standards were principally religious symbols carried by monarchs in the belief that they would impart protection and victory. The renowned cope of St Martin was believed to have brought victory at Vouillé in 507. Philip Augustus (1180–1223) attributed his success at Bouvines (1214) to the oriflamme of St Denis but defeats during the Hundred Years' War, particularly at Agincourt (1415), cast doubts on the efficacy of this sacred relic and it fell into disuse.

The Crusades gave rise to national as opposed to monarchical or royal emblems. At Gisors in 1188, the knights of France, England and Flanders respectively adopted the red, white and green cross as distinguishing marks on their tunics. Under Edward III in 1335, England adopted the red cross, while the French took the white during the reign of Charles V (1364–80). Thenceforth, the white cross became pre-eminently the mark of the French while the red cross of St George has continued as the national flag and emblem of England, appearing on banners around the end of the fifteenth century. It remains the flag of the Royal Navy. During the Hundred Years' War, the principal feudal lords and their vassals began to display individual standards bearing their coats of arms and mottoes. The nomenclature and descriptions of these old banners are very confused. According to Du Cange, knights who had at least fifty men in their pay enjoyed the right to a banner in their capacity as knights banneret. Those knights with smaller followings were knights bachelor or simple and carried only a pennon. When a bachelor could satisfy the conditions required to become a banneret, he handed the pennon to his commander who cut off its point transforming it into a banner. The banner of a prince or a lord was accompanied by a pennon if its owner was an overall commander. The standard was a large banner with two points and indicated the station of the commander. The royal banner was the first to make its appearance. Around 1108, under Louis VI, it was a

gonfalon with three streamers but without decoration. Later, the streamers disappeared leaving a square or rectangular banner. In 1191, G. Giart made the earliest reference to a blue banner 'with its fleur-de-lys portrayed in gold'. St Louis could be seen at Chartres carrying a blue banner decorated with fleur-de-lys. This banner floated above the towers of royal towns, hung from the masts of ships and always preceded the monarch in processions. Members of the nobility and knighthood rapidly adopted similar practices with their own standards and banners.

After the English adoption of St George's Cross, the political junction with Scotland in 1603 and Ireland in 1801 re-

Standard of the 1st Battalion of the Scots Guards, 1685–6, taken from 'The Colour Book of the Army of King James II' (c. 1686). Each company in an infantry battalion had its own colour based on the design of the standard of the colonel's own company.

(The Royal Collection 1993 Her Majesty the Queen)

sulted in the Union flag (Union Jack) in which Scotland's white cross of St Andrew on a blue backround and Ireland's red cross of St Patrick are superimposed on the English flag. Denmark has a legendary symbol in the *Dannebrog* (a white cross on a red background) since this miraculous banner is supposed to have fallen from heaven in 1219. Although it has been the official flag only since 1664, the *Dannebrog* has become firmly identified with the Danish nation. Switzerland has a red flag with a white crucifix, the banner of the canton of Schwyz in the fourteenth century. Although a younger country, the United States has retained the starred flag which it designed during the War of Independence (1775–83); it had thirteen red and white horizontal stripes and, on the blue sector, thirteen stars symbolizing the freed colonies. Later, it became traditional to add a star for every state that joined the Union. Another series of nations, because they have suffered long and turbulent processes of unification, have retained only parts of the numerous symbols that have marked important moments in their history. Germany can show a whole line of nationalities represented by the eagle of Prussia, the horse of Saxony, the key of Bremen, the rhombs of Bavaria and the lion of Swabia. The dominant symbol became the black Prussian eagle which had already appeared on the banner of the Grand Master of the Teutonic Order in the fourteenth century where it had been mounted on large Maltese Crosses transformed into crosses of iron and accompanied by his devices, 'Non soli cedit' and 'Pro gloria et patria'. When unified in 1871, Germany adopted the Prussian colours of black and white but also the red and white of the Holy Roman Empire and the Hanseatic League. The banners of Spain conjoined the red and white coats of arms of Leon and Castile but then, because of the Habsburg association, from the sixteenth century they also displayed the red batons of Burgundy. The year 1785 marked a return to Spanish origins with the red and gold of the counts of Barcelona once more dominating the *bandera*. The final category contains those countries where recent revolutions have swept away many traditions. In the USSR, the double-headed eagle of the tsars was replaced in 1917 by the international red flag of socialism adorned by a hammer and sickle. Revolutionary China has a red flag decorated with five stars.

During the sixteenth and seventeenth centuries, flags became regular features of the emerging standing armies. Each cavalry regiment or infantry battalion possessed the standard, or colour, of its colonel while each troop or company possessed its own flag coloured and decorated according to the theme depicted on the colonel's standard. The colour was carried by the junior commissioned officer in each troop or company, the ensign in the infantry and the guidon or cornet in the cavalry. Towards the end of the eighteenth century, separate company flags gradually disappeared. Austrian infantry battalions were reduced to just two standards in 1748 while French battalions boasted only one after 1776. Cavalry regiments tended to retain one standard per troop or squadron. Also, the various regimental standards became more uniform either by depicting a device common to all, the sun, the royal coat of arms, or a white cross in France, or by adopting a common background colour, green in the Austrian army. After 1804, French infantry flags were identical except for the number of the battalion and in 1808 the battalion flags were replaced by a single regimental standard. Not only did the flags form rallying points in battle but they became icons of regimental tradition and achievement. After the victory at Fleurus in 1690, the French attached a white bow to their flagstaffs. During the eighteenth century, British regiments were allowed to embroider the names and dates of their victorious or glorious actions onto the regimental standard. In Britain and Germany, when new colours were presented, the old flags were frequently hung in the parish church of the regiment's depot town. Superannuated French colours are handed to the army's historical department. In the modern British army, standards continue to play a central role in maintaining regimental identity and morale and the principal public military ceremony is the annual 'trooping of the colour' when the sovereign presents new colours to a regiment on his or her official birthday.

The banner was a square or oblong flag bearing family or personal insignia, borne into action before peers and knights banneret. The ensign was the flag of the knights simple or bachelor. It was triangular, sometimes called a pennon, and flown from the tip of a lance. The guidon was a long tapering cavalry standard, originally carried by a horseman below the rank of knight; it usually bore the national symbol in addition to a badge. The standard was half as long again as the guidon, making it the largest flag. It was stationary and indicated the location of a noble or a monarch in battle. It also flew from houses or castles when the eminent personage was in residence. The streamer or pendant was a naval flag first used during the fifteenth century to distinguish a military from a merchant vessel. Small standards with points, pennants, marked the position of ranks when armies drew up for battle (the 'banner line'). In France, every company possessed a pennant which was entrusted to the sergeant-major. Pennants were also widely used by the quartermasters and commissaries to indicate routes of march, the position of camp sites, strengthened bridges, etc. In the navy, where they were called *jacks*, pennants were larger and flown from the stern of ships. In the British army, the cavalry and dragoons possess guidons, the household cavalry, dragoon guards and infantry have standards, while the hussars are without flags.

Besides their role in the maintenance of morale and the organization of the battlefield, flags have an important function in military signalling. The white flag of surrender was first recorded in 1542 but it has mainly been at sea that flags have found their true *métier* as a signalling medium. As early as 1530, a flag and a single gun were the order for captains to come aboard the flagship for instructions. The first issue of the 'Sailing and Fighting Instructions' in 1653 (printed in 1673) gave a flag signal code for use with the British fleet in the First Anglo-Dutch War. This code was standardized in 1703 and remained in use until 1780 but it was a one-way system for the flagship to pass orders to the fleet and could not be used for the subordinate vessels to send information to the flagship. In 1790, Richard, Earl Howe's numbered system was introduced in which each flag had a number which equalled a specific signal printed in the code book. This was further refined in 1800 by Captain Home Popham's 'dictionary flags' where the numbered flags referred to the letters in a dictionary. The last major revision of the British naval flag codes occurred in 1827 and remained in force despite the advent of morse transmitted by lamp, semaphore and radio. In 1817, Captain Frederick Maryatt introduced his code for use in merchant ships. There now exists an international flag code employing semaphore. *See also* COMMAND; ESPRIT DE CORPS; ETHOS; GLORY; ICONOGRAPHY; MORALE; SIGNAL COMMUNICATION; SYMBOLISM.

P. CHARRIÉ
JOHN CHILDS

FURTHER READING
T. Wise, *Military Flags of the World* (Poole, 1977); G. Campbell and I. O. Evans, *The Book of Flags* (London, 1974); C. King, *The History of British Flags* (London, 1914); L. de Brouille, *Les Drapeaux français* (2nd edn, Paris, 1875; *Flags of the World*, ed. E. M. C. Barraclough and W. G. Crampton (London, 1978).

Vienna, Siege of (14 July–12 September 1683) In 1683, the Ottoman Empire resumed its struggle against the Austrian Habsburgs. Taking advantage of unrest in Hungary and acting within the spirit of plans agreed by Sultan Mehmet IV, Grand Vizier Kara Mustafa Pasha decided upon the capture of Vienna. An army of 80,000 Turks invested Vienna on 14 July which was defended by a garrison under Rüdiger von Starhemberg. Charles V, Duke of Lorraine, commanded the Imperial field army and he withdrew to the north-west of Vienna to await reinforcements from Germany and Poland. John III Sobieski's Polish army joined Lorraine at the end of August and the joint Imperial–Polish army advanced on the Turkish siege camp from the direction of the Kahlenberg on 12 September. The allied forces defeated the Turks decisively, killing at least 15,000 for the loss of only 1,500. The Turks were forced to abandon the siege and withdraw into Hungary. During the ensuing war (1683–99), the Habsburgs regained Hungary and advanced into the northern Balkans. The Siege of Vienna marked the beginning of the Turkish retreat from Central Europe. *See also* AUSTRIA; CHARLES V, DUKE OF LORRAINE; OTTOMAN TURKS; SIEGES; ZENTA.

J. NOUZILLE
JOHN CHILDS

FURTHER READING
John Stoye, *The Siege of Vienna* (London, 1964); Thomas Barker, *Double Eagle and Crescent* (New York, 1967); O. Klopp, *Das Jahr 1683 und der folgende grosse Türkenkrieg bis zum Frieden von Carlowitz 1699* (Graz, 1882).

Vietnam Of all the post-1945 conflicts that have their origins in the anti-colonial struggle the war in Vietnam became the most bloody and protracted. Although it began as a conflict against the French colonial forces it developed, after the defeat of the French, into a civil war between the North and South. This was exacerbated by the international situation. The war in Vietnam became an important part of the United States' stand against what it perceived to be the global spread of Soviet-inspired communism. The Vietnam War encompasses two distinct periods of warfare spanning a period of almost thirty years and its repercussions can be seen in the continuing conflict in the region.

Before the Second World War the territories that composed Vietnam were under French colonial control. The anti-colonial movement began in the 1920s and by the 1930s it was dominated by Ho Chi Minh and his Viet Minh movement. During the war the French forces were ousted and the area came under Japanese domination giving an example to the anti-colonial movement that the European colonial powers could be defeated. In the wake of the Japanese defeat in 1945 and the subse-

quent power vacuum in South-East Asia, Ho Chi Minh was able to found the Democratic Republic of Vietnam. The Republic was short-lived. The Potsdam agreement between the Allied powers in 1945 provided for Vietnam to be liberated by the Chinese from the north and by the British from the south. The British were unable to commit the necessary resources and in order to forestall Chinese influence the French returned to their former colony. After an uneasy peace, conflict between the French and the Viet Minh forces soon broke out with an attempted uprising in Hanoi. The Viet Minh forces, led by Ho Chi Minh and Vo Nguyen Giap, concentrated on guerilla activity harassing the French forces. Giap's troops were especially strong in the northern provinces and an offensive in this area rendered it virtually untenable for the French. With Chinese support the North Vietnamese army grew to over 250,000 soldiers including 60,000 regulars. The guerilla war remained the mainstay of Giap's strategy but the North Vietnamese Army (NVA), as it was now known, proved capable of going over to a full-scale offensive. In 1954 this culminated in the siege of Dien Bien Phu which resulted in heavy French losses in terms of both manpower and prestige. It severely undermined the French will to continue and in July 1954 the Geneva Accords were signed which split Vietnam along the 17th Parallel and granted independence to Laos and Cambodia. The First Indo-China War was over but the Second was not far away.

The Geneva Accords had provided for elections both north and south of the 17th Parallel but in the developing conditions of the postwar world the United States had no confidence that this would not lead to a Soviet–Chinese-backed communist regime over the whole of Vietnam. The United States decided to back South Vietnam as a bastion against communism. The prevailing doctrine of the time was that of the 'domino effect': the loss of one country to communism would be quickly followed by the loss of others.

The South quickly slipped into a state of repression and undemocratic government. By 1957 there were guerilla attacks against government agencies in rural areas by the Viet Cong who had remained behind in the South after 1954. In 1959 the government in the North pledged support to the Viet Cong in South Vietnam and began a policy of large-scale infiltration from the north through Laos and the Central Highlands along what was to become known as the Ho Chi Minh Trail. The communists began to gain control of parts of South Vietnam. President Kennedy, endorsing the domino theory, believed that it was part of a Sino-Soviet conspiracy and began to send large numbers of military advisers to train and equip the Army of the Republic of Vietnam (ARVN). The US advisers developed a policy known as 'strategic hamlets' based on the 'villagization' measures employed by the British in Malaya and Kenya. In Vietnam, however, it was more harshly applied and whole villages were forcibly relocated to fortified settlements. In many areas this alienated the support of the rural peasant classes who were the very people that the South Vietnamese government needed to win over.

In November 1963 a military coup seized power in South Vietnam. The military replaced many provincial governors and local officials. The North saw an opportunity to take advantage of this political upheaval and in December 1963 the North Vietnamese government took the decision to send in regular units of the NVA.

Throughout 1964 there were a number of coups and attempted coups and the United States prepared contingency plans in case of the imminent collapse of the South. Then in August 1964 came an opportunity to increase US involvement. A surveillance patrol came under attack from North Vietnamese patrol boats in the Gulf of Tonkin. The US reaction was swift; President Johnson ordered retaliatory airstrikes in the North and Congress passed the Gulf of Tonkin Resolution. This gave the President a virtual carte blanche to increase US involvement as he saw fit. In South Vietnam the Viet Cong were now attacking US targets and in March 1965 the first US Marine combat ground forces were landed to protect Da Nang, an airbase close to the border. The initial plan was to allow these troops to free ARVN units for more mobile patrols against the Viet Cong. However, US marines were increasingly used in active operations. With the poor performances of the ARVN the United States appeared to have little choice other than to commit additional US forces. By August 1965 there were calls to increase force levels to 125,000. The United States was moving irrevocably away from the low-key 'hearts and minds' approach of the Special Forces.

The first major conflicts between the US forces and the NVA/VC set the pattern for the war. There was very heavy use of US firepower and mobility in the form of airmobile helicopter forces. These were usually brought in to conduct sweeps – 'search and destroy' missions – against areas held by the NVA. These usually resulted in US victories and heavy losses by the NVA but the US forces were never able to consolidate these victories or to follow up and destroy the NVA opposition; the Viet Cong and NVA simply melted away to reappear elsewhere. Trained to perform on a European battlefield dominated by nuclear weapons US forces had considerable difficulty fighting 'area warfare' in which there were no clearly demarcated lines. There were also the political pressures from home which demanded results, pressures that led to the obsession with the 'body count' of NVA/VC casualties.

Nevertheless the United States did appear to be developing a strategy to fight the war. This involved trying to locate NVA bases and forcing it to fight where the United States could concentrate its firepower and inflict heavy attritional losses on the NVA and deter them from mounting offensive operations. In 1966 as force levels grew to 390,000 troops this strategy did appear to offer some hope of success. However, search and destroy operations were only one facet of what was needed to defeat the Viet Cong. The US and South Vietnamese forces also needed to win the support of the population and this required a much broader 'hearts and minds' campaign than was being practised at the time.

Both the US Special Forces teams in the Central Highlands and the Australian forces in Phuoc Tuy province had operated successful hearts and minds campaigns but these were relatively small and self-contained areas. Furthermore the Special Forces campaign in the Central Highlands was with a native group, the Montagnards, who did not necessarily see the aims of the South Vietnamese government as their own.

The combination of search and destroy and large-scale bombing raids against the North, particularly in 1967, led to claims by President Johnson that infiltration by North Vietnamese forces along the Ho Chi Minh Trail had been severely curtailed. Then at the end of January 1968 this claim was firmly rebuked when the NVA launched the Tet Offensive.

Tet is the Vietnamese New Year and the NVA leadership calculated that the ARVN would be at its most relaxed at this time. The NVA leadership were also aware of the political implications of the offensive. They recognized that not only was the ARVN in a weak state but also public opinion in the United States was not committed to the war. The Tet Offensive was not only an attempt to redress the military balance but also an attempt to strike at US prestige.

By 1 February Saigon had been attacked along with the majority of provincial capitals and cities with the attack on Saigon including an attack on the US Embassy. The US forces backed up by the ARVN responded quickly but the cost of the Tet Offensive was very heavy political damage to the United States. It could no longer claim to be winning the war.

In November 1968 Richard Nixon was elected as President on a platform of withdrawal from Vietnam while still continuing to protect the South. The following January peace talks began in Paris. Nixon began the policy of 'Vietnamization' – the increasing use of the ARVN to replace US military forces. This was coupled with the policy of 'Pacification'. This involved the round-up of communist suspects and the reintroduction of democracy at village level through elected councils. This achieved a degree of success as it began to curtail the communist domination of the rural villages. Vietnamization proved harder to achieve.

The size of the ARVN grew from 600,000 to over 1,000,000 and it was supplied with US hardware but it was faced with increasing levels of NVA manpower.

Despite the increasing difficulties of Vietnamization, in 1971 Congress repealed the Gulf of Tonkin Resolution after demonstrations against incursions into Laos by the ARVN and US air and artillery support. Abandonment of the resolution severely curtailed Nixon's power to commit US forces in Vietnam and forced the pace of Vietnamization.

The North was also finding that the war was a drain on its limited resources. It had suffered heavy losses in manpower and considerable damage from US bombing raids. The Pacification programme had also recovered political control of many areas of the South for the South Vietnamese government. In the spring of 1971 North Vietnamese leaders visited the Soviet Union and received promises of substantial aid. By the end of 1971 the NVA had received much modern equipment and was virtually transformed into a modern conventional force. General Giap reassumed command of the NVA and planned a new offensive. Despite almost breaking through in the northern area the attacks were stalled, largely by US firepower, and the NVA was forced to pull back, but it again demonstrated that the United States was in no position to win the war and that the ARVN would not be able to survive without considerable backing from the United States.

Finally, in January 1973, the Paris Peace Accords were signed. The agreement allowed for a withdrawal of US forces and a ceasefire but it left NVA forces in South Vietnamese territory. Nixon promised aid to the South in any future crisis but this was not to be the case as Congress progressively cut the amount of aid allowed to South Vietnam. Without US support the ARVN continued to deteriorate while the NVA was able to carry on its build-up.

In 1975 the NVA launched a general offensive. Without US air support, the ARVN was unable to prevent the NVA advance from the Central Highlands splitting the South in half. At the end of April the NVA entered Saigon.

Since the fall of South Vietnam there has been continuing conflict in the region. Cambodia fell to the Cambodian communists, the Khmer Rouge. The country was renamed Kampuchea and Pol Pot's policy of 'social restructuring' resettled millions from the cities in the countryside killing hundreds of thousands in the process. Many fled to Vietnam and Thailand. Tensions flared between the communists in Vietnam and those in Kampuchea, as much a result of age-old ethnic rivalries as ideological differences. In December 1978, the Vietnamese army invaded Kampuchea and in January 1979 captured Phnom Penh. Pol Pot had Chinese backing and this led to China invading Vietnam in the following month although it withdrew one month later. In September 1989, Vietnam finally withdrew her forces from Kampuchea having failed to secure international recognition for a pro-Vietnamese government. The Khmer Rouge have since launched another offensive in an effort to regain power. *See also* AUSTRALIA; CHINA; COLONIAL WARFARE; DIEN BIEN PHU; GIAP; GUERILLA WARFARE; INDIRECT WARFARE; MAO TSE-TUNG; UNITED STATES.

DAVID WESTON

FURTHER READING
Michael Herr, *Dispatches* (New York, 1978); Stanley Karnow, *Vietnam: a history* (London, 1983); Henry Kissinger, *The White House Years* (Boston, Mass., 1974); Gabriel Kolko, *Vietnam: anatomy of war, 1940–1975* (London, 1986); Michael Maclear, *Vietnam: the ten thousand day war* (New York, 1981); William Shawcross, *Side-Show: Kissinger, Nixon and the destruction of Cambodia* (New York, 1979); Harry G. Summers, *On Strategy: a critical analysis of the Vietnam War* (New York, 1982); Andrew F. Krepinevich, *The Army and Vietnam* (Baltimore and London, 1986).

Villars, Louis Hector, Duke of (1653–1734) Although he was entrusted with diplomatic missions on occasion, Villars was a soldier by temperament. He fought in campaigns from the age of 17 to the age of 81 and was often wounded. He was close to his soldiers and, at the age of 50, he was given command of an army and created Marshal of France. A fine leader of men and a good tactician who knew how to seize opportunities that came his way (e.g. Denain in 1712), he was to distinguish himself in the defensive campaigns of the War of the Spanish Succession between 1705 and 1712. He was badly wounded in the knee at Malplaquet in 1709. In 1733 he devised a plan for a march on Vienna through both Germany and Italy, a scheme which was later taken up by Carnot and implemented by Napoleon. Given the task of putting an end to the Camisard War (1702–5), he completed the work of his predecessor, Montrevel, by a combination of psychological and military action (converging operations and the offer of an amnesty), which achieved the surrender of Jean Cavalier, the Camisards' principal leader. During the Regency (1715–18), he presided over the Council of War which introduced some notable reforms in the artillery, in the rotation of garrisons and in the introduction of a mounted constabulary (*maréchaussée*). Villars was one of the most successful and competent of French generals during the War of the Spanish Succession. *See also* DENAIN; EUGENE OF SAVOY; FRANCE; MALPLAQUET; MARLBOROUGH; VAUBAN.

A. CORVISIER

FURTHER READING
C. Sturgill, *Marshal Villars and the War of the Spanish Succession* (Lexington, Kentucky, 1965); Charles Jean Melchior, Marquis de Vogüé, *Villars d'après sa correspondance et des documents inédits* (2 vols, Paris, 1888).

Vitoria, Francisco de (*c.*1492–1546) A Dominican, Prime Professor of Sacred Theology in the University of Salamanca and a leading figure of the Spanish theologico-juridical school, in company with Bartolomé de Las Casas (1474–1566) and Francisco Suarez (1548–1617), Vitoria was one of the first modern theorists of *Jus inter gentes*, a formula which, when translated by Jeremy Bentham (1748–1832), became 'International Law'. He wrote two books on war, *De Indis* and *De Jure Belli*. In place of the medieval notion of a universal state, he substituted that of *Res publica humana*, a universal society based on equality between states. He recognized the existence and legitimacy of *Res publica humana* on the grounds of the theological notion of humanity. He thus denied the Pope any rights over the temporal domain of princes. Vitoria expounded the theory of just war, which he adopted from St Thomas Aquinas. Hugo Grotius was deeply influenced by the writings of Vitoria. *See also* GENTILI; GROTIUS; LAWS OF WAR; SPINOZA; VATTEL.

A. CORVISIER

FURTHER READING
Francisco de Vitoria, *Political Writings*, ed. Anthony Pagden and Jeremy Lawrance (Cambridge, 1991); G. Livet, *Guerre et paix de Machiavel à Hobbes* (Paris, 1972).

Vo *See* GIAP

W

Waggon-laager The employment of waggons to form a defensive perimeter in battle was first recorded by Julius Caesar. He described how the Helvetii retreated to a waggon-laager after an unsuccessful action against the Romans. In 55 BC, a German force also withdrew into a waggon-laager when attacked by Caesar. At Adrianople in AD 378, the infantry of the Goths occupied a defensive position centred on a waggon-laager, circular in shape according to Ammianus, until the arrival of their cavalry brought victory over the Roman army of the Emperor Valens. The *Leonis Imperator Tactica* of Emperor Leo VI (886–912) indicates that the Byzantine armies frequently used their supply waggons to reinforce the protective entrenchments around their camps. Extensive waggon trains accompanied the armies of the Middle ages, as each 'lance' required at least one vehicle in which to convey its weapons, equipment and supplies. These waggon trains were frequently arranged to protect encampments giving rise to the German expression *wagenburg* (waggon-castle). In action, the *wagenburg* was established behind the battle-line as a refuge should the army be defeated. In this way, the Teutonic Knights retired into their laager at Tannenberg in 1410 after their main forces had been broken by the Polish–Lithuanian army. Jan Ziska (*c.*1370–1424) the Hussite leader, was reputedly present at Tannenberg.

However, the Hussite development of the *wagenburg* into a regular tactical device was not dependent upon Ziska's presence at Tannenberg. Russian armies had regularly employed the *goliaigorod* (moving fortress) against cavalry attack and it was probably this system that Ziska developed for use in the mountainous terrain of Bohemia where his peasant army, weak in horse but strong in foot, was opposed by predominantly German heavy cavalry. For fifteen years (1419–34), the Utraquist Hussite movement in Bohemia held off three 'crusades' aimed at their destruction. Initially using supply carts, the Hussite armies soon constructed special war waggons with high, reinforced sides which could be chained together to form a defensive perimeter, often reinforced with entrenchments. At a word of command, the Hussite waggons could be drawn into a circle, a square or a triangle, the teams disengaged and the vehicles connected with chains. A platoon of twenty men was permanently assigned to each waggon, some armed with missile weapons (bows, crossbows and hand-guns) and the remainder with pikes, spears and flails. The former took position in the waggon to fire down on attackers while the latter stood behind the chain barriers. Nearly a third of the Hussite troops were equipped with firearms and there was a large train of artillery, some of it mounted in waggons. The Hussites achieved prodigious efficiency and speed in forming their laagers from column of march, deploying according to flag signals. These tactics were never satisfactorily countered and even the Battle of Lipan (1434) between the Utraquist Hussites and Roman Catholics on one side and the extreme Hussite Taborites on the other was fought by two armies employing the *wagenburg*. Victory went to the former only because the Taborites advanced beyond their laager into the open field. The Hussite method enabled Ziska and Prokop the Holy to employ the strongest form of military policy: the strategic offensive coupled with the tactical defensive. However, although Hussite tactics demonstrated a means to thwart heavy cavalry with infantry, they would have been fatally vulnerable to attack by artillery. Ziska's methods were devised solely in response to a particular set of circumstances and were largely inapplicable to contemporary military situations in Western Europe.

During the fifteenth century, the Ottoman Turks often deployed their heavy waggons to form a central field fortress (*tabur cengi*) inside which the janissaries and the sultan took station in battle. It is possible that the Ottomans learned this technique from their war against the Hungarian general János Hunyadi (*c.*1387–1456) between 1441 and 1444. However, the waggon-laager was probably a regular tactic of the Turko-Mongols in the steppes of Central Asia well before the fifteenth century. Polish forces in the sixteenth century made use of waggon-laagers (Obertyn in 1531), discovering, like the Russians, that it was one of the few methods of creating a defensive locality in the flat and featureless steppe. As their armies were usually accompanied by long waggon trains, the Cossacks regularly laagered their waggons to protect encampments. At the Battle of Beresteczko (1651), Cossack infantry approached the Polish positions in a long column, defended on either flank by a line of waggons. After their defeat, remnants of the Cossack army retired to a waggon-laager. Both the Polish and the Russian employment of the waggon-laager was only possible because the logistic difficulties in Eastern and Central Europe demanded that large supply trains travelled with the armies. During the later seventeenth and eighteenth centuries, the tactical employment of waggons fell into disuse as supply columns tended to operate further to the rear and were thus unavailable for tactical deployment. Instead, armies turned to entrenchments, earthen redoubts, abatis and other forms of field fortification. However, the use of the waggon to form a defensive perimeter was rediscovered during the nineteenth century by the Boer trekkers in South Africa and white settlers in North America. In both cases, only primitively equipped and organized opponents had to be faced. *See also* ADRIANOPLE; FORTIFICATION, FIELD; LEO VI; POLAND; RUSSIA/USSR; TANKS; TANNENBERG (1410).

JOHN CHILDS

FURTHER READING
R. M. Ogorkiewicz, *Armoured Forces* (London, 1970), pp. 453–6; Charles Oman, *A History of the Art of War in the Middle Ages* (2 vols, London, 1924); Ernest Denis, *Hus et la guerre des Hussites* (Paris, 1930).

Wagram, Battle of (5–6 July 1809)   After fighting brilliant actions against the Austrians (Eckmühl, Regensburg) between 16 and 23 April, Napoleon entered Vienna but failed to cross the Danube, because of insufficient bridging equipment (Battle of Aspern or Essling, 21–22 May). The Archduke Charles of Habsburg took up a position to the north of Vienna with 130,000 men where he awaited the arrival of the Archduke Johann with a further 50,000; Johann had been defeated by Eugène de Beauharnais on the Raab but had escaped his pursuers. To prevent the junction between Charles and Johann, Napoleon crossed the Danube during the night with 160,000 men and attacked the enemy's left, while the Archduke Charles attempted to block off the approach to the French bridges on the right. On 5 July, the outcome of the fighting remained in doubt and action recommenced on the following day. Davout resumed the manoeuvre of the previous day while Napoleon drove in the Austrian centre. Archduke Charles decided upon retreat which was conducted in relatively good order. The Austrians lost 45,000 men, of whom 24,000 were killed and wounded, while the French casualties amounted to 34,000. The Battle of Wagram marked a turning point in the campaigns of Napoleon. Such numbers of men had never before been opposed on a single battlefield. It was very expensive for the French, 21 per cent of their men being rendered *hors de combat* (as opposed to 15 per cent at Austerlitz and 6 per cent at Jena–Auerstädt, though admittedly the figure for Eylau was much higher at 24 per cent). It also showed that Napoleon's adversaries had learned the lessons of the recent campaigns. *See also* AUSTERLITZ; AUSTRIA; CHARLES OF HABSBURG; FRANCE; LEIPZIG; NAPOLEON.

A. CORVISIER

FURTHER READING
D. G. Chandler, *The Campaigns of Napoleon*

(London, 1967); Gunther E. Rothenberg, *Napoleon's Great Adversaries: the Archduke Charles and the Austrian army, 1792–1814* (Bloomington, Ind., 1982).

Wallenstein, Albrecht von, Duke of Friedland (1583–1634) Wallenstein, a complex personality, was one of the last and greatest of the military entrepreneurs of the mid-seventeenth century. Of a minor Bohemian noble family, he made his fortune by marrying an elderly but wealthy widow. He also profited enormously through the purchase of estates confiscated in the aftermath of the Bohemian Revolt (1618–20). Although a cultivated lover of art, he was ambitious, haughty and extravagant. With some previous military experience, in 1625 Wallenstein was appointed to command the new army (30,000 men) raised for the Holy Roman Emperor Ferdinand II. He placed his financial agent, the Antwerp banker Hans de Witte, in charge of logistics, a task made easier by partial access to direct funding from the Emperor's own resources. Wallenstein was a skilful administrator and he imposed an efficient system of contributions on occupied territories in northern Germany. He also produced military equipment, weaponry, bread and foodstuffs from his own Bohemian estates. In return for providing the Emperor with an army, Wallenstein was allowed to appoint his own officers and recover his expenses. Thanks to his system of contributions in cash and kind and the reliable organization of supplies, he maintained better discipline among his troops, reduced the rate of desertion, facilitated recruitment and eased the depredations on the civilian population. However, his contributions were exacted ruthlessly. His growing power caused the German Electors disquiet and he was dismissed in 1630. At this date, his army had a nominal strength of over 150,000 men. From the Emperor's point of view, his removal could not have come at a worse time as Sweden entered the German war in the same year. Wallenstein returned to the Imperial service in 1631. On the death of Tilly in 1632, Wallenstein resumed the chief command of the Imperial armies, enjoying much the same terms as before although he began to operate more as an independent third party within German politics seeking a prominent political and diplomatic role. He had become an uncontrollable political force in personal command of the largest army in Germany. With the connivance of the Emperor and his own generals, he was murdered at Eger in 1634, no longer trusted by any political faction. As much a businessman as a soldier, Wallenstein was a cautious strategist and tactician not wishing to expose his financial and political investment to unnecessary hazard. Although frequently victorious during the 1620s, he was narrowly defeated by Gustavus Adolphus at Lützen in 1632. However, this battle showed that he was beginning to adapt his methods to meet the new Swedish tactics. He was a competent exponent of the war of logistic attrition and manoeuvre. *See also* AUSTRIA; GUSTAVUS II ADOLPHUS; INDIRECT WARFARE; LOGISTICS; LÜTZEN; MERCENARIES; TILLY.

B. KROENER
JOHN CHILDS

FURTHER READING
Golo Mann, *Wallenstein, His Life Narrated* (London, 1976); Fritz Redlich, *The German Military Enterpriser and His Work Force* (2 vols, Wiesbaden, 1964–5).

War economy The study of the war economy has to take into consideration changes which are produced by the existence of a state of war both in the economy in the general sense and in the economic policy of nations. These changes are of two types – passive and active.

Passive changes – both in the economic structure of the state and in society in general – are caused by the mere existence of war, which influences the whole of national life in various ways. The mere presence of war (not to speak of cases where a part of the national territory is lost through enemy invasion) is sufficient to influence production, transport and food supplies, as well as supply and demand – i.e. the market – monetary circulation and revenue. The government of a country at war thus suddenly finds itself obliged to operate in an environment which has profoundly changed for the worse and that environment influences its economic policy insofar as it requires an immediate response in the form of measures which have to be taken without delay.

We thus pass to the field of *active changes* or changes engendered by the conscious activity of the state, which are, in their turn, of two types and directed towards two different objectives, though they are closely related. Above all, the government has to react to the changes referred to above, to bring these under control, in order, as much as possible, to avoid effects which, by seriously damaging the national economy, would hamper the war effort and, by demoralizing the citizens, subject them to tensions which would sap resistance on the home front.

The first problem to be faced in this area is that of ensuring more or less regular supplies, by organizing stocks of essential commodities, by controlling the food market and introducing rationing, by controlling prices and by ensuring that the transport systems reserve at least some of their vehicles or rolling stock for purposes of civil transport – both for people and goods. The second problem is to reconcile this need with the necessity of applying the greatest possible effort to the pursuit of military victory. And it is at this point that we come upon the *active* aspect of the war economy, which consists of all those decisions and measures aimed, as far as possible, at directing all the nation's resources towards the goal of victory (or avoidance of defeat).

The mere fact that the two faces of the war economy interact with one another, and that they often do so in a dangerous way, is clear to everyone: we might even conclude that this distinction between the passive and active aspects of the war economy is in fact the most important research instrument, because it amounts to clarifying the most difficult problem that has to be resolved in this field.

To gain a thorough understanding of this question, we must examine it from the viewpoint of the *active* part, or, in other words, the *voluntary* initiatives of the government. These initiatives can be summed up within a single all-embracing formula:

mobilizing all the productive resources of the country for the economy, while directing them towards sustaining the war effort. Industry, agriculture and transport have to be transformed into a single massive base for the armed forces. Admittedly, this problem (which has always existed to some extent) has become gigantic since the beginning of the Industrial Revolution. The first 'industrial' conflict in history was, without doubt, the American Civil War (1861–5), which saw the first example of total economic mobilization. For the first time, the necessity of making the productive apparatus work to the maximum, while mobilizing human resources for the armies to an unlimited degree, pushed the North (or the United States of America) to bring women into industrial work *en masse*, to militarize the railways and to finance the war through inflation (an experiment which had in fact been tried during the American War of Independence and the French Revolution, though never on such a scale nor with such a degree of planning).

However, the highest degree of economic mobilization took place in the South (the Confederate States of America) where, on the one hand, the level of industrialization was vastly inferior to that of the North and, on the other, the mobilization of human resources was total. All men aged between 17 and 50 were called into the armed forces, while the others served in the territorial reserve. In the end, even slaves who had fought as volunteers in the Confederate Army were given their freedom. The first of the two main problems for the Confederate war economy was to create a war industry almost from scratch and, in order to do this, the government decided to bring all existing industry under its control and to entrust the management of the new installations to the military. A huge industrial machine was also created (including, for example, the biggest explosives factory in the world) and this was entirely state-controlled. In the field of maritime commerce, since the Confederacy received a substantial part of its armaments from Europe, the decision was taken, for the first time in world history, to nationalize foreign trade. Second, a huge state economy was created, which might even be termed collectivist. This was an experiment which was of enormous importance for the future. In passing, we may note that the organization of the war economy ran along lines of centralization and state control which have formed the foundations of twentieth-century dictatorships. The American Civil War marked an end to the days when armies could be supplied without any great change to the normal mode of economic organization and this was the major new development in the field of war economy in this period.

The 1914–18 war provided a striking illustration of the new situation. Germany, whose plans had been based on the expectation of fighting a short war, had very soon to adjust to facing up to a long drawn-out conflict and dealing with economic blockade. In all the belligerent states, peacetime industry soon showed itself quite incapable of meeting the new needs. The German solution was to channel all the available resources and subordinate them to the demands of the war machine; this produced inflation and famine. The military collapse of both Russia and Germany was in large part caused by the bankruptcy of their war economies. Immediately after the end of the First World War, studies were devoted to these problems in an effort to find solutions in case of a recurrence of war. The conclusions which were drawn were of two types. Primarily, it was recognized that *laissez-faire* methods were no longer viable. Private enterprise had to be brought under state control, without the slightest consideration for the economic interests which might be lost by such measures. Second, if inflation was to be prevented, it was necessary to create a market that was strictly controlled by the government. Naturally, this system was enthusiastically adopted by the dictatorships, who hoped, by so doing, both to be victorious and to use this as a means for justifying their monopoly of power. However, the democratic states also had to find a solution for fear that they would otherwise be defeated in another war.

In fact, during the Second World War, with the United States leading the way, the democracies had more success than the dictatorships in organizing a war economy because German aggression enabled the Allies to demand the highest possible level of discipline and sacrifice from their people, while the German government had promised its people a lightning war (blitzkrieg) and had considerable difficulty explaining why the conflict was lasting so long. As for Italy, where war against the former allies from the First World War was never popular, the system of controls proved a total failure. In practice, even the Soviet Union, which was fighting a defensive war, survived thanks in part to economic and material aid from the United Kingdom and the United States. They sent, among other things, 500,000 lorries to the Soviet Union. What was quite new by comparison with the First World War was the highly sophisticated system of taxes, loans and savings campaigns which enabled consent to be won for limitations on prices, wages and profits without resorting to direct state control.

The end of the Second World War, together with the onset of the Cold War and the sense of the probable scale of a future conflict, inspired a number of systematic studies of economic problems in time of war. The stocking of strategic materials was organized; industries were designated for war production; studies were made of how industrial installations could be dispersed for defence against air attack. Admittedly, the existence of nuclear weapons gave the impression that all this was of no avail, since a nuclear war could only last for a very short time. However, though the spectre of nuclear war was a terrible reality, the possibility of a 'conventional' conflict could not be ruled out, and the degree of economic preparedness may, in such a case, make all the difference between victory and defeat.
See also ECONOMIC WARFARE; FINANCES; LOGISTICS; MOBILIZATION; NUMERICAL STRENGTH; TRANSPORT; TRANSPORT, AIR.

R. LURAGHI

FURTHER READING
B. F. Cooling, *War, Business and American Society* (New York, 1977); B. Fairchild and J. Grossman, *The Army and Industrial Manpower; US Army in World War II* (Washington, 1959);

Albert Speer, *Inside the Third Reich* (London, 1970); A. S. Milward, *War, Economy and Society, 1939–45* (London, 1977); G. Hardach, *The First World War, 1914–1918* (Harmondsworth, 1987).

Washington, George (1732–99) An American general and first president of the United States of America, to whose character and ability the ultimate success of the American Revolution has often been ascribed.

When in June 1775 he was chosen by the Continental Congress to be its commander-in-chief, he could draw on the experience of only five years of military service which had ended almost seventeen years previously, when he had been a regimental officer in Virginia's forces during the Seven Years' War. He had been a major at twenty-one (his first appointment) and had served with generals Braddock and Forbes. As a colonel in command of all Virginia's forces he had been responsible for the defence of some 300 miles of mountainous frontier, and had imparted a discipline to his Virginia regiment which had impressed those British officers who saw it. Indeed his greatest wish had been to become a regular officer. His battle experience was limited to the small-scale actions of frontier warfare; he had never commanded cavalry forces nor deployed massed artillery. None the less, in the ensuing struggle for independence (1775–83) he chose to create a regular army on European lines, and both he and his new Continental Line Army became the very embodiment of the revolutionary cause. Subsequently, in 1789, he reluctantly became the first president of the new American Republic and, despite a wish to retire from public life, continued to be active until his sudden death in December 1799.

Washington was a practical soldier who worked hard at his profession. He was no great innovator, leaving no military treatises to posterity. As a field commander he has often been criticized, though the immense difficulties he faced in creating an army at all, while simultaneously fighting a professional enemy, can hardly be overstated. Nor was he unaware of both his own, and his army's, limitations. He believed himself to be inclined to rashness but his boldness was not without skill, imagination and courage, the actions at Trenton (26 December 1776) and Princeton (3 January 1777) in particular winning praise from both Lord Cornwallis and Frederick the Great. Well aware of what was possible he adopted a long-term strategy based on a sort of attrition which avoided a major clash while letting the problems of difficult terrain and great distances wear his opponents down. If a sound strategy, it was also one requiring inexhaustible patience, tenacity and willpower, for he found himself cast not only in the role of a field commander but also in that of an administrator who must solicit the support of both a quarrelsome Congress and a collection of self-minded colonies, while also mediating between them and his fledgling army. For what was required of him, his previous political experience as a Virginian burgess before the revolution was of inestimable value. Perhaps his greatest talent lay in his ability to manage men, in skills which were more political than military. It would be naïve to see Washington as the only man who could have brought the revolution to a successful conclusion but it is difficult to see how, given the circumstances in which he had to act, a more suitable man could have been found.

In the new American Republic Washington's reputation towered above those of his contemporaries and his influence on military affairs correspondingly overshadowed that of others. His personal conduct and preferences did much to shape the military future of his country. He believed (not uncritically) in the superiority of a professional military force formed along European lines and, in a country where many professed an anti-standing-army bias, he advocated the creation of institutions to support a small regular army. But he saw too the necessity of striking the right balance between the discipline and obedience he desired and the reality of American colonial society and, although he had strong reservations about the militia, he acknowledged that it too must be allowed a place. During the revolution he had shown an aversion to an unrestricted partisan style of warfare and he wished to see a compulsory service militia under close regulation, well able to support the republic's small force of regulars. Perhaps most important of all, however, was the influence of his own example in the handling of civil–military relations during the revolutionary war. His respect for civil authority established a precedent which made a professional army more acceptable to Americans. He had shown that the Anglo-American ideal of an army under civil control could be made to work, even under the strain of a long and divisive conflict. *See also* MONONGAHELA; SARATOGA; UNITED STATES; YORKTOWN CAMPAIGN.

G. A. STEPPLER

FURTHER READING
John R. Alden, *George Washington: a biography* (Baton Rouge, 1984); Marcus Cunliffe, *George Washington: man and monument* (London, 1959); John E. Ferling, *The First of Men: a life of George Washington* (Berkeley, 1988); James T. Flexner, *George Washington* (4 vols, Boston, 1965–72); Douglas S. Freeman, *George Washington: a biography* (7 vols, New York, 1948–57); Don Higginbotham, *George Washington and the American Military Tradition* (Athens, Ga, 1985); Dave R. Palmer, *The Way of the Fox: American strategy in the war for America 1775–1783* (Westport, 1975); George Athan Billias, *George Washington's Generals* (New York, 1964).

Waterloo, Battle of (18 June 1815) Having invaded Belgium, where the Prussian army under Blücher and Wellington's Anglo-Dutch forces were converging, Napoleon, with 77,000 men, attacked Blücher, who had 83,000, at Ligny while he gave Ney the task of holding Wellington in check at Quatre-Bras. As a result of a confusion over orders, the 20,000 men of Drouet d'Erlon remained between the two without taking part in the fighting. Blücher beat a retreat but his army was not broken (16 June). The next day, Napoleon sent Grouchy with 33,000 men to pursue Blücher and assembled 72,000 troops to attack the 68,000 of Wellington, who had withdrawn to a defensive position at Waterloo to the south of Brussels. As a storm had soaked the battlefield, Napoleon waited until midday on 18 June before launching his attack. At 4 o'clock, Wellington had to pull back and Napoleon sent his cavalry on a charge which produced no decisive results because he had not dared to commit the Imperial Guard which was needed to cover the imminent arrival of Blücher who had evaded Grouchy. When Napoleon did send in the Guard, without cavalry support, Blücher intervened with 61,000 men. A British counter-attack produced what was undoubtedly a rout, despite self-sacrificing action by squares of the Guard. The French lost 23,000 dead and wounded and 7,000 prisoners. Wellington's casualties amounted to 15,000 men and Blücher's to 7,000. The tactical errors of Napoleon, who no longer had the vigour of youth, and the lack of initiative of his subordinates, in conjunction with the numerical inferiority of the French forces, explain this defeat which, sooner or later, was inevitable. *See also* BLÜCHER; FRANCE; NAPOLEON; WELLINGTON.

A. CORVISIER

FURTHER READING
H. Houssaye, *1815* (3 vols, Paris, 1895–1905); Jac Weller, *Wellington at Waterloo* (London, 1967); John Keegan, *The Face of Battle* (London, 1976).

Weapons The very existence of weapons, their organization and use, are bound up with various dynamically interrelated factors. These can be divided into:

1 *Technical factors* which are inseparable from the development of military science and the related industrial processes. From the beginning, arms manufacture has represented a leading sector of the metal-working industry. However, these factors will only be touched on in broad outline here.
2 *The political, economic and social factors* bearing on the possession of arms and the form of recruitment and composition of the different branches of the services (the individual corps) into which the troops are divided.
3 *The development of state administrative*

structures from the point at which the state has its army firmly under its authority.

4 *Financial resources*, see FINANCES.

Technical Factors Weapons are offensive and defensive instruments used by men on land, sea and air. The major distinction lies between firearms and those which do not rely on fire-power (hand-held or throwing weapons). Weapons may be described as individual when they require only one person to operate them (bow, rifle, sub-machine-gun). They are collective when several men are needed to make them work, a typical example being the cannon, but it would be possible to consider the pike–musket combination as a type of collective weapon of yesteryear. This distinction takes no account of the constraints of maintenance and ammunition supply which made the foot soldier's rifle a collective weapon.

Criteria of effectiveness for weapons are related to their ability to penetrate a body, a breastplate, or a wall; or to the radius over which they act, either through the dispersal of blast or shrapnel from grenades and high-explosive shells; or, more simply, to the weight of weapon necessary to kill one man, which has in some cases exceeded a ton.

Accuracy depends both on the weapon and its user, and is expressed in terms of differences in range or direction. In cases of saturation coverage of an area, though it is important that friendly troops should not be affected, accuracy is not expressly sought. Well-designed weapons have tended to increase in accuracy. More rapid rate of fire partly accounts for the fifteenth-century victory of the longbow over the crossbow. In the eighteenth century, the rate of fire depended on the time it took to load a musket, a problem solved in the twentieth century by the introduction of automatic weapons. However, the possibilities of rapid detection mean that modern cannon can now only fire short bursts from one position.

The increased strength and durability of weapons (fewer cannons exploding) have been achieved by progress in metal-working techniques. Recent technical progress has introduced new components into the situation: electronic measures and counter-measures, detection systems, electro-magnetic impulses and the effect of nuclear blast.

Investment costs have to be taken into account. The turnover of modern weapons is very rapid, but in the past, the turnover time (e.g. from the musket to the rifle) was very much connected with the expenses of undertaking such an operation. Similarly, the supply situation after the First World War explains the backwardness of French arms manufacture until 1935.

The panoply of arms is very great, whether the term is taken to mean offensive or defensive equipment (swords, rifles, cannons, aircraft, ships) or the categories of combatant called to use them (foot soldiers, cavalry, pilots, sailors), and there are a great number of subdivisions of weapons corresponding to particular special areas. Primitive people had only one type of weapon, or two at the most (axes, clubs, bows, assegais, etc.). When they became more advanced they capitalized on their dexterity by specializing in the use of a particular weapon in the service of countries who were aware of the advantages of certain types of arms. Thus it was that Balearic slingshot fighters, Numidian horsemen, Genoese crossbowmen, Swiss infantry and German *Landsknechte* appeared and disappeared from the field of military history as requirements changed. In a similar fashion, master craftsmen were sought: gunners in the first period of fire-powered artillery, engineers from the period when fortification techniques were revived in the sixteenth century. This need for engineers was also experienced in Moscow, by Peter the Great, at the very beginning of the eighteenth century.

What are known as *armes blanches* cover an enormous field if they are defined as those weapons with which man exerts his physical strength. They include throwing weapons, weapons for hand-to-hand combat and protective equipment. Prehistoric weapons were probably little different, at their origins, from hunting or fishing equipment. The beginning of a clear distinction between hunting and fighting weapons seems to have coincided with the development of primitive fortifications (fourth millennium BC). Materials used were hard stone – flint or obsidian – and the bones of dead animals, particularly those of deer. Among the weapons that have been discovered are daggers, axes, clubs and arrowheads. Towards the end of the period in which these weapons predominated, they were joined by weapons made of copper, which in its pure state is too malleable. Harpoon or spear-throwing weapons were still in use in recent times among the Inuit peoples and the aborigines of Australia.

Homer describes weapons and armour of bronze. To the (long) sword and the javelin may be added protective equipment: helmets, breastplates, greaves and very long shields. Archers or slingshots, who were of little account, were not given the benefit of these defensive arms. The javelin was a weapon both for throwing and for close combat. The tradition of heavy defensive armour was preserved by the Classical Greeks – Athenian hoplites and the Theban phalanx – with the latter employing very long lances (Macedonian spears) which could no longer be used as throwing weapons. The Assyrians wore helmets and padded breastplates of plaited esparto grass and were armed with a long broadsword, longbow and javelin. The Gauls wore helmets, had no breastplates but carried a light shield; they were armed with a (defective) sword and an axe. Like the Greeks, the Romans were oriented towards heavy infantry, one third of whom would be pikemen (*hastati*).

Bronze, which is harder than copper, had been known and worked in Egypt from the middle of the second millennium BC. Because of the dearth of tin in Europe, its use remained confined to military needs until the Cornish tin mines came into operation. Nevertheless, bronze would remain in use for the manufacture of cannons throughout the centuries which followed, until iron-working was sufficiently developed.

The first appearance of iron on the battlefield was a failure. The poorly tempered iron swords, used by the Gauls, were apt, until about 450 AD, to bend. However, weapons of quality were being developed from the beginning of the first millennium AD in the Hallstatt region of Switzerland and in Lorestan in Asia Minor, although expansion and know-how did not always go hand in hand. Despite hand-forging, the iron was porous and uneven. In the end, however, the water-driven tilt-hammer and the forge yielded sound products. The barbarians of the Late Empire knew how to weld together bands of soft iron and of iron with a steel inlay (damascening) with steel cutting edges soldered on to the blade. Hand-held cutting weapons could now pierce (with the tip) or slice (with the edge) according to how they were made. Pieces of armour in iron such as helmets or breastplates now also became worthwhile even if their weight restricted their use to horsemen alone. Technical improvements were harder to achieve when it came to firearms. The first iron cannons disintegrated after about ten shots, and so bronze cannons were preferred until about 1840. Barrel-drilling was improved in the eighteenth century, although cannon barrels made of rolled and soldered iron rods were not perfected until the end of that century, when they led to large calibres of up to 18 cm. Nineteenth-century metallurgy, smelting, steelworks, steel and cementation, would give birth to modern weapons and to the armour-plating of fortifications, ships and tanks.

The second millennium before Christ was marked by the advent of the warhorse and mounted bowmen, particularly in the East. War chariots were highly developed throughout the whole of the Middle East where, despite the addition of scythes, they were primarily a rapid means of transport for an archer or a lancer. They virtually disappeared from the battlefield around 350 BC. The camel had occasionally been used in battle, as indeed had elephants, which were still being used by Alexander the Great. But although horses played only a subsidiary role throughout the Roman era, cavalry regained its importance during the Barbarian Invasions. Iron stirrups appeared in Arabia around AD 650 and rapidly spread to other areas. They provided a firm support for archers to fire their arrows and for riders to use their lances and sabres. This development ultimately gave rise to the armoured cavalry who dominated medieval battlefields until the fifteenth century. The collar harnesses which distributed the load on draught animals' shoulders, making them three or four times more effective, date from the ninth century. However, horses were slow to replace oxen for transporting equipment. From about the ninth century, the use of shoes made animals' movements and exertions easier. Until then their hooves had been softened by wet ground or worn out on stony terrain.

Mechanization is a relatively recent phenomenon and the use of motorized vehicles was initially ill-received by those who favoured the horse. Mechanization was first introduced in the 1840s when railways were used for strategic and logistical transport, and from 1866 they were employed in preparations for mobilization. The various uses of the railway were fully exploited in 1914–18. Armoured trains were used only occasionally, except during the Russian Revolution, the American Civil War and the Second Boer War. During the First World War heavy artillery was often mounted on railway trains. Motor vehicles, used as logistical and battlefield transports, experienced a spectacular development during the two world wars, leading to the creation of transport 'arms' or services, which were given different names in the different countries. The tank, which was attached to the artillery on its first appearance in 1916, acquired independent status as a weapon and dominated the Second World War. Although restricted to an observing role in 1914, aircraft quickly joined in the fighting and, with the advent of bombing, acquired a remote-action role; they were, as a consequence, referred to as 'flying artillery'. Already a force to be reckoned with in the Spanish Civil War, they played a major role in the Second World War and subsequent conflicts. All these machines are heavy

consumers of fuel, which causes problems of supply, storage and distribution.

Ancient artillery is known as torsion or neuroballistic artillery, its power resulting from the twisting of animal sinew or hair. Except in the case of ballistas, which launched missiles for up to 450 metres (accurately up to 90 metres), weapons of this type were used in siege warfare. They were far from ineffective. Missiles could be either nets full of stones or single large stones; given a throwing arm of 15 metres and counterweights of 90–140 kg, stones of 25 kg could be thrown for up to 250 metres, and even as far as 450 metres. These weapons – ballistas, mangonels, catapults and trebuchets – remained in use until the appearance of gunpowder-based artillery.

Gunpowder-based artillery goes back to the very beginning of the fourteenth century, when there was no great difference between the design of the light weapons carried by the infantry and the heavier weapons intended for joint actions or sieges. The projectiles were balls weighing less than 3 lb, while the weapon itself was made of iron rods welded together and bound by hoops. These early guns, some of which were breech-loaded, were fired with a red-hot iron rod. No suitable support existed and guns were mounted on specially built wooden frames. At the end of the fourteenth century a distinction began to emerge with the appearance of heavy artillery, which could fire stones of 200 lb in weight. However, these guns were of limited effectiveness as their cannon balls shattered when they came into contact with walls. Improvements were gradually made, though it is impossible to assign precise dates because of the extraordinary circulation of ideas and of processes among the master-casters or gunsmiths who traded their services and skills. Loading was very slow, as was unlimbering the guns.

Though the intervening period saw trials with iron-bound stone cannon balls, grapeshot or incendiary missiles, it was not until the reign of Louis XI (1461–83) that developments in metal-working made the large-scale production of the iron cannon ball possible. Bronze cannon, which were stronger than those of iron, were introduced in the middle of the fifteenth century and survived until well into the nineteenth. Gunpowder production had also been refined so there were now fewer cannon failures and explosions. Most importantly, guns were now attached to carriages. The Swiss carried their lighter weapons on carts. Trunnions also made their appearance during the reign of Louis XI. These were cylindrical appendages affixed to each side of the cannon which distributed the effect of the recoil onto the gun's mount. Artillery was now mobile, making a deep impression at the time of Charles VIII's invasion of Italy. The variation of calibres, expressed in terms of the weight of the ammunition employed, was considerable. The idea behind this was that the enemy should not be able to re-use the enemy's cannon balls. In 1552 Henry II standardized the six French calibres which ranged from the 33- pounder to the 11 oz 'falcon', and also standardized the composition of the bronze. England and the Holy Roman Empire took similar measures during the same period.

Although mortars had been devised fairly early on, they were slow to become established; bombs loaded with explosives presented firing difficulties, and if the angle of fire was greater than 30°, the recoil tore the mounts apart, until the stress was transferred on to a base plate. This problem was overcome in 1634 at the Siege of Lamotte in Lorraine. Also in the middle of the seventeenth century, in England, the howitzer, a cannon which lobbed a hollow missile, or shell, filled with gunpowder, was developed.

Although the artillery was to have a brilliant future, 150 years would be needed to develop its full potential. There was still a slow turnover of systems but this gradually became more rapid; it took fifteen years to substitute Gribeauval's system for that of Vallière, and as long again to introduce rifled artillery and breech loading. Scientists played their part in these first experiments: Galileo discovered parabolic motion, then Benjamin Robins (1707–51) in England, with Newton, introduced considerations of air resistance. After the work of these forerunners, we enter the domain of ballistics as a mathematical science.

Chemicals, in the form of inflammable materials, were in use well before chemistry was constituted as a science. The use of Greek Fire marked a significant step on this path. Incapacitating and blistering poison gases were much used during the 1914–18 war. Although prohibited by international conventions new strains (such as Sarin and Tabun) have been developed.

After the Franco-Prussian War, physics made an unobtrusive appearance on the battlefield in the shape of military telegraphy, while signals – the telephone and radio, etc. – developed during the 1914–18 war, using methods which belonged to the field of applied physics. Not long before 1938, sophisticated detection systems were developed: radar has led to the development of extremely sophisticated electronic and computer-controlled measures and counter-measures.

It was the union of chemistry and physics which gave rise to nuclear weapons. These were first used in 1945, the product of the military application of basic research carried out well before the five-year period that had led to their development. They are almost total weapons, adding contamination from fallout, melting and the disruption of electrical and radio-electrical contacts to the effects of shock and concussion already produced by shells and bombs. Their use has led to the improvement of launch mechanisms – rockets may be fired from silos, ships, submarines or aircraft – and the difficult development of protective measures.

Siege equipment, either for the attack or defence of fortifications, is dealt with under the headings FORTIFICATION and SIEGES.

Before the nuclear age, the history of weapons was characterized by a series of innovations which, though they have been described as revolutionary, might more appropriately be termed evolutionary, given the length of time taken for new developments to be properly appreciated. A few examples will suffice here. The key was for decision-makers to have a mind open to change, to be aware of technical innovations and to have money at their disposal. In the past, discoveries have often been discontinuous and geographically widely spread. Better quality flint, the appearance of missile-throwing devices, the discovery of bronze, iron-working and new explosives all took a long time to develop. More than a century was needed before fire-powdered artillery became really effective. Fashions came and went: the pike, a weapon of the sixteenth century, became the revolutionary weapon for the members of the Convention. And at the end of the last century the conquerors of the colonies found themselves confronted by tribes using slings and assegais with formidable efficiency, weapons thought to have been obsolete since the Stone Age. Similarly, in France, the 1777 musket and Gribeauval's cannons of 1765–72 were still successful weapons in the Revolutionary and Napoleonic Wars. Although in England large muzzle-loading pieces of coastal artillery were still in use in 1890 such an idea would have seemed unthinkable elsewhere. However, the 1914–18 war witnessed the return of muzzle-loading mortars, which were very effective. Two significant revolutions occurred in the nineteenth century, the development of the rifled cannon and of high explosives, both of which took ten years to become established. The latter rendered obsolete all fortifications built before 1875. However, since there were not the financial resources to rebuild them, they continued to be used, at a heavy cost in lives. A true revolution in the field of weaponry is normally produced by a combination of imagination and urgent need, particularly in wartime. The path has usually been prepared by direct and indirect peacetime research.

The history of weapons is punctuated by the eclipse of certain types of weapons and their subsequent reappearance, the most recent case being that of the rocket, which, in its original incarnation, died out around 1880, though another example is the crossbow, used as a sniper's weapon in the wars of decolonization. It is also a history where there is sometimes rapid progress but where, more often, advances come slowly, with periods of stagnation and even of regression. Let us consider a few examples for comparison.

The bow was known in the earliest days of the Ancient World and was used to great effect right up to the sixteenth century. Considered a weapon not for those of noble rank, it was responsible for such victories as Hastings (by indirect fire), Crécy and Agincourt. While the original shortbow was replaced by the Welsh longbow in the eleventh century, simultaneously in the East, the former made a reappearance among the Turkish cavalry. Its chief rival was the crossbow, specimens of which exist dating back to the fourth century. The crossbow enabled a heavier missile (the bolt) to be fired, with a powerful penetrative force. But crossbow strings were very susceptible to rain, as was seen at Crécy, and their rate of fire was slower. Though with the early crossbow, a rate of four shots a minute could be achieved, with a range of about 250 metres, later, heavier models, which necessitated the use of both hands and feet to load, had a rate which fell to two or three shots. In the same period, Edward III's highly trained longbowmen achieved up to twelve shots a minute and could hit their target from 210 metres. Their arrows killed horses but were ineffective against armour and, for this reason, the crossbow continued to be competitive.

Of the cutting and thrusting weapons, the halberd and the pike were extraordinarily popular from the time of Louis XI to that of Francis I, apparently because of the skill shown in their handling by the Swiss. The pike continued to be used until 1640, but was then gradually abandoned in favour of the plug bayonet, though this actually prevented firing, a problem which was not remedied until the socket bayonet came into general use at the end of the seventeenth century. The pike did not completely disappear from European battlefields until 1714. Armour survived in the regulations until well into the reign of Louis XIV, although firearms had made it superfluous, except in trenches during siege warfare, a century earlier.

Light firearms had a difficult gestation. They appeared at the same time as the cannon, during the third quarter of the fourteenth century. Their method of manufacture was similar, iron rods rolled and welded or hooped together, fired from the rear from what was in fact a sort of box held together by corner pieces. It was a long time before they were successful. The bow was still being recommended in England in some quarters at the beginning of the eighteenth century, and when Monluc entered the ranks in 1516 the crossbow was still the favoured weapon among his 'band'. This does, however, seem odd, as in 1476 at Murten 6,000 Swiss 'culverineers' had fought 4,000 of Charles the Bold's arquebusiers. Certainly after 1535, one no longer finds crossbowmen in the French armies. Breech loading was quickly abandoned (for reasons of weather-proofing). The arquebus was invented around 1425: its barrel was longer and the priming powder was held in a receptacle at its side, the priming pan. The slow-match, which needed to be rekindled by human breath, fell onto the priming pan by means of a trigger. It had a range of about 150 metres at the rate of one shot every five minutes, a good deal less than that of the bow or crossbow but it had a greater capacity to wound and led to the disappearance of heavy and costly armour. Most important, a soldier could operate the arquebus with a minimum of instruction whereas a longbowman required years of specialized training. The musket made its appearance around 1520. Initially, it scarcely differed from the arquebus except in its calibre and therefore its weight; it required the support of a forked rest. Firearms particularly benefited from a major invention, the wheel-lock, the slow-match being replaced by a flint or stone held against a rapidly rotated serrated steel wheel; the flint showered sparks onto the pan, which was filled with fine priming powder. This led to the development of the pistol, which was to produce a transformation in cavalry tactics. The pistol used cartridges, and its range reached some 200 metres at a rate of a shot a minute. By 1630, the flintlock musket, which would rule uncontested until the middle of the nineteenth century, was in use. The 'dog' held a flint which struck against a hinged 'steel', producing sparks and uncovering the priming pan. The French 1777 model had a range of 600 metres (and was accurate up to 250 metres), and its useful rate of fire was two or three shots a minute.

Discoveries have occurred more quickly in the modern era, though they have not always been so quickly implemented, whether for reasons of finance or tradition. In 1806, Alexander John Forsyth invented a percussion method of igniting the charge using fulminate of mercury and potassium chlorate and this led to the development of the percussion musket. However, the moveable breech created in 1824 was not introduced into military weapons until after 1850; there followed the multiple-barrelled machine-guns of the 1860s (which had had an early ancestor in 1476), the single-barrelled Maxim gun, down to the automatic rifle, the Bren gun and the machine-pistol. In these final stages it is not range that is sought but density of fire, combined with the use of hand or rifle grenades.

Grooving – or rifling – weapons has a long history. Crossbowmen came to understand that they could increase the accuracy of their aim by arranging the quills on their bolts to make them spin. It was not long before arquebusiers had a small number of spiral grooves made within the barrels of their guns. However, rifling was abandoned with the matchlock and flintlock musket. To engage the lead balls with the rifling required a tight fit which made muzzle-reloading time-consuming and slow. Instead, 'windage' was allowed between the ball and the smooth barrel which enabled more rapid loading but sacrificed accuracy and range. Rifling was not effectively reintroduced into mass military weapons until the development of breech-loading in the mid-nineteenth century. Throughout the ages, the main object of weapons research has been to increase the force of blows delivered, their frequency, and, to a lesser extent, their accuracy.

Political, Economic and Social Factors
The possession and use of a weapon were long considered symbols of individual freedom, while the need to seek one's defence from others was interpreted as a state of political and social dependency. Thus in the earliest city-states, free men called to armed service had to provide

their own weapons. This was still the case with the warriors of the kingdoms of the Ancient World and the high Middle Ages, and it continued to hold for Charlemagne's armies and among feudal troops.

Since the upkeep of weaponry, and particularly of a warhorse, required considerable wealth, the recruitment of the various arms – cavalry, heavy and light infantry, pioneers, oarsmen for the fleet – was organized on the basis of property qualifications (for example, the four classes of Athenian citizenship). In the Carolingian armies, military duties were distributed according to a unit of agricultural exploitation, the *mansus*, though this was often fictive. Depending on the value of their possessions, landowners had to provide a certain number of armed and equipped men, the poorest joining together to provide one soldier. This remained the principle that ruled modern militias. In Sweden, the *Indelta* was based on a unit (*rotar*) covering several estates, which were obliged to maintain the soldier. In medieval times fiefdoms, given in exchange for military service, were used to pay and equip warriors. Arms and social power went together.

However, cities and rulers very quickly had recourse to mercenaries. These might be professionals who possessed their own arms or who bought them with money issued when they entered the ranks. On occasion, however, a wary king preferred to arm them himself leading to the creation of arsenals, examples of which could already be found in Ancient Egypt or Crete (third millennium BC). Another reason for such action on the sovereign's part was the concern, which appeared at an early stage, that cohesion should be achieved among his troops by some degree of uniformity in their weapons. This led to the idea of managing a collective stock of weapons which were distributed to men when they were called to serve in the ranks. However, these ideas ran up against traditions which demanded that free men and, later, nobles possess their own arms. They also ran up against a lack of financial resources on the part of monarchs.

In these conditions, the manufacture, purchase and repair of weapons cost the monarch nothing, except where, by order, men not in his service were forbidden to carry arms. Moreover, the industrial structure was based on craft production, which made it difficult to envisage creating a genuine arms policy. However, in wartime a king might sometimes try to intervene by summary legislation in the manufacture of and trade in arms, for example prohibiting the purchase by private individuals or the sale abroad of raw materials necessary for arms manufacture, banning the export of horses and weapons, granting benefits to armourers, etc. In general, however, these measures had no great effect.

In the Ancient World, the Roman emperors were almost the only rulers to own their troops' weapons. At the end of the Middle Ages, many weapons remained in private hands, feudal lords and professional soldiers hiring out their services collectively or individually, or in the hands of towns. However, after the organization of feudal monarchies, kings often undertook to control the number and quality of the arms of their vassals (Henry II's 1181 Assize of Arms in England) and the weapons of the first regular troops, after these bodies had been formed (inspections or reviews). From the sixteenth century onwards ownership of private weapons declined. Developments in the art of war necessitated the employment of increasingly expensive weapons and the more frequent use of collective weapons (firepower). In addition, kings showed themselves increasingly concerned not to let arms into the hands of private individuals who might be disposed to revolt. In France the turning point was marked by the failure of the Fronde, the last manifestation of local armed forces standing outside the king's power. Henceforth the possession of weapons of war was reserved exclusively to the state.

The Development of the Modern State
Since, in regard to this question, one state is quite different from another, we will restrict ourselves to France.

It was only under Louis XIV and Louvois that control of arms became effective, but it was not until the twentieth century that this control was extended to cover arms manufacture. In the fifteenth century, arms were produced as a craft industry, though their manufacture was already much less dispersed than was the case with other sectors of industrial production. Northern Italy, Spain, Middle Germany and, particularly, Liège already stood out, their role as arms-producing towns decided by the presence of ore, firewood, pure water for tempering the metal, guilds providing highly skilled craftsmen, and finally by the certainty of custom. Specialization appeared (armour in Milan, blades in Toledo) and Liège took a leading place in the manufacture of firearms. There was an international market for good quality weapons as well as regional markets for ordinary weapons. Each captain, or lord, bought the weapons he favoured for his men with the money allocated to him by the king, without worrying too much about models or calibres. Charles VII and Charles the Bold were the first kings to try to establish a little order in this area by creating Masters of Artillery who were responsible for monitoring the equipment of that service. Among them, in the service of France, we find the brothers Bureau. In 1493, Charles VIII created the office of Grand Master of the Artillery, with responsibility for equipment, munitions and recruitment. Galliot de Genouillac held this post with great honour, distinguishing himself at Marignano; he was also involved in the construction of the Arsenal in Paris, the first state arsenal in France. Although it survived to Sully's day, this institution could no longer meet the growing needs of the army after the Thirty Years' War and subsequently declined.

Under Louis XIV the officer of Grand Master of the Artillery was held by a number of rather undistinguished individuals, and it disappeared in 1755. Louvois's energetic action made the War Secretariat effective, while Colbert was conducting a parallel undertaking in the navy. His industrial policy improved the state of the monarchy's weaponry in general. France continued buying arms abroad, but foundries and new arsenals were created, in the Nivernais, at Charleville and Saint-Etienne, made up of small workshops linked with larger manufacturers working under contract for the king under the supervision of inspectors. To regulate manufacture and ensure the maintenance of arms stocks, Louis XIV appointed an *Entrepreneur Général*, Maximilien Titon, to whom was allotted the arms magazine near the Bastille, where weapons were tested before being stored. With the aid of a network of superintendents, Titon was able to manage the successful transfer from the matchlock musket to the flintlock. Six hundred thousand muskets were made in twenty years, which represents a considerable achievement, bearing in mind the capabilities of the time. An 'experimental' regiment, the King's Fusiliers, was used to test innovations. The navy provided itself with a similar organization at Rochefort.

In 1715 the role of *Entrepreneur Général* was abolished for the army, but a factory inspectorate continued to co-ordinate the efforts of the various workshops (Charleville, Saint-Etienne, Tulle, Klingenthal). More-detailed sets of specifications (laid down in the so-called *cahiers des charges*) removed the disparities between weapons. The 1717 musket was the first French example of a standardized weapon and in 1732 the Vallière system reduced the number of artillery calibres to five. In 1735, the First Inspector General took charge of the administration of weapons. Not without difficulty (he was the defendant in a famous trial), Gribeauval succeeded in imposing standardization of equipment so that it could easily be repaired in any location. The Revolution replaced the First Inspector General by the Central Committee of the Artillery. State intervention expanded into manufacture from 1820 onwards, but this continued to be performed under contract. The *Service des Forges* proposed to the Minister where orders for raw materials should be placed and oversaw the execution of contracts in accordance with rules for monitoring procedures which were gradually set in place (1775, 1802, 1803 and 1823), before the rules of 1841 were arrived at, which governed the manufacture of arms for seventy years. Thus, in 1886, the Lebel rifle was manufactured at a rate of 3,000 a day. In 1914, the arms stocks that had been built up with a short war in mind were quickly exhausted and an industrial mobilization was needed such as had never before been seen. In 1918, 226,000 75 mm shells and seven million cartridges were produced each day.

The new forms of warfare necessitated the creation in 1935 of the *Direction des Fabrications d'Armement* (Directorate of Arms Manufacture) within the Ministry of War. In 1948 this became the *Direction des Études et Fabrications d'Armement* (Directorate of Arms Research and Manufacture – DEFA), while in 1936 the arms industry was nationalized. The DEFA was to increase the number of research laboratories, such as the Laboratory for Ballistic and Aerodynamic Research at Vernon and the Experimental Establishment for Military Engineering Equipment at Angers. The *Compte du Commerce* conferred financial autonomy on the Arms Accounts Department (*service financier de l'armement*), which was under the direct authority of the state, allowing it to sell arms abroad, thus making the production of weapons a profitable operation.

The concept of 'Arms system' is recent, incorporating into manufacturing policy and weapons theory the logistical and operational factors which determine how and where a weapon can be used. These factors include the weapon itself, its ammunition, the transporting vehicle, detection and possible counter-measures, all of which are viewed in terms of the needs the weapon is to meet and its desired effects. *See also* AIRCRAFT; ARMOUR PERSONAL; ARMOUR PLATE; ARSENALS; ARTILLERY; BLADE WEAPONS; CAVALRY; CHEMICAL AND BIOLOGICAL WARFARE; DOCKYARDS; EXPLOSIVES; FINANCES; FIREARMS; FORTIFICATION; GUNFIRE; INFANTRY; MOBILIZATION; NAVAL WARFARE; NAVIES; NUCLEAR WARFARE; ORDNANCE; PROPELLANTS; SIEGES; SIGNAL COMMUNICATION.

J.-M. GOENAGA
A. CORVISIER

FURTHER READING
C. J. Ffoulkes, *The Gunfounders of England,* with a List of English and Continental Gunfounders from the XIV to XIX Centuries (Cambridge, 1937); Kelly Devries, *Medieval Military Technology* (Peterborough, Ont., 1992); H. L. Blackmore, *British Military Firearms, 1650–1850* (London, 1961); I. V. Hogg, *A History of Artillery* (London, 1974); S. Bidwell and D. Graham, *Fire-Power* (London, 1982); Maurice Pearton, *The Knowledgeable State* (London, 1982).

Weapons systems *See* WEAPONS

Wellington, Arthur Wellesley, Duke of (1769–1852) There is little evidence that Arthur Wellesley, an Anglo-Irishman of aristocratic connections, took his military career seriously until 1796, when he went to India. With his brother, Lord Mornington, as Governor General, Wellesley was able to regulate political intervention in a way allowed few British soldiers of his day. Furthermore, he learned in the Seringapatam campaign of 1799 the importance of transport and supply. Victory at Assaye (1803) in the 2nd Maratha War cemented his reputation. In 1808 he was given temporary command of the British expeditionary force in Portugal. In the following year, after the defeat and death of Sir John Moore at Corunna, Wellesley returned to the Peninsula and led a British force from Portugal into Spain. His advance was precipitate, but Wellesley fought a successful defensive action at Talavera. He then constructed a series of defensive positions around Torres Vedras. While the British and Portugese forces were supplied from the sea, the French operated in infertile territory, their lengthy communications harassed by Spanish gueril023. In 1810 and 1811 Wellington laid siege to the forts on the Portuguese–Spanish border and, in 1812, after victory at Salamanca, entered Madrid. The reconquest of Spain was completed in 1813, with the defeat of Jourdan at Vitoria, and Wellington (as he now was) crossed the Pyrenees into France. When Napoleon escaped from Elba in 1815, Wellington took command of the Anglo-Dutch army and defeated the French at Waterloo. Here, as elsewhere, his military strengths were tactical and traditional: he chose well-sited positions, and used infantry firepower to break the enemy's initial attacks before himself counter-attacking. Wellington's inclinations were conservative: little of the new military thought generated by the French Revolution found reflection in the British army, and he won his victories by perfecting Frederican systems of warfare. After 1815, his influence proved stultifying for the British army, whose commander-in-chief he was in 1827 and 1828, and again from 1842 to 1852. He was prime minister in 1828–30. *See also* IRREGULAR WARFARE; TORRES VEDRAS; WATERLOO.

HEW STRACHAN

FURTHER READING
Elizabeth Longford, *Wellington: years of the sword* (London, 1969) and *Wellington: pillar of state* (London, 1972); *Wellington*, ed. Norman Gash (Manchester, 1990); Michael Glover, *Wellington as Military Commander* (London, 1968).

Wilkinson, Spenser (1853–1937) Wilkinson began his professional life as a Manchester barrister with an amateur interest in military affairs. In 1881, as an officer in the volunteers, he helped form the Manchester Tactical Society. The publications of the society, his advocacy of the volunteers and his journalistic activities with the *Manchester Guardian* finally found fruit in *Imperial Defence* (1892), written with Sir Charles Dilke. It was a book remarkable for its scope, seeing the empire's needs as a whole, and integrating the roles of the army and the navy. The recognition which it received, and the contact with Lord Roberts which it provided, decided Wilkinson. Military theory became his profession. *The Brain of an Army* (1890) had provided a lucid account of the German general staff. The initial defeats suffered by the British army in the Boer War allowed Wilkinson an active role as reformer, the army accepting his argument that institutional change and an effective organization for command were the basis for military success. In 1909 he became the first holder of the chair in the history of war at Oxford. Military history, and in particular the development of the French army and of Napoleon's style of war, now became his priority. *The French Army before Napoleon* (1915), *The Defence of Piedmont* (1927) and *The Rise of General Bonaparte* (1930) remain excellent accounts, and introduced British readers to the revisionism of Henri Bonnal, Hubert Camon and Jean Colin. *See also* GENERAL STAFF; NAPOLEON; TRAINING.

HEW STRACHAN

FURTHER READING
Jay Luvaas, *The Education of an Army* (London, 1965); Spenser Wilkinson, *Fifty-five years 1874–1929* (London, 1933).

William I King of England, 'the Conqueror' (*c.*1027–87) William succeeded his father as Duke of Normandy in 1035, and his early years on the ducal throne were troubled. He was generally on the defensive against both Norman rebels and external enemies but it was during these difficult times that he acquired a masterly understanding of the art of war. Only when his two main rivals, King Henry I of France and Count Geoffrey of Anjou, both died in 1060 was William able to go over to the attack. In 1063 he conquered Maine. The death of Edward the Confessor in 1066 gave him the opportunity to claim England. A combination of good fortune and William's own strategy of delay enabled him to make an unopposed landing on the Sussex coast. On 13–14 October he then out-generalled King Harold and brought him to battle. Even so, it was only Harold's death that settled the issue. With the English in political disarray, William was able to undertake the conquest of England but it was a long and difficult task requiring both an extensive programme of castle-building and the most brutal ravaging in medieval warfare – the Harrying of the North (1069–70) – before it could be said to have been completed. Not surprisingly, William had made many enemies and after 1076 he was once more on the defensive. Although he suffered a number of setbacks, he ended his days still in control of his conquests. *See also* GREAT BRITAIN; HASTINGS.

JOHN CHILDS

FURTHER READING
D. C. Douglas, *William the Conqueror*

(London, 1964); Frank Barlow, *William I and the Norman Conquest* (London, 1965); John Gillingham, 'William the Bastard at war', in *Studies in Medieval History presented to R. Allen Brown*, ed. C. Harper-Bill (Woodbridge, 1989).

Williams, Sir Roger (*c.*1540–95) Thanks in part to the nineteenth-century belief that he was the model for Shakespeare's Captain Fluellen, Roger Williams is today possibly the best-known Elizabethan military officer. He was one of a number drawn from the impoverished gentry of South Wales and the Marches, a type of background similar to those of many of his Continental contemporaries, Schwendi and Monluc for example. Like Monluc too he was celebrated for his loquacity and bravado. Little is known of his early life. Although he had probably served in previous campaigns, he is first encountered in the English company raised for William of Orange in 1572. When that was disbanded in 1573, he transferred to the Spanish Army of Flanders. Although England and Spain were still at peace, and he was not the only English officer then in the Spanish service, this phase of his career caused Williams considerable later embarrassment. In 1578 he rejoined the English contingent in the Dutch army, and under the Earl of Leicester became sergeant-major of the horse and then a knight in 1586. Williams' most famous moment came in May 1587, when he was hurriedly sent with reinforcements to Sluys in the face of the investment of the port by the Duke of Parma. Although he was forced to surrender on 5 August, his conduct of the defence with an Anglo-Dutch garrison of only 1,600 (of whom 800 were killed) was widely praised. After the death of Leicester, who had been his patron since the 1570s, Williams attached himself to the Earl of Essex, with whom he served in the 'Portugal Voyage' of 1589, and then (as marshal of the field) at the Siege of Rouen in 1591. After Essex was recalled (January 1592), Williams commanded the remaining English troops in Normandy until they in turn were withdrawn in July 1593. Williams was never inhibited in supplying either strategic or tactical advice and in 1584 he began a major work intended to be both a military treatise and a history of the Dutch Wars. Although this was never completed, part of the treatise was published in 1590 as *A Brief Discourse of Warre* and sections of the history appeared in print in 1618 under the title of *The Actions of the Lowe Countries*. As a military commentator, Williams's importance lies in his outspoken assertion that the campaigns in the Netherlands had transformed the conduct of warfare and that the Spanish Army of Flanders was the model to follow: 'no army that ever I saw passes that of the Duke de Parma for discipline and good order.' He was an advocate both of Spanish weapons (particularly advancing the case of the musket against the caliver, arquebus and longbow) and tactics, and of experience and experiment rather than the precepts of classical authors, as argued by Machiavelli and his followers. *See also* DUDLEY, ROBERT; INFANTRY; MACHIAVELLI; MONLUC; PARMA; SCHWENDI.

SIMON ADAMS

FURTHER READING
J. X. Evans, *The Works of Sir Roger Williams* (Oxford, 1972); For Sluys, see G. Mattingly, *The Defeat of the Spanish Armada* (London, 1958), pp. 129–45. For the Normandy campaign, see H. A. Lloyd, *The Rouen Campaign, 1590–1592* (Oxford, 1973); R. B. Wernham, *After the Armada* (Oxford, 1984).

Willisen, Karl Wilhelm (1790–1879) Willisen was a Prussian officer, a military theorist contemporary with Clausewitz but influenced by Jomini. As such, he had a reasonable reputation in his own day but has since been eclipsed. To Moltke and his successors the work of Willisen seemed excessively theoretical and geometric. In the Napoleonic Wars he enjoyed a dramatic career, being wounded at Auerstädt while in the Prussian army, serving at Wagram in the Austrian army, escaping from prison in 1813 to rejoin the Prussian forces, and ending the war on Blücher's staff in 1815. He remained on the staff when peace came. His strategical studies started while he was an instructor at the *Allgemeine Kriegsschule*. Although he wrote commentaries on the principal campaigns of his day – Poland in 1831, Italy in 1848 and 1859 and Austria in 1866 – his central arguments were derived not from particular cases but rested on the assumption that the science of war was unchanging. He stressed the value of surprise, the use of feints and night-marches, and the need to seek a decision through bringing strength against weakness. His main addition to the conceptual framework of war was to distinguish between the strategic offensive or defensive and the tactical, and to recognize that the strategic offensive could be accompanied by the tactical defensive. He made major studies of the role of field fortifications in national defence. In the 1830s he served in Poland, and in 1848 found himself as the intermediary between the Polish revolutionaries and Berlin. In 1850 he assumed command of the army of Schleswig-Holstein in its war with Denmark. Finding himself with inferior numbers, Willisen sallied forth from the security of prepared positions at Idstedt and suffered defeat. His reputation, and his self-esteem, never fully recovered. *See also* CLAUSEWITZ; JOMINI; STRATEGY.

HEW STRACHAN

FURTHER READING
Allgemeine deutsche Biographie (Leipzig, 1898), xliii; Lt. Gen. von Caemmerer, *The Development of Strategical Science during the Nineteenth Century* (London, 1905).

Wolfe, James (1727–59) Wolfe was a British major-general whose death at Quebec in 1759, aged just thirty-two, made him one of Britain's most popular military heroes. The son of a long-serving officer, he was first commissioned in 1741 at the age of only fourteen and, although chronically short of money, nevertheless enjoyed rapid promotion through the patronage of the Duke of Cumberland. Within nine years (in 1750) he had achieved the rank of lieutenant-colonel, having gained experience as a brigade major, and being a veteran of four battles. In 1757 he came to the notice of King George II as a result of the abortive Rochefort expedition and won further distinction at the capture of Louisbourg in the following year. This resulted in his appointment to command the Quebec expedition in 1759 with the local rank of major-general.

Quebec's dramatic fall seized the public's imagination and elevated Wolfe to the status of a national hero. However, opinion about his generalship has always been divided and the fact that Quebec was his only independent command has permitted endless speculation. Although he set a personal example of great energy, he possessed a streak of recklessness, certainly apparent to his contemporaries, which was possibly related to his recurrent ill-health. The capture of Quebec was undoubtedly a formidable task, made worse by his inferior numerical strength, but his initial conduct of the siege seemed to lack strategic insight. Wolfe's reputation has been frequently attacked on account of the precarious situation into which his final stratagem led his small force, but it was not uncalculated and anything less audacious would not have produced the consternation within the city which, in the end, precipitated its fall. Whether a final gamble or not, the thrust came at precisely the right place and moment, when Montcalm had convinced himself that he had successfully foiled the besiegers and saved Quebec.

Posthumously, Wolfe's personal qualities and earlier career as a regimental officer were offered as ideals of the army's paternal style of command. Although the uniqueness of his humanity towards inferiors, and of his serious study of war, would later be greatly exaggerated, his widespread contemporary popularity ensured that his example made a strong impact on the evolution of the British army's ideas on training, discipline and command. *See also* GLORY; ICONOGRAPHY; QUEBEC.

G. A. STEPPLER

FURTHER READING
B. H. Liddell Hart, *Great Captains Unveiled* (London, 1927); W. T. Waugh, *James Wolfe, Man and Soldier* (Montreal, 1928); Beckles Wilson, *The Life and Letters of James Wolfe* (London, 1909); Robert Wright, *The Life of Major-General James Wolfe* (London, 1864); James Wolfe, *General Wolfe's Instructions to Young Officers* (London, 1780, repr. Ottawa, 1967).

Women *See* FAMILIES

X

Xenophon (*c.*428/7–*c.*354 BC) Xenophon, a native of Athens, was a writer and soldier. After a comfortable youth during which he acquired a taste for horse-riding and hunting, and also followed the lessons of Socrates, Xenophon embarked on a soldier's life. His military calling took him first to the Persian Empire where he took part in the famous expedition of the 'Ten Thousand' mercenaries recruited by the Persian prince, Cyrus the Younger, against his brother the king. After the defeat of Cyrus, Xenophon was elected as one of the generals and helped to organize the army's retreat. This campaign is recounted by Xenophon himself in his *Anabasis*. He was exiled, perhaps in 399 in the aftermath of the trial and execution of Socrates in that year. Then, after taking part in the various battles fought in Asia Minor between 399 and 396 by the Spartan expeditionary force under the command of King Agesilaos, he followed the Spartan king back to Europe and even went so far as to fight in the Spartan ranks against Athens at the Battle of Coronea in 394. During his period of exile, which did not end until 366/5, he devoted himself to writing a great number of literary works. Thanks to his extensive military experience, his historical books, especially the *Hellenica* and *Anabasis*, contain invaluable information on the tactics and strategy and also the behaviour of the soldiers in the fourth century BC. He also wrote a number of technical treatises, for example, *Hipparchicus* on the duties of a cavalry commander and *Cynegeticus* on hunting, which are valuable for the light they cast on the training and preparation of Xenophon's contemporaries for war. Lastly, he produced a number of biographical essays, which are generally faithful to their subjects (*Hieron*, *Agesilaos*, *Cyropaedia*), but which mainly provided him with an opportunity to state what he considered to be the essential qualities of the warrior. Despite his limitations as a historian, Xenophon is a very important source for the development of the military art in the fourth century BC. *See also* GREECE, ANCIENT; SPARTA.

R. LONIS

FURTHER READING
Y. Garlan, *War in the Ancient World: a Social History* (London, 1975); J. K. Anderson, *Xenophon* (London, 1974); translation of the *Anabasis* – *Xenophon: the Persian expedition*, introduction by G. L. Cawkwell (Harmondsworth, 1972); translation of the *Hellenica*– *Xenophon: a history of my times*, introduction by G. L. Cawkwell (Harmondsworth, 1979); J. K. Anderson, *Military Theory and Practice in the Age of Xenophon* (Berkeley, 1970).

Y

Yamamoto, Isoroku (1884–1943) Yamamoto joined the Japanese navy at the age of seventeen. His subsequent career was brilliant. After fighting in the Russo-Japanese War, and teaching at the Gunnery School, he served on the General Staff in 1916, before being sent as naval attaché to Washington in 1925. He then participated in both the London naval conferences of 1930 and 1934–5. From 1936 to 1939 he was Deputy Minister for the Navy, and in 1940 he became Commander-in-Chief of the Japanese Imperial Navy. He therefore played a crucial role in the development of Japanese naval forces and the preparation for war with the United States. He strove to build up a balanced fleet of both battleships and aircraft carriers.

As Commander-in-Chief, he is remembered for his direction of three major operations: the attack on Pearl Harbor, the Battle of Midway Island and the actions in Guadalcanal and the Solomon Islands area. After the war, he came in for heavy criticism – for having neglected the political repercussions of Pearl Harbor, for having divided his forces at Midway, and for having refused to commit the main body of the fleet to Guadalcanal. Though it was said of him that he was a better organizer and tactician than a strategist, he none the less enjoyed immense prestige in a navy which adulated him. His death, when his plane was shot down in the Solomon Islands by US aircraft who had been informed of his flight by intelligence, was considered an irreparable loss. *See also* GUADALCANAL; JAPAN; MIDWAY ISLAND; NAGUMO; NAVAL WARFARE; NAVIES; PEARL HARBOR.

P. MASSON

FURTHER READING
Agawa Hiroyuki, *The Reluctant Admiral* (New York, 1979); John D. Potter, *Admiral of the Pacific: the life of Yamamoto* (New York and London, 1965).

Yarmuk, Battle of the River (636)   While the Byzantine emperor Heraclius (610–41) concentrated on the defeat of the Persians, which he had largely achieved by 628, the emerging and expansionist force of Islamic Arabia was virtually ignored. After the death of Mohammed (632), the Caliph Umar (Omar) divided his forces into three columns and raided into Syria in 634. His troops were halted before a Roman fortification on the Yarmuk River, a tributary of the Jordan which runs westwards across the Deraa Gap. A Byzantine army advanced south along the coast to cut off the left-hand column but the Arabs rapidly concentrated their troops and crushed their opponents at Ajnadain, between Gaza and Jerusalem. The Arabs then marched north of the Yarmuk and seized Damascus and Homs as well as besieged Jerusalem.

In 636, Heraclius gathered at Antioch a force supposedly of 80,000 men; whatever its true strength, the Byzantine army outnumbered that of the Arabs. The imperial treasurer, Theodore, was placed in command and duly advanced southwards, the Arabs abandoning Damascus and Homs and falling back to the Yarmuk. From May to April, the Byzantines remained inactive, encamped in the Deraa Gap while the Arabs, under their general Khalid, gathered reinforcements, harried the enemy and probed into the rear of his positions. The Armenian contingent in Theodore's army grew mutinous at the display of inertia. Eventually, the Arabs penetrated into the Byzantine rear and took the bridge over the Wadi-al-Rakkad, one of the key lines of retreat. On 20 August 636, in the thick of a sandstorm which blew into the faces of the Byzantine soldiers, the Arabs charged and trapped Theodore's army, which was destroyed almost to a man. The treasurer was among those slain. By selecting an open battlefield, the Arabs had been able to make use of their own ability to manoeuvre while placing the close order tactics of the Byzantine army at a severe disadvantage.

Syria, including Damascus and Homs, was lost to the Arabs and Jerusalem fell in the following year. The Arabs continued their expansion, occupying the whole of the Near East (Egypt fell in September 642) as far as the Taurus Mountains which blocked their path into Asia Minor. *See also* BYZANTIUM.

G. DAGRON
JOHN CHILDS

FURTHER READING
F. Donner, *The Early Islamic Conquests* (Princeton, 1981); G. Ostrogorsky, *History of the Byzantine State* (3rd edn, Oxford, 1968).

Yorktown campaign (August–October 1781) Although the American Revolutionary War was to continue into 1783, the Franco-American victory at Yorktown proved to be the last significant campaign in North America, ensuring the ultimate success of the Revolution. The Yorktown campaign underscored the key role which naval forces could play in operations along the coastal margins of eastern North America, the regions in which most of the campaigns of the war were conducted.

After abandoning the Carolinas in April 1781 for a campaign in Virginia, General Charles Cornwallis (1738–1805) established a defensive post at Yorktown on the Virginia Peninsula to serve both as a refuge for British ships patrolling the Chesapeake and as a base for future land operations. Learning of the presence of de Grasse's French fleet in the West Indies and of the admiral's willingness to co-operate, Washington marched south from New York on 20 August, together with the French expeditionary force which had been sent by Louis XVI in 1780 under the command of Lieutenant-General Jean-Baptiste de Rochambeau (1725–1807), in the hope of trapping Cornwallis. By mid-September, some 8,800 American regulars and militiamen and 7,800 French

soldiers, equipped with a siege train delivered by sea, were ready to ensnare the British force of 7,000 regulars and American loyalists. The arrival in Chesapeake Bay of de Grasse's fleet surprised the British naval commanders and completed the encirclement. After a siege of three weeks, Cornwallis surrendered on 19 October; a British relief expedition arrived from New York by sea five days too late to save him.

The appearance of de Grasse's unexpectedly large fleet (28 ships of the line and 6 frigates) in North American waters had completely upset British strategic assumptions. Having taken British naval superiority for granted, neither Cornwallis nor Sir Henry Clinton (1738–95) in New York was able to react in sufficient time. The margin of error included in their operational planning had been too slender. Cornwallis's fate was decided at sea and the root cause was the over-stretching of Britain's naval resources. On the Franco-American side, de Grasse had sprung a decisive strategic surprise on the Royal Navy and Washington had seized an opportunity with an imaginative, if tenuous, plan, which, for once, unfolded without complications and brought him a complete triumph. Washington had always been keenly aware of the advantage which superiority at sea gave to British operations; their lateral maritime communications enabled British troops to accomplish in days what American soldiers forced to march overland could only achieve in weeks. In the Yorktown campaign, although Washington's regulars had an overland march of 400 miles, French naval superiority ensured success, lending a literal meaning to the British choice of a martial air to accompany the formalities of the surrender, 'The World turned upside down'. *See also* FRANCE; GRASSE DE TILLY; MAHAN; SARATOGA; UNITED STATES; WASHINGTON.

G. A. STEPPLER

FURTHER READING
Henry P. Johnston, *The Yorktown Campaign and the Surrender of Cornwallis* (New York, 1881); Piers Mackesy, *The War for America,*

1775–1783 (London, 1964); David Syrett, *The Royal Navy in American Waters, 1775–1783* (Aldershot, 1989); Hugh F. Rankin, 'Charles Lord Cornwallis: study in frustration', in *George Washington's Opponents*, ed. G. A. Billias (New York, 1969), pp. 193–232; William B. Willcox, 'The British road to Yorktown: a study in divided command', *AHR*, lii (1946), pp. 1–35.

Ypres, Battles of (1914–17)   Following the Germans' retreat from the Marne and their stand along the Aisne in September 1914, a 'race to the sea' was initiated in which both sides attempted to outflank the other's newly entrenched positions. The process culminated in the attempt by von Falkenhayn, who had replaced the younger Moltke as Chief of the German General Staff, to break through Flanders to the Channel ports at the very moment that the British Expeditionary Force was redeploying from the Aisne into Flanders. The resulting **First Battle of Ypres** (19 October–22 November 1914) together with the preceding action between German and Belgian forces on the Yser (9–15 October 1914), during which the latter inundated much of the countryside to stem the German advance, blunted Falkenhayn's offensive at the cost of *c.*108,000 Allied casualties. However, when the fighting petered out in November the Germans had gained commanding positions along the line of the ridge east of Ypres from Messines in the south to Passchendaele in the north overlooking the 'immortal salient' occupied by the British troops around the town of Ypres itself.

The **Second Battle of Ypres** (22 April–25 May 1915) saw a more limited German attempt to break through the Allied front to the North Sea coast. On the opening day of the offensive, poison gas was used for the first time on the Western Front, around Pilckem and Langemarck. It tore an 8,000-yard gap in the line held by French territorial and colonial troops. The Germans employed gas on eight separate occasions during the battle but their attacks were ultimately unsuccessful, due not least to the tenacity of the Canadian troops who improvised gas masks and plugged the holes left by the terrified French. The Ypres sector also witnessed the first use of a flamethrower when the Germans attacked the positions held by the British 41st Brigade around Hooge on 29 July 1915.

The **Third Battle of Ypres** (31 July–10 November 1917) was a British offensive aimed at seizing the village of Passchendaele before driving on to the supposed German submarine bases at Ostend and Zeebrugge. It followed an earlier limited attack on 7 June 1917, which had secured the Messines sector by the detonation of 19 large mines beneath the German lines. An amphibious assault on the Flanders coast was also contemplated but never materialized. Unfortunately, Haig, the British commander-in-chief, persisted in pursuing the action on a battlefield which had been reduced to a sea of mud by incessant rainfall and the destruction of the natural and artificial drainage systems by artillery bombardment. The British army suffered 238,000 casualties before Passchendaele fell on 6 November. What had become an attritional battle rather than a breakthrough was justified on the grounds that it further weakened German resources and morale but the 'campaign of the mud' has become the enduring image of military futility. *See also* FRANCE; GERMANY; GREAT BRITAIN; HAIG; MARNE.

IAN F. W. BECKETT

FURTHER READING
A. Farrar-Hockley, *Death of an Army* (London, 1967); J. Terraine, *The Road to Passchendaele* (London, 1977); T. Travers, *The Killing Ground* (London, 1987); P. Warner, *Passchendaele* (London, 1987); L. Wolff, *In Flanders Fields* (London 1959).

Z

Zama, Battle of (202 BC) The site of the final battle of the Second Punic War, which brought Hannibal face to face with the Roman commander Publius Cornelius Scipio, cannot be certainly identified. It was in the vicinity of Zama Regia (probably Seba Biar) in Tunisia, about 88 miles south-west of Carthage. Scipio had an army of around 30,000 strengthened by the strong cavalry provided by his ally, Masinissa, a Numidian prince who had previously supported the Carthaginians. Hannibal drew up his army in three lines, with his mercenaries in the first rank, followed by his new levies, and finally his veterans. Eighty elephants were placed in front, with the cavalry on the wings. Scipio placed his cavalry on the flanks and arranged the maniples with gaps between them, to allow the elephants to pass through harmlessly. Then the Romans' cavalry drove the outnumbered Carthaginian cavalry from the field while the infantry broke through the first two ranks of Hannibal's army and engaged his veterans. The battle was still in the balance when the cavalry returned and attacked the rear of the Carthaginian line. This cavalry charge decided the outcome and the Carthaginian losses were so heavy that Hannibal recommended that Carthage immediately seek peace. For his achievement in ending the war, Scipio was known thereafter as 'Africanus'. *See also* CARTHAGE; HANNIBAL; ROME; SCIPIO AFRICANUS.

B. CAMPBELL

FURTHER READING
G. C. Picard, *Hannibal* (Paris, 1967); H. H. Scullard, *Scipio Africanus: soldier and statesman* (London, 1970); J. F. Lazenby, *Hannibal's War: a military history of the Second Punic War* (Warminster, 1978); B. Caven, *The Punic Wars* (London, 1980).

Zenta, Battle of (11 September 1697) The Imperial army of 50,000 men, commanded by Prince Eugene of Savoy, had been ordered to await the arrival of the Turkish army, under Sultan Mustafa II, between the Danube and the Tisza in the vicinity of Peterwardein. His object was to prevent a Turkish invasion of Hungary. Mustafa decided not to attack the strong Imperial army but, instead, marched along the left bank of the Tisza to seize Szeged before raiding into Transylvania. Eugene pursued the Turks. Mustafa, wary of being trapped between Eugene's force and the Imperial garrison at Szeged, crossed the river at Zenta on 11 September by a pontoon bridge, hoping to march into Transylvania via the right bank. With just four hours of daylight remaining, Eugene's cavalry arrived at Zenta to discover the Sultan already on the right bank with all his cavalry, artillery and baggage and the Grand Vizier stranded on the left bank with the infantry protected only by a wall of carts. Eugene deployed his men into a crescent formation and attacked with little preparation. Eugene made use of low water in the Tisza and a sandbank to reach into the rear of the Turkish positions. By nightfall, 20,000 Turks had been killed and another 10,000 drowned in the river. The Sultan fled to Timisoara with his cavalry, abandoning 87 cannon, his war chest and all his baggage. It was too late in the season to exploit the victory by the capture of Belgrade or Temesvár, but Zenta led directly to the Treaty of Carlowitz (1699) by which the Turks surrendered all Hungary and Transylvania to the Emperor of Austria. *See also* AUSTRIA; EUGENE OF SAVOY; OTTOMAN TURKS.

J. NOUZILLE
JOHN CHILDS

FURTHER READING
Derek Mckay, *Prince Eugene of Savoy* (London, 1977); Nicholas Henderson, *Prince Eugen of Savoy* (London, 1964).

Zhukov, Georgi Konstantinovich (1896–1974) Zhukov was born the son of a shoemaker in the village of Strelkova, south-west of Moscow. Zhukov went to work at the age of thirteen. In 1915, he volunteered for the Tsarist army, where he served with bravery and distinction in the 10th Novgorod Dragoons. He was elected a member of the regimental soviet in 1917, and was active in politics throughout that year. In 1918, Zhukov helped to organize the Red Army, and fought throughout the Civil War in the Red cavalry. Here he served under S. K. Timoshenko, a future marshal of the Soviet Union, whose patronage was important for Zhukov's subsequent career. In 1919, Zhukov joined the Communist Party. He remained in the Red Army after the Civil War. After distinguishing himself in various training programmes, he attended the Frunze Military Academy from 1928 to 1931. During the

(Camera Press)

1930s, Zhukov was a specialist in armoured warfare, rising to commander of the 3rd Cavalry Corps by 1936 and Deputy Commander of the Belorussian Military District the following year. In July and August 1939, Zhukov commanded the Soviet forces that defeated the Japanese in Mongolia at the Battle of Khalkin-Gol for which he was made a Hero of the Soviet Union. After serving briefly as Deputy Commander of the Ukrainian Military District, Zhukov became Chief of Staff of the Soviet forces at the end of the Russo-Finnish War. He was promoted to general in May 1940 while commander of the Kiev Special Military District. From February to the end of July 1941, Zhukov was Chief of the General Staff and Deputy Commissar of Defence. During the Second World War, Zhukov acted as Stalin's troubleshooter. Zhukov personally directed the defence of Moscow, and was prominent in the Siege of Leningrad, the Battle of Stalingrad and the defence of the Caucasus. In 1942, he was made Deputy Supreme Commander-in-Chief and First Deputy People's Minister of Defence. In 1943, Zhukov planned the Battle of the Kursk Salient. The following year he devised the major Soviet offensives and took personal command of the Soviet forces in their drive on Berlin. In early 1943, he was made marshal of the Soviet Union. After the war, Zhukov commanded the Soviet occupation forces in Germany until 1946. From that year until 1953, Zhukov was in eclipse, probably because Stalin felt that the marshal's popularity was a threat. As commander of the Odessa and then the Ural Military Districts, Zhukov's career seemed over. Upon Stalin's death, Zhukov was rehabilitated. He was made First Deputy Minister of Defence in 1953 and became a full member of the Central Committee of the Communist Party. Zhukov was a strong supporter of the political career of Nikita Khrushchev. In 1955, Khrushchev made Zhukov Minister of Defence. Two years later, Zhukov's support helped Khrushchev defeat an attempt to oust him as the Soviet leader. Fearing that Zhukov had become overpowerful, Khrushchev subsequently had him removed from his posts in the autumn of 1957. Zhukov remained in obscure retirement until the fall of Khrushchev. From 1965 until his death in 1974, Zhukov was lauded as the most famous and significant of Soviet soldiers. *See also* KONEV; KURSK SALIENT; RUSSIA/USSR; SHAPOSHNIKOV; STALIN.

A. CORVISIER
KEITH NEILSON

FURTHER READING
Otto Chaney, *Zhukov* (Norman, 1971); Georgy Konstantinovich Zhukov, *The Memoirs of Marshal Zhukov* (New York, 1971); John Erickson, *The Road to Stalingrad* (London, 1975); John Erickson, *The Road to Berlin* (London, 1983).

INDEX

Note: references in *italics* denote illustrations; those in **bold** type indicate a separate article on the subject.

gliders, 11, 59
Gloire, La (French warship), 34, 266
glory, **314–16**, 370, 371, 375
Gneisenau, August von, 90, 233, 308, 338, 727
Godley, Sir Alexander, 604
Goebbels, Joseph, 680
Goering, Hermann, 633, 642
Golan Heights, 407
Golden Hinde (Drake's ship), 542
Goltz, Colmar von der, 185, 631, 728
Gordon, Charles George (of Khartoum), 54
Goré, 157
Goring, George, Lord Goring, 492
Gorshkov, Sergei Georgievich, 214
Goths, 9–10, 175, 853
Gournay, B. C., 736
Gouvion-Saint-Cyr, Laurent, Marquis de, 301, 694, 843
Goya y Lucientes, Francisco José de, 374
Gracchus, Gaius, 705
Gracchus, Tiberius, 730
Granada, Siege of, 615, 774
Grandmaison, Louis Loyzeau de, **316**
Grandson, Battle of, 131, **317**, 382, 464–5, 783
Granicus, Battle of, **317**
Grant, Ulysses Simpson, 303, **317–18**, 831
Grasse-Tilly, François-Joseph, Comte de, **318**, 568, 580, 703, 874
Grave, capture of, 626
Gravelines, Battle of, **318–19**, 729
Graves, Thomas, Lord Graves, 318, 580
Graziani, Rodolfo, 413
Great Northern War, 659, 714, 780
Greece, ancient, **325–30**; armour, 32–3, 326; artillery, 39, 351–2; cavalry, 125, 326–7, 656; city-state, 327–8, 550; communications, 745; discipline, 199; economic warfare, 211; elephants, 327; engineering, 218; finances, 238; fortifications, 28; laws of war, 443–4; light infantry, 28, 326, 328, 329; and Macedon, 21, **125–6**, 182; marines, 487; medicine, 494, 495; mercenaries, 215, 327, 328–9, 502; military ethos, 227–8; morale, 534; nationalism, 550; navies, 327, 575–6, 586, 724; pacifism, 635; recruiting, 688; siege warfare, 28, 328, 329, 351–2, (*see also* catapults); slaves, 688; tactical organization, 789; tactics, 794; training, 811; transport, 818; truces, sacred, 635; vexillology, 844; weapons, 81, 326, 861; *see also* Athens; *hoplites*; Macedon; Peloponnesian War; *peltasts*; Persian Wars; phalanx; Sparta; Thebes
Greece, modern, 161, 244; civil war, 665, 699; under Ottomans, 338, 501, 628; resistance, 338, 698, 699; World War II, 12, 55, 89
Greek Fire, 40, 102, 103, 587, 673, 863
Greenwich: Hospital, 6, 648; museum, 542
Grenada, 703
grenades, 252, **330–1**, 385, 409
grenadiers, **330–1**, 334
Grenouillac, Galliot de, 784
Grenzer, Austrian, 57, 289–91
Gribeauval, Jean-Baptiste Vaquette de, 51, **331–2**; artillery system, 43, 75, 284, 331–2, 547, 838, 863, 867; and mining, 220, 331, 521
Grivas, George Theodorou, 160
Gröben, Georg Dietrich von, 735
Grolmann, Karl von, 727
Gros, Antoine Jean, Baron, 374
Gros-Caillou, Hôpital du, 436
Gross-Jägersdorf, Battle of, 711
Grotius, *or* de Groot, Hugo, 305, 320, **332**, 852; on laws of war, 332, 440, 447, 635, 668

Grouchy, Emmanuel, Marquis de, 859
ground, 267, 482, 600, 617, 618
Gruinard, Isle of, 134
Guadalcanal, Battle of, **332–3**, 489, 513, 584, 873
Guadeloupe, 157, 173
Guam, 71, 584, 834
Guantánamo, 71, 89
guards, 77, 330, **333–6**, 402, 408, 529; *see also under* Britain; France; Russia
Guderian, Heinz, 169, 286, **337**, 459, 799
guerilla warfare, **337–9**; Arabs, 337, 510, 512; colonial wars, 162, 510, 512; distinguished from terrorism, 803, 805; Gambiez and, 293; Lawrence on, 442; and laws of war, 451–2; Lenin on, 454; Lettow-Vorbeck, 456–7; Mao Tse-Tung and, 339, 485, 663; Nicephorus II Phocas on, 605; resistance movements, 698; tactics, 796; Wars of Religion, 351; *see also* informal warfare; Peninsular War; popular warfare; *and individual guerilla wars*
Guernica, **339**, 375
guerre de course, 172–3
Guesclin, *see* du Guesclin
Gueux des Bois, 337
Guevara, Ernesto Che, 771
Guiana, French, 157
Guibert, Jacques Antoine Hippolyte, Comte de, 28, **340**, 655, 727, 769, 770; and concentration of fire, 44, 340, 417; influence, 340, 417, 547, 802
Guichen, Lucien Urbain de Bouëxic, Comte de, 703
guidons, 847
Guinea-Bissau, 162
Guines, siege of, 105
Guise, François de Lorraine, 2nd Duke of, 105, 318, **340–1**, 383, 504, 505, 531
Gulf War, 155, **341–3**, 403, 404, 512, 679, 778; command, 168, 169; international force, 23, 56, 414, 452; and laws of war, 452, 671; media reporting, 734; US role, 404, 835
guncarriages, 41, 42, 863
guncotton, 674
gunfire, 45, **343–5**; frontal and lateral, 267–8, 271
gunpowder, 138, 219, 520, 673–4, 862
Gurkhas, 83, 261, 377
Gusev, S. I., 754, 755
Gustavus Adolphus (Gustav II Adolf), king of Sweden, **345–6**; artillery, 42; cavalry, 119; chaplains, 127; composition of army, 779; death, 472; discipline, 200; dragoons, 208; Dutch influence on, 600; engineering, 221; firearms, 248; infantry, 383; influence on Montecucoli, 533; and military law, 440; and morale, 534; staffs, 299; tactical organization, 790; tactics, 779; training, 812; *see also individual battles and campaigns*
Guy d'Anjou, Bishop, 445
Guy de Lusignan, 350, 724

Haarlem, siege of, 20
Habsburg Empire, *see* Austria
Haddington, 739
Hadrian's Wall, 65, 263, 269, *288*
Haganah, 184, 406, 527
Hague Conventions, 136, 196–7, 636, 670
Haiduks, 338, 366, 697
Haig, Douglas, 1st Earl, 168, **347**, 386, 875
Haiphong, 89, 313
Haiti, 173, 338, 555
Haldane, Richard, 324, 812
Halifax (Canada), 205
Halil Pasha, Grand Vizier, 74
Halle, Flanders, 399
Hallstatt culture, 81